THE LAW RELATING TO
PARENT AND CHILD
IN SCOTLAND

THE LAW RELATING TO PARENT AND CHILD IN SCOTLAND

A.B. WILKINSON, Q.C., M.A., LL.B.
Sheriff of Lothian and Borders at Edinburgh

Kenneth McK. Norrie, LL.B., Ph.D.
Professor of Law, University of Strathclyde

SECOND EDITION

by

Kenneth McK. Norrie

With a chapter on Child Support
by

Peter Robson, LL.B., Ph.D.
Solicitor, Professor of Social Welfare Law,
University of Strathclyde

Published under the auspices of
SCOTTISH UNIVERSITIES LAW INSTITUTE LTD

EDINBURGH
W.GREEN
1999

First published 1993
Second Edition 1999

Published in 1999 by W. Green & Son Limited,
21 Alva Street,
Edinburgh, EH2 4PS

Typeset by Trinity Typesetting Ltd
Edinburgh

Printed and bound in Great Britain by
MPG Books Ltd, Bodmin, Cornwall

No natural forests were destroyed to make this product; only farmed timber
was used and replanted

A CIP catalogue record of this book is available from the British Library

ISBN 0414 01251 8

© SCOTTISH UNIVERSITIES LAW INSTITUTE 1999

PREFACE TO SECOND EDITION

It is six years since the first edition of this book was published and since then, of course, the major portion of that area of law with which the book is concerned has undergone radical transformation. The Children (Scotland) Act 1995 not only modernised the law of parent and child but it restructured the very way in which we look at the private aspects of the parent and child relationship. That restructuring has been reflected in the changed format of this edition. Public law aspects of child law were also, in many respects, restructured by the Act though (other than with emergency protection measures) less radically. In addition, those areas of the law which were hardly affected by the 1995 Act, such as international child abduction and (if more affected) adoption, have in both Scotland and England experienced a large increase in court decisions which both clarify many issues and raise many other questions. For these reasons, and others, it is timely to produce a second edition.

There is little doubt that the 1995 Act has resulted in the law of parent and child in Scotland being in a significantly more satisfactory state today than it was in 1993. The courts, in so far as one can tell at this early stage, are applying the principles in the Act in much the way it was intended that they should, this to the benefit of both parents and children in Scotland. The Act, in other words, has been a success. There is, however, still much to be done before the law is entirely fit for the new century. The present statutory law remains vibrant, and while there is already a bank of decisions on the 1995 Act, there will unquestionably be very many more within a short space of years. And the statutory law itself will not remain static. Even as this book goes to press, the Scottish Office are consulting on their discussion paper "Improving Scottish Family Law", which brings together many of the proposals made by the Scottish Law Commission that have not, for a variety of reasons good and bad, yet been implemented. There is likely to be legislation amending parts of the Children (Scotland) Act 1995, though its timescale lies in the hands of the newly elected Scottish Parliament. The system of child support, treated here in far more depth than in the first edition, continues to evolve. The effect that the Human Rights Act 1998 will have on this area of the law is presently as uncertain as it is certain that effect there will be. Nevertheless, it is unlikely that this edition will become so quickly out of date as the first edition did.

As always, a book such as this is the result not only of research and experience but also of many discussions with a variety of people, too numerous to mention. Special thanks must, however, go to Ms Alison Cleland for commenting on an early draft of the new procedure sections, to Mr Al Gordon for bringing to my attention a number of important decisions in which he has been personally involved, and to Mr David Reid whose work as my research assistant helped to ensure that this book appeared timeously. Sheriff A. B. Wilkinson, who shared equal responsibility for the preparation of the first edition, remained as a consultant during the preparation of the second, and his ever-valuable and wise comments, suggestions, and advice have ensured that this edition has a chance of maintaining the standards of his earlier work. One other important difference from the first edition is the addition of a wholly new chapter on child support, written by Professor Peter Robson, and to him thanks are due also.

While most of the preparation of this edition was undertaken in 1997 and 1998, the ever-increasing speed and ease of electronic means of information retrieval has meant that I have been able to take full account of developments in early 1999. Consequently, I have attempted to state the law as at May 6, 1999.

Kenneth McK. Norrie

PREFACE TO FIRST EDITION

There has been no book devoted to a comprehensive treatment of the Scots law of Parent and Child since the third edition of Lord Fraser's classic work was published under the editorship of James Clark in 1906. Some of the law of which Fraser wrote survives, perhaps to a surprising extent, if in a transitional or vestigal form, but the most marked feature of the intervening years has been the radical and far-reaching effect of legislative change. The concept of legitimacy which was central to the older law is obsolescent, the law of guardianship and legal capacity of children has been largely, but not entirely, recast, questions of custody and aliment are governed by new statutory criteria and modern medical technology has given rise to new legal problems in the constitution of the parent and child relationship itself. At the same time the public law regulation of the care and protection of children, the law of adoption and aspects of the law of education now require a place, which they did not previously occupy, in any adequate discussion of the law of parent and child. Questions of boundaries inevitably arise. We have tried to avoid drawing these boundaries narrowly and artificially and to cover all aspects of the law which have a close bearing on the parent and child relationship. We have not, however, discussed, except incidentally, topics which more appropriately fall within the scope of other specialist works. Thus we have dealt, sometimes quite extensively, with questions of succession and criminal liability where that was required by the context but we have not attempted a comprehensive discussion of the cognate aspects of the law of succession or criminal law or revenue and social security law.

There are many to whom gratitude is due. Professor I. D. Willock, Mr J. J. Robertson and Dr Brian Davis generously made available research materials which they had gathered. Mr Simon Bowie, Mr Craig Harvie and Mr Amish Amin provided useful technical assistance. Most of the text was read in an earlier version by the late Lord Dunpark, Dr E. M. Clive and Mr Niall Whitty and we are very grateful to them for the invaluable suggestions they made as we are to Mr Russel P. Meek and Professor J. M. Thomson for comments on the chapters on compulsory measures of care and custody respectively. We are similarly indebted to the Honourable Lord Caplan, Sheriff Mark Sischy and Professor Alastair Bissett-Johnson who read the text in virtually its final form, to successive directors of the Scottish Universities' Law Institute for their guidance and forebearance and, in particular, to the present Director, Professor W. W. McBryde, who was instrumental in bringing about our collaboration and has done much to ease the path to publication. Lord Dunpark gave abundantly not only of his learning and practical judgment but of his interest and support. It is a matter of particular regret that he has not lived to see the publication of a book he did so much to encourage.

We have endeavoured to state the law as at 31st July 1993.

A. B. Wilkinson
Kenneth McK. Norrie

CONTENTS

PART II: ESTABLISHING THE RELATIONSHIP

3. CONSTITUTION OF THE PARENT-CHILD RELATIONSHIP

4. ADOPTION OF CHILDREN

5. PROCEDURAL AND INTERNATIONAL ASPECTS OF ADOPTION

6. SURROGACY AND PARENTAL ORDERS

PART III: PRIVATE LAW CONSEQUENCES OF THE RELATIONSHIP

8. PARENTAL RESPONSIBILITIES AND PARENTAL RIGHTS

9. COURT ORDERS RELATING TO PARENTAL RESPONSIBILITIES AND PARENTAL RIGHTS

10. THE SECTION 11(7) PRINCIPLES

11. INTERNATIONAL ASPECTS OF PARENTAL RESPONSIBILITIES AND PARENTAL RIGHTS

12. EDUCATION OF CHILDREN

13. ALIMENT

14. CHILD SUPPORT

PART IV: PUBLIC LAW CONSEQUENCES OF THE RELATIONSHIP

19. CHILDREN'S HEARINGS

20. INTERIM PROTECTION OF CHILDREN

TABLE OF CASES

TABLE OF STATUTES

TABLE OF STATUTORY INSTRUMENTS

SELECTED ABBREVIATIONS AND AUTHORITIES

A.B.A.Jo.	American Bar Association Journal
A.C.	Appeal Cases (House of Lords)
A.L.R.	Australian Law Reports
All E.R.	All England Law Reports
Balfour	Sir James Balfour of Pittendreich, *Practicks: or a System of the More Ancient Law of Scotland*
Bankton	Andrew McDouall, Lord Bankton, *Institute of the Laws of Scotland in Civil Rights*
Bell	G.J. Bell, *Principles of the Law of Scotland*
B.M.L.R.	Butterworths Medico-Legal Reports
C.F.L.Q.	Child and Family Law Quarterly
C.L.Y.	Current Law Yearbook
C.L.J.	Cambridge Law Journal
Crim. L.R.	Criminal Law Review
D.	Dunlop (Session Cases) (Scotland)
D.L.R.	Dominion Law Reports (Canada)
E.H.R.R.	European Human Rights Reports
Erskine	John Erskine, *An Institute of the Laws of Scotland*
F.	Fraser (Session Cases) (Scotland)
F.C.	Faculty Collection (Scotland)
F.C.R.	Family Court Reports (England)
Fam. L.B.	Green's Family Law Bulletin
F.L.R.	Family Law Reports (England)
Fam. L.R.	Family Law Reports (Scotland)
(20) Fam. L.R	Family Law Reports (Australia) (e.g. vol. 20)
Fraser	Lord Fraser, *The Law of Scotland Relative to Parent and Child*, 3rd ed. (1906)
I.C.L.Q.	International and Comparative Law Quarterly
I.C.R.	Industrial Cases Reports
Imm. A.R.	Immigration Appeal Reports
J.A.M.A.	Journal of the American Medical Association
J.L.S.S.	Journal of the Law Society of Scotland
J.P.	Justice of the Peace Reports
J.R.	Juridical Review
J.S.W.F.L.	Journal of Social Welfare and Family Law
L.G.R.	Local Government Reports
L.Q.R.	Law Quarterly Review
Leg. Stud.	Legal Studies
M.	Macpherson (Session Cases) (Scotland)
Macq.	Macqueen's Appeal Cases (House of Lords)
Med. L.R.	Medical Law Review
Med. Sci. L.	Medicine, Science and the Law
Mod. L.R.	Modern Law Review
Mor.	Morison's *Dictionary of Decisions* (Scotland)
N.I.L.Q.	Northern Ireland Legal Quarterly
N.S.W.L.R.	New South Wales Law Reports
N.T.R.	Northern Territory Reports
N.Z. Uni. L.R.	New Zealand Universities Law Review
N.Z.F.L.R.	New Zealand Family Law Reports
N.Z.L.R.	New Zealand Law Reports
Ox. J. Leg. Stud.	Oxford Journal of Legal Studies
Paton	Paton's Reports (House of Lords)
R.	Rettie (Session Cases) (Scotland)
Rep. L.R.	Reparation Law Reports (Scotland)
S.	Shaw (Session Cases) (Scotland)

S.A.L.R.	South African Law Reports
S.C.	Session Cases (Scotland)
S.C.C.R.	Scottish Criminal Case Reports
Sc. Jur.	Scottish Jurist
S.C.L.R.	Scottish Civil Law Reports
S.C.R.	Supreme Court Reports (Canada)
Sh. Ct. Rep.	Sheriff Court Reports (Scotland)
S.L.G.	Scottish Law Gazette
S.L.P.Q.	Scottish Law and Practice Quarterly
S.L.R.	Scottish Law Reporter
S.L.T.	Scots Law Times
S.N.	Session Notes (Scotland)
Sol. J.	Solicitors' Journal
Stair	Sir James Dalrymple, Viscount Stair, *Institutions of the Law of Scotland*
T.L.R.	Times Law Reports
Tas. L.R.	Tasmanian Law Reports
V.R.	Victorian Reports
W.L.R.	Weekly Law Reports (England)

PART I

PRELIMINARY MATTERS

CHAPTER 1

HISTORICAL INTRODUCTION

GENERAL INTRODUCTION

The parent-child relationship

"Child" may mean (1) the off-spring of particular human parents ("child of **1.01**
X") and in that sense is the correlative of "parent"; and (2) the young of the
human species from birth, or even before, to about the age of adolescence. In
the first sense, age is irrelevant, although for most purposes other than succession
the legal significance of the parent and child relationship ends, or is much
reduced, when the child attains majority. The word "child" when used in the
second sense was not a term of art for the common law which spoke rather of
pupils, *i.e.* children under the legal age of puberty, which was 12 in the case of
a girl and 14 in the case of a boy, and minors between these ages and majority.
The tendency of modern statute has been to apply the term "child" to everyone
under the age of 16,[1] perhaps a rather later age than common usage would
justify, and in some contexts "child" is defined as extending to persons up to
the age of 18[2] or even beyond.[3] That there should be two distinct but related
senses in which the word "child" may be used represents, however, more than
an accident of language. The relationship of parent and child and the extensions
flowing from it provide the primary means to which human societies have looked
for the nurture, care and upbringing of their younger members and that means
may be seen, despite occasional attempts to dispense with it, as founded on
nature. This work takes as its starting-point the legal recognition and regulation
of the relationship of parent and child and goes on to consider legal provision
for substitute and supplementary arrangements for the care and upbringing of
children and associated questions of the management of children's property,
the capacity of children to act and the function of guardianship.

Common law classification

The common law made radical distinctions between (1) legitimate children, **1.02**
i.e. those born or conceived in wedlock or subsequently legitimated,[4] and
illegitimate children; and (2) between pupils and minors in the sense indicated
above. Confusingly, but perhaps more properly, the term "minor" was also often
used to embrace all persons, including pupils, under the age of majority. For
clarity, the expression "minor *pubes*" could be used when the case of a person
between pupillarity and majority was under consideration, to distinguish his or
her position from that of persons under majority generally.

Although for some limited purposes the natural relationship between an **1.03**
illegitimate child and his or her parents was recognised, by imposing an
obligation of aliment on the father and, at least in the later development of the
law, by giving the right of custody to the mother, it was only the relationship
between a legitimate child and his or her parents that was treated as being in the

---

[1] See, *e.g.*, Children (Scotland) Act 1995, ss. 1(2)(a), 2(7) and 93(2)(b).
[2] See, *e.g.*, *ibid.*, ss. 1(2)(b) and 93(2)(a).
[3] See, *e.g.*, Family Law (Scotland) Act 1985, s. 1(5).
[4] See below, paras 1.39–1.59.

1

full sense a relationship of parent and child recognised by law and to which the whole body of common law rules relating to that relationship applied. Legitimate children were subject to the *patria potestas* or paternal power of their father which in the case of pupil children was so extensive that it was called, if slightly misleadingly, a right of dominion. In the case of minors it was much reduced and might be lost by the minor's forisfamiliation.[5] Although on the failure of the father by death or otherwise certain rights which he had exercised as part of the *patria potestas* might accrue or be transferred to relatives, the child's mother or others, the *patria potestas* as such was regarded as vesting in the father alone and was inalienable. The mother's position in respect of custody and guardianship was considerably improved, if in a piecemeal fashion, by a series of enactments from the mid-nineteenth century onwards, but the rule that, in principle, the *patria potestas* belonged to the father alone remained the law until as late as 1973.[6] The guardians who on the failure of the father of a legitimate pupil child might be entrusted with the management of his or her estate and, unless the court ordered otherwise, with his or her personal care and custody were known as tutors. Pupil children had no legal capacity to act or to manage their own affairs. Minors had such capacity, but for many transactions the concurrence of the minor's father, if alive, or if he or she had guardians (known as curators) the concurrence of these guardians, was necessary. In contrast with pupils, however, neither the father nor the curators of a minor could take over the management of his or her estate or act without his or her authority on the minor's behalf. A father had certain but limited powers of personal control over a minor; curators had none. In relation to contracts and legal proceedings fathers were often referred to as tutors of their pupil, and curators of their minor, children; but such language was no more than descriptive of the role and did not imply any distinct office—they so acted by virtue of the *patria potestas*.

Statutory development

1.04   This work treats of a number of topics—local authority involvement in the upbringing of children, emergency child protection measures, transference of parental rights and responsibilities, compulsory measures of supervision, regulation of fostering and child-minding, and adoption—which are the creatures of modern statute designed to address familial and social problems which the common law did not address. They bear on the law of parent and child primarily as remedies for the malfunction of the parent and child relationship or as a means of regulating alternative or substitute provision in the event of its failure. Their legislative history, where it is important for the understanding of the modern law, is given later in its appropriate context. From the mid-nineteenth century onwards there has also been a series of statutes, particularly in the fields of custody, guardianship and the position of illegitimate children, which served to modify, extend and ameliorate the common law in the light of developing perceptions. Although some of these statutes effected fairly radical revision of common law tenets, they left the common law framework substantially in place. Since 1985, however, the effect of legislation such as the Family Law (Scotland) Act 1985, the Law Reform (Parent and Child) (Scotland) Act 1986, the Age of Legal Capacity (Scotland) Act 1991, and culminating in the Children (Scotland) Act 1995, has been to bring about in large measure the replacement of common law by statute. Legitimacy, and with it illegitimacy, has been virtually swept away; the law of aliment and of parental responsibilities and parental rights is embodied in statutory rules; the ancient distinction between

---

[5] See the 1st edition of this book at pp. 44–45.
[6] Guardianship Act 1973, s. 10 (repealed by the Law Reform (Parent and Child) (Scotland) Act 1986, Sched. 2).

pupils and minors *puberes* has been abolished and replaced by a sharp distinction, for the purposes of the legal capacity of persons who have not attained majority, between those under 16 years of age and those of or over that age; tutory and curatory have been abolished, although the former, abolished only in name, has been replaced by legal representation of those under the age of 16. The process is not, however, complete. There is as yet no comprehensive statutory code[7] and even where, as for parental responsibilities and parental rights, and for aliment, the law is entirely, or almost entirely, statutory, it is enacted against a common law background without some knowledge of which the statute law cannot be fully understood. Moreover, common law rules retain some transitional or incidental importance. Although legitimacy has become a largely outmoded concept, its application to heritable titles, coats of arms, honours and dignities, remains in principle part of the law: declarators of legitimacy and illegitimacy are still competent. More importantly, the law on legitimacy still requires to be considered for the purposes of successions opening before the commencement of the Law Reform (Parent and Child) (Scotland) Act 1986[8] and for the construction of deeds executed before that commencement and of references in deeds, even if executed thereafter, to a legitimate and illegitimate person or relationship. Similarly, the law on pupils and minors remains applicable to any transactions entered into before the date of commencement of the Age of Legal Capacity (Scotland) Act 1991.[9]

This chapter contains a brief consideration of historical sources and of the development of some of the major aspects of the parent and child relationship. Thereafter there is a discussion in some detail of the law of legitimacy. **1.05**

HISTORICAL DEVELOPMENT

Historical sources

The main historical sources of the Scots law of parent and child are the civil law (in the sense of the civilian tradition developed from the Roman law of Justinian, *i.e.* the *jus commune*), canon law and to some extent, particularly in questions of tutory and curatory, feudal law. The historical development of the law and the influence of these sources are discussed later in the context of the particular aspects of the modern law to which they are relevant. For a wider discussion, reference should be made to other works which are readily available.[10] Only canon law, because of its importance for doctrines of legitimacy which were central to much of the common law of parent and child and because it has been a subject of some controversy, requires brief separate treatment here. **1.06**

Canon law

In the medieval period questions of status, including legitimacy, were exclusively within the jurisdiction of the ecclesiastical courts, which applied canon law, and these questions were referred to them even if they arose in the course of proceedings in the secular courts.[11] After the Reformation the **1.07**

---

[7] Even the Children (Scotland) Act 1995 does not provide a complete child law code since many important issues, such as adoption, aliment, legal capacity and child abduction, lie mostly outwith its terms.

[8] December 8, 1986.

[9] September 25, 1991.

[10] Baird Smith, "Roman Law", Stair Society Vol. I, pp. 171–182 and "Canon Law", *ibid*. pp. 183–192; Girvan, "Feudal Law", *ibid*. pp. 193–206; Anton,"Parent and Child", Stair Society Vol. 20, pp.116–124; Montgomery, "Guardian and Ward", *ibid*. pp.125–129; Clive, *Husband and Wife* (4th ed.), Chap. 1.

[11] Anton, *op. cit*., p. 116.

jurisdiction of the medieval ecclesiastical courts was taken over by the courts of the commissaries, which continued to apply canon law in so far as it was compatible with statute and Protestant views. But latterly, and well before 1830 when the jurisdiction of the commissaries was transferred to the Court of Session[12] (to which appeal from the commissaries had lain since their institution after the Reformation), it seems to have been a matter of the commissaries' following their own precedents which embodied canon law principles rather than their making direct reference to canon law sources. At least for some time after the Reformation, familiarity with canon law was expected of entrants to the Faculty of Advocates.[13] Against that background it would have been surprising if canon law had not been a formative force in the development of those aspects of Scots law to which it had relevance. It is, however, often difficult, because of the interaction between them, to distinguish clearly between civil law and canon law influences except where civil law influence can definitely be excluded, as in distinctively canonist doctrines such as putative marriage. Also, there was, particularly in the nineteenth century, a tendency to ascribe directly to the civil law doctrines such as legitimation by subsequent marriage which had found their way into Scots law through the canon law. That tendency may have been due to a prejudice which had developed against canon law despite its use by the commissaries and the institutional writers. In 1772 it was referred to in the Court of Session as "a fouler source".[14] By 1811 familiarity with canon law had so declined that in *Brymer v. Riddell*[15] counsel (shortly afterwards to be elevated to the Bench as Lord Gillies) could profess complete ignorance of it. Yet in 1775 Lord President Dundas had said: "The Canon law is in great measure the law of Scotland."[16] Perhaps, however, it is difficult to improve on Lord Hailes' summary: "The Canon law is not the law of Scotland; but the law of Scotland contains much of the Canon law. This is so certain, that in many cases we determine according to the Canon law without knowing it."[17]

Guardianship, legal representation and capacity of children

1.08   Under the common law, the primary incident of the parent and child relationship was the right of tutory or curatory or, as it might be put, of guardianship. This arises out of both the child's natural need for physical protection and his or her legal need to be represented by someone acting on his or her behalf in the conduct of such affairs as the child has. Originally, Scots law followed Roman law in recognising two forms of guardianship over children, the difference lying in the age of the child subject to guardianship. "Tutor" was the name given to the guardian of a pupil child, while the guardian of a child above the age of pupillarity, a minor *pubes*, was known as "curator". The two offices were distinct, and because of the radical difference in respect of capacity and legal competence which the law marked between a pupil and a minor *pubes*, the powers and functions of a tutor differed greatly from those of a curator. When a pupil reached the age of legal puberty, which was 12 for a girl and 14 for a boy, his or her tutor became his or her curator. "Guardian" was not a term of art in Scots law except for certain specific statutory purposes for which it had the meaning ascribed by the particular statute.[18]

[12] Court of Session Act 1830, s. 33.
[13] Baird Smith, *op. cit.*, p. 191.
[14] *Scrutton v. Gray* (1772) *Hailes' Reports*, i, 499.
[15] February 19, 1811, Fergusson's *Consistorial Law*, 212; Robert Bell, *Report on a Case of Illegitimacy* (1825), pp. 102 and 139. Lord Gillies had, it seems, sought to supply the gap in his knowledge from the extensive canon law collection in the Advocates' Library, only to be overcome by the bulk of the material.
[16] *Maxwell v. Gordon* (1775) *Hailes' Reports*, i, 624.
[17] *ibid.*
[18] See, *e.g.* Adoption (Scotland) Act 1978, s. 65; Education (Scotland) Act 1980, s. 135.

The meaning of "tutory" was derived from the Latin *"tueri"*, to protect or defend. It was "a power and faculty to govern the person, and to manage the estate of a pupil".[19] Curatory, derived from the Latin *"curare"*, to care for or look after, was sometimes described as the power of managing a minor's estate.[20] That description was accurate in so far as it omitted any reference to power over the minor's person, for a curator had no such power.[21] It was, however, misleading if the power of management was understood in the same sense as the virtually complete power of management enjoyed by a tutor. The duty of curators was "to see to the minor's affairs, that they get no detriment",[22] but they could not undertake positive acts of management independently of the minor. Their powers were limited to consenting to, or withholding consent from, transactions that required such consent to be legally valid. The parents of a legitimate child (originally only the father) were the primary guardians, whether tutors or curators. Parents could, however, be displaced, though only in limited circumstances. The methods by which a non-parental tutor or curator could be given to a child, and by which a minor child could escape from curatory, were considered in some detail in the first edition of this book,[23] to which reference can be made. An illegitimate child had no guardians unless appointed by the court.

Developments Since 1991
The common law methods of appointing tutors to pupil children were all **1.09** effectively abolished by the Age of Legal Capacity (Scotland) Act 1991, and in the case of factors *loco tutoris* expressly so.[24] So too was the whole notion of curatory of children, for that Act extended the common law notion of tutory to what it called "guardianship" of all children under the age of 16 years, regardless of sex, and provided that no person shall, by reason of age alone,[25] be subject to the curatory of another person.[26] Tutory therefore became the only form of guardianship of children, though the name itself was dropped in place of, simply, "guardianship". The 1991 Act provided no new name to replace "pupil", except to state that any reference in any rule of law, enactment or document to the tutor of a pupil child should be construed as a reference to the guardian of a person under the age of 16 years.[27] Prior to this, section 8 of the Law Reform (Parent and Child) (Scotland) Act 1986 had defined "parental rights" to mean custody, access, tutory and curatory, indicating a distinction between custody and tutory. The 1991 Act replaced the references to tutory and curatory with the single concept of guardianship, while maintaining its separation from custody. Between September 25, 1991 (when the 1991 Act came into force) and November 1, 1996 (the date of commencement of Part I of the Children (Scotland) Act 1995), therefore, "guardianship" was the term for what was known at common law as tutory, that is to say a right of parents which carried both representational and

---

[19] Erskine, I, vii, 1.
[20] *ibid.*
[21] Stair, I, vi, 35; Erskine, I, vii, 1 and 33; Bell, *Prin.*, para. 2090.
[22] Stair, I, vi, 36.
[23] at pp. 38–47.
[24] Age of Legal Capacity (Scotland) Act 1991, s. 5(4). It should perhaps be noted here that tutors–dative and tutors–legitim can still be appointed to mentally *incapax* adults, and indeed the practice has recently been revived: see Ward, "Revival of Tutors-Dative", 1987 S.L.T. (News) 69 and "Tutors to Adults: Developments", 1992 S.L.T. (News) 325; and see *Britton v. Britton's Curator Bonis*, 1996 S.L.T. 1272, *sub nom. Britton v. Johnstone*, 1992 S.C.L.R. 947, in which Lord Abernethy confirmed the competency of an appointment of a tutor-at-law under the Curators Act 1585.
[25] So retaining the law on guardianship of the incompetent.
[26] s. 5(3).
[27] s. 5(1). Since 1995, this provision has read "shall be construed as a reference to the entitlement to act as a child's legal representative": Children (Scotland) Act 1995, Sched. 4, para. 53.

protective powers, but not necessarily custody rights, and which could, in some circumstances, inhere in persons other than the parents. The 1995 Act changed this understanding of guardianship, which is now an office that carries with it full (including custodial) parental responsibilities and parental rights but which is held only by persons *other than* parents. The representational aspect of tutory is found today in the concept of legal representation, which is one of the individual parental responsibilities and parental rights listed respectively in sections 1 and 2 of the Children (Scotland) Act 1995 and inhering equally in parents and in guardians. Guardians themselves, as parent-substitutes, can no longer be appointed in the various ways that tutors could be appointed. The 1991 Act provides[28] that as from the commencement of the Act (September 25, 1991) no guardian of a person under the age of 16 years shall be appointed except under section 7 of the Children (Scotland) Act 1995. The 1995 Act itself, however, permits appointment of a guardian under both section 7 and section 11(2)(h).[29]

Capacity of children: general

1.10   Children require tutors, guardians or legal representatives only for so long as they are legally incapable of acting for themselves. The capacity of persons for legal acts was determined by Roman law according to a refined system of gradation according to age. There were four main stages: infancy, until the age of seven; pupillarity, which lasted from infancy until the age of 12 for boys and 14 for girls; minority, which extended from the end of pupillarity until majority; and majority, which was reached at the age of 25. Within the stage of pupillarity, distinction was made between those *proximi infantiae* and those *proximi pubertati*. Erskine said that the law of Scotland made some difference in respect of each of the stages of life marked by Roman law, but infancy had little legal significance distinct from pupillarity and distinctions within pupillarity were little regarded.[30] The three stages for Scots common law were, in effect, pupillarity, which lasted from birth until 12 in the case of a girl and 14 in the case of a boy; minority, or puberty, which lasted thereafter until majority; and majority, which, under the law obtaining until January 1, 1970 was reached at the age of 21 and thereafter at 18.[31] The word "minority" was also sometimes applied, as in the doctrine of minority and lesion, as a generic term for all those under the age of majority. A sharp distinction, from the standpoint of capacity, marked off each stage from the others.

Capacity of pupils

1.11   It has been asserted in strong and apparently absolute terms that a pupil had no legal personality. Thus Erskine says: "a pupil has no person, in the legal sense of the word. He is incapable of acting, or even of consenting"[32]; and in *Dalgleish v. Hamilton*[33] in 1752 it was said: "the tutor acts for the pupil, who is himself considered nobody".[34] Stair, however, put the matter more guardedly, and, it is submitted, more correctly, when he spoke of the pupil as "not capable of contracting"[35] or as "having no discretion".[36] There are a number of important

---

[28] s. 5(2), as amended by the Children (Scotland) Act 1995, Sched. 4, para. 53.
[29] See below, para. 7.04–7.29.
[30] Erskine I, vii, 1.
[31] Age of Majority (Scotland) Act 1969, s. 1.
[32] I, vii, 14.
[33] (1752) Mor. 2184.
[34] Even in modern times Lord Cameron can be found saying "in our law a pupil is without legal personality": *Finnie v. Finnie*, 1984 S.L.T. 439 at 441.
[35] I, vi, 4.
[36] I, vi, 35.

respects in which legal personality was to be attributed to a pupil. He or she might be the subject of liability in delict and crime and of remedies in recompense; he or she had, if in a highly qualified sense, personality for the purposes of the conduct of legal proceedings; even his or her lack of contractual capacity was not absolute, and he or she had an extensive passive capacity as recipient and title-holder of property.[37] It may be better to say, not that a pupil lacked personality but that in general he or she lacked capacity to act so as to bind him or herself. To put the matter that way has the advantage of directing attention to the purpose of the law, which was to provide for the pupil's protection.

Of the pupil's general incapacity for contracts and legal acts there was no **1.12** doubt. Erskine, however, posited one exception to that incapacity. He said that all deeds or contracts of a pupil at his own hand were null, in respect that they had no effect against him but were obligatory on the other contractors who might be compelled to perform their parts if the contract were judged to be beneficial to the pupil.[38] He explains the rule, while acknowledging it to be contrary to the nature of contracts, as being based in favour of pupils, "to whom the law has not denied the power of making their condition better, though they cannot make it worse" and also "*in poenam* of those who would impose upon their weakness".[39] Erskine's doctrine was adopted by Fraser[40] and, although general observations about the absolute incapacity of pupils in institutional and other writers and judicial dicta can be cited against it, it was judicially approved, albeit *obiter*, in *Drummond's Trustees v. Peel's Trustees*.[41] It consisted with the protective function of the law and is unequivocally vouched by its Roman law origins.[42] Without it, ready money transactions with pupils, which must have occurred often, would have been wholly insecure and difficult to explain. The criticism that the mutuality of obligation in the contract was undermined does not have much weight, as the same argument could be urged against other doctrines for the protection of pupils and minors, such as reduction on proof of minority and lesion, and it was a risk which those who contracted with pupils must be deemed to have undertaken. It was, of course, implicit in this doctrine of *negotium claudicans* that if the pupil sought to enforce the obligation he must himself have been willing to perform his part. The decision to enforce the obligation for the pupil's benefit was therefore a decision which only the tutor could take. Where performance by both parties had taken place at the time of the contract, as in a ready money transaction, the tutor could affirm or reject the bargain, at least if *restitutio in integrum* were possible. The rule accords with the English rule that "an infant's contract is at common law generally voidable at the instance of the infant, though binding upon the other party".[43]

Under the Sale of Goods Act 1979[44] a pupil was liable to pay a reasonable **1.13** price for goods supplied which were necessaries, and which were suitable to the child's condition of life and his or her actual requirements at the time of sale and delivery. A pupil had, therefore, a capacity to contract for such necessaries although

---

[37] Since the commencement of the Age of Legal Capacity (Scotland) Act 1991, the capacity of pupil children has been extended to all children under the age of 16, and s. 1(3)(e) of that Act provides that nothing in it shall "prevent any person under the age of 16 years from receiving or holding any right title or interest". This provision represents, it is submitted, no change in the law.

[38] I, vii, 33.

[39] *ibid.*

[40] (3rd ed.), pp. 205–206.

[41] 1929 S.C. 484.

[42] Inst. I, 21: "*unde in his causis ex quibus obligationes mutuae nascuntur...si tutoris auctoritas non interveniat, ipsi quidem, qui cum his contrahunt, obligantur, at invicem pupilli non obligantur*".

[43] *Halsbury's Laws of England* (4th ed.), p. 168, s. 407.

[44] s. 31 (original text); now amended by the Age of Legal Capacity (Scotland) Act 1991.

whatever the bargain might say he or she would be bound to pay no more than a reasonable price. More generally, where a pupil had benefited from work done or goods supplied under a purported contract which was null because of his or her incapacity, he or she might be liable *quantum lucratus* on principles of recompense.[45]

1.14   As regards the pupil's capacity in judicial proceedings, it was commonly said that a pupil had no *persona standi in judicio*. That could, however, be accepted, if at all, only in a highly qualified sense.[46] There was no radical incompetency in an instance in the name of a pupil. Beyond that the authorities, although reasonably clear in their particular applications, might be thought not to yield any coherent general doctrine. The correct view, it is submitted, was that a pupil had *persona standi* but lacked capacity to enter into *litis contestatio*. For practical purposes, however, the particular rules sufficed, even if they showed some obscurities or inconsistencies in the doctrine they represented. Actions in right of a pupil who had tutors were properly brought by the tutors in their capacity as such. Where the child's tutors were his or her parents, as would usually be the case after 1974[47] where both parents were alive, the instance might be taken in the name of either parent as tutor and administrator-in-law or of both. In other cases of a plurality of tutors, it would be a question of the terms of their appointment whether the action had to be raised in name of all the tutors, or of a majority, or of a quorum. There was, however, no fundamental nullity in proceedings in name of the pupil alone,[48] and where an action had been raised in the pupil's own name, the tutor might subsequently be sisted as pursuer.[49] An instance in the name of the pupil with consent or concurrence of the tutor was not in proper form but had been allowed as substantially sufficient.[50]

Capacity of minors

1.15   There was a marked contrast in respect of legal capacity between a pupil and a minor *pubes*. Whereas a pupil lacked, with certain exceptions which have been noticed, all legal capacity, minors were in principle *sui juris* and capable of legal acts. However, where a minor had curators his or her contractual capacity was with some exceptions dependent on their concurrence (in the case of parents, the concurrence of either parent). Capacity to raise or defend legal proceedings was similarly restricted. The contractual capacity of a minor who had no curators was as extensive as if he or she were major.[51] The only limitation was a practical one: that in some transactions persons might hesitate to contract with a minor because of the risk of reduction on the ground of minority and lesion. The position of a minor whose curators concurred in his or her acts was identical with that of a minor who had no curators. So their concurrence made perfect his or her capacity which without it would have been defective, and he or she could then act with the same freedom as one who was major.

1.16   Where a minor who had curators acted without concurrence in relation to any part of his or her property, the general rule was that the transaction was null.[52] The nullity was, however, pleadable only at the instance of the minor and not of the party with whom he or she had contracted. There was, therefore, a

---

[45] Stair, I, viii, 6.
[46] *Drummond's Trs v. Peel's Trs*, 1929 S.C. 484, *per* Lord President Clyde at 493.
[47] Guardianship Act 1973, s. 10(1), commenced May 8, 1974.
[48] *Drummond's Trs v. Peel's Trs*, above.
[49] Fraser (3rd ed.), p. 208.
[50] *Keith v. Archer* (1836) 15 S. 116. There were a number of situations in which an action would, and should, have been raised in the name of the pupil him or herself, and these are described in the 1st edition of this book, at pp. 56–57.
[51] Stair, I, vi, 32; Erskine, I, vii, 33.
[52] Stair, I, vi, 33. This rule was subject to various exceptions, as detailed in the 1st edition of this book, at pp. 61–62.

negotium claudicans and the minor might if he or she so elected insist on performance. Fraser[53] so states the law, and although in one passage it is contraverted by Bell[54] it is supported by Stair[55] (who says that deeds done without the consent of curators were null by exception in a context which clearly indicates exception at the instance of the minor), as well as by Erskine[56] and Bankton.[57] Where the minor elected to enforce the contract he or she was, of course, obliged to carry out his or her part of the bargain.

Reduction on the ground of minority and lesion

Following the Roman law, the common law of Scotland allowed for the **1.17** reduction of transactions entered into by persons below the age of majority or on their behalf if these transactions resulted in severe prejudice, or "enorm lesion".[58] "Minority" in the term "minority and lesion" meant the whole period of non-age and so relief might be granted against (i) deeds entered into by tutors on behalf of pupils; (ii) deeds of a minor *pubes* where the minor, having no curator, acted alone; and (iii) deeds of a minor *pubes* where he or she had curators and acted with their concurrence. In each case the requirements were the same in principle although where curators had concurred, and also where a tutor had acted on behalf of a pupil, proof of lesion might be more difficult to establish. There was, of course, no need for this remedy where the transaction was absolutely null, as in nearly all contracts of pupils acting alone and most contracts of a minor who had curators but acted without their concurrence.

The transaction had to be challenged before the end of the *quadriennium utile*, **1.18** that is, the four-year period after the attaining of majority, and though there was some conflict of authority as to whether the challenge could be made before majority, reduction was sought before majority, and not denied for that reason, in *McFeetridge v. Stewarts and Lloyds Ltd*,[59] and in *Patrick v. William Baird & Co.*[60] Where a person to whom the privilege was competent died before invoking it, the right to do so passed to his or her representatives.[61] Unless they were themselves minor, they had to take proceedings for reduction within a *quadriennium utile* running from the date of the deceased's death or, if the deceased had passed majority, within the unexpired period of the *quadriennium utile* available to him or her immediately before death; they could not take advantage of any unexpired part of the deceased's minority. Where they were themselves minor, they had the use in their own right of any unexpired portion of their own minority but could take advantage of the *quadriennium utile* only to the extent that it would have been available to the deceased immediately before his or her death.[62]

There were certain circumstances in which transactions could not be reduced **1.19** on the ground of minority and lesion. These were:

(1) where the loss was caused not by the minority of the child but by some extraneous factor, such as *damnum fatale*[63]; (2) where the transaction was in the course of the minor's trade, business or profession[64]; (3) where the

---

[53] (3rd ed.), p. 495.
[54] *Prin.*, para. 2089. But see *Comm.* (7th ed.), Book I, p. 129.
[55] I, vi, 33.
[56] I, vii, 33.
[57] I, vii, 56.
[58] Erskine, I, vii, 34; Fraser (3rd ed.), pp. 498–541.
[59] 1913 S.C. 773.
[60] 1926 S.N. 101.
[61] Stair, I, vi, 44; Erskine, I, vii, 47.
[62] Erskine I, vii, 42.
[63] Stair, I, vi, 44; Bankton, I, vii, 77; Erskine, I, vii, 36; *Edgar v. Executors of Edgar* (1614) M. 8986.
[64] *McFeetridge v. Stewarts and Lloyds Ltd*, 1913 S.C. 773. For particular applications of this rule, see the 1st edition of this book, at p. 64.

transaction created an obligation to tradesmen for necessaries[65]; (4) where the minor induced the other party to enter into the contract by fraud, at least in relation to the minor's age[66]; (5) where the contract was ratified or homologated by the minor after attaining majority in the knowledge of his or her right of reduction[67]; and (6) where the transaction was of its nature unchallengable on this ground alone (*e.g.* the marriage or the testament of the minor could not be reduced on the ground of minority and lesion).

The modern law

1.20   In common with many other aspects of the law of parent and child, guardianship, legal representation and capacity of children have now been put on an almost entirely statutory basis. Capacity is governed by the Age of Legal Capacity (Scotland) Act 1991, while guardianship and legal representation are governed by Part I of the Children (Scotland) Act 1995. The substantive rules contained in these measures are considered in their appropriate contexts later.

Custody of children

Custody at common law[68]

1.21   At common law, custody was properly applicable only to pupil children.[69] The *patria potestas* which belonged to the father and could not in its fullness be conferred on anyone else admitted, however, of such control over minors above the age of pupillarity that they could, if in a somewhat weaker sense than in the case of pupils, be said to be in their father's custody. After remarking that a minor whose father was dead, or was emancipated, was, subject to some qualifications, a person *sui juris* and free to choose his or her place of residence (something inconsistent with being in the custody of another), the consulted judges in *Craig v. Greig and McDonald*[70] said: "No doubt, if his father be alive, and the minor be not emancipated, there is greater restraint upon his personal liberty by reason of the influence of the *patria potestas*... he is not free to choose his place of residence, as a minor is who is subject only to the guardianship of curators." The extent of this paternal restraint on the minor *pubes* was not clearly defined. It grew weaker as the minor advanced in years and discretion but, during the lifetime of the father, it was not completely lost until majority or forisfamiliation. Until then, at least the vestiges of what could be characterised as custody might be said to remain. Accordingly cases are to be found in which a father sought to assert a claim to the custody of his child who was a minor *pubes*.[71] In contrast, however, with a

---

[65] Fraser (3rd ed.), p. 525.

[66] See Stair, I, vi, 44; Gloag, *Contract* (2nd ed.), p. 89.

[67] Stair, I, vi, 44; Bankton, I, vii, 90.

[68] A rather fuller account of the common law than is given here may be found in the 1st edition of this book, at pp. 68–73.

[69] The pupil child was not *sui juris* and so could be subjected not only to the dominion of his or her father but, on the failure of the father, to the custody of others. In contrast, the minor *pubes* was *sui juris* in relation to his or her personal freedom except in so far as that was restrained by the *patria potestas*. The institutional writers are at variance as to how long that restraint was effective to give the father a right of custody. Stair (I, v, 13) thought there was no doubt that, unless the child was forisfamiliated or the father had abused his power, children could be compelled to remain with their parents even after majority. To him therefore only the father's death or forisfamiliation could bring custody to an end; but no later authority supports that view. Erksine (I, vii, 1) thought that the compelling power of the father over his issue lasted only until majority. Bankton (I, vi, 1), while allowing an extensive authority of the father over his children, even if major, so long as they remained in his house, held that the father could not after their pupillarity detain them in his family against their will; custody therefore ended with pupillarity. More (*Notes on Stair*, p. xxxi; *Lectures*, I, p. 87) was of the same opinion as Bankton. By the mid-19th century the question had been resolved as indicated in the text.

[70] (1863) 1 M. 1172, *per* Lord Justice-Clerk Inglis and Lords Benholme and Mackenzie at 1179.

[71] *Harvey v. Harvey* (1860) 22 D. 1198; *Edgar v. Fisher's Trs* (1894) 21 R. 1076.

father's claim to the custody of his pupil children, which might be refused only if to grant it would place the children's moral or physical welfare in serious jeopardy, his claim to the custody of a minor *pubes* might be refused on "good and sufficient grounds" among which the reasonable wishes of the child were a material element.[72]

The pure doctrine of the common law was that the minor *pubes*, again in **1.22** contrast with a pupil child, could not be subjected to the custody of anyone other than his or her father. The source of all claims to custody was in the *patria potestas* which was inalienable. Apart from the *patria potestas* the child's personal freedom was subject to no restraint—once beyond pupillarity *intellegitur venisse in suam tutelam et esse in sua ipsius custodia.*[73] In two cases in the last decade of the nineteenth century[74] applications for the custody of minors were, however, entertained, although in neither was the petitioner the minor's father. They were refused on their merits without consideration of the question of competency. Such willingness as they show to contemplate applications by persons other than the minor's father may be ascribed to an awareness that cases might occur in which there was no alternative consonant with the increased emphasis which was by then placed on the welfare of the child. To take an extreme but apt example, the difficulty was evident of turning away as incompetent a custody application by a relative of a 12-year-old girl which was the only means of saving her from grave moral or physical danger. Yet the court's powers were seen as clearly circumscribed. It needed "a very strong case"[75] to justify intervention against the will of the minor. In general, the opposition even of a 12-year-old girl was a "supreme difficulty".[76]

The effect of the *patria potestas* was such that during the father's lifetime **1.23** there was only very limited scope for custody disputes. His right to custody of his legitimate child could be denied only on proof of serious physical or moral danger to the child.[77] What was true of the father of a legitimate child was, despite the absence of any equivalent of the *patria potestas*, largely true, so far as custody was concerned, of the mother of an illegitimate child.[78] Because of the supremacy of the paternal right questions of who other than the father might be entitled to custody could arise at common law only if the father died or became disqualified as custodian (because to enforce his right would involve serious physical or moral danger to the child) or, on a temporary basis, in the event of his inability or unwillingness to exercise his right. In the event of the father's disqualification or incapacity it was usually to the mother, if she was

---

[72] *Edgar v. Fisher's Trs*, above, *per* Lord McLaren at 1079; Fraser, p. 76, n. 1.

[73] *Newton v. Ker* (1533) Mor. 16218; *Mathieson v. Wedderby* (1534) Mor. 16218 (note); *Graham v. Graham* (1780) Mor. 8934; *Harvey v. Harvey*, above, *per* Lord Justice-Clerk Inglis at 1208; *Craig v. Greig and McDonald*, above, *per* Lord Justice-Clerk Inglis and Lords Benholme and Mackenzie at 1179.

[74] *Flannigan v. Muir* (1892) 19 R. 909; *Morrison v. Quarrier* (1894) 21 R. 1071.

[75] *Flannigan v. Muir*, above, *per* Lord President Robertson at 912.

[76] *Morrison v. Quarrier*, above, *per* Lord President Robertson at 1074.

[77] *Leys v. Leys* (1886) 13 R. 1223; *Lang v. Lang* (1869) 7 M. 445; *Steuart v. Steuart* (1870) 8 M. 821; *Pagan v. Pagan* (1883) 10 R. 1072; *Nicholson v. Nicholson* (1869) 7 M. 1118.

[78] The law as here stated is as laid down in *Corrie v. Adair* (1860) 22 D. 897, especially *per* Lord Justice-Clerk Inglis at 900 and Lord Cowan at 901, and subsequent cases. See also *Simpson v. Cassels* (1865) 3 M. 396; *Grant v. Yuill* (1872) 10 M. 511; *Westlands v. Pirie* (1887) 14 R. 763; *McCarroll v. Kerr* (1877) 15 S.L.R.106; *Brown v. Halbert* (1896) 23 R. 733; *Millar v. Melville* (1898) 1 F. 367; *Moncrieff v. Langlands* (1900) 2 F. 1111. Before that, although the preponderant view was the same, there had been some conflict of judicial opinion. According to one view, the mother's custody of the child was not a matter of law but merely a recognition of the generally appropriate natural arrangement. On that view the mother properly had no right and custody could be regulated according to the circumstances under the general superintendence of the court. Sometimes it was said, with surprising modernity, that the only question was what was best for the child. Therefore the putative father, although he too properly had no right, could apply for custody and, if he could show that he would make superior arrangements, might be preferred. The conflict in judicial opinion is seen in three cases all reported in 4 S.: *Whitson v. Speid* (1825) 4 S. 42;

alive, that custody passed.[79] Beyond that, in cases other than on the death of the father, the law provided no clear rules. Once the *patria potestas* was laid aside there was room for judicial discretion. It consists, however, with the rules applicable on the death of the father that in the event of his disqualification or incapacity, the mother's relatives should, on the failure of the mother, have been preferred in a competition with others.[80] On the death of the father, the general rule was that custody of children under seven years of age passed to the mother.[81] There was a strong presumption on which the rule was based, that that was in the interests of the child. Even over the age of seven, the mother would have custody unless some special cause were shown that to give her custody would be disadvantageous to the child.[82] These rules, however, suffered some exceptions if the mother remarried,[83] and were largely superseded if the father had left directions as to custody. The policy of the law in the latter event was to give effect to the father's wishes and so to give custody to his nominee.[84] By 1845, however, it was doubted whether the father's specific direction must prevail so as to deprive the mother of custody in the case of a child under seven[85] and it was not enough to defeat the mother's claim that the father had nominated tutors.[86] On the failure of the mother, for whatever cause, and in the absence of any express direction by the father, custody passed to the child's tutors. The law took, however, an unsentimental and cautious view of human nature in relation to the custody of tutors. A tutor who was next in succession to the child was deemed to be an admirable guardian of the child's estate which he had every interest to preserve, but to be wholly unfit to be a guardian of the child's person as his interest ran contrary to the continuance of the child in life. Indeed Fraser, borrowing from Blackstone,[87] says that to give custody to such a person would be *"agnum lupo committere ad devorandum"*. Accordingly not only tutors who took office by operation of law in the absence or failure of the father's nomination (tutors-at-law) but also tutors appointed by the court (tutors-dative) and tutors nominated by the father (tutors-nominate) were excluded from custody if they stood next in succession or had the same interest in the ward's estate as a person next in succession would have.[88] Moreover, there was a wider

---

Baxter v. Dougal's Trs (1825) 4 S. 139; and *Fairweather v. Lyall* (1826) 4 S. 614. See also generally *Burges v. Halliday* (1758) Mor. 1357; *Oliver v. Scott* (1778) Mor. 444; *Caldwell v. Stewart* (1773) 5 Mor. Supp. 390; *Kidston v. Smith* (1778) 5 Mor. Supp. 390; *Ballantyne v. Malcolm* (1803) Hume 425; *Wilson v. Bowie* (1810) Hume 426; *Goadby v. Macandys*, July 7, 1815, F.C., 482; *Hunter's Trs v. Speed*, Dec. 2, 1820, F.C., 211; *Keay v. Watson* (1825) 3 S. 561; *Rankine v. AB* (1833) 5 Sc.Jur. 363; *Pott v. Pott* (1833) 12 S. 183; *Weepers v. Heritors of Kennoway* (1844) 6 D. 1166.

[79] *AB v. CD* (1850) 12 D. 1297. *Cf. Cameron, Petr* (1847) 9 D. 1401; *Baillie v. Agnew* (1775) 5 Mor. Supp. 526; *Craig v. Thompson* (1829) 1 Sc.Jur. 201.

[80] For the practice on the father's death and failure of mother and tutors, see *Higgins v. Boyd* (1821) 1 S. 50 and *Gibson v. Dunnett* (1824) 3 S. 249. Even during the father's lifetime cognates might be preferred to agnates because of the latters' interest in succession.

[81] The rule is ancient: *Foreman v. Oliphant* (1527) Mor. 16216; *Durie v. Laird of Dowhill and Lochlevin* (1517) Mor. 16216; *The King and Tullibarden v. Laird of Wedderburne* (1516) Mor. 16216. See also *Scot v. Scot* (1759) 5 Mor. Supp. 872; *Borthwick v. Dundas* (1845) 8 D. 318.

[82] Erskine, I, vii, 7; *Campbell v. Campbell* (1833) 11 S. 544; Fraser, pp. 288 and 289.

[83] Erskine, *ibid.*; *Fulderton v. Boyne* (1675) Mor. 16291; *Langshaw v. Muir* (1629) Mor. 16252; *Finnie v. Oliphant* (1631) Mor. 406; but the rule applied only in a question with tutors qualified to have custody. See *Johnston v. Otto* (1849) 11 D. 718 and *McCallum v. McDonald* (1853) 15 D. 535.

[84] *A v. B* (1553) Mor. 16224; Balfour, CXXIII, p. 336.

[85] *Borthwick v. Dundas* (1845) 8 D. 318, *per* Lords Mackenzie, Fullerton and Jeffrey at 320; *contra, per* Lord President Boyle at 319.

[86] *Borthwick v. Dundas*, above, on this point, in contrast with the earlier rule (*Langshaw v. Muir*, above).

[87] Fraser (3rd ed.), p. 292; Blackstone, I, c., 17; *Robertson v. Elphinstone*, May 28, 1814, F.C. 631, *per* Lord Meadowbank at 636.

[88] Stair, I, vi, 15; Erskine, I, vii, 7; Bankton, I, vii, 28; Craig, II, xx, 6; Reg. Maj., II, xlvii, 4; Balfour, CXXVI, p. 337, citing *Clepan v. Laird & Wymis* (1551) Mor. 16227 and *Dishington v. Hamilton* (1558) Mor. 8913; *Chalmers v. Gadgirth* (1611) Mor. 16239; *Edgar v. Inglis* (1606) Mor. 16237; *Dury v. Dury* (1666) Mor. 16277; *Taylor v. Forrester* (1622) Mor. 16242.

field for the exercise of judicial discretion in the control of the custody of tutors, and in deciding on applications by them in competition with other claimants, than there was for interference with the father's powers during his lifetime.[89] A tutor disqualified from taking actual custody might, nonetheless, be entitled to fix a suitable place of residence for the pupil.[90] If the tutor was disqualified, the nearest cognate was preferred.[91]

The common law had no rules for determining custody on the death or other **1.24** failure of the mother of an illegitimate child. The illegitimate child had no tutors-at-law and it was undecided whether the mother could nominate tutors or other persons to act as custodians after her death.[92] Although neither the father nor, after his death, his relatives[93] had any right to custody during the mother's lifetime, they might make a claim after her death, but were not entitled to any special consideration. The law did not recognise any familial relationship between the illegitimate child and others apart from the natural bond with the mother and the obligation of the father to aliment. In strict contemplation of the law the illegitimate child had no relatives and, in the absence of the mother, responsibility for the care of the child rested, subject to the father's alimentary obligation, with the community as a whole—*filius nullius filius populi*. In the event of claimants for custody coming forward, a choice could, therefore, be made in the free exercise of a judicial discretion.

Statutory modifications of the common law

The common law has now been almost entirely superseded by statute, and **1.25** all issues relating to parental responsibilities and parental rights, including those previously embraced within custody, are now governed by the Children (Scotland) Act 1995. Instead of concentrating on a right of custody, and determining the strengths of competing rights, the law today determines the matter from the child's, rather than the parents', point of view, in particular by applying the welfare principle. This position came about only gradually.

The first inroad on the pre-eminent right of the father of the legitimate child **1.26** was made by the Conjugal Rights (Scotland) Amendment Act 1861, which provided[94] that in any action for separation or divorce the court might make such provision "as to it shall seem just and proper" with respect to the custody, maintenance and education of any pupil children of the marriage.[95] By the Guardianship of Infants Act 1886[96] the court was empowered, on the application of the mother or of the father of any pupil child (later child under the age of 16)[97] to make such order as it might think fit regarding the child's custody, having regard to the welfare of the child and to the conduct of the parents and to the wishes as well of the mother as of the father. These Acts, together with the Custody of Children Act 1891,[98] were all in terms which enlarged the powers of the court in the cases to which they applied so as to enable it, where appropriate, to modify or set aside the rights of the father and give greater weight to *inter*

---

[89] *Black v. Ferguson* (1866) 4 M. 807, *per* Lord Deas at 809.
[90] *Walker v. Walker* (1824) 2 S. 788.
[91] *Higgins v. Boyd* (1821) 1 S. 50; *Gibson v. Dunnett* (1824) 3 S. 249.
[92] *Brand v. Shaws* (1888) 15 R. 449, *per* Lord President Inglis at 454.
[93] *Goadby v. Macandys,* July 7, 1815, F.C. 482.
[94] s. 9.
[95] This provision was amended by the Law Reform (Parent and Child) (Scotland) Act 1986, Sched. 1, para. 2 and re-enacted as s. 20 of the Court of Session Act 1988; s. 20 was itself repealed by the Children (Scotland) Act 1995, Sched. 5.
[96] s. 49 (repealed by the Law Reform (Parent and Child) (Scotland) Act 1986, Sched. 2).
[97] The court's power to make orders as to the custody of (or maintenance or education of, or access to) pupil children was extended to children under the age of 16 by the Custody of Children Act 1939, s. 1(1).
[98] s. 3 (repealed by the Children Act 1989, Sched. 15).

alia the welfare of the child. Although it had been held in the Court of Session that the effect of the 1861 Act was purely jurisdictional and did not give the court any wider powers than it possessed at common law,[99] that view is irreconcilable with the decision and with the preponderance of the speeches in *Symington v. Symington* in which Lord Cairns L.C. said that:

> "the Act of Parliament has given the Court the widest and the most general discretion, and has purposely done so… It must be the duty of the Court in every case to consider the whole of the circumstances of the particular case before it—the circumstances of the misconduct which leads to a separation no doubt, the circumstances of the general character of the father, the circumstances of the general character of the mother, and, above all, it should be the duty of the Court to look to the interest of the children."[1]

In practice, however, after 1861 and even after the decision of the House of Lords in *Symington*, great weight was attached to the father's right and it was often no less conclusive than it would have been at common law.[2] The 1886 Act was more influential than its predecessor both in enlarging the claims of the mother as against the father of a legitimate child and in the stress to be put on the child's welfare to which, unlike the 1861 Act, it explicitly referred. Lindley L.J. could say "the dominant matter for the consideration of the Court is the welfare of the child"[3] and that "it is essentially a mother's Act".[4] These observations were, of course, only true in questions between father and mother which were the questions with which the Act was concerned. After some hesitation[5] a similar view prevailed in Scotland. "The first consideration", the Lord President said in *Reid v. Reid*,[6] "is the welfare of the children, though no doubt the wishes of the spouses are also to be taken into account." The Act so interpreted gave expression to what had in any event been a trend in judicial decision. At common law the rights of the father, although often strictly applied, were open to some latitude of interpretation. Danger to physical or moral welfare was a question of degree. It ordinarily could arise only if there were fault on the part of the father but again culpability was a question of degree. There was occasional opportunity, which some judges took, for what was essentially a welfare judgment. In *Smart v. Smart*[7] Lord Hobhouse ascribed to judicial decision as well as to legislative action and general opinion a tendency in family questions "to bring the marital duty of the husband and the welfare of the children into greater prominence; in both respects diminishing the powers accorded to the husband and the father". That tendency was aided by an indirect influence of the legislation even in cases to which it did not in terms apply. In such a case the statute was not "to be altogether laid aside" but was occasion for administering the law "within temperate limits so as to adapt it to modern views".[8]

1.27   There was, however, a competing line of authority which led to results little different from those of the older cases. Some judges were persuaded that the 1886 Act had made little difference to the common law except, perhaps, in giving the mother a

---

[99] *Lang v. Lang* (1869) 7 M. 445; *cf. Steuart v. Steuart* (1870) 8 M. 821.

[1] (1875) 2 R. (H.L.) 41 at 43.

[2] *e.g. Lang v. Lang*, above; *Steuart v. Steuart*, above; *Bowman v. Graham* (1883) 10 R. 1234; *Beattie v. Beattie* (1883) 11 R. 85. *Cf. Ketchen v. Ketchen* (1870) 8 M. 952, *contra*.

[3] *Re McGrath (Infants)* [1893] 1 Ch. 143 at 148.

[4] *Re A and B Infants* [1897] 1 Ch. 786 at 790. *Cf.* Rigby L.J. at 792: "The Act goes very far indeed in diminution of the rights of the father, and in conferring new rights—I will not say equal rights, but new and important rights—upon the mother."

[5] See *Stevenson v. Stevenson* (1894) 21 R. 430, overruled (1894) 21 R. (H.L.) 96.

[6] (1901) 3 F. 330 at 332.

[7] [1892] A.C. 425 at 432.

[8] *Brand v. Shaws* (1888) 16 R. 315, *per* Lord Shand at 323.

rather stronger claim in a question with the father. That conclusion could be reached by allowing that there had been some development in the common law while, at the same time, interpreting the 1886 Act so as to retain a prominent place for the primary right of the father.[9] And there was, indeed, a view on which even the strictest standards of the common law could be reconciled with the statute. The father's right to custody, although, as part of the *patria potestas*, derived from the Roman law and ultimately from an archaic concept of the family, had for long been justified on the view that it was for the child's welfare. The father, it was held, was the best judge of what was in the interests of the child. The court interfered where the child's welfare was seriously endangered by the father's conduct, not because the law was otherwise neglectful of the interests of the child but because, unless there was clear evidence that the father was abusing his position, interference by the court would be to substitute an inferior for a superior view of where those interests lay.[10] Considerations of that kind were seldom expressly avowed in judicial opinions after 1886 but their persisting influence lurks behind many of the decisions. The law before 1925 presents, therefore, a somewhat confused picture so far as custody disputes between parents of legitimate children are concerned. Statute had opened the way for a wider consideration of the child's welfare and the claims of the mother and judicial dicta had laid some stress on both, but the interpretation had often been such as to retain a strong position for the primacy of the father's right and many of the decisions showed little advance on the common law.

The Guardianship of Infants Act 1886 applied only to disputes between **1.28** parents of legitimate children. In a question with third parties, the father's right was before 1925 unaffected by statute except that, under the Custody of Children Act 1891[11] where a parent had abandoned or deserted his child or allowed his child to be brought up by another person, at that person's expense, for such a length of time and under such circumstances as to satisfy the court that the parent was unmindful of his parental duties, the onus shifted to the parent of showing that he was a fit person to have the custody of the child. In considering whether that onus had been discharged regard had to be had to the welfare of the child. With that exception, there was, before 1925, little move away from the nearly absolute nature of the father's right in a question with third parties.

So far as illegitimate children were concerned, there was also little change before **1.29** 1925. Their position was not affected directly by statute, apart from the 1891 Act.[12] In *Campbell v. Croall*[13] under the 1891 Act and in *Sutherland v. Taylor*[14] at common law (each case at the instance of the mother of illegitimate children) custody was refused on grounds that stressed children's interests as a central consideration but the circumstances of each case were such, in respect of the danger to the children's health, that refusal would have been the likely result even at an earlier period of the law's development. As late as 1921 arrangements for the care of an illegitimate child, which had lasted, without any cause for complaint, for over 10 years, were disturbed and custody granted to the child's mother after some inquiry into whether the mother was in a position to make effectual plans for the child's welfare but without further consideration of where the child's interest lay; and one of the judges was of the opinion that the prayer of the petition ought to have been granted *de plano*.[15]

---

[9] *Sleigh v. Sleigh* (1893) 30 S.L.R. 272; *Mackellar v. Mackellar* (1898) 25 R. 883.

[10] That this is still at least a starting-point can be seen from the following comment of Lord Fraser of Tullybelton in *Gillick v. West Norfolk and Wisbech Area Health Authority* [1985] 3 All E.R. 402 at 412: "Nobody doubts, certainly I do not doubt, that in the overwhelming majority of cases the best judges of a child's welfare are his or her parents."

[11] s. 3.

[12] The Guardianship of Infants Act 1886 "does not apply to illegitimate children": *Brand v. Shaws* (1888) 16 R. 315 at 320 and 323.

[13] (1895) 22 R. 869.

[14] (1887) 15 R. 224.

[15] *Walter v. Culbertson*, 1921 S.C. 490.

1.30   The most significant statutory departure from the common law was the
Guardianship of Infants Act 1925, section 1 of which required that the court
regard the welfare of the child as the first and paramount consideration and also
that it was not to take into consideration whether from any other point of view
the claim of the father was superior to that of the mother or the claim of the
mother was superior to that of the father. As originally enacted, the section also
excluded from consideration, otherwise than from the point of view of the child's
welfare, any right at common law possessed by the father, but that was deleted
as no longer necessary by the Guardianship Act 1973,[16] which gave the mother
equality of parental rights and authority with the father. Not only, therefore,
was consideration of the child's welfare given precedence over all other questions
but, in disputes between father and mother, regard for the welfare of the child
was in future to be the sole basis for giving preference to the one or the other on
general grounds. It appeared, however, that, if only rarely, preference could
still be given to one parent or the other on grounds other than welfare according
to the circumstances of the particular case. Matters such as the conduct of the
spouses to each other or responsibility for the breakdown of the marriage were
primarily to be considered in the context of the child's welfare[17] and usually
that would exhaust the scope for their consideration. Exceptionally, however,
although always postponed to and subject to consistency with the child's welfare,
they were independently taken into account.

1.31   Section 1 of the Guardianship of Infants Act 1925 applied in any proceeding
before any court where *inter alia* the custody or upbringing of a child was in
question. Despite the generality of these words, a number of cases proceeded
on the view, or at least on the assumption, that the section applied only to disputes
between parents of legitimate children.[18] A similar view had been taken in
England.[19] That view was based on the concluding words of the section which
could only be applied to disputes between parents and on the requirement[20] that
the Act be construed as one with the Guardianship of Infants Act 1886 whose
custody provisions were confined to disputes between parents.[21] In *J v. C*,[22]
however, it was held that the words of the section must receive their natural
meanings so as to apply to disputes between parents and third parties as well as
between parents *inter se*. It was applicable, as it says, to any proceedings before
any court where the custody or upbringing of a child is in question irrespective
of whether or not the claimants, or any of them, are parents and irrespective of
whether or not the child is legitimate. Originally the Act only applied to pupil
children[23] but it was later extended to children under 16 years of age.[24] The
1925 Act was repealed by the Law Reform (Parent and Child) (Scotland) Act
1986, section 3 of which gave the court a general power to make such order
relating to parental rights as it thought fit, regarding the welfare of the child as
the paramount consideration and making no order unless it is satisfied that to
do so will be in the interests of the child. Though section 3 is now repealed, this
still represents the modern law.

---

[16] s. 10(8) (repealed by the Law Reform (Parent and Child) (Scotland) Act 1986).

[17] *Christison v. Christison*, 1936 S.C. 381; *McLean v. McLean*, 1947 S.C. 79.

[18] *Hume v. Hume*, 1926 S.C. 1008; *McLean v. Hardie*, 1927 S.C. 344; *Pow v. Pow*, 1931 S.L.T. 485;
Nicol v. Nicol, 1953 S.L.T.(Notes) 67 ("Assuming that s. 1 of the 1925 Act does not apply");
McNaught v. McNaught, 1955 S.L.T. (Sh.Ct) 9; *Macallister v. Macallister*, 1962 S.C. 406.

[19] *In Re Carroll* [1931] 1 K.B. 317, *per* Scrutton L.J. at 335–337, and Slesser L.J. at 355 and 362.

[20] s. 11(2).

[21] That the 1886 Act was so restricted was reasonably clear from its terms. In *Brand v. Shaws*
(1886) 16 R. 315 it was held that the 1886 Act had no application to an illegitimate child.

[22] [1970] A.C. 668.

[23] s. 11, incorporating the Guardianship of Infants Act 1886, s. 8.

[24] Custody of Children (Scotland) Act 1939, s. 1(1).

Custodial rights relating to children whose parents are not married to each **1.32** other have also been modified by statute although less radically than in the case of "legitimate" children. By the Illegitimate Children (Scotland) Act 1930[25] the right of the father of an illegitimate child to meet a claim for aliment by the mother by an offer to assume custody of the child was abolished. By the same Act,[26] the court was empowered on an application by the mother or by the father to make such order as it may think fit regarding custody of an illegitimate child having regard to the welfare of the child and to the conduct of the parties and to the wishes as well of the mother as of the father. Section 1(1) of the Law Reform (Parent and Child) (Scotland) Act 1986 attempted to equalise the position in relation to the two classes of children, by providing that "the fact that a person's parents are not or have not been married to one another shall be left out of account in establishing the legal relationship between the person and any other person; and accordingly any such relationship shall have effect as if the parents were or had been married to one another".

Later developments

In the latter part of the twentieth century a philosophical shift can be detected **1.33** in the law's approach to the parent and child relationship, similar to that of a century previously when the absolute nature of the father's right began to give way to considerations of the child's welfare. Though as late as 1986 statute continued to talk exclusively in terms of parents' rights,[27] these were coming to be seen more as powers, appropriate to parents in order to allow them to fulfil their parental responsibilities, which had come to be recognised as the primary determinant of the parent and child relationship.[28] In addition, greater emphasis was coming to be placed on the notion of children's rights, as recognised by the ratification by the U.K. Government[29] of the United Nations Convention on the Rights of the Child. Most particularly, the right of the child to express a view in legal proceedings the outcome of which would personally affect him or her[30] was recognised as more than simply a factor to be taken into account in determining where the child's welfare lay and was given express, and separate, effect in the Children (Scotland) Act 1995. Part I of this Act contains the modern law of parental responsibilities and parental rights in Scotland, that is to say parental powers and duties in relation to the upbringing of children, the administration of their affairs and the regulation of both by the court. The welfare of the child remains, of course, the court's paramount consideration, and the court is also obliged not to make any order unless it considers that it would be better for the child to make an order than to make no order[31]: there is little substantive difference between this formula and that embodied in section 3 of the 1986 Act. The major innovation of the 1995 Act was to abolish the concepts of custody and access, and to replace them with a more all-embracing notion of parental responsibilities and parental rights. In relation at least to children whose parents are or were married to each other the Act also tries to ensure that the parent and child relationship is not affected by changes in the legal relationship between the parents. The aim of the legislation is to shift the very basis of the argument between parents that was previously before the court, from the issue

---

[25] s. 2(2). The whole Act was repealed by the Law Reform (Parent and Child) (Scotland) Act 1986, Sched. 2.
[26] s. 2(1).
[27] Law Reform (Parent and Child) (Scotland) Act 1986, ss. 3 and 8.
[28] *Gillick v. West Norfolk and Wisbech Area Health Authority* [1986] A.C. 112.
[29] On December 16, 1991.
[30] UN Convention on the Rights of the Child, Art. 12.
[31] Children (Scotland) Act 1995, s. 11(7).

of why one parent should have custody to the issue of why one parent should be denied responsibilities and rights in the upbringing of the child. The change from custody to residence is also of great significance. The concept of custody was thought, perhaps inaccurately,[32] to carry with it almost full upbringing powers, at least in relation to the day-to-day control of the child. A residence order determining that the child is to live with one parent rather than the other will not in itself deny the other the responsibility and right to safeguard and promote the child's health, development and welfare, to maintain personal relations with the child and to act as the child's legal representative. The non-resident parent, in other words, maintains a full legal relationship with the child, involving responsibilities and rights in relation to the upbringing of the child, except in respect of determining where the child is to live and in respect of any other issue for which the court makes express provision.

1.34   As regards children whose parents are not and have not been married to each other, their status is determined in the same way as prior to the commencement of the 1995 Act. The legal relationship between a person and any other person is not affected by the marital status of the person's parents[33] but notwithstanding this provision the nature of a child's legal relationship with his or her father is significantly affected by that issue. Section 3 of the Children (Scotland) Act 1995, re-enacting with little substantive variation section 2 of the 1986 Act, provides that "notwithstanding section 1(1)" of the 1986 Act a child's father shall have parental responsibilities and parental rights only if he is married to the child's mother or was married to her at the time of the child's conception or subsequently. The mother who is not married to the father thus retains the primary role in the child's upbringing, and in the absence of a court order hers is the sole right recognised by law, but the father may make an application for parental responsibilities and parental rights under section 11 of the 1995 Act, which will be determined by the welfare test laid down in section 11(7). In the absence of any such order he remains not entitled to take any part in the upbringing of the child.

Access

Access at common law

1.35   At common law the *patria potestas* was such as to give the father not only the custody of his legitimate child but the control in his discretion of access to the child by others. It was not, however, an arbitrary power and its exercise would ordinarily admit of access to a child by the mother. If, as might happen on separation or divorce, such access were denied, the mother might by application to the court enforce her right of reasonable access. The enforcement of the right was at the discretion of the court and to that extent imperfect, but it was the rule to grant reasonable access unless there was something in the mother's conduct, or in the circumstances of the case (such as a matter affecting the interests of the children), to deprive her of the right.[34] Similarly, on the death of the father, the mother, if she did not have custody, had a right of access.[35] When, on the death of the father, the mother had custody, access might be granted to paternal relatives.[36] Indeed, the court's jurisdiction was by virtue of the broad equitable nature of the *nobile officium* free from any artificial limits as to the

---

[32] See below, para. 8.29.

[33] Law Reform (Parent and Child) (Scotland) Act 1986, s. 1(1).

[34] *McIver v. McIver* (1859) 21 D. 1103, especially *per* Lord Curriehill at 1107; *cf. AB v. CD* (1847) 10 D. 229; *Steuart v. Steuart* (1870) 8 M. 821; *Symington v. Symington* (1874) 1 R. 871; (1875) 2 R. (H.L.) 41; *Lilley v. Lilley* (1877) 4 R. 397.

[35] *Heatlie v. Cathcart* (1827) 5 S. 341; *Borthwick v. Dundas* (1845) 8 D. 318.

[36] *McCallum v. McDonald* (1853) 15 D. 535.

classes of persons in whose favour an award of access might, in a proper case, be made although the father's right to dictate the manner of upbringing of his children was at common law so strong that during his lifetime it would be rare for access to be awarded in favour of anyone other than the mother.[37]

The question of access to an illegitimate child seems seldom to have arisen for consideration at common law, but was also subject to regulation of the *nobile officium*. **1.36**

Statutory modification of the common law

Just as with custody, the history of legislative intervention in relation to access shows a gradual movement away from a concentration on parental rights to a concentration on children's welfare. The Guardianship of Infants Act 1886,[38] whose provisions on custody have already been noticed,[39] provided in the same terms for the regulation of the right of access of either parent. Thus the court could make such order as it thought fit having regard to the welfare of the child and to the conduct of the parents and to the wishes as well of the mother as of the father. These provisions were of less importance in relation to access than they were in relation to custody. On access they did little more than restate the common law. The Guardianship of Infants Act 1925[40] provided for the regulation of the right of access of the surviving father or mother of a child where an order had been made that a testamentary guardian appointed by the deceased parent was to be the sole guardian of the child. The order regulating access could be such as the court thought fit having regard to the welfare of the child. The Illegitimate Children (Scotland) Act 1930[41] provided for the right of access of either parent of an illegitimate child in the same terms as it did for custody (*i.e.* the court could make such order as it thought fit having regard to the welfare of the child and to the conduct of the parents and to the wishes as well of the mother as of the father). Although the 1930 Act referred only to the right of access of either parent it did not, it is submitted, derogate from the power under the *nobile officium* to make orders for access in favour of other persons. These Acts were all repealed in 1986. The Law Reform (Parent and Child) (Scotland) Act 1986 defined "parental rights" to include the right of access,[42] and allowed the court to make such order relating to parental rights as it thought fit, regarding the welfare of the child involved as the paramount consideration and not making any order relating to parental rights unless it was satisfied that to do so would be in the interests of the child.[43] That did not alter the pre-1986 position. Under the Guardianship of Infants Act 1925 access, though not expressly referred to in section 1, was embraced by the custody and upbringing provisions and was thus brought within the matters to be decided by having regard to the welfare of the child as the first and paramount consideration.[44] The matter of access has, **1.37**

---

[37] *S v. S*, 1967 S.C.(H.L.) 46 at 51, *per* Lord Reid.

[38] s. 5 (repealed by the Law Reform (Parent and Child) (Scotland) Act 1986, Sched. 2).

[39] above, para. 1.26.

[40] s. 5(4) (repealed by the Law Reform (Parent and Child) (Scotland) Act 1986, Sched. 2).

[41] s. 2(1) (repealed by the Law Reform (Parent and Child) (Scotland) Act 1986, Sched. 2).

[42] Law Reform (Parent and Child) (Scotland) Act 1986, s. 8.

[43] *ibid.* s. 3(1) and (2).

[44] It was never doubted that, under the Conjugal Rights (Scotland) Amendment Act 1861, s. 9, which did not, as originally enacted, expressly deal with access but with "custody, maintenance and education of any pupil child of the marriage", the court had jurisdiction to deal with access and that was the statutory warrant under which, in actions of separation or divorce, the jurisdiction of the Outer House was consistently exercised before 1986 in questions of access as well as custody (see *S v. S*, 1967 S.C.(H.L.) 46 at 51, *per* Lord Reid). S. 9 was amended by the Law Reform (Parent and Child) (Scotland) Act 1986, Sched. 1, defining the parental rights with which it deals by referring to the definition of "parental rights" contained in s. 8 of the 1986 Act: the provision was later embodied in the Court of Session Act 1988, s. 20, which was repealed by the Children (Scotland) Act 1995, Sched. 5.

therefore, since 1925 been determined entirely by a consideration of the welfare of the child, and the common law rules that limited the court's discretion by reference to parental right or to parental conduct are completely superseded.

1.38   The Children (Scotland) Act 1995 is now the sole source of parental responsibilities and parental rights and is also the source of the court's powers to make orders regulating, conferring or removing such responsibilities or rights. There is no longer any parental right of "access" but if the parent is not living with the child he or she has the parental responsibility and the parental right to maintain personal relations and direct contact with the child on a regular basis[45]; the court may regulate the exercise of this responsibility and right, remove it or confer it upon a person who does not otherwise have it. Unlike access, which in its nature was little more than a qualification to another person's right of custody, the responsibility and right of contact exists, can be exercised and can be regulated independently of any other person's responsibility to safeguard and promote the child's health, development and welfare or right to regulate the child's residence. As with the other parental responsibilities and parental rights, the court's powers to regulate, remove or confer are constrained by the terms of section 11(7), under which the welfare of the child is the court's paramount consideration.

LEGITIMACY AND LEGITIMATION

Significance of legitimacy

1.39   In common with most other European legal systems, a person's status in law, and the nature of the relationship between the person and his or her parents, was for long dependent upon whether that person was legitimate or illegitimate. The reason for this was, according to Fraser,[46] and the same was true in other countries, that: "it is the policy of law to discourage every other connection than that of marriage, by not acknowledging, as to any legal effect, the relations which spring from connections unsanctioned by marriage. The rights and privileges of husband and wife, of parent and child, it reserves for those who are known to the law in these relations." Yet the mere fact of parenthood has always been sufficient in Scotland to give rise to a degree of legal recognition of the parent and child relationship. Although that relationship received, until relatively recently, its full and typical expression only in the case of the legitimate child, there always existed a certain, albeit limited, legal relationship between an illegitimate child and his or her parents and, more particularly, between an illegitimate child and his or her mother. The expression *filius nullius*, although often used, always was an inadequate, and in some degree an inept, description of the status of the illegitimate child.[47] In reference to the authority which parents have over their children, Stair says: "This native authority reacheth all children, whether procreate of lawful marriage or not, so they be truly known to be children."[48] What for Stair was true of authority was also true for him of the whole nexus of rights and obligations between parents and children and had its ground "in the common nature that man hath with other animals".[49] As a

---

[45] Children (Scotland) Act 1995, ss. (1)(c) and 2(1)(c).

[46] (3rd ed.), p. 144.

[47] That the child had a legal relationship with his or her natural parents can be seen, for example, in the rules that the mother of the illegitimate child had the right of custody during pupillarity, and that both parents owed obligations of aliment to the child. Any radical justification for the use of the phrase *filius nullius* in Scotland depended on the making of a somewhat artificial distinction between a legal relationship and the legal recognition of a natural relationship: see *Clarke v. Carfin Coal Co.* (1891) 18 R. (H.L.) 63. The only truly accurate use of the expression was in relation to questions of succession.

[48] I, v, 6.

[49] I, v, 1.

description of the actual state of the law, rather than the dictates of the law of nature on which he took the law of Scotland to be based, Stair's statement puts the matter too broadly, but it sufficiently points the legal recognition of the natural relationship.

At common law the illegitimate child laboured under a number of civil **1.40** disabilities, of which the most important, at least in at all recent times, was a lack of testamentary capacity unless the child had issue of his or her own. That particular disability was removed by the Bastards (Scotland) Act 1836. Moreover, at common law the illegitimate child's legal relationship with his or her parents was sufficiently different from that enjoyed by the legitimate child to add an inferior legal status to the other social disadvantages from which he or she might suffer, and this has taken much longer to disappear from the law. The trend of modern statute has, however, been to assimilate the legal position of legitimate and illegitimate children in very nearly all respects. The most important statute to effect this change was the Law Reform (Parent and Child) (Scotland) Act 1986, the aim of section 1 of which was to rid the law for as many purposes as then possible of the differences between the legitimate and the illegitimate child. Previous statutes had been working towards that aim, though in a piecemeal and partial fashion, and dealing with discrete areas of law.

The treatment of illegitimate children in relation to custody and guardianship, **1.41** and their gradual assimilation with legitimate children, has been noted already. Succession law provided other points of difference. The common law had provided that an illegitimate child could not succeed to the estate of either of his or her parents, nor they to their child's[50]: in this area at least the description of the illegitimate child as *filius nullius* was completely accurate. The first inroad to this principle came with the Legitimacy Act 1926, under section 9 of which an illegitimate child was given the same right of succession to the estate of his or her mother as if he or she had been legitimate, but only if the mother died intestate and without lawful issue; and the mother of an illegitimate child was given the same right of succession to the estate of that child as if the child had been legitimate and she the only surviving parent, but only if the child died intestate. By the Law Reform (Miscellaneous Provisions) (Scotland) Act 1968 illegitimate children were given the same rights of succession in the estates of both parents, though not of remoter ascendants or collaterals, as legitimate children.[51] This did not apply to the construction of deeds executed prior to November 25, 1968. The effect of the Law Reform (Parent and Child) (Scotland) Act 1986 was to remove all distinctions between the legitimate and illegitimate child in relation to succession, except that (i) it does not affect the right of legitim out of, or the right of succession to, the estate of any person who died before the commencement of the Act (December 8, 1986) and (ii) it does not apply to, or affect the succession to or devolution of, any title, coat of arms, honour or dignity transmissible on the death of the holder.

The law of damages also needs to be considered here. There is little authority **1.42** on the question of whether at common law a parent could sue for damages for the negligently caused death of an illegitimate child, or whether an illegitimate child could sue for damages for the negligently caused death of a parent. In relation to loss of support, the question would seem to resolve into the question of whether the one owed an obligation of aliment to the other, for that was the basis of the common law claim in relation to legitimate children.[52] Both parents were alimentary debtors to their illegitimate children[53] and the negligently caused

[50] Erskine, III, x, 8.
[51] Law Reform (Miscellaneous Provisions) (Scotland) Act 1968, ss. 1–3 (amending the Succession (Scotland) Act 1964).
[52] Fraser (3rd ed.), p. 136.
[53] Bankton, I, v, 64; Erskine, I, vi, 56.

death of either parent would seem, in principle, to have given the child a right
of action for loss of support. The illegitimate child owed no obligation of aliment
to the father,[54] and therefore the father could not claim damages for the death of
the child.[55] The position in relation to the mother was at one time more doubtful,[56]
and was never resolved at common law, but it would appear to follow from *Clarke v.
Carfin Coal Co.*[57] that a mother's claim for damages for loss of support would be
incompetent on the same principles as a father's. Statute now governs the matter.
Under the Law Reform (Miscellaneous Provisions) (Scotland) Act 1940
illegitimate children could recover damages from anyone wrongfully causing the
death of either parent,[58] and by the Law Reform (Damages and Solatium) (Scotland)
Act 1962 the parents were given a reciprocal right.[59] The law is today contained
in the Damages (Scotland) Act 1976 which gives the right to sue to "relatives" as
there defined. Parent and child are both within the definition[60] and, in the Act as
originally passed, "an illegitimate person shall be treated as the legitimate child
of his mother and reputed father".[61] This provision has now been replaced by the
requirement to read the Act in accordance with the provisions of the Law Reform
(Parent and Child) (Scotland) Act 1986,[62] under which the fact that a person's
parents are not or have not been married to one another shall be left out of account
in establishing the legal relationship between the person and any other person.[63]
The result is that for the purposes of the Damages (Scotland) Act 1976 the
legitimacy or illegitimacy of the child is irrelevant.

Remaining effects of illegitimacy

1.43   Since 1986 the only significant remaining legal differences between the
legitimate and the illegitimate child, other than those of transitional significance,
concern the child's domicile and the succession to titles, coats of arms, honours
and dignities transmissible on the death of the holder.[64] A child's domicile was
and remains dependent on his or her status of legitimacy or illegitimacy. A
child's domicile of origin is that of the father if the child is legitimate and that
of the mother if the child is illegitimate.[65] In addition, though the marital status
of a child's parents no longer affects the child's status, it does very significantly
affect the child's relationship with his or her father, and the provision whereby
the fact that a person's parents are not or have not been married to one another
shall be left out of account in establishing the legal relationship between the
person and any other person[66] is expressly qualified in section 3 of the Children
(Scotland) Act 1995 which allocates parental responsibilities and parental rights
to the child's mother in all cases but to the father only if he was married to the
mother at the time of the child's conception or subsequently. This fact, taken
together with the effects of illegitimacy in relation to domicile and to succession
to titles, honours and dignities transmissible on death, means that legitimacy
will remain of some significance for some time. Rights vested or acquired before
the 1986 Act came into force will be preserved, and deeds coming into effect

---

[54] *Anderson v. Kirk Session of Lauder* (1848) 10 D. 960; *Corrie v. Adair* (1860) 22 D. 897.
[55] *McNeill v. McGregor* (1901) 4 F. 123.
[56] Fraser (3rd ed.), p. 157.
[57] (1891) 18 R. (H.L.) 63.
[58] Law Reform (Miscellaneous Provisions) (Scotland) Act 1940, s. 2(2).
[59] Law Reform (Damages and Solatium) (Scotland) Act 1962, s. 2.
[60] Damages (Scotland) Act 1976, Sched. 1, para. 1(b).
[61] *ibid.* para. 2(b).
[62] Law Reform (Parent and Child) (Scotland) Act 1986, Sched. 1, para. 15.
[63] *ibid.* s. 1(1).
[64] Law Reform (Parent and Child) (Scotland) Act 1986, s. 9(1)(a) and (c).
[65] *Udny v. Udny* (1869) 7 M. (H.L.) 89, *per* Lord Westbury at 99. A posthumous child takes the
     domicile of his or her mother: Anton and Beaumont, p. 130.
[66] Law Reform (Parent and Child) (Scotland) Act 1986, s. 1(1).

before the final abolition of illegitimacy will continue to be construed according to the law then in force; in addition intentional limitations of rights based on the outmoded concept of illegitimacy will continue to be given effect.

Legitimacy through lawful marriage of the parents

According to Erskine,[67] "lawful children are those who are either procreated in marriage, or who are afterwards legitimated or made lawful". Stair is to like effect, referring to "a lawful child begotten of persons lawfully married".[68] So far as children born legitimate were concerned, Erskine's and Stair's definitions are preferable to Bell's: "a lawful child, according to the law of Scotland, is one born in wedlock, or within a certain time after the dissolution of the marriage",[69] which concentrates attention on birth rather than conception in wedlock as the source of legitimacy and is open to the interpretation that a child born of a married woman is, by operation of law, legitimate and moreover that there is an arbitrary determination of the period of time between dissolution of marriage and the birth of a child which would be consistent with the child's legitimacy. Birth to a married woman gives rise, however, to no more than a presumption, although a very strong presumption, of legitimacy and the legitimacy of a child born after the dissolution of a marriage depends not on the length of time which has elapsed, although that may be relevant to proof, but on whether or not the child was procreated in marriage.[70] Erskine's and Stair's definitions are, however, defective in overlooking the case of the child whose parents married subsequent to his or her conception but before his or her birth. Such cases are not instances of legitimation by subsequent marriage, which is properly applicable only to children born before the marriage of their parents, but the legitimacy of children born of such intervening marriage is undoubted. Nor, it is submitted, is that result affected by the death of the father or the divorce of the parents before the child's birth. A legitimate child can therefore be defined as a child of parents between whom a lawful marriage subsisted at the time of the child's conception or birth or at any intervening time.[71]

1.44

The legitimacy of children conceived as a result of artificial insemination has not been the subject of judicial consideration in Scotland or England. Where insemination was with the semen of the husband, a child so conceived was, however, "procreated in marriage"[72] and "begotten of persons lawfully married"[73] no less than a child conceived in the normal way, and is clearly legitimate. By parity of reasoning, where the donor was a third party the child is illegitimate.[74] It was never doubted that the legitimacy of children conceived as a result of fecundation *ab extra* depends on whether or not fecundation was attributable to the husband and there is no sound principle on which such cases can be distinguished for this purpose from artificial insemination. The provisions deeming paternity contained in the Human Fertilisation and Embryology Act 1990 affect this position in ways explored later.[75]

1.45

---

[67] I, vi. 49.

[68] III, iii, 42.

[69] *Prin.*, para. 1624.

[70] A repute of legitimacy places the onus on those challenging it: *MacDonald of Keppoch*, 1994 S.L.T. (Lyon Ct) 2; *Campbell v. Campbell* (1866) 4 M. 867; Fraser (3rd ed.), p. 22.

[71] *cf.* today the presumption of paternity contained in s. 5(1)(a) of the Law Reform (Parent and Child) (Scotland) Act 1986.

[72] Erskine, *ibid.*

[73] Stair, *ibid.*

[74] That does not detract from the view, affirmed in *MacLennan v. MacLennan*, 1958 S.C. 105, that the artificial insemination of a married woman with the semen of a third-party donor is not adultery. Adultery has no necessary connection with procreation and in cases of adultery the *de quo* is whether there was carnal connection. In questions of legitimacy it is, however, parenthood that is in issue, and the absence of carnal connection is as irrelevant to a question of legitimacy as the absence of procreative, as distinct from copulative, action is irrelevant to adultery.

[75] See below, paras 3.27 *et seq.*

Legitimacy without lawful marriage of the parents

1.46   Although the subsistence of a lawful marriage between parents, whether at the time of conception or at sometime thereafter so as to effect legitimation,[76] was normally a necessary condition of the legitimacy of their off-spring, children of marriages which were declared null could nonetheless be legitimate. That could be so both in the case of a putative but void marriage and in the case of a voidable marriage. It is also possible for children to be legitimate in the complete absence of any marriage on the part of those regarded by the law as their parents.

Putative marriages

1.47   Fraser defines a putative marriage as "one where the parties, or either of them, *bona fide* believing that they could marry, had entered into the contract, while there was an unknown impediment, arising from relationship, previous marriage, or other irritant nullity, which prevented a valid marriage".[77] Although such marriages are null, the effect of the *bona fides* of the parties (or either of them) was to confer the status of legitimacy on children of the union conceived while that *bona fides* subsisted.[78] The application of the doctrine is dependent on the error of one or both parties to the marriage having been made in good faith and, according at least to Fraser,[79] of the marriage having been entered into publicly.[80] On the latter point, it is submitted that Bankton[81] put the matter in proper perspective when he said "such *bona fides* will be the more easily presumed, if the marriage was publicly solemnised than when it was clandestine", and that where the objections to *bona fides* can as a matter of fact be overcome despite the clandestine or irregular nature of the purported marriage, there is no reason that such *bona fides* should not be accepted for the purpose of conferring legitimacy on the children of the union. Due to the common law presumption of legitimacy, the onus of proof lay on the person denying the putative marriage to show the absence of *bona fides*.

1.48   The effect of putative marriage was to confer on the children the status of legitimacy in relation to a parent *in mala fide* as well as the parent *in bona fide*. There was, however, a qualification so far as a parent *in mala fide* was concerned: he or she could not benefit from his or her own wrong. He or she was under all the obligations of a parent of a legitimate child but had none of the parental rights and powers.[82] Thus although he or she had an alimentary liability to the child he or she had no reciprocal right to aliment. The child and the child's issue could succeed to his or her estate and to the estates of ancestors and collaterals traceable through him or her, but no corresponding rights of succession enured to the *mala fide* parent or those who traced their relationship through him or her. It seems that the *mala fide* parent could not even take advantage of the statutory provisions governing parental rights of succession to the estate of an illegitimate child which, since the effect of putative marriage was to confer legitimacy, were inept to cover that case.

---

[76] For which, see below, para. 1.54.

[77] at p. 27. It is convenient to use this definition which postulates the *bona fides* of at least one of the parties, although in ordinary usage the expression "putative marriage" may be applied, irrespective of *bona fides*, to any reputed or supposed but actually invalid marriage.

[78] There was at one time some doubt as to whether the doctrine of legitimacy derived from putative marriage formed part of the law of Scotland, this doubt arising from the division of judicial opinion in *Brymer v. Riddell*, February 19, 1811, Fergusson's *Consistorial Law*, 212; Robert Bell, *Report of a Case of Legitimacy under Putative Marriage*, Hume's *Session Papers*, Vol. CVIII, No. 20. See the 1st edition of this book at pp. 11–12. The matter has been undoubted since *Purves's Trs v. Purves* (1895) 22 R. 513.

[79] (3rd ed.), p. 33.

[80] These matters are explored more thoroughly than is necessary here in the 1st edition of this book, at pp. 12–17.

[81] I, v, 51.

[82] Fraser, *Husband and Wife* (2nd ed.), Vol. I, p. 152.

Cases analogous to putative marriages

An extension of the doctrine of *bona fides* has been canvassed so as to bring **1.49** about the legitimacy (i) of children procreated in incestuous concubinage in the *bona fide* but erroneous belief of their parents that no impediment existed to their subsequent marriage and consequent legitimation of their issue; and (ii) of children born as a result of rape.[83] The former case derived some colour from the circumstances surrounding the succession of Robert III to the throne of Scotland, but neither his succession nor his legitimacy depended on this view of the law.[84] The case of children born of rape was scarcely one of *bona fides* at all but could be advanced out of regard for the innocence of the mother. There is no Scottish authority in point and it may be argued that illegitimacy from putative marriage did not have as its function the providing of a generalised remedy for injustice or wronged innocence in cases of illegitimacy—all illegitimacy may, in a very real sense, be said to be unjust from the standpoint of the child—but the more limited function of approximating the effects of a void marriage, entered into *in bona fide* and under excusable error, to those of a valid marriage. There is, however, some strength in the contrary contention that cases of rape lay, from the mother's standpoint, *a fortiori* of cases of good faith. It is important to remember when one speaks of putative marriage that there is in truth no marriage at all. The doctrine was founded not on respect for purported marriages but on respect for good faith. As Fraser says, "a contrary judgment would, in effect, impose a punishment without a crime, and entail rigorous hardship on individuals, which it is good policy, if possible, to avoid".[85] The victim of rape was a fit beneficiary of that policy no less than the *bona fide* participant in a pretended but invalid marriage. The protection which the law gave to the *bona fides* of the latter could therefore be extended to the innocence of the former. The further advantage would follow that although the perpetrator of the rape would incur liabilities of a father of a legitimate child he would be deprived, on principles discussed above, of any rights in relation to the child. Against these arguments it can, however, be said that they would impose on the mother a legal relationship with her child which might be contrary to her wishes and which in the circumstances she should be entitled to repudiate. If the child was treated as illegitimate, it remained open to the mother after 1930[86] to regularise the relationship, if she so wished, by adoption.

Voidable marriages

Section 4(1) of the Law Reform (Miscellaneous Provisions) Act 1949 provides: **1.50**

> "Where a decree of nullity is granted in respect of a voidable marriage, any child who would have been the legitimate child of the marriage if at the date of the decree it had been dissolved, instead of being annulled, shall be deemed to be their legitimate child."

In England marriage may be voidable on a number of grounds and it was **1.51** primarily with a view to the English position that the legislation was passed. In Scotland the only ground on which marriage is voidable, as distinct from void, is where one of the parties is *incapax copulandi* at the time of the ceremony and that incapacity is permanent and incurable.[87] There will be children of such marriages only where there has been fecundation *ab extra* or artificial insemination with the semen of the husband. In the latter case the children

---

[83] Fraser, pp. 35–36.
[84] *ibid.*
[85] at pp. 27–28.
[86] When the Adoption (Scotland) Act 1930 came into force.
[87] Clive (4th ed.) at pp. 95–100. And see Norrie, "Transsexuals, the Right to Marry and Voidable Marriages in Scots Law", 1990 S.L.T. (News) 353.

would usually have been legitimate in any event on the ground that declarator of nullity is barred by homologation[88]; in some cases of fecundation *ab extra* that will also be so.[89] Even apart from homologation children of a voidable marriage were, however, probably legitimate at common law. They were undoubtedly legitimate as long as the marriage subsisted unchallenged and indefeasibly so once it was dissolved by death or divorce. To allow that status once acquired to be lost would be productive of anomaly. Moreover, such marriages are nearly always entered into in the *bona fide* belief of at least one spouse in their permanent validity (where that is not so there may be personal bar against seeking declarator of nullity), and children of such marriages might therefore have been treated as legitimate on the principle of putative marriage.

Other instances of legitimacy without marriage

1.52   A child may be adopted by an unmarried person and, in that case, the effect of the adoption order is that the child shall be treated as if he or she had been born as a legitimate child of the adopter[90] and as if he or she were not the child of any person other than the adopter.[91] The order legitimates the child, and backdates the legitimation to the child's birth.

1.53   The Human Fertilisation and Embryology Act 1990 permits, in unusual circumstances explored in detail later,[92] that a child may be legally fatherless,[93] though no provision is made in relation to such a child's legitimacy. It would appear to follow that, since legitimacy is primarily dependent on marriage at a time between conception and birth and, *ex hypothesi*, the mother will not be married to the genetic father, the child would be regarded as being illegitimate (even when conceived with the sperm of the mother's deceased husband). It is, perhaps, open to argument that a child without a legal father is not necessarily illegitimate. There is an express provision in the Adoption (Scotland) Act 1978 deeming a child adopted by one person to be not the child of any other person and that making the child legitimate.[94] The considerations behind that rule might be regarded as applying with equal force to a child born as a result of artificial reproductive techniques. Notwithstanding that the issue of legitimacy is expressly dealt with in the adoption legislation but is ignored in the 1990 Act, in both cases the relationship between parent and child is created and governed by statute designed to ease such creation, and the law ought not to be interpreted in such a way as encourages the creation of what, for some purposes at least, may still be called an illegitimate relationship.[95]

Legitimation by subsequent marriage

1.54   Children procreated out of wedlock and illegitimate have for long been able to acquire legitimate status by the subsequent intermarriage of their parents. Though the matter is now governed by statute,[96] the doctrine of legitimation *per subsequens matrimonium* was accepted in the common law, though on slightly different rules from those which apply under the statute.[97] In particular

---

[88] *AB v. CD*, 1961 S.C. 347.
[89] But see Clive (4th ed.) at p. 99.
[90] Adoption (Scotland) Act 1978, s. 39(1)(c)(i).
[91] *ibid.* s. 39(1)(c)(ii).
[92] See below, paras 3.42–3.44.
[93] This is quite different from the situation in which no man is treated as father because he is unknown.
[94] Adoption (Scotland) Act 1978, s. 39(1)(c)(i).
[95] It would seem unquestionable that the legally fatherless child takes his or her mother's domicile as domicile of origin, for there is no other parental domicile to which reference can be made and the domicile of foundlings—the only other possible alternative—introduces a needless complication. The analogy with the posthumous child, who takes the mother's domicile, is apt. The question of such a child's legitimacy, therefore, will have no practical significance.
[96] Legitimation (Scotland) Act 1968.
[97] For a fuller account of the common law doctrine, see the 1st edition of this work, at pp. 18–20.

legitimation was not effected by marriage of the child's parents when there existed an impediment to their marriage at the time of the conception of the child: so "incestuous and adulterine bastards" could not be legitimated.[98] This was a consequence of the canonist theory that the sacramental effects of marriage were fictionally drawn back to the date of conception: this could not occur if a diriment impediment to the marriage at that date existed. The retrospectivity of legitimation that this involved did not survive the Legitimation (Scotland) Act 1968.

Under that Act, rights which had vested or which are ascertainable by **1.55** reference to the law in force before the commencement of the Act were not affected but legitimising effect was given from June 8, 1968 to marriages contracted before that date: (1) where the child had died before the marriage of the parents,[99] and (2) where the marriage did not at common law have the effect of making the child legitimate because of the existence of an impediment at the time of conception.[1] Although in these cases the Act applied to marriages before the commencement of the Act, rights accrue under the Act with effect only from the date of marriage or the date of commencement, whichever was the later.[2] Legitimation cannot be effected at common law from June 8, 1968 but rights may, of course, continue to be enjoyed and to accrue as a result of earlier legitimations at common law and, in relation to intestacies arising or deeds becoming operative before June 8, 1968, with the common law effects.[3]

Section 1 covers all legitimations effected by marriages on or after June 8, 1968 **1.56** other than posthumous legitimations. It enacts that where the marriage is after the commencement of the Act and the child was living at the date of the marriage, the marriage, with effect from that date, renders the child legitimate and confers on him or her the rights and imposes on him or her the obligations of a legitimate person, so long as, at the date of the marriage, the father was domiciled in Scotland. The marriage can be regular or irregular,[4] and (resolving one of the undecided matters at common law) includes putative marriages and voidable marriages.[5] Section 3 caters for and removes any doubts which at common law may have surrounded the case of an illegitimate person who died before the marriage of the parents. In such a case the provisions of the Act apply for the purpose of determining the rights and obligations of any person living at or after the date of the marriage, if that was on or after June 8, 1968, as if the illegitimate person had been legitimated with effect from the date of the marriage. If the marriage was before the commencement of the Act the provisions apply for the purpose of determining the rights and obligations of any person living at or after June 8, 1968 as if that was the effective date of legitimation. The provisions apply irrespective of whether the death of the illegitimate person, or the marriage of the parents, or both, preceded the commencement of the Act, but they do not, of course, apply to successions opening or deeds becoming operative before that date. They do not in any event affect any right which has indefeasibly vested before legitimation, or confer any status or rights or impose any obligation in respect of any time previous thereto.

---

[98] In *Kerr v. Martin* (1840) 2 D. 752, however, it was held that an intervening impediment such as a marriage contracted after the child's conception did not prevent the doctrine from operating after that marriage had terminated.

[99] Legitimation (Scotland) Act 1968, s. 3. This did no more than remove such doubts as there may have been at common law.

[1] *ibid.* s. 4.

[2] *ibid.* ss. 1, 3 and 4.

[3] ss. 3 and 4 are not free from ambiguity on this point but they do not derogate from the general presumption that a statute is not retrospective (*Gardner v. Lucas* (1878) 5 R. (H.L.) 105; *Henshall v. Porter* [1923] 2 K.B. 193).

[4] In which case the date of the marriage for the purposes of the Act, as for other purposes, was the date specified in the decree of declarator or otherwise ascertained by the court.

[5] Legitimation (Scotland) Act 1968, s. 8(1).

1.57   The scope of rights and obligations arising out of legitimation are spelled
out in some detail. Legitimation enures, as at common law, to the benefit not
only of the person legitimated but to claimants whose rights depend on his or
her legitimacy.[6] It is specifically provided that legitimation shall not confer any
status or right, or impose any obligation, on any person in respect of any time
previous to the legitimation[7] and that no one shall be entitled, by virtue of their
own legitimation or the legitimation of any other person, to any right in the
intestate estate or legitim out of the estate of any person dying after the
commencement of the Act and before the date of the legitimation.[8] Legitimation
does not affect any right under a deed coming into operation after the
commencement of the Act if the right has become indefeasibly vested in someone
other than the person legitimated before the date of legitimation.[9] Subject to
that, however, a legitimated person is entitled to any right under a deed coming
into operation after the commencement of the Act, being a right his or her
entitlement to which depends on his or her legitimacy, and a person other than
the legitimated person is entitled to any right under such a deed, being a right
his or her entitlement to which depends on the legitimacy of the legitimated
person.[10] This provision is not restricted to deeds coming into operation after
legitimation and accordingly a legitimated person can acquire rights under deeds
which came into operation before legitimation. The right itself must, however,
be one that vested on or subsequent to legitimation as to hold otherwise would
be to undermine the fundamental principle of the Act that legitimation is effective
only from the date on which it takes place (*i.e.* the date of marriage). Any
reference in any deed coming into operation after the commencement of the
Act to a child, or to issue, of a marriage is to be construed as including a reference
to any child legitimated by that marriage.[11] Where any such reference is to issue,
it is to be construed as including a reference to the issue, being legitimated
persons, of any child of that marriage (including such issue of any child
legitimated by the marriage).[12] The statutory wording "issue, being legitimated
persons" might give rise to the inference that a reference to issue is not to include
issue, being persons born legitimate, of any child legitimated by the marriage,
but that anomalous result is avoided by ordinary rules of construction on the
meaning of issue. It is a common feature of these provisions on the interpretation
of references to children and issue that they should be construed along with
section 4(2) and so, provided there is no prejudice to rights which have
indefeasibly vested, they apply even if the deed came into operation before
legitimation. Special provision is made for the case of rights or obligations,
whether created by operation of law or by any deed coming into operation after
the commencement of the Act, which are conferred or imposed by reference to
the relative seniority of the members of a class consisting of legitimate persons
only. In such a case, a legitimated person ranks as if he or she had been born on
the date of legitimation except that where two or more members of the class are
legitimated persons they rank *inter se* in accordance with their respective times
of birth.[13] This provision applies only to classes consisting solely of legitimate
persons. Where a class is so defined as to include illegitimate persons, legitimated

---

[6] Legitimation (Scotland) Act 1968, s. 2(7).

[7] *ibid.* s. 2(1).

[8] *ibid.* s. 2(2).

[9] *ibid.* s. 2(3).

[10] *ibid.* s. 2(4).

[11] *ibid.* s. 2(5)(a).

[12] *ibid.* s. 2(5)(b).

[13] *ibid.* s. 2(6). The use of the word "time" rather than "date" indicates the application of the rule to
cases where more than one child, as in the case of twins, are born on the same day.

persons rank, as do others, according to time of birth. All provisions of section 2, which deal with the scope of rights and obligations arising on legitimation, are so expressed as to apply only to legitimations by or under the Act or to successions opening or deeds coming into operation after the commencement of the Act and leave the effects of legitimation at common law unaltered in other cases.[14] There is also separate provision by which the common law rules are specifically preserved in relation to deeds which came into operation before the commencement of the Act.[15] The operation of any deed is affected by the Act only in so far as on the construction of the deed no contrary intention appears.[16] Overall, it can be said that despite the change from birth to marriage as the effective date of legitimation, the effects of legitimation under the Act are not, when regard is had to the provisions of the common law regarding vested rights and seniority, materially different from the effects at common law in so far as these were settled.

Titles, honours and dignities

Where a question of succession to or devolution of any title, honour or dignity **1.58** arises after the commencement of the Legitimation (Scotland) Act 1968, the Act has effect in relation to the right in question as if it were a right under, and as if the title, honour or dignity devolved in accordance with, a deed coming into operation after the commencement of the Act.[17] Were it not for this provision, persons who could not have been legitimated at common law but who were legitimated under the Act would have been cut off from succession to titles, honours or dignities created by letters patent or other deeds before the commencement of the Act. This is an exception to the general principle that such succession is governed by the common law.

Other forms of legitimation

In the developed Roman law legitimation could be effected *per rescriptum* **1.59** *principis*.[18] This form of legitimation is usually ascribed to two novels of Justinian,[19] but exceptional instances are to be found earlier. In the medieval papacy letters of legitimation on the Roman imperial model were granted by the popes but were rare in Scotland. It is not clear that they were ever accepted as having civil effect, although it is likely that the ecclesiastical courts recognised them in questions of succession to moveables with which they were concerned. These papal letters of legitimation are to be distinguished from dispensations *de defectu natali* which were common but did no more than exempt from certain ecclesiastical disabilities.[20] Scots law took over the Roman practice although in a highly modified form. The Roman imperial rescript conferred full legitimation and accordingly it was not granted where the parent of the illegitimate child had legitimate issue, for to do so would have been to prejudice their rights. Royal letters of legitimation in Scotland had, however, only a limited effect. They conferred on the illegitimate person no rights of succession and were no more than a waiver of the rights of the Crown. They gave, therefore, capacity to test to an illegitimate person who, until 1836, could not make a will unless he or she had legitimate issue of his or her own and they might also, but only if they contained a special clause to that effect, create rights of intestate succession

---

[14] Legitimation (Scotland) Act 1968, s. 2(1), when read along with s. 2(8) and the references to the commencement of the Act in s. 2(2)–(7).

[15] *ibid.* s. 7(3).

[16] *ibid.* s. 7(1). So in *Wright's Trs v. Callender*, 1993 S.L.T. 556 the House of Lords held that a gift to "lawful children" had to be interpreted as at the date of death of the testator (when the children could not be legitimated) rather than at the date of distribution of the gift (by which time the children had been legitimated).

[17] Legitimation (Scotland) Act 1968, s. 8(4).

[18] Fraser (3rd ed.), p. 51.

[19] Nov. 74, c. 1 and 2; 89, c. 9.

[20] Anton, *Stair Society*, Vol. XX, p. 118.

in the illegitimate's estate.[21] Legitimation *per rescriptum principis* has been regarded as obsolete since illegitimate persons acquired full capacity to test. Although collaterals and ascendants of an illegitimate person, other than his or her parents, had no rights *ab intestato* in his or her estate until 1986,[22] the rescript did not survive as a means of creating rights in intestacy.

Declarators of legitimacy, legitimation or illegitimacy

Jurisdiction and procedure

1.60 A declarator may be raised to determine the legitimacy, legitimation or illegitimacy of any person whose status is in dispute. Jurisdiction is now regulated by statute and subsists if the child was born within the territorial jurisdiction of the court or the alleged or presumed parent or the child (a) is domiciled there when the action is brought or (b) was habitually resident there for not less than one year immediately preceding the bringing of the action or (c) died before the bringing of the action and was domiciled there at the date of death or had been habitually resident there for not less than one year immediately preceding that date.[23]

1.61 An action of declarator without any further conclusion is competent.[24] A declaratory conclusion may, however, be combined with other conclusions and may, in particular, be a preliminary to petitory conclusions.[25] Questions of status, including legitimacy and illegitimacy, may, without declarator, be determined where they arise incidentally to the enforcement of other rights.[26] In that event, jurisdiction is determined by the principal subject-matter and not by the statutory rules just noted. Judgment in such an action will, however, be *res judicata* only between the parties and to the extent necessary for determination of the dispute between them.[27] A declarator will be necessary where it is desired to obtain a judgment *in rem* on the question of status and, generally, where status is a major issue in controversy. Whether that declarator should be sought by means of combining a declaratory conclusion with others or by means of a separate action is dependent on the particular circumstances but, whichever course is followed, the statutory requirements for jurisdiction must be satisfied. A separate action will be appropriate if defenders are to be called to the declarator who would not otherwise be convened to the process or if the question of status would be best disposed of independently of the other issues.[28] A pending action may be sisted to enable a separate declarator to be raised.

1.62 Conclusions for declarator of legitimacy, legitimation or illegitimacy, where it is expedient to do so, may be combined with conclusions for declarator of

---

[21] Erskine, III, x, 7; Stair, III, iii, 45; Hume's *Lectures* I, 201–202; Fraser, pp. 51–52.

[22] Law Reform (Parent and Child) (Scotland) Act 1986.

[23] *ibid.* s. 7(2).

[24] Walker, *Civil Remedies*, p. 116; *Magistrates of Ayr v. Lord Advocate*, 1950 S.C. 102; *McLay v. Farrell*, 1950 S.C. 149; *Fife County Council v. Lord Advocate*, 1950 S.C. 314.

[25] Walker, *op. cit.*, p. 114.

[26] *McDonald v. Mackenzie* (1891) 18 R. 502; *Mackie v. Lyon* (1943) 59 Sh.CtRep. 130 and 133; *Turnbull v. Wilsons and Clyde Coal Co.*, 1935 S.C. 580. In *Hamilton's Trs v. Wright and Sharp* (1880) 7 R. 460 the competency of raising the action in the sheriff court was affirmed on the view that it might be unnecessary to determine the question of status but when, after having been remitted to the sheriff court, the case again came before the Court of Session the sheriff's interlocutor was recalled and the sheriff-substitute's finding on the question of status restored without any discussion of competency. The jurisdiction of the sheriff court to entertain questions of status incidentally to the enforcement of other rights exists at common law independently of s. 5(1) of the Sheriff Courts (Scotland) Act 1907 which is concerned solely with actions of declarator and is to broadly the same effect in relation to them as is the common law rule in relation to other actions. The doctrine has been applied in actions of affiliation and aliment (*Fleming v. Farmer* (1922) Sh.CtRep. 73). For Court of Session practice see *Swinton v. Swinton* (1862) 24 D. 833.

[27] *Turnbull v. Wilsons and Clyde Coal Co.*, above.

[28] *Rackstraw v. Douglas*, 1919 S.C. 354.

marriage or of divorce, as the case may be.[29] A conclusion for putting to silence, normally associated with a declarator of freedom from marriage, is competent against any false claims to personal status and so may be combined with, and follow on, a declarator of illegitimacy.[30] It is available against a parent who makes a false claim to the legitimate relationship as well as against the child.[31] As declarators of marriage and actions of putting to silence remain within the exclusive jurisdiction of the Court of Session, they can, of course, be combined with declarators of legitimacy and illegitimacy only in that court.

Title to sue

Any person who has a legally enforceable interest which turns on a question **1.63** of legitimacy or legitimation has a title to sue a declarator.[32] That parents and the child have such an interest is self-evident. They have a clear title to sue. A declarator must have at least the possibility of present legal consequences and it will not be granted where the sole interest is in some future or contingent right.[33] Accordingly, while the parents and child are all alive, it will be rarely, if ever, that others have a title to sue a declarator of legitimacy or legitimation. On the death of any of them, an interest and consequent title to sue may, however, emerge in others.

International aspects of legitimacy and legitimation

As pointed out above, the remaining effects of illegitimacy in Scotland are by **1.64** and large limited to succession issues. The concept of legitimacy is, however, one that appears in many legal systems and the domestic effects elsewhere differ significantly from those here. Even if illegitimacy were to be abolished completely in Scots law, issues of international private law would continue to arise.[34]

Choice of law: domicile

In the classic formulation of Lord Westbury in *Udny v. Udny*,

> "Civil status is governed universally by one specific principle. Domicil **1.65** or the place of settled residence of an individual is the criterion established by law for the purpose of determining the civil condition of the person, for it is on this basis that the personal rights of the parties—that is, the law which determines his majority or his minority, marriage, succession, testacy or intestacy—must depend."[35]

Questions of legitimacy or illegitimacy are, therefore, determined by the law of the domicile of the person whose status is in issue.

---

[29] *X v. Y*, 1921 1 S.L.T. 79; *Brown v. Brown*, 1972 S.L.T. 143; see also *Jamieson v. Jamieson*, 1969 S.L.T. (Notes) 11.

[30] *Imre v. Mitchell*, 1958 S.C. 439.

[31] *ibid.*

[32] *Shedden v. Patrick* (1849) 11 D. 1333; (1853) 15 D. 379; *Benson v. Benson* (1854) 16 D. 555; *Morley v. Jackson* (1888) 16 R. 78; *Grant v. Countess of Seafield*, 1926 S.C. 274; *Bosville v. Lord Macdonald*, 1910 S.C. 597.

[33] Walker, *Civil Remedies*, pp. 113–114. The rule admits substantial exceptions (see Mackay's *Manual*, p. 375) and where there is a proper contradictor, a future, or even a contingent, legal right can be made the subject of declarator (*Fleming v. McLagan* (1876) 6 R. 588, *per* Lord Young at 598). It is thought, however, that the scope afforded by such exceptions cannot extend to the raising of actions by parties whose sole interest is one which may emerge only on the death of a party having a present and primary interest.

[34] A rather more extensive discussion of the issue than is presented here can be found in the 1st edition of this book, at pp. 28–36.

[35] (1869) 7 M. (H.L.) 89 at 99. That this principle applies to cases of legitimacy as well as to legitimation (which was the issue in *Udny*) is clear from the earlier decision of *Fenton v. Livingstone* (1859) 3 Macq. 497, especially *per* Lord Wensleydale at 547–548.

1.66   Although the principle that choice of law for determining questions of legitimacy, including legitimation, should follow the domicile of the child is clear, the application of that principle has been obscured and to some extent frustrated by the apparent *circulus inextricabilis* involved in ascertaining the domicile of a child before his or her status has been established. That problem was circumvented in a line of English authority, now somewhat discredited and including the much criticised House of Lords case of *Shaw v. Gould*,[36] by the expedient of resolving the question of legitimacy into one of whether or not the child's parents had been validly married. The choice of law rules were, therefore, those applicable to validity of marriage. That device had the advantage of simplicity but the disadvantage that it was applicable only to cases of legitimacy at birth, and not to legitimation, and accordingly required that legitimacy at birth and legitimation be treated on distinct rather than on consonant principles. Whatever its merits or demerits it is in any event clear that it is not part of the law of Scotland, for it allows no place for putative marriage. It has, moreover, been suggested that it relies on notions of the indelibility of bastardy which underlay English judicial thinking on the international private law of legitimacy, at least until the Legitimacy Act 1926, and which have no counterpart in Scots law and are irreconcilable with the long-standing institution of legitimation.[37] In this more than most areas of international private law, English authority is an unsure guide.

1.67   The alternative solution to the *circulus inextricabilis*, favoured by the leading Scottish cases[38] and at least one English case of legitimacy at birth[39] and by the cases in both jurisdictions on legitimation,[40] is to substitute the domicile of the father for the domicile of the child. It is, however, clear both on principle and from the dicta of Lord Westbury cited above that it is the child's domicile which is the ultimate governing factor. The father's domicile is but a route to a goal which might otherwise be unattainable. It is the child's status and not the father's which is in issue.

1.68   For the purposes of the Legitimation (Scotland) Act 1968 a child is, however, legitimated if his or her father was domiciled in Scotland at the date of the marriage,[41] but no corresponding rule is laid down for the recognition of foreign legitimations.[42] It is submitted that the Act applies only to the legitimation of persons domiciled in Scotland.

Legitimacy at birth

1.69   A child is legitimate at birth if this status is conferred by the law of his or her domicile. There is no problem if the domicile of both parents is the same, but no clear rule if their domiciles are different and only one holds the child to be legitimate. In *Smijth v. Smijth*[43] Lord Anderson rejected an argument that the

---

[36] (1868) L.R. 3 H.L. 55; see Cheshire, *Private International Law* (9th ed.), pp. 442–448; Graveson, *Private International Law* (7th ed.), pp. 355 and 367.

[37] Anton and Beaumont (2nd ed.), pp. 486–487.

[38] *Fenton v. Livingstone*, above; *Beattie v. Beattie* (1866) 5 M. 181; *sed contra*, *Smijth v. Smijth*, 1918 1 S.L.T. 156.

[39] *Re Bischoffsheim* [1948] Ch. 79.

[40] *e.g. Bowes v. Bowes* (1871) 6 Paton 645; *Rose v. Ross* (1830), 4 W. & S. 289; *Munro v. Munro* (1840) 1 Rob. 492; *Countess of Dalhousie v. McDouall* (1840) 1 Rob. 475; *McDouall v. Adair* (1852) 14 D. 525; *Maitland v. Maitland* (1885) 12 R. 899; *Re Goodman's Trusts* (1881) 17 Ch.D. 266; *Re Andros* (1883) 24 Ch.D. 667; *Re Grove* (1887) 40 Ch.D. 216; *Re Grey's Trusts* [1892] 3 Ch. 88.

[41] s. 1.

[42] The Scottish Law Commission had recommended that recognition of foreign legitimations be governed by the law of the father's domicile at the time of the marriage and that recommendation was reflected in the Bill. It was, however, dropped—it is believed with the concurrence of the Scottish Law Commission and as a result of the decision of the House of Lords in *Indyka v. Indyka* [1969] 1 A.C. 33 which was seen as opening the door to recognition of decrees determining status on grounds of "real and substantial connection" as well as domicile. Section 5(2) of the Act precludes the court, in a question of recognition, from having regard to the father's domicile at any time prior to the marriage. A person cannot be recognised as having been legitimated from a date earlier than that on which the legitimation occurs (s. 5(3)).

[43] 1918 1 S.L.T. 156.

law of the father's domicile (the law of England under which, at that time, the children would have been illegitimate) should be applied and applied instead the law of Scotland which he took to be the law of the domicile of the children, derived from their mother. Indeed, he regarded that as undoubted and in one passage it seems that the only question which troubled him was the effect of a subsequent change in domicile. The reasoning is not, however, altogether clear. Much stress is placed on considerations of equity and humanity:

> "If this law is not applicable, then the pursuers will never succeed in having the stigma of illegitimacy removed, as I assume that the law of England will not give them the remedy which they seek. When it is kept in mind that the pursuer's claim, if conceded, will not have any patrimonial consequences, that the remedy sought flows from considerations of 'equity and humanity', and that no other law, save that of this country, can be successfully invoked, a strong case for the application of the Law of Scotland is made out."[44]

Consistently with that equitable approach, Lord Anderson acknowledged that it may be that no general rule can be laid down and that the law which is applicable may depend on the facts of the particular case. It is submitted, however, that although equitable exceptions may be allowed in special circumstances, it is unsatisfactory that there should be no general rule. Such a general rule can be found, consistently with the decision in *Smijth v. Smijth* and with the equitable objects Lord Anderson had in mind, in a preference, as between the law of the father's domicile and of the mother's, for the law pointing to legitimacy (*i.e.* the child will be legitimate if that would be the result under either of the two potentially applicable legal systems).

Legitimation

In cases of legitimation by subsequent marriage there may be a question of **1.70** validity of marriage to be determined by the law appropriate to such questions.[45] Given a valid marriage, the question arises as to which system of law determines whether or not the marriage has had legitimising effect. All the authorities affirm that the relevant law is the law of the father's domicile.[46] These authorities are, however, entirely concerned with common law legitimations.[47] In such legitimations, which are retroactive to the time of birth, the father's domicile at the time of marriage would, if legitimation were to be affirmed, necessarily be identical with the child's[48] except in the case, which appears not to have arisen for consideration, of the child's having acquired a separate domicile of choice before the parents' marriage. It can scarcely be maintained that where the child has acquired a domicile of choice at the time of the marriage in a country which does not recognise legitimation by subsequent marriage, he or she is nonetheless to be regarded as legitimate because he or she would be so regarded by the law of the father's domicile at that time.[49] References to the power or capacity or

---

[44] 1918 S.L.T. 160.
[45] *Starkowski v. Att.-Gen.* [1952] P. 135.
[46] See above, n. 40.
[47] See, however, the *obiter* statement of Lord Keith of Kinkel in *Wright's Trs v. Callender*, 1993 S.L.T. 556 at 559L: "It is for the law of Scotland to recognise the status of legitimacy conferred by [the English Legitimacy Act 1959] on the children of fathers domiciled in England at the time of the relevant marriage."
[48] This is a necessary and logical result of the retroactive principle and with an exception for the validity of legal acts which have intervened there is no reason to deny it effect. See *contra*, Anton (1st ed.), p. 168.
[49] "The whole question is, whether he be legitimate or not. The question of his status must be resolved by the law of his own country": *per* Lord Armadale in *Shedden v. Patrick* (1808) 5 Paton 194 at 202.

will of the father to legitimate his children are inept because, according at least to Scottish notions, legitimation does not depend on the father's will, other than his consent to marriage, but is a result that flows *ipso jure* from marriage. It is submitted that in this, as in other questions of status, the law of the domicile of the person whose status is in issue is the sole and sufficient criterion.

1.71   Foreign cases of legitimation by paternal recognition or by letters of legitimation or their equivalent have not been discussed extensively in Scotland. The analogy with legitimation by subsequent marriage suggests that the question should be determined by reference to the law of the child's domicile at the time when paternal recognition took place or the letters of legitimation were granted. There is, however, a stronger argument in cases of paternal recognition than in cases of legitimation by subsequent marriage that, where the father's domicile at the material time differs from the child's, regard should be had to the former as well as, or instead of, the latter. Legitimation by recognition clearly depends on the father's will to recognise, and therefore on his capacity to do so. This thinking clearly lies behind the statement of Lord Dunpark in *Kelly v. Marks*[50] that "As the father has always been domiciled in the Netherlands [where paternal recognition legitimates children], the child's legitimation by Dutch law is recognised by the law of Scotland" (the child having been resident in Scotland all her life). This statement is made, however, with neither reasoning not citation of authority, and it is clearly *obiter* in the context of a custody dispute between parents on the one hand and grandparents on the other, for there was no suggestion that the child's legitimacy would affect either the outcome of the custody dispute, the jurisdiction issue also raised in the case, or indeed the domicile of the child. It is submitted, although with diffidence, that in this case too, regard should be had only to the law of the domicile of the person whose status is in issue. It is sufficient that that law gives effect to the act of recognition.[51] This is not inconsistent with *Kelly v. Marks* since, the child's parents both being domiciled in the Netherlands, that was also the child's domicile notwithstanding her long-established residence in Scotland.

Change of domicile

1.72   Judicial decision has been concentrated on domicile at the time of birth or, in the case of legitimation, at the time of marriage. It is clear that when legitimacy can be affirmed by reference to the law of the domicile at these times, it is unnecessary to have regard to domicile at any other time and that legitimacy, once conferred, cannot be lost by a change of domicile.[52] It is not, however, equally clear that, if notions of indelibility of bastardy are rejected, a child cannot by a change of domicile acquire a status of legitimacy which was not open to him or her by the law of the relevant domicile at the time of birth or, where the parents have subsequently married, at the time of their marriage. Yet, where legitimation is not in issue, questions of legitimacy are once and for all questions to be determined at the time of birth and there is little to be said for invoking a legal system unconnected with domicile at that time. These considerations do not, however, apply to legitimation by subsequent marriage. Marriage has continuing effects. There seems to be no fundamental reason that where the law of the domicile at the time of the marriage does not recognise

---

[50] 1974 S.L.T. 118 at 120.

[51] In *Re Luck's Settlement Trusts* [1940] Ch. 864 the Court of Appeal held by a majority that regard had to be paid to the law of the father's domicile at the time both of the child's birth and of the act of recognition. It is submitted, however, that on the analogy with cases of subsequent marriage the Scottish courts would not have regard to domicile at the time of birth.

[52] *Shedden v. Patrick* (1808) 5 Paton 194, *per* Lord President Campbell at 199.

legitimation by subsequent marriage, it should not be possible, by a subsequent change of domicile during the subsistence of the marriage, to create the status of legitimacy. In the case of legitimation by paternal recognition or by letters of legitimation, the time of the legal act in question can be the only relevant *tempus inspiciendum* and that cannot be affected by a subsequent change of domicile.

Legitimacy as an incidental question

As an exception to the rule that the law of the domicile alone determines **1.73** questions of legitimacy, such questions arising in connection with succession to immoveables are decided by reference to the *lex situs*.[53] Accordingly, a person universally regarded as legitimate for all other purposes may be treated as illegitimate for the purpose of succession to immoveables if the *lex situs* so requires. On the other hand, it will not avail the person that the *lex situs* concedes his or her legitimacy if the *lex domicilii* does not.[54]

The role accorded to the *lex situs* on succession to immoveables raises the **1.74** question of whether issues of legitimacy which arise in connection with succession to moveables should be subsumed to the *lex successionis* (usually the domicile of the deceased). This is the problem of the incidental or subsidiary question.[55] It has been argued that the domestic law should apply,[56] and, despite some criticisms which have been made of it,[57] that argument has force. It is difficult to see why the intestate succession to the estate of someone who died domiciled within the jurisdiction of the forum should be enlarged or reduced by the accidents of foreign law. Similarly, where the law of the forum applies to the construction of a will, there is much to be said for the view that the words of the will should not be construed so as to enlarge or restrict the class of beneficiaries beyond that which these words would have implied in the contemplation of the domestic law of the forum unless, by the ordinary rules of construction, the testator's intention can be shown to have been to the contrary.[58] Some English authority can be cited in support of this view[59] and the failure to appreciate the point explains, it is submitted, the decision of the Inner House in *Wright's Trs v. Callender*[60] which was overruled by the House of Lords.[61] This approach has the advantage of avoiding anomalies which may arise from determining questions of legitimacy by a legal system other than that governing the succession. It has the disadvantages that persons may be regarded as legitimate for one purpose and not for another (perhaps not of practical importance and, in any event,

---

[53] *Fenton v. Livingstone* (1859) 21 D. (H.L.) 10.

[54] *Rose v. Ross* (1830) 4 W. & S. 289.

[55] Anton and Beaumont (2nd ed.), pp. 85–89.

[56] R. S. Welsh, "Legitimacy in the Conflict of Laws" (1947) 63 L.Q.R. 65.

[57] Anton (1st ed.), p. 347.

[58] It is submitted that the sharp distinction between questions of construction and questions of status made by Romer J. in *Re Bischoffsheim* [1948] Ch.79 at 86 ("The only relevant rule of construction is that a bequest in an English will to the children of A means to his legitimate children and that does not carry the matter very far, for the question remains who are his legitimate children, and that is not a question of construction at all, it is a question of law.") and by Kay J. in *Re Andros* (1883) 24 Ch. D. 637 at 639, is artificial. The *de quo* is to give effect to the testator's intention as expressed in his will. If "child" is glossed under rules of construction as meaning "legitimate child" or if the testator expressly says "legitimate child" it is in both cases a question of construction to determine what is meant in context by "legitimate child". Whom did the testator intend to benefit?

[59] *Birtwhistle v. Vardill* (1835) 2 Cl. & Fin. 571 and (1839) 7 Cl. & Fin. 895; *Boyes v. Bedale* (1863) 1 H. & M. 798; *Re Goodman's Trusts* (1880) 14 Ch.D. 619 and (1881) 17 Ch.D. 266; *sed contra Re Andros; Re Bischoffsheim*, above.

[60] 1992 S.L.T. 498.

[61] 1993 S.L.T. 556. See Crawford, "It's a Wise Testator Who Knows His Own Grandchildren", 1994 S.L.T. (News) 225.

already a result of the law regarding succession to immoveables) and that persons may be cut off from the succession on the sole ground that the domestic law of the forum does not recognise a relationship recognised by the only law with which they have any real connection. The rigid application of this view would, for example, exclude children legitimated by paternal recognition and children of polygamous marriages from succession to a domiciled Scotsman, although their relationships with the parent through whom the claim to succession was made was regular and legitimate by their own law. It may be that on balance the arguments for determining legitimacy by the *lex successionis* should be rejected, though in relation to construction of wills, where the prime consideration is to give effect to the wishes of the testator, that balance might well be taken to require a different conclusion.

Children of polygamous marriages

1.75   The legitimacy of children of polygamous marriages requires further consideration. There is no Scottish authority in point but guidance may be obtained from the House of Lords Committee on Privileges, which has accepted polygamous marriages for the purpose of a hereditary qualification to sit as a peer of the United Kingdom as well as by recent English decisions,[62] the consistent trend of which has been to recognise the status of legitimacy derived from polygamous marriage where that was consistent with the law of the domicile.

---

[62] *Sinha Peerage Case* (1939) 171 *Lords Journal* 350; [1946] 1 All E.R. 348; *Baindail v. Baindail* [1946] P. 122; *Bamgbose v. Daniel* [1955] A.C. 107.

CHAPTER 2

ANTE-NATAL ISSUES

INTRODUCTORY

The most significant event in the process that leads to the creation of the **2.01**
parent-child relationship is birth. To the layman it is from the moment of birth
that motherhood or fatherhood commences. The man who says "I have just
become a father" is saying that a child has just been born; the woman who
says "I am going to be a mother" is saying that she is pregnant but has not yet
given birth. The law reflects this to a large (but not exact) degree. The unborn
child has no legal personality in any meaningful sense of that phrase,[1] and so,
for example, it has no capacity to own property, or to sue or to be sued, nor
can legal acts be performed on its behalf. However, the denial of legal
personality is not the denial of all legal consequences to the existence of an
unborn child, and at least certain aspects of the parent-child relationship come
into being as soon as an embryo or foetus[2] comes into being. For example, the
law of Scotland has long recognised that an unborn child[3] has a claim for
legitim from the estate of a parent who dies before the child is born[4]; this is an
aspect of the parent-child relationship since legitim can only be claimed within
the context of that relationship. There is indeed modern statutory authority
for the proposition that at least in some circumstances and for some purposes
the parent-child relationship may come into existence before birth. If a
pregnancy is constituted by means of one of the medical procedures governed
by the Human Fertilisation and Embryology Act 1990 then "the woman who
is carrying or has carried a child...is to be treated as the mother of the child".[5]
If a woman is treated as a mother for all purposes while she is still pregnant
then it might be argued that she has the parental responsibilities and parental
rights of the mother of a born child. However, the courts are unlikely to accept
the full consequences of this ill-thought-out definition.[6]

The parent-child relationship is one of shifting content throughout its **2.02**
subsistence, and many aspects of that relationship are meaningless at particular
times. A parental obligation to aliment a child, for example, or to feed and nurture it,

---

[1] "An unborn person, or foetus, is not a person in the eyes of the law": *per* Lord McCluskey in
Hamilton v. Fife Health Board, 1993 S.L.T. 624 at 629C. "None of the [foreign] decisions to
which we were referred appear to us to provide support for the view that a foetus has a legal
persona, or is otherwise capable of being vested in personal rights for the protection of which the
remedy of interdict may be invoked": *Kelly v. Kelly*, 1997 S.L.T. 896 at 901C. "A foetus is not a
person in any accepted sense of the word": *per* Lord Osborne in *P's Curator Bonis v. Criminal
Injuries Compensation Board*, 1997 S.L.T. 1180, p.1200F. And see Yorke, "The Legal Personality
of the Unborn Child", 1979 S.L.T. (News) 158.
[2] These terms may have precise medical meanings, depending upon the state of development of
the potential human life. They are used here interchangeably to mean any living human entity
between the completion of the process of fertilisation and the completion of the process of birth.
[3] The phrase "unborn child" is here used as shorthand and not as indicating the moral or legal
status imputed to the child before its live birth.
[4] *Jervey v. Watt* (1762) Mor. 8170. See further, below, para. 2.18.
[5] Human Fertilisation and Embryology Act 1990, s. 27(1).
[6] The words "is carrying" were inserted to ensure that the pregnant woman has full control over
the management of the pregnancy, rather than to indicate that she has parental responsibilities
and parental rights before the birth of the child.

is largely meaningless until after the child is born; but that is no more strange than the fact that the parental right to determine a child's religious upbringing has no content for a significant period after birth, or the fact that the parental duty to provide education is directly enforceable only between the ages of five and 16.[7] In English law a parental right to withhold consent to marriage is no right in any meaningful sense until the child is old enough legally to marry. But it is nevertheless a parental right from the moment the relationship is constituted, though for practical reasons it cannot be exercised immediately. When the child attains adulthood most, but not all, of the consequences of the parent-child relationship disappear—consequences that remain include succession rights, and those relating to the laws of incest and the forbidden degrees of marriage.[8] This shifting relationship cannot exist before an embryo comes into being, and it does not survive the death of either the parent or the child, but within that timeframe its consequences vary. The question "When is the parent-child relationship established?" is then ultimately as (legally) meaningless as the question "When does human life begin?" Rather, the question is, what precise consequences does the law recognise as flowing from the existence of particular entities (embryos or foetuses, living children, adults), and the answer to that depends upon the stage of development of the embryo or foetus, or child. The unborn child, no less than the living child, has a developing and changing status in relation to its parents, and to society as a whole. Likewise, a child after birth has a developing and changing status, and varying legal personality, at different ages: so the living child before the age of 16 can own property but cannot normally transact with that property; the child above that age can both own property and transact. There is nothing in principle to deny the child before birth some legal status which has less content than that of the child, just as the pupil had at common law a legal status which had less content than that of a minor. Just like the living human being, the unborn child goes through a number of stages, at each of which its position in law may be quite different from the stage before.

THE STAGE BEFORE PREGNANCY

From production of gametes to fertilisation

2.03   The creation of new human life requires as a first essential the production of gametes of a human male and a human female. The mere production of these, and the making of them available for reproduction through sexual intercourse, has no significance for the law either in relation to any parent-child relationship or in relation to the creation of any entity the existence of which has consequences recognised by the law. The destruction of sperm and eggs that have not yet joined together is legally innocuous.

2.04   However, when sperm and eggs are produced and intended to be used for any form of infertility treatment licensed under the Human Fertilisation and Embryology Act 1990, the person whose body produced them does have certain legally recognised rights of control, in the sense that their consent to such use has to be obtained.[9] The producer of the gametes must give consent if they are to be stored (*i.e.* frozen) either as gametes or after they have been used to create embryos,[10] or if they are to be donated for the treatment of others,[11] or if they

---

[7] Education (Scotland) Act 1980, ss. 30 and 31.

[8] On which see Norrie, "Incest and the Forbidden Degrees of Marriage in Scots Law" (1992) 37 J.L.S.S. 216.

[9] Human Fertilisation and Embryology Act 1990, Sched. 3.

[10] *ibid.* Sched. 3, paras. 2 and 8.

[11] *ibid.* para. 5. The Human Fertilisation and Embryology Authority *Code of Practice* (rev. 1995) provides that gametes should not be taken for the treatment of others from anyone under the age of 18. In specifying this age the Human Fertilisation and Embryology Authority had in mind the age of capacity under English law.

are to be used to bring about the creation of embryos, in which last case the producer must be made aware of whether the embryo is for treatment or for research.[12] When gametes have been donated for any purpose governed by the Act, "proper arrangements" have to be made for their keeping and disposal by the person licensed to keep and use them.[13] Directions as to the keeping of gametes are given to the licence-holder by the Human Fertilisation and Embryology Authority,[14] which was set up by the 1990 Act.

From fertilisation to implantation

Once the sperm and egg have joined together, in the sense of the former **2.05** fertilising the latter, there exists what is variously called (depending upon the stage of development) a fertilised ovum, a zygote, a blastocyst, a pre-embryo, an embryo, a foetus or an unborn child. Whatever it is called, and this is true for the later stages also, its name is irrelevant to its position in law, which depends upon status rather than nomenclature.

Status of the pre-implantation embryo

Once the process of fertilisation has been completed,[15] the embryo must **2.06** find its way, naturally or with medical assistance, to a woman's uterus, and be implanted there. This process in natural conditions takes about a week; the embryo may exist in that state for far longer if it is created *in vitro*, or is removed from the woman's body before implantation. The status of the embryo between its coming into being and the completion of the process of implantation has long given rise to controversy. It has frequently been argued that the pre-implantation embryo cannot be destroyed, because its destruction would infringe the criminal law prohibition of abortion.[16] Whether this is so is undecided in Scotland, although the court might well take the view that, since abortion is concerned primarily with the termination of pregnancy,[17] and pregnancy will not have commenced before implantation, the destruction of pre-implantation embryos will not amount to abortion in Scots law.[18] If this is so, then embryo destruction by means of post-coital contraception or the operation of an intra-uterine contraceptive device would not be illegal as abortion.[19] While there remains some doubt in Scots law as to whether the destruction of a child on the point of being born amounts to homicide,[20] there is no authority to suggest that

---

[12] Human Fertilisation and Embryology Act 1990, para. 6.

[13] *ibid*. s. 17(1)(c).

[14] *ibid*. s. 24(3). These directions may be found in Chap. 3 of the HFEA's *Code of Practice* (rev. 1995).

[15] For the purposes of the Human Fertilisation and Embryology Act 1990 the completion of the process of fertilisation is defined as the moment at which a two-cell zygote appears: s.1(1)(b).

[16] See, *e.g.*, Smith and Hogan, *Textbook on Criminal Law* (6th ed., 1988), p. 367; Tunkel, "Modern Anti-pregnancy Techniques and the Criminal Law" [1974] Crim. L.R. 461 and "Abortion: How Early, How Late and How Legal?" (1979) 2 B.M.J. 253; Keown, "'Miscarriage': A Medico-Legal Analysis" [1984] Crim. L.R. 604. All of these writers were arguing on the basis of the English statutory provisions, which have no analogy in Scotland.

[17] And so in Scotland it is no crime to attempt to abort a woman who is not pregnant: *H.M. Advocate v. Semple*, 1937 J.C. 41; *H.M. Advocate v. Anderson*, 1928 J.C. 1. But these cases do not address the question of the pre-implantation embryo. *Cf.* Gordon, *Criminal Law* (2nd ed.) at p. 812: "Abortion may be committed at any stage between conception and birth". It might be argued (though not, it is submitted, convincingly) that abortion is the ending of the life of a developing entity, of which termination of pregnancy is only the typical example.

[18] This matter is discussed more fully by Norrie in *Family Planning Practice and the Law* (1991) at pp. 48–59. See also Douglas, *Law, Fertility and Reproduction* (1991) at pp. 27–36.

[19] This was the view of the English Attorney-General, expressed to Parliament: May 10, 1983, H.C. Written Answers, Vol. 42, cols 236–237. See further, Norrie, *Family Planning Practice and the Law* (1991), Chap. 4.

[20] See *H. M. Advocate v. McAllum* (1858) 3 Irv. 187; *H. M. Advocate v. Scott* (1892) 3 White 240; Gordon, *Criminal Law* (2nd ed., 1978), p. 727.

human life in its very earliest stages of development is protected by the prohibition on homicide and, indeed, the existence of the crime of abortion suggests otherwise. Whether the High Court would be willing to recognise as criminal the destruction of a fertilised egg as something other than abortion or homicide remains to be seen. It is also undecided whether such destruction can amount to a civil wrong. In the U.S. case of *Del Zio v. Presbyterian Hospital*[21] a civil action for damages was raised against a hospital director who had terminated an infertility treatment programme in which the plaintiffs were taking part, by destroying the embryo that had been created *in vitro* from the husband's sperm and the wife's egg. The couple were awarded damages after the court found that the defendant had acted wrongfully. But on a close examination of the case, it is clear that damages were awarded on the basis of the emotional shock suffered by the plaintiffs (a well-recognised ground of action) and that the destruction of the embryo was merely the medium through which that shock was caused. The question remains, however, of whether persons whose gametes have been used to create an embryo have such an interest in the embryo's continued existence and development as to make its destruction by another an actionable wrong in respect of which, quite apart from any emotional shock, they may sue.

In vitro embryos

2.07   In factual terms we can today distinguish between eggs that have been fertilised naturally in a woman's body, and those fertilised artificially outwith a woman's body and *in vitro*, for, with the former, the woman's interest in her own body supersedes any possibility of mutuality of interest that may characterise the rights, if any, that inhere in *in vitro* embryos. There is also a statutory distinction in that the latter are regulated by the Human Fertilisation and Embryology Act 1990. Section 3(1) of that Act provides that no person may bring about the creation of an embryo[22] or keep or use an embryo except in pursuance of a licence granted by a committee of the Human Fertilisation and Embryology Authority. A licence cannot authorise the keeping or using of an embryo after the appearance of the primitive streak,[23] which is taken to have appeared in an embryo not later than the end of the period of 14 days beginning with the day when the gametes were mixed, not counting any time during which the embryo is stored.[24] To "store" an embryo means to preserve it by cryopreservation (freezing) or in any other way[25]: this presumably means any other way that similarly arrests the development of the embryo. A licence cannot authorise the placing of an embryo in any species of animal.[26] During the period of 14 days the licence-holder may do to the embryo anything that the licence authorises, and in addition to use for infertility treatment, the licence may authorise the creation, keeping and using of embryos for the purposes of a project of research specified in the licence.[27] This, it appears, will include destruction, though that is not stated in so many words in the Act itself (except when human

---

[21] 74 Civ. 3588 (Nov. 14, 1978, U.S. District Court for the Southern District of New York). Substantial portions of the judgment are reproduced in Kennedy and Grubb, *Medical Law: Text and Materials* (1st ed., 1989), pp. 656–660. These are not contained in the 2nd edition (1994).

[22] Which means a live human embryo where fertilisation is complete, and references to an embryo include an egg in the process of fertilisation; fertilisation is not complete for this purpose until the appearance of a two-cell zygote: Human Fertilisation and Embryology Act 1990, s. 1(1).

[23] *ibid*. s. 3(3).

[24] *ibid*. s. 3(4).

[25] *ibid*. s. 2(2). Cryopreservation is the only method possible today by which a living embryo can be stored, but the Act clearly does not wish to inhibit future developments.

[26] *ibid*. s. 3(3)(b).

[27] *ibid*. s. 11(1) and Sched. 2, para. 3(1).

sperm is mixed with the egg of a hamster or other animal in order to test the sperm's fertility, in which case the resulting form must be destroyed when the research is completed and, in any event, not later than the two-cell stage[28]). If a person does something that is not or cannot be authorised by a licence he or she shall be guilty of an offence and liable on conviction on indictment to imprisonment for up to 10 years or a fine or both.[29] It follows that no embryo may lawfully be in existence after 14 days unless it has been implanted into a woman (or was there naturally in the first place).

For a pre-implantation embryo that has been artificially and lawfully created, **2.08** the question arises as to whether the woman whose egg, and the man whose sperm, was used in its creation have any rights or obligations, parental or otherwise, over it or relating to it. That question did not arise for the common law. The common law recognition of children before birth was limited to those described as "*in utero*" or "*en ventre sa mère*", though this represents what was until recently a factual invariability rather than any policy to deny recognition to pre-implantation embryos. The status of pre-implantation embryos has not been discussed by a British court, but the issue has been explored in a number of different contexts elsewhere. The California Court of Appeal held in *Hecht v. Superior Court*[30] that stored sperm was the "property" of the man who produced it and was, therefore, part of his estate for the purposes of succession. For reasons given above, sperm and, *a fortiori*, embryos in the U.K. are not subject to the absolute control that "ownership" would give, and in addition it is almost certainly not possible to have property rights in such human tissue.[31] A quite contrary approach was taken by the Supreme Court of Tasmania in *In Re the Estate of the Late K*[32] where it was held that frozen embryos were entitled to a claim in succession in the estate of the man whose sperm had been used in their creation, by application of the *nasciturus* principle.[33] That result is precluded in this country by section 28(6)(b) of the Human Fertilisation and Embryology Act 1990 which provides that a man who dies before his sperm or an embryo created with his sperm is "used" for infertility treatment is not to be considered for any purpose to be the father of any resulting child.[34] This provision was designed to avoid the possibility of the distribution of an estate being held up perhaps indefinitely until a suitable gestational environment is found in which the foetus can develop into a child.[35] Clearly, an embryo cannot both be "property" and be entitled to succeed to property, and the status of the *in vitro* embryo was again discussed in another context in the case of *Davis v. Davis*.[36] Here the "parents" of seven embryos being cryogenically preserved divorced and each sought "custody" of the embryos. The trial judge held that they were "persons" who could be sujects of a custody decree, but the Tennessee Court of

---

[28] Human Fertilisation and Embryology Act 1990, Sched. 2, para. 3(5).

[29] *ibid.* s. 41(1).

[30] 20 Cal. Rptr. (2d) 275 (1993).

[31] See *Dobson v. North Tyneside Health Authority* [1997] 1 F.L.R. 598. *Cf.* Grubb, "The Legal Status of the Frozen Human Embryo", in A. Grubb, ed., *Challenges in Medical Care* (John Wiley, 1992), pp. 69 *et seq.*

[32] (1996) 5 Tas. R. 365.

[33] For which, see below, para. 2.18.

[34] See further, below, para. 3.43.

[35] Though it does not do so completely, as Grubb points out in a commentary on *In Re the Estate of the Late K* [1997] Med. L. Rev. 121 at 124. He points out that it remains open to a testator to leave his estate to a person who is conceived with his sperm, even when born some years after his death, for all that s. 28(6)(b) does is to deny paternity and not the right to leave property to persons other than one's children. It is competent, subject to the rules on accumulation of income (for which see *Stair Memorial Encyclopaedia of the Laws of Scotland*, Vol. 25, paras 767–770), to leave interests in property to persons not yet in life nor even yet conceived.

[36] 842 S.W. (2d) 588 (1992), Supreme Court of Tennessee.

Appeals held that they were not "persons" but were, rather, the subject of "property rights" held jointly by both parties. The Supreme Court of Tennessee overruled this and held that the embryos were neither persons nor property, and that their disposal had to be determined by weighing the competing interests of the parties.[37]

2.09   In the United Kingdom, rules of conduct for dealing with artificially created embryos are contained in the Human Fertilisation and Embryology Act 1990. By Schedule 3, paragraph 6(1) a person's gametes may not be used to bring about the creation of an embryo *in vitro* unless there is an effective consent by that person to any embryo being used (a) to provide infertility treatment services to that person, (b) to provide infertility treatment services to another person or (c) for the purposes of any research project. Likewise an embryo created *in vitro* cannot be stored without the consent of those whose gametes were used in its creation.[38] An embryo fertilised naturally and taken from a woman cannot be used for any of the above purposes, nor stored, without that woman's consent[39]: in these circumstances the consent of the man whose sperm fertilised the egg is not required. These provisions for consent give the gamete provider certain rights of control though they cannot, of course, be characterised as "parental" rights of consent, because the Act envisages consent to research upon and consequent destruction of embryos up until 14 days. The validity of the exercise of any parental right depends upon the satisfaction of the welfare test,[40] which will usually be incompatible with research and will certainly be incompatible with destruction. The provisions in the 1990 Act are therefore best regarded as imposing statutory control on the use of embryos without in any way creating parental responsibilities or parental rights. It is to be noted that similar consent provisions are laid down for the use and storage of gametes[41] and it cannot be argued that a person has any "parental" control over his or her own gametes. Though not directly addressing the issue, the terms of these provisions are predicated on the assumption that pre-implantation embryos are neither property nor persons.

DURING GESTATION

Introduction

2.10   Once the process of implantation in the uterus has been completed, the embryo attains a very different status in law from the one it had previously, and its existence entails a very large number of consequences. Without question the most important and most contentious of these is that it is protected from destruction by the law prohibiting abortion, and this issue will therefore be discussed first. As will be seen later, however, it is by no means the only consequence.

---

[37] In the event they held that the man's interest in not becoming a father outwith marriage superseded the woman's interest in providing embryos for an infertile couple. See also *Kass v. Kass*, 663 N.Y.S. (2d) 581 (1997), in which the Appellate Division of the Supreme Court of New York held that cryogenically preserved embryos had a status somewhere between property and person and that they should be disposed of in accordance with any pre-existing agreement between the parties whose gametes were used to bring about their creation. For a discussion of these and other cases, see Hibbs in "Assisted Reproduction Technology and the Law" (1997) 2 *Contemporary Issues in Law* 1 at 17–18 and in "Any Frozen Embryos, Mrs Robinson?" (1996) Fam. Law 553.

[38] Sched. 3, para. 8(2). It is to be noted that in this circumstance the right of consent is granted equally to both parties, suggesting a mutuality of interest in which neither one predominates.

[39] *ibid.* paras 7(1) and 8(3).

[40] See below, Chap. 8.

[41] See above, para. 2.04.

Abortion

The nature of abortion

Abortion is the destruction[42] of an unborn child by the termination of **2.11** pregnancy. It is a crime according to the common law of Scotland,[43] though it has been recognised that there may be circumstances in which it is a lawful act such as when it is "a necessary medical operation".[44] Abortion remains a common law crime today. "Abortion in the sense of the criminal law is held to be criminal because its successful accomplishment results in the destruction of potential human life."[45] Potential human life is deemed worthy of protection by the law, though only after a pregnancy has commenced if abortion is defined as the termination of a pregnancy, or the inducing of a miscarriage. The important moment for the commencement of pregnancy is the completion of the process of implantation.[46] This is not to say, however, that the High Court of Justiciary could not declare criminal, even if it be not abortion, the destruction of potential human life before implantation.

Once a woman becomes pregnant, she has the right to seek an abortion **2.12** (though not a right to demand an abortion, as in, for example, the United States of America, where the right to an abortion—if it can be afforded—is currently constitutionally protected as part of the right of privacy[47]) and she must clearly consent to that act being done upon her. The woman's consent to that act is not the exercise of any parental right that she may have over the foetus since the abortion decision will usually be taken for reasons other than the welfare of the unborn child.

Defences to the crime of abortion

The potential human life is protected by the prohibition of abortion, but that **2.13** protection is not absolute, and the embryo may be aborted (that is, destroyed) if carried out by a registered medical practitioner and two registered medical practitioners are of the view, formed in good faith, that one of the grounds laid down in section 1(1) of the Abortion Act 1967[48] is satisfied. The grounds are as follows:

---

[42] It has been argued that abortion does not necessarily pre-suppose destruction and that there may be an ethical duty to carry out the abortion in such a manner as gives the *abortus* the best chance of survival: see McLean, "Abortion Law: Is Consensual Reform Possible?" (1990) 17 J. Law & Soc. 106. If such a duty exists in ethics, it does not exist in law, and, in any case, would apply to only a few very late abortions. A surgeon carrying out an abortion must do so in such a way as serves the best interests of his patient, *i.e.* the pregnant woman: see Norrie, *Family Planning Practice and the Law*, p. 57. The U.S. Supreme Court held in *Thornburgh v. American College of Obstetricians and Gynaecologists*, 106 Sup.Ct. 2169 (1986) that a Pennsylvania statute providing that abortion had to be carried out in the way best designed to give the foetus the greatest chance of survival was unconstitutional since it might involve subjecting the woman to greater risk.

[43] Macdonald, *Criminal Law of Scotland*, p. 114; Gordon *Criminal Law*, p. 812.

[44] Anderson, *Criminal Law of Scotland* (2nd ed., 1904), p. 156; Jones and Christie, *Criminal Law*, p. 188. As a rule of law this view is unsupported by judicial decision but it represents the practice of the prosecuting authorities.

[45] *per* Lord Anderson in *H.M. Advocate v. Anderson*, 1928 J.C.1 at 4.

[46] See Yen and Jaffe, *Reproductive Endocrinology, Physiology, Pathophysiology and Clinical Management* (2nd ed.), p. 200; "Post-Coital Contraception" (1983) 1 *Lancet* 853. This is confirmed for the purposes of the Human Fertilisation and Embryology Act 1990 by s. 2(3) thereof, which provides that "a woman is not to be treated as carrying a child until the embryo has become implanted".

[47] *Roe v. Wade*, 410 U.S. 113 (1973); *Doe v. Bolton*, 410 U.S. 179 (1973). These cases have been affirmed more recently; for example in *Planned Parenthood of Southeastern Pennsylvania v. Casey*, 505 U.S. 833, 120 L. Ed. (2d) 674 (1992).

[48] As amended by s. 37 of the Human Fertilisation and Embryology Act 1990. See also the Abortion Regulations 1991 (S.I. 1991 No. 499).

(1) that the continuance of the pregnancy would involve risk, greater than if the pregnancy were terminated, of injury to the physical or mental health of the pregnant woman or any existing children of her family (though this ground is available only when the pregnancy has not exceeded 24 weeks in duration);

(2) that the termination is necessary in order to prevent grave permanent injury to the physical or mental health of the pregnant woman (in which case there is no limit of time as in (1) above);

(3) that the continuance of the pregnancy would involve risk to the life of the pregnant woman, greater than if the pregnancy were terminated (in which case there is no limit of time as in (1) above); and

(4) that there is a substantial risk that if the child were born it would suffer from such physical or mental abnormalities as to be seriously handicapped (in which case there is no limit of time as in (1) above).

In relation to the first two grounds, account may be taken of the pregnant woman's actual or reasonably foreseeable environment.[49]

2.14   It is important to note that the ground need not exist in fact nor in law: all that is required is that two registered medical practitioners believe in good faith that one or more of the grounds exists, and the court's role is limited to an investigation of that good faith.[50] In *Kelly v. Kelly*[51] Lord Eassie said "Parliament has, in my view, established as the test of legitimacy of the termination, the existence of two *bona fide* medical opinions that termination was appropriate on therapeutic grounds within the parameters laid down in the Act".

Time-limits for the abortion defences

2.15   As originally enacted, the 1967 Act did not contain limits in time to the availability of the abortion defences in Scotland[52] (so long as the destruction was carried out during the subsistence of the pregnancy). That remains the case today in relation to the second, third and fourth of the above-listed grounds. In relation to the first ground, however, the pregnancy must not exceed 24 weeks in duration.[53] This may seem to be a significant tightening-up of the old law, but it is unlikely to be wholly effective since, if a pregnancy is of more than 24 weeks' duration, then it may be possible to use the second or the third ground instead of the first. In relation to the second ground, that is "grave permanent injury", it is to be remembered that account may be taken of the pregnant woman's actual or reasonably foreseeable environment.[54] This was the provision which, after the 1967 Act was originally passed, allowed "social" abortions, and it will continue to do so, notwithstanding the apparent tightening-up of the words, so long as the courts limit their role to a determination of whether or not the doctors granting the required certificates were acting in good faith. In relation to the third ground, that is "risk to life", there is nothing in the Act which expressly qualifies or restricts the interpretation of that phrase given by McNaghten J. in *R. v. Bourne*,[55]

---

[49] Abortion Act 1967, s. 1(2).

[50] *per* Scarman L.J. in *R. v. Smith* [1974] 1 All E.R. 376, at 381; and Baker P. in *Paton v. Trustees of the British Pregnancy Advisory Service* [1978] 2 All E.R. 987 at 991. See also *Rance v. Mid Downs Health Authority* [1991] 1 All E.R. 801.

[51] May 21, 1997, O.H., unreported; see 1997 S.L.T. 896.

[52] Unlike the position in England: for an examination of this and other differences between the two systems between 1967 and 1990, see Norrie, "Abortion in Great Britain, One Act, Two Laws", 1985 Crim. L.R. 475.

[53] The amendments to the 1967 Act are contained in s. 37 of the Human Fertilisation and Embryology Act 1990.

[54] Abortion Act 1967, s. 1(2).

[55] [1938] 3 All E.R. 615.

in which he directed the jury that, life depending upon health, and health including mental as well as physical health, risk to life included risk to physical or mental health. To apply that interpretation to "risk to life" in the Act would, where the risk is to the pregnant woman, subsume the first ground, with its time limit, into the third ground, which has no time-limit.[56] It is submitted that the scheme of the Act is to distinguish between risk to life and risk to health and that a broad interpretation of "risk to life", which would destroy that distinction, should not be adopted.

Another difficulty which the statute creates but does not address is that it **2.16** imposes a time-limit in some circumstances but gives no indication as to when the 24 weeks start running. It might be assumed that this is taken to refer to how the medical profession counts the weeks, but in Britain the medical profession treats a pregnancy as commencing on the date of the woman's last menstrual period, with the result that the pregnancy as a whole is said to run for 40 weeks. This is, of course, factually inaccurate, indeed impossible, and is adopted merely for convenience. A pregnancy "that has not exceeded its 24th week" is a pregnancy that in fact is less than 24 weeks old. The Human Fertilisation and Embryology Act 1990, which introduced this phrase into the 1967 Act, provides in another section that for the purposes of that Act pregnancy commences on implantation of the embryo,[57] which will normally be about a week after fertilisation, and this might indicate that the 24 weeks are to be counted from the completion of implantation. However, medical science is not yet able to determine precisely when implantation in the womb has occurred, not least because the creation of life is a developing process rather than a series of discrete events. A doctor who in good faith certifies that a pregnancy is less than 24 weeks old, using the medically accepted method of counting these weeks, is unlikely to be found to be in breach of the law.[58] It is to be remembered that abortion, being a criminal act, must be proved beyond reasonable doubt, and this standard of proof would have to be satisfied by a prosecutor arguing that an abortion had been carried out too late in law.[59]

Selective reduction

Particularly with infertility treatment, when a number of embryos are **2.17** frequently placed into a woman, in order to maximise the chances of at least one of them implanting successfully, the medical practice known as "selective reduction" is often performed whereby one or more of the implanted embryos is destroyed in order to increase the chance of survival of the remaining embryo or embryos. There had been doubt in English law as to whether this amounted to an offence under the relevant legislation,[60] since the statute prohibits inducing "miscarriage"[61]: this is not wholly appropriate as a description of the destruction of very early embryos *in utero* (which would be absorbed into the woman's body by the process of phagocystosis rather than being expelled out of her

---

[56] See further, Norrie, "British Abortion Rules Altered: Or Are They?", 1992 S.L.T. (News) 41, and McGleenan, "Bourne Again? Abortion Law in Northern Ireland After *Re K* and *Re A*" (1994) 45 N.I.L.Q. 389.

[57] Human Fertilisation and Embryology Act 1990, s. 2(3).

[58] *cf. Rance v. Mid Downs Health Authority* [1991] 1 All E.R. 801. For a further discussion of the difficulty, see Jacob, *Current Law Annotations* of the Human Fertilisation and Embryology Act 1990 (c. 37), s. 37. The same problem appears in the Registration of Births, Deaths and Marriages (Scotland) Act 1965, s. 56(1), as amended by the Still-Birth (Definition) Act 1992, s. 1(2), which provides for the registration of the birth of children still-born after 24 weeks' gestation.

[59] The evidential burden, however, will rest with the accused to set up the defence that the abortion was carried out timeously.

[60] Offences Against the Person Act 1861, ss. 58 and 59.

[61] See Kennedy and Grubb, *Medical Law: Text With Materials* (2nd ed., 1994), pp. 920–922.

body). The matter was put beyond all doubt by the amendment of section 5(2) of the 1967 Act by section 37 of the Human Fertilisation and Embryology Act 1990, and it is now clear that the destruction of any embryo or embryos implanted in a woman is lawful if authorised under section 1 of the 1967 Act.

Succession

2.18   It is in relation to succession that the civil law of Scotland has most clearly recognised that the existence of a conceived but unborn child might have significant consequences. The proposition taken from the *Digest*,[62] in a translation approved by the House of Lords,[63] is wide in its scope: "An unborn child is taken care of just as much as if it were in existence, in any case in which the child's own advantage comes into question; though no one else can derive any benefit through the child before its birth." In Scotland this principle has been expressly applied only in succession matters,[64] but in that field it is widely accepted by the institutional writers and others.[65] The basis of the principle is the presumption that a parent would desire to provide for children conceived but unborn at the date of his or her[66] death, and as such it has the same foundation as the *conditio si testator sine liberis decesserit*.[67] It has extensive application in the law of succession. So, for example, it has been held that a child born subsequently to her father's death was entitled to legitim from his estate,[68] that a legacy in favour of "children" included a child *in utero* but not yet born,[69] and that a posthumous child can in appropriate circumstances take benefit from the application of the *conditio si testator sine liberis decesserit*.[70] A lengthy discussion may be found in what is considered to be the leading decision of *Mountstewart v. Mackenzie*,[71] though that case is ultimately unhelpful since a living heir was allowed to be served before the birth of an unborn child, though subject to holding the estate in trust for a child if born. It is interesting to note that in that case there was no allegation that there was an unborn child, merely that there might be.

2.19   The extent to which the principle can be taken even in the face of apparently unambiguous words in a will can be seen from the case of *Cox's Trs v. Cox*,[72] in which the residue of an estate was directed to be divided between certain "descendants alive at the time of [the testator's] death". Four such descendants were *in utero* at the date of the testator's death. The First Division held that they were included in the gift. Lord Carmont said this:

> "The particular principle, which from a very early time has guided the Courts in this country in regard to the interpretation of such words of

---

[62] 1, v, 7: "*Qui in utero est, perinde ac si in rebus humanis esset, custoditur, quoties de commodis ipsius partus quaeritur: quanquam alii, antequam nascatur, nequaquam prosit.*"

[63] In *Elliot v. Joicey*, 1935 S.C. (H.L.) 57 at 70.

[64] Though in Canada, for example, the same passage was used to justify awarding damages to a child negligently injured while it was *in utero*: see *Montreal Tramways v. Leveille* [1933] 4 D.L.R. 337. In *Cohen v. Shaw*, 1992 S.L.T. 1022, Lord Cullen could see no reason why the principle should be limited to succession.

[65] Stair, III, v, 50; Erskine, III, viii, 76; Bankton, I, ii, 7, p. 47; Bell, *Prin.*, para. 1642; Fraser (3rd ed.), p. 220; McLaren, p. 696; *Stair Memorial Encyclopaedia of the Laws of Scotland*, Vol. 10, pp. 1015–1020 and Vol. 25, pp. 660–662.

[66] Technology now allows a dead woman's corpse to be artificially ventilated in such a way as to provide a gestation environment for her unborn child: *The Independent*, Oct. 17, 1992 reports such a case involving a 15-week-old foetus growing in the ventilated corpse of its deceased mother.

[67] Fraser, *ibid.*; *Stair Memorial Encyclopaedia of the Laws of Scotland*, Vol. 25, p. 751.

[68] *Jervey v. Watt* (1762) Mor. 8170.

[69] *Hardman v. Guthrie* (1826) 6 S. 920. See also *Melrose v. Melrose's Trs* (1869) 7 M.1050.

[70] *Findlay's Trs v. Findlays* (1886) 14 R.167; *Stair Memorial Encyclopaedia of the Laws of Scotland*, Vol. 25, p. 753.

[71] (1707) Mor. 14903.

[72] 1950 S.C. 117.

gift as these, has been favourable to including those children who were *in utero* in order to let them share in such gifts, and that is based upon the view that an equitable interpretation of such words used in such testamentary deeds should be given to them. From Roman times we find that the posthumous child has been given its place along with the other children, and that on the fiction that although not born at the time specified in the settlement the child should be deemed to have been so born."[73]

The qualifications

While the principle itself is well established, equally settled are two qualifications, which are mentioned by nearly all the authorities cited above. The first is that the principle applies only when to do so directly benefits the child him or herself. No one else can claim a right through the child, until such time as the child is born alive. So, for example, in *Elliot v. Joicey*[74] a truster set up a trust for the benefit of her children who were to take the income for 21 years; if any child should die within that period without issue the share would accrue to the other children. One child did die within the 21 years, leaving a child *in utero* (which was later born alive). If that (grand)child had been deemed to be born at the date of his parent's death, then the benefit from his grandparent's estate would go to his parent's estate, and not to the posthumous child himself. The House of Lords held that in these circumstances the principle could not be applied. The fact that the child's parent's estate would be increased, so increasing the child's share in legitim, was too remote and speculative a benefit: "the *commodum* of the posthumous child must be a direct *commodum* to itself resulting from the instrument under construction by virtue of the application to that instalment of the benevolent fiction in question."[75] **2.20**

The second qualification to the principle is that the child must subsequently be born alive. The right to benefit that vests in the child while it is still in the womb is, effectively, a benefit with a resolutive condition attached, which means that it may be subject to defeasance by the child's failure to attain live birth.[76] While there is no Scottish decision turning on this point, this is almost certainly because the position is so well settled, and the qualification unquestioned.[77] Indeed, it may be correct, as Meston suggests,[78] that this second qualification is simply an example of the application of the first. A child who dies in the womb cannot enjoy the benefit it is to take and, clearly, to apply the doctrine in relation to such a child is to apply it for the benefit of someone else. **2.21**

Effect of the Succession (Scotland) Act 1964

The Succession (Scotland) Act 1964 has no effect on this rule,[79] though the Act itself makes no reference to it. Difficulties might arise in relation to section 9, **2.22**

---

[73] 1950 S.C. 117 at 121. The rule was resisted by the court in *Burns' Trs v. Burns*, 1916 2 S.L.T. 318, but that case must now be regarded as no longer good law.

[74] 1935 S.C. (H.L.) 57. See also *Villar v. Gilbey* [1907] A.C. 139 (in which to apply the fiction would have given the child a right to a liferent instead of a right to the fee).

[75] *Elliot v. Joicey*, above, *per* Lord Macmillan.

[76] It is interesting to note that the statutory formulation of the rule found in Quebec was characterised by the Supreme Court of Canada as a suspensive condition, and the argument was rejected that it was a "resolutory" condition: *Tremblay v. Daigle* (1989) 62 D.L.R. (4th) 634 at 656. This was done to answer the proposition that if the right vested before the birth but was subject to a resolutive condition, the foetus would have legal personality. This does not necessarily follow, however. The vesting is as fictional as the unborn child's legal existence, and it can be defeated by the same event as defeats the child's legal existence, *i.e.* its death before live birth.

[77] See, *e.g.*, Bell, *Prin.*, paras 1641 and 1642; Bankton, I, ii, 8; *Stair Memorial Encyclopaedia of the Laws of Scotland*, Vol. 25, p. 662.

[78] "Succession Rights of Posthumous Children" (1970) 15 J.L.S.S. 33.

[79] s. 1(1)(b) provides that a person's intestate succession will devolve according to the rules in that Act and to "any enactment or rule of law in force immediately before the commencement of this Act which is not inconsistent with those provisions". The rule is inconsistent with no provision in the 1964 Act.

which provides that the value of a spouse's prior rights varies depending upon whether the intestate is "survived by issue" or not. It would not, it is submitted, consist with the policy of the Act to hold that a child of the deceased unborn at the date of death but subsequently born alive does not "survive" the deceased. The purpose of differentiating in the value of prior rights according to whether or not issue survive is that, where there are issue, more of the estate should be available for distribution to them. It would be anomalous to deny that benefit to a child *in utero* at the time of death, and a wider interpretation of "survival" may therefore be appropriate for these purposes than would otherwise be the case.

Effect of the Human Fertilisation and Embryology Act 1990

2.23   Under section 14(4) of the Human Fertilisation and Embryology Act 1990 embryos may be stored for up to five years and regulations allow storage for substantially longer[80]; there is no legal limit on how long sperm can be stored. It follows that it is possible for a child to be born many years after the death of his or her genetic father. An embryo in storage is not to be regarded as an embryo *in utero* for the purposes of the law of succession, nor is it to receive the benefit of the civilian fiction described above. If the genetic father of an embryo dies while it is in storage, then the child subsequently born will have no succession rights in that man's estate. This is a consequence of section 28(6)(b) of the 1990 Act, which provides that where the sperm of a man is used after his death, or any embryo created with his sperm is used after his death, that man is not to be treated as the father of the child, "for any purpose"[81] (which includes succession purposes). This avoids the possibility of the distribution of the estate of the genetic father being held up until any potential child is born alive, possibly five or more years after death. This only applies if the sperm or embryo is "used" after his death, which means used to bring about a pregnancy that will continue with normal gestation. So if the father of an artificially created embryo dies during its gestation the subsequently born child will have all normal succession rights, including the benefit of the civilian fiction, even although conception was by a method governed by the 1990 Act; but if the father dies before the woman begins to carry the child (*i.e.* before the embryo has become implanted[82]) then the posthumous child will have no succession rights in his or her genetic father's estate.

2.24   The 1990 Act does not completely obviate succession difficulties, however. In its terms it is limited to denying the genetic father of the child any legal consequence of paternity. It would seem to follow that the Act only cuts off succession rights of the genetic father or to his estate and does not affect other succession claims, for example by grandparents and grandchildren. If this were so, then a trust set up, say, for "all my grandchildren" could benefit a grandchild who was born some years after the death of his or her genetic father (the son of the truster), and an estate in which such a provision were made could not be finally distributed until there are no gametes or embryos in existence capable of producing the truster's genetic grandchild. The easiest way of avoiding this result is to hold that the breaking of the father–child link also breaks any link traced through the father. An analogy with the adoption legislation is apt. The Adoption (Scotland) Act 1978 provides[83] that a child who is subject to an adoption order is in law to be treated as the child of the adopter and of no other person.

---

[80] Human Fertilisation and Embryology (Statutory Storage for Embryos) Regulations 1996 (S.I. 1996 No. 375), reg. 2.

[81] Human Fertilisation and Embryology Act 1990, s. 29(2). See further, below, para. 3.43.

[82] *ibid.* s. 2(3).

[83] Adoption (Scotland) Act 1978, s. 39.

That too in its terms does not affect grandparents, but it has never been suggested that a legal connection for purposes of, *inter alia*, succession between natural grandparents and an adopted child survives the adoption. To apply similar reasoning to the Human Fertilisation and Embryology Act 1990 would consist with the policy of that Act and ought, it is submitted, to be followed. If the genetic father is not to be treated as the father for any purpose, he is not the father for the purpose of any link that might be traced through him.[84]

There is no provision similar to that in section 28(6)(b) made in relation to the **2.25** genetic mother of an embryo, for none is needed since the 1990 Act elsewhere provides that for all purposes of law the woman who carries the child shall be the mother.[85] The child therefore will never have succession rights in the estate of his or her genetic mother if she is not the woman who carries the child during gestation, and her death before the child's birth is therefore legally irrelevant to the child.

Aliment

The physical alimentary needs of the child before birth are, in the nature of **2.26** the case, met by the mother but there is no reason why financial support should not be provided in respect of these needs on the same principles as for a child who has been born. "Inlying expenses" are of an essentially alimentary character and are so recognised by statute. Section 2(5) of the Family Law (Scotland) Act 1985 provides that a woman, whether married or not, may bring an action for aliment on behalf of her unborn child as if the child had been born, but no such action can be heard by the court or disposed of until the child is actually born. Payments in advance of the birth are now no longer possible, as they were under the Illegitimate Children (Scotland) Act 1930.[86] The position of the pregnant woman is therefore rather less protected than it used to be, in that she may be unable to purchase articles for the baby before its birth but the eventual award of aliment may be backdated to the date of bringing of the action or, on special cause shown, to an earlier date. Starting proceedings before the birth may have the effect of preventing the father dissipating his assets in order to defeat the claim for aliment.[87]

Aliment jure representationis

From the point of view of the living child, aliment from his or her parent's **2.27** estate is an entitlement[88]; that entitlement can accrue, like the right to claim legitim, before birth (though defeasibly for the same reasons). So if a parent dies before the child is born, that child is entitled to claim aliment from the parent's estate, so long as he or she is subsequently born alive.[89] In *Spalding v. Spalding's Trustees*[90] the First Division held that an obligation to aliment a child was a debt that was preferred to the beneficiaries under a trust disposition and settlement, and that "it became a debt so soon as the child was begotten".[91] The same conditions will attach to this right as to rights of succession. The action for aliment can be brought on his or her behalf by the parent or guardian of the child, or by a person with whom the child lives or who is seeking a residence order in respect of the child.[92]

---

[84] As always, however, the intention of the testator might indicate a different result—but that is because the issue would be one of whom the testator intended to benefit rather than one of status.

[85] Human Fertilisation and Embryology Act 1990, ss. 27(1) and 29(2).

[86] s. 3(1), repealed by the Family Law (Scotland) Act 1985, Sched. 2.

[87] See Nichols, *The Family Law (Scotland) Act 1985* (2nd ed., 1991), p. 14.

[88] *Beaton v. Beaton's Trs*, 1935 S.C. 187.

[89] *Hastie and Ker v. Hastie* (1671) Mor. 416.

[90] (1874) 2 R. 237.

[91] *per* Lord Deas at 251.

[92] Family Law (Scotland) Act 1985, s. 2(4)(c), as amended by the Children (Scotland) Act 1995, Sched. 4, para. 36.

Aliment of "accepted child"

2.28   Section 1(1)(d) of the Family Law (Scotland) Act 1985 provides that a person owes an obligation of aliment to a child "who has been accepted by him as a child of his family," and the question arises whether a child can be accepted as such before it has been born. The issue is of importance only when such acceptance has become impossible or is purposely retracted by the time the child is born, for example if the putative acceptor has died or has left the family. In England an affirmative answer to that question was given in the case of *Caller v. Caller*.[93] There, a man married a pregnant woman, knowing that she was pregnant and knowing that he was not the father of the child. He deserted the wife before the child was born. The court held that the husband had clearly agreed to take over responsibility for the unborn child, that a "family" had come into (an admittedly brief) existence on the marriage, and that the husband had therefore "accepted [the unborn child] as one of the family" within the terms of the then extant Matrimonial Proceedings (Magistrates Courts) Act 1960. Consequently, the child was entitled to aliment from the husband. This case was not followed in *A v. A (Family: Unborn Child)*,[94] but there the relevant statutory provision[95] involved a child being "treated" rather than being "accepted" as part of the family. Bagnall J. held that the two concepts are quite different, and that "to treat" means "to act or behave towards", which cannot be done in respect of an unborn child.[96] "Acceptance" can be directed towards the other parent, and so can be done before the birth of the child. "Treatment" involves behaviour; "acceptance" involves attitude. The Family Law (Scotland) Act 1985 uses the word "accepted"[97] rather than "treated"[98] and *Caller v. Caller* is therefore the relevant authority.[99] Section 1(1)(d) demands acceptance by a person of the child "as a child of his family", rather than, as the English statute had it, "as a child of the family"[1]; but this change in terminology has no significance and it is submitted that *Caller v. Caller* ought to be followed. There is nothing in the Scottish Act to suggest that the acceptance can occur only after birth. The fact that the Act states that the obligation is owed to a "child" who has been accepted, and that "child" is defined as "a person under the age of 18 years"[2] suggests no more than that the claim for aliment can be made only when the child reaches personhood (*i.e.* on birth[3]) and not that the acceptance as a member of the family has to be done during the child's personhood.

Delict: General

2.29   The existence of an unborn child can have important consequences in the law of delict. The fact that a child is unborn (indeed that it is not conceived) does not prevent a person from owing a duty of care towards it. A duty of care

---

[93] [1966] 2 All E.R. 754.

[94] [1974] 1 All E.R. 755.

[95] Matrimonial Proceedings and Property Act 1970, s. 27(1).

[96] This was followed in later English cases, such as *Re M (A Minor)* (1980) 2 F.L.R. 184, and *Teeling v. Teeling* [1984] F.L.R. 808.

[97] s. 1(1)(d). See *Gallacher v. Gallacher*, 1997 S.C.L.R. 174.

[98] Which is used, for example, in s. 2(1A)(b) of the Marriage (Scotland) Act 1977; s. 17(4) of the Family Law Act 1986; s. 2 of the Criminal Law (Consolidation) (Scotland) Act 1995; and s. 22 of the Matrimonial Homes (Family Protection) (Scotland) Act 1981 (as amended by the Children (Scotland) Act 1995, Sched. 4, para. 30—prior to which the word was "accepted").

[99] *cf. P's Curator Bonis v. Criminal Injuries Compensation Board*, 1997 S.L.T. 1180, where it was held that an unborn child and her father could not be said to be "living together... as members of the same family".

[1] The present English provisions define "child of the family" as any child "who has been treated by both [parties to a marriage] as a child of their family": Children Act 1989, s. 105(1).

[2] s. 1(5)(a).

[3] *cf.* s. 2(5) which provides that an action can be brought before birth, but the action cannot be heard or disposed of until after birth.

can be directed to all those who may foreseeably be harmed by its breach, and there is no requirement that the subject be identified or even identifiable at the time of the breach; nor is there any requirement that the injured person is in existence at that time. Thus the manufacturer of baby food will be liable to the newborn child injured by contaminated food notwithstanding that the food was manufactured before the baby's birth or conception.[4] Whether a defender is liable for injuries inflicted before birth or for breaches of duty committed before birth or before conception is a matter that has given rise to some controversy. It has, however, long been generally accepted in Scotland that the law places no bar to allowing recovery.[5] However, the dearth of direct authority leaves many areas in doubt, such as whether the injured child can sue his or her mother as well as third parties, and whether interdict is ever available to prevent the harm occurring. These (and other) matters will be examined separately in the following paragraphs.

Damages against a third party

2.30 There is no reported Scottish decision in which a child has sued someone in delict for personal injuries suffered before the commencement of the birth process. It has been assumed that, at least where the defender is a third party (*i.e.* not the mother), such a claim would be relevant,[6] and that assumption has been accepted *obiter* in three Outer House decisions and one Inner House decision.[7] Until a case is decided on the precise issue it remains uncertain what the juridical basis of the liability for ante-natal injuries is in Scots law, but there are at least three possibilities.

The civilian fiction theory

2.31 First, one might use an analogy with the civilian fiction applied in the law of succession, discussed above, that in all things to the child's benefit a child not born at the appropriate date is to be regarded as having been born, so long as the child later achieves live birth. This approach has been adopted in some civilian jurisdictions. So in a decision based on the Civil Code of Quebec,[8] damages

---

[4] The statement in the text is one of principle: the precise facts given would now, of course, be governed by the Consumer Protection Act 1987. As an example from the USA, see *Jorgensen v. Meade Johnson Laboratories Inc.*, 483 F. (2d) 237 (1973).

[5] See Scot. Law Com., Report No. 30, *Liability for Antenatal Injury*, Cmnd. 5371 (1973); Walker, *Delict* (2nd ed.), pp. 88–89; Walker, "The Rights of the Unborn Child to Reparation" (1954) 70 S.L.R. 125; Stewart, *Delict* (2nd ed.), p. 189. Oblique statutory recognition that this is correct can be found in s. 35 of the Human Fertilisation and Embryology Act 1990. Due to doubts about the position in English law (see Law Com., *Report on Injuries to Unborn Children*, Cmnd. 5703 (1974)) the Congenital Disabilities (Civil Liability) Act 1976 was passed in order to recognise liability to the unborn child; this Act was not extended to Scotland on the assumption that it would be otiose to do so. The 1976 Act was amended by the 1990 Act: s. 35(1) provides for the obtaining in England of information relating to genetic parenthood when this is required to raise an action under the 1976 Act: s. 35(2) provides for the obtaining in Scotland of information relating to genetic parenthood when this is required to raise any action for damages in which the damages claimed consist of or include damages or solatium in respect of personal injury. This assumes that the common law of Scotland recognises the actionability of ante-natal injuries that was statutorily recognised in England in the 1976 Act. Similarly, s. 44 of the 1990 Act adds into the 1976 Act a new s. 1A, which provides that a child born as a result of infertility treatment can sue if an act or omission in the course of selecting, keeping or using embryos or gametes causes injury to the child when born: again, this is not extended to Scotland, presumably because Scots common law provides a remedy already. And see *P's Curator Bonis v. Criminal Injuries Compensation Board*, 1997 S.L.T. 1180, *per* Lord Osborne at 1186D–E, and at 1197L when he said "it is plain that, in certain circumstances, the law may recognise a pre-conception tort (*sic*). Where avoidable damage has been done to a subsequent foetus or child, no doubt a remedy may be appropriate".

[6] See above, n.5.

[7] *Cohen v. Shaw*, 1992 S.L.T. 1022, *per* Lord Cullen; *Hamilton v. Fife Health Board*, 1992 S.L.T. 1026, *per* Lord Prosser; *McWilliams v. Lord Advocate*, 1992 S.L.T. 1045, *per* Lord Morton of Shuna; *Hamilton v. Fife Health Board*, 1993 S.L.T. 624, *per* Lords McCluskey, Caplan and Wylie. These cases were raised under the Damages (Scotland) Act 1976, and are discussed below at paras 2.49 and 2.54.

[8] *Montreal Tramways v. Leveille* [1933] 4 D.L.R. 337.

were awarded (and upheld on appeal) to a child who suffered injury as a result of the defendant's negligence which caused the child's mother, when pregnant with the plaintiff, to fall while descending from a tram. The passages from the *Digest* which in Scots law have been used to justify an unborn child's claims in succession were founded upon in that case. However, as Rodger points out,[9] the relevant passages[10] are clearly not intended by their authors to be extended into the field of delict. Certainly the rule has been regarded by the judges who have applied it in succession cases as no more than a rule of construction[11] (of wills, trust deeds and statutes). Walker, after stating that the civilian fiction is accepted in Scots law for succession purposes, warns: "it is not, however, safe to infer that the same principle would necessarily apply in a case of reparation."[12] On the other hand, as Winfield points out, "to limit this proposition[13] to property rights is to rate property higher in the scale of legal values than life and limb".[14] While the policy attractions of that statement cannot be denied, the Roman law authority for adopting this approach in Scotland is, at best, fragile. Nevertheless this approach does receive support in *Cohen v. Shaw*,[15] in which Lord Cullen could see no reason in principle why the civilian fiction should be limited to succession cases, and he opined that there was nothing in the law of Scotland to suggest that the fiction should have less than general application. He awarded damages to a child whose father had been killed before the child's birth on the ground that the civilian fiction allowed him to deem the unborn child to be born at the date of death.[16]

The legal personality theory

2.32   Secondly, it might be argued that the unborn child has legal personality and as such can be the subject of a reparable injury. This approach is adopted in some jurisdictions in the USA, where, after an initial reluctance to recognise the competency of claims for ante-natal injuries,[17] such claims are now usually accepted.[18] In some U.S. jurisdictions the constitutional right to life is recognised in, and statutorily granted to,[19] the unborn child, usually from the point of viability,[20] but sometimes even before.[21] This approach cannot, however, be

---

[9] "Report of the Scottish Law Commission on Antenatal Injury", 1974 J.R. 83 at 89–90.

[10] D.1, *v.* 7 and D.1, *v.* 26.

[11] See, in particular, *Villar v. Gilbey* [1907] A.C.139, *per* Lord Loreburn L.C. at 144.

[12] (1954) 70 S.L.R. 125. In England, Dillon L.J. in *Burton v. Islington Health Authority* [1992] 3 All E.R. 833 at 839 considered that it would be open to the English courts to apply the civilian fiction in a claim for damages, but held it unnecessary to do so, since the same result was achieved by adopting the approach whereby the claim crystallises on the birth of the child: see below, para. 2.33.

[13] *i.e.* that in D.1, *v.* 26.

[14] "The Unborn Child" (1944) 8 Camb. L.J. 76 at 90. The Court of Appeal in England seem to have been persuaded by this in *Burton v. Islington Health Authority, De Martell v. Merton and Sutton Health Authority* [1992] 3 All E.R. 833, in which the English common law was said to accept the civilian fiction in the field of tort liability.

[15] 1992 S.L.T. 1022 at 1024F.

[16] See further, below, para. 2.49. Lord Prosser, in *Hamilton v. Fife Health Board*, 1992 S.L.T. 1026 at 1028, accepted this and assumed that the child in *Cohen* would have been unsuccessful without the use of the fiction. However, Lord Morton of Shuna in *McWilliams v. Lord Advocate*, 1992 S.L.T. 1045 at 1048I, did not accept that the civilian fiction was either appropriate or necessary, and Lord Prosser's decision was later overruled: 1993 S.L.T. 624.

[17] See particularly the influential decision of Holmes J. in *Dietrich v. Inhabitants of Northampton*, 138 Mass. 14 (1884) .

[18] The turning point came in the case of *Bonbrest v. Kotz*, 65 F.Supp. 138 (1946).

[19] See, *e.g.*, s. 184 of the California Penal Code which confers on the foetus legal personality for the purposes of the criminal law (allowing it, for example, to be the victim of the crime of murder).

[20] *i.e.* the commencement of the third trimester in the context of the abortion decision in *Roe v. Wade*, 410 US 113 (1973). So in *Jefferson v. Griffen Spalding County Hospital Authority*, 274 S.E. (2d) 457 (1981) the Supreme Court of Georgia held that a viable foetus had legal personality and was entitled to the full protection of the law granted to any other human being.

[21] The U.S. Supreme Court has held that it is not unconstitutional for a state legislature to declare legislatively that human life begins on conception: *Webster v. Reproductive Health Services*, 106 L. Ed. (2d) 410 (1989).

followed in Scotland. There is no constitutionally protected "right to life" guaranteed to an unborn child at any stage of development, and while Article 2 of the European Convention on Human Rights does guarantee "everyone" a right to life, it has been held by the European Commission on Human Rights that the word "everyone" does not encompass the unborn child.[22] Similarly, the UN Convention on the Rights of the Child[23] defines "child" in Article 1 as "every human being below the age of 18 years." The neutral phrase "human being" was chosen to allow individual states to decide whether or not to include the unborn. In Scotland the unborn child, though its existence has legal consequences, has no legal personality.[24] That does not mean that its existence before birth is devoid of legal recognition, nor does it mean that the term "person" may never be used to describe an unborn child, but it does mean that legally protected interests accruing before birth cannot be explained on a theory of legal personality.

The crystallisation of damage theory

Thirdly, it might be argued that an injury caused by a negligent act committed while the child is unborn does not cause any legally recognised loss, injury or damage until such time as the child acquires the capacity (in law) to suffer such loss, injury or damage.[25] It is submitted that this is the approach that ought to be adopted by the Scottish court. It has long been held in Scotland that liability in negligence does not arise simply from the negligent act, but rather from the loss, injury or damage that the negligent act causes. A breach of a duty of care is a continuing wrong, which continues for so long as the wrongful act retains the ability to cause direct or foreseeable hurt. "The ground of any action based on negligence is the concurrence of breach of duty and damage, and I cannot see how there can be that concurrence unless the duty still exists and is breached when the damage occurs."[26] "The fact that the negligent act which caused the injury was not contemporaneous with the injury itself is not a bar to recovery."[27] *Donoghue v. Stevenson*[28] itself provides an example. Given this unchallengeable

2.33

---

[22] *X v. United Kingdom* (1990) 3 E.H.R.R. 408. See also *Trembley v. Daigle* (1990) 62 D.L.R. (4th) 634, a decision of the Supreme Court of Canada, interpreting the Quebec Civil Code to the same effect.

[23] (1989) 28 *International Legal Materials* 1448, adopted Nov. 28, 1989 and ratified by the U.K. on Dec. 16, 1991.

[24] "Prior to being born, a child is not a person", *per* Lord Prosser in *Hamilton v. Fife Health Board*, 1992 S.L.T. 1026 at 1028E. In relation to English law it was said by Baker P. that this proposition "permeates the whole of the civil law of this country": *Paton v. Trustees of the British Pregnancy Advisory Service* [1978] 2 All E.R. 987 at p. 989. This was approved by the Court of Appeal in *Re F (In Utero)* [1988] 2 W.L.R.1288, *per* May L.J. at p.1301. Within the context of English criminal law, Lord Mustill said "It... is established beyond doubt for the criminal law, as for the civil law, (*Burton v. Islington Health Authority*) that the child *en ventre sa mere* does not have a distinct human personality, whose extinguishment gives rise to any penalties or liabilities at common law": *Att.-Gen.'s Reference (No. 3 of 1994)* [1997] 3 W.L.R. 421 at 434G. The definition of "embryo" given in the Human Fertilisation and Embryology Act 1990 is careful to avoid the possibility of including within its terms the status of personhood. See also the Canadian cases of *Trembley v. Daigle*, above, *Re A (In Utero)* (1990) 72 D.L.R. (4th) 722 (Ontario Family Court), and *Winnipeg Child and Family Services (Northwest Area) v. G* (1997) 152 D.L.R. (4th) 193.

[25] This is the conceptual reason why actions for "wrongful life" (see below, para. 2.38) cannot ever succeed, for such actions postulate a duty on the part of the defender to terminate life (or prevent its occurring) before birth, so preventing the claim ever crystallising: the pursuer is effectively founding upon a right not to have his right crystallised. See *P's Curator Bonis v. Criminal Injuries Compensation Board*, 1997 S.L.T. 1180. See further, Norrie, "Wrongful Life in Scots Law: No Right, No Remedy", 1990 J.R. 205.

[26] *per* Lord Reid in *Watson v. Fram Reinforced Concrete (Scotland) Ltd*, 1960 S.C. (H.L.) 92 at 109.

[27] *per* Potts J. in *Burton v. Islington Health Authority* [1991] 1 All E.R. 825 at 831, upheld [1992] 3 All E.R. 833.

[28] 1932 S.C. (H.L.) 31.

fact it can be seen that it is irrelevant when the breach of duty occurs so long as it also causes damage to occur and that damage is visited upon a living person. It would follow that if a child is injured *in utero* by an act committed then or even before its conception, this is, as it were, latent damage which becomes patent when the child attains such legal personality as allows his or her injuries to be recognised, *i.e.* the moment of live birth. If that injury is caused by negligence, liability arises at that moment. This is the approach that the Scottish Law Commission (founding on *Watson*) thought that the courts would adopt.[29] However, Rodger[30] considered this to be "a remarkable feat of redefinition". His argument was that the injury is suffered when the harm is caused and not when title to sue upon it is acquired. In *Cohen v. Shaw*[31] Lord Cullen expressly reserved his opinion as to whether this approach would commend itself to the Scottish court; and in *Hamilton v. Fife Health Board*[32] Lord Prosser dismissed a claim under the Damages (Scotland) Act 1976 on the ground that an ante-natal injury had been "sustained" by a foetus and not by a child at the moment of birth.[33] Both these judges preferred to recognise a child's right to sue on the basis of the civilian fiction as discussed above. On the other hand, Lord Morton rejected the need to rely upon the fiction and accepted the approach postulated here.[34]

2.34   However, this third approach has much, it is submitted, to commend it. Not only is it favoured by the Scottish Law Commission but it has been adopted in cases from other common law jurisdictions. So in *Watt v. Rama*[35] the Supreme Court of Victoria, founding upon *Donoghue v. Stevenson*,[36] allowed a case to go to trial having rejected the argument that the breach of duty was spent by the time the injury was suffered at birth. Two members of the court said this: "On the birth the relationship crystallised and out of it arose a duty on the defendant in relation to the child."[37] This case was followed by the Ontario Court of Appeal,[38] by the Supreme Court of British Columbia,[39] by the Supreme Court of New South Wales, Court of Appeal,[40] and by the English Court of Appeal in *Burton v. Islington Health Authority, De Martell v. Merton and Sutton Area Health Authority*.[41] In *Burton*, a child born in 1967[42] claimed damages from a health authority which had performed an operation upon her mother while pregnant with the plaintiff, which operation allegedly caused her various injuries and allegedly ought not to have been carried out upon a pregnant woman. Potts J. at first instance held that the claim disclosed a reasonable cause of action, for this reason:

> "The circumstances created a contingent or potential duty on the defendants which crystallised on birth of the injured child. The wrong to the child was then complete, she having been born alive physically damaged

---

[29] Scot. Law Com., Report No. 30, *Liability for Antenatal Injury* (1973) at p. 6.
[30] "Report of the Scottish Law Commission on Antenatal Injury", 1974 J.R. 83 at 84.
[31] 1992 S.L.T. 1022.
[32] 1992 S.L.T. 1026.
[33] This decision was, however, overruled: 1993 S.L.T. 624. See below, para. 2.54.
[34] *McWilliams v. Lord Advocate*, 1992 S.L.T. 1045.
[35] [1972] V.R. 353.
[36] 1932 S.C. (H.L.) 31.
[37] at 360, *per* Winneke C.J. and Pape J.
[38] *Duval et al. v. Seguin et al.* (1973) 40 D.L.R. (3d) 666.
[39] *Cherry v. Borsman* (1991) 75 D.L.R. (4th) 668.
[40] *X v. Pal* (1991) 23 N.S.W.L.R. 26; *Lynch v. Lynch* (1991) 25 N.S.W.L.R. 411.
[41] [1992] 3 All E.R. 833.
[42] The case was heard in 1990, but because the birth was in 1967, the Congenital Disabilities (Civil Liability) Act 1976 did not apply. The limitation period does not commence running until child plaintiffs—and pursuers—attain the age of legal capacity. *Cf. McCabe v. McLellan*, 1994 S.L.T. 346, which concerned a child born in 1968 and allegedly injured shortly thereafter.

as a result of the defendants' earlier neglect. On birth, the child acquired legal status and legal rights. Thus her cause of action in negligence was complete and accrued to her when she was a 'legal person who could sue or be sued' and when 'she was a legal person having a legal right' to whom another 'legal person' could owe at that time a corresponding legal duty."[43]

This, and an identical claim, were upheld on appeal.[44] This approach accords with the Scottish view of delict, as exemplified in *Watson v. Fram Reinforced Concrete (Scotland) Ltd* and in *Donoghue v. Stevenson* itself. It also accords with the approach of Scots criminal law.[45] *Donoghue v. Stevenson* was used by Lord McCluskey in *Hamilton v. Fife Health Board*[46] as the basis for actionability and he said that "doctors engaged in the medical work of assisting in the delivery of a child can obviously foresee that a failure to exercise due care and skill by them may result in injuries to the foetus, being injuries which will cause the child to suffer loss". This is an acceptance of the crystallisation of damage theory, as is made plain in this case by Lord Caplan (whose comments are accepted by Lord McCluskey). He stated expressly that injuries can be said to have been "sustained" at the moment of birth even if inflicted before that moment. The civilian fiction was dismissed as unnecessary, and the approach in *Burton* approved. Though these comments were, ultimately, *obiter* they indicate the approach likely and, it is submitted, properly to be followed.

There may be practical difficulties in establishing that an unborn child is a reasonably **2.35** foreseeable subject of negligently caused injury, particularly if the allegedly negligent act occurs before conception[47]; but that is not a conceptual difficulty and there are many situations in which unborn children are as foreseeable as living persons.[48] It should also be noted that if the unborn child dies before its live birth, the damage cannot be suffered, and the breach of duty becomes legally innocuous.[49]

Damages against the mother
    In English law, due to the doubts about whether there ever could be liability **2.36** for ante-natal injury (which doubts were brought to public attention by the Thalidomide tragedy)[50] it was deemed necessary to put the matter on a statutory

---

[43] [1991] 1 All E.R. 825 at 833. It was in relation to this reasoning that Lord Cullen, in *Cohen v. Shaw*, said: "I reserve my opinion as to whether the way in which the question of breach of duty was addressed and answered in that case was one which would commend itself to a Scottish court", 1992 S.L.T. at 1024E.

[44] [1992] 3 All E.R. 833. In *McWilliams v. Lord Advocate*, Lord Morton said "the reasoning of Potts J. commends itself to me": 1992 S.L.T. 1045 at 1048H.

[45] *McCluskey v. H.M. Advocate*, 1989 S.L.T. 175. *McCluskey* was followed in the Supreme Court of New South Wales, Court of Criminal Appeal in *R v. F*, (1996) 24 MVR 436. *Cf. Att. Gen.'s Reference (No. 3 of 1994)* [1997] 3 W.L.R. 425 H.L., in which Lord Hope of Craighead said (at 443G–H): "it is not sensible to say that [a foetus] cannot ever be harmed, or that nothing can be done to it which can ever be dangerous. Once it is born it is exposed, like all other living persons, to the risk of injury. It may also carry with it the effects of things done to it before birth which, after birth, may prove to be harmful."

[46] 1993 S.L.T. 624.

[47] The fact that the negligence occurred before conception is in principle as irrelevant as the fact that it occurred before birth so long as there is a causal link between the negligence and the injuries suffered by the child once born: *Renslow v. Mennonite Hospital*, 367 N.E. 2d 1250 (1977); *Bergstresser v. Mitchell*, 577 F. (2d) 22 (1978).

[48] In *Bourhill v. Young's Exr*, 1941 S.C. 395, Lord Justice-Clerk Aitchison (diss. in the Court of Session) said at 438 that the fact that a woman may be pregnant "is an easily foreseeable fact; it might almost be described as an obvious fact". See also Winneke C.J. and Pape J. in *Watt v. Rama* [1972] V.R. 353 at 360, Potts J. in *Burton v. Islington Health Authority* [1991] 1 All E.R. 825 at 831 and 833 and Lord McCluskey in *Hamilton* to similar effect.

[49] This follows, it is submitted, from the comments of Potts J. in *Burton v. Islington Health Authority* above at 833. See also *Smith v. Fox* [1923] 3 D.L.R. 785 (Ont. Sup. Ct). *Cf. Bagley v. North Herts Health Authority* (1986) 136 New L.J. 1014.

[50] But which doubts proved groundless in the first case raised under the common law: *Burton v. Islington Health Authority*, above; *De Martell v. Merton and Sutton Health Authority* [1992] 3 All E.R. 833.

basis, and this was done with the Congenital Disabilities (Civil Liability) Act
1976. However, that statute contains an important qualification in section 1(1)
by excluding from liability the child's own mother, unless[51] the injuries she
causes the child are caused as a result of her negligent driving of a motor vehicle
while pregnant. (The reason for this exception to the qualification is that
otherwise the child would be denied insurance compensation.[52]) The Act does
not apply in Scotland, but the reasoning behind the maternal exclusion may be
equally applicable here also. The sentiment clearly is that if a child could sue
his or her own mother for injuries she inflicts upon the child during his or her
gestation within her, this would disrupt family harmony and create an unwelcome
adversarial atmosphere between the two.[53] It is to be noted that family harmony
is not so protected by the English statute that a father is also given immunity
from liability.[54] A rather more plausible rationale for excluding a mother's liability
is that otherwise her freedom would be unduly restricted during pregnancy,
with the concurrent effect of over-emphasising women's child-bearing role in
society. This reasoning is not wholly convincing either. We all have duties not
to injure others, with consequent and inevitable restriction on our freedom—
but that is no reason to deny the existence of the duty. Besides, an award of
damages is a retrospective remedy (unlike interdict, which will be discussed
shortly) and the argument that its availability is incompatible with personal
freedom is, for that reason alone, unpersuasive. Alternatively, it could be argued
that if a woman were subject to actions for damages arising from how she
conducts herself during pregnancy, she might be encouraged to avoid the
possibility of liability completely by undergoing an abortion and so preventing
her breaches of duty from causing compensable loss. This argument is not fully
persuasive in a legal system, like Scotland, in which there is no "right" to an
abortion, although it must be accepted that the ease with which abortion can be
obtained here in practice does give it some force. A far stronger argument is that
if the state becomes coercive in its treatment of pregnant women, it will
discourage those who need it from seeking help for fear of the consequences if
they do not conform to expected norms.[55]

The issue has arisen in other countries where, as in Scotland, legislation
gives no guidance. In *Lynch v. Lynch*[56] a child successfully sued its mother for
the injuries it received while *in utero* due to the mother's negligent car driving.
The decision was, however, expressly limited to situations in which there is
compulsory insurance. And in *Dobson v. Dobson*[57] the New Brunswick Court

---

[51] Congenital Disabilities (Civil Liability) Act 1976, s. 2.

[52] Law Com., *Report on Injuries to Unborn Children* (1974).

[53] It was primarily for this reason that the early American cases denied liability in such cases: see,
e.g. Stanford v. St Louis-San Francisco Ry, 214 Ala. 611 (1926). The logic of the maternal exclusion
has been challenged by Brazier in "Parental Responsibilities, Foetal Welfare and Children's
Health" in *Family Law Towards the Millenium: Essays for PM Bromley* (Butterworths, 1997),
(ed. Bridge), at pp. 263–293.

[54] Besides, if family autonomy were so important, this would justify preventing the child suing his
or her parents for post-natal injury, which has never been suggested. In *Young v. Rankin*, 1934
S.C. 499 it was held competent for a minor child to sue his father for damages for personal
injuries caused by the father's negligence; and in *Wood v. Wood*, 1935 S.L.T. 431 a mother was
held entitled to sue her son for damages for personal injuries, this even at a time when spouses
could not sue each other (see *Harper v. Harper*, 1929 S.C. 220). In the latter case the Lord
Ordinary rejected the contention that the claim should be dismissed for reasons of public policy.
Statutorily, husbands and wives are now able to sue each other in delict, as if they were not
married to each other: Law Reform (Husband and Wife) Act 1962, s. 2(1). And children have
always, of course, been able to sue their parents for aliment.

[55] *Winnipeg Child and Family Services (Northwest Area)* v. *G* (1997) 152 D.L.R. (4th) 193, *per*
McLachlin J. at para. 41.

[56] (1991) 25 N.S.W.L.R. 411.

[57] (1997) 148 D.L.R. (4th) 332.

of Appeal held that there was no policy reason to exclude an action against the mother in respect of duties, such as driving carefully, that she owed to everyone, but the court was careful to limit its decision to these facts and it pointed out (as had the court in *Lynch*) that different considerations might apply in cases of alleged duties owed to the child alone, such as refraining from drinking and smoking.[58] Again, the policy is evident that the pregnant woman's freedom to pursue her own lifestyle should not be interfered with unduly. However, if smoking, for example, can found liability for injury suffered by a living person it is difficult to see how or why it should not also found liability for injury suffered by a foetus which is subsequently born alive. There is no authority one way or the other in Scotland on the question, but it is suggested that if liability can be imposed upon a mother by the application of the general principles of delictual liability, then any limitation or denial should come from Parliament. If it is accepted, as was argued above, that there is liability on third parties, it is difficult to see how, in the absence of statute, liability of the mother can be denied.[59] Nor should it be.

Circumstances in which a mother might be held liable

It is disturbingly easy to visualise circumstances in which a pregnant woman **2.37** might act in ways that are likely to cause suffering to her child once it is born. The most obvious example is drug abuse, though alcohol and tobacco usage may also be cited as examples (though with these causation will be somewhat more difficult to prove). In order to establish liability in negligence, the Scottish courts have traditionally demanded proof on the balance of probabilities of the existence of *damnum injuria datum*, or damage wrongfully caused,[60] this being derived from the *lex aquilia*.[61] Damage, following the position with third party defenders described above, is the injury suffered by the child once he or she has been born alive. Wrongfulness lies in the breach of a duty of care owed by the defender to the pursuer. Applying the basic principles of negligence in determining whether there exists a duty of care, it seems undeniable that the foetus in the womb is a "neighbour" of the pregnant woman (or at any rate that the child when born—a foreseeable event to a pregnant woman—is a neighbour) and thus is a person (when born) so closely and directly affected by the woman's acts or omissions that she ought reasonably to have it in contemplation as being so affected when she is directing her mind to the acts or omissions which are called in question.[62] Whether that duty has been breached depends upon whether the woman has taken "reasonable care." Walker says[63] in relation to reasonable care: "It is fixed by what we should expect in the like case from a man of ordinary sense, knowledge, care and prudence, having regard to what such a person must be taken to have known and what he should have foreseen." The test, being objective, must refer to the reasonable pregnant woman, and not the reasonable pregnant drug addict or alcoholic. If the court were to hold

---

[58] *cf. Winnepeg Child and Family Services (Northwest Area) v. G* (1997) 152 D.L.R. (4th) 193 in which the Supreme Court of Canada held that, beyond cases of negligent driving, it would be too great an extension of existing principles to recognise liabilty for "lifestyle choices", such as alcohol and tobacco consumption. The case arose in the context of a pregnant woman who was addicted to solvent abuse.

[59] See further, Whitfield, "Common Law Duties to Unborn Children" (1993) 1 Med. L. Rev. 28.

[60] *Stair Memorial Encyclopaedia of the Laws of Scotland*, Vol. 15, para. 252; Walker, *Delict* (2nd ed.), pp. 17–21, 31–32.

[61] See D. McKenzie and R. Evans-Jones, "The Development of Remedies for Personal Injury and Death" in R. Evans-Jones, ed., *The Civil Law Tradition in Scotland* (1995).

[62] The Supreme Court of Canada accepted that the relationship between a pregnant woman and the foetus she was carrying was sufficiently proximate to found a duty of care (but that policy considerations prevented the recognition of liability for breach of that duty): *Winnipeg Child and Family Services (Northwest Area) v. G* (1997) 152 D.L.R. (4th) 193.

[63] *Delict* (2nd ed.), p. 199.

that a reasonable pregnant woman would not subject her child to risk of injury by taking drugs or alcohol, then for her to do so will be a breach of the duty of care. Causation between that breach and the injury suffered would then have to be established in order to complete the requirements. In most cases this is likely to prove the most difficult element, and would probably deny the child damages based for example on the mother's smoking—while there is scientific evidence to suggest that there is a link between smoking by pregnant women and low birth weight, the pursuer would have to prove that the defender's smoking actually did cause, or at least materially contributed to,[64] his or her own low birth weight (assuming, for the sake of argument, that that would amount to a compensable injury). The same difficulties would be faced if a child alleged that his or her mother's excessive exercise, or sexual activity, or alcohol consumption, led to his or her injury. On the other hand there are situations in which causation might more easily be established. If, for example, the pregnant woman continued to abuse narcotic drugs while she was pregnant, and the child was born with a drug dependency,[65] or if the pregnant woman was an alcoholic and the child was born with foetal alcohol syndrome,[66] then causation might more easily be established. The pain and suffering of such children are clearly of a compensable nature, and for that reason alone it is difficult to see why liability should be denied (if fault can also be proved). There are few examples in which such claims have been successful, but one is *Grodin v. Grodin*,[67] in which a child successfully sued his mother and the manufacturer of a drug which the mother took during pregnancy and which blackened the child's teeth.

"Wrongful life"

2.38   Liability will only be established if the harm to *that particular child* could have been avoided by the mother exercising reasonable care. A mother will not be liable for harm caused to a child through some genetic defect or a disease such as HIV infection that the mother passed on to the child and which she knew or ought to have known that she could pass on. In that situation the child would be claiming that had there been no negligence (*i.e.* had the mother taken sufficient precautions against passing on the defect) he or she would not have been born at all, and possibly that some other child would have been born: this would therefore be an action for "wrongful life," which has been denied in England both at common law[68] and by statute,[69] and in Scotland also.[70] For the same reason, a child born with defects could not sue his or her mother who knew of these defects and refused to abort the child.[71]

Interdict

Interdict against third parties

2.39   While damages is a retrospective remedy designed to provide reparation to the person who has suffered loss, injury or damage as a result of a civil wrong,

---

[64] *McGhee v. National Coal Board*, 1973 S.C. (H.L.) 37.

[65] cf. *D. (A Minor) v. Berkshire County Council* [1987] 1 All E.R. 20, H.L. and *Winnipeg Child and Family Services (Northwest Area) v. G*, (1997) D.L.R. (4th) 193 (Supreme Court of Canada): both cases arose within the context of care and protection proceedings (for which, see further, below, paras 2.62–2.68). The dissenting judgment in the Canadian case contains a detailed description of the physical, psychological and social effects that sustained solvent abuse by a pregnant woman has on the foetus she is carrying.

[66] As in *Re Children's Aid Society for the District of Kenora and J.L.* (1982) 134 D.L.R. (3d) 249.

[67] 301 N.W. (2d) 869 (1980) (Michigan Appeal Court).

[68] *McKay v. Essex Area Health Authority* [1982] Q.B. 1166.

[69] Congenital Disabilities (Civil Liability) Act 1976, s. 4(5).

[70] *P's Curator Bonis v. Criminal Injuries Compensation Board*, 1997 S.L.T. 1180, approving *McKay v. Essex Area Health Authority*. See also *Anderson v. Forth Valley Health Board*, 1998 S.L.T. 588. The matter is fully discussed by Norrie, "Wrongful Life in Scots Law: No Right, No Remedy", 1990 J.R. 205.

[71] This is of course only one of the reasons for this particular conclusion: the overwhelming reason of policy is that there can never be a duty to do something that is prima facie a criminal offence.

interdict is a prospective remedy designed to prevent the injury occurring in the first place. It is, however, wrong to see the two remedies as being different sides of the same coin, and it does not necessarily follow that interdict would have been available in all circumstances to prevent events that give rise to a claim for damages. The remedies are different in a number of respects. First, damages can normally be claimed as of right if the pursuer proves his or her case; interdict, on the other hand, is a discretionary remedy: it is "of the nature of an extraordinary remedy, not to be given except for urgent reasons, and even then not as a matter of right, but only in the exercise of a sound judicial discretion".[72] Secondly, damages is a remedy requiring the court to look to the past; with interdict the court must look to the future. Thirdly, with damages for ante-natal injury the court is granting a remedy to someone already in existence, albeit in relation to events that occurred before the pursuer achieved existence; the court in which an interdict is sought to prevent ante-natal injury is on the other hand being asked to grant a remedy on behalf of someone who has not yet achieved legal existence.

The major difficulty with interdict is whether anyone can seek it when, **2.40** *ex hypothesi*, the "person" who is threatened does not yet have any legal existence.[73] Of course if the interdict is sought against a third party, then this problem can be avoided easily: the pregnant woman will inevitably be affected by any threat to her unborn child, and she would therefore have both title and interest to seek an interdict to prevent the threat eventuating. It must, however, be remembered that in these circumstances she would be suing on her own behalf to prevent injury to her own person. If the pregnant woman were unconscious or otherwise *incapax* and thus unable to raise the action, title would inhere in the guardian of the *incapax*, again because the threat is to be regarded as directed towards the woman and not her unborn child. Even in the (difficult to imagine) situation of a threatened injury that affects the unborn child but not the pregnant woman herself, her right to seek an interdict would be preserved by her own right to be protected from the emotional trauma that injury to her child could cause her[74]; and it may be that a prospective father can seek an interdict against a third party on the same basis.

Interdict against the mother
A far greater difficulty arises when the threat comes from the pregnant woman **2.41** herself, and it is she, therefore, against whom the interdict is sought. In this situation the question—does the unborn child have a right not to be injured?—arises in an acute form. The issue, which requires a highly delicate balance to be struck between the actual rights of the mother and the prospective rights of the foetus, has been extensively canvassed in the context of abortion.[75] These cases, however, may well be *sui generis* and it might not be appropriate to rely upon them in other situations. Abortions in the cases cited were legal acts and their accomplishment would have led to neither criminal penalties nor civil damages. Abortion is the destruction of the unborn child: that child can, therefore,

---

[72] *per* Lord Deas in *Kelso School Board v. Hunter* (1874) 2 R. 228 at 232.
[73] "None of the [foreign] decisions to which we were referred appear to us to provide support for the view that a foetus has a legal persona, or is otherwise recognised as being vested in personal rights for the protection of which the remedy of interdict may be invoked": *Kelly v. Kelly*, 1997 S.L.T. 896 at 901C.
[74] *cf. Re MB (Medical Treatment)* [1997] 2 F.L.R. 426.
[75] *Kelly v. Kelly*, 1997 S.L.T. 896. There are numerous cases from English and Commonwealth court: see, *e.g.* in England, *Paton v. Trustees of the British Pregnancy Advisory Service* [1978] 2 All E.R. 987, *C v. S*, [1987] 2 W.L.R. 1108; in Australia, *Att.-Gen. of Queensland, ex rel. Kerr v. T* (1983) 46 A.L.R. 275; in Canada, *Medhurst v. Medhurst* (1984) 9 D.L.R. (4th) 252, *Medhurst v. Medhurst* (1984) 7 D.L.R. (4th) 335, *Borowski v. Att.-Gen. for Canada* (1987) 39 D.L.R. (4th) 731, (1989) 57 D.L.R. (4th) 231, *Tremblay v. Daigle* (1990) 62 D.L.R. (4th) 634; and in New Zealand, *Wall v. Livingstone* [1982] 1 N.Z.L.R. 734.

never be the subject of legal rights, since the abortion itself will prevent the child acquiring legal personality. In *Kelly v. Kelly*[76] the Second Division said:

> "Whether it is an actionable wrong to the unborn foetus for an abortion to be performed depends entirely on whether Scots law confers on the foetus a right to continue to exist in the mother's womb. Our conclusion is that Scots law recognises no such right in the foetus. It follows that no person can invoke the power of the court to vindicate such a right."

2.42   However, if the threat is to the unborn child's health but not necessarily (in the way that abortion is necessarily) to the unborn child's life, the arguments in the abortion cases do not apply since the act might be a wrong and the possibility of the foetus acquiring legal personality remains. The argument that if an injury to the foetus can later sound in damages then so ought death[77] is flawed (at least in law) since the foetus, lacking legal personality, does not in law "die" (though it may be destroyed). If injured *in utero*, the foetus can sue after being born alive (as discussed above) and will normally do so through a parent or guardian acting as his or her legal representative. If that is so, might the person who will become a parent or guardian seek an interdict to prevent harm eventuating? The Second Division in *Kelly v. Kelly* had "no difficulty in accepting the proposition that the remedy of interdict would be available at the instance of a person or that person's representative to prevent damage being deliberately caused to that person, being damage which, if it occurred, would sound in an award of damages in favour of that person".[78] Though the court did not directly address the point, it would seem to follow from this that the unborn child can, through the person who will be its legal representative, seek protection from injuries even from its mother. The English court has recognised that a breach of duty of care towards an unborn child can create "a contingent or potential duty on the defendants",[79] the entitlement to damages crystallising when the hurt is suffered, *i.e.* on birth.[80] The right to seek an interdict does not need harm before it crystallises—it merely needs a threat. For this reason it is suggested that the court could recognise the contingent or potential existence of the unborn child as giving it a right not to be injured, which right could be the basis of a claim for interdict—even against the mother—so long as the injury, if suffered, would constitute a legal wrong on the part of the person against whom the interdict is sought. The fact that the court would have to predict that the child will later be born alive and so suffer the injury is no more a conceptual difficulty in relation to interdict than the fact that the court always has to predict that the threat it is interdicting would otherwise eventuate.

2.43   A living child has no title to sue until he or she is able to understand what it means to do so.[81] To ascribe to an unborn child even the limited *persona standi in judicio* which, in some circumstances, a child under 16 may have would be to confer on it a legal personality which it does not possess. An interdict against a pregnant woman could only be sought by persons with title to sue either on their own behalves or on behalf of the unborn child. In relation to attempts to prevent pregnant women undergoing abortions, it has been held in England that a husband and potential father had no title to seek an injunction on behalf of the unborn child his wife was carrying[82]; and it has further been held that the "personal

---

[76] 1997 S.L.T. 896 at 901E.
[77] See, *e.g.*, Robertson, "Consider the Foetus", 1997 S.L.T. (News) 319: "If [the foetus] suffers injuries which are not merely debilitating but fatal, no 'right' arises. The greater wrong secures freedom from liability for the wrongdoer and obliterates protection for the foetus. Can this result be just?"
[78] [1997] S.L.T. 896 at 899F-G.
[79] *per* Potts J. in *Burton v. Islington Health Authority* [1991] 1 All E.R. 825 at 833.
[80] See above, para. 2.33.
[81] Age of Legal Capacity (Scotland) Act 1991, s. 2(4A) and (4B). See futher, below, para. 15.11.
[82] *Paton v. Trustees of the British Pregnancy Advisory Service* [1978] 2 All E.R. 987.

interest" of a potential father who was not married to the pregnant woman gave him no independent title to sue in his own name.[83] In relation to these men's title to sue not in their own names but on behalf of the unborn child, it has been held that the foetus has no right to life and therefore no one can sue on its behalf to prevent its abortion.[84] Yet, again, these cases were inextricably linked to the specialities of the abortion situation and even in that context are not wholly persuasive on the question of title to sue. Outwith the abortion situation, a prospective father has, it is submitted, sufficient title and interest to interdict potential harm to a child in respect of whom, if born alive, he would have important responsibilities and rights. The Second Division held, in *Kelly v. Kelly*,[85] that "*if* an abortion is an actionable wrong to the foetus as such, we agree that the father would be able to take proceedings on behalf of the foetus". Though it went on to hold that abortion is not an actionable wrong to the foetus, the statement is nevertheless clear authority for the proposition that the prospective father has title to prevent an actionable wrong against the unborn child. Though the reference to "father" has to be read in the context of the case (which involved a married father and one who would, therefore, have parental responsibilities and parental rights) it is submitted that "father" should not, for the purposes of title to seek a protective remedy, be so limited: otherwise an unborn child's right to protection from his or her mother's actionable wrongs would depend upon the accident of the marital status of the parents.

In the normal case, the court is able to appoint a curator *ad litem* to look after the **2.44** interests of those who, in a court case—and it need not be the parties—cannot look after their own interests. Might the Scottish courts be persuaded to appoint a curator *ad litem* to an unborn child? In South Africa it has been held that a curator *ad litem* could not be appointed over an unborn child in order to prevent its abortion.[86] The Family Court in Nova Scotia did appoint a guardian *ad litem* over an unborn child for just that reason,[87] but that decision is inconsistent with later rulings of the Supreme Court of Canada[88] and clearly can no longer be relied upon. In England it has been held that the wardship jurisdiction does not extend to the unborn child,[89] even in circumstances in which the court considered that the child did need protection from its mother and in which the threat was less than destruction by abortion. These cases are strong and persuasive authority against the existence of a power of the court to appoint a curator *ad litem* over an unborn child. In Scotland the question has never arisen directly, but there is old authority for the proposition that a tutor can be appointed to an unborn child.[90] This case has never been overruled, and is quoted more recently as good authority by Fraser.[91] The report of the case is, however, brief to the point of opacity, and it probably means no more than that a testamentary appointment of a guardian to a posthumous child is as valid as a testamentary gift to a posthumous child. It is likely that the Scottish courts will follow the approach in England, Canada and South Africa in the cases cited above.

---

[83] *C v. S* [1987] 2 W.L.R. 1108.

[84] *Paton,* above; *X v. United Kingdom* (1980) 3 E.H.R.R. 408, in which the European Commission on Human Rights rejected Paton's application based on the unborn child's right to life; *Tremblay v. Daigle* (1990) 62 D.L.R. (4th) 634 (Supreme Court of Canada) in which the court stated *obiter* that if it had held that the foetus did have such a right, the father would be a person with as much right to speak on its behalf as anyone else: at 649. *Cf. Kelly v. Kelly,* 1997 S.L.T. 896.

[85] 1997 S.L.T. 896 at 899G (original emphasis).

[86] *Christian League of Southern Africa v. Rall,* 1981 (2) S.A.L.R. 821.

[87] *Re Simms and H* (1979) 106 D.L.R. (3d) 435.

[88] *Tremblay v. Daigle* (1990) 62 D.L.R. (4th) 634; *Winnipeg Child and Family Services (Northwest Area) v. G* (1997) 152 D.L.R. (4th) 193. The latter, in particular, contains an extensive discussion of why the unborn child may not be protected by interdict.

[89] *Re F (In Utero)* [1988] 2 All E.R. 193.

[90] *Murray v. Merschall* (1555) Mor. 16226 (cited with approval in Balfour's *Practicks* at p. 116). See also D. xxvii, 10, 8.

[91] Fraser (3rd ed.), p. 220.

2.45   One other possibility is that the Lord Advocate, representing the public interest, may raise the action. In a case aimed at preventing an abortion, the Attorney-General of Queensland stepped in on behalf of the public and took over an application for injunction initially raised by the putative father of an unborn child.[92] And in the Republic of Ireland the Attorney-General sought (and at first instance obtained) an injunction preventing a 14-year-old leaving Ireland for the purpose of obtaining an abortion in England.[93] This obviated the title-to-sue problem. In Scotland the Lord Advocate, representing the public interest, might have title to raise an interdict, though he would do so only in the most exceptional of circumstances, in which the public interest is threatened.

2.46   However, even if the title problem could be resolved, for example by the Lord Advocate stepping in, it is by no means certain that an interdict would—or indeed should—be granted. Interdict, as pointed out above, is a discretionary remedy, which the court is not bound to grant if there are policy reasons for withholding it.[94] In the abortion cases[95] the view has consistently been expressed that the granting of a remedy in such circumstances would involve too great a limitation on the pregnant woman's freedom of action, which would be against public policy. So, for example, in *Attorney-General of Queensland, ex rel. Kerr v. T* [96] Gibbs C.J. pointed out that: "There are limits to the extent to which the law should intrude upon personal liberty and personal privacy in the pursuit of moral and religious aims. Those limits would be overstepped if an injunction were to be granted in the present case."

2.47   Due to the very peculiar position of abortion in the law it may well be, as already suggested, that one cannot rely too heavily on these cases, but the same policy considerations have been held determinative in quite different situations. In the English case of *Re F (In Utero)*[97] a local authority, concerned that a pregnant woman who led a nomadic existence, who was mentally disturbed and who they believed to be incapable of caring for her child either after its birth or before, applied for leave to issue a summons making the unborn child a ward of court. The application was refused, and the refusal upheld on appeal. At one level the decision was based merely on the definitional point that an unborn child is not a minor as that term was used in the relevant statute.[98] But there was also a deeper rationale for the decision: it was clear that the court could not exercise the wardship rights, powers and duties over the foetus without controlling the mother's actions, and that the court was not willing to undertake such control. According to May L.J.[99]: "Until the child is actually born there must necessarily be an inherent incompatibility between any projected exercise of wardship jurisdiction and the rights and welfare of the mother." Similarly, Balcolme L.J. said "the only purpose of extending the [wardship] jurisdiction to include a foetus is to enable the mother's actions to be controlled".[1] The Court of Appeal was deeply unhappy about the implications of that. Any conflict between the interests of the child and the interests of the mother would have to be resolved in favour of the child, because the whole aim of the wardship court is to protect the interests of the ward rather than those of the mother. May L.J. pointed out that if an order were

---

[92] *Att.-Gen. of Queensland, ex rel. Kerr v. T* (1983) 46 A.L.R. 275.

[93] *Att.-Gen. v. X* [1992] I.R.L.M. 401.

[94] See above, n. 72.

[95] See above, n. 75.

[96] (1983) 46 A.L.R. 275 at 277–278.

[97] [1988] 2 W.L.R. 1288. See Fortin, "Can You Ward a Foetus?" (1988) 51 Mod. L.R. 768.

[98] Family Law Reform Act 1969, s. 1. It is no longer possible, since the coming into force of the Children Act 1989, for local authorities in England to use the wardship jurisdiction.

[99] [1988] 2 W.L.R. 1288 at 1298.

[1] *ibid.* at 1305. See also Staughton L.J. at 1306.

made concerning the child and the mother disagreed, the order would have to be enforced against her wishes:

> "I think that there would be insuperable difficulties if one sought to enforce any order in respect of an unborn child against its mother, if that mother failed to comply with the order. I cannot contemplate the court ordering that this should be done by force, nor indeed is it possible to consider with any equanimity that the court should seek to enforce an order by committal."[2]

2.48 A court in Scotland (or elsewhere) wishing to interdict a woman whose behaviour constituted a threat to the health, development and welfare of her unborn child would have to be willing to enforce its order, or to imprison a woman who failed to comply with it. It is difficult to visualise the Scottish court being willing to take these sorts of steps.[3] Anything less than real and severe threat would not found an interdict, since the court would have to balance the rights of the pregnant woman with the interests of the child who may potentially be born, and the rights and liberties of a woman are not lost nor even diminished by her becoming pregnant. It is not inconsistent with this policy to accept that if the mother, deliberately, recklessly or negligently causes harm to her child, say by refusing a Caesarean section as a result of which anoxia during the birth process leaves the child living but brain damaged, or by continuing to ingest deleterious substances, she may be held liable to the child in damages *if* her acts or omissions amount to *culpa*.

Suing for the ante-natal death of a parent

2.49 A child who is born alive is entitled to damages for the ante-natal death of his or her parent (by which is normally meant, in practical terms, his or her father[4]). He or she is entitled under section 1(1) of the Damages (Scotland) Act 1976 to reparation as being a relative, which includes a "child of the deceased,"[5] and under section 1(4) to a loss of society award.[6] In *Cohen v. Shaw*[7] the Lord Ordinary (Cullen) held that the word "child" as used in the 1976 Act should on any view be taken as including one in the womb at the time of death, but subsequently born alive. He was unable to envisage any reason that those drafting the 1976 Act might have had for distinguishing the unborn child from surviving children. However, because "relative" is defined to include a person who "was" a child of the deceased, he concluded that the *tempus inscipiendum* was the date of death, and that the pursuer could only be described as a child of the deceased

---

[2] [1988] 2 W.L.R. 1288 at 1301. *Cf.* the Canadian decision of *Re A (In Utero)* (1990) 72 D.L.R. (4th) 722 in which it was held by the Ontario Family Court that a foetus has no status as a legal person and thus no rights to child protection under the Ontario Child and Family Services Act 1984.

[3] In *Kelly v. Kelly*, 1997 S.L.T. 896 the Second Division at 9011 was clearly worried about the policy implications of granting an interdict in any circumstance. It said: "If the foetus had the right to its own protection which could be vindicated on its behalf by interdict there would be no reason why it should be confined to cases of abortion. If such a right existed it could be used as the basis for a father taking legal action with a view to restraining the mother from some form of activity which was claimed to be harmful to the foetus—such as smoking, and certain sports and occupations. There is plainly room for conflicting views as to what would be adverse to the interests of the foetus".

[4] Though not always. It is possible to keep a woman who is brain-dead "alive" with life-support machines until her unborn child has reached term: see the news report in *The Independent*, Oct. 17, 1992, which reports of the corpse of a dead woman being ventilated in order to provide a gestational environment for a foetus of 15 weeks old.

[5] Sched. 1, para. 1(b).

[6] This was the case at common law: see *Moorcraft v. Alexander & Sons*, 1946 S.C. 466; *Connachan v. Scottish Motor Traction Co.*, 1946 S.C. 428; *Leadbetter v. N.C.B.*, 1952 S.L.T. 179; *Riddell v. James Longmuir & Sons Ltd*, 1971 S.L.T. (Notes) 33.

[7] 1992 S.L.T. 1022.

at that date by applying the civilian fiction that in all things to the child's benefit the unborn child is treated as already born. As an alternative approach to the same conclusion, the crystallisation theory discussed above might have been invoked. It is also relevant to note that in some of the other definitions of "relative" a time is expressly stated when the relationship must exist: there is no such time for the relationship of parent and child.[8] However the matter is regarded, it is sufficient that the pursuer was a child of the deceased after birth and the fact that the wrongful act took place before birth is irrelevant for the same reason as that fact is irrelevant when the child is claiming damages for his or her own injuries.[9]

2.50   A child who dies *in utero* or is still-born has no claim for the death of a parent whenever that occurs, because the activation of any right he or she may have is conditional on live birth. A child whose conception was brought about by one of the reproductive techniques governed by the Human Fertilisation and Embryology Act 1990 and whose gestation *in utero* commenced after the death of the genetic father has no claim consequent upon that death, because a man is not to be treated as father of a child for any purpose (this including a claim for damages under the Damages (Scotland) Act 1976) if his sperm or an embryo created with his sperm is used after his death.[10] If the genetic mother is negligently killed before or after the embryo created with her egg is implanted into another woman, the later born child has no claim since the woman who carries the child and no other woman is to be treated as mother for all purposes,[11] including a claim for damages under the 1976 Act.

Suing for the death of a child in utero

At common law

2.51   A quite separate issue to those considered above is that of a parent suing for damages as a result of the death of the unborn child. There are examples from other jurisdictions of damages being awarded to parents for the still-birth of their children, caused as a result of the defenders' negligence.[12] The injury suffered in these cases was nervous shock of the parents. In Scotland damages for nervous shock as a result of the death of another is recognised,[13] though there may be problems in establishing that the killing of a child *in utero* amounts to causing the death of another. However, it is submitted that the later the pregnancy is, the more attached the mother (and indeed the father) is likely to be to the unborn child, and the more foreseeable her (or indeed his) nervous shock at its destruction will be.[14] If the parents of an unborn child which dies *in utero* or is still-born[15] can prove that they have suffered nervous shock as a consequence of that event, it is submitted

---

[8] Damages (Scotland) Act 1976, Sched. 1, para. 1(b), as compared with paras 1(a) and 1(aa).

[9] See above, paras 2.33–2.35.

[10] Human Fertilisation and Embryology Act 1990, ss. 28(6)(b) and 29(2). See further, below, para. 3.43.

[11] *ibid*. ss. 27(1) and 29(2).

[12] See, *e.g.*, the early New Zealand case of *Stevenson v. Basham* [1922] N.Z.L.R. 225, and the more recent American cases of *Giardina v. Bennett*, 545 A (2d) 139 (1988) and *Abdallah v. Callender*, 1 F. (3d) 141 (1993).

[13] See Walker, *Delict*, pp. 671–680; *Brown v. Glasgow Corporation*, 1922 S.C. 527. See also the lengthy discussion by the Second Division in *Bourhill v. Young's Exr*, 1941 S.C. 395.

[14] *cf.* the New York case of *Del Zio v. Presbyterian Hospital*, 74 Civ. 3588 (Nov. 14, 1978) in which damages were recovered by parents of an *in vitro* embryo when they suffered mental shock because the director of the hospital terminated their treatment programme by destroying the embryo. While not suggesting that the Scottish court would go so far, it is to be noted that in *Alcock v. Chief Constable of South Yorkshire* [1991] 4 All E.R. 907 the House of Lords held that the class of persons to whom a common law duty may be owed is not limited by reference to a particular relationship to the deceased, although it must be to someone within the defendant's contemplation.

[15] A still-born child is one that dies *in utero* after 24 weeks' or more gestation: Registration of Births, Deaths and Marriages (Scotland) Act 1965, s. 56(1), as amended by the Still-Birth (Definition) Act 1992, s. 1(2).

that there is no reason why they should not be awarded damages in reparation. The principle to be applied is not the personhood of the medium for the nervous shock, but the foreseeability that that type of harm will follow directly from the defender's action, and there is at least one English case in which damages were awarded for nervous shock suffered as a result of damage to property.[16] In addition, if personal injuries are caused to a pregnant woman as a result of the defender's negligence, she may sue for damages for these personal injuries, and if a miscarriage is caused by these injuries, this would be a relevant head of damages.[17]

A similar claim is illustrated in *Ministry of Defence v. Pope*[18] in which the **2.52** Employment Appeal Tribunal held three women entitled to compensation on the basis of injury to feelings caused by their terminations of pregnancies. The abortions had occurred as a result of the Ministry's unlawful policy of requiring female employees who became pregnant to resign and it was held that this directly caused the injury to feelings of the women who had been forced to choose between their careers and their unborn children. And in a variant on the wrongful birth cases, a Canadian court held that damages could be awarded for (*inter alia*) the depression a woman suffered after undergoing an abortion after her birth control method failed due to the negligence of the defendants.[19]

Under the Damages (Scotland) Act 1976

Section 1 of the Damages (Scotland) Act 1976 provides that "where a person **2.53** dies in consequence of personal injuries sustained" through the delict of another person, then damages will be payable to certain "relatives" specified in Schedule 1 to the Act, which includes any person who was a parent of the "deceased". Damages could be claimed by a parent of an unborn child negligently killed before birth only if the child were within the meaning of the words "person", as used in section 1, and "deceased," as used in Schedule 1. Neither of these words is defined, and their normal meaning is therefore to be ascribed to them: the law regards a "person" as someone who has or has had a living existence independently of his or her mother,[20] and a "deceased" as someone who was in that state and no longer is so. It would follow that damages cannot be claimed under this statute for any delict that causes the unborn child to die *in utero*.

Suing for the post-natal death of a child injured *in utero*

It may happen that a child is injured while *in utero*,[21] but is born alive and **2.54** then dies of its injuries. There had been a conflict of Outer House authority as to whether, in that situation, parents can sue under the Damages (Scotland) Act 1976 for a loss of society award. In *McWilliams v. Lord Advocate*,[22] Lord Morton

---

[16] *Attia v. British Gas plc* [1987] 3 All E.R. 455, CA.

[17] In *Bourhill v. Young*, 1942 S.C. (H.L.) 78 damages were claimed for, *inter alia*, a miscarriage, though that was the result, rather than the cause, of the mental shock (allegedly) suffered in that case. If a miscarriage can found an action of damages when it is the result of mental shock, it should also be able to found an action when it is the cause of the mental shock. Causation might of course prove difficult (as it did in *Bourhill*: see the decision of the Inner House at 1941 S.C. 395, where the evidential difficulties are discussed more fully than in the House of Lords), but that in itself is no reason not to allow the pursuer to attempt to prove his or her case.

[18] [1997] I.C.R. 296.

[19] *Dendaas v. Yackel* (1980) 109 D.L.R. (3d) 455.

[20] "In law a foetus is not yet a person, and is no more a person at [a] late stage than at any other stage from conception onwards": *per* Lord Prosser in *Hamilton v. Fife Health Board*, 1992 S.L.T. 1026 at 1030. Again, "a 'person' denotes someone who is living, not someone who has yet to be born": *per* Woolf L.J. in *D (A Minor) v. Berkshire County Council* [1987] 1 All E.R. 20 at 30.

[21] This is taken to include the child in the course of being born, because of the law's simplistic view of the process of creation: Lord Prosser accepted in *Hamilton v. Fife Health Board*, above, at 1028E, that "at any given moment of time a child must be either born or not born, living or not living, and that prior to being born, a child is not a 'person'". In that case the alleged negligence occurred during the birth process, and the child was treated as not being a person at that point.

[22] 1992 S.L.T. 1045.

of Shuna held that parents could sue for the death of a child as a result of injuries it had sustained *in utero*. He found it unnecessary to depend upon the civilian fiction whereby an unborn child can be treated as having been born when that is to its advantage, holding instead that the terms of the 1976 Act were satisfied: a child who had been born alive and had later died as a result of pre-natal injuries was clearly "a person" at the date of death and, since damage caused before birth crystallised at live birth, the child had at that point "sustained" injury. On the other hand, Lord Prosser in *Hamilton v. Fife Health Board*[23] had held that injuries sustained in the womb could not be said to have been "sustained" by a "person" as required by the 1976 Act, because personality is not achieved until the moment of live birth.[24] Lord Prosser's decision was, however, overturned.[25] The Inner House held that the phrase in the 1976 Act, "personal injury sustained by him" was apt to cover injuries to the person of a child before birth which continue to have effects after birth by impairment of physical condition. Lord Caplan pointed out that it was difficult to identify what policy objectives Parliament could have been trying to achieve if Lord Prosser's view were correct, since it would mean distinguishing parents whose child had died through injury inflicted shortly before birth from those whose child had died through injury inflicted shortly after birth. The result of this decision is that relatives of a child who dies can sue the person responsible for inflicting the fatal injuries, whether those injuries are sustained before or after birth, so long as the child is a living person (i.e. has been born alive) before dying from the injuries. The basis for this liability is not an extended application of the civilian fiction but the terms of the Damages (Scotland) Act 1976.[26]

Parental responsibilities

2.55   As will be seen in detail in Chapter 8, one of the inevitable consequences of the parent–child relationship is the imposition upon parents of various responsibilities, duties and obligations towards their children. Failure in these responsibilities can lead to criminal prosecution[27] and to civil liability in damages. One of the most important of these responsibilities is to safeguard and promote the child's health, development and welfare which, amongst other things, obliges the parent to ensure that the child receives proper medical treatment.[28] A pregnant woman has almost total physical control over the child she is carrying, and the child is in the most fundamental way dependent on her for its health, development and welfare. The question arises whether her parental (or any other) responsibility to care for the child comes into existence on its conception and can be enforced before its birth. This question may be of great importance if, for example, some medical procedure requires carrying out for the welfare of the child before it has an existence independent of its mother, or if the mother adopts a pattern of behaviour that is potentially threatening to her unborn child.

2.56   A pregnant woman is not merely the means of the unborn child's survival (though she is essential for it), and it is submitted that she cannot be forced to do something that infringes her own right to bodily integrity. A threat even to the life of the unborn child would not be sufficient to overcome the woman's personal rights. So if, for example, it were discovered that a woman in the final stages of pregnancy was in a state of complete placenta praevia,[29] with the prognosis that

---

[23] 1992 S.L.T. 1026.

[24] See further, Norrie, "Liability for Injuries Caused Before Birth", 1992 S.L.T. (News) 65.

[25] *Hamilton v. Fife Health Board*, 1993 S.L.T. 624, *per* Lords McCluskey, Caplan and Wylie.

[26] A similar issue arises in relation to criminal liability for the death of a child referable to injuries inflicted before its birth: see *McCluskey v. H.M. Advocate*, 1989 S.L.T. 175 and *Att.-Gen.'s Reference (No. 3 of 1994)* [1997] 3 W.L.R. 421, H.L.

[27] Children and Young Persons (Scotland) Act 1937, s. 12.

[28] See below, para. 8.48.

[29] "The placenta attached...to the lower uterine segment thus impairing the normal delivery of a baby by obstruction and by inevitable haemorrhage": *Faber Pocket Medical Dictionary*.

there was a 99 per cent chance of foetal death and a 50 per cent chance of maternal death if natural childbirth were attempted, and at the same time there was an almost 100 per cent chance of both foetal and maternal survival if the child were delivered by Caesarean section, the woman would be entitled to refuse the invasion of her own bodily privacy that such an operation would constitute, and she would not be in breach of any parental obligation. Treatment without her consent would amount to an assault, and the threat to the unborn child would not be an emergency such as to render her consent unnecessary.[30] It has been said that any other answer would involve the court being willing to contemplate the use of force to manacle a resisting woman on to the hospital bed so that she could be forcibly anaesthetised and then cut open.[31] The example given is not fanciful, and the facts are those of *Jefferson v. Griffin Spalding County Hospital Authority*,[32] a case in which the Supreme Court of Georgia ordered a woman 39 weeks pregnant to undergo a Caesarean section in order to save the life of the child.[33]

No such case has yet arisen in Scotland, though the English courts flirted **2.57** with the approach in *Jefferson* before the Court of Appeal signalled strongly its disapproval. After discussing some of the earlier American cases, Balcombe L.J. in *Re F (In Utero)* said that it would be "intolerable" for the courts to have to make such decisions without statutory guidance as to the principles upon which the decision should be based.[34] He continued: "in such a sensitive field, affecting as it does the liberty of the individual, it is not for the judiciary to extend the law." Nevertheless, in a short and clearly hurried judgment, the President of the Family Division of the High Court in England, Stephen Brown P., granted a declaration that a Caesarean section performed against the wishes of a competent pregnant woman would be lawful if the operation were necessary in the patient's best interests and to protect the vital interests of the unborn child.[35] The case was followed in a number of other first instance decisions,[36] though they all involved patients who were held to lack mental competence to make a healthcare decision.[37] That was also the situation in *Re MB (Medical Treatment)*,[38] in which the Court of Appeal addressed the issue head-on. That case involved a woman 40 weeks pregnant who was advised to undergo a Caesarean section for the benefit of the unborn child but who could not bring herself to agree due to an overwhelming fear of needles. The Court of Appeal held that the evidence was clear that she was suffering from an impairment of her mental functions which temporarily disabled her from making a decision. In these circumstances the decision had to be made in her own best interests, and since she was likely to suffer long-term emotional damage if the child was

---

[30] And in any case emergency can justify medical treatment without consent only when the patient's wishes cannot be ascertained, and not when the patient expressly does not give consent.

[31] It has been reported that this was precisely what happened in a case in Chicago: see Gallagher, "Prenatal Invasions and Interventions: What's Wrong with Fetal Rights" (1987) 10 Harv. Women's L.R. 9 at 9–10.

[32] 274 S.E. (2d) 457 (1981).

[33] At the end of the day, the woman, in defiance of the court order, gave birth naturally, with no ill-effects either for herself or her child. See also *Re AC*, 573 A (2d) 1235 (1990), which backtracked slightly from earlier judgments, but which still held open the possibility that in extreme cases the woman's wishes might have to be overruled.

[34] [1988] 2 W.L.R. 1288 at 1306.

[35] *Re S (Refusal of Medical Treatment)* [1992] 3 W.L.R. 806. The child died.

[36] *Tameside and Glossop Acute Services Trust v. CH* [1996] 1 F.L.R. 762; *Norfolk and Norwich Health Care (NHS) Trust v. W*, [1996] 2 F.L.R. 613; *Rochdale Healthcare (NHS) Trust v. C* [1997] 1 F.C.R. 274. (There are a number of other unreported decisions, mentioned by Butler-Sloss LJ in *Re MB*, below).

[37] See also *Re S's Application for Judicial Review* [1997] Fam. Law 790.

[38] [1997] 2 F.L.R. 426.

to be born handicapped or dead, the Caesarean section was in her best interests, even if it had to be carried out with force. The importance of the case lies not in that result but in the strong endorsement of the propositions (1) that the court has no jurisdiction to take account of the interests of the unborn child and (2) that treatment in a patient's best interests can be forced upon the patient against his or her wishes only if he or she is incompetent to make a decision. Butler-Sloss L.J. put it thus:

> "A competent woman who has the capacity to decide may, for religious reasons, other reasons, for rational or irrational reasons, or for no reason at all, choose not to have medical intervention, even though the consequences may be the death or serious handicap of the child she bears, or her own death. In that event the courts do not have the jurisdiction to declare medical intervention lawful and the question of her own best interests objectively considered does not arise".[39]

Re S, the only case to involve a competent patient,[40] was expressly disapproved.[41]

2.58 There is little possibility that the Scottish courts would adopt a different approach. The American cases are based expressly on the constitutional point that the state has an interest in the life of a viable foetus[42] which justifies intervention by the state, and that is not an argument that can be raised in Scotland. A child in the womb is entitled to certain protections in Scots law, from criminal abortion,[43] from delictual injury,[44] and from parents who misuse or abuse it.[45] But these protections are justified only in so far as they do not conflict with any other important legal principle. To force a woman to undergo an operation upon her body when she does not wish to consent conflicts sharply with the principle of autonomy, which finds legal expression in the right of self-determination in medical treatment. This is so even when the interference is designed to protect the life or well-being of another. It is not true to say that the Abortion Act 1967 subordinates a woman's right of decision to the welfare of the child (*e.g.* by prohibiting abortions over 24 weeks except for certain limited reasons[46]): a woman has no "right" in the abortion situation, for that act remains a criminal offence and all the statute does is provide certain defences. The law in Scotland has for long refused to sanction the idea of compulsory blood-testing in order to determine paternity,[47] this on the ground that it would be an unwarranted invasion of a person's private right; and while the court now has the power to request a party to any civil proceedings to provide a sample of blood or other body fluid or tissue, it may not direct that such be taken and it is limited to drawing such adverse inferences as is appropriate from any refusal.[48]

---

[39] [1997] 2 F.L.R. at 436–437.

[40] Or at any rate a patient whose competency was not called in question.

[41] *Re S* is not, however, without its supporters: see Thorpe L.J., writing extrajudicially in "The Caesarean Section Debate" [1997] Fam. Law 663.

[42] This argument is based, somewhat tenuously (see Gallagher, *op. cit.*, at 5–18, 32–37), on the reasoning in *Roe v. Wade*, which recognised that state interest could prohibit abortion completely during the third trimester of pregnancy (*i.e.* after the foetus has attained viability). Because the argument is based on the state interest in viable foetuses, there is no such case in the USA involving a pre-viable foetus. That this distinction is not made in English or Scots law is made clear in *Re F (In Utero)* [1988] 2 W.L.R. 1288 at 1301, *per* May L.J. and 1304, *per* Balcombe L.J., and in *Kelly v. Kelly*, 1997 SLT 896, *per* Lord Justice-Clerk Cullen at 899F (and indeed is under increasing challenge in the USA).

[43] Above, paras 2.11–2.17.

[44] Above, paras 2.29–2.35.

[45] Below, paras 2.62–2.68.

[46] Above, para. 2.15.

[47] See below, para. 3.56.

[48] Law Reform (Miscellaneous Provisions) (Scotland) Act 1990, s. 70; see below, para. 3.58.

If the Scottish courts are unwilling, indeed unable, to order blood tests, they must be far more unwilling, and equally unable, to order compulsory medical operations of a far more invasive nature. It would follow that in Scotland if an operation upon a competent pregnant woman were necessary in order to save the life or health of her unborn child and she refused consent to that operation, a court could not competently make an order requiring her to undergo the operation, and the unborn child would have to suffer the risk. No breach of parental responsibility would have been committed.

The mentally incapax woman

Slightly different considerations would apply if the pregnant woman were **2.59** for some reason unable to decide whether to provide or withhold consent to medical treatment that is necessary for her unborn child's welfare and which would inevitably involve interference upon her body. It was made plain in *Re MB (Medical Treatment)*[49] that irrationality does not necessarily equate to incompetence, for otherwise patients would be permitted to make only rational choices and the courts would be called upon to assess objective rationality. Nevertheless temporary factors such as fear, confusion and pain may well, the Court of Appeal held, compromise a patient's competence, though it was emphasised that the mere fact of being in labour is clearly insufficient on its own to render a woman incompetent. In *Re MB* the pregnant woman's fear of needles was such as to paralyse her will, rendering her quite incapable of making any decision, rational or otherwise.[50] Courts must be scrupulous to resist the temptation to find incompetency merely to achieve what is seen as the optimal outcome (*i.e.* a live birth to a healthy mother) at the expense of the woman's right to decide what to do with her own body without regard to the interests of the unborn child.[51] It has also been held that the mental health legislation cannot be used against a pregnant woman to achieve a result unrelated to her mental state.[52]

If the woman is incapable in the sense of being unable to comprehend and **2.60** retain material information, or to use and weigh it to arrive at a decision, then the justification for carrying out any medical procedure would be emergency, or immediate necessity facing the woman, and a doctor carrying out such treatment without consent would not be liable in damages for assault.[53] However, this provides a justification for non-consensual medical treatment only when the emergency faces the patient herself, and would provide no help if the emergency faced not her but her unborn child. It could be argued, however, that the woman's own emotional well-being demands that her child's life be saved, and in that sense the emergency could be said to face her also. This line of reasoning was adopted in *Re MB*, where it was held that best interests are to be

---

[49] [1997] 2 F.L.R. 426.
[50] The Court of Appeal explored competency more fully in *Re C (Adult: Refusal of Medical Treatment)* [1994] 1 W.L.R. 290. See also *Re JT (Adult: Refusal of Medical Treatment)* [1998] 1 F.L.R. 48.
[51] It might well be argued that the Court of Appeal in *Re MB*, for all its insistence that the interests of the unborn child were not to be taken into account, failed to resist that temptation. The woman was held to be incompetent to refuse consent to being anaesthetised though it was assumed without argument that she would have been competent to consent to the Caesarean section. This indicates that a decision not to follow medical opinion is regarded as, at the very least, an indication of mental incompetency. See also *St George's Healthcare NHS Trust v. S; R v. Collins and Ors, ex p. S* [1998] 3 All E.R. 673, in which the Court of Appeal overruled the judge at first instance for holding a woman incompetent who had refused to follow medical advice. The case would never have been raised (*i.e.* her competency would never have been questioned) had she been willing to follow medical advice.
[52] *St George's Healthcare NHS Trust v. S; R v. Collins and Ors, ex p. S*, above.
[53] *F v. West Berkshire Health Authority* [1989] 2 All E.R. 545, H.L.

assessed widely and are not limited to best medical interests. However, it is clear that this argument cannot be used in all cases. If the woman were so incompetent that she would never enjoy the existence of her child, it could only be said in the most tenuous of ways that its potential non-existence would be a threat to her well-being.[54] It will, however, seldom be difficult to find a physical benefit to a pregnant woman in performing a Caesarean section which will avoid the dangers of vaginal birth.

Consent on behalf of the unborn child

2.61   It may be doubted whether consent to medical treatment is required on behalf of the unborn child itself, for example to the performance of some surgical procedure while it is still in the womb. Whether such consent is required or not, however, the medical treatment would be justified on the basis of emergency, so long as the emergency faced the unborn child: a doctor performing an operation on an unborn child could not be sued for assault on the ground of lack of consent so long as the treatment were necessary in the sense of being a response to an emergency situation.

Care proceedings and removal of the child

2.62   A further consequence of the existence of a foetus in the womb is that it will be recognised as being entitled to the protection granted to children who have been born, to the extent that if it is not properly looked after, it may be subject to care proceedings and be removed from its parents. Of course this removal can only take place once the child has been born alive, but once it has been born, things done to the child by its parents may justify its removal from their care under the provisions of Part II of the Children (Scotland) Act 1995. There is no reason why the court may not look at matters that occurred before the birth of the child in determining whether it is in need of compulsory measures of supervision.

2.63   Though the matter has not yet been addressed directly in a Scottish case,[55] it has arisen in a number of cases from other jurisdictions. In England, for example, the House of Lords in the case of *D (A Minor) v. Berkshire County Council and Others*[56] was faced with the question of whether a child born suffering from drug withdrawal symptoms, directly attributable to the mother's drug addiction and continued drug-taking during pregnancy, was a child whose proper development was being avoidably prevented by the mother's actions, even although the child had never been in the care of the mother at any time after its birth. A juvenile court had made a care order under section 1(2)(a) of the then extant Children and Young Persons Act 1969 on the ground that the child's proper development was being avoidably prevented or neglected or its health was being avoidably impaired or neglected or it was being ill-treated. This was challenged on the ground that the statute demanded that the child "is being" ill-treated, etc., and that this requirement could never be satisfied once the child had been removed from its parents. The House of Lords held that the phrase "is being" denoted a continuing rather than an instant situation and that

---

[54] *cf. Lausier v. Pescinski*, 226 N.W. (2d) 180 (1975), which involved a proposed kidney transplant from a catatonic man for the benefit of his sister: the survival of the sister would not confer any emotional benefit on a man incapacitated from emotion, and therefore the removal of his kidney could not be said to be in his best interests.

[55] Though it is not uncommon practice for a sheriff to grant a child protection order in relation to a child within hours or days of its birth, expressly founding upon concerns created by the parents' behaviour before the child's birth.

[56] [1987] 1 All E.R. 20. See Bainham, "Protecting the Unborn—New Rights in Gestation?" (1987) 50 Mod. L.R. 361.

the court was entitled to look at the past as well as the present, and indeed at the future, though this last only in a hypothetical way by looking to see whether the situation which began earlier and was still continuing at the point of time immediately before the process of protecting the child was put in motion would, if that process had not been put in motion, have been likely to continue further.[57] Consequently, in the words of Lord Goff of Chieveley,[58] "it can be said that a child is being ill-treated if it has been cruelly beaten in the past, and there is a likelihood that it will continue to be cruelly beaten in the future". He went on:

> "It is not enough that something has avoidably been done or omitted to be done in relation to the child in the past which has, for example, impaired its health, and that the symptoms or effects still persist at the relevant time; for it cannot be said in such circumstances that, at the relevant time, the child's health is being avoidably impaired: all that can be said is that its health has been avoidably impaired in the past."[59]

It is important to note that this case was decided on the precise terms of the English statutory provisions,[60] and this must be borne in mind in reading all such cases. There are similar examples from Commonwealth jurisdictions which again turn on the precise terms of the statute in question. So, for example, in *Re Superintendent of Family and Child Service and McDonald*[61] the question was whether a child born drug addicted was "a child in need of protection" within the context of the British Columbia Family and Child Service Act 1980. The British Columbia Supreme Court said: "It would be incredible to come to any other conclusion than that a drug-addicted baby is born abused. That abuse has occurred during the gestation period"[62]; and it was held that a child "is" in need of protection when it is born drug-addicted and has never been in the care of its parents.[63] All these cases illustrate the proposition that the child, *once born*, can be subject to care proceedings on the basis of events which occurred before his or her birth. A New Zealand court went rather further when, on a question of whether a foetus was a "child" within the terms of the protective provisions contained in the Children, Young Persons and their Families Act 1989, it held that a declaration could be made that an unborn child (at least after attaining the stage of viability) was "a child in need of care and protection".[64] This decision remains unique in Commonwealth jurisdictions and the normal approach is illustrated in *Winnipeg Child and Family Services v. G*[65] where the Supreme Court of Canada held emphatically, in a closely reasoned judgment which contains an extensive review of the issue as it has been tackled in Canada, Australia and England, that the Canadian courts are unable to make an order for the child's welfare before its birth.

In Scotland the relevant statutory provisions are found in Part II of the **2.64** Children (Scotland) Act 1995, section 52(2) of which lays down the conditions

---

[57] *per* Lord Brandon of Oakbrook at 41.

[58] *ibid.* at 44.

[59] *ibid.*

[60] The position under the Children Act 1989 is explored by Wagstaffe, "Harming the Unborn Child—the Foetus and the Threshold Criteria" [1998] Fam. Law 160.

[61] (1982) 135 D.L.R. (3d) 330.

[62] *ibid.* at 335.

[63] See also *Re Children's Aid Society for the District of Kenora and JL* (1982) 134 D.L.R. (3d) 249, in which the Provincial Court of Ontario held that a child born with foetal alcohol syndrome was a "child in need of protection" within the meaning of the Ontario Child Welfare Act 1980.

[64] *In the Matter of Baby P (An Unborn Child)* [1995] N.Z.F.L.R. 577, commented upon at [1997] Med. L. Rev. 143. The facts of this case were, however, very unusual in that the declaration did not seek to limit the rights of the pregnant woman since she consented to it, but it gave protection to the unborn child—and the woman—from the latter's violent boyfriend who had threatened to kill the child.

[65] [1997] 152 D.L.R. (4th) 193.

which have to be satisfied to give rise to the question of whether a child is in need of compulsory measures of supervision (which measures may include the child's removal from his or her parents by the imposition of a supervision requirement requiring the child to reside elsewhere).[66] The reference to "child" in section 52 is, it is submitted, a reference to a living human person with an existence independent of his or her mother. A number of the conditions can, however, be satisfied before birth, though there is no ground of referral until after birth. So, for example, under section 52(2)(c) a child may be in need of compulsory measures of supervision if he or she is likely to suffer unnecessarily or be impaired seriously in his or her health or development due to a lack of parental care. This ground is analogous to, but different in important respects from, the ground involved in the English case of *D (A Minor) v. Berkshire County Council*.[67] The problem in that case was whether a child in the womb could be said to satisfy a ground that it "is being" subject to impairment of health or development. The wording of the Scottish statute, with its emphasis on "likelihood",[68] more clearly refers to a future danger from present or past events; and it has been held in the Inner House that this ground can be satisfied even when the child has never been in the care of the parent[69] (the exact situation in *D (A Minor)* and in the Canadian cases cited above).

2.65   Applying this to drug or alcohol addiction by the mother during pregnancy, it can hardly be denied that such addiction will in some cases clearly amount to habits and modes of life which yield the reasonable inference that the parents are unlikely to care for the child properly. However, it should be noted that the mere suffering of the child from drug withdrawal symptoms or foetal alcohol syndrome will not be sufficient on its own to satisfy this ground. This will be strong evidence, but the test is not the suffering of the child at birth, but whether the lack of parental care is likely to cause the child unnecessary suffering in the future or seriously to impair his or her health or development. "The principal focus of attention is therefore the situation of the now living child and not the mother's behaviour while pregnant."[70] So a woman who is able to break her habit of addiction sometime during the pregnancy, but who has already caused her foetus some impairment in its health or development, might not have the child removed under this ground.[71]

2.66   Under section 52(2)(e) and (f) of the 1995 Act a child may be in need of compulsory measures of supervision if he or she is, or is likely to become, a member of the same household as, respectively, a child who is a victim of or a person who has committed certain offences. The words "is likely to become" are sufficient to include a child who is not yet born but who, once born, would be a member of the same household as the person who committed the offences. Again, the offences could be in the past, and committed at a time when the child was not yet born (nor even conceived).[72]

2.67   As well as compulsory measures of supervision, Part II of the Children (Scotland) Act 1995 also permits the granting by a sheriff of a child protection order, which can authorise the immediate removal of children from their parents and their taking to a place of safety.[73] This provision may be used to authorise the removal of a child immediately on birth, on the basis, established by the

---

[66] See below, para. 19.88.
[67] [1987] 1 All E.R. 20.
[68] See further, below, para. 19.15.
[69] *McGregor v. L*, 1981 S.L.T. 194.
[70] Bainham, *op. cit.*, at 364.
[71] *per* Lord Goff of Chieveley in *D (A Minor) v. Berkshire County Council* [1987] 1 All E.R. 20 at 44–45.
[72] See *A v. Kennedy*, 1993 S.C.L.R. 107.
[73] Children (Scotland) Act 1995, s. 57. See below, paras 20.26–20.50.

parents' past actions, that the child will suffer significant harm if he or she is not removed to and kept in a place of safety.

It follows from the above that parents' actions before the birth of a child can **2.68** be relevant in determining whether that child is in need of compulsory measures of supervision. This does not constitute an untoward limitation on the parents' freedom and liberty, for it is in all senses on a par with the limitations placed on parents whose children have already been born. The fear that to allow the court to look at events before birth would unduly restrict a pregnant woman's liberty is therefore unfounded in this context, since her actions would have to be such as would justify removal of a living child and the procedure could not occur until a living child were in existence. These provisions could not be used to prevent a pregnant woman from, say, smoking tobacco or drinking moderate alcohol, or to ensure that she gave birth in a hospital rather than at home. While arguably failure to follow medical advice might in some cases amount to a lack of parental care, it should be remembered that lack of parental care on its own is not sufficient to activate the care provisions in the Children (Scotland) Act 1995. Rather, it must be established that, due to such lack, "the child is likely to suffer unnecessarily or be impaired seriously in his health or development",[74] or that the child will suffer significant harm if not removed.[75] Evidence that smoking leads to low birth weight might not be sufficient to satisfy this ground, because that may not be considered to be a "serious" impairment of health or development; and in any case causation would have to be established in the sense of showing that the smoking was the likely cause of that particular child being of low birth weight.

THE BIRTH PROCESS

The final stage in the process of the creation of human life is the birth process **2.69** itself. This may be taken to commence at the point when spontaneous or induced labour commences, and to be completed at the moment when the umbilical chord is severed. During that time the child will have somewhat greater protection than that granted during its period of gestation in the womb. Destruction of a child during the process of birth is not abortion in Scots law, but neither is it homicide. In *H.M. Advocate v. McAllum*[76] the panel was accused of murder when she allegedly strangled the child to whom she was giving birth. The Lord Justice-Clerk (Inglis) expressly distinguished between abortion and destruction during birth, but he described them both as "very serious offences".[77] If the destruction of a child in the course of being born is a crime but it is not abortion, then the defences to the crime of abortion laid down in the Abortion Act 1967 cannot be utilised. However, it is likely that the law would recognise a common law defence if the child were destroyed in order to preserve the life of the mother.[78]

As far as the parent-child relationship goes during the birth process, it is **2.70** likely that the most significant consequence of that relationship that practically would arise would be the parental responsibility to safeguard and promote the child's health, development and welfare. This may impose on a woman giving birth the duty to seek medical help if the child's potential life is at risk, and if her failure to do so injures the child she may be sued for damages, and may have the child removed, on the conditions discussed above.

---

[74] Children (Scotland) Act 1995, s. 52(2)(c).

[75] *ibid.* s. 57(1)(a)(ii).

[76] (1858) 3 Irv. 187.

[77] *ibid.* at 200.

[78] In the English case of *R. v. Bourne* [1939] 1 K.B. 687 it was held that this would be a defence to the analogous, statutory, English offence of child destruction. The defence there was given a wide interpretation.

2.71   Once the umbilical chord is severed, the child can be said to have an existence independent of its mother, and if it is alive at that moment, for however short a period, it is a full human person in law, and entitled thereby to all the protections the law affords to human persons. Its destruction will not be countenanced in order to preserve the life of someone else,[79] and it cannot be denied medical treatment because it suffers physical or mental abnormalities.[80] The parent-child relationship will for all intents and purposes be fully constituted and all the normal responsibilities, rights, duties and obligations flowing from that relationship which have not already arisen will come into existence at that moment.

Conclusion

2.72   While for most purposes the parent-child relationship will come into existence at birth, it is to be borne in mind that that relationship exists in law only in the context of the consequences to which it gives rise. Some of these consequences, such as those relating to succession and the right to claim damages, certainly occur before birth (and this is not affected by the live-birth rule); others may possibly occur before birth, such as the imposition of responsibilities of care and nurture. Most will arise on birth, but some will arise only after that, such as the obligation to provide suitable education.[81] After a number of years the relationship will gradually lose significance as the child approaches and eventually reaches adulthood. Though parental responsibilities and parental rights will disappear on the child's attaining adulthood, the relationship will remain one of legal consequence until the death of one of the parties.

2.73   The fear of recognising the existence of the unborn child, and of allowing legal consequences to follow, is that the pregnant woman will thereby be unduly restricted in her own rights and liberties and in her self-determination, which are not to be denied just because she is pregnant. While this risk is certainly real, it is suggested that the balance struck by the law of Scotland—that is, eschewing prospective measures of protection but accepting retrospective remedies—is an acceptable and sensible one. Cases in which a pregnant woman will act against the interests of her unborn child will be few indeed (though they will never be completely unknown in any society in which women of child-bearing age are subject to the risk of drug addiction). If the law protects the child by allowing its removal on birth for actions the woman does during pregnancy, and by allowing the child to sue his or her mother or father or anyone else who causes injury before or after birth,[82] then that is probably sufficient and acceptable deterrent. To go further and to allow a pregnant woman to be interdicted from certain activities, and to enforce such interdict, or to require her to adopt a particular course of action, such as undergoing medical treatment, would be to go too far. It would be too great an interference in the woman's liberties and fundamental freedoms and would reduce the pregnant woman to the status of an incubator for future generations, and to sanction that would be contrary to public policy.

---

[79] *cf. R. v. Dudley and Stevens* (1884) 14 Q.B.D. 273.

[80] *Re B (A Minor)* [1981] 1 W.L.R. 1421; *R. v. Arthur* (1981) 12 B.M.L.R. 1; *Re J (A Minor) (Wardship: Medical Treatment)* [1990] 3 All E.R. 930. The duty to treat is not, however, absolute: see *Re C (A Baby)* [1996] 2 F.L.R. 43.

[81] Education (Scotland) Act 1980, ss. 30 and 31.

[82] Though it must be recognised that in practice the economic vulnerability of most drug and alcohol addicts renders this liability all but worthless.

PART II

ESTABLISHING THE RELATIONSHIP

CHAPTER 3

CONSTITUTION OF THE PARENT-CHILD
RELATIONSHIP

Scope of this chapter

The law of parent and child in Scotland used to be concerned primarily with **3.01** the status of the child as determined by his or her "legitimacy" or "illegitimacy", which in turn was determined by his or her parents' relationship to each other.[1] Fraser opens his work on *Parent and Child*[2] with the statement: "Legitimacy is the status of a party who has been born in a lawful manner, that is, in a manner approved of by the law". Since the coming into force of the Law Reform (Parent and Child) (Scotland) Act 1986, however, it is no longer true that the major concern of the law is with the child's status: in general the thrust of the law is to give all children the same status, which will alter only with age. Nowadays the major concern of the law is the nature of the relationship between the child and his or her parents, how that relationship is constituted, and its consequences in law. The consequences of the parent-child relationship will be examined fully in other parts of this book, and the purpose of this chapter is to show how that relationship will come about in the eyes of the law, other than through adoption.[3]

The concept of "parenthood" is ambiguous and is used, even by the law, in a **3.02** number of different senses. At one time, it was assumed that the law's sole concern was for biological parenthood, and that was certainly so as regards "legitimate" children. Every child has, of course, two biological parents but it has never followed from that fact that the child has full legal relations with these two persons. Recognition of parenthood has a number of automatic consequences, in relation, for example, to succession, to aliment and child support, and to the rules of incest and the forbidden degrees of marriage; and it is also the normal starting point (though neither essential nor sufficient) for claims to a role in the upbringing of the child. However, "the law distinguishes between legal parenthood—the status of being a parent—and parental responsibility—the power to act as a parent".[4] While the question of who should be recognised as having parental responsibilities has for long (at least since the weakening of the full *patria potestas* in the nineteenth century) been seen as a policy matter, the question of who a child's parents are has traditionally been regarded as a matter of fact, or of nature, with no room for the exercise of judicial discretion. Yet even here policy considerations come into play in determining which facts are to be deemed significant to the existence of the parent–child relationship. The legal status of "parent" is no longer necessarily established by proving, to an extent sufficient to satisfy the burden of proof, a genetic parental link between two persons. That may frequently be essential, and will usually be sufficient, but there are now some cases, concerning both maternity and paternity, in which it is not even relevant.

---

[1] Above, paras 1.44–1.58.

[2] (3rd ed., 1906), p. 1.

[3] For a comprehensive examination of this issue in two other legal systems, see Atkin and Bridge, "Establishing Legal Relations: Parents and Children in England and New Zealand" (1996) 17 N.Z. Uni. L.R. 13. See also Douglas and Lowe, "Becoming a Parent in English Law" (1992) 108 L.Q.R. 414.

[4] Barton and Douglas, *Law and Parenthood* (1995), p. 49.

3.03   Very different considerations arise when seeking to establish the legal relationship of mother and child from those which arise when the relationship of father and child is at issue, and consequently they must be considered separately.

ESTABLISHING MATERNITY

3.04 *Mater semper certa est etiamsi vulgo conceperit; pater vero is est, quem nuptiae demonstrant.*[5] The passage from the *Digest* is absolute in its terms but both fact and law admit of a relative judgment. It points, however, to the comparative certainty of proof of maternity, demonstrable as it often is by direct evidence, and the uncertainty of proof of paternity, which until relatively recently had to rely almost entirely on inference. Once maternity is established, all the consequences of parenthood follow automatically , and the mother today has the full complement of parental responsibilities and parental rights in relation to her child, irrespective of her marital status.[6]

Defining maternity
3.05   The certainty which usually attaches to maternity is based on the assumption that a child is conceived of the woman who bears it. Any other view would until recently have seemed absurd. Indeed, it was not so much a question of making an assumption as of drawing a factual inference of unassailable certainty. Modern medical procedures have, however, destroyed the basis of that ancient certainty. It is now possible to take an egg from one woman, to fertilise it externally and to implant it into another woman who will carry it for the necessary gestation period and then give birth to a child. Similarly, it is possible to remove an egg that has been fertilised naturally in one woman from that woman's body and to implant it into another woman, with the same aim and result. These are, respectively, egg donation and embryo transfer, which are two of the technological methods of alleviating infertility that were hardly dreamed of until the later years of the twentieth century. There are many others,[7] but the two mentioned have this in common, that they both result in the genetic mother (*i.e.* the woman whose egg was fertilised to be developed into a child) being different from the "carrying" or "nurturing" or "gestational" mother (*i.e.* the woman in whose uterus the foetus gestates and who goes through the process of giving birth to the child). Where these procedures are employed the question, not previously meaningful, arises of whether it is the woman from whose egg the child has been conceived ("the genetic mother") or the woman who nurtures the foetus in her womb and bears the child ("the gestational mother") who is to be regarded as the child's mother for the purposes of the law. Further complications to the question may arise if the purpose of implantation into a nurturing mother is to create a child not for her to bring up as her own but for another person to bring up as a member of that other person's family. This is referred to as surrogate maternity or "gestational surrogacy"[8] and is considered in some detail below.[9]

---

[5] *Digest*, II, iv, 5: "The mother is always identifiable even if the son has been conceived in promiscuity; the father indeed is declared by the marriage" (Mommsen, Krueger and Watson, eds., 1985).

[6] This is to be compared with the establishment of paternity, considered below, which does not necessarily import the full complement of parental responsibilities and parental rights on the father unless he be married to the mother, though it will automatically give rise to some consequences (such as, for example, succession rights and alimentary obligations).

[7] See the more complete discussion than is possible here in D. J. Cusine, *New Reproductive Techniques: A Legal Perspective* (1988).

[8] Though it is, in fact, only one form of surrogacy. The more usual is when a woman carries a child created by the fertilisation of her own egg, the intention being that she gives up the child on birth to another woman.

[9] See below, Chap. 6.

There has been much academic (and in other countries judicial) discussion of **3.06** the question of defining "mother" in the face of these techniques,[10] and some attempts to identify the criteria adopted by the common law for defining motherhood have been made. In the absence of legislation, there is no obvious answer to the question of whether a woman's genetic contribution to the creation of a child is more or less important than a woman's nurturing contribution: both (like, indeed, a father's genetic contribution) are essential, and no child would come into existence but for the contribution of both. In determining which facts constitute the "natural" mother and child relationship, a number of different approaches could be adopted. On an analogy with establishing paternity, it might be argued that it is the biological or genetic rather than the nurturing or gestational connection that is the determining factor. One may find support for this approach by pointing to the law's preference for "blood-links" in other areas, such as in the law of succession, as well as to the fact that, generally speaking, paternity will depend upon genetic connection. However, it does not necessarily follow from the fact that the father's contribution is solely genetic that that aspect of the mother's dual contribution should be used to the exclusion of her other, gestational, contribution. When the Warnock Committee in the United Kingdom considered the matter,[11] the majority there did not accept the analogy with establishing paternity, and preferred to draw an analogy with sperm donation, which the Committee had previously suggested should be dealt with by severing completely all legal links between the donor and the child[12]: the result would be that the woman who provided the gestational environment would be the legal mother of the child rather than, if different, the woman who provided the genetic material. These are not the only possible approaches, as can be seen from the American case of *Johnson v. Calvert*.[13] Here the Supreme Court of California rejected both genetics and gestation as determining factors and founded instead on the intention of the parties when the child was conceived. *Johnson* was a case of gestational surrogacy in which the gestational mother refused to give up the child, once born, to the genetic mother and her husband (the genetic father). The majority of the Supreme Court held that since the gestational mother had become pregnant with the intent of facilitating the procreation of a child of the genetic parents, such procreation also being their intent, then the law should give effect to that intention.[14] There are a number of flaws in this argument,[15] perhaps the most important being the failure to identify why the gestational mother's intent at the time of conception should be considered more significant than her intent at the time of birth. A minority judgment in the same case argued that the matter should be determined by the best interests of the child, which is yet another approach, but one which seems to confuse the issue of parenthood with the issue of who should bring up the child[16]: one can accept that, for reasons of good policy, children should be brought up by those who will best serve their interests, but parenthood itself cannot be divorced

---

[10] See, for example Cusine, *op. cit.*, at pp. 59–72; Rosettenstein "Defining a Parent: The New Biology and Rebirth of the *Filius Nullius*" (1981) 131 New L.J. 1095; McKenzie, "Who Are a Child's Parents?", 1986 S.L.T. (News) 303; Stumpf, "Redefining Mother: A Legal Matrix for New Reproductive Technologies" (1986) 96 Yale L.J. 187; Douglas, "The Intention to be a Parent and the Making of Mothers" (1994) 57 Mod. L.R. 636.

[11] *Committee of Inquiry into Human Fertilisation and Embryology* (the Warnock Committee), Cmnd. 9314 (1984), paras 6.6–6.8.

[12] *ibid.* para. 4.22.

[13] 851 P (2d) 776, 5 Cal. (4th) 84 (1993) (Supreme Court of California). The earlier decision of the California Court of Appeal in this case was discussed in the 1st edition of this work at p. 122.

[14] This approach was followed in New York in *McDonald v. McDonald*, 608 N.Y.S. (2d) 477 (1994).

[15] Explored by Douglas, in "The Intention to be a Parent and the Making of Mother" (1994) 57 Mod. L.R. 636.

[16] Alternatively, the minority judgment could be read as a denial of any importance to the distinction between genetic parenthood and social parenthood.

from its factual basis. The only two arguable options are, it is submitted, the genetic and the gestational approaches.

3.07   No court in the United Kingdom had to pronounce on the matter,[17] and the proposals of the Warnock Committee were accepted by Parliament, and given effect to in the Human Fertilisation and Embryology Act 1990. Section 27(1) of that Act provides as follows:

> "The woman who is carrying or has carried a child as a result of the placing in her of an embryo or of sperm and eggs, and no other woman, is to be treated as the mother of the child."[18]

This applies whether the woman was in the United Kingdom or elsewhere at the time of the placing in her of the embryo or of the sperm and eggs.[19] The result of section 27 is that the woman who carries the child[20] in her womb and who gives birth to the child will be treated "in law" as the mother of the child "for all purposes",[21] and "references to any relationship between two people in any enactment, deed, or other instrument or document (whenever passed or made) are to be read accordingly".[22] This is not a presumption, but is rather an irrebuttable deeming provision which applies irrespective of the origin of the genetic material which was fertilised to bring about the creation of the embryo that led to the child, and irrespective of how the material was fertilised and implanted. The genetic link between child and egg-producer (like the identity of the eventual carer) is irrelevant to the establishment of maternity, and proof of such a link is meaningless: the donor of the egg, if different from the gestational mother, is not to be treated in law as being the mother of the child for any purpose.[23] It follows that in a situation similar to that in *Johnson v. Calvert* the surrogate would be considered in Scots and English law to be the mother, and the genetic mother would have no legal relationship whatsoever with the child (though she and the genetic father would—if they were married to each other—be entitled to apply for an order under section 30 of the 1990 Act that they be treated as parents).[24]

---

[17] Though the opportunity could have been taken, but was not, in the English case of *Re W (Minors) (Surrogacy)* [1991] 1 F.L.R. 385, in which parentage was held not to be relevant to the issue (an injunction protecting the identity of the parties). And in *Re C (A Minor) (Wardship: Surrogacy)* [1985] F.L.R. 846 the decision solely concerned who should bring up the child.

[18] The same rule applies in, for example, New Zealand where the Children Amendment Act 1987 provides, by s. 9, that the woman who becomes pregnant shall for all legal purposes be regarded as the child's mother rather than, if different, the donor of the egg or embryo. This is also the case under s. 137b of the Austrian *Allgemeines Burgerliches Gesetzbuch*. The same result also follows, though under rather different reasoning, in Art. 374 of the French *Code Civile*.

[19] Human Fertilisation and Embryology Act 1990, s. 27(3). This does not imply extraterritorial effect for the rule in s. 27, but merely that the status of mother conferred will be recognised in the United Kingdom wherever the treatment took place. In *U v. W (Attorney General Intervening)* [1997] 2 F.L.R. 282 embryos had been placed in a woman while she was in Rome, and the Act was held to apply (although, in fact, the gestational mother was shown by tests to be the genetic mother also). There is no requirement that the person seeking recognition of the status of parent through the application of the 1990 Act be domiciled in, national of, or habitually resident in the United Kingdom.

[20] If the embryo has been fertilised within the body of one woman before being removed and implanted into the body of another woman, it is possible to argue that both women have "carried" the child. However, that result is excluded by s. 2(3) which provides that "for the purposes of this Act, a woman is not to be treated as carrying a child until the embryo has become implanted". It is not possible to remove an embryo implanted in the body of one woman from that body for gestation in the body of another woman.

[21] *ibid.* s. 29(1).

[22] *ibid.* s. 29(3). It would, however, remain open to the person executing a deed expressly to exclude from his or her definition of "mother" or "father" persons deemed mother and father by these provisions. S. 29(3) is so worded that nothing short of express terms or necessary implication will, however, suffice. A surrogacy contract, being without legal effect, cannot exclude s. 29(3).

[23] *ibid.* ss. 27(1) and 29(2).

[24] See below, paras 6.05–6.10.

Exceptions

The rule in section 27(1) is not absolute and there are a number of **3.08** qualifications to its application. First, under section 27(2), the woman who carries the child will not be considered in law to be the mother of the child where the child is treated by virtue of adoption as not being the child of any person other than the adopter or adopters.[25] This keeps the law in line with the adoption legislation, which provides that when the adoptive relationship comes into being the child is to be regarded as being the child of no person other than the adopter or adopters.[26]

Secondly, the woman who carries the child but is not the genetic mother **3.09** will not be considered in law to be the mother of the child for the purposes of section 2 of the Human Organ Transplants Act 1989.[27] That Act contains restrictions on organ transplantations between persons who are not genetically related and the purpose of these restrictions would be undermined if any form of genetic parent–child relationship fell outwith their terms. Consequently the parent–child relationship otherwise created by the 1990 Act is deemed not to be effective for the purposes of the Human Organ Transplants Act 1989. It may be noted here that there is no exception made in relation to the laws on incest or the forbidden degrees of marriage,[28] where genetics are otherwise seen as having a significance.[29] This means that a child born through artificial reproductive technology may have lawful sexual intercourse with and may marry a person to whom he or she is genetically closely related.[30] Due to the secrecy that is written into other parts of the 1990 Act it is, in any event, unlikely in the extreme that it would ever be discovered that a child born through these means were genetically related to someone he or she wished to marry or have sex with.

Thirdly, the provision deeming maternity from the fact of gestation does not **3.10** apply to any title, coat of arms, honour or dignity transmissible on the death of the holder thereof or affect the succession thereto or the devolution thereof; and where the terms of any deed provide that any property or interest in property shall devolve along with a title, coat of arms, honour or dignity, nothing in section 27 shall prevent the property or interest from so devolving.[31] This is in line with the general principle that succession to any such title or dignity is governed by the common law of parentage and must be "legitimate"[32] and, in relation to the devolution of these interests, one may assume that the genetic

---

[25] The same rule applies for men deemed fathers under s. 28: s. 28(5)(c).

[26] Adoption (Scotland) Act 1978, s. 39(1). The same result follows, though not expressly, from the application of s. 39(1) to parental orders made under s. 30 of the Human Fertilisation and Embryology Act 1990 after a surrogacy arrangement: Parental Orders (Human Fertilisation and Embryology) (Scotland) Regulations 1994 (S.I. 1994 No. 2804), para. 8.

[27] Human Fertilisation and Embryology Act 1990, Sched. 4, para. 8.

[28] Notwithstanding a plea in the House of Lords from the Chief Rabbi that such an exception be made: H.L. Vol. 513, col. 1074.

[29] Though the extent of that significance can be questioned: see Norrie, "Incest and the Forbidden Degrees of Marriage in Scots Law" (1992) 37 J.L.S.S. 216. An example of when genetic risks did manifest themselves (though not in the context of assisted reproduction) can be seen in the facts of *P's Curator Bonis v. Criminal Injuries Compensation Board*, 1997 S.L.T. 1180.

[30] This may be compared with the adoption legislation which also creates a parent–child relationship in the absence of a genetic link (see Chap. 4). S. 41(1) of the Adoption (Scotland) Act 1978 (as amended by the Incest and Related Offences (Scotland) Act 1986, Sched. 1, para. 5) has the effect of bringing the child and the adopter within the forbidden degrees in respect of the law relating to both marriage and incest, but it does not take the child outwith the forbidden degrees in relation to his or her genetic parents, and other relations.

[31] Human Fertilisation and Embryology Act 1990, s. 29(5).

[32] Legitimation *per subsequens matrimonium* will however suffice. The Legitimation (Scotland) Act 1968, s. 8(4), has the effect of allowing persons legitimated under the Act to succeed to titles and dignities, even although they would not be legitimated at common law: see above, para. 1.58.

Parent and Child

link between the holder and the child remains determinative since this may be taken to be the underpinning philosophy of all hereditary titles.[33] A child born to a woman other than his or her genetic mother will have his or her "legitimacy" determined for this purpose by the nature of the relationship between his or her genetic mother and genetic father. If the gametes from which the child was created have been donated, as will often be the case, proof of "legitimacy" (and therefore the right to inherit titles, dignities and honours) will be almost impossible to establish. That the courts have traditionally favoured presuming "legitimacy" in the absence of evidence to the contrary will seldom save such a child's "legitimacy" for the purposes of succession to hereditary titles and honours since proof that the child developed from an embryo that was created from the gametes of unknown donors will usually be sufficient to rebut the presumption of "legitimacy" (even when strengthened by repute) and will certainly do so if either the nurturing mother or her husband can be excluded as a provider of gametes. In cases in which an embryo has been created using the gametes of a married couple, but carried by a woman other than the donor wife, the gestational mother will be mother for all other legal purposes, including general succession, but the child, being for this purpose the "legitimate" child of his or her genetic parents, will succeed to the titles, coats of arms, honours or dignities transmissible from them, together with any property or interest in property that devolves along with those titles.

3.11   Fourthly, though the matter is not dealt with in the Act, it may be that the mother-child relationship will not be recognised if the question arises incidentally to a question of succession governed by a foreign legal system. Entitlement to succeed to immoveables is generally a matter for the *lex situs*,[34] which will even determine a person's status for that purpose.[35] It would follow from these authorities that if the *lex situs* does not recognise the gestational mother as the legal mother, then she and the child would have no succession rights in each other's immoveable estates. Yet the 1990 Act states that the gestational mother is to be legal mother "for all purposes"[36] which, taken literally, would include succession to immoveables abroad. In this context, then, it may be argued that the 1990 Act has overturned the traditional rule in the international private law of succession. On the other hand, succession to immoveables abroad is not governed by Scots law, and the 1990 Act is part of Scots law. If succession to immoveables is governed by another legal system it is that other legal system that has the power, at the end of the day, to say who succeeds. If the foreign system refers that question back to one of the legal systems which contains the 1990 Act, then section 27 will, on principles of *renvoi* or *envoi*, give the rule, but if the foreign legal system is willing to answer the question itself, then that is the answer that ultimately must be accepted. International private law issues relating to the determination of parentage are discussed at the end of this chapter.

---

[33] This reflects the position under s. 9(1)(c) of the Law Reform (Parent and Child) (Scotland) Act 1986, and s. 37(1)(a) of the Succession (Scotland) Act 1964 which prevents anyone succeeding to such interests through the operation of, respectively, the Law Reform (Parent and Child) (Scotland) Act 1986 (which otherwise removes the distinction between the "legitimate" and the "illegitimate" child) and the Adoption (Scotland) Act 1978 (which creates a parent–child relationship in the absence of any genetic link). It should be noted, however, that the exclusion in the 1990 Act, which covers property or interests devolving along with the title or honour, is rather wider than the exclusion contained in either of these other Acts, which does not include such property or interest. *Cf.* the position under the Legitimation (Scotland) Act 1968, above, n. 32.

[34] Craig, *Jus Feudale*, III, vii, 4; *Fenton v. Livingstone* (1859) 21 D. (H.L.) 10; *Murray v. Earl of Rothes* (1836) 14 S. 1049; Anton and Beaumont, *Private International Law* (2nd ed.), p. 676.

[35] *Fenton v. Livingstone*, above, described by Anton and Beaumont (at p. 676) as the "high water mark" of the general international private law rule.

[36] Human Fertilisation and Embryology Act 1990, s. 29(1).

Proof of maternity

It is only very rarely that, in the absence of the medical procedures previously **3.12** discussed, there is any dispute as to who a child's mother is. Problems do sometimes occur, however, as for example when it is alleged that a child has been infiltrated into a family or that there has been confusion in a hospital at birth. They may also arise if a quest is made for the origins of a child who has been abandoned. And a like effect may follow from deliberate concealment as where, due to the social stigma attaching to "illegitimacy", a child born to a young unmarried girl is brought up by the mother's parents as her brother or sister rather than as her child. It is probable that this practice of familial confusion, once quite common and still not unknown, is motivated more by a desire to avoid the social consequences of birth out of wedlock than as any fraud on the law, but, if persisted in, it may have that effect. Maternity may also be in doubt in immigration cases.[37] If there is any doubt as to maternity, an action of declarator of parentage or non-parentage can now be brought either in the Court of Session or in the sheriff court under section 7 of the Law Reform (Parent and Child) (Scotland) Act 1986.[38] Maternity has to be proved as a fact. In the absence of scientific proof in the form of DNA profiling (when relevant),[39] the best evidence is that of those present at the birth, but reputation or the evidence of the entry in the Register of Births will also be relevant. By statute[40] an extract or abbreviated certificate of birth, duly authenticated,[41] will be sufficient evidence of the facts of the birth, though other evidence, normally oral, will also be required to identify the persons whose relationship is in issue with those named in the record as the mother and child.[42] The lack of reported cases in which maternity has been doubted suggests that this is not a matter that creates many practical problems.[43]

ESTABLISHING PATERNITY

Introduction

Establishing paternity is necessarily less certain and more problematic than **3.13** establishing maternity. In the nature of the case there is no equivalent of gestation or birth from which a conclusion of paternity can be drawn. Nor did the common law find any place for deemed paternity except in the strong but rebuttable presumption that the husband of a married woman was the father of her child. In questions of paternity the quest was always for a genetic link, identifying the male parent to whom procreation was attributable, as both the rules for proof in actions of affiliation of "illegitimate" children and the rules for rebuttal of the presumption *pater est quem nuptiae demonstrant* show. Subject to some statutory

---

[37] Rankin, "DNA Fingerprinting" (1988) 33 J.L.S.S. 124 at 125, describes a case in which a Ghanaian boy born in the U.K. was refused entry into Britain to rejoin his mother because immigration officers suspected that a substitution had occurred and he was not really the child of the woman (the father was unknown). On obtaining the results of scientific tests (to be discussed later) the Home Office conceded the boy the right of entry.

[38] See further, below, para. 3.45.

[39] See below, para. 3.54.

[40] Registration of Births, Deaths and Marriages (Scotland) Act 1965, s. 41(3).

[41] *ibid.* s. 41(1).

[42] See Wilkinson, *The Scottish Law of Evidence* (1986), p. 172. For births abroad, see the Evidence (Foreign, Dominion and Colonial Documents) Act 1933, and for births at sea, the Merchant Shipping (Returns of Births and Deaths) Regulations 1972, made under the Merchant Shipping Act 1970, s. 75.

[43] One of the few Commonwealth cases in which the issue arose was that of *R. v. Jenkins, ex p. Morrison* [1949] V.L.R. 277, decided by the Supreme Court of Victoria. The question arose, though obliquely, in the Scottish case of *Grant v. Countess of Seafield*, 1926 S.C. 274, in which the pursuer sought to prove that he was the son of the Earl of Seafield, and also of the Earl's wife. See also *Douglas v. Duke of Hamilton* (1769) 2 Pat. 143, H.L.

modifications and exceptions, that is still so. Proof of the necessary genetic link had until recently to rely largely on inference. Previously it was impossible to establish by scientific means that, with certainty, a particular man was the father of a particular child though, on the other hand, an exclusion of paternity could sometimes be established beyond any doubt. A positive conclusion could therefore be reached only with the help of inferential evidence such as length of gestation, the alleged father's opportunity for sexual access to the mother, and parental acknowledgment, if any.[44]

Although there has been little occasion for the matter to be considered, the corollary of the common law principles placing paternity for legal purposes on a factual and genetic basis is that the fact that procreation was achieved other than by normal sexual intercourse is irrelevant. So, in relation to children conceived as a result of fecundation *ab extra*, their "legitimacy" depends upon whether or not fecundation is attributable to sperm of the husband of the mother.[45] The same principles, it may be supposed, applied at common law in relation to children conceived by artificial insemination, whether to determine their "legitimacy" or to determine paternity. The technique of donor insemination, whereby a (usually anonymous) donor would provide sperm to a woman for the fertilisation of her egg, is not new,[46] and though in theory the donor was in law the father (and therefore subject to parental obligations such as aliment) the practice of anonymity for donors made proof virtually impossible. Proof became somewhat easier after the development of more accurate means of identification, particularly through DNA profiling[47]; and this, combined with the growing movement to allow children access to information concerning their genetic origins,[48] led to fears that donations of sperm would cease, because potential donors would not wish to be subject to parental obligations. In the true donation situation statute therefore now expressly provides[49] that if a man gives his gametes for the purpose of treatment services of others (*i.e.* if he donates his sperm for the treatment of someone other than himself or for the treatment of persons other than himself and another together[50]) and he gives effective consent to them so being used,[51] then he is not to be treated as the father of any child born as a result of his sperm being so used.[52] The genetic link between the sperm donor and the resultant child is therefore in these circumstances irrelevant in determining legal paternity. In other words, this provision elides all parent–child links between the donor and the child except when the donation is used for the treatment of the donor himself and of his partner.

3.14   Paternity is today still primarily, and in the vast majority of cases, established through a parental genetic link between the child and the putative father. This link can be shown by leading extrinsic evidence, such as the results of scientific tests,[53] though more commonly it is established by relying on one of a number of presumptions that the law provides. In unusual cases, involving artificially

---

[44] For proof of paternity today, see below, paras 3.49–3.53.

[45] See above, para. 1.45.

[46] It was discussed by the Court of Session in the case of *MacLennan v. MacLennan*, 1958 S.C. 105, in which the claim was made (unsuccessfully) that a woman undergoing donor insemination was committing adultery. Donor insemination has been practised by medical practitioners since at least the beginning of the 20th century: see Cusine, *op. cit.* at pp. 12 *et seq*. The same question arose as in *MacLennan* arose (and the opposite conclusion reached) in an Ontario decision in 1921: *Orford v. Orford* (1921) 58 D.L.R. 251. See Smith, "Adultery and AID", 1957 S.L.T. (News) 69.

[47] See below, para. 3.54.

[48] Recognised and accepted by the Warnock Committee, at para. 4.21 (so long as the information given was non-identifying): see now s. 31 of the Human Fertilisation and Embryology Act 1990.

[49] Human Fertilisation and Embryology Act 1990, s. 28(6)(a) and Sched. 3, para. 5.

[50] *ibid.* Sched. 3, para. 5(3).

[51] *ibid.* Sched. 3, para. 5(1).

[52] If his sperm were used without his consent then it would seem that he remains father in both genetics and law: see further, below, para. 3.42.

[53] Discussed below, para. 3.54.

assisted conception, paternity is deemed by the law from certain facts notwithstanding the acknowledged lack of any genetic connection. Before examining how paternity is constituted in law, two points should be noted. First, merely establishing paternity does not in itself establish a full parent–child relationship. Fatherhood alone is insufficient to give the father a legally recognised role in the upbringing of the child, though it is sufficient to impose certain responsibilities (such as the obligation to aliment the child) and to confer certain rights (such as succession rights). Secondly, most fathers rely on legal presumptions for the recognition of their status as such and, though they can be overturned, the main purpose of these presumptions is to avoid the need for court action and the expense of commissioning scientific tests. In the vast majority of cases paternity, though incapable of immediate proof, is never challenged.

Proving paternity by evidence will be considered later[54]; the presumptions and deeming provisions are examined in the immediately following paragraphs.

Marriage to the mother

Section 5(1)(a) of the Law Reform (Parent and Child) (Scotland) Act 1986[55] **3.15** provides that a man shall be presumed to be the father of a child if he was married to the mother of the child at any time in the period beginning with the conception and ending with the birth of the child. This is the statutory re-enactment, with important modifications, of the common law principle *pater est quem nuptiae demonstrant*,[56] which was in truth a presumption of paternity rather than a presumption of "legitimacy" (though it was frequently regarded as the latter, since in many instances that was the legally significant issue). This was a *praesumptio juris* to which, on proof of the basic facts, a court was accordingly bound by law to give effect unless there was evidence sufficiently strong for rebuttal. In terms of the statute the presumption "shall" apply in the relevant circumstances, subject to rebuttal according to the principles shortly to be discussed. The presumption at common law was based on common experience (the majority of children born of married women are procreated by their husbands). The identity of the mother, the existence of the marriage at the appropriate date, and the conception and birth of the child at the relevant time are the basic facts that require to be established before the presumption operates. Proof of these facts will also operate to impose upon the father parental responsibilities and parental rights.[57]

The nature of the marriage

The couple may end the marriage by divorce before the child is born, or one **3.16** party may die, or they may marry before conception or before birth: but so long as there is a marriage at some point between the moment of conception and the moment of birth[58] the presumption will take effect. This applies whether the

---

[54] Below, paras 3.49–3.53.

[55] See Thomson, "The Law Reform (Parent and Child) (Scotland) Act 1986", 1987 S.L.T. (News) 129.

[56] Stair, III, iii, 42; Erskine, I, vi, 49; Fraser, p. 1.

[57] Children (Scotland) Act 1995, s. 3(1)(b).

[58] The statutory formulation also takes into account the previously existing presumption of fact, not of law (*Kerrs v. Lindsay* (1890) 18 R. 365) that where a man marries a pregnant woman he is presumed to be father of the child. The *locus classicus* of this presumption of fact is the opinion of Lord Gifford in *Gardner v. Gardner* (1876) 3 R. 695 at 723: "wherever an avowed and open courtship has taken place, there have been opportunities of access, and thereafter the man marries the woman in an advanced state of pregnancy, knowing that she is so... in such a case the presumption is quite as strong as the mere presumption which arises when a child is conceived during marriage that the husband is the father. Indeed in some aspects it seems to be even stronger, for it has in it the element of express or actual confession or avowal, which does not always arise, or arises with less force, from the mere subsistence of a nuptial tie." (And see (1877) 4 R. (H.L.) 56, *per* Lord Cairns L.C. at 59, Lord Blackburn at 68 and Lord Gordon at 75.) There was no presumption at common law that a man was father when he married the mother of a child conceived and born before the marriage: *James v. McLennan*, 1971 S.C. (H.L.) 77. Nor was (or is) there any presumption that a child born to a woman is her cohabitant's child: *A v. G*, 1984 S.L.T. (Sh.Ct) 65; it will, however, in these circumstances often be easy to draw inferences of fact.

marriage is valid, void, voidable, regular or irregular.[59] At first sight it may seem a little odd to recognise legal consequences of a marriage that is not in law a marriage, but the law has for long done so in recognising that a child of a putative marriage was a "legitimate" child. This provision does no more than presume the relationship between a child and a man, reflecting the fact that the presumption is one of paternity rather than of "legitimacy" (which is more closely linked to the married status of the parents), and the rule can be justified on the ground that the marriage's invalidity does not affect the presumption of fact that if people go through a ceremony of marriage and thereafter have the opportunity for sexual intercourse they will take that opportunity, whether or not the ceremony leads to a valid marriage.[60] In other words a marriage ceremony, whether it leads to a valid marriage or not, is strong presumptive evidence of sexual intercourse. So too is the existence of an irregular marriage, of which the only remaining example is marriage by cohabitation with habit and repute.

The time of conception

3.17   The reference in the statute to the period "beginning with the conception" can lead to difficulties, particularly if the marriage has ended, whether through death or divorce, before the child is born. If the child has been conceived before the end of the marriage then the husband is presumed to be the father, but the date of conception can rarely, if ever, be fixed with precision. At common law, where the *pater est* presumption applied only when there was a marriage at the date of conception, similar difficulties were at one time resolved by reference to fixed periods of time which were held to constitute the minimum and the maximum periods of gestation respectively. The minimum period was six lunar months.[61] There was some divergence of opinion about whether the maximum period should be set at 10 lunar or 10 calendar months.[62] These periods came from the civil and the canon law, which in turn depended on the observations of Hippocrates[63] and they did no more than reflect the medical opinion of the times: they must now give way to advances in medical science. Medical practice today is to count pregnancy from the date of the woman's last menstrual period. But that date is clearly not the date of "conception," which occurs not on fertilisation but on the implantation of the fertilised egg into the woman's uterus.[64] If the marriage has ended before the child's birth, therefore, it is conception that must be proved to have occurred on a date before the ending of the marriage, and the common law cases on possible length of gestation remain relevant. The question was widely canvassed, both in relation to proof of "legitimacy" and in relation to proof of adultery[65]; and although decisions on questions

---

[59] Law Reform (Parent and Child) (Scotland) Act 1986, s. 5(2). There was some authority for the view that at common law the presumption had no application in the case of irregular marriages: Craig, II, xviii, 21; *Swinton v. Swinton* (1862) 24 D. 833, *per* Lord Deas at 838; *Baptie v. Barclay* (1665) Mor. 8413; but Stair, III, iii, 42 and IV, xlv, 20 is explicitly to the contrary. The matter is put beyond doubt by the express terms of the statute.

[60] *per* Lord Neaves in *Ross v. Fraser* (1863) 1 M. 783.

[61] Erskine, I, vi, 50. The corresponding period in Roman law was six solar months, but Scots law from favour of legitimacy put it at six lunar months.

[62] *Sandy v. Sandy* (1823) 2 S. 453, *per* Lord Gillies and Lord Meadowbank. Calculation by calendar months would accord with the favour of legitimacy shown in the calculation of the minimum period. Stair, III, iii, 42 allowed as much as 11 months subject to the qualification that "in these cases, the probability of the circumstances may make the mother's testimony alone sufficient to instruct the bastardy of the child"; but by the time of Erskine it was settled at 10.

[63] *De Septimestri Partu.*

[64] See above, para. 2.11.

[65] *Currie v. Currie*, 1950 S.C. 10 (336 days not impossible, but improbable and went a long way, together with other facts and circumstances, to justify an inference of adultery); *Jamieson v. Dobie*, 1935 S.C. 415 (306 days not impossible—*cf. Williamson v. McClelland*, 1913 S.C. 678); *Doherty v. Doherty*, 1922 S.L.T. 245 (348 days described in medical evidence as "abnormal and extraordinary"—decree of divorce on ground of adultery granted in the circumstances); *Preston-Jones v. Preston-Jones* [1951] A.C. 391 (360 days not impossible); *M-T v. M-T* [1949] P. 331 (340 days not impossible); *Hadlum v. Hadlum* [1949] P. 197 (349 days not impossible).

of fact in individual cases constitute neither precedent nor the material of judicial knowledge, it can probably be said that the fact that gestation of more than 10 months is possible, although highly unusual, is now sufficiently notorious to bring it within judicial knowledge. The maximum period of the older law is therefore superseded even in the absence of medical evidence. In cases involving proof of adultery for the purposes of divorce it has been said that where the period of gestation necessary to maintain consistency with the wife's innocence greatly exceeds the normal period the presumption is inverted and the onus is on the wife to prove that the husband is the father of the child.[66] If that were right the onus would similarly pass, where paternity was directly in issue, to the party asserting paternity and for this purpose anything in excess of 10 months might still be taken as greatly exceeding the normal. The better view, however, is probably that the presumption continues to apply, although with weakened effect, where the period of gestation is abnormally long provided that it is within what is known to be possible.[67] Where the limits of possibility are reached is undecided. In an English case the House of Lords declined to hold that 360 days was an impossible period.[68] That view can be supported by extreme cases known to medical science, but it is submitted that, in the absence of medical evidence pointing to an exceptionally long period of gestation, such extremes should not be taken into account, and that the most which a Scottish court should ordinarily entertain as possible is 11 months. That would accord with the furthest extension warranted by Scottish judicial decision[69] and with institutional authority.[70] The whole matter may, however, be ripe for reconsideration in the light of changed attitudes to the standard of proof. Questions of the application and the rebuttal of the presumption are at this point closely related and the relaxation in the standard of proof for rebuttal (which is now on the balance of probabilities[71]) carries with it occasion for a reconsideration of the attitude which the court should adopt to questions of the maximum period of gestation. Such a reconsideration may well have shifted the emphasis from what is possible to what is probable and may, in any event, lead to the conclusion that in the ordinary case 11 or even 10 months is too long a period to be entertained. The result would be that if a child were to be born, say, 10 months after the ending of a marriage, the party claiming that the ex-husband was the father of the child could not rely on the presumption and would have to lead evidence of circumstances tending to support his paternity.

Conflicting presumptions

One reason why a marriage may be void is because one of the parties thereto **3.18** is a party to a prior subsisting marriage.[72] A result of including the provision to the effect that the presumption in section 5(1)(a) applies in the case of void marriages[73] appears to be that, if the mother is party to a subsisting marriage when she undergoes a later ceremony of marriage, then any child she bears will be presumed to be the child both of her husband and of the man with whom she contracted the later and void "marriage". The same situation would arise in the (less likely) scenario of a woman being validly married twice during the possible gestational period of the child. This is a problem which because of the common

---

[66] *Gray v. Gray*, 1919 1 S.L.T. 163, followed in *McIntosh v. McIntosh*, 1947 S.N. 23.

[67] *Currie v. Currie*, above.

[68] *Preston-Jones v. Preston-Jones*, above. Lord Morton, however, thought than 320 days should be regarded as the maximum.

[69] *Currie v. Currie*, above.

[70] Stair, III, iii, 42.

[71] Law Reform (Parent and Child) (Scotland) Act 1986, s. 5(4). This is also now the standard of proof of adultery: Divorce (Scotland) Act 1976, s. 1(6). Adultery was the issue in many of the cases cited above.

[72] Marriage (Scotland) Act 1977, s. 5(4)(b). See Clive (3rd ed.), pp. 76–77.

[73] Law Reform (Parent and Child) (Scotland) Act 1986, s. 5(2).

law presumption that demanded marriage at the date of conception, (although there was also a certain presumption of fact where marriage intervened between conception and birth) much concerned some of the older writers in the case of a child born of a woman who remarried so soon after the death of her first husband that the child could have been conceived in marriage either by the first or by the second husband. Stair, in an untypical passage which has justly been described as obscure,[74] appears to favour the view that if the child is born within nine months of the dissolution of the first marriage by death, he or she will be presumed to be the child of the first husband unless showing signs of immaturity at birth; conversely, if the child be born more than nine months after the death of the first husband he or she will be deemed to be the child of the second husband. Probability of paternity is not the issue under section 5(1)(a) since the presumption applies for any marriage within the whole gestational period, and will arise simply on proof of the fact of marriage at the relevant time. Probability of paternity is, however, relevant to rebuttal. Where there are two possible fathers it will usually be possible to rebut the presumption in the case of one of them as less likely. In the rare case of equal probability, if the court is not willing to accept that either presumption is rebutted merely by the existence of the other, the result would be that both presumptions should be given effect to until one or other is formally rebutted. A possible alternative to avoid the absurdities that this might create is to hold that when two or more presumptions applies with equal force, they cancel themselves out. The result would be that the person asserting paternity (or indeed denying paternity) has no presumption to assist him or her either way and must lead positive and sufficient evidence to prove his or her own case.[75]

Rebutting the presumption

3.19   The presumption contained in section 5(1)(a) is to the effect that the relevant parental genetic link exists between a man and a child. It is, however, only a presumption, and as such it can be rebutted by showing that the presumed fact is not true. This may be done by leading evidence to the effect that the mother's husband is not (or, which amounts to the same thing, that another man is) genetically related to the child as his or her father. The presumption can be rebutted by proof on a balance of probabilities.[76] How that balance will be struck must, however, depend upon the facts of each particular case. The presumption is not rebutted by showing that either the husband or another man could be the father of the child.[77] Scientific proof, such as DNA profiling,[78] will in most cases be available and will give incontrovertible evidence of where the truth lies, but if it is not available (for example because one of the parties is dead or because appropriate consent is not forthcoming), extrinsic evidence of a number of factors may be led.

---

[74] III, iii, 42, More's annotations.

[75] In some legal systems, the matter is dealt with statutorily: in, for example, Australia the Family Law Reform Act 1975, as amended by the Family Law Reform Act 1995, provides in the new s. 69U(2) that where there are two or more conflicting presumptions the one that prevails is the one that appears to the court to be the more or most likely. This resolves the issue within the context of court proceedings, but of course the major point of presumptions is to recognise the effects of paternity without the need for court action.

[76] Law Reform (Parent and Child) (Scotland) Act 1986, s. 5(4). This alters the common law rule that proof had to be beyond reasonable doubt to rebut the *pater est* presumption: see *Docherty v. McGlynn*, 1983 S.L.T. 645; *Ramsay v. Ramsay's Curator*, 1987 S.L.T. 799. There was previously some doubt as to the full extent of the common law onus (see *Ballantyne v. Douglas*, 1953 S.L.T. (Notes) 10, *per* Lord Justice-Clerk Thomson at 11; *Brown v. Brown*, 1972 S.L.T. 143, *per* Lord Emslie (Ordinary) at 145; *Imre v. Mitchell*, 1958 S.C. 439, *per* Lord President Clyde at p. 462), though that seems to have been resolved by *Docherty* and *Ramsay*. The question is now otiose in the light of s. 5(4) of the 1986 Act. In an action of paternity in which the presumption did not operate, the burden of proof has always been on the balance of probabilities: *A v. G*, 1984 S.L.T. (Sh.Ct) 65.

[77] *Smith v. Greenhill*, 1994 S.L.T. (Sh. Ct) 22.

[78] See below, para. 3.54.

The view was at one time held, and is adopted by Fraser,[79] that the common **3.20** law presumption could be rebutted only by proof of impotence[80] or non-access. The institutional writers do not go as far as that[81] and it is doubtful if it ever was settled law. In *Mackay v. Mackay*,[82] for example, the child had undoubtedly been conceived during marriage and had, moreover, been accepted as a member of the family by her mother's husband in whose house she had continued to live even after her mother's death. Prima facie it was a strong case for giving effect to the presumption. Non-access was out of the question and impotence was not suggested. Yet the presumption was held to be rebutted on evidence of parental declarations that the child was "illegitimate", of the mother's loose character and of general reputation of "illegitimacy". The Lord Ordinary's opinion that "if there be such clear evidence as completely satisfies the tribunal which has to decide the question, that *de facto* a husband is not the father of his wife's child, that child will be held to be illegitimate, although neither impotency nor the utter impossibility of access be established by that evidence" was adopted and approved by the Inner House.[83] When the later case of *Gardner v. Gardner*[84] reached the House of Lords, Lord Gordon, following Lord Gifford in the Court of Session, could say of the common law presumption that "it must yield to evidence, and I think the law of Scotland has always been that the presumption may be overcome, not only by evidence that it was physically impossible that the husband of the mother could be the father of the child, but by every species of moral evidence sufficient to satisfy a reasonable mind that the child was begotten by someone else than the husband".[85] Whatever the historic position may have been, it is now clear in relation to the statutory presumption that not only impotence and non-access (though they remain strong evidence against paternity[86]) but all other facts and circumstances relevant to infer non-parentage may be invoked to rebut the presumption in section 5(1)(a). In an action for declarator of parentage or non-parentage in which it is sought to rebut the presumption, the court is looking for the truth and is not to be limited within artificial bounds of evidence. Other relevant circumstances tending to assist the search for the truth may include, for example, evidence of loose moral character or adultery of the mother,[87] reputation of paternity,[88] declarations of non-parentage

---

[79] Fraser (3rd ed.), p. 5.

[80] As in, for example, *Dundas v. Dundas* (1705) Mor. 4083 and *Sandy v. Sandy* (1823) 2 S. 453. Even then the presumption would not automatically be rebutted if fecundation *ab extra* or artificial insemination by the husband was a possibility. Proof of sterility rather than impotence would have a much more certain effect.

[81] Stair, III, iii, 42 adds a further ground, being the testimony of both the mother and the husband that the child is not the husband's. Erskine, I, vi, 50, describes impotence and non-access as merely "the two principal grounds."

[82] (1855) 17 D. 494.

[83] *per* Lord President McNeill at 500 and Lords Ivory and Deas at 505.

[84] (1877) 4 R. (H.L.) 56.

[85] *ibid.* at 74. *Cf. Montgomery v. Montgomery* (1881) 8 R. 403; *Steedman v. Steedman* (1887) 14 R. 1066; *Coles v. Homer and Tulloh* (1895) 22 R. 716.

[86] Similar to impotency would be evidence of the husband's sterility. In *Re H (Paternity: Blood Test)* [1996] 2 F.L.R. 65 the fact that the husband had had a vasectomy was held relevant (but not conclusive since he had not returned to the hospital to determine the success of the operation).

[87] Craig, II, xviii, 20; Stair, III, iii, 42; Erskine, I, vi, 49. *Cf. Francis v. Francis*, [1960] P. 17; *Cotton v. Cotton* [1954] 2 All E.R 105.

[88] Balfour, p. 240, Craig, II, xviii, 20; Stair, III, iii, 42; Bankton, I, v, 62 and III, iii, 101; Spottiswood, *Practicks*, p. 280; *Roxburghe v. Ker* (1822) 6 Paton 820; *Hamilton v. Hamilton* (1839) 2 D. 89; *Walker v. Walker* (1857) 19 D. 290; *Campbell v. Campbell* (1866) 4 M. 867, (1867) 5 M. (H.L.) 115; *Hirpet v. Scot* (1618) Mor. 2197; *Crawfurd v. Purcels* (1642) Mor. 12636; *Brooke's Exr. v. James*, 1971 S.C. (H.L.) 77; *Tennent v. Tennent* (1890) 17 R. 1205; *Smith v. Dick* (1869) 8 M. 31 (in which reputation was divided but since reputation of illegitimacy was supported by other factors it was that reputation which prevailed).

by the presumptive parents[89] and, in cases free of the risks of fanciful speculation, physical resemblances and family likenesses.[90] None of these elements is conclusive on its own, and the weight to be given to any of them varies with the circumstances, but all are relevant and admissible as tending to establish the probability that someone other than the woman's husband is the father of the child. Scientific evidence will, if available, usually constitute the best evidence as leaving least room for doubt.

Acknowledgment and registration

3.21   Section 5(1)(b) of the Law Reform (Parent and Child) (Scotland) Act 1986 provides that a man who is not married to the mother of the child at the relevant time shall be presumed to be the father of the child if both he and the mother of the child have acknowledged that he is the father of the child and he has been registered in the appropriate register as the father. Though presumed father, the man (not being married to the mother) will not acquire by dint of that presumption parental responsibilities and parental rights in relation to the child[91]: this is a presumption of paternity alone. Like that contained in section 5(1)(a), this presumption has common law antecedents. Craig, Stair and Erskine[92] took over from the canon law[93] the rule that once a child's legitimacy had been acknowledged by his or her parents the parents could not by a subsequent oath deprive the child of the status of legitimacy thereby acquired. The parents were personally barred not only from tendering their own evidence in contradiction of the acknowledgment but also altogether from disputing legitimacy. Under the current statute, there must be both acknowledgment and registration.

Acknowledgment

3.22   Both the mother and the man must acknowledge that he is the father of the child. At common law sworn declarations by both parents were sufficient to establish "illegitimacy",[94] and unsworn statements were relevant evidence and admissible subject to their competency under the rules relating to hearsay.[95] Under the statute, an "acknowledgment" clearly does not have to be sworn, but it does have to be proved. Statements to friends or acquaintances of the relevant facts will probably be sufficient. The declarations required before the man can be registered as father (see the following paragraph) will suffice.

Registration

3.23   Previously, to show that a man was entered as father of a child in the Register of Births was merely one of the elements of evidence used to establish paternity and even now acknowledgment without registration will have no other effect than this. A man cannot be registered as father of a child except (a) at the joint request of the mother and the person acknowledging himself to be the father of

---

[89] Craig, II, xviii, 20; Stair, III, iii, 42; Erskine I, vi, 49.

[90] Though this evidence must be treated with the greatest of care, and, indeed, will normally be excluded: *Rutledge v. Carruthers*, Jan. 20, 1810, F.C. 528; *Grant v. Countess of Seafield*, 1926 S.C. 274; *Slingsby v. Att.-Gen.* (1916) 33 T.L.R. 120, HL, *per* Lord Shaw of Dunfermline at 122; *H.M. Advocate v. Stewart* (1848) Ark. 471 (in which it was held competent to inquire, in a trial for child-murder of a child found to have six toes on each foot, whether this was a family characteristic shared by other members of its family). See also *S v. S*, 1977 S.L.T. (Notes) 65 in which an allegation that the child was "dark-skinned" and that the mother had had a liaison with a man believed to be an Arab was insufficient to discharge the onus on the husband seeking to bastardise the child. And a "coloured" child was born in *S v. S; W v. Official Solicitor* [1972] A.C. 24, which was evidence taken with the mother's association with a Pakistani man that her husband was not the father.

[91] Children (Scotland) Act 1995, s. 3. See below, para. 8.08.

[92] Craig, II, xviii, 20; Stair, IV, xlv, 20: Erskine, I, vi, 49.

[93] Decr. IV, xvii, 3; II, xix, 10.

[94] Craig, II, xviii, 20; Stair, III, iii, 42; Erskine, I, vi, 49.

[95] *Mackay v. Mackay* (1855) 17 D. 494.

the child (in which case the register must be signed by both the mother and the man), or (b) at the request of the mother on the production of both a declaration in the prescribed form made by the mother that that person is the father of the child and a statutory declaration made by that person acknowledging himself to be the father of the child, or on production of a decree by a competent court finding or declaring that person to be the father of the child, or (c) at the request of the man on production of a declaration by him in the prescribed form acknowledging himself to be the father of the child and a statutory declaration made by the mother stating that he is the father of the child.[96] A person under the age of 16 has legal capacity to make such a request or declaration if, in the opinion of the Registrar, that person understands the nature of the request or declaration; and without prejudice to that generality a person 12 years of age or more[97] shall be presumed to be of sufficient age and maturity to have such understanding.[98] It may be noted that this provision does not require an understanding of the nature *and consequences* of the request or declaration,[99] suggesting that all that is required of under-16-year-old parents is that they understand that they will be regarded as parents and not necessarily all the legal consequences of that (in respect, for example, to parental responsibilities and alimentary obligations).

The registration must be in either a register kept under section 13 (the Register **3.24** of Births and Still-births) or section 44 (the Register of Corrections, etc.) of the Registration of Births, Deaths and Marriages (Scotland) Act 1965, or in any corresponding register kept under statutory authority in any part of the U.K. other than Scotland. Registration in a foreign register will not give rise to the presumption, but will be an element in the proof tending to establish paternity, the precise weight to be given to such evidence depending upon the nature of the foreign register, and the applicable rules of registration.

Circumstances in which the presumption applies

The presumption in section 5(1)(b) was designed to deal with the cohabiting **3.25** couple, both of whom acknowledge the man as the father of the child. But its terms are a good deal wider than that. For one thing, there is no requirement that the couple be cohabiting: the only requirements are acknowledgment and registration. It is, however, unclear what other situations are intended to be covered. In particular there are difficulties if the mother is married but she claims that the father is a man other than her husband, and both she and the other man acknowledge this and register the child as such. The difficulty revolves around the opening words of section 5(1)(b): "where paragraph (a) above does not apply". Paragraph (a) deals with the situation of the husband of the mother being presumed father, but it is not clear when it "does not apply". Clearly it "does not apply" when the woman is unmarried; but it is open to question whether paragraph (b) is therefore only applicable when the mother is unmarried. Though this is the interpretation adopted in the annotation of *Current Law Statutes*, it is suggested that the better approach is to see section 5(1) in terms of the man's rather than the mother's marital status. The "he" in paragraph (a) refers to "a man" mentioned in the opening of subsection (1) and paragraph (b) therefore applies whenever he is not married to the mother, rather than when the mother is unmarried. Paragraph (b) should therefore be read as follows: "(1) A man shall be presumed to be the father of a child... (b) [if he is not married to the

---

[96] Registration of Births, Deaths and Marriages (Scotland) Act 1965, s. 18, as amended by Sched. 1, para. 8 to the Law Reform (Parent and Child) (Scotland) Act 1986.

[97] An under-12-year-old parent is possible, but an extreme rarity.

[98] Registration of Births, Deaths and Marriages (Scotland) Act 1965, s. 18(3), as added by s. 99(3) of the Children (Scotland) Act 1995.

[99] *cf.* s. 2(4) of the Age of Legal Capacity (Scotland) Act 1991, concerning capacity to determine medical treatment before the age of 16.

mother of the child] if both he and the mother of the child have acknowledged that he is the father and he has been registered as such". On this interpretation, paragraph (b) will apply either where the woman is unmarried, or where the woman is married but not to the man registered as the father of her child. It follows that, again, there may be conflicting presumptions, though they will be resolved in the same way as two presumptions raised under section 5(1)(a). The words "where paragraph (a) does not apply" do not, for the reasons stated, give preference to the presumption contained therein.[1] Acknowledgment by both the mother and the other man that the other man is the father, and registration to this effect, may well be sufficient in themselves to prove paternity in the face of a conflicting presumption that the husband is the father; they will certainly be sufficient if combined with other factors such as non-access by the husband.

Rebutting the presumption

3.26   As with section 5(1)(a), section 5(1)(b) raises only a presumption that can be rebutted by proof on a balance of probabilities.[2] Such proof will take the form of proof that the man registered as the father is not (or, which amounts to the same thing, that another man is) genetically related to the child as his or her father. The comments made in relation to rebutting the section 5(1)(a) presumption,[3] to which reference should be made, apply equally here.[4]

Assisted reproduction within marriage

3.27   Section 28(2) of the Human Fertilisation and Embryology Act 1990 provides that where a woman has become pregnant as a result of the placing in her of an embryo or of sperm and eggs or of her artificial[5] insemination, and at that time she was a party to a marriage, then the other party to the marriage shall, so long as the embryo was created with sperm that was not his, be treated as the father of the child. This means that he will be treated "in law" as the father of the child "for all purposes",[6] and "references to any relationship between two people in any enactment, deed, or other instrument or document (whenever passed or made) are to be read accordingly".[7] This applies whether the woman was in the United Kingdom or elsewhere at the time of the placing in her of the embryo or

---

[1] We may compare the position under s. 28 of the Human Fertilisation and Embryology Act 1990, discussed below, because alterative provisions there, involving men who are treated as father because of their marriage and men not so treated (s. 28(2) and s. 28(3) respectively) make it quite clear that the rules in s. 28(3) apply whenever the rules in s. 28(2) do not.

[2] Law Reform (Parent and Child) (Scotland) Act 1986, s. 5(4).

[3] Above, at paras 3.19–3.20.

[4] The presumption in s. 5(1)(b) might also be rebutted by challenging the acknowledgement upon which it is based if, for example, it was given as a result of fraud, duress or something of the sort.

[5] s. 28(2)(a) actually talks only of the woman's "insemination", which is to be compared with s. 28(3)(a) which talks of the woman's "artificial insemination." This might suggest that s. 28(2)(a) would also apply when a woman is inseminated naturally, *e.g.* by having sexual intercourse with a man not her husband; but this interpretation is excluded by s. 28(1) which provides as follows: "This section applies in the case of a child who is being or has been carried by a woman as the result of the placing in her of an embryo or of sperm and eggs or of her artificial insemination." The omission of the word "artificial" from s. 28(2)(a), or its addition in s. 28(3)(a), is simply the result of lax draftsmanship. There is, however, no requirement that the artificial insemination be carried out by persons licensed to do so under the Act, and s. 28(2) applies even to informal (but always artificial) inseminations carried out by the parties themselves. *Cf.* s. 28(3) which applies only when the treatment is provided by licensed persons: see below, para. 3.34.

[6] Human Fertilisation and Embryology Act 1990, s. 29(1).

[7] *ibid.* s. 29(3). As with maternity (see above, paras 3.05–3.07), it is open to the person executing a deed to express a different conclusion.

the sperm and eggs or of her artificial insemination.[8] It has been held[9] that, the 1990 Act not having retrospective effect, the status of father is conferred by its terms only in respect of children born after its coming into force.[10] The better rule is probably that the Act applies if the procedure governed by the Act occurs after its coming into force. Section 28(2) does not create a presumption of paternity and still less does it create a presumption of a genetic link (indeed it will only apply when there exists no genetic link[11]). It is, rather, the wholly artificial creation of a father-child relationship, deemed by the law from the husband's presumed consent to the relevant infertility treatment.[12] The donor of the sperm (*i.e.* the genetic father) is not to be treated in law as being the father of the child for any purpose[13] (unless he is otherwise constituted the legal father of the child by an order of the court to that effect under section 30[14]). Unlike the presumption contained in section 5(1)(a) of the Law Reform (Parent and Child) (Scotland) Act 1986, section 28(2) of the 1990 Act cannot be overcome by showing the absence of a genetic link, because its very application depends upon the absence of such a link. Indeed it can be overcome only in the manner later described. Likewise it is not open to another man to claim paternity by showing the existence of the relevant genetic link, for once the provision applies no other person is to be treated as the father of the child,[15] for any purpose.[16]

Nature of the marriage

    The marriage must be subsisting at the time of the placing in the woman of **3.28** the embryo or the sperm and eggs, or at the time of her insemination. The provision does not apply if the marriage was dissolved or annulled at that time, or a judicial separation was in force at that time[17] but includes all valid marriages, including those contracted abroad and entitled to be recognised as valid in this country: an actually or potentially polygamous marriage can be a valid "subsisting" marriage.[18] The provision also applies, though this is not stated,[19] to irregular as well as regular marriages: since irregular marriages are as much valid marriages in Scots law as regular marriages,[20] the normal canons of construction will mean that they are to be regarded as "subsisting marriages".

    The provision also applies to void marriages if either or both[21] of the parties **3.29** reasonably believed at the time of the infertility treatment that the marriage was

---

[8] s. 28(8). This does not imply extraterritorial effect for s. 28(2) but merely ensures that the status of father conferred by the provision is recognised in the United Kingdom wherever the treatment took place.

[9] *Re M (Child Support Act: Parentage)* [1997] 2 F.L.R. 90.

[10] On August 1, 1991.

[11] s. 28(2)(b).

[12] English law had contained a similar provision, though only in relation to artificial insemination, since the passing of s. 27 of the Family Law Reform Act 1987. This is now superseded by s. 28 of the 1990 Act.

[13] s. 28(6)(a), Sched. 3, para. 5, and s. 29(2).

[14] See below, Chap. 6.

[15] s. 28(4).

[16] s. 29(2). This is subject to the exceptions described above, paras 3.08–3.11.

[17] s. 28(7)(a), this including a legal separation obtained in a country outside the British Islands and recognised in the United Kingdom under the terms of Pt II of the Family Law Act 1986: s. 28(9).

[18] See Anton and Beaumont (2nd ed.), pp. 444–450; Matrimonial Proceedings (Polygamous Marriages) Act 1972. A marriage that is voidable "subsists" until it is annulled.

[19] Law Reform (Parent and Child) (Scotland) Act 1986, s. 5(2), makes this clear in relation to the presumptions contained there. But that was a purely Scottish statue, while the 1990 Act is U.K.-wide.

[20] Clive (4th ed.), Chap. 5, Thomson (3rd ed.), p. 15.

[21] *cf.* s. 3 of the Children (Scotland) Act 1995, under which a father acquires parental responsibilities and parental rights from a void marriage only if *both* parties to the marriage believed in good faith that the marriage was valid. So, when a child is born of a couple whose marriage is void but only one believe the marriage to be valid, s. 28(7) deems the husband to be father but s. 3 denies him parental responsibilities and parental rights in Scotland: he is in the same position as the unmarried father who is acknowledged and registered as father. Oddly, through the doctrine of putative marriages, the child is legitimate.

valid; it will be presumed until the contrary is shown that one of the parties to the marriage did reasonably believe at the time of the infertility treatment that the marriage was valid.[22] This form of words follows previous English legislation which preserved the "legitimacy" of children born of invalid marriages where one or both of the parties reasonably believed that the marriage was valid.[23] It was subsequently made clear in the English legislation that the English rule applied when the belief that the marriage was valid was due to a mistake in law as well as a mistake in fact.[24] The equivalent Scottish rule concerned putative marriages, preserves the "legitimacy" of children born of invalid marriages where there is a *bona fide* belief on the part of one or both parties that the marriage was valid. Now, *bona fide* belief is not the same as reasonable belief, and there has been some doubt in Scotland as to whether a mistake in law concerning the validity of a marriage amounts to an error that can be excused and thus save the "legitimacy" of children. Fraser[25] said that only an error of fact could found a putative marriage, and he is followed by Clive[26] and Thomson.[27] However it may be doubted whether this is so. The belief that saves "legitimacy" in Scotland has to be *bona fide* rather than reasonable and a *bona fide* belief may be founded on an error of law, at least where there is a question of *dubium jus*.[28] Reasonable belief, which is here in issue, is not, however, the same as *bona fide* belief. In the context of the previous English legislation "reasonable belief" was held to import an objective test[29] and since this is the formulation used in the present context of the Human Fertilisation and Embryology Act 1990, it is likely that the English approach will be followed in the interpretation of these words in this UK statute. There is no declaration "for the avoidance of doubt" in the 1990 Act (as there now is in the English Legitimacy Act 1976) that error of law as well as error of fact can found a "reasonable belief," but it is thought that in interpreting this U.K. statute the English courts will do as they do for the 1976 Act, and accept errors of law as founding a reasonable belief in appropriate cases. The Scottish courts should, it is submitted, do likewise.

Exceptions

3.30   The four exceptions to the provisions of the 1990 Act deeming maternity are also applicable, *mutatis mutandis*, to section 28(2), and the comments made above[30] should be referred to.

Avoiding paternity—lack of consent

3.31   Unlike a presumption, a deeming provision cannot be rebutted. Section 28(2) of the 1990 Act does not presume any facts but instead provides for the wholly artificial creation of the father–child relationship. Consequences of thus acquiring

---

[22] Human Fertilisation and Embryology Act 1990, s. 28(7). The problem of having more than one "husband" who can be presumed father that may potentially arise with the similar provision in s. 5(1)(a) of the Law Reform (Parent and Child) (Scotland) Act 1986 (see above, para. 3.18) would not arise here, because in practice only one of the competing "husbands" would consent to the treatment of the woman.

[23] Legitimacy Act 1976, s. 1 (and before that the Legitimacy Act 1959, s. 2).

[24] Family Law Reform Act 1987, s. 28(2), which adds a new s. 1(3) to the Legitimacy Act 1976 to this effect, expressly "for the avoidance of doubt". The matter had not been unequivocally decided in *Hawkins v. Att.-Gen.* [1966] 1 All E.R. 392, for, while it appeared to be accepted in that case that an error of law could sometimes found a reasonable belief, it was held that the particular error of law involved in that case did not. The 1987 Act also added the provision (a new s. 1(4) of the Legitimacy Act 1976) presuming that one or both parties reasonably believed the marriage to be valid, this to obviate certain difficulties of proof that had been encountered.

[25] (3rd ed.), p. 34.

[26] *Husband and Wife* (4th ed.), p. 72.

[27] *Family Law in Scotland* (3rd ed.), p. 160.

[28] See *Purves's Trs v. Purves* (1895) 22 R. 513.

[29] *Hawkins v. Att.-Gen.* [1966] 1 All E.R. 392, commented upon by Samuels (1966) 29 Mod. L.R. 559.

[30] at paras 3.08–3.11.

the status of parent follow in relation, for example, to aliment and succession; and because it is the mother's husband at the time of conception who is deemed father under section 28(2) he acquires (under section 3(1)(b) of the Children (Scotland) Act 1995) parental responsibilities and parental rights in relation to the child.[31] The application of section 28(2) can, however, be avoided, not only by showing that it is not applicable in the circumstances (*e.g.* because there is no marriage at the relevant date, or because the husband's sperm was used to bring about the creation of the embryo) but also by showing that the husband did not consent to the infertility treatment. Section 28(2) is stated to apply "unless it is shown that [the husband] did not consent to the placing in [the mother] of the embryo or the sperm and eggs or to her insemination (as the case may be)". This form of words creates a presumption of fact that the mother's husband did consent, with the onus resting on the person seeking to deny the application of the rule in section 28(2)[32] to show, if he or she can, that the husband did not consent to the infertility treatment. The burden of proof on a person claiming that the husband did not consent will, it may be supposed, be on a balance of probabilities. Even when the husband did not in fact consent, this deeming provision will be effective until such time as the presumption of consent has been rebutted. So, until then, the husband of the woman who receives infertility treatment is treated as father for all purposes of law[33] and is subject to parental responsibilities and can exercise parental rights.

Centres licensed to provide infertility services[34] are obliged by their Code **3.32** of Practice, issued by the Human Fertilisation and Embryology Authority (which grants the licences) to take all practicable steps to obtain the husband's written consent, or to obtain written evidence that he does not consent.[35] If a husband (or other person) wishes to deny the validity of his written consent, he must show that it is vitiated for some reason, for example that it was obtained by fraud, or that he did not understand the substance of what he was consenting to. An allegation that he did not understand the legal consequences of paternity will not be sufficient for this purpose if he did understand that his wife might, through the infertility service, become pregnant and give birth to a child.

Effect of section 5(1)(a) of the Law Reform (Parent and Child) (Scotland) Act 1986

The interplay between section 28(2) of the 1990 Act and the presumption of **3.33** paternity contained in section 5(1)(a) of the Law Reform (Parent and Child) (Scotland) Act 1986 is by no means clear. The rule in the 1986 Act is given precedence by section 28(5) of the 1990 Act, which provides that the rules in section 28 do not apply when a person is treated as the child of the parties to a marriage by any enactment or rule of law. Section 5(1)(a) applies whenever a mother is married, unless the presumption contained therein is rebutted, with the result that section 28(2) of the 1990 Act applies only after the 1986 presumption has been rebutted. However, since the 1986 presumption is a presumption of genetic paternity and section 28(2) of the 1990 Act applies only when the absence of a genetic link is established, it follows that proving that the 1990 provision applies will in itself be proof that the 1986 Act does not apply.

---

[31] See *Re CH (Contact: Parentage)* [1996] 1 F.L.R. 569.

[32] Any person with an interest in the child's paternity—including the child—may seek to show this.

[33] Subject to the exceptions discussed above, paras 3.08–3.11.

[34] Under s. 16 of the 1990 Act.

[35] HFEA *Code of Practice* (rev. 1995), para. 5.7. For a study of how the guidelines in this code of practice are variously interpreted in different clinics, see Savas and Treece, "Fertility Clinics: One Code of Practice?" (1998) 3 Med. Law Int. 243.

Yet whichever provision applies, the husband is treated as the father. The difference lies in what requires to be proved. The preservation of the 1986 presumption means, in effect, that whenever a child is born to a married woman, even after donor insemination, her husband can be treated as the father without his having to prove all that is required for section 28(2) to apply—he can rely on section 5(1)(a) and it is only if the presumption in that paragraph is rebutted that he is burdened with the onus of proving that section 28(2) applies.

Assisted reproduction outwith marriage

3.34   If no man is treated as the father of a child by virtue of section 28(2) of the Human Fertilisation and Embryology Act 1990 as discussed immediately above, then a man may be treated as being the father of a child for all purposes of law in accordance with the provisions in section 28(3) of the 1990 Act. This provides that where an embryo or sperm and eggs are placed in a woman, or she is artificially inseminated, and this is done "in the course of treatment services provided for her and a man together" by a person licensed to provide these treatment services under the 1990 Act, then the man shall be deemed, for all purposes,[36] to be the father of the child. In this context, "man" has been held by the European Court of Human Rights not to include a female-to-male transsexual, living in family with a woman who, after donor insemination, gave birth to a child.[37] The rule in section 28(3) applies whether the woman was in the United Kingdom or elsewhere at the time of the placing in her of the embryo or the sperm and eggs or her artificial insemination.[38] As with section 28(2), the deeming provision in section 28(3) applies only when there is no genetic link between the man and the child[39] and is not a presumption of the existence of a genetic link: thus it cannot be avoided by proving the absence of any such link. When it applies, no other person is to be treated as the father of the child[40] for any purpose[41] and it is therefore irrelevant for anyone else to prove a genetic link between the child and any other person. Section 28(3) may apply in any case in which section 28(2) does not, that is to say when the woman is not party to a marriage, or when she is party to a marriage but it can be shown that her husband did not consent to the treatment. If, however, the woman is married, section 28(3) does not apply if her husband is treated as the father by the application of the presumption of paternity in section 5(1)(a) of the Law Reform (Parent and Child) (Scotland) Act 1986.[42] This means that section 28(3) applies only when that presumption of paternity has been rebutted (and that the onus lies on those seeking to rely on section 28(3) of the 1990 Act to rebut the presumption in section 5(1)(a) of the 1986 Act). However, the proof that treatment services have been provided will nearly always be sufficient to rebut the 1986 presumption. In the unlikely event that the mother is a party to a marriage and

---

[36] s. 29(1).

[37] *X, Y and Z v. United Kingdom* (1997) 24 E.H.R.R. 143. The English rule (gleaned from *Corbett v. Corbett* [1970] 2 W.L.R. 1306) that only a biological man can be registered as "father" was considered not to breach Art. 8 (right to family life). For a discussion of that decision, see Bainham, "Sex, Gender and Fatherhood: Does Biology Really Matter?" (1997) C.L.J. 512. *Corbett v. Corbett* may not, however, represent the law of Scotland, for in *Forbes-Sempill, Petitioners*, December 29, 1967 (Lord Hunter) a biological female was held to be male for the purposes at least of the law of succession to a title of honour: see Campbell, "Successful Sex in Succession: Sex in Dispute—The *Forbes-Sempill Case* and Possible Implications", 1998 J.R. 257 and 325.

[38] s. 28(8). This does not imply extraterritorial effect for s. 28(3) but merely ensures that the status of father conferred by the provision is recognised in the United Kingdom wherever the treatment took place.

[39] s. 28(3)(b).

[40] s. 28(4).

[41] s. 29(2).

[42] Human Fertilisation and Embryology Act 1990, s. 28(5).

her husband's sperm was used to bring about the creation of the embryo which is placed in her in the course of treatment services provided for her and a man other than her husband, section 28(5) will prevent the application of section 28(3) since the 1986 presumption (of genetic paternity) preserved thereby will not in these circumstances be capable of rebuttal.

It is noteworthy that, unlike the rule in section 28(2), the rule in section 28(3) **3.35** applies only when the treatment is provided by a person licensed by the Human Fertilisation and Embryology Authority to carry out such treatment.[43]

Treatment must be provided "together"
There is no provision presuming that the man consented to the treatment, nor **3.36** a qualification that the deeming provision will not apply if it can be shown that he did not consent. However, section 28(3) only applies when the treatment is given "for" a woman and a man "together", which presupposes the consent of them both. If consent has not been given, it would be impossible to hold that the treatment had been provided "for" a woman and a man "together". In other words, section 28(3), like section 28(2), can indeed be avoided by showing that the man did not consent,[44] because doing so would show that the treatment was not provided for the woman and the man "together." It should, however, be emphasised that the statutory test for paternity is that of "treatment together" and not of the man's consent. In *Re Q (Parental Order)*[45] it was held that "treatment" had not been provided to a woman and a man together when the woman, as part of a surrogacy arrangement, had been impregnated with an embryo created from the egg of the man's wife and sperm from an anonymous donor (and therefore that the man was not the father). The reason given, that the man himself did not receive any physical treatment, is unconvincing but the decision is probably right. "Treatment together" implies, it is submitted, that the couple intend together to bring up the child, which was not the intention in *Re Q (Parental Order)*. The matter was further discussed in *U v. W (Attorney General Intervening)*[46] in which the evidence was conflicting as to whether the male partner had agreed to the implantation of embryos created *in vitro* into the female partner when only one of them had been created with his sperm. Though the couple had attended various clinics together, the relationship ended as soon as the male partner discovered that the pregnancy had come about with embryos other than the one created with his sperm. The male partner conceded that earlier treatment using his sperm had been provided to the couple "together"[47] (though section 28 would not apply at all if he were the genetic father) but he argued that the treatment using donor sperm (when section 28(3) might apply) was not so provided. On the evidence Wilson J. found that it had been understood by both parties that, as a last resort, recourse might be had to the use of donor sperm. He concluded:

---

[43] In practice, this will mean that s. 28(3) will seldom, if ever, apply when the treatment was provided abroad, notwithstanding the terms of s. 28(8) to the effect that s. 28 applies "whether the woman was in the United Kingdom or elsewhere" at the time of the treatment, since foreign providers of treatment are not licensed by the Human Fertilisation and Embryology Authority. This limitation was held not to breach European Union rules on the free movement of services in *U v. W (Attorney-General Intervening)* [1997] 2 F.L.R. 282. On the other hand, the refusal by the Human Fertilisation and Embryology Authority to allow a widow to take her dead husband's sperm to Belgium for the purposes of treatment there was held to be unreasonable: *R v. Human Fertilisation and Embryology Authority, ex p. Blood* [1997] 2 All E.R. 687.

[44] The onus lies on the person claiming that section 28(3) applies and not on the person claiming that treatment was not provided "together", for there is no presumption that the facts necessary for the application of the subsection exist, as there is with section 28(2).

[45] [1996] 1 F.L.R. 369.

[46] [1997] 2 F.L.R. 282.

[47] As had been the case in *Re B (Parentage)* [1996] 2 F.L.R. 15.

"The test in section 28(3)(a) is not whether the man consented either to be deemed in law to be the father of the prospective child or to become legally responsible for him: it is whether the relevant treatment services were provided for the woman and him together. In my view what has to be demonstrated is that, in the provision of treatment services with donor sperm, the doctor was responding to a request for that form of treatment made by the woman and the man as a couple, notwithstanding the absence of the man of any physical role in such treatment".[48]

3.37   Since section 28 applies only when the man has no genetic connection with the child, the only circumstances in which it could apply are when there was no physical role for the man, and his mental attitude (together with that of the provider) therefore becomes crucial.

3.38   The concept of "treatment together" arises, and has been considered judicially, in another context. The requirement that a man who gives sperm must give written consent to its being used[49] does not apply when the treatment is being provided for his partner and himself "together".[50] In *R v. Human Fertilisation and Embryology Authority, ex p. Blood*[51] it was held that, the donor being dead, treatment could not be said to be "treatment together" when his widow sought to use his sperm for the purposes of becoming pregnant.[52] And in the same context in *Re B (Parentage)* Bracewell J. said: "The attendance at the hospital jointly, with the giving of sperm, waiting a short time at the hospital to ensure the sperm was satisfactory and knowing that the sperm was not used for impregnation that day, can in my judgment only be described as a joint enterprise which encompasses the word 'together'."[53]

3.39   The onus lies on the person founding on section 28(3) to prove the facts upon which its application depends and there is no presumption that treatment was provided together.[54] In the event of it not being shown that the treatment was provided together, but a man and the mother had nevertheless acknowledged the child as his and had registered it as such, the presumption in section 5(1)(b) of the 1986 Act would come into play; but since that presumption can be rebutted on proof of a lack of genetic link, and section 28(3) of the 1990 Act only applies when there is no genetic link,[55] the rebuttal of the 1986 presumption will follow once it is shown that the conception came about by artificial means involving sperm not coming from the woman's partner.

"For all purposes"

3.40   The man who is not married to the mother but to whom section 28(3) applies will be treated in law as the father of the child "for all purposes"[56] (subject to the exceptions referred to in the next paragraph). This means for all purposes applicable to a man not married to the mother of the child. So, for example, he will have the same succession rights and the same alimentary and child support obligations as the father of a naturally conceived child, but he will not have parental responsibilities and parental rights unless he acquires them by other means (such as a parental responsibilities agreement under section 4 or a court order under section 11 of the Children (Scotland) Act 1995). Sections 28 and 29 of the 1990 Act do not confer parental responsibilities and parental rights: they merely deem paternity.

---

[48] [1997] 2 F.L.R. at 295B–C.
[49] 1990 Act, Sched. 3, para. 5(1).
[50] *ibid.* Sched. 3 para. 5(3).
[51] [1997] 2 All E.R. 687.
[52] On the European law implications of this case, see Hervey, "Buy Baby: The European Union and Regulation of Human Reproduction" (1998) 18 Ox. J. Leg. Stud. 207.
[53] [1996] 2 F.L.R. 15 at 21A.
[54] *cf.* s. 28(2) where one element for that provision's application — the husband's consent — is presumed.
[55] s. 28(3)(b).
[56] s. 29(1).

Exceptions

The exceptions to section 28(3) are the same as those to section 28(2), **3.41**
including those discussed in relation to establishing maternity, and the comments
made above should be referred to.[57]

Children with no legal fathers

Apart from cases where no presumption or deeming provision applies and the **3.42**
genetic father is unknown, there are two situations in which a child might be born
with no man being capable of being regarded as his or her legal father (though, of
course, there is no situation in which no person is capable of being given parental
responsibilities and parental rights in relation to the child). First, where the sperm of a
man who has given consent to the use of his sperm for procreative purposes is so used
within the terms of that consent, he is not to be treated as the father of any resulting
child,[58] for any purpose.[59] Unless, therefore, another man is (rebuttably) presumed to
be the genetic father or (irrebuttably) deemed to be the legal father under any of the
provisions discussed above, the child will, legally speaking, have no father for any
purpose whatsoever. On the other hand, if the sperm donation has not been used in a
way licensed under the 1990 Act (*i.e.* the donation has been informal, perhaps between
friends) then the donor remains genetic and legal father since he does not come within
the terms of section 28(6)(a) removing his legal paternity.[60] However, the paragraph is
somewhat wider in effect than that and it will not remove paternity from a sperm
donor who has not consented to his sperm being used to bring about the birth of a
child.[61] While it will be a criminal offence for any person so to use a man's sperm,[62]
that criminality does not elide his paternity. This is harsh on a man whose sperm is
used against or without his consent and, while the policy of encouraging those who
provide infertility services to do so within the terms of the licensing system is sound,
the justice of punishing sperm donors when they do not is elusory.

Secondly, if a man's sperm, or an embryo the creation of which was brought **3.43**
about with his sperm, was "used after his death", then he is not to be treated as
the father of the child,[63] for any purpose.[64] To "use" means, it is submitted, to
use for the purposes of procreation. There is no qualification to this provision
that the use must be in terms of consent given,[65] and the rule is, therefore,
absolute. This provision is designed to avoid any potential succession problems
that some other jurisdictions have faced when a child is created a very long
time after the death of the man who was his or her genetic father,[66] but it is wide
enough to deny any other consequence of the father–child relationship arising

---

[57] at paras 3.08–3.11.
[58] s. 28(6)(a).
[59] s. 29(2). See, for example, *Re Q (Parental Order)* [1996] 1 F.L.R. 369.
[60] *Re B (Parentage)* [1996] 2 F.L.R. 15, *per* Bracewell J. at 21D–E.
[61] Such as, for example, the dying husband in *R. v. Human Fertilisation and Embryology Authority,
ex p. Blood* [1997] 2 All E.R. 687.
[62] s. 4(1)(b) and s. 41(2). One of the difficulties facing the appellant in *Blood* was that the removal
and storage of her deceased husband's sperm without his consent was an offence. See Ferguson,
"Posthumous Conception: Blood and Gametes", 1997 S.L.T. (News) 61; Biggs, "Madonna Minus
Child, Or—Wanted: Dead or Alive! The Right to Have a Dead Partner's Child" (1997) 5 Fem.
Leg. Stud. 225. See also *Re B (Parentage)* [1996] 2 F.L.R. 15.
[63] s. 28(6)(b).
[64] s. 29(2). The issue does not arise in relation to female gametes since the gestational mother is in
all cases the mother recognised by law: see above, para. 3.07.
[65] Though if effective consent is not given, the sperm may not lawfully be used.
[66] Again, it is open to the genetic father to make express provision in his will for a child conceived
after death. In Tasmania it has been held that a frozen embryo would be entitled to succeed to its
genetic father's estate after it had been born alive: *In Re the Estate of the Late K* (1996) Tas. R.
365. This approach creates practical difficulties for executors' duties in winding up estates,
especially in the absence of any requirement to produce a child from a frozen embryo within a
stated time-frame, or indeed to do so at all.

in these circumstances and the child will be legally fatherless unless some other man is deemed or presumed father by the provisions discussed above.

3.44   There is no legal prohibition on providers of infertility treatment making that treatment available in circumstances that will lead to a legally fatherless child.[67] Indeed, the Human Fertilisation and Embryology Act 1990 does not specify any class of person who is ineligible to receive the treatment regulated therein. However, treatment may not be provided "unless account has been taken of the welfare of any child who may be born as a result of the treatment (including the need of that child for a father), and of any other child who may be affected by the birth".[68] This requirement has no direct substantive content[69] and there is no legal rule preventing the birth of legally fatherless children.[70] It can, however, be taken to symbolise the law's disapproval of treatment which will result in children with legal relationships only to one parent.

DECLARATORS OF PARENTAGE OR NON-PARENTAGE

3.45 In circumstances in which parentage is in issue (*e.g.* where none of the above presumptions or deeming provisions is applicable, or a pursuer wishes to challenge the result of one of the presumptions), an action for declarator of parentage or of non-parentage can be brought under section 7 of the Law Reform (Parent and Child) (Scotland) Act 1986. The proof that is required is proof on a balance of probabilities; this in relation both to actions in which the result of a presumption contained in the 1986 Act is being challenged[71] and to actions in which no presumption is applicable.[72] A declarator of parentage will have the same effect as one of the presumptions contained in the 1986 Act, and the effect of a declarator (either of parentage or of non-parentage) is to displace any contrary presumption, however arising.[73] An action of declarator without any further conclusion is competent.[74]

Jurisdiction

3.46   At common law actions of declarator of legitimacy or illegitimacy could be raised only in the Court of Session, because they were consistorial causes which had fallen originally within the exclusive jurisdiction of the Commissaries, before

---

[67] See Hibbs, "Assisted Reproduction Technology and the Law" (1997) 2 *Contemporary Issues in Law* 1 at 8–14.

[68] s. 13(5). It is unclear whether the use of the word "father" in this provision refers to a legal or a social relationship, but the reference to a child's "need" suggests the latter. It may be noted that para. 3.19(a) of the HFEA *Code of Practice* (rev. 1995) suggests that the requirement in s. 13(5) is satisfied by providers considering "whether there is anyone else within the prospective mother's family and social circle who is willing and able to share the responsibility for meeting those needs and for bringing up, maintaining and caring for the child". This is, it is submitted, a sensible interpretation of s. 13(5).

[69] See Douglas, "Assisted Reproduction and the Welfare of the Child" (1993) 46(2) *Current Legal Problems* 53; Blyth, "The United Kingdom's Human Fertilisation and Embryology Act 1990 and the Welfare of the Child: A Critique" (1995) 3 Int. J. Children's Rights 417. The provision does have indirect legal effect in the sense that the HFEA can withdraw the licence of a service provider who does not operate a protocol in which the child's welfare is considered.

[70] A civil claim against the service provider on the part of the child for the denial of a life with a father is, in essence, a claim for "wrongful life" and is, therefore, precluded in Scots and English law: see *McKay v. Essex Area Health Authority* [1982] Q.B. 1166 and *P's Curator Bonis v. Criminal Injuries Compensation Board*, 1997 S.L.T. 1180. The earliest U.S. "wrongful life" cases concerned claims by "illegitimate" children alleging that they had been negligently allowed to be born with that actionable stigma, but none was successful: see *Zepeda v. Zepeda*, 190 N.E. (2d) 849 (1963); *Williams v. New York*, 223 N.E. (2d) 343 (1963), discussed in Norrie, "Wrongful Life in Scots Law: No Right, No Remedy", 1990 J.R. 205.

[71] Law Reform (Parent and Child) (Scotland) Act 1986, s. 5(4).

[72] Where there is no presumption to rebut, proof has always been on this standard: *A v. G*, 1984 S.L.T. (Sh.Ct.) 65.

[73] s. 5(3).

[74] Walker, *Civil Remedies*, p. 116; *Mags of Ayr v. Lord Advocate*, 1950 S.C. 102; *McLay v. Farrell*, 1950 S.C. 149; *Fife County Council v. Lord Advocate*, 1950 S.C. 314.

being transferred to the exclusive jurisdiction of the Court of Session when the consistorial jurisdiction of the Commissaries was abolished by the Court of Session Act 1830.[75] Now, an action of declarator of parentage or non-parentage, legitimacy, illegitimacy or legitimation may be brought either in the Court of Session or in the sheriff court.[76] The action may be raised in the Court of Session if and only if:

(1) the child was born in Scotland, or
(2) the alleged or presumed parent or the child was domiciled in Scotland on the date the action is brought, or
(3) the alleged or presumed parent or the child has been habitually resident in Scotland for not less than one year immediately preceding that date, or
(4) the alleged or presumed parent or the child had died before that date and he or she was either domiciled in Scotland at death or habitually resident in Scotland for not less than one year immediately preceding his or her death.[77]

The action may be raised in the sheriff court if and only if:

(1) the child was born in the sheriffdom, or
(2) the action could have been brought in the Court of Session under the provisions described above and either the alleged or presumed parent or the child was habitually resident in the sheriffdom either on the date when the action is brought or on the date of the parent's death.[78]

"The alleged or presumed parent" in these provisions includes a person who claims or is alleged to be or not to be the parent.[79]

Incidental findings

The court may make in any proceedings an incidental finding as to parentage **3.47** or non-parentage for the purposes of these proceedings,[80] as for example in a declarator of marriage or an action for divorce or in an action for aliment against an alleged father.[81] A conclusion for putting to silence, normally associated with a declarator of freedom from marriage, is competent against any false claims to personal status and so may be combined with, and follow on, a declarator of non-parentage.[82] It is available against a parent who makes a false claim to a relationship as well as against the child.[83]

Title to sue

Any person with a legally enforceable interest that turns on the parentage or **3.48** non-parentage of the child has a title to sue for declarator.[84] That parents (actual, presumed and putative) and the child have such an interest is self-evident: they have a clear title to sue. A declarator must have at least the possibility of present legal consequences and it will not be granted where the sole interest is in some

---

[75] s. 33.
[76] Law Reform (Parent and Child) (Scotland) Act 1986, s. 7(1).
[77] *ibid.* s. 7(2).
[78] *ibid.* s. 7(3).
[79] *ibid.* s. 7(6).
[80] *ibid.* s. 7(5).
[81] *X v. Y*, 1921 1 S.L.T. 79; *Brown v. Brown*, 1972 S.L.T. 143. See also *Jamieson v. Jamieson*, 1969 S.L.T. (Notes) 11.
[82] *Imre v. Mitchell*, 1958 S.C. 439.
[83] *ibid.*
[84] *Shedden v. Patrick* (1849) 11 D. 1333; (1853) 15 D. 379; *Benson v. Benson* (1854) 16 D. 555; *Grant v. Countess of Seafield*, 1926 S.C. 274; *Bosville v. Lord Macdonald*, 1910 S.C. 597. See also *Hogg v. Dick*, 1987 S.L.T. 716.

future or contingent right.[85] Accordingly, while the parents and child are all alive, it will be rarely, if ever, that others have a title to seek a declarator of parentage.[86] On the death of any of them an interest and consequent title may, however, emerge. It was at one time thought that only the Crown or persons whose right was derived from the Crown had a title to seek a declarator of bastardy,[87] probably because the possibility of other interests had not been considered and, as the law then stood, could scarcely arise, but such actions have been entertained, not only at the instance of a parent, but of parties with a remoter interest unconnected with the Crown.[88] Declarators of non-parentage are, in any event, distinct from declarators of bastardy and it may be taken as settled that title to sue for declarator of a person's non-parentage depends, as does jurisdiction, on the same principles as those applicable to declarators of parentage.

Proof of parentage or non-parentage

3.49   In order to establish parentage or non-parentage where no presumption of law is in point, or when an applicable presumption is being challenged, the pursuer must establish, on the balance of probabilities, that there exists or there does not exist (as the case may be) a genetic link between the alleged parent and the child.[89] In the absence of scientific evidence, those matters already discussed in relation to rebutting the *pater est* presumption[90] will be relevant. Scientific evidence may not be available because, for example, appropriate consent cannot be obtained[91] or one of the parties is dead. In an unreported case the alleged father (now deceased) had, during the mother's pregnancy, placed his hand on her stomach and asked after "his baby", had settled out of court an action for aliment shortly after the child's birth, the mother had alleged that she had never had sex with any other man and paternity was held to be established.[92] Proof of maternity has already been considered.[93] Proof of paternity is much more difficult and is, in the absence of scientific evidence, necessarily recondite. It is, however, no longer necessary to provide corroborated evidence[94] (and the doctrine of corroboration by false denial[95] is consequently abolished also[96]), but the court shall not grant decree of declarator unless proof has been established by evidence.[97]

---

[85] Walker, *Civil Remedies*, pp. 113-114. The rule admits substantial exceptions and where there is a proper contradictor, a future, or even a contingent, legal right can be made the subject of declarator (*Fleming v. McLagan* (1879) 6 R. 588, *per* Lord Young at 598). It is thought, however, that the scope afforded to such actions cannot extend to the raising of actions by parties whose sole interest is one which may emerge only on the death of a party having a present and primary interest.

[86] A statutory exception is contained in the Child Support Act 1991, s. 28 of which gives the Secretary of State title to pursue an action of declarator of parentage, and to defend an action of declarator of non-parentage, under s. 7 of the 1986 Act.

[87] Stair, IV, xii, 1, 7 and 8.

[88] *Imre v. Mitchell*, above; *Smith v. Dick* (1869) 8 M. 31.

[89] Note that while such evidence will rebut the presumptions in the Law Reform (Parent and Child) (Scotland) Act 1986 it will have no effect on the deeming provisions contained in the Human Fertilisation and Embryology Act 1990. In relation to mothers, the existence of such a link will be evidence that she carried the child (which is the definition of legal maternity) but is not in all cases conclusive of that fact.

[90] Above, para. 3.19.

[91] *Cameron v. Carr (No. 2)*, 1998 Fam. L.R. 16.

[92] *Antoniewicz v. Barty (Wood's Exr)*, June 27, 1991, in which the alleged father had died four days before he was due to submit to DNA fingerprinting.

[93] Above, para. 3.12.

[94] Civil Evidence (Scotland) Act 1988, s. 1(1).

[95] A doctrine applicable to consistorial and affiliation cases: *Hall v. Hall*, 1958 S.C. 206; *McInnes v. McInnes*, 1954 S.C. 396; *Davies v. Hunter*, 1934 S.C. 10.

[96] Civil Evidence (Scotland) Act 1988, s. 1(2).

[97] *ibid.* s. 8(1).

Proof of intercourse

Proof that sexual intercourse took place at the relevant time will almost always **3.50** be necessary, and an inference of paternity will ordinarily be drawn where there is such proof and nothing more. This is so notwithstanding that evidence of intercourse, apart from the evidence of the parties, is almost always inferential in character, as, in the highest degree, is the answer to the question whether any given act of intercourse led to conception. Moreover, the facts from which the inferences may be drawn are often, in the nature of things, difficult to prove. The specialties of proof flow in the main from the paucity of testimony usually available. In *Jamieson v. Dobie*, Lord President Clyde said: "What was laid down in *Williamson's* case[98] was that, if the pursuer proves connexion at a date such that it is not impossible, according to experience, for the subsequent birth to be connected with it, then the pursuer has done all the pursuer can do to discharge the onus resting on her."[99]

The effect of proof of intercourse with the defender, at a date with which it **3.51** is not impossible for the subsequent birth to be connected, is, in the absence of any evidence to suggest that another man is the father, to raise a presumption of fact which the defender, if he is to escape liability, must displace. Paternity will not, however, be attributed to the defender where acts of intercourse with other men are proved, or seem likely to have occurred, at about the same time as the proved or admitted act of intercourse with the defender, unless there be some special feature pointing to the likelihood that the defender is the father[1]; and *a fortiori* that will be so where the act of intercourse with another man is consistent with resultant conception followed by a normal period of gestation, whereas the act of intercourse with the alleged father would be consistent with his paternity only if an abnormal period of gestation were postulated. The question of the maximum possible period of gestation is the same in principle as in cases of rebuttal of the presumption of paternity,[2] but, where the presumption does not apply, the onus rests on the pursuer to prove that the period of gestation required for consistency with paternity on the part of the alleged father is not impossible and it is submitted that for that reason, if for no other, the court should be less astute than it was in cases when "legitimacy" was in issue to accept periods of gestation that verge on the fanciful. That will, however, be so only where there is no question of intercourse after the last date admitted or proved. If intercourse at a date too remote to be the occasion of conception is admitted or proved and there has been opportunity thereafter at a time consistent with conception, the onus is on the defender, at least if the pursuer speaks to connection then and is credible, to prove that there was not intercourse when opportunity afforded. This principle was applied in a series of cases in which the requirements of *semiplena probatio* were held to be satisfied so as to admit the pursuer's oath in supplement, although the interval between the last act of intercourse admitted or proved and the birth of the child far exceeded the normal period of gestation.[3] The equivalent in modern practice is that the remote act of

---

[98] *Williamson v. McClelland*, 1913 S.C. 678.
[99] 1935 S.C. 415 at 418. Averments of intercourse at specified intervals over a period of time within which conception occurred are relevant: *Farrell v. Brannan* (1921) 37 Sh.CtRep. 75.
[1] *Robertson v. Hutchison*, 1935 S.C. 708; *Sinclair v. Rankine*, 1921 S.C. 933; *Hannan v. Anderson* (1935) 51 Sh.CtRep. 300. The pursuer cannot "choose her victim" (*Robertson v. Hutchison; Butter v. McLaren*, 1909 S.C. 786), but may show reasons for holding the defender rather than another man to be the father. In England it has been held that a refusal by one man to submit to blood testing is such a special feature: see below, para. 3.61.
[2] Above, para. 3.17.
[3] *Brown v. Smith* (1799) Hume 32 (14 months); *Wightman v. Tomlinson* (1807) Mor.App.1 Proof No. 5 (11 months and three weeks); *Leckie v. Lindsay* (1810) Hume 33; *Hunter, Petr*, May 26, 1814, F.C. 614 (one year and 14 days); *Kerr v. Hamilton* (1852) 4 D. 624 (11 months, 15 days). See Fraser (3rd ed.), p. 168. *Cf. Jamieson v. Dobie*, 1935 S.C. 415 (306 days); *Gaw v. McNab* (1933) 49 Sh.CtRep. 55 (320 days); *Gorman v. Smith, ibid.* (315 days).

intercourse should be taken to give rise to a presumption of continuance which, together with the pursuer's evidence of intercourse at a time appropriate for conception, will often be sufficient to establish the pursuer's case. If the evidence is so regarded, there is no real departure from the normal period of gestation as the proper measure. Similar considerations apply where the minimum period of gestation is in issue[4] and in relation to both the minimum and maximum periods regard must be had to the particular facts of the case including the character of the mother. Where there is no question of promiscuity, indulgence may more readily be allowed in considering whether the probable limits have been exceeded.

Other acts of intercourse

3.52   Evidence that the mother had sexual intercourse with other men within the possible period of gestation is admissible because it is directly relevant to the question of whether the alleged father is in fact the father.[5] Evidence of specific acts of intercourse between the mother and men other than the alleged father is, however, in accordance with the general principle which excludes similar fact evidence, inadmissible if the acts fall outwith that period, although it is thought that, on analogy with cases of rape, evidence of the general loose sexual character of the mother may be led.[6] Acts of intercourse between the alleged father and women other than the mother and his loose sexual character are not apt to instruct, except in the most general way, the likelihood of his being the father of the mother's child and so evidence of these matters is inadmissible.[7] The rule excluding similar fact evidence finds, however, an exception in the case of intercourse between the mother and the alleged father falling outwith the possible period of gestation. Evidence of such acts is admitted because the allegations of paternity must be viewed in the light of the whole circumstances of the relationship between the parties and intercourse on occasions other than that which is alleged to have led to conception may be relevant to the character of that relationship.[8] At one time little distinction was made for this purpose between intercourse before and intercourse after the possible time of conception, but it is now recognised that evidence of intercourse before conception has greater evidential force than subsequent intercourse.[9] Where an act of intercourse prior to conception is admitted or proved very little further is required to establish the case; but the contrary is true where the admitted or proved act is subsequent to conception. Once intercourse has taken place, the likelihood, according to ordinary human experience, is that it continues to occur within a continuing relationship.[10] Evidence of an act of intercourse between the parties has accordingly been admitted although it occurred as much as six years before the alleged date of conception.[11] There is not the same strong inferential connection

---

[4] *Elliot v. Scott* (1800) Hume 33 (seven months and four days). *Cf. Watson v. Caine,* (1936) 52 Sh.CtRep. 213.

[5] *Butter v. McLaren,* 1909 S.C. 786. *Cf. Barr v. Bain* (1896) 23 R. 1090. When such acts are founded upon, times, places and names should be specified in the pleadings.

[6] See Walker and Walker, *The Law of Evidence in Scotland,* p. 20. But the analogy with rape may now lead to a different conclusion (Criminal Procedure (Scotland) Act 1995, ss. 274 and 275).

[7] *McDougall v. Balonieri* (1916) 32 Sh.CtRep. 186. See, however, *Whyte v. Whyte* (1884) 11 R. 710, *per* Lord Mure at 711.

[8] *Lawson v. Eddie* (1861) 23 D. 876; *Ross v. Fraser* (1863) 1 M. 783; *McDonald v. Glass* (1883) 11 R. 57; *Scott v. Dawson* (1884) 11 R. 518; *Buchanan v. Finlayson* (1900) 3 F. 245; *Havery v. Brownlee,* 1908 S.C. 424; *Florence v. Smith,* 1913 S.C. 978; *Roy v. Pairman,* 1958 S.C. 334.

[9] *Florence v. Smith,* above; *Havery v. Brownlee,* above.

[10] *Buchanan v. Finlayson,* above, *per* Lord Trayner at 251 and Lord Justice-Clerk Macdonald at 249; *Havery v. Brownlee,* above, *per* Lord Justice-Clerk Macdonald at 425; *Reid v. Storry* (1912) 28 Sh.CtRep. 326.

[11] *Macpherson v. Beaton,* 1935 S.C. 100.

between subsequent intercourse and the probability of intercourse at the time of conception, but it may nonetheless, especially if close in time, cast a light on the relationship of the parties and give a likelihood to the pursuer's evidence which it would not otherwise have.[12]

The defender as witness

In actions for declarator of parentage raised by the mother the pursuer may **3.53** sometimes call the defender as a witness. It is her right to do so; the practice is unobjectionable, at any rate where the defender is adduced immediately before the close of the pursuer's proof, and there is no inference that in doing so the pursuer puts the defender forward as a witness of credit.[13] The problematic case arises where the defender is called as the pursuer's first witness. That is also within the pursuer's rights and it may have tactical advantages, but doubts have been expressed about its propriety and expediency. These doubts have not, however, been uniform. Criticisms in *McArthur v. McQueen*[14] were disapproved in *Darroch v. Kerr*,[15] but repeated in *McWhirter v. Lynch*[16]; and in *Fraser v. Smith*[17] the hope was expressed that this method of conducting cases would thereafter be avoided. It has been said, apparently on the view that to call the defender as the pursuer's first witness is unfair to him, that if the practice is followed the defender should be warned of the importance and possible effect of his answers to material questions[18]; but neither the unfairness nor the necessity for warning is clear. The defender has notice of the case against him on the pleadings and that should protect him from improper surprise. He is bound by his oath to tell the truth and it is difficult to understand the need for any special warning that he should do so. A higher degree of fairness to both parties may be obtained if the defender gives his evidence before he has had an opportunity of measuring the full strength of the pursuer's case as disclosed in the evidence than if he does so at a later stage. The only significant element of unfairness to the defender is that he may not have an opportunity of dealing in his evidence with incidental points that may emerge unexpectedly at later stages of the pursuer's proof; but any prejudice caused by that can be remedied by allowing the defender's recall. If the pursuer remains in court during the defender's evidence, the court may find difficulty in assessing the credibility of her subsequent testimony, but that objection can be elided by the pursuer's voluntary absence during the defender's evidence. Both *McWhirter v. Lynch* and *Fraser v. Smith* show an inadequate appreciation of the cogent considerations advanced by a distinguished bench in *Darroch v. Kerr*, but the weight of adverse judicial opinion is now such that it is probably imprudent to adduce the defender as the pursuer's first witness unless there are special reasons for doing so.

Scientific tests: DNA profiling

The doubts expressed in *Imre v. Mitchell*[19] about the value of scientific **3.54** evidence of blood tests in rebutting the presumption of paternity must be read in the context of the facts of that case[20] and if intended to have a wider application

---

[12] *Ross v. Fraser*, above, *per* Lord Justice-Clerk Inglis at 785 and Lord Neaves at 786; *Florence v. Smith*, above, *per* Lord Dundas at 985–986; *Buchanan v. Finlayson*, *per* Lord Justice-Clerk Macdonald at 249 and Lord Trayner at 251. See also *Lawson v. Eddie*, *per* Lord Benholme at p. 880; *McDonald v. Glass*, above *per* Lord Justice-Clerk Moncrieff at 58 and Lord Young at 59.
[13] *Faddes v. McNeish*, 1923 S.C. 443, *per* Lord Ormidale at 448; *Darroch v. Kerr* (1901) 4 F. 396; *sed contra McArthur v. McQueen* (1901) 3 F. 1010.
[14] above.
[15] above.
[16] 1909 S.C. 112.
[17] 1937 S.N. 67. See also *Finnegan v. Maan*, 1966 S.L.T. (Notes) 47.
[18] *McWhirter v. Lynch*, above, *per* Lord President Dunedin at 113.
[19] 1958 S.C. 439.
[20] The case involved a mother attempting to have her own child declared illegitimate, and this clearly did not elicit much sympathy from the court.

have, in any event, been superseded by the advance of scientific knowledge. The value of such tests is now undoubted,[21] and indeed in the normal case will now be the best evidence available. Until the mid-1980s, the ABO blood grouping system was the main scientific test available, and though it could in the vast majority of cases be used only in an exclusionary manner,[22] the test itself was accepted as being "pretty cast iron" by Lord Cullen in *Russell v. Wood*.[23] In that case the court found a child to be "illegitimate" after being satisfied beyond all reasonable doubt[24] that the mother's husband was not the father: the evidence consisted of the mother's assertion of when she last had sex with her husband, and the result of the ABO blood-grouping test.

3.55   A much more accurate scientific test is now widely available, whereby a person's DNA structure is identified.[25] This test, known as DNA profiling or DNA fingerprinting, can positively identify the parents of a child, to a probability far in excess of what the courts would accept as proof on the balance of probabilities.[26] DNA (deoxyribonucleic acid) is the material from which chromosomes are made. Every (genetically normal) person inherits 23 chromosomes from his or her mother, and 23 from his or her father. The DNA is formed in bands which can be measured and X-rayed. In a dispute concerning, say, paternity, a child's DNA bands can be matched with those of his or her mother. Those bands that do not match with the mother's bands must have come from the father and these bands can then be matched with those of the putative father, giving a positive or a negative result of great accuracy. If this evidence is available, it will clearly be the best evidence of parentage.

Ordering scientific tests

3.56   As a general principle, a party to litigation is not obliged to assist his or her opponent by providing that opponent with the evidence upon which to build a case.[27] At common law the Scottish court took the view that it could not direct parties in civil proceedings to undergo medical examinations such as blood tests, this on the ground that any such order would be an unwarranted invasion of a person's private right and would be inconsistent with the principles upon which litigation is carried out in Scotland. Nor could the court order or authorise tests to be carried out upon children, even to prove their "legitimacy".[28] However,

---

21 *S v. S, W v. Official Solicitor* [1972] A.C. 24, *per* Lord Reid at 41, *Docherty v. McGlynn*, 1983 S.L.T. 645, *per* Lord President Emslie at 648 and Lord Cameron at 650.
22 See Dodd and Lincoln, "An Analysis of 1556 Cases of Doubtful Paternity Submitted for Blood Group Investigation" (1978) 18 Med.Sci.L. 185.
23 1987 S.C.L.R. 207 at 209.
24 *i.e.* to a standard higher than is now necessary.
25 See Bradney, "Blood Tests, Paternity and the Double Helix" (1986) 16 Fam. Law 378.
26 Rankin, "DNA Fingerprinting" (1988) 33 J.L.S.S.124 reports that the chances of error are something in the region of 30,000 million to one, though such accuracy has been challenged: see Macdonald, "DNA Profiling — Less than the Whole Truth?", 1990 S.L.T. (News) 285. In *Torrie v. Turner*, 1990 S.L.T. 718 an Extra Division of the Inner House was told that DNA profiling could establish paternity positively "beyond statistical doubt." In the criminal case of *Welsh v. H.M. Advocate*, 1992 S.L.T. 193 it was held that it was for the jury to determine when the criminal standard had been achieved and that the statistical evidence of the chances of someone other than the accused having blood with the same DNA structure as the accused being 1 in 88 million was sufficient evidence to found a conviction. Challenges to the validity of this method of identification have recently given way to challenges to the rigour (and therefore reliability) of the procedures under which the tests are carried out.
27 *per* Lord Justice-Clerk Thomson in *Whitehall v. Whitehall*, 1958 S.C. 252 at 258–259.
28 *Whitehall v. Whitehall*, above; *imre v. Mitchell*, 1958 S.C. 439; *Torrie v. Turner*, 1990 S.L.T. 718. *Cf.* the position in England where, under different statutory provisions from those obtaining in Scotland, it has been held that while the court cannot require an adult to submit to blood-testing it can require that a child be tested, even in the face of parental refusal: *Re R (A Minor) (Blood Tests: Constraint)* [1998] 2 W.L.R. 796.

this approach was increasingly regarded as unjustified and indeed counter-productive for a number of reasons. First, it was developed at a time when a finding of "illegitimacy" had profound and unfortunate effects on a child's legal status. This is no longer so. Secondly, it was developed at a time when the tests could not positively identify a child's parents, with the result that the person claiming paternity had nothing to gain and everything to lose, while the person denying it had possibly everything to gain and nothing to lose. This too is no longer so, and DNA profiling, by identifying the truth, gives mutual benefits and drawbacks to both sides. Thirdly, the taking of blood samples involves an invasion of a person's bodily integrity, minor it is to be admitted, yet far more than would be required for a DNA test, which can be done using skin scrapings, hair roots or semen.[29] And finally, a principle that was appropriate for litigious proceedings is not necessarily apt in proceedings relating to a child's welfare: there are few situations indeed in which a child's welfare will not best be served by finding out the truth (particularly since that truth cannot now affect the child's own legal status). However, the precedents preventing the Scottish court from ordering tests were clear and the Court of Session was not inclined to accept arguments such as those given above to change its rule.[30] In England the courts were given the power to order scientific tests under the Family Law Reform Act 1969, as amended by the Family Law Reform Act 1987.[31] In Scotland similar (but not identical) powers were given to the court by section 70 of the Law Reform (Miscellaneous Provisions) (Scotland) Act 1990.

This provision was passed as a result of the recommendations of the Scottish Law **3.57** Commission,[32] who had argued that, if the courts were given the power to order DNA testing, "the number of cases of disputed paternity which proceed to a full court hearing would, we suspect, fall dramatically, thus reducing the courts' overall workload. Spurious cases would be prevented and the courts would be able to deal more speedily with those that do proceed".[33] The fall in the number of cases has not, perhaps, been as dramatic as the Scottish Law Commission had envisaged, possibly due to the increase in the number of cases brought by men claiming rather than denying paternity. Nevertheless, though the power has been used infrequently, its existence has generally been welcomed as furnishing the court with the best evidence of where the truth lies.

Section 70 provides that the court[34] may, in any civil proceedings,[35] request **3.58** a party to the proceedings: (a) to provide a sample of blood or other body fluid or of body tissue for the purpose of laboratory analysis; or (b) to consent to the taking of such a sample from a child in relation to whom the party has power to give such consent. Such a request may be made in any civil proceedings brought on or after the date of commencement of section 70, or brought before that date so long as the proof has not yet begun.[36] The court is entitled to make such a request *ex proprio motu* and it does not need to wait for an application by one of the parties;[37] it has, however, no right to request that a person who is not a party

---

[29] Though blood is nearly always used in paternity cases, the amount of blood required for analysis is smaller than that required for ABO grouping.

[30] See *Torrie v. Turner*, above.

[31] There was some disagreement on the extent of the English court's powers at common law: see *S v. S, W v. Official Solicitor* [1972] A.C. 24, *per* Lord Reid at 43, Lord Hodson at 57 and Lord McDermott at 46–47.

[32] Discussion Paper 80, *Evidence: Blood Group Tests, DNA Tests, and Related Matters*, Scot. Law Com. Report No. 120.

[33] *ibid.* para. 3.9.

[34] By which is meant the Court of Session or the sheriff court: Law Reform (Miscellaneous Provisions) (Scotland) Act 1990, s. 70(4).

[35] This is rather wider than the equivalent English provisions, now contained in s. 20(1) of the Family Law Reform Act 1969, for there the court has a similar power only in actions in which a child's parentage falls to be determined.

[36] Law Reform (Miscellaneous Provisions) (Scotland) Act 1990, s. 70(4).

[37] *ibid.* s. 70(1).

to the proceedings provide a sample. So a pursuer in an action for declarator of non-parentage who alleges that someone else not a party to the proceedings is in truth the parent cannot force that person to provide a sample. The person requested need not be an alleged parent of the child, so long as he or she is a "party".[38] Since today testing can provide a positive or a negative identification conclusively, there will generally be no need to involve a third party for the purposes of the question before the court. Allegations that a third party is the parent are sometimes made as an element of proof that the pursuer was not the parent; but proof of, or an allegation of, parentage is not required to found an action of non-parentage.

3.59   Section 70 itself contains no indication as to when it would be appropriate for the court to request a party to provide a sample for analysis, and the matter may be taken to be wholly within the discretion of the court.[39] In England it has been held that, while not paramount, the child's welfare is a relevant consideration in determining whether to order scientific tests[40] and in particular tests ought not to be ordered if the results are likely to disturb the child's security within his or her present family setting with no concomitant benefit.[41] Some caution does, however, require to be shown in relation to these English cases since the issue of parenthood there has significant consequences in relation to title to seek parental responsibilities which are altogether absent in Scots law. In an action for declarator of parentage or non-parentage with no further conclusions the possible outcome of the tests (*i.e.* the truth) ought not to affect whether tests should be requested (*i.e.* whether the truth should be sought); and in the Scottish context neither title to seek an order under section 11 of the Children (Scotland) Act 1995 nor the eventual outcome of any such action is dependent on proof of paternity. The effect of the establishment of paternity is governed by the welfare principle but whether and how paternity is established ought not to be. In any case, the welfare of the child should be accepted as being best served by the establishment of the truth.[42] As Lord Hodson said in *S v. S, W v. Official Solicitor*,[43] "the interests of justice in the abstract are best served by the ascertainment of the truth and there must be few cases where the interests of children can be shown to be best served by the suppression of truth".[44]

Refusal to undergo testing: adverse inferences

3.60   While a request that a party provide a sample of blood or other body fluid or of body tissue for the purposes of laboratory analysis can be made by the court,

---

[38] In *Mackay v. Murphy*, 1995 S.L.T. (Sh.Ct) 30 an action was raised against the executor of the alleged father, now deceased, and it was held that she could be requested to provide a sample (she being the alleged father's mother). *Cf. Cameron v. Carr's Curator ad Litem*, 1998 S.L.T. (Sh.Ct) 22, following *Imre v. Mitchell*, 1958 S.C. 439 and *Docherty v. McGlynn*, 1983 S.L.T. 645, in which the sheriff held that he was unable to request a curator *ad litem* to consent on behalf of a mentally *incapax* person alleged to be parent.

[39] *Cameron v. Carr's Curator ad Litem*, above, *per* Sheriff Fitzsimmons at 26B.

[40] *Re H (Paternity: Blood Tests)* [1996] 2 F.L.R. 65, *per* Ward L.J. at 77G (following *S v. S, W v. Official Solicitor* [1972] A.C. 24.

[41] *Re F (A Minor) (Blood Tests: Paternity Rights)* [1993] Fam. 314; *O v. L (Blood Tests)* [1995] 2 F.L.R. 930. See also *K v. M (Paternity: Contact)* [1996] 1 F.L.R. 312.

[42] This consists with the approach of Temporary Sheriff Principal Coutts in *Petrie v. Petrie*, 1993 S.C.L.R. 391.

[43] [1972] A.C. 24 at 57H.

[44] Art. 7 of the United Nations Convention on the Rights of the Child: "The child... shall have the right from birth to a name, the right to acquire a nationality and, as far as possible, the right to know and be cared for by his or her parents." Art. 8: "States Parties undertake to respect the right of the child to preserve his or her identity, including nationality, name and family relationships as recognised by law without unlawful interference." These international obligations suggest that welfare or other considerations should not be permitted to act as obstacles to the discovery of the truth about a child's origins. Children's rights under the UN Convention are not superseded by the need to protect children's best interests, which is merely "a primary consideration" in the Convention.

the request cannot be enforced, for this would involve a person being subjected to a surgical interference, however slight, without his or her consent: this is perceived to go against an individual's right to physical integrity. A civil case raises different considerations from a criminal case, because the former is more concerned with a balancing of private interest.[45] However, if the court has made a request, but the person requested refuses or fails to comply with it, then "the court may draw from the refusal or failure such adverse inference, if any, in relation to the subject-matter of the proceedings as seems to it to be appropriate."[46] In *Docherty v. McGlynn* Lord Cameron thought, even before the enactment of the statutory power, that a refusal to consent to scientific tests upon oneself could be sanctioned by "the consequential inference to be drawn adverse to the interest of the party in disobedience"[47]; and although he cited no authority for this proposition, a parallel might have been found in the requirement which may be made of a pursuer in a personal injuries action to submit to medical examination. The authority to draw an adverse inference now lies in section 70. The court does not need to draw any adverse inference, but the court will look closely at any proferred reason for refusal.

The matter has been discussed extensively in the English courts, though again caution is required in reading the decisions. The leading case is that of *Re A (A Minor) (Paternity: Refusal of Blood Test)*[48] in which a woman had had a sexual relationship with three different men during the period when conception of her child had taken place. She sought maintenance for the child from one of the men and the court ordered him to submit to blood-testing, which he refused. The Court of Appeal held that if a man chose to exercise his right not to submit to be tested, the inference that he was the father of the child was "virtually inescapable". Waite L.J. said that "he would certainly have to advance very clear and cogent reasons for this refusal to be tested—reasons which it would be just and fair and reasonable for him to be allowed to maintain".[49] The same reasoning was applied in a case involving the reverse situation: in *Re G (Parentage: Blood Sample)*[50] it was held that the presumption of paternity in favour of a mother's husband was rebutted by the presumptive father's refusal to submit to blood testing. According to Ward L.J., "He who obstructs the truth will have the inference drawn against him".[51] And in *Re H (Paternity: Blood Tests)*[52] the same judge held[53] that a refusal to submit to testing *before* the court had ordered it would similarly lead to an adverse inference, though not as strong as when the court's direction is flouted. It seems from these authorities that once the English courts have decided that the truth is in the interests of the child, they will very strongly discourage any person from putting barriers in the way of discovering that truth. Any stated reasons for refusal to submit to blood tests is to be subject to the strictest scrutiny: the court must "look critically at proferred explanation or justification. It should only uphold an explanation that is objectively valid, demonstrating rationality, logicality and consistency. Anything less will usually lead to an adverse inference".[54] The end result is that the

3.61

---

[45] Scot. Law Com., Discussion Paper No. 80, paras 3.20–3.25.

[46] Law Reform (Miscellaneous Provisions) (Scotland) Act 1990, s. 70(2).

[47] 1983 S.L.T. 645 at 650. See also, to similar effect, Lord Denning M.R. in *Re L (An Infant)*, [1968] P. 119 at 159.

[48] [1994] 2 F.L.R. 463, CA.

[49] *ibid.* at 472.

[50] [1997] 1 F.L.R. 360.

[51] *ibid.* at 366H. It is difficult to see how such a principle could apply when it is the mother (as in *Re R (A Minor) (Blood Tests: Constraint)* [1998] 2 W.L.R. 796) or the child itself who is refusing consent. If the mother refuses, it would be arbitrary and inequitable to suggest that the inference should be against whatever position she adopts.

[52] [1996] 2 F.L.R. 65.

[53] *ibid.* at 77C–D.

[54] *Re G (Parentage: Blood Sample)*, above, *per* Thorpe L.J. at 367D.

lower English courts have been given strong and repeated instruction that they should draw inferences from the refusal and that the appropriate inference is that the refuser's claimed position in relation to paternity is false. The matter has been little discussed in Scotland, but it has been held, by Sheriff Principal Nicholson, that section 70 of the Law Reform (Miscellaneous Provisions) (Scotland) Act 1990 gives the court a discretion both as to whether to draw an adverse inference and as to the nature of any inference to be drawn.[55] He found, directly contrary to the holding in *Re G (Parentage: Blood Sample)*, that the defender's refusal to allow her child to be tested did not overcome the presumption that her husband was the father. Rather, the only adverse inference that could possibly be drawn on the facts of the case was that the defender was lying when she denied the possibility of the pursuer being father: that possibility was insufficient to overturn the presumption. This approach, which does not require the court to find against the refuser is, it is submitted, preferable to the English approach. The lack of further direction in the statutory provision suggests that the matter was intended by Parliament to be left at large for the court. An acceptance of the possibility of paternity should not be elevated into a legal certainty in the absence of direct evidence, even when that absence is caused by one party's actions or refusal to act. Otherwise, the law would, in effect, require one party to assist the other. It is, however, appropriate for the court to question the refusing party's motives in determining whether an inference is appropriate in the circumstances, and if so what that inference should be.[56]

Consent on behalf of children

3.62   DNA profiling to establish parentage or non-parentage requires, of course, samples of blood or other body fluid or of other body tissue being taken not only from the putative parents but also from the child concerned. If a person under the age of 16 years is, in the opinion of a qualified medical practitioner, capable of understanding the nature and possible consequences of consenting to the medical procedure of removing a sample, then he or she may provide personal consent thereto.[57] However, if the child is unable to understand then consent can be provided by a person with parental responsibilities and parental rights in relation to the child. In general, such consent is valid only when the treatment or procedure is designed to safeguard and promote the child's health, development and welfare.[58] But if the purpose of the taking of blood or body tissue from the child is to establish that the child is not related to a person (and therefore to deny the child, *e.g.*, the right of aliment or of succession from that person) it is not clear that in all cases this will be in the child's best interests. It was to obviate such doubts that section 6 of the Law Reform (Parent and Child) (Scotland) Act 1986 was passed.[59] This section originally referred only to the taking of blood samples from pupil children, but it has now been extended to cover the taking of other body fluid or of body tissue,[60] and also to apply to all children under 16.[61] Section 6(2)[62] provides that

---

[55] *Smith v. Greenhill*, 1994 SLT (Sh.Ct) 22. Sheriff Fitzsimmons added, in *Cameron v. Carr's Curator ad Litem*, 1998 S.L.T. (Sh.Ct) 22 at 26B, that s. 70 also gives the court discretion as to whether to issue a request at all.

[56] Adverse inferences would not appropriately be drawn against a person who is not mentally competent to understand the nature of the testing nor the consequences of refusal: *cf. Cameron v. Carr's Curator ad Litem*, 1998 S.L.T. (Sh.Ct) 22. Paternity was subsequently established at a later hearing of this case: *Cameron v. Carr (No. 2)*, 1998 Fam. L.R. 16.

[57] Age of Legal Capacity (Scotland) Act 1991, s. 2(4). This applies to "any surgical, medical or dental procedure or treatment" which is amply wide enough to cover the taking of a sample.

[58] See below, para. 8.48.

[59] Discussed by Thomson in "Law Reform (Parent and Child) (Scotland) Act 1986", 1987 S.L.T. (News) 129 at 130.

[60] Law Reform (Miscellaneous Provisions) (Scotland) Act 1990, s. 70(3).

[61] Age of Legal Capacity (Scotland) Act 1991, Sched. 1, para. 42.

[62] As amended by the Children (Scotland) Act 1995, Sched. 4, para. 38(3).

where the sample is sought from a child under 16, consent may be given by any person having parental responsibilities in relation to, or having the care and control of, the child.[63] There is no requirement that the consent be given only if it furthers the child's best interests,[64] and it is for the person empowered to consent on behalf of the child to decide whether the establishing of the truth will outweigh any other, perhaps financial, detriment to the child (*e.g.* by losing a right to aliment from a particular man, or by losing a right to a valuable succession from a particular person's estate[65]). That decision cannot be challenged in a court. In any case, a child's best interests (where relevant) are not to be calculated on a purely financial basis, and the resolving of doubt about his or her parentage, which DNA profiling now conclusively allows, will nearly always weigh more heavily than the protection of rights that may be falsely based.[66]

The court[67] may request a party to any civil proceedings, who has the power **3.63** to give consent on behalf of a child, to give that consent to the taking of a sample of blood or other body fluid or of body tissue.[68] If that party refuses or fails to give the consent, or to take any step necessary for the provision or taking of such a sample, the court may draw from the refusal or failure such adverse inference, if any, in relation to the subject-matter of the proceedings as seems to it to be appropriate.[69] Again, there is no requirement to draw any inference, but the court will look closely at any proferred reason for refusal.[70]

Consent by presumptive father

Where section 6 of the 1986 Act refers to a person having parental **3.64** responsibilities being able to consent on the child's behalf, this includes the man who is presumed father as a result of section 5(1) of the same Act. This may lead to conceptual problems when the man's paternity is the very fact at issue. In *Docherty v. McGlynn*[71] a presumptive father was held entitled to consent to the taking of blood samples from the child, in an action in which the paramour of his wife[72] sought declarator that the child was his rather than the husband's and presumptive father's. The Lord Ordinary, Lord Wylie, held that since the *de quo* in the action was which of the pursuer or defender was in fact (and in law) the father, the presumptive father had no power to consent on behalf of the child. This was overruled by the First Division on the ground that the defender (the presumptive father) enjoyed the benefit of the presumption until it was overturned, and part of that benefit was the right to custody of the child and the right to exercise in relation to the child the *patria potestas* (from which the right to consent flowed). In Lord President Emslie's words: "The presumption and

---

[63] s. 5(1) of the Children (Scotland) Act 1995 provides that a person with care or control of the child may give consent to any surgical, medical or dental treatment or procedure, though this may be limited to circumstances in which it safeguards the child's health, development and welfare (see below, para. 8.16). The phrase "care or control" as it appears in s. 5 of the 1995 Act probably means the same as "care and control" as it appears in s. 6 of the 1986 Act.

[64] *cf.* the position when the court grants consent under s. 6(3) of the 1986 Act (see below, para. 3.66): the court can grant consent only when satified that the taking of the sample would not be detrimental to the child's health.

[65] *Russell v. Wood*, 1987 S.C.L.R. 207.

[66] See *Mackay v. Murphy*, 1995 S.L.T. (Sh.Ct) 30, *per* Sheriff Principal Maguire at 31J.

[67] By which is meant the Court or Session or the sheriff court: Law Reform (Miscellaneous Provisions) (Scotland) Act 1990, s. 70(4).

[68] *ibid.* s. 70(1)(b).

[69] *ibid.* s. 70(2).

[70] See *Smith v. Greenhill*, 1994 S.L.T. (Sh.Ct) 22 in which it was held not appropriate to draw adverse inferences. In *Liggins v. Telfer* (1985) 3 N.Z.F.L.R. 592 a New Zealand court held that the only inference that could be drawn was that the party was unwilling to assist the court.

[71] 1983 S.L.T. 645.

[72] Now deceased: this was why she was not able to provide the requisite consent.

all the rights which flow from it in favour of the first-named defender in this case cannot be defeated unless and until the pursuer has established that he is, and that the first-named defender could not be, the child's father."[73]

3.65   However, the limits of this decision must be recognised. The presumptive father was asserting his right to consent in order to uphold his claim to be father. The case is no authority for the proposition that the presumptive father has the right to consent on behalf of the child in order to deny that he is the father (and therefore to deny that he has the right to consent). In *Imre v. Mitchell*[74] a married woman was attempting to bastardise her child, and it was held that she could not rely on her husband's consent to blood tests[75] for the child when the purpose was to establish that the husband was not the father. This decision was cited with apparent approval by Lord Emslie in *Docherty v. McGlynn*, who described the result as follows: "The pursuer in *Imre's* case, who sought to establish that Mitchell was not the child's father, could not at the same time be heard to assert that Mitchell, as the child's father, was entitled to consent to the sampling and testing of the child's blood."[76] This would suggest that a presumptive father who raises an action of declarator of non-parentage cannot use his presumptive rights in order to acquire evidence to back up his case. Thomson disagrees with this conclusion,[77] and submits that until the presumption of paternity is rebutted, all the rights that flow from that presumption can be exercised by the presumptive father. Though not addressing themselves to this particular point, all three judges in *Docherty* do emphasise that the responsibilities and rights flowing from the presumption apply unless and until it is displaced.[78] *Imre* was not a case in which the presumptive father's capacity to consent was directly in issue, but rather involved the competency of leading evidence already obtained through that consent; and it is suggested that an analysis of the issue in terms of the competency of evidence cannot give a general rule. Rather, it should be accepted that the very point of the presumption of paternity is to allow parental rights to be exercised even when the truth is not unequivocally established: no one would deny that, even during the course of an action to deny his paternity, a presumptive father who raised the action could nevertheless consent to necessary medical treatment of the child. There is a logical consistency in holding that the man presumed father has the parental right to consent until it is proved that another man has that right. Even if the issue is correctly one of the competency of evidence, to hold a presumptive father personally barred from leading evidence derived from consent to the testing of the child could have the effect of denying to the court evidence that is now conclusive. If the action were decided in the absence of such evidence, there might remain a doubt in the parties' minds: the judges of the First Division in *Docherty* were strongly of the view that it would not be in the best interests of the child for such a doubt to remain.[79] It is therefore submitted that the parental right to consent on behalf of a child can be exercised by a presumptive father even in the course of an action he raises to establish that he is not, in fact, the father. This conclusion is, however, difficult to reconcile with *Imre* and the dicta approving it in *Docherty*. It should be noted that in most cases the mother's consent will be competent and available (in *Docherty* the mother had died).

Consent of the court

3.66   Section 6(3) of the 1986 Act gives the court the power to consent to the taking of a sample of blood or other body fluid or of body tissue from a person who is incapable

---

[73] 1983 S.L.T. 645.
[74] 1958 S.C. 439.
[75] At that time she herself had no right to consent.
[76] 1983 S.L.T. 645 at 648.
[77] (3rd ed.), p. 157.
[78] *per* Lord President Emslie at 647, Lord Cameron at 650, and Lord Grieve at 651.
[79] *per* Lord President Emslie at 649, and Lord Cameron at 650.

of giving consent, this in two situations: (a) where there is no person who is entitled to give consent, and (b) where there is a person entitled to give consent but it is not reasonably practicable to obtain his or her consent in the circumstances, or he or she is unwilling to accept the responsibility of giving or withholding consent. These provisions do not permit the court to authorise the taking of samples in the face of parental refusal. Paragraph (a) will cover the situation where either there is no one able to consent on behalf of the child under 16, or a person over 16 is mentally disabled and thus unable to give personal consent: no one could give consent on the basis of parental responsibilities and parental rights in the latter case since these will have disappeared by that age.[80] Paragraph (b) will cover the situation where the person entitled to consent on behalf of the child cannot reasonably be contacted, or that person is unwilling for the purpose stated to give consent. In any of these cases the court itself[81] may consent to the taking of the sample; but it will not do so unless it is satisfied that the taking of the sample would not be detrimental to the health of the person from whom the sample is taken.[82] It is difficult to visualise a case in which the taking of a sample for DNA analysis will prove detrimental to the health of the person from whom it is taken[83]; but the wording of the section suggests that the court cannot simply assume no harm, but must rather be positively persuaded that no harm will be suffered. The test is not the best interests or welfare of the person on whose behalf consent is being given, for that might potentially bring in economic considerations, such as rights to succession and aliment. Rather the test relates solely to the person's health (though this will presumably include mental health as well as physical health). In deciding whether to consent to the taking of blood or other body tissue, the court is not making any order relating to parental responsibilities or parental rights, nor itself exercising any parental rights. It follows that neither the welfare principle nor the no-order presumption contained in section 11(7) of the Children (Scotland) Act 1995 applies to the court's decision. If the court requires to give consent in order to discover the truth, there will in any case seldom be a clash with the child's welfare since, as stated above, it will nearly always be in the child's interests for the truth as to his or her parentage to be established. If, however, on the basis of the declarator made under section 7 of the 1986 Act, the court goes on to make an order under section 11 of the 1995 Act, the latter decision is, of course, governed by the welfare principle in section 11(7).

INTERNATIONAL ISSUES

Introduction

Until recently, international private law issues in relation to parentage (as **3.67** opposed to "legitimacy" and "illegitimacy") could hardly arise. There was no differentiation between legal systems as to the definition of "mother" or "father", for none other than those universally accepted was conceived possible.[84]

---

[80] Children (Scotland) Act 1995, s. 2(7). A curator *ad litem* to such a person has no right to consent since his or her powers are limited to the management of the action: *Cameron v. Carr's Curator ad Litem*, 1998 S.L.T. (Sh.Ct) 22. The powers of a curator *bonis* are similarly constrained. A tutor-dative, or tutor at law may, on the other hand, have the power to consent to the taking of samples from their wards if the terms of their appointment so permit.

[81] Which means the Court of Session or the sheriff court: Law Reform (Parent and Child) (Scotland) Act 1986, s. 8.

[82] *ibid.* s. 6(4).

[83] See Law Com. No 16, *Blood Tests and the Proof of Paternity in Civil Proceedings* (1968) at para. 40: "We are advised by the medical profession that there are hardly any cases where a person's state of health would make it dangerous to have a blood sample taken, though there may be cases, such as with haemophiliacs, where precautions are necessary."

[84] Except in relation to the artificial creation of a parent and child relationship through the process of adoption which leads to different, but complex, problems of international private law. See below, paras 5.40–5.65.

International private law issues might of course, and still may, arise in relation to the consequences of the parent-child relationship and, in so far as they do, such issues are dealt with elsewhere in this work. Legal systems might differ as to the methods of establishing the fact of parentage, but such conflicts affect only questions of proof which are peculiarly within the province of the *lex fori*. That too is still the law, and so Scottish rules of evidence apply to any action of declarator of parentage or non-parentage raised in the Scottish court under section 7 of the Law Reform (Parent and Child) (Scotland) Act 1986[85] and the pursuer must comply with the Scottish requirements for proof and can rely upon the Scottish presumptions contained in section 5 of that Act, notwithstanding that both the child and the alleged parent are domiciled and habitually resident elsewhere and nationals of a foreign country.

Since the development of the reproductive technologies with which the Human Fertilisation and Embryology Act 1990 is concerned, it is now possible for true international private law issues to arise in relation to the determination of parentage, for different legal systems may define the parents of a child born as a result of such techniques differently from the definitions given in the 1990 Act. For example, section 27 of that Act deems the woman who carries a child to be that child's mother, rather than, if different, the woman whose egg was used to bring about the pregnancy.[86] Similarly, section 28(2) provides that where a woman's husband consents to her artificial insemination with the sperm of a donor, that man rather than the donor of the sperm will be deemed to be the father of the child.[87] Other legal systems may define "mother" and "father" in all circumstances as the providers of the genetic material. If the child or parent is domiciled in, habitually resident in, or a national of such other country, the question arises as to which law determines parentage.

3.68   The issue is not directly dealt with in the Human Fertilisation and Embryology Act 1990, except to provide[88] that the rules determining parentage apply whether the infertility treatment is given in the United Kingdom or elsewhere, but they do, of course, only apply when that Act applies, which begs the question. Parentage can be seen either as a matter of the child's status, or as a matter of the relationship between two individuals, and the international private law answer differs depending upon which approach to this issue is taken. There is, of course, no common law authority directly in point one way or the other. What follows is therefore based on principle and analogous authorities and is necessarily somewhat tentative in character.

A question of status?

3.69   Although at common law "an action of affiliation and aliment is essentially, under the affiliation head, of a declaratory nature",[89] it was, unlike a declarator of "legitimacy" or "illegitimacy", not determinative of status[90]—the declaratory crave if used (and it was not necessary[91]) being merely a preliminary to the pecuniary crave for a debt due in respect of a confessedly "illegitimate" child. It has nonetheless some of the elements of an action to determine status.[92] At common law occasion could scarcely arise for a bare declarator of parentage or non-parentage; for such a declarator, cases of affiliation of "illegitimate" children apart, must necessarily have raised and been inextricably identified with

---

[85] The jurisdictional requirements are described above, para. 3.46.
[86] Above, paras 3.49–3.66.
[87] Above, para. 3.27.
[88] ss. 27(3) and 28(8).
[89] Walker, *Civil Remedies*, p. 121.
[90] *McDonald v. Ross*, 1929 S.C. 240; *Silver v. Walker*, 1938 S.C. 595.
[91] *Silver v. Walker*, above.
[92] *Hepburn v. Tait* (1874) 1 R. 875, *per* Lord Neaves at 878; *McDonald v. Ross*, 1929 S.C. 240, *per* Lord Sands at 248.

questions of "legitimacy" and "illegitimacy". There is some attraction in likening the modern declarators of parentage and non-parentage introduced by the Law Reform (Parent and Child) (Scotland) Act 1986[93] to the declaratory crave of an action of affiliation and aliment and so divorcing it from questions of status. If status is "the legal standing or position of a person determined by his membership of some class of persons legally enjoying certain rights or subject to certain limitations",[94] the relationship of parent and child cannot readily be treated as a status in that sense. If one speaks of the "status" of "child of a particular person" in this context it is merely to use a relative term fixing a relationship between two parties and not to use "status" in the sense of fixing the child in a particular legal category.[95] The scheme of the 1986 Act is, however, to assimilate declarators of parentage and non-parentage to declarators of legitimacy, legitimation and illegitimacy.[96] It is difficult (though not, perhaps, impossible) to read the Act in a sense which would admit of the latter being, as is indisputable, concerned with status while the former are not. A similar conclusion is indicated by the relevant provisions of the Civil Evidence (Scotland) Act 1988.[97] And the relevant sections of the Human Fertilisation and Embryology Act 1990 (that is, sections 27 to 30) appear under the headnote "Status". The policy of modern statute seems, therefore, to be to regard parentage as an aspect of status. That consists with the common law under which, as already noticed, parentage is, except in questions of aliment for a confessedly "illegitimate" child, inextricably connected with status. Moreover, both custody[98] and adoption[99] of children have been said on high authority to affect status. If that is so, then questions of parentage, which by their nature are of a more fundamental character than was custody and no less so than is adoption, must also affect status. On the other hand, residence (which in the modern law has replaced custody) is unlikely to be regarded as a matter of status: this might suggest that parentage is today more a matter of relationship (with residence being an incident thereof) than of status. And there are other arguments too against regarding parentage as a matter of status rather than of relationship.[1] If a matter of status, it must be the status of two individuals, the parent and the child, that is in issue, and if status is referred to the (different) domicile of each then the situation might arise that one individual is recognised by their own law as "parent" while the other individual is not recognised by their own law as the "child". The analogy with "legitimacy" is not exact, for that directly concerns the child and only indirectly affect the legal position of the parents. Parentage on the other hand directly affects both the parent and the child. While the essence of status is an individual's membership of a class, parentage points to a relationship between two individuals. A closer analogy than "legitimacy" might well be the relationship of husband and wife. The married state affects a person's status but the major incidents which require recognition concern the relationship between the spouses. And there is an inherent illogicality in regarding parentage as a matter of status. Status is determined by the individual's domicile; an individual's domicile of origin is determined by his or her parentage—parentage, in other words, must be identified before a child's status can be determined and so cannot be determined by that status. Nevertheless, that or any other illogicality cannot stand in the way in attributing parentage to a child.

---

[93] s. 7.

[94] *Shorter Oxford English Dictionary.*

[95] *McDonald v. Ross*, 1929 S.C. 240, *per* Lord Sands at 248.

[96] See s. 7.

[97] s. 8.

[98] *Kitson v. Kitson*, 1945 S.C. 434, *per* Lord Justice-Clerk Cooper at 439.

[99] *J and J v. C's Tutor*, 1948 S.C. 636, *per* Lord President Cooper at 642.

[1] For a full discussion, see Norrie, "Reproductive Technology, Transsexualism and Homosexuality: New Problems for International Private Law" (1994) 43 I.C.L.Q. 757, especially at pp. 761–764.

Status determined by domicile

3.70   A consequence of the view that parentage is a matter of status is that it is to be determined by the law of the domicile of the person whose status is in question as his or her personal law. In matters of parentage the appropriate time for ascertainment of that domicile must be the birth of the child. That raises the problem that in any case of parentage the status of several persons, for example the genetic mother the gestational mother and the child, may be in issue and their domiciles may not coincide. The solution to that problem, it is submitted, is to treat the status of the child as the matter of primary concern and apply the law of his or her domicile. If, however, the domicile of the child turns on the disputed question of parentage, a further problem emerges of how the child's domicile is to be ascertained.

3.71   A practical solution may be achieved by applying the law of Scotland where (1) one of the putative parents is a person to whom the law of Scotland would ascribe parentage, (2) that person was domiciled in Scotland at the time of the child's birth, and (3) the child's domicile would, if parentage were so ascribed, also be Scottish. That can be justified on the ground that the *lex fori* is to be preferred unless a sufficient cause is shown for displacing it. But the problem remains of what is to be done where the law of Scotland is not a potentially applicable system in the sense just considered. It is submitted that in that situation, and perhaps in others, the appropriate course is to apply the potentially applicable system with which the child has the closest connection. A "closest connection" test has been suggested in connection with proposals for reform of the law on domicile of origin.[2] While reform of the law of domicile on these lines may be a matter for legislation rather than judicial decision, there is no bar to developing by judicial decision a "closest connection" test, in a hitherto uncharted field, where a person's domicile cannot be ascertained. Such a test is attended with some uncertainties, and presumptions which could in some contexts be used to resolve these uncertainties may not be available in this, but it is better to address these uncertainties case by case than to adopt an arbitrary solution to an otherwise insoluble problem.

Parentage as an incidental question

3.72   The peculiar difficulties of choice of law in questions of parentage need arise only when parentage has to be considered independently of any other issue. Where a question of parentage arises incidentally to another issue, these difficulties are elided by determining parentage according to the law governing the main issue.[3]

3.73   The problem whether an "incidental question" is to be determined by the same law as governs the main question, or by the law indicated by the conflicts rule governing the question as if it had arisen independently, is a well-known dilemma in international private law.[4] However that dilemma is to be resolved in other contexts, it is suggested that in this context the proper approach is to regard the *lex causae* as determinative of parentage arising as an incidental

---

[2] Law Commissions' *Report on Domicile*, at paras 4.14–4.20.

[3] Indeed it is probable that in the majority of cases parentage will not be a relevant issue. In any aspect of the upbringing of the child the paramount consideration is the welfare of the child, and only rarely will welfare depend upon discovering parentage. See for example *Re W (Minors) (Surrogacy)* [1991] 1 F.L.R. 385 in which it was held unnecessary to determine parentage in a case in which an injunction against publicity was sought, and *Re L (A Minor) (Blood Tests)* [1996] 2 F.C.R. 649 in which the Court of Appeal held that it was unnecessary to determine parentage in order to determine whether the mother's ex-husband should be allowed contact with the child.

[4] See Anton and Beaumont, pp. 85–89; Morris, *The Conflict of Law* (3rd ed.), pp. 489–492; Cheshire and North, *Private International Law* (11th ed.), pp. 53–56.

question. This produces some anomalies, perhaps more apparent than real—for example, that a person can be a parent for some purposes but not for others, or that a person can have different parents according to the issue which arises— but can be justified on the grounds that parentage will most commonly arise as an incidental question rather than independently, that this will normally satisfy the expectations of the parties, and that, as Anton and Beaumont put it,[5] the rules of the *lex causae* derive from the system with which the facts as a whole are likely to be most closely connected.

Practical examples

There are at least two areas in which parentage can readily be envisaged to **3.74** arise as incidental questions. The first is succession. Consider the situation of a man dying intestate, domiciled in a state which *ex hypothesi* retains the rule that paternity is determined purely genetically.[6] He was the identified donor of sperm which, through artificial insemination, led to the conception and birth of a child now living in Scotland; there is moveable property in the estate in Scotland. The child claims a right of succession. At first the child may be met with the argument that by section 28(2) of the Human Fertilisation and Embryology Act 1990 his mother's husband is to be treated as his father "for all purposes,"[7] and that "no other person is to be treated as the father of the child,"[8] this "for any purpose".[9] Additionally it may be argued against the child's claim that section 28(8) provides that "this section applies whether the woman was in the United Kingdom or elsewhere at the time of the infertility treatment". However, such reasoning is predicated upon the false assumption that the 1990 Act applies to all questions within its ambit which come before a Scottish court, no matter how these questions arise. This, it is suggested, is not so. The 1990 Act is applicable only when Scots law or Northern Irish law or English law governs the issue before the court: the rules contained therein are substantive rather than procedural. When an issue of intestate succession to moveable property is before the court, that issue is determined by the law of the deceased's last domicile and that legal system, rather than the law of the forum, should govern the issue of paternity. It would follow in the example postulated that the child would have a right of succession even in the estate of a person who, by our law, is not his or her father (and, it must be accepted, would have a further right of succession in the estate of the person who is, by our law, his or her father if Scots law governed that man's succession).[10]

A second example relates to the law of marriage. If X wishes to marry Y, he **3.75** cannot do so in Scotland if Y is the daughter of his sister (*i.e.* if Y is his niece).[11] However, if X and Y are both domiciled in a country whose definition of parentage results in there being no uncle–niece relationship, and they marry there, then the marriage will be recognised in Scotland.[12] It is nothing to the point that the application of the rules in the Human Fertilisation and Embryology Act 1990 would bring the parties within the forbidden degrees, because Scots law does not govern the question of essential validity of that marriage. The international private law rule on recognition of marriage is applied, rather than a domestic rule relating to parentage.

---

[5] *op. cit.*, p. 89.

[6] The rule which, of course, applied in Scotland before the coming into force of s. 28 of the Human Fertilisation and Embryology Act 1990.

[7] Human Fertilisation and Embryology Act 1990, s. 29(1).

[8] *ibid.* s. 28(4).

[9] *ibid.* s. 29(2).

[10] A further example, relating to succession to immoveable property, is given above, para. 3.11.

[11] Marriage (Scotland) Act 1977, s. 2(1) and Sched. 1.

[12] Public policy could prevent the recognition of some marriages, such as, perhaps, those between what domestic law would consider father and daughter.

Recognition of foreign decrees

3.76   Scots law allows a party to ask the court for a declarator of parentage or non-parentage,[13] but this is not, it is submitted, the only means by which the Scottish court will recognise parentage. If the relationship has been established or recognised by judicial decree from a foreign country, recognition in this country must be governed by the common law principles for the recognition of decrees affecting status, there being no statutory rules in point. These principles would indicate recognition of decrees of foreign courts which would have jurisdiction on grounds similar to those on which Scottish courts assert jurisdiction whether or not the foreign court actually exercised jurisdiction on these grounds[14]—*i.e.* that the child was born within the territorial jurisdiction of the forum, or the alleged or presumed parent or the child was domiciled there when the action was brought or had been habitually resident there for not less than a year immediately preceding the bringing of the action, or, in the case of a parent or child dying before the bringing of the action, had been so domiciled or resident at the date of death.[15] A case can also be made for recognising the decrees of courts with whose jurisdiction the child or putative parent had a close connection.[16] Recognition of a relationship of parent and child said to exist in the absence of a judicial decree is in reality a question of determining status, which is considered above.[17]

---

[13] Law Reform (Parent and Child) (Scotland) Act 1986, s. 7(1).
[14] *cf.* below, paras 5.47–5.52.
[15] Law Reform (Parent and Child) (Scotland) Act 1986, s. 7(2).
[16] See above, para. 3.73.
[17] Above, paras 3.69–3.71.

CHAPTER 4

ADOPTION OF CHILDREN

INTRODUCTORY

History of adoption in Scotland

Before the Adoption of Children (Scotland) Act 1930 there was no legally **4.01** secured means by which, during the lifetime of the father of a legitimate, or the mother of an illegitimate, child the role of parent in relation to the child could be undertaken permanently by someone else. Informal arrangements by which relatives or others took a child into their care and acted as substitute parents were not uncommon and, where they were intended to be permanent, that intention may often, in fact, have been respected. However, an intention of permanency, even if expressed in the most solemn and apparently binding terms, lacked legal sanction. These arrangements were in principle revocable and the natural parents could at any time reassert their parental rights, including, in the case of a pupil child, the right to custody.[1] This lack of any equivalent in Scots law for the Roman law *adoptio* or *adrogatio* has sometimes been thought remarkable in a system which has been heavily influenced by Roman law institutions. The omission is, however, consistent with other legal systems within the Civil law tradition. Adoption was not in use in the Roman-Dutch law[2] which was the principal vehicle for the mediation of the Civil to Scots law during its formative period and it was virtually unknown to pre-Napoleonic French law even within the *pays de droit ecrit*.[3] Moreover, in the Civil law tradition, including modern systems into which adoption has been introduced, adoption was until quite recent times seen principally as a means of providing heirs and thereby overcoming some of the consequences of the restraints on freedom of testation typical of the Civil law.[4] Although Scots law is closer to the Civil law than is the law of England in the restraints that it imposes on freedom of testation, none of these restraints is of a kind that gives rise to the need for adoption

---

[1] *Kerrigan v. Hall* (1901) 4 F. 10; *Macpherson v. Leishman* (1887) 14 R. 780, *per* Lord President Inglis at 782. *Cf. Humphreys v. Polak* [1901] 2 K.B. 385. Even at common law, however, the court would not order redelivery of the child where to do so would involve serious danger to his or her health or morals (*Sutherland v. Taylor* (1887) 15 R. 224; *Mackenzie v. Keillor* (1892) 19 R. 963; *Campbell v. Croall* (1895) 22 R. 869; *Alexander v. McGarrity* (1903) 5 F. 654; *Mitchell* (1903) 43 S.L.R. 429), and a parent's claim might be weakened if the child had been abandoned to the care of others (*Harvey v. Harvey* (1860) 22 D. 1198). The revocability of arrangements entrusting children to the care of persons other than the parents is, short of adoption, still true today, but where a child has been for a long time in the care of someone other than his or her parents the effect of modern statute is to present much more formidable obstacles to recovery by parents than existed at common law (see, for example, *J v. C* [1970] A.C. 668; *Osborne v. Matthan (No. 2)*, 1998 S.L.T. 1264).

[2] Grotius, *Jurisprudence of Holland*, I, vi, 1; Voet 1, vii, 7.

[3] Amos and Walton, *Introduction to French Law* (3rd ed.) p. 78; Dickson, *Introduction to French Law* (1994), p. 225.

[4] In France the *Code Civile*, in its original form, recognised adoption only of adults, and it is only since 1923 that adoption of children has been permitted: Dickson, *op. cit.*

as a means of ameliorating its effects[5]; and when adoption was eventually introduced by statute it had, until the Succession (Scotland) Act 1964, practically no consequences in the law of succession. More remarkable than any departure from Roman law roots is that the prevalence and antiquity of fostering in Scotland did not give rise to any recognition at common law of the custodial rights of foster carers or of the need for at least some degree of permanency in *de facto* adoptions. The introduction of adoption by the Adoption of Children (Scotland) Act 1930 was a radical statutory innovation.

4.02   Changes in the law subsequent to the 1930 Act were consolidated in the Adoption Act 1950 which was in turn replaced by the Adoption Act 1958. The 1958 Act comprehended at the time it was passed practically all the statute law applicable to adoption but additions and amendments were made, in respect of the revocation of adoption orders in the event of legitimation, by the Adoption Act 1960 and the Legitimation (Scotland) Act 1968,[6] and, in respect of certain international questions of adoption, by the Adoption Acts 1964 and 1968. The most important changes effected since 1958 were, however, those contained in the Children Act 1975 by which large parts, but not all, of the 1958 Act were repealed. The whole of the 1958 Act and the relevant Part of the 1975 Act were themselves repealed by the Adoption (Scotland) Act 1978[7] which, as subsequently amended (in particular by Part III of and Schedule 2 to the Children (Scotland) Act 1995), now contains most of the law of adoption in Scotland.[8]

Legal character of adoption

4.03   It is a common feature of the present statutory provisions and their predecessors that adoption involves a radical divestiture of the responsibilities, rights, duties, powers, interests and obligations of the biological parents brought about by operation of law in favour of the adoptive parents. The status of the child and his or her rights and obligations are also thereby affected. A new relationship of parent and child is created which, for practically all legal purposes, replaces the previous relationship. As Lord President Cooper said in *J and J v. C's Tutor*:

> "The Adoption of Children (Scotland) Act 1930 made a serious innovation upon the common law by introducing a novel institution which can not easily be fitted into its setting... The chief elements of the previously inalienable *patria potestas* were made assignable—not by a contract between natural parent and adopter, but by an act of the adopter authorised by the court. All that is required from the natural parent is his consent, and even that consent may be dispensed with."[9]

Adoption is, therefore, not a matter of contract but an act of law.

---

[5]   The testamentary incapacity of bastards had, so long as it subsisted, other remedies, and the rule that heritage could not be the subject of a proper testament could be overcome by the use of a disposition to take effect on death (see Erskine, III, viii, 20). The most important restriction of Scots law on freedom of testation is that constituted by the legal rights of spouses and children. Adoption can and does affect the distribution of the bairns' part in that it brings in a stranger to the rateable prejudice of the children and so to that limited extent may be seen as a possible means of reducing the effects of restriction on the freedom of testation. In addition, if a childless couple adopt a child, a right to legitim is thereby created at the expense of the *jus relicti* or *jus relictae* as well as of the dead's part available for testamentary disposal.

[6]   See above, para. 1.57.

[7]   Adoption (Scotland) Act 1978, Sched. 4. References in this chapter are to this Act, unless otherwise stated.

[8]   The Adoption (Scotland) Act 1978 was brought into force on September 1, 1984 by the Adoption (Scotland) Act 1978 Commencement Order 1984 (S.I. 1984 No. 1050). The 1995 amendments came into force on April 1, 1997.

[9]   1948 S.C. 637 at 641–642.

Competency of revocation

The statutory purpose is that adoption should be permanent and invariable, **4.04** and this differentiates it from, for example, relationships regulated or created by a residence order.[10] It has been described as irrevocable. There are, however, limited circumstances in which specific provision is made for the revocation or supersession of an adoption order.

First, an adoption order may be made notwithstanding that the child is already **4.05** an adopted child,[11] and so an existing adoption order may be effectively superseded by a later order. Secondly, an adoption order made in favour of one natural parent may be revoked by the court which made it if that parent subsequently marries the other natural parent.[12] So too an adoption order in favour of both natural parents, made before the commencement of the Legitimation (Scotland) Act 1968, in respect of a child legitimated by virtue of the terms of that Act, may be revoked.[13] Thirdly, there are special rules (discussed later[14]) for the annulment of overseas adoptions. It is undecided whether these statutory provisions and the ordinary provisions for review, by appeal or reclaiming motion, within the prescribed time-limits, exhaust the means by which an adoption order, once made, can be set aside.

A court order might, in Scotland, be set aside in an action for reduction. It **4.06** has, however, been held that reduction is not open at the instance of adopters who allege essential error or misrepresentation as to the health, physical state or other qualities of the child.[15] It is thought that that will be the case even if the misrepresentation is deliberate. Indeed, any ground that treats adoption as essentially a contract between the natural parents and the adopters will be excluded, for that is to mistake the nature of adoption. Nor will reduction be open where adopters allege a neglect of the statutory prerequisites for the making of an order.[16] That may give a ground of appeal against the order, but not, once the time limits for appeal have passed, a ground of reduction of the decree. However, "the right of review by reduction is", it has been said, "a common law right which has existed for a very long time, and is a mode of review which cannot be taken away except by statutory enactment",[17] and that right will not readily be held to have been taken away by implication.[18] There is no express statutory exclusion of reduction in relation to adoption and no ground on which such exclusion can be said to be necessarily implied. Yet the unique character of adoption proceedings, including the fact that the process of investigation and certification proceeds largely, and in many cases entirely, at the court's own hand, may point to a severe limitation of the grounds on which reduction will

---

[10] *F v. F*, 1991 S.L.T. 357, *per* Lord President Hope at 360E; *C v. S*, 1996 S.L.T. 1387, *per* Lord President Hope at 1395E–G; *D v. Grampain Regional Council*, 1995 S.C. (H.L.) 1.

[11] s. 12(7).

[12] s. 46(1). And see Act of Sederunt (Child Care and Maintenance Rules) 1997 (S.I. 1997 No. 291), r. 2.35.

[13] Legitimation (Scotland) Act 1968, s. 6. The natural parents must at the time of adoption have been married to each other because only the parties to a marriage can adopt jointly. On this issue, see further, the 1st edition of this book at pp. 23–24.

[14] Below, para. 5.43.

[15] *J and J v. C's Tutor*, 1948 S.C. 636. In this case the pursuers sought reduction of an adoption order which they had obtained three years previously on the basis that they had adopted the child under essential error, as to the child's physical condition, induced by the innocent misrepresentation of the adoption agency. The child, who was three months old when adopted, was suffering from brain damage, sustained at birth.

[16] *J and J v. C's Tutor*, above.

[17] *Mathewson v. Yeaman* (1900) 2 F. 873, *per* Lord Trayner at 881.

[18] *Marr & Sons v. Lindsay* (1881) 8 R. 784, *per* Lord President Inglis at 785; *Mathewson v. Yeaman*, above, *per* Lord Justice-Clerk Macdonald at 880.

be entertained, and perhaps to its virtual exclusion. Considerations appropriate to adversarial procedure are not apt to an inquisitorial procedure which, moreover, must turn on the welfare of the child rather than on issues of a kind properly justiciable between parties such as arise in most other types of case. The matter has been discussed in a number of English cases, though these must be read in the light of the different procedural requirements pertaining in that jurisdiction. In *Skinner v. Carter*[19] doubts were expressed by the Court of Appeal as to whether there were any appropriate proceedings in which an adoption order could be set aside, but in subsequent English cases a remedy has been allowed. Certiorari issued in *R. v. Leeds City Justices, ex parte Gilmartin*[20] to quash an adoption order on grounds of procedural irregularity (the concealment of the father's address and the consequent failure to notify him of the proceedings[21]) and in *R. v. Liverpool City Justices, ex parte W*[22] on the ground that the statutory provisions had not been properly considered by the justices making the order. So too in *Re F (R) (An Infant)*[23], *Re RA (Minors)*[24] and *Re F (Infants) (Adoption Order: Validity)*[25] adoption orders were set aside by reason of a failure to effect proper service of the adoption proceedings on a natural parent or by reason of ignorance on the part of the natural parent of the existence of adoption proceedings.[26] In *Re M (Minors) (Adoption)*[27] a father had consented to the adoption of his two daughters by the new husband of the girls' mother. Unknown to him, the mother was at that time suffering from terminal cancer and she died three months after the adoption. The step-father found himself unable to care for the girls adequately and the father, now remarried, resumed the care of his daughters. He then sought leave to appeal out of time against the making of the adoption orders, and this was granted by the Court of Appeal on the ground that his ignorance of the mother's health vitiated his agreement to the adoption orders. All these cases were raised by the natural parent of the adopted child.[28] There is, however, a significant difference between a power of the court to grant leave to appeal out of time to the natural parent (and thereafter to follow the normal appeal procedures) and a general jurisdiction to set aside, at the behest of the adoptive parents,[29] an adoption order validly made and not challenged by appeal while the right to do so was still open. There is nothing in these English cases which suggests that such a general jurisdiction exists.

4.07   The issue was raised in stark form in the leading case of *Re B (Adoption Order: Jurisdiction to Set Aside)*.[30] Here a child born in 1959 to an English mother and a Muslim Arab father was adopted by an Orthodox Jewish couple, they having been informed that the boy was Jewish. After the deaths of the adoptive parents, and some 35 years after the adoption order had been made, the adopted person sought to have the order set aside. The Court of Appeal,

---

[19] [1948] Ch. 387.

[20] [1951] C.L.Y. 1629.

[21] These were the grounds for that decision according to Simon Brown L.J. in *Re B (Adoption Order: Jurisdiction to Set Aside)* [1995] 3 All E.R. 333 at 342.

[22] [1959] 1 All E.R. 337.

[23] [1969] 3 W.L.R. 853.

[24] [1974] 4 Fam. Law 182.

[25] [1977] 2 All E.R. 737.

[26] See also *Re T (A Minor) (Adoption Order: Leave to Appeal)* [1995] 3 F.C.R. 299.

[27] [1991] 1 F.L.R. 458.

[28] A similar conclusion was reached in *Re K (Adoption and Wardship)* [1997] 2 F.L.R. 221 in which a young child orphaned in the Bosnian war was rescued, brought to England and fostered there. The foster carers then adopted the child without any opportunity being given to the child's surviving relatives to recover the child. Leave to appeal out of time was granted to such relatives, and the appeal was upheld.

[29] Who, of course, have no right to appeal against the order they themselves sought.

[30] [1995] 3 All E.R. 333.

following *J and J v. C's Tutor*, held that the court had no inherent power to set aside an adoption order which had been regularly made in accordance with the proper procedure, by reason of a misapprehension or a mistake by the parties as to the race, ethnic origin or religion of the natural parent of the child. Swinton Thomas L.J. distinguished *Re M (Minors) (Adoption)* not only because that case involved an application for leave to appeal out of time rather than a question of general jurisdiction but also on the ground that a mistake or misapprehension as to the race or ethnic origin or parental religion of the natural parents or the child could not amount to a circumstance which would vitiate a consent otherwise freely given.[31] Nevertheless the Court of Appeal did not close the door entirely to setting aside an adoption order once made,[32] and the following propositions may be gleaned from the judgments. First, if the proceedings in which the adoption order was made were so irregular as to amount to a denial of justice (such as an exclusion from the proceedings of the natural parents) then the order might well be set aside.[33] Secondly, if a necessary consent obtained is vitiated by a relevant misapprehension then, so long as it is in the best interests of the adopted child to do so, the order may in exceptional circumstances be set aside[34]; it is not, however, possible for the applicant to rely upon the misapprehensions of the adopters. Thirdly, an adoption order obtained by fraud might be vulnerable to attack.[35] It is unclear whether these propositions were made only in relation to justifying when leave to appeal out of time would be granted, or whether they recognise a general jurisdiction to set aside or, in Scottish terms, to reduce, an adoption order; but if such jurisdiction exists it is submitted that these propositions will be necessary limitations to its exercise and may well be taken to set out the only circumstances in which an application might be successful.

Some assistance may be obtained from the legislation in jurisdictions which **4.08** deal with this problem by specific enactment. In Australia discharge of adoption orders is a matter of express statutory provision in all the States and Territories[36] on the ground that the adoption order, or consent required thereto, was obtained by fraud, duress or other improper reason, or that there is some other exceptional reason why the adoption order should be discharged.[37] In New Zealand an adoption order can be discharged on the basis that it was "made by a mistake as to a material fact or in consequence of a material misrepresentation to the Court or to any person concerned".[38] There are similar provisions in the legislation in some jurisdictions in the United States[39], though in *Allan v. Allan*[40] the Oregon Supreme Court held, in a case in which the adoption agency had allegedly fraudulently failed to notify the adopters of the adopted child's mental condition, that courts in Oregon did not, in the absence of any statutory provision analogous to that in other states, have jurisdiction to annul adoption decrees, and this has

---

[31] [1995] 3 All E.R. at 339E–G.

[32] Swinton Thomas L.J. went no further than to say that "there is no inherent power in the courts *in circumstances such as arise in this case*" (at 341B).

[33] *per* Swinton Thomas L.J. at 338A–B.

[34] *per* Swinton Thomas L.J. at 340J–341B.

[35] *per* Sir Thomas Bingham M.R., at 344C. Swinton Thomas L.J. expressed no opinion on this point other than that it "was not a subject which was relevant to the present appeal", at 338B.

[36] See Adoption of Children Act 1964 (Qld), s. 16; Adoption of Children Act 1965 (N.S.W.), s. 25; Adoption Act 1984 (Vict.), s. 19; Adoption Act 1988 (S.A.), s. 14; Adoption Act 1988 (Tas.), s. 28; Adoption Act 1993 (ACT), s. 26; Adoption Act 1994 (W.A.), s. 9; Adoption of Children Act 1994 (N.T.), s.18.

[37] In the legislation in Victoria and Tasmania it is expressly provided that "some other exceptional reason" or "special circumstances" includes a reference to an irretrievable breakdown in the relationship between the adoptive parents and the adopted child; in the ACT the legislation expressly excludes this from circumstances justifying discharge.

[38] Adoption Act 1955, s. 20(3)(a).

[39] See Note, "When Love is Not Enough: Towards a Unified Wrongful Adoption Tort" (1992) 105 Harv.L.Rev. 1761 at 1766.

[40] 330 P. (2d) 151 (1958).

been the approach of most U.S. jurisdictions which lack express revocation provisions.[41] In the adoption legislation in Scotland and England there has never been express provision except for the limited purposes described above, and this might be taken to indicate a parliamentary intention that adoption be more permanent here than it may be in jurisdictions like Australia and New Zealand. The reasoning in *J and J v. C's Tutor*[42] requires, in any case, that a conservative view be taken of fraud and improper means as a ground of reduction where these have been exercised against the adopters.[43]

4.09   In any question of the reduction of an adoption order, whether under the court's statutory powers or otherwise, the child must be called as a party[44] and, if still under the age of 16,[45] a curator *ad litem* should be appointed. An adoption order is not, so long as it stands unreduced, a nullity because a condition essential to its making (*e.g.* that joint adopters be husband and wife) was not in fact fulfilled and, even on admitted facts, no court can disregard it on that ground.[46] The welfare of the child and also, where practicable, his or her wishes and feelings, are factors to be taken into account in all cases including cases of fraud, duress and improper means. A decision on reduction is a decision relating to the adoption of a child within the meaning of section 6 of the Adoption (Scotland) Act 1978, which requires that the court have regard to all the circumstances but shall regard the need to safeguard and promote the welfare of the child concerned throughout his or her life as the paramount consideration and shall have regard so far as practicable to his or her views and to his or her religious persuasion, racial origin and cultural and linguistic background.[47] The view of a child's welfare, taken in the Australian case of *Re S*,[48] should not, however, be followed. In that case McInerney J., on facts not materially different from those in *J and J v. C's Tutor*, held that an adoption order should be discharged as the adoptive parents were emotionally and economically unable to provide for the child and that his welfare would be better provided for if he were returned to the care of the State. That is to confuse reasons for taking a child, perhaps compulsorily, into the care of the State with reasons for the discharge of an adoption order. There is no reason why adoptive parents should, any more than natural parents, be discharged of their responsibilities merely because the child requires special care. In *Re an Adoption Application*[49] an adopted child[50] was returned to the adoption agency very shortly after the adoption order was made, due to the breakdown in the relationship of the adopters.

---

[41] See Hayes, "Sending Children Back: Efforts to Reverse Adoptions Face Strong Legal Obstacles" (1992) 78 A.B.A.Jo. 88.

[42] 1948 S.C. 636.

[43] "Why should an unexceptional adoption order be reduced merely because the applicants were misled into applying for it?": *per* Lord President Cooper at 644.

[44] *Skinner v. Carter* [1948] Ch. 387.

[45] The legislation in Queensland requires that the application for discharge be made before the child attains the age of 18: 1964 Act, s. 16(1)(a). In the absence of such a statutory limitation, the continued existence of an interest in any party to make the application would be sufficient to allow it, if competent, to be made.

[46] *Skinner v. Carter*, above. See also *Re F (Infants) (Adoption Order: Validity)* [1977] 2 W.L.R. 488 in which the Court of Appeal held voidable but not void adoption orders in favour of joint adopters whose marriage turned out to be void. The court refused to set aside the voidable adoption orders because no one had been aggrieved by them and the interests of justice would not be served by setting them aside.

[47] Although it is manifest that there are decisions relating to the adoption of a child to which such a test cannot be applied (see *Re P (An Infant) (Adoption: Parental Consent)* [1977] Fam. 25), the wide wording of the statute should not be denied effect where, as here, there is no absurdity or inconsistency in doing so.

[48] [1969] V.R. 490. See also *Re Adoption Application No. AD 58/1984* (1986) 11 Fam. L.R. 518.

[49] (1981) 7 F.L.R. 850.

[50] Who, incidentally, suffered from cerebral palsy and required constant care and attention.

The child was then placed with new prospective adopters and the Supreme Court of New South Wales held that it was in the child's interests to discharge the earlier adoption order. In Scotland that effect would be achieved in any case by the making of the second adoption order and the power of discharge is not, therefore, required to deal with this situation. It will seldom, if ever, be in a child's interests to revoke an adoption order in circumstances which will leave the child without anyone who owes him or her parental responsibilities, though the effect of revocation, in the absence of a statutory rule to the contrary, must be to restore any parental responsibilities and parental rights that had been terminated by the adoption order. A revocation will oblige the court, therefore, to ensure the child's future welfare, for example by making an order under section 11 of the Children (Scotland) Act 1995 (just as it must do on the revocation of a freeing order).[51] In *D v. Grampian Regional Council*[52] Lord Jauncey of Tullichettle said, referring to the statutory grounds for revocation, "an adoption order once made is revocable only in circumstances which will have no practical effect upon the child's day to day life".

A delictual remedy?

In the United States of America, revocation of adoption orders is, as here, not **4.10** a realistic option in most states. Nevertheless some courts there have been willing to fashion a remedy for adoptive parents misled as to the health or other attributes of the child they adopt through the so-called tort of "wrongful adoption".[53] So in *Burr v. Board of County Commissioners*[54] the Ohio Supreme Court recognised a cause of action based on the intentional misrepresentations of the adoption agency upon which the adopters relied. In *Michael J. v. Los Angeles County Department of Adoption*[55] the California Court of Appeal extended the cause of action to include cases in which there was an intentional concealment of information. And in *Meracle v. Children's Service Society*[56] the Supreme Court of Wisconsin held that an adoption agency could be liable for its negligent failure to disclose information about the child to the prospective adopters. The issue has been discussed in one Scottish case. In *M and M v. Glasgow Corporation*[57] an action for damages was raised in the sheriff court by adoptive parents whose child was discovered some years after the adoption order to be seriously and permanently brain damaged, due probably to peri–natal anoxia. The pursuers alleged that the adoption agency (the defenders) should have known of this risk and were negligent in placing the child for adoption in ignorance of the facts. The sheriff dismissed the action, holding the pursuers' averments to be irrelevant but, significantly, he did not hold the action incompetent. He held that the defenders had carried out their statutory duties and were not, therefore, negligent but that a claim might relevantly have been pleaded against a doctor who had negligently failed to diagnose the child's problems. He held further that a claim might relevantly be averred against the adoption agency if it could be shown to have "negligently ignored some medical warning in the statutory medical report that a child was medically unsuitable for placing for adoption".[58] This is unlikely to be good law. Liability in damages for "wrongful

---

[51] s. 20(3).

[52] 1995 S.C. (H.L.) 1 at 5H.

[53] See, as representative of the burgeoning and almost univerally supportive literature, Le May, "The Emergence of Wrongful Adoption as a Cause of Action" (1989) 27 J.Fam.L. 475; Note, "When Love is Not Enough: Towards a Unified Wrongful Adoption Tort" (1992) 105 Harv.L.R. 1761; Miller, "Are You Adopting a Child or a Heartache?" (1992) 26 New Eng. L.R. 1145; Bebensee, "In the Best Interests of Children and Adoptive Parents: The Need for Disclosure" (1993) 78 Iowa L.R. 397. The number of actual cases remains tiny.

[54] 491 N.E. (2d) 1101 (1986).

[55] 247 Cal. Rptr. 504 (1988).

[56] 437 N.W. (2d) 532 (1989).

[57] 1976 S.L.T. (Sh.Ct) 45.

[58] *ibid.* at 49.

adoption" is, in its fundaments, based on an understanding of adoption as being designed to confer some benefit on the adoptive parents, which the negligence or fraud denied, and for that reason alone the U.S. cases which recognise the claim are unlikely to be followed here. It ought not to be argued today that any child is "unsuitable for adoption": rather, a placement might be unsuitable for a particularly needy child and though there may be negligence in identifying a suitable placement, considerations of policy, analogous to those in *X v. Bedfordshire County Council*,[59] suggest strongly that any such negligence should not be actionable. If policy considerations are in themselves insufficient to deny liability then the lack of any legally protected interest in the adopters in receiving a child of the "quality" they expect should do so. Nevertheless there is an apparent analogy with the "wrongful birth" cases[60]: these cases are based on the denial of the opportunity to make an informed choice as to whether to commence or to continue with a pregnancy, while "wrongful adoption" cases might be analysed as a denial of the opportunity to make an informed choice as to whether to adopt a child or not. However, the peculiar character of the adoption process, emphasised by Lord President Cooper in *J and J v. C's Tutor*, particularly the investigative role played by the court itself, suggests strongly that the analogy, though superficially close, is not apt. In the wrongful birth cases, the court plays no role in investigating and authorising an act of sterilisation or abortion and the more apt analogy to adoption might well be the cases in which the court grants authority to a tutor-dative to consent to the sterilisation of women unable through mental incapacity to provide their own consent.[61] Damages in these cases would be entirely excluded. In the wrongful birth cases the negligence (generally on the part of a medical practitioner) occurs in attempting to confer some benefit on a patient (the pursuer). In adoption, the aim is to confer benefit not on the adoptive parents (who would be the pursuers) but on the child. For these reasons, any regrets that the adoptive parents have do not, it is submitted, sound in damages under the law of Scotland.

4.11   The New Zealand Court of Appeal was faced with a reverse claim in *Attorney-General v. Prince and Gardner*.[62] There the adopted child sued the adoption agency for placing him with unsuitable adopters, alleging negligence by the social workers involved in failing to identify the prospective adopters' shortcomings. The action was dismissed for policy reasons based on those in *X v. Bedfordshire County Council*, and also because to allow the claim would undermine the finality of the adoption and the integrity of the adoption order. This approach is likely—and, it is submitted, ought—to be followed in Scotland also.[63]

Effects of adoption

Restricted impact on status under earlier legislation

4.12   Although it is clear that adoption affects status it was not, until the Children Act 1975, clear what the exact nature of that impact on status was. Previous

---

59 [1995] 3 All E.R. 353.
60 *Emeh v. Kensington, Chelsea and Westminster Area Health Authority* [1984] 3 All E.R. 1044; *Thake v. Maurice* [1986] 1 All E.R. 479; *Gold v. Haringey Health Authority* [1987] 2 All E.R. 888; *MacFarlane v. Tayside Health Board*, 1998 S.L.T. 307; *Allan v. Greater Glasgow Health Board*, 1998 S.L.T. 580; *Anderson v. Forth Valley Health Board*, 1998 S.L.T. 588; *McLelland v. Greater Glasgow Health Board*, 1999 S.L.T. 543. See also *Sabri-Tabrizi v. Lothian Health Board*, 1998 S.L.T. 607.
61 See, for example, *L v. L's Curator ad Litem*, 1997 S.L.T. 167.
62 [1998] 1 N.Z.L.R. 262.
63 The English courts have held that there is no liability to a foster child who was placed with abusing foster parents: *H v. Norfolk County Council* [1997] 1 F.L.R. 384; *Barrett v. Enfield London Borough Council* [1997] 2 F.L.R. 167. *Cf.*, however, *W v. East Essex County Council* [1998] 2 F.L.R. 278 in which *X v. Bedfordshire County Council* was distinguished and damages were awarded to the children of foster carers who were not informed that the child they looked after on behalf of the local authority constituted a risk (as a sexual abuser) to their own children (the plaintiffs). It would seem that the *Bedfordshire* decision does not close the door entirely to actions for damages against local authorities in the exercise of their child care functions.

legislation had referred to the transfer of "all rights, duties, obligations and liabilities of the parent or parents in relation to the future custody, maintenance and education of the adopted child" so that they should "vest in and be exercisable by and enforceable against the adopter as though the adopted child was a child born to the adopter in lawful wedlock"[64] and had further provided that "in respect of the same matters and in respect of the liability of a child to maintain its parents" the adopted child should stand to the adopter exclusively in the position of a child born to the adopter in lawful wedlock.[65] The 1930 Act did not, but later legislation did, place the adopters and the adopted child within the forbidden degrees of relationship for marriage.[66] Later still, legislation placed the adopter and the adopted child within the forbidden degrees of relationship for the purposes of the crime of incest.[67] The equiparation of the adopted child's status to that of a legitimate child of the adopters was therefore restricted to questions of custody, maintenance, education and marriage and was, moreover, restricted to questions between adoptive parent and adopted child *inter se* and had no wider familial consequences. Questions therefore arose of whether an adopted child might correctly be described as retaining his or her original status, be that legitimate or illegitimate, subject only to some modifications resulting from his adoption, or whether he or she might more aptly be described as the legitimate child of the adopters, subject again to certain modifications, or whether he or she was the subject of some new kind of status, for example adoptive or quasi-legitimate status. All three descriptions were viable, but the first was closest to the immediate legal effects of the statutes, the second closest to common understanding, while the third represented an attempt to do justice to the essentially distinct character of adoption. The question of description was not of importance and in any doubtful practical issue it was unnecessary to do more than to echo or adopt the words of Lord Atkin in *Coventry Corporation v. Surrey County Council*[68] (on a question of construction of a statute in order to ascertain whether it affected adopters and adopted children):

> "It is only necessary to consider whether the statute purports to deal with the rights or obligations of parents or the position of a child in relation to the matters of custody, maintenance, or education. If it does the adopter has the same rights and obligations as though he were the natural parent, and the child is in the same position as though he were the legitimate child of the adopters."

There were, however, practical consequences of the restricted scope of the statutory transfer of rights and obligations. Under the original adoption legislation neither adoptive parent nor adopted child had the right to sue for damages or solatium on the death of the other, although that defect was cured by the Law Reform (Miscellaneous Provisions) (Scotland) Act 1940.[69] It seems that adoptive parents did not have the rights and duties of tutors and curators in relation to the property, contracts and legal acts of their adopted children although in practice this limitation may often have been ignored.[70] The adopted child had no

---

[64] Adoption was, therefore, a means of legitimating a child in the absence of marriage of the parents: see *D, Petr*, 1938 S.C. 223.

[65] Adoption Act 1958, s. 13(1); Adoption Act 1950, s. 10(1); Adoption of Children (Scotland) Act 1930, s. 5(1).

[66] Adoption Act 1958, s. 13(3); Adoption Act 1950, s. 10(3). See now Marriage (Scotland) Act 1977, Sched. 1.

[67] Incest and Related Offences (Scotland) Act 1986, Sched. 1(5), amending Adoption (Scotland) Act 1978, s. 41(1). See now Criminal Law (Consolidation) (Scotland) Act 1995, s. 1.

[68] [1935] A.C. 199 at 206.

[69] s. 2(1). See now Damages (Scotland) Act 1976 and Adoption (Scotland) Act 1978, s. 39(4).

[70] Somewhat anomalously, adoptive parents had the right to appoint guardians, but the rights and duties of such guardians must, it is submitted, have been construed as being confined to those which the adoptive parents themselves had enjoyed unless, perhaps, where the natural parents were dead.

obligation to aliment, nor right to be alimented by, his or her adoptive parents' ascendants. Accordingly, on the death of the adoptive parents the adopted child's only recourse for aliment was against those who were *lucrati* by their succession to the adoptive parents' estate.[71] Equally, the child's natural grandparents retained an obligation to aliment him or her and the right to claim aliment from him or her if need arose.

Status under current legislation

4.13   The anomalies of the previous law were removed by the Children Act 1975 and the current legislation, the Adoption (Scotland) Act 1978, now provides, by section 39(1),[72] that an adopted child shall be treated in law, where the adopters are a married couple or (in the case of a step-parent adoption) a sole adopter is married to a natural parent with parental responsibilities and parental rights, as if he or she had been born as a legitimate child of the marriage and, in any other case, as if he or she had been born a legitimate child of the adopter. The parental responsibilities and parental rights vested in any other person are extinguished, and the child is to be treated as if he or she were not the child of any person other than the adopter or adopters, or (in the case of a step-parent adoption) the adopter and the natural parent who is the adopter's spouse.[73] The child's previous status is thus eliminated and he or she becomes the child of the adoptive parents with all the familial consequences, including for most purposes relationship to siblings and grandparents, which flow from that. Typically, therefore, adoption substitutes new parents for the child's genetic (natural) parents and a new nexus of family relationships for the old. Where a child has been adopted by one of his or her natural parents as sole adoptive parent and the adopter thereafter marries the other natural parent, the child will be treated in law as the child of both his or her natural parents.[74]

4.14   The creation of the relationship of child and parent between adopted child and adopter is not, however, complete. The facts about the child's natural relationships are not altered so that, for example, the natural grandparents of the child retain title to seek a residence order after an order freeing the child for adoption, so long as they can claim an interest on grounds relating to the welfare of the child, and they are not disabled from doing so simply because they were previously related in law to the child.[75] Likewise, the adopter and adopted child come within the forbidden degrees of consanguinity and affinity in relation to the crime of incest and for the purposes of marriage[76]; but the adopted child is not brought within the forbidden degrees with any other adoptive relative. In other words, an adopted child may not marry nor have sexual intercourse with the adoptive parent, but may (in the absence of any other legal prohibition) do so with any of that parent's natural relatives.[77] The adopted child remains within the forbidden degrees in relation to his or her natural parents and other relatives.[78]

---

[71] See *Hutchison v. Hutchison's Trs*, 1951 S.C. 108.

[72] As amended by s. 97(3) of the Children (Scotland) Act 1995.

[73] Adoption (Scotland) Act 1978, s. 39(1).

[74] *ibid.* s. 39(2).

[75] *F v. F*, 1991 S.L.T. 357, *per* Lord President Hope at 361–362. The natural parent, on the other hand, will be barred from seeking any order under s. 11 of the Children (Scotland) Act 1995 after an adoption order or a freeing order has been made: 1995 Act, s. 11(3) and (4)(a) and (b). See also, in relation to the pre-1995 law, *D v. Grampian Regional Council*, 1995 S.C. (H.L.) 1.

[76] Marriage (Scotland) Act 1977, Sched. 3, as amended by the Marriage (Prohibited Degrees of Relationship) Act 1986, Sched. 2; Adoption (Scotland) Act 1978, s. 41, as amended by the Incest and Related Offences (Scotland) Act 1986, Sched. 1, para. 5.

[77] See further, Norrie, "Incest and the Forbidden Degrees of Marriage in Scots Law" (1992) 37 J.L.S.S. 216.

[78] Adoption (Scotland) Act 1978, s. 41(1).

Also, the operation of the British Nationality Act 1981, the Immigration Act 1971, instruments having effect under either, and any other laws determining British citizenship, British Dependent Territories citizenship, the status of a British National (Overseas) or British Overseas citizenship, is unaffected by the status conferred by section 39.[79] However, by section 1(5) and (6) of the British Nationality Act 1981, an adopted child who is not a British citizen acquires British citizenship if that is the citizenship of the adopter or, in the case of joint adoption, of one of the adopters. The child does not lose his or her British citizenship when the adoption order ceases to have effect.[80] British citizenship carries with it the right of abode in the United Kingdom.[81] Citizenship is conferred on an adopted person only if adopted as a "minor" and not if the adoption order is made after the child's 18th birthday[82] for "minor" is defined in section 50(1) of the 1981 Act as "a person who has not attained the age of 18 years". A right of action under the Damages (Scotland) Act 1976 for the death of a natural parent that accrues before the date of the adoption order is not extinguished by the adoption, but a claim for loss of support under that statute cannot take account of any period after the adoption, since the adoptive parent's obligation of support will replace that which is lost.[83] The adoption order itself has no effect on things done or events occurring before the order was made or, in any case, before January 1, 1976.[84]

Effect on parental responsibilities and parental rights

An adoption order has the effect of vesting the parental responsibilities and **4.15** parental rights relating to a child in the adopters, except that such responsibilities and rights are not affected so far as they relate to any period before the making of the order.[85] Conversely, the order will have the effect of extinguishing parental responsibilities and parental rights which before it was made were vested in the child's parent or guardian appointed by deed or order of a court.[86] This is broad enough to cover parental responsibilities and parental rights arising from orders under section 18(5) of the 1978 Act freeing a child for adoption and transferring parental responsibilities and parental rights to an adoption agency, but in its terms would seem not to affect any parental responsibility or parental right vested in a person other than a parent or guardian (such as an unmarried father or a grandparent who has a contact order in his favour) by a section 11 order which does not amount to the conferral of guardianship: such responsibilities and rights would seem therefore to survive the adoption order unless the court makes express provision otherwise.[87] The adoption order will also extinguish any obligation owed to the child to pay or provide aliment or to make any payment arising out of parental responsibilities and parental rights, in respect of any period occurring after the making of the order.[88] However, these obligations

---

[79] s. 41(2).

[80] British Nationality Act 1981, s. 1(6). Citizenship is, however, lost if the order ceases to have effect because it is overturned on appeal: *Re K (Adoption: Non-Patrial)* [1994] 2 F.C.R. 617.

[81] Immigration Act 1971, s. 2(1)(a), as amended by s. 39(2) of the British Nationality Act 1981.

[82] As is permitted under s. 12(1) of the Adoption (Scotland) Act 1978 (as amended by the Children (Scotland) Act 1995, Sched. 2, para. 7) so long as the application is made before the person's 18th birthday.

[83] *Watson & Ors v. Willmott* [1991] 1 All E.R. 473.

[84] Adoption (Scotland) Act 1978, s. 39(4).

[85] *ibid.* s. 12(1) and (2).

[86] *ibid.* s. 12(3)(a), as amended by the Age of Legal Capacity (Scotland) Act 1991, Sched. 2.

[87] The court may make an order under s. 11 of the 1995 Act in any proceedings affecting the child, even when not requested to do so by any party: s. 11(3)(b).

[88] Adoption (Scotland) Act 1978, s. 12(3)(b).

will not be terminated where they have arisen under a deed or agreement which constitutes a trust or which expressly provides that the obligation is not to be extinguished by the making of an adoption order.[89] Also extinguished are the parental responsibilities and parental rights that were transferred to a local authority under a parental responsibilities order made under section 86 of the Children (Scotland) Act 1995.[90] The adoption order does not, however, automatically terminate any supervision requirement to which the child is subject, though the court which makes the adoption order has the power to determine that the child shall forthwith cease to be subject to that requirement on the making of the adoption order, if satisfied that, in consequence of doing so, compulsory measures of supervision in respect of the child are no longer necessary.[91] The decision to terminate a supervision requirement on adoption is "a decision relating to the adoption of a child" and is, therefore, governed by the welfare test in section 6.

Effect on succession

4.16   Until the coming into force of the Succession (Scotland) Act 1964 the questions of succession to, and of legal rights in, the estate of a deceased person were unaffected by adoption. The adopted person retained such rights of succession and the right to legitim as arose from his or her relationship with his or her natural parents and he or she acquired no right to succeed to, or to claim legitim from, the estate of his or her adoptive parents or of the adoptive parents' relatives. Any reference to "child", "children" and "issue" in a will or *inter vivos* deed was construed as not including an adopted person or his or her issue unless the contrary intention appeared. Likewise the adoptive parents, or persons claiming through them, had no rights of succession to the estate of the adopted person. This was wholly altered by the Succession (Scotland) Act 1964, which, for successions opening on or after September 10, 1964, now regulates the law relating to adopted persons in respect of (1) the succession, whether testate or intestate, to a deceased person, (2) legal rights in the estate of a deceased person and (3) the disposal of property by virtue of any *inter vivos* deed. Under that Act, for all purposes relating to succession, whether testate or intestate, to any person who has died on or after September 10, 1964, adopted persons are treated as children of the adopter and not as the children of any other person.[92] The rights of succession so conferred extend to claims for legitim from the moveable estate of a deceased adoptive parent and to representing the adoptive parent in a claim for legitim to which he or she would have been entitled by survivance.[93] If a person has been adopted by a married couple, he or she is treated as a brother or sister of the whole blood of any other child or adopted child of that couple; but in any other cases, where the relationships between an adopted child and another child or adopted child of an adopter is in issue, the children are treated as brothers or sisters of the half blood only.[94] Any reference in a deed to a "child" or "children" is construed as including an adopted child,[95] unless the contrary be expressed or necessarily implied.[96] These

---

[89] Adoption (Scotland) Act 1978, s. 12(4)(a).

[90] Children (Scotland) Act 1995, s. 86(6)(b)(i).

[91] Adoption (Scotland) Act 1978, s. 12(9), as added by the Children (Scotland) Act 1995, Sched. 2, para. 7(d).

[92] Succession (Scotland) Act 1964, s. 23(1). The date of the adoption order is irrelevant: *Salvesen's Trs, Petrs*, 1993 S.C. 14 (in which children adopted after the execution of a trust deed were held entitled to benefit thereunder).

[93] *ibid*.

[94] *ibid*. s. 24(1).

[95] *ibid*. s. 23(2).

[96] As in *Spencer's Trs v. Ruggles*, 1981 S.C. 289. In *Salvesen's Trs, Petrs*, above, s. 23(2) was held to have a limited effect only, that is to say to answer the question of the testator's intention in leaving an earlier deed unaltered, in the knowledge of both the Act and the adoption order. A contrary intention must be expressed if such a testator is not to be taken to intend to include the adopted child in the terms of the deed.

provisions have the effect of equiparating the position of an adopted child to that of a child of the adopters for all purposes of succession including succession to the estate of the adopted person. But where any right is conferred or obligation imposed by reference to the relative seniority of the members of a class of persons then, except in the case of an "illegitimate" child adopted by one of his or her parents, any member of that class who is an adopted person shall rank as if he or she had been born on the date of his or her adoption[97]; if two or more members of the class are adopted persons whose dates of adoption are the same they rank between themselves in accordance with their respective times of birth.[98] In only one situation do adopted children retain full rights of succession in the estate of their natural parents. Where the natural parent has died after August 3, 1966 and the adoptive parent or parents died before September 10, 1964 an adopted person has rights of succession in, and may claim legitim from, the estate of his or her natural parents.[99] The law prior to September 10, 1964, however, still regulates the succession to titles, honours and coats of arms,[1] but not now to the tenancy of crofts.[2]

JURISDICTION AND QUALIFICATIONS OF PARTIES

The child's qualifications

Age and status

In cases in which the adopter is a parent, step-parent or relative[3] of the child, or if **4.17** the child is placed with the applicant by an adoption agency, the child to be adopted must (at the date of the making of the adoption order) be at least 19 weeks old; in all other cases, the child must be at least 12 months old.[4] The child must (at the date of the application for the adoption order) not have attained the age of 18,[5] and must not be or have been married.[6] A person who has already been adopted may be readopted.[7] There is no need to wait until the child is 19 weeks or 12 months old before presenting the petition and as expedition is in the interest of all concerned, not least of the child, it will usually be desirable that the petition should be presented at the earliest opportunity.[8]

Domicile and nationality

There is no requirement as to the domicile or nationality of the child. The **4.18** express jurisdictional tests relating to the domicile of the applicants and the

---

[97] Where a right or obligation arises under a deed, this rule shall apply only if the deed came into operation on or after January 1, 1976.

[98] Succession (Scotland) Act 1964, s. 24(1A), as added by the Children Act 1975, Sched. 2, para. 5.

[99] Law Reform (Miscellaneous Provisions) (Scotland) Act 1966, s. 5.

[1] Succession (Scotland) Act 1964, s. 37(1)(a).

[2] Law Reform (Miscellaneous Provisions) (Scotland) Act 1968, s. 8 and Sched. 2, para. 28.

[3] "Relative" is defined in s. 65(1) (as amended by the Children (Scotland) Act 1995, Sched. 2, para. 29) to mean "a grandparent, brother, sister, uncle or aunt whether of the full blood or half blood or by affinity and includes, where the child is illegitimate, the father of the child where he is not a parent within the meaning of this Act, and any person who would be a relative within the meaning of this definition if the father were such a parent".

[4] s. 13(1) and (2).

[5] s. 65(1) and s. 12(1), as amended by Children (Scotland) Act 1995, Sched. 2, para. 7(a)(ii).

[6] s. 12(5).

[7] s. 12(7).

[8] Except in cases where it is intended to dispense with agreement, it will usually be prudent to wait until the necessary agreements have been given. The agreement of the mother of the child cannot be given less than six weeks after birth (s. 16(4)). Subject to that, the petition may be presented immediately after the child is placed. Section 6 of the Adoption of Children (Regulation) Act 1939 (which required in effect that a petition for adoption might not be presented where arrangements for the placing of the child had been made by a registered adoption society until the expiration of three months from the time when the child was delivered into the care and possession of the prospective adopters but must be made within the following three months if the child had not been returned to the society) has been repealed, but its ghost lingers with detrimental effect.

presence of the child within the jurisdiction,[9] discussed shortly, are exhaustive of the questions of jurisdiction and there is no room for implying a further jurisdictional requirement in relation to the child's domicile. In *Re B(S) (An Infant)*,[10] however, Goff J. treated recognition of the adoption by the law of the child's domicile as a factor to be taken into account in considering whether the making of an adoption order would be for the welfare of the child. Goff J.'s reasoning has been criticised[11] and his views on the ascertainment of domicile and foreign laws are obscure, but it may be accepted that recognition by the law of the domicile is a factor which, in some circumstances, may bear on the welfare of the child. Any importance to be attached to this factor is, however, much reduced by the current provisions. Under the previous law the child's domicile did not change on adoption but since 1975,[12] due to changes in the law affecting status of an adopted child, the child acquires on adoption a new domicile of dependency which, it seems, will be treated as if it were his or her domicile of origin. Recognition of the adoption by the law of the country in which the child was domiciled before the adoption can, therefore, be relevant only on the footing that the courts of that country will take a different view of the child's domicile from that which courts within the United Kingdom are bound to take. That is a consideration to which ordinarily the courts of the forum should pay no regard, but on a question of welfare there may, of course, be the exceptional case in which it cannot be ignored.

Child's residence

4.19   Residence is not a jurisdictional test, but at all times during the 13 weeks preceding the making of the adoption order the child must have had his or her home with the applicants or one of them.[13] Where the placement has not been by an adoption agency and the applicant or one of the applicants is not a parent, step-parent or relative of the child, the 13-week period is extended to 12 months.[14] It is an offence for anyone other than an adoption agency to make arrangements for the adoption of a child, or to place a child for adoption except where the proposed adopter is a relative of the child; and it is also an offence for anyone other than a relative of the child to receive a child for adoption otherwise than from an adoption agency, knowing it is with a view to adoption.[15] Adoption may, however, still follow such illegal placements, provided that the 12-month requirement is satisfied. In order to gain advantage of the shorter period, it is not required that the original placing should have been for the purpose of adoption and, accordingly, foster carers with whom a child has been placed by a local authority or approved adoption society[16] may apply for adoption, and an order may be made in their favour, provided that the child has had his or her home with them for the 13 weeks preceding the making of the order even if adoption was not contemplated when the child was placed. Where, however, the fostering arrangement has been made by someone other than a local authority or approved adoption society, the 12-month period applies. This causes no hardship as, in the ordinary case of a genuine fostering arrangement, more than 12 months will

---

[9] ss. 14(2) and 15(2).

[10] [1968] Ch. 204.

[11] Morris, *The Conflict of Laws* (4th ed.), p. 247.

[12] Children Act 1975, Sched. 2, para. 1. See now Adoption (Scotland) Act 1978, s. 39(1).

[13] s. 13(1).

[14] s. 13(2).

[15] s. 11(1) and (3). Under the equivalent English provisions, a step-parent was held not to be a "relative" for these purposes: *Re MW (Adoption: Surrogacy)* [1995] 2 F.L.R. 759. Though "relatives" includes relatives by affinity, step-parents are implicitly excluded since other parts of the Act (such as s. 13) talks of "step-parent or relative".

[16] *i.e.* by an adoption agency (s. 1(4)).

have expired before the question of adoption arises. There is, however, a danger that placings may be made under cover of fostering so as to defeat the policy of the Act against illegal placements for adoption. The only safeguard is that courts should examine critically, from the standpoint of the child's welfare, all cases in which the applicants are not relatives of the child and the placing has not been by an adoption agency, and particularly so where it appears either that the placing was illegal or that it was done under cover of fostering with a view to circumventing the prohibitions of the Act.

The requirement in section 13(1) of the 1978 Act that the child should have had **4.20** his or her home with the prospective adopters contrasts with the requirement of the 1958 Act that he or she should have been in their continuous care and possession.[17] Although under the previous law a fairly liberal interpretation was allowed of continuous care and possession, the current provisions admit of applications being entertained where formerly they were refused.[18] It may now be possible to make a case that the person to be adopted has had his or her home with the applicants in circumstances in which the making of an adoption order would formerly have been incompetent because of the lack of continuous care and possession (*e.g.* due to absence on military service). It remains essential that the applicants should stand *in loco parentis* to the child to be adopted.[19] They may do so where they exercise quasi-parental control even if the day-to-day care and control is delegated to others.[20] Continuous care and possession was held to be interrupted when the child was allowed, in the course of the statutory period, to stay overnight with his natural mother,[21] but such absence today will affect the competency of the adoption order only if it shows vacillation concerning the home of the child.[22] In the case of applications by spouses an order may competently be made although one of the applicants has been absent (*e.g.* in the course of his or her employment on business or on military or other public service) during the 13-week period, because it is sufficient that the child should have had his or her home with one of the applicants.[23] The court must, however, be satisfied that the adoption agency which placed the child, or in any other case the local authority, has had sufficient opportunities, which need not be within the 13 weeks preceding the order, to see the child with the applicant in the home environment and, where husband and wife jointly apply for adoption, the child must be seen with them both together.[24]

Appropriate court determined by child's presence

If the child is in Scotland an application for an adoption order may be made **4.21** to the Court of Session or to the sheriff court of the sheriffdom within which the child is.[25] The physical presence of the child within the jurisdiction at the time the petition is presented is all that is required: domicile and residence are

---

[17] Adoption Act 1958, s. 3.
[18] *M, Petr*, 1953 S.C. 227; *F, Petr*, 1955 S.L.T. (Sh.Ct) 12. Cases of absence for treatment in hospital (*G, Petr*, 1955 S.L.T. (Sh.Ct) 27) and for the purposes of vocational training with return to the home at weekends and for holidays (*A, Petr*, 1953 S.L.T. (Sh.Ct) 45) in which the statutory requirements were held to have been satisfied will continue to qualify under the current test.
[19] *Re B (An Infant)* [1964] Ch. 1; *Re A (An Infant)* [1963] 1 W.L.R. 231.
[20] *Re B (An Infant)*, above.
[21] *Re CSC* [1961] 1 W.L.R. 304. See also *XY, Petrs,* 1954 S.L.T. (Sh.Ct) 86.
[22] Any substantial contact with the natural parents during the period leading up to the making of an adoption order may, however, make it difficult to assess whether the child has settled down satisfactorily with the proposed adopters and will be, with the possible exception of some adoptions by relatives, from that standpoint a consideration adverse to the making of an adoption order.
[23] Adoption (Scotland) Act 1978, s. 13(1). Under the previous law continuous care and possession had been held *dubitante* to be consistent with absences of one applicant on military service: *A, Petr*, 1958 S.L.T. (Sh.Ct) 61.
[24] s. 13(3).
[25] s. 56(2).

irrelevant. Prospective adopters have an unfettered choice between the Court of Session and the appropriate sheriff court, but past experience has been that most adoption applications are made in the sheriff court. If the child is in England or Wales no Scottish court has jurisdiction.[26] If, however, the child is not in Great Britain the Court of Session, but not the sheriff court, has jurisdiction.[27]

Capacity of applicants to adopt

Age and domicile of applicants

4.22   An adoption order may be made on the application of any person who is domiciled in a part of the United Kingdom or in the Channel Islands or the Isle of Man or was habitually resident in any of these places throughout the period of one year preceding the application; if the application is joint at least one of the prospective adopters must be domiciled there or they must both be habitually resident in any of these places throughout the period of one year preceding the application.[28] The applicant or applicants must have attained the age of 21,[29] or, in the case of a natural parent seeking to adopt jointly with his or her spouse, one must have attained the age of 18 and the other the age of 21.[30] Domicile and age are to be ascertained at the time when the order is made. There is no requirement that the applicant should be domiciled or habitually resident in Scotland: provided that he or she is domiciled or habitually resident in a part of the United Kingdom or in the Channel Islands or the Isle of Man, the jurisdiction of the Scottish court is determined by the whereabouts of the child.[31]

Individuals and married couples as applicants

4.23   Although applications by married couples are the norm, applications by individuals are competent. Only, however, in the case of an application by a married couple may an order be made on the application of more than one person.[32] It is no bar to an application by an individual that he or she is living in a cohabiting relationship with another person who, because the two are not married to each other, cannot join in the application; this is so whether the cohabitation is of a heterosexual[33] or a homosexual nature.[34] It is, however, a bar to an application by an individual that he or she is married, though that general rule is subject to a number of exceptions, which are contained in section 15(1) of the 1978 Act, as amended by the Children (Scotland) Act 1995. First, an application may be made by a married person who is married to a person (1) who is the natural parent of the child concerned and (2) in whom are vested parental responsibilities and parental rights in relation to the child[35]—in other words, step-parent adoption (discussed below). Secondly an application can be made by a married person who cannot make an application under the immediately preceding provision if the court is satisfied that (1) his or her spouse cannot be found, or (2) the spouses have separated and are living apart and the separation is likely to be permanent, or (3) his or her spouse is, by reason of ill-health (whether physical or mental), incapable of making an application for an adoption order.[36] Where reliance is placed on the fact that the spouse cannot be

---

[26] The Adoption Act 1976, s. 62, gives exclusive jurisdiction to stated courts in England and Wales in relation to children present there.

[27] s. 56(3).

[28] s. 14(2) and s. 15(2), as amended by the Children (Scotland) Act 1995, Sched. 2 paras. 8 and 9.

[29] s. 14(1A), as substituted by the Children Act 1989, Sched. 10, para. 33 and s. 15(1).

[30] s. 14(1B), as inserted by the Children Act 1989, Sched. 10, para. 33.

[31] Above.

[32] s. 14(1), (1A) and (1B), as substituted and inserted by the Children Act 1989, Sched. 10, para. 33 and amended by the Children (Scotland) Act 1995, Sched. 2, para. 8.

[33] As in *Re B (Adoption: Joint Residence)* [1996] 1 F.L.R. 27.

[34] As in *T, Petr*, 1997 S.L.T. 724.

[35] s. 15(1)(aa), as inserted by Children (Scotland) Act 1995, s. 97(2).

[36] s. 15(1)(b), as amended by the Children (Scotland) Act 1995, s. 97(2)(b).

found, the court will require that every reasonable step to trace the spouse has been taken.[37] Separation connotes the putting into effect of an intention on the part of at least one of the spouses to cease cohabitation, and "living apart" is the maintenance of that separation. The twin elements of intention and act are essential. The act of separation involves withdrawal from the society of the other but not necessarily living under separate roofs.[38] Cohabitation may have ceased where each is living as if a single person to whom the other is a stranger although their separate accommodation is under the same roof.[39] An adoption application by a spouse who, although separated from the other spouse, is living under the same roof, is, however, unlikely to be successful as such an arrangement almost inevitably would involve some hazard to the welfare of the child.

Parents and step-parents as applicants

Prior to the coming into force of the Children (Scotland) Act 1995, a step-parent could adopt the child of his or her spouse only by means of a joint application with the spouse (the child's natural parent): the spouse, in other words, had to give up his or her parental responsibilities and parental rights obtained by virtue of being a natural parent and reacquire them by means of an adoption order. The amendments to section 15 of the Adoption (Scotland) Act 1978 contained in section 97 of the 1995 Act allow a step-parent to make a sole application if married to the natural parent of the child in whom are vested parental responsibilities and parental rights. This avoids the procedural clumsiness of the natural parent adopting his or her own child and also allows the court to focus more closely on the motives and feelings of the applicant. The term "natural parent" is not defined in the Adoption (Scotland) Act 1978 and, though it appeared in the original section 15 in a number of places it has now been replaced with, simply, "parent".[40] "Parent", on the other hand, is defined,[41] which suggests that "natural parent" has a different meaning, and the only plausible alternative to that given to "parent" is genetic parent, whether or not the natural parent is or was married to the other natural parent and whether or not he or she has parental responsibilities and parental rights in relation to the child. However, since the "natural parent" to whom the applicant is married must have parental responsibilities and parental rights before a sole application by a step-parent is competent, there is little practical difference between "natural parent" and "parent" for the purposes of section 15. If the natural parent to whom the applicant is married does not have parental responsibilities and parental rights then the application must be joint. It is only the spouse of a natural parent who can rely on this provision and competently make a sole application while married. So an adoptive parent (not being a natural parent) who marries again (or, if previously a sole applicant, for the first time) must join in any further adoption application made by his or her new spouse, as must a person who is parent by means of a parental order made under section 30 of the Human Fertilisation and Embryology Act 1990. The position of the man who is deemed father under section 28 of the 1990 Act is slightly less obvious, for section 29(1) of that Act states that a person deemed parent by section 27 or section 28 is to

4.24

---

[37] *cf. Re F (R) (An Infant)* [1970] 1 Q.B. 385 and *S v. M*, 1999 S.L.T. 571 (Extra Div.).

[38] Clive, *Husband and Wife* (4th ed.), p. 401.

[39] See *Lennie v. Lennie*, 1950 S.C. (H.L.) 1, *per* Lord Normand at 5 and Lord Reid at 16. *Cf. Macdonald v. Macdonald*, 1948 S.L.T. 380.

[40] Children (Scotland) Act 1995, Sched. 5.

[41] s. 65(1), as inserted by the Children (Scotland) Act 1995, Sched. 2, para. 29(a)(v): "'Parent' means, irrespective of whether or not they are, or have been, married to each other—(a) the mother of the child, where she has parental responsibilities or parental rights in relation to him; (b) the father of the child where he has such responsibilities or rights; and (c) both of his parents, where both have such responsibilities or rights".

be treated in law as parent for "all purposes". However, a person deemed parent by section 28 of the 1990 Act is not deemed to be the genetic parent and cannot, therefore, be described as the child's "natural parent": the relationship, though recognised and valid for all purposes, is legal and artificial, and not natural. Such a father must, therefore, join the application of his spouse to adopt his child. A woman deemed mother by section 27 of the 1990 Act[42] may have no genetic connection to the child but, having carried and given birth to the child, can, it is submitted, be regarded as the child's "natural" mother: therefore she does not require to join in the adoption application of her husband.

4.25   The 1995 amendments which allow a sole application by a step-parent do not, in their terms, make it incompetent for a natural parent who possesses parental responsibilities and parental rights to join the application and adopt his or her own child and it clearly remains competent for such a parent to make a sole application.[43] Nevertheless it is difficult to see what advantage to the child would follow an adoption order in favour of his or her parents, except in the case of the mother or father who does not possess parental responsibilities and parental rights. Any adoption order, whether obtained by a natural parent who already has parental responsibilities and parental rights or by a step-parent who will thereby acquire parental responsibilities and parental rights, will have the effect of extinguishing any parental responsibilities and parental rights that were vested in the other parent[44] and the child will be treated in law as the child of the adopter (and, in the case of a step-parent adoption, the adopter's spouse) and of no other person.[45] In other words, adoption by one parent or a step-parent, or both, will effectively exclude the other parent from any legal relationship with the child—and, indeed, if that parent previously had parental responsibilities and parental rights, adoption will extinguish their title to seek any such parental responsibility or parental right in the future.[46] Consequently there is a risk that such an adoption might be used as a weapon designed to hurt the other parent by denying parental responsibilities and parental rights rather than to benefit the child; there is also the risk that the adoption will be used to hide from the child the true facts about his or her origins, which may in the long run prove damaging to him or her; and in general it will often be socially and psychologically undesirable to exclude the other parent from contact with the child. There are few valid reasons for adoption by one natural parent today, and single-parent adoptions will therefore normally be inappropriate, especially since parental responsibilities and parental rights can be acquired in ways that do not exclude the other parent, such as obtaining an order conferring them under section 11(2)(b) of the Children (Scotland) Act 1995.

4.26   The law therefore tries to discourage adoption applications by one of the child's parents. By section 15(3) of the Adoption (Scotland) Act 1978,[47] an adoption order is not to be made on the application of the mother or father of the child alone unless the court is satisfied that (1) the other parent is dead, or cannot be found, or there is no other parent by virtue of section 28 of the Human Fertilisation and Embryology Act 1990,[48] or (2) there is some other reason justifying the exclusion of the other parent. These provisions are directed to applications by an unmarried parent or, in the limited circumstances in which one spouse alone can

---

[42] Which provides that a child's mother is for all purposes a woman who is carrying or has carried a child, even when the child is created from the ovum of another woman. See above, para. 3.07.

[43] s. 15(3).

[44] s. 12(3).

[45] s. 39(1), as amended by the Children (Scotland) Act 1995, s. 97(3).

[46] Children (Scotland) Act 1995, s. 11(3) and (4).

[47] As amended by the Human Fertilisation and Embryology Act 1990, Sched. 4, para. 6.

[48] Which defines when a man will be "father" of a child born as a result of an artificial reproductive technique: see above, paras 3.27–3.41.

apply, a parent who although married is not married to the other parent of the child. It does not apply to (and can therefore be avoided by making) a joint application by a step-parent and one of the child's parents. It is unclear whether "other parent" includes fathers of children born out of wedlock. Before the 1995 amendments the phrase used was "other natural parent", which clearly would include the father who did not have parental responsibilities and parental rights. The word "natural", wherever it appeared in section 15(3), has been repealed[49] and "parent" is now defined to exclude the mother or the father who has no parental responsibilities or parental rights.[50] However, the parent–child relationship has more incidents than responsibilities and rights and to exclude from the protection given by section 15(3) a parent affected by these incidents would frustrate in large part the effect of the provision. For that reason, it is submitted that "other" parent, as it appears in section 15(3), should be interpreted in this context[51] to refer to the undefined "mother" or "father" mentioned earlier in the subsection. The natural meaning of "mother" and "father" is "genetic parent" irrespective of whether or not parental responsibilities or parental rights are held, and "other parent" should be taken to mean the genetic parent other than the mother or father who makes the application alone. There is, in these circumstances, a risk that where paternity has neither been admitted nor established in other proceedings, the aim of section 15(3) may be circumvented by falsely attributing paternity to someone who is dead or who cannot be found. There is also a question of what will amount to "some other reason" that would justify excluding the other parent. This would, it is thought, include, for example, a failure to discharge parental responsibilities, failure by either parent to discharge their alimentary or child support obligations,[52] and abandonment, neglect or ill-treatment of the child. There is a clear overlap with the conditions allowing the court to dispense with parental agreement to adoption, but the phraseology used in the present context is significantly less precisely drawn and may well be taken, for that reason, to be wider. Nor is it clear what "the exclusion of the other parent" means. As section 15(3) applies to applications by unmarried mothers and fathers, it cannot mean exclusion from the adoption process because such parents could not make a joint application. The meaning seems to be exclusion from the legal incidents of the relationship between father or mother and child which arise irrespective of the existence of parental responsibilities and parental rights (such as succession rights and alimentary obligations). Where the court is satisfied that there is reason justifying the exclusion of the other parent, that reason must be recorded.[53]

CONSENT AND AGREEMENT

Consent of the child

Children over 12

If the person to be adopted is of or over the age of 12 years his or her consent **4.27** to the order is necessary.[54] A requirement that minor children consent to their own adoption has been a consistent feature of adoption legislation in its application to Scotland[55] and reflects the personal competence and capacity for

---

[49] Children (Scotland) Act 1995, Sched. 5.
[50] Adoption (Scotland) Act 1978, s. 65, as amended by the Children (Scotland) Act 1995, Sched. 2, para. 29.
[51] Remembering that the definition of "parent" in s. 65 is, expressly, "unless the context otherwise requires".
[52] Under, respectively, the Family Law (Scotland) Act 1985 or the Child Support Act 1991.
[53] s. 15(3).
[54] s. 12(8), as substituted by the Age of Legal Capacity (Scotland) Act 1991, s. 2(3).
[55] Adoption of Children (Scotland) Act 1930, s. 2(3); Adoption Act 1950, s. 2(4); Adoption Act 1958, s. 4(1); Children Act 1975, s. 8(6).

legal acts previously imputed by law to a minor as distinct from a pupil child; the requirement was preserved when pupils' incapacities were extended to all children under the age of 16,[56] but the ages equalised at 12 for both boys and girls. The court may dispense with the child's consent where it is satisfied that the child is incapable of giving his or her consent.[57] However, it is provided that a child 12 years of age or more has capacity to give consent,[58] and "incapable" must, therefore, refer to mental incapacity caused other than through age alone. Subject to that exception, the requirement of consent is mandatory.[59] The Adoption Act 1958[60] had required, as had the earlier legislation,[61] that the court should be satisfied that the minor understood the nature and effect of the adoption order for which application was made, but that requirement was repealed by the Children Act 1975[62] and is not repeated in the Adoption (Scotland) Act 1978. It is now presumed that a child 12 years of age or more is of sufficient age and maturity to form a view on any matter relating to his or her adoption,[63] and this presumption will require to be overturned before the court can dispense with the child's consent. Under the previous law the court had refused to give effect to a minor's consent granted in ignorance of his "illegitimacy" until he had been made acquainted with the whole circumstances, including his "illegitimacy", set forth in the petition. Only after that had been done, and he had not withdrawn his consent, was the adoption order made.[64] It is thought that it will still, in general, be sound practice to ensure that the child is aware of his or her parentage.[65]

Children under 12

4.28   The consent of the child is not required if he or she is under the age of 12 years on the date the order is made, but the provision[66] requiring the court to have regard so far as practicable to the child's views has no age limit attached to it[67] and it will be appropriate for the court, or the reporting officer, to consult the child even under the age of 12. Indeed the statutory obligation could hardly be fulfilled without doing so, except in the case of a very young child. In *AB and CB, Petitioners*,[68] the sheriff was criticised for not having satisfied his

---

[56]   Age of Legal Capacity (Scotland) Act 1991, s. 1(1) and (2).
[57]   Adoption (Scotland) Act 1978, s. 12(8). The Adoption of Children (Scotland) Act 1930 had contained a similar power of dispensation (s. 2(4)), but it was omitted from the 1950 and 1958 Acts. In *PQ and RQ, Petrs*, 1965 S.C. 45 it was held, in a question under the 1958 Act, that no adoption order could be granted where the minor child was mentally retarded and unable to understand the circumstances of adoption or sign a form of consent. The omission was supplied by the Law Reform (Miscellaneous Provisions) (Scotland) Act 1966, s. 4 and the 1978 Act repeats what was then enacted.
[58]   Age of Legal Capacity (Scotland) Act 1991, s. 2(3).
[59]   *PQ and RQ, Petrs*, above; *McD and McD, Petrs* (1949) 65 Sh.CtRep. 42.
[60]   s. 7(1)(a).
[61]   Adoption of Children (Scotland) Act 1930, s. 3(a); Adoption Act 1950, s. 5(1)(a).
[62]   Sched. 4.
[63]   s. 6(2), as inserted by the Children (Scotland) Act 1995, s. 95.
[64]   *A, Petr*, 1936 S.C. 255. See, however, *A, Petr*, 1953 S.L.T. (Sh.Ct) 45.
[65]   In the absence of a statutory direction there is room for judicial discretion, but it will only be in highly exceptional circumstances that the court can be satisfied that proper consideration has been given to the child's views when the child is in ignorance of an important issue such as his or her true status or parentage and it is practicable to dispel that ignorance. In considering what is practicable it may, however, be right to give weight to any adverse effect that knowledge of his or her origins would have on the child. That he or she should be kept in ignorance is undesirable but an adoption process may not afford the best occasion for telling him or her the true facts.
[66]   s. 6(1), as amended by the Children (Scotland) Act 1995, s. 95.
[67]   The presumption that a child 12 years of age or more is of sufficient age and maturity to form a view for these purposes (s. 6(2)) does not imply a contrary presumption in the case of a child below that age.
[68]   1990 S.C.L.R. 809.

statutory obligation[69] when he failed to take account of the view of two children aged 11 and 12.[70]

Parental agreement

Except where the procedure of freeing a child for adoption under section 18 **4.29** of the 1978 Act,[71] or the English or Northern Irish equivalent, has been used, it is a prerequisite to the making of an adoption order either that the court should be satisfied that each parent or guardian of the child to be adopted has freely and with full understanding of what is involved agreed unconditionally to the making of the adoption order (whether or not he or she knows the identity of the applicant) or that his or her agreement to the making of the adoption order should be dispensed with on one of the specified statutory grounds.[72] It is the stress laid on parental agreement that, along with permanence, points the character of adoption as distinct from applications for residence orders or other proceedings regulating the care and upbringing of children. As Lord Hailsham of St Marylebone L.C. said in *Re W (An Infant)*[73]:

> "In custody cases what is in question is the custody, care or control of the child, or perhaps the administration of his property, and that is why his interest is the first and paramount consideration. But in adoption cases what is in issue is the parent–child relationship itself and in that relationship the parent as well as the child has legitimate rights."

While the welfare of the child may be relevant to some aspects of dispensing with parental agreement,[74] the withholding of parental agreement may constitute a barrier to the granting of an adoption order even if it can be shown that to grant the order would promote the child's welfare. The primary purpose of the obligation to obtain agreement is to give a right of objection to the parents, rather than to protect the welfare of the child.

Meaning of "parent" and "guardian"

Before the 1995 amendments, the word "parent" was not defined in the **4.30** Adoption (Scotland) Act 1978, and it was unclear whether the requirement of consent applied to all natural parents or only those who had parental rights. In a case decided under the Adoption Act 1950[75] it was held that a putative father who was not a guardian of an "illegitimate" child was not a "parent" within the meaning of the agreement requirement. The decision rested on the basis that the law clearly distinguished between the "legitimate" and the "illegitimate"

---

[69] The unamended s. 6 had required the court to "ascertain the wishes and feelings of the child" and "to give due consideration to them" but the change in wording introduced by s. 95 of the 1995 Act does not, it is submitted, change the nature of the court's obligation.

[70] In *C, Petrs*, 1993 S.L.T. (Sh.Ct) 8 Sheriff Gow held that it was impracticable to ascertain the wishes and feelings of a six-year-old child when the prospective adopters refused to allow her to be interviewed, because they did not want the child to know she was adopted—the wife was the child's natural mother and the husband had married the wife two weeks after the birth. The adoption application was granted. This decision was criticised by Sutherland in "Adoption: The Child's View" 1994 S.L.T. (News) 37 on the basis that it is inconsistent with the spirit of the UN Convention on the Rights of the Child.

[71] See below, paras 4.58 *et seq*.

[72] s. 16(1), as amended by the Children Act 1989, Sched. 10, para. 34. "Agreement" is the term used in place of "consent" in the previous legislation. The purpose is to provide a distinct terminology for the procedure for freeing for adoption. A parent agrees to the making of an adoption order (s. 16(1) and s. 18(1)) but consents to freeing for adoption (s. 18(2)). It is, however, obscure why "agreement" was not used for the new process and "consent" retained in the context in which it had hitherto been used.

[73] [1971] A.C. 682 at 693.

[74] See below, para. 4.45.

[75] *A v. B*, 1955 S.C. 378.

child and that it was only in the case of the former that the term parent could in the full legal sense be applied to a father. That distinction has been modified by subsequent legislation but in relation to parental responsibilities and parental rights important distinctions remain between children of married parents, on the one hand, and of unmarried parents, on the other. The law as contained in the original 1978 Act did not alter this position.[76] "Parent" is now, however, expressly defined for the purposes of the Adoption (Scotland) Act 1978[77] to mean the mother or the father of the child, or both, irrespective of whether or not they are or have been married to each other, so long as she or he, or both, has or have parental responsibilities or parental rights in relation to the child. In other words, parenthood, for the purposes of the 1978 Act, is referable to (1) the appropriate genetic connection, together with (2) the holding of parental responsibilities or parental rights, however they are obtained. The result is little different from the pre-1995 position, for the father who was never married to the mother will not have parental responsibilities and parental rights unless he has obtained an order of the court conferring them or he has entered into an agreement with the mother.[78] Before the 1995 amendments such an order would bring him within the definition of "guardian"; now it brings him within the definition of "parent". It is to be noted that the definition refers to parental responsibilities *or* parental rights, which suggests that holding only parental responsibilities or only parental rights, or any one of them, is enough for a mother or a father to be a "parent". So the parent with nothing more than the responsibility and right to maintain personal relations and direct contact with the child is a "parent" whose agreement to the adoption order is needed. There are some practical advantages in not burdening the adoption process with a requirement of agreement from putative fathers who may have had little or no contact with the child or who may be difficult to trace or whose paternity of the child may be uncertain. Other putative fathers may be able to assert a right to be heard, even although their agreement is not required, and so achieve some protection for their legitimate interests in so far as these are consistent with the welfare of the child. However, it is difficult to see how the exclusion of the male parent from the adoption process on the basis of his lack of parental responsibilities and parental rights, which is itself referable to his marital status, can be held to consist with the decision of the European Court of Human Rights in *Keegan v. Ireland*[79], in which it was held that the exclusion of the unmarried father from the adoption process was a breach of Article 8, which protects the right to family life.[80]

4.31   "Guardian" is defined by section 65 of the Adoption (Scotland) Act 1978[81] to mean a person appointed by deed or will or by a court of competent jurisdiction to be the guardian of the child.[82] The use of the word "guardian" in the definition of "guardian" is unhelpful and it is unclear whether this definition extends only to persons who are specifically appointed to an office designated "guardian". It might be argued that a person upon whom is conferred full parental responsibilities and parental rights by an order under section 11(2)(b) of the Children (Scotland) Act 1995 is in a position in relation to the child that is

---

[76] *A and B v. C*, 1987 S.C.L.R. 514.
[77] s. 65(1), as amended by the Children (Scotland) Act 1995, Sched. 2, para. 29(a)(v).
[78] Under s. 4 of the Children (Scotland) Act 1995.
[79] (1994) 18 E.H.R.R. 342.
[80] Similarly in South Africa a statutory provision dispensing with the requirement for an unmarried father's consent was held unconstitutional in *Fraser v. Children's Court, Pretoria North* (1997) SACLR LEXIS 1.
[81] As amended by the Children (Scotland) Act 1995, Sched. 2, para. 29(a)(iii) and Sched. 5.
[82] On appointment of guardians, see below, paras 7.10–7.21.

indistinguishable from that of a guardian appointed as such under section 11(2)(h) and, therefore, that for the purposes of the Adoption (Scotland) Act 1978 he or she should be treated as a guardian.[83] To hold otherwise is to be a prisoner of terminology. It is, however, difficult to reconcile anything other than an appointment under section 11(2)(h) with the strict terms of the 1978 Act.

Other person's agreement
Persons other than parents or guardians who have parental responsibilities **4.32** and parental rights, however obtained, have no right to grant or withhold agreement to the making of an adoption order, and consequently their agreement should not be sought. So, for example, a person, such as the child's grandparent, upon whom is imposed parental responsibilities and parental rights under section 11(2)(b), or who is granted a residence order under section 11(2)(c), of the Children (Scotland) Act 1995 but who is not appointed as guardian under section 11(2)(h) thereof has no right to grant or withhold agreement unless, as argued above, such a person is, in effect, a guardian. In any case, their relationship with the child will, of course, be a relevant factor in determining the child's welfare. A person other than a parent or guardian who has only limited parental responsibilities and parental rights, such as the responsibility and right of contact or the responsibility and right to act as the child's legal representative, has no right to grant or withhold consent. Also, a local authority to which has been transferred parental rights and responsibilities under a parental responsibilities order made under section 86(1) of the Children (Scotland) Act 1995[84] does not thereby obtain the right to grant or withhold agreement to the making of an adoption order or a freeing order, for that right is expressly excluded from the definition of the parental rights and responsibilities that are thereby transferred.[85] Likewise a local authority which is providing accommodation for the child under section 25 or is otherwise looking after the child in terms of section 17 of the 1995 Act, such as by virtue of a supervision requirement made under section 70(1) of the 1995 Act, has no right to grant or withhold agreement. Nor does a foster carer or the husband of a woman whose child is not his and is the subject of the proceedings. This last case may cause difficulty since the husband will be the presumptive father,[86] and that presumption would have to be overturned if the need for his agreement is to be avoided.

There is no necessary connection between agreement to adoption and the **4.33** right to be heard in the adoption process, except, of course, that a parent or guardian has a right to be heard if there is a question of dispensing with his or her agreement. Persons whose agreement is not required, including some in the categories mentioned in the previous paragraph, may nonetheless have a right to be heard.[87]

Agreement to be given freely and with full understanding
The agreement of the parent or guardian must have been given "freely and **4.34** with full understanding of what is involved".[88] This requirement replaces that in the Adoption Act 1958[89] that the court should be satisfied that the parent or

---

[83] See further, below, para. 9.18.
[84] See below, Chap. 17.
[85] 1995 Act, s. 86(3). The parental responsibilities order ceases to have effect if the child becomes the subject of an adoption or a freeing order: s. 86(6)(b).
[86] See above, para. 3.15.
[87] See below, para. 5.14.
[88] s. 16(1)(b)(i).
[89] s. 7(1)(a). The Adoption of Children (Scotland) Act 1930, s. 3(a), and the Adoption Act 1950, s. 5(1)(a), had been to the same effect.

guardian understood the nature and effect of the adoption order for which application was made and, in particular, that the effect of it would be permanently to deprive him or her of parental rights. The new wording seems to be both less precise and wider than the old, but as a minimum the law would still seem to require an understanding on the part of the parent or guardian that the adoption order would transfer parental responsibilities and parental rights to the adoptive parent. Inability to understand what is involved gives a ground for dispensing with parental agreement,[90] as will refusal to accept the information necessary to bring one to a full understanding[91] but a parent who is not unable and not unwilling to understand must be in possession of sufficient information upon which to make an informed decision, and any agreement in the absence of such information is invalid. The question remains of what knowledge is necessary to constitute understanding. What must the parent know about the adopters and the environment in which the child, if adopted, is to be brought up? It is expressly provided that agreement can be given "whether or not [the parent or guardian] knows of the identity of the applicants".[92] In some cases the identity of the proposed adopters is already known to the natural parents, as in most cases of adoption by relatives, and in others, particularly of adoption of older children, there is increasing recognition that the maintenance of some contact with the natural parents may be advantageous. In many circumstances, however, it is sound and usual practice that the identity of the adopters should not be disclosed, and the rules make provision for achieving that result.[93] The reasons for anonymity in most cases are obvious. As Lord President Normand said in *H and H, Petitioners*: "On both sides it may be recognised that it is best for the future welfare of the child that the natural mother should not have the temptation or the power to interfere between the child and its adoptive parents."[94] The requirement that agreement should have been given freely and with full understanding implies, however, as did the earlier law, that the mother should

> "have had as real an opportunity of making a decision as she would have had if the identity of the adopters had been disclosed to her, and of this also the Court must be satisfied. The names and designations of the adopters are not in themselves material, but it is material that the mother should have such information about their character and circumstances and about the kind of home into which it is proposed to adopt her child as she may desire".[95]

Although the adopters need not, and often should not, be identified, it is essential to the validity of parental agreement that it should have been given in relation to an adoption by proposed adopters distinguished in accordance with the statutory requirements. In *YZ, Petitioners*.[96] it was held that a form of consent which neither named nor distinguished the petitioners was invalid. Under the law as it then stood[97] that result was inescapable and although the requirements of the principal Act have changed the subsidiary rules in their present form point to the same result.[98] A person proposing to present a petition for an adoption order may, before presenting the petition, apply for a serial number to be assigned to him or her and

---

[90] s. 16(1)(a).
[91] s. 16(2)(b); *T, Petr*, 1997 S.L.T. 724 (in which the parent refused to have anything to do with the adoption process and the court held that this amounted to a withholding of agreement which, in the circumstances, was unreasonable).
[92] s. 16(1)(b)(i).
[93] For the Court of Session, see Rules of the Court of Session 1994 (S.I. 1994 No. 1443) (hereinafter RCS 1994), r. 67.20, and for the sheriff court see Act of Sederunt (Child Care and Maintenance Rules) 1997 (S.I. 1997 No. 291), (hereinafter A.S. 1997), r. 2.24.
[94] 1944 S.C. 347 at 352.
[95] *ibid. Cf. C and C, Petrs*, 1936 S.C. 257 and *Re Carroll* [1931] 1 K.B. 317.
[96] 1954 S.L.T. (Sh.Ct) 98.
[97] Adoption Act 1950, s. 4(1). *Cf.* Adoption Act 1958, s. 6(1).
[98] RCS 1994, r. 67.20 and A.S. 1997, r. 2.24.

is therefore sufficiently distinguished for the purposes of the agreement to the making of an order if the document signifying agreement refers to him or her as the petitioner to whom that serial number has been assigned and specifies the year in which, and the court by which, it was assigned. It is, therefore, no objection to agreement to adoption that it was given before the presentation of the petition.[99]

The requirement that agreement be freely given strikes at the validity of any **4.35** agreement obtained by pressure, but the mere existence of pressure will not have that result if it did not in fact affect the agreement.[1] A mother is protected against her ill-considered giving of agreement in the aftermath of birth by the provision that agreement is ineffective if given by the mother less than six weeks after the child's birth.[2] But agreement is not given with full understanding if some factor which will fundamentally affect the child's future upbringing has been withheld from the parent. So in *Re M (Minors) (Adoption)*[3] a father's consent to adoption by the mother and her new husband was held to be vitiated by the fact that he was unaware that the mother was terminally ill and would die within three months. Agreement must be unconditional[4] and a parent can no longer, therefore, as he or she could under the previous law,[5] impose conditions as to the religious upbringing of the child. An adoption agency in placing a child must, however, "have regard (so far as is practicable) to any wishes of the child's parents and guardians as to the religious upbringing of the child",[6] and the court and adoption agency must have regard so far as practicable to the child's own religious persuasion, racial origin and cultural and linguistic background.[7] The court may still, in so far as it can do so consistently with its duty under section 6 of the Adoption (Scotland) Act 1978 to regard the need to safeguard and promote the welfare of the child throughout his or her life as paramount, impose such conditions as it thinks fit,[8] which is clearly broad enough to concern the child's religious upbringing. The wisdom of imposing such restraints on the conscience of adopters is, however, to be doubted, and in the normal case the condition is unenforceable.

Form of agreement and withdrawal

All agreements to the making of an adoption order require to be in writing **4.36** and in the form prescribed by the rules.[9] Agreement must be operative at the very moment when the adoption order is made. Accordingly, it may be withdrawn at any time before then.[10] Any agreement not to oppose the making of an order, however solemnly given, is not binding.[11]

Dispensing with agreement

The modern legislation gives power to dispense on specified grounds but does **4.37** not confer on the court any general discretion to dispense with parental agreement such as had been given by the Adoption of Children (Scotland) Act 1930.[12] A similar

---

[99] RCS 1994, r. 67.20 and A.S. 1997, r. 2.24.
[1] *Re T (An Infant)* (1954) 118 J.P. 139.
[2] s. 16(4).
[3] [1991] 1 F.L.R. 458.
[4] See *B and Anor, Petrs*, 1996 S.L.T. 1370.
[5] Adoption Act 1958, s. 4(2).
[6] Adoption (Scotland) Act 1978, s. 7.
[7] s. 6(1)(b), as substituted by s. 95 of the Children (Scotland) Act 1995.
[8] s. 12(6). In *AH and PH, Petrs*, 1997 Fam. L.R. 84, children of Asian origin were adopted by a white couple, subject to the condition that the adoptive parents "use their best endeavours" to secure that they be brought up with an understanding of their ethnic origins and traditions. See further, below, para. 4.69.
[9] RCS 1994, r. 67.5 and A.S. 1997, r. 2.23.
[10] *Re Hollyman* [1945] 1 All E.R. 290; *Re F (An Infant)* [1957] 1 All E.R. 819.
[11] *Re F*, above.
[12] s. 2(3). Under that subsection the court could dispense with consent if satisfied that the person whose consent was to be dispensed with was a person whose consent ought (in the opinion of the court and in all the circumstances of the case) to be dispensed with. The discretion was probably

discretion had been given in England and Wales by the Adoption Act 1926,[13] but in neither jurisdiction does it appear to have been invoked frequently . Where agreement has not been given, dispensing with it is a judicial act which bears directly not only on the propriety but on the validity of an adoption order and so ought to be recorded in the court's order, preferably as a substantive part of it.[14] An appellate court can interfere with the decision of the court of first instance, not only where there is an error of law but where, on other grounds, it is clear that it has reached a wrong conclusion[15] and where the court of first instance has refused to dispense with agreement an appellate court may do so if, in its view, the facts justify that course.[16] Nevertheless, both because of the experience that courts of first instance commonly have in dealing with questions of adoption and because of the critical role necessarily played by matters of impression, great importance will be attached to the decision of the court of first instance and in the absence of some clear error of fact or law an appellate court will be slow to reverse that decision.[17] Although questions of dispensing with agreement and of whether, given that agreement, an adoption order should be made, may often arise in association, and involve some common factors, they are essentially distinct.[18] The welfare of the child, although central to the decision on the merits of making the adoption order and relevant to the decision of whether to dispense with parental agreement,[19] is not relevant to the determination of whether a ground of dispensation exists, except when agreement is allegedly being unreasonably withheld and even then only in the limited sense that it is a matter which the reasonable parent may be supposed to take into account.[20]

4.38   Questions of dispensation should, however, usually be considered along with the merits. In *Re C(L) (An Infant)*[21] the view had been expressed that a common feature of all the grounds for dispensing with agreement, with the exception of incapacity, and the basis of each of them, was "a callous or self-indulgent indifference [on the part of the parent] to the welfare of the child", using "welfare" in the broad sense and not of mere material advantage; but if by that it was intended to postulate that such indifference was a necessary criterion for invoking any of the grounds, that view must now be rejected.[22]

4.39   The grounds for dispensing with the agreement of a parent or guardian to adoption are now contained in section 16(2) of the Adoption (Scotland) Act 1978, as amended by Schedule 2 to the Children (Scotland) Act 1995. These are that he or she:

(a) is not known, cannot be found or is incapable of giving agreement;
(b) is withholding agreement unreasonably;
(c) has persistently failed, without reasonable cause, to fulfil one or other of the following parental responsibilities in relation to the child—(i) the responsibility to safeguard and promote the child's health, development and welfare or

---

aimed primarily at dispensing with the consent of persons other than parents who were liable to contribute to the support of the child (and whose consent was required under the 1930 Act although they were not parents or guardians) but the wording was wide enough to comprehend dispensation with the consent of parents.
[13] s. 2(3).
[14] *S v. Huddersfield Borough Council* [1975] Fam. 113.
[15] *A and B, Petrs*, 1971 S.L.T. 258, *per* Lord Reid at 259 and Lord Guest at 260.
[16] *S v. Huddersfield Borough Council*, above; *L v. Central Regional Council*, 1990 S.L.T. 818.
[17] *A and B, Petrs*, above, *per* Lord Reid at 259, Lord Guest at 260 and Lord Simon of Glaisdale at 264.
[18] *Re D (A Minor) (Adoption: Parental Agreement)* [1990] F.C.R. 615; *Re E (A Minor) (Freeing for Adoption)* [1995] 1 F.L.R. 382; 1 F.C.R. 65.
[19] That decision being one "relating to the adoption" and so activating the welfare test in s. 6: *per* Lord Justice-Clerk Ross in *P v. Lothian Regional Council*, 1989 S.L.T. 739 at 741G (disapproving the English decision of *Re P (An Infant) (Adoption:Parental Consent)* [1977] Fam. 25).
[20] Below, para. 4.45. *Cf. Re PB (A Minor)* (1985) 15 Fam. Law 198, in which Sheldon J. held the welfare test relevant to a determination of whether the ill-treatment ground had been established or not.
[21] [1965] 2 Q.B. 449, *per* Diplock L.J. at 471.
[22] *Re W (An Infant)* [1971] A.C. 682, especially *per* Lord Hailsham of St Marylebone L.C. at 697.

(ii) if the child is not living with him, the responsibility to maintain personal relations and direct contact with the child on a regular basis;

(d) has seriously ill-treated the child, whose reintegration into the same household as the parent or guardian is, because of the serious ill-treatment or for other reasons, unlikely.

If none of the statutory grounds is established there can be no dispensation, **4.40** while, on the other hand, if a ground is established the facts will often compel a decision in favour of dispensation.[23] However, the question of whether a ground for dispensation exists is separate from the question of whether parental agreement ought to be dispensed with. The existence of any of the grounds for dispensing with parental agreement is primarily a question of fact,[24] while the welfare of the child is central to whether, once a ground has been established, dispensation should be ordered. It has been said:

> "A judge considering whether parental consent to the making of an adoption order should be dispensed with... must proceed by way of two steps. In the first place he must decide whether a ground set out in section 16(2) of the Act has been established. If no such ground is established that is an end of the matter. The application of necessity must be refused. On the other hand, if the necessary ground is established the judge must then proceed to the next stage which is to consider whether in the light of the considerations set out in section 6 of the 1978 Act the order applied for [*i.e.* to dispense with agreement] ought to be made".[25]

Unknown parent, disappearance or incapacity[26]

These are three discrete grounds for dispensation. The usual case of an unknown **4.41** parent is that of the father who is not married to the mother, but he will usually have no right to give or withhold agreement in any case. It is difficult to imagine a situation in which a child's guardian is unknown, and so dispensation based on the fact that the parent or guardian is unknown will in practice be limited to the case of a foundling child. It will not be known whether such a child's parents are married or unmarried and whether, therefore, both have parental responsibilities and parental rights and the court founding on this ground ought to dispense with the agreement of both the foundling's mother and his or her father.

In relation to disappearance of the parent or guardian, it is usually a **4.42** prerequisite for holding that a person cannot be found that his or her whereabouts should be unknown after every reasonable step, by reasonable means, has been taken to trace him or her.[27] Knowledge of the whereabouts of the person whose agreement is required[28] or the failure to use all reasonable means to ascertain them usually therefore excludes dispensation on this ground.[28a] Exceptionally, however, it may be held that a person cannot be found although his or her whereabouts are known. The true test is the reasonable practicability of communication. Thus, in *Re R (Adoption)*[29] it was held that the parents of the

---

[23] It is unusual for agreement not to be dispensed with once a ground has been established, but it is by no means unknown: as an example, see *FB and AB v. AC*, July 10, 1998 (Court of Session, unreported).

[24] *Re P (An Infant) (Adoption) (Parental Consent)* [1977] Fam. 25.

[25] *per* Lords Wylie, Murray and Caplan in *L v. Central Regional Council*, 1990 S.L.T. 818 at 821, approved and reiterated by the First Division in *Lothian Regional Council v. A*, 1992 S.L.T. 858. See also *City of Edinburgh Council v. NB*, March 19, 1999.

[26] s. 16(2)(a).

[27] *Re C, The Times*, April 2, 1957; *Re F(R)* [1970] 1 Q.B. 385; *cf. Clark-Kennedy v. Clark-Kennedy* (1908) 15 S.L.T. 844; *S v. M*, 1999 S.L.T. 571.

[28a] It is reasonable to enquire not only at the person's last known address, but also at the address of known relatives: *S v. M*, 1999 S.L.T. 571.

[28] *Re B* [1958] 1 Q.B. 12.

[29] [1966] 2 All E.R. 613.

person in respect of whom an adoption was sought could not be found when, although their whereabouts were known, they lived under a totalitarian regime in a country from which the person to be adopted had recently escaped.

4.43   Incapacity might be shown in a medical report on the mental and physical condition of the person whose agreement is to be dispensed with. Though it does not say so, the terms of the statute imply that the incapacity be permanent or at least long-term. The deprivation of the right to withold agreement to the adoption of one's child is so significant that it should not be permitted because of a mere temporary or short-term incapacity at the critical time. Although the adoption process is often urgent, it must, it is submitted, await the outcome of an incapacity from which there is a prospect of recovery within a reasonably short space of time, as, for example, until a parent, unconscious after a road accident, recovers consciousness and ability to understand the consequences of agreeing or withholding agreement. Incapacity refers, it is submitted, to mental incapacity and is not referable to age. It must often happen, perhaps more in the past than now, that the parent is less than 16 years old, though the reported cases do not raise the point. The Age of Legal Capacity (Scotland) Act 1991 makes no express provision for granting capacity to a young mother[30] to agree to the adoption of her child, though it is possible to argue that the provision granting capacity to enter into transactions of a kind commonly entered into by persons of her age and circumstances and on terms which are not unreasonable[31] will meet the case.[32] Alternatively it might be argued, though less convincingly,[33] that since the 1991 Act grants children capacity to consent or withhold consent to their own adoptions from the age of 12 years[34] it can be gleaned from this that children of or above that age who are themselves parents have capacity to agree to their children's adoption. In any case, it is suggested that the female who is old enough to bear a child should be regarded as old enough to agree to that child's adoption, until such time as she is shown to be suffering from an incapacity referable to a condition other than her age.[35]

Unreasonable withholding of consent[36]

4.44   By far the most common ground upon which parental agreement is dispensed with is that it is being unreasonably withheld. Where dispensation is sought on this ground, it is commonly the case, at any rate where the proposed adoption is by strangers, that agreement has been once given and subsequently withdrawn. The statutory test is whether at the time of the hearing[37] or, if fresh evidence has been admitted on appeal, at the time of the appeal[38] agreement is being unreasonably withheld and not whether it has been unreasonably withdrawn. The fact that agreement has been given and then withdrawn is, however, relevant

---

[30] The issue of the father under 16 will seldom arise since, in Scotland at any rate, he cannot marry the mother and will not therefore have parental responsibilities and parental rights removal of which will require his agreement. He might, of course, be validly married under a foreign legal system and, though this is unlikely, he might acquire parental responsibilities and parental rights by being appointed guardian to the child. Expressly, a father of any age can acquire parental responsibilities and parental rights by entering into an agreement to that effect with the mother: Children (Scotland) Act 1995, s. 4.

[31] Age of Legal Capacity (Scotland) Act 1991, s. 2(1). The reference to "terms which are not unreasonable" suggest that, if an under-16-year-old mother does have capacity to agree to adoption she does not have capacity to withhold agreement unreasonably.

[32] "Transaction" is defined to include "the giving by a person of any consent having legal effect": Age of Legal Capacity (Scotland) Act 1991, s. 9(d).

[33] The two consents are not different sides of the same coin and it is rational to require more understanding for one than for the other.

[34] Age of Legal Capacity (Scotland) Act 1991, s. 2(3).

[35] *Cf.* the Australian case of *Re Application for Adoption of J* (1990) 71 N.T.R. in which the *Gillick* test was applied to the question in a case involving a 15-year-old mother.

[36] s. 16(2)(b).

[37] *Re L (An Infant)* [1974] 5 Fam.Law 24.

[38] *Re S (An Infant) (Adoption: Parental Consent)* [1973] 3 All E.R. 88. See also *S v. M*, 1999 S.L.T. 571.

to whether agreement is being unreasonably withheld. Vacillation is an element evidencing unreasonable withholding of agreement[39] although little weight will be attached to vacillation under stress.[40]

Whether this ground exists or not is not a matter that is absolutely governed **4.45** by the welfare test as contained in section 6 and section 24(3) of the 1978 Act. However, the welfare of the child is one factor that is always relevant to the reasonableness or otherwise of the withholding of agreement, and thus always relevant to the question of whether this ground exists: it has been said that "a reasonable mother would put the welfare of her child first".[41] This means that "the welfare of the child is a matter to which the reasonable parent must be presumed to give first consideration".[42] It has indeed been held that the question of whether a parent's consent is being unreasonably withheld is not a separate issue from the question of whether adoption would be in the child's best interests.[43] It is submitted that this is to confuse the question of the existence of the ground for dispensing with agreement with the question of whether agreement should be dispensed with. While closely related, the two issues are essentially distinct. An Extra Division of the Inner House has said this:

> "It is, no doubt, a difficult matter for the judge to stand back from his section 6 judgment [concerning whether to dispense with agreement] and make a separate, independent and different judgment from the standpoint of the reasonable parent [concerning whether the ground exists], but that is what the law requires."[44]

The welfare test set out in section 6 and section 24(3) is directly relevant only to the issue of whether dispensation should be granted, but the same considerations as those which these sections describe are matters to be taken into account in determining the reasonableness of the parent's refusal.[45] "The provisions of section 6 of the 1978 Act have a part to play in this analysis, because it must be assumed that the reasonable parent would approach the whole issue in the same way as is required of the court."[46]

It is clear that dispensation will not be granted merely because it is in the **4.46** child's interests to be adopted,[47] for otherwise the court could dispense with agreement every time it was satisfied that adoption was advisable, and "the right of the parent or guardian to refuse to agree to the adoption of the child would be rendered nugatory."[48] "It is perfectly feasible that the court will reach its own view that it would be better that the adoption order should proceed but none the less arrive at the view that a reasonable parent was perfectly entitled to withhold his or her consent to the making of such an order."[49]

---

[39] *AB v. CB*, 1963 S.C. 125, *per* Lord President Clyde at 137 and Lord Sorn at 138.

[40] *Re W (An Infant)* [1971] A.C. 682, *per* Lord Hailsham of St Marylebone at 700F.

[41] *P v. Lothian Regional Council*, above, *per* Lord Justice-Clerk Ross at 742H.

[42] *A v. B*, 1987 S.L.T. (Sh.Ct) 121, per Sheriff Stewart at 125J.

[43] *AB and CB, Petrs*, 1990 S.C.L.R. 809 at 811A.

[44] *Central Regional Council v. M*, 1991 S.C.L.R. 300, *per* Lord McCluskey at 302–303.

[45] *Lothian Regional Council v. A*, 1992 S.L.T. 858, *per* Lord President Hope at 863B. This comment is equally applicable to the amended s. 6 which now governs the issue.

[46] *C v. S*, 1996 S.L.T. 1387, *per* Lord President Hope at 1393A.

[47] *AB v. C*, 1977 S.C. 27, 1987 Fam. L.R. 84, *per* Lord President Emslie at 31; *AH and PH, Petrs*, 1997 Fam. L.R. 84, *per* Lord Marnoch at para. 16.04.

[48] Thomson, *Family Law in Scotland* (3rd ed.), p. 250. See also Lord Hodson in *Re W (An Infant)* [1971] A.C. 682 at 718: "it has been repeatedly held that the withholding of consent could not be held unreasonable merely because the [adoption] order, if made, would conduce to the welfare of the child".

[49] *Central Regional Council v. M*, above, *per* Lord McCluskey at 302.

4.47   There have been a number of cases on this ground,[50] but the two leading cases remain the House of Lords decisions of *A and B, Petitioners*[51] and *Re W (An Infant)*.[52] The central feature of the law as laid down in these two cases is that the reasonableness of the withholding of parental agreement is to be measured by the objective test of whether or not a reasonable parent would in all the circumstances have withheld agreement. The First Division more recently put it as follows: "This question must be looked at objectively and the test will be satisfied if no reasonable parent, in all the circumstances, would withhold agreement to the making of an adoption order."[53] The objective nature of the test means that the matter has to be viewed in the light of all the circumstances of the case even if these were not known to the actual parent. Because *inter alia* of the prospective adopters' right to remain anonymous, important features of the proposed adoption may in fact be unknown to the parent, but the reasonableness of his or her withholding agreement will nonetheless be assessed as if these features, along with all the other circumstances of the case, had been known.[54] An objective assessment will be made of how the interests of the child may be served. These interests will then be held in just balance with the interests of the prospective adopters and of the natural parent, because the reasonable parent, to whose judgment the matter is entrusted, would have regard to all these factors and would, in particular, attach great weight to the interests of the child. The question is viewed through the eyes of the parent but these eyes are endowed with a vision and perspective which the natural parent, by reason of ignorance or otherwise, may have lacked. On the other hand, it does not follow from the objectivity of the test that the court is entitled simply to substitute its own view for that of the natural parent.

> "Two reasonable parents can perfectly reasonably come to opposite conclusions on the same set of facts without forfeiting their title to be regarded as reasonable. The question in any given case is whether a parental veto comes within the band of possible reasonable decisions and not whether it is right or mistaken. Not every reasonable exercise of judgment is right, and not every mistaken exercise of judgment is unreasonable. There is a band of decisions within which no court should seek to replace the individual's judgment with its own."[55]

In that way, but only in that way, and to that extent *A and B, Petitioners* represents a vindication of what has been called the primacy of the natural parent's right.[56] It is better, however, that attention should be concentrated on the words of the statute than on concepts such as primacy of right which, although legitimate as a gloss on the statute, create a risk of introducing extraneous considerations. The statutory extent of the parent's right is that adoption cannot be effected without the parent's agreement unless, on one of the prescribed grounds, the court dispenses with that agreement. That agreement is required from parents

---

[50] See *B and B, Petrs*, 1946 S.L.T.(Sh.Ct) 36; *AB and CB v. X's Curator*, 1963 S.C. 124; *Re W (An Infant)* [1971] A.C. 682; *A and B, Petrs*, 1971 S.C. (H.L.) 129; *Re P (An Infant) (Adoption) (Parental Consent)* [1977] Fam. 25; *Re F (A Minor) (Adoption: Parental Consent)* [1982] 1 W.L.R. 102; *AB v. CB*, 1985 S.L.T. 514; *Re V (A Minor) (Adoption: Consent)* [1986] 1 All E.R. 752; *Re A (A Minor) (Adoption: Parental Consent)* [1987] 1 W.L.R. 153; *Re V (Adoption: Parents' Consent)* (1987) 15 Fam.Law 55; *A v. B*, 1987 S.L.T. (Sh.Ct) 121; *Re C (A Minor) (Adoption: Conditions)* [1988] 2 W.L.R. 474; *P v. Lothian Regional Council*, 1989 S.L.T. 739; *L v. Central Regional Council*, 1990 S.L.T. 818; *AB and CB, Petrs*, 1990 S.C.L.R. 809; *Central Regional Council v. M*, 1991 S.C.L.R. 300; *Lothian Regional Council v. A*, 1992 S.L.T. 858; *D v. F*, 1994 S.C.L.R. 417; *Re E (A Minor) (Freeing for Adoption)* [1995] 1 F.L.R. 382; *C v. S*, 1996 S.L.T. 1387; *B and Anor, Petrs*, 1996 S.L.T. 1370; *T, Petr*, 1997 S.L.T. 724.
[51] 1971 S.C. (H.L.) 129; 1971 S.L.T. 258.
[52] [1971] A.C. 682; [1971] 2 All E.R. 49.
[53] *Lothian Regional Council v. A*, above at 962L. See also *D v. F*, above, and *C v. S*, above.
[54] See Norrie, "Parental Pride: Adoption and the Gay Man", 1996 S.L.T. (News) 321 at 322.
[55] *Re W (An Infant)* [1971] 2 All E.R. at 56, *per* Lord Hailsham of St Marylebone.
[56] *A and B Petrs*, 1971 S.L.T. at 263, *per* Lord Simon of Glaisdale.

with parental responsibilities and parental rights is doubtless a reflection of the primary right of these parents to order the upbringing of their own children; that their agreement can be dispensed with is a qualification of that right. It is not, however, necessary to refer to the concepts of right which may lie behind the statute in order to determine whether a statutory ground for dispensation exists. If the parental withholding of agreement comes within the band of decisions open to a reasonable parent, acting with the knowledge and objectivity mentioned above, there can be no dispensation on this ground and, if it falls outwith that band, the way to dispensation is open. It is not, however, necessary for the court to make an explicit finding that the parent's decision is outwith the band of decisions which could be regarded as reasonable, so long as it looks at the whole matter objectively.[57]

Certain further propositions emerge from *A and B, Petitioners* and *Re W* **4.48** *(An Infant)*. These are to be read in the context of the objective test for assessing the reasonableness of the parental decision and, in the main, as describing, elaborating or explaining that test. The following are the principal among them:

(1) The interests or claims of the child, the natural parents and the prospective adopters all require to be considered.[58]

(2) Other things being equal, it may be in the best interests of a child to be with his or her natural parents but that consideration may be outweighed by other factors, including the merits of his or her new environment with the prospective adopters and, if a substantial time has intervened since the child was placed for adoption, the disruption necessarily involved in removing the child from a home in which he or she is happy and well cared for and into which he or she has been integrated.[59]

(3) The child's welfare is not to be considered exclusively or even primarily in a material sense but extends to all factors which will affect his or her future.[60] Although these factors are not spelt out in *A and B, Petitioners* it seems that the prospect of a stable home environment where he or she enjoys affection and care and may be expected to be happy is foremost among them.

(4) The right of natural parents to bring up their own children is reciprocal on the responsibility which they have to do so.[61] Their affection for a child and their natural claim as parents should not, however, be ignored if they have given up these responsibilities and agreed to adoption under the stress of adverse circumstances and on a change of circumstances have withdrawn that agreement.[62]

(5) The interests of the prospective adopters should not be ignored. By volunteering to perform the duty of bringing up the child they acquire a right to be considered and once they actually enter upon the fulfilment of responsibility towards the child they acquire thereby a further right to be considered. If as a result of the natural parent's actings, they have been brought into a quasi-parental role towards the child they ought not to be displaced without good reason.

(6) The fact that what will, in the long run, be in the child's best interests may often be uncertain is an additional reason for giving considerable weight in proper cases to the claims of the natural parents and of the prospective adopters.

---

[57] *Lothian Regional Council v. A*, 1992 S.L.T. 858 at 865G; *D v. F*, 1994 S.C.L.R. 417 at 423B.

[58] *ibid.* See also *P v. Lothian Regional Council*, 1989 S.L.T. 739; *D v. F*, 1994 S.C.L.R. 417; and *AH and PH, Petrs*, 1997 Fam. L.R. 84.

[59] *A and B, Petrs*, above, *per* Lord Guest at 260. Great stress was laid by Lord Guest on the fact that the child's parents had married after the child was placed for adoption although other factors were held to outweigh that. The main relevance of marriage in the context of the child's welfare is that it may indicate the stability of the home which the natural parents will be able to provide.

[60] *Re W (An Infant)*, above *per* Lord Donovan at 80. *Cf. A and B v. C*, 1977 S.C. 27.

[61] *A and B, Petrs*, above, *per* Lord Simon of Glaisdale at 262.

[62] *ibid. per* Lord Reid at 259.

4.49   The question of whether or not agreement is being unreasonably withheld is primarily one of fact to be determined by the court of first instance according to the circumstances of the particular case.[63] The question is, however, open for review by an appellate court which is entitled to come to a contrary conclusion to that of the court of first instance if the latter is plainly wrong.[64] The court should not treat the case as if it were an appeal against the decision to withhold agreement and thus challengeable only on the basis that it is wholly unreasonable: rather it is for the court to look at the whole matter afresh and to do so objectively in the knowledge that consent is being withheld by the parent, and the question is whether a reasonable parent would in all the circumstances have withheld consent.[65] As a description of how the onus lies, it is still correct to say that it is prima facie reasonable for a parent to withhold agreement to adoption[66] but cases of this kind will rarely be decided on onus. Cases in which, in the absence of culpability, parental agreement is unreasonably withheld are likely to be exceptional[67] but the reasonableness of the decision and not the exceptionality or otherwise of the circumstances remains the test.

4.50   That the position of the natural parent has improved in the interval between agreeing to adoption and withdrawing that agreement is a relevant factor but where, as in *Re W (An Infant)* and *A and B, Petitioners*, a significant period of time has elapsed, that will require to be weighted against the adverse consequences which may follow from disrupting the life of the child.[68] The stability of the home which adoptive parents are able to provide will usually indicate the unreasonableness of withholding agreement if the natural parents have a history of instability or, on other grounds, the child's future with them seems insecure.[69] Other instances of unreasonable withholding of agreement are where it is withheld by one parent in order to spite the other,[70] where the decision is not truly that of the parent[71] and where the decision is based on sentiment rather than substantive considerations.[72] A reasonable parent would not withhold agreement to adoption when he or she has nothing to offer the child,[73] nor any prospect of contact with the child in the foreseeable future,[74] nor when he or she has no accommodation in which the child could reside,[75] nor when the child had never lived with the natural parent and had bonded with the prospective adopters and when it would cause the child trauma and distress to remove the child from the only home he or she had known.[76] Nor would a reasonable parent withhold agreement simply in order to protect his or her own rights of contact, when all other factors point towards adoption being in the interests of the child: in that situation a reasonable parent would regard it as more important that the child enjoy the security which will

---

[63] *Re W (An Infant)*, above, *per* Lord Hailsham of St Marylebone at 56 and Lord Guest at 77; *D v. F*, above.

[64] *A and B, Petrs*, above, *per* Lord Guest at 260.

[65] *D v. F*, above, *per* Lord President Hope at 423B.

[66] *Re W (An Infant)*, *per* Lord Hailsham of St Marylebone at 55; *Re K (An Infant)* [1953] 1 Q.B. 117, *per* Jenkins L.J. at 129–130.

[67] *Re K (An Infant)*, above; *Re F (An Infant)* [1957] 1 All E.R. 819, *per* Harman J. at 825.

[68] *cf. Re L (An Infant)* (1962) 106 Sol. J. 611 and *Re W (Infants)* [1965] 3 All E.R. 231. See also *D v. F*, above.

[69] *Re P (An Infant)* [1976] 3 W.L.R. 924. See also *Re C (A Minor) (Adoption: Conditions)* [1988] 2 W.L.R. 474, *per* Lord Ackner at 484.

[70] *L v. M* (1955) 120 J.P. 27.

[71] *Re P (An Infant)* (1962) 107 Sol.J. 55.

[72] *S v. B* (1973) 4 Fam.Law 75.

[73] *Re D (An Infant) (Adoption) (Parent's Consent)* [1977] A.C. 602; *T, Petr*, 1997 S.L.T. 724.

[74] *Re F (A Minor) (Adoption: Parental Consent)* [1982] 1 W.L.R. 102; *Re E (A Minor) (Freeing for Adoption)* [1995] 1 F.L.R. 382.

[75] *Re H and Anr (Minors) (Adoption: Putative Father's Rights) (No. 3)* [1991] 2 All E.R. 185. See also *Re A (A Minor) (Adoption: Parental Consent)* [1987] 1 W.L.R. 153.

[76] *C v. S*, 1996 S.L.T. 1387.

follow from the making of an adoption order.[77] Parents who have not cared for their child for some years and who remained emotionally unstable were held to be unreasonable in withholding agreement to the child's adoption,[78] as were parents who spoke a different language from their children, who had not looked after their (now seven and eight year old) children since they were eight months and 18 months old, who had not been reliable in keeping access arrangements, with whom rehabilitation attempts had failed and of whom the children were afraid.[79] And a mother who has made it abundantly clear that she has no further interest in her child and no interest in any adoption proceedings in relation to her child is withholding her agreement unreasonably.[80]

Persistent failure to fulfil parental responsibilities[81]

The parent's or guardian's agreement may be dispensed with if the court is **4.51** satisfied that he or she has persistently failed, without reasonable cause, to fulfil either (1) the responsibility of safeguarding and promoting the child's health, development and welfare or, (2) if the child is not living with him or her, the responsibility to maintain personal relations and direct contact with the child on a regular basis. These are not mutually exclusive categories, and the parent who is not living with the child and who maintains regular contact with the child may nevertheless be held to have failed to fulfil the responsibility to safeguard and promote the child's health, development and welfare.[82] This ground for dispensing with parental agreement to adoption encompasses, but is wider than, the ground contained in section 16(2)(c) before the 1995 amendments, that is to say that the parent or guardian persistently failed without reasonable cause to discharge the parental duties in relation to the child. It also includes the previous, and not expressly re-enacted, grounds of abandonment and neglect, since the responsibility to safeguard and promote the child's health, development and welfare clearly includes a duty not to abandon or neglect the child. Abandonment, which is to leave the child to his or her fate, can never have reasonable cause, and unless steps are immediately taken to recover the child the abandonment will be considered to be a persistent failure. It is not relevant that the failure to fulfil parental responsibilities involves no risk to the child, such as when the child is in the care of others who are well able to safeguard and promote his or her health, development and welfare: the question is whether the parent or guardian whose agreement is in issue has been guilty of such failure and not what effect that failure has on the child. The ground clearly refers to past behaviour rather than future prospects: so in *L v. Central Regional Council*[83] the sheriff was overruled for holding that the equivalent ground before the 1995 amendments did not exist because the mother had recently established herself in a more settled environment and was now better able to provide properly for her children.[84] This is a matter relevant to whether consent should be dispensed with because of the ground, rather than to the existence of the ground itself.

A failure in the relevant responsibilities will normally be constituted by neglect **4.52** or inaction (such as failure to provide for or to keep in touch with the child) but positive acts may also amount to this ground for dispensation, at least when it is

---

[77] *AB v. CB*, 1985 S.L.T. 514; *AB and CB, Petrs*, 1990 S.C.L.R. 809; *Re H and Anr (Adoption) (Putative Father's Rights) (No. 3)* above; *Strathclyde Regional Council v. A*, Nov. 3, 1994 (1st Div.); *B and Anor, Petr*, 1996 S.L.T. 1370.

[78] *A and B, Petrs*, 1971 S.C. (H.L.) 129; see also (in another context) *Glasgow City Council v. M*, February 12, 1999 (Extra Div.).

[79] *AH and PH, Petrs*, 1997 Fam. L.R. 84.

[80] *T, Petr*, 1997 S.L.T. 724.

[81] s. 16(2)(c).

[82] *Angus Council, Petr*, June 12, 1998, unreported, *per* Lord Penrose.

[83] 1990 S.L.T. 818.

[84] *cf. R v. Lothian Regional Council*, 1987 S.C.L.R. 362, Sh.Ct, in which a mother claimed that her alcoholism was beaten.

the responsibility to safeguard and promote the child's health, development and welfare that is in issue. The duty to safeguard the child's health, for example, includes the duty not to visit acts of physical violence upon the child just as much as the duty to provide appropriate medical attention when needed. Neglect of the appropriate responsibilities is when the parent shows

> "want of reasonable care—that is, the omission of such steps as a reasonable parent would take, such as are usually taken in the ordinary experience of mankind... provided the parent had such means as would enable him to take the necessary steps."[85]

The omission of any reference to unnecessary suffering or likelihood of injury to health means that conduct which would not be criminal is not excluded in principle from the category of failure to fulfil parental responsibilities in the context of adoption. In order to be obnoxious to the statute, the failure must, however, be significant in kind and degree; it must relate to an aspect of the child's well-being to which a reasonable parent would attach importance and be of such seriousness as reasonably to cause concern for its adverse effects on the child. Not only neglect of physical welfare but also emotional neglect and rejection may be in point. Although there is in the adoption legislation no express provision corresponding to section 12(2)(a) of the Children and Young Persons (Scotland) Act 1937 relating to failure to provide adequate food, clothing, medical aid or lodging such failure falls, it is submitted, within the ordinary meaning of failure to fulfil the responsibility to safeguard and promote the child's health, development and welfare. The two qualifications to the failure to fulfil the appropriate parental responsibilities are (1) that the failure be without reasonable cause and (2) that the failure be persistent.

4.53   The lack of necessary means on the part of the parent to fulfil the parental responsibilities does not in itself give reasonable cause to fail to do so, and the parent may nonetheless be guilty of a failure to fulfil his or her responsibilities if he or she does not take reasonable steps to remedy that defect (as, *e.g.*, by taking advantage of the provisions of the welfare legislation). In *A v. B*[86] the sheriff held that a failure to aliment the child was not without reasonable cause when the parent had no earnings with which to fulfil the obligation. The position might, however, be different if the lack of resources had come about deliberately, for then the cause of the failure to fulfil parental responsibilities could hardly be described as being reasonable. In this connection the case of a parent serving a long term of imprisonment is problematic. The lack of opportunity to fulfil the parental responsibility to safeguard and promote the child's health, development and welfare is imputable to the prisoner's fault; however, against that it can be said that he or she has not willed the lack of opportunity of which the proximate cause is his or her imprisonment and any fault on his or her part is therefore too remote to characterise the failure as being without reasonable cause. There is much to be said for the view that the words "without reasonable cause" are designed to limit the ground of dispensing with agreement to the parent who has in some way forfeited the right to give consent through lack of caring. This may not necessarily be the case with the imprisoned parent. Dispensing with an imprisoned parent's agreement may often come more appropriately under the heading of unreasonable withholding of agreement. Additionally, since the child will not be living with the imprisoned parent, that parent will be under the duty to maintain contact with the child, and the ground will be established if the parent has failed to utilise such means of communication with the child as are open to him or her. It may well be reasonable cause for failing to fulfil the responsibility to safeguard and promote the child's health, development and welfare that the parent or guardian

---

[85] *R. v. Senior* [1899] 1 Q.B. 184, *per* Lord Russell C.J. at 291.
[86] 1987 S.L.T. (Sh.Ct) 121.

who lives apart from the child is not permitted by the residence parent to have any practical input or influence in the child's life, but he or she retains the responsibility to maintain personal relations and direct contact with the child on a regular basis and a failure in that responsibility will constitute this ground for dispensation. (This was probably the position under the previous law in any case[87] but the statute now puts it beyond doubt.[88]) Reasonable cause to fail in the responsibility to maintain contact might likewise be constituted by the residence parent's refusal to allow the child contact with the other parent, at least when the other continues to assert his or her rights. A parent whose child has been placed for adoption will nearly always thereby have reasonable cause for failure to maintain contact.[89] Where the child has been placed with strangers, it will usually be impracticable to maintain contact and, even in other cases, it may be desireable that the child should be given an opportunity to settle down in his or her prospective adoptive home without the conflict which may ensue from maintaining contact with the natural parent.

As well as being without reasonable cause, the failure must be persistent. **4.54** "Persistently" has been glossed as the equivalent of "permanently".[90] It is, however, submitted that to say this is to read words into the statute that are not there. In order to be characterised as persistent, the failure must endure over a substantial period of time though, unlike some Commonwealth legislatures,[91] Parliament has not prescribed a minimum period. The length of time required to constitute persistent failure is, therefore, a question of circumstances,[92] but if there has been failure over what can properly be regarded as a substantial period, it is submitted that it is irrelevant that it lacks or has lacked permanency because of interruption by periods of virtue or because of the prospect of reformation. Lord Coulsfield, speaking for the Inner House, put it thus: "clearly the failure must not be merely a temporary or excusable one, nor one whose effects are limited or transient. It must be a failure of enduring significance, at the time when the court is considering whether or not to dispense with consent. Each case, however, has to be judged on its own circumstances".[92a] No mental element is required to establish the existence of "persistent failure". In *Central Regional Council v. B*[93] the sheriff was overruled by an Extra Division of the Inner House because, *inter alia*, he had held that the adverb "persistently" imports *animus*. If this were also the case in the present context—and the statutory wording is so similar that a different construction could hardly be justified—then it would be irrelevant (to the question of whether the failure is persistent) whether the parent's failure were deliberate or wholly outwith his or her control.

Whether there has been a persistent failure without reasonable cause to fulfil **4.55** parental responsibilities has been discussed in a number of cases.[94] A father

---

[87] See *A v. B*, 1987 S.L.T. (Sh.Ct) 121, *per* Sheriff Stewart at 123.

[88] s. 16(2)(c)(ii).

[89] *Re M (An Infant)* (1965) 109 Sol. J. 574. *Quaere* whether there is reasonable cause when the terms of a supervision requirement to which the child is subject contains a condition of no contact between the child and parent. Such a case would probably turn on the reasons why the children's hearing felt it appropriate to make such a condition.

[90] *Re D (Minors) (Adoption by Parent)* [1973] 3 All E.R. 1001, *per* Sir George Baker P. at 1005.

[91] For example the various states of Australia, which require that there should be a failure to discharge the obligations of a parent or guardian for a period of not less than one year: Adoption of Children Act 1964 (Qld), s. 25(1)(d); Adoption of Children Act 1965 (NSW), s. 32(1)(d); Adoption Act 1984 (Vict.), s. 43(1)(e); Adoption Act 1988 (S.A.), s. 18(1)(d); Adoption Act 1988 (Tas.), s. 37(1)(e); Adoption Act 1993 (ACT), s. 35(1)(d); Adoption Act 1994 (W.A.), s. 24(2)(b) (in which a period of two years is specified); Adoption of Children Act 1994 (N.T.), s. 35(d).

[92] In *Re M (An Infant)* (1965) 109 Sol. J. 574 it was doubted if six months was long enough to constitute persistent failure.

[92a] *G and G, Petrs*, Feb. 26, 1999.

[93] 1985 S.L.T. 413 (interpreting the phrase "persistent failure" as it appeared in s. 16 of the Social Work (Scotland) Act 1968).

[94] The previous statutory formulation at issue, that the parent has persistently failed to discharge parental duties, is so similar to the effect of the current wording that these cases remain relevant.

who, after separation from his wife, saw the young children of the marriage only occasionally and who, after divorce, did not see or maintain them, although he maintained some contact by sending presents, was held by the Divisional Court in England not to have persistently failed to discharge the obligations of a parent.[95] Likewise, there was no persistent failure without reasonable cause where a mother, in a six-month period following the placing of the child for adoption, did not maintain contact with him,[96] and it is generally reasonable for a parent not to maintain contact with a child placed for adoption although it may be reasonable to make inquiries if, after a lapse of time, steps in the adoption process are not taken. Where, however, a mother handed her children over to foster carers soon after their birth, and thereafter, although for much of the time she had accommodation for them, showed little interest in them, visiting them only seldom and paying little towards their maintenance although drawing family allowances for them, it was held that there was persistent failure without reasonable cause.[97] A father who neither claims residence nor aliments a child of his marriage born after separation from his wife and placed by her for adoption may be said to have persistently failed in his duty.[98]

Serious ill-treatment[99]

4.56   The final ground upon which a parent's or guardian's agreement to adoption can be dispensed with is that he or she has seriously ill-treated the child, whose reintegration into the same household as the parent or guardian is, because of the serious ill-treatment or for other reasons, unlikely. Ill-treatment is an echo of section 12(1) of the Children and Young Persons (Scotland) Act 1937 but there is no requirement that the ill-treatment amounts to an offence before it will justify dispensing with parental agreement to adoption: so the likelihood of unnecessary suffering or injury to health is irrelevant, except in so far as it indicates seriousness. Conduct resulting in "agitation of mind, astonishment and disgust",[1] may be ill-treatment for this purpose although not for the purposes of a criminal offence. There need not be a physical element in the conduct and threats, language or conduct calculated to create terror in the child, or verbal abuse, may be enough. The age, health and constitution of the child and his or her history require to be taken into consideration and what may be innocuous in the case of a healthy, well-cared-for child may be ill-treatment "if applied to a child already enfeebled and suffering from previous ill-usage".[2]

4.57   For this ground for dispensing with parental agreement to exist there must be something that justifies the explicit qualification of ill-treatment by the epithet "serious". Ill-treatment that amounts to an offence will nearly always be serious, as will any treatment whose deleterious consequences last for more than a very short period of time. In addition, it is only where the reintegration of the child within the household of the parent or guardian is unlikely that the ground exists, and, while it is not necessary that the unlikelihood of reintegration should be because of the ill-treatment, the prospects of reintegration will in most cases afford a good indication of whether or not the ill-treatment was serious. The use of the word "reintegration" should not, it is submitted, be taken to imply that this ground is inapplicable when the child has never been a member of the household of the parent or guardian, for there is no reason to limit the ground to

---

[95] *Re D (Minors) (Adoption by Parent)* [1973] 3 All E.R. 1001. As noted above, however, it is to be doubted if this proceeds on a sound view of the law.
[96] *Re M (An Infant)* (1965) 109 Sol. J. 574.
[97] *Re P (Infants) (Adoption) (Parental Consent)* [1962] 1 W.L.R. 1296.
[98] *Re B (S) (An Infant)* [1968] 1 Ch. 204. See further *Re H (Minors)*, *The Times*, Nov. 26, 1974; *Re M and M* (1976) 6 Fam.Law 172; *H and H, Petrs*, 1976 S.L.T. 80; *A and B v. C*, 1977 S.L.T. (Sh.Ct) 55; *L v. Central Regional Council*, 1990 S.L.T. 818.
[99] s. 16(2)(d).
[1] *R. v. Hatton* [1925] 2 K.B. 322 at 324.
[2] *Farquharson v. Gordon* (1894) 21 R. (J.) 52, *per* Lord Justice-Clerk Macdonald at 53.

cases in which the child was once, but is no longer, a member of the parent's or guardian's household. It is conceivable that a parent who has always lived apart from the child can seriously ill-treat the child, and if integration of the child into that person's household is, for whatever reason, unlikely, the ground for dispensing with that person's agreement exists.

Freeing for adoption

The question of the parent's or guardian's agreement to adoption, or **4.58** dispensation therefrom, can be dealt with in the same process as the making of the adoption order itself, and the discussion so far has assumed that this will be so. However, it has been possible since the coming into force of the Adoption (Scotland) Act 1978 for the issue of the parent's or guardian's agreement to be examined and, if appropriate, dispensed with in a separate and earlier process in which the court makes an order declaring the child free for adoption.[3] This has the practical advantage that the parent's agreement can be obtained earlier than otherwise, thus reducing the risk of the parent changing his or her mind at a late stage: for while in the normal case agreement is not binding and can be withdrawn at any time until the adoption order is made, its retraction after a freeing order is without effect and the only way the parent can later prevent the adoption is to have the freeing order revoked.[4] Prospective adopters, with whom the child is placed, obtain thereby a greater sense of security. And it has the further advantage that the natural parent can give his or her final agreement earlier and so drop out of the picture earlier and thus be free from prolonged trauma and further inquiry.[5]

The court may make an order declaring a child free for adoption on an **4.59** application by an adoption agency which is a local authority,[6] if satisfied either (1) that each parent or guardian[7] of the child has freely and with full understanding of what is involved agreed generally[8] and unconditionally to the making of an adoption order, or (2) that the parent's or guardian's agreement to the making of an adoption order should be dispensed with on any of the grounds listed in section 16(2) and described above.[9] The application to free the child for adoption is competent only when made with the consent of a parent or guardian of the child, or alternatively, when the child is in the care of the adoption agency, the adoption agency is applying for dispensation of the agreement of each parent or guardian of the child.[10] Though the same considerations apply to dispensation of parental agreement both to the adoption order and the freeing order, the orders do achieve different things and it is possible that withholding agreement to one order is unreasonable but withholding agreement to the other is reasonable.[11] The court is directed by section 18(1) to make the order when applied for if satisfied that the appropriate agreements have been given or dispensed with, subject only to the requirement that the child over 12 years of age consents to the order. However, there is little doubt that a decision in a

---

[3] See 1985 S.L.T. (News) 1 at 1–4.

[4] On revocation, see below, paras 4.64–4.67.

[5] Though in practice the freeing procedure is used most frequently to secure a dispensation of parental agreement at an earlier stage than would otherwise be possible. A further advantage, which played a part in *Re W (A Minor)* [1997] 3 All E.R. 620 is that if parental agreement is to be dispensed with, this is done at the behest of a local authority rather than the prospective adopters.

[6] Prior to the 1995 amendments, any adoption agency, whether local authority or private adoption society, could apply for a freeing order. See the Children (Scotland) Act 1995, Sched. 2, para. 11(a).

[7] Defined as above, para. 4.31.

[8] s. 12(1) (agreement to adoption) does not require "general" agreement. Its use in the context of s. 18(1) (agreement on freeing for adoption) reflects the fact that it is not required that the parent or guardian agree to a particular adoption, but that they agree to the child's eventual adoption.

[9] s. 18(1).

[10] s. 18(2).

[11] See *Re H (A Minor) (Adoption Proceedings)* [1994] 2 F.C.R. 437.

freeing application is a "decision relating to the adoption of the child", thereby activating section 6. The decision is also, expessly, governed by the rule in section 24(3) that "the court shall regard the welfare of the child as its paramount consideration and shall not make the order in question unless it considers that it would be better for the child that it should do so than that it should not". The court is, therefore, able to refuse to make the order, even when all the conditions in section 18(1) are satisfied, if it is not persuaded that the order would be in the child's interests. The structure of the provisions indicates that a freeing order should be made only where an adoption is likely to take place within 12 months or shortly thereafter.[12] Though the grounds of dispensation are the same as under section 16(2), there is a further requirement in the freeing process, that is, that no agreement can be dispensed with unless the child is already placed for adoption or the court is satisfied that it is likely that the child will be placed for adoption.[13] As with an application for adoption, the agreement of a mother to the making of a freeing order is ineffective if given less than six weeks after the child's birth[14] and the consent of a child of or over the age of 12 years is required, except that where the court is satisfied that the child is incapable of giving consent to the making of the order, it may dispense with that consent.[15]

4.60   Before making an order freeing a child for adoption, the court must satisfy itself, in relation to each parent or guardian of the child who can be found, that he or she has been given an opportunity of making, if he or she so wishes, a declaration that he or she prefers not to be involved in future questions concerning the adoption of the child.[16] In the case of a child whose father is not and has not been married to the mother and who does not have any parental responsibilities or parental rights in relation to the child (and is not therefore considered a parent in the adoption process itself[17]), the court must, before making the order, satisfy itself in relation to any person claiming to be the father that either (1) he has no intention of applying for, or, if he did so apply, it is likely that he would be refused, an order under section 11 of the Children (Scotland) Act 1995; and (2) he has no intention of entering into an agreement with the mother under section 4 of the 1995 Act, or, if he has such an intention, that no agreement under that section is likely to be made (*i.e.* the mother is unlikely to agree).[18] "It is a condition of the application of that provision that there is a person who is actively asserting a claim to be the father of the child in question."[19]

4.61   Where the child is subject to a supervision requirement the court making a freeing order may, if satisfied that, in consequence of making the order, compulsory measures of supervision in respect of the child are no longer necessary, determine that the child shall forthwith cease to be subject to that requirement.[20] The decision whether to make such a determination is governed by the welfare test contained in section 6. Conditions may not be attached to a freeing order, in the way that they can be with an adoption order.[21]

---

[12] *per* Lord Browne-Wilkinson in *Re G (A Minor)* [1997] 2 All E.R. 534 at 541C.

[13] s. 18(3).

[14] s. 18(4).

[15] s. 18(8), as amended by the Age of Legal Capacity (Scotland) Act 1991, s. 2(3). It is notable, though probably without substantive effect, that s. 2(3) confers capacity on children above the age of 12 years to consent to an adoption order but does not expressly confer capacity to consent to a freeing order. Capacity, it is submitted, is carried with the requirement to obtain consent and, in relation to the adoption order, s. 2(3) is for the avoidance of doubt only.

[16] s. 18(6). This decision may be withdrawn at any time in relevant form: RCS 1994, r. 67.12; A.S. 1997, r. 2.10(5).

[17] s. 65(1), as amended by the Children (Scotland) Act 1995, Sched. 2, para. 29.

[18] s. 18(7), as substituted by the Children (Scotland) Act 1995, Sched. 2, para. 11(c).

[19] *Angus Council, Petr*, June 12, 1998, unreported, *per* Lord Penrose.

[20] s. 18(9), as inserted by the Children (Scotland) Act 1995, Sched. 2, para. 11(d).

[21] See below, paras 4.77–4.79.

Effect of a freeing order

On the making of an order freeing a child for adoption the parental **4.62** responsibilities and parental rights in relation to the child are transferred to the adoption agency (*i.e.* the local authority which applied for the freeing order).[22] Thereafter, when the adoption application itself comes to be considered, there is no need to obtain the further agreement of the parent or guardian, or to dispense with their agreement[23]: apart from that feature, the effect of a freeing order is very similar to a parental responsibilities order made under section 86 of the Children (Scotland) Act 1995.[24] There is no effect on the child's status (which does not change until the adoption order) and so, for example, the child retains after a freeing order succession rights in the estate of the natural parent.

The parent does, however, retain certain rights in the adoption process, even **4.63** after the making of the freeing order. First, within 14 days following the date 12 months after the making of the freeing order the adoption agency to which parental responsibilities and parental rights were transferred by the order shall, if it has not already done so, inform the "relevant parent"[25] whether an adoption order has been made in respect of the child and, if no such order has been made, whether the child has his or her home with a person with whom he or she has been placed for adoption.[26] If an adoption order has not been made at the time when the relevant parent is to be given notice, the adoption agency must thereafter give notice to the parent of the making of an adoption order (if and when made) and meanwhile give notice whenever the child is placed for adoption or ceases to be placed with a person with a view to his or her being adopted by that person.[27] None of these requirements applies if, before the expiry of the 12-month period, the agency has informed the relevant parent that an adoption order has been made[28] or if the parent has made a declaration that he or she does not wish to be involved in further questions concerning the adoption of the child[29] (unless, in that latter case, the declaration has been withdrawn). Secondly, the parent retains title to seek a revocation of the freeing order.

Revocation of freeing order

An order freeing a child for adoption may be revoked on the application of the **4.64** relevant parent[30], on the ground that he or she wishes to resume parental responsibilities and parental rights.[31] An application is competent, however, only if (a) no adoption order has been made in respect of the child and (b) the child does not have his or her home with a person with whom he or she has been placed for adoption.[32] It is sufficient

---

[22] s. 18(5), as substituted by the Children (Scotland) Act 1995, Sched. 2, para. 11(b).

[23] s. 16(1)(a).

[24] See below, Chap. 17. An order under s. 86 transfers all parental rights and responsibilities to the local authority, except the right to grant or withhold agreement to the making of an adoption order or a freeing order, which right remains with the parent or guardian in respect of whom the parental responsibilities order has been made: s. 86(3). One important difference is that an order under s. 86 does but a freeing order does not make the child a child who is "looked after" by a local authority in terms of s. 17(6) of the Children (Scotland) Act 1995.

[25] *i.e.* each parent or guardian who must be given the opportunity under s. 18(6) of declaring that he or she prefers not to be involved in future questions concerning the adoption of the child: s. 19(1).

[26] s. 19(2).

[27] s. 19(3), as amended by the Children (Scotland) Act 1995, Sched. 2, para. 12(c). For a discussion of the analogous English provision (s. 19(3) of the Adoption Act 1976), see *R. v. Derbyshire County Council, ex p. T and Anr* [1990] 1 All E.R. 792.

[28] s. 19(2)(a).

[29] s. 19(4)(b), as amended by the Children (Scotland) Act 1995, Sched. 2, para. 12(d).

[30] *i.e.* each parent or guardian who must be given the opportunity under s. 18(6) of declaring that he or she prefers not to be involved in future questions concerning the adoption of the child: s. 19(1). The application cannot be made by any other parent: *Re C (Adoption: Freeing Order)* [1999] 1 F.L.R. 348.

[31] s. 20(1), as amended by the Children (Scotland) Act 1995, Sched. 2, para. 13.

[32] *ibid.*

that the applicant is willing to resume parental responsibilities and parental rights and there is no requirement that the applicant should him or herself be able to provide a home for the child. The application can be made by the relevant parent at any time more than 12 months after the making of the order, and it must specify detailed proposals for the future well-being of the child.[33] In addition, the adoption agency may, at any time after the making of the order, apply to the court for an order revoking the freeing order, so long as no adoption order has been made in respect of the child and the child does not have his or her home with a person with whom he or she has been placed for adoption.[34] The court is not, however, bound to grant the application and in reaching its decision it must have regard to all the circumstances and apply the rules in section 6.[35] The court may appoint a curator *ad litem* who shall have regard to the welfare of the child as his or her paramount duty and who shall further (i) investigate the facts contained in the minute of application to revoke, (ii) investigate the circumstances and care of the child with regard to the promotion of his or her welfare throughout his or her life, and (iii) ascertain from the child whether he or she wishes to express a view and, where the child indicates such a wish, ascertain that view.[36] A report in writing must be made to the court within four weeks of the appointment of the curator, or within such period as the court allows.[37]

4.65   In relation to the equivalent provision in the English legislation,[38] it was said that "the requirement in section 20 of the Act of 1976 that the parent can apply for revocation 'on the grounds that [the former] parent wishes to resume parental responsibility' does not postulate that the former parent must wish for sole and unfettered parental responsibility".[39] This was in the context of a finding under the 1976 Act that on revocation it is open to the court to make a public law order such as a care order under section 31 of the Children Act 1989. Under the Scottish legislation it is equally true that the parent can apply for a revocation order without seeking the restoration to him or her of full parental responsibilities and parental rights, but the structure of the Scottish legislation suggests that, contrary to the English position, there is no power to make a public law order such as a parental responsibilities order under section 86 of the Children (Scotland) Act 1995. The revocation of a freeing order revokes the local authority's parental responsibilities and parental rights in relation to the child, and the court which revokes the order must then determine on whom are to be imposed the parental responsibilities and to whom are to be given the parental rights in relation to the child; it is directed to make an order under section 11 of the Children (Scotland) Act 1995 giving effect to that determination.[40] This obligation is mandatory and it would seem that the court cannot revoke a freeing order without also making a section 11 order. This replaces the previous rule that on revocation of the freeing order parental rights and duties were vested in those who had them before they were vested in the local authority. The current provision is designed to be more flexible and also to ensure that the court directs its mind to the position of the child after the freeing order is revoked. It is not

---

[33] A.S. 1997, r. 2.15(1). There is no equivalent in the Rules of the Court of Session.

[34] s. 20(1A), as inserted by the Children (Scotland) Act 1995, Sched. 2, para. 13(b).

[35] *Re G (A Minor)* [1997] 2 All E.R. 534, *per* Lord Browne-Wilkinson at 539J. It is to be noted that the rules in s. 24(3) do not apply to the decision to revoke a freeing order.

[36] A.S. 1997, rr. 2.16 and 2.17. RCS 1994, r. 67.14(5) lists rather different duties for curators *ad litem* appointed by the Court of Session.

[37] *ibid.*

[38] Adoption Act 1976, s. 20(1).

[39] *per* Lord Browne-Wilkinson in *Re G (A Minor)* above, at 541E.

[40] s. 20(3), as substituted by Children (Scotland) Act 1995, Sched. 2, para. 13(d). See also RCS 1994, r. 67.15A.

the case, as it was in the previous law, that an application for revocation carries the connotation that parental responsibilities and parental rights are to vest in the applicant, and in making the section 11 order the court is, of course, bound by the principles in section 11(7).[41] However, since the parental responsibilities and parental rights controlled by section 11 can be held only by natural persons[42], it is not possible, on revocation of a freeing order, to make an order in favour of a local authority such as a parental responsibilities order. The result is that, on revocation of a freeing order, the child is released from public law involvement and if such involvement remains necessary the local authority must commence public law proceedings anew.[43] If such release is not in the child's interests then the only course is for the court to refuse to revoke the freeing order.[44]

While the application for revocation is pending the adoption agency retains **4.66** the parental responsibilities and parental rights but is prohibited from placing the child for adoption without the leave of the court.[45] There is no indication of what the consequences of the granting of leave are in relation to the application for revocation but it seems that it does not automatically fall when leave is granted or even if the child is thereafter placed for adoption. It is, of course, superseded by an adoption order which might competently be made following such a placement and before the revocation proceedings were completed, for a child remains free for adoption although such proceedings are pending. It is, however, unlikely that a court would grant an adoption order in these circumstances, and still less so if a child were placed without leave and therefore in contravention of the statutory prohibition.

If an application for revocation made by the relevant person is dismissed on **4.67** the ground that to allow it would contravene the principles embodied in section 6 of the Adoption (Scotland) Act 1978, the applicant is precluded from making any further application for revocation without leave of the court.[46] The court may grant such leave only if it appears that, because of a change in circumstances, or for any other reason, it is proper to allow the application to be made. Unless the court grants leave to make a further application, the failure of the application releases the adoption agency from the duty of complying with the statutory requirement on progress reports, so far as the applicant in question is concerned.[47] Leave is not required for a further application if the application is dismissed on grounds other than those embodied in section 6. Leave will not therefore be required when the application is dismissed on the ground of incompetency (*e.g.* because the required period of time has not elapsed since the freeing order was made, or because, when the application is made, the child remains placed with

---

[41] *i.e.* that the welfare of the child is the court's paramount consideration and that no order should be made unless it is better to make the order than not to do so, and that the child's views should be taken appropriately into account. Since, however, s. 20(3) of the 1978 Act obliges the court to make an order under s. 11 of the 1995 Act, the no order presumption in s. 11(7) would seem to be of no effect here.

[42] Children (Scotland) Act 1995, s. 15(4).

[43] It is to be noted that in revocation proceedings the court has no power to refer the child to the reporter, specifying that a ground of referral to the children's hearing exists. Section 54(2)(c) is applicable only to "proceedings for an adoption order... or for an order under s. 18". Revocation proceedings take place under s. 20.

[44] This is contrary to the holding of the House of Lords in *Re G (A Minor)* [1997] 2 All E.R. 534, but the new statutory wording of s. 20(3), introduced by the Children (Scotland) Act 1995, Sched. 2, para. 13(d), creates a very different regime from that in the English legislation, under which there is no requirement that the court make a private law order on revocation of the freeing order.

[45] s. 20(2), as amended by the Children (Scotland) Act 1995, Sched. 2, para. 13(c).

[46] s. 20(4)(a) and (5).

[47] s. 20(4)(b).

a person with whom he or she had been placed for adoption), or when the application is dismissed of consent or is abandoned. Leave will, however, be required whenever an application is dismissed on its merits as every such decision to dismiss must be governed by section 6.[48]

DECISION ON MERITS OF ADOPTION

The rules in section 6 and section 24(3)

4.68   When the conditions precedent to the making of an adoption order have been satisfied, the decision on the merits of whether or not an order should be made is governed by section 6 of the Adoption (Scotland) Act 1978, as substituted by section 95 of the Children (Scotland) Act 1995, and section 24(3), as added by paragraph 16 of Schedule 2 to the 1995 Act. Section 6 provides:

> "(1) Without prejudice to sections 12(8) and 18(8), in reaching any decision relating to the adoption of a child, a court or adoption agency shall have regard to all the circumstances but—
> > (a) shall regard the need to safeguard and promote the welfare of the child concerned throughout his life as the paramount consideration; and
> > (b) shall have regard so far as practicable—
> > > (i) to his views (if he wishes to express them) taking account of his age and maturity; and
> > > (ii) to his religious persuasion, racial origin and cultural and linguistic background.
>
> (2) Without prejudice to the generality of paragraph (b) of subsection (1), a child twelve years of age or more shall be presumed to be of sufficient age and maturity to form a view for the purposes of that paragraph".

This wording is different in a number of significant respects from that which was contained in section 6 before the 1995 amendments.[49] The original section 6 had been repeated from section 3 of the Children Act 1975 and had not added significantly to the law before that. The Adoption Act 1958 had required, as had its predecessors, that a court before making an adoption order should be satisfied that the order if made would be for the welfare of the child[50] and that due consideration should be given to the wishes of the child, having regard to his age and understanding.[51] There was, it is true, no specific requirement to relate a consideration of the child's welfare to the duration of his or her childhood or life but, despite the difficulties of prediction which were experienced and will remain, it had never been supposed that, in a case of adoption, welfare could be judged on a short-term basis. This has now been made explicit, with the requirement to treat as paramount the need to safeguard and promote the welfare of the child throughout his or her life. Though assessment of welfare becomes necessarily more speculative the longer the timeframe involved, the change in wording is an overdue recognition that some of the consequences of adoption (such as those relating to succession, nationality and forbidden degrees) extend beyond the child's childhood. It will be appropriate to adopt a child very close

---

[48] The principles embodied in s. 6 are, it is thought, exhaustive of the principles governing a decision on the merits. (S. 24(3) is expressly limited to decisions under s. 18(1) on the granting and not on the revocation of a freeing order.) It is to be noted that these principles include having regard to all the circumstances.

[49] Section 6 originally read as follows: "In reaching any decision relating to the adoption of a child, a court or adoption agency shall have regard to all the circumstances, first consideration being given to the need to safeguard and promote the welfare of the child throughout his childhood; and shall so far as practicable ascertain the wishes and feelings of the child regarding the decision and give due consideration to them, having regard to his age and understanding."

[50] Adoption Act 1958, s. 7(1) and (6).

[51] *ibid.* s. 7(2).

to his or her 18th birthday in order to obtain the benefits of the parent–child relationship other than the upbringing powers over a child inhering in a parent: in the totality of the circumstances welfare beyond childhood is always a relevant, and may in some cases be a determining, consideration.[52] The change in the place of welfare from "first consideration" (as s. 6 was orginally worded) to "paramount consideration" (as s. 6 says after the 1995 amendments), which was necessitated by the U.K.'s ratification of the UN Convention on the Rights of the Child,[53] means that the child's welfare will always be the determining factor (see below), but it does not mean that other factors may not be taken into account (otherwise the words in s. 6(1)(b) would have no effect). It means rather that factors are relevant in so far as they indicate wherein the child's interests lie and that the court is prohibited from making a decision relating to adoption which will go against the child's welfare. The interests of the natural and of the prospective adoptive parents are relevant and should be taken into account, as should all the circumstances of the case, but are subservient to the welfare of the child.

The requirement to have regard to the views of the child, and to the child's **4.69** religious persuasion, racial origin and cultural and linguistic background, is a requirement to take these factors into account in assessing wherein the child's welfare lies. They are, however, matters subsidiary to the child's welfare, which is paramount. Any consideration is relevant only in so far as it affects the child's welfare, and section 6(1)(b) effectively directs the court to treat these matters as relevant. There is no requirement to accept and follow the child's views and still less is there a requirement to place or even to attempt to place the child with prospective adopters of the same racial origin or cultural and linguistic background as the child. The child's welfare requires, rather, that the court be sensitive to any child's needs to be aware of his or her origins.[54] The reference to religious persuasion is to the child's and not his or her natural parents' religious persuasion. As such it is not a relevant consideration in cases of children who are too young to adhere to any religious faith; and for the older child it does not amount to a requirement that the prospective adopters be of the same faith as the child. Rather, it indicates that a factor telling against a successful adoption would be the prospective adopters' unwillingness to permit a believing child to continue with the religious observances to which he or she has become accustomed. Similarly, while it will seldom be in a child's best interests to be placed with prospective adopters who do not speak the language in which the child is most fluent, this is not determining and, in exceptional cases, there may well be other factors (such as the child's attachment to the prospective adopters and the lack of suitable alternatives) which outweigh language difficulties and make it, in all the circumstances of the case, for the welfare of the child to be adopted by such applicants.

Section 24(3) to some extent repeats the welfare principle contained in **4.70** section 6. It provides that "In considering whether to make an adoption order or any order under section 18(1), the court shall regard the welfare of the child concerned as its paramount consideration and shall not make the order in question unless is considers that it would be better for the child that it should do so than that it should not". This provision, unlike section 6, is limited to decisions on the

---

[52] See *Re D (A Minor) (Adoption Order: Validity)* [1991] 3 All E.R. 461. But *cf. Re A (An Infant)* [1963] 1 All E.R. 531 in which an adoption order was refused when the child was one month short of majority but in which avowedly the only reason for the adoption was to confer British nationality on the child. On that issue, see further, below, para. 4.76.

[53] Art. 21.

[54] See the discussion of these issues in *AH and PH, Petrs*, 1997 Fam. L.R. 84 (a case decided before the 1995 amendments to s. 6 gave them legislative recognition) and in *Re N (A Minor) (Adoption)* [1990] 1 F.L.R. 58. See also Hayes, "The Ideological Attack on Transracial Adoption in the USA and Britain" (1995) 9 Int. J. Law and Fam. 1.

making of the adoption order itself and the making (but not the revoking) of a freeing order, and its application is further limited to courts making such decisions. The welfare principle is no different from that contained in section 6 (though worded slightly differently) and it adds nothing to the law contained therein. The second clause is more significant as it requires the court to make a positive decision that adoption would be better for the child than not to be adopted.[55] In the context of section 11 orders, this has been referred to as "the no-order presumption".[56] However, adoption cases will seldom be decided by applying presumptions and the provision probably amounts to little more than an exhortation to the court to be satisfied that adoption is indeed the most appropriate method of securing the child's welfare before making an adoption order. There is no requirement that the court make a positive finding that adoption is more appropriate than a residence order[57] (or, indeed, than no order), and the application of the welfare test will nearly always resolve a dispute as to which if any order is more appropriate. The question has often arisen of what advantage an adoption order gives over, for example, long-term fostering secured by a residence order and it has been said, "To that the answer is always the same—and it is always a good answer—adoption gives us total security and makes the child part of our family and places us in parental control of the child; long-term fostering leaves us exposed to changes of view of the local authority, it leaves us exposed to applications, and so on, by the natural parents".[58] The "no order" principle also applies to conditions attached to the adoption order, so that conditions should not be so attached unless the court is satisfied that it would be better for the child to attach conditions than not to do so.[59]

Meaning of "welfare"

4.71   In deciding the merits of making an order, as in assessing the reasonableness of the withholding of parental agreement, a broad view should be taken of the child's welfare.

> "One must look at the whole future of the child; not to mere temporary unhappiness or grief, however acute, if it is transient; not to mere material affluence in childhood or a better chance through educational advantages, to achieve affluence later."[60]

Disruption in a child's life should not, however, be lightly dismissed as likely to be transient in its effects, and has to be regarded in the light of the increased recognition given to the importance of continuity for the secure and stable upbringing of a child.[61] Medical evidence may be of assistance in assessing the

---

[55] Prior to its repeal by Sched. 5 to the Children (Scotland) Act 1995, s. 53 of the Children Act 1975 had required the court to treat as a custody application any adoption application in which the court considered that a custody order would be more appropriate than an adoption order. The new s. 24(3), together with the power of the court to make a s. 11 order even when not asked to do so, rendered that provision unnecessary.

[56] See below, paras 10.36—10.40.

[57] *C v. S*, 1996 S.L.T. 1387.

[58] *Re H (Infants) (Adoption: Parental Consent)* [1977] 2 All E.R. 339, *per* Ormrod L.J. at (1982) 3 F.L.R. 386 and 388. See also *C v. S*, above and *B and Anor, Petrs*, 1996 S.L.T. 1370. In *G and G, Petrs*, Feb. 26, 1999, the underlying hope of the mother (whose consent was dispensed with) to recover full-time care of the child was held to be a destabilising factor which favoured the granting of an adoption order rather than a residence order.

[59] *Re T (A Minor) (Contact After Adoption)* [1995] 2 F.C.R. 537. Part of the reasoning in this case was that attaching no conditions relating to contact did not deprive the natural mother of her right later to seek contact. That line of reasoning does not apply in Scotland (Children (Scotland) Act 1995, s. 11(3) and (4)(a)) but the principle that a condition should be shown to be better for the child than not making the condition remains sound.

[60] *Re C(L)* [1965] 2 Q.B. 449, *per* Diplock L.J. at 471.

[61] See *J v. C* [1970] A.C. 668; *A and B, Petrs*, 1971 S.C.(H.L.) 129; *Re B (MF) (An Infant), Re D (SL) (An Infant)* [1972] 1 W.L.R. 102; *Re M (An Infant) (No. 2)* (1964) 108 Sol. J. 1031.

effects of disruption,[62] but even in the absence of such evidence the court is entitled to reach the conclusion that disruption is likely to have serious adverse effects.[63] "Welfare" comprehends every factor likely to affect the physical, mental and emotional development of the child, including "educational, general surroundings, happiness, stability of home and the like",[64] and is not restricted, or even mainly directed, to material considerations.[65] Stability in the child's life is sometimes the only advantage that adoption will give, but that is sufficient to justify the making of the order.[66] A principal merit of adoption—indeed its primary aim—is that it provides the child with a normal family background which, in most cases, he or she would otherwise lack, and it is usually thought that that can be achieved only if there is a complete break of links with the natural parents.[67] In some instances, especially of adoption by relatives, there may, however, be benefits in maintaining contact with the natural parents,[68] and even where there are no specialities pointing to the advantage of maintaining contact the fact that contact will be maintained is not necessarily a factor that is conclusive against adoption.[69] The court is not required, as it had been by the Adoption Act 1958[70] but not by previous legislation, to have regard to the health of the applicants. Serious chronic illness affecting capacity to care for the child, or of an infectious character, are, however, obvious factors to be taken into account.[71] Stress was previously laid on the advantage of adoption in removing the stigma of illegitimacy,[72] which was commonly considered to be its practical effect, although until the Children Act 1975 it did not in the full sense legitimise an "illegitimate" child.[73] This is probably a far less potent consideration now that the legal status of illegitimacy has all but disappeared. The character of the applicants is necessarily an important consideration, but a conviction for an offence against a child is not an automatic disqualification if a long interval of time during which the applicant had a blameless record has elapsed since the conviction.[74] In residence cases it has been held that a religious upbringing is essential to the welfare of a child[75] and the reasoning adduced in support of that view is in the main also applicable to adoption. It is not, however, in practice applied to questions of residence where there is no dispute and it seems to be equally inapplicable to uncontested adoptions. When regard is had to other factors affecting the welfare of the child its role, even in contested cases, will nearly always be small. In placing a child for adoption, an adoption agency is required to have regard, so far as is practicable, to any wishes of the child's parents and guardians as to the religious upbringing of the child[76] and, if the matter is raised, the court should be satisfied that that duty has been conscientiously discharged, but apart from that the wishes of the parents in this regard is not a matter the court is bound to consider. When a parent with strong religious conviction

---

[62] As in *Re B (MF) (An Infant)*, above.
[63] *Re W (An Infant)* [1971] A.C. 682, *per* Lord Hailsham of St Marylebone at 703–704.
[64] *Re B* [1971] 1 Q.B. 437, *per* Davies L.J., approved in *Re W (An Infant)*, above *per* Lord Hodson at 719.
[65] *A and B v. C*, 1977 S.C. 27.
[66] *Re C (A Minor) (Adoption: Conditions)* [1988] 2 W.L.R. 474.
[67] *Re B (MF) (An Infant)*, above.
[68] *Re J (Adoption Order: Conditions)* [1973] Fam. 106; *Re S (A Minor) (Adoption Order: Conditions)* [1975] 1 All E.R. 109.
[69] *Re G (DM) (An Infant)* [1962] 1 W.L.R. 730.
[70] s. 7(2).
[71] See *G and G, Petrs*, 1949 S.L.T. (Sh.Ct) 60.
[72] *Re E(P)* [1969] 1 All E.R. 323; *Re C* (1969) 113 Sol. J. 721.
[73] See above, para. 4.12.
[74] *Re G (DM) (An Infant)*, above.
[75] See below, para. 10.30.
[76] s. 7.

withholds agreement to adoption because the child is to be brought up in a different system of religious belief, or in none, it will usually be right to respect these convictions and give them considerable weight in assessing the reasonableness of the parental attitude. Where a child has been accustomed to a pattern of religious observance it will often be desirable that that should be continued and, in matters of this kind, the wishes of older children must be taken into account.[77] If these considerations have been taken into account the scope for questions of religious upbringing in decisions on adoption, if not exhausted, is very largely fulfilled.[78]

4.72   The issue of the prospective adopter's sexual orientation is not to be regarded as a "fundamental question of principle". Rather, it is a factor, like the applicant's race, gender and age, which is relevant to the satisfaction of the test in sections 6 and 24(3). The court must, however, be careful to make its judgment on this matter on the basis of the evidence as to how it affects the particular child to be adopted and not on the basis of "preconceptions about homosexuality".[79] In the case cited[80] an adoption order was made in favour of a male petitioner who lived in a cohabiting relationship with another man, the First Division having been directed to a number of research studies on the effect on children of being brought up by homosexual parents and finding in them no evidence to suggest that adoption was not in the best interests of the child in the instant case.[81] Similarly, the fact that a sole applicant cohabits with another person who will in practice share in the upbringing of the child is a relevant factor, and the character, health and experience of the cohabitant are matters which should be brought to the attention of the court. It will generally be considered more advantageous than disadvantageous that the applicant has support and assistance in rearing the child. The cohabitant of the applicant will, indeed, be subject to legal responsibilities in relation to the child,[82] and this factor should also be taken into account by the court in making its judgment on the child's welfare. So the cohabitant who in fact shares with the child's upbringing will be subject to the responsibility under section 5 of the Children (Scotland) Act 1995 to do what is reasonable in all the circumstances to safeguard the child's health, development and welfare; and he or she as a "relevant person"[83] will be obliged to attend any children's hearing to which the child's case is referred. It is open to the court to give a more formal recognition to the position of the adopter's cohabitant by granting a residence order in his or her favour if, as always, this is for the welfare of the child. In *Re AB (Adoption: Joint Residence)*[84] the English court made an adoption order in favour of a male cohabitant and at the same time made a residence order in favour of a female cohabitant because this reflected the reality that both would be caring for the child and because to do so gave the added

---

[77] s. 6(1)(b)(ii).
[78] On some of the problems of religious upbringing which may arise see, however, *Re E (An Infant)* [1964] 1 W.L.R. 51; *Re G (An Infant)* [1962] 2 Q.B. 141; and *H and H, Petrs*, 1949 S.L.T. (Sh.Ct) 68. See also *AH and PH, Petrs*, 1997 Fam. L.R. 84.
[79] *T, Petr*, 1997 S.L.T. 724, *per* Lord President Hope at 735L.
[80] Discussed in Norrie, "Parental Pride: Adoption and the Gay Man" 1996 S.L.T. (News) 321. The case was followed in England: *Re W (A Minor) (Adoption: Homosexual Adopter)* [1997] 3 All E.R. 620.
[81] See also *Re K and B* (1995) 125 D.L.R. (4th) 653 (discussed by Sandor in (1997) 11 Aust. J. Fam. L. 23) and *Re E (Adoption: Freeing Order)* [1995] 1 F.L.R. 382. In relation to the place of homosexuality in applications for section 11 orders, see below, para. 10.27
[82] If the cohabitant has "charge of or control over" the child he or she will be a relevant person for the various purposes of Pt II of the 1995 Act.
[83] That is to say a person who ordinarily has charge of, or control over, the child.
[84] [1996] 1 F.L.R. 27.

protection of providing security were some untoward mishap to befall the adoptive parent. There is no reason why, in appropriate cases, the Scottish court should not follow this approach.

Merits of applications by parents

As has been seen,[85] special restrictions apply to applications by the mother **4.73** or father of the child alone. Applications by both parents are incompetent if they are unmarried because only a married couple may present a joint application and, in the case of married parents, a joint application will usually be refused because adoption will have no effect on the legal relationships between parent and child. The latter objection will apply even where some collateral benefit is to be achieved by adoption, as where the child has been registered as "illegitimate" in a foreign register of births.[86] Where, however, the child's status is to be determined by the law of a country that does not recognise legitimation *per subsequens matrimonium*, or which imposes restrictions which would prevent legitimation in the particular case, it is submitted that an adoption application by parents who have married since the birth of the child may be entertained[87] if its effect, if granted, would be to confer legitimate status by the law of that country.

Merits of applications by relatives or step-parents

Adoption applications at the instance of relatives or step-parents are common, **4.74** especially with the latter, but they require particular caution as they may be influenced by considerations ulterior to the welfare of the child or lack the assurance of permanency characteristic of adoption. In these circumstances contact with the natural mother or father is often maintained and, although that is not necessarily inimical to adoption, it may produce tensions that will be harmful for the child or prevent the child forming a satisfactory relationship either with the natural or with the adoptive parents. In most cases in which relatives seek an adoption order, both the welfare of the child and the objects which the relatives have in view can be best served by the making of a residence order rather than by adoption. There is, however, no longer a rule that where an application for an adoption order is made by a relative or step-parent of the child and the court is of the opinion (1) that the child's welfare would not be better safeguarded and promoted by the making of an adoption order than it would be by the making of a custody order, and (2) that it would be appropriate to make a custody order, the court is required to direct that the application for adoption be treated as if it had been made for the custody of the child.[88] Nevertheless it remains the duty of the court to refuse to make an adoption order on the ground that that is not the best or most appropriate means of serving the child's interests,[89] and section 11(3)(b) of the Children (Scotland) Act 1995 allows the court to make an order under section 11(2) of that Act even when no application has been made to it to do so. The court may be of the opinion that an adoption order would further the child's welfare rather than a residence order if, for example, the child were settled with his or her grandparents and there is no likelihood of the child going to live with someone else.[90] The permanence of

---

[85] Above, para. 4.26.
[86] *Y and Y, Petrs* (1950) 66 Sh.CtRep. 22; *M and M, Petrs,* 1950 S.L.T. (Sh.Ct) 3.
[87] Accordingly, there may be circumstances in which it will be competent to entertain applications for a convention adoption order (see below, paras 5.35–5.39) at the instance of a married couple who are the parents of the child.
[88] Children Act 1975, s. 53, repealed by the Children (Scotland) Act 1995, Sched. 5.
[89] s. 24(3).
[90] This was the state of affairs in *Re O (Minor) (Adoption by Grandparents)* (1984) 15 Fam. Law 305.

adoption may then be preferred over a variable or revocable residence order.[91] Applications for adoption at the instance of the relatives of the child sometimes follow the breakdown of the marriage of the child's parents and it has been said that the test in such cases is whether the separation of the parents is final[92]; but the sound view, it is submitted, is that that is only one of the factors to be taken into account in determining what is for the welfare of the child. Where a step-parent has become the real "father figure" or "mother figure" in the child's life[93] and has been so from an early age, it may be right to give formal recognition to the actual relationship by means of an adoption order in favour of the step-parent; though it should be noted that in such cases adoption will confer little tangible advantage and its intangible results will often be either vague and uncertain or ambivalent.[94] Adoption by a step-parent excludes, as shown above,[95] the non-resident parent and, unless there is some clear advantage to the child in formalising the step-parent's relationship with the child, to do so would be justified only when it could be shown to be in the interests of the child that the non-resident parent be so excluded.

Specialities affecting applications by one applicant alone

4.75   The law in force before 1975 had required that an adoption order should not be made in respect of a female child if the sole applicant were a man unless the court were satisfied that there were special circumstances justifying the making of the order as an exceptional measure.[96] That requirement was repealed in 1975[97] and has not been re-enacted in the Adoption (Scotland) Act 1978. Its intention seems to have been to provide special safeguards against sexual corruption although, if so, it overlooked the risk of homosexual corruption and indeed of such corruption (heterosexual or homosexual) by a sole female applicant. All such risks are now subsumed into a consideration of the need to safeguard and promote the welfare of the child throughout his or her life which will often be best served by his or her being brought up in a home in which he or she has adoptive parents with whom he or she can identify as fulfilling the role of father and mother respectively. That consideration will, however, play little part in the decision if it is an ideal rather than a practicality in any particular case. Adoptions at the instance of one person may well be conducive to the child's welfare, such as where a connection already exists between that person and the child. It will be more difficult (though by no means impossible) to reconcile with the child's welfare adoption on the application of a sole applicant who is a stranger to the child[98] but the making of an adoption order may be justified, for example, where the child has been placed with a married couple one of whom has died in the interval between the placement and the hearing of the adoption application[99] or a sole applicant is relevant to a child with special

---

[91] For a comparison of the place of welfare in adoption as opposed to residence cases, see Lord President Hope in *F v. F*, 1991 S.L.T. 357 at 360, and Lord Justice-Clerk Ross in *Borders Regional Council v. M*, 1986 S.L.T. 222 at 225.

[92] *LH, Petrs*, 1951 S.L.T. (Sh.Ct) 46.

[93] As in *Re S (A Minor)* (1975) 5 Fam. Law 88.

[94] *Re S (Infants)* [1977] 2 W.L.R. 919, although decided on statutory provisions that have no Scottish counterpart, contains a useful discussion of the issues which the court requires to take into account in cases of step-parent adoptions.

[95] Above, para. 4.24.

[96] Adoption of Children (Scotland) Act 1930, s. 2(2); Adoption Act 1950, s. 2(2); Adoption Act 1958, s. 2(3). See *R. v. Liverpool City Justices, ex p. W* [1959] 1 W.L.R. 149; *AB, Petrs*, 1959 S.L.T. (Sh.Ct) 49; *H, Petr*, 1960 S.L.T. (Sh.Ct) 3.

[97] Children Act 1975, Sched. 4.

[98] At one time it was not the practice of adoption agencies to make placements with one person alone, but, except in the case of very young children, such placements are no longer uncommon.

[99] *AB, Petr*, 1976 S.L.T. (Sh.Ct) 49.

needs[1] or, particularly in the case of the older child, there is no alternative other than the child remaining in local authority care.

Collateral considerations

It is against public policy to make an adoption order where the applicants do **4.76** not truly stand *in loco parentum* to the person to be adopted and the application is made solely for a collateral purpose such as conferring on him or her British nationality.[2] In *Re B (Adoption Order: Nationality)* an adoption order had been made over a16-year-old Jamaican girl in favour of her grandparents, with whom she was living in England on a temporary visa. [The Court of Appeal had recalled this order on the basis that since the child's relationship with her mother remained secure, there were no benefits to the adoption order other than that it would permit the girl to remain in England permanently. The House of Lords overruled this decision and held that the benefits of nationality were clear and direct benefits to the child and as such required to be taken into account in applying the welfare test. However, they were careful to point out that these benefits accrued in the present case during the child's childhood, which was the term relevant to welfare in the English legislation,[4] and they indicated that the position might well have been different had the benefits accrued only after the child attained adulthood. So in *Re K*[5] where the adoption order was made eight days short of the child's 18th birthday, the minimal benefits were insufficient to justify making the orders. This decision was approved by the House of Lords in *Re B*.] The extension (in Scotland) of the paramountcy of welfare to the whole of the child's life[6] suggests that considerations other than the need for the proper upbringing of the child will, in future, be afforded greater weight than previously. Nevertheless the policy considerations against allowing adoption to be used as a means of circumventing the naturalisation legislation remain valid and the adoption must, it is submitted, continue to give some benefit referable to the parent–child relationship created thereby. It is, however, no objection that one of the objects of the application is to secure British nationality for the person to be adopted, if there is a genuine intention to create the relationship of parent and child and the order would confer social, legal and psychological benefits as well as the benefit of British nationality.[7] The fact that the main object of the application is a collateral one is not, it is thought, a reason for refusing to make an order if the collateral object is consistent with the welfare of the child and there is no public policy objection.[8] In an application by a step-father it is not a sufficient reason for refusing to make an order that the main object of the application is to promote the welfare of the mother if there is no possibility of conflict between her welfare and the interests of the child.[9] Where the child to be adopted is domiciled abroad, that is a factor to be taken into account in assessing the welfare of the child but it has no further significance and that is so even if adoption is not possible by the law of the domicile.[10] The *bona fides* of a proposed adoption requires careful

---

[1] See for example *T, Petr*, 1997 S.L.T. 724; *Re E (A Minor) (Freeing for Adoption)* [1995] 1 F.C.R. 65.

[2] *Re A (An Infant)* [1963] 1 W.L.R. 231; *Re K (A Minor) (Adoption Order: Nationality)* [1994] 2 F.L.R. 557.

[3] [1998] 1 F.L.R. 965, CA, overruled March 11, 1999.

[4] Adoption Act 1976, s. 6.

[5] Above, n. 2.

[6] Children (Scotland) Act 1995, s. 95.

[7] *Re R (Adoption)* [1967] 1 W.L.R. 34; *Re H (Adoption: Non-Patrial)* [1996] 2 F.L.R. 187; *Re J (Adoption: Non-Patrial)* [1998] 1 F.L.R. 225; *Re I (Adoption: Nationality)* [1998] 2 F.L.R. 997.

[8] See *W, Petrs* (1945) 61 Sh.CtRep. 130.

[9] *Re S (A Minor)* (1975) 5 Fam. Law 88.

[10] *Re B (S) (An Infant)* [1968] 1 Ch. 204.

scrutiny where it is associated with the intention of one of the parents of the child to enter into a second marriage.[11] Similar scrutiny requires to be applied to the use of adoption as a means of "shifting about", as part of a family arrangement, a child who has already been adopted. The duties owed by adoptive parents to the child in such circumstances are the same as they would owe to their natural child.[12]

Terms and conditions attached to the order

4.77   Section 6 is to be read in conjunction with section 12(6), which provides that "an adoption order may contain such terms and conditions as the court thinks fit". These words give the court a wide discretion, for as Lord Ackner said,

> "it seems to me essential that, in order to safeguard and promote the welfare of the child throughout his childhood, the court should retain the maximum flexibility given to it by the Act and that unnecessary fetters should not be placed upon the exercise of the discretion entrusted to it by Parliament".[13]

4.78   The English courts have frequently used the analogous English provisions[14] to impose a condition of access or contact in favour of a natural parent or other relative, where this has been shown to be in the interests of the child,[15] and the House of Lords have accepted this as a proper, and unqualified, usage to which section 12(6) can be put.[16] The discretion of the court is unfettered in relation to the terms or conditions the court can impose,[17] though it is only in exceptional cases that conditions about matters arising after the making of the adoption order, such as contact, should be made. In the words of Lord President Hope:

> "The guiding principle is that adoption provides complete security to the child by making the child part of the adopting parent's family. Conditions expressed in favour of third parties, which might make it necessary for the court to become involved in the making of further orders with a view to the child's welfare, will not be appropriate except in the very rare cases where the child's welfare might be prejudiced if a condition to that effect were not to be made."[18]

---

[11] *F, Petr* (1951) 67 Sh.CtRep. 45; *EO, Petrs*, 1951 S.L.T. (Sh.Ct) 11. See also *Re DX (An Infant)*, [1949] Ch. 320.

[12] *B, Petr*, 1951 S.L.T. (Sh.Ct) 48.

[13] *Re C (A Minor) (Adoption Order: Conditions)* [1989] A.C. 1 at 17.

[14] Adoption Act 1976, ss. 6 and 12(6) (and previously the Children Act 1975, ss. 3 and 8(7)).

[15] *Re J (A Minor) (Adoption Order: Conditions)* [1973] Fam. 106 (access granted in favour of putative father); *Re G(DM) (An Infant)* [1962] 1 W.L.R. 730 (natural mother); *Re B (MF) (An Infant)* [1972] 1 W.L.R. 102 (parents); *Re S (A Minor) (Adoption Order: Access)* [1976] Fam. 1 (natural father); *Re C (A Minor) (Wardship and Adoption)* [1981] 2 F.L.R. 177 (elder brother and grandparents).

[16] *Re C (A Minor) (Adoption Order: Conditions)* above. In *AB v. CB*, 1985 S.L.T. 514 the sheriff had considered it incompetent to impose such a condition, and the Inner House did not consider it necessary to decide the point. In the light of the House of Lords decision in *Re C (A Minor) (Adoption Order: Conditions)*, on identical statutory wording, the sheriff's view must now be considered to be mistaken.

[17] In *AH and PH, Petrs*, 1997 Fam. L.R. 84, Lord Marnoch made adoption orders and imposed conditions that the adoptive parents use "their best endeavours" to secure that the children be brought up with an understanding of their ethnic origins and traditions.

[18] *B and Anor, Petrs*, 1996 S.L.T. 1370 at 1377H. See also *Re T (A Minor) (Contact After Adoption)* [1995] 2 F.C.R. 537.

In *Re S (A Minor) (Adoption: Blood Transfusions)*[19] an adoption order had **4.79**
been made in favour of applicants who were Jehovah's Witnesses, with a
condition that if ever the child needed a blood transfusion the adopters would
seek a ruling from the High Court. The Court of Appeal held that this condition
was inappropriate, since the best interests of the child are nearly always served
by putting the child in as near the position of a natural child of the adopters as
possible, and the general law has adequate means of ensuring that the children
of Jehovah's Witnesses, natural or adopted, receive appropriate medical
treatment. As well, any condition imposed must not be inconsistent with the
fundamental concept of adoption itself: thus it would not be a valid exercise of
the power to make an adoption order subject to the condition that the child
should remain in or be passed into the care and control of some person other
than the adopter.[20] The terms and conditions must, the English Court of Appeal
has held, concern the parental responsibilities and parental rights affected by
the adoption order itself, and cannot concern something entirely extrinsic thereto.
So in *Re D (A Minor) (Adoption Order: Injunction)*[21] it was held that the court
had no power to issue an injunction under the Adoption Act 1976 to restrain the
natural mother of the child from having contact with him after he reached the
age of majority.[22] In Scotland an adoption order has the effect of depriving the
natural parents of such parental responsibilities and parental rights as they
possessed and conferring full responsibilities and rights on the adoptive parents.
It hardly seems appropriate to qualify the adoptive parents' responsibilities and
rights with conditions attached to the natural parents, and it is submitted that
section 12(6) of the Adoption (Scotland) Act 1978 gives no authority to impose
an interdict on persons other than the adopters. (Doubtless, however, if there is
an apprehended wrong against the adoptive parents' or the child's interests,
they can be protected by interdict at common law against apprehended wrong
at the hands of a natural parent or third party.)

The problem remains as to how enforceable any condition attached to an **4.80**
adoption order is. There is no doubt that breach of a condition attached under
section 12(6) does not affect the validity of the order itself. In appropriate cases
it might be possible to characterise breach as contempt of court, though in the
usual case no purpose would be served in doing so. In addition, some conditions,
such as conditions relating to contact, give individuals an interest to seek
enforcement and it is competent to include, as an integral part of the terms to be
included in the adoption order, the opportunity to apply to the court in the same
process for any further order as might be needed from time to time.[23]

---

[19] [1995] 2 F.C.R. 177.

[20] *Re C (A Minor) (Adoption Order: Conditions)*, above, *per* Lord Ackner at 14–15.

[21] [1991] 3 All E.R. 461.

[22] cf. *Re F (A Minor) (Adoption Order: Validity)* [1990] 3 All E.R. 580, which may now be taken to
be overruled.

[23] *B and Anor, Petrs*, 1996 S.L.T. 1370. In *W v. R*, 1987 S.L.T. 369 Lord Cullen had accepted at
370H counsel's submission that an attempt to vary an adoption order was "incompetent". If the
procedure in *B and Anor, Petrs* is followed, then at least conditions attached to the order can be
kept open for variation. It would not seem possible to seek the imposition of conditions after the
order has been made.

CHAPTER 5

PROCEDURAL AND INTERNATIONAL ASPECTS
OF ADOPTION

INTRODUCTORY

The Scottish Adoption Service

5.01   The Adoption (Scotland) Act 1978 contemplates, and in large measure prescribes, that except where the child is to be adopted by one of his or her relatives, placement of children for adoption should be made by an adoption agency (*i.e.* a local authority or an approved adoption society).[1] The aim is that throughout Scotland there should be a comprehensive adoption service known as "The Scottish Adoption Service" to be provided by local authorities acting in conjunction with approved adoption societies in their areas, so that help may be given where needed in a co-ordinated manner and without duplication, omission or avoidable delay.[2] The service is designed to meet the needs of children who have been or may be adopted, parents and guardians of such children and persons who have adopted or may adopt a child. The facilities to be provided include arrangements for assessing children and prospective adopters and placing children for adoption, and counselling and assistance to children who have been adopted and to persons who have adopted a child.[3] A duty is placed on local authorities to provide these facilities or secure that they are provided by approved adoption societies[4] and this is to be done in conjunction with the local authorities' other social services so that the whole social work functions of a local authority, and in particular its functions concerning the care of children,[5] are integrated with the adoption service.[6] Although the duties are laid on local authorities the service is seen as national in its extent, and accordingly the approval of adoption societies is entrusted to the Secretary of State who must be satisfied, before giving approval, that a society is making, or is likely to make, an effective contribution to the Scottish Adoption Service.[7]

Placement of child by adoption agency

5.02   In arranging the placement of a child for adoption and in taking any other decisions relating to the adoption of a child, an adoption agency is under the same duty as is the court in deciding the merits of making an adoption order. It must therefore have regard to all the circumstances but shall regard the need to safeguard and promote the welfare of the child concerned throughout his or her

---

[1] Adoption (Scotland) Act 1978, ss. 1(4) and 65(1). All references in this chapter are to this Act, unless otherwise stated.

[2] s. 1(3).

[3] s. 1(2), as amended by the Children (Scotland) Act 1995, Sched. 2 para. 2.

[4] s. 1(1).

[5] See s. 2.

[6] s. 1(3).

[7] See ss. 3, 4 and 5 (as amended by the Children (Scotland) Act 1995, s. 94 and Sched. 2, para. 3) for the detailed provisions on approval, and withdrawal of approval, of adoption societies.

life as the paramount consideration; and it must, so far as practicable, have regard (i) to the views of the child (if he or she wishes to express them) taking account of his or her age and maturity, and (ii) to the child's religious persuasion, racial origin and cultural and linguistic background.[8] In complying with its duties under section 6, the adoption agency must, before making any arrangements for the adoption of a child, consider whether adoption is likely best to meet the needs of that child or whether for him or her there is some better, practicable, alternative; and if it concludes that there is such an alternative it is obliged not to proceed to make arrangements for the adoption of the child[9] (and, presumably, to pursue the alternative). In addition to these duties contained in the 1978 Act, the adoption agency is also obliged to comply with special statutory regulations.[10] It must ensure that the parent or guardian of the child is furnished with a memorandum in the prescribed form explaining the effect of the making of an adoption order on his or her rights as parent or guardian and calling attention to the statutory provisions relating to the agreement of parents or guardians to the making of adoption orders.[11] Before the child can be regarded as having been placed at the disposition of the agency for adoption the parent or guardian must sign a document in the prescribed form certifying that he or she has read and understood the memorandum.

Inquiries

Inquiries must be made and reports obtained in relation to the child and the **5.03** prospective adopters for the purpose of ensuring, so far as may be possible, the suitability of the child and the proposed adopters respectively. An interview with the prospective adopters is obviously necessary and must, in any event, be held.

Notice and investigations

If the placement has not been by an adoption agency the prospective adopters **5.04** must give notice to the local authority within whose area they have their home of their intention to apply for an adoption order; no adoption order can be made until after the expiry of three months from the giving of notice.[12] This requirement applies not only to illegal third-party placements and to non-agency placements which were originally for some purpose other than adoption but to all non-agency placements including placements with relatives and cases where parents or step-parents wish to adopt. The local authority to which notice has been given must then investigate the matter and submit to the court a report of its investigation.[13] That investigation shall, in particular, include an examination of (i) so far as is practicable, the suitability of the applicant and any other matters relevant to the operation of section 6 of the 1978 Act (*i.e.* the duty of the court in relation to the welfare and views of the child), and (ii) whether the child was placed in contravention of the statutory prohibitions contained in section 11.[14] Children placed with prospective adopters by adoption agencies are not subject to local authority visitation under this provision. It is, however, expected that

---

[8] s. 6(1), as substituted by s. 95 of the Children (Scotland) Act 1995. For an examination of the terms of this section, see above, paras 4.68–4.70.

[9] s. 6A, as inserted by s. 96 of the Children (Scotland) Act 1995.

[10] See Adoption Agencies (Scotland) Regulations 1996 (S.I. 1996 No. 3266).

[11] *ibid*, r. 14 and Sched. 4.

[12] s. 22(1).

[13] s. 22(2).

[14] s. 22(3); see also (for the sheriff court) Act of Sederunt (Child Care and Maintenance Rules) 1997 (S.I. 1997 No. 291 (S. 19))—hereinafter "A.S. 1997"—r. 2.21(4).

the adoption agency will visit the prospective adopters and supervise the child's welfare between his or her being placed for adoption and the making of an adoption order; and a duty is placed on the agency of reporting to the court on the suitability of the applicant and any other matters relevant to the operation of section 6, and the agency must assist the court in any matter the court may direct.[15]

5.05   The report to be drawn up by the local authority or the adoption agency under these provisions must include the following matters:

   (1) information about how the needs of the child came to the notice of the agency;
   (2) the family circumstances of the child;
   (3) where the child was placed for adoption by an adoption agency, a description of the physical and mental health of the child (including any special needs) and his or her emotional, behavioural and educational development;
   (4) an account of the discussion with the parents or guardians of the child and, if appropriate, with the child about their wishes and the alternatives to adoption;
   (5) the position of other relatives or persons likely to be involved;
   (6) an account of the search for a parent or guardian who cannot be found;
   (7) information about the mutual suitability of the petitioner and the child for the relationship created by adoption and the ability of the petitioner to bring up the child including an assessment of the personality of the petitioner and, where appropriate, that of the child;
   (8) particulars of all members of the household of the petitioner and their relationship to the petitioner;
   (9) a description of the accommodation in the home of the petitioner;
   (10) in a petition by one of two spouses, why the other spouse has not joined in the petition;
   (11) whether the petitioner understands the nature and effect of an adoption order and in particular that the order, if made, will make the petitioner responsible for the maintenance and upbringing of the child;
   (12) whether the means and standing of the petitioner are such as to enable him or her to maintain and bring up the child suitably, and what right or interest in property the child has;
   (13) whether any payment or other reward in consideration of the adoption, other than an approved adoption allowance, has been received or agreed upon;
   (14) what insurance has been offered on the life of the child;
   (15) the religious persuasion, if any, of the petitioner and the religious persuasion, if any, racial origin and cultural and linguistic background of the child;
   (16) considerations arising from the difference in age between the petitioner and the child if this is more or less than the normal difference in age between parents and children;
   (17) whether adoption is likely to safeguard and promote the welfare of the child throughout his or her life;
   (18) any other information which may be of assistance to the court.[16]

---

[15] s. 23.
[16] A.S. 1997, r. 2.21(3); the Rules of the Court of Session 1994 (S.I. 1994 No. 1443)—hereinafter "RCS 1994"—r. 67.21 are substantially the same.

Before making any order, the court must also consider any report received in terms of section 73(14) of the Children (Scotland) Act 1995[17], that is to say a report drawn up by a children's hearing at a review of a supervision requirement to which the child is subject, arranged because a freeing order has been applied for or the child has been placed for adoption or an application for an adoption order has been made.

Return of child to agency

Once a child has been placed in the care and possession of prospective **5.06** adopters by an adoption agency, the return of the child to the agency is subject to statutory control. On the one hand, the prospective adopters may give notice in writing to the adoption agency of their intention not to retain the care and possession of the child. On the other hand, the agency may give notice in writing to the prospective adopters of their intention not to allow the child to remain in the prospective adopter's care and possession.[18] However, once an application for an adoption order has been made the adoption agency cannot give such notice except with the leave of the court.[19] Where notice is given, whether by the adoption agency or by the prospective adopter, or where an application for an adoption order is refused or withdrawn, or where the probationary period under an interim order expires without an adoption order having been made, then the prospective adopter must, within seven days, return the child to the adoption agency and the agency must receive the child.[20] Where an adoption order is refused the seven-day period may, if the court thinks fit, be extended to a period not exceeding six weeks[21] but with that exception there is no jurisdiction to extend the period within which the child must be returned.[22] Where notice of intention to apply for an adoption order is given in respect of a child who is, for the time being, in the care of a local authority but who has not been delivered into the care and possession of the person by whom the notice is given in pursuance of an adoption placement, *i.e* where the child has been placed with the applicant for a purpose other than adoption, the provisions affecting return of the child apply as if the child had been so delivered except that where the adoption application is refused or withdrawn the child need not be returned to the local authority unless the local authority so requires.[23] Once such notice has been given, any right of the local authority to require the child to be returned, otherwise than in pursuance of the above provisions, is suspended pending disposal of the adoption application and, while the child remains in the care and possession of the person by whom the notice is given, the liability of any person to make contributions in respect of the child as being a child looked after by a local authority[24] is suspended until the expiry of 12 weeks since the giving of the notice without the application being made or until the application is refused or withdrawn.[25]

The power granted to adoption agencies to require the return of the child **5.07** cannot be exercised indiscriminately and section 6 of the 1978 Act governs their actions here as in other respects. There are conflicting decisions in England

---

[17] A.S. 1997, r. 2.28(7); RCS 1994, r. 67.5A and, in relation to freeing applications, A.S. 1997, r. 2.11(5); RCS 1994, r. 67.5A.
[18] s. 30(1).
[19] s. 30(2).
[20] s. 30(3) and (4).
[21] s. 30(6).
[22] *Re CSC (An Infant)* [1960] 1 All E.R. 711, *per* Roxburgh J. at 715.
[23] s. 31(1).
[24] Social Work (Scotland) Act 1968, s. 78.
[25] s. 31(3).

as to whether the agency's decision is open to challenge in the courts. The Court of Appeal held that the decision, having been placed by Parliament on the adoption agency, was not open to review by the courts.[26] But in a later case[27] Scott Baker J. stated that this applied only when the adoption agency was acting lawfully, and that the court could hear a challenge that it had been acting unlawfully. The matter has not arisen for decision in Scotland, where the statutory provisions are, in substance, the same. But it is submitted that a challenge to the adoption agency's actions here, as elsewhere, would be competent. Otherwise the application of the rules in section 6 to adoption agencies would be without sanction.

THE ADOPTION APPLICATION

Petitions—Productions

5.08   Applications for adoption are made by petition in the prescribed form.[28] Along with the petition there require to be lodged:

(1) an extract of the entry in the Register of Births relating to the birth of the child;

(2) in the case of a joint petition by a married couple, an extract of the entry in the Register of Marriages relating to their marriage;

(3) where the child was not placed for adoption with the applicant by an adoption agency, three copies of a medical report showing the physical and mental health of the child (including any special needs) and his or her emotional, behavioural and educational development;

(4) any report by the local authority required by section 22(2) of the Act[29] (*i.e.* on the investigation upon receipt of notice of intention to apply for an adoption order);

(5) any report by the adoption agency required by section 23 of the 1978 Act[30] (i.e. on the suitability of the applicant);

(6) where appropriate, an extract of the order freeing the child for adoption; and

(7) any other document founded upon by the petitioner in support of the terms of his or her petition.[31]

All documents lodged in process, including the reports of the curator *ad litem* and the reporting officer, are to be treated as confidential and are not to be made available to anyone except the court, the curator *ad litem*, the reporting officer and the parties.[32]

---

[26] *Re C and F* [1997] 1 F.L.R. 190, following and approving *Re W (A Minor) (Adoption Agency) (Wardship)* [1990] 2 All E.R. 463.

[27] *R v. Devon County Council, ex p. O'Brien* [1997] Fam. Law 390.

[28] A.S. 1997, r. 2.21 and Form 11 (sheriff court); RCS 1994, Form 67.22 (Court of Session). Most adoption petitions are sheriff court petitions, and the details in the text relate thereto. Any differences in Court of Session petitions are adverted to in the footnotes.

[29] See above, paras 5.04–5.05.

[30] See above, paras 5.04–5.05. If no such report as is mentioned in paras (d) or (e) is available to be lodged along with the petition, the sheriff must pronounce an interlocutor requiring the adoption agency or the local authority concerned to prepare and lodge such a report within four weeks or within such other period as the sheriff in his discretion may allow: A.S. 1997, r. 2.21(5).

[31] A.S. 1997, r. 2.21(2). RCS 1994, r. 67.22 has a rather different list of productions. If the application is for a freeing order, there must be lodged an extract of the entry in the Register of Births relating to the child, a report of the adoption agency dealing with various specified matters, and any other document founded upon by the petitioner in support of the terms of the petition: A.S. 1997, r. 2.5; and see the different list in RCS 1994, r. 67.9.

[32] A.S. 1997, r. 2.30(1); RCS 1994, r. 67.3.

Anonymity

Anonymity as between adoptive parents and the natural parents or guardians   **5.09**
is usually an advantage. Any petitioner who desires that his or her identity should
not be disclosed to the parent or guardian of the child may apply for a serial
number to be assigned to him or her for the purpose of the petition and, in that
event, the document signifying the agreement of the parent or guardian shall
not name the petitioner but shall identify him or her by reference to the serial
number.[33]

Appointment and duties of reporting officer and curator *ad litem*

On presentation or lodging of the petition for adoption, a reporting officer   **5.10**
must in all cases be appointed to the child, though if an order freeing the child
for adoption has previously been made the role of the reporting officer is limited
to witnessing any agreement executed within the United Kingdom by a parent
or guardian of the child to the making of the adoption order and lodging the
agreement in process.[34] If the petition is in the sheriff court a curator *ad litem*
must also be appointed[35]; and if in the Court of Session, the court has a
discretionary power to appoint a curator *ad litem* where it appears desirable in
the circumstances of the case in order to safeguard the interests of the child, and
in any case must appoint a curator *ad litem* where the child is not free for adoption
and it appears that a parent or guardian of the child is unwilling to agree to the
making of the adoption order.[36] The same person may be appointed as curator
ad litem and reporting officer in the same petition if the sheriff considers that
doing so is appropriate in the circumstances.[37] Though there is some overlap of
functions and matters to be reported on, the offices are essentially distinct. The
reporting officer's report will, among other things, examine the issues relevant to
the natural parent or guardian of the child; the curator's report will be more focused
on the issues directly relating to the child, including in particular the position of the
petitioners. The duties of the reporting officer are largely administrative, while the
duties of the curator *ad litem* are to provide the court with evidence of the history of
the child, his or her parents, the current situation and the prospects for the adoption.[38]
All information obtained by the reporting officer and the curator *ad litem* in the
exercise of their duties must be treated as confidential and must not be disclosed to
any person except where necessary for the proper discharge of their duties.[39]

Duties of reporting officer

When he or she is appointed by the sheriff[40] the reporting officer is obliged to do   **5.11**
the following, and to report in writing thereon to the sheriff within four weeks of his or
her appointment or within such period as the sheriff in his discretion may allow:

    (1) witness any agreement executed within the United Kingdom by a parent
        or guardian of the child to the making of an adoption order in respect
        of the child and lodge the agreement in process;

---

[33] A.S. 1997, r. 2.24; RCS 1994, r. 67.20.
[34] A.S. 1997, r. 2.25(1) and (2); RCS 1994, r. 67.23. On cause shown a reporting officer may be
appointed prior to the lodging of the petition: A.S. 1997, r. 2.25(4) and, in relation to a freeing
application, r. 2.7(3); RCS 1994, rr. 67.23 and 67.10.
[35] A.S. 1997, r. 2.25(1). This statutory power does not displace the sheriff's common law power to
appoint a curator *ad litem* to any other party, such as a natural parent: *Strathclyde Regional
Council*, 1996 S.L.T. (Sh.Ct) 65; 1996 S.C.L.R. 109.
[36] RCS 1994, r. 67.23(1)(c).
[37] A.S. 1997, r. 2.25(1).
[38] RCS 1994, r. 67.24, *Greens Annotations*.
[39] A.S. 1997, r. 2.30(2) and, in relation to freeing applications, r. 2.12(2); RCS 1994, r. 673.
[40] A.S. 1997, r. 2.26(1) and, in relation to a freeing application, r. 2.7(1). The duties of a reporting officer
appointed by the Court of Session are slightly different and are laid out in RCS 224(1), (2) and (3).

(2) ascertain that each parent or guardian who is not a petitioner and whose agreement is required or may be dispensed with understands the effect of the adoption order[41];

(3) where a parent or guardian whose agreement is required or may be dispensed with can be found, ascertain whether alternatives to adoption have been discussed with him;

(4) ascertain whether there is any person other than those mentioned in the petition upon whom notice of the petition should be served;

(5) ascertain whether the child is subject to a supervision requirement:[42] and

(6) confirm that each parent or guardian whose agreement is required understands that he or she may withdraw that agreement at any time before the adoption order is made.

When the petition is one for an order declaring the child free for adoption the reporting officer must[43]:

(1) witness any consent to the making of an application for an order freeing a child for adoption executed within the United Kingdom by a parent or guardian of the child and shall lodge the consent in process;

(2) witness any agreement executed within the United Kingdom by a parent or guardian of a child to the making of an adoption order in respect of the child and lodge the agreement in process;

(3) ascertain that each parent or guardian who can be found understands that the effect of an adoption order would be to extinguish his or her parental responsibilities and rights;

(4) ascertain from any parent and guardian who can be found, whether alternatives to adoption have been discussed with him or her;

(5) ascertain whether there is any person other than those mentioned in the petition upon whom notice of the petition should be served;

(6) ascertain whether the child is subject to a supervision requirement[44];

(7) confirm that each parent or guardian who can be found understands the implications of an order freeing the child for adoption;

(8) confirm that each parent or guardian who has given his or her agreement and can be found understands that he or she may withdraw that agreement at any time before an order under section 18(1) of the 1978 Act is made;

(9) confirm that each parent or guardian who can be found is aware that he or she may in certain circumstances apply to the court for revocation of the order freeing the child for adoption and of the appropriate procedure for such an application;

(10) confirm that each parent or guardian who can be found has been given an opportunity to make a declaration of preference not to be involved in further questions concerning the adoption of the child and, where

---

[41] Earlier rules had imposed this duty on the curator, but that was somewhat anomalous since the curator was and is appointed to the child and it is the child's interests that the curator has to protect. The present rule would seem to oblige the reporting officer to attempt to communicate with the parent or guardian to ascertain their understanding, but the process is not to be frustrated by the parent refusing to respond to any communication: *T, Petr*, 1997 S.L.T. 724.

[42] If the child is so subject, the local authority must refer the case to the children's reporter for a review of that supervision requirement: Children (Scotland) Act 1995, s. 73(5).

[43] A.S. 1997, r. 2.8; see also the slightly differently worded RCS 1994, r. 67.11(1).

[44] If so, the child's case must be referred to the reporter for a review: Children (Scotland) Act 1995, s. 73(4).

such a declaration is made, witness the declaration and explain to the parent or guardian the consequences of signing it[45]; and

(11) in the case of a child whose father is not married to the mother, consider the likelihood of any person claiming to be the father of the child (a) applying for or being refused an order under section 11 of the Children (Scotland) Act 1995 or (b) entering into an agreement with the mother in terms of section 4(1) of the 1995 Act under which he would acquire parental responsibilities and parental rights.

Duties of curator ad litem

The curator *ad litem* is a judicial officer as well as a guardian of the child's **5.12** interests.[46] The curator's duty is to investigate as fully as possible and to report to the court on all the circumstances of the child and petitioners and all other matters relevant to the proposed adoption. This report must be made within four weeks of the curator's appointment or within such other period as the sheriff in his discretion may allow; expedition is, however, always important. Nothing in the more specific points of investigation which are entrusted to the curator is intended, or should be taken, to detract from the generality of his or her duty as just described or from the centrality of his or her duty to regard the need to safeguard and promote the welfare of the child throughout his or her life as the paramount consideration: that is the viewpoint from which the investigations of the curator are to be directed. The curator must further:

(1) generally safeguard the interests of the child whose adoption is the subject of the petition;

(2) where the child in respect of whom an adoption order is sought is over the age of 12 years, witness any consent to the order executed by him or her in the United Kingdom and lodge the consent in process;

(3) ascertain whether the facts stated in the petition are correct and, if not, establish the true facts;

(4) obtain particulars of the accommodation in the home of the petitioner and the condition of the home;

(5) obtain particulars of all members of the household of the petitioner and their relationship to the petitioner;

(6) in the case of a petition by only one of two spouses, ascertain the reason of the other spouse for not joining in the application[47];

(7) ascertain whether the means and status of the petitioner are sufficient to enable him or her to maintain and bring up the child suitably;

(8) ascertain what rights or interests in property the child has;

(9) establish whether the petitioner understands the nature and effect of an adoption order, and in particular that the making of the order will render him or her responsible for the maintenance and upbringing of the child;

(10) where appropriate, ascertain when the mother of the child ceased to have the care and possession of the child, and to whom care and possession was then transferred;

---

[45] A.S. 1997, r. 2.10.

[46] *Drummond's Trs* v. *Peel's Trs*, 1929 S.C. 484, *per* Lord President Clyde at 498; *T, Petr*, 1997 S.L.T. 724, *per* Lord President Hope at 730L.

[47] This information is required not only because it may bear on the interests of the child but because an application by one of two spouses is incompetent unless certain conditions are satisfied. The curator should therefore direct his or her attention, in particular, to matters on which the court has to be satisfied if the competency of the petition is to be sustained. It is, however, for the court rather than the curator *ad litem* to determine the competency of the petition, and the curator is not to be criticised if he or she reports on all the matters the rules require but does not make any conclusions on competency: *T, Petrs*, 1997 S.L.T. 724, *per* Lord President Hope at 731C–F.

(11) ascertain whether any payment or other reward in consideration of the adoption has been given or agreed upon;

(12) establish whether the adoption is likely to safeguard and promote the welfare of the child throughout his or her life;

(13) ascertain whether the life of the child has been insured, and if so for what sum;

(14) ascertain whether it may be in the interests of the welfare of the child that the court should make any interim order, or make the adoption order subject to particular terms and conditions, or require the petitioner to make special provision for the child and, if so, what provision;

(15) where the petitioner is not ordinarily resident in the United Kingdom, establish whether a report has been obtained on the home and living conditions of the petitioner from a suitable agency in the country in which he or she is ordinarily resident;

(16) establish the reasons of the petitioner for wishing to adopt the child;

(17)   establish to which religion, if any, the petitioner subscribes and the religious persuasion, if any, racial origin and cultural and linguistic background of the child;

(18) assess the considerations which might arise where the difference in age as between the petitioner and the child is greater or less than the normal difference in age between parents and their children;

(19)   consider such other matters, including the personality of the petitioner and, where appropriate, that of the child, which might affect the suitability of the petitioner and the child for the relationship created by adoption and affect the ability of the petitioner to bring up the child;

(20) ascertain whether it would be better for the child that the court should make the order than it should not make the order; and

(21) ascertain from the child whether he or she wishes to express a view and where a child indicates his or her wish to express a view, ascertain that view.[48]

5.13   When the petition is one for an order declaring the child free for adoption, the curator *ad litem* shall have regard to the welfare of the child as his or her paramount duty and shall further:

(1) generally safeguard the interests of the child and ensure that consideration has been given to the interests of the child for the purposes of section 6 of the 1978 Act;

(2) ascertain whether the facts stated in the petition are correct except where investigation of such facts falls within the duties of the reporting officer;

(3) where the child who is sought to be freed for adoption is over the age of 12 years, witness any consent to the order executed by the child in the United Kingdom and lodge the consent in process;

(4) ascertain from the child whether he or she wishes to express a view and where a child indicates his or her wish to express a view, ascertain that view;

(5) ascertain whether an order freeing the child for adoption would safeguard and throughout his or her life promote the welfare of the child;

(6) ascertain whether it would be better for the child that the court should make the order than that it should not make such order; and

(7) report on the current circumstances and care of the child.[49]

---

[48] A.S. 1997, r. 2.26(2); see also the slightly different rules in RCS 1994, r. 67.24(2).
[49] A.S. 1997, r. 2.8(2); see also the slightly differently worded RCS 1994, r. 67.11(2).

The statutory hearing

Upon receipt of the reports of the reporting officer and the curator *ad litem* a **5.14** date for the hearing will be fixed.[50] Before the 1978 Act came into force a hearing was not essential and it was unusual in uncontested cases. Now, however, there must be a hearing in any petition to adopt a child where the child has not previously been freed for adoption, and to free a child requires a hearing[51]: the result is that no child can ever be adopted without some form of court hearing. The petitioner must intimate the diet to every person who can be found and whose agreement or consent to the making of such an order is required to be given or dispensed with.[52] If he considers it appropriate the sheriff may ordain the petitioner to serve notice of the date of the hearing on (a) any person or body having the rights and powers of a parent of the child or having the custody or care of the child or a local authority having the child committed to its care; (b) any person liable by virtue of any order or agreement to contribute to the maintenance of the child; (c) the local authority to whom the petitioner has given notice of his or her intention to apply for an adoption order; and (d) any other person or body who in the opinion of the sheriff ought to be served with notice of the hearing.[53] In relation to this last category, what is required for the welfare of the child, and the effect which the making of an adoption order may have on the interests (which need not in this context be construed in a narrow patrimonial sense) of third parties, should be the guiding consideration. It is a question of circumstances including such connection with, and interest in, the child, as the father has maintained, as to whether the court should under this general power order notice to be served on a man who is not married to the child's mother but who is the putative father and who does not fall under one of the specific headings considered above. Some circumstances will be strong for service of notice, for example where he ordinarily has charge of or control over the child, where he has applied for or wishes to apply for a residence or contact order, or where, although willing to contribute to the child's maintenance, his contributions have been refused by the mother. In other cases a putative father's continuing connection with the child may have been so tenuous that he can have no representations of value to make on the child's welfare or claims to put forward which can be given practical effect. Even so, service of notice on him may be prudent unless there is some contrary indication or it is shown that he acquiesces in the petition, but delay should not be caused by attempts to trace putative fathers whose identity or whereabouts is unknown.[54]

Form and conduct of hearing

All proceedings before the court will be heard and determined in private, **5.15** unless the court otherwise directs.[55] There is no rule about the form which the hearing should take.

> "Adoption proceedings are *sui generis*, uniquely devised to effectuate a new statutory institution, and incapable of being forcibly compressed into any of our pre-existing categories of forms of action."[56]

Natural justice must be observed but there is no right to a proof at large. If, however, the court is not satisfied that the facts stated in the petition are supported

---

[50] A.S. 1997, r. 2.28; RCS 1994, r. 67.25.

[51] A.S. 1997, r. 2.11; RCS 1994, r. 67.13.

[52] A.S. 1997, r. 2.28(3); RCS 1994, r. 67.25(3).

[53] A.S. 1997, r. 2.28(4); see the slightly differently worded RCS 1994, r. 67.25(3).

[54] *Re Adoption Application (41/1961)* [1962] 1 W.L.R. 866, *per* Wilberforce J.

[55] s. 57. See *Strathclyde Regional Council*, 1996 S.L.T. (Sh.Ct) 65; 1996 S.C.L.R. 109.

[56] *J and J v. C's Tutor*, 1948 S.C. 636, *per* Lord President Cooper p. 642; approved in *A and B, Petrs*, 1971 S.L.T. 258, per Lord Reid at 249.

by the documents lodged or by the reports of the curator *ad litem* and reporting officer or for any other reason the court considers appropriate, the court may order further production of documents or appoint oral evidence to be led.[57] It may interview privately the petitioner and the child or either of them, or any person on whom a notice of the hearing has been served. It may remit to a reporter to investigate facts[58] and may rely on reports, documents and interviews in substitution for the ordinary methods of proof. It may order the curator *ad litem* or the reporting officer to be questioned on matters arising from their reports. In general, the court may adopt any form of inquiry which is consistent with the maintenance of justice to the parties and with the statutory objects to which the inquiries must be directed and among which the need to safeguard and promote the welfare of the child is paramount. If no person appears at the hearing who is entitled to do so, the sheriff may grant the adoption order on the motion of the petitioner; but if a person entitled to appear does appear and wishes to be heard, the sheriff may hear him or her or may order a further diet to be fixed.[59] Where anyone claiming, contrary to what appears *ex facie* of the petition, to be a parent or guardian of the child is heard in support of that claim, the consequence of success is of course that his or her agreement to the making of an adoption order must either be given or be dispensed with on one of the statutory grounds. With that qualification, the fact that a person is heard, even of right, in an adoption proceeding, is in no sense to be equiparated with a requirement for his or her agreement. Any objections he or she offers to the making of an adoption order, or support for it, will, unless in so far as they bear on proof of one of the prerequisites, be relevant only in the context of the child's welfare or as one of the other circumstances to which the court may give consideration in reaching a decision on the merits of whether or not an adoption order should be made.

Views of the child

5.16   Before making an adoption order the court must have regard, so far as practicable, to the views of the child concerned (if he or she wishes to express them) taking account of the age and maturity of the child, and without prejudice to that generality a child 12 years of age or more is presumed to be of sufficient age and maturity to form a view for this purpose.[60] Where the child has indicated his or her wish to express views the court may order such procedural steps to be taken as it considers appropriate to ascertain the views of the child and it may not make any order unless an opportunity has been given for the views of the child to be obtained or heard.[61] Where the views of the child have been recorded in writing (whether in the report of the curator *ad litem* or otherwise) the sheriff may direct that such a written record shall be sealed in an envelope marked "Views of the child—confidential", that it be available to a sheriff only, that it not be opened by any person other than a sheriff and that it not form a borrowable part of the process.[62] This is an exception to the rule that all documents lodged in process including reports are to be made available to the parties.[63] In England, where there is no such statutory exception, the House of Lords held that there was a strong presumption in favour of disclosing to the parties all reports,

---

57 A.S. 1997, r. 2.29; RCS 1994, r. 67.6. See *AB v. CD*, 1970 S.C. 268.
58 *A and B, Petrs*, above.
59 A.S. 1997, r. 2.28(5) and (6) and, in relation to freeing applications, r. 2.11(3) and (4).
60 s. 6(1)(b)(i) and (2), as substituted by s. 95 of the Children (Scotland) Act 1995.
61 A.S. 1997, r. 2.27(1) and, in relation to freeing applications, r. 2.9(1); RCS 1994, r. 67.5A.
62 A.S. 1997, r. 2.27(2) and, in relation to freeing applications, r. 2.9(2).
63 A.S. 1997, r. 2.30(2) and, in relation to freeing applications, r. 2.12(2).

including those containing the child's views.[64] The curator may, if he or she considers it appropriate, convey the views of the child to the sheriff orally.[65]

PROHIBITIONS

The Adoption (Scotland) Act 1978 creates a number of criminal offences, which **5.17** are designed to ensure that, so far as possible, the whole adoption process is carried out by persons or bodies properly experienced and acting for proper motives. The statute does not, however, prevent an adoption order from being made when any of these offences have been committed, for the aim of the offences is to punish wrongdoers and not to inhibit the court from making decisions that are in the best interests of the child.

Illegal placements
It is illegal for anyone other than an adoption agency to make arrangements **5.18** for the adoption of a child or place a child for adoption except where the proposed adopter is a relative of the child.[66] It is also an offence to receive a child placed in contravention of the statutory prohibitions.[67] This represents a tightening of the earlier law which had prohibited arrangements for adoption made by any body of persons other than an adoption agency but had permitted them when made by individuals (*e.g.* the parents themselves, friends, relatives, doctors or ministers of religion). Such arrangements (commonly called "third-party placements") were thought to be undesirable for at least two reasons: (1) the persons who made them did not usually have the knowledge, experience or means of investigation necessary to ensure, so far as possible, that the welfare of the child was safeguarded; and (2) the placements were sometimes made in circumstances which left open the possibility of contact between the natural parent and child when that was undesirable and thus endangered the security of the child and adoptive parents which is normally necessary for the success of adoption and the well-being of the child. The same objection can in some degree be made where the child is placed with a relative, but the character of such adoptions is necessarily rather different from that of adoption by strangers and there is less need to guard against the maintenance of contact with the natural parent which, in these cases, may sometimes be beneficial. Third party arrangements are illegal only where they are for adoption and, in any given case, it may be difficult to prove that adoption rather than some arrangement for care or fostering was the original purpose. Moreover, where there has been an illegal placement or where there has been a placement which is legal only because adoption was not its original purpose, an adoption application may nonetheless be made and an order granted. In such cases, however, the child must have had his or her home with the adopters for a period of 12 months preceding the making of the adoption order.[68]

Restrictions on removal of child
It is essential, both for the orderly disposal of adoption applications and **5.19** also, as a general rule, for the welfare of the child, that the child should, while the proceedings are pending, remain undisturbed in the home of the prospective

---

[64] *Re D and Anor (Minors) (Adoption Reports: Confidentiality)* [1995] 4 All E.R. 385.

[65] A.S. 1997, r. 2.26(3) and, in relation to freeing applications, r. 2.8(3).

[66] s. 11(1). A children's hearing requiring a child to reside at a particular place (for example with prospective adopters) is not thereby "making arrangements" for that child's adoption: s. 65(3), as amended by s. 27 of the Law Reform (Miscellaneous Provisions) (Scotland) Act 1985 and the Children (Scotland) Act 1995, Sched. 2, para. 29(b).

[67] s. 11(3).

[68] s. 13(2).

adopters. Except where the child has had his or her home with the prospective adopters for the five years preceding the application, parents or guardians who have not agreed to adoption may, however, seek to recover a child during that time. A general prohibition against their so doing would create the hazard that an adoption application would be used as a weapon in a residence dispute or as a means of preventing or delaying the recovery of a child illegally removed. These considerations do not, however, apply where a parent has agreed to adoption even if he or she subsequently withdraws that agreement. In these circumstances it is undesirable that he or she should be able to embarrass or frustrate the proceedings by removing the child. Accordingly, where an adoption agency has placed a child with a person with a view to the child being adopted by that person and the consent of each parent or guardian has been obtained to that placement, such parent or guardian may not remove the child from the care and possession of the person with whom he or she has been placed except with the leave of either the adoption agency or the court.[69] Removal in contravention of this prohibition is a criminal offence.[70] Where parents or guardians authorise others to remove the child they no doubt commit an offence no less than if they remove the child themselves, but there is no statutory prohibition against the removal of the child by third parties (*e.g.* grandparents or other relatives) acting without the parent's authority, even if in what they conceive to be the parent's interests; nor is it clear that in these circumstances the crime of *plagium* is committed.[71]

5.20   The prohibition against removal of a child from prospective adopters is more extensive where the child has had his or her home with them for the five years preceding the application. In these circumstances no person is entitled, against the will of the prospective adopters, to remove the child from their care and possession without the leave of the court or under authority conferred by any enactment or on the arrest of the child.[72] The protection applies not only while the application is pending but also in the interval between the giving of notice of intention to apply for an adoption order and the presentation of the petition.[73] The purpose is to strengthen the position of foster carers who have had children in their long-term care and who wish to adopt but are inhibited from doing so by parental unwillingness to agree. In such cases there may be a strong *prima facie* case for adoption. The prohibition is against removal by any person and that extends to the local authority in whose care the child is.[74] Removal "under authority conferred by any enactment" is ostensibly far-reaching but it does not extend to the statutory provisions relating to the return of the child placed for adoption by adoption agencies.[75] Children may, however, be removed where the removal is authorised by a children's hearing in terms of Part II of the Children (Scotland) Act 1995 or by a justice of the peace acting under section 61 or under the terms of a child protection order granted under section 57 thereof.

---

[69] s. 27(1), as substituted by the Children (Scotland) Act 1995, Sched. 2, para. 19. And see A.S. 1997, r. 2.36; RCS 1994, r. 67.28.

[70] s. 27(3), as amended by the Children (Scotland) Act 1995, Sched. 2, para. 19.

[71] See below, para. 9.81.

[72] s. 28(1). And see A.S. 1997, r. 2.36; RCS 1994, r. 67.28.

[73] s. 28(2).

[74] s. 28(3). Questions arise as to the consequences of this. If a child is being looked after by a local authority, the authority may be impeded from making decisions for the welfare of the child and thus discharging its statutory duties. If parental responsibilities and parental rights have been transferred to the authority the exercise of these rights may also be frustrated. If a foster carer refuses to return a child, pending an adoption application, he or she may be in breach of the fostering agreement but if the local authority seeks to enforce its rights it may be in contravention of the statutory prohibition and will commit an offence.

[75] s. 28(3).

Foster carers or others who have had a child in their care for less than five years have, in a question with natural parents who do not agree to adoption, no direct means of securing the continued residence of the child with them while the adoption application is pending other than by first making an application for a residence order under section 11 of the Children (Scotland) Act 1995. Foster carers with whom a child has been boarded out by a local authority may, however, with the co-operation of the authority, obtain security against the removal of the child by parental responsibilities and parental rights being transferred to the local authority or, when the child is subject to a supervision requirement, by a children's hearing attaching a condition of residence with the foster carers on to the supervision requirement.

Where a child has been removed in contravention of either of these statutory **5.21** prohibitions, the court before whom the application for an adoption order or for an order freeing the child for adoption is pending may, on the application of a person from whose care and possession the child has been removed, order the return of the child to the applicant. Where there is no pending application but the child has been removed after the giving of notice of intention to adopt by a person with whom the child has had his or her home for the preceding five years, the Court of Session or the sheriff court of the sheriffdom within which the child is may make such an order.[76] The order must be directed to the person who has removed the child and so, where that person has handed on the child to another, an action of delivery may be necessary in order to secure the return of the child. Where there are reasonable grounds for believing that someone intends to remove a child in contravention of the statutory prohibition, an order may be made directing that person not to do so.[77] This does not seem to add anything to the remedy of interdict which would, in any event, be available, but when proceedings are pending there may be some convenience in seeking an order in the adoption process rather than making a separate application for interdict.

Removal of children for adoption abroad

Except under the authority of an order transferring parental responsibilities **5.22** and parental rights in relation to a child to a person who is not domiciled in England and Wales or Northern Ireland or Scotland,[78] it is unlawful to take or send a child who is a British subject or a citizen of the Republic of Ireland out of Great Britain to any place outside the United Kingdom, the Channel Islands and the Isle of Man with a view to the adoption of the child by anyone who is not a parent or guardian or relative[79] of the child; and it is also unlawful to take part in any arrangement for transferring the care and possession of a child to any person for that purpose.[80]

Prohibition on payments

In order to prevent trafficking in children for gain it is necessary to prohibit **5.23** the exchange of money or other valuable consideration in relation to an adoption. It is, accordingly, unlawful to give to anyone any payment or reward in respect

---

[76] s. 29(1) and s. 56(2). And see A.S. 1997, r. 2.36; RCS 1994, r. 67.28.

[77] s. 29(2).

[78] s. 49: see below, para. 5.33.

[79] "Relative" is defined in s. 65(1). The definition includes an uncle, and it has been held in this context under the equivalent English legislation not to include a great-uncle *(Re C and Anor (Minors) (Wardship: Adoption)* [1989] 1 All E.R. 395), nor a step-parent *(Re MW (Adoption: Surrogacy)* [1995] 2 F.L.R. 759. *Cf. Monteith v. Cape Insulation,* 1999 S.L.T. 116 in which a mother-in-law was held to be within the phrase "immediate family" as it appears in the Damages (Scotland) Act 1976.

[80] s. 50(1), as amended by the Children Act 1989, Sched. 10, para. 43.

of (1) the adoption by that person of a child, or (2) the granting by him or her of any agreement or consent required in connection with the adoption of a child, or (3) the transfer by him or her of the care and possession of a child with a view to adoption, or (4) the making by him or her of any arrangements for the adoption of a child.[81] To do so is a criminal offence and the court may, irrespective of any other power it has, order that the child be removed to a place of safety until he or she can be restored to his or her parents or guardians or until other arrangements can be made for him or her.[82] Special allowances paid to adopters for the aliment of the child are generally thought to fall within the prohibition. That special allowances should not be paid is consistent with the general principle of adoption law that the relationship between adoptive parents and their adopted children should, so far as possible, be the same as that between natural parents and their children. However, the rigid application of that doctrine has the unfortunate result that handicapped children and other children who are "hard to place", including large families of children, remain in institutional care when adoptive homes might be found for them if payments to compensate the adopters for the exceptional expenditures which they will incur could be made. Foster carers who wish to adopt a child who has been in their care for a long time may, moreover, not be able to do so because they cannot afford to be without the boarding-out allowance, although adoption would be in the best interests of the child. Provision is accordingly made for the approval by the Secretary of State of schemes submitted to him by adoption agencies for the payment by the agency of allowances to persons who have adopted, or intend to adopt, a child. Payments made under such schemes will not offend against the prohibition.[83]

5.24   There are two other circumstances in which the prohibition does not apply. First, it does not apply to any payment by a parent or guardian or prospective adopter made to an adoption agency in respect of expenses reasonably incurred by the agency in connection with the adoption, or to any payment or reward authorised by the court.[84] In *C v. S*[85] the sheriff held that a sum of £8,000 paid to a surrogate mother could not be said to represent expenses reasonably incurred, and that conclusion was not challenged on appeal; in the same case the First Division held that in determining whether retrospectively to authorise the unlawful payment or reward the court had to have regard to section 6 of the 1978 Act and to the degree of blame to be attached to the petitioners who made the payment.[86] And secondly, the prohibition does not apply to any payment made by an adoption agency to (1) the prospective adopter in respect of legal or medical expenses incurred by that person in connection with the adoption application, (2) another adoption agency in consideration of the placing of the child for adoption, or (3) an approved voluntary organisation as a fee for services in putting the agency in contact with another agency for the making of an adoption arrangement.[87] Even outwith these exceptions, the prohibition, being a matter of criminal law, does not have extraterritorial effect.[88] It has been held[89]

---

[81] s. 51(1).

[82] s. 51(2), as amended by the Children (Scotland) Act 1995, Sched. 2, para. 24.

[83] s. 51(5) and s. 51A; Adoption Allowance (Scotland) Regulations 1996 (S.I. 1996 No. 3257).

[84] s. 51(3). Authorisation may be prospective or retrospective: *Re An Adoption Application (Surrogacy)* [1987] 2 All E.R. 826; *Re MW (Adoption: Surrogacy)* [1995] 2 F.L.R. 759.

[85] 1996 S.L.T. 1387.

[86] *ibid.* at 1399C–E, *per* Lord Weir. *Cf. Re C (A Minor) (Adoption Application)* [1992] 1 F.C.R. 337; [1993] 1 F.L.R. 87 in which Booth J. refused to authorise a payment which had been made to encourage the mother to adhere to a deception as to the child's provenance. To do otherwise, she said, would be to sweep aside the protection given by the Adoption Act to children and would, in effect, amount to ratifying the sale of children for adoption.

[87] s. 51(4).

[88] *Re A (Adoption: Placement)* [1988] 1 W.L.R. 229.

[89] *C v. S*, above. See also *Re an Adoption Application (Surrogacy)* [1987] 2 All E.R. 826.

that payments made under a surrogacy arrangement[90] do not fall within the prohibition even when they do fall within the analogous prohibition in the surrogacy legislation.[91] This is so, however, only when the payments are made in consideration of the making of or giving agreement to a parental order following a surrogacy arrangement and not an adoption order. The two prohibitions are usually mutually exclusive, but it is possible to conceive of a situation in which a single payment could be held to have breached both.

Prior to the coming into force of the amendments to the adoption legislation **5.25** contained in the Children (Scotland) Act 1995, the court was forbidden from making an adoption order if the prohibition against payments had been infringed. That rule has now been reversed and the court may make an adoption order even where it is found that the applicants have contravened section 51.[92] The welfare of the child is the paramount consideration and there may well be circumstances in which the child's interests are furthered by being adopted by applicants who have breached the criminal law in this, as in other, respects.[93]

Restrictions on advertising

Further protection against trafficking and other abuses in connection with **5.26** adoption is provided by the restriction on advertisements. It is unlawful to publish any advertisement indicating that the parent or guardian of a child desires to cause the child to be adopted or that anyone desires to adopt a child or that anyone, other than an adoption agency, is willing to make arrangements for the adoption of a child.[94] Advertisements by an adoption agency that it has children, or even specified children, whom it wishes to place for adoption do not, it is thought, contravene this provision because such an advertisement does not carry any necessary implication that the parent or guardian of a child desires to cause the child to be adopted. Such advertisements, although controversial, may be of assistance in finding homes for children who are hard to place.

FURTHER PROCEDURAL MATTERS

Interim orders

Instead of making a final adoption order, it is open to the court to make an **5.27** interim order. The effect of an interim order is to give parental responsibilities and parental rights to the petitioners for a probationary period not exceeding two years upon such terms for the aliment of the child, and otherwise, as the court thinks fit.[95] Where an interim order specifies a period of less than two years the court may, by a further order, extend the period to a duration not exceeding two years in all.[96] Such orders are rare. They appear to be used where the court is not fully satisfied but it is nevertheless felt that doubts or difficulties may be resolved after the passage of time.[97] A better course may often be to

---

[90] See below, Chap. 6.

[91] *i.e.* the Human Fertilisation and Embryology Act 1990, s. 30(7).

[92] s. 24(2), as substituted by the Children (Scotland) Act 1995, Sched. 2, para. 16.

[93] It may, however, be noted in contrast that a parental order under s. 30 of the Human Fertilisation and Embryology Act 1990 remains incompetent if payment has been made in breach of the equivalent prohibition under s. 30(7). This is subject to the qualification that court authorisation may be granted and, one assumes, it may be granted retrospectively, so the difference between the adoption and the surrogacy provisions is not great.

[94] s. 52(1).

[95] s. 25(1), as amended by the Children (Scotland) Act 1995, Sched. 2, para. 17. *Cf.* the Adoption Act 1958, s. 8. For a case in which conditions were imposed, see *S v. Huddersfield Borough Council* [1974] 3 All E.R. 296, in which a condition of access by a natural parent was imposed.

[96] s. 25(2).

[97] An example from England is *Re AW (Adoption Application)* [1993] 1 F.L.R. 62; [1992] 2 F.C.R. 641.

adjourn the application. Such need as there has been for interim orders may be largely obviated by the power which the court now has to make a residence order under section 11 of the Children (Scotland) Act 1995 on an application for adoption,[98] but an interim order has the advantage that the matter remains subject to automatic review by the court and that during the probationary period the adoption agency and the reporting officer and the curator *ad litem* may remain in touch with the prospective adopters. It is a prerequisite of the making of an interim order either that the child should be free for adoption or that parental agreement to adoption has been given or dispensed with[99]; and where not an adoption agency placement, three months' notice must have been given to the local authority of the prospective adopter's intention to apply for the order.[1]

Appeals

5.28   Formerly adoptions in the Court of Session were Inner House petitions and so the only appeal was to the House of Lords. They are now heard in the Outer House and interlocutors in an adoption process may be reclaimed to the Inner House and appeal taken from there to the House of Lords in accordance with the rules generally applicable to Court of Session causes. Appeals in cases originating in the sheriff court also follow the ordinary rules. Decisions in adoption cases, and in particular decisions on dispensation with parental agreement, are not properly discretionary and so review is not confined to the well-recognised grounds on which an appellate court may interfere with the exercise of a discretion.[2] At any rate, where the decision depends on facts ascertained by reporting officers the matter is at large on appeal. Great importance is, however, to be attached to the opinion of the trial judge and while the appellate court is well entitled to come to a contrary conclusion if it thinks he is wrong, it will be slow to do so unless he has misdirected himself in law or is otherwise clearly in error.[3] Because adoption proceedings are not essentially adversarial and because of the paramountcy attached to the need to safeguard and promote the welfare of the child, additional evidence will be admitted on appeal with greater liberality than in ordinary causes and that may include evidence of facts occurring since the date of the order.[4] The power to direct that proceedings be heard in open court, which in practice is never exercised in proceedings at first instance,[5] may often, without disadvantage, be exercised for the hearing of an appeal.

Registration and disclosure

5.29   Every adoption order must contain a direction to the Registrar-General to make in the Adopted Children Register an entry recording in prescribed form the adoption.[6]

5.30   The entry in the Adopted Children Register is, without further or other proof, received as evidence of the adoption to which it relates and of the date of birth and country of birth of the adopted person.[7] The original entry of the child's

---

[98] s. 11(3)(b).

[99] s. 25(1) and s. 16(1).

[1] s. 25(1) and s. 22(1).

[2] *A and B, Petrs*, 1971 S.L.T. 258, *per* Lord Guest at 260. On the appellate court's power to interfere with the trial judge's discretion in residence cases, see *Jordan v. Jordan*, 1983 S.L.T. 539; *Britton v. Central Regional Council*, 1986 S.L.T. 207; and *Early v. Early*, 1990 S.L.T. 221; *Brixey v. Lynas*, 1994 S.L.T. 847; *Sanderson v. McManus*, 1997 S.L.T. 629; *Osborne v. Matthan*, 1997 S.L.T. 811.

[3] *A and B, Petrs*, above; *cf. per* Lord Reid at 259 and Lord Simon of Glaisdale at 264.

[4] *Re Adoption Act 1950, The Times*, July 29, 1958. If agreement has been dispensed with on the ground that a parent cannot be found and then the parent reappears after the decision but before the appeal, that ground for dispensation becomes spent, though reappearance is not in itself the ground of appeal. See *S v. M*, 1999 S.L.T. 571.

[5] *cf. Strathclyde Regional Council*, 1996 S.L.T. (Sh.Ct) 65; 1996 S.C.L.R. 109.

[6] Sched. 1, para. 1(1).

[7] s. 45(2).

birth in the Register of Births is marked "Adopted" and where the child has been previously adopted the entry then made in the Adopted Children Register is marked "Re-adopted".[8] The Registrar-General must keep registers and books so as to record and make traceable the connection between any entry in the Register of Births which has been marked "Adopted" and any corresponding entry in the Adopted Children Register, but these registers and books are not to be open to public inspection or search and no information contained in them may be furnished to any person unless a court so orders or an adopted person who has attained the age of 16 years seeks such information relating to himself.[9] The right of an adopted person, who has attained the appropriate age, to trace the records of his or her birth has been a feature of the Scottish legislation on adoption since it was introduced in 1930.[10] On furnishing information from the Register of Births to an adopted person, the Registrar-General is now obliged to advise him or her that counselling services are available from the local authority for the area where he or she lives or, if the adoption was arranged by an approved adoption society, from that society; and it is the duty of local authorities and approved adoption societies to provide counselling in these circumstances.[11] Where counselling is provided, an extract of the entry relating to the adopted person in the Register of Births will be furnished from the Register of Births to the authority or society carrying out the counselling as well as to the adopted person.[12] The statute does not lay down any guidance as to when it would be appropriate for a court to order disclosure of information to a person other than the adopted person, but it has been held in England, on similar statutory wording, that this may be done only in exceptional circumstances.[13] So in *Re H (Adoption: Disclosure of Information)*[14] a court ordered disclosure to an adoption counselling service almost 50 years after the adoption since the adopted person's half-sister was suffering from a genetic disease early treatment of which could arrest its development and disclosure was necessary in order to trace the adopted person.

The court which pronounced the adoption order has power (1) to amend an **5.31** adoption order within one year from the date of the order by adding any new name given to, or taken by, the adopted person or substituting such a name for a name in the order, and (2) to revoke any direction for the marking of an entry in the Register of Births or the Adopted Children Register where that direction has been wrongly included in the order.[15] If an adoption order is so amended, or a direction revoked, the entry in the Adopted Children Register or in the Register of Births is to be cancelled or amended accordingly.[16] The power to revoke is a wide one which is not restricted to the correction of clerical errors.[17]

No extract of an adoption order may be issued except by authority of the **5.32** court obtained by petition setting forth the reasons for which the extract is required.[18] Where such an extract is issued then immediately on its issue, or

---

[8] Sched. 1, para. 1(5) and (6).

[9] s. 45(4) and (5), as amended by the Children (Scotland) Act 1995, Sched. 2, para. 22.

[10] The Court of Appeal in England held that the right, though in statutory terms unqualified, was not in fact absolute and that the Registrar-General could refuse to make available records if to do so would place a person named therein at serious risk of injury: *R. v. Registrar-General, ex p. Smith* [1991] 2 All E.R. 88.

[11] s. 45(6), (6A) and (6B), as substituted and inserted by the Children Act 1989, Sched. 10, para. 41.

[12] s. 45(7).

[13] *D v. Registrar-General* [1997] 1 F.L.R. 715 (interpreting s. 50(5) of the Adoption Act 1976, which is the equivalent of s. 45(5) of the 1978 Act).

[14] [1995] 1 F.L.R. 236.

[15] Sched. 1, para. 4(1); A.S. 1997, r. 2.34(1) and RCS 1994, r. 67.29.

[16] Sched. 1, para. 4(2).

[17] See *R. v. Chelsea Juvenile Court (Re an Infant)* [1955] 1 W.L.R. 52.

[18] A.S. 1997, r. 2.32(2) and (3); RCS 1994, r. 67.31.

otherwise immediately after the communication to the Registrar-General of any adoption order or its amendment or revocation, the adoption process must be sealed and cannot thereafter be opened up or made accessible to any person within 100 years after the date of the order except:

(1) to an adopted person to whom the order refers and who has attained the age of 16 years;
(2) to the sheriff clerk on the written application of an adoption agency made with the consent of the adopted person for the purpose of ascertaining the name of the agency, if any, responsible for the placement of that person and informing the applicant of that name;
(3) to a person, on an application made by him or her to the court setting forth the reason for which access to the process is required;
(4) to a court, public authority or administrative board (none of which need be within the United Kingdom) having power to authorise an adoption, on petition by it to the court which granted the original order requesting that information be made available from the process for the purpose of discharging its duties in considering an application for adoption and specifying the precise reasons for which access to the process is required; or
(5) to a person who is authorised by the Secretary of State to obtain information from the process for the purposes of such research as is intended to improve the working of adoption law and practice.[19]

In addition, the Court of Session on appeal from the sheriff may in exceptional cases grant its own authority to the sheriff to issue an extract of the adoption order to named individuals in order to provide them with a basis upon which to return to the court if further orders, such as relating to contact with the child, might be required at some time in the future.[20]

INTERNATIONAL ASPECTS OF ADOPTION

Adoption of children abroad

5.33   The general rule is that a child who is a British subject may not be taken out of the country in order to be adopted abroad.[21] However, where a person who is not domiciled in England and Wales or Scotland or Northern Ireland intends to adopt a child under the law of, or within, the country in which he or she is domiciled, the court may make an order transferring to him or her the parental responsibilities and parental rights in relation to the child.[22] The result of such an order is to enable the child to be taken out of the country for the purpose of adoption. The main provisions of the adoption legislation apply to such orders but they do not have the full effect on status which an adoption has and they do not affect citizenship and rights of succession.[23] An interim order cannot be made.[24] A petitioner must, in addition to complying with the other requirements relating to an adoption petition, adduce evidence of the law of adoption in the

---

[19] A.S. 1997, r. 2.33(2) and, in relation to freeing orders, r. 2.14(2); see also the differently worded RCS 1994, r. 67.32(2).
[20] *B, Petr*, 1996 S.L.T. 1370. The exceptional nature of this case was emphasised by the court and it does not lay down any general rule that can be commonly relied upon.
[21] s. 50. See above, para. 5.22.
[22] s. 49(1), as amended by the Children Act 1989, Sched 10, para. 42 and the Children (Scotland) Act 1995, Sched. 2, para. 23.
[23] The definition of "adoption order" given in s. 65(1), *i.e.* the orders which have the effects mentioned in the text, does not include orders under s. 49.
[24] And there is no equivalent for an order freeing a child for adoption (see further s. 49(2)).

country in which he or she is domiciled. Such evidence may take the form of an affidavit sworn by a person conversant with that law and who practises, or has practised, law in that country or is a duly accredited representative of the government of that country in the United Kingdom.[25] For purposes of registration the words "proposed foreign adoption" or "proposed foreign re-adoption" take the place of "adopted" or "re-adopted".[26]

The prerequisites for the making of these orders differ from those of **5.34** adoption orders in that the child must be at least 32 weeks old (rather than 19 weeks) and have had his or her home with the applicants, or one of them,[27] for at least 26 weeks (rather than 13 weeks) preceding the making of the order.[28]

Convention adoption orders

Convention adoption orders were introduced by the Adoption Act 1968 **5.35** following the Hague Convention on Adoption of Children 1965,[29] and the law applicable to them is now contained in section 17 of the Adoption (Scotland) Act 1978[30] which substantially re-enacts the provisions of the 1968 Act. Their purpose is to facilitate adoption where the nationality or country of habitual residence of the prospective adopters is different from that of the child. As the test for jurisdiction in adoption is ordinarily that of the domicile or habitual residence of the prospective adopters and not of their nationality, cases may occur where there is jurisdiction to make both a convention order and an order in ordinary form. The extent of that overlap is restricted by the exclusion of a convention order where the applicant or applicants and the child are all United Kingdom nationals living in British territory[31] but that in turn leaves a gap where the applicants and the child all fall into that category and the applicants are domiciled abroad. In such a case there is no jurisdiction to make an adoption order although an order, discussed in the preceding section, transferring parental responsibilities and parental rights for the purposes of adoption in the country of the prospective adopters' domicile may be made.[32] Where there is an overlap of jurisdiction the applicants can choose which type of order to apply for. However, if the application is for a convention order then a convention order must be made so long as the conditions for making it are satisfied both at the time of application and at the time the order is made.[33]

Apart from the rule that the applicants and the child must not all be United **5.36** Kingdom nationals living in British territory the conditions relating to nationality and residence are as follows:

---

[25] A.S. 1997, r. 2.22; RCS 1994, r. 67.27(3). In the Rule of Court evidence that the child in respect of whom the application is made may be adopted under the law of or in the country in which the petitioner is domiciled may be given by a signed statement by a person qualified in the law of that country.

[26] s. 49(3).

[27] See *Re M (An Infant) (Adoption: Child's Removal from Jurisdiction)* [1973] Fam. 66.

[28] s. 49(2).

[29] The Hague Convention on Jurisdiction, Applicable Law and Recognition of Decrees Relating to Adoption, signed on Nov. 15, 1965.

[30] For comment on the Hague Convention, see Graveson, Cmnd. 2615, also printed at (1965) 14 I.C.L.Q. 558; Graveson, *Conflict of Laws* (7th ed., 1974), pp. 532–538; Lipstein [1965] Camb.L.J. 224; Unger (1965) 28 M.L.R. 463. For comment on the 1968 Act see McClean and Patchett (1970) 19 I.C.L.Q. 1 and Blom (1973) 22 I.C.L.Q. 109.

[31] s. 17(3).

[32] s. 49.

[33] s. 17(1).

(1) The child must be a United Kingdom national or a national of a convention country and must habitually reside in British territory or a convention country.[34]
(2) If the application is by a married couple *either* (a) each must be a United Kingdom national or a national of a convention country and both must habitually reside in Great Britain, *or* (b) both must be United Kingdom nationals and each must habitually reside in British territory or a convention country.[35]
(3) If the application is by one person, *either* (a) he or she must be a United Kingdom national or a national of a convention country and must habitually reside in Great Britain, *or* (b) he or she must be a United Kingdom national and must habitually reside in British territory or a convention country.[36]

A convention country is any country outside British territory designated by an order of the Secretary of State as a country in which the Hague Convention is in force.[37] "British territory" means Great Britain, the Channel Islands, the Isle of Man and any colony, being a country designated for the purposes of this provision by order of the Secretary of State or, if no country is so designated, any of those countries; "United Kingdom national" means a citizen of the United Kingdom and colonies satisfying such conditions, if any, as the Secretary of State may specify for the purpose of a convention order.[38] The term "habitual residence" is not defined, but it will have the meaning ascribed to it in other areas of international private law.[39]

5.37   In order to make a convention adoption order, the following further conditions must be satisfied:

(1) The child must not be or have been married.[40]
(2) If, in the case of an application by a married couple, they are both nationals of the same convention country, or if, in the case of an application by one person, he or she is a national of a convention country, the adoption must not be prohibited by a specified provision of the internal law of that country.[41] By "specified provision" is meant a provision of the law of the foreign country which has been notified to the United Kingdom government in pursuance of one of the provisions of the Hague Convention and has, as a result, been specified in a statutory instrument.[42]
(3) If the child is not a United Kingdom national the consents must be obtained and consultations carried out which are required by the internal law of the child's nationality and the court must be satisfied that each person who consents in accordance with that internal law does so with full understanding of what is involved.[43] This restriction does not, however, apply to any provision of the foreign law requiring consents by, or consultations with, the family of the prospective adopter, including his or her spouse. Where the foreign law provides for

---

[34] s. 17(2)(a) and (b).
[35] s. 17(4).
[36] s. 17(5).
[37] To date, only the U.K., Austria and Switzerland have ratified the Hague Convention: see Convention Adoption (Austria and Switzerland) (Scotland) Order 1978 (S.I. 1978 No. 1442).
[38] s. 65(1).
[39] In relation to "habitual residence" for the purposes of the Hague Child Abduction Convention, see below, para. 11.21.
[40] s. 17(2)(c).
[41] s. 17(4) and (5).
[42] s. 17(8).
[43] s. 17(6).

dispensation with consent, the court shall be treated as the authority by whom that dispensation may be made and the adoption effected.[44]

Only the Court of Session has jurisdiction to make a convention adoption order.[45] **5.38**

A convention adoption order is an adoption order in the statutory sense and **5.39** not an independent species of order. Accordingly, with the exception of the statutory requirements on the domicile or habitual residence of applicants,[46] the general law of adoption applies, subject to the conditions noted above, to applications for a convention adoption order as it does to other applications. Among the advantages of the provision for convention adoption orders is that the jurisdiction of British courts is enlarged to comprehend cases with an international aspect which would not otherwise be open while, at the same time, the simplicity of retaining the internal rules of the forum for such cases is largely maintained. As has been seen, the law of the nationality of the child is, however, respected so far as questions of consent and consultation are concerned, as is the law of the nationality of prospective adopters in relation to prohibitions on adoption.

Recognition of foreign adoptions

General

An adoption order made in England and Wales, Northern Ireland, the Isle of Man **5.40** or the Channel Islands is an adoption order within the meaning of the same statutory provisions as is a Scottish adoption order,[47] and is entitled to the same recognition and to be given the same effect. Beyond that, the recognition of non-Scottish adoptions depends in part on special statutory provisions, and in part on the common law. The statutory and common law rules constitute independent systems and the fact that recognition is not available under statute is no bar to recognition at common law.

Statutory recognition

All adoptions that take place outside British jurisdiction are entitled to be **5.41** recognised by the Scottish courts as long as they come within the definition of "overseas adoptions".[48] Recognition entails that the adoption is to be treated in every way as if it had been granted under the domestic legislation in Scotland. The result is that the effect given to an overseas adoption may be different from that which it would have received in the country in which the adoption took place. Where the succession to an estate is governed by the law of Scotland a child adopted under an overseas adoption will, therefore, have the succession rights which a Scottish adopted child would have even if the system of law under which he or she was adopted did not confer such rights.[49]

An overseas adoption is an "adoption of such a description as the Secretary **5.42** of State may by order specify, being a description of adoptions of children appearing to him to be effected under the law of any country outside Great Britain".[50] In effect, therefore, provided that the description specified by the Secretary of State is one that can be applied to the adoption of children, any order falling within that description is an overseas adoption. Determinations of competent overseas authorities in relation to overseas adoption, whether authorising, reviewing or annulling the adoption, must receive effect.[51]

---

[44] s. 17(7).
[45] s. 56(4).
[46] ss. 14(2)(b) and 15(2)(b).
[47] s. 38(1)(c).
[48] ss. 38(1)(d) and 65(2).
[49] Succession (Scotland) Act 1964, s. 23, as amended by the Adoption (Scotland) Act 1978, Sched. 3, para. 4. See *Salvesen's Trs, Petrs*, 1993 S.C. 14.
[50] s. 65(2).
[51] s. 53(1), as amended by the Children Act 1989, Sched. 10, para. 44.

5.43   While the general rule is that overseas adoptions will be recognised and
determinations in relation to overseas adoptions will be given effect, this suffers
an exception in terms of section 47(2) of the Adoption (Scotland) Act 1978,
which allows the Court of Session to order that the adoption or determination
shall cease to be valid on the ground that it is contrary to public policy or that
the authority which purported to authorise the adoption or make the determination
was not competent to entertain the case. Similarly, any court in Great Britain
may, for the purposes of proceedings before it, treat an overseas adoption as
invalid on either of these grounds.[52] In addition, where the overseas adoption is
regulated by the Hague Convention (*i.e.* broadly, was effected in a country which
is a party to the convention under provisions corresponding to those laid down
for convention adoption orders in this country) it may be annulled by the Court
of Session (a) on the ground that it was prohibited by a notified provision of the
law of the adopters' nationality, (b) on the ground that it contravened the consent
requirements of the internal law of the nationality of the adopted person or (c)
on any other ground on which it could be impugned in the country in which it
was effected.[53] With these exceptions the validity of an overseas adoption or
determination may not be impugned in any court.

5.44   Statutory (or indeed common law) recognition of overseas adoptions does not
depend on reciprocity nor is it necessary that the country whose adoptions are
recognised should have been a party to the Hague Convention from which the
legislation flows. Adoptions made in and under the law of many Commonwealth
countries, the United States of America, and all western European countries, have
now been specified as overseas adoptions.[54]

5.45   Overseas adoptions have effect as respects anything done or any event occurring
on or after February 1, 1973. An exception, however, must be made in questions
of succession: an overseas adoption will be recognised for the purpose of
successions opening before, as well as on or after, that date because section 23 of
the Succession (Scotland) Act 1964, which puts adopted children in the same
position, for succession purposes, as natural children, includes "overseas
adoptions" in its definition of "adoption order"[55] and consequently no distinction
is to be made between overseas adoptions and domestic adoptions for this purpose.[56]

Common law recognition

5.46   There is no Scottish authority directly in point on questions of common law
recognition[57] and no English authorities other than in relation to succession and
immigration. The Adoption (Scotland) Act 1978 assumes that adoptions can be
recognised in Scotland by means other than that discussed in the preceding
paragraph,[58] but it gives no indication of the grounds upon which such recognition
is based. A number of propositions are, however, open in principle and these
are discussed in the following paragraphs.

---

[52] s. 47(3).

[53] s. 47(1).

[54] Adoption (Designation of Overseas Adoptions) Order 1973 (S.I. 1973 No. 19) (as subsequently
amended).

[55] Succession (Scotland) Act 1964, s. 23(5).

[56] *Salvesen's Trs, Petrs*, 1993 S.C. 14, *per* Lord President Hope at 19.

[57] In *Salvesen's Trs, Petrs*, above, Lord President Hope at 18 cited *Re Valentine's Settlement* [1965]
Ch. 831 for the proposition that in 1968 "the courts in this country would only recognise an adoption
made in another country if the adopting parents were domiciled there and the child was ordinarily
resident there at the time of the adoption". This was not, however, an issue that required to be
decided in the case, and it was doubted by Dicey and Morris whether that proposition (particularly
its reference to the child's habitual residence) correctly expresses the *ratio decidendi* of *Re Valentine's
Settlement*: see Dicey and Morris, *The Conflict of Laws* (12th ed., 1993), p. 894.

[58] s. 38(1)(e).

Jurisdictional parity

A foreign adoption will, it is submitted, be recognised if it took place in a **5.47** country in which, had rules corresponding to the Scottish rules for jurisdiction being applied, there would have been jurisdiction to make an adoption order. As Lord President Robertson said in a different but relevant context: "It seems difficult to the degree of impossibility for this Court to decline on principle to recognise if done abroad, what it is itself bound to do and does daily at home."[59] It is sufficient that the jurisdictional basis should be substantially the same[60]; and it is not required that principles of recognition must be "a mirror image of our own law or that the pace of recognition must be geared to the haphazard movement of our legislative process".[61] A broad correspondence will take account of the general trend of legislative development.

The ordinary jurisdictional requirement for a Scottish adoption order is that **5.48** the applicant or, in the case of a joint application, one of the applicants should be domiciled, or both should be habitually resident, in the United Kingdom, the Channel Islands or the Isle of Man. A foreign adoption should therefore be recognised if the adoptive parent, or one of two adoptive parents, were domiciled, or both were habitually resident, at the time the adoption took place, in the country in which it took place[62] (or, where that country forms part of a larger national unit, were domiciled or habitually resident in one of the component parts of that unit). As a Scottish adoption order, other than a convention adoption order, may be made irrespective of the child's domicile, habitual residence or nationality and, so far as the Court of Session's jurisdiction is concerned, largely irrespective of his or her whereabouts, there is no need to import any of these factors into a decision on recognition where the adopters satisfy the domiciliary or residence test for jurisdiction.

That attention should be directed to the domicile of the adopters is supported **5.49** by authority and borne out by the statutory provisions on transferring parental responsibilities and parental rights for the purpose of adoption abroad.[63] These provide for an order being made in favour of an applicant who intends to adopt a child under the law of, or within, the country in which the applicant is domiciled. It would be anomalous if recognition were to be denied to adoptions following on such orders and valid by the law of the domicile. The fundamental reason for using the law of the adopter's domicile as the basis for recognition is, however, that the domicile of the applicants for adoption is the basis upon which Scottish courts ordinarily exercise jurisdiction.[64] Where, therefore, as is now the case, alternative grounds of jurisdiction may be invoked (such as habitual residence, or in relation to convention adoption orders), recognition of foreign adoptions should follow if jurisdictional tests corresponding to those other tests are satisfied in the country in which the adoption took place.

---

[59] *Obers v. Paton's Trs*, (1897) 24 R. 719 at 732. This view is difficult to reconcile with *Warden v. Warden*, 1951 S.C. 508, in which Lord Strachan said: "I doubt whether Scots law recognises without qualification the general proposition thus contended for, viz., that in the recognition of foreign decrees the Scots Courts must concede to foreign Courts any ground of jurisdiction which they claim for themselves." *Warden v. Warden* is, however, in turn difficult to reconcile with *Travers v. Holley* [1953] P. 246, which was approved in *Indyka v. Indyka* [1969] 1 A.C. 33. See also *Galbraith v. Galbraith*, 1971 S.C. 65; *Bain v. Bain*, 1971 S.L.T. 141; Anton and Beaumont, *Private International Law* (2nd ed.), p. 468. For a criticism of *Warden v. Warden* see Gow (1954) 3 I.C.L.Q. 152.

[60] *Travers v. Holley*, above.

[61] *Indyka v. Indyka*, above, *per* Lord Wilberforce at 106.

[62] It was assumed in *Spencer's Trs v. Ruggles*, 1981 S.C. 289 that a Scottish adoption granted when the adopter was domiciled in Scotland would be given effect to in a Scottish succession.

[63] s. 49.

[64] "Our courts should recognise a jurisdiction which *mutatis mutandis* they claim for themselves": *Re Valentine's Settlement* [1965] Ch. 831, *per* Lord Denning M.R. at 842.

5.50   Questions remain as to whether on the principles under discussion
recognition can be granted where, although on Scottish grounds of jurisdiction
there would have been jurisdiction in the courts of a foreign country, (1) the
foreign court, in fact, exercised jurisdiction on other grounds, or (2) the
adoption was not the subject of judicial proceedings but was effected in that
country by an administrative agency or by contract, or (3) the adoption did
not take place in, but would be recognised by the law of, the country in question.
There are arguments against recognition in all these cases. That the Scottish
courts claim jurisdiction on one ground is, it may be said, no reason that they
should recognise the jurisdiction of a foreign court claimed on another. *A
fortiori* of that, there is no reason to recognise the results of administrative
procedures to which jurisdictional tests in the proper sense do not apply at all,
while contract is both alien to Scottish principles of adoption and invites the
application of international private law rules in which the observance of
jurisdictional parity plays no part. And to say that one should recognise an
adoption recognised by, as distinct from taking place in, the country, for
example, of the domicile, is illogical. That recognition is accorded to an
adoption under the law of the adopters' domicile, because that law is indicated
by Scottish jurisdictional tests, is no reason for recognising an adoption which
that law would recognise by invoking other tests. These arguments have force
but under none of the heads under consideration is the argument against
recognition conclusive.

5.51   Considerations of policy, that is a favour which the law may show to
adoption as it did to legitimacy because of the beneficial results which follow,
point to a more liberal view. An analogy with recognition of foreign divorces
at common law[65] is of assistance. In *Robinson-Scott v. Robinson-Scott* it was
said:

> "It is not essential for recognition by this court that the foreign court
> should assume jurisdiction on the grounds laid down [by English domestic
> legislation]. It is sufficient that facts exist which would enable the English
> courts to assume jurisdiction."[66]

So when divorce was recognised on the ground of its validity according to
the law of the husband's domicile, a basis of recognition which had for long
been accepted, it was never required as a condition of recognition that the
foreign court should, in fact, have asserted jurisdiction on that ground. The
foreign basis of jurisdiction is irrelevant. It is submitted that the analogy
with adoption is apt and, therefore, that it is sufficient for the recognition of
a foreign adoption that the adopters were domiciled where the adoption took
place, or that another relevant Scottish jurisdictional test could have been
satisfied, regardless of the basis for jurisdiction actually invoked in the
foreign country. As in the case of extrajudicial divorces at common law[67]
the extrajudicial character of the adoption process, whether contractual or
administrative, is also, it is submitted, irrelevant. In the case of an
administrative process that argument takes added force from the fact that
the court's function in a Scottish adoption bears a ministerial as well as a
judicial aspect. The comparison with divorce also supports the view that
adoptions recognised in the foreign country should be regarded in the same
light as adoptions which actually take place there.[68]

---

[65] That issue is now wholly governed by statute: see the Family Law Act 1986, Pt II.
[66] [1958] P. 71 at 88, *per* Karminski J.
[67] *Har-Shefi v. Har-Shefi (No. 2)* [1953] P. 220.
[68] *Armitage v. Att.-Gen.* [1906] P. 135.

The general view of recognition indicated above can be reconciled with *Re* **5.52** *Marshall*[69] and *Re Valentine's Settlement*[70] and derives considerable support from the latter.[71] It can also be reconciled with *Re Wilson*[72] in which it seems that Vaisey J. would have recognised the adoption had it taken place according to the law of the adopters' domicile. It cannot be reconciled with *Re Wilby*,[73] which was, however, overruled by *Re Valentine's Settlement.*

Child's domicile

In addition to the ground for recognition considered above, a foreign adoption **5.53** will, it is submitted, also be recognised if made according to the law of the child's domicile at the time the adoption took place. It is no objection that Scottish jurisdictional rules make no requirement regarding the child's domicile. The absence of such a requirement is a positive feature, enlarging the scope of adoption, which should not be given the negative effect of denying recognition which the law of the child's domicile would confer.

The reason for this is that adoption affects status,[74] and that will be so in **5.54** practically all legal systems, although the exact nature of the impact on status may vary greatly from one system to another.[75] The grand rule in questions of status is that they should be determined by the law of the domicile of the *propositus*. It therefore follows that adoption valid by the law of the child's domicile should be recognised because, and in so far as, it affects his or her status.

It has been suggested that before an adoption valid by the law of the child's **5.55** domicile can be recognised it must also be valid by the law of the adopter's domicile.[76] It is, however, the child's status that is primarily in issue and the child should not, because of conflict with the law of the adopters' domicile, be denied the protection which adoption confers on him or her by the law of his or her domicile or the benefit of rights enforceable by that law against adopters who have freely entered into an adoptive relationship with him or her. Similarly, there is no reason that the child should not be subject to obligations imposed by the law of his or her domicile.

Succession may be thought to be a special case pointing to the adopter's **5.56** domicile but that view is increasingly difficult to maintain in the light of the availability of British adoption processes to petitioners who are not domiciled in this country.[77] It is therefore submitted that reference should not be made to the law of the adopters' domicile as an additional requirement.[78] There is also no reason for taking into account jurisdiction over the genetic parents of the child. Scottish domestic law makes no jurisdictional requirements in relation to the genetic parents, and there is no reason that its rules of international private law should do otherwise. The legitimate interests of genetic parents are sufficiently protected by considerations of morality and public policy which, if

---

[69] [1957] Ch. 507.

[70] [1965] Ch. 831.

[71] In *Patel v. Visa Officer, Bombay* [1990] Imm. A.R. 297 the Immigration Appeal Tribunal read *Re Valentine's Settlement* to mean that the adoptive parents had to be domiciled in the country of the adoption. This is, with respect, too limited an interpretation of the case.

[72] [1954] Ch. 733

[73] [1956] P. 174.

[74] *J and J v. C's Tutor*, 1948 S.C. 636.

[75] The effect of a Scottish adoption on status is now practically complete, but has not always been so. See above, para. 4.12.

[76] See Cheshire and North, *Private International Law* (12th ed., 1992), pp. 767–769.

[77] Convention adoption orders (for which see above, paras 5.35–5.39). Moreover, where an adoption in ordinary form is by a married couple only one of them need have the requisite domiciliary qualification. It is therefore difficult to argue that the requirements of the law of an adopter's domicile must be met before adoption can impinge on succession or, indeed, on other rights.

[78] See *Re Valentine's Settlement*, above, *per* Salmon J at 850–851.

contravened, would lead to refusal of recognition and also by the coincidence that will usually obtain between their domicile and the domicile of the child.

5.57   The proposition which is here put forward can be reconciled with *Re Valentine's Settlement*[79] and *Re Wilson*[80] only on the view that in these cases the domicile of the child was not proved. There is nothing in the opinions to suggest that that was the controlling factor, and in both cases it seems likely that the child was, in fact, domiciled in the country in which the adoption took place. In *Re Valentine's Settlement*, moreover, Lord Denning M.R. expressly rejected the domicile of the child as even among the criteria to be considered: "You do not", he said, "look to the domicile of the child; for that has no separate domicile of its own. It takes its parent's domicile. You look to the [adopting] parents' domicile only."[81] There is, however, a fallacy in that reasoning. It is true that a child will not normally have a domicile separate from that of one or other of his or her genetic parents (or other persons regarded by the law as parents) but his or her domicile may well not coincide with that of the adoptive parents. That may be so after as well as before adoption if, under the relevant legal regime, adoption does not effect a change in domicile. Even where that change takes place, it is only if the adoption is recognised that the child's domicile can, in the contemplation of the forum, become the same as that of the adopters; and to exclude consideration of the child's domicile because it will be the same as theirs is therefore to beg the question of recognition. It is submitted that the proposition is, despite the conflict with *Re Valentine's Settlement*, sound in principle.

Real and substantial connection

5.58   Lastly, it is further submitted that a foreign adoption may be recognised where any of the parties had, at the time of the adoption, a real and substantial connection with the jurisdiction under which the adoption took place. This proposition is derived, again by analogy with the common law on recognition of foreign decrees of divorce, from *Indyka v. Indyka*.[82] "Real and substantial connection" is not defined and, indeed, it is of the essence of its utility that it should be at large for the court. As Lord Wilberforce said:

> "The courts are well able to perform the task of examining the reality of the connection... In so acting, I am convinced that they are more likely to reach just, and to avoid artificial, results."[83]

5.59   It is, however, possible to identify as among the factors that may play a part in establishing the appropriate connection the parties' nationality, domicile (although not necessarily in the technical sense of the forum), and residence (which again need not be in the sense of "habitual residence" or "ordinary residence" as these have come to be understood in the forum). *Indyka* has, of course, been superseded by statute so far as recognition of foreign divorces is concerned but similar thinking underlies the Law Commissions' proposals on domicile,[84] whereby the domicile of an individual is to be determined by looking at the place with which he or she is most closely connected and is also reflected in (i) the rules relating to the inferred proper law of the contract[85] and (ii) the

[79] [1965] Ch. 831.
[80] [1954] Ch. 733.
[81] [1965] Ch. at 842.
[82] [1969] 1 A.C. 33. For a discussion of this case and the principle of recognition on the ground of real and substantial connection which emerges from it, see Graveson, *Conflict of Laws* (7th ed.), pp. 311–318. The case was followed in Scotland in *Galbraith v. Galbraith and Ors*, 1971 S.C. 65 and in *Bain v. Bain and Ors*, 1971 S.C. 146.
[83] [1969] 1 A.C. at 106–107.
[84] Scottish Law Commission No. 107; Law Commission No. 168 (1987).
[85] See Anton and Beaumont, pp. 268–270.

principle of the proper law of the trust whereby, if the truster has not chosen a legal system to govern the trust, it will be governed by the law with which it is most closely connected.[86]

As a test for recognition of foreign adoptions this outlook accords well with **5.60** the dissenting judgment of Salmon L.J.[87] in *Re Valentine's Settlement*, where he said:

> "Our law... develops in accordance with the changing needs of man. These have always been ascertained by experience rather than by the rigid application of abstract theory. Experience has shown that there are sound sociological reasons for recognising an adoption in circumstances such as these. Adoption—providing that there are proper safeguards— is greatly for the benefit of the adopted child and of the adoptive parents, and also, I think, of civilised society, since this is founded on the family relationship. It seems to me that we should be slow to refuse recognition to an adoption order made by a foreign court which applies the same safeguards as we do and which undoubtedly had jurisdiction over the adopted child and its natural parents."[88]

The last words, if taken out of their context, may seem to beg some questions **5.61** of jurisdiction, but, read in context, it seems that Salmon L.J. had in mind the domicile of the child and the natural parents and the real connection with the country where the adoption took place which arose from that. A caveat may, however, be entered against too strict an interpretation of Salmon L.J.'s reference to the application of "the same safeguards as we do". In the United Kingdom the safeguards are as stringent as almost anywhere else in the world, and if an exact equivalence were required there would be little scope for recognition of foreign adoptions at common law with the exception of a few countries whose adoptions are, in any event, recognised under statute. In so far as the safeguards relate to the welfare of the child their importance may, moreover, vary according to the purpose for which recognition is sought. It is an important matter where the purpose is the assertion of parental rights and powers, but in questions of succession it can often be discounted.

Limitations on recognition

Limitation by reference to purpose

As has been seen, an overseas adoption to which statutory recognition is **5.62** accorded is valid in this country for all purposes. The same is not true of common law recognition. Whether or not a foreign adoption should be recognised at common law may vary according to the purpose for which recognition is sought.[89] Thus, an objection on the ground of public policy may be apt for certain purposes of recognition and inept in others. What is offensive where parental responsibilities and parental rights are at stake may not be so in relation to succession or property. The limits of adoption under the foreign law may also limit the purposes for which it should be recognised in this country. To take any other view is to become a prisoner of terminology. There is, despite some similarities, no common international understanding of the nature and effects of adoption such as there is, say, of marriage (other than polygamous marriage),

---

[86] Hague Convention on the Law Applicable to Trusts and their Recognition, Art. 7, imported into Scots and English domestic law by the Recognition of Trusts Act 1987.
[87] See Anton and Beaumont, pp. 268–270.
[88] [1965] Ch. at 852.
[89] *Re Wilson* [1954] Ch. 733, *per* Vaisey J. at 738.

and the basis for all-purpose recognition that exists in relation to marriage is therefore lacking in the case of adoption.[90] The foreign adoption should receive recognition only to the extent, broadly conceived and with regard to substance rather than technicality or form, that it corresponds with the Scottish understanding of adoption (or the understanding of the appropriate *lex causae* if not Scottish), for it is only to the extent that it reflects that understanding that the label "adoption" can properly be applied to it. That is consistent with and, it is submitted, a correct interpretation of what was said on a question of testate succession in *Re Marshall*,[91] that "only those who are placed by adoption in a position, both as regards property rights and status, equivalent, or at all events substantially equivalent, to that of the natural children of the adopter can be treated as being within the scope of the testator's contemplation". That does not derogate from, but gives effect to, the primacy of the law governing the succession. That law determines whether or not an adopted child should succeed (or whether claims to succession should transmit through him or her), but the law of the adoption determines whether or not the *propositus* has, for the purposes of succession, been adopted.

5.63　　　An inevitable consequence of recognition according to purpose is a piecemeal effect and the creation of "limping adoptions", good for one purpose but not for another. Carried to excess, that would be a serious disadvantage but, at some cost in consistency and flexibility, the scope for that is much reduced by the Adoption (Scotland) Act 1978. Part IV, which regulates the status conferred by adoption for practically all purposes other than succession and property, applies to any adoption recognised by the law of Scotland.[92] Within the boundaries of the Act discrimination according to purpose is, therefore, excluded. It is doubtful whether the result is restrictive or enlarging. Does a foreign adoption which satisfies the principles for common law recognition but by its own law effects only a very limited transfer of parental responsibilities and parental rights still qualify for recognition? If it does qualify it must, despite the limitations imposed by its own law, receive effect for all the purposes of the Act; for the only alternative is to deny it recognition altogether. The question of what is meant by "adoption" where the Act refers to "any other adoption recognised by the law of Scotland"[93] cannot be answered merely by reference to whether "adoption" or its foreign language equivalent is the name employed, but must involve some consideration of the incidents and effects of the foreign institution. It is thought that the statute envisages a broad correspondence between the effects of adoption under the foreign law and under the law of Scotland as a condition of recognition.

5.64　　　As questions of succession and property are excluded from Part IV of the 1978 Act room for discrimination remains between recognition decisions affecting succession and property, on the one hand, and other features such as status and parental responsibilities and parental rights, on the other. That distinction is preserved if the relevant provisions of the Succession (Scotland) Act 1964 and Part IV of the Adoption (Scotland) Act 1978 are construed in a restrictive but, it is submitted, correct sense.[94] In view of the disparate nature of the issues raised in questions of succession and property and in questions of

---

[90] See, for example, *Re G (Adoption: Parental Agreement)* [1996] 1 F.C.R. 495; [1995] 2 F.L.R. 534 where a Paraguayan "simple adoption" had a very limited effect on the responsibilities and rights of the natural parents. The issue arose in relation to the question of whether the natural mother's consent remained required for the child to be adopted again in England.

[91] [1957] Ch. 507 at 523.

[92] s. 38(1).

[93] s. 38(1)(e).

[94] Adoption (Scotland) Act 1978, ss. 38 and 44; Succession (Scotland) Act 1964, s. 23(5), as amended by the 1978 Act, Sched. 3, para. 4.

parental responsibilities and parental rights the distinction accords with sound policy.

Other limitations on recognition

One general constraint on recognition of foreign adoptions remains to be **5.65** noticed. Foreign adoptions which are *contra bonos mores* or contrary to public policy in the forum will not be recognised.[95] The principles which have been discussed are to be read always subject to that qualification. Nor will a foreign adoption be recognised at common law if to do so would offend against section 6 of the Adoption (Scotland) Act 1978. A decision on recognition is, it is submitted, "a decision relating to the adoption of a child" so as to bring section 6 into operation, and the considerations which have led to a restrictive application of that section do not in general apply to questions of common law, as distinct from statutory, recognition. Accordingly the court must regard the need to safeguard and promote the welfare of the child concerned throughout his or her life as the paramount consideration and must have regard, so far as practicable, to the child's views, if he or she wishes to express them, taking account of his or her age and maturity. There are, however, two qualifications. First, there is a fundamental inconsistency between the welfare test contained in section 6 and the principles governing the law of succession and property. So section 6 is excluded if recognition is sought in that context. Secondly, the operation of section 6 is purely negative. Positive principles of recognition are, it is thought, like principles of jurisdiction, anterior to the operation of section 6 which serves only to exclude recognition which would otherwise be accorded. So if the grounds of recognition discussed above are lacking, regard for the welfare of the child or his or her views cannot in itself supply the gap.

---

[95] See *Re Valentine's Settlement* [1965] Ch. 831, *per* Lord Denning M.R. at 842.

CHAPTER 6

SURROGACY AND PARENTAL ORDERS

Introduction

6.01   Cusine states:

> "it is important to define the term 'surrogacy' as covering any situation
> in which one woman agrees to carry a child for another. This includes
> a case where a couple decide to hand over their child to another couple;
> also an arrangement whereby a woman is artificially inseminated with
> semen by a man who, with his wife or partner, will be the child's
> 'parents'; and finally a situation in which a woman has another couple's
> embryo implanted in her, on the understanding that she will surrender
> the child to the couple who produced the embryo, or possibly to
> someone else".[1]

He goes on to list 19 different permutations of the surrogacy arrangement.[2]
At common law, a surrogacy arrangement that involved the woman who
gives birth to a child surrendering that child to another would not be criminal,
but neither would the agreement be enforceable. It had been held in England
that an agreement to surrender a child would not be enforced against a mother
who changed her mind,[3] and almost certainly if the agreement were carried
out the law would not pay any regard to it (with the result that the mother
remained "mother" for the purposes of the law[4]). In Scotland, although
fostering of children has had a much longer history than in England, the law
is to similar effect. The person who receives the child can be compelled to
return him or her to the mother; but the agreement itself is legally recognised
in the sense that its incidents may receive effect in so far as they do not
encroach on parental responsibilities or parental rights.[5] Redelivery of the
child would not be ordered at common law if this would involve serious
danger to his or her health or morals[6] and such questions must now be decided
on the basis that the child's welfare is the paramount consideration. Such an
agreement, even where redelivery is not sought or is refused, cannot,
however, create a complete parent–child relationship, affecting, for example,
succession rights. Adoption is needed to effect such a radical shift in

---

[1] Cusine, *New Reproductive Techniques: A Legal Perspective* (1988), p. 143. There has been a
burgeoning literature on this subject. Scottish articles include Norrie "The Parental Orders (Human
Fertilisation and Embryology) (Scotland) Regulations 1995" 1995 Fam. L.B. 13/3; Biondi,
"Surrogate Parency and the Law", 1995 Scolag 54; Willock, "Caring for the Offspring of Surrogacy",
1995 S.L.T. (News) 41.

[2] at p. 209.

[3] See *Humphrys v. Polak* [1901] 2 K.B. 385; *A v. C* (1978) 8 Fam. Law 170; (1984) 14 Fam. Law 241;
[1985] F.L.R. 445.

[4] In *Humphrys v. Polak*, above, it was held that a mother could not give up her right of custody,
because that right was conferred only to allow her to fulfil her parental duties.

[5] See *Kerrigan v. Hall* (1901) 4 F.10; *Macpherson v. Leishman* (1887) 14 R. 780, in which Lord
President Inglis expressed regret that the arrangement was being brought to an end (this on the
basis of the welfare of the child).

[6] *Sutherland v. Taylor* (1887) 15 R. 224; *Mackenzie v. Keillor* (1892) 19 R. 963; *Campbell v.
Croall* (1895) 22 R. 869.

relationships. In the typical surrogacy arrangement it is the intent of the parties that such a parent–child relationship be established. But of course intent does not make law.[7]

Statutory control of surrogacy

When the Warnock Committee examined the issue of surrogacy, it could not **6.02** reach a unanimous conclusion. The majority wanted to criminalise the setting-up or operating of surrogacy agencies whether they were profit-making or not,[8] while a minority saw some place for State-controlled surrogacy.[9] Due to intense public disquiet on the issue, which arose as a result of the case reported as *Re C (A Minor)*[10], the Government felt that it could not give the time for the consultation and consideration afforded to the other issues raised in the Warnock Committee Report, and shortly after that report was published it rushed through Parliament the Surrogacy Arrangements Act 1985. This renders criminal any act designed to establish a surrogacy arrangement[11] if that arrangement is made on a commercial basis, by which is meant if money or money's worth is passed as a consequence.[12] A person or an organisation can be guilty of this offence. Advertising in connection with surrogacy, commercial or otherwise, is also a criminal offence.[13]

The 1985 Act has only limited application. It is designed to proscribe the **6.03** agencies who operate for profit by bringing together infertile couples and women willing to act as surrogate mothers. Agencies who do so on a non-profit basis are not breaching the law. Likewise, merely to enter into a surrogacy arrangement is not *per se* a criminal act. Nor is the paying of money or money's worth to a woman or for her benefit in respect of the carrying of the child.[14] So, the infertile couple and the surrogate mother herself do not commit any offence if they enter into a private arrangement, even when money passes.[15] It is only those who seek to make profit by bringing them together, or who advertise, who are covered by these provisions. In particular, the 1985 Act says nothing about the legal status of the child, which, until the passing of the Human Fertilisation and Embryology Act 1990, depended on the genetic link (proved or presumed) that existed between the child and his or her parents.

The issue of enforceability of the contract was expressly avoided, with **6.04** section 1(9), as originally passed in 1985, weakly providing that the offence was committed "whether or not" the arrangement itself was enforceable. The Human Fertilisation and Embryology Act 1990 repealed these words,[16] and added a new section 1A to the 1985 Act, to the effect that "no surrogacy arrangement is enforceable by or against any of the persons making it".[17] Surrogacy

---

[7] But see *Johnson* v. *Calvert*, 851 P. (2d) 776 (1993), discussed above, para. 3.06, in which the Supreme Court of California defined a child's "natural mother" in a case of gestational surrogacy as the woman who was intended by the parties when the surrogacy arrangement was made to be the social mother of the child.

[8] *Report of the Committee of Inquiry into Human Fertilisation and Embryology*, Cmnd. 9314 (1984) (the "Warnock Committee Report"), para. 8.18.

[9] *ibid.* Expression of Dissent "A".

[10] [1985] F.L.R. 846.

[11] Defined (s. 1(2) and (3), as amended by the Children Act 1989, Sched. 13, para. 56) as one involving a "surrogate mother", which is defined as "a woman who carries a child in pursuance of an arrangement (a) made before she began to carry the child and (b) made with a view to any child carried in pursuance of it being handed over to, and parental responsibility being met (so far as practicable) by, another person or other persons".

[12] Surrogacy Arrangements Act 1985, ss. 1(8) and 2(3).

[13] *ibid.* s. 3.

[14] *per* Lord President Hope in *C* v. *S*, 1996 S.L.T. 1387 at 1390D.

[15] s. 2(3) provides that payments to or for the benefit of a surrogate or prospective surrogate do not fall within the prohibition.

[16] Human Fertilisation and Embryology Act 1990, s. 36(2)(b).

[17] *ibid.* s. 36(1).

arrangements, then, are permitted by the law[18] and will sometimes (see below) lead to a reallocation of parental status, but they are not encouraged and if the parties to the arrangement disagree on any matter (for example the mother refuses to give up the child on birth,[19] or the commissioning couple refuse to take the child at birth, or the pregnant woman seeks an abortion, or the commissioning couple seek recovery of any payments made) the law will resolve the disagreement in accordance with pre-existing rules and the arrangement itself will not be taken to have affected the legal rights or obligations of any party.

Parental orders in favour of gamete donors

6.05   The Human Fertilisation and Embryology Act 1990 also makes provision for the parentage of children born as a result of surrogacy arrangements. The general position is that parentage will be determined, as usual, by the genetic connection, or by utilising one of the presumptions or deeming provisions discussed above in Chapter 3. In addition, however, the court[20] is given the power to make an order providing for a child born as a result of a surrogacy arrangement to be treated in law as the child of the couple who commissioned the surrogate mother to carry the child.[21] The effect of such an order, known as a "parental order", is almost identical to the effect of an adoption order, and the similarity to adoption is reflected in the regulations,[22] which apply many of the provisions in the Adoption (Scotland) Act 1978[23] to applications for a parental order under section 30.

Effect of the order

6.06   The effect of a parental order made under section 30 is that the child is to be treated in law as the child of the parties to the marriage who applied for the order,[24] which means that the child who is the subject of the order shall be treated as from the date of the order (a) as if he or she had been born as the child of the parties to that marriage and (b) as if he or she were not the child of any person other than the parties to that marriage.[25] The parental rights and duties relating to the child are vested in the husband and wife, except in so far as they relate to any period before the making of the order,[26] and the making of the order operates to extinguish

> (a) any parental right or duty relating to the child which, immediately before the making of the order, was vested in a person (not being either

---

[18] The HFEA *Code of Practice* (rev. 1995), para. 3.20 directs licence-holders that "the application of assisted conception techniques to initiate a surrogate pregnancy should only be considered where it is physically impossible or highly undesirable for medical reasons for the commissioning mother to carry the child".

[19] As in *A v. C*, [1985] F.L.R. 445 and in *Re P (Minors) (Wardship: Surrogacy)* [1987] 2 F.L.R. 421.

[20] By which is meant the Court of Session or the sheriff court of the sheriffdom within which the child is: s. 30(8)(b).

[21] s. 30(1). This section was added to the legislation at a late stage. For a discussion, see Hogg, "Surrogacy—Nobody's Child" [1991] Fam.Law 276; Douglas and Lowe, "Becoming a Parent in English Law" (1992) 108 L.Q.R. 414; Blyth, "Section 30—The Acceptable Face of Surrogacy" (1993) J. Soc. Wel. and Fam. L. 248.

[22] Parental Orders (Human Fertilisation and Embryology) (Scotland) Regulations 1994 (S.I. 1994, No. 2804).

[23] As it applied before the amendments contained in the Children (Scotland) Act 1995. The Parental Orders Regulations have not been amended to take account of the new rules in the adoption legislation.

[24] s. 30(1).

[25] Adoption (Scotland) Act 1978, s. 39, as applied to parental orders by the Parental Orders (Human Fertilisation and Embryology) (Scotland) Regulations 1994, Sched. 1, para. 8. This applies for the construction of enactments or instruments passed or made before or after the date of coming into force of the 1994 Regulations unless the context otherwise requires: s. 39(3), as so applied.

[26] Adoption (Scotland) Act 1978, s. 12(1) and (2), as applied to parental orders by the Parental Orders (Human Fertilisation and Embryology) (Scotland) Regulations 1994, Sched. 1, para. 3.

the husband or the wife) who was (i) the mother or father of the child by virtue of section 27 or 28 of the 1990 Act, or otherwise, or (ii) a guardian of the child appointed by a deed or by the order of a court;

(b) any duty owed to or by the child (i) to pay or provide aliment in respect of any period occurring after the making of the order; and (ii) to make payment arising out of parental rights and duties in respect of such a period.[27]

The order does not, however, extinguish any duty arising under a deed or agreement which constitutes a trust or which expressly provides that the duty is not to be extinguished by the making of a parental order; nor does it in itself terminate the appointment or functions of any judicial factor *loco tutoris* or curator *bonis* appointed to administer the whole or any part of the child's estate.[28] The parental order may contain such terms and conditions as the court thinks fit.[29]

The child who is the subject of a parental order shall be treated for the **6.07** purposes of the forbidden degrees of marriage and for the law of incest as if (a) he or she were the child of the parties to the marriage and (b) he or she were also the child of any other person who, prior to the making of the parental order, was the mother or the father of the child.[30] Curiously, this form of wording does not quite reflect the much more precise (and more limited) rules in relation to adopted children. With the latter, children are brought within the forbidden degrees for the purposes of marriage and the crime of incest only in relation to their adoptive (or former adoptive) parents, and they are not removed from the forbidden degrees in relation to their genetic parents.[31] However, it would seem that to treat a child subject to a parental order as if he or she were the child of the parties to the marriage requires that he or she be so treated in respect of relationships traced through the parties to the marriage, such as their siblings. If this is correct then, while an adopted person may marry, for example, the genetic child of his or her adoptive parents, a person who is the subject of a parental order may not.

Conditions for making the order

The Human Fertilisation and Embryology Act 1990 lays down a number of **6.08** conditions, each of which must be satified before a parental order can be made.

(1) The applicants must be married, and the order cannot be made in favour of a cohabiting couple, nor of a married or a single person on his or her own. This may be compared with the adoption legislation which allows, in some circumstances, persons other than a married couple to adopt.[32] The nature of the marriage is not specified in the Act, though it may be taken from the absence of any provision to the contrary that the marriage must be valid and subsisting at the time of the making of the order (and possibly at the time of the application as well). An irregular marriage would, in Scotland, suffice, as would a voidable marriage. It is likely, on an analogy with adoption,[33] that if the marriage is proved to be invalid after the making of a parental order, the order itself retains effect.

---

[27] s. 12(3), as so applied.
[28] s. 12(4), as so applied.
[29] s. 12(5), as so applied.
[30] Adoption (Scotland) Act 1978, s. 41, as applied to parental orders by the Parental Orders (Human Fertilisation and Embryology) (Scotland) Regulations 1994, Sched. 1, para. 9.
[31] See above, para. 4.14.
[32] See above, para. 4.23.
[33] See above, para. 4.09, n. 6.

(2) The child must have been carried by a woman other than the wife of
     the marriage, as a result of the placing in her of an embryo or sperm
     and eggs or her artificial[34] insemination[35]; and either the sperm of the
     husband or the egg of the wife, or both, must have been used to bring
     about the creation of the embryo.[36] (In other words, at least one of the
     parties to the marriage must be the genetic parent.)

(3) The order must have been applied for within six months of the birth of
     the child, or, in the case of a child born before the coming into force of
     the Act, within six months of its coming into force.[37]

(4) Both at the time of the application and of the making of the order the
     child's home must be with the married couple,[38] and either one or both
     of the married couple must be domiciled in a part of the United
     Kingdom or in the Channel Islands or the Isle of Man.[39] Where the
     application for a parental order is pending, the person who is either
     the mother or the father of the child or any guardian of the child is not
     entitled against the will of the person with whom the child has his or
     her home to remove the child from the care and possession of that
     person except with the leave of the court.[40]

(5) Both husband and wife must have attained the age of 18 at the time of
     the making of the order.[41] The application itself must be made within
     six months of the child's birth (see above) though it may be competent
     for the court, on receiving the application, to delay the making of the
     order until such time as the applicants are both 18 years of age.

(6) The man and woman who would otherwise be father and mother but
     for the making of such an order (including a man or woman who would
     be father or mother through the application of any of the other
     provisions of the 1990 Act[42]) must have freely and with full
     understanding of what is involved agreed unconditionally to the making
     of the order.[43] Difficulties may in practice arise in identifying who is
     the appropriate person to give agreement as the father, but in principle
     paternity is determined in the ways described earlier in this chapter. It
     follows from this that, if the surrogate mother is married and her
     husband agreed to the treatment which led to her becoming pregnant,
     he will be the father whose agreement is necessary.[44] So will the man
     to whom treatment is provided together with the woman (for, though

[34] Thus excluding from section 30 children conceived naturally but nevertheless as the intended
     subject of a surrogacy agreement. There is, however, no requirement that the surrogate pregnancy
     be achieved under the direction of a person licensed by the Human Fertilisation and Embryology
     Authority.
[35] s. 30(1)(a). This applies whether the woman was in the United Kingdom or elsewhere at the time
     of the placing in her of the embryo or the sperm and eggs or of her artificial insemination.
[36] s. 30(1)(b). It is not sufficient that the husband can claim paternity by other means (*cf. Re Q
     (Parental Order)* [1996] 1 F.L.R. 369). This provision expressly requires a genetic link.
[37] s. 30(2). This part of the 1990 Act came into force on November 1, 1994 (Human Fertilisation
     and Embryology Act 1990 (Commencement No. 5) Order 1994 (S.I. 1994 No. 1776)) and so
     after May 1, 1995 all applications must be within six months of birth.
[38] s. 30(3)(a).
[39] s. 30(3)(b).
[40] Adoption (Scotland) Act 1978, s. 27(1), as applied to parental orders by the Parental Orders
     (Human Fertilisation and Embryology) (Scotland) Regulations 1994, Sched. 1, para. 6. If a child
     has been removed in breach of this provision the court may on the application of a person from
     whose care and possession the child has been removed order the person who has so removed the
     child to return him or her to the applicant: s. 29(1), as similarly applied by Sched. 1, para. 7.
[41] s. 30(4).
[42] See *Re Q (Parental Order)* [1996] 1 F.L.R. 369.
[43] s. 30(5).
[44] *Re Q (Parental Order)*, above, *per* Johnson J. at 372D.

not married to the mother, he is "the father by virtue of section 28 of this Act" whose consent is, expressly, required).[45] The "commissioning father" will sometimes be the genetic (and therefore legal) father, such as when the surrogate mother is unmarried and the treatment was not provided to her and a man other than the genetic father "together", but his consent is implicit in his making the application and is not otherwise required[46]. In other circumstances (*e.g.* when the surrogate mother's husband did not consent or donated sperm was used to impregnate a single woman) the child will be legally fatherless, in which case no paternal consent is required to the making of the order under section 30.[47] The requirement for agreement is absolute, subject only to two qualifications: (a) the agreement of a person who cannot be found or is incapable of giving agreement is not required and (b) the agreement of a woman who has carried the child is ineffective if given by her less than six weeks after the birth of the child.[48] It is to be noted that, other than the first of these qualifications, there is no provision in the Act allowing the court to dispense with the agreement of the parents.

(7) The court, before making the order, must be satisfied that no money or other benefit (other than for expenses reasonably incurred) has been given or received by the husband or the wife for or in consideration of (a) the making of the order, (b) any agreement required by the Act, (c) the handing over of the child to the husband and the wife or (d) the making of any arrangements with a view to the making of the order; the court does, however, have the power to authorise any such payment.[49] These rules are closely analogous to the prohibition of payments contained in the adoption legislation.[50] However, it should be noted that a payment that breaches the adoption legislation does not for that reason alone breach the surrogacy legislation, and vice versa. A payment made in consideration for adoption is not a payment made in consideration for surrogacy, and it is therefore important to identify the motives with which the payments have been made.[51] Expenses "reasonably incurred" do not breach the prohibition in section 30 of the 1990 Act,[52] but if the payments do breach the prohibition the court cannot grant the parental order unless it first authorises the payments. Authorisation can be granted retrospectively.[53] In *Re Q (Parental Order)*[54] payment of £8,280 was authorised, £5,000 of that being referable to the surrogate mother's lost earnings. And in *C v. S*[55] payment of £8,000 would have been authorised (had the order sought been a parental order) due to the absence of bad faith on the part of the parties. In determining whether to authorise payments which breach the prohibition, the welfare

---

[45] A surrogacy arrangement on these facts would be rare, but might arise if it is entered into after the pregnancy commences.
[46] s. 30(5).
[47] *Re Q (Parental Order)*, above.
[48] s. 30(6). *Cf.* the Adoption (Scotland) Act 1978, s. 16(4).
[49] s. 30(7).
[50] See above, para. 5.23–5.25.
[51] *C v. S*, 1996 SLT 1387. See especially Lord President Hope at 1396A–B.
[52] In *Re an Adoption Application (Surrogacy)* [1987] 2 All E.R. 826 it was held that payments which did not cover the surrogate mother's expenses or lost earnings did not breach the prohibition in the adoption legislation.
[53] *Re an Adoption Application (Surrogacy)*, above; *Re MW (Adoption: Surrogacy)* [1995] 2 F.L.R. 759; *Re Q (Parental Order)* [1996] 1 F.L.R. 369.
[54] above.
[55] 1996 S.L.T. 1387.

of the child, and the effect the order would have on the child, are relevant factors and if there is no deliberate attempt to bypass the law's protections authorisation will usually be granted in cases in which it is in the child's interests to do so.[56]

6.09 The permissive "may" is used in section 30 which indicates that the making of the order is a discretionary power of the court, as is the case with adoption. That discretion must be exercised by the court having regard to all the circumstances, first consideration being given to the need to safeguard and promote the welfare of the child throughout his or her childhood, and having so far as practicable ascertained the wishes and feelings of the child concerned regarding the decision and given due consideration to them, having regard to the child's age and understanding.[57] The court may not determine an application for a parental order where a previous application for such an order, made in relation to the same child by the same persons, was refused by any court, unless (a) in refusing the previous application the court directed that this rule should not apply or (b) it appears to the court that because of a change in circumstances or for any other reason it is proper to proceed with the application.[58] If an order is refused (whether, it would seem, on its merits or because a condition precedent has not been satisfied) the court may, if it appears to the court that there are exceptional circumstances making this desirable, order that the child be under the supervision of a specified local authority or, if there are exceptional circumstances making it impracticable or undesirable for the child to be entrusted either to the person who is the mother or the father of the child by virtue of section 27 or 28 of the 1990 Act, or otherwise, or to any other individual, the court may commit the child to the care of a specified local authority.[59]

6.10 If section 30 cannot, due to the failure to satisfy any of the conditions, be relied upon, it remains open to the commissioning couple (or even to one of them) to seek a residence or contact order and that matter will, of course, be determined on the basis of the best interests of the child.[60] Alternatively, the commissioning couple might seek to adopt the child, for an inability to satisfy the criteria for a parental order does not preclude adoption. If, for example, parental consent is withheld, the parental order cannot be made but seeking an adoption order instead opens the way to dispensing with agreement.[61]

Procedure

6.11 An application for a parental order under section 30 is to be made by means of petition, and there must be lodged in process:

---

[56] Lord Weir in *C v. S*, above, at 1399 was careful to point out that the child's welfare should not be used to undermine public policy. He was thinking in particular of the policy of discouraging child-trafficking.

[57] Adoption (Scotland) Act 1978, s. 6, as applied to parental orders by the Parental Orders (Human Fertilisation and Embryology) (Scotland) Regulations 1994, Sched. 1, para. 2. The application must be made within six months of the child's birth, so the requirement to ascertain the child's wishes and feelings is inept.

[58] Adoption (Scotland) Act 1978, s. 24(1), as applied to parental orders by the Parental Orders (Human Fertilisation and Embryology) (Scotland) Regulations 1994, Sched. 1, para. 4.

[59] Adoption (Scotland) Act 1978, s. 26, as applied to parental orders by the Parental Orders (Human Fertilisation and Embryology) (Scotland) Regulations 1994, Sched. 1, para. 5. This provision in the Adoption (Scotland) Act 1978 was repealed by the Children (Scotland) Act 1995, Sched. 5 and the provision currently being considered remains the only circumstance in which the care of a child can be committed to a local authority.

[60] See *Re C (A Minor)* [1985] F.L.R. 846 (decided before the passing of the 1990 Act) in which the commissioning couple were awarded care and control of the child and allowed to remove him from the jurisdiction, and *Re H (A Minor)* [1993] Fam. Law 205 in which a residence order was made in favour of one of the commissioning couple. A parental order would have been unavailable since the commissioning couple were both women.

[61] See, for example, *Re MW (Adoption: Surrogacy)* [1995] 2 F.L.R. 759; *C v. S*, 1996 S.L.T. 1387.

(a) an extract of any entry in the Register of Births relating to the child; (b) extracts of any entry in the register of births relating to the birth of each of the petitioners; (c) an extract of any entry in the Register of Marriages relating to the marriage of the petitioners, and (d) any other document founded on by the petitioners in support of the terms of the petition.[62]

Before determining the cause, the sheriff may order production of further documents (including affidavits) or parole evidence.[63] On the presentation of the petition the sheriff shall appoint a reporting officer and a curator *ad litem* and the same person may be appointed to both offices in the same petition if the sheriff considers that doing so is appropriate in the circumstances.[64] The duties of both are set out in the regulations.[65] On receipt of the reports prepared by the reporting officer and the curator *ad litem* the sheriff shall fix a hearing,[66] which must be intimated by the petitioners to every person whose whereabouts are known to them and whose agreement is required to be given, to the reporting officer and the curator *ad litem* and to any person on whom the sheriff has ordered intimation.[67]

At the hearing (which must be in private unless the court otherwise directs[68]), **6.12** the petitioners, the reporting officer and the curator *ad litem* shall, if required by the sheriff, appear and may be represented; any other person required by the sheriff to attend shall, and any person on whom intimation has been made may, appear and may be represented.[69]

Applicants who wish to prevent their identity being disclosed to any person **6.13** whose agreement is required may, before presenting a petition, apply to the sheriff clerk for a serial number to be assigned to them, and where a serial number is assigned the record of the serial number and the persons to whom it relates shall be treated as confidential and be disclosed only to the sheriff; any agreement shall refer to the petitioners only by the serial number; and the serial number shall be used to name or design the petitioners for all purposes connected with the petition.[70] There are similar rules in relation to adoption[71] but, in relation to section 30, it is difficult to see when and how they will apply. In a surrogacy arrangement the identity of the commissioning couple will nearly always be known to the woman who will carry and give birth to a child on their behalf; and in any situation in which the identity of the applicants is not known and the mother wishes to discover that identity, all she need do is withhold agreement until she is given the information she wants. As stated above, there is no requirement that agreement be withheld reasonably, nor any means of dispensing with agreement unreasonably withheld, nor any means of forcing the mother to give agreement in any circumstance in which she is not wholly satisfied with her position.

---

[62] Act of Sederunt (Child Care and Maintenance Rules) 1997 (S.I. 1997 No. 291) (S.19), r. 2.47; Rules of the Court of Session 1994 (S.I. 1994 No. 1443), r. 81.3. The sheriff court rules are given in the text, and Court of Session references in the footnotes.

[63] A.S. 1997, r. 2.49; RCS 1994, r. 81.6.

[64] A.S. 1997, r. 2.51(1); RCS 1994, r. 81.10.

[65] A.S. 1997, r. 2.53; RCS 1994, r. 81.11.

[66] A.S. 1997, r. 2.54(1); RCS 1994, r. 81.12.

[67] A.S. 1997, r. 2.54(2) and (3); RCS 1994, r. 81.12.

[68] Adoption (Scotland) Act 1978, s. 57, as applied to parental orders by the Parental Orders (Human Fertilisation and Embryology) (Scotland) Regulations 1994, Sched. 1, para. 13.

[69] A.S. 1997, r. 2.54(4); RCS 1994, r. 81.12.

[70] A.S. 1997, r. 2.50; RCS 1994, r. 81.18.

[71] See above, para. 4.34.

6.14   If a parental order is made, the interlocutor shall be sent by the sheriff clerk to the Registrar-General in a sealed envelope marked "confidential"[72]; and the sheriff clerk shall forthwith thereafter place the whole process in an envelope bearing only (i) the name of the petitioners; (ii) the full name of the child to whom the process relates; and (iii) the date of the order; and shall seal the envelope and mark it "confidential".[73] Thereafter the person in respect of whom the parental order was made may open the process or inspect its contents after he or she has reached the age of 16 years.[74] The order must be registered, in accordance with the rules laid down in Schedule 1 to the Adoption (Scotland) Act 1978, as applied to parental orders by the Parental Orders (Human Fertilisation and Embryology) (Scotland) Regulations 1994.[75]

---

[72] A.S. 1997, r. 2.57; RCS 1994, r. 81.16.

[73] A.S. 1997, r. 2.59(1); RCS 1994, r. 81.18.

[74] A.S. 1997, r. 2.59(2). Access to the process may also be given under this rule (a) to any person or body entitled under a modified s. 45(5) of the Adoption (Scotland) Act 1978 (but only with the written authority of the person in respect of whom the parental order was made); (b) by order of the court in an application made by petition presented by another court or authority (whether within the United Kingdom or not) having power to make a parental order, for the purpose of obtaining information in connection with that purpose; (c) by order of the court on an application made by petition presented by any person; and (d) to any person who is authorised in writing by the Secretary of State to obtain information from the process for the purpose of research designed to improve the working of human fertilisation and embryology law and practice.

[75] Parental Orders (Human Fertilisation and Embryology) (Scotland) Regulations 1994, Sched. 1, para. 18.

CHAPTER 7

GUARDIANSHIP OF CHILDREN

INTRODUCTION

As has already been pointed out,[1] "guardianship" was not a term of art in **7.01**
the common law of Scotland which talked rather of tutory and curatory.
These offices were, properly, held by persons other than parents, though it
was common to refer to the parental role as including the rights of tutory
and curatory; this usage received statutory sanction in 1986.[2] In that usage,
the parental right to represent children in legal transactions was the meaning
given to tutory and (in a qualified sense) to curatory and the right to custody
was regarded as distinct. The office of tutor, however, as enjoyed by a
person other than a parent comprehended custody although that aspect of
tutory might be, and often was, separately regulated by the court. With the
coming into force of the Age of Legal Capacity (Scotland) Act 1991, tutory
became "guardianship" and, as such, a separate concept from custody.[3]
"Guardianship" under the Children (Scotland) Act 1995 acquired a different
meaning again, though one which more closely reflects the popular
understanding of the word, for it now imports responsibilities and rights
over both the child's property and person. Today, a child's guardians are
persons expressly appointed to that office and who have thereby the
responsibilities and rights to act in substitution for or, occasionally, in
addition to the child's own parents. It creates a quasi-parent and child
relationship in which the guardian acts as a parent-substitute. The purpose
of guardianship is to provide the child with persons who can take over the
upbringing role when the parents are unable to fulfil that role, whether
through death or otherwise. It is a means whereby the private ordering of
the child's upbringing can be ensured without the necessity to involve the
public authorities. That involvement remains available in situations in
which state control or regulation of the child's upbringing is desirable,
and the rules and procedures applicable to those situations will be
considered later.[4] The benefit of guardianship, however, is that it allows
parents to make provision for the upbringing of their children on their
deaths according to their wishes, without the uncertainties which might
otherwise occur.

Another alternative to guardianship as a means of providing for the **7.02**
upbringing of children on the failure of the parents is adoption, also considered
in detail elsewhere.[5] Guardianship differs from adoption in that its only effect is

---

[1] Above, para. 1.08.
[2] The Law Reform (Parent and Child) (Scotland) Act 1986, s. 8 (as originally enacted) defined
"parental rights" to mean *inter alia* "tutory, curatory, custody or access". The Age of Legal
Capacity (Scotland) Act 1991 amended s. 8 so that "parental rights" were defined to include
"guardianship, custody or access".
[3] That custody and guardianship were different concepts was confirmed in the opinion of Lord
Justice-Clerk Ross in *L v. H*, 1996 S.L.T. 612.
[4] See below, Chaps 16–20.
[5] See above, Chaps 4 and 5.

to impose parental responsibilities and confer parental rights in relation to the upbringing of children: it grants to the guardian the authority of a parent without in any way creating, as adoption does, a full parent-child relationship. So there are no succession consequences to guardianship, nor are the parties brought within the forbidden degrees of relationship for the purposes of marriage; the relationship terminates on the exhaustion of parental responsibilities and parental rights and has no continuing, lifelong, consequences. It is, of course, open to a guardian to effect these consequences by adopting the child, but unless this is done the parent-substitution of guardianship is limited to the upbringing of the child, that is to say the fulfilling of those parental responsibilities and the exercising of those parental rights listed in sections 1 and 2 respectively of the Children (Scotland) Act 1995.

Scope of this chapter

7.03   The treatment in this chapter is confined to guardianship as a distinct office held by persons who are appointed thereto in the place of or in addition to parents. It will consider the circumstances affecting the appointment of guardians, the persons who may be so appointed, and the duration of their office and its termination. The exercise and legal control of parental responsibilities and parental rights is no different with guardians from that relating to parents and gives rise, therefore, to no specialities requiring separate treatment here.

APPOINTMENT OF GUARDIANS

7.04 Section 5(2) of the Age of Legal Capacity (Scotland) Act 1991 (as amended)[6] provides as follows:

> "Subject to section 1(3)(f) above, as from the commencement of this Act no guardian of a person under the age of 16 years shall be appointed as such except under section 7 of the Children (Scotland) Act 1995."

Section 1(3)(f) preserves the court's power to appoint a curator *ad litem* or a curator *bonis* to persons under the age of 16[7]: these are no longer true examples of guardianship since guardians became parent-substitutes. Guardians may also be appointed by the court under section 11(2)(h) of the 1995 Act,[8] so that the two basic methods by which a person can become guardian are appointment by parent or guardian, and appointment by the court. Before considering these two methods of appointment, however, the question of disability from the office of guardian will be treated, for the principles involved apply however the appointment to the office is made.

Disqualification from office

7.05   The general rule is that every person *sui juris* and of sane mind is eligible for appointment to the office of guardian.[9] That general rule admits, however, of a few exceptions.

---

[6] By the Children (Scotland) Act 1995, Sched. 4, para. 53(5).
[7] See below, paras 15.59–15.65.
[8] The apparent conflict with s. 5(2) of the 1991 Act can be reconciled with s. 11(2)(h) only by restricting the former to appointments by parents and guardians.
[9] Fraser (3rd ed.), p. 449; Erskine, I, vii, 12; Bankton, I, vii, 18.

Age

Under the Roman law no one under the age of 25, the Roman age of majority, **7.06**
could hold the office of tutor. In Scotland that rule was applied to tutors-legitim
by statute[10] until the Age of Majority (Scotland) Act 1969 substituted the age of
18.[11] Erskine[12] says that tutors-nominate and tutors-dative[13] could be received
at 21 but, in saying that, he had the age of majority in mind. Bankton[14] refers to
21 years in the context of majority and More[15] expressly refers to the years of
majority. Eighteen, the modern age of majority, might, therefore, be taken to be
the qualifying age for guardians today. However, the terms of the Age of Legal
Capacity (Scotland) Act 1991 throw considerable doubt on this, and an argument
can be sustained that the qualifying age is now 16. Section 1(1)(b) of the 1991
Act confers legal capacity upon persons of or over the age of 16 years to enter
into any transaction. "Transaction" is given a wide meaning[16] and includes the
bringing or defending of, or taking any step in, civil proceedings, as well as
acting as trustee. If a 16-year-old has this capacity to act as trustee then it is
difficult to see on what principle capacity to act as guardian can be denied, for
trusteeship requires a person to act on another's behalf just as guardianship
does. The age of majority was adopted because it was the age at which a person
left the curatory of another and became fully *sui juris*. That rationale no longer
exists in relation to the age of 18 and can be applied now to the age of 16.
Indeed it is provided that any reference in any enactment to a person under
legal disability by reason of non-age shall be construed as a reference to a person
under the age of 16 years.[17] It is further provided[18] that nothing in the 1991 Act
shall prevent any person under the age of 16 years from exercising parental
responsibilities and parental rights in relation to any child of his. The result of
these provisions is, it is submitted, that there is no age limit on an unmarried
father being appointed guardian to his own child (subject only to a court
appointment being made in the child's best interests), and that the age limit on
a person being appointed guardian to other than his or her own child is now
16.[19] It remains obscure how a person under 16, who has no legal capacity, can
exercise such capacity in relation to his or her own child, and it may be doubted
whether the legislature intended to grant that capacity.

Sex and marriage

Under the Roman law, which accounted tutory an *officium virile*, no woman, **7.07**
with the exception of certain classes of mother of the child, could be appointed
tutor. That doctrine was accepted by the institutional writers only in the case of
tutors-legitim and women could be appointed tutors-nominate or tutors-dative.
Married women were, however, absolutely excluded on the view that it was
illogical to give guardianship of others to persons who were themselves under

---

[10] Tutors Act 1474, c. 6 (APS II, 106) (repealed by the Age of Legal Capacity (Scotland) Act 1991,
Sched. 2).
[11] s. 1.
[12] I, vii, 5.
[13] The differences between tutors-legitim, -dative and -nominate are described in the 1st edition of
this book, at pp. 38–40.
[14] I, vii, 18.
[15] *Notes on Stair*, p. xxxv, n. D, para. 1.
[16] Age of Legal Capacity (Scotland) Act 1991, s. 9.
[17] *ibid.* s. 1(2).
[18] *ibid.* s. 1(3)(g), as amended by the Children (Scotland) Act 1995, Sched. 4, para. 53(2).
[19] s. 2(1) of the 1991 Act confers legal capacity on persons under the age of 16 to enter into
transactions "of a kind commonly entered into by persons of his age and circumstances." It is
unlikely to be considered common for a person under 16 to be appointed guardian to anyone
other than his own child.

guardianship (*i.e.* the curatory of their husbands). That reflects the requirement that tutors be persons who are themselves *sui juris*.[20] The theoretical basis for the rule was, therefore, abrogated by the abolition of the husband's curatory[21] and with its abolition the exclusion of married women is obnoxious to the Sex Disqualification Removal Act 1919 which provides that a person shall not be disqualified by sex or marriage from being appointed to, or holding, any civil office. This today will certainly include guardianship, for which sex or marriage is therefore no longer a disqualification.

Other disabilities

7.08   There is old authority that aliens are incapable of being tutors.[22] Fraser[23] gives as the reasons for this disability that it attaches to the alien on account of his connection with a foreign country and his incapacity to hold heritable property within the United Kingdom. The former reason seems insubstantial and the latter no longer corresponds with the law[24]: the prohibition may therefore be taken to be obsolete. Residence in a foreign country is no objection.[25] It has been held that a partnership may not be appointed tutors,[26] and the same reasoning would apply to corporations.[27] It is now expressly provided that any reference in Part I of the Children (Scotland) Act 1995 to a person being appointed a guardian is to a natural person only,[28] and since guardians can be appointed only under the provisions in that Part, there is no room for appointment of corporations or other non-natural persons by other means. This provision did not effect any change in the law. Under the law of Justinian, although not of the older Roman law, creditors and debtors of the child were incapable of holding the office of guardian,[29] but Erskine says that that is not the law of Scotland.[30] Disabilities on the ground of religious profession should be regarded as obsolete.[31]

Effect of disqualification

7.09   If persons disqualified from the office of guardian are nominated in a parent's or guardian's testamentary deed their purported appointment is null and the deed will be read under deletion of their names so that the nomination of other

---

[20] Erskine I, vii, 12.

[21] Married Women's Property (Scotland) Act 1920, s. 2; Law Reform (Husband and Wife) (Scotland) Act 1984, s. 3.

[22] *Donaldson v. Brown* (1627) Mor. 4647; *Miller v. Allen* (1792) Mor. 4651. The objection is not merely on the ground of residence outwith the jurisdiction, because someone resident in England may be appointed (*Sim v. Robertson* (1901) 3 F.1027, but *cf. Fergusson v. Dormer* (1870) 8 M. 426; *Fenwick v. Hannah's Trs* (1893) 20 R. 848; *Napier, Petr* (1902) 9 S.L.T. 375 at 439).

[23] (3rd ed.), 236.

[24] This disability was abolished by the Naturalisation Act 1870, s. 2.

[25] *Sim v. Robertson*, above: *Fenwick v. Hannah's Trs*, above; *Rob v. Rob*, Dec. 22, 1814 F.C. 117; *Bell v. Henderson* (1784) Mor. 16374; More's *Notes on Stair*, p. xxxv. Appointment may, however, be refused or annulled where residence outwith the jurisdiction makes the appointment inexpedient (More, *ibid.*).

[26] Fraser, p. 236. The only authority Fraser gives is *De Mazar v. Pybus* (1799) 4 Ves. Jun. 644 and there is no Scottish authority in point, but the exclusion of partnerships seems consistent with the personal character of guardianship. The matter is put beyond doubt by s. 15(4) of the Children (Scotland) Act 1995.

[27] *cf.* the court's dislike of appointing corporate trustees to private trusts which involve the exercise of discretion in personal matters: *Ommanney, Petr*, 1966 S.L.T. (Notes) 13. It is otherwise in England: see Norrie and Scobbie, *Trusts*, pp. 62–63.

[28] Children (Scotland) Act 1995, s. 15(4).

[29] Nov. 94, cl.

[30] I, vii, 12.

[31] Stair does not treat of the matter and the only religious disability of which Erskine takes notice is the statutory disability attaching to professed or suspected papists and abolished by the Roman Catholic Relief Act 1829. More, *Notes on Stair*, D 24, points out that apart from a doubt expressed in *Burnet v. Burnet* (1670) 2 Mor. Supp. 462 there is no authority for Bankton's doctrine excluding pagans and persons of reprobated religions.

persons properly qualified can take effect.[32] It had previously been suggested that the only exception to that was where a minor had been nominated, in which event his appointment was merely suspended until majority.[33] If the proposition above relating to age is correct, then this exception is qualified so that appointments of those under 16 are suspended until that age is reached.

Testamentary appointment by parent or guardian

A child's parent may appoint a person (who is not subject to the disqualif- **7.10** ications discussed above) to be guardian of the child in the event of his or her death.[34] There is no requirement that the appointment be made having regard to the child's welfare as the paramount consideration, though if it is in the child's interests to have the appointee removed then this can be done by an application under section 11 of the Children (Scotland) Act 1995.[35] The decision is, however, a "major decision which involves exercising a parental right",[36] with the result that in making the appointment the parent is obliged by section 6 of the 1995 Act to have regard so far as practicable to the views (if he or she wishes to express them) of the child concerned, taking account of his or her age and maturity, and also to the views of any other person who has parental responsibilities or parental rights in relation to the child.[37] A failure in this obligation to consult is, however, unlikely in itself to render the appointment invalid, for the child's consent to the appointment of a guardian is not a condition precedent in the way that the consent of a child of 12 or over is to adoption.

In order to be effective, the appointment must be in writing and be signed **7.11** by the parent,[38] and the parent at the time of his or her death must have been entitled to act as the child's legal representative, or would have been so entitled if he or she had survived until after the birth of the child.[39] So, for example, a father who does not have parental responsibilities or parental rights over the child at the time of his death (*e.g.* because he has never had them or because he has been deprived of them by due process, such as adoption of the child or the making of a parental responsibilites order transferring parental rights and responsibilities to a local authority) cannot appoint a guardian. It would seem that a parent with only limited parental responsibilities and parental rights can make the appointment, so long as they have the responsibility and right of legal representation: the appointment is not, however, limited to the responsibilities and rights that the appointer had. In addition to the parent, and in a change to the pre-1995 law, a guardian of the child may appoint a person to take his or her place as guardian in the event of his or her death, so long as the appointment is in writing and signed by the person making it.[40] The guardian too is obliged to take account of the views of the child and of any other person with parental responsibilities or parental rights in making the appointment. There is no express requirement that the guardian making a testamentary appointment be entitled to act as the child's legal representative, but this is implicit in the office of

---

[32] Erskine I, vii, 3; *Baird* (1711) Mor. 7431. And see s. 7(4) of the Children (Scotland) Act 1995.

[33] More, *Notes on Stair*, DD4; Fraser, p. 235.

[34] Children (Scotland) Act 1995, s. 7(1).

[35] See below, paras 9.17–9.18.

[36] Children (Scotland) Act 1995, s. 7(6).

[37] *ibid.* s. 6(1). A child 12 years of age or more is presumed to be of sufficient age and maturity to form a view for these purposes.

[38] *ibid.* s. 7(1)(a)(i). At common law tutors-nominate could be appointed by any writing, formal or informal, that sufficiently indicated the parent's wishes. This remains the case under the statute and the only requirement is that the deed be signed by the parent.

[39] *ibid.* s. 7(1)(a)(ii).

[40] *ibid.* s. 7(2).

guardian.[41] Whether it is a parent or a guardian who makes the appointment it does not take effect until accepted by the appointee, either expressly or impliedly by acts which are not consistent with any other intention.[42] Nor, being testamentary, can the appointment take effect before the death of the person making the appointment. The appointment can come into effect posthumously, so that it remains effective even if the parent or guardian making the appointment dies before the child in respect of whom it is made is born.[43]

Effect of appointment

7.12   Unless qualified by court order a person appointed as a child's guardian by a parent's or guardian's testamentary deed has, in respect of the child, the responsibilities imposed on a parent by section 1 and the rights conferred on a parent by section 2 of the Children (Scotland) Act 1995, these sections applying to guardians as they do to parents.[44] It would seem that, court order being the only specified means of qualifying the effect of sections 1 and 2, the deed of appointment itself cannot limit the responsibilities and rights conferred.[45] This is qualified in the case of joint appointments, considered below.

7.13   The appointment is not (unless its terms so provide) postponed, as it is in England,[46] until the other parent dies or loses parental responsibilities. Before the coming into force of the Law Reform (Parent and Child) (Scotland) Act 1986, which was in similar terms to the Children (Scotland) Act 1995 on this issue, there had been detailed provision to deal with the situation of the appointed guardian acting along with a surviving parent who remained tutor or curator of the child.[47] These provisions were repealed in 1986 and replaced with the simpler rule, now contained in section 2(2) of the Children (Scotland) Act 1995, that where two or more persons have a parental right as respects a child, each of them may exercise that right without the consent of the other or, as the case may be, of any of the others, unless any decree or deed conferring the right, or regulating its exercise, otherwise provides. Because parental rights exist in order to enable the holder of the right to fulfil his or her parental responsibilities in relation to the child[48] the principle in section 2(2) applies to the fulfilling of responsibilities as well as to the exercise of rights; and in any event it is in the nature of parental responsibilities that they inhere in individuals independently of their inherence in anyone else. In addition, it is now expressly provided[49] that any parental responsibilities or parental rights (or the right to appoint further guardians) which a surviving parent has in relation to the child shall subsist with those which, by, under or by virtue of Part I of the 1995 Act, the appointee so has.

---

[41] It is, however, possible for the court to remove the right of legal representation from a guardian, or to appoint a guardian under reservation of that right and responsibility. In such circumstances there would seem to be nothing to prevent such a guardian from appointing another guardian, though that has the anomalous result that the guardian's powers of appointment are less qualified than those of a parent.

[42] Children (Scotland) Act 1995, s. 7(3). See further, below, paras 7.24–7.26.

[43] *Murray v. Merschall* (1555) Mor.16226. But the pregnancy must have commenced before the appointer dies, otherwise he will not be the father of the child (Human Fertilisation and Embryology Act 1990, s. 28(6)(b)).

[44] Children (Scotland) Act 1995, s. 7(5).

[45] Though the terms of s. 8(5) suggest that the duration of the appointment can be so limited: see below, para. 7.33.

[46] Children Act 1989, s. 5(8).

[47] Guardianship of Infants Act 1925, ss. 4 and 5. Under these provisions parents could act independently of each other, but where there was a guardian appointed and a surviving parent, and where there were more than one guardian appointed, they had to act jointly.

[48] Children (Scotland) Act 1995, s. 2(1).

[49] *ibid.* s. 7(1)(b).

Delegation of appointment

Because the nomination of guardians belongs personally to parents and **7.14** guardians, it is not delegable nor, on the death or incapacity of the parent or guardian, can it be exercised by anyone in their place. So where a testator conferred on the trustees, under his testamentary settlement, power to assume new trustees and appointed the trustees "named or to be named or assumed" tutors of his pupil children, the appointment of assumed trustees as tutors was held to be invalid.[50] The matter is put beyond doubt by section 5(2) of the Age of Legal Capacity (Scotland) Act 1991 which, as amended, provides that a guardian may be appointed only in terms of section 7 of the 1995 Act.

Nomination of plurality of guardians

There is no limitation on the number of guardians who may be appointed by **7.15** a parent or guardian to act in his or her place on his or her death and section 7(4), indeed, presupposes that it is competent to appoint "two or more persons" to act as such. If this occurs then, unless the appointment expressly provides otherwise, any one or more of those nominated is entitled to accept office even if one or more of the other nominees do not.[51] This was the position at common law.[52] The reason is the respect accorded to the will of the parent (and now guardian) and his or her *delectus personae*.[53]

> "The ultimate decision and choice by the father is to be preferred in all cases where any portion of it remains, and where even one part of it remains, though the other part is taken away. Though you may say, *non constat*, that he should have appointed one, if the other had not been added, yet it was for him to state the difference—it was for him to state the jointure—it was for him to say *sine quo non* or *sine quibis non*; and as he has not said so, the Court will assume that he preferred even one of those, if all could not be had, to any other person whom the law might appoint, or whom the Court might appoint."[54]

So express words are required for a joint appointment under which each guardian is *sine quo non*. Where such words are used, the result is that if one of the nominees fails the whole appointment falls.[55] The general rule is that that will be so whether the failure is due to death after acceptance or to non-acceptance. There is, however, authority for the view that if one of the nominees predeceases the parent making the joint nomination, the appointment nonetheless subsists in the others.[56] The general rule may, of course, be modified by the terms of the particular appointment. The words "whom failing" will, if unqualified, be construed as referring to failure on any ground; and where one group is nominated whom failing another, the substitution will not be effected until all those in the first group have failed.

Where a number of guardians are appointed each may act, as already pointed **7.16** out, without the consent of the others unless the decree or deed appointing them directs otherwise.[57] The deed may require that guardians, or guardians and remaining parent, act jointly in the sense of all agreeing before undertaking any particular act. If the deed provides for a quorum, any act of the guardians requires

---

[50] *Walker v. Stronach* (1874) 2 R.120.

[51] s. 7(4).

[52] Stair, I, vi, 14; Bankton I, vii, 20.

[53] *Scot v. Stewart* (1834) 7 W. & S. 211, *per* Lord Brougham at 236–237.

[54] *ibid.* at p. 241.

[55] Erskine I, vii, 30; *Drummond v. Feuars of Bothkennel* (1671) Mor. 14694.

[56] *Scott v. Scott* (1775) Mor. 16371.

[57] Children (Scotland) Act 1995, s. 2(2).

the consent of a number sufficient to satisfy the quorum and is valid only if that consent is obtained. Similarly, one or more of a number of guardians may be appointed *sine quibis non* with the result that his, her or their consent is essential to any act of administration. In the event of a failure of a quorum, or of a guardian *sine quo non*, through death, non-acceptance or resignation, the whole appointment falls.[58] That result has been doubted in the case of the failure of a quorum[59] but its logic seems clear and is authoritatively affirmed in *Drumore v. Somervil*.[60] Equally, the whole appointment falls if all the guardians, except those appointed *sine quibis non*, fail, because an appointment *sine quo non* implies the existence of other guardians with less powers.[61] Again, where there has been a joint appointment of guardians, the whole appointment falls on the failure of one:

> "The reason in all these cases is the same, that the father seems to have put no trust in the rest without the quorum or without the *sine quo non*, or in any one or more of tutors named jointly without the whole".[62]

The appointment does not, of course, fall if express provision to the contrary has been made, as by a declaration that the guardian should subsist after the failure of a guardian *sine quo non*, or of a quorum or of a joint guardian.[63] The ultimate test is the parent's or guardian's intention as disclosed in the deed. In the case of joint guardians in the strict sense unanimity is essential for any administrative act, but, if they are unable to agree on any question affecting the welfare of the child, any of them may apply to the court for an order in relation to guardianship and the court may make such order as it thinks fit taking account of the welfare of the child as its paramount consideration and of the views of the child.[64]

7.17   These rules, developed at common law in relation to tutors, can be applied without difficulty to the representational aspect of modern guardianship, but it is only with some awkwardness that they can be applied to the other aspects of parental responsibilities and parental rights which are now inherent in guardianship. Often a decision has to be made in relation to the upbringing of the child where maintaining the status quo is not an option (such as deciding how a child who has reached five years of age is to be educated). Applications to the court, though always competent, are likely to prove impractical in terms of time and costs in many cases, and it is submitted that terms in a deed appointing guardians which require each to consent to any act of guardianship are to be interpreted as limited to the representational duties of guardianship and that they may safely be ignored, at least in the absence of challenge, where the proper upbringing of the child might otherwise be jeopardised.

Revocation of appointment

7.18   Being of a testamentary nature, the appointment is ambulatory and can be revoked in the same way as a will can before the parent's death.[65] Any revocation

---

[58] Erskine, I, vii, 29; *Montrose v. Tutors* (1688) Mor. 14697.

[59] More's *Notes on Stair*, D. 5 and cases cited therein.

[60] (1742) Mor. 14703.

[61] *Primrose v. Roseberry* (1715) Mor. 16335; *Blair v. Ramsay* (1735) Mor. 14702; 5 Mor. Supp. 633. The reasoning seems to be open to question. The issue is not whether the existence of others is implied but whether their acceptance of and continuance in office is (by implication) essential.

[62] *Drumore v. Somervil*, above.

[63] *Drumore v. Somervil*, above; *Scott v. Scott* (1775) Mor. 16371; *Aikenheads v. Durham* (1703) Mor. 14701.

[64] Children (Scotland) Act 1995, s. 11.

[65] Stair, I, vi, 6; Erskine, I, vii, 2.

will not take effect unless it is in writing and is signed by the person making the revocation.[66] An appointment made in a will or codicil is revoked if the will or codicil itself is revoked.[67] An appointment (other than one made in a will or codicil) is revoked if, with the intention of revoking the appointment, the person who made it either (i) destroys the document by which it was made or (ii) has some other person destroy that document in his or her presence.[68] It is unclear whether these are the only methods of revocation or whether, for example, later writing can achieve revocation of an earlier deed. It is suggested that other methods which unequivocally indicate an intention to revoke will be sufficient. An appointment of a guardian made under section 7(1) or (2) revokes any earlier appointment made by the same person in respect of the same child (including one made in an unrevoked will or codicil), unless it is clear (whether as a result of an express provision in the later appointment or by any necessary implication) that the purpose of the later appointment is to appoint an additional guardian.[69]

Appointment of guardian by the court

Development of the law

    The Court of Session in the exercise of the *nobile officium* had at common **7.19** law the power to appoint tutors-dative to pupil children.[70] This power was enlarged in some respects by various statutes. Under the Guardianship of Infants Act 1925[71] if one parent of a pupil child died, survived by the other parent, without nominating tutors, or if the tutors nominated by the deceased parent were dead or refused to act, the court could, if it thought fit, appoint a tutor to act jointly with the surviving parent. Under the same Act as later amended,[72] where a pupil child had no parent, no guardian of the person and no other person having parental rights with respect to him or her, the court, on the application of any person, could, if it thought fit, appoint the applicant to be the child's tutor. That provision added nothing to the substantive law as it stood before it was passed, except that, where a tutor-legitim had not served, it could enable a tutor-dative to be appointed in preference to a tutor-legitim and without the necessity of waiting for the expiry of a year and a day from the death of the latter of the two parents to die. Jurisdiction was, however, enlarged in that under the Guardianship of Infants Act 1925 an appointment could be made in the sheriff court. Under the Agricultural Holdings (Scotland) Act 1949[73] where a landlord or tenant was a pupil or a minor who did not have a tutor, curator or other guardian, the sheriff, on the application of any person interested, could appoint to him or her a tutor or curator for the purposes of the Act and could recall the appointment and appoint another as the occasion required. Under the Merchant Shipping Act 1894[74] where, by reason of nonage, any person interested in any ship or any share therein is incapable of making any declaration or doing anything required or permitted by the Act to be made or done in connection with the registry of the ship or share, any court having jurisdiction in respect of the property of incapable persons may appoint a person to make such declaration and do

---

[66] Children (Scotland) Act 1995, s. 8(2).
[67] *ibid.* s. 8(4).
[68] *ibid.* s. 8(3).
[69] *ibid.* s. 8(1).
[70] See the 1st edition of this book at p. 40.
[71] s. 4(1) and (2) (repealed by the Law Reform (Parent and Child) (Scotland) Act 1986, Sched. 2).
[72] s. 4(2A), added by the Children Act 1948, s. 50 (repealed as above).
[73] s. 84 (repealed in so far as it related to children by the Age of Legal Capacity (Scotland) Act 1991, Sched. 2). See now the Agricultural Holdings (Scotland) Act 1991, s. 77.
[74] s. 55(1), as amended by the Age of Legal Capacity (Scotland) Act 1991, Sched. 1, para. 24.

such act or thing in the name and on behalf of the incapable person. This last is limited to the performing on behalf of the child of a specific act and though it does contemplate a representational power it does not amount to the appointing of a guardian for the child. In 1986 the court was given the power to make such order relating to parental rights as it thought fit,[75] though it was not to make any order unless satisfied that to do so would be in the interests of the child.[76] This power was originally in addition to any other power that the court might have, but in 1991 it was provided[77] that the only means by which the court can appoint a guardian was under section 3 of the 1986 Act (now section 11 of the Children (Scotland) Act 1995).[78] There is therefore no longer any room for the Court of Session to appoint guardians in the exercise of its *nobile officium*.

Appointment under section 11

7.20   The court may appoint a person[79] as guardian of a child under section 11(2)(h) before the child reaches the age of 18 years, though from the age of 16 the only role of the guardian will be to provide the child with guidance under section 1(1)(b)(ii) of the 1995 Act. The "court" means the Court of Session or the sheriff.[80] The court's decision to appoint a guardian must be made regarding the welfare of the child as its paramount consideration[81] and it must not make the appointment unless it considers that it would be better to do so than that no order should be made at all.[82] The court must also, taking account of the child's age and maturity, so far as practicable, (i) give the child an opportunity to indicate whether he or she wishes to express his or her views, (ii) if he or she does so wish, give him or her an opportunity to express them and (iii) have regard to such views as the child may express.[83] On the same basis, the court may remove a person as guardian of the child.[84]

7.21   Title to seek an appointment of a guardian follows the normal rules for title to make an application for a section 11 order.[85] Questions of title coalesce to a large extent with questions relating to the merits of the case, and it is likely that the courts will be slow in placing artificial limitations on who can make an application. Anyone who can make out a prima facie case that the guardianship arrangements he or she proposes will be for the child's welfare will, it is submitted, possess title to seek an order under section 11. In response to the application the court may make "such order... as it thinks fit". Indeed the court may appoint a guardian, or make any other section 11 order, even when not asked to do so but when it considers that it should make such an order.[86] So the court may appoint the applicant, or some other person, to be guardian. For example, in an action raised by the child's maternal grandparents to be appointed guardians (say, after the death of the unmarried mother) the court may appoint the child's father who does not otherwise have parental responsibilities and

---

[75] Law Reform (Parent and Child) (Scotland) Act 1986, s. 3(1).
[76] *ibid.* s. 3(2).
[77] Age of Legal Capacity (Scotland) Act 1991, s. 5(2) (as originally enacted).
[78] Children (Scotland) Act 1995, Sched. 4, para. 53(5), amending s. 5(2) of the 1991 Act.
[79] That is to say, a natural person: Children (Scotland) Act 1995, s. 15(4).
[80] Jurisdiction depends upon the habitual residence of the child within Scotland on the date of the application (for the Court of Session) or within the sheriffdom (for the sheriff court): Family Law Act 1986, s. 16(1). It is arguable, however, that this special rule applies only to the representational role of the guardian: see below, para. 9.24.
[81] *cf.* testamentary appointments under s. 7 when welfare considerations do not have to be taken into account.
[82] Children (Scotland) Act 1995, s. 11(7)(a). See further, Chap. 9.
[83] *ibid.* s. 11(7)(b).
[84] *ibid.* s. 11(2)(h) and (13).
[85] See below, paras 9.51–9.58.
[86] Children (Scotland) Act 1995, s. 11(3)(b).

parental rights, if this is held to be in the child's best interests (perhaps because this is the person with whom the child is living). Nor is there any limitation on the number of guardians appointed, nor on whether they take office only on the death of the remaining parent. The court may make such order as it thinks fit, and it is therefore competent for the court to appoint any number of guardians, consistent with the child's welfare and, if that welfare so demands, these guardians can take office even when there remains a parent with parental responsibilities and parental rights. Any one guardian (or parent with responsibilities and rights if such remains) may exercise parental rights in fulfilling parental responsibilities without the consent of the other,[87] and for that reason, together with general administrative convenience, it will seldom be in the child's interests for provision to be made for more than two guardians to be in office at any one time. The court may make the appointment joint, in which case the considerations discussed above in relation to joint appointments by parents or guardians will be relevant, but in the absence of express provision in the court order, the appointment will not be joint, either in a question with other appointees or with a remaining parent who has parental responsibilities and parental rights.

Effect of appointment

There is no provision in the 1995 Act setting out the responsibilities and **7.22** rights of a guardian appointed under section 11(2)(h), but a guardian appointed by a parent or guardian under section 7 has full parental responsibilities and parental rights[88] and there is no sound principle upon which it can be argued that a court appointee has, in the absence of express provision in the court order, any less. The court can, however, make any order it thinks fit and is able, therefore, to qualify the terms of the appointment in appropriate cases. If it is intended that the appointment carries only some parental responsibilities or parental rights, for example those of legal representation, then the better approach to appointing a guardian under section 11(2)(h) with limited powers would probably be to impose and confer such parental responsibilities and parental rights under section 11(2)(b) as are appropriate in the circumstances.

The father as guardian

A father who is married to the mother of the child or was married to her at the **7.23** time of the child's conception or subsequently has parental responsibilities and parental rights,[89] and therefore does not need to be appointed guardian of the child and, as parent, ought not to be. His authority to exercise parental responsibilities and parental rights comes from his paternity rather than from his holding any separate office,[90] and any necessary alteration in his responsibilities and rights ought to be achieved by an order under section 11(2)(b) rather than through the concept of guardianship. If he is not and never has been married to the mother of the child he will not be automatically entitled to parental responsibilities and parental rights and would have to apply to the court under section 11(2)(b) of the 1995 Act to obtain them. A father who does not have parental rights has no better claim (in law) to receive parental responsibilities and parental rights than a stranger to the child, for any applicant under section 11(2) must satisfy the court that it will be in the interests of the child that he be so appointed and paternity on its own will not enhance that claim.[91]

---

[87] Children (Scotland) Act 1995, s. 2(2).

[88] *ibid.* s. 7(5).

[89] *ibid.* s. 3(1)(b).

[90] See below, para. 15.31.

[91] *Porchetta v. Porchetta*, 1986 S.L.T. 105, approved in *Sanderson v. McManus*, 1997 S.L.T. 629, *per* Lord Hope of Craighead at 635A–B.

Entry into office

Acceptance

7.24   In Roman law, tutory was a *munus publicum* with the result that persons
appointed might be compelled to act unless they were in some exempt category.
Scots law, however, has not followed the Roman model in that respect. In the
case of testamentary appointments, there is a statutory rule that the appointment
shall not take effect until accepted, either expressly or impliedly by acts which
are not consistent with any other intention,[92] and while there is no statutory rule
to this effect in relation to court appointments, these will follow the common
law rule that acceptance of the office of guardian by the nominee or appointee
is, in every case, required before the duties of the office attach.[93] Problems of
whether or not there has been acceptance arise mainly in the case of guardians
nominated in testamentary deeds, because the court is unlikely—even, it may
be, unable—to appoint a person guardian unless it is satisfied that that person is
willing and able to take on the role of parent-substitute. Acceptance may be
inferred from actings that are not consistent with any intention other than
acceptance; because the consequences of acceptance may be onerous, it will
not be implied unless the actings are unequivocal.[94] A person nominated by a
parent or guardian to act as a guardian cannot, of course, be held to have accepted
by implication if he or she had no knowledge of the nomination. So if, in
ignorance of the appointment, he or she acts in a way suggestive of management
of the child's affairs, he or she will not be held, on that ground, to have impliedly
accepted office although he or she may, by these actings, incur certain liabilities
in respect of the acts themselves. Where the acts are weighty and such as would
ordinarily be undertaken only by an accepting guardian, the onus, however,
will be on the nominee to show his or her lack of knowledge.[95] But even after he
or she knows of the appointment, not every act relating to the child's affairs will
infer acceptance. There will be no such inference from anything which can be
fairly attributed to friendship or to a humane concern for the child's unprotected
condition.[96] Acceptance will, however, be inferred from actings which can only
be referable to guardianship management, such as giving up inventories *habile
modo*,[97] or taking the oath *de fideli administratione*,[98] or signing deeds, or taking
receipts in which he or she is designated as guardian, or authorising legal
proceedings at his or her instance *qua* legal representative.[99] Ordinarily, of course,
there should be no need to have resort to implication. Express acceptance is
affixed by any writing signed by the guardian which is to that effect or necessarily
bears that construction.[1] The usual form is by a minute or declaration endorsed
on the deed by which the guardian is nominated. Where a guardian, who is also
a trustee under the parent's testamentary settlement, has intromitted with the

---

[92] Children (Scotland) Act 1995, s. 7(3).

[93] Erskine, I, vii, 20; *Scrimgeour v. Kingheny* (1675) Mor. 6357. It is otherwise in England where,
    under s. 6(5) of the Children Act 1989 appointment is automatic unless it is expressly disclaimed
    in formal writing.

[94] Erskine, above. He says: "Acceptance, as it may draw severe consequences after it, is not to be
    inferred by implication", but it is clear from the discussion that follows that he means that only
    of persons who handle the child's affairs in ignorance that they have been nominated as tutors.

[95] *Beatson v. Beatson* (1678) Mor. 16298.

[96] Erskine, above; *Beatson*, above.

[97] *Watson v. Watson* (1714) Mor. 3244.

[98] *Kirktoun v. Hunthill* (1662) Mor. 16268; *Napier v. Wood* (1669) Mor. 16280.

[99] Erskine, above; Stair, I, vi, 6; *Seton v. Seton* (1668) Mor. 2185 and 12767; *Cunningham* (1684)
    Mor. 16305; *Murrays v. Murray* (1832) 10 S. 276.

[1] Erskine, above.

child's property, it is a question of circumstances whether acceptance of the office of guardian, as well as that of trustee or executor, will be inferred. In *Mollison v. Murray*[2] Lord Gillies said:

> "The same deed which named them trustees also named them tutors. They accepted and acted under that deed. They did not limit their acceptance to the one character of trustee, and express their repudiation of the other character of tutor. They acted generally under the deed, and this, in all the circumstances, I hold to infer their acceptance generally of the deed. I consider therefore that they cannot now repudiate the character of tutors."

Where, however, there is appointment as trustee or executor and guardian, acceptance of the former will not necessarily infer acceptance of the latter,[3] and effect will be given to a clause in the deed that acceptance of the office of trustee is not to imply acceptance of the office of guardian.[4]

Refusal, if not express, will be inferred only from very clear circumstances.[5] **7.25** Mere delay in acceptance does not have any effect on the guardian's right. Accordingly he or she may accept office and enter into the management of the child's affairs even if the acceptance has been delayed for a period of years.[6] As the freedom of the guardian to delay is obviously productive of abuse, an action may be raised by anyone having an interest, which will certainly include the child, to put the appointee to his or her election as between acceptance and refusal.

In the case of a guardian appointed by the court, the appointee's having **7.26** consented to his or her name being put forward will be sufficient evidence of acceptance as will, *a fortiori*, the appointee having expressly solicited the office by raising the action him or herself.[7] It is only where the appointee has not allowed his or her name to be put forward or has not him or herself been the applicant that it will be necessary to have recourse to express or implied acceptance much as in the case of a guardian appointed by a parent. As in that case, any act by a guardian subsequent to his or her appointment by the court that impinges on the management of the child's affairs may be taken to be referable to the appointment.

Caution and inventories

Tutors-dative were required to find caution and to make up inventories before **7.27** they were vested in their office and could lawfully intromit with the pupil's affairs. Neither the Children (Scotland) Act 1995 nor the Law Reform (Parent and Child) (Scotland) Act 1986 before it lays this down as a requirement to the appointment of a guardian either by a parent or by the court, but since the court may make any order it thinks fit, it remains competent for the court to require that its appointee finds caution. It is likely to do so only when the major purpose of the guardianship is to provide protection to the child's estate rather than to provide for the child's upbringing, and even then only when the estate is extensive. If the court order does require the guardian to find caution, then the principles evolved at common law remain applicable.[8]

---

[2] (1833) 12 S. 237 at 240.
[3] *Paterson v. Moncrieff* (1866) 4 M. 706; *Hill v. City of Glasgow Bank* (1879) 7 R. 68, *per* Lord President Inglis at 76.
[4] *Hunter v. Matthew* (1844) 16 Sc.Jur. 337.
[5] *Ramsay v. Dalhousie* (1699) Mor. 16313.
[6] *Auchterlony v. Oliphant* (1631) Mor. 16258; Erskine, I, vii, 3.
[7] Erskine I, vii, 20.
[8] For details, see the 1st edition of this book, at pp. 392–394.

TERMINATION OF GUARDIANSHIP

7.28 Termination of guardianship may be brought about in a number of different ways, to be discussed in the following paragraphs. However it occurs, a guardian's powers cease immediately on the termination of office.[9] Equally, his or her duties come to an end and he or she is not bound to attend to the management of any matter which is incomplete at that time.[10]

The child's attaining the age of 18

7.29 The natural termination of a guardian's office occurs when the child reaches the age of 18 years.[11] This age is absolutely fixed and termination of guardianship cannot be postponed beyond that age even by the direction of a parent purporting to give to guardians powers of guardianship for an extended period.[12] It should be noted, however, that while the office of guardianship remains until the child is 18, all parental responsibilities and parental rights except the responsibility to give guidance terminate on the child's 16th birthday.[13]

Death of child or guardian

7.30 The office of guardian terminates on the death of the child or the guardian.[14] The death of the child brings an end to all parental responsibilities and parental rights in relation to that child and there are no ongoing consequences of guardianship, such as succession rights. On the death of a guardian, the office did not, even under the older law, pass to his heir; and it does not do so today. The proper course in modern practice is for a new guardian to be appointed by the court under section 11(2)(h) of the 1995 Act, though that will not always be necessary if there remains a guardian in office or a parent with parental responsibilities and parental rights, or if the deceased guardian has appointed another guardian in terms of section 7(2).

Removal of guardians by court

7.31 Superintendence of guardians belonged at common law to the Court of Session as *parens patriae* in the exercise of its *nobile officium*. By virtue of these powers of superintendence a jurisdiction to remove guardians, where that was necessary for the protection of the child's estate, has been in use from early times (at any rate in relation to tutors of pupil children). By an Act of 1555,[15] jurisdiction to remove was extended to any judge ordinary and in the seventeenth century it was held that tutors-dative might be removed by the Court of Exchequer[16] on whose authority the Crown gift of tutory proceeded to them and so might be recalled. Long before the abolition of the Court of Exchequer as a separate court, it had, however, come to be accepted that jurisdiction to remove tutors pertained exclusively to the Court of Session.[17] The grounds for removal

---

[9] *Lockhart v. McKenzie's Trs* (1826) 5 S. 136, affd (1829) 3 W. & S. 481. See also *Bruce v. Sinclair* (1610) Mor. 16239; *Foster v. Foster* (1610) Mor. 16238 and *Forbesses v. Forbes* (1683) Mor. 16287.

[10] *Cass v. Ellis* (1672) Mor. 16285. See also *A v. B* (1533) Mor. 16218; Balfour, *Practicks*, p. 121, No. 135.

[11] Children (Scotland) Act 1995, s. 8(5)(a).

[12] *Graham v. Graham* (1780) Mor. 8934, *per* Lord Braxfield (referring to the attainment of the age of puberty bringing tutory to an end).

[13] Children (Scotland) Act 1995, ss. 1(2) and 2(7).

[14] *ibid.* s. 8(5)(b).

[15] c. 8. (APS II, 493).

[16] *Mersington v. Fletcher* (1694) 4 Mor. Supp. 272.

[17] Erskine, I, vii, 29.

were always wide, embracing neglect as well as positive acts of maladministration or fraud, but the court sometimes showed a reluctance to go as far as
removal and instead appointed a curator to act along with the tutor and control
his administration.[18] A number of other statutes had been superimposed on the
common law without greatly modifying or adding to it. By the Judicial Factors
Act 1849[19] the court was empowered, on cause shown, to remove any guardian
and to appoint a curator *bonis* in his room. By the Trusts (Scotland) Act 1921 a
guardian, being within the definition of "trustee" for the purpose of this and the
other Trusts Act, could be removed if he was or became insane or incapable of
acting, by reason of physical or mental disability, or was absent from the United
Kingdom, or had disappeared, for at least six months.[20] Both these statutes limited
the power to remove to the Court of Session, but under the Law Reform (Parent
and Child) Scotland Act 1986, power to remove was extended to the sheriff
court also.[21] Today, section 11(2)(h) of the Children (Scotland) Act 1995, which
allows the court[22] to make an order removing as well as appointing a person to
be a child's guardian, is the only authority for the removal of guardians by the
court[23]; procedure follows the normal rules for any application for a section 11
order.[24]

Section 11(7) applies to the removal of guardians as it does to any proceedings **7.32**
under section 11 and, as a result, the welfare of the child is the paramount
consideration by which the merits of removal must be decided and the court is
prohibited from making an order removing a person as guardian unless it
considers that it would be better for the child that the order be made than that
none should be made at all.[25] In addition, appropriate account must be taken of
the views of the child.[26] Clearly it will seldom, if ever, be better for a child to
have a guardian removed than not when there is no other person with parental
responsibilities and parental rights and the court must therefore ensure before
removing a guardian that proper provision is in place for the child's continued
care and upbringing. Subject to section 11(7) of the 1995 Act, the common law
grounds for removal of a guardian are still of relevance. The general principle
is that a guardian is suspect if by act or omission he or she has given rise to
injury or reasonable apprehension of the risk of injury to the child's health,
development or welfare. Evil intention is not required. The maxim applies *non
solum dolus vel lata negligentia suspectum reddit tutorem, verum etiam levior
culpa.*[27] Even that maxim is, however, too narrow. Although usually there will
be fault, *culpa* is not always necessary. Failure to fulfil the parental
responsibilities inherent in the office, or evident ground for fearing that they
will not be fulfilled in the future, is the test and it matters not whether the cause
is evil intent, negligence or some entirely innocent circumstance such as disability
or incapacity. Particular instances include delay in defending the child's

---

[18] Erskine, I, vii, 29; *McBrae v. McLaine* (1667) Mor. 16278; *McBrair v. McBrair* (1667) Mor. 16279; *A v. B*, (1534) Mor. 16219.
[19] s. 31 (as amended by the Age of Legal Capacity (Scotland) Act 1991, Sched. l, para. 11 and Sched. 2). The inclusion of "guardian" within the terms of this provision was removed by the 1995 Act, Sched. 4, para. 2(6) and Sched. 5.
[20] Trusts (Scotland) Act 1921, s. 23. The Children (Scotland) Act 1995, Sched. 4 para. 6 amended the definition of "trustee" in s. 2 of the 1921 Act, so that guardians are no longer included.
[21] Law Reform (Parent and Child) (Scotland) Act 1986, s. 8.
[22] *i.e.* the sheriff court or the Court of Session: s. 11(1).
[23] Children (Scotland) Act 1995, s. 8(5)(c).
[24] See below, paras 9.38 *et seq.*
[25] Children (Scotland) Act 1995, s. 11(7)(a).
[26] *ibid.* s. 11(7)(b).
[27] Inst. I, 22, 6; D. xxvi 10, 3, 5; Code v, 43, 9.

rights,[28] wilful omission to state a valid defence, abandonment of the administration, refusal of necessaries for the child's aliment and education where there are sufficient funds in hand to provide them, embezzlement of the child's funds, failure to institute necessary actions, insolvency of the guardian or of his cautioner,[29] wastage or neglect of the child's means,[30] violation of an order made by the court, clandestine or unwarrantable removal of the child from the jurisdiction,[31] and employment of the child's means for the guardian's own trade or business.[32]

Terms of the appointment

7.33   The satisfaction of a condition on which the guardian's appointment is dependent also brings the office to an end. The mere satisfaction of the condition is enough to have that effect by operation of law without the necessity of declarator or other legal proceedings.[33] Examples of this occur when a parent or guardian, in appointing a guardian under section 7 of the 1995 Act, has provided that the office should last for a fixed period or until the occurrence of a certain event. Also in this class are appointments of guardians subject to a quorum, of guardians *sine quibus non* and of joint guardians.[34] The power to specify a limited period of appointment in a testamentary provision is not constrained by welfare considerations and the only means by which an appointee can continue as guardian after the testamentary appointment ends is by court order under section 11. The court too, in appointing a guardian under section 11(2)(h), can make the appointment on any terms and conditions as it thinks fit, including specifying when the appointment will come to an end, short of the child's attaining 18 or of the death of either the child or guardian. Such a condition in a court appointment must, of course, satisfy the welfare test and for that reason it will be rare for the court to limit the length of the appointment to a period less than its natural duration. This might, however, be appropriate if the need for a parent-substitute will predictably persist only for a limited period of time (such as temporary illness, incarceration or absence abroad of the parent).

Resignation

7.34   Under the older law, the tutor of a pupil child might resign if he had accepted office but had not entered on the management of the estate. But any intromission with the estate deprived him of that liberty and he could, thereafter, resign only with leave of the court.[35] Nor did the liberty to resign apply to a guardian who had accepted any legacy or bequest or annuity expressly given on condition that he accept the office of guardian, nor to any guardian appointed on the footing of receiving a remuneration for his services. By the Trusts (Scotland) Act 1921,[36] under which guardians were, for the purposes of that Act, assimilated to trustees, power was given to any trustee to resign office unless the contrary

---

[28] See generally D. xxvi, 10, 3 (5, 12, 14, 15, and 17); 10, 7(1); Erskine, I, vii, 29; *Mersington v. Fletcher* (1694) 4 Mor. Supp. 272.

[29] *McLaurin, Petr* (1831) 3 Sc.Jur. 550; *Mersington v. Fletcher*, above.

[30] *Heriot v. Livverton* (1564) Mor. 16229.

[31] *Stuart v. Moore* (1860) 22 D. 1504; *Reoch v. Robb*, Nov. 14, 1817, F.C. 388; *Gordonston's Trs v. Gordon* (1708) 4 Mor. Supp. 725. *Cf.*, however, *Edgar v. Fisher's Trs.* (1893) 21 R. 325. See also *Harris, Petr* (1893) 1 S.L.T. 254 at 257.

[32] *Dewar* (1853) 16 D. 163 and 489.

[33] *Et sic quidem etiam ipso jure sine facto hominis finitur tutela*: Inst, I, xxii, 2 and 5; D. xxvi, 1, 14 (3 and 5).

[34] See above, paras 7.15–7.17.

[35] Fraser (3rd ed.), pp. 408–410 and authorities cited therein.

[36] s. 2.

had been expressed in the deed or decree from which his powers were derived.[37] The definition of "trustee", however, no longer includes any person who, within the meaning of Part I of the Children (Scotland) Act 1995, is entitled to act as the legal representative of the child.[38] Guardians in the sense of parent-substitutes are so entitled and are not, therefore, "trustees" for the purposes of the Trusts Acts, and so can no longer trace a right to resign to these Acts. It would seem, however, that it is open to a parent or guardian appointing a guardian by testamentary deed expressly to provide for the freedom to resign and, if so, the guardian is not inhibited from doing so by considerations of the welfare of the child. The court might similarly grant the freedom to resign in its appointment under section 11(2)(h), but in that case could do so only when it would be in the interests of the child for such a provision to be included in the terms of the appointment. The court might, of course, remove a guardian from office on his or her own application.

---

[37] s. 3(a). See also the Judicial Factors Act 1849, s. 31, under which the court had a general power to accept the resignation of any guardian coming under the provisions of the Act, but only "on cause shown". "Guardians" are no longer within the terms of the 1849 Act: Children (Scotland) Act 1995, Sched. 4, para. 2(6).

[38] Children (Scotland) Act 1995, Sched. 4, para. 6, amending s. 2 of the Trusts (Scotland) Act 1921.

PART III

PRIVATE LAW CONSEQUENCES OF THE RELATIONSHIP

PARENTAL RESPONSIBILITIES AND
PARENTAL RIGHTS

INTRODUCTORY

Scope of this chapter

8.01   Parental responsibilities and parental rights concern the obligations that parents and those who stand in the place of parents have towards their children and the powers they possess in order to fulfil these obligations. This chapter will examine the concepts of parental responsibilities and parental rights, together with the questions of who may exercise these responsibilities and rights, how they are conferred and how they are terminated; it will then look in some detail at the particular parental responsibilities and parental rights listed in the Children (Scotland) Act 1995, and some of those which, while not expressly mentioned, are nevertheless implicit in the terms of that Act. Some consequences of the parent–child relationship, which may rationally, though misleadingly, be described as parental rights, such as the right to succeed on death, fall quite outwith the scope of this work; other statutory responsibilities, such as the duty to aliment the child and the duty to attend a children's hearing, are dealt with in their appropriate places. Court orders in relation to parental responsibilities and parental rights are examined in the immediately following chapter, and this chapter is limited to a consideration of such responsibilities and rights in the absence of court order.

Judicial character of parental responsibilities and parental rights

8.02   The modern law on parental responsibilities and parental rights is contained in Part I of the Children (Scotland) Act 1995, one of the major purposes of which was to put the whole of the law in this area on to a statutory basis. So section 1 lists the parental responsibilities that parents owe to their children, and section 2 lists the parental rights that parents have in relation to their children; it is provided that these responsibilities and rights supersede any analogous duties imposed on, and analogous rights enjoyed by, a parent at common law (this without prejudice to any other responsibility or right imposed or enjoyed by or under any other statutory provision).[1] Notwithstanding the importance of the 1995 Act in reformulating these responsibilities and rights, their judicial character is little different under the statute from what it was at common law. For Stair, the primary consequence of the parent and child relationship was one of obligation.

> "That there are natural obligations betwixt parents and children, not proceeding from the consent of either party, or from the constitution of any human law, but from the obedience man oweth to his Maker, who hath written this law in the hearts of parents and children, as to their interests and duties, with capital letters, is evident by the common consent of all the nations of the world, how barbarous soever."[2]

---

[1] Children (Scotland) Act 1995, ss. 1(4) and 2(5).
[2] Stair, I, v, 1.

These obligations were "placed in the common nature that man hath with other animals, and so are given as an evident instance of the law of nature".[3] The power of parents over their children which went with this nexus of interest and obligation was "the only natural authority and government" from which all authority, public and private, civil and criminal, was derived.[4] It is, then, in the context of obligation inherent in the natural relation that parental power was seen. The matter was put succinctly by Erskine. "Parents lie under the strongest obligations, from nature itself, to take care of their issue during their imperfect age, *in consequence of which*[5] they are vested with all the powers over them which are necessary for the proper discharge of their duty."[6] Parental powers were seen by Erskine to flow directly from the natural obligation of parents and were to be used for the proper discharge of that obligation. Parental responsibilities and parental rights can thus be seen as different aspects of the same principle, which is that parents are obliged to protect and nurture their children and necessarily have the power to do so. This was recognised judicially in more recent times. In *Humphrys v. Polak*[7] it was held that the parent and child relationship was one founded on duty, and in *Gillick v. West Norfolk and Wisbech Area Health Authority*[8] the relationship between the parent's duty and right was described as follows: "[parental rights] exist for the benefit of the child and they are justified only in so far as they enable the parent to perform his duties towards the child"[9]; "Parental rights are derived from parental duty and exist only so long as they are needed for the protection of the person and property of the child."[10] Under the Children (Scotland) Act 1995, the primary determinant of the parent and child relationship remains, as it was for Stair and Erskine, one of responsibility[11]; "parental rights" are recognised too but, following Erskine, only "in order to enable [the parent] to fulfil his [or her] parental responsibilities in relation" to the child.[12] It follows that a parent is entitled to exercise a parental right only in so far as it is directed towards the fulfilment of one or other of the parental responsibilities. Though the term "parental rights" is commonly used, and continues to have statutory sanction, the term "parental power or privilege" is jurisprudentially more accurate. The rights of parents are not enforceable merely because they are recognised, nor are they such that if inhibited or infringed the right-holder can claim damages as compensation for breach.[13] Rather, parental right is more in the nature of entitlement or privilege, whereby the law will recognise the parent's abilities competently to perform certain acts in relation to and on behalf of the child, and will give legal force and effect to these acts.

---

[3] *ibid.*
[4] I, v, 6.
[5] Emphasis added.
[6] I, vi, 53.
[7] [1901] 2 K.B. 385.
[8] [1985] 3 W.L.R. 830.
[9] *ibid.* at 841, *per* Lord Fraser of Tullybelton.
[10] *ibid.* at 853, *per* Lord Scarman. See also *L v. H*, 1996 S.L.T. 612.
[11] Children (Scotland) Act 1995, s. 1(1).
[12] s. 2(1).
[13] *F v. Wirral Metropolitan Borough Council* [1991] 2 All E.R. 648 (damages denied in an action for breach of the parent's right to be asked to consent to child's adoption); *McKeen v. Chief Constable of Lothian and Borders Police*, 1994 S.L.T. 93 (damages denied for loss of society following allegedly wrongful removal of child from lawful custodian).

Exercise of parental responsibilities and parental rights

8.03   Parental power is, then, limited by the requirement that its exercise must be directed towards the fulfilment of one of the statutory responsibilities, such as the responsibility to safeguard and promote the child's health, development and welfare. The decision in a case like *Macpherson v. Leishman*[14] would not be reached today. There, the mother of an "illegitimate" child raised an action for delivery of her child against the defender whom she had previously allowed to care for the child. The court ordered delivery of the child, on the ground that the mother had the "right" of custody; but it expressed regret at having to do so, on the ground that the child's welfare would be better served by leaving the child where it was. Today, this matter would be determined by the welfare test embodied in section 11(7) of the Children (Scotland) Act 1995.[15] It would, however, be wrong to say that parents have power only to do that which is best for their children, for, in truth, in the fulfilment of their responsibilities parents have far more discretion than that.[16] In exercising their rights and powers parents may do things that are neutral or even mildly disadvantageous,[17] so long as their actions are not clearly against the interests of the child. So, for example, while it may be best for a child to be vaccinated, the law will permit the parent to refuse consent thereto for whatever reason, because that refusal does not positively and directly harm the child; but a refusal of a blood transfusion that is necessary to prevent injury to the child is not permitted by the law.[18] In exercising such discretion as the parent has within the confines of the obligation to safeguard and promote the child's health, development and welfare, a person must, in reaching any major decision which involves his or her fulfilling parental responsibilities or exercising parental rights, have regard, so far as practicable, to the views (if he or she wishes to express them) of the child concerned, taking account of the child's age and maturity, and of those of any other person who has parental responsibilities or parental rights in relation to the child (and wishes to express those views).[19] A child 12 years of age or more is presumed to be of sufficient age and maturity to form a view. This obligation, which can be traced to the UN Convention on the Rights of the Child,[20] is unenforceable in the sense that any decision made remains valid even although the person making it did not consult the child or other parent. Any transaction entered into in good faith by a third party and a person acting as legal representative of the child is not challengeable on the ground only that the child, or a person with parental responsibilities or parental rights in relation to the child, was not consulted or that due regard was not given to his or her views before the transaction was entered into.[21]

---

[14] (1887) 14 R. 780.

[15] See *J v. C* [1970] A.C. 668 and *Osborne v. Matthan (No. 2)*, 1998 S.L.T. 1264 in which the application of the welfare test led to the child remaining with non-parental carers; and *Re M (Child's Upbringing)* [1996] 2 F.L.R. 441 in which the application of that test required the child's return to his parents.

[16] See the interesting discussion by McCall Smith, "Is Anything Left of Parental Rights?" in *Family Rights, Family Law, and Medical Advance* (eds. Sutherland and McCall Smith) (1990). He argues that while parental rights are usually presented as designed to benefit the child, in practice their rationale lies more often in the protection of an interest of the parent. The examples he gives are the right to the child's society and the right to determine the child's religious upbringing.

[17] For example piercing the ears of baby girls, circumcising baby boys for non-therapeutic reasons, subjecting the child to an unhealthy (but not seriously detrimental) diet, exposing it to unpopular religious beliefs, giving it a ridiculous name and, generally, acting in a way which may not be best for the child or may result in some unhappiness, provided it stops short of cruelty or neglect.

[18] *Finlayson, Applicant*, 1989 S.C.L.R. 601. *Cf. Re B. (A Minor) (Wardship: Medical Treatment)* [1981] 1 W.L.R. 1412; *Re D (A Minor) (Wardship: Sterilisation)* [1976] 1 All E.R. 326.

[19] Children (Scotland) Act 1995, s. 6(1).

[20] Art. 12: "States Parties shall assure to the child who is capable of forming his or her own views the right to express those views freely in all matters affecting the child, the views of the child being given due weight in accordance with the age and maturity of the child."

[21] Children (Scotland) Act 1995, s. 6(2).

A further limitation on the exercise of parental responsibilities and parental **8.04**
rights is contained in section 3(4) of the 1995 Act, under which the fact that a
person has such responsibilities and rights does not entitle that person to act in
any way that would be incompatible with any court order relating to the child or
the child's property, or with any supervision requirement made by a children's
hearing. This provision is for the avoidance of doubt only and makes no change
from the pre-1995 position.

Inalienability of parental responsibilities and parental rights

The *patria potestas* of the common law was usually said to be inalienable,[22] **8.05**
but that proposition always required some qualification. In its fullness the *patria
potestas* belonged only to the father and could be transferred to no one else; it
could not be surrendered, although its exercise could be delegated.[23] So, it was
incapable of voluntary alienation. But in its major aspects, it might be alienated
by judicial order. If custody of the child was taken away from the father and
given to another, direction of the child's education left in the hands of the
custodian or separately regulated by the court, and the father superseded in the
management of the child's estate by a judicial factor—all courses of action which,
however rare, were competent long before modern statute intervened—the father
was left with little but a shadow of the *patria potestas*. If, in the modern law,
one is still to speak of parental responsibilities and parental rights as inalienable,
considerably greater qualification must be made. Adoption, orders under
section 30 of the Human Fertilisation and Embryology Act 1990 and procedures
for transferring parental rights and responsibilities to local authorities effect a
transfer of parental power which is virtually complete and the scope for the
removal of parental responsibilities and parental rights both in the care of the
child and in the management of the child's estate has been much enlarged. It
remains the case, however, that parental responsibilities and parental rights
cannot irrevocably be alienated, during the life of the parent who has them, by
voluntary act unsupported by judicial order. The provision in section 10(2) of
the Guardianship Act 1973 to this effect was repealed by Schedule 2 to the Law
Reform (Parent and Child) (Scotland) Act 1986 and was not there re-enacted.[24]
In its *Report on Family Law*,[25] however, the Scottish Law Commission considered
that it would be a helpful restatement to have the matter put on a statutory basis
once more, in pursuit of the aim to provide a comprehensive statutory code of
parental responsibilities and parental rights which leaves virtually nothing to
the common law. Consequently, it is now provided that a person who has parental
responsibilities or parental rights in relation to a child shall not abdicate those
responsibilities or rights to anyone else but may arrange for some or all of them
to be fulfilled or exercised on his or her behalf; without prejudice to that
generality, any such arrangement may be made with a person who already has
parental responsibilities or parental rights in relation to the child concerned.[26]
Any agreement that parental responsibilities and parental rights be exercised
by another person may, in principle, be revoked although whether the
consequences of revocation should receive effect is now a question to be
determined with regard to the welfare of the child as the paramount

---

[22] *J and J v. C's Tutor*, 1948 S.C. 636, *per* Lord President Cooper at 642.
[23] *Kerrigan v. Hall* (1901) 4 F.10; *Craig v. Greig and Macdonald* (1863) 1 M. 1172 at 1179.
[24] This was on the basis that this was the position at common law in any case: according to the
    Scottish Law Commission "parental rights are *extra commercium* and cannot be validly renounced
    or transferred by mere private agreement": Scot Law Com. No. 82, *Report on Illegitimacy*, p. 131.
[25] Scot. Law Com. No. 135 (May 1992).
[26] Children (Scotland) Act 1995, s. 3(5).

consideration. Parental responsibilities cannot, short of adoption, a parental order or a parental responsibilities order, competently be transferred. While it is possible for a parent to arrange for his or her parental responsibilities to be met by other persons acting on the parent's behalf, that does not affect any legal liability of the parent arising from a failure to fulfil parental responsibilities[27] except, where the care of a child has been delegated, in respect of the immediate duties incumbent on a person having care of a child[28]; and that only to the extent that the delegation was reasonable when regard is had to the character and competence of the delegate and any circumstances affecting risk of harm to the child, for ultimate responsibility cannot be delegated.

Who may exercise parental responsibilities and parental rights

8.06   For the vast majority of children there will be either one or two persons, usually their parents, who possess parental responsibilities and parental rights. Sometimes there will be no such person and occasionally there will be more than two such persons. Parental responsibilities and parental rights can be acquired by operation of law, by private deed or by court decree. Whenever there is more than one person who possesses parental rights at any one time then whoever possesses a particular parental right may exercise that right without the consent of any other person who has the same right unless the deed or decree conferring the right, or regulating its exercise, otherwise provides.[29] It is in the nature of parental responsibilities that they be owed individually and so the same rule applies to them also.

Parents

8.07   Parental responsibilities and parental rights are the natural consequence of the parent and child relationship. This was recognised, as was seen at the start of this chapter, by the institutional writers, and it is of interest that they speak of parental, not paternal, power. That they should do so was consistent with the interrelation of power and obligation: if it were from parents' duties to their children that all powers over them were truly derived, then the mother, no less than the father, could enjoy powers correlative to her duties. Nevertheless it was in the father of the "legitimate" child that parental power or authority was "chiefly discovered".[30] He had, in effect, the *patria potestas* taken over, though in modified form, from the Romans even if it was seen as originating in the parental relation which both parents shared with the child. In relation to "legitimate" children, for most purposes of legal consequence, that power vested solely in him and from it he had the right of custody of the child, together with the right to be the child's tutor or curator. By the Guardianship Act 1973, however, the mother of a "legitimate" child was given the same rights and authority as the law allowed to the father,[31] and so the participation of both parents in parental power acquired a reality that it previously lacked. The "illegitimate" child was treated quite differently, and the father had no power over the child but was regarded, rather, as a stranger to the child except in so far as he was the subject

---

[27] Children (Scotland) Act 1995, s. 3(6).
[28] Such a person has the responsibility to do what is reasonable in all the circumstances to safeguard the child's health, development and welfare and in fulfilling that responsibility the person may, in particular, give consent to any surgical, medical or dental treatment or procedure: *ibid.* s. 5(1).
[29] *ibid.* s. 2(2).
[30] Stair, I, vi, 53.
[31] s. 10, repealed by Sched. 2 to the Law Reform (Parent and Child) (Scotland) Act 1986.

of certain burdens and restrictions.[32] "A bastard has in law no father; and the person so-called is he who, from contact with the mother, is liable in the burdens of paternity without any of the privileges."[33] The mother of the "illegitimate" child had the right of custody,[34] and her rights as custodian were little different in relation to the child's person and upbringing from the parental powers over a "legitimate" child. She did not, however, have the right to be tutor or curator, and any right solely to guardianship did not, therefore, vest in her.

The Law Reform (Parent and Child) (Scotland) Act 1986 provides that the **8.08** fact that the child's parents are not or have not been married to one another shall be left out of account in establishing the legal relationship between the child and any other person; and accordingly any such relationship shall have effect as if the parents were or had been married to one another.[35] This provision survived the passing of the Children (Scotland) Act 1995. The child's "illegitimacy" is therefore irrelevant for the purpose of his or her being subject to parental responsibilities and parental rights. It is not, however, irrelevant to the question of who can possess and exercise these responsibilities and rights. It is now provided that a child's mother has parental responsibilities and parental rights in relation to the child whether or not she is or has been married to the child's father[36] but, notwithstanding section 1(1) of the Law Reform (Parent and Child) (Scotland) Act 1986, the child's father has such responsibilities and rights in relation to the child only if married to the mother at the time of the child's conception or subsequently.[37] In order that the father acquires parental responsibilities and parental rights, his marriage to the mother may be valid (regularly or irregularly constituted), voidable, or void so long as both parties[38] believed in good faith (whether by error of fact or of law) at the time of the marriage that it was valid.[39] If the father is never married to the mother at a time after the conception of the child then he has no parental responsibilities or parental rights until such time as he acquires them under a parental responsibilities and parental rights agreement made with the mother under section 4,[40] or they are conferred upon him by order of the court under section 11(2) of the Children (Scotland) Act 1995.[41] Parental responsibilities and parental rights will vest in the mother as soon as the natural parent and child relationship is created, that is on birth[42]; they will vest in the father on the child's birth or the father's marriage to the mother if he acquires responsibilities and rights by virtue of section 3(1)(b) or,

---

[32] *Clarke v. Carfin Coal Co.* (1891) 18 R. (H.L.) 63. The burden was that of aliment; the restrictions related to the law of marriage (see now the Marriage (Scotland) Act 1977, s. 2 and Sched. 1 as amended by the Marriage (Prohibited Degrees of Relationship) Act 1986, Sched. 2) and the law of incest (see now the Criminal Law (Consolidation) (Scotland) Act 1995, s. 1).

[33] *Weepers v. Heritors and Kirk Session of Kennoway* (1844) 6 D. 1166, *per* Lord Jeffrey at 1173.

[34] See above, para. 1.23.

[35] s. 1(1).

[36] Children (Scotland) Act 1995, s. 3(1)(a).

[37] *ibid.* s. 3(1)(b). On proof of the time of conception, see above, para. 3.17.

[38] Prior to 1995, the father obtained parental rights through a void marriage only if he believed in good faith that the marriage was valid: Law Reform (Parent and Child) (Scotland) Act 1986, s. 2(2)(b). Now his good faith is irrelevant if the mother is in bad faith. The reason why fathers are prejudiced by the bad faith of mothers is elusory. Since the doctrine of legitimacy through putative marriage applies on the *bona fide* belief of its validity by only one of the parties to the marriage (see above, para. 1.47) it follows that a child may be "legitimate" but nevertheless not be owed parental responsibilities and parental rights by his or her father.

[39] Children (Scotland) Act 1995, s. 3(2).

[40] See below, paras 8.10 *et seq.*

[41] *Montgomery v. Lockwood*, 1987 S.C.L.R. 525; *Sanderson v. McManus*, 1997 S.L.T. 629 (claims for access by unmarried fathers made under the pre-1995 legislation). *Cf. Re C and Anr (Minors)* [1992] 2 All E.R. 86.

[42] While the existence of an unborn child can have legal consequences, discussed above at Chap. 2, these are not (for reasons explored there) to be seen as parental responsibilities and parental rights.

if that provision is inapplicable, on the date of registering in the Books of Council and Session an agreement made under section 4, or if he acquires them by court order on the date of the decree or any other date the court may determine. Article 18(1) of the UN Convention on the Rights of the Child[43] provides that "States parties shall use their best efforts to ensure recognition of the principle that both parents have common responsibilities for the upbringing and development of the child". This article is to be read in conjunction with Article 2 under which the rights in the Convention are to be respected "irrespective of the child's or his or her parent's... birth or other status". In Scots law, the father is absolved of his responsibilities if his status is that of a man not married to the child's mother. The United Kingdom is, therefore, in breach of its international obligations under Article 18(1). The European Court of Human Rights has held, however, that the equivalent provision under the 1986 Act[44] did not breach the non-discrimination requirements in Article 14 of the European Convention on Human Rights since that provision was designed to identify "meritorious" fathers, that is those who deserved to have "parental rights", and that the discrimination between married and unmarried fathers was not disproportionate to that aim.[45] The 1995 Act moves away from the terminology of "parental rights" to that of "parental responsibilities" and it is open to argument that the aim of the provision is no longer to identify fathers who merit rights but to identify those who ought to have obligations towards a child. If this is so then, taking account of Articles 2 and 18 of the UN Convention, it can be argued that to absolve unmarried fathers of their responsibilities does not serve that aim and is therefore contrary to the European Convention on Human Rights.

8.09   For most children parental responsibilities and parental rights are vested in both parents. In that case, the rights and authority of mother and father are equal and exercisable by either without the other.[46] So each enjoys parental power severally. Some advantage is thereby given to the parent who takes the initiative. His or her acts are effective regardless of the attitude of the other parent. Both do, however, have an (imperfect) obligation to consult the other in making "major decisions" on the fulfilment or exercise of parental responsibilities or parental rights,[47] and in the event of disagreement application may be made to the court for an order relating to parental responsibilities, parental rights, guardianship or the administration of the child's property. The court may make any such order as it thinks fit,[48] though in doing so it must regard the welfare of the child concerned as its paramount consideration and must not make any such order unless it considers that it would be better for the child that the order be made than that none should be made at all.[49] Court orders in relation to parental responsibilities and parental rights are examined in some detail in the immediately following chapter.

---

[43] 28 *International Legal Materials* 1448, ratified by the U.K., December 16, 1991.

[44] Law Reform (Parent and Child) (Scotland) Act 1986, s. 2(1).

[45] *McMichael v. United Kingdom* (1995) 20 E.H.R.R. 205. *Cf. Kroon v. The Netherlands* (1995) 10 E.H.R.R. 263 in which it was held that a Dutch legal provision which denied the biological father of the right to prove his paternity unless the mother's husband first denied his paternity breached Art. 8. See also the decision of the Constitutional Court of South Africa in *Fraser v. Children's Court, Pretoria North*, 1997 SACLR LEXIS 1 where the different treatment accorded married and unmarried men in the adoption process was held to be unconstitutional discrimination.

[46] Children (Scotland) Act 1995, s. 2(2).

[47] *ibid.* s. 6(1).

[48] *ibid.* s. 11(2).

[49] *ibid.* s. 11(7).

Parental responsibilities and parental rights agreements

Where the father does not have parental responsibilities and parental rights **8.10** because he is not, and has not since the conception of the child been, married to the mother, he and the mother may enter into an agreement under which he shall have such responsibilities and rights as he would have if married to the mother.[50] The agreement must be in prescribed form[51] and must be registered in the Books of Council and Session at a time when the mother still has the parental responsibilities and parental rights that she had when the agreement was made.[52] The agreement comes into effect when it is so registered.[53] Registration is automatic and there is no requirement that it satisfies the welfare test before being recognised as valid. Such an agreement is not open to negotiation between the parents, and the father cannot acquire only one or some of the parental responsibilities and parental rights. Nor can the mother attach conditions or time-limits to the father's acquisition of responsibilities and rights. Entering into the agreement is an entirely voluntary act by both parties and the mother cannot be forced to do so, nor is there any provision for dispensing with her agreement if she refuses. The father is similarly entitled to refuse to enter into the agreement and to evade thereby the responsibilities that he would otherwise have in relation to his child. And, since a mother's decision to share parental responsibilities and parental rights with a father is certainly a major decision involving the fulfilment of parental responsibilities and the exercise of parental rights, the mother is obliged to have regard, so far as practicable, to the views (if he or she wishes to express them) of the child concerned, taking account of the child's age and maturity, and to those of any other person who has parental responsibilities and parental rights[54] in relation to the child and who wishes to express these views.[55] If she is married, then her husband will require to be consulted, if he is presumptively the father.

The agreement may be entered into only if the mother retains the full range of **8.11** parental responsibilities and parental rights that she has by virtue of section 3(1)(a), and if she has been deprived of some or all of them then the father thereby loses this means of acquiring parental responsibilities and parental rights. "Deprived" means, it is submitted, deprived permanently or at least indefinitely. So, for example, the mother is unable to enter into a parental responsibilities and parental rights agreement if she has been deprived of all of her parental responsibilities and parental rights by the making of an adoption order, or an order freeing the child for adoption, or a parental order made under section 30 of the Human Fertilisation and Embryology Act 1990. Likewise, a parental responsibilities order made under section 86 of the Children (Scotland) Act 1995 transferring parental rights and responsibilities to a local authority will deprive the mother of the ability to enter into such an agreement with the father. And if the court makes an order under section 11(2)(a) of the 1986 Act depriving the mother of some or all of her parental responsibilities or parental rights she will lose the ability to enter into this agreement. It is to be noted that this result follows even if the mother is deprived only of one of her responsibilities or rights. So, for

---

[50] Children (Scotland) Act 1995, s. 4(1). See Sutherland, "Parental Responsibilities and Rights Agreements: Better Half a Loaf than None at All?" 3 S.L.P.Q. 265.

[51] See Parental Responsibilities and Parental Rights Agreement (Scotland) Regulations 1996 (S.I. 1996 No. 2549).

[52] Children (Scotland) Act 1995, s. 4(2).

[53] *ibid.* s. 4(3).

[54] If the mother is unmarried then only in the case of a court order will any person other than she have parental responsibilities and parental rights.

[55] Children (Scotland) Act 1995, s. 6(1).

example, if a residence order is made by a court doing no more than requiring the child to live somewhere other than with the mother, the mother loses thereby her right to regulate the child's residence but she retains her full parental responsibilities and her rights to maintain contact, to control, direct and guide the child's upbringing and to act as the child's legal representative; nevertheless she is unable thereafter to enter into an agreement under section 4. The temporary suspension of parental responsibilities and parental rights, such as through the implementation of a child protection order or a warrant under which the child is required to stay away from home, does not "deprive" the mother of her parental responsibilities and parental rights—rather it puts them in abeyance for the short period during which the order is effective. The same is true, it is submitted, for a supervision requirement made by a children's hearing with a condition of residence, even although that may last very much longer than a child protection order or a warrant. Any such condition suspends the mother's right to regulate the child's residence but suspension is not deprivation, for her right will automatically be restored if the requirement is terminated before the child reaches the age of 16 (which is not the case with the termination of adoption orders or orders transferring parental rights and responsibilities to local authorities) and therefore the mother of a child subject to a supervision requirement may enter into a section 4 agreement with the father during the requirement's currency.[56]

8.12   An agreement under section 4 may be entered into by parents no matter whether they are above or below the age of 16,[57] though a parent under the age of 16 does not, by entering into the agreement, acquire thereby a capacity to act on behalf of the child which he would not otherwise have. The agreement can only be made between the parents of the child. It is not open, for example, to a guardian taking office on the death of the mother to enter into an agreement with the father. Nor is it open to the mother to enter into an agreement under section 4 with any person other than the father, such as her husband or cohabitant, even if that person has adopted a fathering role and may even owe the child an obligation of aliment.[58] "Father" for these purposes will usually be the child's genetic father, but it might also be the man deemed father under section 28(3) of the Human Fertilisation and Embryology Act 1990.[59] It will also include the man presumed father under section 5(1)(b) of the Law Reform (Parent and Child) (Scotland) Act 1986, until that presumption is overturned, and it may be supposed that if that presumption is overturned after a parental responsibilities and parental rights agreement has been registered the agreement will lose its effect even without being revoked. It is entirely unclear under the legislation whether a man must prove himself to be father or be able to rely on a statutory provision presuming or deeming him to be father before the agreement will be effective. It may be that the agreement, once registered in the Books of Council and Session, will receive effect until shown to be invalid (for example by proof that the man does not satisfy the description of "father") but registration does not create a "presumption" of paternity such as is contained in section 5 of the Law Reform (Parent and Child) (Scotland) Act 1986 which would hold good for purposes other than the exercise of parental responsibilities and parental rights, such as succession, aliment and child support. And if an agreement is

---

[56] By giving him parental responsibilities and parental rights, the father becomes thereby a "relevant person" for the purposes of Pt II of the 1995 Act: s. 93(2)(b).

[57] s. 4(1).

[58] To acquire parental responsibilities and parental rights, such a man must either adopt the child or seek an order under s. 11(2)(b).

[59] *i.e.* the man who is "treated together" with a woman to whom he is not married who undergoes infertility treatment: see above, paras 3.34–3.41.

entered into with one man while another is deemed or presumed to be father then it is submitted that the agreement must be presumed to be ineffective (which presumption may be overturned on proof that the party to the agreement is, indeed, the father). The existence of a parental responsibilities and parental rights agreement may go some way to displace the presumption that the husband is father, but without court action to that effect it cannot on its own do so.[59a]

Once registered the agreement cannot be revoked by the parties.[60] It lasts **8.13** for as long as the parental responsibilities and parental rights last,[61] unless terminated earlier by court order. The court may revoke the order in any case in which it makes an order under section 11(2)(a) (depriving a person of some or all of his or her parental responsibilities or parental rights) or under section 11(2)(b) (imposing parental responsibilities on, or giving parental rights to, a person).[62] It would seem from the words of this provision that the court could not entertain an independent application to revoke the agreement, even although the effect would be the same as an order under section 11(2)(a). The revocation is available only in connection with an order under section 11(2)(a) or (b). This is not, however, a real limitation on the court's power since it can achieve the same effect by making an order under section 11(2)(a) in any case in which it considers it necessary to do so, even when not asked to do so.[63] It may be noted that there is no provision for the revocation of the agreement in circumstances in which it becomes otiose, such as when the father subsequently marries the mother, or is appointed the child's guardian.[64] But in such cases revocation would achieve as little as the agreement itself. Revocation of the agreement, because it will have the effect of removing a person's parental responsibilities and parental rights, should be ordered by the court on the same basis as it would make any other order removing these responsibilities and rights.[65]

Guardians

When the guardian was little more than what would today be called the child's **8.14** legal representative, his powers and obligations were, unless he had custody also, virtually confined to the management of the ward's estate. The education of a pupil child whose father had died was, however, at common law, subject to the direction of the tutor (*i.e.* guardian) even if the tutor did not have custody. Accordingly, the mother's custody of the child might be disturbed in so far as was necessary to give effect to the tutor's scheme of education, although, in the event of dispute, the court could adjudicate between mother and tutor and determine

---

[59a] In *Aberdeen City Council, Petitioners*, Feb. 11, 1999, the appellant had entered into "what purported to be a parental rights agreement" with the wife of his brother, in respect of a child she bore, allegedly to him. Lord Justice-Clerk Cullen, speaking for the court, held that the appellant had locus to appear in an application for an order freeing the child for adoption. The basis of this holding seems to be that any court in which the question is relevant can find a presumption of paternity to be overturned if the evidence before the court suggests that another man is father, even without an application to that effect under the 1986 Act. In the instant case, the fact that all the parties treated the appellant as the father, together with the fact that he and the mother had entered into a parental responsibilities and parental rights agreement was treated as sufficient for the court to regard him, for the purposes of the adoption legislation, as a man claiming to be the father.

[60] s. 4(4).

[61] See ss. 1(2) and 2(7).

[62] s. 11(11).

[63] s. 11(3)(b).

[64] *cf.* revocation of an adoption order when the parents marry: Adoption (Scotland) Act 1978, s. 46(1).

[65] *Re P (Terminating Parental Responsibility)* [1995] 1 F.L.R. 1048. See also *Re G (Child Case: Parental Involvement)* [1996] Fam. Law 459.

the preferable course of education.[66] The law on these matters is, however, now obsolete. On the death of either parent the surviving parent acts alone, or along with any guardian nominated by the deceased parent or appointed by the court.[67] The guardian appointed by the deceased parent has, in respect of the child, the responsibilities imposed and the rights conferred on a parent by sections 1 and 2 of the 1995 Act and these sections apply in relation to a guardian as they apply in relation to a parent.[68] Each parent or guardian can act independently of the other,[69] and disputes are to be resolved in accordance with the welfare principle embodied in section 11(7) of the Children (Scotland) Act 1995. The position is, it is thought, little different on the death or other failure of both parents.

Persons with children in their care or control

8.15   The responsibilities and rights of persons, other than parents and guardians, who have children in their care will vary considerably according to circumstances. In this category may be included foster carers, persons who have or share actual day-to-day care and control unsupported by a residence order or other legal title, persons (such as relatives, friends or neighbours) to whose care parents have temporarily entrusted their children, child-minders, persons in whose charge children are for purposes of medical care, school teachers, leaders of organised groups of children, and generally anyone into whose care or control[70] a child, in fact, passes. A person may have care or control of a child either alone or with another person, and this is not affected by the fact that the other person has parental responsibilities and parental rights in relation to the child. So, for example, a step-parent, or a cohabitant of a parent, may in fact have care or control even while the parent has and exercises parental responsibilities and parental rights in relation to the child. The general duty of a person with care or control of a child is to do what is reasonable in all the circumstances to safeguard the child's health, development and welfare.[71] It is the content of that duty, and in particular what it is reasonable to do, that will vary with the circumstances. Often it will be enough to take reasonable measures to protect the child from harm. But a person in whose care a child is must see that, while in his or her care, the child does not suffer from neglect and, where care is continuous and extended over a period in which the child may be expected to grow and develop, there may be a more positive duty of nurture and promotion of health, development and welfare such as a parent or guardian has. This is so notwithstanding that the statutory formulation of the duty is limited in its terms

---

[66] Fraser (3rd ed.), p. 295 and cases cited there.

[67] See above, paras 7.04 *et seq.*

[68] s. 7(5).

[69] s. 2(2).

[70] There is little, if any, substantive distinction between a person with care, on the one hand, and a person with control, on the other hand, of the child, for he who has control of a child has a duty to care for the child, and he who owes obligations to care for the child has thereby such control as is necessary to allow the fulfilment of these obligations.

[71] s. 5(1). In fulfilling this duty, the obligation under s. 6(1) to have regard to the views of the child and of any other person with parental responsibilities and parental rights applies. The statutory duty does not apply to persons who have care or control of a child in a school (s. 5(2)) but common law duties flowing from the *in loco parentis* relationship continue to apply: these are not "parental responsibilities and parental rights" and so are not abolished by the terms of ss. 1(4) and 2(5). It is open to argument that, the responsibilities in s. 5 not being "parental responsibilities" as defined in s. 1, non-natural persons such as local authorities, churches or other institutions into whose care or control a child temporarily passes, are subject to s. 5. Section 15(4) says that only natural persons can have "parental responsibilities" but says nothing of the responsibilities imposed by s. 5. However, the fact that the responsibilities are imposed on "a person who has attained the age of 16 years" indicates, it is submitted, an implicit limitation on the application of s. 5 to natural persons only.

to safeguarding.[72] A person who has the care of a child has the same duties to secure the child's education as are laid on a parent by the Education (Scotland) Act 1980,[73] and is subject to the same criminal sanctions for neglect as a parent.[74] From this obligation to attend to the child's nurture and well-being and, in some cases, to the child's education, the person with care or control of the child has in a certain, if limited, sense[75] a duty to aliment the child. He or she must at least see that what is immediately necessary for the child's physical support is supplied, whether the need be for food, clothing, medicine and medical treatment or shelter. But, although certain immediate responsibilities for aliment may rest on the person with care or control, to the extent that if the child should be neglected as a result of failure in these responsibilities he or she cannot plead in defence that he or she was not given the means by those on whom the alimentary obligation ultimately lay, that does not derogate from the obligation of those ultimately responsible. A person with care or control is, therefore, entitled to relief from the parent or other person on whom the alimentary obligation properly lies for necessary expenditure by him or her in respect of the child's aliment.[76] He or she may also sue on behalf of the child for an award of aliment to cover future expenditure.

The powers of a person with a child in his or her care are those that are necessary **8.16** for the exercise of his or her duties towards the child. Thus, the person who has the care of the child may restrain and control him or her and exercise discipline to the extent that is necessary for that purpose. He or she stands, if but temporarily and for limited purposes, *in loco parentis* and has the powers of a parent so far as reasonably required for the discharge of his or her duties and the achievement of the legitimate purposes for which the child is in his or her care. Where the child has been entrusted to a person by a parent, the parent may, by delegation, enlarge that person's duties and powers but cannot thereby absolve him or her from the duty to care for the child nor withhold the powers necessary for the exercise of that duty because these arise, independently of delegation, from the *in loco parentis* relationship. Consent to medical treatment was previously a problematic issue. Before 1995, a person in whose temporary care a child was had, in general, no powers in relation to medical treatment; but he or she may have had a duty to secure that such medical treatment was made available as was practicable and the occasion demanded. If the child did not have the legal capacity to provide consent him or herself,[77] the treatment could nevertheless be provided without consent, but only in so far as there existed an emergency,

---

[72] *cf.* s. 1(1)(a) which obliges a parent to "safeguard and promote".

[73] s. 30, as applied to a person who has parental responsibilities in relation to, or has care of a child by s. 135(1), as amended by Children (Scotland) Act 1995, Sched. 4, para. 28(5).

[74] Children and Young Persons (Scotland) Act 1937, s. 12(1).

[75] *i.e.* a sense other than that of the Family Law (Scotland) Act 1985 (discussed below, Chap. 13).

[76] Under the Family Law (Scotland) Act 1985 an action for aliment for a child may be brought by the child him or herself or on his or her behalf if under 18 by (1) the parent or guardian of the child; or (2) a person with whom the child lives or who is seeking a residence order in respect of the child (s. 2(4), as amended by the Age of Legal Capacity (Scotland) Act 1991, Sched. 2 and the Children (Scotland) Act 1995, Sched. 4, para. 36) and an award of aliment may be backdated to the date of commencement of the proceedings or on special cause shown to an earlier date (s. 3(1)(c)). It is therefore open to the child's *de facto* carer to obtain relief for past expenditure by means of a backdated award in an action for aliment, and that remedy will be available in an action at the instance of the residence parent against the other parent. The requirement that special cause be shown may, however, present an obstacle in many cases. In such cases a *de facto* carer who is not a parent will have a remedy by way of an action for payment founded on the obligation of relief against the parent or other person properly liable for aliment.

[77] *i.e.* was not, in the opinion of a qualified medical practitioner, capable of understanding the nature and possible consequences of the procedure or treatment: Age of Legal Capacity (Scotland) Act 1991, s. 2(4).

that is, an immediate necessity to act in order to save the life, or avoid serious permanent impairment of the health, of a child. Where there was no emergency, and the child could not give personal consent, reference would usually have to be made to the parent or person with equivalent powers. Difficulties arose if such a person was not immediately available and was likely to remain so for a considerable time. The Children (Scotland) Act 1995 now provides for such situations. A person over the age of 16[78] who has the care or control of a child under that age but who has no parental responsibilities or parental rights in relation to the child may, in fulfilling his or her obligation to do what is reasonable in all the circumstances to safeguard the child's health, development and welfare, give consent to any surgical, medical or dental treatment or procedure.[79] This may only be done where (a) the child is not able to give such consent on his own behalf (through incapacity as a consequence of age[80]) and (b) it is not within the knowledge of the person who has care or control of the child that a parent of the child would refuse to give the consent in question. There is, however, an overlap here with cases of emergency, in which no consent at all may be required. It is submitted that treatment in the absence of consent may be justified by emergency only when there is no person immediately available to give that consent, and that if such a person is available then consent must be obtained and treatment without that consent will be an assault. Though the wording of the provision suggests the consent may be given to "any surgical, medical or dental treatment or procedure", this is limited, it is submitted, by its protective purpose and consent is valid only if the proposed treatment or procedure is reasonably necessary in all the circumstances to safeguard the child's health, development and welfare. So elective, cosmetic or experimental treatment may not be consented to under this provision.

Other persons

8.17   Parental responsibilities and parental rights may vest in other persons as a result of various statutory provisions. In relation to adoption, parental responsibilities and parental rights are vested in the adoptive parent or parents when the adoption order is made.[81] When a child is freed for adoption, vesting in the adoption agency takes place on the making of the freeing order.[82] A parental responsibilities order made under section 86 of the Children (Scotland) Act 1995 has the effect of transferring the "appropriate parental rights and responsibilities" to the local authority. In addition, the court may make such order relating to parental responsibilities or parental rights as it thinks fit under section 11(1) of the 1995 Act, which includes conferring such responsibilities and rights on a person who does not otherwise have them.[83] Any responsibilities imposed or rights conferred will vest on the making of the order, or at any other time determined by the court. If a residence order is made which requires that a child lives with a person who, immediately before the order is made, does not

---

[78] This whole section applies only to persons over the age of 16, but persons under that age may well retain common law duties towards children in their care, analogous to the responsibility laid down in s. 5(1). The only practical effect of specifying persons of or above the age of 16 is in relation to the power to consent to medical treatment.

[79] s. 5(1).

[80] Incapacity through, say, unconsciousness of a child otherwise capable of consenting to medical treatment does not reactivate a parent's power to consent on his or her behalf and will not, therefore, activate the present provision either. Treatment can be provided to an unconscious but otherwise competent child only on the basis of emergency.

[81] Adoption (Scotland) Act 1978, s. 12(1) and (2).

[82] *ibid.* s. 18(5).

[83] Children (Scotland) Act 1995, s. 11(2)(b).

have in relation to the child the responsibilities and rights mentioned in section 1(1)(a), (b) and (d)[84] and in section 2(b) and (d)[85] then the making of the residence order will confer upon that person these responsibilities and rights.[86] The court may, of course, qualify the effect of that provision by varying the terms of the residence order in any way it thinks fit.

Termination of parental responsibilities and parental rights

Natural termination

Parental responsibilities and parental rights are extinguished naturally by **8.18** death either of the parent or guardian or of the child. They are also terminated by the child's attaining the age of 16 or, in relation to the responsibility to provide guidance to the child, the age of 18.[87] Other statutory responsibilities and rights will terminate according to the rules in the statutes that create them.

Legal termination

Parental responsibilities and parental rights may be terminated by court order. **8.19** Most obviously the making of an adoption order has this effect,[88] as does the making of an order freeing a child for adoption[89] and an order under section 30 of the Human Fertilisation and Embryology Act 1990. The Court of Session or the sheriff court has the power to make such order relating to parental responsibilities or parental rights as it thinks fit[90] and in particular it may make an order depriving a person of some or all of his or her parental responsibilities or parental rights in relation to a child.[91] In addition, the sheriff, on application by a local authority, may make a parental responsibilities order which will have the effect of transferring from the child's parents and guardians to the local authority the appropriate parental rights and responsibilities in relation to the child.[92]

Renunciation and forfeiture

In addition to the circumstances already discussed, release from parental power **8.20** could be obtained at common law by express renunciation by the parent or by conduct on the parent's part amounting to forfeiture. Renunciation could be inferred, as from "an apparent intention to abandon" the parental power and leave the child to his or her own guidance.[93] Forfeiture could be by "atrocity" or otherwise dealing unnaturally with the child or showing an unwillingness to discharge parental obligations.[94] Here again, the interrelation of power and obligation, responsibility and right, can be seen and renunciation today would not relieve the parent of his or her legal liabilities.[95] In the modern context, renunciation and forfeiture are likely to arise only as elements in a welfare decision made by a court.

---

[84] *i.e.* the responsibility to safeguard and promote the child's health, development and welfare, to give direction and guidance, and to act as the child's legal representative.
[85] *i.e.* the rights to control, direct and guide the child's upbringing, and to act as the child's legal representative.
[86] s. 11(12).
[87] Children (Scotland) Act 1995, ss. 1(2) and 2(7): the position could perhaps have been put more clearly, but the proposition given in the text follows from these provisions defining "child" to mean a person under the age of 16 (or, as the case may be, 18).
[88] Adoption (Scotland) Act 1978, s. 12(3).
[89] Adoption (Scotland) Act 1978, s. 18(5).
[90] Children (Scotland) Act 1995, s. 11(2).
[91] *ibid.* s. 11(2)(a).
[92] *ibid.* s. 86. See below, Chap. 17.
[93] Fraser (3rd ed.), p. 88; *Harvey v. Harvey* (1860) 22 D. 1198, *per* Lord Justice-Clerk Inglis at 1208; *Fraser v. Robertson* (1867) 5 M. 819.
[94] Stair, I, v, 13.
[95] Children (Scotland) Act 1995, s. 2(5) and (6).

SPECIFIED PARENTAL RESPONSIBILITIES AND PARENTAL RIGHTS

Introduction

8.21   The parental responsibilities owed to children and the parental rights enjoyed over children are set out in sections 1 and 2 respectively of the Children (Scotland) Act 1995, as follows:

> "**1.**—(1) Subject to section 3(1)(b) and (3) of this Act,[96] a parent has in relation to his child the responsibility—
>> (a) to safeguard and promote the child's health, development and welfare;
>> (b) to provide, in a manner appropriate to the stage of development of the child—
>>> (i) direction;
>>> (ii) guidance,
>> to the child;
>> (c) if the child is not living with the parent, to maintain personal relations and direct contact with the child on a regular basis; and
>> (d) to act as the child's legal representative.
>
> ...
>
> **2.**—(1) Subject to section 3(1)(b) and (3) of this Act,[97] a parent, in order to enable him to fulfil his parental responsibilities in relation to his child, has the right —
>> (a) to have the child living with him or otherwise to regulate the child's residence;
>> (b) to control, direct or guide, in a manner appropriate to the stage of development of the child, the child's upbringing;
>> (c) if the child is not living with him, to maintain personal relations and direct contact with the child on a regular basis; and
>> (d) to act as the child's legal representative."[98]

These parental responsibilities and parental rights supersede any analogous duties imposed and rights enjoyed at common law, with the result that, apart from express duties and rights recognised by statute, there are no other parental responsibililities and parental rights upon which a parent can rely and to which a child is subject.[99] It follows that any responsibility or right that existed at common law exists today only if it can be located within the terms of sections 1(1) or 2(1) as quoted above, or within the terms of another statutory provision. Though listed severally, the parental responsibilities and parental rights are to be read together and are to be seen as different aspects of the same principle. The rights exist, as explained above, in order to enable the parent to fulfil his or her responsibilities in relation to the child, and it follows that the exercise of any particular parental right is valid only in so far as it is directed towards the fulfilment of one or more of the parental responsibilities. The right to have the child living with the parent or otherwise to regulate the child's residence exists, then,

---

[96] Under which a father who is not and has not been married to the mother of the child is absolved of his responsibilities towards the child.

[97] Under which a father who is not and has not been married to the mother of the child is denied rights in relation to the child.

[98] The thinking behind these provisions can be found in Scot. Law Com. 135, *Report on Family Law* (May 1992), Pt II.

[99] ss. 1(4) and 2(5).

in order to give the parent the practical power to fulfil his or her responsibility to safeguard and promote the child's health, development and welfare; the right to control, direct or guide the child's upbringing exists in order to allow the parent the opportunity to fulfil his or her responsibility to provide the child with direction and guidance; the right to maintain personal relations and direct contact with the child on a regular basis exists in order to allow the parent to fulfil his or her responsibility to do so; and the right to act as the child's legal representative is granted in order to allow the parent to fulfil his or her responsibility so to act. Nor are the individual responsibilities or individual rights severable one from the other, and the right, say, to maintain personal relations and direct contact with the child is to be exercised not only in a manner that fulfils the responsibility to do so but also in a manner that is not inconsistent with the safeguarding and promotion of the child's health, development and welfare. Or again, the exercise of the right of legal representation is valid in so far as it fulfils the responsibility to act as the child's legal representative, but also only in so far as it safeguards and promotes the child's health, development and welfare. And the parental responsibilities are owed to a child only in so far as their fulfilment is practicable and in the interests of the child.[1] It follows that in determining whether a claimed right is being validly exercised, a two-stage analysis must be adopted: (1) is the claimed right expressly listed in section 2(1) or can it be traced to one of the rights listed there?; and (2) if so, is its exercise directed towards the fulfilment of one or other of the responsibilities listed in section 1(1) without being inconsistent with any? For example, the right of the father recognised at common law to direct the child's religious upbringing exists today as an aspect of the parent's right to control, direct or guide the child's upbringing, but its exercise is now valid only in so far as it is directed towards the responsibility to provide the child with direction and guidance and is not inconsistent with the duty to safeguard and promote the child's health, development and welfare. This approach may be adopted to test the existence of any claimed right or the validity of its exercise.

The responsibility to safeguard and promote the child's health, development and welfare

The fundamental parental obligation is to safeguard and promote the child's **8.22** health, development and welfare.[2] The various parental duties which parents have, although often and conveniently considered separately, are largely subsumed under this heading and it is from this obligation that most of the powers of parents, as necessary for its discharge, flow. The responsibility to safeguard the child's welfare is fundamental in the sense of being both the minimum that is expected of a parent and the most general formulation of the parent's obligations. This responsibility can be traced at least as far back as Erskine's conception of the parent's duty to "preserve and protect" the child and to provide for his or her child "in bed, board and clothing, and all the necessaries of life".[3] But the obligation extends beyond the provision of material support to a positive duty of care and nurture in all things that concern the child's welfare in so far as that is required in accordance with the child's age and understanding. Promotion is, it is conceived, a more active aspect of the duty than safeguarding, and imports encouragement and development and the provision of opportunities as well as protection. Within the terms of section 1(1)(a) are found particular duties. The obligation to promote the child's health clearly imposes a duty to ensure proper

---

[1] s. 1(1).
[2] Children (Scotland) Act 1995, s. 1(1)(a).
[3] Erskine, I, vi, 56.

medical treatment, in its widest sense, as well as a duty to provide a healthy environment in which the child is raised; the obligation to promote the child's development includes a duty to make proper educational provision for the child. Both medical treatment and education are considered below in detail. More generally, the obligation is to ensure that the child's upbringing is such that his or her good health, proper development and appropriate welfare are both protected and enhanced.

8.23   In its more intangible aspects, the duty is usually incapable of legal enforcement. It comprehends, however, a duty to protect the child which if breached in the case of a child under 16 may amount to the criminal offence of neglect.[4] If such breach results in personal injury to the child, it would seem also to be civilly actionable and the child, or any person acting on his or her behalf, has title to sue in respect of parental responsibilities.[5] This is, however, so only in so far as it is practicable and in the interests of the child that the responsibility that was neglected be fulfilled. So a parent is not in breach of this statutory duty when, through illness, incarceration or absence overseas, he or she is unable to safeguard the child's well-being. There are few cases in which children or their legal representatives have sued their own parents for a failure to fulfil their parental responsibilities and the matter is better illustrated in the case of persons having temporary care *in loco parentis* rather than of parents themselves.

Duty of care—liability for negligence

8.24   The duty of care owed by persons who have children in their charge is, apart from criminal neglect, best illustrated by cases on liability for negligence of schoolteachers and authorities responsible for schools. The general principle is that a schoolteacher is bound to take such care of his or her pupils as a reasonably careful and prudent parent would take of his or her own children.[6] That principle which follows from the *in loco parentis* relationship is, it is conceived, applicable to all cases of persons having children in their care. It requires, however, some elaboration, and even modification, according to circumstances. A parent usually attaches great importance to the safety and well-being of his or her children, although he or she will also recognise that as they grow up some risks must be run either because, in a practical sense, risks are inevitable or because they are to be balanced against the damage inherent in overprotection. The general principle may say no more than that schoolteachers and others with children in their care are expected to be guided by the same fundamental consideration. Beyond that it may often be difficult to apply the principle to the particular situations which persons other than parents having children in their care have to face, particularly where a sizeable group of children is concerned. The exigencies of the classroom or the laboratory, even of the gymnasium or the playing field or a children's hostel, may often not be those that a parent ordinarily encounters. The remoteness of the general principle becomes even more marked when the question at issue is not the care required of a person immediately in charge of a child or group of children, but of the care to be shown in the management of a large institution.[7] So, "the standard is that of a reasonably prudent parent judged not in the context of his own home but in that of a school, in other words, a person exhibiting the responsible mental qualities of a prudent

---

[4] Children and Young Persons (Scotland) Act 1937, s. 12(1). See *H v. Lees, D v. Orr*, 1994 S.L.T. 908; *M v. Orr*, 1995 S.L.T. 26; *McF v. Normand*, 1995 S.C.C.R. 380.

[5] Children (Scotland) Act 1995, s. 1(3).

[6] *Williams v. Eady* (1893) 10 T.L.R. 41, *per* Lord Esher M.R. at 42.

[7] *Beaumont v. Surrey County Council* (1968) 66 L.G.R. 580, *per* Geoffrey Lane J.

parent in the circumstances of school life".[8] If, therefore, it is borne in mind that a person who has the care of children should be animated by the same fundamental considerations as a careful and prudent parent, the test for negligence may often appropriately be put in terms reflecting those applicable to other relationships in which a duty of care arises: whether he or she took such care as a reasonable person placed in the circumstances in which he or she was placed would have taken to protect the children in his or her care from reasonably foreseeable harm.

The ambit of the duty of care is as wide as the circumstances demand but **8.25** the matters covered usually fall under one or more of three main heads: safety of premises and equipment, organisation of activities, and supervision. In relation to all of them, account has to be taken of the propensities of children, "the ordinary nature of young boys, their tendency to do mischievous acts, and their propensity to meddle with anything that came in their way".[9]

Safety of premises and equipment

Because the duty flows from the relationship of care and not merely from **8.26** the occupation of premises it may be higher in a question of safety of premises than that incumbent on an occupier under the Occupier's Liability (Scotland) Act 1960.[10] As, however, the Act reformulates the duty of reasonable care the difference may not be material provided that appropriate weight is given to the relationship between the child and the occupier as among the circumstances affecting the duty. A person with children in his or her care may, however, have a duty in respect of the safety of premises although he or she is not the occupier. In the case of schools and other educational establishments under the management of an education authority, there is a further statutory duty to secure that the premises and equipment conform to the standards and requirements laid down in regulations made by the Secretary of State and that they are maintained in such a condition as to conduce to the good health and safety of all persons occupying or frequenting the premises or using the equipment.[11] It has been held on the corresponding words of English legislation that the duty so imposed is absolute and that breach resulting in damage is civilly actionable at the instance of a pupil or other person whom the statutory provision is designed to protect.[12] Injuries arising from holes in the floor of a playshed,[13] from glass panels in a door which proved to be too thin[14] and from a swing door which, because of its weight and the strength of the spring, was unsafe for young children,[15] are among those for which damages have been recovered.

Elements of negligence

What constitutes negligence on the part of those having the care of children **8.27** is a question of degree which may vary according to the age and personal characteristics of the children. To leave a knife accessible to a child of four would be negligence,[16] but in the case of children of 11 it has been held to be

---

[8] *Lyes v. Middlesex County Council* (1962) 61 L.G.R. 443, *per* Edmund Davies J. *Cf. Jacques v. Oxfordshire County Council* (1968) 66 L.G.R. 440, *per* Waller J.

[9] *Williams v. Eady*, above, *per* Lord Esher M.R. at 42.

[10] *Lyes v. Middlesex County Council*, above.

[11] Education (Scotland) Act 1980, s. 19(2).

[12] *Ching v. Surrey County Council* [1910] 1 K.B. 736; *Morris v. Carnarvon County Council* [1910] 1 K.B. 840; *Lyes v. Middlesex County Council*, above; *Reffell v. Surrey County Council* [1964] 1 All E.R. 743.

[13] *Ching v. Surrey County Council*, above.

[14] *Lyes v. Middlesex County Council* and *Reffell v. Surrey County Council*, above.

[15] *Morris v. Carnarvon County Council*, above.

[16] *Williams v. Eady* (1893) 10 T.L.R. 41, *per* Cave J.

sufficient precaution that knives were kept in an unlocked cupboard.[17] Where the use of articles to which a degree of danger attaches is necessary for some educational purpose, appropriate safeguards should be taken and dangerous substances, when not in use, should be kept in a secure place having in mind the tendency of children to do mischievous acts and their propensity to meddle with anything that comes their way.[18] A distinction is, however, to be made between things dangerous in themselves[19] in which case the greater the danger the higher the standard of diligence the law exacts,[20] and things, in ordinary use, which are not in their essential character dangerous but become a source of danger only on the occurrence of certain circumstances of negligence or mischance.[21] In the latter case there is negligence in not taking safeguards only if an occurrence occasioning danger could reasonably have been foreseen.[22] What is required in the way of supervision is to be measured by what harm may reasonably be anticipated if supervision is not exercised. The standard is, however, high. "It is a headmaster's duty, bearing in mind the known propensities of boys and indeed girls between 11 and 17 or 18, to take all reasonable and proper steps to prevent any of the pupils under his care from suffering injury from inanimate objects, from the action of their fellow pupils, or from a combination of the two."[23] A schoolteacher is not, however, expected to exercise such a degree of care that his pupils could never get into mischief.[24] It is reasonable, not constant, supervision that is required,[25] and the test for professional negligence laid down in *Hunter v. Hanley*[26] has been applied to schoolteachers.[27] What is reasonable is, of course, a question of circumstances and there may be circumstances in which only constant supervision could meet the test of reasonableness. It has, however, been held not to be necessary to provide continuous supervision for a group of 50 children aged between about six and 10 while in the playground during a school break,[28] and not to be negligence to leave the supervision of well-disciplined pupils to prefects,[29] nor to fail to assist every child in a school gymnasium to perform every exercise[30] nor to fail to supervise children leaving the school premises at the end of the day when this was not a standard procedure.[31] Physical activities that can ordinarily be carried out without serious injury are not to be regarded as dangerous merely because an accident can happen,[32] but there will be negligence where a person in charge of such an activity does not act promptly to avert a danger of which he or she should be aware.[33] Failure to observe a possibly dangerous happening does not,

---

[17] *Suckling v. Essex County Council, The Times*, Jan. 27, 1955.

[18] *Williams v. Eady*, above.

[19] *ibid.* (bottles of phosphorous in a conservatory).

[20] *Sullivan v. Creed* [1904] 2 I.R. 317, *per* Gibson J, cited with approval in *Wray v. Essex County Council* [1936] 3 All E.R. 97.

[21] *Chilvers v. London County Council* (1916) 80 J.P. 246; *Dixon v. Roper, The Times*, Feb. 3, 1922; *Wray v. Essex County Council*, above.

[22] *Wray v. Essex County Council*, above.

[23] *Beaumont v. Surrey County Council* (1968) 66 L.G.R. 580.

[24] *Ricketts v. Erith Borough Council* [1943] 2 All E.R. 629.

[25] *Clark v. Monmouthshire County Council* (1954) 52 L.G.R. 246.

[26] 1955 S.C. 200.

[27] *Scott v. Lothian Regional Council*, 1999 Rep. L.R. 15.

[28] *Ricketts v. Erith Borough Council*, above. *Cf. Price v. Carnarvon County Council, The Times* Feb. 11, 1960.

[29] *Jacques v. Oxfordshire County Council* (1968) 66 L.G.R. 440.

[30] *McDougall v. Strathclyde Regional Council*, 1996 S.L.T. 1124.

[31] *Wilson v. Governors of the Sacred Heart Roman Catholic School* [1998] 1 F.L.R. 663.

[32] *Jones v. London County Council* (1932) 96 J.P. 371.

[33] *Gibbs v. Barking Corporation* [1936] 1 All E.R. 115.

however, necessarily indicate negligence on the part of a person in charge of a group of children,[34] nor is there negligence in such a person failing to prevent an unexpected and unforseen misfortune.[35] Compliance with a general practice successfully followed over a period of years affords evidence that there was no negligence.[36] Although legislation on safety in factories does not apply to schools, failure to meet the requirements of that legislation may be an indication of negligence in the safety arrangements made by persons responsible for comparable technical processes in schools.[37]

The right of residence

Custody and residence compared

In order to enable the parent to fulfil his or her parental responsibilities in relation to the child, and in particular the obligation to safeguard and promote the child's health, development and welfare, the parent has the right to have the child living with him or her, or otherwise to regulate the child's residence.[38] There are obvious parallels between this right and the common law right of custody, and while the right of residence is clearly more limited than the right of custody, the change to the law introduced by the Children (Scotland) Act 1995 from custody to residence is, perhaps, less radical than is sometimes assumed. Both are founded in obligation. "Custody" means keeping or guarding, though the obligation which the custodian of a child owed was not merely to preserve the child in life and keep him or her from harm but more positively to care for him or her and promote his or her welfare. With that gloss, the stress on keeping and preserving as a matter of obligation was apt, and remains so today. Questions of the custody of children most often arose from claims made by potential custodians and envisaged powers to be exercised; and the lawful custodian, of course, had certain powers over the person of the child and the right to exercise these powers to the exclusion of others. But the primary character of custody, in contemplation of the law, was as a source of obligation. He who had the custody of a child thereby undertook obligations to which such rights and powers as he had were ancillary. So too with residence in the modern law: the right to have the child living with the parent or otherwise to regulate the child's residence exists in order to enable the parent to fulfil the parental responsibility to safeguard and promote the child's health, development and welfare, and to provide the child with direction and guidance. **8.28**

In English law custody, prior to the coming into force of the Children Act 1989, was a term of wide scope and some ambiguity. Although capable of a more restricted meaning, it may have gone so far as to embrace the "whole bundle of rights" and powers vested in a parent or guardian.[39] In Scots law, on the other hand, the amplitude of the concept of parental power, derived from the ancient *patria potestas*, and the institutions of tutory and curatory, obviated the need for such a wide-ranging concept. There is no Scottish authority for giving to custody anything other than its ordinary meaning. It was the "cure and keiping" or "keiping and custodie" or simply "keiping" of the person to which the old cases refer.[40] The rights and powers which it conferred were, therefore, **8.29**

---

[34] *Clarke v. Bethnall Green Borough Council* (1939) 55 T.L.R. 519.
[35] *Gow v. Glasgow Education Authority*, 1922 S.C. 260.
[36] *Wright v. Cheshire County Council* [1952] 2 All E.R. 789.
[37] *Butt v. Inner London Education Authority* (1968) 66 L.G.R. 379.
[38] s. 2(1)(a).
[39] *Hewer v. Bryant* [1969] 3 All E.R. 578, *per* Sachs J. at 585, approved by Lord Scarman in *Gillick v. West Norfolk and Wisbech Area Health Authority* [1985] 3 W.L.R. 830 at 854.
[40] See the cases cited in Balfour, CXXIII to CXXXI, pp. 336–338, *sub nom*, "of keiping of minoris persounis".

those of physical control and the regulation of everyday life which goes with that control, and it was not strictly necessary to imply anything further. However, the common understanding of custody, influenced in all likelihood by a mistaken assumption that the Scottish concept was no different from the English, was that it carried with it the full gamut of rights and powers in relation to the upbringing of the child—these to be exercised, many thought, exclusively and certainly to the exclusion of any losing party in a custody dispute. The gradual weakening of the concepts of tutory and curatory gave strength to this perception of custodial rights. Tutory and curatory have now developed into the more limited responsibility of legal representation[41] and the replacement of custody with residence has served to clarify that the essence of the right, in so far as it is divorced from the corresponding responsibility, is little more than to determine where the child is physically to be.

The nature of the right of residence

8.30   The right of residence, like the other parental rights, does not exist independently of the parental responsibilities. No one, not even a parent, can have, for the purpose of judicial proceedings, a right of residence which, if it were to receive effect, would conflict with the child's welfare.[42] Except where there is, by the standard of the child's welfare, an even balance among the claimants all questions of "right" to have the child living with the claimant, whether parent or otherwise, are altogether excluded. That is true not only of questions between parents *inter se* but also of questions between parents and strangers.[43] Moreover, in a question between parents, where both have automatic vested rights,[44] the effect of equating the parents is that there is no priority attaching to one parent rather than the other from the standpoint of residual right. There are, however, two, and only two, senses in which it may be permissible to speak of a right inherent in a parent to have the child living with him or her. First, there is a right of residence which is prima facie in the sense that, where there is no court order regulating residence, the right that arises by operation of section 3(1)(a) (for mothers) or section 3(1)(b) (for fathers) of the Children (Scotland) Act 1995 is entitled to legal respect and protection unless, and until, there is a court order to the contrary. Mothers always do and fathers may have such prima facie rights (unless their parental responsibilities and parental rights have been removed by legal process, for example, by an adoption order or an order made under section 11 or section 86 of the 1995 Act). One practical application of the recognition of such prima facie rights is in relation to the Hague Convention on International Child Abduction, under which a child will be ordered to be returned to the jurisdiction of his or her habitual residence if removed from that jurisdiction in breach of the parent's right to determine the child's place of residence.[45] In a question, however, between parents, or between parents' nominees, neither party has a higher right than the other pending resolution of the dispute by judicial decision. Secondly, in a question between parents and others, parents have a right to be preferred where there is an even

---

[41] See below, paras 5.29–5.31.

[42] Thus the case of *Macpherson v. Leishman* (1887) 14 R. 780 is no longer good law. In that case the "right" of a mother to custody of her illegitimate child was enforced, notwithstanding that the judges considered this to be against the interests of the child.

[43] *J v. C* [1970] A.C. 668, which, as a decision on the interpretation of a U.K. statute (the Guardianship of Infants Act 1925) must, it is submitted, be taken as superseding earlier Scottish authorities to the contrary. See *Cheetham v. Glasgow Corporation*, 1972 S.L.T. (Notes) 50. See also *Osborne v. Matthan (No. 2)*, 1998 S.L.T. 1264.

[44] Under s. 3(1)(a) and (b) of the Children (Scotland) Act 1995.

[45] See below, paras 11.19 *et seq.*

balance from the standpoint of the child's welfare between them and the other claimant or claimants. That was the effect of the common law as amended by the Guardianship Act 1973 and, to that very limited extent, is unaffected by the Children (Scotland) Act 1995. On the same principle, after the death of both parents, the nominee of either of them is probably entitled to a preference if the balance from the standpoint of the child's welfare is even as between that person and other claimants who are not nominees. It is, however, necessary to emphasise that the rights of parents or their nominees, even in the very limited sense under discussion, are entirely subordinated to a consideration of the welfare of the child and for this reason it may be misleading and unhelpful to express the principle in terms of "right". Although the terms of section 3 of the Children (Scotland) Act 1995 lend support to the view that it will normally be assumed that a child will benefit from living with his or her parent, the validity of that assumption in any particular case must be tested by reference to the evidence.[46] There is no rule of law which gives the parent a preference if that does not consist with the welfare of the child. Indeed the law is rather the reverse; the child's welfare must prevail against any consideration which is seriously in conflict with it.

Apart from welfare considerations, there is one other constaint to the exercise **8.31** of the parental right to regulate a child's residence. While the general rule is that where two or more persons have parental rights they may each exercise them without the consent of the other,[47] this is qualified by the additional rule that no parent is entitled to remove a child habitually resident in Scotland from, or to retain the child outwith, the United Kingdom without the consent of the other parent, where they both have and are exercising either the right to regulate the child's residence or the right to maintain personal relations and direct contact with the child on a regular basis.[48] This provision is not as broad as may have been intended, for it is limited in its terms to the case of two parents with parental responsibilities and parental rights. It prevents removal abroad by one parent against the wishes of the other (or, at least, renders such removal unlawful and "wrongful"[49]) but does not cover the situation where two persons have parental responsibilities and parental rights but only one, or neither, is the child's parent. In that case, each may exercise the power to regulate the child's residence independently of the other,[50] and each may rely on his or her own consent to remove the child from the United Kingdom. Similarly, a third party may remove the child with the consent of one person with parental responsibilities and parental rights even against the wishes of another such person, so long as they are not both parents. The prohibition is without prejudice to any court order, which may provide a remedy to a parent against a guardian or third party, though in many cases such an order will be too late to prevent removal. Court order will more commonly be sought to authorise removal by one parent when the other parent refuses consent.[51] Permanent removal of the child may be permitted by

---

[46] *Osborne v. Matthan (No. 2)* above, *per* Lord President Rodger (referring to the pre-1995 position, though the principle continues to apply today).

[47] s. 2(2).

[48] s. 2(3) and (6). For a discussion of this provision, see Norrie, "The Hague Convention, Rights of Contact, and s. 2(3) and (6) of the Children (Scotland) Act 1995", 1997 S.L.T. (News) 173. If consent is not forthcoming, the child may be removed from the jurisdiction only with the authority of the court, by way of a specific issue order made under s. 11(2) of the 1995 Act. Such an order is made regarding the child's welfare as paramount and not making any order unless it is better for the child that the order be made than that no such order is made at all. As an example (where authority was not granted), see *Fourman v. Fourman*, 1998 Fam. L.R. 98.

[49] For Hague Convention purposes: see Norrie, *sup. cit.*

[50] s. 2(2).

[51] Such order is, presumably, sought as a specific issue order under s. 11(2)(e): see below, para. 9.14.

the court, even in circumstances in which that would frustrate the other parent's ability to fulfil his or her responsibility (which in any case would thereby be rendered impracticable), and to exercise his or her right (which ceases to exist once the responsibility ceases) to maintain personal relations and direct contact with the child.[52]

Other residence rights

8.32   Persons other than parents may sometimes have residual rights of residence. First, where a child has been placed by an adoption agency with a person with a view to his or her being adopted by that person, and the parents and guardians of the child have agreed to the making of the order, such parents or guardians are not entitled to remove the child from the care and possession of the person with whom the child has been placed, without the leave of either the adoption agency or the court.[53] Secondly, while an adoption application is pending in respect of a child having been made by the person with whom the child has had his or her home for the preceding five years, no person may remove the child from the applicant's care and possession except with leave of the court.[54] Thirdly, a local authority which has provided accommodation to a child for more than six months may continue to do so (for a limited period) against the wishes of a person with parental responsibilities and parental rights who is willing and able to provide accommodation for the child.[55] Fourthly, where an application is pending in any court for a residence order in relation to a child who has been in the care and possession of the applicant for at least three years, it is an offence to remove the child from the applicant against the wishes of the applicant without authority of the court or statutory provision.[56] More generally, persons who do not have a specifically recognised legal right of residence, but into whose actual care and control a child has lawfully passed, may, in a question with persons with no better title, be entitled to retain that care and control pending judicial determination on the view that they hold under the licence, express or tacit, of the person with the right to regulate the child's residence or that, in the absence of sufficient cause to the contrary, the status quo should be preserved pending judicial decision. On the latter view, it may be lawful to retain care and control even in a question with a person with a better title if there is immediate danger of serious harm to the child should he or she be removed.[57]

8.33   Prima facie rights of the kind under consideration may be of importance in the extrajudicial resolution of disputes, but by their nature can seldom require consideration in judicial proceedings. They may, however, be relevant where *plagium* is alleged or in other proceedings for the wrongful detention of a child.

---

[52] *Huddart v. Huddart*, 1961 S.C. 393; *Fourman v. Fourman*, above. See also *Johnson v. Francis*, 1982 S.L.T. 285. "Relocation cases" have proved highly problematic in large jurisdictions such as Canada, Australia and the USA. The approach, however, is always the same: the paramount consideration is the child's welfare and it is accepted that this might suffer if the residence parent is prevented from moving outwith commuting distance from a person with the right of contact. See *Poel v. Poel* [1970] 1 WLR 1469; *Tyler v. Tyler* [1989] 2 F.L.R. 158; *Re H (Application to Remove from Jurisdiction)* [1998] 1 F.L.R. 848 (England); *Gordon v. Goertz* (1996) 134 D.L.R. (4th) 321 (Supreme Court of Canada); *Stadniczenko v. Stadniczenko* [1995] N.Z.F.L.R. 493 (New Zealand Court of Appeal); *B v. B* (1997) 21 Fam. L.R. 676 (Full Court of the Family Court of Australia). For a discussion of the last-mentioned case, see Norrie, "The Australian Children (Scotland) Act 1995" (1998) 3 S.L.P.Q. 15.
[53] Adoption (Scotland) Act 1978, s. 27, as substituted by the Children (Scotland) Act 1995, Sched. 21, para. 19.
[54] Adoption (Scotland) Act 1978, s. 28.
[55] Children (Scotland) Act 1995, s. 25: see below, paras 16.07–16.17.
[56] Children Act 1975, s. 51, as amended by the Children (Scotland) Act 1995, Sched. 4, para. 26.
[57] Any person with care or control of a child in fact, whether or not sustained by legal provision, is subject to the responsibility to safeguard the child's health, development and welfare under s. 5 of the Children (Scotland) Act 1995: see above, paras 8.15–8.16.

The child's right to determine his or her own residence

Because of the parent's right under section 2(1)(a) of the Children (Scotland) **8.34**
Act 1995 to regulate the child's residence, which exists until the child is 16, a
child who is under 16 is not free to determine his or her own residence, though
if he or she has capacity to enter into transactions to give effect to an intention
to reside other than where the parent determines, it would seem that the child
might in some circumstances do so. At common law (which contemplated a
custodial regime for all pupil children although some, in the absence of judicial
decree, might not in fact have been subject to custody) it could be said with
some confidence that a pupil child could not choose his or her own residence. A
minor, on the other hand, whose parents were dead could, if he or she were not
the subject of a custody order, determine his or her own place of residence.[58]
The question, therefore, turns on the effect of modern statute, particularly, the
Age of Legal Capacity (Scotland) Act 1991 and the Children (Scotland) Act
1995. Under the former, the position of the child under 16 became in many
respects that of the common law pupil, which might suggest that the pupil's
inability to determine his or her own residence was extended to all children
under 16. It is, however, submitted that this is not so. The inability of pupils
rested on practical as well as legal considerations; today it may in some cases
be practicable for a child below 16 to live away from his or her parents, and the
1991 Act may be open to the interpretation that, in some circumstances, he or
she has the legal capacity to enter into transactions for that purpose.[59] While
conflict between the child's wishes and the parent's right has to be resolved
with regard to the welfare of the child as the paramount consideration, the same
is not true of a conflict between the child's capacity and the parent's rights.
There is logic in holding that when the child attains capacity to choose his or
her own residence the parent loses the right to do so, but that conclusion is
difficult to reconcile with the terms of the 1995 Act. The provision in the 1995
Act[60] whereby a parent's right comes to an end when the child attains capacity—
avoiding thereby any conflict ever arising—is limited to the right to act as the
child's legal representative. In any case, the question of the extent of the parent's
right is in some degree an economic and practical one measured in the light of
the parent's obligations. In considering the child's welfare, the parent must have
regard to the child's reasonable requirements in the way of education or of
following his or her occupation or employment, but the parent is not in all
circumstances bound to follow the child's wishes even where he or she can
afford to do so and the child is mentally mature. The parent's obligation of
aliment is to provide such support as is reasonable in the circumstances having
regard *inter alia* to the needs and resources both of the child and of him or
herself.[61] It is in that context that choice of residence has to be seen. So, often
the child will have little real choice. Where he or she is dependent on his or her
parents the child must accept what the parent provides, either in the family
home or elsewhere, if that is indicated by his or her needs and provided it is
reasonably adequate in the circumstances. If, on the other hand, the child is able
to maintain him or herself, there is authority for the view that the child above
the age of common law pupillarity may even during the parents' lifetime choose

---

[58] *Graham v. Graham* (1780) Mor. 8934.
[59] Nichols suggests that for a child who is afraid of his or her parents to enter into a contract with a
shelter to live there would be a "reasonable transaction commonly entered into" by someone in his
or her circumstances, and therefore one that the child has legal capacity to undertake: "Can They or
Can't They?" 1991 S.L.T. (News) 395 at 397–398. The Children (Scotland) Act 1995 envisages
that a child under 16 has the capacity to seek refuge in local authority accommodation: s. 38.
[60] s. 15(5).
[61] Family Law (Scotland) Act 1985, ss. 1(2) and 4(1).

his or her residence if of sufficient maturity and understanding to do so.[62] There
is nothing in the Age of Legal Capacity (Scotland) Act 1991 which limits this
power.[63] The right conferred on parents of children under 16 by section 2(1)(a)
of the Children (Scotland) Act 1995 does not alter the pre-existing law since
custody was long a right over children under 16.[64] It would follow that if a
child, even when below 16, has the means to live other than with his or her
parent (or is given the means by others), and has the maturity to understand the
consequences of such independence, the parent would not have the right to
insist that the child resides where the parent chooses unless he or she could
show that it was in the interests of the child's welfare that the child's choice
should, despite this maturity, be overridden; the benefits in not frustrating a
mature child's wishes in this or other matters are a relevant consideration in
that welfare judgement. The only remaining problematic case from a legal
standpoint would seem to be that of the child below 16 who has the means to
maintain him or herself but lacks the requisite maturity and understanding to
choose his or her own residence. It would not be "reasonable" (in terms of s.
2(1) of the 1991 Act) for such a child to choose his or her own residence and he
or she would, therefore, lack capacity to do so. Such a case must fall within the
scope of the parental right and the parent may regulate the child's residence in
accordance with his or her general obligation to safeguard and promote the
child's health, development and welfare.

Control, direction and guidance

8.35   Parents have the responsibility to provide the child, in a manner appropriate
to the stage of development of the child, with direction and guidance and in
order to allow them to fulfil this parental responsibility they have the right to
contol, direct or guide the child's upbringing.[65] This responsibility and right
contains within it many of the upbringing duties and powers that were previously
contained within the concepts of custody and tutory. At common law, custody
was generally the right to determine the manner in which the child was brought
up as well as with whom; tutory included the duty to protect the child's welfare.
Both were inextricably connected with, and gave power to direct, the child's
upbringing. Custody was originally a right exercisable only over the pupil child,
and even when custody was extended to all children under the age of 16,[66] it

---

[62] Bankton, I, vi, 1, p. 153 thought that a minor was without qualification free to choose his own
     residence, and that view is followed by More (*Lectures*, p. 87, *Notes on Stair*, C., pp. xxxi and
     xxxii), under reference to *Graham v. Graham*, above, *Marshall v. McDowell* (1741) Mor. 8930
     and *Anstruther v. Murray* (1694) 1 Foutainhall 613, but these are cases in which the father was
     dead and so paternal power was extinguished. More's argument for the minor's freedom to
     marry immediately on the expiry of pupillarity is, however, cogent. Erskine, I, vi, 53, although
     often cited for the contrary view, is consistent with the minor's freedom to leave home and set up
     his own residence. Stair, I, v, 4 and 13 takes a larger view of the parental powers than would now
     be accepted. It is, however, reasonably clear from *Harvey v. Harvey* (1860) 22 D. 1198, *Edgar v.
     Fisher's Trs* (1894) 21 R. 1076 and *Craig v. Greig and McDonald* (1863) 1 M. 1172 that a
     minor's choice of residence was subject to some parental restraint to be exercised in the light of
     the minor's maturity and understanding and with regard to his welfare.
[63] See Nichols, *op. cit.* S. 1(2) of the 1991 Act does not affect the matter because it does no more
     than provide a rule of statutory interpretation and, unlike other provisions of the Act, has no
     bearing on the common law position of the child except in so far as that has been modified by the
     statute.
[64] Custody of Children (Scotland) Act 1939, s. 1; Law Reform (Parent and Child) (Scotland) Act
     1986, s. 8. Prior to the 1939 Act, custody was a right which could be exercised only over pupil
     children.
[65] Children (Scotland) Act 1995, ss. 1(1)(b) and 2(1)(b).
[66] Custody of Children (Scotland) Act 1939, s. 1.

remained a right far more apt for the pupil child than the minor child. In relation to the latter there was no right of dominion and so the power had not the comprehensive, and, within the welfare principle, absolute character that it had in the case of a pupil. Although there continued to be some right of control, the emphasis was not on control but on counsel and aid. Curatory, the restricted form of guardianship applicable to children over the age of puberty, was essentially an advisory office. The extension of the capacity, or rather lack of it, of the pupil child to all children under the age of 16,[67] together with the extension of the right of custody[68] and now the right to control, direct or guide to parents of all children below the age of 16,[69] might be taken to extend the dominion custody gave over pupil children to all children under 16; but it is submitted that this would misinterpret the effects of both the 1991 Act and the 1995 Act. The 1991 Act extends the child's lack of capacity rather than the parent's dominion. And the statutory formulation under the 1995 Act of the parental right to control, direct or guide expressly contains within it the qualification that parental power diminishes as the child grows older: the right may be exercised only "in a manner appropriate to the stage of development of the child".[70] This was also implicit in custody, which had been described as "a dwindling right which the courts will hesitate to enforce against the wishes of the child, the older he is. It starts with a right of control and ends with little more than advice".[71] This was true for Scots, no less than for English, law, at least in the case of children over pupillarity. Today, the right to counsel and aid the child or, in modern terms, to provide guidance to the child, which characterised the custodial right over the minor child before 1991 may be all that remains of the parental right to control, direct and guide a particular child who has acquired the mental maturity, practical ability and in some respects the legal capacity to determine his or her own lifestyle. This may perhaps best be illustrated in relation to religious upbringing: in the early years of childhood a parent has the right (subject to the normal welfare qualification) to control and direct the religious observances of the child, but in later years (the commencement of which cannot be subject to strict legal rule) the religious beliefs of the child are a matter for the child him or herself. The parent may provide guidance on this matter but for practical more than legal reasons is unable to exercise control. This is also, though for different reasons, the case with medical treatment: the parent may decide, subject to the child's welfare, when the child cannot decide himself, but when the child acquires legal capacity to give personal consent to medical treatment the parent's right becomes little more than one to advise.[72] Custody was, therefore, and the right to control, direct or guide is, a diminishing right whose content dwindles as the

---

[67] Age of Legal Capacity (Scotland) Act 1991, s. 1(2).
[68] Custody of Children (Scotland) Act 1939, s. 1; Law Reform (Parent and Child) (Scotland) Act 1986, s. 8.
[69] Children (Scotland) Act 1995, s. 2(7).
[70] The responsibility and right to provide the child with direction and guidance may be traced to the UN Convention on the Rights of the Child, Art. 5 of which obliges States Parties to respect the responsibilities, rights and duties of parents and others "to provide, in a manner consistent with the evolving capacities of the child, appropriate direction and guidance in the exercise by the child of the rights recognised in the present Convention". Implicit, therefore, in the parent's obligation to direct and guide is the recognition that the child may make independent decisions but, due to his or her inexperience and lack of knowledge, will need assistance in making these decisions.
[71] *per* Lord Denning M.R. in *Hewer v. Bryant* [1969] 3 All E.R. 578 at 582, approved in *Gillick v. West Norfolk and Wisbech Area Health Authority* [1985] 3 W.L.R. 830, per Lord Fraser at 843.
[72] The right to advise does not include the right to be consulted in all cases: see Norrie, *Family Planning Practice and the Law* (1991), pp. 102–105; *contra*, Thomson, "The Gillick Case and Parental Rights in Scots Law: Another View", 1985 S.L.T. (News) 223.

child grows older and acquires personal beliefs and philosophies and the practical ability to put them into effect by adopting their own lifestyle. Scots law no longer adopts, if it ever, in truth, did, a strict dichotomy between full dominion before and minimal control after puberty. In the case of real dispute between the parent and the child, concerning some aspect of his or her upbringing, either may apply to the court for an order under section 11 of the Children (Scotland) Act 1995, but in that case, as we will see later, the matter is not determined by analysing whose "right" is greater, but rather by the court's obligation to give priority to the interests of the child as the paramount consideration.[73]

8.36   It is to be noted that the terms of the right as specified in section 2(1)(b) are different from the terms of the corresponding responsibility as specified in section 1(1)(b). The right is to "control" as well as to direct and guide, while the responsibility is limited to direction and guidance. And the right is specifically to control, direct and guide the child's upbringing, while the responsibility is to provide direction and guidance to the child him or herself. However, given the interrelation between all the rights and all the responsibilities adverted to earlier,[74] it is unlikely that these terminological inconsistencies make any practical difference. A further peculiarity is that the responsibility to provide direction lasts until the child reaches the age of 16 (as does all the parental rights) while the responsibility (but not the right) to provide guidance lasts until the child reaches the age of 18.[75] There is a difference between direction and guidance in that the former imports command while the latter imports advice. The duty to provide advice in general may well continue to have legal content even after the right to provide advice in relation to the child's upbringing has come to an end. In many cases of professional negligence, liability has been based on a failure to provide appropriate advice in circumstances in which there was a duty to do so[76] and it may be that an analogous claim is now open to children who suffer due to their own inexperienced decisions, made as a result of a failure of their parents in the parental responsibility to provide them with appropriate guidance.[77] The standard of appropriate advice to be given by parents is, one assumes, the standard of the reasonable parent in the circumstances of the actual parties.

Contact
8.37   If the child is not living with the parent, the parent has the responsibility and the right to maintain personal relations and direct contact with the child on a regular basis.[78] This is the modern manifestation of, but is by no means equivalent to, the common law right of access. Contact is as much an obligation on the part of the parents as it is their right, and failure in the obligation may have legal consequences beyond indicating to the court in a section 11 application wherein the welfare of the child lies. So, for example, the persistent failure on the part of

---

[73] Children (Scotland) Act 1995, s. 11(7)(a).

[74] Above, para. 8.02.

[75] Children (Scotland) Act 1995, s. 1(2).

[76] *Sidaway v. Bethlem Royal Hospital* [1985] 1 AC 871; *Moyes v. Lothian Health Board*, 1990 SLT 444; *Cosgrove v. Lothian Health Board*, March 9, 1990; *McFarlane v. Tayside Health Board*, 1998 S.L.T. 304. Though these cases all involved medical negligence, the principle is not limited to that situation.

[77] A 16-year-old child may, for example, enter into a contract which is disadvantageous without being "prejudicial" in the sense that would allow its setting aside under s. 3 of the Age of Legal Capacity (Scotland) Act 1991. In that circumstance a failure on the part of the parent to advise against the contract might open him or her to liability to the child for breach of statutory duty.

[78] Children (Scotland) Act 1995, ss. 1(1)(c) and 2(1)(c).

a parent who is not living with the child to maintain personal relations and direct contact with the child on a regular basis provides the court with a ground upon which to dispense with that person's agreement to the child's adoption[79] or to the making of a parental responsibilities order.[80] And if the child is being provided with residential accommodation in a hospital or nursing home and has had no parental contact for a period of three months, the body providing the accommodation must inform the local authority who must then determine whether to exercise any of their functions under Part II of the Children (Scotland) Act 1995.[81]

The responsibility and right of contact is based on the assumption that it is a **8.38** benefit to the child that he or she maintain links with both parents[82] and it gives effect to the right of the child, recognised by the UN Convention on the Rights of the Child,[83] to maintain personal relations and direct contact with both his or her parents. Like residence, contact is a concept of both fact and of law. It is a concept of fact since clearly all children have and may benefit from regular contact with persons other than those subject to the legal responsibility and enjoying the legal right of contact, and it is a concept of law in that an enforceable legal obligation and recognised right is vested in some people. In the latter context it is sometimes convenient, to avoid ambiguity, to speak not simply of contact but of the parental responsibility and parental right of contact. It is the legal responsibility and right that is governed by sections 1 and 2 of the 1995 Act, though both the legal and the factual concept can be subject to an order under section 11[84]; contact in fact, though not the parental responsibility and parental right of contact, might be regulated under another Part of the Act,[85] though such regulation does not create the parental responsibility and parental right of contact as understood in this legal sense.[86] It is with the legal

---

[79] Adoption (Scotland) Act 1978, s. 16(2)(c)(ii).

[80] Children (Scotland) Act 1995, s. 86(2)(b)(iii).

[81] *ibid.* s. 36.

[82] *Sanderson v. McManus*, 1997 S.L.T. 629 (though that case is *not* authority for the view that this is a presumption that affects the onus of proof); *Donnelly v. Green*, 1998 Fam. L.R. 12; *Davidson v. Smith*, 1998 Fam. L.R. 21. In the last-mentioned case the Second Division said this: "[the sheriff] was entitled and indeed bound to take account of the fact that it is normally in the best interests of a child to maintain contact and relations with the natural parent with whom the child is no longer living. That may be judged as a benefit without the need for evidence from experts or otherwise".

[83] Art. 9(3): "States Parties shall respect the right of the child who is separated from one or both parents to maintain personal relations and direct contact with both parents on a regular basis, except if it is contrary to the child's best interests." Art. 2 of the Convention requires that this right be respected irrespective of the child's or the parent's sex or marital status. By limiting the responsibility to fathers who are or have been married to the mother of their child, s. 3 of the 1995 Act is a direct infringement of Art. 9(3).

[84] See below, paras 9.11–9.13.

[85] The sheriff in making a child assessment order under s. 55 requiring a child to be kept in a specified place may attach directions "as to the contact which the child shall be allowed to have with any other person" (s. 55(5)); the sheriff in making a child protection order under s. 57 may give a direction as to the contact between the child and parent, person with parental responsibilities, or any other specified person or class of person (s. 58(1)); the children's hearing in making or varying a supervision requirement may attach a condition regulating the contact between the child and any specified person or class of person (s. 70(5)(b)); and the sheriff in making an exclusion order may make an order regulating the contact between the child and the named person (s. 77(3)(f)). In addition, a court making an adoption order may make the order subject to such terms and conditions as it thinks fit (Adoption (Scotland) Act 1978, s. 12(6)), which might include conditions relating to contact (*Re C (A Minor) (Adoption Order: Conditions)* [1989] 1 A.C. 1).

[86] So, for example, a person who acquires what might be described as a right to have contact with a child under any of the provisions mentioned in n. 85 above does not by that order alone acquire the right to consent to the child being removed outwith the United Kingdom under s. 2(3) and (6); nor the right to be consulted under s. 6(1) by a person with parental responsibilities and parental rights who is making a major decision in relation to the child; nor the right to attend a children's hearing under s. 45(8) or to deny grounds of referral under s. 65(7) or to appeal a decision of the children's hearing under s. 51(1) as a relevant person (defined in s. 93(2)(b) as a person with parental responsibilities or parental rights).

responsibility and right, and its recognition and regulation under Part I, that this chapter is concerned: judicial regulation of contact in fact by provisions other than those in Part I is dealt with in appropriate places elsewhere. There remains room for confusion, however, since the ordinary factual meaning of "contact" is reflected in the terms of sections 1(1)(c) and 2(1)(c) which describe the legal concept. It is clear both from judicial orders regulating contact on terms which envisage the child's being taken away by, or even residing for short periods with, the person entitled to contact, and with the statutory reference to maintaining personal relations, that a right of contact may extend beyond the visiting of the child which the ordinary meaning would suggest. This is true no less for the right of contact which is unsupported by court order. The lack of precise definition seems to have given rise to little practical difficulty. In a broad sense the meaning of "contact" is well understood and the terms of a court order, or of agreement between the parties, will afford more specific information in the circumstances of a particular case. There remains some vagueness, particularly on the relation between the right of contact and the parental responsibilities, though it is unlikely that the right to contact alone implies anything other than the power to fulfil the corresponding parental responsibility to maintain personal relations and direct contact with the child. In particular, a person with no other parental right in respect of the child than the right of contact probably has no responsibility to promote the child's development except that, if he or she has the factual care and control of the child during a period of contact, he or she will have the responsibility to safeguard the child's health, development and welfare. That responsibility comes, however, from section 5 of the 1995 Act[87] rather than from section 1.

Access and contact compared

8.39   Common law access could be understood only in terms of its relation to common law custody. Access was something much weaker than custody: it was "the lesser and more restricted right" compared with the greater right of custody.[88] It was in essence no more than a burden or restriction on the custodian's right of control over the child.[89] Indeed, as a "right" it only really came into existence through court order as a qualification to custody.[90] This cannot be said in relation to contact, which is a right that exists in the statute independently of either a court order under section 11(2)(d) or the right of residence recognised by section 2(1)(a).[91] The responsibility and right of contact, recognised under sections 1(1)(c) and 2(1)(c) are activated not by court order but by the fact that the parent is not living with the child. When the parent is living with the child the responsibility and right to maintain personal relations and direct contact with the child is subsumed into the more general right of residence. The independent responsibility and right of contact arises whenever and for whatever reason the parent and child are no longer living together and it may exist alongside

---

[87] "It shall be the responsibility of a person who has attained the age of sixteen years and who has care or control of a child under that age, but in relation to him... does not have the parental responsibility mentioned in section 1(1)(a) of this Act [*i.e.* the responsibility to safeguard and promote the child's health, development and welfare], to do what is reasonable in all the circumstances to safeguard the child's health, development and welfare."

[88] *Stokes v. Stokes*, 1965 S.C. 246 at 251, *per* Lord President Clyde.

[89] "Access is a modification of a party's legal right to have care and control of a child", *per* the Second Division in *D v. Strathclyde Regional Council*, 1985 S.L.T. 114 at 116. See also the sheriff's judgment in *Girvan v. Girvan*, 1988 S.L.T. 866 at 869J–K.

[90] *Porchetta v. Porchetta*, 1986 S.L.T. 105. See further, the 1st edition of this book, at pp. 229–231. See also Thomson, "Whither the Right of Access?", 1989 S.L.T. (News) 109.

[91] See further, Clive, *Husband and Wife* (4th ed.), pp. 499–500.

other rights such as residence. There is nothing in sections 1 or 2 to suggest that a parent with the right to regulate the child's residence may not also have, in appropriate factual circumstances, the responsibility and right of contact: a child may, for example, be sent to live with a grandparent as an exercise of the parental right to determine where the child is to live and in that situation the parent will certainly remain subject to the duty to maintain personal relations and direct contact with the child. Before the 1995 Act it made no sense to say that the custodian had a right of access; now a residence parent may well have a responsibility and right of contact.

Exercise of the right of contact
The responsibility and right of contact qualifies, as access did, the powers **8.40** of the parent with the right to determine the child's residence, in particular that person's responsibility to control, direct and guide the child's upbringing, in so far as he or she has an obligation not to interfere with the fulfilment of another person's responsibility of contact. This, of course, is always subject to the assumption that contact is for the welfare of the child, and the onus will be on the residence parent wishing to deny or restrict contact to prove that it is against the child's interests. The residence parent must exercise his or her rights in a way that admits of contact and that must often mean that he or she temporarily yields immediate control. Moreover, if there is a court order regulating contact, the residence parent is obliged to persuade and encourage the child to see the person entitled to contact and allow contact to take place in the way for which the order provides.[92] If he or she fails to do so and, more seriously, if he or she seeks to influence the child against contact, the residence parent may be guilty of contempt of court. He or she is not, however, obliged physically to force the child to enable contact to take place.[93] Conversely, the right of contact should not be exercised in such a way as unreasonably restricts the residence parent's freedom, provided that he or she acts consistently with the welfare of the child. In the event of dispute between the person with the responsibility and right of contact and the person with the right of residence, the welfare of the child is, as always, the court's paramount consideration and the court must not make any order unless it considers that it would be better for the child that the order be made than that none should be made at all.[94] Accordingly, a contact order may be varied even to the extent that it is in effect recalled, if a change of residence consistent with the child's welfare means that it is no longer practicable for it to receive effect; and that is so even if, as a result, the child is taken outwith the jurisdiction.[95]

Effect of agreement
Although contact is often, and conveniently, arranged by agreement between **8.41** the parents, any agreement about contact cannot be enforced unless it satisfies both the welfare test and the "no-order presumption" contained in section 11(7) of the 1995 Act. Moreover, just as, at common law, any agreement by a parent (or, it is submitted, by any other lawful custodian) to surrender custody was revocable, so any agreement to burden the residence parent's rights with contact is, by parity of reasoning, revocable. Although, therefore, agreement may be relevant background it can never in itself be a sufficient basis for an enforceable right of contact. Though a person with parental responsibilities and parental

---

[92] *Brannigan v. Brannigan*, 1979 S.L.T. (Notes) 73; *Blance v. Blance*, 1978 S.L.T. 74.
[93] *ibid.*
[94] Children (Scotland) Act 1995, s. 11(7).
[95] *Huddart v. Huddart*, 1961 S.C. 393. See also *Johnson v. Francis*, 1982 S.L.T. 285.

rights is permitted to arrange for some or all of them to be fulfilled or exercised on his or her behalf, including by the other parent,[96] the inherently personal nature of the responsibility and right to maintain direct contact and personal relations with the child on a regular basis suggests that this particular responsibility and right cannot be so delegated. If this is so, then a consequence is that a parent's agreement to the making of an adoption order or a parental responsibilities order can be dispensed with if he or she fails to maintain personal relations even although he or she has arranged for some other person to do so.[97]

Legal representation

8.42   The parent or guardian of a child who has parental responsibilities and parental rights has the responsibility and the right to act as the child's legal representative.[98] This matter is examined in detail in a later chapter.[99]

SECONDARY PARENTAL RESPONSIBILITIES AND PARENTAL RIGHTS

Introduction

8.43   The responsibilities and rights considered so far have been those which are expressly mentioned in sections 1 and 2 of the Children (Scotland) Act 1995. These sections are, however, broad enough in their terms to contain other responsibilities and rights than those specifically referred to. Because there are no parental responsibilities or parental rights other than those drawn from the Children (Scotland) Act 1995 or other statutory provision,[1] any right which a parent claims to exercise must be contained in such statutory provision and its exercise must, as explained above,[2] be directed towards the achievement of one of the parental responsibilities expressly listed in section 1. The most important of the parental responsibilities and parental rights which are not expressly mentioned in sections 1 and 2 are examined below.

Education

Parental power to determine education

8.44   An important aspect of the parental responsibility to promote the child's development, and the responsibility and right to provide direction and guidance, is to ensure that the child receives a suitable education[3]; this carries the right to determine the form that the education of a child under 16 is to take. So the parent may choose whether the child is to be educated within the state system, or, if he or she has the means to afford it, by other provision amounting to efficient education. As long as his or her choice meets the requirements of the Education Acts, is consistent with the promotion of the child's health, development and welfare, and is suitable to the child's needs and position in life, it cannot be challenged. Within these constraints the parent may choose what kind of education the child is to receive. The older the child is, however, the more the child's own wishes and aspirations are to be taken into account.

---

[96] s. 3(5).
[97] s. 86(2)(b)(iii) of the 1995 Act and s. 16(2)(c)(iii) of the Adoption (Scotland) Act 1978 permits dispensation on this ground.
[98] Children (Scotland) Act 1995, ss. 1(1)(d) and 2(1)(d).
[99] See below, Chap. 15.
[1] Children (Scotland) Act 1995, ss. 1(4) and 2(5).
[2] Above, para. 8.02.
[3] See UN Convention on the Rights of the Child, Arts 28 and 29.

This is because the more mature the child is the greater the weight that is properly to be accorded to his or her wishes within the context of the welfare principle. In addition, choice of education is a "major decision" in the fulfilment of parental responsibilities, with the result that the parent has an obligation to have regard so far as practicable to the views (if he or she wishes to express them) of the child concerned, taking account of the child's age and maturity (a child 12 years of age or more being presumed to be of sufficient age and maturity to form a view).[4] Clearly, however, where the child's wishes make demands on the financial support of parents, their reasonableness from that standpoint will be a critical factor in a reconciliation with parental choice; and it is noteworthy that the governing legislation dealing with state provision for school education is concerned to respect parental choice rather than the wishes of the child.[5]

Parental obligation to provide education

The exercise of parental power in determining a child's education is closely related to the question of whether there is a common law duty to provide education and to the duty of aliment on which that question largely turns. In an early case "it occurred to the court that the *patria potestas* is such, that a peer may breed his son a cobbler, and after putting him in business with a competent stock is relieved from all further aliment".[6] Even that view postulates a certain, if very limited, duty to provide an education in preparation for adult life. Erskine, however, put the parental duty higher and, it is thought, more accurately. Among parental duties he includes giving children "an education suitable to their rank, in their younger years".[7] Despite what occurred to the court in *Scot v. Sharp*, just quoted, it has not been much disputed that there is a duty such as Erskine asserts. Controversy has centred rather on whether the duty is legally enforceable or merely imperfect.[8] Erskine considered it to be enforceable. Education was part of the obligation of care, protection and aliment, which was not merely natural, "for if they [the parents] refuse to discharge it, they may be compelled to performance by the civil magistrate, according to their station of life and the measure of their fortune".[9] And it is difficult to see why that should not be so. Contrary views turn not on any special feature of the duty to educate rendering it inherently incapable of enforcement, but on the unassailability of the father's discretion in the exercise of the *patria potestas*.[10] Such views are now obsolete. Essentially the question is one of the extent of the parent's duty of aliment, of whether it extends to the maintenance of a child while he or she is undergoing education and of the provision of the costs of that education. Even at common law the obligation of aliment, although regulated on an economical footing, extended beyond the provision of bare subsistence. It was a question of the relief of want,[11] but want was determined according to the circumstances and condition in life of the claimant.[12] So, Stair juxtaposed the obligation of aliment to the obligation of education. "The main obligations", he says, "are education

8.45

---

[4] Children (Scotland) Act 1995, s. 6(1).
[5] Education (Scotland) Act 1980, s. 28(1).
[6] *Scot v. Sharp* (1759) Mor. 440.
[7] I, vi, 56.
[8] Hume, *Lectures*, Vol. I, p. 219.
[9] Erskine, *ibid*.
[10] Hume, *ibid*.
[11] *Maule v. Maule* (1825) 1 W. & S. 266.
[12] The term "necessity" "has a relative meaning; relative to the situation of the person who is said to be in want. A person who has received the education of a gentleman... would not be placed above the reach of want by getting the relief of a parish pauper": *Thom v. Mackenzie* (1864) 3 M. 177, *per* Lord Justice-Clerk Inglis at 179.

and provision. The education of children consisteth not only in the care and entertainment of them during infancy, but especially in breeding of them for some calling and employment according to their capacity and condition."[13]

8.46   Now, under statute, the obligation of aliment is conceived, more broadly than at common law, in terms of reasonableness in the circumstances having regard to the needs, resources and earning capacities of the parties.[14] That it may extend to the provision by a parent of education for a child is borne out by the extension of the obligation beyond majority to the age of 25 where the child is reasonably and appropriately undergoing instruction at an educational establishment or training for employment or for a trade, profession or vocation.[15] So far as children under school leaving age are concerned any general duty of educational provision is, of course, now supplemented and largely superseded by the specific requirements of the Education Acts. For such children, the statutory requirements will, it is submitted, usually provide the measure of what is required because, within the bounds of reasonableness, the parent is entitled to discharge his or her duty in an economical fashion and it will be only in an exceptional case, if at all, that education within the state system can be said to be inappropriate to the needs of the child or unreasonable.[16]

Religious upbringing

8.47   The right to determine the religious upbringing of children is part of the parental power which can be traced to the responsibility and right to provide the child with direction and guidance. The place of religious considerations in residence disputes, including such disputes after the death of the parents, is considered elsewhere.[17] Although that is the most likely area of conflict, questions may arise in other contexts. As between parent and child the right of the former is virtually absolute during the early years, though this is so more for practical than for legal reasons. The only exception to that would seem to be where the religious upbringing favoured by the parent can be shown to be detrimental to the child. As with other aspects of parental power, the right does, however, progressively diminish as the child matures in mind and comes to have the ability to make personal judgements. Perhaps in this respect more than in others, the wishes of the child, if based on conviction, are entitled to respect, and in any event are protected by Article 14 of the UN Convention on the Rights of the Child,[18] which obliges States Parties to "respect the right of the child to freedom of thought, conscience and religion". The same article also protects the "rights and duties of the parents... to provide direction to the child in the exercise of his or her rights in a manner consistent with the evolving capacities of the child". The right and duty to provide direction cannot be enlarged into a power of determination. *Religio sequitur patrem* is a maxim grounded in the nature of the *patria potestas* but the father's wishes, with which the mother's must now be put in parity, decline in importance with the weakening of the parental power, and that decline may be more rapid in this matter than in others because of its inseparability from the child's personal convictions. It has been remarked that "in Scotland not a great deal of weight seems to be attached to the question of the father's religion"[19] and in *Kincaid v. Quarrier*,[20] a case that arose after the

---

[13] I, v, 6.
[14] Family Law (Scotland) Act 1985, ss. 1(2) and 4(1).
[15] *ibid.* s. 1(5).
[16] Provision of education is discussed more fully in Chap. 12.
[17] Below, paras 10.29 *et seq.*
[18] 28 *International Legal Materials* 1448, adopted Nov. 20, 1989, ratified by the U.K. Dec. 16, 1991.
[19] Fraser, p. 190.
[20] (1896) 23 R. 676.

parent's death, the most that Lord Kyllachy was prepared to say was: "It may be—I express no opinion to the contrary—that *prima facie* the father's religion is the religion in which a child should be brought up."[21] What was then said of the father must now of course be said equally of the mother. In disputes that reach the court the question is to be decided with regard to the welfare of the child as the paramount consideration,[22] but if the dispute is purely about religious upbringing and no other interests are affected the application of the welfare principle is attended with difficulties which are examined in detail elsewhere.[23] Where the dispute is between parents, no preference can, in principle, be given to either the father or the mother, although the particular facts of the case, such as the greater interest shown by one parent in the child's religious upbringing may, of course, afford a ground of preference. An agreement by a parent to give up his or her rights in relation to a child's religious upbringing is unenforceable, as is the case with agreements to surrender any aspect of parental responsibility or right, unless it forms part of a separation agreement, and even then it will not be enforced if it will not be for the benefit of the child to give effect to it; but such an agreement may afford evidence of the parent's attitude. Where other aspects of the child's welfare are not in issue a high premium will be put on continuity of religious upbringing and on the wishes of the older child. Here, perhaps more than in any other area, if a dispute is brought before the court the no-order principle might aptly be invoked: apart from an order designed to protect the child's right of freedom of religion from interference by parents or others, it is difficult to visualise a case in which it would be better for the child that a court order be made governing his or her religious observances than that none should be made at all.

Medical treatment
    Parental duty in relation to the child's medical treatment can readily be traced **8.48** to the parental responsibility to safeguard and promote the child's health, development and welfare,[24] but it is less apparent which parental right gives the parent power to fulfil that duty. Providing the child with medical treatment is not an aspect of regulating the child's residence, nor of maintaining personal relations and direct contact with the child. And it can only with some awkwardness be described as an aspect of the right to control, direct or guide the child's upbringing. The appropriate parental right is, it is submitted, that of legal representation. References in Part I of the Children (Scotland) Act 1995 to a person acting as a child's legal representative include references to that person giving consent to any transaction,[25] "transaction" being a "transaction having legal effect".[26] To give consent to medical treatment is to perform a transaction having legal effect since it provides the medical practitioner with a defence to what would otherwise amount to an assault. A child who lacks capacity to give personal consent requires that act to be performed on his or her behalf and juridical acts are performed on behalf of incapable children by their legal representatives.[27] That medical consent is an aspect of legal representation is implicit in the terms of section 5 of the Children (Scotland) Act 1995, for there is it provided that a person who does not have the parental right of legal representation may nevertheless, if he or she has care or control of a child, give

---

[21] (1896) 23 R. 676 at 681.
[22] Children (Scotland) Act 1995, s. 11(7).
[23] Below, paras 10.29 *et seq.*
[24] s. 1(1)(a).
[25] s. 15(5).
[26] s. 15(1), referring to the definition given in s. 9 of the Age of Legal Capacity (Scotland) Act 1991.
[27] See further, below, Chap 15.

consent to the child's surgical, medical or dental treatment or procedure in certain circumstances.[28] This aspect of legal representation must be exercised in such a manner as safeguards and promotes the child's health, development and welfare.

The mentally immature child

8.49   Beyond the statutory guidance that now exists, there is little in Scottish case law to indicate how the parental power in relation to medical treatment is to be exercised over a child who does not have legal capacity to determine his or her own medical treatment.[29] It is within the parental power to determine what medical treatment the child is to receive, subject as always to the requirement that the parent exercises the power in a manner directed towards the fulfilment of his or her parental responsibilities in relation to the child, and in particular the responsibility to safeguard and promote the child's health, development and welfare. While it is in the nature of medical "treatment" to safeguard and promote the child's health, development and welfare, and can therefore safely be consented to by the parent, this is not true for all medical "procedures". The transplantation of organs, such as kidneys, gives rise to particularly anxious questions. In such cases, the donor invariably suffers a significant physical detriment which will be permanent and it is doubtful if parental consent can, in the ordinary case, justify an operation on a mentally immature child as donor. There may, however, be exceptions where the potential recipient is a sibling or other person with whom the child has a strong connection.[30] It may be supposed, in such cases, that the child, if adult, would have wished to consent, but that is necessarily a speculative judgment, and in any case this is not the basis upon which the legality of medical treatment of children is normally based.[31] Among the factors to be weighed in assessing whether the proposed treatment is likely

---

[28] See further, above, para. 8.16

[29] The issue arose obliquely in *Docherty v. McGlynn* 1983 S.L.T. 645, which involved the question of consent to blood tests of the child in an action of paternity, and rather more relevantly in *Finlayson, Applicant*, 1989 S.C.L.R. 601, where the parental refusal to consent to medical treatment was held to be a ground for referral to a children's hearing and in *Houston, Applicant*, 1996 S.C.L.R. 943 which involved an application by a mental health officer for the compulsory detention of a 15-year-old patient who was withholding consent to treatment and whose mother apparently wished to consent on his behalf (*cf. V v. F*, 1991 S.C.L.R. 225). For an insightful comment on *Houston*, see Grubb [1997] 5 Med. L. Rev. 237.

[30] In a number of cases from the United States organ transplantation has been approved on the basis that the *incapax* would receive benefit from the continued existence of the recipient of the donation: see *e.g., Hart v. Brown*, 289 A. (2d) 386 (1972) (kidney transplantation between seven-year-old twins); *Strunk v. Strunk*, 35 A.L.R. (3d) 683 (1969) (kidney transplant from a 27-year-old incapax to his brother); and see cases cited in Curran, "A Problem of Consent: Kidney Transplantation in Minors" (1959) 34 N.Y.U.L.R. 891. In *Lausier v. Pescinski*, 226 N.W. (2d) 180 (1975) authorisation for the transplant was refused from an institutionalised catatonic schizophrenic man for donation to his sister, on the ground that the sister's previous lack of interest in her brother suggested that her survival would not be likely to benefit the donor. See further Norrie, "Human Tissue Transplants: Legal Liability in Different Jurisdictions" (1985) 34 I.C.L.Q. 442; Price and Garwood-Gowers, "Transplantation from Minors: Are Children Other People's Medicine?" (1995) 1 *Contemp. Issues in Law 1*.

[31] In U.S. jurisdictions this is known as the "substituted judgment" test, and some courts have applied it, though in quite different contexts from the one under consideration here. So, for example, it was applied in *Re Quinlan*, 70 N.J.10, 355 A. (2d) 647 (1976) in which the Supreme Court of New Jersey held that life-support treatment could be terminated once it was shown that this is what the patient would have wanted had she been competent to make a judgment, and in *Re Grady*, 85 N.J. 235, 426 A. (2d) 467 (1981) in which the same court permitted the sterilisation of a mentally disabled woman on the same basis. These particular issues are determined in England and in Scotland not on the basis of what the patient would have wanted but on the basis of the best interests of the patient: see, *e.g., F v. West Berkshire Health Authority* [1989] 2 All E.R. 545, HL; *Re B. (A Minor) (Wardship: Medical Treatment)* [1981] 1 W.L.R. 1412, CA; *Airedale N.H.S. Trust v. Bland* [1993] 1 All E.R. 821, HL; *Law Hospital N.H.S. Trust v. Lord Advocate* 1996 S.L.T. 848; *Re S (Medical Treatment: Adult Sterilisation)* [1998] 1 F.L.R. 944. In Scotland the courts do not themselves authorise sterilisation of mentally handicapped adults, but will grant authority to tutors dative to consent to such treatment on behalf of the patient: see, *e.g., L, Petr*, 1996 S.C.L.R. 538.

to safeguard and promote the child's health, development and welfare are the prospects of success of the transplant, the possibility of alternatives, and, importantly, any indirect benefit that may be supposed to accrue to the child donor, such as, for example, the emotional benefit brought by a sibling restored to health.[32] It is probably not necessary, in order to justify parental consent, that benefit to the child be shown but merely that what is done is consistent with the child's welfare. If, however, the court should be asked to regulate the matter by way of a specific issue order granted under section 11(2)(e) of the Children (Scotland) Act 1995, the court would require to regard the welfare of the child concerned as its paramount consideration and could not make an order unless it considered that it would be better for the child that the order be made than that none should be made at all.[33] The requirement to take account of the child's views is subject to the child's age and maturity[34] and if the child is deemed immature for the purpose of granting his or her own consent to medical treatment, little if any importance need be attached to his or her views on whether the treatment should be given. However, even very young children are likely to have views on the nature of their relationship with siblings and others. It should perhaps be emphasised that it will only be in highly unusual cases that the test of consistency with the child's welfare, far less positive benefit, could be satisfied by the removal of non-regenerative organs such as kidneys. Regenerative tissues such as skin, bone marrow or blood are on the other hand less problematical and there is therefore, it is submitted, no obstacle to parents consenting to procedures such as the donation of blood for transfusion in which there is no appreciable risk to the child and no permanent detriment.

The mentally mature child

In relation to the child who has legal capacity to determine his or her own **8.50** medical treatment[35] there is a substantial difference between Scots and English law. In England the matter is, in part, determined by the Family Law Reform Act 1969[36] but only in respect of minors who have attained the age of 16 years, and common law rules remain relevant in the case of younger minors and also, for some purposes, of those who have attained that age.[37] The common law of England, although not free from doubt and controversy, appears to be that the question of the minor's capacity to consent to medical treatment or other medical procedure is a factual one of his or her ability to understand and to make a

---

[32] *cf. Re Y (Mental Incapacity: Bone Marrow Transplant)* [1996] 2 F.L.R. 787, in which the court authorised the removal of bone marrow from an elderly incompetent in order to save the life of her sister. The mother of both would be adversely affected by the death of the recipient, which would have deleterious consequences for the incompetent, who was reliant on the mother.

[33] Children (Scotland) Act 1995, s. 11(7)(a).

[34] *ibid.* s. 11(7)(b).

[35] See below, para. 15.09.

[36] s. 8.

[37] There has been a burgeoning literature on this topic, particularly since the decision of the House of Lords in *Gillick v. West Norfolk and Wisbech Area Health Authority* [1986] A.C. 112 As representative but by no means exhaustive of this literature, see Skegg, "Consent to Medical Procedures on Minors" (1973) 36 Mod.L.R. 370; Williams, "The *Gillick* Saga" (1985) 135 New L.J. 1156, 1179; Drane, "Competency to Give an Informed Consent" (1984) 252 J.A.M.A. 925; Kerr, "Medical Treatment of Children" [1984] 35 N.I.L.Q. 185; Skegg, *Law, Ethics and Medicine* (1984), pp. 58–71; Kennedy and Grubb, *Medical Law: Text with Materials* (2nd ed., 1994), pp. 252–276; Bridgeman, "Old Enough to Know Best?" (1993) 13 Leg. Stud. 69; Edwards, "The Right to Consent and the Right to Refuse: More Problems with Minors and Medical Consent", (1993) J.R. 52; Brazier and Bridge, "Coercion or Caring: Analysing Adolescent Autonomy", (1996) 16 Leg.Stud. 84; Bridge, "Parental Powers and the Medical Treatment of Children", in Bridge, ed., *Family Law Towards the Millenium: Essays for P.M. Bromley* (1997).

decision,[38] and that a parent can consent on behalf of a minor who does not have that ability, at least where the decision can be defended as not detrimental to the minor's welfare. In addition, the Court of Appeal has held (1) that in exercising its wardship jurisdiction the High Court (and the parent[39]) has the power to consent to medical treatment of a minor who is competent to consent but who refuses consent, and (2) that the wardship court or the High Court exercising its inherent protective jurisdiction has an overriding power to refuse consent or forbid treatment to which the minor (below or over 16) has consented but which the court deems not to be in the child's welfare; natural parents do not have this right of veto.[40] In Scotland at common law the power of dominion, which a parent enjoyed in relation to a pupil child, would seem to have been such that a parent could validly give consent to any medical procedure in respect of such a child, provided that the procedure was consistent with the object for which the power existed, *i.e.* the welfare of the child.[41] It was implicit in the power of dominion that it would prevail irrespective of whether or not the child, in fact, had ability to understand and decide although, in a doubtful case, it would be right for the parent to have regard to the wishes of a child capable of forming a rational judgement. The Age of Legal Capacity (Scotland) Act 1991 extends pupillarity to all children under the age of 16 years, but it also makes express provision concerning the child's capacity to consent to medical treatment:

> "A person under the age of 16 years shall have legal capacity to consent on his own behalf to any surgical, medical or dental treatment or procedure where, in the opinion of a qualified medical practitioner attending him, he is capable of understanding the nature and possible consequences of the procedure or treatment."[42]

---

[38] *Gillick v. West Norfolk and Wisbech Area Health Authority*, above. It is unclear from that case whether mental maturity is all that is necessary to confer competence (the approach of Lord Scarman) or whether, in addition, it must be shown that the treatment is in the child's best interests (the approach of Lord Fraser). For a discussion, see Norrie, "*Gillick* Again: The House of Lords Decides," 1986 S.L.T. (News) 69.

[39] Though this aspect of *Re R*, below, was supported only by Lord Donaldson, M.R.

[40] *Re R (A Minor) (Medical Treatment)* [1991] 4 All E.R.177; *Re W (A Minor) (Medical Treatment)* [1992] 4 All E.R. 627. For a discussion, see Bainham, "The Judge and the Competent Minor" (1992) 108 L.Q.R.194; Edwards, "The Right to Consent and the Right to Refuse," 1993 J.R. 52; Bridgeman, "Old Enough to Know Best?" (1993) 13 Leg.Stud. 69. These decisions probably have to be read in the light of their own facts. *Re R* involved a 15-year-old child who suffered from a psychotic illness and who refused consent to drug treatment of that psychosis during one of her lucid intervals. The Court of Appeal held that her competence was not to be judged purely on her state of mind during a lucid interval, which amounts to a holding that the child in that case was incompetent—rendering the comments concerning competent children obiter. *Re W* involved a 16-year-old suffering from *anorexia nervosa* and it was found that one of the peculiarities of this disease is that the disease itself creates a wish not to be cured: again this raises doubts as to the girl's competence to decide (see particularly the judgment of Balcombe L.J.). See also *Re E (A Minor)* [1993] 1 F.L.R. 386, in which Ward J. authorised a transfusion of blood to a 15-year-old boy who, together with his parents, were Jehovah's Witnesses and who refused to consent to the treatment. The boy was a ward of court and for that reason the court could do no other than decide on the basis of the child's best interests. *Re S (A Minor) (Consent to Medical Treatment)* [1994] 2 F.L.R. 1065 involved a 15-year-old whose parents were Jehovah's Witnesses. She was found not to be competent to refuse life-saving treatment and the court authorised the treatment on the basis of emergency. In *Re T* [1993] Fam. 95 the Court of Appeal overrode the decision of a 22-year-old woman to refuse life-saving treatment on the ground that her decision had been unduly influenced by her parent's religious beliefs—again challenging competency. In no case has a patient's decision been overridden without some challenge to his or her competency or at the very least complete ability fully to understand all the implications of refusal.

[41] See Norrie, "The *Gillick* Case and Parental Rights in Scots Law", 1985 S.L.T. (News) 157. Thomson has argued that this power flowed from the right of custody rather than the right of tutory and therefore existed until the child was 16: "The *Gillick* Case and Parental Rights in Scots Law: Another View", 1985 S.L.T. (News) 223.

[42] Age of Legal Capacity (Scotland) Act 1991, s. 2(4), discussed further, below, para. 15.09.

This provision grants capacity to the child but there is nothing in its terms indicating what effect that has on the parent's responsibility and right to determine the child's medical treatment as an aspect of the responsibility to safeguard and promote the child's health, development and welfare. The matter remained in doubt until the passing of the Children (Scotland) Act 1995, section 15(5) of which provides that any reference to a legal representative is to a person, in the interests of the child, acting in or giving consent to any transaction where the child is incapable of acting or consenting on his or her own behalf. The effect of this, though it could have been expressed more clearly, is that a legal representative can act only when the child cannot, and that when the child acquires capacity to transact the legal representative loses the authority to do so. Whether this principle applies to medical consent is, however, open to question since "transaction" is defined for these purposes as it is in section 9 of the Age of Legal Capacity (Scotland) Act 1991 with the express exception of paragraph (d) thereof (*i.e.* the giving by any person of consent having legal effect).[43] However, the definition is general and includes, even for present purposes, "a transaction having legal effect", which is wide enough to cover medical consent. The exclusion of paragraph (d) of section 9 of the 1991 Act from the definition of "transaction" for the purposes of the rule in section 15(5) of the 1995 Act does no more, it is submitted, than avoid the tautology that would otherwise be inherent.[44] In other words, once a child acquires capacity to consent in terms of section 2(4) of the 1991 Act, this gives the child capacity to determine his or her own medical treatment, including (1) the right to refuse proposed treatment, even when the treatment is, objectively, in the interests of the child and (2) the right to go against parental wishes in this respect. This interpretation consists with *obiter* comments in the only Scottish reported decision in which the issue is mentioned. In *Houston, Applicant*,[45] even before the coming into force of the 1995 Act, Sheriff McGowan said this:

> "It seems to me illogical that on the one hand a person under the age of 16 should be granted the power to decide upon medical treatment for himself but his parents have the right to override his decision. I am inclined to the view that the minor's decision is paramount and cannot be overridden. The [1991] Act itself does not provide any mechanism for resolving a dispute between the minor and the guardian but it seems to me that logic demands that the minor's decision is paramount".

This interpretation also follows both the approach of Lord Scarman in *Gillick*[46] and the logic of the 1991 Act, which deliberately avoids reference to the child's welfare in favour of the child's capacity on achieving maturity. This means that the doctor cannot rely upon the consent of the parent to override a refusal of the child, even when to do so would consist with the child's welfare. In most cases, of course, to override the mature child's wishes would compromise the child's welfare: so for example to force, say, an abortion, or a kidney removal, from a resisting mentally mature child can be argued never to be within the child's welfare, even although some benefits might be gained by doing so.[47]

---

[43] Children (Scotland) Act 1995, s. 15(1).

[44] Section 15(5) would read in part "giving consent to [the giving by a person of any consent having legal effect]".

[45] 1996 S.C.L.R. 943 at 945D.

[46] *Gillick v. West Norfolk and Wisbech Area Health Authority* [1985] 3 All E.R. 402, in which Lord Scarman says (at 422) "parental right yields to the child's right to make his own decisions when he reaches a sufficient understanding and intelligence to be capable of making up his own mind on the matter requiring decision" and (at 423) "parental right to determine whether or not their minor child below the age of 16 will have medical treatment terminates if and when the child achieves a sufficient understanding and intelligence to enable him [to give personal consent]".

[47] See Feenan, "Abortion and Minors" (1992) 37 J.L.S.S. 111 and Herring, "Children's Abortion Rights" (1997) 5 Med.L.Rev. 257.

8.51   If, however, a court were requested to resolve a dispute between a parent and a competent child on the matter of medical treatment, it is open to argument that welfare considerations could—and should—be brought in. An application for a specific issue order made under section 11(2)(e) of the Children (Scotland) Act 1995 would have to be decided by reference to section 11(7), under which the welfare of the child is paramount and a parent might wish to argue that a proposed form of medical treatment that the child is refusing is necessary for the child's welfare. However, it is submitted that any such application should be dismissed as incompetent once the child has been determined to be of sufficient mental maturity to have capacity under section 2(4) of the Age of Legal Capacity (Scotland) Act 1991. An application under section 11 of the 1995 Act is competent only in relation to parental responsibilities, parental rights, guardianship or the administration of a child's property. If the child has capacity under the 1991 Act to perform a legal transaction on his or her own behalf then the parent has no right under the 1995 Act to act in that transaction as the child's legal representative.[48] The dispute is, therefore, not one relating to parental responsibilities and parental rights and not one to which section 11(7) applies.

Remedies for failure to provide consent

8.52   The parent's power in respect of medical treatment arises from his or her obligation to safeguard and promote the child's health, development and welfare. Failure to ensure that the child receives appropriate medical treatment may amount to a criminal offence.[49] The sanctions of the criminal law may, however, be inadequate, or come too late, to provide protection for the child. In such cases, the child can be referred to a children's hearing on the ground that lack of parental care is likely to cause the child unnecessary suffering or seriously to impair his or her health or development,[50] but that does not in itself provide a remedy where the difficulty is the parent's refusal, perhaps on religious grounds, to consent to medical treatment in a case in which that consent is required. The making of a supervision requirement by the children's hearing, perhaps with a condition attached requiring the child to submit to any medical or other examination or treatment,[51] will have the effect of determining how the parent is to fulfil his or her duty to safeguard and promote the child's health, development and welfare, but both this and the application of criminal sanctions will usually be a circuitous and cumbersome procedure in cases of this kind.

8.53   In an emergency a doctor is justified in applying treatment that is clearly necessary,[52] even in the absence of parental consent, but he may be denied the opportunity. In England the wardship jurisdiction affords a remedy for such problems unless the child is the subject of a care order,[53] in which case the local authority can apply to the court for leave to make an application for the exercise of the inherent jurisdiction of the High Court.[54] In Scotland the court has an undoubted jurisdiction to control the exercise of parental power, but examples of its use are virtually exhausted by the making of orders under section 11 of the

---

[48] Children (Scotland) Act 1995, s. 15(5).
[49] *cf. R. v. Instan* [1893] 1 Q.B. 450; *R. v. Stone* [1977] Q.B. 354.
[50] Children (Scotland) Act 1995, s. 52(2)(c). See *Finlayson, Applicant* 1989 S.C.L.R. 601.
[51] Children (Scotland) Act 1995, s. 70(5)(a).
[52] *per* Lord Scarman in *Gillick v. West Norfolk and Wisbech Area Health Authority* [1985] 3 All E.R. 402 at 424; Lord Donaldson M.R. in *Re R (A Minor) (Wardship: Medical Treatment)* [1991] 4 All E.R. 177 at 184. See also *F v. West Berkshire Health Authority* [1989] 2 All ER 545; *Marshall v. Curry* (1933) 3 D.L.R. 260; *Murray v. McMurchy* (1949) 2 D.L.R. 442.
[53] *Re L* [1968] P. 119; *B(BR) v. B.(J)* [1968] P. 466; *M(DK) v. M(SV) & G* [1969] 1 W.L.R. 843; *Re B (A Minor) (Wardship: Medical Treatment)* [1981] 1 W.L.R. 1412; *Re R (A Minor) (Wardship: Medical Treatment)*, above. See the Children Act 1989, s. 100(2)(c).
[54] Children Act 1989, s. 100(3).

1995 Act. However, the control of parental power is based on the *nobile officium* of the Court of Session which acts as *parens patriae* as does the High Court in England in its wardship jurisdiction and is, in principle, no less extensive.[55] It would therefore be open to the Court of Session in exercise of its *parens patriae* jurisdiction to make orders authorising or prohibiting medical treatment.[56] Moreover, both the Court of Session and the sheriff court have a statutory power to make a specific issue order under section 11(2)(e) of the Children (Scotland) Act 1995 which might be used to require a parent to exercise his or her parental rights in a particular manner. Either of these two procedures seems, therefore, to be amply sufficient to provide remedies in appropriate cases. Where necessary, delivery of the child may be ordered to enforce compliance with the order authorising treatment. Applications to the *nobile officium* are to be determined on the basis of the best interests of the patient,[57] and applications under section 11(2)(e) are to be determined by regarding the welfare of the child concerned as the paramount consideration and by making no order unless it is considered that it would be better for the child that the order be made than that none should be made at all.[58]

Discipline

A further, and contentious, aspect of the parental right to control, direct or **8.54** guide the upbringing of children is that parents may exercise "that degree of discipline and moderate chastisement upon them, which their perverseness of temper or inattention calls for".[59] This aspect of parental power was not easily reconciled with dicta on the nature of that power in relation to minors at common law, but it was never suggested that it ended with pupillarity although, according to the circumstances of the case, the age and maturity of the child were among the factors relevant to the reasonableness of its exercise. If discipline is a power that flows from the right to control, direct or guide then it must now end when that right ends, that is at age 16[60]; in all cases, however, its exercise will have to be qualified by practical considerations.[61] The right to discipline a child is valid only if exercised in a manner that satisfies the responsibility to direct and guide the child and is not inconsistent with the responsibility to safeguard and promote the child's health, development and welfare. So the welfare of the child "while it sanctions, also limits the right".[62] Punishment must therefore be moderate and reasonable in relation to its end, and its end must, it is conceived, be educative or developmental in nature. Even control can be exercised only for the purpose of safeguarding and promoting the child's health, development and welfare. If punishment is moderate and reasonable in relation to this legitimate end then, even when physical, that end constitutes a defence to a charge of cruelty to the child,[63] to a charge of criminal assault,[64] and to a claim for damages for civil assault.[65] If it is not directed towards the safeguarding and promoting of the

---

[55] *Law Hospital NHS Trust v. Lord Advocate*, 1996 S.L.T. 848. Lord President Hope at 857E approved this statement as it appeared in the 1st edition of this book, "subject to the point that in my opinion the origin of the tutory jurisdiction lies in the power of the Sovereign as *parens patriae* rather than in the residual power of the court in the exercise of the *nobile officium*".
[56] *ibid.*
[57] *ibid.*
[58] Children (Scotland) Act 1995, s. 11(7).
[59] Erskine, I, vi, 53.
[60] Children (Scotland) Act 1995, s. 2(7).
[61] "A mother, for example, may find difficulty in disciplining her son for refusing to dry the dishes if he is a 15-year-old, 12-stone prop forward": Thomson, *Family Law in Scotland* (3rd ed.), p. 203.
[62] Fraser (3rd ed.), p. 83.
[63] Children and Young Persons (Scotland) Act 1937, s. 12(7).
[64] Wallington, "Corporal Punishment in Schools", 1972 J.R. 124 at 128–134. See *Peebles v. MacPhail* 1990 S.L.T. 245.
[65] See, *e.g.*, *Muckarsie v. Dickson* (1848) 11 D. 4; *Ewart v. Brown* (1882) 10 R. 163.

child's health, development and welfare then, however moderate and apparently reasonable, the physical chastisement of a child is not a legitimate exercise of any parental right and in the absence of any other defence will be an assault, criminal and civil.[66]

Delegability of disciplinary power

8.55   It has been argued that because what is at stake is a privilege and not a right, the exercise of a parental power of discipline cannot be delegated.[67] It can be accepted that there is no right to exercise discipline in the strict sense of an enforceable claim in respect of which there is a corresponding duty to satisfy the claim and that, on such an analysis, classification as a privilege is apt. It is also true that the powers of those *in loco parentis* arise from their quasi-parental relationship with the child and not from delegation. As a consequence, where the *in loco parentis* relationship arises independently of contract express or implied, a parent has no right to control the reasonable exercise of disciplinary power such as he or she would have in the case of a delegate.[68] That does not, however, mean that delegation is excluded. Generally privileges are not delegable, but an analysis on the basis of claims with correlative duties, which leads to the conclusion that a privilege is involved, is not really appropriate to questions of this kind. It is not a right in the strict sense but parental responsibility that is in issue and there is no reason for excluding delegation of its exercise in this aspect any more than in general nurture or education.[69] A person with parental responsibilities and parental rights now has an express statutory power to arrange for some or all of them to be exercised on his or her behalf by another person.[70] A widow or other single mother with an unruly son would, therefore, have the power to authorise, say, the boy's uncle or grandfather to discipline him.

Purpose

8.56   The authorities even before the 1995 Act bring out clearly that the power of discipline is related to and limited by the purposes for which a person has a child in his or her care and the resultant duties. The parental power to discipline a child flows from the duty to promote the child's development and welfare and, importantly, to educate the child. For this reason, the power vests in schoolteachers, though only as part of their educative functions. "There is no doubt that a school teacher is vested with disciplinary powers to enable him to do his educational work and to maintain proper order in class and in school."[71] "It is clear that a teacher of a public school, being bound to see that the pupils behave correctly, is entitled to administer chastisement when the pupils deserve it."[72] So the power of discipline is often said to rest on the relationship between teacher and pupil.[73] No peculiar significance attaches, however, to that particular

---

[66] See Sheriff Kelbie's editorial comments on the case of *G v. Templeton*, 1998 S.C.L.R. 180 at 185-186.

[67] Wallington, *op. cit.*, at 128–134.

[68] See Wallington, *op, cit.* at 143–144 and, among cases there cited, especially *McShane v. Paton*, 1922 J.C. 26 at 31, *per* Lord Salvesen. *Cf. Byrd v. Wither*, 1991 S.L.T. 206, in which the sole question was whether the force used by the cohabitant of a child's mother was reasonable or not: it seems to have been assumed that the accused, who "acted as a father on a day to day basis to the child", had the power to chastise the child.

[69] The decision in *Stewart v. Thain*, 1981 J.C. 13 can be interpreted as an example either of a teacher acting *in loco parentis* or of a teacher acting as the agent exercising powers delegated from the parents.

[70] Children (Scotland) Act 1995, s. 3(5).

[71] *Gray v. Hawthorn*, 1964 J.C. 69, *per* Lord Guthrie at 75.

[72] *Muckarsie v. Dickson*, above, *per* Lord President Boyle at 5.

[73] *McShane v. Paton*, above, *per* Lord Salveson at 31; *Brown v. Hilsom*, 1924 J.C. 1, *per* Lord Cullen at 5. The power of teachers to "administer punishment" is recognised in s. 12(7) of the Children and Young Persons (Scotland) Act 1937.

relationship which must now, in any case, be seen in the light of the abolition of the right to administer corporal punishment to pupils in State and other prescribed schools.[74] It is but an instance of the *in loco parentis* relationship which anyone with children in his or her care and control enjoys. The schoolteacher's power of discipline is, therefore, the analogue of the parental power and arises from the quasi-parental character of the relationship.[75] Section 48A(1) of the Education (Scotland) Act 1980[76] provides that where in "any proceedings" it is shown that corporal punishment has been given to a pupil by a teacher in a public school, the giving of such punishment cannot be justified on the ground that it was done in pursuance of a right exercisable by the teacher by virtue of his position as such. This does not affect the right to discipline that inheres in anyone *in loco parentis*, otherwise than as a teacher in a public school. Despite the generality of the words "any proceedings" in section 48A(1), this is limited by section 48A(4) to civil proceedings, for it is provided there that anything which previously would have been reasonable chastisement, were it not for section 48A(1), is not an offence. The result of this is that reasonable chastisement by a teacher remains a defence to a criminal charge of a assault but is no longer a defence to a civil claim for damages. Again, however, the criminal defence remains available to anyone who can trace their power to the parental power, and it is not a defence limited to teachers alone.

European Convention on Human Rights

The infliction of corporal punishment has raised questions under the **8.57** European Convention on Human Rights,[77] which, by Article 3, prohibits inhuman and degrading punishment. In no Scottish case has the exercise of disciplinary powers over children been held to contravene that prohibition, but the developing jurisprudence of the European Court of Human Rights may influence views of reasonableness.[78] The convention also requires respect for the religious and philosophical views of parents and that too may have consequences, if indirect, for the exercise of disciplinary powers by persons *in loco parentis.*[79]

---

[74] Education (Scotland) Act 1980, s. 48A, as inserted by Education (No. 2) Act 1986, s. 48 and as amended by the Education Act 1993, s. 294. For a discussion, see Phillips, "Teachers, Corporal Punishment, and the Criminal Law: A Retrospect and Prospect", 1992 J.R. 3.

[75] *Stewart v. Thain*, above, at 18, *per* Lord Justice-Clerk Wheatley.

[76] See Phillips, *op. cit.*, pp. 14–16.

[77] See *Campbell and Cosans v. U.K.* [1982] 4 E.H.R.R. 293; *Costello-Roberts v. U.K.* (1995) 19 E.H.R.R. 112; *A v. U.K.*, [1998] Fam.L.R. 118; [1998] 2 F.L.R.959.

[78] In *Costello-Roberts*, above, though the majority (five to four) held that corporal punishment by "slippering" a seven-year-old child was not inhuman and degrading punishment when the parents had not indicated any opposition to corporal punishment, they were careful to point out that their judgment was not to be taken to approve in any way the retention of corporal punishment as part of the discipline regime of a school. In *A v. U.K.*, above, the court held that ill-treatment had to attain a minimum level of severity before it breaches the prohibition on torture or inhuman or degrading treatment or punishment, but that what that level was depended on the nature and context of the treatment, its physical and mental effects, and the age, sex and health of the child. In its *Report on Family Law* (Scot. Law Com. No. 135), the Scottish Law Commission proposed that it should not be regarded as moderate and reasonable chastisement ever to strike a child (1) with a stick, belt or other object of whatever description, or (2) in such a way as causes injury, or pain or discomfort which lasts for more than a very short time. This proposal was not, however, accepted by the government at the time and it did not appear in the Children (Scotland) Act 1995. It is not, however, inconsistent with the guidelines given by the E.C.H.R. in *A v. U.K.*

[79] The U.K. was held in breach of this provision in *Campbell and Cosans v. U.K.*, above, and that led directly to the passing of the Education (No. 2) Act 1986. *Cf.* Art. 28 of the UN Convention on the Rights of the Child (28 *International Legal Materials* 1448, ratified by the U.K., Dec. 16, 1991) which states that school discipline must be "administered in a manner consistent with the child's human dignity and in conformity with the present Convention". (See also Art. 37 prohibiting cruel, inhuman and degrading treatment or punishment.)

Reasonable and moderate chastisement

8.58   The problematic cases in the exercise of the power of discipline have been
cases on the use of corporal punishment. This is because this form of discipline
would, without the justification of being a parental right, amount to a civil or
criminal wrong, which, for example, imposing extra homework, or withholding
pocket money, would not.[80] It is only reasonable and moderate chastisement
that is permitted, and doubt may now hang over the traditional Scottish methods
of corporal punishment within schools. What is today acceptable punishment
by parents may well be limited to slaps and the like that do not cause injury,
extensive bruising or long-lasting pain. Excess, judged objectively, constitutes
an assault.[81] Standards of reasonableness and moderation are subject to
development, and for that reason the older cases may form an imperfect guide.
Striking a child with a stick, belt or other object, or with a clenched fist, may
not now be considered to be reasonable. What constitutes excess may, in any
event, vary according to the circumstances of the case including the age,[82] sex[83]
and any known disabilities or weaknesses of the child.[84] Factors such as the
nature and context of the punishment, the manner and method of its execution,
its duration and its physical and mental effects are all to be taken into account.
It has been said that "to slap a child of two years old on the face, knocking him
over, is an act as remote from reasonable chastisement as one can possibly
imagine",[85] and that "it may be debated whether a blow of considerable force
applied by an adult male to the face of a girl could ever be justified as reasonable
chastisement".[86] Unforeseen injury does not itself show that there was excess,[87]
but punishment which is intended to cause significant physical injury or which
is inflicted in disregard of a readily foreseeable risk of such injury is clearly
excessive. The fact that the parent is angry when punishing the child does not in
itself turn moderate chastisement into an unreasonable punishment inflicted
vindictively and with the *mens rea* necessary to constitute an assault.[88] Cases of
emotional injury are more difficult to categorise and so less susceptible of proof,
but it is thought that punishment that goes beyond the reasonable objects of
discipline and is degrading or grossly humiliating is excessive.[89] As in the case
of children suffering from physical disability so known cases of serious emotional

---

[80] Keeping a child locked in a bedroom might, conceivably, amount to wrongful imprisonment, if
it were for an unreasonable length of time, or in unreasonable conditions. It has been held in
England that a parent with parental rights can be guilty of this wrong: see *R. v. Rahman* (1985)
81 Crim.App.Rep. 349. If unnecessary suffering or injury to health were likely it would, in any
event, be an offence under s. 12(1) of the Children and Young Persons (Scotland) Act 1937 and if
forseeable harm resulted it would be a civil wrong even if the description "unlawful imprisonment"
be thought inappropriate.
[81] *G v. Templeton*, 1998 S.C.L.R. 180.
[82] *Peebles v. MacPhail*, 1990 S.L.T. 245 (two-year-old child).
[83] See *Scorgie v. Lawrie* (1883) 10 R. 610, *per* Lord Young at 613.
[84] For a short review of the cases, see Ness, "Assault and Reasonable Chastisement", 1995 S.L.T.
(News) 185.
[85] *Peebles v. MacPhail*, above at 246H, *per* Lord Justice-General Emslie and Lords Cowie and
Clyde.
[86] *G v. Templeton*, above, *per* Sheriff Principal Risk at 184B.
[87] *Scorgie v. Lawrie*, above; *Mansell v. Griffin* [1908] 1 K.B. 160.
[88] *G v. Templeton*, above; *B v. Harris* 1990 S.L.T. 208; *C v. Harris*, 1989 S.C.L.R. 644; *Guest v.
Annan*, 1988 S.C.C.R. 275. But see *Kennedy v. A*, 1993 S.L.T. 1134, in which it was held that a
father who intended to strike blows which caused extensive bruising on the buttocks of a
five-month-old child possessed the necessary *mens rea* for assault "in the absence of justification
or other exoneration" (*per* Lords Murray, Osborne and Wylie).
[89] Humiliation that is not degrading may however be part of legitimate punishment, whether the
humiliation is public or private: *Stewart v. Thain*, 1981 J.C. 13 at 18, *per* Lord Justice-Clerk
Wheatley. And see the majority judgment of the European Court of Human Rights to like effect
in *Costello-Roberts v. U.K.* (1995) 19 E.H.R.R. 112.

disturbance or mental defect may give rise to special considerations. Normally the court will not enter into a consideration of whether or not a punishment, not excessive in degree, was justified because in that matter a large discretion is allowed to the parent or guardian.[90] Where, however, a punishment is inflicted without any justification at all, or is entirely out of proportion to the triviality of the offence, it may be wrongful and constitute an assault although the actual physical results would not otherwise have been excessive. Such punishment shows a motive that is inconsistent with the purpose for which the power to discipline exists. The power is abused and so cannot protect the parent or other person with children in his or her care if the motive is not a disciplinary one but flows from malice, caprice or rage. So where there had been a succession of punishments by a teacher with little or no just reason for some of them so as to amount to what the sheriff said he could only describe "as a degree of unjust persecution", a conviction for assault was sustained.[91] An objectionable method of punishment may also constitute excess irrespective of whether physical harm results. Thus, in *Ewart v. Brown*,[92] although the action failed because a causal connection between the condition from which the pursuer suffered and the assault was not proved, the action of the defender in striking a pupil on the head with a blackboard pointer was clearly considered to amount to a wrong. And in *Ryan v. Fildes*[93] Tucker J. said of a teacher who had struck a boy on the side of his head with her hand, "the blow struck was moderate in the sense that it was not a very violent blow, but, as punishment, it was not moderate punishment, because I do not think that the proper way of punishing a child is to strike it on the head or the ear". In *Ewart v. Brown* the main reason for the condemnation of the punishment seems to have been that the punishment was inherently dangerous.[94] The court will not sanction, as moderate or reasonable, punishment which carries with it an appreciable risk of injury even if that injury does not materialise or is not shown. That consideration may also have played some part in *Ryan v. Fildes* but references in that case to what was usual in a school and what "the parent of the child might expect that the child could receive if it did wrong" suggest that the motive for the punishment may also have been in question. In any event it appears that there are certain methods of punishment that are to be regarded as in themselves improper,[95] and that blows to the head, generally, come into that category.

Ambit of disciplinary power

It appears that the power of discipline exists as long as the child is in the **8.59** care of the person exercising it and may be applied, at least in some circumstances, in respect of acts committed outwith that care as well as within it. Thus, it has been held in England that a schoolteacher might inflict punishment on a boy for an offence committed away from school and outwith school hours and that although the boy's father had permitted the conduct in question.[96] It

---

[90] *Gray v. Hawthorn*, 1964 J.C. 69 at 75, *per* Lord Guthrie.

[91] *ibid.* at 76.

[92] (1882) 10 R. 163.

[93] [1938] 3 All E.R. 517 at 520.

[94] See especially Lord Young at 169: "The defender, who will thus prevail, is a wrongdoer—in fact, it cannot be reasonably disputed that what he did was a highly imprudent thing, because it never can be known for certain what will be the result of beating a boy on the head with a stick, even when the striker is not in a passion."

[95] See also *McShane v. Paton*, above, where Lord Salvesen refers, at 31, to "proper instruments of chastisement," an expression that carries the implication that others may be improper.

[96] *R. v. Newport (Salop) Justices, ex p. Wright* [1929] 2 K.B. 416. *Cf. Cleary v. Booth* [1893] 1 Q.B. 465. And see *Stewart v. Thain*, above. By contrast, however, punishment for failure to do homework has been held to be wrongful where there was no statutory power to require homework to be done and the child's parents had forbidden it: *Hunter v. Johnson* (1884) 13 Q.B.D. 225.

may be that schoolteachers are in a stronger position in this respect than others because of their general responsibility for education in conduct. A person who punishes a child for acts that do not in any way affect the purposes for which he or she has the child in his or her care cannot, it is thought, be said to exercise a power of discipline legitimately.

Local authority regulations

8.60   Local authority regulations sometimes lay down how discipline within schools is to be exercised, or prohibit certain aspects of discipline, such as corporal punishment of foster children by local authority foster carers. Breach of these regulations may give rise to questions between the teacher or foster carer and the authority which employs or otherwise contracts with him or her, but is *res inter alios acta* and so cannot directly affect the legitimacy of the punishment in a question between the teacher and the child or the child's parents. Similarly, breach of regulations (other than regulations imposing criminal sanctions) or breach of contract cannot, in general, affect criminal liability. There may, however, be circumstances in which such a breach throws some light on questions of motive.

Naming the child

8.61   Article 7(1) of the UN Convention on the Rights of the Child provides that "The child shall be registered immediately after birth and shall have the right from birth to a name, the right to acquire a nationality and, as far as possible, the right to know and be cared for by his or her parents". Having a name is one of the most fundamental elements of a person's sense of self and personal identity, which itself makes an essential contribution to his or her psychological development and well-being. For this reason the parental responsibility to safeguard and promote the child's health, development and welfare includes an obligation to provide the child with a name.[97] The corresponding right to name the child can be traced to the right to control or direct the child's upbringing. Under section 14(1) of the Registration of Births, Deaths and Marriages (Scotland) Act 1965, parents have an obligation to give information concerning the particulars of the child's birth, including the name that has been given to the child. In Scots law, however, the name under which a child has been registered is of little real legal significance and a person, generally, has the name by which he or she is known. For most children, it lies within the practical power of parents to make a child known by a particular name, and though it has been held (under pre-1995 legislation) that this is not a matter of parental right,[98] an element of such right probably does exist since "right" and "power" in relation to parents cannot readily be separated. Apart from the sheriff court decision just mentioned the matter has not troubled the Scottish courts, possibly due to the lack of legal significance attaching to the name of the child.

8.62   As well as giving the child a name on birth, parents also have the power to change the child's name, at least in the early years. A change of name may be registered under the Registration of Births, Deaths and Marriages (Scotland) Act 1965,[99] though only on the application of both parents if they both have parental responsibilities in relation to the child, or on the application of one if there is only one, or on the application of any other person with parental responsibilities if neither parent has such responsibilities. Again, however,

---

[97] Confirmation that this is a parental responsibility is found in s. 43 of the Registration of Births, Deaths and Marriages (Scotland) Act 1965, as amended, whereby persons with parental responsibilities can register a change in the child's name.

[98] *Flett v. Flett*, 1995 S.C.L.R. (Sh.Ct) 189.

[99] s. 43, as amended by the Children (Scotland) Act 1995, Sched. 4, para. 12(3).

registration has little legal effect and one parent will often have the practical power to change the name by which a child is generally known even against the wishes of the other. This happens most frequently after the separation of parents, and particularly when the parent with whom the child resides enters into a new relationship and wishes to change the child's name to that of the new partner.[1] Though there is little legal consequence there may be significant social or emotional consequences in a change of a child's name particularly, perhaps, for the parent. In *Flett v. Flett*[2] the sheriff held that the matter of the child's name was not open to judicial regulation but that decision was expressly based on the terms of the Law Reform (Parent and Child) (Scotland) Act 1986.[3] Under the Children (Scotland) Act 1995, the naming of a child can, for reasons given above, be located within the parental responsibilities and parental rights and may, therefore, be subject to an order under section 11(2).[4] If this is so then the matter is determined, of course, by the court regarding the welfare of the child concerned as its paramount consideration and not making any order unless it considers that it would be better for the child that the order be made than that none should be made at all.[5] In England it has long been held that the child's name is open to judicial regulation and there are a number of decisions on the issue.[6] Caution must be shown in reading the English cases since the registration of a child's name has greater legal significance there than in Scotland, and a change in the child's registered name can be achieved where the parents do not agree only by authority of the court in an application under section 13(1) of the Children Act 1989. However, because that authority is given on the basis of the welfare test, the English cases do give indication of the factors relevant to the application of that test in this context. The typical dispute involves a mother with whom children continue to reside after divorce and who marries again and now wishes to change the children's name to that of her new husband.

The presumption is that a child's welfare is served by his or her retaining **8.63** the name by which he or she has hitherto been known, so that if there is no significance to the change the court will not authorise it.[7] A factor that proved decisive in earlier cases was the weight to be attached to the security of the child within a new family unit: taking the name of the new family unit helps the child to perceive him or herself as a full member thereof.[8] More recent cases have emphasised the benefits to be gained from the child's sense of identity and background as the natural father's child.[9] This has been held to be of sufficient significance to supersede the wishes even of older children: in *Re B (Change of Surname)*[10] children aged 16, 14 and 12 expressed a strong desire to take the

---

[1] Before doing so, the parent is obliged to take account of the views of the child concerned, a child of 12 years of age of more being presumed capable of forming views for this purpose, as well as the views of any other person with parental responsibilities or parental rights (Children (Scotland) Act 1995, s. 6(1)); it is difficult to see, however, what legal effect a failure in this duty would have.

[2] 1995 S.C.L.R. 189.

[3] Sheriff Bell's reasoning was that, a child's name not being a matter of "parental rights", it was incompetent to seek an order over the child's name under s. 3 of the 1986 Act which dealt only with "orders relating to parental rights".

[4] A specific issue order might be sought to grant authority to a parent to cause the child to be known by a particular name, or an interdict may prevent one parent from doing so without the consent of the other.

[5] s. 11(7).

[6] See the discussion by Herring, "Name this Child" [1998] C.L.J. 266.

[7] *Re F (Child: Surname)* [1994] Fam. Law 12.

[8] *Re B (Child: Surname)* [1977] 1 W.L.R. 1256; *D v. B (Otherwise D) (Surname: Birth Registration)* [1979] Fam. 38.

[9] *W v. A (Child: Surname)* [1981] Fam. 14; *R v. R (Child: Surname)*, (1982) F.L.R. 345; *Re B (Change of Surname)* [1996] 1 F.L.R. 791; *Re T (Change of Surname)* [1998] 2 F.L.R. 620.

[10] above.

name of their step-father rather than retain that of the father with whom they had had little contact for some years. The court held that to allow such a change would convey the inappropriate message to the children that the natural father belonged wholly to their past and had no place in their present. On the other hand, if a connection with the past is not served, then there is no benefit in insisting that the child retains an old name. In *Re C (Change of Surname)*[11] children who stayed with their father in practice used his surname, though for what were described as "official purposes" they were known by their mother's maiden name. The father sought to change their "official" name but this was opposed by the mother. She, however, had ceased using her own maiden name and the court held that the continued use of that name by the children served no purpose in retaining the link between the children and their mother and therefore it authorised the change.[12] The issue arose in a rather different way in *Dawson v. Wearmouth*.[13] Here a child had been born to a woman whose husband was not the father, though his registered name was the husband's. The relationship between the mother and the father broke down shortly after the child's birth and the father, who was awarded a contact order, sought as well a specific issue order that the child should henceforth be known by his rather than the husband's name. Though the judge at first instance granted the order sought, the Court of Appeal overturned the decision and the House of Lords affirmed the Court of Appeal, on the basis that it was not in the child's best interests to have a name different from that of his mother (who had retained her ex-husband's name) and his half-siblings. This decision is important in emphasising that any notion of parental "right" in a child's name is entirely out of place and that the sole consideration in such cases is the welfare of the child.[14]

---

[11] [1998] 1 F.L.R. 549.

[12] See also *Re P (Parental Responsibility)*, [1997] 2 F.L.R. 722; *Re C (Change of Surname)* [1998] 2 F.L.R. 656 and *Re S (Change of Surname)* [1999] 1 F.L.R. 672..

[13] [1997] 2 F.L.R. 629 affirmed by the House of Lords on March 25, 1999.

[14] In Scotland the only remedy for someone in the position of the plaintiff in *Dawson v. Wearmouth* would be an action for putting to silence any person who was falsely claiming that he was the father of the child: merely naming the child after a man is unlikely in itself to amount to a claim to paternity.

CHAPTER 9

COURT ORDERS RELATING TO PARENTAL RESPONSIBILITIES
AND PARENTAL RIGHTS

Scope of this chapter

Section 11 of the Children (Scotland) Act 1995 permits the Court of Session or the sheriff court to make orders in relation to parental responsibilities, parental rights, guardianship or the administration of a child's property. This chapter will examine the particular orders in relation to these matters that are open to the court to make, the jurisdiction of the court to make such orders, and the procedure to be followed. In addition, the issue of conflict between different court orders will be addressed. How the court determines whether to make an order under section 11 and, in particular, the principles upon which the court bases its decision, are considered in detail in the immediately following chapter.[1]   **9.01**

THE AVAILABLE ORDERS

Introduction

Prior to the coming into force of the Children (Scotland) Act 1995, the court was empowered to make any order relating to parental rights as it thought fit.[2] "Parental rights" was defined to mean "guardianship, custody and access and   **9.02** any right and authority relating to the welfare or upbringing of the child conferred on a parent by any rule of law".[3] Not only did this formulation protect the validity of "right and authority" emanating from the common law, but the content of the specified parental rights, such as custody and access, was also determined by the common law. Parental responsibilities and parental rights under the 1995 Act are, on the other hand, entirely creatures of statute, both in terms of their content[4] and in terms of their regulation by court order. That regulation is governed by section 11. Orders are made under section 11(1), in proceedings in the Court of Session or the sheriff court, either (a) on the application made by a person with title to do so[5] or (b) although no such application has been made, the court (even if it declines to make any other order) considers it should make such an order.[6] There is no limitation to the nature of the proceedings in which the court is able to make an order under section 11(1) though some issue must, it is submitted, be competently before the court. Apart from applications made specifically under section 11(1), the typical instance of an action in which the court is likely to make an order under that subsection will be a divorce action in which the parties themselves do not seek an order relating to parental responsibilities and parental rights but in which the court nevertheless considers

---

[1] For the background to matters, see Scot. Law Com. No. 135, *Report on Family Law* (May 1992), Pt V.

[2] Law Reform (Parent and Child) (Scotland) Act 1986, s. 3(1).

[3] *ibid.* s. 8.

[4] See above, Chap. 8.

[5] See below, paras 9.50 *et seq.*

[6] Children (Scotland) Act 1995, s. 11(3). This was the case at common law in relation to custody, at least in the Court of Session: *Symington v. Symington* (1874) 1 R. 871; (1875) 2 R. (H.L.) 41.

that it should make such an order.[7] The wording of section 11(1) and (3) is designed to ensure maximum flexibility in the court making an order whenever it comes to its attention that an order should be made and it follows that even in proceedings under Part II of the 1995 Act, a section 11 order might competently be made in addition to any order made under that Part. So, for example, in making a child protection order under section 57 the court may, in addition to giving directions in relation to contact and the exercise of parental responsibilities and parental rights under section 58, make a specific issue order under section 11(2)(e) dealing with a matter that cannot be dealt with under section 58. It is likely, however, that the power to make an order under section 11 in proceedings under Part II is limited to orders that cannot be made under the provisions in Part II. A contact order under section 11(2)(d) cannot, if this is correct, be made when a child protection order is being made since contact during the subsistence of child protection orders is expressly dealt with, according to its own rules, in section 58,[8] and any order should be made under that section rather than section 11. Nor can a section 11 order be used by a court in Part II proceedings to achieve that which is prohibited by or inconsistent with a provision in Part II.[9]

9.03 There is one situation in which the court is obliged to make an order under section 11. If a child has been freed for adoption, parental responsibilities and parental rights are thereby transferred from the child's parents and guardians to the adoption agency.[10] If, thereafter, the freeing order is revoked under section 20 of the Adoption (Scotland) Act 1978[11] the adoption agency loses these responsibilities and rights but they are not automatically revested in the parent or guardian. In order to ensure that the child is not left with no one who has parental responsibilities and parental rights in relation to him or her, the court that revokes the freeing order must make an order under section 11 of the Children (Scotland) Act 1995 determining on whom are to be imposed the parental responsibilities and to whom are to be given the parental rights in relation to the child.[12]

9.04 The wording of section 11 is careful to avoid so far as possible the impression that court orders grant "rights": rather they "regulate" matters, appoint persons to offices, and remove or confer parental responsibilities and parental rights. Informal arrangements between parents, if they work well, do not require the sanction of a section 11 order[13] and any order may be made only when the court considers that it would be better for the child that the order be made than that

---

[7] In actions for divorce, judicial separation or declarator of nullity of marriage, the court must consider whether to make a s. 11 order in respect to any child of the family under the age of 16, or to refer the child to the reporter under s. 54: s. 12(1): see further, below, para. 19.10.

[8] See below, para. 20.35.

[9] So, for example, a sheriff who makes a child protection order cannot bypass the prohibition on appointing a safeguarder at that time (s. 41(2)) by purporting to do so as a specific issue order under s. 11(2)(e). Nor can he require a child to undergo an assessment under s. 11 on grounds other than those laid down for child assessment orders in s. 55. It was conceded by counsel in *Osborne v. Matthan (No. 2)*, 1998 S.L.T. 1264, that s. 11 cannot be used to require a local authority to supervise a child's upbringing. This must be correct since local authorities' supervisory powers are both defined and delimited by Pt II of the 1995 Act. It would seem, however, that it is open to the court to make a contact order subject to a condition of supervision, to be provided by the local authority, so long as this does not require the local authority to provide the supervision: see, for example, the order made by the sheriff in *Senna-Cheribbo v. Wood*, Nov. 19, 1998 to that effect, which passed without comment in the Inner House.

[10] Adoption (Scotland) Act 1978, s. 18(5), as substituted by the Children (Scotland) Act 1995, Sched. 2, para. 11.

[11] See above, para. 4.64.

[12] Adoption (Scotland) Act 1978, s. 20(3), as substituted by the Children (Scotland) Act 1995, Sched. 2, para. 13.

[13] They are, indeed, sanctioned by s. 3(5).

none should be made at all.[14] So orders under section 11 are available only in cases of dispute which cannot otherwise be resolved, and the onus is on the applicant to establish that making the order is better for the child than not making the order. If an order is made, then the fact that a person has parental responsibilities and parental rights does not entitle that person to act in any way which would be incompatible with the order.[15]

Without prejudice to the generality of the court's power in section 11(1) to **9.05** make an order in relation to parental responsibilities, parental rights, guardianship or the administration of a child's property, section 11(2) lists a number of particular orders that the court may make, which are discussed in the paragraphs below. It remains open to the court to make an order under section 11(1) in relation to the specified matters other than one of those listed in section 11(2), though any order regulating any specific question which has arisen, or may arise, in connection with parental responsibilities, parental rights, guardianship or the administration of a child's property will fall within the terms of a specific issue order as defined in section 11(2)(e). An example of an order not mentioned in section 11(2) but competent under section 11(1) might be a declarator of entitlement to exercise parental responsibilities and parental rights.

Orders removing parental responsibilities or parental rights

The court may make an order depriving a person of some or all of his or her **9.06** parental responsibilities or parental rights in relation to a child.[16] The order requires to be explicit which responsibilities and rights are being removed, for an order under section 11 has the effect of depriving a person of a parental responsibility or a parental right only in so far as the order expressly so provides and only to the extent necessary to give effect to the order.[17] It is competent to remove only one or some of the parental responsibilities and parental rights without affecting any of the others,[18] but since parental rights exist only in order to enable a person to fulfil his or her responsibilities it is probably incompetent to remove a right without also removing the corresponding responsibility. So the court could not, it is submitted, remove the right of a parent to act as the child's legal representative without also removing the responsibility of the parent to do so. For the same reason the removal of a responsibility implicitly includes the removal of the right to act for the fulfilment of the responsibility. The court may also remove particular responsibilities and rights that are referable to, rather than expressly listed in, section 2 though particular issues are more tidily dealt with under specific issue orders, considered below.

Orders imposing parental responsibilities and parental rights

The court may make an order imposing parental responsibilities and giving **9.07** parental rights to any person,[19] and again the order must be explicit as to which responsibilities and rights are being conferred. It is competent to confer only one or some of those listed in sections 1 and 2 though it is probably incompetent to impose a parental responsibility without also conferring the corresponding parental right necessary for its fulfilment. The court may confer a parental "right" other than one of those expressly listed in section 2 only if the right can be gleaned from the terms of one of those listed: for example the right to determine

---

[14] s. 11(7): see further, below, paras 10.38–10.40.
[15] s. 3(4).
[16] s. 11(2)(a).
[17] s. 11(11).
[18] Any reference in the Act to a person having parental responsibilities or parental rights includes a reference to a person having any of those responsibilities or rights: s. 103(1).
[19] s. 11(2)(b).

a child's education might be conferred on a person as a limited part of the right to control, direct or guide the child's upbringing. If all the parental responsibilities and parental rights are to be conferred on a person who is not a parent, then the order is more appropriately one appointing the person as guardian, *i.e.* as parent-substitute, under section 11(2)(h).[20] It should be noted here that an order conferring parental responsibilities and parental rights does not confer the status of parenthood (for the purposes, for example, of succession or the obligations of aliment and child support) but merely imposes some of the consequences of the parent and child relationship.

9.08   It is open to the court to impose parental responsibilities and confer parental rights on any person, whether the applicant or otherwise, but the recipient must be a natural person and not, for example, a local authority or an incorporated body. This follows, though it could have been expressed more clearly, from the rule of interpretation that any reference in Part I of the 1995 Act to a person having parental rights or responsibilities, acting as a legal representative or being appointed a guardian is to a natural person only.[21] Another limitation, found in section 11(2)(b) itself, is that, with one exception, the person obtaining parental responsibilities and parental rights by court order must be aged 16 years or more. The one situation in which it is competent to confer parental responsibilities and parental rights on a person below that age is when the person is the child's parent. This usually means the child's father since mothers of whatever age have parental responsibilities and parental rights automatically[22] (unless they have been removed by court order). It will, however, be an unusual case in which a father under the age of 16 years is granted parental responsibilities and parental rights: though there is no age limit on a mother automatically acquiring those rights, that acquisition is an inevitable legal consequence of maternity with which the child's welfare is irrelevant, while any court order must, as we will see, be made on the basis that the child's welfare is the court's paramount consideration. Any order granting parental responsibilities and parental rights will not in itself affect any lack of personal capacity from which the father under the age of 16 suffers and section 11 cannot, it is submitted, be used to increase a parent's capacity from that which he has under the Age of Legal Capacity (Scotland) Act 1991.[23]

Residence orders

9.09   The court may make an order, known as a residence order, regulating the arrangements as to (i) with whom, or (ii) if with different persons alternatively or periodically, with whom during what periods, a child under the age of 16 years is to live.[24] The wording of the paragraph should be noted carefully. Residence orders are not made "in favour of" one parent or the other,[25] for it is to be remembered that mothers and most fathers will already have the right to have their children living with them in any case: the order will not be made simply to confer upon a parent that which he or she already has.[26] Rather, the

---

[20] See further, below, paras 9.17–9.18.

[21] s. 15(4).

[22] Under s. 3(1)(a).

[23] See further, below, para.15.26.

[24] s. 11(2)(c).

[25] As, it was held, custody orders were: *T v. T*, 1987 S.L.T. (Sh.Ct) 74, in which it was held incompetent for a pursuer to seek a custody order "in favour of" the defender. The Act is quite deliberate in its move away from this terminology: see Scot. Law Com. No. 135, *Report on Family Law* (May 1992), para. 5.37.

[26] To do so would have no effect and making such an order would therefore breach the requirement in s. 11(7) that the court "shall not make any... order unless it considers that it would be better for the child that the order be made than that none should be made at all".

order is primarily designed to regulate, for the benefit of the child, the arrangements under which parents can exercise their pre-existing rights. Unless there is, in addition to an order under this paragraph, an order removing or qualifying the non-resident parent's[27] parental responsibilities and parental rights, the making of a residence order under which the child is to live with only one parent does not affect the pre-existing parental responsibilities and parental rights of the other parent (other than the right to determine where the child is to live); nor does it increase those of the parent with whom the child is to live. Though the residence parent will now have the exclusive rather than shared right to determine where the child is to live, he or she remains under the obligation to have regard to the views of the other on this, as on other, matters.[28] The non-resident parent, in other words, has a right to be consulted on the residence parent's exercise of the right to determine where the child is to live. If a child ceases in fact to reside with a person with parental responsibilities and parental rights, then that person acquires the additional responsibility and right to maintain direct contact and personal relations with the child: that effect follows not from any court order but from the fact of the parent not living with the child.

As well as regulating how pre-existing residence rights are to be exercised, **9.10** a residence order might require the child to live with someone who does not have parental responsibilities and parental rights in relation to the child. This might be an unmarried father, another relative, or any other person. If the residence order requires the child to live with such a person then the residence order itself, without any additional order under section 11(2)(b), confers on that person the parental responsibilities to safeguard and promote the child's health, development and welfare, to provide direction and guidance to the child, and to act as the child's legal representative, together with the parental rights to control, direct or guide the child's upbringing, and to act as the child's legal representative.[29] The order may permit the child to live with different persons alternatively or periodically, and a residence order in such terms might overlap to some degree with a contact order which permits or requires the child to stay overnight with another person. There is, however, an important difference between a residence order requiring the child to live periodically with a person who did not have parental responsibilities and parental rights, on the one hand, and on the other hand a contact order requiring the child to stay overnight with such a person on regular occasions: the rule in section 11(12) carrying parental responsibilities and parental rights to such a person applies only with a residence order. As Sheriff Kelbie pointed out in *McBain v. McIntyre*,[30] a residence order is appropriate only when it truly requires the child to "live with" the person, which is qualitatively different from "staying with" a person even regularly overnight. The terms of section 11(2)(c) recognise, however, that it is possible in certain circumstances for a child to "live with" two people who live apart, such as when he or she lives during the week with one parent and lives during the weekend with the other. This might occur if the child has his or her own room at the house of both parents, keeps separate clothes at each, and separate toys, books, school work, interests and friends.[31] A court asked to make an order regulating these arrangements might make either a residence order or a

---

[27] *i.e.* the parent with whom the child is not or will not be living.

[28] s. 6(1).

[29] s. 11(12). For this reason, a "residence order" should not be used to achieve purposes other than requiring the child to live with someone who has or will have parental responsibilities and parental rights over the child.

[30] 1997 S.C.L.R. 181.

[31] This seems to have been the situation of the child in *McKiver v. McKiver*, 1995 S.L.T. 790 (a Hague Convention case).

contact order: there is no practical difference if both parties already have parental responsibilities and parental rights, but if only one does then a residence order would give the person the advantage of parental responsibilities and parental rights, while a contact order would not.

Contact orders

9.11   The court may make an order, known as a contact order, regulating the arrangements for maintaining personal relations and direct contact between a child under the age of 16 and a person with whom the child is not, or will not be, living.[32] The careful wording of this paragraph is designed to emphasise that the order will not confer any "right" to contact but will, rather, regulate the arrangements for contact between a child and any person with whom the child is not living. As previously explained,[33] contact is both a legal and a factual concept, and both concepts can be regulated by an order under this provision. The order may regulate how a person whose responsibility and right of contact, recognised by sections 1 and 2 and activated by the fact that he or she is not living with the child, is to fulfil that legal responsibility. But in addition, the terms of the paragraph are wide enough to allow the court to regulate contact as a concept of fact between the child and a person without any such responsibility or right.[34] This might include a child's siblings, friend, relative, ex-foster carer or any other person whose continued relationship with the child serves his or her welfare. Regulating factual contact does not confer any "right" of contact and if the "parental responsibility" and "parental right" of contact is sought by a person who does not have that responsibility or right then the order sought must be one under section 11(2)(b) rather than section 11(2)(d).[35] If an order is made under the latter provision it does not follow that the person whose personal relations with the child are regulated by the order becomes thereby a "person with parental responsibilities and parental rights" for the purposes of, for example, the power to consent to the child's removal from the United Kingdom,[36] or the requirement to be consulted by a parent making major decisions relating to the child,[37] or becoming a "relevant person" within the children's hearing system.[38] These effects follow only if an order is made under section 11(2)(b) (imposing parental responsibilities and parental rights) or section 11(2)(c) (requiring the child to live with a person which, as explained above, will sometimes carry with it the parental responsibilities and parental rights).

9.12   The extent of the regulation of contact, whether as a legal or as a factual concept, is entirely at the discretion of the court (subject to the application of the principles in section 11(7)[39]) and the court may be as specific or as fluid in the arrangements it makes as it deems necessary in the interests of the child. Times, dates and places may be specified, if it serves the child's interests to do so, as may whether the contact is to be supervised, and if so by whom.

---

[32] s. 11(2)(d).

[33] Above, para. 8.38.

[34] It has been suggested (Scott, *Butterworths Scottish Family Law Service*, para. C. 567) that the court may simply recognise in another person the responsibility and right of direct contact and personal relations without necessarily regulating the arrangements for their fulfilment and exercise. An order that does not "regulate arrangements" is not a contact order within the terms of s. 11(2)(d), though the terms of s. 11(1) allow orders to be made other than those specified in s. 11(2).

[35] See *Re CB (A Minor) (Parental Responsibility Order)* [1993] 1 F.L.R. 920 in which it was held that contact and parental responsibility were entirely separate and distinct questions to be examined from quite different perspectives.

[36] s. 2(3) and (6).

[37] s. 6.

[38] It is open to the court, for example, to regulate the contact arrangements between the child and a younger sibling under s. 11(2)(d) without this giving the sibling the "parental responsibility" of contact.

[39] See below, Chap. 10.

Being little more than a qualification to custody,[40] access at common law was **9.13**
not recognised as a right unless it was capable of being physically exercised at the
instant time. Nor was the right granted by the court unless that condition was
satisfied. So in *D v. Strathclyde Regional Council*[41] the Second Division held that
it was incompetent for a parent (or anyone else) to seek access to a child during
the subsistence of a supervision requirement. The reason for this was that access,
being operable at the instant time, could not be suspended by the supervision
requirement in the way that custody could be,[42] with the result that ordering access
during the subsistence of a supervision requirement would interfere with the
discretion granted to the local authority under the supervision requirement.[43] It is
unlikely that this remains the case in relation to contact. An order regulating contact
is a section 11 order and section 11(4), which removes title to seek a section 11
order from various persons,[44] does not mention persons whose responsibilities
and rights have been suspended by a supervision requirement. Physical contact
may well be as ephemeral as access, but the obligation is wider than that and is
more properly to maintain personal relations and direct contact. Personal relations
between the parent and the child is an ongoing concept, not dependent on actual
fulfilment at the instant time for its existence, and is as permanent an obligation
as the other parental responsibilities. A contact order is not "directed against" the
party with the right of residence (as an access order was in relation to the
custodian[45]) but is rather an order regulating the contact arrangements between
the child and a person with whom the child is not living.[46] Thus, to make a contact
order in respect of a child who is subject to a supervision requirement does not
qualify the local authority's responsibility and right to control who has contact
with the child and it inhibits the children's hearing's decision-making powers to
no greater extent than a residence order (which can unquestionably be made during
the subsistence of a supervision requirement) would. A contact order is not,
therefore, necessarily inconsistent with a supervision requirement. It follows, it is
submitted, that there is nothing to prevent the court making a contact order under
section 11(2)(d) during the subsistence of a supervision requirement.[47] Of course,
if the terms of the order are inconsistent with the terms of the supervision
requirement then the former is suspended until the latter is varied or terminated. It
remains open to a children's hearing to make contact arrangements different from
those in a pre-existing court order, in which case the terms of the supervision
requirement are again given precedence.

Specific issue orders
The court may make an order, known as a specific issue order, regulating **9.14**
any specific question which has arisen, or may arise, in connection with parental
responsibilities, parental rights, guardianship or the administration of a child's

---

[40] See above, para. 8.39.
[41] 1985 S.L.T. 114.
[42] *Aitken v. Aitken*, 1978 S.C. 297.
[43] *D v. Strathclyde Regional Council*, above; *A v. G*, 1996 S.L.T. (Sh.Ct) 123. See also *Henderson v. Adamson*, 1998 S.C.L.R. 365.
[44] Those whose parental responsibilities and parental rights have been (a) extinguished on the making of an adoption order, (b) transferred to an adoption agency on the making of an order declaring a child free for adoption, (c) extinguished by the making of an order under s. 30 of the Human Fertilisation and Embryology Act 1990 and (d) transferred to a local authority by a parental responsibilities order.
[45] See *A v. G*, above, at 125K.
[46] s. 11(2)(d) and s. 93(1).
[47] It should be noted that this conclusion is the reverse of that reached, without proper recognition of the effect of the 1995 Act, in an earlier work: Norrie, *Children's Hearings in Scotland* (1997), p. 118. The sheriff in *Russell v. W*, 1998 Fam. L.R. 25 was, it is respectfully submitted, mistaken in concluding likewise that the 1995 Act did not change the principle laid down in *D v. Strathclyde Regional Council*, above, and followed in *A v. G*, above.

property.[48] This is very wide and might be used to allow the court to determine wherein the child's welfare lies in any situation in which that is in dispute, for example in relation to medical treatment, schooling, religious instruction, name or any other aspect of the child's upbringing. The only limitation is that the order must regulate a matter concerning parental responsibilities, parental rights, guardianship or the administration of the child's property. The child's medical treatment, being a matter of the parental responsibility to safeguard and promote the child's health, development and welfare, is an issue that can be regulated by a specific issue order and the English courts have been much exercised in this area of the law.[49] A specific issue order might, for example, authorise a person to withhold consent to medical treatment, or authorise the child's medical treatment,[50] or allow the child to be known by a new name,[51] or authorise a person to sign a passport application form on behalf of the child when the parent refuses to do so,[52] or authorise a child to live away from his or her parents,[53] or require the delivery of the child to any person,[54] or authorise one parent to remove the child from the jurisdiction, either temporarily or permanently, against the wishes of the other parent.[55] A specific issue order cannot, it is submitted, deal with matters covered by other statutory provisions, such as the exclusion of a person from the child's home,[56] for that would be to sidestep the different statutory requirements contained in these other provisions.[57] It is open to question whether a specific issue order can grant to a person a right to attend, and title to appeal against decisions of, children's hearings.[58] It is difficult to see why—other than for their own benefit—any person should have these rights when they do not have any of the other, specified, parental responsibilities and parental rights and it is suggested that a specific issue order should not be used for this means. The order may be made only on the basis that the child's welfare is paramount and any interest of another person to attend a children's hearing is, in this context at least, entirely subsumed into that consideration. If it is appropriate to allow a person standing in the children's hearing system then a better approach than a self-standing specific issue order is to grant one or more of the parental responsibilities or parental rights under section 11(2)(b), thus

---

[48] s. 11(2)(e).

[49] See, *e.g.*, *Re B (A Minor)* [1981] 1 W.L.R. 1421; *Re B (A Minor)* [1988] A.C. 199; *Re E (A Minor)* [1991] 2 F.L.R. 585; *Re C (A Minor)* [1989] 2 All E.R. 782; *Re J (A Minor)* [1990] 3 All E.R. 930; *Re R (A Minor)* [1991] 4 All E.R. 177; *Re W (A Minor)* [1992] 4 All E.R. 627; *Re S (A Minor) (Consent to Medical Treatment)* [1994] 2 F.L.R. 1065; *Re T (A Minor) (Wardship: Medical Treatment)* [1997] 1 All E.R. 906; *Re C (Detention: Medical Treatment)* [1997] 2 F.L.R. 180; *Re C (A Minor) (Medical Treatment)* [1998] 1 F.L.R. 384. Few of these cases, even after the coming into force of the Children Act 1989, were dealt with by the making of a specific issue order.

[50] *Re R (Minor)* (1993) 15 B.M.L.R. 72; *Re R (A Minor) (Blood Transfusion)* [1993] 2 F.L.R. 757; *Northampton Area Health Authority v. the Official Solicitor and the Governors of St Andrews Hospital* [1994] 1 F.L.R. 162.

[51] *Dawson v. Wearmouth* [1997] 2 F.L.R. 629, affirmed by the House of Lords on March 25, 1999; *Re T (Change of Surname)* [1998] 2 F.L.R. 620; *Re C (Change of Surname)* [1998] 2 F.L.R. 656. *Cf. Flett v. Flett*, 1995 S.C.L.R. 189.

[52] See *City of Edinburgh District Council v. M*, 1996 S.L.T. (Sh.Ct) 112. This case failed on a question of title, though if the application were made by a person with good title, the order could competently be made.

[53] *Re C (A Minor) (Leave to Seek Section 8 Orders)* [1994] 1 F.L.R. 26.

[54] *Re B (Minors) (Residence Order)* [1992] 3 All E.R. 867.

[55] This will be the court order referred to in s. 2(3), which otherwise prohibits one parent from so removing the child without the consent of the other parent. See, *e.g.*, *Fourman v. Fourman*, 1998 Fam. L.R. 98.

[56] So it was held in England in *Pearson v. Franklin* [1994] 1 F.L.R. 246.

[57] In *Re J (Specific Issue Order: Leave to Apply)* [1995] 1 F.L.R. 669 it was held that a specific issue order could not declare a child to be "in need" for the purposes of local authority support and that the local authority's decision that a child was not in need could be challenged only by way of judicial review.

[58] This question was raised but not answered in *Russell v. W*, 1998 Fam. L.R. 25. This was held incompetent in *M v. Lothian Regional Council*, 1989 S.L.T. 429 and *Paton v. Paton*, March 4, 1999, Glasgow Sheriff Court.

making the person a "relevant person" for these purposes. The question of attendance at a children's hearing might not be considered to be a matter of parental responsibilities or parental rights or guardianship or the administration of a child's property, in which case there would be no power to make a specific issue order on that point in any case.

Interdicts

The court may make an order prohibiting the taking of any step of a kind **9.15** specified in the interdict in the fulfilment of parental responsibilities or the exercise of parental rights relating to a child or in the administration of a child's property.[59] It is noticeable that there is no reference here to guardianship, but an interdict against a guardian exercising any of the guardianship powers necessarily involves the fulfilment of parental responsibilities or the exercise of parental rights in any case. An interdict under this provision might be granted, for example, against a parent or guardian consenting to, and doctors from performing, any medical procedure that the court does not consider to be in the interests of the child.[60] Or the court might interdict the legal representative from selling or dissipating a child's property, or putting it to improper purposes, or prohibiting the removal of the child from the jurisdiction,[61] or prohibiting a person from exercising their right of contact with the child.[62] Again, however, an order under this provision should not be used to bypass any of the procedures in Part II of the 1995 Act or under any other statutory provision, though it may be used to achieve similar effects in situations in which doing so can properly be said to supplement rather than to avoid the other statutory provisions. In making this, or any, section 11 order, the court is exhorted to "endeavour to ensure that any order that it makes, or any determination by it not to make an order, does not adversely affect the position of a person who has, in good faith and for value, acquired any property of the child concerned, or any right or interest in such property".[63] So, for example, a parent who, as legal representative, is improperly disposing of the child's property may be interdicted from doing so, though the court might protect the validity of contracts already entered into. This consideration is to be balanced against that which is always the court's paramount consideration, that is to say the welfare of the child, and the requirement to "endeavour" to protect third party rights does not, for that reason, create an absolute obligation.

Appointing a judicial factor

The court may make an order appointing a judicial factor to manage a child's **9.16** property or remitting the matter to the Accountant of Court to report on suitable arrangements for the future management of the property.[64] This deals with the situation of a child who owns property, cannot for some reason administer that property him or herself, and there is reason to supersede his or her legal representative in that administration. Sections 9 and 13 provide the court with similar powers, the former requiring applications to the Accountant of Court for directions, the latter allowing the court to appoint a judicial factor to deal with awards of damages to the child. The situation envisaged by an order under section 11(2)(g) is that of a child who already owns and possesses property, and it is in the interests of the child that some appropriate person be appointed to manage that property on the child's behalf.

---

[59] s. 11(2)(f).
[60] *cf. Re D (A Minor)* [1976] 1 All E.R. 326.
[61] See also s. 35(3) of the Family Law Act 1986.
[62] See *Re H and Ors (Minors) (Prohibited Steps Order)* [1995] 4 All E.R. 110.
[63] s. 11(8).
[64] s. 11(2)(g).

Appointing or removing a guardian

9.17   The court may make an order appointing or removing a person as guardian of the child.[65] There is no provision indicating the effect of such an appointment, but it is submitted that a person appointed guardian under section 11(2)(h) will have all the parental responsibilities and parental rights conferred on a parent by sections 1 and 2, and will become, in effect, a parent-substitute. This is the effect of an appointment of a guardian by testamentary deed under section 7,[66] but is not stated in so many words here. However, there is nothing in the Act to indicate that the powers, duties, liabilities and role of guardian are different depending upon whether the person comes into that office by means of a court order under section 11(2)(h) or by testamentary appointment under section 7, and had Parliament intended to change the law in that respect it would surely have done so expressly. The court can, of course, make the appointment of guardian subject to such terms, conditions and qualifications as it thinks fit.

9.18   There is an apparent overlap here with section 11(2)(a) and (b), under which the court may make an order removing or conferring parental responsibilities or parental rights. If the full range of responsibilities and rights is conferred on a person under section 11(2)(b) then there is, for the purposes of Part I of the 1995 Act, no practical difference between such a person and a guardian appointed under section 11(2)(h). However, there are various provisions contained in other statutes which make a clear distinction between a guardian appointed as such and a person with parental responsibilities and parental rights. The most obvious example is in relation to adoption, where agreement to the adoption order must be obtained from all "parents and guardians",[67] "guardian" being defined as "a person appointed by deed or will or by a court of competent jurisdiction to be the guardian of the child".[68] It is difficult (though not, perhaps, impossible) to argue that a person given full parental responsibilities and parental rights by an order under section 11(2)(b) is "appointed to be guardian of the child". However that may be, courts making an order under section 11(2)(h) must be clear as to why they are appointing a guardian rather than conferring full parental responsibilities and parental rights under section 11(2)(b). Since, for reasons discussed elsewhere,[69] parents are never "guardians", section 11(2)(a) and (b) should be utilised when dealing with parents[70]; the orders in these paragraphs should also be utilised when making an order which concerns something less than the full range of parental responsibilities and parental rights. On the other hand, it is suggested that section 11(2)(h) is the appropriate provision when the person being appointed is not a parent but the aim is to give that person the full range of parental responsibilities and parental rights. The only qualification to this is when the purpose of the order lacks the permanency that is characteristic of guardianship: if a person is to be awarded the full range of parental responsibilities and parental rights, though only for a limited period of time, then probably the order should be made under section 11(2)(b) rather than section 11(2)(h).

---

[65] s. 11(2)(h).

[66] s. 7(5).

[67] Adoption (Scotland) Act 1978, s. 16(1)(b).

[68] *ibid.* s. 65(1). Another, undefined, example of "guardian" having legal effect is in the Foster Children (Scotland) Act 1984. Local authorities are obliged to ensure the well-being of, and to visit, foster children in their area, foster children being defined as children whose care is undertaken by a "person who is not a relative or guardian of his" or hers (1984 Act, s. 1). A person who is looking after a child and has been awarded parental responsibilities and parental rights under s. 11(2)(b) is not a guardian and the child is therefore a foster child for the purposes of the 1984 Act. This was assumed without discussion in *Osborne v. Matthan (No. 2)*, 1998 S.L.T. 1264 (though that case involved an award of custody under s. 3 of the Law Reform (Parent and Child) (Scotland) Act 1986).

[69] See above, para. 7.23

[70] The unmarried father, for example, would become a "parent" for the purposes of agreement to adoption by being awarded parental responsibilities or parental rights: Adoption (Scotland) Act 1978, s. 65(1). He would not have to rely on being a "guardian" since he would then be a "parent with parental responsibilities and parental rights".

Interim orders

The court may make any of the above orders in the form of an interim order and **9.19** it may make an order varying or discharging an order made under section 11(1).[71]

JURISDICTION

Jurisdiction before 1986

The Court of Session

Common law jurisdiction in custody and related questions, including access, **9.20** rested entirely on the *nobile officium*[72] and as such was exercised by the Inner House. The court acted as *parens patriae* and its jurisdiction could be compared with the wardship jurisdiction exercised at one time by the Court of Chancery in England and later by the Chancery, and now the Family, Division of the High Court.[73] Although its incidents were less well developed in detail it was, in principle, as extensive as the English wardship jurisdiction. The various statutes regulating the rules of custody were sometimes referred to as if they were separate sources of jurisdiction, but the better view is probably that all jurisdiction in custody before 1986, although extended and regulated by statute, flowed from the *nobile officium*. In cases outwith the Conjugal Rights (Scotland) Amendment Act 1861[74] procedure in the Court of Session was by petition to the Inner House, except that in vacation it was at one time competent for the Lord Ordinary on the Bills to exercise all the powers and prerogatives of the court.[75] It was later provided that petitions for the custody of children brought under any Act of Parliament or at common law could be presented in the Outer House.[76]

The sheriff court

No order for custody was truly permanent. It could be recalled or varied by **9.21** the court for sufficient cause. A distinction could, however, be made between, on the one hand, an order that was permanent in the sense of having in its contemplation the regulation of the child's custody unless occasion for recall or variation emerges or until, by operation of the law, the child ceased to be subject to it and, on the other hand, an interim or temporary order that had as its purpose the regulation of custody in an emergency, or during the dependence of an action or for like reasons of a temporary kind until a permanent order was made. Because the regulation of custody involved the exercise of the *nobile officium* the sheriff court had, with one possible exception, no jurisdiction at common law to regulate custody on a permanent basis. As judge ordinary of the bounds the sheriff could, however, make temporary orders in an emergency so as to regulate custody until the matter was decided by the supreme court.[77] There is also some authority—the exception just referred to—for the view that the sheriff

---

[71] s. 11(13). See further, below, paras 9.59–9.63.
[72] *S v. S*, 1967 S.C. (H.L.) 46. See also Jamieson, *Parental Responsibilities and Rights* (1995), pp. 157–159.
[73] *McLean v. McLean*, 1947 S.C. 79 at 84, *per* Lord Justice-Clerk Cooper; *Stuart v. Stuart* (1861) 4 Macq. 1 at 60, *per* Lord Campbell L.C. and 66, *per* Lord Cranworth. Though the English courts lost by statute their *parens patriae* jurisdiction over adults (*Re F (Mental Patient: Sterilisation)* [1990] 2 AC 1; *Airedale NHS Trust v. Bland* [1993] A.C. 789) that still subsists in the Court of Session: *Law Hospital NHS Trust v. Lord Advocate*, 1996 S.L.T. 848.
[74] Repealed in relevant part by the Court of Session Act 1988, Sched. 2.
[75] *Edgar v. Fisher's Trs* (1893) 21 R. 59; *Buchan v. Cardross* (1842) 4 D. 1268; Fraser (3rd ed.), p. 294.
[76] 1965 Rules of Court, r. 189(a)(XX), as inserted by Act of Sederunt of January 30, 1970 (S.I. 1970 No. 134). See *Syme v. Cunningham*, 1973 S.L.T. (Notes) 40.
[77] *Speid v. Webster* (1821) 1 S. 221; *Hood v. Hood* (1871) 9 M. 449; *Brand v. Shaws* (1888) 15 R. 449; *Mackenzie v. Keillor* (1892) 19 R. 963; *Gillan v. Barony Parish Council* (1898) 1 F. 183.

could make a permanent order if its sole effect was to support a legal right to custody[78]; there was in such a case no appeal to the *nobile officium* which was exercised only when custody rights were curtailed.

9.22   In 1886 the sheriff court jurisdiction was extended to applications by a mother of a legitimate child[79] and in 1907, more generally, to actions regulating the custody of children.[80] The jurisdiction thereby given to the sheriff court was not limited to cases under statute but extended to those in which direct appeal was made to the *nobile officium*.[81] The custody jurisdiction of the sheriff court therefore became co-extensive with that of the Court of Session and so the sheriff could deal with disputes to which persons other than parents were parties, including disputes between parents (or a parent) and a third party, as well as with disputes between parents *inter se*.[82]

Grounds for jurisdiction today: Family Law Act 1986

9.23   Part I of the Family Law Act 1986, following the recommendations of the Law Commission and the Scottish Law Commission in their joint report *Custody of Children—Jurisdiction and Enforcement Within the UK*,[83] entirely superseded the previously existing rules of jurisdiction[84] in relation to custody and access and, as amended by the Children (Scotland) Act 1995,[85] the 1986 Act now contains all the jurisdictional rules for "Part I Orders", as defined in the following paragraph. It had long been felt unsatisfactory that the jurisdictional rules in Scotland were different from those in England, not least because of the potential conflicts to which this might give rise in questions of recognition and enforcement. As early as 1959 there had been recommendations to harmonise the jurisdictional rules in relation to custody for all the parts of the United Kingdom,[86] but it was not until proposals from the Council of Europe and the Hague Conference, aimed at dealing with the problems of recognition and enforcement of foreign custody decrees, and the return of children taken abroad in breach of "rights of custody",[87] were nearing enactment into United Kingdom domestic law that the Law Commissions recommended the changes in the law that were *inter alia* incorporated into the Family Law Act 1986. The purpose of Part I of this Act is twofold: first, to lay down a uniform system of jurisdiction throughout the United Kingdom, which aims to ensure, so far as possible, that there is only one court at any one time with jurisdiction to make orders relating to parental responsibilities and parental rights over a child, these jurisdictional rules being, so far as possible, the same throughout the United Kingdom; and secondly to provide for the automatic recognition and speedy enforcement of such orders made in one part of the United Kingdom throughout the other parts of the United Kingdom. Recognition and enforcement will be dealt with later[88]; this part of this chapter will consider the grounds of jurisdiction of the Scottish courts.[89]

---

[78] *Murray v. Forsyth*, 1917 S.C. 721 at 724, *per* Lord Skerrington; *Brand v. Shaws* (1888) 15 R. 449; 16 R. 315. See, however, the reservations expressed in *Harvey v. Harvey* (1860) 22 D. 1198, *per* Lord Justice-Clerk Inglis at 1209, and in *Hood v. Hood* (1871) 9 M. 449 at 455. See also Fraser, p. 94, n. 2 citing *Herd v. Ellis* (1864) 3 Scot. Law Mag. (N.S.) 143.

[79] Guardianship of Infants Act 1886, ss. 5 and 9 (repealed by the Law Reform (Parent and Child) (Scotland) Act 1986, Sched. 2).

[80] Sheriff Courts (Scotland) Act 1907, s. 5(2) (as originally enacted).

[81] *Murray v. Forsyth*, above.

[82] *ibid.*

[83] Law Com. No. 138, Scot. Law Com. No. 91, Cmnd. 9419 (1985).

[84] s. 8.

[85] Sched. 4, para. 41.

[86] *Report of the Committee on Conflicts of Jurisdiction Affecting Children*, Cmnd. 842 (1959) ("the Hodson Report").

[87] See below, Chap. 11.

[88] Below, paras 11.03–11.09.

[89] See further, *Stair Memorial Encyclopaedia of the Laws of Scotland*, Vol. 10, paras 1314–1318; Balfour, "Family Law—Cross-Border Child Abduction" (1989) 34 J.L.S.S. 96; Jamieson, "Custody of Children and the Family Law Act 1986", 1991 S.L.T. (News) 438.

"Part I orders"

Chapter III of Part I of the Family Law Act 1986 provides the rules governing **9.24** the jurisdiction of courts in Scotland to make "Part I orders".[90] In relation to orders made by a court in England or Wales, Part I orders are defined as any order made under section 8 of the Children Act 1989, other than an order varying or discharging such an order.[91] In relation to orders made in Scotland, the position is rather more complicated, for Part I orders are defined[92] as orders "made by a court of civil jurisdiction in Scotland under any enactment or rule of law with respect to the residence, custody, care or control of a child, contact with or access to a child or the education or upbringing of a child", subject to certain specified exceptions.[93] Most of these exceptions relate to public law orders governed by statutory provisions other than those contained in Part I of the Children (Scotland) Act 1995,[94] but while all "Part I orders" can now be made under section 11 of the 1995 Act it would be a mistake to conclude from this that all orders made under section 11 are necessarily Part I orders. That section is wide in its terms and allows the court to make orders relating to parental responsibilities, parental rights, guardianship or the administration of a child's property; the definition of Part I orders in section 1(1)(b) of the 1986 Act, which was amended by the 1995 Act, is in significantly different terms. For one thing, administration of children's property, while not expressly excluded from the definition of Part I orders, is subject to its own jurisdictional rule in section 14 of the Children (Scotland) Act 1995. This provides (i) that the Court of Session shall have jurisdiction to entertain an application for an order relating to the administration of a child's property if the child is habitually resident in, or the property is situated in, Scotland and (ii) that the sheriff shall have jurisdiction to entertain such an application if the child is habitually resident in, or the property is situated in, the sheriffdom.[95] The appointment under section 11(2)(g) of a judicial factor to manage a child's property is a section 11 order but is unlikely to be considered to be a Part I order.[96] Also, "orders relating to the guardianship of a child" are expressly excluded from the definition of Part I orders for the purposes of the Family Law Act 1986 and a special rule is laid down in section 16 of that Act, to the effect that the Court of Session has jurisdiction if, on the date of the application, the child is habitually resident in Scotland and the sheriff has jurisdiction if, on the date of the application, the child is habitually resident in the sheriffdom; that rule is in addition to any other ground of jurisdiction

---

[90] The same rules are applied to actions for delivery of the child taken by one parent against the other, or by one of the parties to a marriage against the other in relation to a child of their family: Family Law Act 1986, s. 17, as amended by the Children (Scotland) Act 1995, Sched. 4, para. 41.

[91] Family Law Act 1986, s.1(1)(a).

[92] *ibid.* s. 1(1)(b).

[93] *i.e.* (i) an order committing the care of a child to a local authority or placing a child under the supervision of a local authority; (ii) an adoption order as defined in s. 12(1) of the Adoption (Scotland) Act 1978; (iii) an order freeing a child for adoption made under s. 18 of the said Act of 1978; (iv) an order giving parental responsibilities and parental rights in relation to a child made in the course of proceedings for the adoption of the child (other than an order made following the making of a direction under s. 53(1) of the Children Act 1975); (v) an order made under the Education (Scotland) Act 1980; (vi) an order made under Pt II or III of the Social Work (Scotland) Act 1968; (vii) an order made under the Child Abduction and Custody Act 1985; (viii) an order for the delivery of a child or other order for the enforcement of a Pt I order; and (ix) an order relating to the guardianship of a child.

[94] *cf. Re M (Care Orders: Jurisdiction)* [1997] 1 F.L.R. 456 in which the English court held that the jurisdictional rules contained in the 1986 Act did not apply to public law proceedings.

[95] Children (Scotland) Act 1995, s. 14(1) and (2).

[96] It may be noted that while most s. 11 orders are subject to the procedural rules for "family actions" in the Sheriff Court Ordinary Cause Rules 1993, excluded from the definition of "family actions" are orders made under s. 11(2)(g) and (h) (appointment of judicial factors and guardians): OCR 1993, r. 33.1.

applicable to actions relating to guardianship.[97] Though the 1986 Act contains no definition of "guardianship", it is open to argument that the word there does not import the same meaning as in section 11 of the Children (Scotland) Act 1995. Section 16 continues to appear under the headnote "Tutory and Curatory" and, as originally enacted, it applied to orders "relating to the tutory or curatory of a pupil or minor". Since the coming into force of the Age of Legal Capacity (Scotland) Act 1991, section 16 has referred to "guardianship" rather than to "tutory and curatory"[98] but it continues, it is submitted, to refer to the previous understanding of that legal concept, that is to say legal representation, rather than the concept of parent-substitution that guardianship has now developed into.[99] It follows that an order made under section 11 of the 1995 Act relating to guardianship is, because it concerns the upbringing of the child and not just the legal representation of the child, a Part I order as defined in section 1(1)(b) of the 1986 Act.[1] An order made under section 11 relating to legal representation is, on the other hand, not a Part I order and jurisdiction is governed exclusively by section 16 of the 1986 Act. Any other order made under section 11, such as for example a specific issue order under section 11(2)(c), will be a Part I order for the purposes of the 1986 Act only if it concerns residence, care or control, contact, education or upbringing of the child. It should be noted, however, that section 11 of the 1995 Act allows the court to make any section 11 order in any proceedings that are competently before it, and the role of the 1986 Act is limited to determining the competency, from the point of view of jurisdiction, of an applicant for such an order raising the action in a court in Scotland. If proceedings are already competently before the court, the 1986 Act does not cut down the court's power under the 1995 Act to make such order as it thinks fit.[2]

Existence of matrimonial proceedings

9.25   The pre-eminent ground of jurisdiction for Part I orders is the existence of matrimonial proceedings to which orders made under section 11 of the Children (Scotland) Act 1995 are ancillary. This is the result of the terms of section 11 of the Family Law Act 1986, which excludes the other, subsidiary, grounds of jurisdiction (except the emergency ground under section 12) when, on the date of an application for a Part I order, there are continuing in a court in any part of the United Kingdom matrimonial proceedings in respect of the marriage of the parents of the child.[3] This has been particularly important since the coming into force of the Children (Scotland) Act 1995, under which the Court of Session or the sheriff is obliged in any action for divorce, judicial separation or declarator of nullity to consider whether to make an order under section 11 thereof in respect of a child of the family.[4]

---

[97] Family Law Act 1986, s. 16(1) and (3).
[98] *ibid.* s. 16, as amended by the Age of Legal Capacity (Scotland) Act 1991, Sched. 1, para. 45.
[99] See above, paras 1.08–1.09 and below, paras 15.29–15.30.
[1] The importance of the point, given that the jurisdictional test for "guardianship" in s. 16 is identical to that for Pt I orders in s. 9, is that if matrimonial proceedings are continuing then s. 11 deprives the court of the habitual residence of jurisdiction to make a Pt I order, but not to make an order relating to "guardianship" in the sense of legal representation.
[2] So, for example, the sheriff might make a s. 11 order in an application by a reporter under s. 68 of the 1995 Act to establish grounds of referral to the children's hearing, or under s. 85 to review the establishment of these grounds, notwithstanding that matrimonial proceedings are continuing in another court. Similarly, and expressly, the court that revokes an order freeing a child for adoption must make a s. 11 order determining on whom are to be imposed the parental responsibilities and to whom are to be given the parental rights in relation to the child: Adoption (Scotland) Act 1978, s. 20(3), as substituted by the Children (Scotland) Act 1995, Sched. 2, para. 13(d). There is no room to argue that the court's jurisdiction to do so is compromised by the existence of matrimonial proceedings involving the child's parents in another court, whether in Scotland or elsewhere in the U.K.
[3] Family Law Act 1986, s. 11(1). For "parents of the child", see s. 42(4), discussed below, para. 9.31.
[4] Children (Scotland) Act 1995, s. 12(1).

"Matrimonial proceedings" are defined[5] to mean "proceedings for divorce, **9.26** nullity of marriage or judicial separation". It is therefore to the rules of jurisdiction in relation to matrimonial proceedings, which are found in the Domicile and Matrimonial Proceedings Act 1973, that we must turn to determine the pre-eminent ground of jurisdiction in relation to Part I orders.[6]

The Court of Session has jurisdiction to entertain an action for divorce or **9.27** separation if (and only if) either of the parties to the marriage in question (a) is domiciled in Scotland on the date when the action is begun; or (b) was habitually resident in Scotland throughout the period of one year ending with that date.[7] It has jurisdiction to entertain an action for declarator of nullity of marriage if (and only if) either of the parties to the marriage (a) is domiciled in Scotland on the date when the action is begun; or (b) was habitually resident in Scotland throughout the period of one year ending with that date; or (c) died before that date and was either domiciled in Scotland at death or had been habitually resident in Scotland throughout the period of one year ending with the date of death.[8] The sheriff court has jurisdiction to entertain an action for divorce or separation[9] if (and only if) (a) either party to the marriage in question is domiciled in Scotland at the date when the action is begun, or was habitually resident there throughout the period of one year ending with that date, and (b) either party to the marriage was resident in the sheriffdom for a period of 40 days ending with that date, or had been habitually resident in the sheriffdom for a period of not less than 40 days ending not more than 40 days before the said date and has no known residence in Scotland at that date.[10]

Continuance of matrimonial proceedings

Matrimonial proceedings, once commenced, are deemed to be "continuing" **9.28** in the court they are taken until either (i) the child concerned reaches the age of 16,[11] (so that even after, say, a divorce has been pronounced, the court that granted that decree retains jurisdiction to make a Part I order in relation to children of the family at some later date), or (ii) the proceedings have been dismissed or decree of absolvitor granted before then.[12] In the latter case the court retains jurisdiction only if the application for a Part I order was made on or before the dismissal or the granting of the decree of absolvitor.[13] There are a number of practical difficulties with the rule that the court in which matrimonial proceedings took place is the court with primary jurisdiction until the child is 16. For one thing, the parties and the child may have lost all connection with that court district shortly after the proceedings took place. Or the parent with whom the child resides may remarry and divorce again, giving rise to a second matrimonial court. Or the matrimonial court, applying the principle in section 11(7)(a) of the Children (Scotland) Act 1995, might have made no order in relation to the child, while at the same time granting the matrimonial decree sought. Or a dispute may arise involving one of the parties to the matrimonial proceedings in which the other party takes no part (or indeed in which neither of the parties

---

[5] Family Law Act 1986, s. 18(1).
[6] For a more detailed discussion of jurisdiction in matrimonial proceedings than is necessary here, see Clive, *Husband and Wife* (4th ed.), pp. 572–579.
[7] Family Law Act 1986, s. 7(2). See *Spence v. Spence*, 1995 S.L.T. 335.
[8] *ibid*. s. 7(3).
[9] The sheriff court has no jurisdiction to entertain a declarator of marriage or of nullity of marriage.
[10] Domicile and Matrimonial Proceedings Act 1973, s. 8(2) (as amended by the Divorce Jurisdiction, Court Fees and Legal Aid (Scotland) Act 1983, Sched. 1, para. 18).
[11] Or 18, in the case of proceedings in England or Wales or in Northern Ireland: s. 42(2), as amended by the Family Law Act 1996, Sched. 8, para. 37(10).
[12] Family Law Act 1986, s. 42(3).
[13] *ibid*. s. 13(2), as amended by the Children (Scotland) Act 1995, Sched. 4, para. 41(3).

takes part). It is not obvious why, in any of these circumstances, the parties should have to return to the original court, and the problem is compounded when the order is sought by a third party, who will have no standing to enter the process in the earlier matrimonial proceedings.[14] In all such circumstances the correct procedural approach is to seek an order from the original court declining jurisdiction to make a Part I order. The court may make such an order if both the following conditions are satisfied: (a) it appears to the court that, but for the existence of matrimonial proceedings, another court in Scotland or in another part of the United Kingdom would have jurisdiction; and (b) the court considers that it would be more appropriate for Part I matters relating to that child to be determined in that other court or other part.[15] The court may recall an order made under this provision.[16]

Conflict of jurisdiction between matrimonial courts

9.29   As pointed out above, if a decree of separation has been granted by one court then that court will usually retain jurisdiction to entertain an application for a Part I order until the child reaches the age of 16.[17] However, there is no rule that a divorce may be obtained only from the same court that previously granted a legal separation, and if after one court grants a decree of separation, an action for divorce or nullity of marriage is raised in another court, both courts would be able to claim jurisdiction over the children of the marriage on the basis of the existence of matrimonial proceedings. It was considered that in that situation the divorce or nullity court should take precedence, and so the court that granted the decree of separation is deprived of jurisdiction to entertain an application for a Part I order if, on the date of that application, proceedings for divorce or nullity of marriage in respect of the marriage concerned are continuing in another court in the United Kingdom.[18] This, however, is qualified if the court in which divorce or nullity proceedings are continuing has declined jurisdiction in favour of the court that granted the decree of separation[19]: in that case the court that granted the decree of separation will retain jurisdiction.

Refusal of the matrimonial decree

9.30   The court that made a Part I order in matrimonial proceedings but refused to grant the principal (*i.e.* the matrimonial) remedy sought does not have jurisdiction to entertain an application for the variation of the Part I order if, on the date of the application, matrimonial proceedings in respect of the marriage concerned are continuing in another court in the United Kingdom.[20] This, however, is qualified if the court in which matrimonial proceedings are continuing has declined jurisdiction in favour of the court that made the original order[21]: in that case the original court does have jurisdiction to vary the order.

"Treated" child

9.31   The court in which matrimonial proceedings are continuing in respect of the marriage of the parents of a child has, to the exclusion (subject to section 12) of

---

[14] See Scott, "Jurisdiction to Make Orders Relating to Children After Divorce" 1994 Fam. L.B. 9–4 and in *Butterworths Scottish Family Law Service*, para. C.606.

[15] Family Law Act 1986, s. 13(6).

[16] *ibid.* s. 13(7).

[17] *ibid.* s. 42(3).

[18] *ibid.* s. 13(3). (The other court could be in Scotland, or in another part of the United Kingdom.)

[19] *ibid.* s. 13(5) and (6).

[20] *ibid.* s. 13(4) (as amended by the Children (Scotland) Act 1995, Sched. 4, para. 41(3)). This supersedes the normal rule (s. 15(2)) that the court that had jurisdiction to make a Pt I order will have jurisdiction to vary and recall the original order, even when it no longer has jurisdiction to make the original order.

[21] *ibid.* s. 13(5) and (6).

any other court, jurisdiction to entertain an application for a Part I order in respect of any child who is either (i) a child of both parties to the marriage or (ii) not a child of both parties but has been treated by both parties as a child of their family except in the case of a child who has been placed with these parties as foster parents by a local authority or a voluntary organisation.[22] In the latter case there is no requirement that the child be the genetic or adopted child of either party to the marriage.[23] Whether the child has been treated by both spouses as a child of their family is a question of fact, the answer to which is usually to be inferred from the circumstances. The mere fact of marriage is insufficient to give rise to an inference that both spouses treated the child as a child of their family. Nor is the fact sufficient that the parties were looking after the child, even for a substantial period.[24] "Treatment" requires an *actus reus* rather than a state of mind, as the previous test of "acceptance" did. It suggests some action directed towards the child which indicates that the non-parent spouse (or spouses) regarded the child as part of the family centred around the marriage. It would seem not to matter whether the non-parent has ceased treating the child as a child of the family by the time of the court action, for the relationship is established as soon as the child "has been treated", and these words imply an action in the past rather than a continuing state of affairs. A typical situation is where a man marries and "sets up home with his wife, the children [of the wife] come to live there, he treats them as his own and does his best to make them not only members of the family, but to feel that they are members of the family".[25] The test is an objective one: "the independent outside observer has to look at the situation and say: Does the evidence show that the child was treated as a member of the family?"[26] It has been held that a child *in utero* could be "accepted" as one of the family, even when the spouses separate before the child is born.[27] However, acceptance (which remains relevant for aliment) is different from treatment, which is here at issue, and it is unlikely that a child can be "treated" as a child of the family before it is born.

Habitual residence

If matrimonial proceedings are not continuing in a court in any part of the United Kingdom in respect of the marriage of the parents of the child, then an independent application for a Part I order may be entertained (a) by the Court of Session if, on the date of the application, the child concerned is habitually resident in Scotland or (b) by the sheriff if, on the date of the application, the child concerned is habitually resident in the sheriffdom.[28] Habitual residence has the meaning ascribed to it in other areas of international private law.[29] If the child is removed from or retained outside or him- or herself leaves or remains outside a part

9.32

---

[22] Family Law Act 1986, s. 11(1) and s. 42(4). This is also the definition of "child of the family" given in s. 12 of the 1995 Act, which obliges the matrimonial court to consider whether to make a s. 11 order. Prior to the coming into force of the Children (Scotland) Act 1995, "child of the family" was defined as "any child of one of the parties who has been accepted as one of the family by the other party" (s. 42(4), as originally enacted). This was amended by the 1995 Act, Sched. 4, para. 41(9).

[23] In *Bradley v. Bradley*, 1987 S.C.L.R. 62 the sheriff held that the terms of s. 42(4), as then in force (see n. 22 above), required that the child be the genetic child of at least one of the parties. The current wording of the subsection contains no requirement to this effect.

[24] In *Re A (Child of the Family)* [1998] 1 F.L.R. 347, grandparents who had assumed the care of their grandchild when her mother became unable to do so were held, on an objective examination of the circumstances, to have treated their granddaughter as a child of their family.

[25] *Bowlas v. Bowlas* [1965] P. 450, *per* Salmon L.J. at 461.

[26] *D v. D (Child of the Family)* [1981] 2 F.L.R. 93, *per* Ormrod L.J. at 97. See also *M v. M (Child of the Family)* [1981] 2 F.L.R. 39; *W v. W (Child of the Family)* [1984] F.L.R. 796; *Carron v. Carron* [1984] F.L.R. 805; *Teeling v. Teeling* [1984] F.L.R. 808; *Re A (Child of the Family)*, above.

[27] *Caller v. Caller* [1966] 2 All E.R. 754. See further, above, para. 2.28.

[28] Family Law Act 1986, s. 9. See *Scullion v. Scullion*, 1990 S.C.L.R. 577.

[29] See below, para. 11.21.

of the United Kingdom in which he or she was habitually resident before the change of residence, and this is done (a) without the agreement of the person or all persons having the right to determine where the child is to reside or (b) in contravention of an order made by a court in any part of the United Kingdom, then the child shall be treated as continuing to be habitually resident in that part of the United Kingdom for a period of one year after his or her removal, etc.,[30] or until he or she reaches the age of 16, if sooner, or until the person or persons whose agreement was not obtained subsequently agrees and this is not in contravention of any United Kingdom court order, if sooner.[31] The purpose of this provision is to prevent the objective of the Act being frustrated simply by removing the child to another jurisdiction, but if this happens and the state of affairs persists for more than one year the child might be held to have acquired a new habitual residence, which can found jurisdiction in the court in the new part of the United Kingdom.[32] It is undecided whether this result will follow even when the removal is in contravention of a court order but given the factual nature of habitual residence[33] such contravention should not, in principle, prevent a new habitual residence from being acquired.

Presence

9.33   If matrimonial proceedings are not continuing in a court in any part of the United Kingdom in respect of the marriage of the parents of the child, then an independent application for a Part I order may be entertained (a) by the Court of Session if, on the date of the application, the child concerned is present in Scotland and is not habitually resident in any part of the United Kingdom, or (b) by the sheriff if, on the date of the application, the child is present in Scotland and is not habitually resident in any part of the United Kingdom and either the pursuer or the defender in the application is habitually resident in the sheriffdom.[34] This section is intended to act as a safety net to ensure that jurisdiction exists over children physically present in Scotland and over whom it is felt that there should be jurisdiction, even though there is no emergency facing the child.[35] It will allow the Scottish court to make an order under section 11 of the Children (Scotland) Act 1995 over a child brought from abroad as soon as he or she enters Scotland,[36] and this is so even when the child is subject to a foreign order entitled to recognition here.[37] This jurisdiction is limited to cases in which the child is not habitually resident in any part of the United Kingdom (including Scotland), and thus there is no overlap with the previous ground of jurisdiction. Nevertheless it may well be correct that given the emergency jurisdiction described in the next paragraph, this ground based on mere presence "smacks of exorbitancy."[38]

---

[30] Family Law Act 1986, s. 41(1) and (2). See *Rellis v. Hart*, 1993 S.L.T. 738; *Morris v. Morris*, 1993 S.C.L.R. 144; *D v. D (Custody: Jurisdiction)* [1996] 1 F.L.R. 574.

[31] Family Law Act 1986, s. 41(3).

[32] Clive has pointed out that there is no case in the reported decisions in which a person has been held not to be habitually resident in a place where he or she has in fact resided for more than one year: "The Concept of Habitual Residence", 1997 J.R. 137 at 141.

[33] See Clive, *op. cit.*

[34] Family Law Act 1986, s. 10.

[35] This was the case at common law in Scotland: *Kelly v. Marks*, 1974 S.L.T. 118. See also *Babington v. Babington*, 1955 S.C. 115 at 121 and 124; *Calder v. Calder*, 1960 S.L.T. (Notes) 52.

[36] See, *e.g.*, *Hill v. Hill*, 1991 S.L.T. 189.

[37] *Calleja v. Calleja*, 1997 S.L.T. 579, *per* Lord Osborne (Ordinary) at 594D.

[38] Anton and Beaumont, *Private International Law* (2nd ed.), p. 515. The English Court of Appeal applied this provision to found jurisdiction in *Re M (Minors: Residence Order: Jurisdiction)* [1993] 1 F.L.R. 495 but was criticised for doing so by an eminent commentator: see Cretney, "Fresh Life for Presence?" (1993) 109 L.Q.R. 538. See also *Re F (Residence Order: Jurisdiction)* [1995] 2 F.L.R. 518 in which Singer J. held that the English court would have jurisdiction due to the child's presence in England at the relevant date, however that presence came about, but that in the instant case the court should decline jurisdiction because the child had since been returned to her habitual residence under the terms of the Hague Convention and it would therefore be absurd for the court to exercise its jurisdiction. Perhaps the absurdity lies in the ground itself.

Emergency

Notwithstanding that any other court, whether within or outwith Scotland, **9.34** has jurisdiction to entertain an application for a Part I order, the Court of Session or the sheriff has jurisdiction to entertain such an application if (a) the child concerned is present in Scotland or, as the case may be, in the sheriffdom on the date of the application; and (b) the Court of Session or the sheriff considers that, for the protection of the child, it is necessary to make such an order immediately.[39] This emergency jurisdiction supersedes all other grounds, including jurisdiction based upon the existence of matrimonial proceedings, and it was enacted to give effect to the Law Commissions' recommendation that "the ability to invoke the jurisdiction of the court on this basis should [never] be excluded by reason of the fact that some other basis of jurisdiction may be available".[40] The Law Commissions did not specify what nature of necessity has to exist before the section is operable, except to state that it must be immediate and it is, therefore, a matter to be decided by the court in each particular case. The sorts of emergency that, at common law, justified the Court of Session in exercising its inherent protective jurisdiction included threats of the child being abducted from his or her parents[41] and threats of "injury, physical or moral, to the child".[42] A more modern phraseology would be "risk of exposing the child to any form of physical or psychological harm".[43] At common law the basis of the emergency jurisdiction was the welfare of the child[44] and that, doubtless, remains the basis of the exercise of the jurisdiction under the statutory provisions. It follows from the emergency nature of this basis of jurisdiction that it cannot be invoked to deal with issues (such as, in the normal case, contact) which do not require determination as a matter of urgent necessity.[45] Even a residence order, because it will usually deal with the child's long-term future, will seldom require to be decided on an emergency basis. It is more likely that this jurisdiction will be relied upon when the application is for a specific issue order under section 11(2)(e) or an interdict under section 11(2)(f) of the Children (Scotland) Act 1995.

Refusal of application and sisting of proceedings

Notwithstanding that the court has jurisdiction to entertain an application **9.35** for a Part I order, it may refuse the application in any case where the matter in question has already been determined in other proceedings.[46] The other proceedings may be in Scotland, elsewhere in the United Kingdom, or in a foreign country. Various issues relating to the upbringing of a child, such as his or her residence or with whom he or she is to have contact are never, in principle, "determined" in the sense of a dispute being finally and for all time coming resolved[47] and they are always, therefore, open to be revisited. It follows that this provision is limited to proceedings which come to a final conclusion in a one-off dispute (such as, for example, whether a child should be subjected to a particular form of medical treatment or procedure, or should be allowed to leave the jurisdiction for a short holiday).

---

[39] Family Law Act 1986, s.12.
[40] Law Com. No. 138, Scot. Law Com. No 91, Cmnd. 9419 (1985), para. 4.99.
[41] *Murray v. Forsyth*, 1917 S.C. 721.
[42] *Westergaard v. Westergaard*, 1914 S.C. 977, *per* Lord Justice-Clerk Macdonald at 981. See also *McShane v. McShane*, 1962 S.L.T. 221; *Oludimu v. Oludimu*, 1967 S.L.T. 105; *Woodcock v. Woodcock*, 1990 S.L.T. 848.
[43] *Calleja v. Calleja*, 1997 S.L.T. 579, *per* Lord Coulsfield (speaking for the First Division) at 603E.
[44] *Stuart v. Moore* (1861) 23 D. 902, *per* Lord Campbell L.C. at 908.
[45] See *B v. B (Scottish Contact Order: Jurisdiction to Vary)* [1996] 1 F.L.R. 688.
[46] Family Law Act 1986, s. 14(1).
[47] So a plea of *res judicata* is never available.

9.36   In addition, the court to which application has been made may sist the proceedings at any stage if it appears to it that proceedings in relation to matters to which the application relates are continuing outside Scotland or in another court in Scotland[48] or where it appears to the court that it would be more appropriate[49] for those matters to be determined in proceedings outside Scotland or in another court in Scotland, and that such proceedings are likely to be taken there.[50] This provision was enacted to avoid doubt as to whether the court could decline its essentially protective jurisdiction in cases involving children; but in any case in deciding whether to sist the proceedings before the Scottish court, the welfare of the child is the paramount consideration.[51] The exercise of the power to sist proceedings is a matter of judicial discretion, which cannot be interfered with on appeal just because the appellate court would have decided otherwise.[52]

Jurisdiction to vary or recall orders

9.37   A court in Scotland which has made a Part I order may make an order varying[53] or recalling that order, even when it no longer has jurisdiction to make the original order,[54] unless it lost jurisdiction through the application of section 13(3)[55] or (4).[56] And if the original order has ceased to have effect because a court of competent jurisdicition has subsequently made an inconsistent Part I order or an order from a court outside the United Kingdom relating to parental responsibilities or parental rights has been recognised in Scotland[57] then the court that made the original order loses jurisdiction to vary it.[58]

PROCEDURE

9.38 Procedure for family actions is governed, for the sheriff court,[59] primarily by Chapter 33 of the Ordinary Cause Rules[60] and, for the Court of Session, by Chapter 49 of the Rules of the Court of Session.[61] "Family actions" are defined to include actions or applications for or in respect of an order under section 11

---

[48] Family Law Act 1986, s. 14(2)(a). See *Hill v. Hill*, 1991 S.L.T. 189; *B v. B*, 1998 S.L.T. 1245.
[49] For what is envisaged by this, see Law Com. No. 138, Scot. Law Com. No. 91, para. 4.97. For comment on the equivalent English rule contained in s. 5, see Cretney, "Conventions and Convenience" (1993) 109 L.Q.R. 363. See also *T v. T (Custody: Jurisdiction)* [1992] 1 F.L.R. 43; *Re S (Jurisdiction to Stay Application)* [1995] 1 F.L.R. 1093.
[50] Family Law Act 1986, s. 14(2)(b).
[51] *Hill v. Hill*, above, *per* Lord McCluskey at 192B; *Calleja v. Calleja*, 1997 S.L.T. 579, *per* Lord Osborne (Ordinary) at 594G-H. This was, however, doubted by Lord Maclean in *B v. B*, 1998 S.L.T. 1245 at 1246K.
[52] See *Messenger v. Messenger* 1992 S.L.T.(Sh.Ct) 29.
[53] An order varying a Pt I order means any subsequent Pt I order made with respect to the same child: s. 15(3).
[54] Family Law Act 1986, s. 15(2). The rules require that the application for the variation or recall of a s. 11 order be made by minute in the process of the action to which the application relates: OCR 1993, r. 33.44; RCS 1994, r. 49.41.
[55] Separation court losing jurisdiction in favour of divorce or nullity court.
[56] Matrimonial court losing jurisdiction in favour of later matrimonial court.
[57] s. 15(1).
[58] s. 15(2). See *A v. A (Forum Conveniens)* [1999] 1 F.L.R. 1.
[59] See further Macphail, *Sheriff Court Practice* (2nd ed., 1998), Chap. 22.
[60] Act of Sederunt (Sheriff Court Ordinary Cause Rules) 1993 (S.I. 1993 No. 1956), as amended by Act of Sederunt (Family Proceedings in the Sheriff Court) 1996 (S.I. 1996 No. 2167 —hereinafter "OCR 1993".
[61] Act of Sederunt (Rules of the Court of Session) 1994 (S.I. 1994 No. 1443), as amended by Act of Sederunt (Rules of the Court of Session Amendment No. 5) (Family Actions and Miscellaneous) 1996 (S.I. 1996 No. 2587)—hereinafter "RCS 1994".

of the Children (Scotland) Act 1995 with the exception of (for the sheriff court) an application for the appointment of a judicial factor under section 11(2)(g)[62] and an application for the appointment or removal of a person as a guardian under section 11(2)(h),[63] and (for the Court of Session) a petition for the appointment of a judicial factor.[64] The court being under a mandatory duty to regard the welfare of the child as its paramount consideration, some examination of the facts and circumstances of the case is necessary even if the case be undefended: "it is not normally appropriate, where the welfare of the child is involved, to dispose of an application for an order relating to parental rights solely on the pleadings. Once the point is in issue the court ought not to dispose of the matter, except on a point of law only, without conducting some kind of an inquiry into the facts."[65]

Applications in actions of divorce, separation or nullity

In actions of divorce, legal separation or (in the Court of Session) declarator **9.39** of nullity of marriage, applications for a section 11 order (or for an order for aliment for a child) are to be made by a crave in the initial writ or conclusion in the summons, or defences or, where the application is made by a person other than the pursuer or defender, by minute in that action.[66] An application by a party in an action depending before the court for, or for variation of, an order for interim aliment for a child under the age of 18 or for a residence order or a contact order shall be made by motion.[67] In actions of divorce, judicial separation and declarator of nullity of marriage,[68] where there is a child of the family who has not reached the age of 16 years at the date when the question first arises, the court is obliged to consider whether to make an order under section 11 or under section 54 (referral to the principal reporter).[69] The implication is clear, though it is not stated, that if the court considers it necessary to make such an order then it must do so. Where the court is of the opinion that the circumstances of the case require, or are likely to require, it to exercise any power under section 11 or section 54, but it is not in a position to exercise that power without giving further consideration to the case, and there are exceptional circumstances which make it desirable in the interests of the child that it should not grant decree in the action until it is in a position to exercise such a power, then the court must postpone its decision on the granting of decree in the action until it is in such a position.[70] The previous law[71] had precluded the court from granting decree unless and until it was satisfied about the arrangements for the care of the

---

[62] Procedure for such applications is governed by Pt I of the Act of Sederunt (Judicial Factors Rules) 1992 (S.I. 1992 No. 272).

[63] Procedure for such applications is governed by para. 4 of the Act of Sederunt (Family Proceedings in the Sheriff Court) 1996 (S.I. 1996 No. 2167)

[64] OCR 1993, r. 33.1(1)(h) and RCS 1994, r. 49.1(1)(j).

[65] *O v. O*, 1995 S.L.T. 238, *per* Lord President Hope at 240H–I. OCR 1993, r. 33.31 permits the sheriff to pronounce decree in an undefended action "after such inquiry as the sheriff thinks fit". In *Sanderson v. McManus*, 1997 S.L.T. 629 Lord Clyde said, at 635K that the requirement on the court to be satisfied that the order it makes will be in the interests of the child "does not necessarily involve the formal leading of evidence. The particular circumstances will dictate what is or is not required to satisfy the court in particular cases".

[66] OCR 1993, r. 33.39; RCS 1994, r. 49.36.

[67] OCR 1993, r. 33.43; RCS 1994, r. 49.40 (which also provides for Court of Session actions that written intimation of a motion shall be given to every other party not less than seven days before the date on which the motion is enrolled).

[68] *N.B.*: *not* declarator of marriage.

[69] Children (Scotland) Act 1995, s. 12(1).

[70] *ibid.* s. 12(2).

[71] Matrimonial Proceedings (Children) Act 1958, s. 8, repealed by the Children (Scotland) Act 1995, Sched. 5.

children, though little attention was paid to that provision in practice. The current wording indicates that the matrimonial decree will be granted, even when the court is not satisfied as to the arrangements made for the care of the children and that only in exceptional circumstances must it postpone its decision until in a position to determine whether an order in relation to the children should be made. There is no indication in the Act as to what these exceptional circumstances might be, though it is reasonably clear that the aim of the change in wording was to separate as much as possible the matrimonial dispute from any arrangements that might have to be made for the care and future upbringing of the child: only if the one cannot realistically be separated from the other should the court postpone its decision until it can deal with both issues.

9.40   There is no Scottish authority on the consequences of decree being granted where the court, through ignorance of a child's existence, has failed to give consideration to the question of whether to exercise the powers under sections 11 or 54. If the parties have knowingly misled the court, that would be a contempt but no positive duty is placed upon the parties and so mere failure to disclose circumstances which might indicate to the court that it should exercise these powers would not appear to attract any sanction. With provisions in England similar to the pre-1995 Scottish rule,[72] it was at one time held that the decree was void,[73] but the authorities to that effect were later overruled in favour of the view that the decree is voidable.[74] There is, however, no statutory warrant for treating the decree as void or voidable and unless both parties have been guilty of a fraud on the court, it is difficult to see on what principles of Scots law the decree could be reduced.

Applications in independent actions

9.41   In applications for a section 11 order other than in matrimonial proceedings, the application must be made (i) by an action for a section 11 order or (ii) by a crave in the initial writ or conclusion in the summons or defences in any other family action (other than matrimonial proceedings) or (iii) where the application is made by a person other than a party to the action, by minute in that action.[75] In an action for a section 11 order the pursuer must call as a defender (a) the parents or other parent of the child in respect of whom the order is sought, (b) any guardian of the child, (c) any person who has treated the child as a child of his or her family,[76] (d) any person who in fact exercises care or control in respect of the child; and (e) in any case where there is no person falling within paragraphs (a)–(d) the Lord Advocate.[77]

Applications after final decree

9.42   An application after final decree for, or for the variation or recall of, a section 11 order is to be made by minute in the process of the action to which the application relates.[78] There was some dispute under the previous rules (which were in similar but not identical terms) as to the competency of seeking a custody or access order other than by minute in the existing process. The dicta from the First Division in *Girvan v. Girvan*[79] that the welfare of the child was the paramount

[72]   Matrimonial Proceedings (Children) Act 1958, s. 2.
[73]   *B v. B* [1961] 1 W.L.R. 856; *N v. N* (1964) 108 Sol.J. 99.
[74]   *F v. F* [1971] P. 1; *P v. P and J* [1971] P. 217, in which the principle in *F v. F* is approved and *B v. B* and *N v. N* overruled.
[75]   OCR 1993, r. 33.61; RCS 1994, r. 49.59.
[76]   On which, see above, para. 9.31.
[77]   OCR 1993, r. 33.62; RCS 1994, r. 49.60.
[78]   OCR 1993, rr. 33.44 and 33.65; RCS 1994, rr. 49.41 and 49.63.
[79]   1988 S.L.T. 866.

consideration even in the interpretation of procedural rules which made no reference to that consideration were founded upon by some sheriffs who were on that basis willing to allow fresh and independent proceedings in courts different from the one that granted a previous decree, though not all sheriffs who were faced with the issue adopted that approach.[80] In *Sangeelee v. Smith*, Sheriff Principal Nicholson was not persuaded that considerations of the welfare of the child could justify departing from the clear terms of the rule, but he nevertheless allowed an appeal against a decision that a separate action was incompetent for just that reason (finding support for this approach in *Girvan v. Girvan* while at the same time expressing the hope that the Inner House would reconsider its decision in that case). The present rules in both the sheriff court and the Court of Session might make the problem more acute in that they expressly cover all applications for a section 11 order after a section 11 order has been made and not only those seeking to vary or discharge the earlier order. However, the nature of section 11 orders has changed significantly from custody and access orders. As was pointed out in a commentary on *Sangeelee v. Smith*,[81] it would be a ludicrous interpretation of the rules to require that an application for a residence order be made in the same process (and necessarily in the same court) as that in which a specific issue order had been made on a quite different point some years previously, merely because it related to the same child. The aim of the rules is clearly to prevent the child being subjected to an unnecessary duplication and proliferation of court processes, but if the issue to be dealt with is quite different from that determined by an earlier decree there will often be no disadvantage to the child in allowing the action to proceed in a different court. If protection of the welfare of the child is the underlying purpose of the rules then they should not be interpreted in such a way as subjects a child to an inappropriate jurisdiction. It is submitted that when the issue before the court is substantively different from that determined by an earlier section 11 order then it can be considered not to relate to the action, with the result that there is no requirement that the new application is to be made in the previous process. It is less clear that this is the case when the issue is the same or substantially so. The welfare of the child being the determining feature, no universal rule can be laid down but there will again be circumstances in which that feature will suggest that a new and independent action be allowed to proceed: the rules do not, it is submitted, make this incompetent.

Pleadings and intimation

A party who makes an application in a family action for a section 11 order **9.43** must include in his or her pleadings averments giving particulars of any other proceedings known to him or her, whether in Scotland or elsewhere and whether concluded or not and in addition, if the action is other than an action of divorce or separation, averments giving particulars of any proceedings known to him or her which are continuing, whether in Scotland or elsewhere, and which relate to the marriage of the parents of that child; the defences or minute lodged by any party may correct such particulars or give such further particulars as are known to the party.[82] Intimation is governed by OCR 1993, r. 33.7 and RCS 1994, r. 49.8. Importantly, in any action which includes a crave or conclusion

---

[80] See *McGuire v. McGuire*, 1987 S.C.L.R. 378; *Wilson v. Hislop*, 1992 S.C.L.R. 185; *Fisher v. Fisher*, 1993 S.C.L.R. 39; *Sangeelee v. Smith*, 1997 S.L.T. (Sh.Ct) 97.

[81] As reported in 1997 Fam. L.R. 89 at 94 (commentary by A. J. Loudon).

[82] OCR 1993, r. 33.3; RCS 1994, r. 49.3 (applying also to actions of declarator of nullity of marriage). "Child" includes a child of the family, as defined in s. 42(4) of the Family Law Act 1986, for which see above, para. 9.31.

for a section 11 order, there must be intimation to the child in the appropriate form.[83] This is to ensure that the child's statutory right to express views[84] is given effect to, but there is a lacuna in the statutory provisions. The form must be sent to the child only in cases in which a section 11 order is sought, whereas the court is entitled to make such an order even when it is not sought.[85] The court must of course take account of the child's views in that situation also, but the procedure is in place for ensuring the child that opportunity only when an order is expressly sought by one or other of the parties. This lacuna is perhaps most evident in relation to divorce actions, for even although there is no crave or conclusion for a section 11 order, the court is obliged to give consideration to the question of whether to make a section 11 order: yet there is no requirement to notify the child of any divorce action involving his or her parents.[86] If the pursuer considers that to order intimation to the child would be inappropriate he or she can seek to dispense with intimation and the court may do so or make such other order as it thinks fit.[87] Intimation might be considered inappropriate due to the child's age, or likelihood of distress or confusion. The onus is on the party seeking dispensation to show to the court that intimation would be inappropriate. Courts should, however, be slow to dispense with intimation given the child's rights to express views.

Child welfare hearings and options hearings

9.44 In defended actions in the sheriff court (but not in the Court of Session) a child welfare hearing must take place not sooner than 21 days after the lodging of notice of intention to defend (or earlier if the sheriff so directs) whenever (i) the initial writ seeks or includes a crave for a section 11 order and the defender wishes to oppose any such crave or order or seeks the same order as that craved by the pursuer, (ii) the defender seeks a section 11 order which is not craved by the pursuer, or (iii) in any other circumstances in a family action the sheriff considers that a child welfare hearing should be fixed and makes an order (whether at his own instance or on the motion of a party) that such a hearing shall be fixed.[88] The hearing may be held in private and the sheriff may order such steps to be taken or make such order if any or order further procedure as he thinks fit. This means that, if the sheriff is satisfied on the information he competently has before him that he is in a position to do so, he may make a section 11 order immediately, without the necessity of going to proof or following any further procedure.[89] Indeed a proof is inappropriate if there are no issues of fact to be resolved.[90] All parties (including a child who has indicated a wish to attend) must, except on cause shown, attend the hearing personally. It is the duty of the parties to provide the sheriff with sufficient information to enable him to conduct the hearing[91]: this means, to enable him to achieve its purpose, which is to allow the sheriff to identify the issues in relation to the child that are in dispute, and to seek to secure the expeditious resolution of such disputes by ascertaining from the parties what these matters are and any information relevant to that dispute and its resolution.

---

[83] OCR 1993, r. 33.7(1)(h) and Form F9; RCS 1994, r. 49.8(1)(h).

[84] As detailed below, para. 9.49.

[85] Children (Scotland) Act 1995, s. 11(3)(b).

[86] Unless a crave for a section 11 order is included: OCR 1993, r. 33.7(1)(h); RCS 1994, r. 49.8(1)(h). However, the rule is general that the court must not grant any s. 11 order unless an opportunity has been given for the views of the child to be obtained and heard: OCR 1993, r. 33.19; RCS 1994, r. 49.20.

[87] OCR 1993, r. 33.7(7); RCS 1994, r. 49.8(8). See *Gallacher v. Gallacher*, 1997 S.L.T. (Sh.Ct) 42.

[88] OCR 1993, r. 33.22A. See further, Ross, "Reforms in Family Proceedings in the Sheriff Court: Raising Conflicts in Civil Justice?" (1998) 3 *Contemp. Issues in Law* 1.

[89] *Hartnett v. Hartnett*, 1997 S.C.L.R. 525, *per* Sheriff Principal Risk. This is subject to the *caveat* that evidence must be recorded before a final decision can be made, in order to safeguard the appeal process.

[90] *Morgan v. Morgan*, 1998 S.C.L.R. 681, *per* Sheriff Principal Risk.

[91] OCR 1993, r. 33.22A(6).

The aim behind the introduction of this procedure was to allow the sheriff **9.45**
the opportunity to address the issues relating to the child separately from the
other issues in dispute (such as issues relating to the breakdown in the relationship
between the parents), for in many cases the identification of the issues over
which there is real dispute will show that the issues relating to the child are
susceptible to agreement between the parties: for the sheriff to encourage such
agreement is consistent with the no-order principle in section 11(7)(a) of the
Children (Scotland) Act 1995. It is envisaged that the sheriff will take a more
active role in the hearing than would be appropriate at other stages in the
procedure.[92]

An options hearing[93] will follow the child welfare hearing if the application **9.46**
remains defended and the matters relating to the child have not been resolved,
whether by the sheriff making a section 11 order or otherwise.[94] The purpose of
this hearing is for the sheriff to seek to secure the expeditious progress of the
case.[95] The options hearing is, unlike the child welfare hearing, purely procedural
and the sheriff has no power to make final orders.[96] In an explanatory note, the
Sheriff Court Rules Council said,[97] "The primary purpose of the options hearing
will be to enable the sheriff to ascertain the state of the pleadings following
adjustment and to make an informed decision on the next step in procedure. It
is anticipated that in most cases he will close the record at the options hearing
and appoint the cause to a proof." The sheriff might, however, take the
opportunity during the options hearing to assist the parties to resolve their dispute
relating to the child without court order, and to facilitate this there is a special
rule for family actions that all parties are required to attend in person at the
options hearing, except on cause shown.[98] The sheriff must be given sufficient
information to allow him to conduct the options hearing: the conduct of both
hearings ought to ensure that the issue at any proof is focused and that neither
party will be surprised by non-disclosed information if the case does proceed to
proof.

Local authority and other reports

Where the court is considering any question relating to the care and **9.47**
upbringing of a child (which necessarily includes—but is not limited to—
considering whether to make a section 11 order) the court may appoint an
appropriate local authority to investigate and report on all the circumstances of
the child and on the proposed arrangements for the care and upbringing of the
child.[99] That power is without prejudice to the court's power to appoint any
other person not being an officer of the relevant authority. This power is
particularly useful when interim orders are being sought before a full
consideration of all the facts and circumstances is possible.[1] If, on a consideration
of the report the court, either *ex proprio motu* or on the application of any person

---

[92] See Neilson, "It's Good to Talk", 1997 Fam. L.B. 27–3; *Hartnett v. Hartnett*, above, *per* Sheriff
   Principal Risk at 529C.
[93] OCR 1993, r. 9.12. See Neilson, "Sheriff Court Options Hearings: Beware the Ides of March"
   (1993) 38 J.L.S.S. 425.
[94] See *Henderson v. Adamson*, 1998 S.C.L.R. 365.
[95] See Neilson, "It's Good to Talk", 1997 Fam. L.B. 27–3.
[96] *Hartnett v. Harnett*, above.
[97] (1993) 38 J.L.S.S. 334 at 335.
[98] OCR 1993, r. 33.36.
[99] Matrimonial Proceedings (Children) Act 1958, s. 11; OCR 1993, r. 33.21, RCS 1994, r. 49.22.
   Cf. the rather wider power granted to the English court by s. 37 of the Children Act 1989. In *Re
   H (A Minor) (Section 37 Direction)* [1993] Fam. Law 205 a report on the applicant's mental
   health was ordered: this would not be appropriate under the Scottish legislation.
[1] See *Hardie v. Hardie*, 1993 S.C.L.R. 60.

concerned, thinks it expedient to do so it may require the person who furnished the report to appear and to be examined.[2] Any expenses incurred in connection with the preparation of the report form part of the expenses of the cause and are to be defrayed by such party to the action as the court may direct.[3] Where a local authority or other person has been appointed to investigate and report, an application for a section 11 order may not be determined until the report has been lodged.[4] Reports are not, however, the only nor in the ordinary case the primary means by which the court obtains the information necessary to determine wherein the child's welfare lies. The pursuer in the action has an interest and a corresponding responsibility to obtain adequate information about the circumstances of the child involved and that is so even if he or she does not seek a residence order and avers that satisfactory arrangements have been made by the defender or a third party. It is, therefore, for the pursuer to lead evidence (for which a report is no substitute) and to take all reasonable steps to ensure that it is adequate for the purpose.[5] In an uncontested case of that kind the court will not usually accede to a motion for a remit to a local authority for reports. Where the reporter is not examined the court may accept the statements of fact made in the report and consider them along with any relevant facts proved in the case.[6]

Mediation

9.48   In any family action in which an order in relation to parental responsibilities or parental rights is in issue, the court may, at any stage of the action, where it considers it appropriate to do so, refer that issue to a mediator accredited to a specified family mediation organisation.[7] The Court of Session has, on occasion, indicated to the sheriff that he should consider whether mediation is appropriate[8] but the appeal court cannot direct a sheriff to refer the case to a mediator. No information of what occurred during family mediation between two or more individuals relating to various matters[9] is admissible as evidence in any civil proceedings, unless one of the specified exceptions applies.[10] Exceptions include when the parties agree to admit such evidence, when a local authority or a voluntary organisation is a party to civil proceedings relating to a child's care or protection, and when the proceedings are under Chapters 2 or 3 of Part II of the Children (Scotland) Act 1995 in connection with a children's hearing.

Taking the views of the child

9.49   Section 11(7)(b) of the Children (Scotland) Act 1995 provides that in considering whether or not to make a section 11 order the court shall, taking account of the child's age and maturity, so far as practicable, (i) give the child an opportunity to indicate whether he or she wishes to express his or her views; (ii) if the child does so wish, give him or her an opportunity to express these views, and (iii) have regard to such views as the child may express. A child who

---

[2] Matrimonial Proceedings (Children) Act 1958, s. 11(4). This is unusual in practice.
[3] *ibid.* s. 11(5); OCR 1993, r. 33.21(2), RCS 1994, r. 49.22(2).
[4] OCR 1993, r. 33.21(6); RCS 1994, r. 49.22(6).
[5] See *Kristiansen v. Kristiansen*, 1987 S.C.L.R. 462; *Oliver v. Oliver* 1988 S.C.L.R. 285; *Hardie v. Hardie*, above.
[6] *Wallace v. Wallace*, 1963 S.C. 256 at 257–258; *Hunter v. Hunter*, 1979 S.L.T. (Notes) 2.
[7] OCR 1993, r. 33.22; RCS 1994, r. 49.23.
[8] See, *e.g.*, *Harris v. Martin*, 1995 S.C.L.R. 580.
[9] *i.e.* (i) the residence of a child; (ii) the regulation of personal relations and direct contact between a child and any other person; (iii) the control, direction or guidance of a child's upbringing; (iv) the guardianship or legal representation of a child; or (v) any other matter relating to a child's welfare.
[10] Civil Evidence (Family Mediation) (Scotland) Act 1995, ss. 1 and 2.

is 12 years of age or more is presumed to be of sufficient age and maturity to form a view for these purposes.[11] The child (of whatever age) will be sent an appropriate form[12] and if this is returned or the child otherwise indicates a wish to express views, the court shall order such steps to be taken as is considered appropriate to ascertain the views of that child; and it is obliged not to grant any order unless an opportunity has been given for the views of that child to be obtained or heard and due weight has been given by the court to the views expressed by that child, having regard to his or her age and maturity.[13] In the sheriff court[14] where a child expresses a view on a matter affecting him or her whether expressed personally to the sheriff or to a person appointed by the sheriff for that purpose or provided by the child in writing, the sheriff, or the person appointed by the sheriff, shall record the views of the child in writing and he may direct that such views, and any written views, given by the child shall (a) be sealed in an envelope marked "Views of the child—confidential", (b) be kept in the court process without being recorded in the inventory of process, (c) be available to a sheriff only, (d) not be opened by any person other than a sheriff, and (e) not form a borrowable part of the process.[15] It is to be noted that the sheriff has to make a decision that the child's views are to be kept confidential: this will seldom, it is submitted, be appropriate if these views are, in the sheriff's opinion, determinative for otherwise the parties to the action will be unable to challenge the sheriff's finding.

Title to sue

Title prior to the Children (Scotland) Act 1995

Even before the shift in focus from rights to responsibilities that characterised **9.50** Part I of the Children (Scotland) Act 1995, a discussion of parental rights subsumed the question of title to sue. Custody decisions were, after 1925,[16] determined entirely on the welfare principle. At first impression, however, that principle appeared to be concerned with the question of to whom custody should be given (the award) rather than of who may apply (title to sue) and these questions, although they often coalesced to an extent that they could be separated only with some awkwardness, were in principle, and sometimes in practice, distinct. The same difficulty was apparent with the Law Reform (Parent and Child) (Scotland) Act 1986: section 3(1) provided that "any person claiming interest may make an application to the court for an order relating to parental rights", while section 3(2) directed the court to regard the welfare of the child involved as the paramount consideration "in any proceedings relating to parental rights". It followed that any person who claimed interest had title to sue, and that the court had to determine any application consistently with the welfare test. However, any conflict inherent in that formulation was removed by a liberal interpretation of what constituted interest. A trend in the direction of liberality for questions of title to sue had been apprehended even before 1925 by the sheriff-substitute in *Samson v. Samson*,[17] when he said: "In this class of cases, *i.e.* for custody of children, the ordinary test of title to sue, viz. a prima facie right and an interest, seems subject to modification; some prima facie right no

---

[11] Children (Scotland) Act 1995, s. 11(10).
[12] Form F9 in the sheriff court and Form 49.8–N in the Court of Session. See comments above, para. 9.43.
[13] OCR 1993, r. 33.19; RCS 1994, r. 49.20.
[14] There is no equivalent rule in the Court of Session.
[15] OCR 1993, r. 33.20.
[16] Guardianship of Infants Act 1925, s. 1.
[17] 1922 S.L.T. (Sh.Ct) 34.

doubt there must be, but interest in the pursuer gives place to what is really the true principle—the welfare of the children." This statement is consistent with the fact that the common law does not appear to have imposed any close restriction by way of title to sue. Applications have been entertained at the instance of a tutor-at-law,[18] a tutor-nominate,[19] testamentary trustees of the father of an illegitimate child,[20] a judicial factor,[21] a step-mother,[22] a great-aunt,[23] and there are numerous instances, both before and after the Law Reform (Parent and Child) (Scotland) Act 1986, of applications by grandparents.[24] These are, however, only illustrations. There is no indication in the authorities of limitation of title to sue to these classes or, indeed, of any other limitation.[25] In *Syme v. Cunningham*[26] Lord Keith was relying on the common law rather than statute when he said: "In my opinion, the court has power under the *nobile officium* to entertain and deal with an application for custody of an illegitimate child at the instance of any person who can qualify a proper interest."[27] Although expressed in relation to an illegitimate child, the same principle applied to legitimate children, at least after 1986 and very probably before. On this matter there was little or no conflict between the common law and section 3(1) of the Law Reform (Parent and Child) (Scotland) Act 1986 and it can be asserted with some confidence that their combined effect was to free title to sue in custody proceedings from any artificial limitation.[28] This is so notwithstanding the apparent limitations of title contained in section 47(2) of the Children Act 1975,[29] for that provision was required to be read together with the welfare test in section 3(2) of the Law Reform (Parent and Child) (Scotland) Act 1986, with the

---

[18] *Walker v. Walker* (1824) 2 S. 788.

[19] *Low, Petr*, 1920 S.C. 351.

[20] *Whitson v. Speid* (1825) 4 S. 42.

[21] *AB v. CD* (1837) 9 Sc.Jur. 536; *Paul* (1838) 16 S. 822; *Denny v. Mcnish* (1863) 1 M. 268; *Muir v. Milligan* (1868) 6 M. 1125; *Gulland v. Henderson* (1878) 5 R. 768—all cases at the instance of a judicial factor against the mother of a fatherless legitimate child—*Moncreiff* (1891) 18 R. 1029 (a judicial factor against the father of a legitimate child).

[22] *Stewart v. Brodie* (1887) 3 Sh.CtRep. 405 (step-mother against aunt).

[23] *Girvan, Petr*, 1985 S.L.T. 92.

[24] e.g. *Erskine v. Connolly* (1916) 32 Sh.CtRep. 163 (grandmother against father of legitimate child); *Law v. Elrick* (1939) 55 Sh.CtRep. 253 (grandmother against stranger for custody of illegitimate child); *Richardson v. Burns*, 1963 S.L.T. (Sh.Ct) 26 (grandmother against father of legitimate child); *Cochrane v. Keys*, 1968 S.L.T. (Notes) 64 (maternal grandmother against father of legitimate child); *Klein and Anr, Petrs*, 1969 S.L.T. (Notes) 53 (paternal grandparents against mother of legitimate child); *Syme v. Cunningham*, 1973 S.L.T. (Notes) 40 (grandmother against father of illegitimate child); *F v. F*, 1991 S.L.T. 357 (grandparents against prospective adopters). See also *MacInnes v. Highland Regional Council*, 1982 S.C. 69, in which grandparents sought access, and *M v. Lothian Regional Council*, 1989 S.L.T. 426, in which grandparents sought (unsuccessfully) to be appointed tutors to allow them to make representations to a children's hearing.

[25] In *Hunter's Trs v. Speed*, Dec. 2, 1820, F.C. 211, the court expressed doubt on the petitioners' title to sue when confronted with an argument on their behalf that "it does not seem very material by whom the application is made, provided it be made by a person who, in some shape or other, has some kind of interest in the child", but in subsequent proceedings (*Whitson v. Speid* [sic] (1825) 4 S. 42) went on to grant an application at the instance of the same parties (testamentary trustees of the father of an illegitimate child).

[26] 1973 S.L.T. (Notes) 40.

[27] at 40. Although reference to the *nobile officium* was made a distinction between the Court of Session and the sheriff court in respect of title to sue would be anomalous in view of the broad terms in jurisdiction over children given to the sheriff court. The reference to the *nobile officium* did not, in this context, confine what was said to the Court of Session because the sheriff court has long exercised the powers of the *nobile officium* in cases involving children.

[28] "The apparent purpose of [s. 3 of the 1986 Act] was to remove any restriction or doubt as to title to apply by enacting that it was sufficient that the applicant claimed an interest," *per* Lord Cullen in *M v. Lothian Regional Council*, 1989 S.L.T. 426 at 428, approved 1990 S.L.T. 116, and by Lord President Hope in *F v. F*, 1991 S.L.T. 357 at 361H.

[29] See the 1st edition of this book, pp. 205–206. In *Osborne v. Matthan (No. 2)*, 1998 S.L.T. 1264, the First Division was not prepared to accept, as was suggested there, that s. 47(2) was, effectively, meaningless. See, especially, Lord Caplan at 1278B.

result that sufficient cause (the requirement under the 1975 Act) was shown if the court was satisfied on a balance of probabilities that the welfare of the child requires that the order be made in the child's best interests.[30] Section 47 of the Children Act 1975 was repealed by the Children (Scotland) Act 1995.[31]

Title under the Children (Scotland) Act 1995

In *Beagley v. Beagley*[32] the House of Lords held that a person who had lost **9.51** parental rights by means of a resolution vesting parental rights and powers in a local authority[33] had no title to seek their restoration by way of a custody application; and in *Borders Regional Council v. M*[34] the Inner House came to the same conclusion when parental rights were removed by an order freeing a child for adoption.[35] These decisions predated the Law Reform (Parent and Child) (Scotland) Act 1986, with its reference to "any person claiming interest". In *D v. Grampian Regional Council*,[36] the speeches in which were handed down during the passage of the Bill that became the Children (Scotland) Act 1995, the House of Lords held that the removal of parental rights by an adoption order or by an order freeing a child for adoption under the Adoption (Scotland) Act 1978 removed title to seek an order relating to parental rights under the 1986 Act. The extent of this decision was, however, unclear since it was based very firmly on an analysis of the law of adoption, and it did not address the question of whether the same result would be reached in other situations in which parental rights had been removed by public law process (such as that now contained in section 86 of the Children (Scotland) Act 1995, that is to say the making of a parental responsibilities order). Amendments to the Bill were tabled to take account of the decision in *D v. Grampian Regional Council* and to clarify a number of issues that it had raised without answering, and these appear as subsections (3)–(5) of section 11. The structure of these provisions indicates that an application for a section 11 order can be made only by persons who come within one of three separate classes, and not by persons who come within any of certain specified exceptions. The law has never liked quite to admit that anyone can seek an order in relation to a child, but the included classes are drawn so widely, and reflect the pre-1995 position of eschewing artificial limitations, that the substantive effect would appear to be that any person has title to seek a section 11 order unless they fall within one of the stated exceptions. The three specified classes of person with title are as follows.

First, a person may make an application for a section 11 order if he or she **9.52** does not have, and never has had, parental responsibilities or parental rights in relation to the child but nevertheless "claims an interest".[37] Some pre-1995 dicta, notably of Lord Keith in *Syme v. Cunningham*,[38] stipulate the need for an applicant for custody to qualify a proper interest but this does not serve to cut down title. The underlying notion is one of legitimate concern for the welfare of the child. The father of the child, though without parental responsibilities and parental rights in relation to the child due to a lack of marital status in

---

[30] *F v. F*, above, *per* Lord President Hope at 362. See also Wilkinson, "Children Act 1975", 1976 S.L.T. (News) 221; Edwards, "Who Has Interest to Appy for Parental Rights?" 1994 S.L.T. (News) 321.
[31] Sched. 5.
[32] 1984 S.C. (H.L.) 69.
[33] Under s. 16 of the Social Work (Scotland) Act 1968.
[34] 1986 S.C. 63.
[35] Under s. 18 of the Adoption (Scotland) Act 1978.
[36] 1995 S.L.T. 519.
[37] Children (Scotland) Act 1995, s. 11(3)(a)(i).
[38] 1973 S.L.T. (Notes) 40.

relation to the mother, will always have legitimate concern and, therefore, title.[39] There is no reason why siblings, or other natural relatives like grandparents, should not have title, even after the child has been adopted.[40] Usually a prior connection with the child will be necessary to found such concern, but there may be exceptional cases in which the welfare principle requires that a sufficient interest is qualified where, even without prior connection with the child, an applicant can show a prima facie case that the order he or she seeks will be for the child's welfare. In any event, the requisite interest is, it is submitted, possessed by anyone who has lawfully had the child in his or her care and control for any material length of time. Accordingly, foster carers have title to sue.[41] Indeed, title and interest are probably possessed by practically any *bona fide* applicant. In *Beagley v. Beagley*[42] the child's schoolmaster and a close friend of the family are given as examples.[43]

9.53 "Person" for these purposes expressly includes the child him or herself.[44]

9.54 The second category of person with title to make an application for a section 11 order consists of persons who have parental responsibilities or parental rights in relation to the child.[45] This includes any person who has such responsibilities and rights automatically under section 3 or has acquired them by any other means, whether by court order under section 11, agreement under section 4, or testamentary deed under section 7 of the 1995 Act. It includes a person who has one particular responsibility or right but not them all, such as a person with only the responsibility or right to maintain contact with the child. It does not include a person with care and control of the child and, thereby, responsibilities under section 5 of the 1995 Act, though such a person will be able to claim interest and come within the preceding category.

9.55 The third category is any person who used to have but no longer has parental responsibilities or parental rights, unless these have been removed by the specified means described in the following paragraph.[46] A person who has lost parental responsibilities and parental rights by any other means, such as a court order made under section 11(2)(a), or some of them, for example under the terms of a supervision requirement, retains title to seek their restoration or to seek any other section 11 order.

Persons with no title

9.56 There are four categories of natural person who cannot seek a section 11 order. These are persons whose parental responsibilities and parental rights have been removed by court order under: (i) section 12(3) of the Adoption (Scotland) Act 1978 on the making of an adoption order; (ii) section 18(5) of the 1978 Act on the making of an order freeing a child for adoption; (iii) section 30(9) of the Human Fertilisation and Embryology Act 1990 on the making of a parental order after a surrogacy arrangement; and (iv) section 86(1) on the making of a parental responsibilities order transferring those rights and responsibilities to a local authority.[47] It may be assumed that these categories are, *expressio unius*

---

[39] *Sanderson v. McManus*, 1997 S.L.T. 629, *per* Lord Hope of Craighead at 634B.
[40] *cf. AB, Petr*, 1988 S.L.T. 652; *F v. F*, 1991 S.L.T. 357.
[41] See *M v. Lothian Regional Council*, 1990 S.L.T. 116 and *F v. F*, above.
[42] 1984 S.L.T. 202, *per* Lord Fraser of Tullybelton at 206.
[43] It is unnecessary to seek a declarator of interest before making an application under s. 11: *McBain v. McIntyre*, 1997 S.C.L.R. 181, *per* Sheriff Kelbie at 182E.
[44] Children (Scotland) Act 1995, s. 11(5). Capacity of the child to raise a court order is determined by s. 2(4A) and (4B) of the Age of Legal Capacity (Scotland) Act 1991: see below, para. 15.11.
[45] Children (Scotland) Act 1995, s. 11(3)(a)(ii).
[46] *ibid.* s. 11(3)(a)(iii).
[47] *ibid.* s. 11(4).

est exclusio alterius, exhaustive. The purpose of these exceptions is to ensure that so far as possible the child is not subjected to different court processes, and that one process is not used to defeat the aims of another process. It is to be remembered that this does no more than deny these persons title to make an application under section 11. It does not prevent a court from making a section 11 order in their favour, if the application has been made by a person who does have title (such as, for example, the child him or herself) and if the welfare of the child requires it.

The only other "person" who is expressly denied title to seek a section 11 order **9.57** is a local authority.[48] The reason is to reflect the fact that Part I of the 1995 Act deals exclusively with private law matters, in respect of which local authorities have no standing. There were conflicting sheriff court decisions under the previous legislation on the question of whether a local authority could nevertheless seek to rely on a principle or rule such as is now contained in Part I of the 1995 Act in a case competently before the court. In *M v. Dumfries and Galloway Regional Council* a local authority was held entitled to rely upon section 3(2) of the Law Reform (Parent and Child) (Scotland) Act 1986 to resist an action for delivery of a child whom they were keeping under no other statutory authority. This decision was, however, expressly departed from by the sheriff principal in *City of Edinburgh Council v. M*,[50] though that case involved an attempt by a local authority to make an application under section 3 of the 1986 Act which would now be incompetent under express provision. The underlying principle is that the rights and powers of local authorities to become involved in the upbringing of children are governed by Part II of the 1995 Act, which both specifies and limits their power and role. It would subvert the very structure of the Act, and also run the risk of procedural confusion, if local authorities were able to found upon principles in Part I to achieve ends that they are incapable of achieving under Part II, whether as pursuers or as defenders.[51]

Apart from local authorities, no other non-natural person is excluded. While **9.58** the typical applicant for a section 11 order will be a natural person there is nothing to prevent an application by a corporate body which claims an interest. So, for example, an NHS Trust might seek a specific issue order to regulate the child's medical treatment over which some argument has arisen, or a private school might seek an order relating to a particular aspect of the child's education. Attention must be paid to the terms of section 15(4), under which only natural persons can have parental responsibilities and parental rights. Though it could have been made clearer, the effect of this is, it is submitted, that the court cannot grant parental responsibilities or parental rights to a non-natural person, nor make a non-natural person the child's legal representative or guardian: the provision does not, however, prevent such persons from applying for other section 11 orders nor, it would seem, for orders which affect the parental responsibilities or parental rights of natural persons.

Interim orders

A court with the power to make a section 11 order also has the power to **9.59** make an interim order.[52] The terms of the statutory provision are wide enough

---

[48] Children (Scotland) Act 1995, s. 11(5).
[49] 1991 S.C.L.R. 481.
[50] 1996 S.L.T. (Sh.Ct) 112.
[51] Nor can local authorities be brought in by any other means under s. 11, such as making a contact or residence order subject to supervision by the local authority. This was possible prior to the Children (Scotland) Act 1995 (see s. 12 of the Matrimonial Proceedings (Children) Act 1958 and s. 11 of the Guardianship Act 1973) but both these provisions were repealed by Sched. 5 to the 1995 Act. In *Osborne v. Matthan (No. 2)*, 1998 S.L.T. 1264, the First Division accepted counsel's concession that such a condition attached to a s. 11 order would be incompetent.
[52] Children (Scotland) Act 1995, s. 11(13).

to allow any section 11 order to be made on an interim basis. Orders for interim residence and for interim interdict designed to prevent disturbance of the existing arrangements for care of the child, or to avoid prejudice to the eventual disposal of the case, are among those most commonly encountered. It has been pointed out[53] that interim orders have great practical significance in that their effect can be to establish a status quo which will be a major influence on the final outcome of the case. This does not, however, mean that after a proof in which the parties seek interim orders the court may pronounce a decree disposing of the whole dispute.[54]

9.60   As a section 11 order, an interim order may be made only after the provisions in section 11(7) have been satisfied. So the welfare of the child is the court's paramount consideration, but in making an interim order that consideration is necessarily constrained by the short-term aim of the order. In *Osborne v. Matthan*[55] the sheriff was criticised for purporting to "decide the issue of interim custody after a very limited proof, but by reference to the long-term interests of the child which were not, and could not be, adequately explored in the type of proof which he heard".[56] Different considerations might be relevant if a full and detailed proof were held. In relation to interim interdict, the general test, *i.e.* the balance of convenience, remains appropriate but has to be applied in the context of the welfare of the child as the paramount consideration. The requirement that the court makes no order unless it considers that it would be better for the child that the order be made than that none should be made at all applies to interim no less than to final orders, but at the stage of an interim order no issue of standard of proof arises. It is a question of whether the court is satisfied on the information before it.[57] The child's views must be given an appropriate regard before making an interim order.

9.61   The Family Law Act 1986 makes specific provision for interdict or interim interdict prohibiting the removal of a child from the United Kingdom or any part of the United Kingdom or out of the control of the person in whose care the child is.[58] An application for interim interdict can be made (a) at any time after the commencement of proceedings[59] in connection with which the court would have jurisdiction to make a Part I order[60], or (b) in any proceedings in which it would be competent for the court to grant an interdict prohibiting the removal of a child from its jurisdiction.[61] The court can be the Court of Session or the sheriff[62] and the application can be at the instance of any party to the proceedings, the guardian of the child concerned, and any other person who has or wishes to obtain the care of the child.[63] The court may grant interim interdict if satisfied that there is a likelihood that the child will be removed.[64] Whether the court, once satisfied of that, should grant interim interdict is a matter of discretion to

---

[53] Scott, *Butterworths Scottish Family Law Service*, para. C.646.
[54] *Osborne v. Matthan*, 1997 S.L.T. 811 at 813B.
[55] 1997 S.L.T. 811.
[56] *ibid*. at 814F–G.
[57] *Armstrong v. Gibson*, 1991 S.L.T. 193.
[58] Family Law Act 1986, s. 35(3), as amended by the Children (Scotland) Act 1995, Sched. 4, para. 41(8). S. 37 allows the court to require any person to surrender any United Kingdom passport that has been issued to, or contains particulars of, the child.
[59] "Commencement" is defined as meaning, in the Court of Session, when a summons is signeted or a petition is presented and, in the sheriff court, when the warrant of citation is signed: Family Law Act 1986, s. 35(5).
[60] For the definition of "Part I order", see above, para. 9.24.
[61] Family Law Act 1986, s. 35(3).
[62] *ibid*. s. 35(5).
[63] *ibid*. s. 35(4).
[64] Interdict *ad interim* was refused in *Woodcock v. Woodcock*, 1990 S.L.T. 848 because there was no evidence that the mother was likely to remove the child furth of the United Kingdom: at 853A.

be determined with regard to the welfare of the child as the court's paramount consideration. The risk of temporary prejudice to the child's welfare may, however, have to be balanced against the need for interim interdict if conditions are to be preserved that will enable the eventual disposal of the case in accordance with the welfare principle.

The Child Abduction and Custody Act 1985 also provides that, where an **9.62** application has been made to the Court of Session under the Hague Convention for an order for the return of a child wrongfully removed to Scotland,[65] or under the European Convention for the registration or enforcement of a foreign custody order,[66] the court may give such interim directions as it thinks fit for the purpose of securing the welfare of the child or of preventing changes in the circumstances relevant to the determination of the application.[67]

Although these statutory provisions on interim interdict may, by specification, **9.63** contribute to clarity, it is doubtful if they add anything to the general powers of the court under section 11 of the Children (Scotland) Act 1995 to make such order, including an interim order,[68] as it thinks fit.

Remission from sheriff court to Court of Session

The sheriff has a discretion, exercisable at any stage of the action, to remit **9.64** the cause to the Court of Session.[69] Although parties may no doubt invite the sheriff to exercise his discretion, it is essentially a power to be exercised *ex proprio motu* and neither its exercise nor the failure or refusal to exercise it is subject to review.[70] That is, however, without prejudice to the right of a party to any ordinary cause to move the sheriff to remit the cause to the Court of Session because its importance or difficulty makes it appropriate to do so and a decision to remit or not to remit on such a motion is subject to appeal to the Court of Session.[71] As the matter is entrusted to the discretion and opinion of the sheriff, it would seem that it is only if he has failed to give the matter proper consideration or has proceeded on some improper ground, that an appeal will be successful.

Enforcement

If the court makes an order under section 11 requiring the child to live with **9.65** a particular person, a separate action for delivery is not necessary. If the process in which residence, for example, was regulated is still in dependence, the court may, on a motion made in that process, ordain the person with actual possession of the child to deliver him or her to the person with whom the child is to live.[72] A delivery order may be sought by one parent against the other although its purpose is not to implement a residence or other similar order: jurisdiction to make such an order follows the same rules as jurisdiction to make other section 11 orders,[73] and the principle upon which a section 11 order will be granted also

---

[65] See below, paras 11.19 *et seq.*

[66] See below, paras 11.10 *et seq.*

[67] Child Abduction and Custody Act 1985, s. 5 (Hague Convention); s. 19 (European Convention).

[68] Children (Scotland) Act 1995, s. 11(13).

[69] Sheriff Courts (Scotland) Act 1971, s. 37(2A), as inserted by Law Reform (Miscellaneous Provisions) (Scotland) Act 1980, s. 16 and as amended by the Children (Scotland) Act 1995, Sched. 4, para. 18.

[70] Sheriff Courts (Scotland) Act 1971, s. 37(3), as substituted by the Law Reform (Miscellaneous Provisions) (Scotland) Act 1980, s. 16(c).

[71] Sheriff Courts (Scotland) Act 1971, s. 37(1)(b) and (3)(b), as inserted or substituted by the 1980 Act, s. 16(a) and (c).

[72] *Brown v. Brown*, 1948 S.C. 5 at 11; *Fowler v. Fowler (No. 2)*, 1981 S.L.T. (Notes) 78. It is a contempt of court to fail to comply (*Muir v. Milligan* (1868) 6 M. 1125; *Leys v. Leys*, (1886) 13 R. 1223; *Brown v. Brown*, above).

[73] Family Law Act 1986, s. 17.

governs the court's decision to make (or not to make) a delivery order. Alternatively a specific issue order may be made under section 11(2)(e) requiring the person in possession of the child to deliver him or her up to another person. In addition warrants may be granted to messengers at arms, or sheriff officers, to search for and seize the child so that he or she may be delivered to the person with the right of residence.[74] Individual sanctions such as sequestration of trust income may also be used and have sometimes proved successful.[75]

9.66   An ancillary conclusion for delivery is strictly appropriate in all cases in which the claimant seeks possession with a view to the child's removal from the person with whom the child currently resides. Actions or petitions for delivery alone were at one time common at the instance of the person legally entitled to custody— usually the father—against anyone not so entitled in whose control the child was.[76] The enhancement of the mother's rights has made such proceedings inappropriate in disputes between parents when they both have parental responsibilities and parental rights, unless where a residence order is already in force.[77] The general weakening of parental rights so that, in the absence of a court order, they can now be asserted only in a prima facie sense,[78] may also have contributed to a decline in actions for delivery unless combined with conclusions for custody or now residence. An application for delivery alone is in favour of the applicant but the enforcement procedures of the original process cannot be used because it is no longer in dependence or where the order has been made by a court of pre-eminent jurisdiction outwith Scotland. If the application is defended, the applicant's right of care and control is necessarily put in issue and that question must be resolved by having regard to the welfare of the child as the paramount consideration. Where, however, the matter has already been determined by a court of competent jurisdiction, a fresh inquiry may not be necessary.[79]

9.67   The Family Law Act 1986 confers on the court the power to order any person who it has reason to believe may have relevant information as to the child's whereabouts to disclose that information to the court in any proceedings for or relating to a Part I order.[80] A person cannot be excused from complying with

---

[74] *Muir v. Milligan*, above; *Nicolson v. Nicolson* (1869) 7 M. 1118; *Marchetti v. Marchetti* (1901) 3 F. 888; *Low, Petr*, 1920 S.C. 351 (recommendation to English magistrates to lend their aid). For circumstances in which warrant was refused, see *Robertson, Petr*, 1911 S.C. 1319. Fraser (3rd ed.), p. 294, says that the warrant may also cover apprehension of the person violating the order. It has been said that only the Inner House can exercise this power (*Guthrie v. Guthrie* (1906) 8 F. 545), but it is submitted that it is no more than an aspect of the old custody jurisdiction which is now vested in the Outer House and the sheriff court which "impliedly carries with it all the powers which are necessary for its proper exercise" (*Sanderson v. Sanderson*, 1921 S.C. 686, *per* Lord Skerrington at 693). The wide scope of the sheriff court jurisdiction (*Murray v. Forsyth*, 1917 S.C. 721), together with the facts (i) that the Inner House no longer exercises any original jurisdiction in residence matters and (ii) that the sheriff court and the Court of Session have conterminous jurisdiction to make s. 11 orders, afford grounds for considering the dicta in *Guthrie* to be obsolete even if they were well founded at the time they were made.

[75] *Ross v. Ross* (1885) 12 R. 1351; *Edgar v. Fisher's Trs* (1893) 21 R. 59 and 325; *Fisher v. Edgar* (1894) 21 R. 1076.

[76] *A v. B* (1870) 42 Sc.Jur. 224; *Ketchen v. Ketchen* (1870) 8 M. 952; *Markey v. Colston* (1888) 15 R. 921; *Hutchison v. Hutchison* (1890) 18 R. 237. If the right to custody were not clear, the claimant would, however, seek an order dealing with custody as well as with delivery (*Reilly v. Quarrier* (1895) 22 R. 879) and sometimes even fathers of "legitimate" children thought it prudent to seek an order for custody in support of their claim for delivery (*Pagan v. Pagan* (1883) 10 R. 1072; *Beattie v. Beattie* (1883) 11 R. 85).

[77] *Brown v. Brown*, 1948 S.C. 5 at 11.

[78] See above, para. 8.02.

[79] *Sargeant v. Sargeant*, 1973 S.L.T. (Notes) 27; *Campbell v. Campbell*, 1977 S.C. 103; *Lyndon v. Lyndon*, 1978 S.L.T.(Notes) 7; *Thomson, Petr*, 1980 S.L.T.(Notes) 29.

[80] Family Law Act 1986, s. 33(1), and see *Abusaif v. Abusaif*, 1984 S.L.T. 90. "Any proceedings" includes those for the enforcement of an order made outside the U.K. which is recognised in Scotland: s. 33(3).

such an order on the ground that to do so may incriminate him or his spouse of an offence, though any statement or admission made in compliance with the order will not be admissible in evidence against either spouse in proceedings for any offence other than perjury.[81]

CONFLICTS WITH OTHER ORDERS

Conflict between section 11 orders

A foreign order relating to parental responsibitilities and parental rights in **9.68** relation to a child cannot be enforced in Scotland without the intervention of the Scottish courts.[82] There can, therefore, be no conflict between an order made by a Scottish court under section 11 and an equivalent foreign order. There may, however, be a conflict between one Scottish order and another Scottish order or an order made by a court in another part of the United Kingdom. As section 11 orders in general are seldom, and residence and contact orders never, truly permanent,[83] a subsequent application to the court is not subject to the plea of *res judicata*[84] and so there may be a succession of orders. There is no formal requirement regulating the conditions on which a second or subsequent application will be entertained, but making repeated applications would seem to be an abuse of process in the absence of a material change in circumstances.[85] Section 11 of the Children (Scotland) Act 1995, which entitles the court to make any order relating to parental responsibilities, parental rights, guardianship or the administration of a child's property as it thinks fit, expressly includes the right to vary or discharge an earlier order.[86] Further, section 15(2) of the Family Law Act 1986 provides that a Part I order made by a Scottish court may be varied or recalled by a subsequent order of that court provided the original order has not ceased to have effect and notwithstanding that the court no longer has the jurisdiction on which the original order proceeded. Cases may, however, occur despite those ample provisions, in which a section 11 order is made without variation or recall of an earlier inconsistent order. This may be because an action has been raised in a sheriff court different from the sheriff court in which an earlier order was made and either the parties did not realise this or the sheriff has taken the view that rule 33.44 of the Ordinary Cause Rules does not prevent him from hearing the case.[87] In such cases the principle, that a subsequent order has the effect of varying or revoking a prior order inconsistent with it, applies. Accordingly, where, for example, it appears that a child has been the subject of more than one residence order, it is the last in point of time that is effective. That was the rule at common law, at any rate where the later order was pronounced by a court of equivalent or superior jurisdiction, and is now statutorily so[88] when the later order is competently made by another court, even of inferior jurisdiction, in any part of the United Kingdom, or is made outside the United Kingdom[89] and is recognised in Scotland according to the rules discussed

---

[81] Family Law Act 1986, s. 33(2).
[82] See below, paras 11.02 *et seq.*
[83] *Sanderson v. McManus*, 1997 S.L.T. 629, *per* Lord Hope of Craighead at 631J.
[84] Though the court does have a discretion under s. 14(1) of the Family Law Act 1986 to refuse to entertain an application for a Pt I order where the matter has already been determined in other proceedings: see above, para. 9.35.
[85] But see *S v. S*, 1965 S.L.T. 131 at 132–133.
[86] Children (Scotland) Act 1995, s. 11(13).
[87] See the discussion of the competency of this in *Sangeelee v. Smith*, 1997 S.L.T. (Sh.Ct) 97. And see above, para. 9.42.
[88] Family Law Act 1986, s. 15(1).
[89] See, *e.g.*, *T v. T (Custody: Jurisdiction)* [1992] 1 F.L.R. 43 and *S v. S (Custody: Jurisdiction)* [1995] 1 F.L.R. 155 in which subsequent English orders were held to deprive earlier Scottish orders of effect.

later.[90] It is also provided by statute[91] that where an order under section 11 of the Children (Scotland) Act 1995 (or under any earlier enactment relating to the custody, care or supervision of a child, or access to a child) has been pronounced by the Court of Session in connection with an action of divorce, separation or declarator of nullity of marriage it may be varied or recalled in the sheriff court. Apart from that provision, it is doubtful if, before the Family Law Act 1986, a Court of Session decree could be superseded by a decree in the sheriff court. That is no longer so but if an application should be presented in the sheriff court which is in conflict with an existing decree of the Court of Session to which the specific statutory exception does not apply, the proper course may still often be removal or remission to the Court of Session.[92]

Conflict with other types of order

General

9.69   An apparent conflict may sometimes arise between a section 11 order relating to the residence of or contact with a child and measures taken under the statutory provisions for the protection and welfare of children under Part II of the Children (Scotland) Act 1995. The measures in question are supervision requirements made by a children's hearing under section 70, child protection orders made by a sheriff under section 57, parental responsibilities orders made under section 86, and warrants granted under various sections of the 1995 Act. The conflict in such cases is apparent rather than real. The guiding principle is that the effect of a section 11 order is subject to such other lawful measures as may be taken in relation to the child.[93] A residence order, for example, gives the person with whom the child lives responsibilities and rights over the child which he or she may vindicate in a question with others only if they have no lawful authority to interfere: the Part II provisions mentioned above grant that very authority. Nearly all children under 16 are subject to the parental responsibilities and parental rights of some person and, in the great majority of cases, that position is not regulated by any court order. The position of children in respect of whom section 11 orders have been made does not, in principle, differ from the position of those who are subject to parental responsibilities and parental rights which are neither created nor regulated by any court order. In both cases, it is evident that statutory measures may modify the effect of parental responsibilities and parental rights. If that were not so, the statutory provisions would be reduced to a nullity. While the statutory provisions may affect particular parental responsibilities or parental rights they do not affect other responsibilities and rights whose exercise would not be inconsistent with the terms of the order or the statutory purposes.[94]

Conflict with supervision requirements

9.70   A supervision requirement made by a children's hearing is a compulsory measure of supervision under which the child is treated as being, for certain purposes, looked after by a local authority.[95] The child may, nonetheless, often remain at home and parental responsibilities and parental rights are affected only in so far as is necessary to give effect to the supervision requirement. It is provided by statute that the fact that a person has parental responsibilities and parental rights in relation to a child does not entitle that person to act in a way

---

[90]   Below, paras 11.10–11.18.
[91]   Law Reform (Miscellaneous Provisions) (Scotland) Act 1966, s. 8. For procedure, see OCR 1993, rr. 33.84–33.86.
[92]   See above, para. 9.64.
[93]   See, in relation to the pre-1995 position, Thomson, "Parental Rights and Children in Care: A 'Confusing Overview'", 1991 S.L.T. (News) 379.
[94]   Thomson, *op. cit.*
[95]   Children (Scotland) Act 1995, s. 17(6)(b).

which would be incompatible with any supervision requirement made under section 70.[96] So for example the right to determine the child's residence is affected only if a residential condition is attached to the supervision requirement. In that event, the effective exercise of residence rights is suspended so long as the residential stipulation remains in force but revives as soon as the requirement, or the residential element in it, comes to an end.[97] So residence orders (and residence rights traced to section 2 and not regulated by court order) may have their effect suspended by a supervision requirement, even to the extent that the child is obliged to reside with a person denied the right of residence under the terms of a section 11 order. Similarly, a residence order made while a supervision requirement is in force (and the requirement does not affect title to seek a section 11 order) receives effect subject to the requirement, and the rights conferred by such an order are inhibited for so long as the requirement subsists.[98] It has, however, been said that "it would seldom be appropriate for an order for custody [now residence] to be pronounced in favour of persons who could not in practice exercise those rights for the time being",[99] but exceptional cases are not outwith the bounds of imagination. Similarly (though this is not expressly provided for in the 1995 Act), warrants granted by a children's hearing[1] will temporarily suspend the parent's right to determine where the child is to be for the very limited periods of time that these warrants are in force.

Conflict with child protection orders

A child protection order made by a sheriff under section 57 of the Children **9.71** (Scotland) Act 1995 may authorise the removal of the child by the applicant to a place of safety and the keeping of the child at that place, on the satisfaction of certain conditions.[2] The sheriff may attach to the order a direction as to the contact that certain persons are to have with the child, and, if requested, may give a direction in relation to the exercise or fulfilment of any parental responsibility or parental right in respect of the child concerned.[3] Keeping the child in a place of safety will clearly suspend the exercise of the parent's residence rights, and making a contact direction will clearly supersede the exercise of the responsibility and right of contact, even when regulated by an extant section 11 order. However, as in the case of a supervision requirement, the right of residence or contact revives as soon as the detention ends or the contact direction ceases to have effect. It would seem clear that the other parental responsibilities and parental rights are unaffected in so far as they are not inconsistent with the terms of the child protection order. So while the parent or guardian will not be entitled to have the child living with him or her during the currency of the child protection order, he or she retains the right, for example, to consent to medical treatment or to act as the child's legal representative.[4]

Conflict with parental responsibilities orders

The transfer of parental rights and responsibilities to a local authority under **9.72** the terms of a parental responsibilities order does not abrogate the jurisdiction of the court to make a section 11 order.[5] The parent or guardian in respect of

---

[96] Children (Scotland) Act 1995, s. 3(4).
[97] *Aitken v. Aitken*, 1978 S.C. 297, though decided under the previous legislation in relation to custody, remains in principle good law.
[98] *ibid.* at 302, *per* Lord President Emslie.
[99] *F v. F*, 1991 S.L.T. 357, *per* Lord President Hope at 363.
[1] Under ss. 45, 63, 66 or 69 of the 1995 Act.
[2] See below, paras 20.27–20.31.
[3] Children (Scotland) Act 1995, s. 58(4).
[4] Unless the sheriff makes a direction dealing with the issue under s. 57(5)(a).
[5] *Aitken v. Aitken*, above; *Beagley v. Beagley*, 1984 S.L.T. 202; *M v. Lothian Regional Council*, 1989 S.L.T. 426.

whom the order was made has, however, no title to apply for a section 11 order.[6] His or her remedies are restricted to reduction, if grounds for that exist. Applications made by any other person are to be determined with regard to the welfare of the child as the paramount consideration[7] but, unless there is evident abuse, the court will, it is thought, be slow in such a case to go against the judgment of the child's welfare formed by the court which made the parental responsibilities order. If a section 11 order is already in force under which the child was required to reside with a parent or guardian whose parental rights and responsibilities have been transferred to a local authority, that order is superseded by the parental responsibilities order because the right to determine the child's residence is among the rights which are transferred. The responsibilities and rights which were transferred will be restored if the order is subsequently discharged but not if it terminates for any of the other reasons specified in section 86(6).[8]

Conflict with local authority's duty to accommodate children

9.73   No question of conflict arises when a child, in respect of whom a section 11 order is in force, is provided with accommodation by a local authority under Chapter 1 of Part II of the Children (Scotland) Act 1995.[9] Such provision of accommodation is voluntary and parental responsibilities and parental rights are unaffected. The return of the child may be requested at any time. If, however, the child has been accommodated by the local authority for six months or more, 14 days' notice is required if the child is to be removed without the consent of the authority.[10] To that extent there is a limited suspension of residence rights, but not of any other parental responsibility or parental right. There is no objection to the making of a section 11 order while a child is being accommodated under section 25.

Conflicts concerning contact orders

9.74   Much the same principles apply to contact orders as to other section 11 orders but contact orders may, in their nature, be more amenable than, say, residence orders to reconciliation with the purposes of statutory measures. The responsibility and right of contact, however acquired, may continue to be exercised in so far, but only in so far, as that exercise is consistent with the statutory measure in question. Thus, a parent's or guardian's responsibility and right to maintain personal relations and direct contact with the child will not be affected by a supervision requirement made by a children's hearing unless, as in the case of a requirement with a condition relating to contact, there is conflict with the terms of the requirement.[11] Under the previous legislation it was held that, where there is potential for such conflict, while a custody order could be granted, although with suspended effect, during the currency of a supervision requirement, an access order could not be so granted, because access, being a right instantly operable, could not have its effects suspended in the way that custody could.[12] Nor was it deemed appropriate to grant access against a local

---

[6] Children (Scotland) Act 1995, s. 11(3)(a)(iii) and (4)(d).

[7] *ibid.* s. 11(7)(a).

[8] See below, paras 17.29–17.34.

[9] See further, below, Chap. 16.

[10] Children (Scotland) Act 1995, s. 25(7).

[11] One of the matters that children's hearings must always consider is whether to impose a condition relating to contact on the supervision requirement: Children (Scotland) Act 1995, s. 70(2) and (5)(b).

[12] *D v. Strathclyde Regional Council*, 1985 S.L.T. 114; *A v. G*, 1996 S.L.T. (Sh.Ct) 123.

authority which would be exercisable only once the local authority care came to an end.[13] It is likely that this no longer represents the law.[14]

Previously, rights of access were usually granted in a question with the **9.75** custodian, and they were considered to be a qualification of the custodian's rights.[15] It followed that they were not exigible against third parties into whose care the child lawfully passed: it was for the custodian in such a case to see that access was enabled. So where a child was the subject of a supervision requirement with a residential condition, an access order granted in a question with the person who, apart from the requirement, was the child's custodian was of no avail against any other person, with whom the child had to reside under the requirement. This has now changed. The responsibility and right to maintain personal relations and direct contact with the child on a regular basis, and rights of contact created and regulated by a section 11 order, can no longer be regarded as being merely a qualification to another person's right to determine the child's residence. Contact is a responsibility and right which exists independently of the right to determine where the child is to live, and an order which either creates or regulates contact rights is, as explained earlier in this chapter, self-standing with no necessary connection to another person's right of residence. There is no reason in principle, therefore, that a contact order cannot be made during the currency of a statutory order that precludes its immediate exercise. In any case, the contact that the child is to have with any person is a matter that must be considered by a children's hearing that imposes or continues a supervision requirement and it may be the subject of a condition attached to a warrant granted by the children's hearing under sections 63, 66 or 69 or by the sheriff under section 67, or of a direction made by a sheriff in the context of a parental responsibilities order. The specific granting of the power to deal with the issue of contact by the bodies making these orders minimises the possibility of conflict between contact responsibilities and rights and these orders, though even when no regulation of the exercise of contact is specified, the responsibilities and rights cannot be exercised in such a way as is inconsistent with the terms of the order or which would conflict with the proper exercise by the authority in which they have vested and to whose care the child is entrusted. A parent or guardian whose parental responsibilities and parental rights have been transferred to a local authority by means of a parental responsibilities order has no title to apply for a contact order.[16] A parent or guardian is not, however, deprived of title during the currency of a supervision requirement and the court may, it is submitted, competently make an order regulating contact though any order that it does make will be suspended until the requirement terminates if it is in terms that are inconsistent with the requirement.[17]

OFFENCES

Children Act 1975

Where a person has applied for a residence order in relation to a child and **9.76** the child has been in the care and possession of the applicant for a period or periods, before the making of the application, which amount to at least three years, it is an

---

[13] *D v. Strathclyde Regional Council*, above, at 116.
[14] See further, above, para. 9.13.
[15] See the 1st edition of this book, at pp. 229–230.
[16] Children (Scotland) Act 1995, s. 11(3)(a)(iii) and (4)(d). This was the position prior to the coming into force of these provisions: *D v. Strathclyde Regional Council*, above; *Beagley v. Beagley*, 1984 S.L.T. 202 (dealing with the equivalent process to the parental responsibilities order, governed by s. 16 of the Social Work (Scotland) Act 1968).
[17] Since only "relevant persons" (see below, para. 19.07) can seek a review of a supervision requirement it follows that the only method available to other persons seeking contact with the child is by means of a s. 11 order. On the competency of doing so, see above, para. 9.13.

offence to remove the child from the care and possession of the applicant against the applicant's will while the application is pending.[18] The prohibition applies to removal by a local authority even if the child was being looked after by the local authority before he or she began to have his or her home with the applicant and continues to be so looked after. In such a case, however, the Act provides for removal with the leave of the court or in accordance with an order made, or authority or warrant granted, under Chapter 2 or 3 of Part II of the Children (Scotland) Act 1995.[19] The primary purpose of the legislation creating this offence was to give long term foster carers security in pursuing applications for custody and now residence without risk of disturbance whether from the natural parents or from the placing authority,[20] but it is capable of wider application, including disputes between parents. The penal provisions are reinforced by power given to the court (1) to order the person who has removed the child to return the child to the applicant, and (2) to interdict removal of the child from the applicant's care and possession on the application of any person who has reasonable grounds for believing that such removal is intended.[21] "Child" means a person who has not attained the age of 18 years.[22]

Child Abduction Act 1984

9.77   Under the Child Abduction Act 1984 it is an offence for "a person connected with a child under the age of 16 years" to take or send the child out of the United Kingdom:

> (a) "without the appropriate consent" if there is, in respect of the child either (i) an order of a court in the United Kingdom awarding custody to any person or naming any person as the person with whom the child is to live, or (ii) an order of a court in England, Wales, or Northern Ireland making the child a ward of court; or
>
> (b) if there is any order of a court in the United Kingdom prohibiting the removal of the child from the United Kingdom or any part of it.[23]

A person is connected with a child if (i) he or she is a parent or guardian, (ii) there is in force an order of a court in the United Kingdom awarding custody to him or her or naming him or her as the person with whom the child is to live (whether solely or jointly), or (iii) in the case of a child whose parents are not and have never been married to one another, there are reasonable grounds for believing that he is the father of the child.[24] "Appropriate consent" in relation to the crime under (a) means either (i) the consent of each person who is a parent or guardian or to whom custody has been awarded or who is named as the person with whom the child is to live by an order of a court in the United Kingdom, or (ii) the leave of that court.[25] Alternative (i) is not, however, available where a wardship order is in force.[26] Consent is no defence to the crime under (b) above.[27] Where more than one custody, residence or wardship order is in force in relation to a child, the leave of any court which has made such an order suffices.[28] Taking, or sending, a child out of the United Kingdom means (a) causing

---

[18] Children Act 1975, s. 51, as amended by the Children (Scotland) Act 1995, Sched. 4, para. 26.

[19] *ibid.* s. 51(2).

[20] See *Report of the Departmental Committee on the Adoption of Children*, Cmnd. 5107 (1972), recommendation No. 36, para. 126.

[21] Children Act 1975, s. 52, as amended by the Children (Scotland) Act 1995, Sched. 4, para. 26.

[22] *ibid.* s. 107.

[23] Child Abduction Act 1984, s. 6(1), as amended by the Children (Scotland) Act 1995, Sched. 4, para. 34.

[24] *ibid.* s. 6(2), as amended by the Children (Scotland) Act 1995, Sched. 4, para. 34.

[25] *ibid.* s. 6(3), as so amended.

[26] *ibid.*

[27] See *Deans v. Deans*, 1988 S.C.L.R. 192 (Sh.Ct).

[28] Child Abduction Act 1984, s. 6(3).

or inducing the child to accompany the person charged with the offence or any other person, and (b) causing the child to be taken or sent.[29] "Guardian" means a person appointed by deed or will or by order of a court of competent jurisdiction to be the child's guardian.[30]

It is a defence for the accused person to show that, at the time of the alleged **9.78** offence, he or she had no reason to believe that a custody, residence or wardship order was in existence in relation to the child.[31] Except where the child is a ward of court, an offence is not committed if the person taking or sending the child (a) did so in the belief that each person who is a parent or guardian or has custody of the child, or is named as the person with whom the child is to live either had consented, or would have consented if he or she were aware of all the relevant circumstances, or (b) has taken all reasonable steps to communicate with each such person but has been unable to do so.[32]

Put briefly, the effect of the above provisions of the Child Abduction Act **9.79** 1984 is to apply a criminal sanction, where a custody, residence or wardship order or an interdict against removal is in force, in order to prevent the removal of the child outside the United Kingdom at the instance of a parent, guardian, custodian or person with the right of residence unless the other interested persons have consented or the court has granted leave. The Act, therefore, strikes at acts by persons with an established connection with the child that are in defiance of, or would circumvent the purpose of, a court order. A typical situation is where a parent who does not have the right of residence takes the child abroad with a view to defeating the rights under a residence order in favour of the other parent; but it is to be noted that the residence parent is also subject to the Act and may commit an offence if, for example, he or she takes the child abroad in order to defeat the other parent's right to contact.[33] Although it will usually be prudent to obtain all relevant consents, the temporary removal of a child for a short period, without such consent, for a holiday or for educational or medical purposes may often be justified on the ground that it was done in the belief that the person whose consent was required would have consented if he or she were aware of all the relevant circumstances. That justification would not, however, be available where the child is a ward of the English, or Northern Irish, courts.

Plagium and abduction

The provisions of the Child Abduction Act 1984 applicable to England and **9.80** Wales are, in a number of respects, different from their Scottish counterparts. There is no Scottish equivalent at all for the English provision under which anyone not connected with the child commits an offence if, without lawful authority or reasonable excuse, he or she takes or detains a child under 16 so as to deprive anyone entitled thereto of lawful control.[34] The reason may be that such acts were thought to be criminal in Scotland at common law. The relevant common law crimes, *plagium* and abduction, are, however, inexact counterparts.[35]

---

[29] Child Abduction Act 1984, s. 6(6).

[30] *ibid.* s. 6(7) (as amended by the Age of Legal Capacity (Scotland) Act 1991, Sched. 2, restoring the subsection to its original wording).

[31] *ibid.* s. 6(5).

[32] *ibid.* s. 6(4).

[33] Under s. 2(3) and (6) of the Children (Scotland) Act 1995 a parent may not take a child habitually resident in Scotland abroad without the consent of the other parent when they both have parental responsibilities and parental rights.

[34] Child Abduction Act 1984, s. 2.

[35] The Scottish Law Commission has recommended that *plagium* be abolished, but that abduction be retained: Scot. Law Com. No. 102, *Report on Child Abduction* (1987). And see Kelly, "Child Abduction", 1991 S.L.T. (News) 53.

9.81   It is the crime of *plagium* to take a pupil child[36] away from the custody (by
which is understood today the care and control) of his or her parents or those to
whom the parents have entrusted the child, whether or not the child is willing to
go.[37] A parent can be guilty of this crime.[38] To take someone of any age away
against his or her will or, probably, by obtaining consent through deception, is
to commit the crime of abduction unless it is done with lawful authority.[39] These
crimes leave, however, three areas of possible doubt so far as children are
concerned. First, is it criminal to remove a child below the age of common law
pupillarity from a person who has the care and control of the child but who is
someone other than the child's parents or the person to whom the parents have
entrusted him or her? It is submitted that the answer is plainly affirmative
although there may be some doubt whether the crime is *plagium* or abduction.
It is perhaps better treated as abduction because a person who has care and
control of the child, other than a parent, does not have the rights of *dominium*
which, if on rather outmoded reasoning, underlie *plagium*.[40] Although abduction
usually involves overcoming the will of the person abducted, it is entirely
consistent with the legal understanding of pupillarity, at least at common law,
that the pupil child's will should be regarded as irrelevant to a question of his or
her abduction[41] and that the will of the carer should be the relevant consideration.

9.82   Secondly, is it criminal to remove the child against his or her will but with
the consent of a person with parental responsibilities and parental rights? It is
implicit in the concept of the parental right to regulate the child's residence that
the right-holder has authority to move the child from place to place, and, although
the extent of that authority was at common law, and still may be, subject to
substantial qualification in the case of a minor *pubes*, it is difficult to envisage
that the person with that parental right could be guilty of abduction. If that is
correct, it must follow that those who act on his or her authority or with his or
her consent are in a like position.

9.83   Thirdly, is it abduction to take a child above the age of common law
pupillarity away, with his or her consent freely given, if that is against the will
of the person with the parental right to regulate his or her residence? The relative
freedom of a minor *pubes* at common law was, it is submitted, such that his or
her consent validated his or her being taken away without the necessity of
obtaining the custodian's prior approval. Today it may be argued that the
dominium exercised over pupils at common law has been extended to age 16,
i.e. is now co-terminous with the right to regulate residence, and that the right-
holder's consent is therefore always required for the child's removal. The Age
of Legal Capacity (Scotland) Act 1991 does not, however, affect the previously
existing criminal law in any way[42] and it is submitted that the definition of child

---

[36] *i.e.* a boy below 14 or a girl below 12. This remains the case although for most purposes pupillarity
is now in effect extended to 16 (Age of Legal Capacity (Scotland) Act 1991), for s. 1(3)(c) of that
Act provides that nothing in it shall affect the criminal responsibility of any person: it cannot
therefore be taken to have extended the crime of *plagium* to all children under 16.

[37] Hume, I, 84; Alison, I. 280; Macdonald, 21; *H.M. Advocate v. Cairney or Cook and Anr* (1897) 2
Adam 471; *H.M. Advocate v. Mary Millar or Oates* (1861) 4 Irv. 74; *H.M. Advocate v. Helen Wade*
(1844) 2 Broun 288; *H.M. Advocate v. Rachel Wright* (1809) 1 Hume 84; *H.M. Advocate v. Janet
Douglas* (1817) 1 Hume 85; *H.M. Advocate v. Marion Rosmond or Skeoch* (1855) 2 Irv. 234.

[38] *Downie v. H.M. Advocate*, 1984 S.C.C.R. 365; *Hamilton v. Mooney*, 1990 S.L.T. (Sh.Ct) 105;
Hamilton v. Wilson, 1994 S.L.T. 431; and see John M. Fotheringham; "Plagium: the Sins of the
Father *v.* the Rights of the Parent" (1990) 35 J.L.S.S. 506.

[39] Macdonald, p. 124.

[40] It is because parental rights over a pupil child were characterised at common law as a right of
dominium that *plagium* can be regarded—if misleadingly—as a species of theft.

[41] *cf. plagium*, to which the pupil's will is clearly irrelevant.

[42] s. 1(3)(c).

in section 2(7) of the Children (Scotland) Act 1995, as a person under the age of 16 years, does not affect the content of the parental rights and, in any event, applies only for the purposes of that Act and does not affect criminal liability. A child above the age of pupillarity was free, in a way in which a pupil was not, to form purposes of his or her own and assume responsibility for his or her actions. Whatever other remedies may be available, he or she commits no offence if, in pursuit of these purposes, the minor child moves out of the control of those who have parental responsibilities and parental rights.[43] In that situation it is difficult to see how someone who merely co-operates with the child over the age of common law pupillarity but below the age of 16, or who facilitates his or her movements, is guilty of abduction and there is no authority for the view that, in the absence of fraud, any common law offence is thereby committed.

It is, however, an offence to take or cause to be taken an unmarried girl **9.84** under 18 out of the possession of her father or mother or any other person having lawful care and charge of her with intent that she should have unlawful sexual intercourse with men or with a particular man.[44] It is essential to the commission of the offence that the taking away should have been against the will of the person having care and charge. There must be an actual taking, or causing to be taken, and it is not an offence merely to consent to the girl's leaving or to fail to return her if she leaves.[45] Nor, as unlawful sexual intercourse means intercourse outwith marriage,[46] is it an offence to take a girl away with a view to marriage.[47] The consent of the girl is no defence if she is actually taken rather than leaves without active involvement by the accused amounting to taking.[48] But it is a defence that the accused had reasonable cause to believe that the girl was of or above the age of 18[49] or that he did not know that the girl was in the possession of her parents or in anyone's care and charge.[50] It is obscure to what extent a child over 16, and thus free from the constraints of parental rights, can be said to be in the possession of anyone.

---

[43] Nichols points out that the Age of Legal Capacity (Scotland) Act 1991 may well have conferred capacity on a child to determine his or her own residence: "Can They or Can't They?", 1991 S.L.T. (News) 395 at 397–398. And see above, para. 8.34.

[44] Criminal Law (Consolidation) (Scotland) Act 1995, s. 8.

[45] *R. v. Jarvis* (1903) 20 Cox. C.C. 249; *R. v. Olifier* (1866) 10 Cox C.C. 402.

[46] *Mohamed v. Knott* [1969] 1 Q.B. 1.

[47] *R. v. Chapman* [1959] 1 Q.B. 100.

[48] *R. v. Manktlow* (1853) 6 Cox C.C. 143; *R. v. Jones* [1973] Crim. L.R. 621.

[49] Criminal Law (Consolidation) (Scotland) Act 1995, s. 8(2). For the meaning of "reasonable cause", see *H.M. Advocate v. Hoggan* (1893) 1 Adam 1, *per* Lord Justice-Clerk Macdonald at 3–4; and *H.M. Advocate v. Macdonald* (1900) 3 Adam 180, *per* Lord Mclaren at 182.

[50] *R. v. Hibbert* (1869) L.R. 1 C.C.R. 184.

CHAPTER 10

THE SECTION 11(7) PRINCIPLES

Introduction

10.01   Other than the requirement to regard the child's welfare as the first and paramount consideration and the injunction not to take into consideration whether from any other point of view the claim of the father was superior to that of the mother or the claim of the mother was superior to that of the father,[1] the Guardianship of Infants Act 1925 gave no guidance to the court in determining whether to make an order relating to the child's upbringing or custody and, if so, what form that order should take. The Law Reform (Parent and Child) (Scotland) Act 1986 provided that the court could make such order relating to parental rights as it thought fit, but also that it had to regard the welfare of the child as the paramount consideration and could not make any order relating to parental rights unless to do so was in the interests of the child.[2] No indication was given of the factors that might be relevant to the child's welfare, nor the weight to be given to any particular factor. It was—and is—considered better to allow the court dealing with each individual child to determine on the particular facts and circumstances of each case how the decision should be made. The Children (Scotland) Act 1995 adopts the same approach and, though a conscious effort was made to take account of (some of) the principles laid down in the UN Convention on the Rights of the Child (which led to one new factor—the views of the child—being expressly specified as a matter to which the court must have regard), the effect of the current legislation is little different from that under the 1986 Act. In determining whether to make an order under section 11 of the 1995 Act, and if so what sort of order, the court is left with the flexibility that characterised the pre-1995 law to make such order as, in the light of the circumstances of the individual case, it thinks fit.[3] The English approach, found in section 1(3) of the Children Act 1989,[4] whereby statute provides a "welfare checklist", that is a list of factors which the court must at least give consideration in making its welfare judgement,[5] has been rejected.[6]

10.02   The 1995 Act does, however, give some guidance to the court in considering whether or not to make a section 11 order: it must have regard to the three principles, often referred to as "the overarching principles",[7] which are set out in the two paragraphs in section 11(7). That provides as follows:

---

[1] Guardianship of Infants Act 1925, s. 1.
[2] Law Reform (Parent and Child) (Scotland) Act 1986, s. 3(1) and (2).
[3] Children (Scotland) Act 1995, s. 11(1) and (2).
[4] See also the Family Law Act 1996, s. 11 of which specifies other factors relevant to the child's welfare in the context of matrimonial proceedings.
[5] The court is obliged to give consideration to these factors only if the application is opposed, or if the application relates to a care or supervision order.
[6] See Scot. Law. Com. No. 135, *Report on Family Law* (1992) at paras 5.20–5.23. Such checklists have, however, found favour elsewhere: see, *e.g.*, the Australian Family Law Act 1975, as amended by the Family Law Reform Act 1995, introducing s. 68F, discussed in Norrie, "The Australian Children (Scotland) Act 1995" (1998) 3 S.L.P.Q. 15.
[7] For they are found repeated, though in different terms, in other parts of the Children (Scotland) Act 1995, such as in ss. 16, 17 and 95.

"Subject to subsection (8) below, in considering whether or not to make an order under subsection (1) above and what order to make, the court—

(a) shall regard the welfare of the child concerned as its paramount consideration and shall not make any such order unless it considers that it would be better for the child that the order be made than that none should be made at all; and

(b) taking account of the child's age and maturity, shall so far as practicable—

    (i) give him an opportunity to indicate whether he wishes to express his views;

    (ii) if he does so wish, give him an opportunity to express them; and

    (iii) have regard to such views as he may express."

Scope of this chapter

This chapter will examine the three principles contained in section 11(7), **10.03** that is to say (1) the welfare principle, (2) the no-order presumption, and (3) the requirement to take appropriate account of the child's views. Of these three, the predominant—the paramount—principle is the child's welfare. Laying down the no-order presumption in the same paragraph indicates the inextricable connection between that principle and the child's welfare: the presumption, in other words, is that the child's welfare will be better protected and advanced by making no order than by making an order under section 11. This chapter will therefore concentrate on the welfare principle, its meaning and effect, and the factors which are usually relevant to its application, including the no-order principle. Following that there will be a rather briefer consideration of the requirement to take account of the child's views.

THE WELFARE PRINCIPLE

Introduction

In considering whether to make an order under section 11(1), the court is **10.04** required, as pointed out above, to regard the welfare of the child concerned as its paramount consideration and also to make no such order unless it considers that it would be better for the child that the order be made than that none should be made at all.[8] The court is therefore barred from making any section 11 order unless it is satisfied that to do so will be in the interests of the child: the effect of this is that the onus will always be on the applicant to prove the satisfaction of the welfare test, and that failure to do so will result in the applicant losing the case.[9] The standard of proof that the applicant must satisfy is the normal standard of proof on the balance of probabilities.[10]

---

[8] Children (Scotland) Act 1995, s. 11(7)(a).

[9] See *Porchetta v. Porchetta*, 1986 S.L.T. 105; *Montgomery v. Lockwood*, 1987 S.C.L.R. 525; *Russell v. Russell*, 1991 S.C.L.R. 429; *M. v. Lothian Regional Council*, 1989 S.L.T. 426, *per* Lord Cullen at 429G; *Sanderson v. McManus*, 1997 S.L.T. 629, *per* Lord Hope of Craighead at 634E; *Osborne v. Matthan*, 1998 S.C.L.R. 691.

[10] *per* Lord President Hope in *F v. F*, 1991 S.L.T. 357 at 362, approving the sheriff in *Sloss v. Taylor*, 1989 S.C.L.R. 407, and disapproving the sheriff in *McEachan v. Young*, 1988 S.C.L.R. 98; *Sanderson v. McManus*, above, *per* Lord Hope of Craighead at 634E. See also *Armstrong v. Gibson*, 1991 S.L.T. 193. The House of Lords has held that to prove that there is at least a risk of harm to the child is proof that his or her welfare is threatened and that actual harm is not required before the standard of proof is satisfied: per Lord Oliver of Aylmerton in *Re KD (A Minor) (Ward: Termination of Access)* [1988] 2 W.L.R. 398 at 408.

10.05   As well as being the court's paramount consideration whenever it is asked to make, or is considering making under its own hand, a section 11 order, the welfare of the child is also the court's paramount consideration in other applications relating to children, such as those under Part II of the Children (Scotland) Act 1995. It is, however, necessary to be aware of the limitations to the application of the welfare principle. Most importantly, it applies only when an issue is before the court. The state cannot interfere in the private upbringing of a child merely because that upbringing is not the best that can be expected. As was said in the (English) DHSS *Review of Child Care Law*[11]; "taken to its logical conclusion, a simple 'best interests' test would permit the state to intervene whenever it could show that the alternative arrangements proposed would serve the children's welfare better than those proposed by the parents". None of the applications under Part II of the Children (Scotland) Act 1995 can be founded purely on the ground that it is in the interests of the child to be subject to one or other of the orders permitted under that Part. There is less limitation on the making of an application under Part I, but the welfare principle seldom extends beyond such applications.[12] It has to be remembered that the welfare principle does not apply in every case involving a child, even when the decision to be made will have profound effects on the child's life or his or her upbringing.[13] It does not assist, for example, in the resolution of disputes of fact. Nor, perhaps less obviously, does it apply when the dispute does not concern the extent or exercise of parental responsibilities and parental rights, the administration of a child's property, guardianship or legal representation.[14] Not every statutory or other rule of law which affects the child is to be applied in such a way as furthers the child's interests. The Education Acts provide an example where other considerations, particularly parents' rights of choice, underlie the legislation. Again, issues of children's capacity, except when qualified by concepts such as reasonableness, do not depend upon nor are cut down by considerations of the child's welfare. So a child over 12 years of age may withhold consent to his or her own adoption,[15] notwithstanding that every agency involved with the child, including the court, considers that it would further the child's welfare to be adopted. That proposition might, of course, be analysed in terms that consist with the application of the welfare principle: it might persuasively be argued that it is never in the interests of a child to be adopted by persons to whom the child objects. But in other circumstances, such as those involving medical treatment, the argument that it is never in the interests of a child to go against his or her wishes is not persuasive.[16] The point of conferring capacity is that it

---

[11] (HMSO, 1985), para. 2.13.

[12] See *Re X (A Minor) (Wardship: Jurisdiction)* [1975] Fam. 47 in which the Court of Appeal held, in an application to restrain the publication of a book about a child's deceased father, that even although the child was a ward of court, her interests were not the paramount consideration. See also *Re Z (A Minor) (Freedom of Publication)* [1996] 1 F.L.R. 191.

[13] See Lowe, "The House of Lords and the Welfare Principle", Chap. 4 in Bridge, ed., *Family Law Towards the Millenium: Essays for P.M. Bromley* (1997), pp. 150–162.

[14] The welfare principle was held not to apply in England in a dispute relating to ownership or occupancy of the matrimonial home in *Richards v. Richards* [1984] A.C. 174; *K v. K (Minors: Property Transfer)* [1992] 2 F.L.R. 220; *Gibson v. Austin* [1992] 2 F.L.R. 437; nor to the question of whether a mother in contempt of court for failing to abide by the terms of a contact order should be imprisoned: *A v. N (Committal: Refusal of Contact)* [1997] 1 F.L.R. 533.

[15] Age of Legal Capacity (Scotland) Act 1991, s. 2(3).

[16] In some situations this will undoubtedly be so (such as, *e.g.*, when a 14-year-old girl is pregnant and a decision has to be made whether to continue to or to terminate the pregnancy) but in other circumstances (refusal of life-saving blood transfusion, for example) any objective assessment of welfare may well give a different answer from the child's own wishes.

allows the child that freedom which adults have to go against their own interests. And there is one statutory qualification to the paramountcy of the child's welfare in relation to section 11 orders. The court must endeavour to ensure that any order which it makes, or any determination by it not to make an order, does not adversely affect the position of a person who has, in good faith and for value, acquired any property of the child concerned, or any right or interest in such property.[17] This will be limited to questions involving the administration of the child's property. It is to be noted that in terms of the provision the court must "endeavour" to ensure that the position of third parties is protected and it is not "required" so to ensure. This suggests that the obligation is not absolute and that the court is required merely to balance the claims of the child against the claims of the third party, in which balance the welfare of the child is not necessarily determining.

Nevertheless, the welfare principle is the dominant determinant in most issues **10.06** that will reach the court concerning the child's upbringing. Even when statute does not expressly refer to that principle the court will apply it if, in the circumstances, it is considered that the underlying purpose of the statutory rule is to protect the child's interests. So in *Girvan v. Girvan* the First Division, faced with a question involving jurisdiction between sheriff courts to hear an access claim, said this:

> "The important point however is not the correct interpretation of Rule 129,[18] but the welfare of the child, Ryan. In a case such as this when the welfare of a child is the paramount consideration procedural and legal niceties must give way to common sense and reality."[19]

But the point remains good that not every rule of law that affects children **10.07** has as its underlying purpose the protection of the child's interests. Those that do, together with those that expressly require the application of the welfare principle, will be applied regarding that principle as the paramount consideration.

Meaning of "paramount consideration"

The court is directed to regard the child's welfare as its paramount **10.08** consideration.[20] This requirement, which has been part of Scots law since 1925,[21] gives a higher regard to the child's interests than is required under the UN Convention on the Rights of the Child, Art. 3(1) of which provides that the best interests of the child are to be "a primary consideration" in all court proceedings. It has been said that paramount does not mean exclusive and so considerations, other than the welfare of the child, may enter into the decision.[22] That is probably still the law[23] but paramountcy is to be understood in a strong sense and the fact that it does not mean exclusive does not detract from the overriding importance of the child's welfare as against any consideration inconsistent with it. The claims of an "unimpeachable parent" or "the essential justice of the case" cannot

---

[17] s. 11(8), to which s. 11(7) is expressly subject.

[18] Sheriff Courts (Scotland) Act 1907, Sched., Sheriff Court Rules (as amended).

[19] 1988 S.L.T. 866 at 871D.

[20] Children (Scotland) Act 1995, s. 11(7)(a).

[21] Guardianship of Infants Act 1925, s. 1; Law Reform (Parent and Child) (Scotland) Act 1986, s. 3(2).

[22] *Re O (Infants)* [1962] 1 W.L.R. 724; *Re L (Infants)* [1962] 1 W.L.R. 886.

[23] And is expressly so in relation to the protection of third party property rights: Children (Scotland) Act 1995, s. 11(8).

prevail against it.[24] The course to be followed will be that which is most in the interests of the child's welfare "when all the relevant facts, relationships, claims and wishes of parents, risks, choices and other circumstances are taken into account and weighed". The child's welfare "is the first consideration because it is of first importance and the paramount consideration because it rules upon or determines the course to be followed".[25] If the child's welfare rules upon, or determines, the course to be followed it follows that all the circumstances must be viewed in that context and that no consideration can receive effect in the decision unless it is related to the child's welfare. The only exception to that can be where regard for the child's welfare does not afford a basis of choice because either, or any, of the courses available would serve that interest equally well. Only when, from the welfare standpoint, there is an equal balance can other considerations come into play. That equality of balance should not, however, be regarded in too narrow or closely structured terms. Welfare judgments often embrace a choice among risks, depend on contingencies, and are based upon uncertain opinions. No consideration, however cogent it may otherwise be, can prevail against what is clearly for the child's welfare. Where, however, there is uncertainty there is some scope for giving weight to other considerations, always provided that they are not prejudicial to the child's welfare. Since 1925 no intrinsic merit or demerit has attached to the conduct or wishes of one parent as against the other although a preference may be exercised according to the circumstances of the given case. It was said in a custody case under the 1925 Act that where the welfare considerations are equally balanced weight may still be attached to the position of the father as head of the family,[26] but that is difficult to reconcile with the equality of parental authority, created by the Guardianship Act 1973.[27] The terms of the 1995 Act do not indicate any principle upon which such a preference in a residence or any other section 11 dispute can be based. Responsibility for the breakdown of the marriage is an aspect of conduct which used frequently to be taken into account in custody cases.[28] The court is not, however, concerned, in an application for a section 11 order, to penalise spouses for failure in marital duty.[29] In a question between parent and stranger, consideration may have to be given, and weight attached according to circumstances, both to a natural parental desire for the society of a child and to the reluctance of persons who have cared for a child over a period of time to see a bond of affection broken. Such matters are, however, always to be entirely subordinated to the regard due to the child's welfare and, in general, it is only in that context that the conduct and claims of parents or others should be assessed.[30] If a single case involves the interests of two children, which are in conflict, the court's decision must attempt to balance out the interests of both.[31] The House

---

[24] *S v. S* (1975) 5 Fam. Law 148 in which *Re L*, above, is treated as overruled by *J v. C* [1970] A.C. 668. The proposition that "paramount" does not mean "exclusive", if understood in the sense indicated in the text, is not, however, inconsistent with *J v. C. Hume v. Hume*, 1926 S.C. 1008 and *M v. M*, 1926 S.C. 778, in which a larger scope was claimed for considerations other than the child's welfare, must be regarded as overruled by *J v. C.*

[25] *J v. C* [1970] A.C. 668, *per* Lord MacDermott at 711. At that time, the Guardianship of Infants Act 1925 provided that the child's welfare was "the first and paramount consideration". The words "first and" were dropped in 1986 as being subsumed into and adding nothing to "paramount consideration": see Scot. Law Com. No. 82 (1984), para. 9.17.

[26] *Douglas v. Douglas*, 1950 S.C. 453.

[27] s. 10, repealed by the Law Reform (Parent and Child) (Scotland) Act 1986, Sched. 2.

[28] *Hume v. Hume*, 1926 S.C. 1008 at 1010; *Christison v. Christison*, 1936 S.C. 381; *Christie v. Christie*, 1945 S.L.T. 300; *Spicer v. Spicer*, 1946 S.L.T. (Notes) 24; *Douglas v. Douglas*, 1950 S.C. 453; *Stevenson v. Stevenson*, 1967 S.L.T. (Notes) 7.

[29] *McLean v. McLean*, 1947 S.C. 79, *per* Lord Justice-Clerk Cooper at 85.

[30] *Christison v. Christison*, above; *McLean v. McLean*, above; *J v. C*, above.

[31] *Re T and E (Proceedings: Conflicting Interests)* [1995] 1 F.L.R. 581.

of Lords has held, in the context of care proceedings in England, that if the parent is herself a child, her interests do not need to be taken into account as part of this balance.[32] It is submitted that this applies also in private law proceedings. The "child" referred to in section 11(7), whose welfare is paramount, is the child in respect of whom an order is sought. So if, for example, an application is made to remove the parental responsibilities and parental rights of a 15-year-old parent in respect of her child, the parent's interests are relevant but no more so than in a case in which she is not a child. It is the welfare of the parent's child which is the court's paramount consideration in any application relating to parental responsibilities or parental rights.

Meaning and application of the welfare principle

The welfare principle offers an admirable ideal for the regulation of disputes **10.09** relating to the upbringing of children, but its protean character gives rise to difficulties in application. Extreme cases are clear. Confronted with squalor, cruelty, neglect or exposure to depravity on the one hand, and a wholesome environment on the other, there is no problem in determining where the child is to live. More often, however, the decision will turn on more subtle and debatable factors on which there may be wide latitude of opinion. These factors may take on quite different colour depending both upon the issue before the court and upon whether welfare is to be assessed in its short-term or in its long-term sense. Section 11(7), in sharp contrast with other provisions in the 1995 Act, gives no indication of the length of future time the court should take into account.[33] The Scottish courts have seldom been asked to weigh immediate, though transient, happiness against long term opportunities and advantages, though cases in which the two could give different answers are not hard to visualise.[34] Are benefits which might reasonably be expected to accrue only in adulthood more important than benefits that are real and immediate but will invariably become more ephemeral as the child grows older? Clearly there is no one answer to such questions that is "right" for every child, and one can say no more than that neither type of benefit is to be ignored. Common experience, however, suggests that the maintenance of an immediately satisfying and rewarding relationship is likely to lay the foundations of long-term psychological health. If this is so, then it may well be impossible in most cases to distinguish between the short- and the long-term aspects of welfare.[35]

In light of the difficulties in predicting with confidence which of various **10.10** options will best protect the child's welfare, it may be objected that the welfare principle leaves matters of the highest importance to child, parent and others in the hands of a virtually unfettered discretion; that such well verified insights into a child's welfare as we have, whether from ordinary lay experience or from scientific knowledge, should be embodied in rules, even if only of a presumptive

---

[32] *Birmingham City Council v. H (No. 3)* [1994] 2 A.C. 212. See Douglas, "In Whose Best Interests?" (1994) 110 L.Q.R. 379.

[33] *cf.* s. 16, which makes the child's welfare "throughout his childhood" the paramount consideration in any matter governed by Pt II of the Act, and s. 95 which amends s. 6 of the Adoption (Scotland) Act 1978 to make the child's welfare "throughout his life" the paramount consideration in adoption matters.

[34] One example is the sheriff's decision in *Brixey v. Lynas*, 1996 S.L.T. 908, where he removed a very young child from her mother's care on the ground that as a member of her father's family she would have "all the advantages of comfort, education and a strong and stable moral framework which they can offer... I have come to the view that I should not deprive the child of the advantages which the accident of her paternity make available to her". For other reasons, the decision was overruled. And in *Osborne v. Matthan*, 1997 S.L.T. 811 the sheriff was criticised for purporting to assess a child's long-term welfare when making an interim order.

[35] In *Senna-Cheribbo v. Wood*, Nov. 19, 1998 the Inner House accepted that a first instance decision on welfare would be open to challenge if it were based on a "limited outlook" of the present and ignored the long-term future.

character; and that, beyond rules so derived, our views of welfare form a dubious basis for decision.[36] Judicial decision has compensated to some extent but unevenly for the fluidity and uncertainty of the welfare principle. There is a marked reluctance on the part of appeal courts to interfere with the conclusions on welfare reached by judges at first instance who heard at first hand the parties and their witnesses and gained thereby a perceived advantage in assessing where the child's interests lie: an appeal court will disturb a trial judge's conclusions only if it is demonstrated that he failed to take sufficient account of a significant factor or that he reached a conclusion which was so plainly wrong as to demonstrate that he had not properly exercised his discretion.[37] Nevertheless, on some, though only on some, aspects of welfare a pattern has been set by leading cases into which subsequent decisions fall. Occasionally cases are treated at least as persuasive, if not as binding, authorities,[38] but more often it is a question of a practice developing by way of reaction to broadly similar situations.[39] A decision on welfare is a matter of informed and properly directed discretion. What is for the welfare of the child is essentially a question of fact. But in some cases it is clearly a matter of judgment, the making of which is influenced by socio-political considerations. A rare judicial admission of this is to be found in the judgment of Brennan J in *Secretary, Department of Health and Community Services v. JWB and SMB*[40] when he said, "It must be remembered that, in the absence of legal rules or a hierarchy of values, the best interests approach depends upon the value system of the decision-maker. Absent any rule or guideline, that approach simply creates an unexaminable discretion in the repository of the power". Decisions of superior courts may indicate factors to which much or little weight should ordinarily be given, but too much depends on the individuality and variety of circumstances of every case for them to rule subsequent decisions. Rarely do they establish strict precedents or lay down rules of law on what is best for the child.[41] The following discussion of the operation of the welfare principle must be understood in that sense. One rule can, however, be laid down, with both certainty and force. It is that the child's

---

[36] There has been quite extensive academic criticism of the indeterminacy, subjectivity, cultural bias and unpredictability of the welfare test: see, *e.g.*, Bala, "Judicial Discretion and Family Law Reform in Canada" (1986) 5 Can. J. Fam. L. 15; Dupaix, "Best Interests Revisited: In Search of Guidelines" (1987) 3 Utah L.R. 651; Montgomery, "Rhetoric and Welfare" (1989) 9 Oxford J. Leg. Stud. 395; Parker, "The Best Interests of the Child: Principles and Problems" (1994) 8 Int. J. L. and Fam. 26; Reece, "The Paramountcy Principle: Consensus or Construct?" (1996) 49 Current Leg. Prob. 267 and, in the context of child protection, Baskin, "State Intervention Into Family Affairs: Justifications and Limitations" (1974) 26 Stanford L. Rev. 1383; Walter, Isenegger and Bala "'Best Interests' in Child Protection Proceedings: Implications and Alternatives" (1995) 12 Can. J. Fam. L. 367. Cretney and Masson, *Principles of Family Law* (6th ed., 1997), p. 730, talk of the judge's "unexaminable discretion", drawing attention to appeal courts' reluctance to interfere with the welfare judgment made by judges at first instance who heard the evidence. Despite attempts, however, none of these writers has been able to suggest any all-embracing principle that might rationally replace the welfare principle (though, to be fair, some suggest that the search for such a principle is, of necessity, vain).

[37] *Thomas v. Thomas*, 1947 S.C. (H.L.) 45, *per* Lord Macmillan at 59; *Jordan v. Jordan*, 1983 S.L.T. 539; *Britton v. Central Regional Council*, 1986 S.L.T. 207; *Early v. Early*, 1990 S.L.T. 221, *per* Lord Cowie at 223; *Brixey v. Lynas*, 1994 S.L.T. 847, *per* Lord Morison at 849F; *Sanderson v. McManus*, 1997 S.L.T. 629, *per* Lord Hope of Craighead at 631F; *Osborne v. Matthan*, 1997 S.L.T. 811.

[38] *Gray v. Gray*, 1961 S.L.T.(Notes) 83, following *McAllister v. McAllister*, 1947 S.L.T.(Notes) 9; and *McClements v. McClements*, 1958 S.C. 286, following *Mackay v. Mackay*, 1957 S.L.T. (Notes) 17.

[39] See *Povey v. Povey* [1972] Fam. 40, *per* Sir Jocelyn Simon, P. at 49: "Judges exercising a given discretion consistently in order to do justice will tend to react similarly to similar situations; so that a practice will develop."

[40] (1992) 106 A.L.R. 385 (High Court of Australia).

[41] *Townsend v. Townsend* (1973) 4 Fam. L. 127, *per* Davies L.J. at 128.

welfare is to be understood comprehensively, embracing material, physical, intellectual, emotional, psychological, moral and, so far as it admits of assessment, spiritual well-being. It has for long been recognised that that is so. In *Re McGrath* in 1892, Lindley L.J. said:

> "The welfare of the child is not to be measured by money only, nor by physical comfort only. The word welfare must be taken in its widest sense. The moral and religious welfare of the child must be considered as well as its physical well-being. Nor can the ties of affection be disregarded."[42]

Some of these factors receive separate consideration in the paragraphs that follow. They are, however, to be regarded as interacting with each other so as to constitute a totality. It is error to concentrate on one to the exclusion of the others.[43]

Factors relevant to welfare: general

10.11 The welfare principle has no meaning except in the context of the particular dispute that it is employed to resolve. The aim of the court, in considering whether to make a section 11 order, is to make a decision on a dispute before it that is, in the circumstances, the best available option for the child. This may, of course, involve making an order that is not asked for, or making no order. The nature of the dispute, and the order sought or considered appropriate, clearly affects the assessment of individual factors and the weight they should be given in indicating how the particular dispute is to be resolved. To take an obvious example, a parent's homelessness will usually be the determining consideration in denying the right to have the child reside with him or her, but it will be of far less significance in determining whether that parent should have contact with the child; again it will gain in significance in determining how contact is to be regulated. Most of the following factors have greatest but not sole relevance in disputes as to where the child is to live, but it is right to concentrate on that question since, though it does not in itself affect the parental responsibilities and parental rights except in relation to the child's residence, that is the issue that has most immediate significance to, and long-term influence on, the child in respect of whom the decision is being made. Many of the factors will, however, have relevance in other issues, such as contact, guardianship and the administration of the child's property.[44]

Material needs

10.12 There is a minimum level at which provision for the material needs of a child is fundamental if only because, without it, his or her physical welfare and probably also his or her emotional, intellectual and even moral development will be prejudiced. In some of the older cases the inability of an applicant for custody to make such minimum provision was the ground of decision.[45] In modern conditions, however, State social security support should nearly always remove the need to deny an otherwise suitable claimant on this ground. Beyond

---

[42] [1893] 1 Ch. 143 at 148.

[43] *Allen v. Allen* [1948] 2 All E.R. 413, in which it was held that to stress the supposed moral welfare of the child to the exclusion of other factors was to apply the wrong test. The welfare of the child, both moral and physical, was the paramount consideration. *Cf. Bevan v. Bevan* (1973) 3 Fam. Law 126.

[44] A useful table collecting together custody cases in which particular factors predominated is to be found in Jamieson, *Parental Responsibilities and Rights* (1995), pp. 297–300. A similar table for access cases is at pp. 301–302.

[45] *Campbell v. Croall* (1895) 22 R. 869; *Alexander v. McGarrity* (1903) 5 F. 654; *Mitchell v. Wright* (1905) 7 F. 568.

such minimum provision, there is little evidence that Scottish courts are influenced in residence decisions by the material wealth or comfort of the potential environment. That, in general, corresponds well with a proper understanding of the welfare principle. Once minimum conditions are satisfied the material advantages or disadvantages of a child's surroundings are likely to be less important from the standpoint of welfare than other less tangible, but nonetheless vital, qualities in the relationship between the child and the person with whom he or she resides.[46] Moreover, in many cases, and especially in questions between parents, it will be possible, by an appropriate award of aliment, to reduce or remove any disadvantages accruing from requiring the child to live with a party in relatively poor financial circumstances. So, although differences in material wealth should not altogether be excluded from consideration they will usually be of comparatively minor importance. They may, however, attain rather greater importance than would ordinarily be the case if a potential applicant for residence, who, if not awarded a residence order, has no alimentary obligation, can make better material provision for the child than would be afforded on any alternative disposal. That will be particularly so where the potential advantages do not lie solely in immediate material benefits but offer the child the prospect of better opportunities in his or her future life. Thus, in *Huddart v. Huddart*[47] the court entertained, if only peripherally, the somewhat speculative question of the potential advantages of life in Australia as compared with Scotland.[48] Such considerations cannot, it is submitted, ever justify disturbing a secure and satisfying relationship but, where other considerations are equal or nearly so, may play a prominent, or even a decisive, role.

Physical and emotional welfare

10.13   Physical and emotional welfare are interrelated and the one may strongly affect the other. There is an obvious and extreme sense in which physical welfare is the more fundamental. A modicum of physical well-being is essential for life and, therefore, a prerequisite of any consideration of life's quality. Beyond such extreme cases, it is, however, impossible to say whether the physical or the emotional welfare of the child is the more important. The court should not contemplate making an order, whether regulating residence or contact, which exposes the child to circumstances that seriously endanger either.[49] Because of the interrelation between physical and emotional welfare, factors which bear on the one will often bear on the other. Where they are in conflict, stress may sometimes be laid on physical welfare because it is a prerequisite or because it is the more easily assessed. On the other hand, emotional welfare will often play a more critical role because physical welfare is relatively easily secured and there may be little to choose between one placement and another on that account while the child's emotional welfare depends on the quality of particular relationships which are less likely to be evenly balanced. Some physical risks,

---

46 In *Brixey v. Lynas*, 1996 S.L.T. 908, HL the sheriff (G. L. Gordon, Q.C.) had found that the father was "comfortably middle-class" while the mother had had none of the educational and social advantages which he had had but that that was not sufficient reason for separating the child from her mother and sister (he did, however, find other reasons—though his decision was eventually overturned).

47 1961 S.C. 393. See also *Johnson v. Francis*, 1982 S.L.T. 285.

48 *cf. Re Weston's Settlements* [1968] 3 All E.R. 338, in which, on a question of whether a variation of a trust was for the benefit of a child beneficiary, Lord Denning M.R. pointed out (at 342) that the court should not consider merely financial benefit, but also educational and social benefits. One of the things in life "more worthwhile than money", he said, was "to be brought up in this our England, which is still 'the envy of less happier lands'".

49 In relation to physical welfare, this has long been recognised: *Lang v. Lang* (1869) 7 M. 445 at 447; *Stewart, Petr,* (1870) 8 S.L.R. 279; *Bloe v. Bloe* (1882) 9 R. 894.

such as the risk of communicable disease, need seldom determine a residence or contact dispute as they can usually be overcome by temporary arrangements. Defects of character or capacity which put the child's physical welfare in jeopardy may exist even where there is a warm bond of affection with the child conducive to his or her emotional development, and, even in such cases, these defects can scarcely be ignored. On the other hand, a competent and conscientious person, likely to provide in every way for the child's physical welfare, is not to be preferred in a residence dispute if he or she cannot form a relationship with the child that would satisfy the child's emotional needs.

Beyond observations of that kind, perhaps largely self-evident, there is little **10.14** that can be said of general application. The circumstances of particular cases are infinitely variable and what is for the welfare of the child, whether physical or emotional, requires an assessment of the individual case which will turn very largely on its own peculiar facts. Medical evidence may be of assistance[50] and, if its intendment is clear, cannot, especially in a question of physical welfare on which the conclusions of medical science are well established, lightly be disregarded, but it may have to be weighed along with other matters not susceptible of medical assessment and, in any event, it does not rule the decision.[51] There are, however, a few considerations of more or less general application which can be identified as playing a prominent role in judicial assessment of the child's physical or emotional welfare, and these are considered below.

Mother's possession of child of tender years
There is no settled rule of law that a child, even of tender years, should be **10.15** left in the care and control of his or her mother.[52] Where there have been grounds for removing the mother's residence rights, any presumption there may be in favour of her retaining residence has been treated as not being a major, far less a conclusive, consideration.[53] It is not sufficient ground for disturbing an existing satisfactory relationship with someone else.[54] Nonetheless, some place remains for the view that the mother will often be the person best equipped to look after the child on a day-to-day basis and in other cases, where the issues may have been more evenly balanced, a certain preference for her on that ground may be detected.[55] In England too it is recognised that there is no rule of law in favour of the mother but it is the practice to allow very young children, and particularly young girls, to reside with her unless there are reasons to the contrary.[56] To do so has been said to be a dictate of nature[57] or "one of the facts of nature which

---

[50] *Gibson v. Gibson* (1894) 2 S.L.T. 71; *Mitchell v. Wright* (1905) 7 F. 568; *Pow v. Pow*, 1931 S.L.T. 485.

[51] *M v. M*, 1926 S.C. 778.

[52] *Whitecross v. Whitecross*, 1977 S.L.T. 225; *Re B (An Infant)* [1962] 1 All E.R. 872; *Aldous v. Aldous* (1974) Fam. Law 152; *Brixey v. Lynas*, 1996 S.L.T. 908.

[53] *M v. M*, 1926 S.C. 778; *Brown v. Brown*, 1948 S.C. 5; *Stevenson v. Stevenson*, 1967 S.L.T. (Notes) 7; *Whitecross v. Whitecross*, above; *Jordan v. Jordan*, 1983 S.L.T. 539; *MacMillan v. Brady*, 1997 Fam. L.R. 29. *Cf.* before the 1925 Act, *Campbell v. Campbell*, 1920 S.C. 31.

[54] *Whitecross v. Whitecross*, above.

[55] *McLean v. Hardie*, 1927 S.C. 344; *Christison v. Christison*, 1936 S.C. 381; *McLean v. McLean*, 1947 S.C. 79; *Nicol v. Nicol*, 1953 S.L.T.(Notes) 67. *Cf.* before the 1925 Act: *Reid v. Reid* (1901) 3 F. 330; *Robertson, Petr*, 1911 S.C. 1319. In *Jordan v. Jordan*, above, Lord Stott in the Inner House quoted, without comment, the Lord Ordinary's view that *"prima facie* a mother is better qualified than a father to bring up two young girls".

[56] *Re S (A Minor) (Custody)* [1991] 2 F.L.R. 388, *per* Butler-Sloss L.J. at 390F; *Re A (A Minor) (Custody)* [1991] 2 F.L.R. 394, *per* Butler-Sloss L.J. at 400A; *Re W (A Minor) (Residence Order)* [1992] 2 F.L.R. 332.

[57] *G v. G* (1975) 6 Fam. Law 43, *per* Stamp L.J. The Inner House has disapproved of relying on "nature" in support of a mother's claim: "it is not nature but the welfare of the child which is the material matter", *per* Lord Walker in *Hannah v. Hannah*, 1971 S.L.T. (Notes) 42 at 43.

always weighed heavily in considering what was in the welfare of children".[58] Some criticisms have been made of the English decisions on the view that they represent role expectations based on an idealised view of motherhood. It has been said that a legal presumption in favour of the father has been turned into a moral presumption in favour of the mother.[59] In the absence of a full survey, it is impossible to say whether Scottish decisions show, with any consistency, a similar pattern and whether they might be open to a similar criticism. In the case of very young children a certain preference for the mother, although one which must yield to any weighty consideration to the contrary is, it is submitted, in any event defensible. Children of either sex may benefit from the presence of parents or parent substitutes of both sexes at all stages of their development, but in the early years the need for the mother, or substitute mother, at any rate on an emotional level, is almost certainly the stronger. As Lord Morison put it in *Brixey v. Lynas*[60] "It has been and remains the practice of the courts in Scotland to recognise as an important factor which has to be fully taken into account in a dispute concerning custody between the mother and father of a very young child, that during his or her infancy the child's need for the mother is stronger than the need for a father... There is a generally recognised belief that a mother is ordinarily better able, for whatever reason, to minister to a very young child's needs than is a father". In a question between the mother and father it may therefore be better, especially where the mother has until the dispute arose had the child in her care,[61] for the child to live with the mother rather than to embark on the risks inherent in the father's fulfilling a maternal role or in the creating of a new relationship in which there will be a substitute mother. There are, however, two objections to that view. One is that, once it is allowed, it may be given greater weight than it merits, but that objection is met if there is a sound exercise of judicial discretion. Lord Jauncey of Tullichettle put it thus in *Brixey v. Lynas*:

> "The advantage to a very young child of being with its mother is a consideration which must be taken into account in deciding where lie its best interests in custody proceedings in which the mother is involved. It is neither a presumption nor a principle but rather recognition of a widely held belief based on practical experience and the workings of nature. Its importance will vary according to the age of the child and to the other circumstances of each individual case such as whether the child has been living with or apart from the mother and whether she is or is not capable of providing proper care. Circumstances may be such that it has no importance at all. Furthermore it will always yield to other competing advantages which more effectively promote the welfare of the child."

An example of when other competing advantages did prevail is provided by the case of *MacMillan v. Brady*.[62]

---

[58] *P v. P* (1975) 6 Fam. Law 75, *per* Sir John Pennycuik at 76. *Cf. Southgate v. Southgate* (1978) 8 Fam. L. 246; *P v. McK (Formerly P)* (1973) 3 Fam. Law 172.

[59] See Oster "Custody Proceedings—A Study of Vague and Indefinite Standards" (1965) 5 J.F.L. 21 at 25–26. For an analysis of similar trends in Canada, see Bradbrook: "The Role of Judicial Discretion in Child Custody Adjudication in Ontario" (1971) 21 Univ.Tor.L.J. 402 at 405. This, it has been said, amounts to a "maternal bias in custody decisions" (letter in New L.J., Feb. 28, 1980, criticising the decision of the English Court of Appeal in *L v. L* (1980) 124 Sol.J. 203. See also Sutherland, "Mother Knows Best", 1994 S.L.T. (News) 375, criticising the First Division's approach in *Brixey v. Lynas*, 1994 S.L.T. 847.

[60] above, at 849I, affd 1996 S.L.T. 908.

[61] Thomson, *Family Law in Scotland* (3rd ed.), p. 226, explains the preference some judges show towards mothers as doing no more than reflecting a preference for the status quo, coupled with the fact that on the break-up of most parental relationships, young children tend to go with their mother.

[62] 1997 Fam. L.R. 29 (Inner House).

The second objection is that although residence decisions, in contrast with **10.16**
adoption orders, are in principle readily open to review, a residence order once
made is, in practice and for good reason, usually very difficult to disturb and
that the court should take a long view rather than be influenced by transient
considerations applicable only to the early years of a child's life.[63] That is an
important objection to which weight should be given where it can be said with
confidence that the long-term welfare of the child will be better served by
placement with the father. The long view may, however, be speculative and in
such cases it may be right to give effect to the general preference for the mother
in order to secure the immediate benefits which may be expected to accrue.[64] To
do so accords with the solution preferred in the vast majority of cases in which
the relationship between the parents has broken down but the parties nevertheless
succeed in agreeing about the arrangements for the care of their children. It
appears that any judicial expectations there may be concerning the maternal
role are widely shared throughout society. Even if these expectations are
culturally determined[65] they may nonetheless be valid in prevailing social
conditions. In the case of older children, however, it is difficult to justify a
placement with the mother on the grounds of any prima facie preference. Agreed
placements with the mother in these cases may be dictated less by any perception
of what is for the child's welfare than by the fact that the mother is, more often
than the father, willing to undertake the responsibilities of care or that, in an
amicable agreement where both parties are willing and other considerations are
equal, the father is commonly expected, and may himself expect, to "yield"
residence to the mother. The expedient occasionally adopted in the case of older
children of requiring the boys to reside with the father and requiring the girls to
reside with the mother, even to the extent of splitting the siblings in the case of
families of boys and girls,[66] may be justified in the circumstances of a particular
case but does not, it is thought, have any justification on general grounds.[67]

Maintenance of the status quo

In *Re Thain, Thain v. Taylor*[68] Eve J. said, with reference to the removal of a **10.17**
child from the care of an uncle and aunt by whom she had been brought up for
some years,

---

[63] See *M v. M*, 1926 S.C. 778 at 786. In *Hastie v. Hastie*, 1985 S.L.T. 146 Lord Davidson awarded
custody to the mother, after the child had been looked after by the father and the father's mother
for four years, this notwithstanding admitted short-term difficulties, on the ground that awarding
custody to the father could cause greater, long-term difficulties.

[64] Another criticism made of the sheriff's decision in *Brixey v. Lynas*, above, to award custody to
the (very young) father was his failure to have regard to the consequences of material changes
which were likely to occur in the future, such as the father's moving out of his parents' home, or
his marrying.

[65] See Sutherland, "Mother Knows Best" 1994 S.L.T. (News) 375; Edwards, "Mother Still Knows
Best", 1996 Fam. L.B. 23–5.

[66] As in *Symington v. Symington* (1874) 1 R. 871, (1875) 2 R. (H.L.) 41 which, although before the
1925 Act, turned on a consideration of welfare.

[67] So prevalent is the preference for wives in disputes between husbands and wives that it has
indeed been suggested that "since wives will, under most circumstances, be awarded custody
regardless of the statutory standard, and since it seems wise to discourage traumatic custody
contests whenever it is possible to do so, the Act should discourage those few husbands who
might wish to contest by establishing a presumption that the wife is entitled to custody. The
presumption resolves several value conflicts: it may well be true that because of the presumption
some fathers who would be better custodians than their wives will either fail to seek custody or
will be denied custody following a contest, but that disadvantage has a lower 'social cost' than
the disadvantages of any alternative statutory formulation—more contested cases (with the trauma
that contests seem to produce), more risk of a custody award to a father who will be only marginally
better than the mother or even much worse": Ellsworth and Levy (1969) 4 Law and Society
Review 167, at 203.

[68] [1926] Ch. 676 at 684.

"it is said that the little girl will be greatly distressed and upset at parting from Mr and Mrs Jones. I can quite understand it may be so, but, at her tender age, one knows from experience how mercifully transient are the effects of partings and other sorrows, and how soon the novelty of fresh surroundings and new associations effaces the recollection of former days and kind friends, and I cannot attach much weight to this aspect of the case."

A similar attitude was adopted by the Lord Justice-Clerk in *Begbie v. Nichol*,[69] in which he described as irrelevant an averment regarding the disturbance caused to a child of seven who had been in the care of foster parents for practically the whole of her life. So too in *Minto v. Minto*[70] the effects of disruption were discounted. *Minto v. Minto* was decided before the passing of the Guardianship of Infants Act 1925 and in *Begbie v. Nichol* only Lord Jamieson referred to the paramountcy of the welfare of the child, the other judges apparently taking the view, in accordance with the indications given in *Hume v. Hume*[71] that the 1925 Act applied only to disputes between parents of a legitimate child. That view must now be regarded as mistaken, and in any case is obsolete. Neither case, therefore, offers any sure guidance in a context in which the child's welfare is paramount. They may, however, be taken to reflect a judicial attitude which, because the effects were thought likely to be transient, regarded disruption of relationships as of little enduring significance for the child's welfare. Modern authorities by contrast stress the importance of continuity which has, in many cases, proved the decisive factor. In *J v. C*[72] Lord MacDermott had *Re Thain, Thain v. Taylor* in mind when he said:

"Some of the authorities convey the impression that the upset caused to a child by change of custody is transient and a matter of small importance. For all I know that may have been true in the cases containing dicta to that effect. But I think that a growing experience has shown that it is not always so and that serious harm even to young children may, on occasion, be caused by such a change. I do not suggest that the difficulties of this subject can be resolved by purely theoretical considerations, or that they need to be left entirely to expert opinion. But a child's future happiness and sense of security are always important factors and the effects of a change of custody will often be worthy of the close and anxious attention which they undoubtedly received in this case."

In that case the House of Lords refused to order the return to unimpeachable parents of a child who, for a protracted period, had been in the care of foster parents. Although a number of factors entered into the decision, the dangers of disruption were prominent among them and probably played a determinative part.[73] A similar emphasis in the related field of adoption can be seen in *A and B, Petitioners*.[74] And in *Brixey v. Lynas*[75] it was the sheriff's failure to take account of the benefit to be gained by leaving the child in her present environment that

---

[69] 1949 S.C. 158 at 164.

[70] 1914 2 S.L.T. 381.

[71] 1926 S.C. 1008 at 1014.

[72] [1970] A.C. 668 at 715.

[73] *cf.*, however, *Re M (Child's Upbringing)* [1996] 2 F.L.R. 441, in which a 10-year-old boy was returned to his parents in South Africa after spending four years in the care of a family in England. The major determinant in that case was the need to ensure the black child received a Zulu upbringing.

[74] 1971 S.C. (H.L.) 129.

[75] 1994 S.L.T. 847.

gave the Inner House the opportunity to overturn his decision.[76] It accords with a widely expressed and increasing recognition of the importance of the continuity of relationships.[77] In some literature, derived in the main from psychoanalytic sources,[78] that has been pressed to the extent of saying that no existing relationship should be disturbed unless there is positive evidence both that the existing relationship is detrimental to the welfare of the child and that an alternative placement would be less detrimental. That may take the matter too far. As was pointed out by the Lord Justice-Clerk in *Begbie v. Nicol*, changes may sometimes be inevitable. Most children are capable of adapting to change and damage is not an inevitable result of the adaptation.[79] Sometimes change, even from a favourable environment, may be beneficial. Much, no doubt, depends on the reasons for the change, the child's perception of them and the quality of the new relationships flowing from the change. When every allowance has been made for that, however, disturbance of an existing satisfactory relationship for a new one, whose benefits must always in some degree be speculative, involves risks, including the risk that a trauma which might be expected to be transient may become permanent; and these risks are particularly high when the disturbance comes about in the circumstances of contentious litigation. Despite earlier dicta to the contrary, Scottish decisions, both before and after *J v. C*, show considerable respect for the continuity of relationships.[80] The courts do not, of course, hesitate to disturb existing arrangements if required by the welfare of the child,[81] but there seems little doubt that continuity in a child's life is seen as a factor that enhances his or her welfare, with the result that the longer a settled environment has lasted, the more that will be required to persuade the court that alteration in the child's present circumstances will better enhance his

---

[76] In affirming the Inner House's decision, Lord Jauncey of Tullichettle said this: "Given that the mother's care of K was not criticised the sheriff undoubtedly erred in not addressing the advantages of the status quo when considering the advantages of an upbringing in the father's family" (1996 S.L.T. at 911I). See also *Sanderson v. McManus*, 1997 S.L.T. 629, in which Lord Hope of Craighead said (at 631H) "the greater the interval between the taking of the evidence from the witnesses and the hearing of each appeal... the stronger will be the argument that the appellate court should not disturb the status quo". And see Lord Weir in the Inner House in the same case, 1996 S.L.T. 750 at 765H–I.

[77] See "Alternatives to 'Parental Rights' in Child Custody Disputes Involving Third Parties" (1964) 73 Yale L.J. 151 at 159 *et seq.*; Michaels, "The Dangers of a Change of Parentage in Custody and Adoption Cases" (1967) 83 L.Q.R. 547 at 549.

[78] *e.g.*, famously, Goldstein, Freud and Solnit, *Beyond the Best Interests of the Child* (1973), reprinted as *The Best Interests of the Child: The Least Detrimental Alternative* (New York, Free Press, 1996). For a trenchant criticism of this work, see Freeman "The Best Interests of the Child? Is *The Best Interests of the Child* in the Best Interests of Children?" (1997) 11 *Int. J. Law, Policy and the Family* 360.

[79] In *Osborne v. Matthan (No. 2)*, 1998 S.L.T. 1264 Lord President Rodger accepted that to move the child from her home in Perth to a new home in Jamaica with her mother would cause her "some distress" but said that "if the move were otherwise required in the interests of Fiona, such temporary distress would not be a sufficient argument for preventing the defender [the mother] from taking her with her to Jamaica".

[80] *Macallister v. Macallister*, 1962 S.C. 406 at 413; *Cheetham v. Glasgow Corporation*, 1972 S.L.T. (Notes) 50; *Wincentzen v. Wincentzen*, 1974 S.L.T. (Notes) 26; *Robertson v. Robertson*, 1981 S.L.T. (Notes) 7. In the last-named case legal custody was awarded to the father on the understanding that the child was to remain in the care of the mother, with whom the child had been living. Since the coming into force of the Children (Scotland) Act 1995, this effect will be the result in very many more cases: a child will be required to reside with one parent but that will not affect, unless the court additionally so orders, the decision-making responsibilities of the other parent. In *Sinclair v. Sinclair*, 1988 S.L.T. 87 Lord Prosser held, in effect, that the onus of proving that current arrangements should be disturbed lay with the party claiming it: see 89I. See also *Breingan v. Jamieson*, 1993 S.L.T. 186.

[81] See, *e.g.*, *Hastie v. Hastie*, 1985 S.L.T. 146; *Early v. Early*, 1990 S.L.T. 221; *MacMillan v. Brady*, 1997 Fam. L.R. 29.

or her welfare. This consideration is also important in contact disputes, though other factors such as the assumption that the maintenance of a parental link is good for a child, will often be held to be more important.[82] If a child has not been used to contact with a person seeking it then the court must give careful consideration to the question of how the child is to be introduced into regular contact.[83]

Relationships with parents, siblings and others

10.18   The welfare of the child is intimately connected with the relationships which he or she has formed and will form.[84] Probably, once minimum standards of physical care and provision have been met, no aspect of the child's welfare is more important than the child's relationship with the persons with whom the child lives and spends, therefore, most of his or her time. Usually it will be the critical factor on which a residence dispute turns, and the relationship between the child and a person seeking contact will have equal importance in determining whether contact is or is not in the child's best interests. Unfortunately it may be one of the most difficult factors to assess. The child's views give an indication but not the only, nor indeed always the most reliable, indication of what the relationship is likely to be. It is, moreover, easier to ascertain the qualities of an existing relationship than to predict the effects of a change. Relationships with the wider family, and indeed with the wider community, although less important than the relationship with those with whom the child resides, may have a considerable bearing on the child's welfare. It is no doubt generally true that children benefit from the companionship of other children,[85] from the "rough and tumble of family life"[86] rather than seclusion, and from being in one family unit with their brothers and sisters,[87] but these generalities admit of exceptions.[88] In this, as in other matters, an assessment has to be made in relation to the particular child and the particular circumstances of the case. The general social environment will usually be only a minor factor, but it may assume importance if the child is likely to be exposed to hostility in the form of acute social, religious, racial or ethnic prejudice.[89] The drawbacks of appearing to yield to prejudice must be subordinated to the paramountcy of the child's welfare.[90]

---

[82] See *Donnelly v. Green*, 1998 Fam. L.R. 12 and *Davidson v. Smith*, 1998 Fam. L.R. 21.

[83] *Henderson v. Henderson*, 1997 Fam. L.R. 120; *Perendes v. Sim*, 1998 S.L.T. 1382.

[84] See the discussion of this point in Kaltenborn and Lempp, "The Welfare of the Child in Custody Disputes After Parental Separation or Divorce" (1998) 12 Int. J. Law & Fam. 74. In *Hill v. Hill*, 1991 S.L.T. 189 it was held that a relevant consideration in determining welfare was that the granting of custody to one parent would terminate the child's relationship with the other (since the mother lived in Scotland and the father lived in Canada). The same is true of contact: in *Breingan v. Jamieson*, *Herald*, March 3, 1992 Lord Penrose allowed a father access to his seven-year-old daughter so that she could act as a flower girl at his wedding, this because attendance at the wedding would allow her to identify herself as a member of the new family unit being created. In a later action custody was granted to the child's aunt, with whom she lived: 1993 S.L.T. 186.

[85] *Christison v. Christison*, 1936 S.C. 381 per Lord Anderson at 385–386.

[86] *Begbie v. Nichol*, 1949 S.C. 158, *per* Lord Justice-Clerk Thomson at 164.

[87] *Steuart v. Steuart* (1870) 8 M. 821; *Morrison v. Quarrier* (1894) 21 R. 1071; *Mackellar v. Mackellar* (1898) 25 R. 883; *Nicol v. Nicol*, 1953 S.L.T. (Notes) 67; *Douglas v. Douglas*, 1950 S.C. 453 at 457; *Reynolds v. Reynolds* (1974) 4 Fam. Law 193; *Early v. Early*, 1989 S.L.T. 114, affd 1990 S.L.T. 221. See also *Campins-Coll, Petr*, 1989 S.L.T. 33; *Urness v. Minto*, 1994 S.L.T. 988.

[88] See *Johnson v. Johnson*, 1972 S.L.T. (Notes) 15, and *Barr v. Barr*, 1950 S.L.T. (Notes) 15, for cases in which the separation of siblings may be accepted.

[89] On the importance of racial or ethnic considerations, see below, para. 10.37.

[90] But see Montgomery, "Rhetoric and Welfare" (1989) 9 Ox.J.Leg.Stud. 395. This question has been considered in the USA. See *Fountaine v. Fountaine*, 57 A.L.R. (2d) 675 (1956), discussed by Clive, *Husband and Wife* (3rd ed.), p. 543. This may go some way to explaining the decision in *Early v. Early*, 1989 S.L.T. 114.

Maintaining relationships in contact disputes

The question of the maintenance of relationships is particularly significant **10.19** in contact disputes. There is an increasing acceptance[91] that a child's welfare is more likely to be enhanced than compromised by maintaining contact with both parents even after they separate.[92] In English law this now has the status of a presumption. In *Re M (Contact: Welfare Test)*[93] Wilson J in the Court of Appeal referred to the "fundamental emotional need of every child to have an enduring relationship with both of his parents". Sir Thomas Bingham, M.R., said, in a case involving unmarried parents who had separated prior to the child's birth, "where parents of a child are separated and the child is in the day-to-day care of one of them, it is almost always in the interests of the child that he or she should have contact with the other parent".[94] The result of these, and other, cases is that there is a strong presumption in favour of contact between a child and his or her parents, both when the parents are or were married to each other and when they are unmarried; in the former case the presumption has added statutory force.[95] Latey J., in a judgment endorsed by Balcome L.J. in *Re H (Minors) (Access)*[96] eloquently explained the basis of this presumption:

> "Where the parents have separated and one has the care of the child, access by the other often results in some upset in the child. Those upsets are usually minor and superficial. They are heavily outweighed by the long-term advantages to the child of keeping in touch with the parent concerned so that they do not become strangers, so that the child later in life does not resent the deprivation and turn against the parent who the child thinks, rightly or wrongly, has deprived him, and so that the deprived parent loses interest in the child and therefore does not make the material and emotional contribution to the child's development which that parent by its companionship and otherwise would make."

The question for the English court in all cases in which a parent seeks contact **10.20** is this: "Are there any cogent reasons why this father should be denied access to his children?"[97] The onus is very clearly on those seeking to deny parental contact, and the English courts have resisted allowing the implacable hostility of the residence parent[98] or even the effect that contact would have on the residence

---

[91] See the research material referred to in Weyland, "Judicial Attitudes to Contact and Shared Residence Since the Children Act 1989" (1995) 17 J. Soc. Wel. & Fam. L. 445. For earlier acadmic support, see Eekelaar, "What Are Parental Rights?" (1973) 89 L.Q.R. 210 at 218–219; Eekelaar, "The Wardship Jurisdiction, Children's Welfare and Parents' Rights" (1991) 107 L.Q.R. 386; Thomson, "Whither the 'Right' of Access?", 1989 S.L.T. (News) 109.

[92] UN Convention on the Rights of the Child, Art. 9(3): "States Parties shall respect the right of the child who is separated from one or both parents to maintain personal relations and direct contact with both parents on a regular basis, except if it is contrary to the child's best interests". That the Scottish courts have long attached weight to the retention of the link between parent and child can be seen in a number of cases, including *Blance v. Blance*, 1978 S.L.T. 74; *Cosh v. Cosh*, 1979 S.L.T. (Notes) 72; *Brannigan v. Brannigan*, 1979 S.L.T. (Notes) 73. In *Sanderson v. McManus*, 1996 S.L.T. 750 (Extra Division), Lord McCluskey at 761E (dissenting) adopts the language of the UN Convention when he criticises the sheriff and the sheriff principal for failing to give any real weight to the child's "right" to know his own father.

[93] [1995] 1 F.L.R. 274 at 278.

[94] *Re O (Contact: Imposition of Conditions)* [1995] 2 F.L.R. 124 at 128E. See also *Re W (A Minor) (Contact)* [1994] 2 F.L.R. 441; *Re P (Contact: Supervision)* [1996] 2 F.L.R. 314.

[95] Family Law Act 1996, s. 11(4)(c).

[96] [1992] 1 F.L.R. 148 at 151A.

[97] *ibid.*

[98] *Re S (Minors: Access)* [1990] 2 F.L.R. 166; *Re J (A Minor) (Contact)* [1994] 1 F.L.R. 729; *Re S (Contact: Grandparents)* [1996] 1 F.L.R. 158; *A v. N (Committal: Refusal of Contact)* [1997] 1 F.L.R. 533. But see *Re D (A Minor) (Contact: Mother's Hostility)* [1993] 2 F.L.R. 1. See also *Donnelly v. Green*, 1998 Fam. L.R. 12.

parent[99] to be regarded as a "cogent reason" which will satisfy the onus on those seeking to deny contact.[1] These are relevant factors but are to be assessed in the light of the weight of the presumed benefits that contact with the non-resident parent will bring the child.

10.21   The position in Scotland appears to be rather different. In a dissenting opinion in *Sanderson v. McManus*,[2] an access case decided under the Law Reform (Parent and Child) (Scotland) Act 1986, Lord McCluskey followed the English approach when he expressed the view that the link between the child and each of his or her parents was so important in itself, with an intrinsic value quite independent of any supposed "right" that it should be preserved, by an appropriate award of access, unless there were very strong reasons to the contrary. However, in the House of Lords, upholding the majority of the Extra Division, Lord Hope of Craighead said that, if that had been the effect of the common law, section 3(2) of the 1986 Act had removed any such rule or principle, and he expressly approved the approach of Lord Dunpark in *Porchetta v. Porchetta*[3] that a father with no statutory right to access can only acquire that right if the court is satisfied that that is in the best interests of the child, the onus to show this being on the father seeking access.[4] That position remains unaltered by the Children (Scotland) Act 1995, notwithstanding a shift in emphasis from parental rights to parental responsibilities. The Act recognises that it is for the welfare of the child that a person with parental responsibilities and parental rights maintain personal relations and direct contact with the child when that person is not or is no longer living with the child,[5] and an order under section 11 may regulate how that responsibility and right is to be exercised. The onus lies on the person seeking an order regulating contact to show why it is necessary to have an order rather than leaving the details to be worked out by the parties themselves; if a person wants the court to remove the responsibility and right completely then similarly the onus is on the applicant to show why it would be in the interests of the child for the court to make such an order. In that sense there is a clear presumption in favour of continued contact. But no presumption can be gleaned from the terms of the 1995 Act that this is so in relation to a person, such as a father who is not and has not been married to the mother, who does not have parental responsibilities and parental rights. Such a person too, therefore, has the onus of showing why an order granting him contact rights would be in the interests of the child, and why it would be better for the court to make such an order than to make no order at all.[6] The assumption underlying this position (to which the English courts have given no credence) would seem to be that the unmarried father will not already have an established relationship with the child at the time of the court hearing. When that assumption is factually correct, the requirement on the father to prove that contact will be beneficial is defensible, for it is the social relationship rather than the genetic link that justifies a presumption of benefit. However, the existence (or otherwise) of parental responsibilities and parental rights is but a crude indication of whether or not

---

[99] *Re F (Minors) (Contact: Mother's Anxiety)* [1993] 2 F.L.R. 830.

[1] For a criticism of the English court's approach here, see Wallbank, "Castigating Mothers: The Judicial Response to 'Wilful' Women in Disputes over Paternal Contact in English law" (1998) 20 J.Soc. Wel. & Fam. L. 357.

[2] 1996 S.L.T. 750.

[3] 1986 S.L.T. 105.

[4] *Sanderson v. McManus*, 1997 S.L.T. 629 at 634L–635B.

[5] Children (Scotland) Act 1995, ss. 1(1)(c) and 2(1)(c).

[6] In relation to the unmarried father, it may be that Scots law, in placing the onus this way, is contrary to the UN Convention on the Rights of the Child, for the terms of Art. 9(3) (see n. 92 above) suggest that the presumption is that contact is beneficial and that the onus is on the person seeking to show that it is contrary to the child's best interests. And Art. 2 requires that those rights be respected without discrimination on the basis of either the child's or the parents' race, sex or other status.

the holder of the responsibilities and rights has an established relationship with the child which ought to be preserved. In applications for an order conferring the right of contact, or regulating the exercise of a pre-existing right of contact, or removing that pre-existing right, though the onus lies on the applicant in all cases, courts should nevertheless endeavour to make their decisions on the basis of the evidence rather than on the issue of onus. If an unmarried father, or any other person, does have an established relationship with the child then, although the formal onus remains with him, the acceptance of the importance of the child maintaining contact with those with whom he or she has an established relationship should make it easier for him to discharge the onus of showing that the child's welfare will be advanced by allowing him contact. Support for this can be found in the House of Lords decision in *Sanderson v. McManus*, where Lord Hope of Craighead said this:

> "The relationship between the father and the child can never be dismissed as irrelevant. The natural relationship is a fact of life which it will always be proper to take into account. But the importance which is to be attached to it must vary according to the circumstances. This is a matter which must be decided not by applying any presumption but upon an evaluation of the evidence. As with any other factor which the court is asked to take into account, the question is whether contact with the parent has something to offer which is likely to be of benefit to the child's welfare. This question must be examined from the point of view of the child. It may normally be assumed that the child will benefit from continued contact with the natural parent. But there may be cases where it is plain on the evidence that it has nothing to offer at all. There may be other cases where the evidence will show that continued contact is likely to be harmful. Whatever the view which is taken on this matter in the light of the evidence, the child's welfare is paramount."[7]

The discharge of a formal onus is made easier, in the case of a father without **10.22** parental responsibilities and parental rights, by the acceptance by the Inner House of the proposition that courts deciding questions of contact are

> "entitled and indeed bound to take account of the fact that it is normally in the best interests of a child to maintain contact and relations with the natural parent with whom the child is no longer living. That may be judged as a benefit without the need for evidence from experts or otherwise".[8]

The natural relationship in residence disputes

The existence of the natural parent and child relationship is always a relevant **10.23** factor to be taken into account in determining the child's welfare, but the weight to be given to that factor varies according to the context of the dispute before

---

[7] *Sanderson v. McManus*, 1997 S.L.T. 629, *per* Lord Hope of Craighead at 635C–F. Compare *Henderson v. Henderson*, 1997 Fam. L.R. 120 where the maintenance of the paternal link was held to be outweighed by the dangers posed by the pursuer's mental illness and the 10-year-old child's clearly expressed views, with *Davidson v. Smith*, 1998 Fam. L.B. 31–4 in which contact with an unmarried father was permitted where the factors against it were the mother's opposition and the fact that the child had not seen her father (that is to say, had not been permitted by her mother to see her father) for some years. Neither consideration was deemed strong enough to justify refusing contact.

[8] *Davidson v. Smith*, 1998 Fam. L.R. 21. See also *Donnelly v. Green*, 1998 Fam. L.R. 12; *Lamont v. Lamont*, 1998 Fam. L.R. 62, *per* Sheriff Principal Hay. *Cf. Rashid v. Rashid*, 1998 Fam. L.R. 91. Edwards, "Life After *Sanderson v. McManus*: What Next?", 1998 S.L.T. (News) 299 at 302 claims that this approach is "clearly wrong".

the court. There is no necessary correlation between the weight to be accorded to the natural relationship in a contact dispute and that to be accorded the same factor in a residence dispute, for the purpose of a court order regulating residence is very different from the purpose of a court order regulating contact. The resolution of a residence dispute will more commonly compromise one of the parties' parental responsibilities and parental rights than will the resolution of a contact dispute. The English cases on the matter are reviewed in the opinion of Lord President Rodger in *Osborne v. Matthan (No. 2)*,[9] the most recent of which was *Re M (Child's Upbringing)*.[10] That case involved a child from South Africa who had been permitted by his parents to reside with an English woman and, subsequently, to be brought to England. When the English woman sought to adopt the child after he had been in her care for some years, his natural parents sought his return to their care in South Africa. In ordering the return of the child Waite L.J. said:

> "In my judgment that strong supposition, other things being equal, that it is in the interests of the child to be brought up by his natural parents, is a guide to the resolution of the competing claims in this case... I agree that this is not determinative of the conclusion for it must be subservient to the paramount consideration, which the court always has in mind, that is to say, the welfare of the child".[11]

This formulation of a strong supposition acting as a guide for the court is worded rather more cautiously than the presumption that applies in the English contact cases discussed above, and is more in line with the principles that may be extracted from the Scottish contact case of *Sanderson v. McManus*. Though he did not distinguish contact cases from residence cases, the Lord President in *Osborne v. Matthan (No. 2)* doubted whether the approach in *Sanderson* was materially different from that adopted in the English residence cases such as *Re M (Child's Upbringing)*. In the instant residence case, he concluded that:

> "While... it may normally be assumed that a child will benefit from being in her mother's custody,[12] the validity of that assumption in any particular case must be tested by reference to the evidence. That evidence may strengthen the assumption or weaken it or even in an extreme case negative it entirely."

Lord Caplan, after referring to what Waite L.J. had said in *Re M (Child's Upbringing)*, as quoted above, said:

> "I think it goes without saying that the claim of a natural mother to bring up her child will always be carefully considered by the court and that she will only be deprived of her parental rights if it is clear that the

---

[9] 1998 S.L.T. 1264.

[10] [1996] 2 F.L.R. 441.

[11] at 456B–C. In a rather different context (that of local authority care) the Court of Appeal elevated the strong supposition into a presumption. In *Re D (Care: Natural Paternal Presumption)* [1999] 1 F.L.R. 134 it was held that in a residence dispute between a parent (who, in that case, had parental responsibilities and parental rights) and another person, the question for the court was whether there were any compelling factors which overrode the prima facie right of a child to an upbringing by its surviving parent. It was wrong, they held, simply to compare the parent's care with that of the other potential carer. Rather the correct approach was first to consider whether the parent was fit as a potential carer and to override that presumption only when other factors pointed to the child's particular needs being best met elsewhere. This approach may not be of general application since a stronger case of parental unfitness needs to be made out before a local authority can take over care of a child than when the dispute is purely private and between different family members.

[12] The case was decided under the Law Reform (Parent and Child) (Scotland) Act 1986.

child's welfare requires this. There is no doubt that society recognises that, all other things being equal, it is an important element in the welfare of a child, and a benefit, to be brought up by its natural parents. However, Scottish courts, in particular, have resisted the temptation to elevate the primacy of the parental claim into anything approaching a principle, far less a rule. This emerges clearly in the House of Lords in *Sanderson v. McManus*".

Lord Wylie distinguished *Re M (Child's Upbringing)* on the basis that in that case there was nothing about the natural parents which militated against the boy being returned to South Africa, while in the instant case there were various such factors. Interestingly, however, in neither case was the issue of maintaining the status quo considered significant (which distinguishes both from *J v. C*[13]). However, the weight accorded that factor in most cases clearly remains greater than the weight to be accorded the natural link which appears to do little more than tilt the balance when all other things are equal. Things are not equal when the child is settled in a safe and secure and loving environment.

Moral welfare
    The moral welfare of the child has always been an important consideration **10.24** and has often been associated with moral judgments on a parent's behaviour. At common law immoral conduct on the father's part opened the door to judicial intervention.[14] Sometimes, as in cases of drunkenness or cruelty, the conduct, although reflecting on the father's moral character, was not primarily moral in its effect but bore as much, or more, on the child's physical as on his or her moral welfare. In these cases interference with the father's powers was, therefore, necessary for the protection of the child's health. Danger to the child's moral development was, however, usually an additional element in such decisions and was an independent and, even where it stood alone, a sufficient ground for removing a child from the father's control.[15] It was in these cases with the effect, or possible effect, and the likelihood of its continuance that the court was primarily concerned rather than with the father's conduct as such. So in *Lang v. Lang*[16] Lord Neaves could say: "It is not that he has committed faults, but that he teaches, or is likely to teach, evil to [the children], and to corrupt their morals, that can alone entitle us to interfere." Changes in accepted standards of conduct, particularly in sexual matters, and changes in the law have made the content of much of the older decisions obsolete, but the concentration of attention on actual, or prospective, moral or psychological harm arising from the parent's or guardian's influence, rather than on past misconduct as such, is even more apt now than it was at common law. A welfare judgment looks to the present and the future although the inferences on which it is based must be drawn from past events. But subtle influences, to which past conduct and its effects can be the only guide, will often be more important than express teaching. The problems of whether past patterns of conduct are likely to repeat themselves and of what effect, if any, they have had or are likely to have on the moral formation of the children are problems for the modern, as they were for the older, law. The older cases, however, were little troubled by questions of what constituted morality.

---

[13] [1970] A.C. 668.
[14] *Baillie v. Agnew* (1775) 5 Mor. Supp. 526; *Craig v. Thomson* (1829) 1 Sc.Jur. 201; *Cameron, Petr* (1847) 9 D. 1401.
[15] See, *e.g.*, *McFarlane v. McFarlane* (1847) 9 D. 904, *per* Lord Jeffrey: "Unless the health or morals of the child be affected by allowing its father to have the custody, we must just submit to that general rule which delivers the child to him." Cruelty to the children justified the court's intervention in *Baillie v. Agnew*, above, but cruelty to a wife (and mother of the children), as in *McFarlane v. McFarlane*, was not usually considered enough.
[16] (1869) 7 M. 445 at 447.

They proceeded on an assumption of moral consensus. The growth, or wider recognition, of moral pluralism raises questions of the meaning of moral welfare. In what does the child's moral welfare consist?

10.25   The difficulties which may arise in some controversial areas do not justify a radical moral scepticism. Divergence of view on some issues does not preclude a broad consensus on others. There may be arguments about the importance or desirability of taking the child's moral welfare into consideration,[17] but there is no doubt that the law does require it to be considered[18] and the difficulties in giving it effective meaning are, outside some areas of controversy, largely academic rather than real. Moral assumptions underlie both the civil and the criminal law and, provided the limitations of the judicial function in judging of moral welfare are kept in mind,[19] afford sufficient guidance. The court's function is essentially protective. The court may prefer one moral regime to another as the more likely to achieve generally acceptable standards or even as the more likely to cultivate them to a higher degree, but it has never been suggested, nor is it practicable, that it should distinguish between them on the positive merits of the goals at which they aim where neither is objectionable by the standards of the forum. Because it is the child's moral welfare and not the moral character of those who bring up the child which, as such, is at stake, it is no answer that the person who looks after the child has no alternative and is, him or herself, free from fault if the surroundings into which he or she would bring the child expose the child to risk of moral harm. On the other hand, the culpability of those with whom the child lives can, so far as the question of welfare is concerned, be disregarded if there is no consequential risk of moral harm to the child. Thus, little weight need be attached to an isolated conviction for dishonesty.[20] The question always is: what are the risks for the moral welfare of the child and what weight is to be given to these risks when considered in the totality of circumstances affecting welfare? The risks which require to be so considered include that the child may be led into ways of criminality, dishonesty, irresponsibility, violence, deceit, the intentional or reckless harming of others, and the moral abuses associated with the abuse of alcohol and drugs and with sexual promiscuity.[21] Often practical necessity will constrain the inquiry into moral welfare within these negative limits. Occasionally, however, cases may present, in a more positive form, questions of what is the more wholesome

---

[17] Concern with moral welfare may be said to put a premium on conformity and prejudice unfairly the innovative or idiosyncratic (*cf.* the decision in *Early v. Early*, 1990 S.L.T. 221, where the risk of a child being teased at school as a result of his unusual family circumstances was held to be a relevant factor). That is a serious objection, in principle, and it has practical force in some cases of conflict between established views and the beliefs and conduct of minority groups. With these exceptions it is, however, in existing conditions of tolerance only a marginal problem. Even where the problem is real, it has to be balanced against society's interest in the reflection, in the moral formation of children, at least of certain minimum standards of conduct and the state's interest to promote that. It can also be argued that virtue is an integral part, or even the highest form, of the child's well-being and even if judicial regulation of the child's residence can do little to promote that it can at least contribute to the avoidance of evil.

[18] *Hume v. Hume*, 1926 S.C. 1008.

[19] See *T, Petr*, 1997 S.L.T. 724 at 735–736 for an exposition of the role of the judge in such cases.

[20] *AC v. BC* (1902) 5 F.108. Great weight was however attached to a conviction and long history of drug abuse in *F v. F*, 1991 S.L.T. 357 at 363. On the other hand, in *MacMillan v. Brady*, 1997 Fam. L.R. 29 the Inner House upheld the sheriff's decision to remove a three year old child from his mother and award custody to the father, "a man of bad character who takes drugs" (including cocaine the day before the proof) and who had at least eight convictions, many for dishonesty. The risks to the child from the mother's neglect outweighed the risks from the father's bad character, as he was now married in a stable relationship and could offer a secure environment.

[21] *Hume v. Hume*, above; *Gray v. Gray*, 1961 S.L.T. (Notes) 83; Stuart, "Consistorial Actions Involving Criminal Offenders," 1973 J.R. 43 at 56–58.

environment from the standpoint of the promotion of generally accepted moral goals and when that is so, the comprehensive regard for the welfare of the child which the statute envisages requires that that be taken into account.

Parents' sexual behaviour
Problems of standards of sexual conduct are, perhaps, particularly acute. **10.26** The double standard has gone which, under the older practice, looked more leniently, in custody disputes between the parents of legitimate children, on the sexual misdemeanours of the father than of the mother. That double standard, although largely based on the moral notions of the time, could be explained on the view that, according to the law as it then was, more was required to deprive a father of custody which, subject to some qualifications, was his right than to withhold it from a mother to whom custody could be awarded, if at all, only as a matter of discretion.[22] Adultery, by either spouse, is generally no longer an obstacle to making a residence order in favour of the adulterer[23] and, even where it is an element taken into consideration it is often as an aspect of conduct that may influence the decision independently of the child's welfare where the welfare considerations are evenly balanced.[24] Unless it has taken some gross or promiscuous form there seems to be no ground in the modern authorities for regarding adultery by a parent as having a close, or necessary, bearing on the child's moral welfare. Occasionally it may be relevant to the child's emotional welfare if it is associated with or shows instability or indifference to the family. Other aspects of sexual conduct do, however, remain controversial, as reflected in changing attitudes to extramarital sexual relations and to homosexuality, and the proper response from the standpoint of the child's welfare is problematic. The child's moral welfare, although always an important, is never an isolated, consideration and regard for the child's welfare as a whole may resolve many practical difficulties. Where that is not so, the court must make the best judgment it can according to what are deemed to be the prevailing moral notions in the forum. To expose the child to a sexually promiscuous environment, or to the risk of sexual corruption or exploitation, whether heterosexual or homosexual, would be considered inconsistent with welfare, and in the case of exploitation manifestly so. As always, the real issue before the court is the effect on the child of the parent's sexual behaviour. In *Re L (Contact: Transsexual Applicant)*[25] the court adjourned the father's application for a contact order on his accepting that contact with his daughter while he was undergoing gender realignment surgery would disturb her and on the mother's agreeing to allow indirect contact by letters and the sending of presents. The father's other application, to be awarded parental responsibility, was granted with no hesitation (on the basis that the applicant had been closely involved in the child's nurture and upbringing in the early years of her life and there was a clear continuing commitment).

---

[22] *cf. Lang v. Lang* (1869) 7 M. 445; *Symington v. Symington* (1875) 2 R. (H.L.) 41; *AB v. CD* (1847) 10 D. 229; *Bowman v. Graham* (1883) 10 R. 1234; *Shirer v. Dixon* (1885) 12 R. 1013. See also *McIver v. McIver* (1859) 21 D. 1103.

[23] *Christie v. Christie*, 1945 S.L.T. 300; *Johnston v. Johnston*, 1947 S.L.T. (Notes) 26; *Nicol v. Nicol*, 1953 S.L.T. (Notes) 67; *McClements v. McClements*, 1958 S.C. 286; *Zamorski v. Zamorska*, 1960 S.L.T. (Notes) 26. Even before the 1925 Act the importance attached to adultery as a factor adverse to an award of custody had declined: see *Stewart v. Stewart*, 1914 2 S.L.T. 310; *McCurdie v. McCurdie*, 1918 2 S.L.T. 250; *Allan v. Allan*, 1919 2 S.L.T. 88.

[24] See *Hume v. Hume*, 1926 S.C. 1008.

[25] [1995] 2 F.L.R. 438. See also, on similar facts, *Re F (Minors) (Denial of Contact)* [1993] 2 F.L.R. 677 and *C v. D* [1992] N.Z.F.L.R. 537.

Sexual orientation of parents

10.27   There is authority, if controversial and a product of its time, for the view
that even at the cost of permanent separation a reasonable parent would not
wish his or her child to be subject to homosexual influences,[26] and, if that is so,
such influences would be regarded as contrary to the child's welfare. Social
attitudes to homosexuality have altered considerably in the two decades since
that decision and judicial attitudes, though slow to respond, reflect these changes.
In *Early v. Early*[27] a child was removed from the mother with whom he had
lived for some years and custody awarded to the father, after the mother had
entered into a lesbian relationship and set up home with another woman. There
was no allegation that the child was exposed to any sexual or moral danger. The
court, however, took the view that the environment in which the child lived was
unsuitable because it lacked any male role-models for the child (which seems
insubstantial, given that such lack is not otherwise a significant factor when a
single or divorced mother is left with sole care and control), and because it
might expose him to teasing and other difficulties at school (which was
speculative, given the absence of any evidence that the child was suffering or
would suffer that disadvantage).[28] The "stigmatisation" argument has been used
in a number of English decisions.[29] Homosexuality is not, of course, an automatic
bar but it is an important factor to be taken into account. The Court of Appeal
explained this on the basis of the "normally held view" that the ideal environment
for the upbringing of a child is the home of caring parents and that when that
was not possible the environment that came closest to that ideal should be
preferred.[30] In *Hill v. Hill*[31] a child was returned to his father, who lived openly
in a homosexual relationship, this against the wishes of the mother, who had, in
breach of the father's custody rights, removed the child from Canada to
Scotland.[32] The mother here alleged that the child would be exposed to "harmful
influences" (but again led no evidence as to what harm the child would be
exposed to). Access was permitted to a homosexual father in *Meredith v.
Meredith*,[33] the sheriff making plain that contact should be as natural as possible
with the result that the father's male partner should not be excluded from contact
with the children. Some local authorities have long been willing to place children
with foster carers in stable homosexual relationships[34] and many adoption

---

[26] *Re D (An Infant) (Adoption: Parent's Consent)* [1977] A.C. 602. Though this was an adoption case,
where the question was one of the reasonableness of the parent withholding consent to adoption
rather than the child's welfare, the views there expressed have obvious application in other cases.

[27] 1990 S.L.T. 221. See also *C v. C* [1991] 1 F.L.R. 223 (Court of Appeal).

[28] There were, however, other factors that pointed to the child's welfare being better served by custody
with the father, in particular the fact that the other children of the marriage lived with the father, and
the fact that the father had a more balanced and mature view as to what was best for the child.

[29] *S v. S*([1978] 1 F.L.R. 143; *Re P* (1982) 4 F.L.R. 401; *C v. C* [1991] 1 F.L.R. 223. In *B v. B
(Minor) (Custody, Care and Control)* [1991] 1 F.L.R. 402 it was found that fears of taunting or
ostracism were not supported by research, though the judge nevertheless held that it was a factor
which must take its place in the balancing exercise. Fears for the effect on the child's own sexual
orientation in being brought up by his lesbian mother were also discounted on the basis that no
research evidence suggested any foundation for such fears.

[30] *C v. C*, above. This reasoning has been subject to trenchant and persuasive criticism. See Caffey
(1992) J. Soc. Wel. & Fam. L. 249 and Boyd, "What is a 'Normal' Family?" (1992) 55 M.L.R. 269.

[31] 1991 S.L.T. 189.

[32] The basis of this decision was that the Canadian court was a more appropriate forum to decide
the issue of custody than the Scottish court, but the court accepted (at 192C) that homosexuality
is not, nor is living openly as such, an automatic bar to an award of custody. It cannot be while
the paramount consideration is the welfare of the child. See Bates, "Unravelling the Tangled
Web", 1990 S.L.T. (News) 69 for a discussion of *Early v. Early* and other cases involving
homosexual parents from the Australian and U.S. courts.

[33] 1994 Fam. L.B. 11–6.

[34] See, *e.g.*, *Re W (A Minor) (Wardship: Freedom of Publication)* [1992] 1 All E.R. 794 (though
this would not be permitted under Scottish statutory provisions).

agencies place for adoption children in such environments. Within that latter context, the issue was fully explored in *T, Petitioner*[35] in which an adoption order was made in favour of a homosexual applicant, the First Division making plain that there was no point of principle preventing the making of an order in such circumstances. The matter in adoption, as in an application for a section 11 order, must be dealt with on the basis that the welfare of the particular child is the paramount consideration and from that point of view the applicant's sexual orientation is relevant only in so far as it affects the child's welfare. Though the dicta in *Re D (An Infant)* were not expressly disapproved by the First Division in *T, Petitioner*, it is difficult to see what relevance they retain. It remains, of course, true that the reasonable parent would not want to expose his or her child to harmful influences but *T, Petitioner* warns against courts relying on preconceived notions of homosexuality or founding on prejudices. The result of that is, it is submitted, that the court should not assume homosexual influences are harmful in any particular case.[36] If these or other influences can be shown to be harmful to the particular child then of course they will weigh heavily in the court's decision.[36a] Residence orders have been made in England under which the child was to live with homosexual parents,[37] with homosexual couples, one of whom is the parent,[38] and indeed with an individual homosexual person who was not the parent of the child.[39]

Education

10.28   The promotion of a child's skills and aptitudes, his or her capacities for work and recreational pursuits, and his or her intellectual and artistic development, forms an integral part of his or her welfare. No general rule can be laid down on such problems of choice as may arise except that leaving scope for the maximum development of the child's potential is always an important consideration. These elements of welfare will often be associated with the child's emotional and moral development and sometimes with his or her religious upbringing. All may be comprehended under the heading of "education" broadly conceived. The need for choices to depend on educational considerations is somewhat reduced so far, at least, as provision for formal instruction is concerned,

---

[35] 1997 S.L.T. 724: see above, paras 4.23 and 4.72.
[36] There is a burgeoning legal and psychological literature on this issue. The legal literature includes the following: Goodman, "Homosexuality of a Parent: A New Issue in Custody Disputes" (1979) 5 Monash University L.R. 305; Bradley, "Homosexuality and Child Custody in English Law" (1987) 1 Int. J. Law and the Family 155; Ross, "Attitudes to Sexual Orientation in Adoption Law" (1997) 1 Edin. L.R. 370. Among the psychological literature are the following: Golombok *et al.*, "Children in Lesbian and Single-Parent Households: Psychosexual and Psychiatric Appraisal" (1983) 24 J. Child Psychology and Psychiatry 551; Tasker and Golombok, "Children Raised by Lesbian Mothers: The Empirical Evidence" [1991] Fam. L. 184; "Adults Raised as Children of Homosexual and Heterosexual Single Mothers" (1993) 23 *Child Psychiatry and Human Development* 235 and "Do Parents Influence the Sexual Orientation of Their Children? Findings From a Longitudinal Study of Lesbian Families" (1996) 32 *Developmental Psychology* 3. Much of the psychological literature is reviewed in *Re K and B* (1995) 125 D.L.R. (4th) 653 (Ontario Court, Provincial Division).
[36a] The same reasoning was adopted in a quite different context in *Re W (Residence Order)* [1999] 1 F.L.R. 869, where it was held that neither a parent's nudity in front of her children nor the fact that her partner bathed with her children implied any charge of abuse to the children.
[37] *B v. B (Minors) (Custody, Care and Control)* [1991] Fam. Law 174, [1991] 1 F.L.R. 402 (in which the judge felt about to award custody to a mother on being assured that she was not a "militant lesbian who tries to convert others to her way of life"); *Re P* (1983) 4 F.L.R. 401 (in which the mother, again, was found to be "discreet as to her homosexuality").
[38] *Re C* [1994] Fam. Law 468.
[39] *Re H (A Minor)* [1993] Fam. Law 205. See also *G v. F (Contact and Shared Residence: Applications for Leave)* [1998] 2 F.L.R. 799 in which a lesbian couple had separated and one sought leave to seek a contact or residence order in respect of the other's child (English law requiring leave when the applicant is not the child's parent). It was held that the fact that the applicant was a lesbian was part of the background circumstances to be taken into account but was nothing in itself to reflect against the applicant.

by the power of the court to make orders with respect to education independently of residence. In many cases it has, however, to be accepted that the child's residence will profoundly influence the educational possibilities for the child.

Religious or spiritual welfare

10.29   In the seventeenth century, when religious controversy and confidence in the rightness of sectional religious opinions ran high, robust views were sometimes entertained of State powers of interference in the religious upbringing of children. In 1665 the Scottish Privy Council, from which the Court of Session's jurisdiction in matters relating to the upbringing of children is derived,[40] ordered the children of Scott of Raeburn and his wife "being infected with the error of Quakerism" to be taken from them and, later in the same year, the young Marquis of Huntly was taken from the custody of his mother and guardians "they being Popishly inclined" and entrusted to the care of the Protestant Archbishop Sharp of St Andrews under a direction that "no person Popishly inclined have liberty to serve or attend him".[41] By an Act of 1661[42] "All children under Popish tutors or curators" were taken from their care, and by an Act of 1700[43] not only professed Papists but also those suspected of popery were declared incapable of the offices of tutory or curatory unless they signed a prescribed formula purging themselves of that taint. Roman Catholics were therefore precluded from claiming custody *qua* tutors, and that disability remained until repealed in 1829.[44] Even in the seventeenth century interference with custody on the ground that the custodian's religious beliefs were objectionable seems to have been exceptional and no reported Scottish cases thereafter have been traced.[45] Nor is interference on the ground of lack of religious belief well attested by the older authorities, although Fraser[46] considered that the court would interfere if the government of the father was calculated to engender irreligious or atheistical opinions.

10.30   Two modern Scottish cases take substantially the same view as Fraser and apply it in the context of the paramountcy of the child's welfare. In *Mackay v. Mackay*[47] custody was given to an atheist father, but only on an understanding which provided for the child's religious instruction. Lord President Clyde said that it would be almost impossible for a court in Scotland to award custody to an atheist with the prospect of the child's being brought up without the solace and guidance of any religious teaching at all "for atheism and the child's welfare

---

[40] See Jamieson, *Parental Responsibilities and Rights* (1995), 157–159.
[41] Fraser, pp. 90–91.
[42] 1661 c. 37 (APS 7, 26).
[43] 1700 c. 3 (APS 10, 215).
[44] Roman Catholic Relief Act 1829, s. 10.
[45] Courts throughout the Commonwealth have in the 20th Century been punctilious in refusing to weigh the merits of different forms of religion: see, *e.g.*, *Re Carroll* [1931] 1 K.B. 317, *per* Scrutton L.J. at 336; *McNaught v. McNaught*, 1955 S.L.T. (Sh.Ct) 9; *In the Marriage of Paisio (No. 2)* (1978) 5 Fam. L.R. 281, *per* Full Court of the Family Court of Australia at 283; *P v. K*, [1983] 2 N.Z.F.L.R. 27, *per* McAloon J. at 29; *Young v. Young* [1994] 108 D.L.R. (4th) 193, *per* L'Heureux-Dube at 252. For a discussion, see Van Praagh, "Religion, Custody and a Child's Identity" (1997) Os. Hall L.J. 309.
[46] at 90. This view has some support in English authority: see *Re Besant* (1878) 11 Ch.D. 508, in which the refusal of the mother to allow the child to receive religious instruction was an element in the decision. See also *Shelley v. Westbrooke* (1817) Jac. 266; *Re Agar-Ellis* (1878) 10 Ch.D. 49, *per* Malins V.C. at 56–57. These cases may, however, now require to be understood as instances of religious opinion manifesting itself in conduct which the law regards as vicious and immoral (*Re Carroll* [1931] 1 K.B. 317, *per* Slesser L.J. at 354), and in any event the decision in *Re Agar-Ellis* has been characterised in the House of Lords as "so out of line with present-day views that it should no longer be treated as having any authority": *per* Lord Fraser of Tullybelton in *Gillick v. West Norfolk and Wisbech Area Health Authority* [1985] 3 All E.R. 402 at 412. Lord Scarman at 419 described the decision in *Re Agar-Ellis* as "horrendous".
[47] 1957 S.L.T. (Notes) 17.

are almost necessarily mutually exclusive, according at least to our standards of civilised society".[48] In *McClements v. McClements*[49] an atheist father was refused custody and given access only on condition that he did not attempt to influence the child's religious beliefs. The decision can be justified, so far as the custody award is concerned, on grounds independent of the question of religious beliefs including the expressed preference of the child and the lack of any sufficient ground for disturbing the interim arrangement under which the child had been in the custody of the mother. Among the reasons given for the decision were, however, that the child "ought not to be denied the opportunity of being brought up in the generally accepted religious beliefs of the society in which he lives".[50] That view seems to have been expressed on general grounds as there is no indication that lack of religious belief would have created particular problems in the locality or surroundings in which the child would have lived had he been entrusted to his father's custody.

10.31 The dicta in these cases are surprising. There must be many cases in which residence or contact orders are made in favour of a person of atheistic or agnostic opinions if only because both parties are opposed or indifferent to a religious upbringing for the child and neither, therefore, puts it in issue. Nor was it the practice of the court, when under a statutory duty to consider the arrangements for the care of the children of the marriage before granting decree of divorce or nullity of marriage or separation,[51] to make particular inquiries about religious upbringing. And there must, of course, be many children whose residence is never the subject of judicial regulation who are brought up by parents who have no religious beliefs. If the views expressed in *Mackay* and *McClements* are sound they merit a wider application than the fairly few cases in which a religious, as opposed to an atheistic or agnostic, upbringing is raised as a matter of controversy by the parties; yet it is to such cases that it seems they must be confined. However, *Mackay* and *McClements* lay down, it is submitted, no rule of law. In so far as the preference they indicate is accepted, it can only be as an element in the totality of circumstances affecting welfare. In view of the difficulties in applying it, the part it will play must usually be small. It should too be seen in the context of tolerance as a widely held moral value affecting religious belief and one to which the court might properly have regard in connection with the child's moral welfare.[52] Exposure to narrow and bigoted religious influence on the one hand, whether Christian or otherwise, or to a militant and uncompromising atheism, on the other, may be seen as detrimental to the child's welfare. Regarded as warnings against the latter danger, *Mackay* and *McClements* can be more readily accepted than on any other ground but, even on that view, they seem to go too far in elevating the matter into a necessarily critical factor in the decision.

10.32 It is submitted that there are at least two assumptions which it is reasonable to make without thereby embarking on an examination of the merits of any given form of religious upbringing. The first is that the child's religious welfare will be best served by respect for his or her autonomy as an individual.[53] The second is that it will be promoted by allowing progressive development without externally imposed change. From the first it follows that weight should be given

---

[48] 1957 S.L.T. (Notes) 17.
[49] 1958 S.C. 286.
[50] *ibid.* at 289, *per* Lord Justice-Clerk Thomson.
[51] Matrimonial Proceedings (Children) Act 1958, s. 8, repealed by the Children (Scotland) Act 1995, Sched. 5.
[52] *Re T (Minors)*, Dec. 10, 1975, unreported, *per* Scarman L.J., quoted in *Re H (A Minor)* (1980) 10 Fam. Law 248 at 249.
[53] Bearing in mind that autonomy is a concept that matures with the child.

to the child's wishes and sentiments, even to a degree which would be inappropriate in other contexts. Although much must depend on age and ability for
choice, that is a particularly important factor where the child has strongly held
convictions.[54] From the second it follows that patterns to which the child has
become accustomed should not readily be disturbed. A purely formal religious
connection is, however, of little importance.[55] These conclusions indicate, of
course, only how the child's religious or spiritual welfare may be determined
and not how these aspects of welfare are to be weighed in relation to other
aspects. They have, however, the merit that they accord with criteria used in
other aspects of welfare and will often tend to promote harmony in a total
assessment. Where conflict between the child's religious welfare so considered
and other aspects does emerge, it seems that the disposal indicated by the latter
must be preferred at least where the arguments in favour of it are strong. The
child's physical, emotional or moral well-being can scarcely be jeopardised for
the sake of continuity of religious upbringing or even out of respect for the
child's own convictions. In such a case the separate regulation of religious
upbringing may have to be considered.[56]

10.33   The religious upbringing of the child is usually considered as a matter bearing
on the court's decision in relation to residence for the understandable reason
that the residence parent is likely to be the strongest influence on the child's
religious and spiritual development. Because of that, and of the risks of conflict
which may arise, the courts have been reluctant to make orders regulating
religious upbringing as a matter separate from residence (previously custody).[57]
In *Mackay v. Mackay*,[58] however, the court imposed what was in effect a condition
on custody in order to secure separate provision for the child's religious
upbringing. There is no doubt that such regulation by orders specifically dealing
with upbringing is competent.[59] That may sometimes be a convenient and
appropriate way, especially in the case of older children, of securing the
continuity of their religious upbringing or of giving effect to their wishes while
at the same time enabling a residence order to be made in favour of a person of
different religious persuasion. That will, however, only be so where the risk
that tension will thereby be introduced into the relationship with the person
with whom the child is to live is small. Perhaps more than most, a child's religious
upbringing is an issue where no enforceable court order will usually be better
than making an order, if for no other reason than that the child's every-increasing
maturity renders it ever more inappropriate for the matter to be regulated by
anyone other than the child him or herself.

10.34   It is relevant to note that while regard for the child's religious persuasion
(*inter alia*) is a matter that must be taken into account by a court in determining
an adoption issue,[60] and by a local authority in determining how to fulfil its
various duties towards the child,[61] that consideration does not expressly appear

---

[54] See *Re M (Infants)* [1967] 1 W.L.R. 1479.
[55] *Re C (M.A.) (An Infant)* [1966] 1 W.L.R. 646.
[56] *Re E (An Infant)* [1964] 1 W.L.R. 51; *J v. C* [1970] A.C. 668, in which the order at first instance
      of Ungoed Thomas J., for the separate regulation of religious upbringing, was not disturbed.
[57] *Barr v. Barr*, 1950 S.L.T. (Notes) 15; *McNaught v. McNaught*, 1955 S.L.T. (Sh.Ct) 9. *Cf. Zamorski v.
      Zamorska*, 1960 S.L.T. (Notes) 26, in which the child's education and religious upbringing were
      treated as, or assumed to be, dependent on the decision on custody.
[58] 1957 S.L.T. (Notes) 17.
[59] There are a number of English examples of the separate regulation of religious upbringing: *Re E
      (An Infant)*; *J v. C*, above, but the dangers of resultant tension within the family have also been
      recognised in *B(M) v. B(R)* [1968] 1 W.L.R. 1182.
[60] Adoption (Scotland) Act 1978, s. 6, as amended by the Children (Scotland) Act 1995, s. 95.
[61] Children (Scotland) Act 1995, s. 17(4).

in relation to applications for an order under section 11 of the Children (Scotland) Act 1995. This reflects the fact that in the vast majority of section 11 applications the issue of the child's religious beliefs will not be relevant to a determination of his or her best interests within the context of the question that the court has to answer.

Harmful effects of some religious influences

Questions may sometimes be raised about the harmful effect of a particular **10.35** form of religious upbringing. These are properly questions not of the child's religious or spiritual welfare but of the impact of a particular religious environment on his or her moral, emotional, educational or even physical welfare.[62] They are therefore to be resolved by a consideration of the seriousness of that impact assessed by the criteria relevant to the aspects of welfare which are endangered in the context of the child's welfare as a whole. There are several English cases illustrative of the problems which arise. In *Hewison v. Hewison*[63] a father who was a member of the Exclusive Brethren was deprived of custody and a custody order made in favour of the mother who did not belong to that sect. The judgment turned materially on the harmful influence that an upbringing in the Exclusive Brethren would have had.

> "The mode of life and code of behaviour enforced by the sect upon its members and their children is [it was said] harsh and restrictive. The children are greatly deprived of normal social contacts with the vast majority of other children. They are handicapped in respect of further education, professional qualification and opportunities for academic life and technical skills. They are taught to regard themselves as different and separate from the rest of the children."[64]

Among other matters referred to were that members of the sect were required to associate with other members of the sect and avoid any close friendships outside it, were not permitted to go to the cinema or theatre or visit the homes of families outside the sect or watch television or listen to radio and were controlled to some extent in the books they read and music they listened to. In *T v. T*,[65] in which the mother was said to be obsessed with the Jehovah's Witnesses, Stamp L.J. took notice of the fact that growing up in the narrow world of the Jehovah's Witnesses "would lead the children into isolation from the rest of the world, socially and intellectually and would deprive them of some of the sweet and wholesome joys of life";[66] but that was only an element in the decision which turned, primarily, on the mother's mental instability. Membership of the Church of Scientology was, however, given greater weight in the case of *Re B and G (Minors) (Custody)*.[67] And in *Re R*[68] a father who had been excluded from the Exclusive Brethren was granted a residence order in respect of his nine-year- old

---

[62] Some writers, however, deny the validity of this distinction, arguing that belief, environment and welfare are so inextricably linked that it is entirely false to attempt to extricate the one from the other: see Mucci, "The Effect of Religious Beliefs in Child Custody Disputes", (1986) 5 Can.J.Fam.L. 353 at 359–360; Bainham, "Religion, Human Rights and the Fitness of Parents" [1994] C.L.J. 39 at 40. It may well be so that, from the parents' point of view, there is no distinction that can properly be made between their beliefs and the effects of their beliefs, but the matter must be looked at with the child's welfare as paramount and in that context it is not difficult to distinguish between the parent's beliefs and the effects these beliefs have on the child.

[63] (1977) 7 Fam. Law 207.

[64] *ibid*. at 208.

[65] (1974) 4 Fam. Law 190.

[66] *ibid*. at 191.

[67] [1985] F.L.R. 134.

[68] [1993] 2 F.L.R. 163.

son, although that involved removing the boy from a couple he regarded as his grandparents, who had looked after him ever since his father's expulsion, and against the expressed wishes of the boy to remain with them and within the fellowship. Contact was allowed with other relatives, subject to their giving an undertaking not to discuss religious or spiritual matters with the child. Caution has, however, been sounded against exaggerating, because a sect may be unpopular or some of its practices unusual, the harmful effect on a child's welfare of an upbringing in an unconventional religious environment.

> "We live in a tolerant society. There is no reason at all why the mother should not espouse the beliefs and practice of Jehovah's Witnesses. There is nothing immoral or socially obnoxious in the beliefs and practice of the sect. There is a great risk, because we are dealing with an unpopular sect, in overplaying the dangers to the welfare of these children inherent in the possibility that they may follow their mother and become Jehovah's Witnesses."[69]

10.36   Accordingly custody has been awarded to a Jehovah's Witness mother who was "moderate in her religious attitude", and was prepared to undertake that she would not take the children proselytising with her, that she would allow access to the father so as to enable Christmas, Easter and birthdays to be celebrated and that she would accept and use a certificate signed by the father consenting to a blood transfusion if ever the child needed one.[70] In general, English courts, while recognising that certain aspects of the way of life of Jehovah's Witnesses may seem "somewhat awkward, difficult and not very good for children", treat these matters as of relatively light weight in decisions concerning where the child is to live.[71] Similar considerations apply, it is submitted, to other sects or religions that are not immoral or socially obnoxious. The weight to be given may, however, vary according to the other circumstances of the case. The restrictive and inhibiting influences exerted by some forms of religious upbringing may be of little weight against grounds for maintaining a residence arrangement in which the child is settled and which is otherwise satisfactory, but yet constitute a substantial objection to a placement which would subject a child to these influences for the first time. In every case, however, courts must avoid assumptions about the harmful effects of minority and unpopular religions.[72] Freedom of religion is protected by the European Convention on Human Rights and that freedom is infringed when residence issues are determined on the basis of a parent's religious beliefs without evidence of the harm to the child that these beliefs might cause.[73] It is doubtless the case that "an insistence on clear evidence of harm from the religious practice at

---

[69] *Re T (Minors)*, Dec. 10, 1975, unreported, *per* Scarman L.J., cited in *Re H (A Minor)* (1980) 10 Fam. Law 248.

[70] *Re H (A Minor)*, above. See also the decision of the Supreme Court of Canada in *P(D) v. S(C)* [1993] 4 S.C.R. 141. In *Jane v. Jane* (1983) 13 Fam. Law 209 custody was granted to the father so that he could consent to medical treatment, while care and control was given to the Jehovah's Witness mother. *Cf. McKechnie v. McKechnie*, 1990 S.L.T. (Sh.Ct) 75, in which the father was a Jehovah's Witness and custody was awarded to the mother, one of the relevant factors mentioned being the possibility of difficulties in the event of the child requiring a blood transfusion. The issue of blood transfusion arose in another context in *Finlayson, Applicant*, 1989 S.C.L.R. 601, for there both parents refused to consent to blood transfusions for their haemophiliac son, though this was due to fear of the son contracting the HIV infection rather than for religious reasons. Their refusal was held to be a ground establishing that the child was in need of compulsory measures of care under the then extant s. 32 of the Social Work (Scotland) Act 1968: on that issue, see Chap. 19.

[71] *Re C (Minors) (Wardship: Jurisdiction)* [1978] Fam. 105, *per* Ormrod L.J. at 119.

[72] As it must do with minority forms of sexual orientation: see above, para. 10.27.

[73] *Hoffman v. Austria* (1994) 17 E.H.R.R. 293.

issue is the best way to ensure that parents of minority faiths are not unfairly prejudiced by the best interests standard".[74] This thinking underlies the approach of the First Division in a context that is quite different but raises similar issues.[75]

Racial origin, cultural and linguistic background
    In contrast with other Parts of the Children (Scotland) Act 1995,[76] there is **10.37** no express requirement in section 11 on the court to have regard to the racial origin, cultural or linguistic background of the child, and though the matter has seldom been discussed in the Scottish courts, there is little doubt that this will be a relevant factor in some cases in which a section 11 order is being considered. It has long been recognised that a child's sense of self and personal identity form an important part of his or her psychological development and well-being and that identity is closely bound to cultural origins. The right to preserve personal identity is protected by the UN Convention on the Rights of the Child,[77] and the right to information concerning one's personal origins is provided for in the adoption legislation.[78] In the context of adoption, the issue of racial origin, cultural and linguistic background caused some difficulty in *AH and PH, Petitioners*,[79] which was only partially resolved by imposing a condition on the adoption order that the adopters should use their best efforts to secure that the children be brought up with an understanding of their ethnic origins and traditions.[80] In *Osborne v. Matthan (No. 2)*[81] the Inner House touched upon but did not explore in depth the difficulties a child of Caribbean origin would have in being brought up by a white Scottish woman who had no connection with her family. It was accepted that the child would suffer difficulties caused by her racial origin and the court dealt with these by accepting undertakings from the pursuer that she would encourage and maintain contact between the child and the child's mother and shoulder responsibility for minimising such difficulties as the child would face. In *Perendes v. Sim*,[82] in a claim for access by a Greek Cypriot father to children of a white Scottish mother, Lord Osborne was minded to award access against both the strong opposition of the mother and the expressed opposition of the children. He considered it "particularly important" that the children retain contact with their father since they were the product of an ethnically mixed relationship. He said: "I consider that it would be of considerable value to the children that they should come to understand and appreciate the Greek Cypriot element in their makeup"[83] (this particularly in light of the fact that the children had been the victims of some racially oriented abuse at school).[84] As always, this is only one factor amongst many that, in

---

[74] Ahdar, "Religion as a Factor in Custody and Access Disputes" (1996) 10 Int. J. Law & Fam. 177.
[75] *T, Petr*, 1997 S.L.T. 724.
[76] s. 17(4)(c) (imposing a duty on local authorities making any decisions in respect of children whom they are looking after) and s. 95 (amending s. 6 of the Adoption (Scotland) Act 1978 requiring courts and adoption agencies to consider certain matters).
[77] Art. 8: "(1) States parties undertake to respect the right of the child to preserve his or her identity, including nationality, name and family relations as recognised by law without unlawful interference. (2) Where the child is illegally deprived of some or all of the elements of his or her identity, States Parties shall provide appropriate assistance and protection, with a view to speedily re-establishing his or her identity".
[78] See above, paras 5.29–5.32.
[79] 1997 Fam. L.R. 84. See further, above, para. 4.69.
[80] *Quaere* how such a condition could be enforced.
[81] 1998 S.L.T. 1264. See earlier proceedings reported at 1997 Fam. L.R. 70 (sheriff court) and 1998 S.L.T. 811 (Inner House).
[82] 1998 S.L.T. 1382.
[83] *ibid.* at 1384G.
[84] In the event, because the difficulties of reintroducing the petitioner to the children had not yet been resolved, Lord Osborne felt unable to make an order immediately. See also *Re P (A Minor) (Contact)* [1994] 2 F.L.R. 374.

cases in which it is relevant, requires to be taken into account. There is certainly no presumption, for example, that a black child will be better served living with a black relative rather than a white stranger,[85] nor indeed that cultural links should be preserved, through an appropriate contact arrangement, at all costs. Linguistic links, once lost, can seldom be satisfactorily re-established[86]; the wishes of the child involved will frequently be held to reflect the child's welfare better than maintenance or re-establishment of cultural links already broken.[87]

The no-order presumption

10.38   The structure of section 11(7)(a) indicates that the requirement on the court to make no order unless it considers that it would be better for the child that the order be made than that none should be made at all is a factor relevant to the identification of the child's welfare. This is not, in other words, a principle to be applied independently of the welfare principle, but instead creates a presumption that making no order will better serve the child's welfare than making a section 11 order. It emphasises that the onus rests with the person seeking an order to show to the satisfaction of the court that the child's welfare will be in some way enhanced by making the order sought. To put it simply, the court should subject children to orders under section 11 only when to do so is likely to do some good. This is not new law. Under section 3(2) of the Law Reform (Parent and Child) (Scotland) Act 1986 it was provided that the court "shall not make any order relating to parental rights unless it is satisfied that to do so will be in the interests of the child". These words placed the onus on the applicant for what was then a section 3 order to satisfy the court that the order sought would be in the interests of the child.[88] If the applicant was unable to discharge that onus then the proper course was to make no order.[89] Nevertheless there was a perception, both before and after the 1986 Act, that too many children were being subjected to unnecessary court orders. This perception was borne out by the strikingly large numbers of custody awards made in favour of mothers in respect of their own children under section 3 of the 1986 Act, notwithstanding the fact that no decree was necessary to give them custody since all mothers had that parental right under section 2 of the 1986 Act in any case. The real reason such awards were made was not to grant mothers a right they did not have but to remove that right from some other person, leaving the mother free to exercise her rights exclusively. The law, by thus appearing to do one thing while aiming to achieve another, ran the risk of falling into disrepute, as well as subjecting more children than was necessary to regulation of their lives by court order. For these reasons, the Scottish Law Commission recommended strengthening the words in section 3(2)[90] and their recommendations are now embodied in section 11(7)(a) of the Children (Scotland) Act 1995.

---

[85] The Court of Appeal, however, held that there was a strong supposition that, other things being equal, it was in the interests of the child to be brought up by his natural (i.e. his biological) parents rather than psychological parents and that since "Zulu development" was better for a child of Zulu origin than an "Afrikaans or English development", the child should be returned to his Zulu parents in South Africa within a few weeks, after having spent almost four years in England and being then 10 years of age: *Re M (Child's Upbringing)* [1996] 2 F.L.R. 441. *Cf. Re B (Residence Order)* [1998] 1 F.L.R. 520.

[86] *cf. AH and PH, Petrs*, above.

[87] *AH and PH, Petrs*, above; *Perendes v. Sim*, above.

[88] *Porchetta v. Porchetta*, 1986 S.L.T. 105; *Montgomery v. Lockwood*, 1987 S.C.L.R. 525; *Russell v. Russell*, 1991 S.C.L.R. 429; *O v. O*, 1995 S.L.T. 238; *Sanderson v. McManus*, 1997 S.L.T. 629, *per* Lord Hope of Craighead at 634F.

[89] *Potter v. Potter*, 1992 S.C.L.R. 788; *Patterson v. Patterson*, 1994 S.C.L.R. 166; *Ross v. Ross*, 1997 Fam. L.R. 77; *Henderson v. Henderson*, 1997 Fam. L.R. 120.

[90] Scot. Law Com. No. 135, *Report on Family Law* (1992), paras 5.16–5.18.

The application of the no-order presumption is general, and it applies both **10.39** whenever a section 11 order is sought and whenever the court is considering *ex proprio motu* whether to make such an order. The presumption is that no such order will be made.[91] This is based on the supposition that the arrangements that parents make for the upbringing of their children are likely to be better (from the point of view of the child's welfare) than any arrangements that the court is able to make, or any arrangements backed up with the legal formality of an enforceable order; it also has the advantage of encouraging parents to make their own suitable arrangements. Of course if the parents cannot agree, or if the arrangements they propose are not suitable,[92] or in any other circumstances in which the court considers it would be better for the child to make an order, then the court is free to make such order as it thinks fit,[93] and it may come to the view that the presumption has been overturned even without a party seeking to discharge a formal onus resting with him or her to that effect. The no-order presumption applies to all section 11 orders. So, in a case where the dispute is between two parents both of whom have parental responsibilities and parental rights, the court will presume that it should not make an order regulating with whom the child is to live, or how the non-resident parent is to fulfil his or her responsibility and right to maintain contact with the child. Similarly, though perhaps more strongly, the court will presume that it should not make an order granting or removing (rather than simply regulating) any parental responsibilities or parental rights, or grant an interdict or make a specific issue order.[94] The presumption will prevent a residence order being made in favour of a person who already has the right to determine the child's residence without anything further: such an application is likely to be considered incompetent or, at best, irrelevant. If a parent with parental responsibilities and parental rights seeks to have these responsibilities and rights on an exclusive basis then the application is properly for an order removing the other person's responsibilities and rights under section 11(2)(a). The decision whether to grant any parental responsibility or parental right can be taken independently of the decision of how they are to be exercised,[95] and so it is not necessary that the court granting parental responsibilities and parental rights make any further order regulating how they are to be exercised.

One consequence of the no-order presumption which is not altogether **10.40** satisfactory is that any particular decision may be made according to how the question comes before the court rather than in terms of its own merits. The presumption is that the unregulated position is better for the child than a position

---

[91] For a discussion of the similar principle contained in the English legislation, see Bainham, "The Children Act 1989: Welfare and Non-Interventionism" [1990] Fam. Law 143.

[92] The fact that parents have agreed as to the upbringing of their child after their separation does not in itself mean that no order should be made. The welfare of the child, rather than encouraging parental agreement, is the court's paramount consideration: *cf. S v. E (A Minor) (Contact)* [1993] Fam. Law 407.

[93] See *Re S (Contact: Grandparents)* [1996] 1 F.L.R. 158 in which the court at first instance made no order granting grandparents contact even although it found the application had "overwhelming merit" and that the child would be at risk of significant harm if contact were denied, this on the basis that the mother who had sole residence rights might change her mind and allow contact to which, presently, she was opposed. The Court of Appeal, finding no evidential basis for this hope held that it was an inappropriate application of the no-order principle.

[94] See *Fourman v. Fourman*, 1998 Fam. L.R. 98 in which the sheriff very clearly required a mother who sought a specific issue order authorising her to remove her children to Australia against the wishes of their father to show why this would be better for the children than not making the order. She failed to do so and the order was not made. According to the sheriff, the evidence showed no more than that the mother wanted the children to go to Australia because she wanted to go there, rather than because it was in their best interests to go there.

[95] *Harris v. Martin*, 1995 S.C.L.R. 580.

regulated by court order. While this leads to innocuous results in residence and contact disputes, and in these contexts merely reflects the emphasis long placed on preserving the status quo, the results are rather more anomalous if a specific issue order or an interdict is sought. An order may be sought by either party to a dispute, though in opposing terms. For example, parents may seek to interdict a foster carer from taking the child on holiday abroad; or the foster carer may seek a specific issue order requiring the parent to sign a passport application form on behalf of the child to allow the trip abroad.[96] In either case the presumption is in favour of the court making no order and, if the onus on the party seeking the order cannot be discharged, the decision will go in favour of the person opposing the order: the foster carer in the first case and the parent in the second, notwithstanding that the substantive issue is effectively the same in both. Such a difficulty may be more apparent than real. Questions involving the care or upbringing of children will seldom turn on the issue of formal onus and the evidence before the court will nearly always allow the court to assess wherein the child's interests lie, irrespective of who, by making the application, has the onus. Nevertheless the no-order presumption does give a benefit to the party who takes the initiative, and in many cases the ability or inability to do so will be purely fortuitous.

VIEWS OF THE CHILD

10.41 The UN Convention on the Rights of the Child provides that the child's views must be taken into account in any decisions affecting him or her.[97] Moreover, respect for the child as a person requires that some account be taken of his or her views, wishes, and feelings. Residence disputes provide the typical example of court decisions that affect a child in a most fundamental way, but the obligation is general and applies to all decisions affecting the child (including, *e.g.*, a divorce action in which no section 11 order is sought[98]). It has long been the practice in Scotland for courts to place a high regard on the wishes expressed by older children. Pupils at common law were probably considered to be too young to have proper views on any matter, but in so far as a minor *pubes* could be the subject of custody at common law it required a strong case to justify an award against his or her expressed wishes.[99] Though the attributes of pupillarity were extended to all children under the age of 16 by section 5(1) of the Age of Legal Capacity (Scotland) Act 1991, this did not deny the minor child under that age the capacity to express views. The 1991 Act is based upon an acceptance that, in various different circumstances, effect can and should be given to decisions made by children under 16 who are deemed capable of making those decisions on a rational basis. If that is so then it is difficult to argue that children under 16 are not capable of holding rational views on matters relating to parental responsibilities and parental rights, and the courts, even before the 1995 Act, took these views into account, though strictly as a matter affecting the welfare

---

[96] *cf. City of Edinburgh Council v. M*, 1996 S.L.T. (Sh.Ct) 112.

[97] Art. 12: "States Parties shall assure to the child who is capable of forming his or her own views the right to express those views freely in all matters affecting the child, the views of the child being given due weight in accordance with the age and maturity of the child."

[98] Scots law fulfils its international obligations in this respect not by requiring that the child be given an opportunity to express views in the divorce action itself but by requiring parents to have regard so far as practicable to the views of the child in reaching any major decision relating to parental responsibilities and parental rights: Children (Scotland) Act 1995, s. 6. Divorce invariably affects the practical exercise of these responsibilities and rights.

[99] *Harvey v. Harvey* (1860) 22 D. 1198; *Fisher v. Edgar* (1894) 21 R. 1076 at 1078. *cf. Flannigan v. Inspector of Bothwell* (1892) 19 R. 909, *per* Lord President Robertson at 912; *Morrison v. Quarrier* (1894) 21 R. 1071 at 1075.

judgment that they had to make. However, though the child's wishes were an important element in the welfare judgment, neither the Guardianship of Infants Act 1925 nor the Law Reform (Parent and Child) (Scotland) Act 1986 (in contrast with the provisions relating to adoption)[1] explicitly required the court, as a matter of procedural obligation, to give the child an opportunity to express views. That has now changed. Section 11(7)(b) of the Children (Scotland) Act 1995 provides that the court shall, taking account of the child's age and maturity, so far as practicable: (i) give the child an opportunity to indicate whether he or she wishes to express his or her views, (ii) if the child does so wish give him or her the opportunity to express them, and (iii) have regard to such views as the child expresses.[2] This provision is strengthened by the court rules which prohibit the court from making any order when the child has indicated a wish to express views unless due weight has been given to these views.[3] A failure on the part of the court either to give the child an opportunity to express views or to have due regard to such views as are expressed will give a ground of appeal against the court's decision on the basis of procedural irregularity.

The obligation on the court to have appropriate regard to the child's views **10.42** exists independently of its further obligation to regard the welfare of the child as its paramount consideration.[4] Nevertheless, the matters are not entirely distinct and it remains the case that an important factor to be weighed in the balance in determining the child's welfare is whether the decision to be made consists with the child's own wishes and feelings. The welfare principle has been given a role predominant over the parent's rights and it retains its predominance over the child's rights: the child's wishes in relation to the making of a section 11 order can, therefore, never be given effect to if this is not consistent with his or her interests.[5] The question is not so much one of how strong the case to the contrary must be before the child's wishes can be denied, but whether his or her wishes can be given effect in a manner consistent with regard for his or her welfare as the paramount consideration. In the event of conflict the course indicated by the child's welfare must, in the last resort, prevail.

The circumstances in which the child's views are expressed and their **10.43** background and origin are relevant to the weight that the court will give them. If a child expresses a view, for example, that he or she does not wish contact with a parent then, so long as the resistance is genuine and free from external pressure it would normally be inappropriate to require contact.[6] It has been said that the child's resistance must also be reasonable[7] and that, no doubt, usually affords a good indication of whether the child's views are genuine and independent, but if they are, and are strongly held, it is unattractive to compel a child to act against them merely because to the adult mind they appear irrational. Views may be genuinely held even when based on a lack of understanding and the effect of these views on the child is no less significant than when the child's feelings are both rational and reasoned. Where negative reactions such as fear

---

[1] Adoption (Scotland) Act 1978, s. 6, as originally enacted and now as amended by the Children (Scotland) Act 1995, s. 95.

[2] On the procedure for fulfilling this obligation, see above, para. 9.49.

[3] RCS 1994, r. 49.30(3); OCR 1993, r. 33.19(3).

[4] *cf.* the Children Act 1989, s. 1(3)(a) in which "the ascertainable wishes and feelings of the child concerned" are factors in the "welfare checklist" which the court must consider in making its welfare judgment.

[5] It will be different if the question before the court concerns something other than the making or the content of a s. 11 order, such as an issue of capacity under the Age of Legal Capacity (Scotland) Act 1991.

[6] *Blance v. Blance* 1978 S.L.T. 74, *Cosh v. Cosh*, 1979 S.L.T. (Notes) 72, *Brannigan v. Brannigan*, 1979 S.L.T. (Notes) 73.

[7] *Cosh v. Cosh*, above.

or hostility underlie the child's views, they afford, unless there are both a cogent and satisfactory explanation and good grounds for believing that the negative reaction can be overcome, compelling reasons for giving the child's wishes effect. In *Russell v. Russell*[8] a child of five had, through the illegitimate influence of her mother, strongly negative feelings about her father, which manifested themselves in signs of extreme distress whenever the suggestion was made to her that her father have contact with her. However unfair this was on the father, the child's reaction indicated clearly that her interests lay in disallowing contact. On the other hand, in *Perendes v. Sim*[9] Lord Osborne felt able to afford the views of children aged 11 and 10 little significance because he found that they had been unduly influenced by their mother against contact with their father. Nevertheless he postponed a decision on whether to make a contact order until the matter of reintroducing the children back to their father had been explored, and he accepted that if this proved not possible, or detriminental to the children, then he would be reluctantly compelled to refuse to make a contact order.[10]

Presumption of age and maturity

10.44   A child aged 12 years or more is presumed to be of sufficient age and maturity to form a view for the purposes of the court's obligation to have regard to any view the child wishes to express.[11] There is a noticeable circularity in "presuming" a child aged 12 or more to be of sufficient "age". It is submitted, therefore, that the phrase "age and maturity" must be taken as a single unified concept the content of which is mental capacity, so that a child aged 12 years or more is presumed to have the mental capacity to form a view on a section 11 application. This applies to any decision, however far-reaching, that the court is asked to make, though the more complex the decision is, in terms of its effects on the child, the easier it will be to overturn this presumption. It is, however, difficult to imagine a situation in which the matter would be analysed in terms of overturning the presumption of age and maturity. More likely, the courts will "have regard" to any view expressed, but will be more willing to depart from the expressed wishes of a child in cases in which more in the way of mental capacity is required to understand the significance of the decision that has to be made. But the presumption of age and maturity is a strong one. In *Gover v. Gover*[12] Lord Thomson said: "When the child is a minor it would be, in my opinion, quite unrealistic, and indeed wrong, for the Court, in an issue of custody or access, to do other than place very great and usually decisive weight on the wishes of the child."[13] "Minor" in this dictum may now be read as "child of or over the age of 12 years". The primary matter is not an abstract regard for the legal status of the child, although that is entitled to respect, but the recognition that to enforce, for example, a residence or contact order against the wishes of an adolescent is likely to be detrimental and that a right to a measure of choice between alternatives is appropriate to the later stages in personal development. The older child's desires are always a matter relevant to the determination of

---

[8] 1991 S.C.L.R. 429.

[9] 1998 S.L.T. 1382.

[10] See also *Marshall v. Marshall*, 1996 S.L.T. 429 in which a 13-year-old child's views were disregarded. This was, however, a Hague Convention case in which the circumstances have to be exceptional before the court can refuse to order the return of the child to his or her habitual residence, and the insubstantiality of the child's reasons for wishing to remain in Scotland meant that the circumstances were not sufficiently exceptional.

[11] Children (Scotland) Act 1995, s. 11(10).

[12] 1969 S.L.T. (Notes) 78 at 78.

[13] *cf. Hannay, Petr*, 1947 S.L.T. (Notes) 55; *Klein and Anr, Petrs*, 1969 S.L.T. (Notes) 53; *Johnson v. Johnson*, 1972 S.L.T. (Notes) 15.

where his or her interests lie and should, therefore, be at the forefront of the court's consideration.

Rather different considerations are appropriate in the case of a child below **10.45** the age of 12. There is no presumption that he or she is of sufficient age and maturity to form a view, but the obligation to take account of expressed views applies to children below as it does to children above the age of 12 years. The presumption of mental capacity for the 12-year-old child is expressly "without prejudice" to the generality of the obligation to have regard for the views of the child, taking account of his or her age and maturity.[14] This means, it is submitted, that the court must give every child, except those who are too young to understand what is being offered, the opportunity to express views, but that the regard to be had to these views will vary depending upon the actual mental capacity of the individual child. How that opportunity is afforded will, of course, vary with the age of the child. But the views of every child who can form views are clearly relevant to his or her welfare and it is submitted that to deny a hearing to a child of sufficient understanding, even when under the age of 12, would amount to a failure to observe the duty laid upon the court by section 11(7)(b) of the 1995 Act. A young child should not, however, be disturbed by choices beyond his or her capacity: there may well be a "right not to have to make a decision",[15] and this is doubtless why the obligation in section 11(7)(b) is structured into three distinct parts.[16] Though technically the child is not, of course, making a choice, courts and those charged with finding out the views of the child must be sensitive to the fact that the child may not fully appreciate the difference between making a choice and expressing a view while at the same time being perfectly able to form and to express a view. It will usually be right to ascertain the feelings of even very young children, so long as they are of sufficient age that it can properly be accepted that they have views.

It is further submitted that the word "views" as it appears in the various **10.46** statutory provisions, primary and secondary, should be given a wide interpretation and should not be limited to a sense of "reasoned opinion". Views should, rather, be held to encompass wishes and feelings, at least in relation to the application of the welfare principle.[17] Even the very youngest children have been observed to express feelings of discomfort, distress, fear, comfort, contentment or happiness and these are all relevant to the determination of welfare. These feelings are, in a very real sense, "views" although not the result of a rational or logical pattern of thought. Whether these "views" are based on a valid understanding of the situation is hardly relevant to the question of whether they are genuinely held, and it is their genuineness rather than their rationality that most closely links them to the child's welfare. But the interpretation to be put on a child's wishes and feelings and the effect, if any, to be given to them will, necessarily, vary greatly from case to case.[18]

---

[14] Children (Scotland) Act 1995, s. 11(10).

[15] *M v. M* [1973] Fam. Law 17. See also *Adams v. Adams* [1985] 5 F.L.R. 768, *per* Dunn L.J.

[16] Giving the child the opportunity to indicate whether he or she wishes to express views; if so giving the child the opportunity to express these views; taking due account of any views expressed.

[17] The obligation to give the child an opportunity to indicate whether he or she wishes to express views suggests a requirement that the child be capable of coming to a "view", in the narrow sense, on this point.

[18] See *Pow v. Pow*, 1931 S.L.T. 485 (girl of 10, boy of eight); *Hannay, Petr*, 1947 S.L.T. (Notes) 55 (boy of 12); *Johnson v. Johnson*, 1972 S.L.T. (Notes) 15 (children between ages of seven and 14); *Fowler v. Fowler*, 1981 S.L.T. (Notes) 9 and 78 (girl of 10); *Hay v. Hay*, 1997 Fam. L.B. 28–6 (boy of eight). *Cf. Nicol v. Nicol*, 1953 S.L.T. (Notes) 67, in which the wishes of children of 11 and 10 were considered but did not receive effect. For a view stressing the risks of undue emphasis on giving effect to the child's wishes, see Plant, "The Psychiatrist Views Children of Divorced Parents" (1944) 10 Law and Cont. Prob. 807 at 815.

CHAPTER 11

INTERNATIONAL ASPECTS OF PARENTAL RESPONSIBILITIES AND PARENTAL RIGHTS

CHOICE OF LAW

11.01 In relation to parental responsibilities and parental rights there is little room for choice of law questions in the pure sense of choosing a legal system to govern the issue before the court. An order may be made under section 11 of the Children (Scotland) Act 1995 in proceedings in the Court of Session or in the sheriff court whether or not either of the parties seeks such an order and, while it is expressly provided that any question that concerns parental responsibilities or parental rights or the responsibilities or rights of a guardian must be determined by the law of the place of the child's habitual residence at the time when the question arises,[1] it is further provided that nothing in that provision shall affect the application of section 11(7) of the 1995 Act.[2] It follows that whatever the provisions of any potentially applicable foreign legal system may be, the case before the Scottish court has to be decided with regard to the welfare of the child as the court's paramount consideration. Usually, therefore, the rules of foreign legal systems will require to be considered only in so far as they bear on the child's future welfare, though once the welfare test has been satisfied, account should, in principle, be taken of any preferences which the law of the child's habitual residence may indicate. If the question before the court concerns the immediate protection of the child, that question must be determined by the law of the place where the child is when the question arises,[3] but since it is difficult to imagine a case in which the Scottish court would be asked to determine a question concerning the "immediate protection" of a chid who is not then present in Scotland, the result in most cases will be the application of Scots law. And if the question is one concerning whether a person is validly appointed or constituted guardian of a child, that question is to be determined by the law of the child's habitual residence at the date when the appointment was made or the event constituting the guardianship occurred.[4] Though the principles in section 11(7) apply in both these situations no less than in cases concerning parental responsibilities and parental rights the role these principles can play is much circumscribed in relation to the appointment (as opposed to the powers) of guardians. The recognition of the appointment is automatic in terms of section 14(3)(c) if valid by the law of the child's habitual residence and that recognition cannot be resisted on the ground that to do so would be against the child's welfare, or that the child was denied the opportunity of expressing any views about the appointment, or that the appointment was unnecessary. But section 14(3)(c) is in its terms limited to recognition of the appointment, and the content and exercise of the office is expressly governed by section 14(3)(a) (*i.e.* the law of the child's

---

[1] Children (Scotland) Act 1995, s. 14(3)(a).
[2] *ibid.* s. 14(4).
[3] *ibid.* s. 14(3)(b).
[4] *ibid.* s. 14(3)(c). Testamentary appointments are deemed to be made on the date of death of the appointer.

habitual residence when the question arises) and that content or exercise can clearly be cut down or qualified by the application of the principles in section 11(7).[5]

RECOGNITION AND ENFORCEMENT OF NON-SCOTTISH ORDERS

Introduction

The responsibilities and rights of parents or guardians in relation to **11.02** the upbringing of children conferred by legal systems other than Scots law, and the orders regulating these responsibilities and rights made by courts outwith Scotland, are statutorily subject to three distinct regimes of recognition rules, depending upon the country of origin, and upon whether and to what extent that country is party to certain international conventions and agreements:

(1) In relation to orders from courts in other parts of the United Kingdom, the court in Scotland will recognise and give effect to them according to the rules laid down in chapter V of Part I of the Family Law Act 1986.[6]

(2) In relation to responsibilities and rights, and the court orders governing them, emanating from countries outside the United Kingdom that are party to the European Convention on the Recognition and Enforcement of Decisions Concerning Custody of Children, or the Hague Convention on the Civil Aspects of International Child Abduction, the court in Scotland will recognise and give effect to them according to the rules in these conventions, insofar as they are brought into United Kingdom law by the Child Abduction and Custody Act 1985.[7]

(3) In relation to responsibilities and rights, and the court orders governing them, emanating from countries outside the United Kingdom that are not party to either the European Convention or the Hague Convention, or which are not in the circumstances covered by the conventions,[8] the court in Scotland will recognise and give effect to them according to the rules developed at common law and modified by section 26 of the Family Law Act 1986.[9]

Recognition and enforcement of Part I orders within the United Kingdom

The Family Law Act 1986 laid down, as we have already seen,[10] the rules **11.03** governing the jurisdiction of the Scottish courts in relation to "Part I orders", as defined in section 1(1) of that Act. Comparable rules, similarly based on matrimonial proceedings, habitual residence, presence and emergency, are laid down in that Act for England and Wales[11] and for Northern Ireland.[12] Not only

---

[5] The same result follows in relation to parenthood, which is recognised or not by principles other than the child's welfare but whose legal consequences are governed by welfare considerations.

[6] See below, paras 11.03–11.09.

[7] See below, paras 11.10–11.15 for the European Convention and paras 11.19 *et seq.* for the Hague Convention.

[8] See , *e.g.*, *Hill v. Hill*, 1991 S.L.T. 189, in which, though the child had been brought from Ontario, where both conventions apply, the European Convention was inapplicable since the removal had taken place before the making of a custody order. (It seems not to have been realised in that case that the Hague Convention would not be inapplicable for this reason alone.)

[9] See below, paras 11.16–11.18.

[10] Above, paras 9.23 *et seq.*

[11] Family Law Act 1986, ss. 2–7.

[12] *ibid.* ss. 19–24.

does the Act lay down uniform rules for jurisdiction to make Part I orders throughout the United Kingdom, but it also provides the basis for recognition and enforcement in each part of the United Kingdom of the Part I orders made by courts in any other part of the United Kingdom. The harmonisation of the rules on jurisdiction has allowed for the general principle to be enacted that the orders relating to the upbringing of children made by a court in one part of the United Kingdom will be recognised in all other parts without any further procedure. If the order is to be enforced in a part other than the part where the order was made, then a certain, though minimal, procedure requires to be followed. Because of the way that the jurisdictional rules operate it will generally not be possible, once a residence order has been made in one part of the United Kingdom, to seek a fresh residence order in another part instead of applying for recognition and enforcement of the existing order.

Recognition

11.04   Section 25(1) of the Family Law Act 1986 provides that where a Part I order made by a court in any part of the United Kingdom is in force with respect to a child, then the order shall be recognised in any other part of the United Kingdom as having the same effect in that other part as if it had been made by the appropriate court in that other part and as if that court had had jurisdiction to make it. The "appropriate court" in relation to Scotland means the Court of Session.[13] "Child" means a child under the age of 16 years.[14] It follows, for example, that a residence order or a contact order granted by an English court that had jurisdiction to do so according to the English jurisdictional rules in the 1986 Act will be recognised in Scotland automatically, and it will have the same effect in Scotland as if a residence order or a contact order had been made in relation to the child by the Court of Session. Scottish orders will be recognised in England and Wales, and in Northern Ireland, under identical rules. If the order includes provision as to the means by which the rights conferred by the order are to be enforced, then that provision of the order is to be ignored,[15] for the Act itself lays down the enforcement procedure that must be followed.

11.05   While enforcement of a Part I order is another issue (about to be discussed), its recognition alone will give the person in whose favour the order is made certain rights. For example, an order conferring parental responsibilities and parental rights upon a person other than the child's parents will entitle that person to provide legally effective consent to the medical treatment of the child, or to enter into valid contracts on behalf of the child, anywhere in the United Kingdom. If, however, the exercise of any rights under the order is challenged, or the holder of the rights wishes to enforce them, in a part of the United Kingdom other than the part in which they were granted, the procedure described in the next paragraph has to be adopted.

Enforcement

11.06   A court in a part of the United Kingdom in which a Part I order from another part is recognised in accordance with the provision described above cannot enforce the order unless it has been registered in that part of the United Kingdom under section 27 of the Family Law Act 1986 and proceedings for enforcement are taken in accordance with section 29.[16] If a Part I order is to be enforced in a part of the United Kingdom other than the part in which it was granted, then the

---

[13] Family Law Act 1986, s. 32(1).
[14] *ibid.* s. 25(1).
[15] *ibid.* s. 25(2).
[16] *ibid.* s. 25(3).

person on whom rights are conferred by the order may apply to the court that made the order to have it registered in another part of the United Kingdom.[17] On receiving an application to have its order registered in another part of the United Kingdom, the court has no discretion and must grant the application, unless it appears that the order is no longer in force[18] (*e.g.*, because the child subject to the order has since it was granted attained the age of 16 years). On receiving the application the court that made the order must cause to be sent to the appropriate court (a) a certified copy of the order, (b) where the order has been varied, prescribed particulars of any variation that is in force, and (c) a copy of the application and of any accompanying documents. The appropriate court is, if the order is to be enforced in Scotland, the Court of Session or, if the order is to be enforced in England and Wales or Northern Ireland, the High Court.[19] When the prescribed officer of the appropriate court receives the certified copy of the order he must forthwith cause the order, together with particulars of any variation, to be registered in that court.[20] Registration cannot be refused, unless the order is in respect of a child who has attained the age of 16, and the registration of an order shall cease to have effect when the child attains that age.[21] Registration can be cancelled where the order ceases to have effect in the part of the United Kingdom in which it was made, cancellation being on the court's own motion or on the application of any person who appears to the court to have an interest.[22]

The effect of registration is that the court in which the order is registered has **11.07** the same powers in relation to enforcement of the order as if it had itself made the order and had jurisdiction to make it.[23] Accordingly, an English residence order or contact order registered in the Court of Session can be enforced in Scotland by following the procedures appropriate for the enforcement of an equivalent order made by the Court of Session.[24] Where the order ceases to have effect in the part of the United Kingdom in which it was made, or it has ceased to have effect in Scotland as a result of the making of an order in proceedings outside the United Kingdom, then, if enforcement proceedings are brought in Scotland in accordance with section 29, any person who appears to the court to have an interest in the matter may apply for the proceedings to be dismissed.[25] If in either case the court is satisfied that the registered order has ceased to have effect then it must dismiss the proceedings for enforcement.[26]

Notwithstanding that the procedure laid down by the 1986 Act has been **11.08** followed, an ultimate discretion in relation to enforcement lies with the Court of Session, because the Act "has not elided the limited protective jurisdiction of the Court of Session to refuse to give effect to the custody order of a foreign court... which the Court of Session may always exercise if it is satisfied that enforcement of the foreign decree would result in physical or moral injury to

---

[17] Family Law Act 1986, s. 27(1). The procedure for such applications in the Court of Session is governed by Chap. 71 of the Rules of the Court of Session 1994 (S.I. 1994 No. 1443) and in the sheriff court by Chap. 4 of the Act of Sederunt (Child Care and Maintenance Rules) 1997 (S.I. 1997 No. 291).

[18] *ibid*. s. 27(3).

[19] *ibid*. s. 32(1).

[20] *ibid*. s. 27(4).

[21] *ibid*. s. 27(5). It is competent for the courts in England and Wales and in Northern Ireland to grant residence orders over children until the age of 18. They will not be recognised in Scotland, nor enforced, after the child reaches the age of 16 years.

[22] *ibid*. s. 28.

[23] *ibid*. s. 29(1).

[24] See RCS 1994, r. 71.7.

[25] Family Law Act 1986, s. 31(1) and (2).

[26] *ibid*. s. 31(3).

the child".[27] It is submitted that it is only in exceptional circumstances that this limited protective jurisdiction should be invoked; otherwise the whole basis of this part of the 1986 Act would be placed in jeopardy.[28]

Interim directions and sisting of enforcement proceedings

11.09   Where an application for the enforcement of an order registered under section 27 is made the court may, at any time before the application is determined, give such interim directions as it thinks fit for the purpose of securing the welfare of the child concerned and of preventing changes in the circumstances relevant to the determination of the application.[29] Where proceedings for enforcement are taken, any person who appears to the court to have an interest may apply for the proceedings to be sisted on the ground that he or she has taken or intends to take other proceedings the result of which may be that the order will cease to have effect, or have a different effect, in the part of the United Kingdom in which it is registered.[30] So, for example, in *Woodcock v. Woodcock*[31] a father obtained from the Family Division in England an order against the mother for the delivery of a child to him. This order was registered in the Court of Session in accordance with section 27(1) and the father petitioned the court for an order for delivery of the child in accordance with section 29. The mother successfully moved the court to sist the proceedings on the ground that in a divorce action in England the delivery order against her might be lifted.[32] If, having granted a sist, it appears to the court that there has been unreasonable delay in the taking of the other proceedings, or that the other proceedings are concluded and the registered order is still in force, the court may recall the sist.[33]

Recognition and enforcement under the European Convention

11.10   In relation to those countries that have ratified the European Convention on Recognition and Enforcement of Decisions Concerning Custody of Children,[34] and in circumstances in which the convention is applicable, orders made by courts outwith the United Kingdom relating to the upbringing of children will be recognised and enforced in Scotland in accordance with the terms of the Child Abduction and Custody Act 1985, in Schedule 2 to which the convention is reproduced, in so far as it is adopted into United Kingdom law.[35]

11.11   The European Convention provides for the mutual recognition between contracting states of any "decision relating to custody", which is defined to mean a decision "of an authority in so far as it relates to the care of the person of the child, including the right to decide on the place of his residence, or to the right of access to him".[36] "Child" means a person of any nationality, so long as

---

[27] *Woodcock v. Woodcock*, 1990 S.L.T. 848, *per* Lord President Hope, Lords Dunpark and Milligan at 853B: this opinion was expressed "for future guidance".

[28] See Edwards, "A Domestic Muddle: Custody Orders in the United Kingdom" (1992) 41 I.C.L.Q. 444.

[29] Family Law Act 1986, s. 29(2). This requires some inquiry by the court into whether it would be in the child's best interests to give directions: *Woodcock v. Woodcock*, above, at 852F.

[30] *ibid.* s. 30(1).

[31] 1990 S.L.T. 848.

[32] See also *Cook v. Cook*, November 5, 1996, OH.

[33] Family Law Act 1986, s. 30(3). This provision is without prejudice to any other power of the court to recall a sist: s. 30(4).

[34] A list of current signatories and dates of accession to the European Convention can be found in Norrie, *Scottish Family Law Legislation*, para. A.662.1.

[35] The provisions set out in the schedule have the force of law: s. 12(2). See Jones, "Council of Europe Convention on Recognition and Enforcement of Decisions Relating to the Custody of Children" (1981) 30 I.C.L.Q. 467.

[36] European Convention, Art. 1(c).

he or she (1) is under 16 years of age and (2) has not the right to decide on his or her own place of residence under the law of his or her habitual residence, the law of his or her nationality, or the internal law of the state addressed. Both of these conditions must be satisfied: if a child has capacity to determine his or her own residence before the age of 16—as, arguably, a child in Scotland might[37]—then any court order purporting to regulate that child's residence would not be entitled to recognition or enforcement under the terms of the European Convention.

The fundamental principle in the European Convention is contained in Article 7, which **11.12** provides that "a decision relating to custody given in a contracting state shall be recognised and, where it is enforceable in the state of origin, made enforceable in every other contracting state". The courts of contracting states must therefore recognise and enforce the decisions of courts and administrative bodies in other contracting states, subject only to the exceptions shortly to be discussed. The provisions of the convention apply to decisions made before the child was removed to another country, and to decisions made afterwards if they contain a declaration that the removal was unlawful.[38] The Scottish court has the power to make such a declaration in relation to children taken out of the United Kingdom.[39]

The procedure for recognition and enforcement by the Scottish courts of decisions **11.13** covered by the European Convention is laid down in the body of the Child Abduction and Custody Act 1985.[40] Recognition, as the convention itself demands, is automatic unless refused on an application made to the court.[41] The person on whom rights are conferred by the decision relating to custody may apply to have the decision registered in the appropriate court,[42] which in Scotland is the Court of Session.[43] It is only if the decision is registered that it can be enforced,[44] though recognition alone does have legal effects (*e.g.* on the validity of acts taken under the authority of the decision). An application to register the decision must be granted by the court (subject to what is said below) and the decision can then be enforced as if it were a decree of the Court of Session, the court having the same powers for the purpose of enforcing the decision as if it had been made by that court.[45] If one of the grounds for refusing recognition (shortly to be discussed) exists, the court must refuse to register the decision,[46] as it must do if the decision is not, in the opinion of the court, covered by the convention,[47] or if an application under the Hague Convention, discussed later, is pending.[48] If the decision is varied or revoked in the country in which it was made, the person on whose behalf it was registered in Scotland must notify the Court of Session,[49] which will then vary or cancel the registration accordingly.[50] The court may also do this on the application of any person appearing to the court to have an interest in the matter.[51]

---

[37] See Nichols, "Can They or Can't They?", 1991 S.L.T. (News) 395 at 397-398, and above, para. 8.34.
[38] Art. 12. See, *e.g.*, *Re S (A Minor) (Custody: Habitual Residence)* [1997] 4 All E.R. 251, HL; *Re S (Abduction: European Convention)* [1996] 1 F.L.R. 660.
[39] Child Abduction and Custody Act 1985, s. 23(2).
[40] *ibid.* ss. 12–24.
[41] *ibid.* s. 15(2)(a).
[42] *ibid.* s. 16(1).
[43] *ibid.* s. 27(2). For the procedure, see RCS 1994, r. 70.9–70.14.
[44] *ibid.* s. 15(2)(b).
[45] *ibid.* s. 18.
[46] *ibid.* s. 16(4)(a).
[47] *ibid.* s. 16(4)(b).
[48] *ibid.* s. 16(4)(c). See, *e.g.*, *Re R (Abduction: Hague and European Conventions)* [1997] 1 F.L.R. 663.
[49] Child Abduction and Custody Act 1985, s. 17(1).
[50] *ibid.* s. 17(2) and (3).
[51] *ibid.* s. 17(4). See RCS 1994, r. 70.14.

11.14   Any person who has obtained in a contracting state a decision relating to the custody of a child and who wishes to have that decision recognised or enforced in another contracting state may, if he or she needs help in so doing, submit an application to the central authority of any contracting state.[52] In Scotland the central authority is the Secretary of State,[53] and in England and Wales and in Northern Ireland it is the Lord Chancellor.[54] Applications can be made to any central authority (or to none) and if an application is made to an authority in a country different from that in which the applicant seeks to have the order recognised or enforced, the authority addressed must directly and without delay send the documents to that other central authority.[55] The purpose of the central authorities is to provide such assistance as is required to the person in whose favour the decision relating to custody was made, in tracing the child if necessary, taking action to have the order recognised and enforced, and in arranging for the return of the child.[56]

Grounds for refusing recognition and enforcement

11.15   The general principle is that recognition of the decision relating to custody will be automatic, and it is provided expressly that "in no circumstances may the foreign decision be reviewed as to its substance".[57] However the convention, as enacted in the 1985 Act, requires the courts in the state addressed to refuse recognition of orders on grounds laid down by Articles 9 and 10.[58] These Articles provide that recognition and enforcement may be refused in the following circumstances:

(1) In the case of a decision given in the absence of the defendant or his or her legal representative, if the defendant was not duly served with the document that instituted the proceedings in sufficient time to enable him or her to arrange his or her defence. This ground cannot, however, be used if the failure to effect service was a result of the defendant having concealed his or her whereabouts from the person who instituted the proceedings.[59]

(2) In the case of a decision given in the absence of the defendant or his or her legal representative, if the competence of the authority giving the decision was not founded (i) on the habitual residence of the defendant, (ii) on the last common habitual residence of the child's parents, at least one parent still being habitually resident there, or (iii) on the habitual residence of the child.[60]

(3) If the custody decision is incompatible with a decision relating to custody which became enforceable in the state addressed before the removal of the child, unless the child has had his or her habitual residence in the territory of the requesting state for one year before his or her removal.[61]

---

52 Art. 4.

53 On whose behalf the functions are performed by Scottish Courts Administration.

54 Child Abduction and Custody Act 1985, s. 14(1).

55 Art. 4(3).

56 Art. 5.

57 Art. 9(3). This means that the court asked to register the order cannot vary it in any way, or recognise it only in part. See *Re A (Foreign Access Order: Enforcement)* [1996] 1 F.L.R. 561.

58 Child Abduction and Custody Act 1985, s. 16(4)(a). The convention itself allowed the Art. 9 grounds to be applied only when the application was made within six months of a removal of the child from the jurisdiction in which the order was made to another. The convention as enacted by the 1985 Act makes no distinction between the grounds under Art. 9 and Art. 10: *i.e.* they apply whenever the application is made.

59 Art. 9(1)(a).

60 Art. 9(1)(b).

61 Art. 9(1)(c).

(4) If it is found that the effects of the decision are manifestly incompatible with the fundamental principles of the law relating to the family and children in the state addressed.[62] In Scotland this would entitle the court to refuse to recognise or enforce a decision that is contrary to the interests of the child, the welfare principle being fundamental in child law in Scotland. However, it has been suggested that this ground is not satisfied just because a Scottish court would have reached a different conclusion from that of a foreign court as to where the child's welfare lies.[63] This must be so, otherwise the court would be breaching the injunction not to review the foreign decision as to its substance.[64]

(5) If it is found that by reason of a change in the circumstances including the passage of time but not including a mere change in the residence of the child after an improper removal, the effects of the original decision are manifestly no longer in accordance with the welfare of the child.[65] This is not simply the welfare test, for the standard of proof to be met by a party founding on this provision is "a very high one".[66] Lord MacFadyen in *Dehn, Petitioner* said that "manifestly" means "clearly, plainly or obviously". In making a decision under this head the court is obliged to ascertain the child's views unless this is impracticable having regard in particular to his or her age and understanding.[67]

(6) If at the time when the proceedings were instituted in the state of origin (i) the child was a national of the state addressed or was habitually resident there and no such connection existed with the state of origin or (ii) the child was a national both of the state of origin and of the state addressed and was habitually resident in the state addressed.[68] This ground justifies refusal of recognition and enforcement when stronger connections exist between the child and the state asked to recognise the order than between the child and the state in which the order was originally made.

(7) If the decision is incompatible with a decision given in the state addressed or enforceable in that state after being given in a third state, pursuant to proceedings begun before the submission of the request for recognition or enforcement, and if the refusal is in accordance with the welfare of the child.[69] Both conditions must be satisfied before this ground can be used to refuse recognition and enforcement.

---

[62] Art. 10(1)(a).

[63] *Stair Memorial Encyclopaedia of the Laws of Scotland*, Vol. 10, para. 1329.

[64] Art. 9(3).

[65] Art. 10(1)(b).

[66] *Campins-Coll, Petr*, 1989 S.L.T. 33 at 36L, *per* Lord Kirkwood. In this case, that standard was satisfied, particularly due to the fact that the child, a boy of 15-and-a-half, whom the judge described as an "intelligent and level-headed boy who knows that he wants to do with his life", expressed an adamant refusal to return to Spain. It was held that it would be manifestly contrary to his welfare to force him to return against his will and thereby separate him from his brother (who was 17) and also thereby further disrupt his education. In *F v. F (Minors) (Custody: Foreign Order)* [1989] Fam. 1, the passage of 21 months, together with the father's changed attitude towards contact, was held to constitute a change of circumstances in the lives of children aged five and three at the time of the hearing, and thus recognition and enforcement was refused under this ground. In *Dehn, Petr*, November 26, 1997, the irresponsible behaviour of the petitioner in relation to an older child was held to create a change of circumstances in relation to two younger children who, as a result, were afraid to return to Germany where access had previously taken place. See also *Re A (Foreign Access Order: Enforcement)* [1996] 1 F.L.R. 561; *Re R (Abduction: Hague and European Conventions)* [1997] 1 F.L.R. 663.

[67] Art. 15(1).

[68] Art. 10(1)(c).

[69] Art. 10(1)(d). See *Campins-Coll, Petr*, above, in which a Spanish decree in favour of the father, granted in 1982, was not enforced as it was incompatible with a Scottish decree in favour of the mother, dated 1977.

These grounds are the only grounds upon which registration of a foreign decision can be refused. Enforcement is, however, another matter.[70] Section 18 of the 1985 Act provides that a registered order will be enforceable as if it were an order made by the Court of Session but it does not limit the grounds upon which the Court of Session can refuse to enforce an order.[71] In particular the court may refuse to enforce an order that it considers contrary to the welfare of the child even after it has been registered, for the court would never enforce its own order once persuaded that it was contrary to the welfare of the child to do so. In making its decision on enforcement, the court must take appropriate account of the views of the child.

Recognition of other foreign orders

11.16   At common law the Scottish court would recognise foreign custody decrees if granted by the court of the child's domicile.[72] That was justified on the view that custody affected status[73] in which the grand rule is that it "is governed universally by one single principle", namely that of domicile.[74] A status, when created by the law of the domicile, "is, or ought to be, judicially recognised as being the case everywhere, all the world over".[75] So judgments of the courts of the domicile, and only those judgments, had the character of judgments *in rem*.[76] While the strength of that conclusion in purity of principle can be acknowledged, a rigid adherence to it, particularly if it meant that judgments of courts other than those of the domicile were disregarded, could have unfortunate consequences in some cases. The use of domicile as the jurisdictional test, though logical, could lead to anomalies. Domicile is more easily applied retrospectively to the situation of the *propositus* at a fixed time in the past than in the fluid context of an ongoing dispute. It could also be uncertain and require elaborate proof when expedition and concentration on other issues were important. Sometimes, especially when a domicile of origin was revived after having been lost, it could be an artificial concept lacking any real connection with the child. The concept of habitual residence was increasingly perceived as more appropriate than domicile for custody cases, and, indeed, in the context of family law in general.[77] In 1986 the common law rule was altered so that, where domicile of the child was previously the ground for recognising custody orders made outside Scotland, habitual residence of the child was to be the ground for recognising custody orders made outside the United Kingdom.[78] This was amended by the Children (Scotland) Act 1995 to take account of the abolition of the concept of custody, and the rule was applied to all orders relating to parental responsibilities or parental rights. Now, any such order made outside the United Kingdom, if not governed by the Child Abduction and Custody Act 1985, will be recognised in

---

[70] In *Re H (A Minor) (Foreign Custody Order: Enforcement)* [1994] 1 All E.R. 812 it was held by the Court of Appeal that the phrase "recognition and enforcement" in Art. 10 as it appears in Sched. 2 to the 1985 Act should be read disjunctively.

[71] See Jamieson, *Parental Responsibilities and Rights* (1995) at p. 216.

[72] Anton and Beaumont, *Private International Law* (2nd ed.), p. 521, suggest, and the principle seems sound, that the common law rules apply to recognition of foreign rights arising by operation of law as well as those arising from a court decree.

[73] *Kitson v. Kitson*, 1945 S.C. 434, *per* Lord Justice-Clerk Cooper at 439.

[74] *Udny v. Udny*, (1860) 7 M. (H.L.) 89, *per* Lord Westbury at 99.

[75] *Re Luck* [1940] Ch. 864, p. 891, *per* Scott L.J.

[76] *Kitson v. Kitson*, above at 439; *Radoyevitch v. Radoyevitch*, 1930 S.C. 619 at 624; *Ponder v. Ponder*, 1932 S.C. 233 at 236.

[77] See Anton and Beaumont, *Private International Law* (2nd ed.), pp. 150–152.

[78] Family Law Act 1986, s. 26, as originally enacted. See the Lord Ordinary's judgment in *Calleja v. Calleja*, 1997 S.L.T. 579.

Scotland if the order was made in the country where the child was habitually resident.[79] Habitual residence is to be determined on the date the order was made.

However, foreign judgments relating to the upbringing of children, even **11.17** from courts of competent jurisdiction, will not be recognised or enforced automatically, for the question of enforcement is secondary to the question of the welfare of the child. Since 1925 the child's welfare has by statute been the paramount consideration in any proceedings before the court in which the custody or upbringing of the child was in question.[80] It has consequently been held that an order of a foreign court of competent jurisdiction is entitled to "grave consideration" but not to automatic enforcement[81]; that a foreign order cannot inhibit the Scottish court from reaching an independent conclusion on the merits where the child's welfare so requires[82]; and that there is no presumption that the order of the court of the habitual residence (previously domicile) should be followed.[83] The Scottish court will give effect to an order of a foreign court of competent jurisdiction, provided it is shown that that can be done without injury to the interests of the child and, with orders granting a right of residence, that the party with whom the child is, under the order, required to reside is in a position to make arrangements for the child's welfare. An inquiry into welfare is not always necessary. It is entirely a question of the circumstances of each case but it will often be evident, especially where the foreign order is recent and supported by documents showing that it was based on a full consideration of the child's welfare, that the child could be entrusted to the person in whose favour the foreign order was made without further inquiry.[84]

If a foreign court has been seized of jurisdiction the Scottish court is not **11.18** inhibited from making an order under section 11 of the Children (Scotland) Act 1995 if it has jurisdiction under the Family Law Act 1986.[85] However, in these circumstances the approach of the English court, accepted by the Lord Ordinary in *Calleja v. Calleja*,[86] is likely to be followed as being consistent with the Scottish common law recognition of orders of the court of the habitual residence. The English court has accepted that in cases in which neither the European nor the Hague Convention applies, similar principles to those contained in these conventions should be adopted by the court.[87] The welfare of the child, the Court of Appeal held in *Re F (A Minor: Abduction: Jurisdiction)*, normally requires that the child not be removed from his or her habitual residence, and it

---

[79] Family Law Act 1986, s. 26, as amended by the Children (Scotland) Act 1995, Sched. 4, para. 41(6). It is to be noted that this rule applies only to orders relating to parental responsibilities and parental rights and not to all "Part I orders" as defined in the 1986 Act for the purposes of jurisdiction.

[80] Guardianship of Infants Act 1925, s. 1; Law Reform (Parent and Child) (Scotland) Act 1986, s. 3(2); Children (Scotland) Act 1995, s. 11(7)(a).

[81] *McKee v. McKee* [1951] A.C. 352, P.C., *per* Lord Simonds at 365. *Cf. Radoyevitch v. Radoyevitch*, above; *McLean v. McLean*, 1947 S.C. 79; *Girvan, Petr*, 1985 S.L.T. 92, *per* Lord Stewart at 93–94; *Sinclair v. Sinclair*, 1988 S.L.T. 87, *per* Lord Prosser at 89C.

[82] *Campins v. Campins*, 1979 S.L.T.(Notes) 41; *Radoyevitch v. Radoyevitch*, above; *McKee v. McKee*, above; *Sinclair v. Sinclair*, above.

[83] *Sinclair v. Sinclair*, above, *per* Lord Prosser at 89.

[84] *Sargeant v. Sargeant*, 1973 S.L.T. (Notes) 27; *Campbell v. Campbell*, 1977 S.C. 103; *Lyndon v. Lyndon*, 1978 S.L.T (Notes) 7; *Thomson, Petr*, 1980 S.L.T. (Notes) 29.

[85] See above, paras 9.23 *et seq.*

[86] 1997 S.L.T. 579.

[87] *Re F (A Minor: Abduction: Jurisdiction)* [1990] 3 All E.R. 97; *D v. D (Child Abduction: Non-Convention Country)* [1994] 1 F.L.R. 137; *Re M (Abduction: Non-Convention Country)* [1995] 1 F.L.R. 89. This is also the approach of the Full Court of the Family Court of Australia: *Re the Marriage of Barrios and Sanchez* (1989) 13 Fam. L.R. 477. See, however, *Re P (Abduction: Non-Convention Country)* [1997] 1 F.L.R. 780.

follows from this that the British court asked to make an order when a child has been brought here from his or her habitual residence or against the order of the court of the habitual residence should normally refuse to make any order other than to require the child's immediate return back to his or her habitual residence. It has been made clear, however, that this is so only when the courts of the habitual residence similarly regard the welfare of the child as paramount, and that the court should not assume without some evidence that the court in a non-convention country would so regard the welfare of the child. In unusual cases the ordinary need for the court of the habitual residence to decide the child's future might not be of sufficient benefit to outweigh the other risks inherent in ordering the return of the child.[88] In non-convention cases the welfare of the child is the sole consideration.[89] That consideration is not qualified before a court can refuse to order the child's return as it is in the European Convention by the need for a change of circumstances or as it is in the Hague Convention by a need to show a grave risk that the child will suffer physical or psychological harm or otherwise be placed in an intolerable situation. In that respect, though the underlying principles in the conventions are to be applied in non-convention cases, the rules in the conventions do not govern.

RETURN OF THE CHILD UNDER THE HAGUE CONVENTION

Introduction

11.19   The Hague Convention on the Civil Aspects of International Child Abduction sets out a scheme not for the recognition and enforcement of foreign court orders but for the practical enforcement of "rights of custody" which are being inhibited in an international context. It was brought into legal force in Scotland by the Child Abduction and Custody Act 1985, in Schedule 1 to which the convention is reproduced, in so far as it is adopted into United Kingdom law.[90] The convention is a good deal wider than the European Convention, and not just in its geographical extent. Most significantly, it is not restricted in its terms to "decisions relating to custody", but includes "custody" and "access" rights, whether these rights flow from an order of a court or by operation of law.[91] The Hague Convention on International Child Abduction has proved to be one of the most successful conventions ever produced by the Hague Conference on Private International Law, in terms both of the numbers of countries who have ratified it[92] and of its practical effect, and it has generated a plethora of case law from a number of jurisdictions. It is a procedural and jurisdictional convention which does not attempt to lay down internationally adopted standards or criteria for the resolution of custody or residence disputes; rather it identifies the appropriate jurisdiction within which these disputes are to be resolved. The aim of the Hague Convention is to ensure the "immediate and summary return"[93] of

---

[88]   *Re JA (Child Abduction: Non-Convention Country)* [1998] 1 F.L.R. 231.

[89]   *Re P (Abduction: Non-Convention Country)* [1997] 1 F.L.R. 780.

[90]   The provisions set out in the Schedule have the force of law (s. 1(2)). The full text of the Hague Convention may be found in (1981) 15 Fam.L.Q. 149. See also Anton, "The Hague Convention on International Child Abduction" (1981) 30 I.C.L.Q. 537; Eekelaar, "International Child Abduction by Parents" (1982) 32 Univ.Tor.L.J. 281; Sachs, "Child Abduction" (1988) 18 Fam. Law 81; Crawford, "International Child Abduction" (1990) 35 J.L.S.S. 277.

[91]   Art. 3.

[92]   A full list of signatories and dates of accession to the Hague Convention is to be found in the website of the Hague Conference on Private International Law, with details at http://www.hcch.net/e/status/abdshte.html.

[93]   *MacMillan v. MacMillan*, 1989 S.L.T. 350 at 355A.

children who have been taken across international borders[94] in breach of "rights of custody" granted or recognised by the law of the child's habitual residence.[95] This is achieved by requiring the court or authority in the state in which the child is present to order the return of a child who has been wrongfully removed to or retained in a country other than that in which he or she was habitually resident to the country of his or her habitual residence. In this way a parent will gain no benefit from attempting to seek out a more sympathetic forum than the court of the habitual residence is perceived to be. Return is correctly ordered back to the country of the child's habitual residence and not necessarily back into the possession of the person holding the rights of custody that have been breached.[96] Return must be ordered "forthwith", which means with the minimum of delay[97]: the courts are indeed directed by the convention to "act expeditiously".[98] In addition, the convention aims to assist in the promotion of the peaceful enjoyment of access rights,[99] though breach of a right of access does not oblige the court to order the child's return to his or her habitual residence.[1] The convention ceases to apply when the child attains the age of 16 years.[2]

Cases from countries that are not signatories to the Hague Convention are **11.20** likely to be dealt with by applying analogous principles, as discussed above in relation to non-European Convention cases.[3]

Meaning of "habitual residence"

The convention applies to children who were habitually resident in a **11.21** contracting state immediately before the breach of custody or access rights.[4] "Habitual residence" is for all practical purposes the same as the concept of ordinary residence.[5] It is not a term of art with a special meaning but is to be understood according to the ordinary and natural meaning of the words. It is a residence which is being enjoyed voluntarily[6] for the time being and with the settled intention that it should continue for some time[7]; there is no requirement

---

[94] To remove a child in breach of custody rights from, say, Dumfries to Thurso would not activate the Hague Convention, and domestic enforcement measures would have to be adopted. The Hague Convention is concerned only with international abduction, *i.e.* that in which the child is taken across borders. A child removed from one part of the U.K. to another is dealt with under the provisions of the Family Law Act 1986, discussed above, paras 11.03–11.09.

[95] "The objects of the Convention are—(a) to secure the prompt return of children wrongfully removed to or retained in any contacting State; and (b) to ensure that rights of custody and of access under the law of one contracting State are effectively respected in the other contracting States": Art. 1, Hague Convention.

[96] *Re A (Minor) (Abduction)* (1988) 18 Fam. Law 54; *A v. Central Authority for New Zealand* [1996] 2 N.Z.L.R. 517 at 524, line 20.

[97] *per* Lord President Hope in *Dickson v. Dickson,* 1990 S.C.L.R. 692 at 701B. In *Viola v. Viola,* 1988 S.L.T. 7 it was held that "forthwith" meant as soon as practicable and not necessarily immediately on the conclusion of the court proceedings. The court in that case also decided that the requirement in Art. 13 to consider social background reports could not be used to delay the proceedings until such reports are available. See also *MacMillan v. MacMillan,* 1989 S.L.T. 350, in which the Lord Ordinary was criticised by the Inner House for delaying his decision to see if arrangements could be made to avoid the risk to the child that would have justified refusal of return.

[98] Art. 11.

[99] Art. 21.

[1] See below, para.11.36.

[2] Art. 4.

[3] Above, paras 11.16–11.18.

[4] Art. 4. For a discussion, see Crawford, "'Habitual Residence of the Child' as the Connecting Factor in Child Abduction Cases: A Consideration of Recent Cases", 1992 J.R. 177.

[5] *R. v. Barnet London Borough Council, ex p. Shah* [1983] 2 A.C. 309. The same conclusion was reached by the U.S. Court of Appeals (6th Circuit) in *Friedrich v. Friedrich,* 983 F. (2d.) 1396 (1993).

[6] The Second Division in *Cameron v. Cameron,* 1996 S.L.T. 306 were less convinced that habitual residence required in all cases the element of voluntariness, giving as examples Robinson Crusoe and Nelson Mandela who, they said, might be considered to be habitually resident on their respective islands. In any case it is always rather false to talk of voluntariness in the case of young children.

[7] *Dickson v. Dickson,* 1990 S.C.L.R. 692 at 703A, *per* Lord President Hope.

that the residence be intended to be permanent or indefinite.[8] It may be for a limited period[9] and it is sufficient that there is an intention to reside for an appreciable period.[10] The question whether a person is or is not habitually resident in a specified country is a question of fact to be decided by reference to all the circumstances of any particular case.[11] In the case of a child who can form no intention of his or her own, the child's habitual residence is the residence chosen for him or her by his or her parents. If the parents are living together with the child they will all have their habitual residence in the same place, and if the parents separate the child's habitual residence cannot be changed by one parent without the consent of the other.[12] In *Findlay v. Findlay (No. 2)*[13] a child had been brought by his father from Ontario to Scotland on the separation of his parents, the mother having agreed that the child come to Scotland for four months. The father retained the child in Scotland at the end of that period and argued that the child, now living in Scotland, was habitually resident here at the date of the retention. Lord Cullen, following *Dickson v. Dickson*,[14] found that the mother had agreed to the child coming temporarily to Scotland but not to a change in his habitual residence, which remained in Ontario. The retention was therefore wrongful and return of the child was ordered. The situation might well have been different had the agreement been to allow the child to come to Scotland for a substantially longer period than four months and there are circumstances in which this might be interpreted as an agreement to alter the child's habitual residence.[15] So in *Cameron v. Cameron*[16] a minute of agreement that the children were to remain in France for a number of years was held to amount to an agreement that their habitual residence be changed to France, notwithstanding a clause in the agreement that it be reviewed after six months.[17] Similarly, in *Watson v. Jamieson*[18] an agreement that the children spend alternative two year periods with each parent allowed their habitual residence to change during these periods.[19] Agreement can be inferred from the facts and circumstances, including

---

[8] *Cameron v. Cameron*, 1996 S.L.T. 306.

[9] *Moran v. Moran*, Aug. 25, 1995, OH, approved in *Cameron* at 313H

[10] In *Cameron*, three months was held sufficient and in *V v. B (A Minor) (Abduction)*, [1991] 1 F.L.R. 266 a residence of two months was held sufficient to be described as habitual. In *Department of Health and Casse* (1995) 19 Fam. L.R. 474 the Family Court of Australia held that a parental intention to remain permanently plus slightly more than two months actual residence in Australia was sufficient to fix the children's habitual residence there. See also *Robertson v. Robertson*, March 18, 1997, OH and *Re S (A Minor)* [1997] 4 All E.R. 251.

[11] *Re J (A Minor) (Abduction: Custody Rights)* [1990] 2 A.C. 562, *per* Lord Brandon of Oakbrook at 578G.

[12] *per* Lord President Hope in *Dickson v. Dickson*, 1990 S.C.L.R. 692 at 703B–C. This does, however, rather detract from the view that habitual residence is purely a question of fact. See also *Re J (A Minor) (Abduction: Custody Rights)* [1990] 2 A.C. 562 (*sub nom. C v. S (Minor: Abduction: Illegitimate Child* [1990] 2 All E.R. 961); *Re S (Minors) (Abduction: Wrongful Retention)* [1994] 2 W.L.R. 228; *Re KM (A Minor) (Habitual Residence)* [1996] 2 F.C.R. 333, CA.

[13] 1995 S.L.T. 492.

[14] 1990 S.C.L.R. 692.

[15] Agreement to a change in the child's habitual residence is not in itself consent which amounts to a defence to a "wrongful removal" (see below, paras 11.30–11.31) but it will have the same effect if the new habitual residence is where the child is taken to since the court of that place need not then order return of the child to the country of his or her previous habitual residence.

[16] 1996 S.L.T. 306.

[17] In *Re S (Minors)*, above, an agreement that the children go to England for a year was held not to change the children's habitual residence. *Cf. F v. F (Abduction: Habitual Residence)* [1993] Fam. Law 199, in which there was an agreement between the parents to move the children's habitual residence to England: in these circumstances the Hague Convention could not be relied upon before the English courts.

[18] 1998 S.L.T. 180.

[19] *cf.* the very similar case from Sweden, *Johnson v. Johnson*, mentioned by Clive in "The Concept of Habitual Residence", 1997 J.R. 137 at 140.

the actions of the parties, and it does not have to be express or written. However, it is for the person alleging an agreement to establish its existence and it is the parties' actual state of mind rather than others' perceptions of their state of mind which is relevant to whether agreement has been reached.[20]

Meaning of "rights of custody"

It is only a breach of rights of custody that obliges the court to order the **11.22** child's return. "Rights of custody" are defined in the convention to include "rights relating to the care of the person of the child and, in particular, the right to determine the child's place of residence".[21] They may arise by operation of law or by reason of a judicial or administrative decision, or by reason of an agreement having legal effect under the law of the country of the habitual residence.[22] The phrase does not include the *de facto* care that a parent might be exercising without legal authority.[23] These rights must be granted by or at least recognised under the law of the country of the habitual residence, so an examination of that country's laws is unavoidable. When the convention was first drafted most English speaking countries used the word "custody" in their domestic laws, with the consequent risk of confusion between the domestic definition and the convention meaning of the word, the latter of which was generally somewhat wider than the former. "The purposes of the Hague Convention were, in part at least, humanitarian. The objective is to spare children already suffering from the effects of breakdown in their parents' relationship the further disruption which is suffered when they are taken arbitrarily by one parent from their settled environment and moved to another country... The expression 'rights of custody' when used in the Convention therefore needs to be construed in the sense that will best accord with that objective. In most cases, that will involve giving the term the widest sense possible".[24] More and more countries are dropping the terms "custody" and "access" in favour of terms like "residence" and "contact".[25] Sometimes the amending legislation makes plain that the new terms are to be understood as including "rights of custody" in the Hague Convention sense.[26] The Children (Scotland) Act 1995 contains no such provision but there is little doubt that a person who, in Scotland, has the parental right in section 2(1)(a) of the 1995 Act to have the child living with him or her or otherwise to regulate the child's residence has "rights of custody" protected by the Hague Convention. "Rights of custody" are, however, wider than this and a person in Scotland without the parental right in section 2(1)(a) may nevertheless sometimes be able to rely upon the Hague Convention to have the child returned to Scotland. The court asked to order return must look beyond the form and terms of the parental right being founded upon in order to determine

---

[20] *Robertson v. Robertson*, May 7, 1997, IH.

[21] Art. 5(a).

[22] Art. 3.

[23] *Re J (A Minor) (Abduction: Custody Rights)* [1990] 2 A.C. 562 (*sub nom. C v. S (Minor: Abduction: Illegitimate Child)* [1990] 2 All E.R. 961, *per* Lord Brandon of Oakbrook at 577H; *Re W (A Minor) (Abduction)* [1996] 1 F.C.R. 46. But see *Re B (A Minor) (Abduction)* [1995] 2 F.C.R. 505 in which an unmarried father who had sole *de facto* care with the agreement of the sole legal custodian (the mother) was held to have "rights of custody". Peter Gibson L.J. dissented on the ground that the agreement could not be said to have legal effect.

[24] *per* Waite L.J. in *Re B (A Minor) (Abduction)* [1995] 2 F.C.R. 505 at 517F.

[25] See, *e.g.*, Children Act 1989 (England); Children (Scotland) Act 1995; Family Law Reform Act 1995 (Australia).

[26] See, *e.g.*, s. 42 of the Family Law Reform Act 1995 in Australia, which amended s. 111B of that country's Family Law Act 1975 and provides that each parent of a child should, subject to any court order, be regarded for the purposes of the Hague Convention as having custody of the child, as should any person in whose favour a residence order is made or who is responsible under a specific issue order for the day-to-day care, welfare and development of the child.

whether the right recognised or granted by the law of the child's habitual residence amounts to "rights of custody" within the meaning of the convention. So in *Gross v. Boda*[27] the New Zealand Court of Appeal held that where a mother had been given by an American court "sole care and custody" and the father given "reasonable rights of visitation", the father's right amounted to "rights of custody" for the purposes of the convention. Custody and access were held not to be mutually exclusive, and one of the father's remaining rights was to give agreement to a change in the child's residence: it followed that the parents had jointly the right to determine where the child was to live, with the result that removal of the child by the mother without the father's consent was a breach of the father's "rights of custody". Similarly, it has been held in England that a parent who does not have the day-to-day care and control of the child may nevertheless have "rights of custody" if he or she is entitled to prevent the child being removed to another jurisdiction. In *C v. C*[28] in which an Australian court had granted "custody" to the mother and "joint guardianship" to both her and the father, the Court of Appeal held that, since an aspect of "guardianship" in Australia was that the father had the right to withhold consent to the child's removal from Australia, he had thereby "rights of custody". The same result follows where there is no court order governing the matter but the parents agree that they will both have the right to determine the child's residence or they agree that the parent with whom the child lives will not remove the child from the jurisdiction without the consent of the other.[29] This is so even although no such agreement is in its terms directly enforceable as if it were a binding contract. On the other hand, breach of a right merely to have contact with the child ("rights of access") does not require the court to order return, because that right alone does not carry with it the right to determine the child's place of residence.[30] However, in some legal systems, the right of contact carries with it the right to withhold consent to the child's removal from the jurisdiction. So in New York State, for example, the rule is that the custodial parent cannot move the child's residence such a distance that the other parent's visitation rights are frustrated, without the other parent's consent.[31] In such cases, the holder of the right of contact will be able to seek the child's return if removed without his or her consent. Under English law a residence parent cannot remove a child from the jurisdiction without the written consent of every person with parental responsibilities or the leave of the court.[32] In *Thorne v. Dryden-Hall*[33] the British Columbia Court of Appeal held that a father with a contact order from an English court had a "right of custody" as protected by the Hague Convention because this provision gave him the right to prevent the removal of the child from the jurisdiction. Scots law has a similar rule in section 2(3) and (6) of the Children

---

[27] [1995] 1 N.Z.L.R. 569.

[28] [1989] 2 All E.R. 465.

[29] *Bordera v. Bordera*, 1995 S.L.T. 1176. And see *David S v. Zamira*, 574 NYS (2d) 429 (1991) in which the parents agreed that the mother was to retain day to day care and control of the child but that she was not to relocate away from Toronto. When she took the child to New York, the court there ordered the child's return on the basis that the father's "rights of custody" had been breached. See also *Re B (A Minor) (Abduction)* [1995] 2 F.C.R. 505.

[30] cf. *Pirrie v. Sawacki*, 1997 S.L.T. 1160 in which Lord Coulsfield held that a divorced father who had exercised significant access did not, according to the law of Scotland as it then stood, have any right to determine the child's place of residence, which rested solely with the custodial mother. Since the coming into force of the Children (Scotland) Act 1995, this result would stand (as Lord Coulsfield recognised) only where there was a court order expressly removing the father's parental responsibilities and parental rights, including his right of contact with the child.

[31] See *C v. C (Minors) (Child Abduction)* [1992] 1 F.L.R. 163.

[32] Children Act 1989, s. 13.

[33] (1997) 148 D.L.R. (4th) 508.

(Scotland) Act 1995 which provides, in language reflecting that used in the convention, that where both the child's parents have and are exercising *either* the right to have the child living with him or her or otherwise to regulate the child's residence *or* if the child is not living with him or her the right to maintain personal relations and direct contact with the child on a regular basis, then no one may remove the child from or retain the child outwith the United Kingdom without the consent of both such parents.[34] It is indeed in many circumstances a criminal offence to do so.[35] This right to prevent the child's removal amounts, according to the case law discussed above, to "rights of custody", with the result that a Scottish parent with only the right of contact can require the return of the child to Scotland if removed by the residence parent outwith the United Kingdom.[36] In addition, it sometimes happens that the contact between the child and a parent is so extensive that, even in the absence of any formal parental rights, "rights of custody" can be held to exist. In *Re B*[37] an unmarried father who, according to the law of Western Australia, had no parental rights in relation to his child, assumed the role of primary carer of the child with the consent of the English-resident mother who was drug addicted and therefore unable to look after the child. The father's role as primary carer of the child was held by the Court of Appeal to give him a "settled status... which any court would be bound to uphold" and was therefore a status "which falls properly to be regarded as carrying with it rights [of custody] in the convention sense, breach of which by unauthorised removal would be rendered unlawful within the terms of Articles 3 and 5".[38] In *MacKiver v. MacKiver*,[39] a nine-year-old Australian boy lived much of his time after his parents' divorce with his mother, but spent at least two days each week with his father. He had his own room and clothes in both establishments. There was no court order regulating custody and the mother claimed that the father only had access. Lord Cameron of Lochbroom held that the father, in allowing the child to live with the mother for much of the week, was exercising his right to determine the child's residence. As a result, the mother's removal of the child to Scotland was an infringement of his "rights of custody".[40]

Wrongful removal or retention

The convention applies only when there has been a "wrongful removal or retention" of the child from his or her habitual residence. The wrongfulness that the convention seeks to prevent lies in the removal of the child from the jurisdiction rather than removal from his or her parents.[41] It follows that both parents may be jointly guilty of a wrongful removal or retention.[42] In determining whether there has been a wrongful removal or retention the court must have regard to the purpose of the convention, and its provisions may be brought into

11.23

---

[34] A flaw in these difficult provisions would seem to be that they give a veto only to a parent with the right of contact and not to another person with such a right; and they do not seem to give a veto to a parent with the right of contact if the right of residence lies with a non-parental carer.

[35] Child Abudction Act 1984, s. 6.

[36] See further, Norrie, "The Hague Convention, Rights of Contact, and s. 2(3) and (6) of the Children (Scotland) Act 1995", 1997 S.L.T. (News) 173.

[37] [1995] 2 F.C.R. 505.

[38] *per* Waite L.J. at 518D–E.

[39] 1995 S.L.T. 790.

[40] See further, Bailey, "The Right of the Non-Custodial Parent to an Order for Return of a Child under the Hague Convention" (1996) 13 Can.J.Fam.L. 287.

[41] *per* Lord Brandon of Oakbrook in *Re H and Anor (Minors) (Abduction: Custody Rights)* [1991] 3 All E.R. 230 at 240. And see Lord Justice-Clerk Ross in *Findlay v. Findlay*, 1994 S.L.T. 709 at 713D.

[42] See, *e.g.*, *Ontario Court v. M and M (Abduction: Child's Objections)* [1997] 1 F.L.R. 475.

effect if the removal or retention is prima facie wrongful.[43] It is for the petitioner to establish a wrongful removal or retention. The removal need not have been effected by a parent of the child from whom return is sought and might even, in some circumstances, be instigated by the child him or herself.[44] It is for the court asked to order return to determine whether there has been a wrongful removal or retention and the parties cannot confer jurisdiction on the court by agreeing that there is.[45]

11.24   "Removal" and "retention" are mutually exclusive events, removal occurring when a child who has previously been in the state of his or her habitual residence is taken across the frontier of that state, retention occurring where a child, who has previously been for a limited period of time outside the state of his or her habitual residence, is not returned to that state on the expiry of such limited period.[46] Wrongful retention can also occur before the expiry of the limited period if the parent with possession of the child intimates a decision, or even comes to the unintimated decision, not to return the child at the expiry of the period.[47] Wrongful retention also properly occurs when the child has instigated his or her own removal from the habitual residence and the parent then refuses to return the child (in which case the date of the wrongful act is probably the date the parent fails immediately to send the child home). If wrongful removal is pleaded, the court cannot grant the petition for return on the ground that wrongful retention has been established by the evidence.[48] "Retention", like "removal", is an event (being the initial retention) rather than a continuing state of affairs, otherwise there would be no point from which the one year mentioned in Article 12[49] could be measured.[50] Consequently, a child removed from his or her habitual residence to another country before the convention comes into force between the two countries is not wrongfully retained if he or she is retained after its coming into force.[51] Because of the different nature of access, however, a retention after a removal from a particular country before the convention comes into force there may breach current access rights.[52] Though removal and retention are separate and mutually exclusive, both can occur on the facts in relation to the same child at different times[53] and a lawful retention may, through a change in circumstances, become a wrongful retention.[54] So in the case cited a father who had no rights of custody when a child was removed and originally retained in England and who later acquired by an English court order rights of custody was held able to require the child's return on the basis of a wrongful retention.

---

[43] *per* Lord Murray, giving the opinion of the court in *Perrin v. Perrin*, 1995 S.L.T. 81 at 85E.

[44] The use of the word "abduction" in the title to the convention is, for this reason, misleading. *Cf. Marshall v. Marshall*, 1996 S.L.T. 429 in which a 13-year-old girl willingly flew from Ireland to Scotland in the company of her aunt, to be met in Edinburgh by her father.

[45] So held the Supreme Court of Canada in *W(V) v. S(D)* (1996) 134 D.L.R. (4th) 481.

[46] *per* Lord Brandon of Oakbrook in *Re H and Anor (Minors) (Abduction: Custody Rights)* [1991] 3 All E.R. 230 at 240.

[47] *per* Wall J. in *Re S (Minors) (Abduction: Wrongful Retention)* [1994] 2 W.L.R. 228 at 239C.

[48] *Findlay v. Findlay*, 1994 S.L.T. 709.

[49] See below, para. 11.34.

[50] *per* Lord Brandon of Oakbrook in *Re H and Anor (Minors)*, above at 240.

[51] *Kilgour v. Kilgour*, 1987 S.L.T. 568, followed by the House of Lords in *Re H and Anor (Minors) (Abduction: Custody Rights)*, above, and by the Full Court of the Family Court of Australia in *Re Murray and Tam* (1993) 16 Fam. L.R. 982.

[52] *B v. B (Minors: Enforcement of Access Abroad)* [1988] 1 All E.R. 652 (though the applicant in this case was ultimately unsuccessful since it had not been established that the child was habitually resident in a contracting state before his or her removal).

[53] *per* Lord Slynn of Hadley in *Re S (A Minor)* [1997] 4 All E.R. 251 at 262B.

[54] *ibid.*

Removal or retention is considered to be wrongful where (a) it is in breach **11.25** of rights of custody attributed to a person, an institution or any other body,[55] either jointly or alone, under the law of the state in which the child was habitually resident immediately before the removal or retention and (b) at the time of the removal or retention those rights were actually being exercised, either jointly or alone, or would have been so exercised but for the removal or retention.[56]

Breach of rights of custody

The "rights of custody" must be granted or recognised by the law of the **11.26** habitual residence rather than by the law of the forum, though whether they are breached within the meaning of the convention is an issue for the court of the forum.[57] It is a breach of "rights of custody" to act in such a way that these rights cannot be exercised, even when the abducting parent is ostensibly exercising his or her own rights. "Where the law concedes, or the court grants, joint custody rights, the removal of a child by one parent without the consent of the other would clearly be a wrongful removal in the sense of article 3".[58] This is because the removal by one parent, exercising his or her own rights of custody by determining a child's residence, may well have the effect of denying the other parent of the practical power to exercise their rights. The true question is whether there has been a breach of the right recognised in the Hague Convention and an act that prevents a person exercising recognised rights is a breach within the meaning of the convention even when it is otherwise lawful. This is put beyond doubt in relation to Scots law by section 2(3) and (6) of the Children (Scotland) Act 1995, which provides that no person shall remove a child who is habitually resident in Scotland from the United Kingdom, or retain any such child outwith the United Kingdom, unless with the consent of both parents (if both have the parental rights of either residence or contact). Removal or retention by one

---

[55] In some countries it has been held that when a court has the power to determine a child's residence then the court has "rights of custody". So in, *e.g.*, *Thomson v. Thomson* (1994) 119 D.L.R. (4th) 253 the Supreme Court of Canada held that the Court of Session, having been seised in a custody dispute, itself had "rights of custody" until such time as the case was disposed of: consequently when the mother removed the child from Scotland to Canada in breach of the interim custody order in her favour, there was a wrongful removal. And in *B v. B* [1993] 2 All E.R. 144 it was held that a court seised of the matter had the right to determine custody and thereby had "rights of custody" under the convention, at least until it made its decision (see also *Re W, Re B (Child Abduction: Unmarried Father)* [1998] 2 F.L.R. 146). This was doubted by Lord Prosser in *Seroka v. Bellah*, 1995 S.L.T. 204. Even if a court determining a child's custody does have such a right (being a right to determine the child's place of residence) it is difficult to see how a court could ever "exercise" that right. In any case it could not be argued that a Scottish court, having made a residence order, retained a right to determine the child's residence because it retains the power to vary the order.

[56] Art. 3.

[57] *Re F (A Minor) (Abduction: Risk if Returned)* [1996] 1 F.C.R. 379. The habit of wronged parents in seeking a declarator from the court of the habitual residence is problematic since such a declarator will not bind the court asked to order the child's return to accept that there has been a wrongful removal.

[58] Anton and Beaumont, *Private International Law* (2nd ed.), p. 531. See *C v. C* [1989] 2 All E.R. 465; *Gross v. Boda* [1995] 1 N.Z.L.R. 569; *Re F (A Minor) (Abduction: Risk if Returned)* [1996] 1 F.C.R. 379. In *Taylor v. Ford*, 1993 S.L.T. 654 a father who had removed a child from Canada was found to be not guilty of a wrongful removal since the mother failed to establish that she too had custody rights in the child.

parent without the consent of the other is a breach of section 2(3) and (6) which, as explained above, creates "rights of custody" and is therefore "wrongful".[59]

Actual exercise of rights

11.27   If the rights of custody were not actually being exercised at the time of the removal or retention, there is no wrongfulness, and the convention can be relied upon only by those who are actually exercising their rights (or would be but for the wrongful act) and not by those who allow others to do so.[60] This causes some difficulty for a parent who has separated from the other parent and the child before the removal or retention from the jurisdiction, for such a person may be vulnerable to the challenge that he or she is not actually exercising his or her "rights of custody". It would frustrate the aims of the convention if a parent, by preventing all contact between the child and the non-resident parent before removal from the jurisdiction were thereby able to deny the non-resident parent's rights under the convention. The courts have recognised this and have been willing to accept that a person can exercise their "rights of custody" even when they do not have and cannot exercise day-to-day care and control of the person of the child. The most extensive discussion of this question is found in a decision of the U.S. Court of Appeals (6th Circuit). That court considered that, in the absence of any definition in the convention of "exercise", it would be inappropriate for any domestic court to attempt a definition to be applied in its own country. "The only acceptable solution", they concluded, "is to liberally find 'exercise' whenever a parent with *de jure* custody rights keeps, or seeks to keep, any sort of regular contact with his or her child".[61] If, for example, a person with *de jure* rights asserts his or her rights or seeks to vindicate them in legal proceedings, he or she will be regarded as exercising "rights of custody": in other words, attempts to exercise custody rights are sufficient.[62] Indeed, a person can be said to be exercising a right to determine the child's place of residence by permitting residence with the other parent[63] and it is to be noted that Article 5 defines "right of custody" to include in particular the "right to determine the child's place of residence" rather than "the right to have the child living with the right-holder". This suggests that no actual residence of the child with the petitioner is required to establish that the petitioner is actually exercising custody rights. So long as the petitioner has a legal right to prevent the removal of the child then, so long as that right is not abandoned or, *a fortiori*, if refusal has been expressed, it can be said that "rights of custody" are being exercised.[64] Likewise if there is some continuing positive act, such as the attempt to vindicate

---

[59] A guardian's consent would seem not to be required by this provision. A parent can remove the child in the exercise of his or her own parental rights, satisying the requirement in s. 2(3) that the consent of "a person" with parental rights be obtained; s. 2(6) is limited to requiring the consent of "both the child's parents". Nevertheless if a non-parental guardian has the right in s. 2(1)(a) to have the child living with him or her or otherwise to regulate the child's residence, then that guardian has "rights of custody" since s. 7(5) provides that a person appointed guardian under that section has all the responsibilities and rights imposed and conferred by ss. 1 and 2 with the result that a removal without the guardian's consent will be a breach of the guardian's "rights of custody". In the reverse situation when a guardian removes a child against the wishes of a parent who has the right of contact, there is no breach of rights of custody since the right of contact carries with it a veto on the child's removal only in the case of two parents (see Norrie, 1997 S.L.T. (News) 173).

[60] Art. 3(a).

[61] *Friedrich v. Friedrich (No. 2)*, 78 F. (3d) 1060 (1996), *per* Boggs C.J. at 1065.

[62] *Urness v. Minto*, 1994 S.L.T. 988.

[63] *Re W (A Minor) (Abduction)* [1996] 1 F.C.R. 46. *Cf. MacKiver v. MacKiver*, 1995 S.L.T. 790; *Bordera v. Bordera*, 1995 S.L.T. 1176.

[64] *Police Commissioner of South Australia v. Temple* [1993] F.L.C. 79–819; *MacKiver v. MacKiver*, 1995 S.L.T. 790.

custody rights as in *Urness v. Minto*[65] or regular though limited residential contact as in *MacKiver v. MacKiver*[66] then "rights of custody" are being exercised. The U.S. Court of Appeals concluded that "if a person has valid custody rights to a child under the law of the country of the child's habitual residence, that person cannot fail to 'exercise' those custody rights under the Hague Convention short of acts that constitute clear and unequivocal abandonment of the child"[67] and, if the purposes of the convention are not to be frustrated by the abducting parent preventing all contact between the child and the other parent before the removal from the jurisdiction, this test may well commend itself to the Scottish courts also.

Central authorities

Like the European Convention, the Hague Convention establishes central **11.28** authorities[68] (being the same as those established under the European Convention) which can be (but do not need to be) approached for assistance by persons whose rights have been breached, and which have various duties in relation to discovering the whereabouts of the child, to prevent harm to the child, to ensure his or her safe return, for the raising of proceedings with a view to securing the return of the child and in co-operating with other central authorities.[69]

Grounds for refusing to order return

The grounds upon which a Scottish court, asked to order the return of a **11.29** child under the Hague Convention, can refuse to do so are a good deal narrower than the grounds under the European Convention for the refusal of recognition or enforcement of custody decisions. It is provided under the Hague Convention that the judicial or administrative authority of the state to which the child has been taken is not bound to order the return of the child to his or her habitual residence if the person who opposes the return establishes—and the onus is always on the respondent to the petition[70]—one or more of the four situations[71] shortly to be discussed. The court has the discretion and is not bound to refuse return even when one of the grounds for refusal has been established.[72] A two-stage process must therefore be followed. First, the court must decide whether the respondent has established that a ground for refusal to order return exists or not. This is an issue of fact, which is not determined by consideration of the welfare of the child. If no ground is found to exist the court's obligation to grant the petition and order the child's return to the country of his or her habitual residence is mandatory. If, on the other hand, one or more of the grounds is found to exist the court must then move to the second stage, which is to determine whether to order return or to refuse the petition for return. That decision is to be made by balancing the requirements of the convention on the one hand with the

---

[65] 1994 S.L.T. 988.
[66] 1995 S.L.T. 790.
[67] *Friedrich v. Friedrich*, 78 F. (3d.) 1060 (1996) at 1066.
[68] Child Abduction and Custody Act 1985, s. 3(1).
[69] Art. 7. See Bruch, "The Central Authority's Role under the Hague Child Abduction Convention: A Friend in Deed" (1994) 28 Fam. L.Q. 35.
[70] *per* Lord Justice-Clerk Ross in *Urness v. Minto*, 1994 S.L.T. 988 at 997. See also the opening words of Art. 13.
[71] The Hague Convention itself contains a fifth ground for refusing to order return: Art. 20, that return would be inconsistent with the fundamental principles of the requested state relating to protection of human rights and fundamental freedoms. This ground has not generated the case law in countries accepting it that the other grounds have.
[72] Art. 18.

interests of the child on the other, and it is only in exceptional cases that the court should refuse to order the immediate return of the child once a wrongful removal or retention has been established.[73] In all cases in deciding whether to exercise its discretion to refuse return, the child's welfare as a general factpor must be given consideration.[74] Even when a ground for refusing to order return exists, the presumption will be in favour of ordering such return. In an unusual decision, *Clarke v. Carson*,[75] the High Court of New Zealand seemed to take account of the likely outcome of the action in the court of the habitual residence in deciding not to return the children. The father accepted in the New Zealand court that he would only be seeking access in the court of the habitual residence (in the U.S.) and would permit the children to reside in New Zealand. In these circumstances the New Zealand court (having found a ground for refusing return to exist) held that it would serve no purpose other than disruption in the children's lives to return them to the U.S. for what would almost certainly be a very limited period of time. In most cases, however, the possible outcome of the custody or residence dispute will have no bearing on whether the child should be returned to the country where that dispute is to be resolved.

The grounds for refusal to order return are as follows.

Consent or acquiescence

11.30 The court is not bound to order the return of the child if the person opposing the return establishes that the person, institution or other body having the care of the person of the child was not actually exercising the custody rights at the time of removal or retention, or had consented to or subsequently acquiesced in the removal or retention.[76] The first limb of this provision simply reflects the definition of wrongful removal or retention as discussed above. The second limb concerns consent or acquiescence to the removal by the person seeking return (that is to say, the petitioner). Consent can be express, or by necessary implication (though most examples of implied consent will more properly be regarded as acquiescence). Whether or not the petitioner has consented to the child's removal is a question of fact and it has been held in England that the evidence to establish consent requires to be clear, compelling and positive.[77] In *Zenel v. Haddow*[78] the First Division, by a majority, rejected the contention that when the convention talks of consent "to the removal", this means consent to the specific act of removal being complained about rather than a more general consent to removal at some future time. Lord Morton of Shuna dissented on the basis that the convention clearly refers to the particular removal in question and that otherwise the consent, once given, could never be revoked. It is submitted, with respect, that this conclusion does not follow the premise and that all that a respondent, seeking to persuade a court that this ground for refusal exists, need show is that the removal occurred at a time when there was consent to removal which had not been revoked.

---

[73] *Urness v. Minto*, above, *per* Lord Penrose at 993G–J, and authorities cited there; *Marshall v. Marshall*, 1996 S.L.T. 429 at 433E–F; *Singh v. Singh*, 1998 S.L.T. 1084 at 1095B.

[74] *Singh v. Singh*, above, at 1095D–E. The court here took account of "social, educational and psychological benefit" in the child's remaining in Scotland. These matters are, with respect, better left to the court of the habitual residence to assess.

[75] [1996] 1 N.Z.L.R. 349.

[76] Art. 13(a).

[77] *Re W (A Minor) (Abduction)* [1996] 1 F.C.R. 46.

[78] 1993 S.L.T. 975, discussed by Maher in "Consent to Wrongful Child Abduction under the Hague Convention", 1993 S.L.T. (News) 281.

Acquiescence will generally be an implication drawn from the petitioner's **11.31** acts or failure to act, though the circumstances in which that implication may be drawn created some controversy in England. In *Re A and Anor (Minors) (Abduction: Acquiescence)*, the Court of Appeal held that acquiescence can be either (1) active acceptance of the removal or retention, signified by express words of consent or by conduct inconsistent with an intention to insist on legal rights or (2) passive acquiescence inferred from silence and inactivity for a sufficient period in circumstances where different conduct was reasonably to be expected on the part of the aggrieved parent.[79] This was interpreted to mean that acquiescence depended not on the wronged parent's subjective state of mind but on his or her conduct, viewed objectively.[80] The House of Lords, however, warned against drawing a rigid distinction between active and passive acquiescence, which was not to be found in the words of the convention. They held instead that "acquiescence", as used in Article 13, refers to the subjective state of mind of the wronged parent rather than the outside world's perception of his or her intentions, though that state of mind can be inferred from the outward and visible acts of the wronged parent.[81] Lord Browne-Wilkinson, with whom the other four members of the Judicial Committee agreed, laid down the following principles:

> "(1) For the purpose of Article 13 of the Convention, the question whether the wronged parent has 'acquiesced' in the removal or retention of the child depends upon his actual state of mind. As Neill L.J. said in *Re S (Minors)*[82] 'the court is primarily concerned, not with the question of the other parent's perception of the applicant's conduct, but with the question whether the applicant acquiesced in fact'.
> (2) The subjective intention of the wronged parent is a question of fact for the trial judge to determine in all the circumstances of the case, the burden of proof being on the abducting parent.
> (3) The trial judge, in reaching his decision on that question of fact, will no doubt be inclined to attach more weight to the contemporaneous words and actions of the wronged parent than to his bare assertion in evidence of his intention. But that is a question of the weight to be attached to evidence and is not a question of law.
> (4) There is only one exception. Where the words or actions of the wronged parent clearly and unequivocally show and have led the other parent to believe that the wronged parent is not asserting or going to assert his right to the summary return of the child and are inconsistent with such return, justice requires that the wronged parent be held to have acquiesced."[83]

The exception, which appears to be a form of personal bar, will only arise in "strictly exceptional cases", in which "the words or actions of the wronged party show clearly and unequivocally that the wronged parent is not insisting on the summary return of the child: they must be wholly inconsistent with a request for the summary return of the child".[84] In the instant case, the father's

---

[79] *Re A and Anor (Minors) (Abduction: Acquiescence)* [1992] 1 All E.R. 929, approved in *Souci v. Souci* 1995 S.L.T. 414; *Clarke v. Carson* [1996] 1 N.Z.L.R. 349 (High Court of New Zealand).
[80] *Re AZ (A Minor) (Abduction: Acquiescence)* [1993] 1 F.L.R. 682; *Re S (Minors) (Abduction: Acquiescence)* [1994] 1 F.L.R. 819.
[81] *Re H and Ors (Minors)* [1997] 2 All E.R. 225.
[82] [1994] 1 F.L.R. 819.
[83] [1997] 2 All E.R. at 237D–G.
[84] *ibid.* at 236H–J.

recourse to a religious court in Israel (the children's habitual residence) rather than immediately to the English court to order return was held to be far from satisfying that test. Similarly, attempts to negotiate with the abducter after the child has been removed rather than immediately invoking the convention in-court should not be interpreted as acquiescence[85]: "to do so could lead lawyers to refuse to talk or negotiate at all for fear of creating the impression of acquiescence, and could encourage litigation at the expense of a more amiable resolution."[86] So there was no acquiescence when an American father wrote to the abducting mother indicating that he would not do anything to remove the child and suggesting a reconciliation.[87] Nor will requests for access do anything more than show the wronged parent's desire to preserve contact with the child.[88] Inactivity that can be explained will not give rise to an inference of acquiescence (at least not if the explanation is reasonable and is believed). In *Souci v. Souci*[89] the petitioner's delay in seeking return of his child was explained by refusal of legal aid followed by bad legal advice in his attempts to seek the return of his children. Both the Lord Ordinary and the Inner House had little difficulty in finding in these circumstances that an inference of acquiescence could not be drawn.[90]

Grave risk of harm or intolerable situation

11.32	The court is not bound to order the return of the child if the person opposing the return establishes that there is a grave risk that the child's return would expose the child to physical or psychological harm or otherwise place the child in an intolerable situation.[91] The *tempus inscipiendum* in assessing the risks is the present time, but account can be taken of facts in the future in forming a picture of what would happen if the child were returned.[92] It is not enough to establish this ground of refusal that it would be against the best interests of the child to be sent back: the matter before the court is restricted to determining whether or not the party opposing the return has established the existence of a grave risk of the kind specified.[93] The child's welfare is to be determined by the court of the habitual residence and courts have been impatient with evidence which may be relevant to resolution of the "custody" dispute but which does not indicate harm of the nature required to refuse return. Were it otherwise, the whole convention would be nullified and the matter dealt with according to the domestic law of Scotland.[94] "Grave" risk means a "weighty" risk, of "substantial

---

[85] In *Re H and Ors (Minors)* [1997] 2 All E.R. 225 at 235J, Lord Browne-Wilkinson said this: "I would suggest judges should be slow to infer an intention to acquiesce from attempts by the wronged parent to effect a reconciliation or to reach an agreed voluntary return of the abducted child". See, further, *P v. P (Abduction: Acquiescence)* [1998] 2 F.L.R. 835.

[86] Silberman, "Hague Convention on International Child Abduction" (1994) 28 Fam. L.Q. 9 at 26.

[87] *Re R (Minors: Child Abduction)* [1995] 2 F.C.R. 609. Nor was there acquiescence when a German father agreed to the children remaining with the mother in the U.S. during a reconciliation attempt: *Warringer v. Warringer* 850 F. Supp. 78 (1994); see also *Currier v. Currier*, 845 F. Supp. 918 (1994).

[88] *Re H and Ors (Minors) per* Lord Browne-Wilkinson at 236J–237A. *Cf.*, however, *Re S (Abduction: Acquiescence)* [1998] 2 F.L.R. 115.

[89] 1995 S.L.T. 414.

[90] The same result was reached on similar facts by the Court of Appeal in *Re S (Minors) (Abduction: Acquiescence)* [1994] 2 F.C.R. 945. And in *Re B (Minors) (Hague Convention) (No. 2)* [1994] 1 F.C.R. 394 it was held that acquiescence could not be inferred from an agreement for the child to remain in the U.K. for the duration of the court proceedings. See also *P v. P (Abduction: Acquiescence)* [1998] 1 F.L.R. 630 and *Re D (Abduction: Acquiescence)* [1998] 2 F.L.R. 335.

[91] Art. 13(b).

[92] *per* Lord Prosser in *McCarthy v. McCarthy*, 1994 S.L.T. 743 at 746C.

[93] *Viola v. Viola*, 1988 S.L.T. 7 at 10, *per* Lord McCluskey.

[94] "When we trust the court system in the abducted-from country, the vast majority of claims of harm—those that do not rise to the level of gravity required by the Convention—evaporate": *Friedrich v. Friedrich (No. 2)*, 78 F. (3d.) 1060 (1996) at 1068.

and not trivial" harm.[95] It is a high and strict test that the respondent faces in establishing this ground.[96] The ground was held to be not established on the basis that a child, if returned, would be looked after by an elderly grandfather who spoke no English,[97] nor when the father to whom return was opposed suffered from a diabetic condition, abused alcohol and had only a limited ability to cope with stress.[98] Lord Prosser held in the latter case that the evidence showed that the situation was "less than ideal", but that this fell far short of what was required to satisfy this ground of refusal. And in *Re K (A Minor) (Abduction: Psychological Harm)*[99] it was held that there was no grave risk of harm to the child in being returned to the United States even although the mother could not provide the child with a home there and would indeed not be permitted to remain under immigration rules, for the evidence showed that the child would have a home with the father's grandmother, with whom the child had previously lived, until the American court made its decision on custody. When a mother, who had wrongfully removed her child from his habitual residence in Australia, refused to return to Australia if the child were sent back there it was held that there was not an intolerable position even although the mother's presence was deemed necessary for the child's welfare.[1] As Butler-Sloss L.J. put it, "If the grave risk of psychological harm to a child is to be inflicted by the conduct of the parent who abducted him, then it would be relied on by every mother of a young child who removed him out of the jurisdiction and refused to return. It would drive a coach and four through the convention, at least in respect of applications relating to young children".[2] This was followed by the Inner House in *Whitley, Petitioner*,[3] and by Lord Abernethy in *Starr, Petitioner*[4] holding that an unsubstantiated allegation of sexual abuse did not create an intolerable situation. Stress to the child caused by his or her wrongful removal and the continuing stress that a further dislocation will invariably cause cannot be used to found this ground for refusing to return the child.[5] On the other hand, return was refused under this ground in *MacMillan v. MacMillan*[6] because the father, from whom the mother had wrongfully removed the child, had a long history of alcoholism and depression; and in *Urness v. Minto*[7] return was refused because it would have meant splitting up the children, which in the circumstances (described below) was considered to be intolerable. In *Re F (A Minor)*[8] return was refused when serious allegations of violence against the mother were not

---

[95] *Re A (Minor) (Abduction)* (1988) 18 Fam. Law 54, *per* Nourse L.J. See also *Whitley, Petr,* 1998 Fam. L.R. 7.

[96] *C v. C* [1989] 2 All E.R. 465; *B v. B* [1993] 2 All E.R. 144. In the U.S., the enacting legislation, the International Child Abduction Remedies Act 1988, 42 U.S.C. ss. 11601 at ss. 11603(e)(2)(A), provides that grave risk or intolerable situation must be established by "clear and convincing evidence".

[97] *Viola v. Viola,* 1988 S.L.T. 7.

[98] *McCarthy v. McCarthy,* 1994 S.L.T. 743.

[99] [1996] 1 F.C.R. 24.

[1] *C v. C (Abduction: Right of Custody)* [1989] 2 All E.R. 465.

[2] *ibid.* at 471.

[3] 1998 Fam. L.R. 7.

[4] 1998 S.C.L.R. 775.

[5] *Clarke v. Carson* [1996] 1 N.Z.L.R. 349, *per* Elias J. at 353. In *Friedrich v. Friedrich (No. 2),* 78 F. (3d.) 1060 (1996) at 1068 the U.S. Court of Appeals (6th Circuit) said this: "Under the logic of the Convention, it is the *abduction* that causes the pangs of subsequent return. The distruption of the usual sense of attachment that arises during most long stays in a single place with a single parent should not be a 'grave' risk of harm for the purposes of the Convention".

[6] 1989 S.L.T. 350.

[7] 1994 S.L.T. 988.

[8] [1996] 1 F.C.R. 379.

[9] *cf. Re SS and DK Bassi* (1994) 17 Fam. L.R. 571 in which similar allegations were made but return was nevertheless ordered by the Family Court of Australia since the mother had allowed the allegedly violent father access to the children and there was no evidence to suggest that he might direct violence towards them.

denied by the father.[9] And in *Re G (Child Abduction: Psychological Harm)*[10] return was refused when an abducting mother established that return would cause a serious deterioration in her own physical and psychological well-being, which in turn would affect the children. This is a particularly liberal interpretation of the defence, which sits uneasily with earlier English decisions, but it may be explained by the very young ages of the children in the case.[11] A somewhat stricter approach is apparent in the judgment of the United States Court of Appeals in *Friedrich v. Friedrich*[12] where it was held that this ground can be satisfied in only two situations: "First, there is a grave risk of harm when return of the child puts the child in imminent danger *prior* to the resolution of the custody dispute—*e.g.* returning the child to a zone of war, famine or disease. Second, there is a grave risk of harm in cases of serious abuse or neglect, or extraordinary emotional dependence, when the court in the country of the habitual residence, for whatever reason, may be incapable or unwilling to give the child adequate protection." This strict approach has much to commend it.[13]

Mature child's objection

11.33   The court may also refuse to order the return of the child if it finds that the child objects to being returned and has attained an age and degree of maturity at which it is appropriate to take account of his or her views.[14] A child aged 12 years or more is presumed by the law of Scotland to be capable of forming and expressing views on many matters[15] and while none of these provisions is expressed to apply to decisions under the Child Abduction and Custody Act 1985[16] nevertheless a presumption of fact that a child of 12 years or more has reached a sufficient maturity would not, it is submitted, be inappropriate in the present context. There are three questions which the court requires to consider when dealing with this ground for refusing to order return: (1) whether the child objects to being returned, (2) if so whether the child has attained an age and degree of maturity at which it is appropriate to take account of his or her views and (3) if so whether the court is prepared to exercise its discretion to refuse to order the return of the child.[17] The first two issues are matters that can be determined only on a case-to-case basis, and are matters of fact; the third is a matter for the court's discretion to be exercised in favour of refusal only in exceptional cases, and taking account of the child's welfare. "Maturity" refers to mental maturity. In *Urness v. Minto*[18] two boys, aged 12 and nine, had been wrongfully removed from California to Scotland. The Lord Ordinary found that the older child was of an age and maturity that his views should be taken into account, but that the younger child was not. The older child objected to being sent back to California, and it was held that in these circumstances it would put the younger in an intolerable situation to be sent back alone, therefore

---

[10] [1995] 2 F.C.R. 22, upheld on appeal Dec. 19, 1994.

[11] See also *Re F (Minor: Abduction)* [1995] 3 All E.R. 641.

[12] 78 F. (3d.) 1060 (1996) (6th Circuit) at 1069.

[13] This approach can be seen also in the Court of Appeal in New Zealand in *A v. Central Authority for New Zealand* [1996] 2 N.Z.L.R. 517.

[14] Art. 13.

[15] See, *e.g.*, Children (Scotland) Act 1995, ss. 6(1), 11(10) and 16(2); Age of Legal Capacity (Scotland) Act 1991, s. 2(4A); Adoption (Scotland) Act 1978, s. 6(2).

[16] Any order for return is made under the 1985 Act and is not an order under s. 11 of the 1995 Act, notwithstanding that it concerns parental responsibilities and parental rights, otherwise the Scottish court's views of the child's welfare would have to be regarded as being paramount.

[17] *Marshall v. Marshall*, 1996 S.L.T. 429 at 433D–E.

[18] 1994 S.L.T. 988.

neither was returned: this approach was held to be proper by the Inner House.[19] The court does not have to accept the child's views, and it should pay regard to the child's motives for expressing an objection. In *Marshall v. Marshall* the Lord Ordinary ordered return of a 13-year-old girl who objected to being returned to Ireland on the ground that there was no sufficient substance in the reasons given for her objection to returning, and that therefore the circumstances were not sufficiently exceptional to justify a departure from the general aim of the convention. This was upheld on appeal.[20] Also, and in particular, the court will give little weight to the expressed views of a child if it seems that he or she has been influenced by the abducting parent or because the objection to return is based on no more than a wish to remain with the abducting parent.[21] These matters, concerning as they do the weight to be accorded to the child's expressed views, are for the court of the habitual residence to take into account in making the custody or residence decision, rather than the court determining whether or not to order return. On the other hand, an order for return was discharged by the Court of Appeal in the unusual case of *Re M (Child Abduction: Child's Objection to Return)*[22], in which a 13-year-old child appealed in his own name against the order for his return. He alleged that he had suffered physical and psychological abuse for many years at the hands of his mother and her cohabitant and the Court of Appeal held that these objections to return[23] were sufficiently weighty to allow them to exercise their discretion to refuse to order return.[24]

Settlement in new environment

In a case in which a period of more than one year has elapsed from the date **11.34** of the wrongful removal or retention,[25] the court must order return unless it is demonstrated by the respondent that the child is now settled in his or her new environment.[26] The whole purpose of the convention is to minimise disruption in the life of the child, and this ground for refusal to order return is based on the assumption that to unsettle the child more than is necessary will invariably be against his or her welfare—as always, the parent's "right" to custody or residence takes second place to the welfare of the child. This ground for refusing return is available only when the proceedings are commenced more than one year after the removal or retention: it cannot be pleaded when proceedings commence before but are not completed until after the year. In *Souci v. Souci*[27] Lord Sutherland, delivering the opinion of an Extra Division, said this:

---

[19] The same result was reached on substantially similar facts in *Re SS & DK Bassi* (1994) 17 Fam. L.R. 571 (Fam. Ct Aust.) and in *Singh v. Singh*, 1998 SLT 1084. *Urness* was approved in the High Court of Australia in *De L v. Director General, New South Wales Department of Community Services* (1996) 139 A.L.R. 417, in which is contained a useful discussion of this ground for refusing to order return. The case itself is usefully discussed by Nygh in (1997) 11 Aust.J.Fam.L. 1. See also *B v. K (Child Abduction)* [1993] Fam. Law 17.

[20] 1996 S.L.T. 429. *Cf.* the English case of *Re B (Abduction: Child's Objections)* [1998] 1 F.L.R. 667 where the objections of 12- and seven-year-old boys prevented the court ordering their return to Ireland to a father they disliked and of whom they had unhappy memories. See also *Matznick v. Matznick*, Nov. 9, 1994, OH.

[21] *Re S (A Minor) (Abduction: Custody Rights)* [1993] Fam. 242, CA.

[22] [1995] 1 F.C.R. 170.

[23] Backed up by evidence that he had been received into care on a number of occasions while in his mother's custody.

[24] *cf. Re HB (Abduction: Child's Objections) (No. 2)* [1998] 1 F.L.R. 564, where the English court was clearly not happy with a 12-year-old child being a litigant in the case. In *Re P (Abduction: Minor's Views)* [1998] 2 F.L.R. 825 a 13-year-old with very clearly expressed views was given leave to appeal against an order for return.

[25] Remembering that retention is an act referable to a specific date: see above, para. 11.24.

[26] Art. 12.

[27] 1995 S.L.T. 414.

"having regard to the context we consider that the proper question is whether the child is so settled in her new environment that the court would be justified in disregarding an otherwise mandatory requirement to have the child returned. This is another way of saying that the interest of the child in not being uprooted is so cogent that it outweighs the primary purpose of the convention, namely return of the child to the proper jurisdiction so that the child's future may be determined in the appropriate place... What must be clearly shown is that the settlement in a new environment is so well established that it overrides the otherwise clear duty of the court to order the return of the child."[28]

11.35   In general terms, the longer the lapse of time after the expiry of the year the more likely it is that the child will be found to have settled in a new environment, and if the time is very short, a matter of days or weeks, the quality of the evidence relied upon to establish settlement would have to be good.[29] There are two important constituent elements of "settlement": a physical element of relating to a community and an environment, and an emotional element denoting security and stability.[30] In *Perrin v. Perrin*[31] a child removed from France had been in Scotland for 14 months (out of 23 months of life) but had been settled in her new home for only three or four months. In these circumstances it was held that there was no "settlement" for the purposes of this defence. The Family Court of Australia has held that mere presence in a country for over a year does not raise any presumption of settlement.[32]

Access
11.36   "Rights of access", which are defined to include "the right to take a child for a limited period of time to a place other than the child's habitual residence"[33] are protected by Article 21, though that protection is a good deal less than that afforded to rights of custody.[34] A breach of rights of access does not oblige the court to order the return of the child,[35] for "it is not wrongful, within the meaning of the Convention, to remove or retain a child in circumstances which frustrate the enjoyment of rights of access".[36] Article 21 merely requires the central authorities to promote the peaceful enjoyment of access rights and the fulfilment of any conditions to which the exercise of those rights may be subject. Central authorities must also take steps to remove, as far as possible, all obstacles to the exercise of such rights and may (but are not obliged to[37]) initiate or assist proceedings to vindicate access rights. An application to make arrangements for organising or securing the effective exercise of rights of access may be presented to the central authorities in the same way as an application for the return of the child. The rights of access that are protected in this way are rights granted or recognised by the law of the child's habitual residence, and it is not

---

[28] 1999 S.L.T. 414 at 417–418.

[29] *per* Lord Murray in *Perrin v. Perrin*, 1995 S.L.T. 81 at 85.

[30] *per* Bracewell J in *Re N (Minors) (Abduction)* [1991] 1 F.L.R. 413 at 418, accepted by the Inner House in *Perrin v. Perrin*, above.

[31] 1995 S.L.T. 81.

[32] *Graziano v. Daniels* (1991) 14 Fam. L.R. 697.

[33] Art. 5.

[34] See Lowe, "Problems Relating to Access Disputes Under the Hague Convention on International Child Abduction" (1994) 8 Int. J.L. and Fam. 374.

[35] See *W(V) v. S(D)* (1996) 134 D.L.R. (4th) 481 (Sup. Ct Canada).

[36] *per* Lord MacFadyen in *MD, Petr*, March 3, 1999.

[37] Lowe, however, (*op. cit.* at p. 385 n. 32) suggests that an argument can be made that "may" means "shall" on the basis that the apparent discretion in Art. 21 should be read with the obligation in Art. 7 to take "all appropriate measures" to initiate the institution of proceedings.

necessary to show that the child has been wrongfully removed before invoking Article 21[38]: a consequence of this is that a change in the child's habitual residence does not affect the applicability of Article 21, which can still be invoked even when the child is now habitually resident in the country where the enforcement proceedings are raised.[39] Article 21 does not in itself create any right which a party can enforce in a court, but merely obliges central authorities to initiate or assist proceedings for the recognition of access rights under the rules of the forum; the remedy for any failure by the central authority to comply with its obligations under Article 21 is judicial review.[40] It follows that if the child has been taken to a country other than his or her habitual residence, the direct enforcement of rights of access can be achieved by raising normal proceedings for access or contact in the courts of the country where the child is.[41] In most Hague Convention countries, the child's welfare will be regarded as the paramount consideration, and in assessing welfare it would consist with the philosophy of the convention for courts to pay regard to any rights of access under the law of the child's previous habitual residence. However, "the weight which will be accorded to the foreign order will be a matter of the circumstances of the particular case".[42] And it is to be remembered that access decisions from European Convention countries can be recognised and enforced in terms of that Convention.[43]

---

[38] "Wrongful removal" is an Art. 3 concept, limited to rights of custody. If, however, there has been a "wrongful removal" the wronged parent can insist on return even if his or her motivation for doing so is merely to enforce rights of contact. See, *e.g.*, the facts of *Clarke v. Carson* [1996] 1 N.Z.L.R. 349, as discussed above, para. 11.29.

[39] *Re G (A Minor) (Hague Convention: Access)* [1993] 3 All E.R. 657.

[40] *ibid.*

[41] *Re T (Minors) (Hague Convention) (Access)* [1993] 2 F.L.R. 617. In *MD, Petr*, March 3, 1999, Lord MacFadyen accepted that, in addition to an application for a contact order under s. 11(2)(d) of the Children (Scotland) Act 1995, governed by r. 49.1(1)(j) of the Rules of the Court of Session, r. 70.5(2) of the Rules additionally permits application by way of petition when the application was made under the Hague Convention. He opined, however, that this additional procedure was unnecessary (given that the need for speedy resolution, essential in custody cases, did not apply in access cases) and unhelpful (given that a perfectly satisfactory procedure existed under r. 49.1).

[42] *per* Lord McFadyen in *MD Petr*, above.

[43] See above, paras 11.10–11.15.

CHAPTER 12

EDUCATION OF CHILDREN

Scope of this chapter

12.01   It has long been held to be part of a parent's duty towards a child to provide him or her with education. Originally, as with other aspects of the parental duty, this attached to the father alone, but now of course it attaches to both parents. In the earlier law, this was seen as an aspect of the obligation to maintain the child, for that included an obligation to make the child able to take his or her place in society and to earn his or her own living[1]; but today the obligation to educate the child is better seen as arising from the responsibility under the Children (Scotland) Act 1995 to promote the child's development and to provide direction and guidance,[2] independent of the obligation to aliment and governed by the Education (Scotland) Act 1980.[3] The discussion in this chapter is limited to the duty of parents to educate their children, their right to determine the form of the child's education, and the subsidiary duties of local authorities to make provision to allow parents to fulfil their responsibility and to exercise their right. This book is not the place for a comprehensive description of the governance and control of schools, public or private, nor their funding, and these issues are not dealt with except peripherally in so far as they affect the parental obligation.[4]

THE OBLIGATION TO EDUCATE CHILDREN

Statutory duty of parents

12.02   Under the Education (Scotland) Act 1980,[5] it is the duty of the parent of every child of school age to provide efficient education for him or her suitable to his or her age, ability and aptitude, either by causing the child to attend a public school regularly or by other means. Subject to certain adjustments by reference to school commencement dates and school leaving dates,[6] a child is of school age if he or she has attained the age of five years and has not attained

---

[1] See Erskine, I, vi, 56.
[2] Children (Scotland) Act 1995, s. 1(1)(a) and (b).
[3] References in this chapter relate to the Education (Scotland) Act 1980, unless otherwise stated.
[4] Details of the early statutory law may be found in Roxburgh, *The Law of Education in Scotland* (W. Hodge & Co., 1928). A general account of the post-1980 position can be found in Marr and Marr, *Scots Education Law* (W. Green, 1995).
[5] s. 30.
[6] s. 31. A child who does not attain the age of five years on a school commencement date is deemed not to have attained that age until the school commencement date next following his or her fifth birthday (s. 32(3)). A child whose 16th birthday is on or after March 1, but before October 1, in any year is deemed to have attained the age of 16 on the summer leaving date (May 31) in that year, and a child whose 16th birthday is on or after October 1 in any year, but before March 1 in the following year is deemed to have attained the age of 16 on the intervening winter leaving date (the first day of the Christmas holiday period for a pupil in attendance at school and December 21 in any other case) (s. 33). School commencement dates are fixed by the local authority (s. 32(1) and (2)) which must also fix an appropriate latest date on or before which a child must attain the age of five years in order to come within the category of children whom the authority consider of sufficient age to commence attendance at a public primary school (s. 32(4)). Children who are under five at the commencement date but

the age of 16 years. An exemption from the obligation to attend school, so as to enable him or her to give assistance at home, may however be granted in respect of a child over 14 years of age if, after due inquiry, the education authority are satisfied that by reason of any circumstances existing at his or her home it would cause exceptional hardship to require the child to attend school.[7] The exemption may be on such conditions, if any, as to the amount and manner of further attendance at school until the child reaches the upper limit of the school age as the authority think fit. The exemption is not to extend beyond the date for commencing school attendance next following the date upon which the exemption was granted but it may be renewed. When an exemption is in force the parent of the child cannot be prosecuted or be the subject of any other proceeding under the Act for neglecting to provide for the child's education.[8]

Meaning of "parent"

The parent's duty to provide efficient education for his or her child is the **12.03** primary principle of the Act. The duty laid on the education authority to secure adequate and efficient school education[9] is merely an ancillary means by which the parent's duty may be carried into effect. "Parent" is defined to include guardian and any person who is liable to maintain, or has parental responsibilities (within the meaning of section 1(3) of the Children (Scotland) Act 1995) in relation to, or has care of, a child or young person.[10] "Guardian" is not defined but must, it is submitted, mean a person who has been appointed to that office either by testamentary deed under section 7, or by court order under section 11(1), of the Children (Scotland) Act 1995. A person liable to maintain a child or young person will include both parents, whether or not they have parental responsibilities in relation to the child and any person, such as a spouse or partner of a parent, who has accepted the child as a member of his or her family, for these persons owe obligations of aliment by virtue of the Family Law (Scotland) Act 1985.[11] "Parental responsibilities", as understood under section 1(3) of the Children (Scotland) Act 1995, arise by virtue of sections 3, 4, 7 or 11 of that Act, and by no other means. The duty rests on both parents and it is no defence in the event of failure that the child was in the care of a third party.[12] Equally it would seem to be no defence for either parent that the child was effectively in the care of the other.[13] Nor is the parent's duty elided because

---

have attained that age by the appropriate latest date may, therefore, be enrolled in a public primary school but will not be subject to the compulsory provisions of the Act until the arrival of the commencement date next following. The period between an appropriate latest date and the next following school commencement date applicable to the same school must not be more than six months and seven days (s. 32(7)).

[7] s. 34.

[8] s. 34(3).

[9] s. 1(1).

[10] s. 135(1), as amended by the Children (Scotland) Act 1995, Sched. 4, para. 28(5).

[11] 1985 Act, s. 1(1).

[12] *London School Board v. Jackson* (1881) 7 Q.B.D.502. The case was one of failure to comply with an attendance order and may turn on the fact that the parent was the person against whom the order was made, but the principle that liability is not elided by the fact that the child is in the care or actual custody of someone else is capable of wider application.

[13] The view that the mother was not included in the term "parent" where father, mother and child were living together with the result that liability attached solely to the father (*London County Council v. Stansell* (1936) 154 L.T. 241) was later doubted (*Plunkett v. Alker* [1954] 1 Q.B. 421) and in any event is difficult to reconcile with the equality of parental responsibilities and parental rights created by the Guardianship Act 1973 and now the Children (Scotland) Act 1995. It does not today represent the law.

there is a residence order requiring the child to live with someone else, whether
the other parent or a third party, because such an order merely regulates where the
child is to live and does not, unless it specifically so provides, detract from any
of the parental responsibilities that the non-resident parent owes to the child.
On the other hand, the parent's duty does lapse in the event of adoption, on the
making of a parental order under section 30 of the Human Fertilisation and
Embryology Act 1990, or on the transfer of parental rights and responsibilities
effected by the making of a parental responsibilities order.

Alternatives to State education

12.04   Instead of securing the regular attendance of the child at a public school, a
parent is free to perform his or her duty by "other means".[14] There is no
requirement as to what these means should be. It is enough that they enable the
parent to perform his or her duty. The parent may, therefore, choose to send the
child to an independent school or have him or her attend, or take by
correspondence, a variety of courses, or provide tuition for the child at home
either personally or by another, or indeed proceed in any way the parent thinks
fit provided an efficient education suitable to the child's age and aptitude is
thereby attained. The generality of these words leaves much to parental
discretion. "Efficient instruction in some other manner" (the phrase used in the
Elementary Education Act 1874) was interpreted as meaning "efficient
instruction in the subjects of the curriculum approved for elementary schools",[15]
but the standard of state schools, although it may afford a guide, does not
determine the matter.[16] For a mother with no educational qualifications to have
her children at home, encouraging them to follow any subject which interests
them but without any lessons and without any prescribed course of study,
probably does not meet the test,[17] but the lack of structure or formal instruction
should not in itself be an objection if it can be shown that it is, in the result,
efficient in affording an education suitable to the age, ability and aptitude of the
child concerned.

Enforcement of parental duty

12.05   The method of enforcing the parental duty varies according to whether or
not the child has attended a school, called in the Act "public school",[18] within
the State system. Such attendance is the mark of the parent's election to use the
State system rather than other means as the way of performing his or her duty.
Beyond that, there is no formal requirement that the parent give notice of his or
her election. Where a child has once attended a public school the child's parent
can fail in his or her duty to provide efficient education suitable to the child's
age, ability and aptitude only if thereafter the child does not attend regularly.[19]
In such a case the method of enforcement of the parental duty is by proceedings
in respect of the parent's failure to secure the child's regular attendance at
school.[20] The parent's election to use the State system is not, however, irrevocable.
A child may, with the consent of the education authority, be withdrawn from a

---

[14] s. 30.
[15] *Osborne v. Martin* (1927) 138 L.T. 268, *per* Avory J. at 269.
[16] *Osborne v. Martin*, above; *Bevan v. Shears* [1911] 2 K.B. 936.
[17] *Baker v. Earl* [1960] Crim.L.R. 363.
[18] "Public school" is defined as meaning "any school under the management of an education
       authority": s. 135(1).
[19] This is implicit in s. 37 under which the education authority's powers where they are not satisfied
       that a parent is providing efficient education arise only where a child of school age has not
       attended a public school or has attended such a school and has been withdrawn or excluded. In
       other cases s. 36 applies.
[20] s. 36.

public school which he or she has attended and, in that event, the sanctions for failure to secure regular attendance cease to apply.[21] Moreover, the education authority's consent is not to be withheld unreasonably. In view of the primacy of the parental duty to provide efficient education and the corresponding parental right of choice, it would seem that the authority's withholding of consent would be unreasonable wherever means of providing efficient education outwith the State system were available and the reason for withdrawal was the parent's wish to make use of these means. Where a parent has elected to use such means, but has failed thereby to provide an efficient education, or where a parent has altogether neglected the duty to provide an efficient education, the method of enforcement, whether the child has never attended a public school or has attended such a school and been withdrawn with the consent of the authority, is by attendance order.[22]

Enforcement in relation to children at public schools

Where a child of school age who has attended a public school on one or **12.06** more occasions fails, without reasonable excuse, to attend regularly at that school, then, unless the education authority has consented to the withdrawal of the child from the school, the child's parent is guilty of an offence.[23] Where a child has attended more than one public school the school in question would seem to be that which he or she last attended. Regular attendance connotes attendance in accordance with arrangements lawfully made by the education authority and for the whole time for which these arrangements provide. "A parent is not obliged to avail himself of the free education provided by the State, if he prefers to provide privately for his child's education; but if he does avail himself of it, he must take it as a whole."[24] So a parent is guilty of an offence if the child attends a public school for only part of the time stipulated even if the parent provides education by other means and at other times and the education so provided, when considered along with the child's part-time attendance at a public school or even by itself, is sufficient to amount to efficient education suitable to the child's age, ability and aptitude. Thus, a child may not, unless with the consent of the education authority, be withdrawn for a period during school hours so as to obtain independent instruction in a particular subject.[25] Similarly lateness, at least if more than *de minimis*, may amount to non-attendance and, if persistent, to failure to attend school regularly.[26] A child does not attend school if he or she is refused admission after being sent in a condition in which it is known that he or she will not be admitted.[27]

---

[21] s. 35(1).
[22] s. 37(2). Attendance orders may, however, also be used in the event of a failure of a child to attend a public school regularly (s. 36(2)).
[23] s. 35(1).
[24] *Osborne v. Martin*, above, *per* Slater J.
[25] *ibid.*
[26] *Hinchley v. Rankin* [1961] 1 All E.R. 692.
[27] *Spiers v. Warrington Corporation* [1954] 1 Q.B. 61; *Saunders v. Richardson* (1881) 7 Q.B.D. 338; *Fox v. Burgess* [1922] 1 K.B. 623. In contrast with the law of England as laid down in *Spiers v. Warrington Corporation* it is open to a Scottish court to take account of any circumstances which in its opinion afford a reasonable excuse (s. 42(1)(c)). So, while a child does not attend school if he or she is refused admission after being sent in a condition in which it is known that he or she will not be admitted, there may be a reasonable excuse for non-attendance if it can be shown that for some reason pertaining to the child it was reasonable that he or she should be sent to school in the condition in which he or she was sent.

Meaning of "reasonable excuse"

12.07   There is deemed to be a reasonable excuse for non-attendance if:

(a) there is within two miles of the child's home, in the case of a child under eight, and within three miles in the case of any other child, measured in both cases by the nearest available route, no public or other school the managers of which are willing to receive the child and to provide him or her with free education, and either (i) no arrangements have been made by the education authority for enabling the child to attend an appropriate school, or for the provision of transport or the payment of travelling expenses, or (ii) any arrangements so made are such as to require the child to walk more than two miles or three miles as the case may be in the course of any journey between his or her home and school, or

(b) the child is being prevented by sickness from attending school or receiving education,[28] or

(c) there are other circumstances which in the opinion of the education authority or the court afford a reasonable excuse.[29]

12.08   Where, however, a child has, in consequence of a placing request,[30] been placed in a school other than a school in which the education authority proposed to place him or her in accordance with their arrangements, the provisions of the Act relating to walking distance between the child's home and school do not apply—provided that, where the school in which the authority proposed to place the child is more than walking distance from the child's home, the authority offered to make suitable arrangements under which the child would not require to walk more than walking distance to that school.[31]

12.09   Under paragraph (c) above, the parent will not be guilty of an offence if there are "other circumstances which in the opinion of the education authority or the court afford a reasonable excuse". A wide range of matters may be considered here, but the excuse must be one that affects the child and is reasonable in relation to him or her; the defence is established if the child has a reasonable excuse for failing to attend school regularly, rather than if the parent has a reasonable excuse for failing to secure the child's regular attendance.[32] Thus, it has been held to be no defence to a prosecution that an invalid parent reasonably required the services of a child at home.[33] (Where, however, an exemption from attendance at school has been granted in respect of a child over 14, to enable the child to give assistance at home, the parent is, as mentioned above,

---

[28] This does not include "sickness" which is self-induced as a result of a deliberate course of conduct on the part of the child. "Sickness" as used in the statute means something unavoidable: *Kiely v. Lunn*, 1983 S.L.T. 207.

[29] s. 42(1) and (4).

[30] See below, para.12.29.

[31] s. 42(1A), as inserted by the Education (Scotland) Act 1981, s. 2(1).

[32] In *Skeen v. Tunnah*, 1970 S.L.T. (Sh.Ct) 66 the sheriff fell, it is submitted, into error in acquitting a parent who had failed to send his children (aged eight and five) to school in circumstances in which he had a reasonable excuse for so failing.

[33] *Jenkins v. Howells* [1949] 2 K.B. 218. The words there under construction were "unavoidable cause" and in *Spiers v. Warrington Corporation*, above, Lord Goddard C.J. who had been a party to the decision in *Jenkins*, said, at 68, that it was "a very hard case, but we felt that the statute was too strong; we could not go into the question of reasonableness". The *ratio* of *Jenkins* appears however to be that "unavoidable cause" must be construed in relation to the child and affect the child. The reason for non-attendance given in that case affected, it was held, the mother and not the child. On that reasoning it seems that reasonable excuse too must affect the child and there may be sound policy for that. To open up a consideration of family excuses might by its breadth and uncertainty defeat the purposes of the Act. Certain cases of exceptional hardship are covered by s. 34.

immune from prosecution.[34]) Similarly, a *bona fide* and reasonable belief on the part of the parent that the child was attending school when, in fact, he or she was not, affords no defence.[35] And it has been held that a child's illness, due to his solvent abuse, does not provide a reasonable excuse, notwithstanding that the child rather than the parent was thereby responsible for the failure to attend.[36] So the offence is treated as one of strict liability in relation to the parent.[37] That view may, however, take too little account of the reservations on the creation of offences of strict liability expressed by the House of Lords in *Sweet v. Parsley*[38] in which Lord Diplock said that it was

> "a general principle of construction... that even where the words used... would not in any other context connote the necessity of any particular mental element, they are nevertheless to be read as subject to the implication that a necessary element of the offence is the absence of a belief, held honestly and upon reasonable grounds, in the existence of facts which, if true, would make the act innocent".[39]

There may also be some room for the maxim *impotentia excusat legem* **12.10** where it is physically impossible for the parent to secure the child's attendance, as in the case of a parent in hospital in a condition in which he or she is incapable of giving directions for the child's care. But it may be argued against the application of that maxim, and of the doctrine in *Sweet v. Parsley*, that criminal liability does not, on the wording of the Act, arise from any act or omission of the parent and so it is irrelevant whether he or she was incapable of acting or whether his or her failure to act was based on honest and reasonable belief. On that view liability attaches to the parent on the occurrence of an event, i.e. the child's failure to attend school regularly without reasonable excuse, and no connection between the parent and the event need exist.[40] To say that is, however, to ignore the substance of the matter which is that the parent should secure the child's regular attendance. A duty to secure readily falls within the ratio of *Sweet v. Parsley* and, it is submitted, should not be so construed as to give rise to liability where through no fault of the parent performance by him or her was impossible.

Effect of exclusion on reasonable excuse
Where a child has been required to discontinue for any period his or her **12.11** attendance at a school on account of a parent's refusal or failure to comply with the rules, regulations or disciplinary requirements of the school, the child is, unless the court otherwise determines, deemed to have failed without reasonable excuse to attend regularly.[41] The power of the court to determine otherwise

---

[34] s. 34(3).
[35] *Crump v. Gilmore* (1969) 113 Sol.J. 998. On the other hand, in *MacIntyre v. Annan*, 1991 S.C.C.R. 465 an accused parent was charged that she did "fail, without reasonable excuse, to secure the regular attendance" of her son. The justices found that she had been unaware of the child's absences and had no reason to believe that he was not attending school, but nevertheless convicted her on the basis that she had no reasonable excuse. On appeal, this conviction was quashed, though not on the basis that s. 35(1) provided her with a defence if she had a reasonable excuse. Rather, she had been charged with having no reasonable excuse and such a charge, having no basis in the terms of the statute, was not a relevant charge.
[36] *Kiely v. Lunn*, 1983 S.L.T. 207.
[37] See also *Montgomery v. City of Glasgow Council*, January 19, 1999 where the child did not attend school because she was being bullied. This was held to afford no reasonable excuse when the child had failed to report the bullying or to identify the bullies.
[38] [1970] A.C. 132.
[39] *ibid.* at 163.
[40] This seems to underpin the reasoning of the judges in *MacIntyre v. Annan*, 1991 S.C.C.R. 465.
[41] s. 35(2).

appears to open the way to a consideration of the reasonableness of the exclusion and of the rules, regulations or disciplinary requirements in question. Where a child believed to be infested with vermin or in a foul condition has been excluded until examination or cleansing can be carried out,[42] the exclusion constitutes a defence to any proceedings in respect of the child's failure to attend school on any day on which he or she is excluded unless it is proved that the issue of the exclusion direction was necessitated by the wilful default of the parent.[43]

Prosecution of parent

12.12   An education authority which considers that a parent has committed an offence in respect of a child's failure to attend school regularly is not, on that account, empowered to take steps forthwith to institute prosecution of the parent. A notice must be served on the parent requiring him or her, within a specified time, not less than 48 hours nor more than seven days from the service of the notice, to appear with or without the child before the authority and explain the reason for the absence of the child from school.[44] If the parent fails to satisfy the authority that the child[45] had a reasonable excuse, the authority may then instruct that the parent be prosecuted forthwith or may warn the parent and postpone, for a period not exceeding six weeks, a decision on whether to prosecute. In the latter event the authority may make an attendance order requiring the parent to cause the child to attend the public school which he or she has been attending or, if the child has changed his or her residence, a school attended by children residing in the same neighbourhood.[46] It is not clear what is gained by the making of an attendance order in these circumstances except that if the child's non-attendance should recur during the period of postponement the parent may be prosecuted for failure to comply with the attendance order as well as for the child's original failure to attend school regularly. The Act is silent about the basis on which a decision as to whether to prosecute is to be taken at the end of the period of postponement: it is however to be supposed that if the child has, in the interval, attended regularly no further proceedings will be taken while if his or her non-attendance without reasonable excuse has recurred a prosecution will be instituted. Whether or not a prosecution is instituted or a decision thereon postponed the education authority may, even although there is no requirement to do so,[47] provide the children's reporter with information concerning a child of school age who has failed to attend a public school regularly.[48] If a prosecution is brought and in these proceedings it appears to the court that any of the conditions for referral to the children's hearing, other than that the child has committed an offence (and not just that the child has failed without reasonable excuse to attend school regularly) the court may refer the matter to the reporter, specifying the condition.[49] Such a referral may be made whether or not the parent is convicted and where the reporter, in consequence of the referral, arranges a children's hearing the condition specified will be treated as if it were

---

[42] See below, para.12.48.
[43] s. 58(6).
[44] s. 36(1).
[45] The statute says: "If the parent fails to satisfy the authority that he had a reasonable excuse, the authority may instruct that he be prosecuted..." The first "he" refers, it is submitted, to the child (who is the only person who requires a reasonable excuse in terms of the offence in s. 35(1): *MacIntyre v. Annan*, 1991 S.C.C.R. 465 (*cf.* s. 41)) while the second refers to the parent.
[46] s. 36(2).
[47] Under s. 53(1) of the Children (Scotland) Act 1995, under which a local authority must give the reporter information if they are satisfied that compulsory measures of supervision may be necessary in respect of the child.
[48] s. 36(3), as amended by the Children (Scotland) Act 1995, Sched. 4, para. 28(2).
[49] Children (Scotland) Act 1995, s. 54(1) and (2)(d).

a ground of referral established before the sheriff.[50] Alternatively, the court may make an attendance order requiring the parent to cause the child to attend the public school which he or she has been attending, or, if the child has changed residence, a school attended by children residing in the same neighbourhood.[51] The onus is on the parent to satisfy the court that there was a reasonable excuse for the child's non-attendance.[52]

Exclusion of pupil

There was no common law right to exclude a child from school.[53] Regulations **12.13** now, however, provide that an education authority shall not exclude a pupil from a school under their management to which he or she has been admitted except where (a) they are of the opinion that the parent of the pupil refuses or fails to comply, or to allow the pupil to comply, with the rules, regulations, or disciplinary requirements of the school, or (b) they consider that in all the circumstances to allow the pupil to continue his or her attendance at the school would be likely to be seriously detrimental to order and discipline in the school or the educational well-being of the pupils there.[54]

The latter ground of exclusion does not refer only to the educational well-being **12.14** of the pupil in question but also to that of other pupils at the school. It may therefore be used where the presence of a child would cause a hazard to others. The regulations merely prescribe that exclusion is unlawful unless one of the grounds for exclusion is satisfied. They do not lay down that satisfaction of one of these grounds necessarily justifies exclusion. Accordingly, questions of the reasonableness of the authority's actings may remain. There is a further specific statutory ground of exclusion where a medical officer, authorised by the education authority, or a person authorised by him, has reason to believe that the body or clothing of any pupil is infested with vermin or in a foul condition but action for examination or cleansing cannot immediately be taken.[55] In such a case the medical officer, or authorised person, is to advise the authority which may, if they consider it necessary to do so in the interests either of the pupil or of other children in attendance at the school, direct that the pupil be excluded from the school until the examination or cleansing can be carried out.

Review of exclusion

Where by decision of the education authority a child is excluded from a **12.15** school under the authority's management which he or she attends, the child's parent may refer the authority's decision to an appeal committee which may confirm or annul the decision and, if it confirms a decision excluding a child until certain conditions are complied with, may modify the conditions.[56] It is noticeable that the child has no right to challenge the exclusion under the statute unless he or she is a young person (*i.e.* a person over school age but under 18). However, it is arguably open to a child who, before then, has legal capacity to instruct a solicitor,[57] to seek judicial review of the decision to exclude. The decision of the appeal committee and the reasons for it must be notified in

---

[50] Children (Scotland) Act 1995, s. 54(3).

[51] s. 44(2), as amended by the Children (Scotland) Act 1995, Sched. 4, para. 28(3).

[52] *Buchanan v. Price*, 1982 S.C.C.R. 534; *Neeson v. Lunn*, 1985 S.L.T. 409. See also *Lanarkshire County Clerk v. Vincent*, 1976 J.C. 5 and *Ross v. Simpson*, 1995 S.L.T. 956.

[53] Cleland, "Exclusion of Children From School" (1995) Fam.L.B. 18–2.

[54] Schools General (Scotland) Regulations 1975 (S.I. 1975 No. 1135), reg. 4, as amended by S.I. 1982, No. 56 and S.I. 1982, No. 1735. See *Wyatt v. Wilson*, 1994 S.L.T. 1135.

[55] s. 58(6).

[56] s. 28H, as inserted by the Education (Scotland) Act 1981, s. 1(1).

[57] See Age of Legal Capacity (Scotland) Act 1991, s. 2(4A) and (4B). See below, para. 15.11 .

writing to the parent and to the education authority. The authority must comply with the decision of the appeal committee. The parent has a right of appeal to the sheriff having jurisdiction where the school is situated. There is no corresponding right of appeal for the education authority against a decision of the appeal committee annulling the authority's decision. The sheriff's powers on hearing and disposing of the appeal are similar to those of the appeal committee. The provisions on the form of application, the time within which it must be lodged, hearing in chambers, expenses and finality of the sheriff's judgment apply to appeals in relation to the exclusion of a child from a school as they apply to appeals to the sheriff in relation to decisions on placing requests.[58] In contrast, however, with cases arising from decisions on placing requests, no criteria are prescribed for deciding appeals whether by the appeal committee or by the sheriff and the matter would seem to be at large for them. Among the matters to be considered, however, must be whether there were grounds for exclusion in terms of the regulations and whether the decision to exclude was reasonable in the circumstances.

Enforcement in relation to children outwith the State system

12.16   Where a child is not attending a public school the education authority have certain powers and duties designed to ensure that the child receives an efficient education. These powers and duties arise if a child of school age (a) has not attended a public school, or (b) has attended such a school and has been withdrawn with the consent of the education authority, or (c) has attended such a school and has been excluded by the education authority, and in any of these cases the authority are not satisfied that the child's parent is providing efficient education for him or her suitable to his or her age, ability and aptitude.[59] The authority must then serve a notice on the parent requiring him or her, within a specified time not less than seven nor more than 14 days from the service of the notice, either (a) to appear (with or without the child) before the authority and to give such information as the authority may require regarding the means, if any, he or she has adopted for providing education, or, in the parent's option, (b) to give such information to the authority in writing. If the parent fails to satisfy the authority, either that he or she is providing efficient education, or that there is a reasonable excuse for the failure to do so, the authority must make an attendance order.[60]

12.17   An attendance order is an order in writing requiring the parent of a child to cause the child to attend the school named in the order.[61] The school need not be a public school but may be any school the managers of which are willing to receive the child. A school at which the parent will be required to pay fees must not, however, be named except at the parent's request and a special school must not be named unless the child has been recorded in a Record of Needs as having pronounced specific or complex special educational needs.[62] Before making an attendance order, the authority must consider any views expressed by the parent as to the school which he or she desires his or her child to attend.[63] At that stage the authority is not required to do any more than consider these views and, provided such consideration is given, does not, it seems, require to justify failure

---

[58] For which, see below, para. 12.29.
[59] s. 37(1).
[60] s. 37(2).
[61] s. 38(1).
[62] s. 38(2). See below, paras 12.49 *et seq.*
[63] s. 38(3). Though there is no requirement on the education authority to consider the child's views, the parent is obliged to have regard to them: Children (Scotland) Act 1995, s. 6(1).

to give them effect. The parent may, however, at any time while the attendance order is in force, apply to the authority requesting that another school be substituted for that named in the order and the authority must amend the order in compliance with that request unless it is of the opinion that the proposed change of school is unreasonable or inexpedient in the interests of the child.[64] It seems also that notwithstanding that an attendance order is in force, a parent may make a placing request.[65] The authority must cause a copy of the attendance order to be served upon the parent and it then becomes the duty of the parent, subject to an appeal to the sheriff, to cause the child to attend regularly at the school named in the order.[66] An appeal to the sheriff is to be taken within 14 days and the sheriff, whose decision is final, may confirm, vary or annul the order.[67]

Amendment of attendance order by education authority

At any time while an attendance order is in force the education authority **12.18** which made the order may amend it by substituting the name of another school for that named in the order and where a child, in respect of whom an attendance order is in force, moves his or her residence the education authority of the area to which the child has moved may amend the order by substituting for the name of the school appearing in the order the name of a school attended by children residing in the same neighbourhood as the child.[68] Amendment is effected by a decision of the authority to that effect following service upon the parent of a notice of intention to amend. The parent may, within 14 days of service of the notice, intimate in writing to the authority objections to the proposed amendment and the amendment cannot be made until after the expiry of that period and consideration by the authority of any objections the parent has made.[69] The same restriction as to schools that can be named apply to the amendment of an order as apply to its making. As in the case of the original order, a copy of the amended order must be served on the parent and, thereafter, the parent has a duty to comply with the amended order. The parent has the same right of appeal against the amendment of an order as against its making.

Revocation of attendance orders

At any time while an attendance order is in force a parent may apply to the **12.19** authority by whom the order was made or amended requesting that the order be revoked on the ground that arrangements have been made for the child to receive efficient education suitable to his or her age, ability and aptitude at a school other than that named in the order, or elsewhere than at a school.[70] On such an application the authority must revoke the order unless they are of the opinion that the arrangements made for the education of the child are not satisfactory. A parent aggrieved by a failure of the authority to reach a decision upon his or her application within one month, or by the authority's refusal to comply with his or her request, whether for amendment or revocation, may appeal to the sheriff. The sheriff, on an appeal being made, is to give such direction as he or she thinks fit.[71]

---

[64] s. 39(4).
[65] See below, para. 12.29.
[66] s. 38(4).
[67] s. 38(5).
[68] s. 39(1) and (2).
[69] s. 39(3).
[70] s. 39(4).
[71] *ibid.*

Duration

12.20   An attendance order, unless revoked or annulled, continues in force as long as the child is of school age.[72] If, however, a record of needs of a child who had pronounced specific or complex special educational needs falls to be discontinued by virtue of any enactment, any attendance order requiring the attendance of that child at a special school is deemed to be annulled.[73]

Non-compliance

12.21   If an attendance order is in force and is not complied with after a copy has been served on the parent, the parent is guilty of an offence unless he or she satisfies the court that he or she has a reasonable excuse.[74] The parent's duty is "to cause the child to attend" the school named in the order.[75] In the event of non-compliance the parent's acts and omissions are, therefore, directly in issue. The question of whether this is an offence of strict liability, noticed earlier in connection with the failure of a child to attend a public school regularly, is again raised and perhaps in sharper form. Reasonable excuse appears in this context to include reasons personal to the parent as well as those directly affecting the child, for what is in issue is whether there is reasonable excuse for the parent's failure to cause the child to attend. The fact that an application has been made to the education authority to amend or revoke the attendance order, or that an appeal to the sheriff is pending, is not to be deemed to be a reasonable excuse.[76] Subject to these qualifications, the statutory provisions on reasonable excuse are the same in relation to non-compliance with attendance orders as to failure to attend a public school regularly. Where a public school has been named in the order, the offences of non-compliance with the order and of the child's failure to attend regularly at the school may both arise from the same facts. A prosecution cannot, however, be brought for both offences without contravening the prohibition against double jeopardy. But where it appears to the court, before which a prosecution is brought for non-compliance with an attendance order, that any of the conditions for referral to a children's hearing other than that the child has committed an offence (and not just that the child has failed without reasonable excuse to attend regularly at the school named in the order) the court may refer the matter to the reporter, specifying the condition.[77] Such a referral may be made whether or not the parent is convicted and, where the reporter, in consequence of the referral, arranges a children's hearing the condition specified will be treated as if it were a ground of referral established before the sheriff.[78]

EDUCATION AUTHORITY'S DUTY

Provision of education

12.22   The UN Convention on the Rights of the Child requires that "States Parties recognise the right of the child to education", and in particular that they make primary education compulsory and available free to all and make different forms of secondary education available and accessible to every child.[79] The United Kingdom fulfils its obligations under this provision by imposing duties to provide

---

[72] s. 40.
[73] Proviso to s. 40, added by the Education (Scotland) Act 1981, Sched. 2, Pt II, para. 6 and Sched. 8.
[74] s. 41.
[75] s. 38(1).
[76] s. 42(2).
[77] Children (Scotland) Act 1995, s. 54(1) and (2)(d).
[78] *ibid.* s. 54(3).
[79] Art. 28.

primary and secondary education on local authorities. Under the Education (Scotland) Act 1980 it is the duty of every education authority (that is a council constituted under section 2 of the Local Government etc (Scotland) Act 1994[80]) to secure that there is made for their area adequate and efficient provision of school education and further education.[81] The duty to provide adequate and efficient education is owed to every child individually and not to children in general, and in determining how to fulfil the duty wholly objective educational criteria are to be used.[82] By school education is meant progressive education appropriate to the requirements of pupils in attendance at institutions for the provision of primary and/or secondary education whether that institution be a public school, a grant-aided school, a self-governing school or an independent school, and includes a nursery school and a special school.[83] It includes education by special methods appropriate to the requirements of pupils whose physical, intellectual, emotional or social development cannot be adequately promoted by ordinary methods of education ("special education"). It also includes the teaching of Gaelic in Gaelic-speaking areas and nursery education for pupils who are under school age, but although there is a power, there is no duty to provide nursery schools or classes. Further education, which education authorities may but are not obliged to provide,[84] includes voluntary part-time or full-time courses of instruction for persons over school age, and also various forms of social, cultural and recreative activities and physical education and training for persons over school age.[85] The word "pupil" where used in the Act means a person of any age for whom education is, or is required to be, provided under the Act[86] and does not, therefore, carry the special meaning (child under the legal age of puberty) previously associated with it in the general law of Scotland. In addition to providing school and further education, every education authority is obliged to provide, for their area, a psychological service in clinics whose function includes (a) the study of children with special educational needs, (b) the giving of advice to parents and teachers as to the appropriate methods of education for such children, (c) in suitable cases the provision of special education for such children in clinics, and (d) the giving of advice regarding the assessment of the needs of any child for the purposes of the Social Work (Scotland) Act 1968 or any other enactment.[87]

---

[80] s. 135(1), as amended by the Local Government etc. (Scotland) Act 1994, s. 180(1) and Sched. 13, para. 118(9).

[81] s. 1(1). S. 70 of the Act (as amended by the School Boards (Scotland) Act 1988, Sched. 4, para. 6) provides for complaint to the Secretary of State if a person considers that the education authority or managers of the school or other educational establishment have failed in their duties to provide adequate and efficient education. This provision does not exclude the court's right to hear an application for judicial review of the carrying out of these duties: *Walker v. Strathclyde Regional Council (No. 1)* 1986 S.L.T. 523.

[82] *R. v. East Sussex County Council, ex p. Tandy* [1998] 2 All E.R. 769. In that case the statutory provision (s. 298 of the Education Act 1993—now s. 19 of the Education Act 1996) was in rather different terms and the House of Lords held that the decision of an education authority to cut the hours of home tuition of a pupil who was unable to attend school, for financial rather than educational reasons, was unlawful. In so far as the case turns on an issue of statutory interpretation it is of limited value in Scotland, though the point relating to what criteria are relevant to how the duty (once defined) is to be satisfied is good here also.

[83] ss. 1(5)(a) and 135(1).

[84] s. 1(2A).

[85] s. 1(5)(b).

[86] s. 135(1).

[87] s. 4. The promotion of the welfare of children in need is governed generally by the Children (Scotland) Act 1995, Pt II, Chap. 1.

12.23   It is the duty of an education authority, in the performance of the above functions, to provide for their area sufficient accommodation in public schools, and other educational establishments under their management to enable them to perform these functions. Subject to certain exceptions, school education provided by an education authority is to be provided without payment of fees,[88] and books, writing material, stationery, mathematical instruments, and other articles necessary to enable the pupils to take full advantage of the education provided are to be made available free of charge.[89]

Self-governing schools

12.24   The existence of self-governing schools in the education authority's area, the boards of management of which have a duty to provide "suitable and efficient school education",[90] does not detract from the authority's obligation to provide "adequate and efficient school education" for children in their area, although their duty to maintain the self-governing school is superseded on the incorporation of the board of management by an equivalent duty of the Secretary of State.[91] In carrying out their obligations under the Education (Scotland) Act 1980 owed to all children, whether at a public school or a self-governing school, the education authority are not to distinguish, as regards the benefits or services provided or as regards the terms on which they are provided, between the pupils in the different categories of school.[92]

Religious observance

12.25   It is unlawful for an education authority or the board of management of a self-governing school to discontinue religious observance or the provision of instruction in religion in a public school unless in pursuit of a resolution duly passed by the authority and approved by a majority of the local government electors for the area of the authority voting at a poll taken for that purpose.[93] Every public school, every grant-aided school, and every self-governing school must, however, be open to pupils of all religious denominations.[94] Any pupil may be withdrawn by his or her parent from any instruction in religious subjects and from any religious observance, and no pupil is to be placed at any disadvantage with respect to secular instruction by reason of the denomination to which the pupil or his or her parents belong or by reason of the child being withdrawn from instruction in religious subjects.[95] An education authority must, if requested to do so by the parent of any pupil who is a boarder at any public school or other educational establishment under the management of the authority or board of management of a self-governing school, make arrangements for affording to the pupil reasonable opportunities for attending worship on Sundays or other days exclusively set apart for religious observance by the religious body to which his or her parent belongs or for receiving religious instruction or practising religious observance outside the working hours of the school or other establishment.[96] Where a denominational school has been transferred to an

---

[88] s. 3.
[89] s. 11(1). The same rule applies for self-governing schools, who must provide the stated items free of charge: Self-Governing Schools Etc. (Scotland) Act 1989, s. 11(3)(a). A self-governing school may, however, charge for articles of clothing provided which are suitable for physical exercise or for any activities of the school for which special clothing is desirable: s. 11(3)(b).
[90] Self-Governing Schools Etc. (Scotland) Act 1989, s. 7(1).
[91] *ibid.* s. 1.
[92] *ibid.* s. 25(1).
[93] Education (Scotland) Act 1980, s. 8(2).
[94] s. 9.
[95] *ibid.*
[96] s. 10.

education authority, the time set apart for religious instruction or observance must be not less than that set apart according to the use and wont of the former management of the school, and all teachers appointed to the staff must be approved as regards their religious belief and character by representatives of the church or denominational body in whose interest the school has been conducted.[97]

Duty to have regard to parental wishes

The Education (Scotland) Act 1980 requires the Secretary of State and **12.26** education authorities, as had previous legislation, to have regard to the general principle that, so far as is compatible with the provision of suitable instruction and training and the avoidance of unreasonable public expenditure, pupils are to be educated in accordance with the wishes of their parents.[98] The provision does not, by itself, oblige either the Secretary of State or an education authority to give parents an opportunity of making representations regarding any proposed exercise of the Secretary of State's or the authority's powers and functions under the Act, but if representations come to their notice they are bound to consider them. It has been said that the corresponding legislation in England and Wales refers, on its true construction, to the wishes of particular parents in respect of their own particular children and not to the wishes of parents generally,[99] but it is submitted that that should not be understood as meaning that where a decision may affect all the school children in a locality, or any large number of school children, it may on account of its generality be made without regard to the wishes of the parents of the children affected. There is no authority in the section for any such restriction nor for restricting its application to questions of curricula, the provision of religious instruction, and whether or not a school should be co-educational.[1] The section bears rather to apply, without qualification, to the exercise and performance by the Secretary of State and the education authorities of their powers and functions under the Act and would seem, therefore, to comprehend all such powers and functions to which the wishes of parents may be relevant. The section does not, however, require that the wishes of parents should receive effect. It only lays down a general principle to which the Secretary of State and the education authority must have regard,[2] and if they do so, the fact that the education authority comes to a view different from that of the parents does not raise a presumption that the authority disregarded the parent's views.[3] Unless it can be shown that parental wishes were wholly disregarded, or were overborne by some improper consideration, or that the authority paid to the parents' wishes a degree of regard less than any reasonable authority would have paid, it would seem to have little enforceable content. The general principle is to be taken into account so far as is compatible with the provision of suitable instruction and training and the avoidance of unreasonable public expenditure, and there had been some conflict of sheriff court authority on whether these considerations exhausted the matters which it was competent for an education authority to balance against parental wishes.[4] The preponderance of recent

---

[97] s. 21(2C).
[98] s. 28.
[99] *Wood v. Ealing London Borough Council* [1967] Ch. 364, *per* Goff J.
[1] *ibid.*
[2] *Watt v. Kesteven County Council* [1955] 1 Q.B. 408; *Keeney v. Strathclyde Regional Council*, 1986 S.L.T. 490.
[3] *Harvey v. Strathclyde Regional Council*, 1989 S.L.T. 612, HL.
[4] That the specified conditions are exhaustive is supported by *Huckstep v. Dunfermline District Education Sub-Committee*, 1954 S.L.T. (Sh.Ct) 109 and *Kidd v. Newkilpatrick School Council*, 1978 S.L.T. (Sh.Ct) 56. See also *Brown v. Lothian Regional Council*, 1980 S.L.T.(Sh.Ct) 14.

decision, supported by English authority, was that a duty to have regard to the general principle admitted of considerations other than those specified being taken into account.[5] The matter was put beyond doubt in *Harvey v. Strathclyde Regional Council*,[6] in which the House of Lords affirmed the decision of the First Division[7] which proceeded, *inter alia*, on the view that an education authority would be entitled to have regard to relevant considerations other than those expressly mentioned, and indeed that there might be exceptions to the general principle.

Parental choice of school

12.27   In relation to choice of school, the duty under section 28 to have regard to parental wishes was subsequently supplemented by sections 28A to 28H (introduced by the Education (Scotland) Act 1981). These sections greatly enhance parental rights in choosing a particular school to which a parent can send his or her child. The provisions about to be described refer to public schools; analogous provisions contained in the Self-Governing Schools Etc. (Scotland) Act 1989[8] deal with self-governing schools. The choice of a child's school is a "major decision" in the fulfilment of a parental responsibility, with the result that in making the choice the parent is obliged to have regard so far as practicable to the views (if he or she wishes to express them) of the child concerned, taking account of the child's age and maturity, and to those of any other person who has parental responsibilities or parental rights in relation to the child (and wishes to express these views); a child 12 years of age or more is presumed to be of sufficient age and maturity to form a view.[9] A failure in this duty to consult does not, however, render the parent's choice void.

Information

12.28   Every education authority must publish, or otherwise make available, information as to their arrangements for the placing of children in schools under their management.[10] Where a child falls in accordance with those arrangements to be placed in a school under the authority's management, the authority must, where they propose to place the child in a particular school, inform the child's parent of that school and in every case must inform the parent of the general effect of section 28A and of the parent's right to make a placing request.[11] The duty to inform of the general effect of section 28A and of the right to make a placing request applies, however, only where the existence of the child and the fact that he or she falls to be placed in a school under the authority's management is known to the authority.[12] In addition, the authority must, in making arrangements for the performance of their functions under the Act, formulate guidelines to be followed by them as respects placings in schools generally or, if they think it necessary, in any particular school. The authority must also, on request, supply a parent with certain prescribed information about any school under their management.

---

[5] *Edwards v. Lothian Regional Council*, 1980 S.L.T.(Sh.Ct) 107; *Sinclair v. Lothian Regional Council*, 1981 S.L.T.(Sh.Ct) 13; *Watt v. Kesteven Council*, above; *Cumings v. Birkenhead Corporation*, [1972] Ch. 12. See also *Parlane v. Perth and Kinross J.C.C.*, 1954 S.L.T. (Sh.Ct) 95; *Grieve v. Lothian Regional Council*, 1978 S.L.T. (Sh.Ct) 24; and *Keeney v. Strathclyde Regional Council*, 1986 S.L.T. 490.

[6] 1989 S.L.T. 612.

[7] 1989 S.L.T. 25.

[8] s. 10 and Sched. 2.

[9] Children (Scotland) Act 1995, s. 6(1).

[10] s. 28B.

[11] s. 28B(1).

[12] s. 28B(4).

Placing request

Where a parent makes a written request to an education authority to place **12.29** his or her child in a school specified in the request, being a school under the authority's management, it is the duty of the authority to place the child accordingly.[13] If two or more schools managed by the authority are specified, the duty applies in relation to the first-mentioned such school.[14] The specification of a school outwith Scotland is not an effective request.[15] The duty does not apply:

(a) if placing the child in a specified school would (i) make it necessary for the authority to take an additional teacher into employment, (ii) give rise to significant expenditure on extending, or otherwise altering, the accommodation at, or facilities provided in connection with, the school, (iii) be seriously detrimental to the continuity of the child's education, (iv) be likely to be seriously detrimental to order and discipline in the school, or (v) be likely to be seriously detrimental to the educational wellbeing of pupils attending the school;

(b) if the education normally provided at the specified school is not suited to the age, ability or aptitude of the child;

(c) if the education authority have already required the child to discontinue his or her attendance at the specified school;

(d) if, where the specified school is a special school, the child does not have special educational needs requiring the education or special facilities normally provided at that school; or

(e) if the specified school is a single-sex school and the child is not of the appropriate sex.[16]

Nor does the duty apply where the acceptance of a placing request in respect of a child who is resident outwith the catchment area of the specified school would prevent the education authority from retaining reserved places at a specified school or in relation to any particular stage of education at the school.[17]

These exceptions qualify the duty but do not restrict the powers of the **12.30** education authority. Accordingly, the authority may place a child in the specified school notwithstanding that one or more of the exceptions to the duty applies. The authority must inform the parent, in writing, of their decision on the placing request and where they decide to refuse the request must give the parent written reasons for the decision and inform the parent of his or her right to refer it to an appeal committee.[18] If the parent is not informed in writing of the authority's decision within a prescribed period the placing request is deemed to have been refused.[19]

---

[13] s. 28A(1).

[14] s. 28A(2).

[15] *Lamont v. Strathclyde Regional Council*, 1988 S.L.T. (Sh.Ct) 9.

[16] s. 28A(3), as amended by the Education (Scotland) Act 1996, s. 33(3). For self-governing schools, see Self-Governing Schools Etc. (Scotland) Act 1989, Sched. 2, para. 2.

[17] s. 28A(3A), as inserted by the Education (Scotland) Act 1996, s. 33(4). This ground does not entitle the education authority to refuse a placing request where they manage another equivalent school within two miles' walking distance in the case of primary education and three miles walking distance in any other case: s. 28A(3B), as so inserted. "Reserved places", "catchment area" and "equivalent school" are defined in s. 28A(3C), (3D) and (3E) respectively.

[18] s. 28A(4).

[19] s. 28A(5), and Education (Placing in Schools—Deemed Decisions) (Scotland) Regulations 1982 (S.I. 1982 No. 1733), reg. 4.

Appeal

12.31   Except where the authority's refusal was in respect of the placing of a child
in a nursery school or nursery class, a parent whose placing request has been
refused may refer the authority's decision to an appeal committee.[20] If a reference
has previously been made in respect of the same child no further reference is
competent during the period of 12 months beginning with the day on which the
immediately preceding reference was lodged.[21] The reference must be lodged
within 28 days of the receipt by the parent of the decision of the education
authority but the committee may, on good cause being shown, hear a reference
notwithstanding that it was not lodged within that time.[22]

12.32   The appeal committee may confirm the education authority's decision only
if it is satisfied both (a) that one or more of the grounds of refusal specified in
the Act exist and (b) that in all the circumstances it is appropriate to do so.[23]
Otherwise it must refuse to confirm the authority's decision and require the
authority to place the child in the specified school. Where the authority's decision
is not confirmed and the specified school is a special school, the appeal committee
may, if the authority has decided not to record the child as having pronounced
specific or complex special educational needs, require the education authority
to reconsider their decision.[24] The appeal committee's decision must be notified
in writing together with the reasons for it to the parent who made the reference,
and to the education authority, and where the authority's decision is confirmed
the parent must be informed of his or her right to appeal to the sheriff.[25] Where
the appeal committee refuses to confirm the authority's decision, the authority
must give effect to the placing request.[26] Where the appeal committee's decision
is inconsistent with any decision of the authority refusing a placing request in
respect of another child, the authority must review its decision so to refuse and
must inform the parent of the other child, in writing, of its decision upon that
and the reasons for it.[27] If, upon such a review, the authority decides not to
reverse its decision, the parent of the other child may refer that decision to an
appeal committee and the appeal procedure follows thereon as if the decision
on the review were a decision refusing a placing request.[28]

12.33   A parent who has referred an education authority's decision to an appeal committee
is entitled to a hearing before the committee at which he or she may be accompanied
by up to three friends, including someone representing him or her.[29] As an alternative
the parent may lodge written representations and choose not to appear before the
committee. The hearing of two or more references concerning different children and
parents may be combined if they concern decisions in relation to placing requests all
of which relate to the same stage of education at the same school and, in the committee's
opinion, have been refused for substantially the same reasons. The parties may call
evidence and question persons giving evidence and there is provision for the submission
of information relevant to the decision by either party and for the inspection, by a
party, of documents submitted in evidence by the other party.[30]

---

[20] s. 28C. For self governing schools, see Self-Governing Schools Etc. (Scotland) Act 1989, Sched.
       2, paras 3–7.

[21] s. 28C(3).

[22] s. 28C(4).

[23] s. 28E(1).

[24] s. 28E(2).

[25] s. 28E(3).

[26] s. 28E(4).

[27] s. 28E(5).

[28] s. 28E(6).

[29] Education (Appeal Committee Procedures) (Scotland) Regulations 1982 (S.I. 1982 No. 1736),
       reg. 13(4).

[30] *ibid.* reg. 11.

A parent who has referred the refusal of a placing request to an appeal **12.34** committee may appeal to the sheriff having jurisdiction where the specified school is situated against the decision of the appeal committee.[31] There is no corresponding right of appeal for the education authority. The education authority may be, and the appeal committee shall not be, a party to the appeal.[32] The appeal, which is by way of summary application, must be lodged within 28 days from the date of receipt of the decision of the appeal committee[33] but on good cause being shown the sheriff may hear an appeal notwithstanding that it was not lodged within that time.[34] The appeal is to be heard in chambers and the sheriff's powers in deciding the appeal are governed by similar provisions to those applying to the appeal committee's decision.[35] There are also similar provisions relating to the review by the authority of a decision, whether confirmed by the appeal committee or not, refusing a placing request in respect of another child which is inconsistent with the sheriff's judgment on the appeal and for the consequences of refusal to reverse that decision.[36] The sheriff's judgment on the appeal is final,[37] unless the challenge is to competency.[38] The sheriff may make such order regarding expenses as he thinks proper.[39]

Choice of school by young person

The provisions of the Education (Scotland) Act 1980 on choice of school **12.35** have so far been considered in relation to children not over school age and their parents. They apply, however, equally to any young person over school age but under 18 who is a pupil (*i.e.* a person for whom education is, or is required to be, provided under the Act) with the difference only that in their application to such a young person reference to the parent of a child as well as references to the child him or herself are to be construed as references to the young person.[40]

Assistance in taking advantage of educational facilities

Education authorities have a number of powers and duties designed to assist **12.36** persons to take advantage of educational facilities. Some of these powers and duties apply specifically to school education but others have a wider or different application. The beneficiaries may, unless it is otherwise stated or the context so requires, be of any age. Where the reference is to a "pupil" it means a person of any age for whom education is, or is required to be, provided under the Act,[41] and therefore comprehends anyone who is receiving education provided by the education authority.

Allowances, bursaries and scholarships

An education authority has power for the purpose of enabling persons to **12.37** take advantage, without hardship to themselves or their parents, of the facilities for school education available to them, and to pay allowances for the purpose of defraying in whole or in part:

---

[31] s. 28F(1).
[32] s. 28F(2).
[33] s. 28F(3).
[34] s. 28F(4).
[35] s. 28F(3)(c) and (5).
[36] s. 28F(6) and (7).
[37] s. 28F(9).
[38] *Lamont v. Strathclyde Regional Council*, 1988 S.L.T. (Sh.Ct) 9.
[39] s. 28F(8).
[40] s. 28G. For self-governing schools, see Self-Governing Schools Etc. (Scotland) Act 1989, Sched. 2, para. 8.
[41] s. 135(1).

(a) such expenses of a person's attending any school as may be expedient to enable him or her to take full part in the activities of the school;

(b) the fees and expenses payable in respect of persons attending schools at which fees are payable; and

(c) the maintenance expenses of persons over school age who are attending schools.[42]

The authority also has power to make payment of bursaries, scholarships or other allowances to persons over school age attending courses of full-time or part-time education whether held in Scotland or elsewhere which are not courses of school education, or, in the case of courses outside Scotland, are not courses of education comparable to school education in Scotland.[43]

Arrangements for exceptional circumstances

12.38   Where, in the opinion of an education authority,

(a) any pupil is, owing to the remoteness of his or her home or the conditions under which he or she is living or other exceptional circumstances, unable to receive the full benefit of school education unless special arrangements are made for him or her, or

(b) school education suitable to the age, ability and aptitude of any pupil can best be provided for him or her at any particular school,

the authority shall, after consultation with the parent, make such arrangements of either a temporary or a permanent character as it thinks best suited to the purpose of enabling that pupil to attend an appropriate school.[44] These arrangements may include (a) the provision of travelling facilities or the payment of travelling expenses, (b) the accommodation of the pupil at a boarding school or in a hostel, home, or other institution, (c) other provision of board and lodging provided that, so far as practicable, effect is given to the wishes of the parent with respect to the religious denomination of the person with whom the pupil is to reside, or (d) provision for travelling, board and lodging of teachers.[45] If a child or young person is provided with residential accommodation for the purposes of being in attendance at a school the education authority or managers of the school are under the duty to safeguard and promote the welfare of the child or young person while he or she is so accommodated.[46]

Transport and other facilities

12.39   Such arrangements, as the education authority considers necessary, are to be made for the provision of the following facilities in respect of pupils attending schools or other educational establishments:

(a) for the conveyance of pupils, without charge, for the whole or part of the journey between their homes and the schools or other educational establishments which they are attending. If after the requirements of these pupils have been met, there are vacant places in a vehicle used

---

[42] s. 49(2). References to attending school are to attending schools in Scotland and in other parts of the United Kingdom (s. 49(2A), as inserted by the Self-Governing Schools Etc. (Scotland) Act 1989, Sched. 10, para. 8).

[43] s. 49(1). A local authority may also make grants to persons over school age but under 21 who were being looked after by a local authority when he or she ceased to be of school age, in order to enable him or her to meet expenses connected with his or her receiving education or training: Children (Scotland) Act 1995, s. 30.

[44] s. 50(1).

[45] s. 50(2).

[46] s. 125A, as inserted by the Children (Scotland) Act 1995, s. 35.

for their conveyance it is the duty of the authority to allow such places to be used without charge by other pupils to be selected by them;

(b) for making bicycles, or other suitable means of transport, available to pupils, or to their parents for the use of pupils, upon such terms and conditions as may be arranged, or for paying money allowances in lieu thereof;

(c) for paying the whole or any part, as the authority think fit, of reasonable travelling expenses.[47]

Any arrangement made in respect of any pupil may make provision for more than one of these facilities. The authority may moreover pay the whole or part of the expenses of attendance for examination or interview where these are necessarily incurred by anyone whose attendance is required as a condition of admission to any educational institution. In considering whether to make such arrangements, an education authority is obliged to have regard to the safety of the pupils affected.[48]

Board and lodging

Where board and lodging are provided by the authority under section 50 of **12.40** the Act no sum is recoverable from the parent or young person in respect of that provision.[49] In any other case, however, an education authority, who have provided a pupil with board and lodging whether at a school, hostel or elsewhere may, in its discretion, require the parent to pay such sum not exceeding the cost of such board and lodging as, in the opinion of the authority, he or she is able without financial hardship to pay.[50] Where the board and lodging have been provided for a young person in an educational establishment in connection with which the authority has provided a hostel the authority, if satisfied that the young person is in a financial position to pay, may instead recover from him or her the whole or any part of the sum recoverable from his or her parent.[51]

School meals

An education authority may provide milk, meals or refreshment for pupils **12.41** in attendance at public schools and other educational establishments under its management, either on the premises or elsewhere, and such facilities as the authority considers appropriate are to be provided for the consumption of any meals or other refreshments brought to the school or other educational establishment by pupils.[52] The authority must, subject to what is said in the next sentence, charge for anything provided by it in the way of milk, meals and other refreshment and must charge every pupil the same price for the same quantity of the same item.[53] In relation to a pupil whose parents are in receipt of income support or of an income-based jobseeker's allowance or who is him or herself in receipt of that benefit, an authority shall exercise the power to provide milk, meals and other refreshment in a way that ensures that such provision is made to the pupil in the middle of the day as appears to the authority to be requisite and shall make that provision for him or her free of charge.[54] These provisions

---

[47] s. 51(1) and (2), as amended by the Self-Governing Schools Etc. (Scotland) Act 1989, Sched. 6, para. 1.
[48] s. 51(2C), as inserted by the Education (Scotland) Act 1996, s. 36 and Sched. 5, para. 2.
[49] s. 52.
[50] *ibid.*
[51] *ibid.*
[52] s. 53(1).
[53] s. 53(2), as amended by s. 77 of the Social Security Act 1986.
[54] s. 53(3), as amended by s. 77 of the Social Security Act 1986, and the Jobseekers Act 1995, s. 41(4) and Sched. 2, para. 5.

apply in relation to pupils in attendance at a self-governing school and the board of management of that school as they apply in relation to pupils in attendance at a public school and the education authority that manages it.[55] Where special arrangements have been made for a pupil to receive education elsewhere than at an educational establishment he or she may, at the discretion of the authority, be deemed to be in attendance at a public school under its management for the purpose of these provisions.[56]

Clothing

12.42   When it is brought to the notice of an education authority that a pupil attending either a school under its management or a self-governing school is unable, by reason of the inadequacy or unsuitability of his or her clothing, to take full advantage of the education provided, the authority is to make such provisions for the pupil as it deems necessary, for the purpose of ensuring that he or she is sufficiently and suitably clad.[57] That provision is to be made during such period while the pupil is attending school, including days when the school does not meet, as the authority may determine. The expense thereby incurred may be recovered from the parent of the pupil in whole or in such part as the parent is, in the opinion of the authority, able without financial hardship to pay.[58] Without prejudice, however, to its other powers, an education authority may provide clothing free of charge for any pupil who is a boarder at a school or for any pupil in attendance at a nursery school or nursery class under the management of the authority, or for any pupil who is a boarder at a self-governing school.[59] For all purposes connected with the provision of clothing, a pupil on attaining the age of five years is, pending his or her admission to school, deemed to be attending a school under the management of the authority in whose area he or she is ordinarily resident and a pupil for whom it is the duty of an education authority to provide special education is deemed to be attending a school under the management of that authority.[60]

Meals and clothing at independent schools

12.43   An education authority may, with the consent of the managers of any school in their area which is not a public school and upon such financial and other terms, if any, as may be agreed, make arrangements for securing the provision for pupils in attendance at the school of milk, meals and other refreshment; and, except in relation to self-governing schools, where any such pupil is unable, by reason of the inadequacy or unsuitability of his or her clothing, to take full advantage of the education including physical exercise provided by the school, the authority may provide such clothing as is necessary for the purpose of ensuring that he or she is sufficiently and suitably clad while he or she remains a pupil at the school.[61]

Rights in relation to clothing provided

12.44   Provision of clothing by an education authority under any of its powers conferred by the Act may be made so as to confer, at the option of the authority, either a right of property in the clothing or a right of use only.[62]

---

[55] s. 53(3A), as inserted by the Self-Governing Schools Etc. (Scotland) Act 1989, Sched. 10, para. 8.
[56] s. 53(4).
[57] s. 54(1), as amended by the Self-Governing Schools Etc. (Scotland) Act 1989, Sched. 6, para. 1. See *Shaw v. Strathclyde Regional Council*, 1987 S.C.L.R. 439.
[58] s. 54(2).
[59] s. 54(3), as amended by the Self-Governing Schools Etc. (Scotland) Act 1989, Sched. 6, para. 1.
[60] s. 54(4).
[61] s. 55, as amended by the Self-Governing Schools Etc. (Scotland) Act 1989, Sched. 6, para. 1.
[62] s. 56.

Assisted places at independent schools

For the purpose of enabling pupils, who might otherwise not be able to do **12.45** so, to attend and receive education at independent schools, the Secretary of State was previously entitled to establish and operate a scheme whereby participating schools remit fees that would otherwise be chargeable in respect of pupils admitted to assisted places under the scheme and the Secretary of State reimbursed the schools for the fees that were remitted.[63] This scheme was phased out as from the 1997–1998 school year.[64]

Grants by Secretary of State and industrial scholarships

The Secretary of State may, in accordance with regulations made by him, **12.46** apply such sums as he thinks necessary or expedient for the purpose *inter alia* of the payment of allowances to or in respect of persons attending courses of education.[65] He may also award industrial scholarships or make payments in respect of the award of such scholarships by other persons.[66] An industrial scholarship is a scholarship tenable by persons undertaking full-time courses of higher education provided by a university, college, or other institution in the United Kingdom which are relevant to a career in industry.[67] A course is full-time for this purpose although full-time study alternates with associated industrial, professional or commercial experience.[68]

Health and cleanliness

Medical and dental inspection

An education authority or board of management of a self-governing school **12.47** may require the parent of any pupil in attendance at any school under their management to submit the pupil for medical or dental inspection in accordance with arrangements made by the appropriate health board in agreement with the authority or board of management.[69] The authority or board of management may similarly require any young person in attendance at any educational establishment under their management to submit him or herself for medical or dental inspection.[70] Anyone who fails without a reasonable excuse to comply with a requirement so made may be guilty of an offence.[71]

Examination for cleanliness

An education authority or board of management of a self-governing school **12.48** may, by directions in writing, issued with respect to all schools and other educational establishments under its management or any of them, authorise a medical officer to cause examination to be made of the bodies and clothing of all, or any, of the pupils whenever, in the medical officer's opinion, such examinations are necessary in the interest of cleanliness.[72] Any such examination

---

[63] s. 75A, as inserted by the Education (Scotland) Act 1981, s. 5(1). For details, see the 1st edition of this book, at pp. 343–344.

[64] Education (Schools) Act 1997, s. 5.

[65] s. 73(f).

[66] s. 76(1).

[67] s. 76(2).

[68] s. 76(3).

[69] s. 57(2), as amended by the Self-Governing Schools Etc. (Scotland) Act 1989, Sched. 6, para. 1.

[70] *ibid.*

[71] s. 57(3). *Quaere* whether refusal of a child with capacity to consent to medical treatment to submit to inspection would amount to reasonable excuse. It is submitted that, at least in relation to the parent, there is reasonable excuse since once the child acquires capacity the parent loses the power to consent: see above, para. 8.50.

[72] s. 58(1).

is to be made by the medical officer, or by a person authorised in writing by him or her, and no female is to be examined or cleansed except by a registered medical practitioner or by a woman authorised for that purpose.[73] If the body or clothing of any pupil is then found to be infested with vermin or in a foul condition, the authority or board of management may serve a notice upon the parent or, in the case of a young person, upon the young person him or herself. The notice must inform the person on whom it is served that cleansing will be carried out under arrangements made by the education authority or board of management unless, within the period limited by the notice and not more than 24 hours after its service, the body and clothing of the pupil are cleansed to the satisfaction of the medical officer or authorised person specified in the notice.[74] If the medical officer or authorised person is not then satisfied that the body and clothing of the pupil have been properly cleansed an order may be issued which will be sufficient authority for compulsory cleansing and which carries with it powers to convey and detain for that purpose. The parent's or child's consent or refusal to this procedure would appear to be irrelevant and the authority to carry out the procedure is the statutory provision itself. It is an offence if, after cleansing has been carried out in compliance with a notice or compulsorily, the body or clothing of the pupil is again found to be infested with vermin or in a foul condition at any time while he or she is in attendance at a school or other educational establishment; provided that it is proved that the condition of his or her body or clothing is due to neglect on the part of the parent, or of the young person, as the case may be.[75]

SPECIAL EDUCATIONAL NEEDS

Introduction

12.49   It is the duty of an education authority:

(a)   to disseminate in its area information as to the importance of the early discovery of special educational needs and the opportunity for assessment available;

(b)   to establish which of those children in its area, who are (i) of school age or (ii) under school age but being at least two years of age have come to the attention of the authority as having special educational needs, have pronounced specific or complex special educational needs such as require continuing review; and

(c)   to keep a record of needs of each such child.[76]

The authority also has a power but not a duty to establish which children in its area under school age (not otherwise covered), and which young persons (those over school age but under 18) who are receiving school education, have such

---

[73] s. 58(2) and (7).
[74] s. 58(3), as amended by the Self-Governing Schools Etc. (Scotland) Act 1989.
[75] s. 58(5).
[76] s. 60(1) and (2) as substituted by the Education (Scotland) Act 1981, s. 4(1), and as amended by the Self-Governing Schools Etc. (Scotland) Act 1989, s. 72(1). Special educational needs are needs caused by a learning difficulty which calls for special provision, *i.e.* where (a) a child or young person has significantly greater difficulty in learning than the majority of children or young persons of his or her age, or (b) suffers from a disability which either prevents or hinders him or her from making use of educational facilities of a kind generally provided for children or young persons of his or her age, or (c) in the case of a child under the age of five, he or she is or would be if provision for special educational needs were not made for him or her, likely to be in such need if over the age of five (s. 1(5) (d) as added by the Education (Scotland) Act 1981, s. 3(1)). A child or young person is not, however, to be taken as having a learning difficulty solely because the language in which he or she is or will be taught is different from a language, including a form of the teaching language, spoken in his or her home (*ibid.*).

needs; and to open and keep a record of needs in respect of each of them. In relation to a young person, the power is exercisable only on a request by the young person or his or her parent.[77]

The record is to include four parts containing respectively (a) a summary of **12.50** the child's or young person's impairments, (b) a statement of the special educational needs arising from those impairments, (c) a statement of the measures proposed by the education authority to meet those needs and (d) where appropriate, the nomination of a school to be attended by the person recorded.[78]

Examination and assessment

It is not lawful to establish and record a child's needs unless the child has **12.51** undergone a process of assessment, including a medical and a psychological examination and a report by any teacher in the authority's employment who has been concerned in his or her education.[79] The authority must, by notice in writing, invite the child's parent to submit the child for examination and if a parent of a child to whom the authority owe a duty in terms of section 60(2) fails, without reasonable excuse, to comply the authority may, by notice in writing, require him or her to do so.[80] Failure of the parent to comply with the latter notice absolves the authority from its duty to establish and record the child's needs,[81] and if the failure is without reasonable excuse the parent is guilty of an offence.[82] If the parent of any child requests the education authority, for the area to which the child belongs, to make arrangements for the child to undergo assessment the authority must comply with that request unless in its opinion the request is unreasonable.[83]

It is not lawful for an education authority to establish that a young person **12.52** has pronounced specific or complex special educational needs and to record him or her unless the young person has undergone a process of assessment and he or she or, where the education authority are satisfied that the young person is not capable of expressing his or her views, his or her parent has been invited by the authority to express views as regards these needs and the measures required to meet them.[84]

Decision to record

In deciding whether or not to record a child or young person, an education **12.53** authority must take into consideration the advice given to them in consequence of the process of assessment, any views expressed by the parent or by the young person, any reports or other information with respect to the child or young person obtained from the managers or teachers of any school which he or she has attended, and any other reports or information relevant to his or her educational needs which the authority are able to obtain.[85] The decision of the authority, the reasons for the decision and the terms in which the authority propose to record the child or young person, must be intimated forthwith by a notice in writing to the parent, or, in the case of a young person capable of expressing his or her views, to the young person.[86] Within 14 days of that notice, the parent or young

---

[77] s. 60(5).
[78] s. 65D(2).
[79] s. 61(1).
[80] *ibid.*, as amended by the Self-Governing Schools Etc. (Scotland) Act 1989, s. 72(2).
[81] s. 61(5).
[82] s. 61(4).
[83] s. 61(6).
[84] s. 61(7).
[85] s. 62(1).
[86] s. 62(2).

person may express to the authority views on the terms on which the record should be made and, in recording the child or young person, the authority must have regard to these views. Thereafter, the authority must notify the parent or young person of (a) their decision as to the terms, (b) the parent's or young person's right of appeal, and (c) the name and address of the person to whom application may be made for advice and information about the child's or young person's special educational needs. The authority must then ensure that the provision made by them for the recorded child or young person includes provision for his or her special educational needs.[87]

Appeals

Reference to appeal committee

12.54   The parent of a recorded child may refer to an appeal committee any of the following decisions made by an education authority[88]:

(a) A decision to record the child, or, following a review, to continue to record him or her.

(b) A decision of an education authority not to record the child or not to continue to record the child.

(c) A decision as to the terms on which a summary of the child's impairments or a statement of his or her special educational needs arising from those impairments are recorded; and any such decision following a review.

(d) A decision as to nomination of a school to be attended by the child or young person or any such decision following a review. A reference to the appeal committee is competent under this heading, however, only if a placing request has been made and no other such reference has been made in respect of the child within the previous 12 months.

(e) A decision refusing a placing request in respect of the child provided no reference under this heading, or under heading (d) above, has been made within the previous 12 months.

A young person, or, where the authority was satisfied that the young person was not capable of expressing views, his or her parent, may refer to an appeal committee decisions of the education authority corresponding to the decisions (b), (c), (d) and (e) above.[89]

12.55   Any reference to an appeal committee must be lodged within 28 days of receipt of the notification of the decision of the education authority as to the terms in which it recorded the child or young person but the appeal committee has power, on good cause being shown, to hear a reference notwithstanding that it was not lodged within that time.[90] Regulations may make provision (a) requiring the authority to make information relevant to a decision available to the appeal committee and to the parent or young person, and (b) for deeming an appeal committee to have confirmed the decision of the education authority if the committee's decision has not been notified within a prescribed time.[91]

Reference to the Secretary of State

12.56   Where the reference relates (a) to a decision to record, or to continue to record, a child or (b) to the terms in which the summary of a child's or young

---

[87] s. 62(3), as amended by the Self-Governing Schools Etc. (Scotland) Act 1989, s. 72(3).

[88] s. 63(1).

[89] s. 63(2).

[90] s. 63(5).

[91] s. 63(6). See Education (Appeal Committee Procedures) (Scotland) Regulations 1982 (S.I. 1982 No. 1736).

person's impairment, and a statement of the special educational needs arising from those impairments, are to be recorded, the appeal committee must refer the reference to the Secretary of State.[92] Also, where an appeal committee considers that it cannot deal with a reference which relates to the education authority's decision as to the nomination of a school, without having the decision of the Secretary of State on the question of whether or not a child should be recorded or the terms in which the summary of impairments and statement of special educational needs should be recorded, it must refer that question, or so much of the reference as relates to those terms, to the Secretary of State. When any of these matters has been referred to him, the Secretary of State shall then (a) confirm or refuse to confirm the education authority's decision to record or continue to record the child, (b) confirm with or without modification the terms in which the summary of impairments and statement of special educational needs are recorded.[93] Where, however, the reference has been made to the Secretary of State because the appeal committee considered that without having his decision it could not deal with the reference to it of an education authority's decision as to the nomination of a school to be attended by a child or young person, the Secretary of State is not to make his decision unless he has first obtained and taken into consideration the views of the parent or young person who made the reference to the appeal committee.[94] Where the Secretary of State refuses to confirm an education authority's decision to record or to continue to record a child, he shall direct the authority to discontinue the record of the child and the authority must comply with that direction.[95] Where the Secretary of State confirms an education authority's decision with modifications as to the terms in which the summary of impairments and statement of special educational needs are to be recorded, he must direct the authority to modify the record accordingly and the authority must comply with that direction.[96] The Secretary of State's decision is to be notified to the appeal committee, the person who made the reference to the appeal committee, and the education authority.[97]

Decision of appeal committee
    The effect of the above provisions is that references of decisions to record, **12.57** or to continue to record, a child and of decisions as to the terms in which the summary of impairments and statement of special educational needs are to be recorded, are, in effect, references to the Secretary of State and also that questions relating to these matters, which arise in connection with the reference of other decisions, are to be decided by the Secretary of State. The references which remain for decision by the appeal committee are those relating to the nomination of a school to be attended by the child or young person and decisions refusing a placing request. As a decision on the nomination of a school can be referred only if there has been a placing request,[98] all the decisions taken by the appeal committee are essentially decisions on placing requests. The appeal committee may confirm the education authority's decision as to nomination of a school or refusing a placing request only if it is satisfied that (a) in relation to the placing request one or more of the specified grounds of refusal, as they apply to recorded

---

[92] s. 64(1).
[93] s. 64(4).
[94] s. 64(7).
[95] s. 64(5).
[96] s. 64(6).
[97] s. 64(8).
[98] s. 63(3).

children or young persons, exist, and (b) it is, in all the circumstances, appropriate to do so.[99] Otherwise the appeal committee must refuse to confirm the authority's decision and require it to place the child or young person in the school specified in the placing request. If the specified school is an independent school, the appeal committee is to require the authority to meet the fees and other necessary costs of the child's or young persons's attendance at that school and the authority must comply with that requirement.[1] Where the appeal committee has referred the reference, or any part of it, to the Secretary of State, they are not to dispose of so much of the reference as relates to the school to be attended by the child or young person until the Secretary of State's decision upon the matter referred to him is notified to the appeal committee; and the appeal committee is to reach its decision as respects the child or young person in the light of the Secretary of State's decision.[2]

12.58   The appeal committee's decision and the reasons for it are to be notified in writing to the person who made the reference and to the education authority, and where the authority's decision as to the nomination of a school, or refusing a placing request, has been confirmed, the person who made the reference is to be informed of his or her right of appeal to the sheriff.[3] Where the authority's decision is not confirmed, the authority must place the child or young person in the specified school and amend accordingly any nomination in his or her record of a school to be attended by him or her.[4]

Appeal to sheriff

12.59   There is an appeal to the sheriff against a decision of an appeal committee on references relating to an education authority's decision on the nomination of a school or refusing a placing request in respect of a recorded child or young person.[5] The appeal is at the instance of the person who made the reference. The education authority have no corresponding right of appeal. The provisions of the Act on parties to appeals, the form of appeal, the time within which it must be lodged, hearings in chambers, and expenses, apply to these appeals as they do to appeals in respect of placing requests.[6] Where the sheriff considers that he cannot deal with the appeal without having the decision of the Secretary of State on the question of whether or not the child should be recorded, or on the terms in which the summary of impairments and statement of special education needs should be recorded, he may refer that question or those matters to the Secretary of State.[7] He can, however, perhaps surprisingly, do so only on the motion of a party to the appeal, and he is not to refer to the Secretary of State if there has already been a reference to him by the appeal committee.[8] The sheriff's powers and the grounds on which he is to confirm, or refuse to confirm, the decision of the education authority, are the same as those of the appeal committee[9] Where there has been a reference to the Secretary of State, either by himself or by the appeal committee, the sheriff is to dispose of the appeal in the light of the Secretary of State's decision.[10]

---

[99] s. 64(2).
[1] s. 64(3).
[2] s. 64(9).
[3] s. 64(10).
[4] s. 64(11).
[5] s. 65(1).
[6] s. 65(2). See above, para.12.29.
[7] s. 65(3).
[8] s. 65(5).
[9] s. 65(6).
[10] s. 65(8).

Review and reports

It is the duty of an education authority to keep under consideration the cases **12.60** of all recorded children and young persons belonging to their area and to review the decision to record whenever they think it expedient or when requested to do so by notice in writing given by the parent of the child or by the young person, or by the parent of a young person who in the opinion of the authority is not capable of expressing his or her views.[11] The parent of a recorded child, the recorded young person, or, as the case may be, the parent of a recorded young person, is not, however, entitled to request a review of the decision to record at an interval of less than 12 months from the date of that decision, or its most recent review, whichever is the later, nor of the information entered in the record at an interval of less than 12 months from the date of the commencement of the record or the most recent review of the information, whichever is the later.[12] It is also the duty of an education authority to consider, during the period beginning two years before a recorded child ceases to be of school age and ending nine months before then, what provision would benefit the child after he or she ceases to be of school age and to make a report thereon.[13] That consideration may be carried out in conjunction with a review in relation to the child.[14] The report is to include the authority's recommendation as to whether the child would benefit from school education after he or she ceases to be of school age and, if it does so recommend, whether or not his or her record should be discontinued.[15] A copy of the report is to be sent to the child's parent, who is to be informed of his or her right to have the record discontinued. In any case where it considers it appropriate to do so, the education authority is also to send a copy of the report to the health board for the area in which the child resides and, with the consent of the child's parent, any other body making provision from which the child might benefit and the local authority as education authority shall also ensure that the local authority for the purposes of Part II of the Children (Scotland) Act 1995 receive a copy.[16] A copy of the report sent for this purpose is, where possible, to be sent not later than six months before the child or young person to whom the report relates is expected to cease receiving school education.[17]

Discontinuance of record

An education authority is to discontinue the record of a young person if **12.61** requested to do so by him or her, or, where the young person is incapable of expressing a request, by his or her parent.[18] Subject thereto the record of a child who ceases to be of school age, but as a young person receives school education, is to be continued for so long as he or she receives such education.[19]

Provision of special educational needs outwith the United Kingdom

Without prejudice to the powers described above, an education authority **12.62** also has the power to make such arrangements as it thinks fit to enable a child or young person to attend an establishment outwith the United Kingdom if that establishment makes provision wholly or mainly for persons with pronounced,

---

[11] s. 65A(1).
[12] s. 65A(2).
[13] s. 65B(1) and (2).
[14] s. 65B(4).
[15] s. 65B(5).
[16] s. 65B(6), as amended by the Children (Scotland) Act 1995, Sched. 4, para. 28(4).
[17] s. 65B(7).
[18] s. 65C(3).
[19] s. 65C(1).

specific or complex special educational needs.[20] It is not necessary that there be a record of needs in relation to the child.[21] The arrangement may include defraying, wholly or partly (a) the fees payable for the child's or young person's attendance and his or her travelling, maintenance and other expenses in respect of that attendance; and (b) the expenses of the child's or young person's parent, parents or other person where in the opinion of the authority it would be to the advantage of the child or young person to be accompanied by such parent or other person.[22]

[20] s. 65G(1), as inserted by the Self-Governing Schools Etc. (Scotland) Act 1989, s. 71.
[21] s. 65G(2).
[22] s. 65G(3).

CHAPTER 13

ALIMENT

THE OBLIGATION TO ALIMENT

Nature of the alimentary obligation

"The main obligation of a parent is to aliment the child."[1] When questions **13.01** of enforcement arise the obligation is seen nearly always in terms of payment of money, but the money payment is but a substitute for, or a means of effecting, provision in kind. Aliment is that part of the general duty of nurture—itself an aspect of the statutory responsibility to safeguard and promote the child's health, development and welfare—that can be met by material provision. It is a parent's duty to provide his or her children "in bed, board, and clothing, and all the necessaries of life"[2] and that duty will often be fulfilled, at least in large part, by entertainment of the child in the family home without any question of money payment. So to provide for the child is the characteristic performance of the duty and, unless need for other provision arises, its sufficient discharge.

The obligation of aliment is not based on implied contract and so cannot be **13.02** irrevocably discharged[3] nor is it based on the parental right to have the child living with the obligant because it subsists although that parental right be lost,[4] and might at common law devolve on those who did not have that right. It is rather an "evident instance of the law of nature"[5] based on the parental relationship in lines of descent and ascent. So at common law the duty was enforceable *ex debito naturali* not only against parents but on their failure against descendants and remoter ascendants. The natural tie giving rise to the obligation was not, however, seen as embracing collaterals although persons who did not have a natural obligation to provide aliment, including collaterals, might fall under an obligation *ex jure representationis* as successors to the estate of a person bound *ex debito naturali*.[6]

The Family Law (Scotland) Act 1985

The common law was superseded in virtually all its aspects by the Family **13.03** Law (Scotland) Act 1985.[7] In relation to alimentary claims from the executors of a deceased person or from any person enriched by the succession to a deceased person's estate (that is to say the liability *ex jure representationis*) the common

---

[1] Hume, *Lectures*, Vol. I, p. 206.

[2] Erskine, I, vi, 56.

[3] Fraser, pp. 99 and 121; Stair, I, v, 1.

[4] This was certainly the case at common law, and receives statutory recognition by the Child Support Act 1991, s. 1(1) of which provides "each parent of a qualifying child is responsible for maintaining him"; s. 3 defines "qualifying child" to be one whose parent or parents do not live in the same household as the child.

[5] Stair, *ibid.*

[6] Fraser, pp. 102 and 103, and see below, paras 13.17 *et seq.*

[7] ss. 1–7. See Nichols, *The Family Law (Scotland) Act 1985* (2nd ed., 1991), Chap. 2.

law rules have, however, been expressly preserved[8] and in some other respects reference may still have to be made to the common law principles for assistance in the interpretation of the Act or for the solution of questions that are left open. Most of the previous statute law on the substance of the alimentary obligation is repealed and the law is now contained in the 1985 Act. Before the repeal of the Guardianship of Infants Act 1925[9] the welfare of the child, at least when a pupil, was the first and paramount consideration in questions of aliment as in other questions relating to the upbringing of the child. Welfare is now the paramount consideration only in actions relating to parental responsibilities, parental rights, guardianship and the administration of a child's property,[10] which covers the parental obligation of aliment in so far as it is an aspect of the responsibility to safeguard and promote the child's health, development and welfare. In any case, the terms of the 1985 Act are sufficiently wide to enable the court to observe the spirit of the welfare principle, though its application would not justify the court awarding a child aliment when the child is not otherwise entitled thereto.[11] Statutory rules for enforcement are largely unaffected by the 1985 Act.

The main features of the statutory obligation of parents to aliment their children are described in the following paragraphs.

Obligants

13.04　　Liability for aliment now attaches only to:

> (a) the spouse of the person to be alimented;
> (b) the father or mother of the person to be alimented; or
> (c) a person who has accepted the child to be alimented as a child of his or her family.[12]

In the last case, the obligation does not, however, apply where the child has been boarded out with the acceptor by a local authority. A grandparent or other ascendant therefore has no obligation now unless he or she has accepted the grandchild as a child of his or her own (immediate) family,[13] and the rule under which liability might attach to children and remoter descendants has also been abolished. The alimentary obligation of spouses lies outwith the scope of this book[14] and is considered here only in so far as it impinges on the parental obligations. Categories (a) and (b) are usually questions of fact and will seldom lead to difficulties, though the validity of the marriage (which sometimes affects the question) is, of course, a question of law. "Father" and "mother" are sometimes matters of law, as when the person satisfies the description only by application of the terms of the Human Fertilisation and Embryology Act 1990.[15] Category (c) is more problematic, and will depend on a number of circumstances that may differ in each case. The concept of "child of his family" is not restricted, as

---

[8] Family Law (Scotland) Act 1985, s. 1(4).

[9] By Sched. 2 to the Law Reform (Parent and Child) (Scotland) Act 1986.

[10] Children (Scotland) Act 1995, s. 11.

[11] *cf.* s. 2 of the Child Support Act 1991, which provides that the Secretary of State or a child support officer "shall have regard to the welfare" of the child in exercising any discretionary power under that Act. There is no requirement to further welfare, nor to regard it as paramount, and the section does no more than oblige the Secretary of State or the child support officer to take account of the child's welfare.

[12] Family Law (Scotland) Act 1985, s. 1(1).

[13] *cf. Re A (Child of the Family)* [1998] 1 F.L.R. 347 which raised the question of whether grandparents who had assumed the care of their grandchild had "treated" her as a child of their family.

[14] For details in that context, see Clive, *Husband and Wife* (4th ed.), Chap. 12.

[15] See above, Chap. 3.

it previously was in relation to jurisdiction in custody,[16] to the child of one spouse being accepted as one of the family by the other spouse,[17] and it can therefore include a child who is the child of neither spouse.[18] There is indeed no need for the family into which the child is accepted to be based on marriage, or to consist of two adults. "Family," as used in the Act, includes a one-parent family.[19] Acceptance as a child of the family probably requires an intention for the arrangement to be permanent, or at least indefinite, and the temporary looking after of a child, even if the child is treated in all respects alike with the natural children of a family, will be insufficient to impose the alimentary obligation.[20] "Acceptance" is primarily a state of mind, though it may be shown by words or actions. Some interpretative help may be obtained from the cases decided on (now repealed, though similar) provisions relating to jurisdiction in custody.[21] The acceptance must be after the coming into force of the Act[22] before the obligation in the Act can be founded upon,[23] but acceptance is, it is submitted, a continuing concept so that a family that is established before the relevant date and continues after that date could found acceptance and thus an obligation under the Act. Categories (b) and (c) would appear to be mutually exclusive, the former being a matter of fact and the latter being a state of mind, with the result that a parent will never come within category (c): it follows from this, it has been held, that a person who believes himself to be a parent, but who is not, cannot be held to have accepted the child to be a member of his family.[24]

Status irrelevant

No distinction is now made for the purposes of aliment between legitimate **13.05** and illegitimate children. It is paternity or maternity[25] that imposes the obligation, and a child can be an obligee in relation to aliment whether or not his or her parents have ever been married to one another.[26] This alters the common law and consists with section 1 of the Law Reform (Parent and Child) (Scotland) Act 1986, under which the fact that a person's parents are not or have not been married to one another is to be left out of account in establishing the legal relationship between two persons. An adopted child is for this, as for other, purposes in the same position as a child born of the obligant.[27] The biological parent of an adopted child is not subject to the obligation of aliment.

---

[16] See above, para.9.31.
[17] Though this will be the typical example of its application, and, indeed was the intendment of the now repealed s. 7 of the Matrimonial Proceedings (Children) Act 1958, under which the court in divorce proceedings could order aliment to be paid by a spouse to his or her stepchildren.
[18] *Bradley v. Bradley*, 1987 S.C.L.R. 62 (Sh.Ct) was decided on different statutory words, which required the child of one spouse to be accepted by the other: the case related to jurisdiction in custody.
[19] Family Law (Scotland) Act 1985, s. 27. In another context (transmission of tenancies) it was held by the English Court of Appeal that "family" does not (yet) include a relationship based on homosexual cohabitation: *Fitzpatrick v. Sterling Housing Association* [1997] 4 All E.R. 991.
[20] See *Inglis v. Inglis*, 1987 S.C.L.R. 608; *Watson v. Watson*, 1994 S.C.L.R. 1097.
[21] *Bowlas v. Bowlas* [1965] P. 450; *Holmes v. Holmes* [1966] 1 W.L.R. 187; *R v. R* [1968] P. 414; *Dixon v. Dixon* [1968] 1 W.L.R. 167. The English legislation upon which these cases were based, and the Scottish equivalent, has now been changed (to the concept of a child "treated" rather than "accepted" as a member of the family), but the wording in the Family Law (Scotland) Act 1985 remains the same as that upon which these cases were decided.
[22] On September 1, 1986.
[23] *Forbes v. Forbes*, 1991 S.C.L.R. 389.
[24] *Watson v. Watson*, 1994 S.C.L.R. 1097.
[25] On the establishment of which, see above, Chaps 3, 4 and 6. This often has to be proved before aliment can be claimed: see *Torrie v. Turner*, 1990 S.L.T. 718.
[26] Family Law (Scotland) Act 1985, s. 27, as amended by the Law Reform (Parent and Child) (Scotland) Act 1986, Sched. 1, para. 21.
[27] Adoption (Scotland) Act 1978, s. 39(1).

How amount of aliment is to be determined

13.06   Aliment is such support as is reasonable in the circumstances having regard to the needs and resources of the parties, their earning capacities and, generally, all the circumstances of the case.[28] Both present and foreseeable needs and resources are to be taken into account[29] and a consideration of earning capacity clearly entitles the court to have regard not only to present earned income and opportunities in present employment but, more generally, to the potential income which it may be within a party's capacity to earn. Reasonable choices of employment are, however, it is submitted, to be respected and although unemployment, where it is voluntary and avoidable, no doubt needs to be justified there may be cases, as of a student obligee, or a retired obligant, where it is, in the circumstances, right to have regard to present earnings rather than those of which the party may be capable.

Plurality of obligants

13.07   Where there are two or more obligants there is no order of liability.[30] In deciding how much, if any, aliment to award against any one obligant the court is, however, to have regard, among the other circumstances of the case, to the obligation of aliment owed by any other person.[31] And in an action brought by or on behalf of a child under the age of 16 years, the court in assessing the amount may award such provision as it considers to be in all the circumstances reasonable in respect of the expenses incurred wholly or partly by the person having care of the child for the purposes of caring for the child[32] (*e.g.* that if the child is being cared for by one parent only, the other parent's liability to the child may be increased to reflect the expenses of the caring parent).[33] A consequence would seem to be that liability for aliment is not joint and several and that a claimant should, therefore, direct his or her claim against all parties subject to the obligation and that the court will make, not an apportionment *inter se* but a separate award against each obligant.[34] A further consequence of there being no order of liability—and perhaps its major intendment—is the abrogation of the rules that the obligation of aliment rested primarily on the child's father, that as long as the father's means were sufficient to enable him adequately to aliment the child no decree for aliment could be pronounced against any other person and that it was unnecessary and incompetent to consider the ability of any other person, including the child's mother, to provide aliment.[35] The mother now stands in like position to the father and, in determining the amount of aliment to be paid by each parent, the court is to have regard to both parents' respective needs, resources and earning capacities and all the circumstances of the case.[36] Yet another consequence, perhaps more surprising, of the complete abolition of any order of liability is that the parental obligation

---

[28] Family Law (Scotland) Act 1985, ss. 1(2) and 4(1). This can include awards previously made under other provisions: *Jowett v. Jowett*, 1990 S.C.L.R. 348, and the conduct of the defender in attempting to conceal his financial position: *Walker v. Walker*, 1991 S.L.T. 649. S. 4(3)(b) provides that the court shall not take account of the conduct of any party in determining the amount due unless it would be "manifestly inequitable to leave it out of account."

[29] Family Law (Scotland) Act 1985. s. 27(1).

[30] *ibid.* s. 4(2).

[31] *Inglis v. Inglis*, 1987 S.C.L.R. 608.

[32] Family Law (Scotland) Act, s. 4(4), as inserted by the Child Support Act 1991, Sched. 5, para. 5.

[33] This provision is, it is submitted, somewhat illogical, particularly because the award of aliment goes to the child and not to the caring parent who suffers the expenses that increase the obligant's liability.

[34] See Nichols, *op. cit*, pp. 11–12.

[35] *Dickinson v. Dickinson*, 1952 S.C. 27.

[36] *Scully v. Scully*, 1989 S.C.L.R. 757.

to aliment a married child is no longer, as a matter of law, postponed to the obligation of a spouse.[37] The scheme of the Act is such that questions of amount of aliment and extent of liability are interrelated[38] and it would seem that it opens up a comparison at large between the needs and means of the child to be supported, of his or her spouse, and of his or her parents in determining both the appropriate amount of aliment and the extent, if any, to which the spouse or the parents should contribute. A parent whose means are greater than a spouse's may, therefore, be called upon to make the greater or even the sole contribution; but it is of the nature of marriage that spouses should look to each other rather than to a parent for support and it is submitted that in the circumstances of most cases that consideration should place a restraint on the extent of parental liability.

Duration of obligation

The parental obligation to aliment a child subsists only until the child reaches **13.08** the age of 18 years or, where he or she is reasonably and appropriately undergoing instruction at an educational establishment or training for employment or for a trade, profession or vocation, until he or she reaches the age of 25 years.[39] Doubts about the obligation to aliment a child who was able to earn a livelihood but was instead undergoing education or training are thus removed and a limit put on the duration of the obligation; but doubts may yet remain, though of a different nature, of whether education or training is undertaken "reasonably and appropriately".[40] At the same time, the common law rule disappears that the obligation to aliment a child unable to earn his or her livelihood or otherwise support him- or herself subsisted throughout his or her incapacity even if that incapacity were lifelong.[41] Except when under 25 and undergoing education or training, a person who is over the age of majority and unable to earn a livelihood must look to his or her spouse or to State schemes of assistance and not to his or her parents so far as any legally enforceable claim for support is concerned; and that is so even if his or her inability is due to physical or mental incapacity. The death of either obligant or obligee ends the obligation of aliment, as does the ending of the parental relationship by adoption.[42] Express provision is, however, made for the recovery of contributions to the maintenance of children looked after by local authorities[43] made by persons who have parental responsibilities in relation to the child.[44]

Common law principles

The common law rules on the nature and purpose of aliment are now entirely **13.09** replaced by the statutory definition of the alimentary obligation.[45] That definition is, however, so wide that an outline of the common law rules may serve to give it content although they cannot detract from its generality or from the freedom of comparison and evaluation which the statute gives. A number of principles evolved at common law that are not inconsistent with the Family Law (Scotland) Act 1985.

---

[37] Fraser (3rd ed.), p. 124 and cases cited therein (nn. 2 and 3).

[38] Family Law (Scotland) Act 1985, ss. 1 and 4.

[39] *ibid*. s. 1(1)(c) and (d) and (5). See *Jowett v. Jowett*, 1990 S.C.L.R. 348. In *Fleming v. Fleming*, 1995 S.L.T. 100 it was held that the obligation continued even beyond the terms of a court decree, because it was dependent on the Act and not on the decree.

[40] See Nichols at p. 6. In *McBride v. McBride*, 1995 S.C.L.R. 1021 an adult training centre for mentally and physically disabled adults was held to be an "educational establishment" within the terms of the Act.

[41] Erskine, I, vi, 56.

[42] Adoption (Scotland) Act 1978, s. 39(1).

[43] See below, Chap. 16.

[44] Social Work (Scotland) Act 1968, ss. 78–81. That such "contributions" are different in kind from alimentary obligations is clear from the fact that the obligant is any person with parental responsibilities and not just a parent or person who has accepted the child as a member of his or her family.

[45] Family Law (Scotland) Act 1985, s. 1(2).

Economy of provision and relevance of obligant's means

13.10   In *Maule v. Maule*[46] it was held by the House of Lords that aliment extended to no more than "support beyond want; and all that is beyond that, is left to paternal affection". That decision, made in the early nineteenth century, requires, however, to be interpreted in the light of changing social perspectives. The court is not bound by ancient concepts. The rules of law relating to aliment are fluid and vary with social conditions.[47] In any event, "want" is a relative term. It does not mean bare subsistence but is relative to the situation of the party who made the claim. So "a person who has received the education of a gentleman... would not be placed above the reach of want by getting the relief of a parish pauper".[48] Such comments require adaptation to modern conditions but they indicate an award that is a reasonable but economical provision for the applicant in the light of his or her condition and circumstances. Provided the applicant's needs so measured can be met by the obligant without depriving him or her of proper support for him- or herself or others for whom he or she has a prior responsibility, the means of the obligant are, it has been said, irrelevant.[49] In most cases the statutory test will now point to a similar result but the scope for taking account of the obligant's needs and means is wider while, on the other hand, it is no longer necessary, within the bounds of what is reasonable, to have special regard to economy of provision.[50]

Obligee's means

13.11   Because the common law was that the need of the person to be alimented had to be established before the obligation to aliment him or her became exigible, it was a bar to any claim that the claimant already had the means of his or her own aliment.[51] These principles are consistent with the Family Law (Scotland) Act 1985 and, in particular, with the reference to needs as among the matters to which the court is to have regard.[52] The Act gives wider discretion according to circumstances and comparative means and needs of parties, but in general it will remain the case that there can be no valid claim for aliment where the claimant's income whether earned or derived from property or obtained as State benefits[53] would be sufficient to provide his or her aliment, and the possession of capital capable of sale will usually bar a claim where the proceeds of sale would provide sufficient aliment. At one time, the father's position in relation to the aliment of his children constituted an exception. He might not encroach on the child's capital nor it seems use the child's income for the purpose of the child's aliment, so long at least as the child was not major and not forisfamiliated and the father had sufficient means to provide aliment. In *Fairgrieves v. Hendersons* Lord President Inglis said: "the father's obligation to aliment his children is absolute and unconditional; he is not in a position to say that the children shall maintain themselves out of any money they may have before he is called upon".[54] It was, however, settled before the 1985 Act that a child's estate might be applied to his or her aliment in relief of the father's obligation

---

[46] (1825) 1 W. & S. 266.

[47] *Polland v. Sturrock's Exrs*, 1952 S.C. 535, *per* Lord Justice-Clerk Thomson at 544–545.

[48] *Thom v. Mackenzie* (1864) 3 M.177, *per* Lord Justice-Clerk Inglis at 179.

[49] *ibid.*; Erskine, I, vi, 56; Stair, I, v, 7; Fraser, pp. 109 and 110.

[50] In determining the extent of the obligant's liability, his or her income is to be assessed net of tax: *Begg v. Begg*, 1987 S.C.L.R. 704; *Wiseman v. Wiseman*, 1989 S.C.L.R. 757; *Pryde v. Pryde*, 1991 S.L.T.(Sh.Ct) 26.

[51] Erskine, I, vi, 53; Stair I, v, 7.

[52] s. 4(1)(a).

[53] *McBride v. McBride*, 1995 S.C.L.R. 1021.

[54] (1885) 13 R. 98 at 99–100, *sed contra Hutcheson v. Hoggan's Trs* (1904) 6 F. 594; *Polland v. Sturrock's Exrs*, above.

even where the father was of sufficient means and that, at least in some circumstances, the father might be justified in encroaching on the child's capital for that purpose.[55] That view can readily be reconciled with the Act and the freedom with which it can be applied is enlarged, but it may still be the law that encroachment on a child's capital by a father, or now by a mother, for the purpose of alimenting the child is to be regarded as exceptional, and will not be justified where the parent's means are ample and the child's resources are small.

Effect of establishment in trade, business or profession

Again at common law, no aliment was due where a child had been established **13.12** in a business, trade, profession or other way of life and had as a result means sufficient to support him- or herself.[56] But the mere attainment by a child of a qualification which could, given the opportunity, be applied in the earning of a livelihood did not relieve the parent of liability. If the child was unemployed and could not with reasonable diligence secure employment the parent remained liable and if the child, having been gainfully employed, fell into unemployment or if his or her business failed so that he or she was no longer able to support him- or herself, the parental liability revived.[57] The extent to which a parent was required to go in setting up the child in a business, trade or profession was not well settled. Stair speaks of "breeding of them for some calling and employment according to their capacity and condition"[58] and in *Polland v. Sturrock's Executors*,[59] Lord Justice-Clerk Thomson referred to "the obligations and duties of a father under modern conditions, especially in regard to a daughter's education and training for earning her own living".[60] Much depended on circumstances, including the parents' means and assistance available from State and other sources, but where the parents' means so considered were sufficient it seems to be clear that the duty extended to providing for an education and training reasonably suited to the child's abilities and aptitudes. If the child's needs, including the need for education and training, so required, liability to provide aliment continued after the child attained majority and, in the case of a child incapable of earning a living because of physical or mental infirmity or other insuperable cause, subsisted throughout the child's life.[61] But where a child had once been established in a suitable way of earning his or her livelihood he or she could not make further demands for aliment unless having fallen into necessitous circumstances from which he or she had no means of retrieving him- or herself.[62] The obligation was, therefore, perpetual in the sense that it was never fully discharged and might at any time become exigible in the event of necessity. The Act has now put a term on the duration of the parental obligation, but, within that term, it contains nothing that affects the principle that an alimentary obligation that has lapsed may revive. So a child who at 16 became self-supporting may, if need arises, again call upon his or her parents for aliment at any time before attaining majority or, if reasonably and appropriately undergoing education or training, before attaining the age of 25. And the law does not require that in order to make such a claim the child must have fallen

---

[55] *Polland v. Sturrock's Exrs*, above.
[56] Erskine, I, vi, 53; Stair, I, v, 7; Fraser, p. 121.
[57] *ibid.*
[58] I, v, 6.
[59] 1952 S.C. 535.
[60] at 544.
[61] See Hume, *Lectures*, Vol. 1, pp. 214 and 215 and cases discussed therein and in the editorial footnotes.
[62] *AB v. CD* (1848) 10 D. 895; *Hunter's Trs v. Macan* (1839) 1 D. 817; *Maule v. Maule* (1825) 1 W. & S. 266.

into necessitous circumstances from which he or she cannot extricate him- or herself. So a child who has been established in a way of livelihood may give it up and call upon his or her parents to support him or her until the age of 25 in education or training which he or she has reasonably and appropriately undertaken. Whether parents are obliged to meet such a claim is a question of what is reasonable in the circumstances having regard to the factors which the Act lays down.

Obligant's discretion in discharge of obligation

13.13 Subject to the constraints imposed by the obligee's need, the obligant had at common law a wide discretion in the provision of aliment.[63] He or she might implement the obligation in the way he or she considered most economical provided the legitimate needs of the person to be alimented were not thereby jeopardised. So, a parent might insist on the child living in family with him or her as the most economical way of alimenting the child.[64] On the other hand a child could not complain if a parent chose to discharge the obligation by providing separate accommodation, provided that that was consistent with relief of the child's needs.[65] But in the case of a child who had not been established in a way of earning a livelihood, a parent could be required to provide aliment such as to enable the child to live in separate accommodation if that were necessary for the purpose of his or her education or training or for the early stages of his or her employment before he or she was in a position to earn sufficient to maintain him- or herself. Under a long line of authority of considerable antiquity, a parent who had ill-treated his children could not, whatever their age, require them as a condition of aliment to live in family with him; in such cases aliment would be decreed sufficient to enable separate provision to be made.[66]

13.14 In the circumstances of many cases a parent will still be entitled to implement the alimentary obligation in the way he or she considers most economical because it is reasonable to allow him or her to do so, but it is now a question of reasonableness rather than of right. The stress of the common law on economical discharge is lessened. The Act does, however, make specific provision which, although still invoking the test of reasonableness, goes some way to protect the parent's position. It is a defence to an action for aliment by or on behalf of a person other than a child under the age of 16 that the defender is making an offer, which it is reasonable to expect the person concerned to accept, to receive that person into his or her household and to fulfil the obligation of aliment.[67] For that purpose, however, the court is to have regard to any conduct, decree or other circumstances which appear to be relevant.[68] The rule is, therefore, in effect preserved that a parent may by ill-treatment forfeit any right to require his or her children, as a condition of aliment, to live in family with him or her. No provision is required in relation to children under 16 because questions of their residence will be determined by having regard to their welfare as the paramount consideration.[69]

---

[63] *Bell v. Bell* (1890) 17 R. 549.
[64] Erskine, I, vi, 56.
[65] In *Kirklands v. Kirklands* (1685) Mor. 403 it had, however, been found that a mother was bound *jure naturali* to aliment the younger children *in familia* and the modern law even before the 1985 Act would undoubtedly have considered the aliment of minor children in separate accommodation from the standpoint of the welfare of the child.
[66] Erskine I, vi, 56; Bankton I, vi, 14; and cases cited in Erskine.
[67] Family Law (Scotland) Act 1985, s. 2(8).
[68] *ibid.* s. 2(9).
[69] Children (Scotland) Act 1995, s. 11(7)(a).

Plurality of obligees

If a parent had means sufficient to aliment some but not all with a claim **13.15**
upon him or her, those children who remained under the parental protection
were, at common law, to be preferred to those who had been forisfamiliated.[70]
There is now no fixed rule that children who stay in the parental home are to be
preferred in this way.

Agreements on aliment

It followed from the perpetual character of the common law alimentary **13.16**
obligation that no conventional discharge, however conclusive and
comprehensive in its terms, could bar a later demand in the event of need
reviving. Agreements to exclude future liability for aliment or to restrict the
right to sue for aliment are, however, now subject to specific statutory regulation
under which they are of no effect unless fair and reasonable in all the
circumstances of the agreement at the time it was entered into.[71] Courts may be
reluctant to interfere with arrangements between parties of full age in so far as
they affect themselves but may be expected to look critically at any exclusion
of children's future aliment.[72] An agreement on aliment will not prevent any
party from applying for a maintenance assessment under the Child Support Act
1991,[73] and any provision purporting to restrict that right is void.[74] Agreements
to pay aliment may be varied at the instance of the obligant or of the person to
whom the obligation is owed on the occurrence of a material change of
circumstances.[75]

Representational liability

The general principle

Erskine says that "a father is not barely bound to maintain his children during **13.17**
his own life; he ought so to provide for all of them, that they may be able to live
comfortably after his death".[76] The obligation so stated is moral rather than
legal and so "is left entirely upon the conscience, without being enforced by
any civil sanction". The law, however, goes further and provides that where on
the death of a parent a child is left with insufficient means to support him- or
herself he or she may claim aliment from the parent's estate.[77] The claim is
prestable against executors but, as executors and trustees are not bound to retain
funds sufficient to meet it on a continuing basis, it is good against them only
prior to the period of distribution. The right to claim aliment transmits thereafter
against those who have succeeded to the parent's estate. The liability thus
incurred arises purely *ex jure representationis* and so is subject to rather different
principles from those applicable to direct liability.[78]

---

[70] Stair, I, v, 9.
[71] Family Law (Scotland) Act 1985, s. 7(1).
[72] See Nichols, *op. cit.*, p. 19.
[73] See below, Chap. 14.
[74] Child Support Act 1991, s. 9(4).
[75] Family Law (Scotland) Act 1985, s. 7(2); see Nichols at p. 20. And see *Mackenzie v. Mackenzie*, 1987 S.C.L.R. 671; *Woolley v. Strachan*, 1997 S.L.T. (Sh.Ct) 88. It is a material change of circumstances that a maintenance assessment under the Child Support Act 1991 has been made in respect of the child: s. 7(2A), as inserted by S.I. 1993 No. 660.
[76] I, vi, 58; *cf.* Stair, I, v, 7.
[77] Erskine, *ibid.*; *Beaton v. Beaton's Trs*, 1935 S.C. 187. The Scottish Law Commission have, however, recommended that aliment *jure representationis* be abolished: see *Report on Succession*, Scot. Law Com. No. 124 (1990), para. 9.5; this on the ground that the new rules of succession proposed there would obviate the need for such alimentary liability.
[78] Fraser, p. 128.

Preservation by the Act of representational liability

13.18   This common law representational liability is preserved by the Family Law (Scotland) Act 1985, which provides that

> "nothing in this section shall affect... any rule of law by which a person who is owed an obligation of aliment may claim aliment from the executor of a deceased person or from any person enriched by the succession to the estate of a deceased person".[79]

The provision is unhappily expressed. Section 4, which governs the amount of aliment, applies to representational liability but section 1(2), which defines the obligation of aliment and is to be read along with section 4, is excluded. The statutory definitions of the persons to and by whom the obligation of aliment is owed (which occur in section 1) are also excluded: with the result, it would seem, that these persons are to be ascertained by the common law rules. The apparent difficulties and anomalies which might ensue are, however, largely elided if the representational character of liability is kept in view. The representative can be liable only for a debt for which the deceased would have been liable had he or she been alive and liability is limited to the extent of the estate falling under the succession or, in the case of a person who has been enriched by the succession, to the extent of his or her enrichment. Despite the preservation of common law definitions of the person to whom the obligation is owed, there cannot therefore be liability to the ascendants of the deceased or to his or her grandchildren because, although there could, at least on some authorities and in some circumstances, have been such liability at common law, the result of the Act is that the deceased him- or herself would not have been liable to them. Nor, although for a different reason, can there be liability to a child accepted into his or her family by the deceased: under the Act the deceased might have had a liability to such a child but his or her representative has none because he or she has no liability at common law and the Act, while preserving the common law rule, creates no new representational liability.

Extent of representational liability

13.19   The statutory rules on determining the amount of aliment[80] apply, but the manner of their application is obscured by the omission of the reference to what is "reasonable in the circumstances"[81] as the basis on which the criteria are to be applied. In any event common law rules inherent in the nature of representational liability may still play a controlling role. Not only is the liability of the successor restricted to the extent of his or her enrichment by the succession but, within that restriction, equity in the distribution of the estate may limit the extent of his or her liability at least where the successor stands in the same relationship to the deceased as do the claimants. Representational liability has been seen as designed to compensate as far as necessary to meet alimentary need for the inequitable distribution of the estate—for example where the heritable part of the estate is large and has not passed to the deceased's children or has been distributed unequally among them, while the moveable estate is small.[82] Accordingly, it has been held that a successor is under no liability to aliment a brother or sister who has taken a corresponding benefit from the same succession.[83] The equity of that view may be questioned if it is strictly applied

---

[79]   Family Law (Scotland) Act 1985, s. 1(4).

[80]   *ibid.* s. 4.

[81]   *ibid.* s. 1(2).

[82]   If the moveable estate is large the children's claim to legitim will usually be sufficient provision for their aliment.

[83]   *Mackintosh v. Taylor* (1868) 7 M. 67.

in all cases and the Act may open the way for reconsideration. If the estate has been divided equally among the children but the share of one of them, perhaps much younger than the others, is insufficient when taken along with his or her other resources to meet his or her alimentary needs, the priority of the alimentary claim over rights of succession would suggest that he or she should be entitled to pursue a claim against his or her brothers and sisters *qua* successors to the extent that they have been enriched by the succession and have a surplus over their own alimentary needs. It is also doubtful whether considerations of equity of distribution have any necessary limiting role in a claim against a successor who is not a brother or sister of the claimant. There can, however, be no question but that full account must always be taken of anything received from the deceased's estate whether by way of legitim or of succession before a claim to aliment can arise against the deceased's representatives.

Classes of representative liable

Erskine discusses liability *ex jure representationis* as attaching only to heirs **13.20** in heritage,[84] but it is settled that it attaches also to those who have succeeded to the moveable estate of the deceased.[85] The alimentary interests of the children disadvantaged by the division of the moveable estate—and children are now the sole class of claimants—will often, however, be sufficiently protected by their claims for *legitim*. The claim for aliment is competent both where the estate has passed by the testamentary conveyance of the parent and where succession is on intestacy,[86] but in the latter event questions are unlikely now to arise in view of the equitable division of both heritable and moveable estate among children affected by the modern law of intestate succession.[87] The cases have been mainly concerned with claims by one or more of the deceased parent's children against relatives, but neither principle nor authority support Fraser's view[88] that the doctrine cannot be applied where property is left to a stranger.

Duration of representational liability

Unlike common law liability *ex debito naturali*, liability *ex jure representationis* **13.21** subsists only until the majority of the child to be alimented[89] and in some cases an earlier period has been fixed on the view that by then the child should be able to earn a livelihood.[90] The reason appears to be that there are insufficient grounds for extending liability further where it is based on positive rather than natural law. Where, however, there is a mental or physical incapacity to earn a livelihood aliment may be continued beyond majority.[91] But even in these cases liability will now normally come to end at majority because the representative's liability cannot be more extensive than the parent's, *i.e.* it will extend beyond majority only if the child is undergoing reasonable and appropriate education or training and in that event it will end at 25.[92] The cases are obsolete in which

---

[84] I, vi, 58.

[85] *Scot v. Sharp* (1759) Mor. 440; *Thomson v. Wilkie* (1678) Mor. 419; *Stokers v. Moubray* (1632) 1 Mor. Supp. 332. See also Ivory's note to Erskine, *ibid.*

[86] *Spalding v. Spalding's Trs* (1874) 2 R. 237; *Ormiston v. Ormiston's Trs* (1838) 11 Sc. Jur. 232; *Drummond v. Swayne* (1834) 12 S. 342; *Fenton v. Scott* (1832) 4 Sc.Jur. 457; *Riddell v. Riddell* (1802) Mor. App. 1 Aliment 4; *Scot v. Sharp*, above; *Hastie and Ker v. Hastie* (1671) Mor. 416 and 5922.

[87] See Succession (Scotland) Act 1964.

[88] p. 132. The cases Fraser cites (*Riddell v. Riddell*, above, and *Scot v. Sharp*, above) do not vouch his proposition.

[89] Erskine, I, vi, 58; Bankton, I, vi, 16; *Hunter's Trs v. Macan* (1839) 1 D. 817, *per* Lord Ordinary; *Strathmore v. Strathmore* (1825) 1 W. & S. 402; *Douglasses v. Douglass* (1739) Mor. 425.

[90] *Seatons v. The Heir* (1764) Mor. 431; *Don v. Don* (1697) Mor. 420; *Hastie and Ker v. Hastie* (1671) Mor. 416.

[91] *Thomson v. Wilkie* (1678) Mor. 419.

[92] Family Law (Scotland) Act 1985, s. 1(5)(b).

it was held that the obligation to aliment ladies of rank might extend beyond majority until their marriage—"for the daughters of gentlemen can do as little for themselves after as before majority, 'til they get a husband to provide for them".[93] Marriage before majority cuts off the claim.[94] If the claimant is also a beneficiary of the deceased's estate, the vesting of payment of whose share has been postponed, aliment is due only until the term of payment[95] and if in the interval he or she is entitled to interest, that must be applied to his or her aliment and any aliment due by the heir as representative reduced accordingly.[96]

Order of liability between representatives and others

13.22   The statutory provision that there shall be no order of liability[97] applies in a question with representatives of deceased parents. Accordingly, in determining the amount of aliment which he or she should pay, a representative is to be considered along with other obligants and, subject to the limitation that his or her liability cannot exceed the amount by which he or she has been enriched by the succession, his or her other resources, earning capacity and needs are to be taken into account. These will fall on the representative of a deceased parent to the exclusion of the surviving parent.[98] In such a case the surviving parent's obligation may become prestable on the expiry of the representative's liability, as on the majority of a child not mentally or physically incapable who is continuing to undergo education or training.

Posthumous children and aliment ex jure representationis

13.23   The obligation to aliment a child is a debt that becomes a debt "so soon as the child was begotten".[99] It follows that a child born after the death of his or her parent can claim aliment from the deceased's estate or his or her representatives in the same way as surviving children can. This issue was discussed more fully earlier in this book.[1]

Reimbursement of aliment paid

13.24   Where a child is living in family with a parent or other person, he or she will usually be alimented as part of the family provision even if he or she is of sufficient means him- or herself. In that and other cases in which a person is alimented in kind or expenditure is incurred for his or her aliment, questions of reimbursement may arise. Whether a parent or other person under alimentary obligation can be compelled to provide aliment without looking for reimbursement is now a question of what is reasonable in the circumstances,

---

[93] *Douglasses v. Douglass*, above. *Cf.* Erskine, I, vi, 58; *Dalziel v. Dalziel* (1788) Mor. 450; *Bissets v. Bisset* (1748) Mor. 413.

[94] *Maxwell v. Maxwell* (1711) Mor. 423. This is settled only in the case of the marriage of daughters, but it is thought that the same view would be taken of the marriage of the son of the deceased. Although at common law as now under statute a parent might in certain circumstances be liable for the aliment of a married son (or of a married daughter) the marriage of a son or daughter is in a question with the heir an assertion of independence which frees the latter from liability.

[95] *MacNeil v. MacNeil* (1749) Mor. 426; *Straitons v. Lauriston* (1679) Mor. 418; *Children of Lawriston v. Lawriston* (1677) Mor. 418; *Stuart and Innes v. Rosyth* (1668) Mor. 415; *Frazer v. Frazer* (1663) Mor. 415; *Otter v. Otter* (1663) Mor. 414.

[96] *Dudgeon v. Arnot* (1830) 9 S. 36; *Gordon v. Maitland* (1757) Mor. 11161.

[97] Family Law (Scotland) Act 1985, s. 4(2).

[98] The mother's heirs have a representational liability at common law (Bankton I, vi,16; *Scot v. Sharp*, above; *Thomson v. Wilkie*, above). In a question between the heir to the father's estate and the mother, the mother's liability was postponed to the heirs (Erskine, I, vi, 58; *Douglasses v. Douglass*, above) and was activated only if the heir's estate did not afford a sufficient aliment for himself as well as for the other children (Ivory's *Note* on Erskine, *ibid.*; *Bissets v. Bisset*, above).

[99] *Spalding v. Spalding's Trs* (1874) 2 R. 237, *per* Lord Deas at 251.

[1] Above, paras 2.26–2.28.

having regard to the respective means and resources of the parties. At common law a parent might contract for payment of board with a child living at home who was earning a sufficient livelihood,[2] and that is probably still the law.[3] Anyone not under an alimentary obligation who provides aliment may, of course, freely contract with the recipient for reimbursement provided the recipient has contractual capacity; and if notice is given that reimbursement is expected a contract will be inferred from the continued acceptance of the provision. We are, however, here concerned with cases in which there is no contract. Stair lays down the principle:

> "in all cases aliment or entertainment, given to any person without paction, is presumed a donation, if the person was major, and capable to make agreement. But entertainment to minors or weak persons doth ever infer recompense according to the true value of the benefit received. And in the case of those, who are in use to furnish provision for money, the presumption ceaseth, and recompense is due."[4]

That aliment to minors (*i.e.* in this context all persons below, now, the age of 18) "doth ever infer recompense" admits, however, of exceptions where the aliment is provided by a relative, as examples given by Stair show. In such cases there may be a question of some delicacy whether aliment was given *ex pietate* or on conditions of reimbursement. It has been held that in the absence of contract the ordinary presumption against donation does not always apply and that, on the contrary, there may be a certain presumption in favour of gift *ex pietate*.[5] Where, however, the person alimented is in receipt of income the relative providing aliment is entitled to reimbursement from any income the recipient had during the period he or she was alimented unless it appears that the provision was made with a contrary intention.[6] Moreover it is doubtful if, except in the case of aliment by parents, a presumption in favour of gift *ex pietate* survives the abolition of the alimentary obligation of relatives other than parents. Similarly, authorities in which it was held that a relative could not insist on repayment from a child out of the child's capital, at least where the property was small, unless a contract had been made with the child or his or her administrators-at-law,[7] are now obsolete because they proceed on a view of the relative's obligations which can now be applied only to parents or persons who have accepted a child as a child of their family. In *Polland v. Sturrock's Executors*[8] it was held that in a proper case a father, although of ample means, might be entitled to be recompensed out of the capital of his children's estate, and that must apply *a fortiori* to persons not under an alimentary obligation. A contention that aliment was given *ex pietate*, and thus that no recompense is due, is strongest where the provision was made by a parent because he or she has an obligation to aliment, but a brother or sister, or even a more distant relative, may be held on a consideration of all the facts to have acted *ex pietate*.[9]

---

[2] Erskine, I, vi, 53.

[3] The child would have contractual capacity to enter into such a contract under ss. 1(1)(b) and 2(1) of the Age of Legal Capacity (Scotland) Act 1991.

[4] Stair, I, viii, 2.

[5] *ibid.*; *Gordon v. Lesly* (1680) Mor. 11426; *Guthrie v. Mackerston* (1672) Mor. 10137; *Hamilton v. Symington* (1667) Mor. 382; *Ludquharn v. Gight* (1665) Mor. 11425; Bankton, I, ix, 22.

[6] *Steven v. Simpson* (1791) Mor. 11458; *Hutcheson v. Hoggan's Trs* (1904) 6 F. 594; *Webb v. Cleland's Trs* (1904) 6 F. 274; *Duke of Sutherland, Petr* (1901) 3 F. 761; *Seddon, Petr* (1893) 20 R. 675; *Muir v. Muir's Trs* (1887) 15 R. 170.

[7] *Galt and Ors* (1830) 8 S. 332.

[8] 1952 S.C. 535.

[9] *Drummond v. Swayne* (1834) 12 S. 342; *Cuningham v. McGachan* (1831) 9 S. 472; *Rig v. Rig* (1676) Mor. 11426. *Cf. McGaws v. Galloway* (1882) 10 R. 157 and *Chisholm v. Steedman* (1703) Mor. 11428.

Reimbursement by obligant for expenditure by others

13.25   Questions of reimbursement may also arise where a relative or a stranger
aliments a child in place of a parent or other person with an alimentary obligation,
as where a grandparent keeps a child in his or her home while the child's parents
are alive and have sufficient means to provide aliment. Where in such a case a
child has been brought up by a person other than a parent and the parent seeks
to regain possession of the child, the court could previously, in its discretion, if
it ordered the child to be given up to the parent, further order that the parent pay
to the person who had brought up the child the whole of the costs properly
incurred in bringing him or her up, or such portion of them as seemed to the
court to be just and reasonable having regard to all the circumstances of the case.[10]
The court no longer has this power, and the general rule in a claim at the instance
of a relative is that, as the parties were free to make a contract and had not done
so, there is in the absence of contract or of necessity no claim for recompense.[11]
The general rule admits, however, of an exception. Where a parent has, whether
expressly or by clear implication, been called upon to fulfil his or her alimentary
obligation and has refused or neglected to do so, as where a grandparent requires
that a parent take a child home and the parent does not do so, the presumption
of donation *ex pietate* is in these circumstances rebutted, with the result that
recompense may be claimed.[12] It seems, moreover, that if a relative aliments a
child for whom the primary liability rests on someone else *ex jure
representationis*, there is a good claim for reimbursement without the necessity
of contract. *Pietas* has, it has been said, no weight where the question is with
extraneous heirs.[13] Nor does *pietas* have any place where the aliment has been
provided, whether by accommodation in his or her home or in money or in
kind, by a stranger and the claim for recompense is at his or her instance. The
having of a child in a person's care is sufficient to impose obligations upon the
carer.[14] The presumption against donation will then apply but, except where
the person acts from necessity, the circumstances may often be such as to rebut the
presumption. Recompense for relief of necessity is best illustrated where
tradesmen supply food, clothing or other necessaries to a child in need whose
parent has failed to provide them. In such a case the parent is liable to the
tradesmen.[15] "Necessaries to a person's wife or child are necessaries to himself".[16]
The doctrine applies as long as the child has no property or means of earning a
livelihood. It is for the tradesman to satisfy himself that the child is in need, and
he will have no remedy where the parent has in fact provided a competent
allowance or otherwise arranged for the child's necessaries to be supplied.[17]
Ex hypothesi of the case, the tradesman looks to the parent for payment and has
no action against the child unless perhaps where the child has misrepresented
his or her true situation.[18] As the action lies for relief of necessity, nothing
extravagant will be allowed, but necessity will be related to what is suitable to
the child's station in life.[19] An action on this ground is to be distinguished,

---

[10] Custody of Children Act 1891, s. 2, repealed by the Children Act 1989, Sched. 15.
[11] Fraser, p. 120; *Ludquharn v. Gight* (1665) Mor. 11425; *Barclay v. Berry*, (1700) 4 Mor. Supp.
491.
[12] *Gordon v. Lesly* (1680) Mor. 11426.
[13] *Gourlay v. Urquart* (1697) Mor. 11438; *Wilkie v. Morison* (1675) Mor. 5923; *Stirling v. Ottar*
(1663) Mor. 11432.
[14] See above, para. 8.15.
[15] Erskine, I, vi, 57.
[16] Fraser p. 111 quoting Evans' *Pothier*, II, p. 29.
[17] Erskine, I, vi, 57.
[18] *Hamilton v. Forrester* (1825) 3 S. 572; *Gray v. Purves* (1816) Hume 411; *Crichton v. Kilmarnock*
(1744), Elchies, *Minor*, No. 11; *Lamb v. Tweedie* (1623) Mor. 13424; *Anderson v. Craig, ibid.*
[19] Erskine, I, vi, 57.

although the distinction is not always attended, from an action on the ground of the parent's implied mandate. In the latter case, which may arise from a course of dealings between the child and the tradesman in which the parent has accepted responsibility for the child's transaction, but not in the former, the parent's liability will cease on his or her giving notice to the tradesman to that effect.[20] On the other hand, a case based on relief of necessity will always be confined to necessaries, whereas a case on implied mandate, although normally similarly confined, may extend beyond that if the circumstances justify the implication.

Parent's right to child's earnings

Stair and Erskine lay it down that as long as children are living in family with **13.26** their parents and alimented by them the children may be obliged to employ themselves for the common benefit of the family and that profit or earnings arising therefrom belong not to the children but to the parents.[21] It seems that they held, as did Bankton, that the parental right to the fruits of the childrens' labour subsisted until forisfamiliated even if the child was major. Stair attributed this right to the parental power, but Bankton says that the father "has right to their service for their entertainment, if they are not able otherwise to recompense him".[22] The father's right to insist that his child work for him must now be regarded as obsolete, but it is no doubt still the law that if called upon, a child must, in so far as is reasonably within his or her power, recompense a parent by whom he or she is being alimented. The child's obligation is limited to what is required for recompense, and in that respect Bankton accurately reflects the modern principle. So, when a child earning a wage or salary is living in family with his or her parents, the parents are entitled to payment for board and accommodation provided[23] but not to any surplus of his or her earnings. The child may, however, have no liability for recompense in respect of aliment before the demand for payment was intimated, on the view that aliment prior thereto is taken to have been provided *ex pietate*.

JURISDICTION AND PROCEDURE

Jurisdiction: Introduction

Actions for aliment of a child are personal actions for payment. The ordinary **13.27** jurisdictional rules for such actions are, however, supplemented by a number of specialities. The Civil Jurisdiction and Judgments Act 1982[24] is now the primary context for consideration of these matters.

The jurisdictional provisions of the Civil Jurisdiction and Judgments Act 1982 **13.28** fall into three categories, which may be broadly described as (1) jurisdiction in the United Kingdom where the person sued is domiciled in a "contracting state," that is a state (including in some cases certain dependent territories) which was a party to or subsequently acceded to the Brussels Convention on Jurisdiction and the Enforcement of Judgments in Civil and Commercial Matters 1968 (the "1968 Convention"), *i.e.* a member of the European Union; (2) allocation of jurisdiction among the several parts of the United Kingdom; and (3) the enactment of a new and comprehensive code of civil jurisdiction in Scotland. The effect of the Act on questions of aliment requires consideration under each of these hearings.

---

[20] Fraser, pp. 114–115; *Knox v. Hay* (1813) Hume 351; *Samson v. Goldie* (1808) Hume 425; *Barclay v. Douglas* (1758) Mor. 9624; Stair, I, *v.* 7.

[21] Stair, I, v, 6 and 8; Erskine, I, vi, 53.

[22] I, vi, 1, p. 153.

[23] Erskine, I, vi, 53.

[24] The reader is referred to Anton and Beaumont, *Civil Jurisdiction in Scotland* (2nd ed., 1995), for a full discussion of the Act. Only the special provisions on aliment and such other matters as are necessary to put those provisions in context are considered here.

Jurisdiction as between contracting states

13.29   One of the effects of the Civil Jurisdiction and Judgments Act 1982 is to make the 1968 Convention part of the law of Scotland.[25] As the jurisdictional provisions of the convention apply solely to cases where the person sued is domiciled in a contracting state, the rules here under consideration have no application where the defender is domiciled in a country outwith the European Union. The meaning of domicile is, however, different from that usually attributed to it in Scottish rules of international private law.[26] The fundamental jurisdictional principle of the convention is that persons domiciled in a contracting state are, irrespective of nationality, to be sued in the courts of that state and not of any other contracting state.[27] Jurisdiction, in other words, follows the domicile of the defender. This applies to alimentary actions as it does to others. So, a person domiciled in Scotland may be sued for aliment in the Scottish courts and, generally speaking, a person domiciled in a contracting state other than the United Kingdom may not be so sued. However, to the general rule there are a number of exceptions, one of the most important of which concerns aliment, in relation to which the pursuer's as well as the defender's position may be used to found jurisdiction. It is provided that in matters relating to aliment there is jurisdiction in the courts of the place where the alimentary creditor is domiciled or habitually resident, or, if the matter is ancillary to proceedings concerning status, in the courts which, according to its own law, has jurisdiction to entertain those proceedings.[28] So, although the defender is domiciled in another contracting state, an action for aliment may be raised in the Scottish courts if the pursuer is domiciled or habitually resident in Scotland; and where a question of aliment arises as an ancillary matter in a Scottish action of divorce, separation, nullity of marriage or in an application for an order under section 11 of the Children (Scotland) Act 1995, the Scottish court has jurisdiction to determine it despite the domicile in another contracting state of the person against whom the claim for aliment is directed. In an action for aliment, as in other actions, there may also be jurisdiction by prorogation.[29]

13.30   Neither the Act nor the convention contains specific provision for jurisdiction in the revocation or variation of alimentary decrees. In all the contracting states it would be accepted that a court has power to vary or revoke its own decrees as long as it retains jurisdiction to pronounce the decree in question. However, in contrast with the general understanding in the United Kingdom, the law of most of the contracting states seems to be that if jurisdiction to pronounce a decree is lost the power to vary or revoke it is lost at the same time, and the convention is probably to be interpreted to that effect.[30] For the alimentary creditor there is

---

[25] Civil Jurisdiction and Judgments Act 1982, s. 2(1) (as amended by the Civil Jurisdiction and Judgments Act 1991, Sched. 2, para. 1). For ease of reference the 1968 Convention and the amendments thereto occasioned by later accessions are set out in Scheds 1–3B to the Act, as substituted and added by Civil Jurisdiction and Judgments Act (Amendment) Order 1990 (S.I. 1990 No. 2591).

[26] Civil Jurisdiction and Judgments Act 1982, s. 41(2) provides that an individual is domiciled in the United Kingdom if, and only if (a) he or she is resident in the United Kingdom and (b) the nature and circumstances of his or her residence indicate that he or she has a substantial connection with the United Kingdom. Art. 52 provides that in order to determine whether a person is domiciled in another contracting state the court is to apply the law of that state. S. 41 (7) provides that an individual is domiciled in a state other than a contracting state if, and only if, (a) he is resident in that state and (b) the nature and circumstances of his or her residence indicate that he or she has a substantial connection with that state.

[27] *ibid.* Sched. 1, Art. 2.

[28] *ibid.* Sched. 1, Art. 5(2).

[29] *ibid.* Sched. 1, Arts. 17 and 18.

[30] Anton and Beaumont, *Civil Jurisdiction in Scotland* (2nd ed.), p. 106.

little problem; if he or she seeks to vary the decree he or she merely follows the jurisdictional rules which the convention supplies and which he or she can readily invoke. The position of the alimentary debtor seeking variation or revocation is more problematic. It has been suggested that if the court which pronounced the decree is no longer seised of jurisdiction the only courts to which he or she can go are those of the domicile of the alimentary creditor.[31] The habitual residence of the alimentary creditor is, it is submitted, available as an alternative, provided always he or she is domiciled in a contracting state, but, with that exception, the alimentary debtor is driven back to the general principle that jurisdiction rests on the domicile of the person sued in the application under consideration.[32] He or she cannot rely on his or her own domicile, or habitual residence, as a source of jurisdiction in the way in which the alimentary creditor can. The absence from the convention of any uniform scheme for variation and revocation and the potential jurisdictional conflict which that absence entails are major weaknesses of the convention and so of the Act.

The convention contains a saving provision for any other conventions to **13.31** which the contracting states are, or will be, parties and which, in relation to particular matters, govern jurisdiction or the recognition or enforcement of judgments.[33] So far as jurisdiction is concerned there are at present no applicable conventions to which the United Kingdom is a party. It should also be noted as applicable to alimentary, as well as to other, proceedings that under the 1968 convention application may be made to the courts of a contracting state for such provisional, including protective, measures as may be available under the law of that state, even if under the convention, the courts of another contracting state have jurisdiction as to the substance of the matter.[34]

Jurisdiction as between parts of the United Kingdom

In relation to jurisdiction in the United Kingdom the Act follows the general **13.32** provisions for the allocation of jurisdiction discussed above in relation to the European Union. The 1968 Convention is modified for application within the United Kingdom and is enacted in this modified form in Schedule 4 to the Civil Jurisdiction and Judgments Act 1982. Again the general rule refers to the domicile of the defender (with the special definition of domicile[35] being applied). So it is provided that persons domiciled in a part of the United Kingdom are to be sued in the courts of that part; this applies to proceedings for aliment of children as it does to other civil proceedings.[36] To the general rule there are again a number of exceptions, including one relating to aliment, and it is provided that there is to be jurisdiction in the court for the place where the alimentary creditor (*i.e.* the pursuer) is domiciled or habitually resident, or, if the matter is ancillary to proceedings concerning status, in the court which, according to its own law, has jurisdiction to entertain those proceedings.[37] The rules on allocation of jurisdiction do not, however, apply (a) to proceedings under section 80 of the Social Work (Scotland) Act 1968 (contributions in respect of children being looked after by a local authority) or section 81 of that Act (applications for or for variation of affiliation orders in respect of children being so looked after)[38] nor (b) to proceedings brought in pursuance of any statutory provision which

---

[31] Anton and Beaumont, *Civil Jurisdiction in Scotland* (2nd ed.), p. 106.
[32] Civil Jurisdiction and Judgments Act 1982, Sched. 1, Art. 2.
[33] *ibid.* Sched. 1, Art. 57.
[34] *ibid.* Sched. 1, Art. 24.
[35] See above, para. 13.29.
[36] Civil Jurisdiction and Judgments Act 1982, Sched. 4, Art. 2.
[37] *ibid.* Sched. 4, Art. 5(2).
[38] *ibid.* s. 17 and Sched. 5, para. 5(a) and (b).

either implements an international convention protected by Article 57 of the 1968 Convention, or makes provision with respect to jurisdiction in any field to which such a convention relates, nor to any rule of law so far as it has the effect of implementing any such convention.[39] There is also a general exception for "any enactment which confers jurisdiction on a Scottish court in respect of a specific subject-matter on specific grounds."[40] The effect of these words is not free from doubt, but it would seem that jurisdictional rules specifically laid down by statute or statutory instrument for actions of aliment remain in force. Some of the jurisdictional provisions of the Maintenance Orders Act 1950 are, however, repealed.[41]

General rules on jurisdiction in Scotland

13.33   Subject to the rule concerning the allocation of jurisdiction as between the contracting states and also as between the several parts of the United Kingdom the new jurisdictional code for Scotland determines "in what circumstances a person may be sued in civil proceedings in the Court of Session or in the sheriff court".[42] This code applies to persons not otherwise governed by the provisions described above, though the rules in each situation are closely similar. The general rule of the code is that a person is to be sued in the courts for the place where he or she is domiciled, or, where he or she has no fixed residence, in a court within whose jurisdiction he or she has been personally cited, and this applies to alimentary actions as to others.[43] In addition, there is a special rule which, in matters relating to aliment, vests a concurrent[44] jurisdiction in the courts for the place where the alimentary creditor (*i.e.* the pursuer) is domiciled or habitually resident or, if the matter is ancillary to proceedings concerning the status of a person, in the court which has jurisdiction to entertain those proceedings.[45] It is, however, provided that an action for affiliation and aliment is not to be treated as a matter ancillary to proceedings concerning the status of a person.[46] Jurisdiction may be prorogated.[47] Existing rules on variation and recall are preserved[48] with the result that, where this code applies, a court retains power to vary or revoke its own decrees even if it no longer has jurisdiction in respect of the original decree.

Procedure and remedies

13.34   Actions for aliment present some procedural specialties in addition to those associated with enforcement which are noted later. An action of, or application for or in respect of, aliment is a "family action" to which the rules in Chapter 49 of the Rules of the Court of Session 1994 and Chapter 33 of the sheriff court Ordinary Cause Rules 1993 apply[49] with the addition that any conclusion for

---

[39] Civil Jurisdiction and Judgments Act 1982, s. 17 and Sched. 5, para. 6.
[40] *ibid.* s. 17(1).
[41] *ibid.* Sched. 14.
[42] *ibid.* s. 20(1).
[43] *ibid.* Sched. 8, paras 1 and 2(1). See *O'Neill v. Tebbett*, 1994 S.L.T. 752.
[44] Sched. 8, r. 2 is clearly to the effect that the special jurisdictions are concurrent with that conferred by the general rule, because it states that a person may "also" be sued in certain courts in the special circumstances. *Cf.* the wording in Sched. 1, Art. 5 and Sched. 4, Art 5, which, though less clear, also confer a concurrent rather than an exclusive jurisdiction: Anton and Beaumont at p. 547.
[45] Civil Jurisdiction and Judgments Act 1982, Sched. 8, para. 2(5).
[46] *ibid.*
[47] *ibid.* Sched. 8, para. 5. And see *British Steel Corporation v. Allivane International Ltd*, 1989 S.L.T. (Sh.Ct) 57 (not followed in *Jenic Properties Ltd v. Andy Thornton Architectural Antiques*, 1992 S.L.T. (Sh.Ct) 5).
[48] Civil Jurisdiction and Judgments Act 1982, s. 23(1)(a).
[49] RCS 1994, r. 49.1; OCR 1993, r. 33.1.

aliment must contain averments indicating upon which basis the court retains jurisdiction to make an award of aliment over and above any maintenance assessment made under the Child Support Act 1991.[50]

In an undefended action of aliment the pursuer shall, on enrolling or lodging **13.35** the motion, lodge all documentary evidence of the means of the parties available to him or her in support of the amount of aliment sought, and the sheriff may require the appearance of the pursuer.[51] An application for, or for the variation of, an order for interim aliment in an action of aliment depending before the court shall be made by motion.[52] A person to whom an obligation of aliment is owed and in whose favour an order for aliment was made in an action of aliment while he or she was under the age of 18 and who has now reached that age and seeks an order for aliment against the person against whom the earlier order was made, shall apply by minute in the process of that action.[53]

An application after final decree for, or for the variation or recall of, an **13.36** order for aliment for a child shall be made by motion or by minute in the process of the action to which the application relates; and if by motion in the Court of Session the motion must include a brief statement of the reasons for the order sought and must be intimated by registered post or the first class recorded delivery service to any person concerned or a solicitor known to be acting on behalf of that person, not less than 14 days before the date on which the motion is enrolled.[54]

A claim for aliment only (whether or not expenses are also sought) may be **13.37** made in the Court of Session or the sheriff court.[55] Unless the court considers it inappropriate in any particular case a claim for aliment may also be made in proceedings:

(a) for divorce, separation, declarator of marriage, or declarator of nullity of marriage;
(b) relating to orders for financial provision;
(c) concerning parental responsibilities or parental rights or guardianship in relation to children;
(d) concerning parentage or legitimacy;
(e) of any other kind where the court considers it appropriate to include a claim for aliment.[56]

An action for aliment of a child may be brought (a) by the child him- or herself, (b) by the curator *bonis* of an *incapax* child, (c) on behalf of a child under 18 by the parent or guardian of the child or by a person with whom the child lives or who is seeking a residence order under section 11(2) of the Children (Scotland) Act 1995 in respect of the child.[57] A woman, whether married or not, may bring an action for aliment on behalf of her unborn child as if the child had been born, but no such action can be heard or disposed of prior to the birth of the child.[58] Any person qualified to bring an action for aliment of a child may give a good receipt for aliment paid under the decree in the action.[59]

---

[50] RCS 1994, r. 49.6; OCR 1993, r. 33.6.
[51] RCS 1994, r. 49.55; OCR 1993, r. 33.57.
[52] RCS 1994, r. 49.56(1); OCR 1993, r. 33.58(1).
[53] RCS 1994, r. 49.56(4); OCR 1993, r. 33. 58(3). See also RCS 1994, r. 49.44 and OCR 1993, r. 33.46.
[54] RCS 1994, r. 49.43(1) and (2); OCR 1993, r. 33.45(1).
[55] Family Law (Scotland) Act 1985, s. 2(1).
[56] *ibid.* s. 2(2), as amended by the Children (Scotland) Act 1995, Sched. 4, para. 36.
[57] *ibid.* s. 2(4), as amended by the Age of Legal Capacity (Scotland) Act 1991, Sched. 1, para. 40 and Sched. 2 and the Children (Scotland) Act 1995, Sched. 4, para. 36.
[58] Family Law (Scotland) Act 1985, s. 2(5). And see above, para. 2.26.
[59] *ibid.* s. 2(10).

13.38   Where a person for, or on behalf of, whom aliment is claimed is living in the same household as the defender it is a defence to the action that the defender is fulfilling the obligation of aliment and intends to continue doing so.[60] And, as already noticed, it is a defence to an action for aliment by, or on behalf of, a person other than a child under the age of 16 years that the defender is making an offer which it is reasonable to expect the person concerned to accept to receive that person into his or her household and to fulfil the obligation of aliment.[61] In considering whether it is reasonable to expect a person to accept such an offer the court is, however, to have regard among other things to any conduct, decree or other circumstances which appear to the court to be relevant.[62]

13.39   The powers of the court in granting decree in an action for aliment extend to (a) ordering the making of periodical payments whether for a definite or indefinite period or until the happening of a specified event, (b) ordering the making of alimentary payments of an occasional or special nature, including payments in respect of inlying, funeral or educational expenses, (c) the backdating of an award of aliment to the date of the bringing of the action or to such later date as the court thinks fit, or on special cause shown to a date prior to the bringing of the action, and (d) the award of an amount less than that claimed even if the claim is undisputed.[63] There is also provision for awards of interim aliment payable until disposal of the action or until such earlier date as the court specifies, and for the variation or recall, but not the backdating, of such awards.[64]

Variation and recall

13.40   A decree granted in an action for aliment may, on an application by or on behalf of either party to the action, be varied or recalled by the court if, since the date of the decree, there has been a material change of circumstances.[65] Amongst other things, the making of a maintenance assessment with respect to the child under the Child Support Act 1991[66] is a "material change in circumstances" for these purposes.[67] The change in circumstances does not require to be unexceptional or unexpected. It might include an increase on the costs of maintaining the child as the child grows older,[68] at least if such increase has not been taken account of in the original award.[69] A change of circumstances is not constituted by showing that the court at the time of the earlier award proceeded upon a different hypothesis which turned out to be incorrect.[70] However, showing that the obligant had, in law, no obligation of aliment under section 1 of the 1985 Act will be a material change of circumstances permitting variation (to nil) or recall. In *Watson v. Watson*[71] the obligant was found some time after an award of aliment had been made against him not to be the father of the child, and it was held that he had not accepted the child as a member of his family. In these circumstances the award of aliment was varied to nil.[72] Pending

---

[60] Family Law (Scotland) Act 1985, s. 2(6) and (7).
[61] *ibid.* s. 2(8).
[62] *ibid.* s. 2(9).
[63] *ibid.* s. 3.
[64] *ibid.* s. 6.
[65] *ibid.* s. 5(1).
[66] See below, Chap 14.
[67] Family Law (Scotland) Act 1985, s. 5(1A), as inserted by S.I. 1993 No. 660.
[68] *Skinner v. Skinner*, 1996 S.C.L.R. 334.
[69] *Kirkpatrick v. Kirkpatrick*, 1993 S.C.L.R. 175.
[70] *Walker v. Walker*, 1995 S.L.T. 375. *Dickinson v. Dickinson*, 1952 S.C. 27 is no longer good law on this point.
[71] 1994 S.C.L.R. 1097.
[72] Making an application under s. 5 in these circumstances is an alternative (often cheaper) to an appeal which may, in any event, be out of time.

the determination of an application for variation or recall, the court may make such interim order as it thinks fit and where it backdates an order for variation or recall it may order any sums paid under the decree to be repaid.[73]

INTERNATIONAL ISSUES

Choice of law

In *Macdonald v. Macdonald*[74] it was held that the law of the mother's domicile **13.41** governed her liability to aliment her son, and in *Rosses v. Sinhjee*[75] that a claim for aliment for an illegitimate child depended on the law of England which was the law of the mother's domicile and also, following that, of the child's. The correct principle would seem to be that liability for aliment should be dependent on its being exigible by the proper law of the debt. That will be the law with which the relationship has the closest and most substantial connection. The law of the child's domicile will have a strong, but not a conclusive, claim and the domicile of the person against whom the claim is directed will also be relevant. Where the child him- or herself is not the claimant, the domicile of the parent or other person who seeks payment in respect of the child's aliment is, as such, an adventitious factor which will normally be of no account. There would, however, be a good deal of convenience and probably little risk of injustice in a rule which, without consideration of domicile or other connecting factors, allowed choice of law to follow jurisdiction and so applied Scots law where the Scottish court was competently seised of the case. That consideration has particular force where aliment is ancillary to an action of divorce, separation or nullity of marriage and was followed in the comparable field of financial relief between spouses.[76] The Scottish Law Commission has suggested[77] that this position be put on a statutory basis.

Recognition and enforcement: general

Decrees for payment of aliment for children are, in principle, enforceable in **13.42** the same way as other decrees for the payment of a debt. Enforcement at common law of foreign decrees (including English and Northern Irish decrees) was, however, obstructed by the rule that only final decrees could be the subject of a decree conform.[78] As alimentary decrees are usually subject to variation or recall, they did not meet that test and so could not be enforced except for arrears and even arrears could not be recovered if they were subject to variation or recall under the foreign decree.[79] The same difficulty did not arise on the face of the Judgments Extension Act 1868 or the Inferior Courts Judgments Extension Act 1882,[80] which provided an improved means of enforcement of judgments for debt within the United Kingdom but these Acts were not much used for the enforcement of alimentary decrees, perhaps because it was thought that a restriction as to finality should be implied, and it was not until 1950 that, by the Maintenance Orders Act of that year, procedures were supplied specifically adapted to the enforcement of alimentary decrees within the United Kingdom. Today, alimentary decrees from outwith the United Kingdom are recognised

---

[73] s. 5. See further, Nichols at pp. 17–19.
[74] (1846) 8 D. 830.
[75] (1891) 19 R. 31.
[76] Divorce (Scotland) Act 1976, s. 5.
[77] Scot. Law Com. No. 135, *Report on Family Law*, May 1992, para. 18.5, and draft Bill, cl. 43.
[78] Anton, *Private International Law* (1st ed.), pp. 586–587; Morris, *Conflict of Laws* (3rd ed.), p. 224.
[79] Morris, *op. cit.*.
[80] Both of these statutes were repealed by the Civil Jurisdiction and Judgments Act 1982, Sched. 14.

and enforced here, and Scottish alimentary decrees are recognised and enforced outside the United Kingdom, in accordance with a number of different regimes, depending upon whether the other country is

(1) a Member State of the European Union, *i.e.* a "contracting state" for the purposes of the Civil Jurisdiction and Judgments Act 1982;

(2) one of a number of Commonwealth and ex-Commonwealth states and thus a "reciprocating country" for the purposes of Part I of the Maintenance Orders (Reciprocal Enforcement) Act 1972;

(3) one of a number of foreign and Commonwealth countries that is a "convention country" for the purposes of Part II of the 1972 Act; or

(4) another country with which the United Kingdom has entered into a bilateral agreement under Part III of the 1972 Act.[81]

13.43 In relation to countries subject to none of these regimes, the common law or the procedures under the Administration of Justice Act 1920 or the Foreign Courts (Reciprocal Enforcement) Act 1933 remain.[82] Before looking at each of these different statutory regimes, the position within the United Kingdom, governed by the Maintenance Orders Act 1950, will be examined.

Enforcement as between different parts of the United Kingdom

13.44 The normal means for the enforcement, in one part of the United Kingdom, of judgments of the courts of another part are contained in the Civil Jurisdiction and Judgments Act 1982, but the provisions of that Act do not apply to an order to which section 16 of the Maintenance Orders Act 1950 applies.[83] The result is that the 1950 Act continues to regulate the enforcement, within the United Kingdom, of maintenance orders made by Scottish, English or Northern Irish courts. Also, where an alimentary judgment of a foreign court has been registered in the United Kingdom and falls to be treated for the purposes of enforcement as a judgment of a court of law in the United Kingdom, the rules for its enforcement remain those contained in the legislation providing for its registration whether under Part II of the Administration of Justice Act 1920, or Part I of the Foreign Judgments (Reciprocal Enforcement) Act 1933, or Part I of the Maintenance Orders (Reciprocal Enforcement) Act 1972, or section 4 or 5 of the 1982 Act itself.[84]

13.45 Part II of the Maintenance Orders Act 1950 provides for the enforcement, in parts of the United Kingdom other than that in which the order was made, of maintenance orders made by courts in England and Wales, Scotland, and Northern Ireland.[85] Maintenance order is defined so as to include any decree for payment of aliment for children and similar orders, of an alimentary nature, for payment of weekly or periodic sums, including orders under the Social Work (Scotland) Act 1968 and the Social Security Administration Act 1992 as well as the corresponding English or Northern Irish orders.[86] Procedure is by registration. A maintenance order made in one part of the United Kingdom may be registered in another if it appears that the person liable to make payments

---

[81] A very brief layman's guide to this complex area of law is found in *Obtaining Maintenance From Abroad*, published by Scottish Courts Administration. A more detailed exposition written for lawyers is given by Jamieson in *Butterworths Scottish Family Law Service* at paras D1001–1123.

[82] For a full discussion thereof, see Anton and Beaumont, *Private International Law* (2nd ed.), pp. 219–247.

[83] Civil Jurisdiction and Judgments Act 1982, s. 18(5)(a).

[84] *ibid.* s. 18(7).

[85] Maintenance Orders Act 1950, s. 16(1). See also Act of Sederunt (Child Care and Maintenance Rules) 1997 (S.I. 1997 No. 291), rr. 5.6–5.13 and 5.24 –5.28.

[86] *ibid.* s. 16(2), as frequently amended. See *Tayside Regional Council v. Thaw*, 1987 S.L.T. 69.

under the order resides there and it is convenient that the order should be enforceable there.[87] The decision as to residence and convenience rests with the court that made the order or its prescribed officer and not with the court in which the order was registered.[88] Orders have to be registered with the court of corresponding jurisdiction within which the defender appears to be.[89] There is no discretion to refuse registration.[90] Once registered, the order is enforceable in all respects as if it had been made by the court in which it is registered and as if that court had had jurisdiction to make it.[91] The application for registration should be made to the court by which the order was made.[92] Arrears which have accrued before registration may be recovered if supported by a statutory declaration or an affidavit or by certificate of an officer of the court to, or through whom, payments were required to be made.[93] Variation or discharge of the order remains a matter for the court which made it and not for the court in which it is registered, except that an order registered in the sheriff court or in a magistrates' court may be varied as the court thinks fit in respect of the rate of payments under the order, provided the liability thereby imposed does not exceed any maximum authorised by law in the part of the United Kingdom in which the order was made.[94] Registration may be cancelled on application by, or on behalf of, the person entitled to payment, to the prescribed officer of the court in which the order is registered provided no proceedings for variation are pending; and the person liable to make payments under the order may apply to the court by which the order was made to have registration cancelled on the ground that he or she has ceased to reside in the part of the United Kingdom in which the order is registered, and if it appears to that court, or its prescribed officer, that that is so, registration will be cancelled on the sending of a notice to that effect to the registering court.[95] A registered order cannot be enforced otherwise than under the provisions of Part II of the Act and so is unenforceable so long as the registration remains in force in that part of the United Kingdom in which the order was made.[96]

Enforcement as between European Union states

The rules of the Civil Jurisdiction and Judgments Act 1982 on recognition **13.46** and enforcement within one European Union state of the alimentary judgments of the courts of another[97] afford only a few points of distinction from those applicable to civil judgments generally.[98] An application for enforcement, instead of being, as in the case of other civil judgments, submitted directly to the Court of Session is, in Scotland, to be submitted to the sheriff court on transmission by the Secretary of State.[99] The relevant sheriff court is to be determined by reference to the place of domicile of the person against whom enforcement is sought, or, if he or she is not domiciled in Scotland, by reference to the place of enforcement.[1] The application is to be determined in the first instance by the

---

[87] Maintenance Orders Act 1950, s. 17(2).
[88] *ibid.* s. 17(1).
[89] *ibid.* s. 17(3).
[90] *ibid.* s. 17(4).
[91] *ibid.* s. 18.
[92] *ibid.* s. 17(1).
[93] *ibid.* s. 20.
[94] *ibid.* ss. 21 and 22.
[95] *ibid.* s. 24.
[96] *ibid.* s. 18(6).
[97] Civil Jurisdiction and Judgments Act 1982, s. 5.
[98] *ibid.* s. 4, and 1968 Convention, as set out in Sched. 1.
[99] *ibid.* s. 5(1) and Art. 32 of the Convention. See also Act of Sederunt (Child Care and Maintenance Rules) 1997 (S.I. 1997 No. 291), rr. 5.38–5.43.
[1] *ibid.*

sheriff clerk, from whose decision there is an appeal to the court.[2] Where enforcement is authorised to any extent, the order is to that extent to be registered in that court.[3] An order so registered is for the purposes of its enforcement of the same force and effect, the registering court has in relation to its enforcement the same powers, and proceedings with respect to its enforcement may be taken, as if it had been originally made by the registering court.[4] Corresponding procedures are available for the enforcement of Scottish alimentary decrees in other contracting states.[5]

13.47　　The 1982 Act applies only to recognition and enforcement in the United Kingdom of the judgments of the courts of contracting states.[6] In such cases it supersedes all rules of law inconsistent with it except where Article 57 has the effect of permitting their continued application. Article 57 provides that the convention shall not affect any other convention to which the contracting states are parties and which, in relation to a particular matter, governs jurisdiction or the recognition or enforcement of judgments. It is of more consequence in questions of recognition and enforcement than it is in jurisdiction. Accordingly, where means of recognition and enforcement of alimentary judgments is afforded by United Kingdom legislation referable to an international convention, these means remain available in addition to those provided by the 1982 Act and the 1968 Convention. Procedures under the Reciprocal Enforcement of Maintenance Orders (Hague Convention Countries) Order 1993,[7] and under the Reciprocal Enforcement of Maintenance Orders (Republic of Ireland) Order 1993[8] are therefore available in cases to which they apply as alternatives at the option of the party seeking enforcement.[9]

Enforcement as between "reciprocating countries"

13.48　　Part I of the Maintenance Orders (Reciprocal Enforcement) Act 1972[10] provides, on a reciprocal basis, for the enforcement in the United Kingdom of maintenance orders made by courts in foreign or Commonwealth countries, and for the enforcement in these countries of orders made by courts in the United Kingdom. It is the main means for such enforcement except that for the enforcement in the United Kingdom of judgments of courts of Member States of the European Union it is largely superseded by the Civil Jurisdiction and Judgments Act 1982, and procedures available under the 1968 Convention will be the usual vehicle for enforcement of Scottish decrees in these countries.[11] Procedures under the Administration of Justice Act 1920 or the Foreign

---

[2] Civil Jurisdiction and Judgments Act 1982, s. 5(2) and Arts. 37 and 40. There is a single further appeal to the Inner House of the Court of Session on a point of law (s. 6(3)).

[3] *ibid.* s. 5(3).

[4] *ibid.* s. 5(4).

[5] Title III of the Convention (set out in Sched. 1). This raises no question of Scots law as the procedure is governed by the law of the state in which enforcement is sought (Art. 33).

[6] *ibid.* s. 2(1) and Arts. 25, 26 and 31.

[7] Below, paras 13.81–13.85.

[8] Below, paras 13.76–13.80.

[9] On the relative priorities between the provisions contained in the 1982 Act and those contained in the other provisions, see Anton and Beaumont, *Private International Law* (2nd ed.), pp. 562–563.

[10] An outline of the Act is given in the following pages. For a more detailed discussion the reader is referred to Clive, *Husband and Wife* (4th ed.) at pp. 182–209, Jamieson, *op. cit.* and Anton and Beaumont at pp. 551–555.

[11] No Member State of the European Union is, in fact, a reciprocating country for the purposes of the Act, but some (Denmark, Germany, Finland, France, Ireland, Italy, Luxembourg, the Netherlands, Portugal and Sweden) participate, as does Norway, in reciprocal arrangements to which a modified version of the Act applies under the Reciprocal Enforcement of Maintenance Orders (Republic of Ireland) Order 1993 and the Reciprocal Enforcement of Maintenance Orders (Hague Convention Countries) Order 1993.

Judgments (Reciprocal Enforcement) Act 1933 or at common law remain as alternatives to the extent that they are applicable to alimentary decrees but will seldom be appropriate where the 1972 Act applies.

For the purposes of the Act, a maintenance order is an order that provides **13.49** for the periodic payment of sums of money towards the maintenance of anyone whom the payer (the person liable to make payments under the order) is liable to maintain according to the law of the place where the order was made.[12] It therefore comprehends all decrees for payment of aliment for children. In the case of affiliation orders it includes an order for the payment, by the father, of expenses incidental to the child's birth, or, where the child has died, of his or her funeral expenses.[13] The procedures which the Act provides are available only between the United Kingdom and reciprocating countries or territories as designated by Order in Council.[14] A country may be designated either as regards maintenance orders generally or as regards a specified class or classes of orders and is to be regarded as a reciprocating country only as regards orders of the class to which the designation extends.[15]

Two forms of procedure are laid down by the Act. The first is for the transmission **13.50** for the purposes of enforcement in a reciprocating country of a maintenance order made by a court in the United Kingdom and for registration in the United Kingdom of such orders made by courts in reciprocating countries. The second form provides for the making of provisional orders in the United Kingdom with a view to their confirmation and enforcement in reciprocating countries and for the confirmation and registration in the United Kingdom of provisional orders made in reciprocating countries. It will be convenient to consider the operation of these procedures in relation to (1) the enforcement in reciprocating countries of Scottish decrees, and (2) the enforcement in this country of orders made in reciprocating countries.

Transmission of Scottish maintenance orders

Where the person liable for payment under a Scottish alimentary decree or **13.51** other maintenance order is residing in a reciprocating country, the payee may apply for the order to be sent to that country for enforcement.[16] This procedure does not apply in relation to a provisional order or to an order made under Part II of the Act.[17] The application is to be made to the Deputy Principal Clerk of Session in the case of a Court of Session order, or, in the case of a sheriff court order, to the sheriff clerk of the court which made the order who, if satisfied that the payer is residing in a reciprocating country, is to send to the Secretary of State (a) a certified copy of the order, (b) a a statement of arrears, (c) a statement giving information as to the whereabouts of the payer, (d) a statement for facilitating the identification of the payer, and (e) where available, a photograph of the payer.[18] The Secretary of State is then to transmit these documents to the responsible authority in the reciprocating country if he is satisfied that the statement relating to the whereabouts of the payer gives sufficient information to justify that being done. It should then be possible for the order to be enforced in the reciprocating country under provisions of its

---

[12] Maintenance Orders (Reciprocal Enforcement) Act 1972, s. 21.
[13] *ibid.*
[14] *ibid.* s. 1(1). See Reciprocal Enforcement of Maintenance Orders (Designation of Reciprocating Countries) Orders 1975 (S.I. 1975 No. 2187), 1979 (S.I. 1979 No. 115) and 1983 (S.I. 1983 No. 1125).
[15] *ibid.* s. 1(2).
[16] *ibid.* s. 2(1).
[17] For which see below, paras 13.67–13.73.
[18] Act of Sederunt (Child Care and Maintenance Rules) 1997 (S.I. 1997 No. 291), r. 5.14.

laws similar to those under which corresponding orders of its courts are enforceable in this country.

Transmission of Scottish provisional orders

13.52   The direct method of transmission just described enables a Scottish decree to be enforced abroad without further judicial process. Procedure by way of provisional order, on the other hand, contemplates a judicial act of confirmation in the foreign jurisdiction. If, in any action, (a) the sheriff has jurisdiction by virtue of the domicile or habitual residence of the maintenance creditor in the sheriffdom or because the question of maintenance is ancillary to proceedings concerning status, and (b) the defender resides in a reciprocating country, any maintenance order granted by the sheriff is a provisional order.[19] There is no corresponding provision for Court of Session alimentary decrees. An action in which a provisional order is sought may commence and proceed without the necessity of citation of any person and so without notice to the payer.[20] No decree can, however, be granted unless the grounds of action have been substantiated by sufficient evidence and the evidence is to be recorded even if the action is a summary cause.[21] The sheriff's power of remit to the Court of Session is excluded.[22]

13.53   Where a provisional order is made, the sheriff clerk must send to the Secretary of State (a) a certified copy of the order, (b) a document setting out, or summarising, the evidence given in the proceedings, (c) a certificate of the grounds on which the making of the order might have been opposed by the payer, (d) a statement of such information as was available to the court as to the whereabouts of the payer, (e) a statement of such information as the sheriff clerk possesses for facilitating the identification of the payer, and (f) where available, a photograph of the payer.[23] The Secretary of State is then to transmit these documents to the responsible authority in the reciprocating country in which the payer is residing if he is satisfied that the statement relating to the payer's whereabouts gives sufficient information to justify that being done.[24] The order will then be subject to confirmation procedure in the reciprocating country and, if confirmed by a competent court, is to be treated for all purposes as if it had never been provisional and had been made by the sheriff in the form in which it is confirmed.[25]

Enforcement, variation and revocation of Scottish orders

13.54   So far as the Scottish court's power of enforcement, variation or revocation of Scottish orders is concerned, it is immaterial whether the order sent to the reciprocating country is a plenary or a provisional order. Whichever procedure has been used, transmission of any subsequent process to the reciprocating country does not affect the powers of United Kingdom courts to enforce or revoke or vary the order.[26] As long, however, as the payer is residing in a reciprocating country, a provisional order is the only means by which the court can, on the application of the payee, vary the order by increasing the rate of the payments thereunder. The Act also envisages extensive scope for the use of

---

[19] Maintenance Orders (Reciprocal Enforcement) Act 1972, s. 4(1) as substituted by the Civil Jurisdiction and Judgments Act 1982, Sched. 12, Pt II, para. 3(1).
[20] *ibid.* s. 4(4)(a).
[21] *ibid.* s. 4(4)(b).
[22] *ibid.* s. 4(5).
[23] *ibid.* ss. 3(5) and 4(6) and S.I. 1974 No. 939.
[24] *ibid.*
[25] *ibid.* s. 3(6).
[26] *ibid.* ss. 2(5) and 3(6).

provisional orders by a court in a reciprocating country for varying or revoking Scottish maintenance orders. Indeed it is to be anticipated that, except in certain prescribed and very limited circumstances[27] revocation or variation of a Scottish maintenance order by a foreign court will always be by means of a provisional order. Where a certified copy of such provisional order, together with a document setting out or summarising the evidence given in the proceedings in which the provisional order was made, is received by the Scottish court which made the maintenance order, that court may confirm or refuse to confirm the provisional order.[28] If the provisional order relates to variation the Scottish court may confirm it with such alterations as it thinks reasonable. Confirmation must be preceded by intimation to the payee that the provisional order has been received and that unless appearance is entered within the prescribed period it will be confirmed.[29] Variation, whether by a foreign or a United Kingdom court is effective from the date on which the varying order is made and, where the varying order is a provisional order which has been confirmed, it has effect as if it had been made in the form in which it was confirmed and had never been a provisional order.[30] It seems that the confirmed order takes effect retroactively from the date on which the provisional order was made.

The provisions on the effect of revocation are similar to those on variation. **13.55** The maintenance order is deemed to have ceased to have effect as from the date on which the revoking order was made, but this is subject to the exception that arrears due under the maintenance order at the date of revocation remain exigible.[31] Where revocation is by means of a provisional order made by a foreign court and confirmed by a court in the United Kingdom, it seems that revocation takes effect from the date on which the provisional order was made.

A provisional order is not appropriate to the revocation by a United Kingdom **13.56** court of a Scottish maintenance order. A United Kingdom court which has power to vary a Scottish maintenance order may, however, do so by provisional order and is required to do so where the rate of payment under the maintenance order is increased.[32] Where a United Kingdom court makes a provisional order varying a maintenance order the prescribed officer of the court must send to the court in a reciprocating country having power to confirm the provisional order a certified copy of that order, together with a document setting out or summarising the evidence given in the proceedings.[33] It is not necessary for the payee to intimate to any person the making by him or her of an application for such a provisional order varying the maintenance order by increasing the rate of payments[34] and, *a fortiori* of that, intimation must be unnecessary where the rate of payment is not to be increased.

Registration of foreign orders

Enforcement in Scotland of maintenance orders made in reciprocating **13.57** countries depends on registration. Where a certified copy of the foreign order is received by the Secretary of State and it appears to him that the payer under the order is residing or has assets in Scotland, he is to send the copy of the order to the sheriff clerk of the court within whose jurisdictions the payer is residing.[35]

---

[27] Such as apply under s.9(2) and (3) to the variation or revocation by a Scottish court of a maintenance order made by a court in a reciprocating country.
[28] Maintenance Orders (Reciprocal Enforcement) Act 1972, s. 5(5).
[29] *ibid.* s. 5(6).
[30] *ibid.* s. 5(7).
[31] *ibid.* s. 5(8).
[32] *ibid.* s. 5(2) and (3).
[33] *ibid.* s. 5(4).
[34] *ibid.* s. 5(3A).
[35] *ibid.* s. 6(2), as amended by the Civil Jurisdiction and Judgments Act 1982, Sched. 11, para. 10. See also Act of Sederunt (Child Care and Maintenance Rules) 1997 (S.I. 1997 No. 291), rr. 5.29–5.33.

The sheriff clerk is then to take such steps as he thinks fit for the purpose of ascertaining whether the payer is residing or has assets within the court's jurisdiction; if after taking these steps he is satisfied that the payer is not so residing and has no assets within the jurisdiction of the court, he is to return the certified copy of the order to the Secretary of State with a statement giving such information as he possesses as to the whereabouts of the payer.[36] In any other case he must register the order.[37] A maintenance order for the purpose of these provisions includes a provisional order which has been confirmed by a court in another reciprocating country, but not an unconfirmed provisional order.[38]

Confirmation and registration of foreign provisional orders

13.58   Where the Secretary of State receives a certified copy of a provisional order made by a court in a reciprocating country together with (a) a document setting out or summarising the evidence given in the proceedings in which the order was made and (b) a statement of the grounds on which the making of the order might have been opposed by the payer, he is, if it appears to him that the payer is residing in Scotland, to send the copy of the order and accompanying documents to the sheriff clerk of the court within whose jurisdiction the payer is residing.[39] The sheriff clerk must then intimate to the payer that the order has been received and will be confirmed unless appearance is entered within the prescribed period.[40] If such intimation cannot be given, the sheriff clerk is to return the copy order and accompanying documents to the Secretary of State with a statement giving such information as he possesses as to the whereabouts of the payer.[41] If the case proceeds the sheriff is to apply with respect to sufficiency of evidence the law in force in the country in which the order was made[42] and the statement received from the foreign court of the grounds on which the making of the order might have been opposed by the payer is to be conclusive evidence that the payer might have raised a defence on any of these grounds.[43] If the payer appears and establishes any such defence as he or she might have raised in proceedings in which the order was made, the court must refuse to confirm the order.[44] In any other case it must confirm the order either without alteration or with such alterations as it thinks reasonable. If the order is confirmed the sheriff clerk is to register the order in the Maintenance Orders (Reciprocal Enforcement) Act 1972 Register kept by him for that purpose.[45] If the court refuses to confirm the order he is to return the certified copy order and the accompanying documents to the Secretary of State.

---

[36] Maintenance Orders (Reciprocal Enforcement) Act 1972, s. 6(4), as similarly amended.

[37] *ibid.* s. 6(3).

[38] *ibid.* s. 6(1).

[39] *ibid.* s. 7(1) and (2).

[40] *ibid.* s. 7(4) (as applied to Scotland by s. 7(7)).

[41] *ibid.* s. 7(6) (as so applied).

[42] *ibid.* s. 7(7). The Act is silent on how the foreign law on sufficiency of evidence is to be ascertained. A remit under s. 14(5) to the foreign court may be competent but otherwise the foreign law must be proved by evidence. Either expedient seems unnecessarily burdensome but if the presumption that the foreign law is the same as Scots law is applied, the statutory provision is deprived of much of its force. In any event it is extremely unlikely that the foreign law makes the requirement of corroboration previously made by Scots law and, indeed, the contrary may, with safety, be presumed. In *Killen v. Killen*, 1981 S.L.T. (Sh.Ct) 77 Sheriff Macphail took judicial notice (at 82) that "a general rule of law requiring corroboration in civil actions is peculiar to the laws of Scotland and, perhaps, Portugal", and it is submitted that that was a sound course. On the other hand, foreign systems may have requirements for proof unknown to Scots law and the statute clearly envisages that they should be ascertained and applied.

[43] Maintenance Orders (Reciprocal Enforcement) Act 1972, s. 7(3).

[44] *ibid.* s. 7(2).

[45] *ibid.* s. 7(5); Act of Sederunt (Maintenance Orders (Reciprocal Enforcement) Act 1972 Rules, 1974 (S.I. 1974 No. 939), para. 13.

Enforcement of foreign registered orders

A foreign order registered under the Act may be enforced in the United Kingdom **13.59** as if it had been made by the registering court and as if that court had had jurisdiction to make it; and proceedings for or with respect to the enforcement of the order may be taken accordingly.[46] In any enforcement proceedings a certificate of arrears sent to the sheriff clerk is sufficient evidence of the facts stated therein.[47] Sums payable under the order are payable from the date on which the order was made, except that the court confirming a provisional order may direct that the sums payable under it shall be deemed to have been payable from such date, being a date later than the date on which the order was made, as it may specify.[48] Subject to any such direction, a provisional order which has been confirmed shall be treated as if it had been made in the form in which it was confirmed and as if it had never been a provisional order.

Variation or revocation of foreign registered orders

The registering court has like power to vary or revoke a registered order as **13.60** if it had itself made and had had jurisdiction to make the order.[49] It may do so on the application of the payer or payee. Variation must be by a provisional order unless:

(a) both the payer and the payee are for the time being resident in the United Kingdom; or

(b) the application is made by the payee; or

(c) the courts in the country in which the order was made do not have power according to their own law to confirm provisional orders varying maintenance orders and the variation (i) consists in a reduction of the rate of payment and (ii) is made solely on the grounds that there has been a change in the financial circumstances of the payer since the order was made or, in the case of a provisional order, since it was confirmed.[50]

Revocation must be by provisional order unless both the payer and the payee are for the time being residing in the United Kingdom.[51] The registering court cannot vary or revoke a registered order if neither the payer nor the payee is resident in the United Kingdom.[52]

It is unnecessary for the payer to intimate to anyone the making by him or **13.61** her of an application for a provisional order varying or revoking a registered order.[53] Intimation would seem to be necessary in the limited classes of case in which variation or revocation can be otherwise than by a provisional order. The law to be applied to the revocation of a registered order is the law applied by the reciprocating country in which the order was made (which may not necessarily be the law of that country).[54] That law need not, however, be applied where both the payer and the payee are for the time being residing in the United Kingdom and in such a case it would seem that Scots law can be applied if the order is registered in a Scottish court. Where a foreign law has to be applied the court

---

[46] Maintenance Orders (Reciprocal Enforcement) Act 1972, s. 8(1).
[47] *ibid*. s. 8(6).
[48] *ibid*. s. 8(7) and (8).
[49] *ibid*. s. 9(1).
[50] *ibid*. s. 9(2).
[51] *ibid*. s. 9(3).
[52] *ibid*. s. 9(1B).
[53] *ibid*. s. 9(4A).
[54] *ibid*. s. 9(4). By virtue of the international private law rules of the reciprocating country the law applied by the courts for that country may be a system other than the domestic law of the forum.

may make a provisional order if it has reason to believe that the ground on which the application is made is a ground on which the order could be revoked according to the law applied by the reciprocating country, notwithstanding that it has not been established that it is such a ground.[55] The Act is silent on the law to be applied to an application for variation. The law applied by the reciprocating country would seem to be the appropriate law, but Scots law may be applied on the view that if it differs from that law, the necessary adjustment can, in the case of a provisional order, be made by the foreign court in deciding on confirmation.[56] Where the registering court makes a provisional order varying or revoking a registered order the sheriff clerk must send to the court that made the registered order a certified copy of the provisional order together with the document setting out or summarising the evidence given in the proceedings.[57]

13.62 The initiative in the variation or revocation of the registered order need not always be taken in the country in which the order is registered. It may often be taken, particularly at the instance of the payee, in the courts of the country in which the order was made. In some cases of variation the foreign court will proceed by way of a provisional order, a certified copy of which will be transmitted to the registering court together with a document setting out or summarising the evidence given in the proceedings in which the provisional order was made. On receipt of the certified copy the sheriff clerk must intimate to the payer that the provisional order has been received and will be confirmed unless appearance is entered within the prescribed period.[58] The court may thereafter (i) confirm the order either without alteration or with such alterations as it thinks reasonable, or (ii) refuse to confirm the order.[59]

13.63 Where a registered order has been varied by an order (including a provisional order which has been confirmed) made by a Scottish court or by a competent court in a reciprocating country, the registered order is to have effect as varied from the date on which the varying order was made; and where the varying order was a provisional order it is to have effect as if that order had been made in the form in which it was confirmed and as if it had never been a provisional order.[60] Where a registered order has been revoked (a) by an order made by a Scottish court (including a provisional order which has been confirmed by a competent court in a reciprocating country), or (b) by an order made by a competent court in a reciprocating country, the registered order is deemed to have ceased to have effect as from the date on which the revoking order was made with the exception that any arrears due under the registered order at that date remain exigible.[61] The sheriff clerk is to register any order varying a registered order other than a provisional order which is not confirmed.[62]

Cancellation of registration of foreign order

13.64 The registration of an order registered in a Scottish court is to be cancelled if (1) the order is revoked by the order of a competent court, or (2) the payer ceases to reside or have assets in Scotland. These two grounds of cancellation require separate consideration:

---

[55] Maintenance Orders (Reciprocal Enforcement) Act 1972, s. 9(4).
[56] In the limited circumstances in which a registered order can be varied otherwise than by a provisional order, it seems that the law of Scotland should be applied.
[57] Maintenance Orders (Reciprocal Enforcement) Act 1972, s. 9(5).
[58] *ibid.* s. 9(7).
[59] *ibid.* s. 9(6).
[60] *ibid.* s. 9(8).
[61] *ibid.* s. 9(9).
[62] *ibid.* s. 9(10).

(1) A registered order is to be cancelled where it is revoked by (i) an order made by the registering court, or (ii) a provisional order made by the registering court and confirmed by a court in a reciprocating country, or (iii) an order made by a court in a reciprocating country.[63] In the case of (ii) and (iii) cancellation is effected on receipt by the registering court of notice of confirmation or revocation respectively. Any arrears due at the date of cancellation continue to be recoverable as if the registration had not been cancelled.

(2) Where the sheriff clerk of the registering court is of the opinion that the payer under a registered order is not residing within the jurisdiction of that court and has no assets within that jurisdiction against which the order can be effectively enforced he is to cancel the registration and send the certified copy of the order to the Secretary of State along with a certificate of arrears signed by him, a statement giving such information as he possesses as to the whereabouts of the payer, and the nature and location of the payer's assets, and any other relevant documents in his possession.[64] If it appears to the Secretary of State on receipt of the certified copy order that the payer is residing or has assets in the United Kingdom he is to transfer the order to the appropriate court by sending the certified copy and related documents to the prescribed officer of that court (in Scotland the sheriff clerk).[65] The prescribed officer is then to take such steps as he thinks fit for the purpose of ascertaining whether the payer is residing or has assets within the jurisdiction of the court.[66] If he is then satisfied that the payer is not so residing and has no assets within the jurisdiction of the court, he is to return the certified copy order and relevant documents to the Secretary of State, along with a statement giving such information as he possesses as to the whereabouts of the payer.[67] In any other event he must register the order. Where it appears to the Secretary of State on receipt by him of the certified copy of the order, whether from the court in which it was registered or on its being returned from another court to which it was sent by him, that the payer has ceased to reside and has no assets in the United Kingdom, he is to send to the responsible authority in the reciprocating country from which the order was received (a) a certified copy of the order and of any order varying it, (b) a certificate of arrears signed by the prescribed officer, (c) a statement giving such information as the Secretary of State possesses as to the whereabouts of the payer and the nature and location of his or her assets, and (d) any other relevant documents in his possession.[68] Alternatively, if having regard to all the circumstances he thinks it proper to do so, he may send the certified copy of the order and the other documents to the responsible authority in another reciprocating country.[69] Where the certified copy order and documents are sent to the responsible authority in a country other than that in which the order was made, the Secretary of State is to inform the responsible authority in the country in which the order was made of what he has done.[70]

---

[63] Maintenance Orders (Reciprocal Enforcement) Act 1972, s. 10(1).
[64] *ibid.* s. 10(2) and (7).
[65] *ibid.* s. 10(5).
[66] *ibid.* s. 10(6).
[67] *Ibid.* s. 10(6) and (7).
[68] *ibid.* s. 11(1).
[69] *ibid.*
[70] *ibid.* s. 11(2).

Appeals

13.65   No appeal lies from a provisional order made by a Scottish court,[71] but where a Scottish court confirms or refuses to confirm a provisional order made by a court in a reciprocating country, whether the provisional order was a maintenance order or an order varying or revoking a maintenance order, the payer or payee has the like right of appeal from confirmation or refusal to confirm as he or she would have if the order were not a provisional order.[72] Where a Scottish court makes or refuses to make an order varying or revoking a maintenance order made by a court of a reciprocating country then, provided the varying or revoking order is not a provisional order, the payer or payee has the right of appeal from the varying or revoking order or from the refusal to make it as he or she would have if the maintenance order had been made by a Scottish court.[73] These provisions do not affect any right of appeal conferred by any other enactment.[74]

Enforcement after provisional revocation

13.66   Where the sheriff has made a provisional order revoking a registered maintenance order, it is incompetent except with the leave of the sheriff to enforce, whether by diligence or otherwise, the payment of any arrears which accrue after the making of the provisional order.[75] On an application for leave the sheriff may refuse leave or grant it subject to such restrictions and conditions (including conditions as to the allowing of time for payment or the making of payment by instalments) as he thinks appropriate, or remit the payment of the arrears or of any part thereof.[76]

Enforcement as between "convention countries"

13.67   Part II of the Maintenance Orders (Reciprocal Enforcement) Act 1972 is not concerned with the enforcement of judgments as such but is a method of facilitating the pursuit of actions of aliment where the pursuer is in one country and the defender is in another. It gives effect to the United Nations Convention on the Recovery Abroad of Maintenance Orders 1956[77] and applies as between countries or territories ("convention countries") specified by Order in Council to which that convention extends.[78]

Transmission of claims to foreign countries

13.68   An applicant in the United Kingdom who claims to be entitled to recover aliment from a person who is subject to the jurisdiction of a convention country may apply to the Secretary of State to have his or her claim for recovery of aliment transmitted to that country.[79] Likewise, if he or she seeks to vary any provision made in a convention country for payment of aliment to him or her by a person for the time being subject to the jurisdiction of that country, he or she

---

[71] Maintenance Orders (Reciprocal Enforcement) Act 1972, s. 12(1).
[72] *ibid.* s. 12(2).
[73] *ibid.* s. 12(3).
[74] *ibid.* s. 12(4).
[75] *ibid.* s. 20.
[76] *ibid.*
[77] New York, June 20, 1956 (Cmnd. 6084).
[78] Maintenance Orders (Reciprocal Enforcement) Act 1972, s. 25. For the countries presently specified, see Recovery Abroad of Maintenance (Convention Countries) Orders (S.I. 1974, No. 423, S.I. 1978 No. 279, S.I. 1982 Nos 1423 and 1530, and S.I. 1996 No. 1925). Pt II of the Act is applied with a minor procedural modification to many of the states of the United States of America by the Recovery of Maintenance (United States of America) Order 1993 (S.I. 1993 No. 591). The appropriate states are specified in the Schedule to the order.
[79] Maintenance Orders (Reciprocal Enforcement) Act 1972, s. 26(1).

may apply to the Secretary of State to have his or her application for variation transmitted to that country.[80] In either case the application is made through the sheriff clerk or sheriff clerk depute of the sheriff court within whose jurisdiction the applicant is residing and he is to assist the applicant in completing an application which will comply with the law applied by the convention country; the application is then sent to the Secretary of State together with such other documents as are required by the law of the convention country.[81] On receipt of the application and documents the Secretary of State is to transmit them to the appropriate authority in the convention country unless he is satisfied that the application is not made in good faith or that it does not comply with the requirements of the law applied by that country.[82] The Secretary of State may in that connection request the sheriff clerk to obtain from the court which he serves specified information relating to the application, and it is the duty of the court to furnish the Secretary of State with that information.[83] If the application is transmitted to a convention country, it will follow procedures similar to those applicable in this country to applications received from convention countries.

Receipt of foreign claims and registration of consequent forms

On receipt from the appropriate authority in a convention country, of an **13.69** application by a person in that country for the recovery of aliment from another person for the time being resident in Scotland, the Secretary of State is to send the application together with any accompanying documents to the Secretary of the Law Society of Scotland, who is in turn to send the application and documents to a solicitor practising in the sheriff court of the jurisdiction within which the person against whom the claim is directed is residing, or to such other solicitor practising in Scotland as appears to the Secretary to be appropriate, this for the purpose of enabling the solicitor to take such steps on behalf of the applicant as appear to him appropriate.[84] These steps would seem normally to include proceedings for the recovery of aliment, and any order made by the sheriff in such proceedings containing a provision requiring the payment of aliment is to be registered in the Maintenance Orders (Reciprocal Enforcement) Act 1972 Register.[85]

Transfer and cancellation of registration

Where the sheriff clerk or sheriff clerk depute of the registering court is of **13.70** the opinion that the payer under a registered order has ceased to reside in Scotland, he is to send a certified copy of the order and related documents to the Secretary of State unless he is of the opinion that the payer has ceased to reside in the United Kingdom, in which case he is instead to send a notice to that effect to the Secretary of State.[86] On receipt of a certified copy of the order the Secretary of State, if it appears to him that the payer is still residing in the United Kingdom, is to transfer the order to the appropriate court by sending the copy order and related documents to the prescribed officer of that court.[87] The prescribed officer is then to take such steps as he thinks fit for the purpose of ascertaining whether the payer is residing within the jurisdiction of the court; if after taking those steps he is satisfied that the payer is not so residing he is to return the certified

---

[80] Maintenance Orders (Reciprocal Enforcement) Act 1972, s. 26(2).
[81] *ibid.* s. 26(3).
[82] *ibid.* s. 26(4).
[83] *ibid.* s. 26(5).
[84] *ibid.* s. 31(1), as amended by the Legal Aid (Scotland) Act 1986, Sched. 3, para. 1.
[85] s. 31(2).
[86] *ibid.* s. 32(1).
[87] *ibid.* s. 32(3).

copy order and related documents to the Secretary of State, together with a statement giving such information as he possesses as to the whereabouts of the payer.[88] In any other case he must register the order and give notice of registration to the prescribed officer of the court in which immediately before that it was registered and to the Secretary of State.[89] The previous registration is then to be cancelled,[90] and the Secretary of State is to send a copy of the registered order and related documents to the Secretary of the Law Society of Scotland for transmission to a solicitor practising in the registering court or to such other solicitor practising in Scotland as appears to the Secretary to be appropriate, this with a view to his taking, on behalf of the person entitled to the payments for which the order provides, such steps as appears to him appropriate to enforce the order.[91]

Enforcement of registered order

13.71   An order registered in a court other than that by which it was made may be enforced as if it had been made by the registering court and as if that court had had jurisdiction to make it.[92] For the purpose of enforcement a certificate of arrears signed by the prescribed officer of the court in which the order was previously registered is sufficient evidence of the facts stated therein.[93] So long as the order is registered in a Scottish court any provision is of no effect by which payments are required to be made through or to any officer or person on behalf of the person entitled to the payments.[94] Part II of the Maintenance Orders Act 1950 does not apply to an order registered under these provisions.[95]

Variation and revocation of registered order

13.72   An order registered in a court other than that by which it was made may be varied or revoked by the registering court as if it had been made by it and as if that court had had jurisdiction to make it; and no other court shall have power to vary or revoke the order.[96] There is a like right of appeal against variation or revocation of a registered order or refusal to vary or revoke as there would be in respect of an order made by the registering court.[97] On revocation the registration is to be cancelled.[98]

13.73   On receipt from the appropriate authority in a convention country of an application by a person in that country for variation of a registered order, the Secretary of State is to send the application and accompanying documents to the Secretary of the Law Society of Scotland for transmission to a solicitor practising in the registering court or to such other solicitor practising in Scotland as appears to the Secretary to be appropriate, this with a view to the solicitor's taking on behalf of the applicant such steps as appear to him appropriate.[99]

Arrangements with the Republic of Ireland, Hague Convention countries and the United States

13.74   Part III of the Maintenance Orders (Reciprocal Enforcement) Act 1972 envisages the United Kingdom entering into bilateral agreements with other countries not otherwise covered, for the reciprocal recognition and enforcement

---

[88] Maintenance Orders (Reciprocal Enforcement) Act 1972, s. 32(4).
[89] *ibid.* s. 32(3) and (6).
[90] *ibid.* s. 32(7).
[91] *ibid.* s. 32(7A), as inserted by the Legal Aid (Scotland) Act 1986, Sched. 3, para. 1(2).
[92] *ibid.* s. 33(1).
[93] *ibid.* s. 33(5).
[94] *ibid.* s. 32(7B), as inserted by the Legal Aid (Scotland) Act 1986, Sched. 3, para. 1(2).
[95] *ibid.* s. 33(6).
[96] *ibid.* s. 34(1).
[97] *ibid.* s. 34(4).
[98] *ibid.* s. 34(2).
[99] *ibid.* s. 34(3), as substituted by the Legal Aid (Scotland) Act 1986, Sched. 3, para. 1(3).

of maintenance orders.[1] In pursuance of this, such agreements have been entered into with the Republic of Ireland,[2] with the countries to which the Hague Convention on the Recognition and Enforcement of Decisions Relating to Maintenance Obligations 1973 is in force,[3] and with the United States of America.[4] In relation to each, a modified version of Part I of the Maintenance Orders (Reciprocal Enforcement) Act 1972 is adopted. There is a certain overlap between the modified provisions and those already discussed, at least in relation to some countries, and parties would seem to be free to choose whichever provisions they prefer to rely upon.

The modifications to Part I of the Act follow a similar pattern in each order. **13.75** A central common feature is the absence of any provisional order procedure,[5] with the result that all alimentary decrees to which the orders apply are directly enforceable in the country to which they are transmitted without the necessity of confirmation, or, subject to certain safeguards, other judicial process. The orders should be read in conjunction with the provisions of Part I of the 1972 Act as described above.

Republic of Ireland

The modifications to Part I of the 1972 Act contained in the reciprocal **13.76** enforcement arrangements with the Republic of Ireland, all of which are related to the absence of provisional order procedure, can be considered under four main headings: (1) jurisdiction, (2) registration, (3) restrictions on enforcement and (4) variation and revocation. Heading (1) is relevant to the making of orders in Scotland and their transmission to Ireland, while headings (2) and (3) relate to making Irish orders effective in Scotland. Heading (4) is relevant to both Scottish and Irish orders.

(1) Jurisdiction and restriction on granting decree

Because of the changes in grounds of jurisdiction introduced by the Civil **13.77** Jurisdiction and Judgments Act 1982 the extension of sheriff court jurisdiction, for which the original 1974 Order[6] had provided, is no longer necessary. If, however, it appears that the defender is residing in the Republic of Ireland and the judgment is to be enforceable there, decree cannot be granted unless (a) a copy initial writ and warrant for citation has been sent to the appropriate authority in the Republic of Ireland for service on the defender, (b) a copy initial writ has been served in accordance with the requirements of Irish law in sufficient time to enable the defender to arrange his or her defence, and (c) the grounds of action have been substantiated by sufficient evidence. The purpose of these provisions and of those noted in heading (2) below is to protect the defender from prejudice as a result of the absence of any need for the order to be confirmed in the Republic of Ireland.[7] Procedure is governed in the Court of Session by

---

[1] Maintenance Orders (Reciprocal Enforcement) Act 1972, s. 40.
[2] Reciprocal Enforcement of Maintenance Orders (Republic of Ireland) Order 1993 (S.I. 1993 No. 594).
[3] Reciprocal Enforcement of Maintenance Orders (Hague Convention Countries) Order 1993 (S.I. 1993 No. 593). The relevant countries are listed in Sched. 1 thereto.
[4] Reciprocal Enforcement of Maintenance Orders (United States of America) Order 1995 (S.I. 1995 No. 2709). The specified states within the United States are listed in Sched. 1 thereto.
[5] Sched. 1 to the Republic of Ireland Order contains references to provisional orders (paras 2 and 3) but these do not apply to Scotland (para. 19).
[6] Reciprocal Enforcement (Republic of Ireland) Order 1974 (S.I. 1974 No. 2140), repealed by the current Order (S.I. 1993 No. 594).
[7] S.I. 1993 No. 594, Sched. 1, para. 4(4) and Sched. 2, para. 4(4).

the Reciprocal Enforcement of Maintenance Orders (Republic of Ireland) Order 1974 Rules 1975[8] and in the sheriff court by the Child Care and Maintenance Rules 1997.[9]

(2) Registration

13.78 Special provisions apply to the registration of an Irish maintenance order in this country. The order will not be registered (i) if registration is contrary to public policy, (ii) if the payer did not appear in the proceedings in the Republic of Ireland and was not served, in accordance with the law of his or her place of residence, with notice of the institution of the proceedings in sufficient time to enable him or her to arrange for his or her defence, or (iii) if the order is irreconcilable with a judgment given in the United Kingdom in proceedings between the same parties. Otherwise the order must be registered. Notice must be given to payer and payee if the order is registered, and to the payee if it is not registered. If the order is registered the payer may, within one month, apply to the court in which it was registered to set the registration aside. The grounds of challenge of registration are limited to the three grounds on which registration might have been refused. If the order is not registered, the payee may within one month apply to the sheriff to set aside the decision not to register it.[10]

(3) Restriction on enforcement

13.79 A registered Irish order is unenforceable for the one month period during which the payer can apply for registration to be set aside. If an application to set the order aside is made, the only measures of enforcement that can be taken against the property of the payer pending a decision on the application are such as are designed "to protect the interests of the payee".[11] Poinding and arrestment are, therefore, competent during that time but not sale or furthcoming.

(4) Variation and revocation

13.80 The powers of revocation and variation of an order remain exclusively with the courts of the country in which the order was made. A Scottish order, although transmitted to Ireland, can therefore be varied or revoked by a Scottish court and proceedings for variation or revocation will not be entertained by an Irish court. A Scottish court will, however, vary or revoke an order on the application of the pursuer only if the defender has been given notice of the proceedings and had an opportunity to defend.[12] No application for variation or revocation of an Irish order will be entertained by the Scottish courts.[13]

Hague Convention countries

13.81 The scheme of the Hague Convention Order[14] is similar to that of the Republic of Ireland Order.[15] The main points of distinction relate to (1) restrictions on the recognition of certain types of orders, (2) conditions of registration, and

---

[8] S.I. 1975 No. 475.
[9] S.I. 1997 No. 291, r. 5.15.
[10] *ibid.* Sched. 1, para. 6 and Sched. 2, para. 6.
[11] *ibid.* Sched. 1, para. 8 and Sched. 2, para. 8.
[12] *ibid.* Sched. 1, para. 4(2) and (4) and Sched. 2, para. 4(2) and (4).
[13] *ibid.* Sched. 1, para. 9 and Sched. 2, para. 9 provide the sole means of revocation or variation of Irish orders.
[14] S.I. 1993 No. 593.
[15] S.I. 1993 No. 594. Procedure for transmission of order to Hague Convention countries is governed in the Court of Session by the Reciprocal Enforcement of Maintenance Orders (Hague Convention Countries) 1980 (S.I. 1980 No. 291) and in the sheriff court by the Child Care and Maintenance Rules 1997 (S.I. 1997 No. 291) rr. 5.16–5.17.

(3) variation and revocation. Under the Hague Convention a country which is party to the convention may nonetheless reserve the right not to recognise or enforce a maintenance order (i) in so far as it relates to a period of time after a maintenance creditor attains the age of 21 years or marries (except where he or she is the spouse of the maintenance debtor), (ii) in favour of collaterals of the payer or persons related by affinity to him or her, and (iii) not providing for the periodical payment of maintenance. The United Kingdom has reserved the right not to recognise or enforce orders in category (iii) and also orders in category (ii) other than those in favour of a child of the family (for the purposes of the law of England and Wales and Northern Ireland) or of a child of the payee who has been accepted as a child of the family by the maintenance debtor (for the purposes of the law of Scotland). Where a maintenance order made in a Hague Convention country is of a description which that country or the United Kingdom has reserved the right not to recognise or enforce it is not a maintenance order for the purposes of the Hague Convention Order.[16] Accordingly, it cannot be enforced in the United Kingdom under the provisions of the order.

Variation and revocation

Scottish courts retain power to vary or revoke Scottish alimentary decrees **13.82** although transmitted to a Hague Convention country. Whether or not the decree can be varied or revoked by a court in that country is a matter for the foreign law but the Hague Convention Order, in contrast with the Republic of Ireland Order, envisages that that can be done.[17] If a Scottish alimentary decree transmitted to a Hague Convention country is varied or revoked by a competent court there it will have an effect in Scotland subject to the variation or, if revoked, will cease to have effect except in relation to arrears.[18]

If an order made in a Hague Convention country, but transmitted to Scotland, **13.83** is varied or revoked by a court in the country in which it is made the variation order will, on transmission, be registered in Scotland and the original order will have effect subject to the variation. Equally, however, the Scottish court may vary or revoke the order and it has like power to do so on application by either payer or payee as if the order had been made by a Scottish court with jurisdiction to make it. That power can be exercised, however, only if (i) the payer had his or her habitual residence in the United Kingdom at the time when the proceedings for variation were instituted or (ii) the party against whom the application for variation is directed has prorogated the court's jurisdiction.[19]

Registration

The conditions on which registration of an order made in a Hague Convention **13.84** country may or must be refused resemble those aplplicable to Irish orders, but the provisions are more extensive and even where there is a resemblance the resemblance is not exact. Registration may be refused by the sheriff clerk in the following circumstances:

(i) if the court in the Hague Convention country did not have jurisdiction to make the order on any of the prescribed grounds of jurisdiction;
(ii) if registration is manifestly contrary to public policy;
(iii) if the order was obtained by fraud in connection with a matter of procedure;

---

[16] S.I. 1993 No. 593, Sched. 2, para. 21(2) and Sched. 3, para. 21(1).
[17] *ibid.* Sched. 2, paras 5(9), (10) and (11) and Sched. 3, paras 5(9), (10) and (11).
[18] *ibid.* paras 5(9) and (10).
[19] *ibid.* Sched. 2, para. 9 and Sched. 3, para. 9.

(iv)　if proceedings between the same parties, and having the same purpose, are pending before a court in Scotland and those proceedings were the first to be instituted; or

(v)　if the order is incompatible with an order made in proceedings between the same parties and having the same purpose either in the United Kingdom or another country provided that the latter order itself fulfils the conditions necessary for its registration and enforcement under Part I of the 1972 Act.

In addition the prescribed officer must refuse to register unless (i) the payer appeared in the proceedings in the Hague Convention country in which the order was made or (ii) notice of the institution of the proceedings, including notice of the substance of the claim, was served on him or her in accordance with the law of that country and having regard to the circumstances he or she had sufficient time to enable him or her to defend the proceedings.[20]

Application to set registration aside

13.85　　The payer has, as under the Republic of Ireland Order, one month in which to apply for registration to be set aside but, in contrast with the Republic of Ireland Order, the payee's application to have refusal to register set aside is subject to the same time-limit.[21]

The United States of America

13.86　　The provisions of the Reciprocal Enforcement (United States of America) Order 1995 modify Part I of the Maintenance Orders (Reciprocal Enforcement) Act 1972 in ways similar to the modifications for Hague Convention countries, as just considered. Provisions for registration of American orders[22] are simpler and there is no discretion, as there is with orders from Hague Convention countries, to refuse registration. Other differences are minor, though close attention requires to be paid to the precise terms of the order and, in particular, the states that are specified and to which, therefore, the order applies. Procedure for the transmission to specified states from either the Court of Session or the sheriff court is governed by the Act of Sederunt (Reciprocal Enforcement of Maintenance Orders) (United States of America) 1995.[23]

---

[20]　S.I. 1993 No. 593, Sched. 2, para. 6 and Sched. 3, para. 6.
[21]　*ibid.*
[22]　Reciprocal Enforcement of Maintenance Orders (United States of America) Order 1995 (S.I. 1995 No. 2709), Sched. 3, para. 6.
[23]　S.I. 1995 No. 3345, rr. 5–10.

CHAPTER 14

CHILD SUPPORT

INTRODUCTORY

Aliment

The role of the courts in relation to aliment discussed in the previous chapter **14.01**
has been drastically altered and only remains in a residual form.[1] From April 1,
1993 maintenance in respect of children has been largely the province of the
Child Support Agency, operating a controversial piece of legislation applying
to children throughout Great Britain the Child Support Act 1991. This provides
for the determination of maintenance due to the child by applying a complex
set of formulae treating like cases exactly the same and involving minimal
discretion. The long-term future of this approach is in the balance at the end
of 1998.[2]

Background to the scheme

Policies in relation to families headed by lone parents have developed as the **14.02**
number of such families has risen in Great Britain from under 8 per cent in
1971 to 23 per cent in 1994.[3] As regards the aliment of children in such families
there appear to have been two distinct but related policies behind the reforms of
the 1990s. First, there was a recognition of the ineffectiveness of the existing
court-centred system of assessment and collection. The number of parents
receiving maintenance fell from 50 per cent in 1980 to 25 per cent in 1989.[4]
Secondly, there was a strong desire to shift the burden of support from the
community in general to the absent parent and to make public expenditure
savings. The number of lone parents forced to rely on income support[5] rose
from 37 per cent in 1971 to 59 per cent in 1986,[6] and to 70 per cent in 1989.[7]

A considerable number of studies into the lives of those living in households **14.03**
headed by a lone parent have been carried out from 1976 onwards. The stress
has varied from how mothers coped with bringing up children on their own[8] to
the impact of measures to assist low-income families.[9] Research has suggested

---

[1] See above, paras 13.03–13.08.
[2] November 30, 1998 was the final date for comments on the Green Paper of July 1998 and almost
    1,600 responses were received—two-thirds from the point of view of the absent parent. The
    Government indicated in March 1999 that the new scheme was unlikely to be introduced before
    2001.
[3] *General Household Survey*, Office for National Statistics 27 (1997), Social Trends, fig. 2.9.
[4] *Children Come First*, Cm. 1264 (1990).
[5] This means-tested benefit ensures that no one falls below the poverty line in Britain and is
    payable to those whose resources, income and capital are below a certain level. For details see
    National Welfare Benefits Handbook (CPAG Guide). It was known as "supplementary benefit"
    until 1986.
[6] Jonathan Bradshaw and Jane Millar, *Lone Parent Families in the UK* (DSS Research Report No.
    6, 1991), Chap. 6.
[7] *ibid.*
[8] Angie Hopkinson, *Single Mothers:The First year—A Scottish Study of Mothers Bringing Up
    Their Children On Their Own* (Scottish Council for Single Parents, 1984).
[9] Martin Evans, *Giving Credit Where it's Due? The Success of Family Credit Reassessed* (LSE,
    1996) (research period covered prior to the introduction of the Child Support Act).

that policies of financial support for children through the benefits system in the era of the Welfare State have been concerned to maintain a differential between wages and benefits as well as to restrain public expenditure.[10] Studies have shed light on life on benefits in general[11] and the difficulties for lone-parent families in particular. As for maintenance payments, the pattern of the receipt of these seemed to follow the course of contact with children by the absent parent. They lessened soon after separation and dwindled over the next 15 months.[12] Those in work were more likely to be in receipt of maintenance. They had better qualifications and a greater ability to pursue maintenance claims.[13] The reasons for lone parents ceasing to claim the means-tested benefit available for those in low-waged work reveal the relative unimportance of court maintenance in this process.[14] The role of child maintenance from ex-partners did not figure in lone parents' decisions about returning to work. Reliable child care and good wages were seen as most important.[15] The overall nature of support for children and the differential impact of lone parenting were the focus of research.[16] The issue of the source of child maintenance did not figure extensively in this work.[17]

14.04   There was no direct investigation into how the public perceived the extent to which lone parents had a legitimate claim to collective support.

14.05   The thrust of the Child Support Act 1991, however, reflects a shift of approach from the concerns of the research with the problems of lone-parent families. The legislation rather proceeds from the assumption that such families are problematic and that collective support is to be residual rather than central.

14.06   The background to the British approach was discussed by various writers prior to the introduction of the legislation.[18] Maclean suggested that a combination of economic pressure and impatience with what the Conservatives perceived as a "nanny state culture of dependency" helped create a political climate in which maintenance recovery arrangements were deemed worthy of strengthening.[19] The problem was exacerbated by court decisions such as *Delaney v. Delaney*[20] in which the judge reduced a maintenance award in order to enable an absent father and his new partner to get started on their new life, leaving the first family on social security.

---

[10] Joan C. Brown, *Children in Social Security* (Policy Studies Institute, 1984).

[11] Roy Sainsbury, Sandra Hutton and John Ditch, *Changing Lives and the Role of Income Support* (DSS Research Report No. 45, 1996) (research period covered prior to the introduction of the Child Support Act).

[12] Anna Leeming, Judith Unell and Robert Walker, *Lone Mothers* (DSS Research Report No. 30, 1994), Chap. 7 (research period covered prior to the introduction of the Child Support Act).

[13] Stephen McKay and Alan Marsh, *Lone Parents and Work* (DSS Research Report No. 25, 1994) (research period covered prior to the introduction of the Child Support Act).

[14] Alex Bryson and Alan Marsh, *Leaving Family Credit* (DSS Research Report No. 48, 1996), Chap. 3 (research period covered prior to the introduction of the Child Support Act).

[15] Reuben Ford, Alan Marsh and Stephen McKay, *Changes in Lone Parenthood 1989–1993* (DSS Research Report No. 40, 1995).

[16] Bradshaw and Millar, *op. cit.*

[17] Jonathan Bradshaw, John Ditch, Hilary Holmes and Peter Whiteford, *Support for Children—a comparison of arrangements in fifteen countries* (DSS Research Report No. 21, 1993); Jo Roll, *Lone Parent Families in the European Community* (European Family and Social Policy Unit, 1992).

[18] M. Maclean and J. Eekelaar, "Child Support: the British solution" (1993) 7, *International Journal of Law and the Family*, 205; see also G. Barton and G. Douglas, *Law and Parenthood* (Butterworths, London,1995), Chap. 9.

[19] Mavis Maclean, *The origins of Child Support in Britain and the Case for a Strong Child Support System in Private Lives and Public Responses*, ed. R. Ford and J. Millar (Policy Studies Institute, 1998).

[20] [1990] 2 Fam. 457.

Maclean also suggested that, with the loss of legal aid in divorce settlements, **14.07** the continuation of court-based maintenance payments would have become "problematic".[21] Jacobs and Douglas have opined that the 1991 Act formed the third plank in the Thatcher Government's programme to stress the importance of parental responsibilities. They refer to the introduction in England and Wales of (1) the Children Act 1989, with its concept of parental responsibility; and (2) the Criminal Justice Act 1991, with its emphasis on parental responsibility for the delinquent behaviour of their children.[22] As far as Scotland is concerned the Children (Scotland) Act 1995 likewise placed an emphasis on parental responsibilities as the foundation of parental rights.[23] The Scottish legislation, however, did not slavishly mirror that in England and Wales. The extensive reforms of the Scottish criminal justice system in Scotland during the 1990s, for instance, did not include any equivalent to the parental responsibility sections of the Criminal Justice Act indicated.[24] It is also worth noting that other legal systems have grappled with the broader social development in the breakdown and formation of family relationships. The same kind of conflicts between support for parental responsibility and the reality of changing patterns of living exist in those systems examined.

THE CHILD SUPPORT ACT 1991

Introduction

Whatever governmental motives may have been, the resulting legislation **14.08** was complex and inaccessible. Critical debate was inhibited by the general nature of the Act, with extensive reference to regulations for substantive details of how the system would work.[25] The original Child Support Bill published on February 14, 1991, contained over 100 regulation-making powers. The Bill was passed, virtually unchanged, by July 1991 and received the Royal Assent on July 25, 1991. The one area of extensive debate was the proposal to restrict benefit paid to those women who did not wish to reveal the identity of the father of any children for whom they were claiming. This concern was not surprising since by 1991 75 per cent of single parents were claiming income support. The debates in the Commons and Lords centred on this issue.[26] A compromise was reached whereby the legislation retained the reduced benefit direction. During the passage of the legislation there was accepted an exemption from the requirement to co-operate where an application for maintenance from the absent parent would put the parent or any child living with her at "risk of harm or undue distress". In addition it was enacted that the welfare of children should be taken into account when discretionary decisions, such as reducing benefit, were being taken.

The transition to the new system was facilitated by the setting up of a Child **14.09** Support Unit in April 1992 to improve the service to customers of the DSS Benefits Agency for whom child maintenance was an issue.[27] The legislation itself was launched on April 5, 1993 without the benefit of any actual pilot studies being carried out as to possible teething troubles. Whilst the legislation

---

[21] Mavis Maclean, *op. cit.*, n. 19
[22] *Child Support: The Legislation* (Sweet & Maxwell, 1993).
[23] Lockyer and Stone, *Juvenile Justice in Scotland* (T & T Clark, 1998), pp. 107 *et seq.*
[24] ss. 46–49.
[25] Wilson, "The Bairns of Falkirk: The Child Support Act 1991", 1991 S.L.T. (News) 417.
[26] House of Lords, Official Report, February 25, 1991, col. 817 for a critical perspective, *per* Lord Simon.
[27] Mark Speed, Christine Roberts and Kai Rudat, *Child Support Unit National Client Survey 1992* (DSS Research Report No. 14, 1993).

had come on to the statute book in July 1991, less time was available to evaluate the operation of the new formula basis. The key regulations were introduced in July 1992, leaving a short familiarisation period for what were immensely complex issues.[28] In this text it is proposed to outline the system that was introduced in 1993 and then to discuss the way the system has been perceived and the problems for the future. The basic structure—support derived from applying a fixed formula—remains intact. While the changes have been significant, unless indicated otherwise the system remains as it was enacted in 1993.

Alternative approaches

14.10 There are several models of a formula-based system. The system which the Australian Child Support Agency[29] operates involves a straight percentage, as does that of the New Zealand Child Support Agency.[30] The antipodean formulae take the gross income of the absent parent, usually based on the previous full tax year's income, and deduct a figure for exempt income based on current family commitments. A percentage of the remaining figure is then calculated, based on the number of children for whom child support is being assessed.[31] This system is also found in the American state often used as a model for experiments in reducing welfare: Wisconsin.[32]

14.11 Other common law jurisdictions operate court-based discretionary models for assessing the appropriate sum which an absent parent requires to pay to maintain any children remaining with the other parent. The problem of enforcing such court orders continues to exercise parents with care and official statistics suggest that this method of approach does not necessarily lead to higher numbers of absent parents paying.[33] There are individual systems of State support and sanction in the United States.[34] The disincentives for non-payers include in certain states loss of driving licence[35] as well as negative publicity on the television of "deadbeat dads".[36] Collection devices have included using marriage licence statutes,[37] linking support rights with inheritance[38] and allowing mothers on welfare to keep all their child support payments from the father.[39] In addition to state and county enforcement bodies,[40] there is a Federal Office of Child Support Enforcement.[41] There are also a significant number of private agencies who

---

[28] It is not intended in a work of this kind to deal with all the immensely complex calculation issues raised by the 1991 Act. For such a treatment see *Butterworth's Scottish Family Law Service* and Child Support Handbook (CPAG). The Appendix contains typical examples of how in the appeal papers to a child support appeal tribunal the calculations under the 1991 Act and regulations are presented.

[29] H.C. 470 (1993–94) Fifth Report from the Social Security Committee at 81; S. Parker, "Child support in Australia: children's rights or public interest?" (1991) 5 Int. J. Law and Fam. 24; M. Harrison, "The reformed Australian child support: an international policy comment" (1991) 12 J. Fam. Issues 430.

[30] *ibid.*; M. Henaghan and B. Atkin, *Family Law Policy in New Zealand* (1992).

[31] *loc cit* at para. 57: Australia: one child, 18%; two, 27%; three, 32%; four, 34%; five +, 36%; New Zealand: one, 18%; two, 24%; three, 27%; four +, 30%.

[32] Discussed in G. Davis, N. Wikeley, R. Young, J. Barron and J. Bedward, *Report of a Study of the Child Support Agency* (Nuffield Foundation, 1997) p. 6.

[33] J. Pearson, "Legislating adequacy: the impact of child support guidelines" (1989) 23 Law and Soc. Rev. 569.

[34] S. Abel and E. Sussman, "Child support guidelines: a comparison of New York, New Jersey and Connecticut: a synopsis" (1995) 33 Fam. and Conciliation Courts Rev. 426; J. Pearson, "Child Support in the United States: the experience in Colorado" (1992) 6 Int. J. Law and Fam. 321.

[35] M. Ray, "Child Support: Class Biases, State Interests and the Judicial Response" (paper delivered at the Law and Society Annual Meeting, June 1994).

[36] *ibid.*

[37] M. Rogers, "Use of the Texas marriage licence statutes as a child support collection device does not violate equal protection" (1996) 48 Baylor L. R. 1153.

[38] P. Monopoli, "'Deadbeat dads': should support and inheritance be linked?" (1994) U. Miami L. R. 257.

[39] "Where Wisconsin goes, can the world follow?" *The Economist*, Nov 1 1997, p. 25.

[40] Such as Marion County prosecutor's Office Child Support Division, Indianapolis, Indiana—charging a one off $25 dollar fee for non-welfare clients .

[41] R. Landers, "Prosecutorial limits on overlapping federal and state jurisdiction", *Annals of the American Academy of Political and Social Science* (1996) Vol. 543, p. 64.

engage to recover child support and arrange for increases. They do this by charging a percentage of the sums recovered.[42]

The issue of child support has been raised in the context of changes in divorce **14.12** laws in the 1990s across a range of western states including France,[43] Sweden[44] and Canada.[45] In Norway the *bidragsfogd* has, reportedly, impressive performance figures. It obtains payments from 90 per cent of the men liable to make child support payments and recoups some 80 per cent of the interim payments made by the State to families where there is an absent parent.[46]

Aliment by an absent parent

The Child Support Act 1991 provides the basic structure for the existing child **14.13** support regime applicable in most situations where one of the parents is absent. The courts do not have any power to make, vary or revive any maintenance order against an absent parent in relation to a "qualifying child". They do, however, retain jurisdiction in a number of specified discrete areas. Claims for aliment may be made:

(a) by a child against his or her step-parent[47];
(b) by a child against an adult who has accepted the child as a child of the family[48];
(c) by a child in excess of the formula laid down in the legislation[49];
(d) for expenses of a child's education or training[50];
(e) for expenses in connection with child's disability[51] where the child is in receipt of disability living allowance or is disabled in terms of section 8(9)[52];
(f) for aliment by a child against the parent with care[53];
(g) for aliment by a child where the child, the absent parent or the parent with care is habitually resident outwith the United Kingdom[54];
(h) for aliment by a child aged 19 or over[55];
(i) for aliment by a child aged 16 or over but under 19[56] who is not in receipt of full-time education;

---

[42] The organisations have official-sounding names and include the Child Support Assistance Network, the Child Support Network and the National Child Support Network.
[43] M. Fine and D. Fine, "An examination and evaluation of recent changes in divorce laws in five western countries: the critical role of values" (1994) 56 *Journal of Marriage and the Family* 249.
[44] *ibid.*
[45] E. Zweibel, "Child support policy and child support guidelines:broadening the agenda" (1993) 6 Can. J. Women and the Law 371.
[46] MR = AG – CB: the algebra of care, *The Guardian*, May 15, 1998.
[47] Child Support Act ("1991 Act"), s. 3(1); Family Law (Scotland) Act 1985: "child of the family" includes step-children and provided for the courts fixing their maintenance; jurisdiction continues as step-children not included in CSA definition of "qualifying child".
[48] *ibid.*
[49] 1991 Act, s. 8(6); see below, paras 14.15–14.24.
[50] *ibid.* s. 8(7)—typically where the maintenance assessment was modest compared with the absent parent's income—father with gross income of £26,000 required to pay £25 per week maintenance ordered to pay half of annual school fees of £4,200: [1994] N.L.J. 702; see also *MacLachlan v. MacLachlan*, January 31, 1997, OH.
[51] 1991 Act, s. 8(8).
[52] Defined as "blind, deaf or dumb or is substantially or permanently handicapped by illness, injury, mental disorder or congenital disorder or congenital deformity or such other disability as may be prescribed".
[53] 1991 Act, s. 8 (10).
[54] *ibid.* s. 44; habitual residence is not defined in the Act. Commissioners' decisions have covered the nature and degree of past and continuing connection with the United Kingdom (Isle of Man and Channel Islands excluded). Mere absence abroad does not destroy habitual residence, as where an immigration official employed in India for three years and expected to remain there for a further two years was deemed to still be habitually resident in the U.K. [CCS/7395/1995].
[55] *ibid.* s. 55(1).
[56] *ibid.* s. 55(1)(b); Child Support (Maintenance Assessment Procedure) Regulations 1992 (S.I. 1992 No. 1813) (CS (MaP) Regs 1992), Sched. 1.

(j) for aliment by a child aged 16 or over but under 18 who does fall within category (i) and satisfies prescribed conditions; and

(k) for aliment by a child who is or has been married.[57]

Parental responsibility

14.14　　The legislation made the obligation of the child's parents clear. Each parent of a "qualifying child" was to be responsible for maintaining that child.[58] The parent with care of the child was assumed, through the act of living with the child, to be providing maintenance. Although the financial split between the parents will be specified using the formula adopted under the Child Support Act 1991 (hereinafter "the 1991 Act") there is no machinery provided in the legislation to ensure that the parent with care expends such sums. They represent notional rather than actual expenditures of time, albeit that they are real and are likely to be much less than the equivalent professional child care costs. The 1991 Act only applies to "qualifying" children. A qualifying child is defined as one where either one or both of the parents are "absent parents".[59] This leaves certain children whose rights are covered by the previous court-centred regime[60] or special cases such as where both parents are absent.[61] Although this was (presumably) never intended, there was a whole host of transitional cases which it was not appropriate for the Child Support Agency to process.[62]

The basic formula

14.15　　The Child Support Act 1991 puts the principle of parental responsibility into effect through a series of complex formulae. These formulae are outlined in the Act. Provision is made for regulations to provide such details as may be likely to change. Typically, the amount of child support maintenance is to be fixed by a maintenance assessment. This is to be determined in accordance with the terms of Schedule 1 to the 1991 Act. Schedule 1 itself lays out the elements which enable a maintenance assessment to be made. These consist of a "maintenance requirement", the "basic rule", the "basic element" and the "additional element". The Schedule also introduces the key concepts of "assessable income", "protected income" and the "minimum amount of child support maintenance". Within the definitions of each of these elements there are references to "regulations made by the Secretary of State for the purposes of this sub-paragraph". Hence in relation to calculating the "additional element" there is a formula involving three separate parts: A and C, Z and Q. A and C are defined in the Schedule, Z is "such number as may be prescribed,[63] and Q is defined partly in the Schedule and partly in regulations.[64]

14.16　　Although its status was initially regarded as likely to be limited, there is a child welfare principle within the Act. Where the exercise of a discretionary power by the Secretary of State or any child support officer is involved, the decision-maker in question must have regard to the welfare of any child likely to be affected by the decision.[65] It is important to stress that this does not provide

---

[57] 1991 Act, s. 4(10),7(10) and 8(3A), added by Child Support Act 1995, s. 18; *McGilchrist v. McGilchrist* 1997 S.C.L.R. 800.

[58] s. 1(1).

[59] s. 3(1).

[60] See above, Chap. 13.

[61] Child Support (Maintenance Assessments Special Cases) Regulations 1992 (S.I. 1992 No. 1815) (CS (MASC) Regs 1992), Pt III, Special Cases deals with a range of non-standard child care arrangements where the formula does not apply.

[62] See T. Mullen in Thomson, *Family Law in Scotland* (Butterworth, 1995), p. 187.

[63] CS (MASC) Regs 1992, reg. 6 (2)(a), as amended by reg. 43 of the Amendment Regulations 1995.

[64] See App. 1.

[65] s. 2.

a fall-back position against which to measure whether or not the legislation as a whole is operating for the welfare of children. Much of the legislation involves no exercise of discretion. Thus, for instance, there is a provision that there is a minimum payment which must be made by an absent parent who is existing on the official poverty line payment: income support.[66] The fact that paying out 10 per cent of this figure takes an individual below the poverty line and might have an impact on any children living with him is not a relevant consideration since there is no element of discretion in operating this section of the legislation. By contrast, one important area which is discussed below does involve child support officer ("CSO") discretion. This occurs where there is a proposal to reduce the benefit as a result of non-co-operation with the Child Support Agency.[67] In addition the Secretary of State has discretion in relation to collection and enforcement of maintenance.[68]

Maintenance requirement[69]

14.17 The objective factor in the level of financial support regime is found in the concept of the "maintenance requirement". This lays down the level of support which the individual child should receive, assuming a reasonable level of income of the absent parent. The figure derives from adding together income support personal allowances for the qualifying children to those for the person with care together with family premium and (where the person with care is a single parent) a lone parent premium.[70] From this is deducted the amount payable by way of universally available child benefit.[71] The resultant figure represents what the State regards as the appropriate level of maintenance for a child in the average family. The calculation seems to involve taking account of the parent with care and has led to resentment from absent parents that they are not simply paying for the children but for their ex-partner.

Maintenance assessment[72]

14.18 The basis of the level of financial support required in an individual case from the absent parent comes from the child support officer making a "maintenance assessment". Using the information obtained from the parent with care in her maintenance assessment form ("MAF") and that from the absent parent in his maintenance enquiry form ("MEF")[73] the maintenance assessment figure is arrived at. This involves comparing the "maintenance requirement" and the "assessable income" of the child's parents. Where the assessable income is less than or equal to the "maintenance requirement", the level of support payable by the absent parent is half that parent's "assessable income".[74] Where the "assessable income" exceeds the fixed assumed cost of bringing up that child a two-stage calculation is carried out to arrive at the "maintenance requirement". The initial calculation takes 50 per cent of the absent parent's

---

[66] At November 1998 for an adult aged 25 or more £50.35 plus housing costs. For up-to date details see the annually updated *National Welfare Benefits Handbook* published by the Child Poverty Action Group.

[67] See below, para. 14.28.

[68] See below, para. 14.35.

[69] 1991 Act, Sched. 1, para. 1; see also App. 1.

[70] Sched. 1, Pt 1, para. 1(1), (2).

[71] CS (MASC) Regs 1992, reg. 3.

[72] 1991 Act, Sched. 1, para. 2.

[73] The MAF and MEF forms resemble tax self-assessment forms. The MAF is obtainable by post only from the Child Support Agency rather than in Post Offices etc as other social security forms have traditionally been.

[74] Sched. 1, para. 2(2).

assessable income.[75] To this is added, in effect, a further 25 per cent of the absent parent's additional income to reach the total figure provisionally available for the maintenance of the "qualifying" children.[76]

Assessable incomes[77]

14.19   The 1991 Act and regulations attempt to make a distinction between certain kinds of income and expenses. The idea is to prevent subsequent "commitments" and "illegitimate" expenses swallowing up the cash which is available for the support of the absent parent's children. The income to be taken as available for the support of the absent parent's children encompasses the parent's income net of tax, National Insurance payments and half of pension payments.[78]

14.20   The formula identifies certain sums which are to be exempt. These are such sums as will allow a person to live and include the single person's income support allowance and any relevant income support premiums and their housing costs.[79] There is a ceiling placed on the amount that is accepted for housing costs, to prevent absent parents leaving nothing available for child support.[80] Where absent parents are in receipt of wages the regulations specify that the "relevant week" for calculating wages for the initial assessment is immediately *prior* to when the maintenance assessment form is sent to the absent parent.[81] The appropriate period for determining the parent's earnings are five consecutive weeks (for those paid weekly) and two consecutive months (for those paid monthly) ending in this "relevant week".[82] This looking backwards is to combat abuse where absent parents might otherwise seek to arrange their earnings to minimise their income during the period for which the calculation is made. There is, in addition, provision for a different period to be selected where the standard specified period does not accurately reflect the normal amount of earnings. This includes taking account of the duration and pattern of earnings so that, for instance, one might want to look over a six month period for a worker whose pattern of work was "three weeks on, three weeks off", or a period of 12 months where it was standard to receive an annual bonus in one month's wages.[83]

Basic element[84]

14.21   As indicated, the intention of the legislation is that absent parents should contribute a fixed proportion of their income to support their children where their earnings are average.[85] A formula puts this notion into practice. This provides that half of the minimum amount necessary to maintain a child is to be provided by the absent parent.[86]

---

[75] 1991 Act, Sched. 1, para. 2(2).

[76] Sched. 1, para. 2(3).

[77] 1991 Act, Sched. 1, para. 5; see also App. 1.

[78] CS (MASC) Regs 1992, Sched. 1, para. 1(3).

[79] *ibid.* reg. 9.

[80] Initially £80 per week or half the assessable income of the absent parent—CS (MASC) Regs 1992, reg. 18 on "excessive housing costs".

[81] CS (MASC) Regs 1992, reg 1.

[82] *ibid.* Sched. 1, para. 2.

[83] *ibid.* Sched 1, para. 2 (4): the same kind of flexibility allows the CSO to look at the income of self-employed people over a longer period .

[84] 1991 Act, Sched. 1 para. 3; see also App. 1.

[85] *Children Come First* Cm 1264.

[86] Sched. 1, para. 2(1)—$(A + C) \times P$ where A and C are the assessable incomes of the parents; P is prescribed by CS (MASC) Regs 1992, reg. 5(b) at 0.5.

Additional element[87]

For those with higher incomes the legislation provides that a further 25 per cent **14.22** slice of that higher income is to be made available for the support of the children. The underlying notion is that the child is entitled to support at something like the level they would have received had the parent not ceased to reside with the other parent. There is, however, a ceiling on how much of this higher income is to be made available under the formula. This ceiling is expressed in another version of the additional element formula. The additional element available was not to exceed this second formula.

Protected income[88]

The formula assumes that the level of support to which children are entitled **14.23** is to be based on income support levels. The concept of "protected income" and its calculation endeavours to protect absent parents on low incomes being left with highly restricted discretionary income. The impact on the child and parent with care is that they receive less income than the community assesses a child requires. This shortfall may be met through such means-tested benefits as income support. Where the parent with care is engaged in waged work this would be met by family credit, provided that that parent otherwise qualifies.[89] The amount allowed to the absent parent is the income support levels for him and any other dependants together with housing costs, council tax, travel to work costs above a specified limit, and an earnings disregard. In addition, to provide (according to Jacobs and Douglas) an incentive to stay at work, the absent parent is allowed 15 per cent of the amount by which his income exceeds "disposable income".[90] It is in the calculation of what amounts to "disposable income" that the income of any new partners is factored into the formula.

Maintenance payable

In order to obtain assistance from the CSA the parent with care will have **14.24** completed a maintenance application form giving details of her financial circumstances and those of the absent parent, in so far as they are known. The CSA then obtains further information from the absent parent. The maintenance is fixed using this information. The date at which payment becomes due is fixed in relation to the sending of the maintenance enquiry form to the absent parent. This date, known as the "effective date", was originally fixed as the date the absent parent received the relevant forms from the CSA.[91] From April 18, 1995 this date can be fixed eight weeks after receipt by the absent parent of the maintenance enquiry form. The absent parent must, however, return the form within four weeks of receiving it.[92] In the early days arrears built up and this recommendation was made in the first report on the operation of the legislation in 1993.[93] The actual maintenance payable to the parent with care for the qualifying child(ren) is the sum reached after applying the appropriate formulae. Interestingly, the original formula actually contained two elements designed to

---

[87] 1991 Act, Sched. 1, para. 4; see also App. 1.

[88] *ibid.* Sched. 1, para. 6; see also App. 1.

[89] The principal restrictions are on income as well as capital and hours worked: for details consult the current *CPAG Handbook* published annually.

[90] *Child Support: The Legislation* Edward Jacobs and Gillian Douglas (Sweet & Maxwell, 1997), p. 11.

[91] CS (MAP) Regs 1992, regs 1 and 30: there is also provision for the CSO fixing the effective date when the absent parent has deliberately avoided receipt of the maintenance enquiry form or MEF.

[92] *ibid.* reg. 30(2)(a).

[93] HC (1993) *The Operation of the Child Support Act*, HC 69 House of Commons Social Security Committee First Report 1993-94, London: HMSO .

ensure that no payment should be made above a certain figure and that absent parents would be left with at least 70 per cent of their net income after meeting their maintenance assessments. As noted, there was the "protected income" element as well as the ceiling produced by the alternative formula for the "additional element". Research, however, indicated that around 20 per cent of absent parents were left with less than the 70 per cent figure.[94] Accordingly a fixed statutory maximum was introduced in 1995 whereby no absent parent has to pay more than 30 per cent of net income as child support. [95]

14.25   There is a minimum maintenance payable[96] where the formula produces a figure less than the prescribed minimum.[97] The Government, when outlining the new scheme in 1990, was keen to ensure that parents on low incomes should, in principle, meet their "legal and moral obligations" as parents and pay a "nominal" 5 per cent of income support.[98] The figure for those existing at the official poverty level in receipt of income support has been doubled since 1996. Their contributions are met through deductions from benefit.[99] This figure is almost exactly 10 per cent of the income support personal allowance figure.[1] There are a small number of groups exempt from paying the minimum[2]:

(1) those in receipt of certain specified benefits (21 health-related benefits or pensions are currently specified, such as incapacity benefit, attendance allowance and disability living allowance[3];
(2) those who have family premium in the calculation of estimated or protected income[4] (*i.e.* have at least two days care per week);
(3) where the absent parent is a child[5];
(4) prisoners[6];
(5) income less than minimum amount.[7]

Obligation to co-operate

14.26   As indicated above, one of the concerns of the Government in the early 1990s was the cost to the community of single parents living on income support.[8] The legislation lays an obligation on parents with care who are receiving income support, family credit or any prescribed benefit to authorise the Secretary of State to recover maintenance from the absent parent.[9] This requirement does not apply where there are reasonable grounds for believing that if the parent were required to authorise recovery "there would be a risk of her, or of any child living with her, suffering harm or undue distress as a result".[10] In order to make the recovery likely the parent with care can be asked to provide information to enable the absent parent to be traced. The principal issue that has emerged in this area is whether or not the parent with care has grounds for suspecting that

---

[94] *Improving Child Support* Cm. 2745 (HMSO, 1995).
[95] Child Support (Miscellaneous Amendment) Regulations 1995 (S.I. 1995 No. 123).
[96] 1991 Act, Sched. 1, para 7.
[97] CS (MASC) Regs 1992; reg. 13—amended by S.I. 1996 No. 481—this expresses the amount as 5% of the income support personal allowance multiplied by a variable—in 1998 this was fixed at 2.
[98] *Children Come First* Cm 1264, para. 3.29.
[99] 1991 Act, s. 43(2) and Social Security Administration Act 1992, s. 5(1)(t).
[1] £51.40 for someone aged 25 or over from April 1999.
[2] CS (MASC) Regs 1992, reg. 26.
[3] *ibid.* Sched. 4.
[4] *ibid.* reg. 26(1)(ii).
[5] *ibid.* reg. 26(1)(iii)—as defined within s. 5 of the Act.
[6] *ibid.* reg. 26(1)(iv).
[7] *ibid.* reg. 26(1)(v).
[8] See above, para. 14.08.
[9] s. 6 (1).
[10] s. 6 (2).

there are fears for her own or her children's safety in the event that the absent parent is contacted by the Child Support Agency. The courts in England have made it clear that when deciding about the question of the welfare of the child there is no obligation on the CSA to make inquiries of the absent parent.[11] As for the general question of the relationship between the social security and child support systems the Court of Appeal has indicated that the claim that parents with care may not be entitled to income support was not the crucial issue. There was authority for action under section 6 by the Secretary of State on the basis of what was "actually" paid not what was "lawfully" paid by way of the relevant social security benefits.[12]

In order to ensure co-operation by the absent parent there exists the possibility **14.27** of a standard assessment to be made to encourage compliance by, in effect, charging a high maintenance assessment. This mechanism is known as an "interim maintenance assessment". There are four kinds of interim maintenance assessments: categories A, B, C and D. Category A occurs where the absent parent has failed to provide information about wages or housing costs required by the CSO to enable an assessment to be made.[13] The amount of maintenance is fixed as 1.5 multiplied by the maintenance requirement.[14] A Category B interim maintenance assessment will be made where information is required about the income of the absent parent's partner or other member of the family of the absent parent or parent with care. If the CSO is prevented by lack of information from making the necessary calculation on the question of exempt income and protected income then no allowance will be made for the partner. This will occur where a partner is expected to maintain a joint child of either absent parent or parent with care or where the absent parent's family income is unknown.[15] A category C interim maintenance assessment applies to self-employed absent parents who are unable to provide information about earnings. In such cases the amount of child support maintenance is £30 unless the CSO decides, after hearing representations from the parent with care,[16] that a lower amount (including a nil amount) is reasonable in all the circumstances.[17] In such circumstances the protected income calculation does not apply.[18] Category D assessments are available where the CSO is of the view, on the basis of the information available, that the amount of an existing Category A may be less than the maintenance assessment using the standard formula.[19] The Category D assessment operates the formula except that there is no protected income, no 30 per cent restriction, no housing costs allowed, the exempt income is limited to the adult personal allowance and there is no pension disregard.[20]

Reduced benefit direction
Where the parent with care fails to co-operate with the CSA a written notice **14.28** may be served requiring either compliance or reasons to be given for failing to do so.[21] The CSO must at the end of the specified six-week period for reasons, consider any reasons given. They may act after two weeks if there is no response

---

[11] *R. v. Secretary of State for Social Security, ex p. Lloyd* [1995] 1 F.L.R. 856, QBD.
[12] *Secretary of State for Social Security v. Harmon, The Times,* June 10, 1998.
[13] CS (MAP) Regs 1992, reg. 8(3)(a).
[14] *ibid.* reg. 8A (1).
[15] *ibid.* reg. 8A (2), (3) and (4).
[16] *ibid.* reg. 8A (8).
[17] *ibid.* reg. 8A (6).
[18] *ibid.* reg. 8A (7).
[19] *ibid.* reg 8 (3)(d).
[20] *ibid.* reg. 8A (9).
[21] s. 46(3).

from the parent with care. If it is considered that there are no reasonable grounds
then a reduced benefit direction may be given.[22] This reduces the amount of
benefit payable by a specific percentage. Originally this was set at 20 per cent
for the first six months and then 10 per cent for the next 12 months.[23] Initially
this was for a fixed maximum period of 18 months,[24] though this was extended
to an indefinite reduction from October 1996 at a higher level of 40 per cent.[25]

14.29   In terms of determining whether there is good cause for a parent with care
to refuse to co-operate with the authorities, Commissioners' decisions have
discussed what amounts to a risk of harm or undue distress. The test is not
whether it is certain or definite that the harm or undue distress *will* occur but
whether this *might* occur.[26] The correct test involves whether "there is a realistic
possibility" of harm or undue distress being suffered. The risk does not require
to be "substantial" but must be real rather than imagined. "Distress" must,
however, be "undue". Guidance is also available from the Secretary of State. It
suggests that the withdrawal of informal financial assistance would not in itself
amount to good cause nor that the parent with care fears that the absent parent
will want contact with the child. Nor, it is suggested, is distress to the absent
parent who might not want a new partner to know of the child.[27]

14.30   In the first year good cause was raised in some eight per cent of cases where
application forms were issued.[28] The number of good cause requests rose from
65,000 to 190,000 between 1993–94 and 1996–97 and the acceptance rate fell
from 49 per cent to under 20 per cent. Benefit penalties were only imposed in
about one-third of cases where good cause was refused partly because of the
welfare of the child consideration.[29] Nonetheless the number of reduced benefit
directions has been considerable. Eighteen thousand were issued in the first
two years of the Act's operation and in 1995–96 27,478 were issued. In evidence
to the Social Security Committee the Child Support Agency indicated that some
50,000 reduced benefit directions were issued in the first four years of the Act's
operation.[30] The number revealed in its other material amounts to 65,000.[31]

14.31   The numbers of parents with care who have accepted, or at least not appealed
against, a reduced benefit direction increased from 4.3 per cent in 1994–95 to
nine per cent in 1995–96.[32] Large numbers of parents with care were seen as
being able to opt out of the child support scheme. Governmental concern was
expressed at the number of situations where it was suspected there had been
collusion between the parent with care and the absent parent so that women
were refusing to co-operate and shifting the burden of child support from their
ex-partners onto the community for no good reason. This was looked into in an
in-house Report by the Department of Social Security[33] and by the Social Security

---

[22] s. 46(5).

[23] CS (MAP) Regs 1992, reg. 36.

[24] *ibid.*

[25] CS (MAP) Regs 1992, reg. 36 (as amended).

[26] CCS/1037/1995 (starred 10/96).

[27] But see CCS/12609/1996 (starred 78/96)—good cause where daughter knew her father but not
that he had another family.

[28] Child Support: Good Cause and the Benefit Penalty, Social Security Committee, Fourth Report
(1995–96) HC 440 at vii.

[29] E. Knights, J. Blackwell, S. Cox and A. Garnham, *Child Support Handbook* CPAG (6th ed.
1998), p. 93.

[30] Child Support: Good Cause and the Benefit Penalty, Social Security Committee, Fourth Report
(1995-96) HC 440 at vii.

[31] E. Knights, J. Blackwell, S. Cox and A. Garnham, *Child Support Handbook* CPAG (6th ed.,
1998), 93.

[32] *ibid.*

[33] *The Requirement to Co-operate: A Report on the Operation of the 'Good Cause' Provisions,*
DSS April 1996—referred to extensively in n. 28.

Committee.[34] The latter recommended that the changes to the regulations extending the benefit penalty should be supplemented by regular interviews and a consideration of whether fraud investigations should commence. The government extended the benefit penalty to 40 per cent in line with the penalty imposed in relation to failing actively to seek work.

Shared care

Where the absent parent shares care with the parent with care there is **14.32** recognition of this in the financial assessment provided that, on average, over the year the care amounts to a minimum of two nights per week. Whilst there is no definition of "shared care" itself the term "day-to-day care" means care of not less than 104 nights during the 12-month period ending with the relevant week.[35] This means that where the level of care is less than the average of two nights per week there is no recognition of this care contribution in the formula. It is possible to use a different period from the full year where, for instance, this is more representative of the care arrangements,[36] although the two days out of seven ratio must remain the same.[37] A future period cannot be used as the regulations require that the computation period end with the "relevant week".[38] The crucial aspect of day-to-day care is care during the night[39] rather than continuous care during the day. Evidence may be required to establish the level of care and some lawyers have advised their clients to keep a diary of the dates of overnight visits.[40]

Disputed parentage

Although it does not apply to Scotland it is worth noting the situation that **14.33** operates in England and Wales where there is disputed parentage. It has an impact on decisions which may come before the Scottish courts. Where a man denies that he is one of the child's parents the child support officer must not make a maintenance assessment on the assumption that the alleged parent is one of the child's parents unless the case falls within a number of categories specified in the legislation.[41] These are six in number[42]: where the person alleged to be a parent is a parent by virtue of (1) having adopted the child; (2) a parental order in favour of a gamete donor; (3) a court declarator or declaration and no subsequent adoption of child; (4) a section 27 declaration, with no subsequent adoption; (5) the child being habitually resident in Scotland to whom one or other of the presumptions in section 5(1) of the Law Reform (Parent and Child) (Scotland) Act 1986 applies and no subsequent adoption; or (6) affiliation proceedings which have found the alleged parent to be the father of the child and no subsequent adoption.

Where an application for a maintenance assessment has been made or is in **14.34** force and the alleged parent denies he is the parent and the CSO is not satisfied that any of these situations outlined applies[43] then the Secretary of State or the person with care may apply to the court for a declaration as to whether the

---

[34] Child Support: Good Cause and the Benefit Penalty, Social Security Committee, Fourth Report (1995–96) HC 440.
[35] CS (MASC) Regs 1992, reg. 1(2) as amended by Child Support and Income Support (Amendment) Regulations 1995, reg. 41(2)(i).
[36] *ibid.* CCS/6/1994 (starred 7/95).
[37] 52 nights—6 months; 26 nights—3 months; 13 nights—2 months; 9 nights a month.
[38] CCS/499/1995 (starred 7/95); CCS/7171/1995 (starred 55/96).
[39] CS (MASC) Regs 1992, regs 1(2) & 20(1); CCS/499/1995 (starred 69/96).
[40] CCS/11728/1996 (starred 69/96).
[41] 1991 Act, s. 26(1).
[42] *ibid.* s. 26(2).
[43] *ibid.* s. 27(1).

alleged parent is one of the child's parents.[44] If satisfied that the alleged parent is or is not the parent it is to make a declaration to that effect.[45]

Collection and enforcement

14.35   Rather than leave collection in the hands of parents with care, part of the remit of the Child Support Agency has been to provide a cheap collection and enforcement service. It has not, however, been an unqualified success. The delays have been considerable and the main function of the Agency has been to collect payments from "soft targets" like men in salaried and waged employment rather than the self-employed. In addition a major target has been those on benefit. Those on benefit amounted to 97 per cent of the maintenance claims dealt with by the CSA in the first year of the operation of the Act.[46] In reality private applicants were in the first five years of the Child Support Agency's existence treated as marginal to their core activity of achieving benefit savings for the Treasury.[47]

14.36   The 1991 Act introduced a flat fee for those who opted to use their collection services[48] as well as where parents with care have no option as recipients of State benefits.[49] This collection fee is payable by the absent parent.[50] The Act specifies that the CSA collects any child support maintenance payable in accordance with a maintenance assessment where the person with care is on benefit[51] or where there has been a request for such collection by a private client.[52] They have played a much greater role in relation to those with care on benefit than for private clients.[53]

14.37   The CSA has a range of different alternatives available to it to collect and enforce decisions about the maintenance assessment.[54] These include the possibility, in the event of non-compliance with orders, of a deduction from earnings order. Decisions about enforcement are for the Secretary of State and, although this involves discretion, enforcement issues cannot be raised on appeal before the Child Support Appeal Tribunal.[55] As discretionary issues, they require the Secretary of State, prior to making a deduction from earnings order or liability order, to have regard to the welfare of any child likely to be affected.[56] A challenge on this issue can only be made through judicial review.[57] Where a deduction from earnings order is not appropriate either because the absent parent is not in waged work or it has not proved effective the CSA can take court action and obtain a liability order in the sheriff court.[58] The court is limited to dealing with whether or not the payments have become payable and whether or not they have been paid.[59] It was not possible, moreover, according to the Court of Appeal,

---

[44] 1991 Act, s 27(1A).
[45] *ibid.* s. 27(2).
[46] A. Garnham and E. Knights (1994) *Child Support Handbook* (2nd ed.) CPAG.
[47] G. Davis, N. Wikeley, R. Young, J. Barron and J. Bedward, *Report of a Study of the Child Support Agency* (Nuffield Foundation, 1997), Chap. 4, p. 49.
[48] Basic fee of £44 per year—Child Support Fees Regulations 1992 (S.I. 1992 No. 3094), reg. 4(3).
[49] s. 29 (1).
[50] Child Support Fees Regulations 1992, reg. 3(3).
[51] *ibid.* s 19(1)(a); Child Support (Collection and Enforcement) Regulations 1992 (SI 1992 No. 1989) (CE), reg 2.
[52] 1991 Act, s. 6 (CE), reg. 2.
[53] See below, para. 14.83.
[54] 1991 Act, s. 37 makes provision for regulations providing that where the sheriff has made a liability order and it remains unpaid, in whole or in part, the absent parent must supply relevant information to the CSA—not in force at the time of writing.
[55] 1991 Act, s. 31(2).
[56] s. 2.
[57] *R. v. Secretary of State for Social Security, ex p. Biggin* [1995] 1 F.L.R. 851.
[58] s. 33 and Act of Sederunt (Child Support Rules) 1993.
[59] 1991 Act, s. 33(3); *Secretary of State v. Shotton* [1996] 2 F.L.R. 241.

for the CSA to prevent a person from disposing of his assets in terms of the 1991 Act.[60] The question of disposal of assets has now been addressed indirectly by the 1995 Act and may feature in a request for a departure direction.[61]

Deduction from earnings orders

There is, as indicated, a discretionary power for the Secretary of State, acting **14.38** through the Children (Scotland) Act 1995, to make a deduction from earnings order to secure the payment of any sum due under a maintenance assessment.[62] It is challengeable by way of judicial review.[63] If the order is defective there is authority from England which suggests that the CSA cannot be ordered by the courts to repay money paid under the defective order.[64] This order may be made to secure the payment of arrears of child support maintenance, as well as future amounts, or a combination of both.[65] A deduction from earnings order must be directed at the employer of the liable person and has effect from the date specified in the order.[66] The order operates as an instruction to the employer to make deductions from the liable person's earnings and pay the amounts deducted to the Children (Scotland) Act 1995.[67] The earnings deduction order must be served on the person who appears to be the employer of the liable person as well as the liable person.[68] There is a prescribed form for use by employers.[69] Where an earnings deduction order has been made and a copy has been served on the liable person's employer it is the duty of the employer to comply with the order. There is a seven day period of grace for compliance.[70] This is likely to be used as a last resort after agreements have failed and it seems that the CSA is less than enthusiastic to get involved in these methods of money recovery.[71] It has concentrated instead on simpler assessments to boost performance targets.[72]

Liability orders

Where a liable person fails to make one or more payments and it appears **14.39** to the CSA that it is inappropriate to make a deduction from earnings order against him (because, *e.g.*, he is not employed) or, although such an order has been made, it has provided ineffective as a means of securing that payments are made in accordance with the maintenance assessment in question[73] then the CSA may apply to the sheriff for a liability order against the liable person.[74]

It is competent for a departmental official to sign the application in place of **14.40** the Secretary of State.[75] Where the CSA applies for such a liability order the

---

[60] *Department of Social Security v. Butler* [1995] 4 All E.R. 195; [1995] 1 W.L.R. 1528, CA.
[61] See below, para. 14.70
[62] 1991 Act, s 31(2).
[63] *ex p. Viette*, March 28, 1996, QBD.
[64] *Secretary of State for Social Security v. Shotton* [1996] 2 F.L.R. 241.
[65] 1991 Act, s 31(3).
[66] *ibid.* s 31(4).
[67] *ibid.* s 31(5).
[68] *ibid.* s 31(6).
[69] CE, reg. 19(1) and Sched. 1.
[70] 1991 Act, s 31(7).
[71] G. Davis, N. Wikeley, R. Young, J. Barron and J. Bedward, *Report of a Study of the Child Support Agency* (Nuffield Foundation, 1997), Chap. 4.
[72] HC 50 The Performance and Operation of the Child Support Agency, House of Commons Social Security Committee, Second Report 1995-96 London: HMSO, p. xi—of 46,000 assessments completed between April and August 1995, 20,700 were for £2.35 or less—45% of the total.
[73] 1991 Act, s. 33(1).
[74] *ibid.* s. 33(2).
[75] *Secretary of State for Social Security v. Love*, 1996 S.C.L.R. 535, Sh.Ct.

fact that an appeal has been lodged with a child support appeal tribunal (CSAT) is to be ignored.[76]

14.41   The liability order, in turn, may be rendered operative by poinding and sale and an arrestment and action of furthcoming or sale.[77] Should the CSA choose to enforce an assessment it is important to note that there is no equivalent to regulation 37 of the Social Security (Claims and Payments) Regulations 1987.[78] This provides that there is suspension of enforcement pending an appeal under section 25 of the Social Security Administration Act 1992. Under the 1991 Act the sheriff must make an order if satisfied that the payments in question have become payable by the liable person and have not been paid.[79] Where there is an application the sheriff cannot question the maintenance assessment under which the payments of child support come to be made.[80] This limits the sheriff to ascertaining that (1) the sums in question have become payable and (2) those sums have not been paid. This test is determined by the Child Support (Collection and Enforcement) Regulations 1992[81] where regulation 4 requires the CSA to specify the day and interval when payments of child support maintenance are to be made. As indicated, where the subject-matter of the application is under appeal to a Child Support Appeal Tribunal the sheriff must grant the order irrespective of the appeal and this is different from situations where there is an appeal outstanding against a judicial decision.[82]

14.42   Hence the familiar common law rule that an appeal suspends the order of a lower court[83] does not apply where the 1991 Act is concerned. The reasoning behind this stems from the fact that provision is made for a CSO to make adjustments in any case of overpayments[84] as well as that no express provision was made in the child support legislation for a suspension pending appeal. The power and duty to grant the order is expressly conferred by Parliament.[85]

Enforcement of liability orders by diligence

14.43   In Scotland where a liability order has been made against a person the order is a warrant for a charge of that amount and recovery through poinding and sale and for an arrestment (other than arrestment of earnings) and action of furthcoming or sale.[86] Regulations provide that any liability order made by a court in England and Wales or any corresponding order made by a court in Northern Ireland may be enforced in Scotland as if it had been made by the sheriff.[87]

Committal to prison

14.44   Whilst it has been suggested that Parliament has made it plain that the power to imprison for debts was a power "to be used exceedingly sparingly and only as a last resort",[88] the power does, nonetheless, exist. This is because any sum

---

[76] *Secretary of State for Social Security v. Nicol (No. 2)*, 1997 S.L.T. 572 (2nd Div).
[77] s. 38 (1)(a).
[78] S.I. 1987 No. 1968.
[79] 1991 Act, s. 33(3).
[80] S.I. 1992 No. 1989.
[81] *Secretary of State for Social Security v. Nicol (No. 2)*, above.
[82] *Macleay v. Macdonald*, 1928 S.C. 776, 1928 S.L.T. 463; *Kennedy v. M* 1995 S.L.T. 717; *Stirling v. D*, 1995 SCLR 460; 1995 S.L.T. 1089, IH.
[83] *Stirling v. D*, 1995 S.C.L.R. 460 at 464.
[84] Child Support (Arrears, Interest and Adjustment of Maintenance Assessments) Regulations 1992 (S.I. 1992 No. 1816), reg. 10.
[85] *Secretary of State for Social Security v. Nicol (No. 2)* 1997 S.L.T. 572 (2nd Div.); *Department of Social Security v. Butler* [1995] 4 All E.R. 195; [1995] 1 W.L.R. 1528, CA.
[86] 1991 Act, s. 38.
[87] *ibid.* s. 39.
[88] *R. v. Luton Magistrates' Court, ex p. Sullivan* [1992] 2 F.L.R. 196 at 201.

payable under a liability order is to be treated as a sum decerned for aliment for the purposes of the Debtors (Scotland) Act 1880 and the Civil Imprisonment (Scotland) Act 1882.[89] Where a liability order has been made the CSA is regarded as the creditor and may exercise all the powers of a creditor for the purposes of section 4 of the Civil Imprisonment (Scotland) Act 1882, and this includes imprisonment for failure to obey decree for an alimentary debt.[90]

Arrears of child support maintenance

Where the CSA has the power to recover child support maintenance and the **14.45** absent parent has failed to make one or more payments due in accordance with that assessment there was originally provision for the charging of interest[91] at a prescribed rate—1 per cent above median bank rate.[92] Interest payments were suspended and replaced after April 1997 with late payment penalties.[93] This did not affect past liabilities.

Where the CSA recovers arrears it may in prescribed circumstances retain **14.46** them if satisfied that the amount of certain means-tested benefits paid to the person with care of the child(ren) would have been less had the absent parent not been in arrears with payments of child support maintenance.[94] The benefits specified are income support and jobseeker's allowance.

Research indicates that arrears are often ignored in practice. One of the **14.47** problems identified in studies of the operation of the Child Support Agency's work is that the system, for all its concern to avoid the variation of decisions between individuals judges, is in reality highly discretionary when it comes to collection and enforcement. Variations are common and delays and negotiations are the key to what happens to clients in arrears.[95]

Review

One of the difficulties with a system which seeks to obtain a proportion of the **14.48** absent parent's income by way of maintenance is how to make sure that the sums due relate to changing financial circumstances. One of the key assumptions to the effective operation of the 1991 formula is that the population is static, enjoys fixed employment and that relationship status is not fluid.[96] The legislation allows for income to be examined over periods which are representative of the absent parent's normal income.[97] It also provides for the review of assessments on a periodic basis. This was initially to be every 52 weeks[98] but has been extended to every two years.[99] There is also provision for review where there is a change of circumstances.[1] This includes such matters as increases in wages or benefits. It should be noted, however, that in order for a reassessment to take place the change must normally satisfy one of several financial thresholds between £1 and £10.[2] This is to avoid constant trivial revisions. In addition there may be review at the instigation of the child support officer.

---

[89] 1991 Act, s. 40(13).
[90] *ibid.* s. 40(14).
[91] *ibid.* s. 41(3).
[92] *ibid.* s. 41(4); Child Support (Arrears, Interest and Adjustment of Maintenance Assessments) Regulations 1992 (S.I. 1992 No. 1816) (AIAMA), reg. 6.
[93] Child Support (Miscellaneous Amendments) Regulations 1995 (S.I. 1995 No. 123).
[94] 1991 Act, s 41(2); AIAMA, reg. 8 (as amended).
[95] G. Davis, N. Wikeley, R. Young, J. Barron and J. Bedward, Report of a Study of the Child Support Agency (Nuffield Foundation, 1997), pp. 44 *et seq.*
[96] *ibid.* 95.
[97] MASC, Sched. 1, para. 2(4).
[98] CS (MAP) Regs 1992, reg. 17 (1)(ii) .
[99] *ibid.* as amended by Child Support (Miscellaneous Amendments) (No. 2) Regulations 1995 (S.I. 1995 No. 3261), reg. 24 (2).
[1] s. 17.
[2] CS (MAP) Regs 1992, reg. 20, as amended by Child Support (Miscellaneous Amendments) (No. 2) Regulations 1995 (S.I. 1995 No. 3261), regs 27 and 28.

14.49   Decisions by a child support officer on matters other than reduced benefit
direction are not immediately subject to appeal. Instead there is provision for
further review by the child support officer, known as a second-tier review.[3]

Periodical review

14.50   Complementing the notion of reviews when there is either a change of
circumstances or where the CSO discovers that some kind of error has occurred,
there is provision for reviews on a periodical basis.[4] These are to be conducted
as if a fresh application for a maintenance assessment had been made.[5] The
regulations provide that assessment must be reviewed after it has been in force
for a period of 52 weeks (in the case of an assessment whose effective date is on
or before April 18, 1994) or 104 weeks (where the effective date is after April
18, 1994).[6] On completion of the review the CSO must make a fresh assessment
unless satisfied that the original assessment has ceased to have effect or should
be brought to an end.[7] Regulations prescribe circumstances (*e.g.* where a
maintenance assessment is about to terminate) where a CSO may decide not to
conduct a review.[8] It provided that where such a review would cease to have
effect within 28 days of the effective date of the fresh assessment the CSO may
decide not to conduct a review.[9] The relevant persons must be given 14 days'
notice of the proposed review.[10]

14.51   Information or evidence as to current circumstances may be requested from
relevant persons[11]—that is the person with care or the absent parent.[12] This may
not occur where:

    (1) income support is payable[13];

    (2) it is a "special case"[14];

    (3) a periodical or change of circumstances review has taken place on
another maintenance assessment in relation to that person[15];

    (4) notification of an assessment has been made within 13 weeks[16]; or

    (5) the CSO has no reason to believe that there has been a change in that
person's circumstances.[17]

Where a notice of change of circumstances review is given less than eight
weeks prior to a periodical review being due and there is no change in the
assessment this review is treated as if it had been a periodical review.[18]

Review on change of circumstances

14.52   One of the issues which the research has identified as confusing parties
involved in appeals has been the role of change of circumstances reviews.
Typically, appellants find that their applications for such reviews are suspended

---

[3] s. 18.

[4] 1991 Act, s. 16(1).

[5] *ibid.* s 16(3).

[6] CS (MAP) Regs 1992, reg. 17(1) (as amended by the Child Support and Income Support
(Amendment) Regulations 1995 (S.I. 1995 No. 1045), reg. 34).

[7] 1991 Act, s. 16(4).

[8] *ibid.* s. 16(6).

[9] CS (MAP) Regs 1992, reg. 17(3).

[10] *ibid.* reg. 17(4).

[11] *ibid.* reg. 17(5).

[12] *ibid.* reg. 1(2).

[13] *ibid.* reg. 17(6).

[14] *ibid.* reg. 17(7)(a) specifying CS (MASC) Regs 1992, regs 22 and 23.

[15] *ibid.* reg. 17(7)(b).

[16] *ibid.* reg. 17(7)(c).

[17] *ibid.* reg. 17(7)(7)(d).

[18] *ibid.* reg. 18.

awaiting the outcome of an appeal which is in effect seeking to get the CSA to deal with a change of circumstances.[19] The legislation provides that where a maintenance assessment is in force the absent parent, parent with care or child concerned may make an application for review of that assessment.[20] Such an application may be made only on the ground that the amount of maintenance payable by the absent parent would be significantly different at the later date.[21] The CSO must not proceed unless, on the information available, it is likely that a fresh maintenance assessment will result from the review.[22] Prior to conducting a review, notice of 14 days[23] must be given to the relevant persons.[24] There is no power to backdate an assessment where there has been a change of circumstances. Thus where employment is lost, for instance, the commencement date for any variation is the date upon which notice is given to the agency rather than the date when the employment is lost, if there is a delay in communication.[25] As in periodical reviews information or evidence as to current circumstances may be requested from relevant persons.[26] This may not occur where the same situations apply as specified in relation to periodical reviews.[27]

Reviews must be conducted as if a fresh application had been made by the **14.53** person in whose favour the original assessment was made.[28] On completing any such review the CSO must make a fresh assessment unless satisfied

    (a) that the original assessment has ceased to have effect or should be brought to an end[29];

    (b) that the difference between the amount of the new and old assessments is less than £10 per week[30]; or

    (c) that where protected level income is concerned[31] or different qualifying children are concerned the effect would be a change of less than £1.00 per week.[32]

Reviews at the instigation of a child support officer

There is also a proactive role for the Child Support Officer to instigate a **14.54** review at his or her own instance. This occurs where the CSO is satisfied that a maintenance assessment in force is defective because it has been made in ignorance of a material fact, is based on a mistake as to a material fact or is wrong in law: in these circumstances he or she may make a fresh assessment as if there had been an application by the affected party.[33] In addition the CSO has power to make an assessment as if an application had been made on grounds of change of circumstances or against refusal to make or review an assessment where satisfied that application for such a review would be appropriate.[34] Notice of a prescribed period must be given to the prescribed persons prior to making

---

[19] G. Davis, N. Wikeley, R. Young, J. Barron and J. Bedward, Report of a Study of the Child Support Agency (Nuffield Foundation, 1997), Chap. 5.

[20] 1991 Act, s. 17(1).

[21] *ibid.* s. 17(2).

[22] *ibid.* s. 17(3).

[23] *ibid.* s. 17(4).

[24] CS (MAP) Regs 1992, reg. 19(1).

[25] *Secretary of State for Social Security v. Bacon* (December 20, 1994, unreported).

[26] CS (MAP) Regs 1992, reg. 19(2).

[27] See above, para.14.50.

[28] 1991 Act, s. 17(5).

[29] *ibid.* s 17(6)(a); CS (MAP) Regs 1992, reg. 20.

[30] MAP, reg. 10(1).

[31] 1991 Act, s. 17(6)(b); CS (MAP) Regs 1992, reg. 20(2).

[32] *ibid.* s 17(6)(b); CS (MAP) Regs 1992, reg. 20(3).

[33] *ibid.* s. 19(1).

[34] *ibid.* s 19(2).

such an assessment.[35] The result of such review must be given immediately to the relevant person so far as is reasonably practicable.[36]

Second-tier review

14.55   In order to avoid the system being clogged up with expensive and unnecessary appeals there is provision for an internal review of a refusal to review or to make a maintenance assessment. A person aggrieved by the refusal of the CSO to make a maintenance assessment or to undertake a change of circumstances review may apply to the Secretary of State for review of such a refusal.[37] Where a maintenance assessment is in force there may be application for review by the absent parent, the person with care, or the child.[38] Cancellation of a maintenance assessment[39] or refusal to cancel a maintenance assessment[40] are subject to review by the Secretary of State. Applicants for such reviews must give their reasons for making the application.[41] The applications must be made within 28 days of the notification to the applicant of the decision sought to be reviewed.[42] This period may be extended if the Secretary of State is satisfied that there was an unavoidable delay in making the application.[43]

14.56   Review applications made to the Secretary of State must be referred to the CSO. Review must be conducted by the CSO unless there are no reasonable grounds for supposing that the refusal, assessment or cancellation in question was made in ignorance of a material fact, was based on a mistake as to a material fact or was wrong in law.[44] The CSO charged with review must have played no part in the original decision under review.[45]

14.57   The relevant persons must be given 14 days' notice of the intention to conduct a review.[46] The applicant's reasons must be sent to the relevant persons[47] and representations either in person or in writing must be invited from them on any matter relating to the review.[48] Where, within 14 days of the notice being given, the CSO conducting the review receives no notice from a relevant person that he or she wishes to make representations in person or where he or she fails to keep any appointment the CSO may complete the review in the absence of representations from that person.[49] If the CSO is satisfied there were good reasons for the appointment not being kept he must provide for a further opportunity for the making of representations before completing the review.[50] Similarly, where written representations are not received within 14 days from any relevant person the CSO may go ahead and complete the review without such representations.[51] Confidentiality must be maintained as to address and information which could threaten anonymity.[52] Reviews involving more than one application may be dealt with together.[53]

---

[35] 1991 Act, s. 19(3).
[36] CS (MAP) Regs 1992, reg. 10(1).
[37] 1991 Act, s. 18(1).
[38] *ibid.* s. 18(2).
[39] *ibid.* s. 18(3).
[40] *ibid.* s. 18(4).
[41] *ibid.* s. 18(5).
[42] CS (MAP) Regs 1992, reg. 24(1).
[43] *ibid.* reg. 24(2).
[44] 1991 Act, s. 18(6).
[45] *ibid.* s. 18(7).
[46] CS (MAP) Regs 1992, reg. 25(1).
[47] *ibid.* reg. 25(2)(a).
[48] *ibid.* reg. 25(2)(c).
[49] *ibid.* reg. 25(3).
[50] *ibid.* reg. 25(4).
[51] *ibid.* reg. 25(5).
[52] *ibid.* reg. 25(6).
[53] *ibid.* reg. 26.

Appeals

As already indicated,[54] the CSO may refuse to conduct a second-tier review if **14.58** in his or her view there are no reasonable grounds for supposing that the decision in question was made in ignorance of a material fact, or was based on a mistake as to a material fact or was wrong in law.[55] There is provision for appeal to a child support appeal tribunal ("CSAT") by any person aggrieved by a decision of a CSO on review or against a refusal to review.[56] Child Support Appeal Tribunals are part of the Appeals Service (formerly the Independent Tribunal Service) and are chaired by legally qualified chairmen. Until 1998 it was necessary for there to be two wing members. This requirement was deemed unnecessary[57] and was dispensed with under the Social Security Act 1998 and chairmen and chairwomen may now sit alone. In addition provision is made for "paper hearings" although any party can insist on an oral hearing.[58] Appeal from the CSAT lies to the Child Support Commissioner on a point of law and thereafter to the Court of Session or High Court. This alternative is in line with social security appeal practice as the basic legislation applies throughout the United Kingdom.[59]

Appeal may not be brought more than 28 days after the date on which **14.59** notification of the decision in question was given, except with the leave of the CSAT chairman.[60] Successful appeals must be remitted to the CSA for the matter to be dealt with by a CSO[61] subject to such directions as the CSAT considers appropriate.[62]

Child Support Appeal Tribunals are to hear and determine appeals under **14.60** regulations as to procedure made by the Secretary of State.[63] Some issues do not permit anything other than a right answer, for example, the maintenance requirement stems from a fixed formula centred on social security rates etc. Other areas, however can give rise to disputes. A major area of dispute is assessable icome. This often centres on disputes as to the variable components in this area, *i.e.* income and housing costs. The original decision may have been reviewed in ignorance of a material fact, a mistake as to a material fact or been wrong in law.

The income of those who are solely self-employed or who are both waged **14.61** and self-employed should come under particular scrutiny. There may well be disagreements as to the amounts claimed. It is not formally laid down that Inland Revenue assessments must be accepted by the CSO although this is a practice widely followed. There is provision for a profit and loss account and, where appropriate, a trading account or balance sheet, or both. The CSO, however, retains a significant discretion "where a calculation would... produce an amount which in the opinion of the CSO, does not accurately reflect the normal amount of earnings of the person in question".[64] A different time period may be selected. This is based on, amongst other things, the "expected duration and pattern of employment of that person". Notional income is a concept familiar in social security law which also operates under the Child Support Act. This involves the CSO

---

[54] Above, para. 14.56.
[55] s. 18(6).
[56] 1991 Act, s. 20(1).
[57] Department of Social Security *Improving Decision-making and Appeals in Social Security* Cmnd. 3328 London HMSO pp 67-68.
[58] Child Support Appeal Tribunals (Procedure) Regulations 1992 (S.I. 1992 No. 2641) (CSAT) (P) Regs 1992) 11(1B).
[59] But see Jamieson, "The Child Support Act and the Act of Union" (1992) 37 J.L.S.S. 484.
[60] 1991 Act, s. 20(2).
[61] *ibid.* s. 20(3).
[62] *ibid.* s. 20(4).
[63] *ibid.* s 21(2); CSAT(P) Regs 1992.
[64] CS (MASC) Regs 1992, Sched. 1, para. 2(4).

deciding whether any income normally received has not been received and if there are reasonable grounds for believing it will be received then it is treated as if it had been received.[65]

14.62   In addition, a person might wish to dispute a finding about housing costs. Currently loans for acquisition and repairs are included in permitted housing costs.[66] There may be disagreement as to whether the repair is "necessary to maintain the fabric of the home". The regulations specify certain matters as well as what "other improvements the child support officer considers reasonable in the circumstances".

Procedural issues

14.63   Appeals must be brought within 28 days from the date on which notification of the decision in question was given or sent to the applicant.[67] An appeal is treated as having been made on the day it is received at the CSA Central Office.[68] Applications to set aside must be made within three months beginning with the date on which notification of the decision in question was given or sent to the applicant.[69]

14.64   The chairman may extend the time-limits for appeal or applications to set aside for special reasons.[70] Any appeal or application made out of time is deemed to include an application for an extension of time. If no reasons are initially put forward the chairman may provide the applicant a reasonable opportunity to give reasons.[71] Although there is no provision for renewal of an appeal against a refusal to set aside, a chairman may set aside a refusal if it appears just to do so on specified grounds.[72] These cover late or non-arrival of a document, absence of one of the parties at the hearing where notice had been given, or the occurrence of some other procedural irregularity or mishap.[73]

14.65   The nature of the appeal must make it possible to identify the decision appealed against.[74] This does not seem to be an unduly onerous requirement. There is provision for the chairman to direct the applicant to provide further particulars to enable the decision to be identified.[75] The grounds of appeal or for an application to set aside must be stated except where an extension of time is sought.[76] Every appeal must have the option of an oral hearing and where there are applications to set aside, there may also be oral hearings.[77] A minimum of 10 days' notice must be given of the time and place of any hearing to every party to the proceedings.[78] The notice period begins on the day on which it is given to a person entitled to it, and the hearing may proceed only with that person's consent.

14.66   Parties are entitled to be present at any hearing and to be heard.[79] Such a person may address the tribunal, give evidence, call witnesses and put questions directly to any other party to the proceedings, to any representative of the CSO

---

[65] MASC, Sched. 1, Pt V.
[66] *ibid.* regs 14–18, Sched. 3.
[67] CSAT(P) Regs 1992, reg. 3(3).
[68] *ibid.* regs 3(2) and 2(1).
[69] *ibid.* reg. 3(4).
[70] *ibid.* reg. 3(6).
[71] *ibid.* reg. 3(7).
[72] *ibid.* reg. 3(8).
[73] *ibid.* reg. 15(1).
[74] *ibid.* reg. 3(9).
[75] *ibid.* reg. 3(11).
[76] *ibid.* reg. 3(10).
[77] *ibid.* reg. 11(1).
[78] *ibid.* reg. 11(2).
[79] *ibid.* reg. 11(3).

or any other person called as a witness.[80] A tribunal has the power to require any witness to give evidence on oath or affirmation.[81] Where a party fails to appear at the hearing the tribunal may, having regard to all the circumstances including any explanation offered for absence, proceed with the appeal in that party's absence. Alternatively it may give such direction as it thinks proper.[82]

Decisions

Traditionally decisions of tribunals have been by a majority,[83] unless, of **14.67** course, the chairman is sitting alone.[84] Decisions are to be recorded in writing by the chairman[85] and must include a statement of the reasons for the decision, the findings of the tribunal on questions of fact material to it and any directions given.[86] A copy of the decision must be sent as soon as practicable to every party to the proceedings together with information concerning appeals to a Commissioner.[87] Where a CSO to whom a case is referred after a successful appeal is uncertain how to deal with the case in terms of the decisions and any directions contained in it, he or she may apply to the tribunal or another tribunal for directions.[88] The tribunal may give such directions or further directions as it thinks fit. The clerk to the tribunal must send a copy of such an application for directions by a CSO to all the parties to the proceedings who must be given a reasonable opportunity to make representations on it before any directions are given.[89]

No address of any of the parties nor any other information which could **14.68** reasonably be expected to lead to a person being located is to be disclosed except with the written consent of the person to whom the information relates. Such a person has 21 days to indicate he or she does not consent to such disclosure.[90]

Child support commissioners

The appellate role of specialised Commissioners is one which is encountered **14.69** throughout the social security field since the Beveridge Reforms after the Second World War. Their rank is broadly equivalent to that of Outer House judges. Their decisions and precedents form the bulk of the working "case law" in social security areas. There is provision for a Chief Child Support Commissioner and a number of child support commissioners[91] to be appointed from advocates or solicitors in Scotland of 10 years' standing.[92] Hearings before the Child Support Commissioners are in public except in so far as the Commissioner for special reasons directs otherwise.[93] A considerable jurisprudence has built up from the Child Support Commissioners covering a range of issues. The decisions of Commissioners are legally binding on CSATs, CSOs and the Secretary of State. They in turn are bound by the judgments of the House of Lords and the Court of Session. Commissioners are not bound by their own decisions or those

---

[80] CSAT(P) Regs 1992, reg. 11(4).
[81] *ibid.* reg. 11(5).
[82] *ibid.* reg. 11(6).
[83] *ibid.* reg. 13(1).
[84] *ibid.* regs 11A and 13(3F) (added by DDCA, regs 59 and 60(3)).
[85] *ibid.* reg. 13(2)(a).
[86] 1991 Act, s. 20(4); CSAT(P) Regs 1992, reg. 13(2)(b).
[87] *ibid.* reg. 13(3).
[88] *ibid.* reg. 13(4) (substituted by DDCA, reg. 60(4)).
[89] *ibid.* reg. 13(5).
[90] *ibid.* reg. 17 (substituted by Child Support (Miscellaneous Amendments) Regulations 1996 (S.I. 1996 No.1945), reg. 2).
[91] 1991 Act, s. 22(1).
[92] *ibid.* s. 22(2).
[93] *ibid.* s. 22(4).

of other Commissioners. There are also decisions of greater weight given by a tribunal of Commissioners which will normally be followed. Appeal on a point of law, with the leave of the Commissioner who gave the decision, lies to the Court of Session or the Court of Appeal.[94] The Child Support Commissioner specifies the appropriate court[95] having regard to the circumstances of the case and in particular the convenience of the persons who may be parties to the appeal.[96] If the Commissioner refuses leave to appeal the appropriate court may grant such leave.[97]

Departures from the formula

14.70 A major break with the concept of the formula approach was introduced with "departures directions" by the Child Support Act 1995 following consideration of the problems encountered both by parents with care and absent parents with the inflexible formula approach adopted in the 1991 Act.[98] These provided an element of flexibility and an opportunity for the individual circumstances of an individual to be looked at. There are two aspects to the concept of "departures". First, it permits individuals with certain special expenses to have allowances made for these. Secondly, it allows evidence to be introduced which indicates that the declared income of a person is incorrect. A pilot system was tested during 1996.

14.71 The current departures system came into effect in December 1996.[99] Certain special expenses not taken into account in the standard assessment may be taken into account. Six kinds of costs are specified in the regulations:

(1) costs incurred in travelling to work[1];
(2) costs incurred in maintaining contact with a child or children covered by the maintenance assessment[2];
(3) costs attributable to a long-term illness or disability of the applicant or dependant of the applicant[3];
(4) debts incurred before the absent parent became an absent parent where these debts were for the joint benefit of both parents or for the benefit of the child involved[4];
(5) pre-1993 financial arrangements from which it is impossible for the parent concerned to withdraw or from which it would be unreasonable to expect the parent to withdraw[5]; and
(6) costs incurred by a parent in supporting a child who is not his child but who is part of his family.[6]

14.72 The other areas where there had been complaints from users of the Child Support system was in the apparent ability of some absent parents and, to a lesser extent, some parents with care to live a comfortable life with very low declared income. The departure direction allows the Child Support Officer to

---

[94] 1991 Act, s. 25(1).
[95] *ibid.* s. 25(3A).
[96] *ibid.* s. 25(3A).
[97] *ibid.* s. 25(3B).
[98] *Improving Child Support*, Cm. 2745 (1994).
[99] Child Support Departure Direction and Consequential Amendments Regulations 1996 (S.I. 1996 No. 2907).
[1] *ibid.* reg. 13.
[2] *ibid.* reg. 14.
[3] *ibid.* reg. 15.
[4] *ibid.* reg. 16.
[5] *ibid.* reg. 17.
[6] *ibid.* reg. 18.

depart from the formula where the parent's overall lifestyle requires a substantially higher income than the amount on which the maintenance assessment is based.[7] There may still be situations where the income and the lifestyle are incompatible but where there can be no departure direction as where the lifestyle is paid for either out of capital or by the new partner. This is a cause of much resentment against the authorities. There may, however, be an increase in the assessment where the CSO determines that it is appropriate for the partner to contribute to the housing costs.[8] Related to this issue is the suspicion that a parent may be underusing assets which could produce income or which could reasonably be sold.[9] Provided that there is a minimum of £10,000 involved there may be a direction that such assets be regarded as having a notional income.

There may also be departures where a parent has unreasonably diverted **14.73** income such as by paying a partner a salary but receiving nothing directly.[10] In addition, where a parent is exempt from the ceiling on housing costs, departure may be applied where the housing costs are unreasonably high.[11] Finally where travel costs allowed under the formula are unreasonably high then there may be departure from the formula figure.[12]

CHILD SUPPORT IN CONTEXT

Child support and social security benefits

Those parents with care in low-waged work who are entitled to means- **14.74** tested family credit and who receive child support payments from the absent parent are entitled to have up to £15 of this sum disregarded.[13] The same disregard applies for those disabled workers in the waged workforce who are in receipt of the means-tested benefit disability working allowance.[14]

Those on income support originally had no change in their income if the **14.75** absent parent contributed child support. Payments are treated as income and no disregard has been made for such payments. From April 1997, however, a person in receipt of either income support or income-based jobseeker's allowance[15] can build up a bonus at the rate of £5 per week. This is payable as a lump sum when the parent with care is no longer in receipt of income support or income-based jobseeker's allowance and has taken up employment of at least 16 hours a week. It is also available where the hours worked exceed 16[16] or wages increase[17] disentitling the parent with care to income support. There is a maximum specified in 1998 at £1,000. The parent with care must have the qualifying child living with her,[18] be under 60 (women) or 65 (men on income-based jobseekers' allowance)[19] and be entitled to either income support or income-based jobseekers' allowance.

---

[7] Child Support Departure Direction and Consequial Amendments Regulations 1996, reg. 25.
[8] *ibid.* reg. 25(3).
[9] *ibid.* reg. 23(2)(a).
[10] *ibid.* reg. 24.
[11] *ibid.* reg. 26.
[12] *ibid.* reg. 27.
[13] Family Credit (General) Regulations 1987 (S.I. 1987 No. 1973), Sched, 2, para. 47.
[14] Disability Working Allowance (General) Regulations 1991 (S.I. 1991 No. 2887), Sched. 3, para. 13.
[15] The verbal sleight of hand introduced to minimise the political impact of replacing a 12-month insurance benefit with a six-month benefit and avoid using the term "income support".
[16] Social Security (Child Maintenance Bonus) Regulations 1996 (S.I. 1996 No. 3195), reg. 3 (1)(d).
[17] *ibid.* reg. 3 (1)(c).
[18] Social Security (Child Maintenance Bonus) Regulations 1996 (S.I. 1996 No. 3195)—a temporary absence of up to 12 weeks does not affect entitlement—reg. 4.
[19] *ibid.* reg. 8.

Simplifying the formula

14.76   The recognition of the limitations of the formula in the context of Britain in the late 1990s was recognised in the General Election of 1997. No political party was committed to the retention of the Child Support Agency and its abolition was widely predicted. The problem of an alternative, however, was also evident. The previous court-centred system was arbitrary and dependent on the whims of a range of different sheriffs and judges with divergent views on what level of financial support was appropriate in different circumstances. The role of the liable relative officer where benefit claimants were involved had also not been productive of a consistent approach to child support recovery.

14.77   The Green Paper published in July 1998, *Children First: A New Approach to Child Support*,[20] suggests that the 1993 scheme "is a mess"[21] and that the proposed child maintenance system should be much simpler. It proposed to replace the complicated formula with liability based on slices of net income. Absent parents would pay 15 per cent of their net income for one child, 20 per cent for two children and 25 per cent for three or more children. Reductions from these figures would be available for those on lower incomes who will be asked to pay the same fixed minimum amount of child support as those on income support.[22] Those who had second families would have the amount of net income used to calculate maintenance liability reduced by a percentage to cover the child(ren) of the second relationship.[23] This reduction would be at the rate of 15 per cent if there were one child of the second relationship rising to 20 per cent for two children and 25 per cent for three or more children. The minimum period for the shared care to be reflected in the level of financial support is reduced to one day per week on average. Exceptional expenses would also be allowed. A number of administrative changes were proposed to allow individuals access to local fieldworkers to deal with their cases on a face-to-face basis. As is noted below, child support legislation depends for its effectiveness on how it is perceived within the community. Child support ran the risk of becoming the poll tax of the 1990s. The timetable indicated for the introduction of the new system suggests that the 1991 system will continue for a number of years.

Collective financial support

14.78   In addition to the possibility of obtaining aliment from parents either through the Child Support Agency or through the courts, any person in Great Britain is entitled to support through a range of benefits. These benefits were available before the introduction of the Child Support Act 1991. At that time the Department of Social Security sought to offset the cost of providing support through the work of the liable relative officer in terms of the Social Security Act 1986.[24] Their task was to secure such support from the "liable relative" as was reasonable having regard to new family obligations.[25] The benefits available for family support include universal benefits paid to all irrespective of means such as child benefit.[26] This is available for all children and is normally paid to the mother. In addition there is a scheme for paying a six-month benefit to those who are out of work called contribution-based jobseekers' allowance.[27] Those who have not worked or have insufficient contributions may be entitled to the means-

---

[20] Cm. 3992 (1998)—the comment period lasted until November 30.
[21] Foreword by Prime Minister Blair at 1.
[22] 10% of income support for those aged 25 or more at the time of writing.
[23] No mention is made of subsequent relationships and how these might affect the income available.
[24] s. 26(3).
[25] *Support for Lone Parents*, HC 328 (1990) National Audit Office.
[26] See *Rights Guide to Non-Means-Tested Benefits* CPAG—published annually.
[27] See *Jobseeker's Allowance Handbook* CPAG—published annually.

tested benefit, income-based jobseekers' allowance or income support. Finally there is a means-tested benefit payable to those with dependent children in low-waged work, family credit.[28]

Monitoring the performance of the Child Support Agency

Any discussion of the changes and developments in relation to the Child Support **14.79** Act 1991 need to take account of the plethora of administrative problems which have been encountered by those operating the Act. These were encountered right from the beginning of the operation of the legislation in April 1993 and were particularly serious in the first year. The first information indicated that the introduction of the legislation had not been without problems.[29] There was a shortfall in the expected saving of some £112m.[30] Only 14 per cent of monitored assessments were correct in the first year of the CSA.[31] This rose to 29 per cent in the second year.[32] Administrative problems bedevilled the operation throughout the first five years of its operation.[33]

During the first year a series of minor issues were drawn to the Government's **14.80** attention by the Social Security Committee in December 1993.[34] They made various recommendations.[35] These led to minor changes in the operation of the formula.[36] Further recommendations were made by the Committee in October 1994.[37] A number of the 23 recommendations were put into effect, the most significant being the treatment of capital agreements made prior to the introduction of the 1991 Act.[38] The Social Security Committee continued to monitor the performance of the Agency during 1995.[39] The issue of the benefit penalty was looked at in 1995 and the Social Security Committee's views were sought on the question of the duration and level of benefit penalty for failure to co-operate.[40] The Committee supported the draft changes which the government had produced extending the length and depth of the penalty.[41]

During the rest of the 1990s things did not improve appreciably and the **14.81** reports of the House of Commons Social Security Committee[42] recorded a range

---

[28] See *National Welfare Benefits Handbook* CPAG — published annually.
[29] HC 983 (1993) *The Operation of the Child Support Act* Social Security Committee First Report, Session 1992–93, London: HMSO.
[30] HC (1994) The Operation of the Child Support Act: Proposals for Change HC 470, House of Commons Social Security Committee, Fifth Report 1993–94, London: HMSO.
[31] Annual Report of the Chief Support Officer 1993–94, London: HMSO 1994.
[32] Annual Report of the Chief Support Officer 1994–95, London: HMSO 1995.
[33] G. Davis, N. Wikeley and R. Young with J. Barron and J. Bedward, *Child Support in Action* (Oxford, Hart, 1998), Chap. 4.
[34] First Report of the Social Security Committee, 1993–94, Cm. 2469, London: HMSO 1994.
[35] (i) the £8 element in the protected income be increased to either £20.,30 or even £40 - to allow paid absent parents to work, to increase incentives to work and not to be restricted to particular categories of expenses; (ii) payments of assessments should be phased in over a period of up to 2 years; (iii) allowance to be made for stepchildren in calculation of exempt income; (iv) consideration to be given to reduction of care element in maintenance requirement once children reached age of 11; (v) there was no sensible way of calculating current values of past capital settlements in order to take account of them in the formula; (vi) if absent parents return to the ME forms within 2 weeks of issue liability for maintenance should begin from the date of assessment; (vii) amendments to the citizen's charter for the Agency should include a 28-day appeal period.
[36] HC (1993) *The Operation of the Child Support Act*, HC 69 House of Commons Social Security Committee First Report 1993–94, London: HMSO.
[37] HC (1994) *The Operation of the Child Support Act: Proposals for Change* HC 470, House of Commons Social Security Committee, Fifth Report 1993–94, London: HMSO, p. 81.
[38] *ibid.*
[39] HC 303 (1994–95) *The Operation of the Child Support Act.*
[40] HC 440 (1996) *Child Support: Good Cause and the Benefit Penalty*, Social Security Committee Fourth Report, Session 1995-96, London: HMSO.
[41] *ibid.* at v.
[42] HC 50 *The Performance and Operation of the Child Support Agency*, House of Commons Social Security Committee, Second Report 1995–96, London: HMSO.

of administrative problems. The first report[43] noted that performance had not always measured up to the high standards the Agency had set out to achieve.

14.82   The Ombudsman[44] for his part was highly critical. He pointed out that maladministration leading to injustice was likely to arise when a new administrative task was not tested first by a pilot project. In his January 1995 Report, the Ombudsman looked at the structural problems of the CSA, drawing on a representative sample of cases remitted to him by MPs. The kinds of issues identified were delays, erroneous requests and misidentifications, as well as general errors in administration.[45] The chorus of critics was joined by the National Audit Office.[46] The Child Support Agency had four Chief Executives during its first five years. It is little wonder that staff, after five years of operating this system, were reported as feeling unable to cope with the pressure.[47]

Assessing child support

14.83   Those studies which were carried out prior to the 1991 Act found a reasonable degree of satisfaction with those claimants using the DSS services to assess and collect child maintenance.[48] One goal of the Government at the time was that the Child Support Act should encourage parents back to work by making dependence on income support less attractive. This hope was not borne out by early studies into the operation of the legislation.[49] The broad message of the early studies was that the Act did not provide adequate policies to achieve its goals. It reduced women's access to the social security safety net and transferred women's dependence to both the labour market and men. There were, however, no corresponding policies to strengthen the capacity of the labour market to deal with women's work needs. Nor, tellingly, was any work done in relation to increase the willingness or ability of men to provide financial support.[50] The Liverpool study suggested that there was also little support for the Act by parents with care. Its implementation was perceived as coercive and intrusive. For low income parents with care there was little incentive to co-operate with the Child Support Agency.[51] Initial national research suggested that the scheme had limited financial impact on the vast majority of women. Seventy-two per cent were no better nor worse off. Eight per cent were worse off and 20 per cent better off. The impact on men

[43] CSA, *The First 2 Years*.

[44] Parliamentary Commissioner for Administration (1995) *Investigation of Complaints against the Child Support Agency*, Third Report, Session 1994-95, London: HMSO.

[45] HC (1995a) *Investigation of Complaints against the Child Support Agency*, Parliamentary Commissioner for Administration, Third Report, 1994-95, London: HMSO; HC (1995b) The Child Support Agency, Select Committee on the Parliamentary Commissioner for Administration, Third Report 1994-95, London, HMSO.

[46] NAO (1995) Child Support Agency Memorandum by the Comptroller and Auditor General to the House of Commons Public Accounts Committee, within Committee of Public Accounts First Report on the Child Support Agency (HC 31, 1995).

[47] G. Davis, N. Wikeley, R. Young, J. Barron and J. Bedward, *Report of a Study of the Child Support Agency*, Nuffield Foundation (1997), p. 50.

[48] *Child Support Unit National Client Survey 1992* Mark Speed, Christine Roberts and Kai Rudat (DSS Research Report No 14,1993).

[49] P. Daniel and E. Burgess (1994) *The Child Support Act: The Voice of Low Income Parents with Care*, London: Social Responsibility Department, Diocese of Southwark; K. Clarke, G. Craig, C. Glendinning and M. Thompson (1994) *Children Come First? The Child Support Act and Lone Parent Families*, London: Barnardo's, Children's Society, NCH, NSPCC, SCF ; National Council for One Parent Families (1994) *The Child Support Agency's First Year:The Lone Parent Case*, London, NCOPF; National Association of Citizen's Advice Bureaux (1994) *Child Support:One Year On*, London NACAB.

[50] D. Abbott, *The Child Support Act 1991: the lives of parents with care living in Liverpool* (1996) 18 JSWFL 21.

[51] *ibid.* at 33; see also E. Kempson, A. Bryson and K. Rowlingson, *Hard Times? How Poor Families make Ends Meet* (1994) London: Policy Studies Institute.

was somewhat different. Forty-seven per cent were the same, with 15 per cent better off and 48 per cent worse off. The impact on the community was that in 51 per cent of cases the result was the same to the Treasury, 37 per cent saving to the public purse and 12 per cent extra expenditure.[52]

The concentration on the reduction of the social security bill by targeting **14.84** of parents with care on benefit seems to have compromised the legislation's other objectives.[53] These included the arbitrary nature of the use of discretion to determine maintenance awards, the absence of regular systematic increases in maintenance payments and the apparent ease of avoiding complying with court orders.[54] The Department of Social Security had opined in 1990 that the pre-Child Support Act system of maintenance was "unnecessarily fragmented, uncertain in its results, slow and ineffective".[55] The concern to reduce public expenditure undermined potential popular support,[56] more frequently encountered in other legal systems.[57] By contrast, the political and media campaign against the legislation during the 1990s did not feature the voices of low income parents. Rather it was dominated by what Richard Collier described as "middle-class male angst"[58] as men complained about the sudden shift to being required to make a contribution to their children's upkeep more in tune with the actual costs of such care than what courts had previously awarded. In practice the lack of investigative powers in the CSA combined with its actual performance and policy towards enforcement has led it to be dubbed a toothless dragon—or "vegetarian tiger".[59] A related structural problem implicit in the formula approach was the assumption about the nature of the population: static, enjoying fixed employment and non-fluid relationships.[60] These may be the aspirations of those concerned with "traditional family values". They do not correspond with the lives that people actually led in the documented research.

The problems which have been encountered both by absent parents and **14.85** parents with care have led to a situation where those who can avoid the CSA do so just as the courts were avoided before the 1991 Act. Researchers have noted the prevalence of private agreements struck between absent and caring parents. Whereas according to the Nuffield study "parents used to bargain in the shadow of the courts, many now bargain in the shadow of the CSA".[61] The major change has been the weakening of the bargaining position of men since absent parents have more to fear from the levels of maintenance set (if not actually enforced) by the CSA. The result has been that the CSA has shifted the focus away from society having a primary concern with children's welfare. This rests clearly with parents and to that extent it can be said that responsibility for maintaining children has been privatised.[62]

---

[52] G. Davis, N. Wikeley and R. Young with J. Barron and J. Bedward, *Child Support in Action* Oxford: Hart (1998).
[53] C. Glendinning, K. Clarke and G. Craig, *Implementing the Child Support Act* (1996) 18 JSWFL 273.
[54] *ibid.* at 275.
[55] *Children Come First* Cmnd 1264 Vols. I and II, London HMSO Vol I at para 1.5.
[56] C. Glendinning, K. Clarke and G. Craig, *Implementing the Child Support Act* (1996) 18 JSWFL 273.
[57] See above, para. 14.11.
[58] R. Collier, *The Campaign Against the Child Support Act: "errant fathers" and "family men"*, (1994) Fam. Law 384.
[59] G. Davis, N. Wikeley, R. Young, J. Barron and J. Bedward, *Report of a Study of the Child Support Agency* Nuffield foundation (1997) at p. 64.
[60] *ibid.* at p. 95.
[61] *ibid.* at p. 69.
[62] *ibid.* at p. 95.

The future

14.86 Extreme consequences have stemmed from the work of the Child Support Agency. In the early days the tabloids documented a series of suicides and attempted suicides which were claimed to be the result of stress caused by the operation of the formula and the heavy-handed approach of the Agency.[63] One conviction was reported in mid-1998 where a woman hired a contract killer to do away with her husband. She feared the Child Support Agency would threaten her lifestyle and result in her losing her Mercedes.[64] The legislation arouses powerful emotions and has prompted severe reactions.

14.87 Pressure groups have campaigned and commented on the impact of legislation on low-income groups and families such as the National Association of Citizens Advice Bureaux,[65] the Child Poverty Action Group,[66] the National Council for One Parent Families[67] and a range of major children's charities.[68] They have carried out work on the Child Support Act as they affect their client groups. In addition a range of organisations has emerged with a particular perspective on the Child Support legislation. These include groups whose aim has been to repeal the legislation: Network Against the Child Support Act and the Campaign Against the Child Support Act and the National Campaign for Fair Maintenance as well as groups with a concern that the legislation operate equitably such as Legal Action for Women.[69]

14.88 The concern with the operation of the formula and the performance of the Child Support Agency bore fruit in the publication of a Consultation paper, *Children First* in July 1998.[70] The National Association for Child Support Action expressed concern that the simple formula approach had the potential to "allow ministers to pitch figures sufficiently low to defuse opposition, while designing in the opportunity to increase levels with impunity in the years ahead".[71]

14.89 A range of alternative options has also been suggested which address the issue of embedding child support more firmly within popular culture by ensuring that increases in payments go to the children rather than in Treasury savings.[72] The same imperative of saving the costs of welfare was the stimulus for the American policy[73] and was suggested as the main goal in Britain too.[74] American research also noted that where women have a strong political base the

---

[63] R. Collier, *The Campaign Against the Child Support Act: "errant fathers" and "family men"*, (1994) Fam. Law 384.

[64] *The Express* Tuesday June 30 1998 "Ex-wife hired hitman to keep up life of luxury"—the wife was sentenced to three-and-a-half years for soliciting to murder.

[65] NACAB (1994) *Child Support: One Year On* London: National Association of Citizens Advice Bureaux.

[66] *Putting the Treasury First* CPAG (1994).

[67] NCOPF (1994) *The Child Support Agency's First Year: the Lone Parent Case*, London: National Council for One Parent Families.

[68] K. Clarke, C. Glendinning and G. Craig (1994) *Losing Support: Children and the Child Support Act*, Barnardo's, The Children's Society, NCH Action for Children, National Society for the Prevention of Cruelty to Children, Save the Children.

[69] All gave evidence to the prior to the publication of the Green Paper *Improving Child Support*. See also *Men behaving sadly*, Julia Brosnan, *New Statesman and Society* (1995) Vol. 8, August 4 1995, p. 16 on the formation of the Cheltenham Group to have the Child Support Act repealed.

[70] Above, para. 14.77.

[71] Nacsa News, 1998 Issue 2, Milton Keynes.

[72] K. Clarke, *Supporting Children? the Impact of the Child Support Act on Lone Mothers and Children*; C. Glenndinning and G. Craig (in *Private Lives and Public Responses*, eds R. Ford and J. Millar, Policy Studies Institute, 1998).

[73] J. Josephson, *Public policy as if women mattered: improving the child support system for women on AFDC* Women and Politics (1997) Vol 17 p. 1.

[74] P. Bingley, G. Lanot and E. Symons, *The Child support reform and the labor supply of lone mothers in the United Kingdom* (1995) 30 J. Human Resources 256.

bureaucracy responds to this and increases its enforcement.[75] This supported the transformation of the equivalent Federal legislation in the United States introduced in 1974. Initially it was highly contentious and passed Congress by only one vote. When the legislation came to be renewed 10 years later this was done unanimously.[76]

14.90 In policy terms there is a concern that support and policy in relation to lone-parent families is in danger of being separated from issues relating to support for all families with children and the integration of policy in relation to income support, housing and childcare has been urged.[77] Further, the Child Support Act has been criticised for casting women in their traditional dependent role[78] and seeking to reproduce traditional family and gender relationships.[79] The difference in the way financial issues are seen by both parties has also been the subject of analysis.[80] A more child-centred approach would involve a guaranteed minimum income for single parents linked with a tax on absent parents based on their incomes and liabilities.[81]

14.91 The form and nature of future child support would seem to depend on a number of factors, both local and global. Does the breakthrough of women in politics in Britain's election of May 1997 represent a critical mass which will provide an effective counter-weight to the male perspective on providing adequate financial support to children? Given a series of governments with a shared strategy of withdrawal of the State from key areas of social welfare in favour of market solutions, is the future of children in poverty anything but bleak? In the longer term how will patterns of work affect the nature and levels of support which globalising business and the community judge reasonable to provide for an increasingly female workforce?

---

[75] L. Keiser, *The influence of women's political power on bureaucratic output: the case of child support enforcement* (1997) 27 B. J. Political Science 136.

[76] MR = AG − CB: the algebra of care *The Guardian*, May 15, 1998.

[77] J. Millar and R. Ford, *Lone Parenthood and Future Policy* (in *Private Lives and Public Responses*, eds R. Ford and J. Millar, Policy Studies Institute, 1998).

[78] S. Millns, *Legislative constructions of motherhood* (1996) 49 Parliamentary Affairs 161.

[79] J. Millar, *State, family and personal responsibility: the changing balance for lone mothers in the United Kingdom* (1994) Fem. Rev. 24; L. Harding, *Family, State and Social Policy* (1996) Macmillan, Basingstoke.

[80] Bob Simpson, *On gifts, payments and disputes: divorces and changing family structures in contemporary Britain* (1997) 3 Journal of the Royal Anthropological Institute 731.

[81] G. Davis, N. Wikeley, R. Young, J. Barron and J. Bedward, *Report of a Study of the Child Support Agency*, Nuffield Foundation (1997), p. 95.

CHAPTER 15

CAPACITY AND LEGAL REPRESENTATION
OF CHILDREN

Introduction

15.01   Legal capacity is the ability to perform on one's own behalf juridical acts such as entering contracts and raising or defending actions. For long Scots law, following the Roman law, adopted a gradualist approach to the acquiring of legal capacity which reflected, if somewhat crudely, the fact that children's physical and mental capacities increase with age and experience.[1] There was, as explained more fully in a previous chapter, a radical difference between the capacity of pupils (boys below 14 and girls below 12) and that of minors (children above pupillarity but below majority[2]), the former having, generally speaking, no legal capacity and the latter having full legal capacity subject, for most acts, to the need, if they had curators, for their curators' concurrence. The old rules were replaced in respect of transactions occurring on or after September 25, 1991 by a whole new framework, contained in the Age of Legal Capacity (Scotland) Act 1991.[3] That Act lays down, in general, that persons under the age of 16 years have no legal capacity (subject to certain exceptions) while persons of or above that age have full legal capacity (subject to certain protections). It also provides[4] that "any reference in any enactment to a pupil (other than in the context of education or training) or to a person under legal disability or incapacity by reason of nonage shall, insofar as it relates to any time after the commencement of this Act, be construed as a reference to a person under the age of 16 years". The statutory rules governing the legal capacity of pupils before the commencement of the 1991 Act apply after the date of commencement, in so far as they are capable of being reconciled with the Act, to all persons under the age of 16. A brief description of the legal capacity of pupil children before the 1991 Act came into force is given in Chapter 1, to which reference should be made. Unlike the statutory rules, the common law rules relating to pupils (with the exception of some rules relating to civil proceedings) are not expressly preserved, but are largely replaced by the provisions of the 1991 Act and applied to persons under the age of 16. This chapter will examine, first, the details of the 1991 Act; it will then consider a number of other issues of legal capacity and incapacity for children and young persons; and finally it will examine the law of legal representation, through which legal acts can be performed on behalf of those persons under 16 who do not, for that reason, have legal capacity.

---

[1] See above, paras 1.08–1.20.

[2] Originally 21, now 18: Age of Majority (Scotland) Act 1969.

[3] Any transaction entered into prior to that date is governed by the previous law (for which see the 1st edition of this book, at pp. 52–68): Age of Legal Capacity (Scotland) Act 1991, s. 1(3)(a).

[4] Age of Legal Capacity (Scotland) Act 1991, s. 1(2).

Calculation of age

At common law a person aged *de momento in momentum* and so attained an **15.02** age at the precise moment on the relevant anniversary of his or her birth.[5] This remains the rule for anniversaries occurring before September 25, 1991. Since that date,[6] however, a person attains a particular age at the beginning of the relevant anniversary of his or her date of birth.[7] When a person has been born on February 29 the relevant anniversary in any year other than a leap year shall be taken to be March 1.[8]

CAPACITY UNDER THE AGE OF LEGAL CAPACITY (SCOTLAND) ACT 1991

General incapacity of persons below 16

Section 1(1)(a) of the Age of Legal Capacity (Scotland) Act 1991 provides **15.03** that, as from the commencement of the Act, a person under the age of 16 years shall, subject to certain stated exceptions (discussed below), have no legal capacity to enter into any transaction. This does not affect the child's legal personality which, amongst other things, enables the child to receive or hold any right, title or interest.[9] "Transaction" is defined to mean

"a transaction having legal effect, and includes:
(a) any unilateral transaction;
(b) the exercise of testamentary capacity;
(c) the exercise of any power of appointment;
(d) the giving by a person of any consent having legal effect;
(e) the bringing or defending of, or the taking of any step in, civil proceedings;
(f) acting as arbiter or trustee;
(g) acting as an instrumentary witness".[10]

A transaction entered into by a person under 16 which he or she has no legal **15.04** capacity to enter into is void,[11] and such a transaction has to be undertaken by the person entitled to act on the child's behalf. Legal representation of the child is examined in some detail below.[12] If a person under 16 purports to perform a legal transaction, such as entering into a contract, but that transaction is void, then any remedy accruing to the other party will be determined by the general law. So if the person under 16 has committed a fraud, for example in misrepresenting his or her age, then delictual remedies will be available to the person injured thereby.[13] In other cases the principle of unjust enrichment may afford a remedy.[14]

Exceptions to incapacity

While the general rule is that a person under 16 has no legal capacity, this is **15.05** qualified by the enactment of a number of specific exceptions, and one general exception. A transaction entered into by a person under the age of 16 which is

---

[5] Stair, I, vi, 33; Erskine, I, vii, 36.
[6] When the Age of Legal Capacity (Scotland) Act 1991 came into force.
[7] Age of Legal Capacity (Scotland) Act 1991, s. 6(1).
[8] *ibid.* s. 6(2).
[9] *ibid.* s. 1(3)(e).
[10] *ibid.* s. 9.
[11] *ibid.* s. 2(5).
[12] Below, paras 15.28 *et seq.*
[13] The child's capacity for delict is considered below, para. 15.18.
[14] Stair, I, viii, 6.

valid by the application of any of these exceptions is unchallengeable on the ground of that person's age. The previous rules whereby valid transactions entered into by or on behalf of a young person can be set aside on the grounds of minority and lesion are abolished[15] and replaced with a more limited rule allowing for the setting aside of prejudicial transactions entered into by 16- and 17-year-olds.[16] It might appear anomalous that a transaction entered into by a 15-year-old cannot be set aside on the ground of prejudice while a transaction entered into by a 16-year-old can be, but if the 15-year-old's transaction is one capable of being described as prejudicial then, as will be seen in the immediately following paragraph, it is void in any case as being on unreasonable terms.[17] (The 16-year-old's prejudicial transaction is not void, but voidable). It is likely that the common law on adoption of void contracts continues to apply, subject to the qualification that adoption can now be effected once the child reaches the age of 16 (rather than, as before, majority).[18]

Transactions commonly entered into

15.06   A person under the age of 16 years has legal capacity to enter into a transaction (a) of a kind commonly entered into by persons of his or her age and circumstances and (b) on terms that are not unreasonable.[19] Condition (a) builds in a recognition that there are different levels of understanding at different ages, and it is designed to allow even very young children to enter into some minor transactions, such as purchasing sweets or comics, while at the same time prohibiting them from entering into more major transactions. A five-year-old might validly buy a packet of sweets, a 10-year-old might purchase a cinema ticket, and a 15-year-old might enter into a contract for part-time employment. The terms of the condition are capable of covering any type of transaction, whether a unilateral transaction, or a contract of purchase or of lease or of services or of employment,[20] or any other transaction having legal effect. The condition is designed to be tailored to the individual child's particular circumstances and in that respect it imports a subjective test. The words "transaction of a kind commonly entered into" are, however, attended by difficulties. "Transaction" is defined for the purposes of the Act as "a transaction having legal effect". As a transaction cannot have legal effect unless the parties have capacity to enter into it, condition (a), if strictly construed, is reduced to a meaningless tautology. That result can be avoided only at the cost of some violence to the language of the statute. It is, however, submitted that condition (a) can, and should, be read, on a liberal construction, to the effect that a person under 16 "shall have legal capacity to enter into a transaction *so as to give it legal effect* if that transaction (read in its ordinary sense and without any necessary legal connotation) is of a kind". That construction gives the condition an intelligible meaning and has the further advantage of leaving open the possibility of development according to changing circumstances in the kind of transactions which may satisfy the condition. Parliament no doubt intended that persons under 16 should have

---

[15] Age of Legal Capacity (Scotland) Act 1991, s. 1(5).

[16] *ibid.* s. 3(1). See below, paras 15.12–15.14.

[17] But see the odd case of *Bell's C.B., Noter*, 1998 S.C. 365 where Lord Gill at 371A–C assumed that a settlement made by a paraplegic 14-year-old's curator *bonis* might be open to challenge under s. 3 of the 1991 Act. The terms of that provision are, it is submitted, clearly to the effect that challenge is only possible against transactions entered into by a young person between the ages of 16 and 18.

[18] Gloag, *Contract* (2nd ed.) at p. 546 points out that the adoption of a void contract is, in effect, the entering into a new contract.

[19] Age of Legal Capacity (Scotland) Act 1991, s. 2(1).

[20] Though under the Children and Young Persons (Scotland) Act 1937, s. 28(1)(a) a person under the age of 13 may not be in employment.

capacity to transact in circumstances in which one would ordinarily expect them to have such capacity but unless some such device as is here suggested is adopted that intention must fail. The words "commonly entered into" do not refer to numerical frequency but rather to the unexceptionality of the act in question. Condition (b) makes plain that a person under 16 does not have capacity to enter into a transaction whose terms are unreasonable, however common it is for a person of that age and circumstance to enter into a transaction of that nature: an unreasonable transaction will be void.[21] An unreasonable transaction is, it is submitted, one which an adult, exercising reasonable prudence, would not have entered into in the circumstances of the child; it does not need to have caused the child prejudice before it can be termed unreasonable.

Testamentary capacity

At common law testamentary capacity, like many other capacities, was acquired when the child became minor *pubes*. Indeed the capacity of minors in this respect was not limited in any way by the existence of curators, with the result that minors could test even without the consent of their curators.[22] This capacity was, however, restricted to wills over moveables: "for in order to alter the legal succession of heritage, there must be a deliberate *animus* in the granter of the deed, which cannot be presumed in a minor; and it would be most dangerous to allow the consent of curators to supply that defect".[23] By section 28 of the Succession (Scotland) Act 1964, a minor was given the like capacity to test on heritable property as he or she had on moveable property, which meant an unlimited right to do so with no requirement that the curator's concurrence be obtained. Though this section was repealed in 1991[24] the old law did not revive and the position is now governed by section 2(2) of the Age of Legal Capacity (Scotland) Act 1991, which provides "A person of or over the age of 12 years shall have testamentary capacity, including legal capacity to exercise by testamentary writing any power of appointment". No difference is made between heritable and moveable property, and no role is given to the legal representative of the child under 16. **15.07**

Consent to adoption

A person of or over the age of 12 years has legal capacity to consent to the making of an adoption order over him or her or an order freeing him or her for adoption.[25] The adoption legislation[26] had previously provided that the consent of minor children was necessary for their own adoption, and this provision preserves that position while equalising the age of consent for boys and girls. The child's consent may be dispensed with where the court is satisfied that the child is incapable of giving consent[27] but that incapacity must be referable to something other than the child's age. **15.08**

Consent to medical treatment

It is provided that: **15.09**

> "A person under the age of 16 years shall have legal capacity to consent on his own behalf to any surgical, medical or dental procedure or treatment where, in the opinion of a qualified medical practitioner

---

[21] Age of Legal Capacity (Scotland) Act 1991, s. 2(5).
[22] Erskine, III, ix, 15; McLaren, *Wills and Succession* (3rd ed.), pp. 262–263.
[23] Erskine, I, vii, 33.
[24] Age of Legal Capacity (Scotland) Act 1991, Sched. 2.
[25] *ibid.* s. 2(3).
[26] Adoption (Scotland) Act 1978, ss. 12 and 18.
[27] *ibid.* ss. 12(8) and 18(8). See further, above, para. 4.27.

attending him, he is capable of understanding the nature and possible consequences of the procedure or treatment."[28]

Capacity to consent is therefore a purely factual question of the child's ability to understand, this to be determined by the medical practitioner attending the child. There is no requirement that the proposed procedure or treatment be in the child's best interests or indeed that it in any way enhances his or her welfare. This is logical: once the child understands, he or she will understand the risks involved and will be able to determine him- or herself whether or not to take these risks, which the law should allow him or her the opportunity to do.[29] The words "surgical, medical or dental procedure or treatment" are intended to cover all such procedures or treatments, including examination, diagnosis, treatment, and procedures not amounting to treatment in a strict sense.[30] The words "qualified medical practitioner" are intended to be wider than registered doctors (for which "registered medical practitioner" is the normal statutory wording[31]); it is submitted that it will cover doctors, dentists, anaesthetists, nurses, chiropodists, midwives, and all health professionals qualified to do that which they are doing. A matter of some controversy in England has been the question whether capacity to consent necessarily carries with it capacity to refuse consent, and the preponderance of judicial authority there is that it does not.[32] However, if the right to consent is an aspect of individual autonomy, then the only point in asking a patient to consent to medical treatment is to give the patient the opportunity to refuse and for that reason the capacity to consent carries with it, it is submitted, capacity to refuse. "In logic there can be no difference between an ability to consent to treatment and an ability to refuse treatment."[33] Some support for this position can be found in the structure of the Age of Legal Capacity (Scotland) Act 1991. Section 2(3) grants children over 12 years of age capacity to consent to their own adoption and as with s. 2(4) capacity to refuse is not mentioned. Yet it has never been suggested in this context that capacity to refuse is not carried by the words granting capacity to consent to adoption. Capacity to consent to medical treatment is conferred by section 2(4) and it would be difficult to argue that refusal is implicit in section 2(3) but not in section 2(4).

The child over 16

15.10   At common law a minor above the age of pupillarity was free from the right of dominion which the law gave to the parent of a pupil child and so would seem, prima facie at least, to have been free to consent to medical procedures.[34] The curatorial role of the parent has now been abolished[35] and it would follow that there is no limitation on the 16- and 17-year-old's right to consent or to

---

[28] Adoption (Scotland) Act 1978, s. 2(4).

[29] The Scottish Law Commission, in suggesting this legislation, expressly rejected the addition of a welfare test: see Scot. Law Com. No. 110, *Report on the Legal Capacity and Responsibility of Minors and Pupils*, 1987, at para. 3.77, citing Lord Scarman's speech in *Gillick v. West Norfolk and Wisbech Area Health Authority* [1985] 3 All E.R. 402, and Norrie, 1985 S.L.T. (News) 157.

[30] This is to be compared with the situation in England, where s. 8 of the Family Law Reform Act 1969 grants a right to consent to persons above 16 to "surgical medical and dental treatment": in *Re W (A Minor) (Medical Treatment)* [1992] 4 All E.R. 627 it was held that this did not cover organ or blood donation since these are not "treatment". They are, however, "procedures" and therefore covered by the Scottish statute.

[31] See, *e.g.*, the Abortion Act 1967, s. 1.

[32] See particularly the judgments of Lord Donaldson, MR, in *Re R (A Minor) (Medical Treatment)* [1991] 4 All ER 177 and *Re W (A Minor) (Medical Treatment)*, above, discussed above, para. 8.50.

[33] *per* Balcombe L.J. in *Re W (A Minor) (Medical Treatment)* above, at 643.

[34] For another view, see Thomson, "The Gillick Case and Parental Rights in Scots Law: Another View", 1985 S.L.T. (News) 223.

[35] Age of Legal Capacity (Scotland) Act 1991, s. 5(3).

refuse consent to medical treatment. Such a patient has complete autonomy in the matter of medical treatment, in contradistinction to the position of the 16- or 17-year-old in England.[36] Section 1(1)(b) of the Age of Legal Capacity (Scotland) Act 1991 puts the matter beyond doubt by providing that a person of or above the age of 16 years shall have legal capacity to enter into any transaction, "transaction" being defined to include "the giving by a person of any consent having legal effect".[37]

Civil proceedings
A person under the age of 16 years has legal capacity to instruct a solicitor in **15.11** connection with any civil matter, where that person has a general understanding of what it means to do so; and without prejudice to the generality of this rule a person 12 years of age or more shall be presumed to be of sufficient age and maturity to have such understanding.[38] A person who by virtue of this rule has legal capacity to instruct a solicitor also has legal capacity to sue, or to defend, in any civil proceedings.[39] Expressly, these rules are without prejudice to any question of legal capacity to instruct a solicitor in connection with any criminal matter.[40] For these purposes it is submitted that proceedings in respect of a referral to a children's hearing are to be regarded as civil proceedings, even when the ground of referral is that the child has committed an offence. These rules do not, however, affect the court's power to allow civil proceedings to be brought or defended, or any step in civil proceedings to be taken, in the name of the child where the child has no legal representative or the legal representative is unable (whether by reason of conflict of interest or otherwise) or refuses to bring or defend such proceedings or take such step.[41] The court may still appoint a curator *ad litem* or curator *bonis* to a person under 16 notwithstanding their capacity in this respect.[42]

Persons above 16 and below 18
Section 1(1)(b) of the Age of Legal Capacity (Scotland) Act 1991 provides **15.12** that, as from the commencement of the Act, a person of or over the age of 16 years shall have legal capacity to enter into any transaction.[43] Such a person does not need a legal representative to undertake any legal transaction on his or her behalf nor to consent thereto, and accordingly curatory on the ground of age is abolished.[44] Transactions by persons in this age group are therefore valid and

---

[36] See Balcombe L.J. in *Re W (A Minor) (Medical Treatment)*, above, at 643C.
[37] Age of Legal Capacity (Scotland) Act 1991, s. 9. Consent to medical treatment has the legal effect of providing a doctor with a defence to a charge of assault.
[38] *ibid.* s. 2(4A), as inserted by the Children (Scotland) Act 1995, Sched. 4, para. 53(3).
[39] Age of Legal Capacity (Scotland) Act 1991, s. 2(4B). It has been suggested that one of the unforeseen consequences of this new rule might be that the period of limitation in, *e.g.*, a personal injuries case will begin to run from the date the child acquires legal capacity rather than from his or her 16th birthday: Dunlop, "Possible Repercussions of the Children (Scotland) Act 1995 in Reparation Cases" (1997) 42 J.L.S.S. 370. The argument is as follows: s. 17(3) of the Prescription and Limitation (Scotland) Act 1973 provides that in the computation of the *triennium* "there shall be disregarded any time during which the person who sustained the injuries was under legal disability by reason of nonage", but the rules introduced by the 1995 Act mean that the child with capacity is no longer under legal disability by reason of nonage. Against this it might be argued that the child remains under legal disability for the purpose of the 1973 Act notwithstanding that for limited purposes the child has capacity to perform particular and clearly delineated acts. Such an interpretation would, it is submitted, be preferable to one that required the *triennium* to begin to run from a moment that is impossible to determine precisely—especially retrospectively—that is to say the moment at which the child achieves a "general understanding" of what it means to instruct a solicitor.
[40] *ibid.* s. 2(4C).
[41] *ibid.* s. 1(3)(f)(i).
[42] *ibid.* s. 1(3)(f)(ii) and (iv).
[43] "Transaction" being defined in the same way as in relation to persons below the age of 16: s. 9.
[44] Age of Legal Capacity (Scotland) Act 1991, s. 5(3).

binding. The law does, however, recognise that a person aged 16 or 17 may be inexperienced and might in some circumstances require some protection from that inexperience. Though a person aged 16 or 17 no longer has a curator who must consent to the person's transactions, nevertheless the person's parent retains the parental responsibility to provide guidance until the person reaches the age of 18 years.[45] In addition, the 1991 Act provides[46] that a person who entered into a transaction while he or she was of or over the age of 16 years but under the age of 18 years may make an application to the court to set aside the transaction on the ground that it is a prejudicial transaction.[47] This right of challenge has to be exercised by the person before attaining the age of 21 years,[48] otherwise challenge on this ground is forever thereafter barred. There is, however, no requirement that the young person be over 18 before raising the action: indeed his or her general capacity from the age of 16 to raise and defend legal proceedings gives a person above that age the right to apply for the setting aside of his or her own transactions any time after they are undertaken. Power to seek the setting aside of a transaction on this basis rests solely with the young person (or his or her successors[49]) and not with the other party. This provision is in addition to any other ground for seeking reduction that the general law provides (such as, for example, coercion, fraud or misrepresentation): the setting aside is justified by the injury to the young person caused by his or her own inexperience and does not depend upon proof of intrinsic nullity.

15.13   A "prejudicial transaction" is defined to mean a transaction which "(a) an adult, exercising reasonable prudence, would not have entered into in the circumstances of the applicant at the time of entering into the transaction, and (b) has caused or is likely to cause substantial prejudice to the applicant".[50] Both conditions must be satisfied. The first condition is so worded as to exclude transactions which in the event prove to be prejudicial after having been entered into, such as for example the purchase of shares shortly before an unexpected stock-market crash.[51] "Substantial prejudice" has some affinity with the doctrine of enorm lesion, which provided a similar ground for challenge at common law. As with the common law doctrine, "substantial prejudice" is not susceptible to exact definition and much will depend upon the facts of each individual case. In relation to the common law doctrine, Lord President Dunedin said that "lesion, in the sense of the authorities, must not be trifling, but must be enorm, which means that the consideration which the minor got must be immoderately disproportionate to what might have been got".[52] Lord Adam in the same case said "the point to be considered is not whether the bargain has turned out well for the pursuer, but whether at the date of the agreement it was a proper and reasonable one for him to make".[53] Proof of lesion was achieved if the minor

---

[45] Children (Scotland) Act 1995, s. 1(1)(b)(ii) and (2)(b).
[46] *ibid.* s. 3(1).
[47] It is undecided whether transactions entered into by curators of incompetent young persons are open to challenge under this provision. Lord Gill assumed that they were in *Bell's Curator Bonis, Noter*, 1998 S.C. 365 at 371A–C, but the passage is flawed by his additional assumption that s. 3 applies to children under the age of 16.
[48] *ibid.* That age is attained at the beginning of the 21st anniversary of the person's birth: s. 6(1). The rule at common law was that reduction had to be sought during the *quadriennium utile*, which was calculated *de momento in momentum*: Stair I, vi, 44; Bankton, I, vii, 74; Erskine I, vii, 35.
[49] Age of Legal Capacity (Scotland) Act 1991, s. 3(4).
[50] *ibid.* s. 3(2).
[51] Erskine I, vii, 36 postulates a similar example in the context of the common law of reduction on the ground of minority and lesion.
[52] *Robertson v. S. Henderson & Sons Ltd* (1905) 7 F. 776 at 785.
[53] *ibid.* at 786.

proved that he had not benefited to the full value of the consideration given for the obligation.[54] So, for example, a bond granted by a sister in favour of her brother in consideration of the latter's trouble and expense in connection with legal proceedings on her behalf was reduced as going beyond proper recompense, while any claim that the brother might properly have was reserved.[55] Some care requires to be shown, however, in applying the principles enunciated in the older cases to the new statutory rules. Substantial prejudice should not be seen as the statutory equivalent of the common law doctrine of enorm lesion, for the 1991 Act is designed to provide a whole new statutory regime: in particular the difference is that challenge under the 1991 Act is to transactions undertaken by the young person on his or her own behalf without concurrence of any adult person while challenge on the ground of minority and lesion was frequently to transactions which tutors had undertaken or curators had consented to. There were some situations in which lesion would be irrebuttably presumed and others in which there was a rebuttable presumption.[56] In the absence of statutory provision to that effect it is submitted that it is not open to the court to presume substantial prejudice for the purposes of the 1991 Act. Having said which, however, there will clearly be situations (gift of a large portion of the person's estate would seem an obvious example) in which the court might readily hold that there has been substantial prejudice.

Where an application to set aside a transaction can be made or could   **15.14** have been made under this provision by a person below the age of 21, such an application can be made instead by that person's executor, trustee in bankruptcy, trustee acting under a trust deed for creditors or curator *bonis* so long as the challenge is made at any time prior to the date on which that person would have attained or does attain the age of 21 years.[57] The application can be made in the Court of Session or in the sheriff court, either as a separate action or as an incidental application in other proceedings in these courts.[58] The court may set aside the transaction and make such further order, if any, as seems appropriate to the court in order to give effect to the rights of the parties.[59] This last rule replaces the common law position that mutual and complete restitution should follow reduction so far as possible.[60] The matter is now at large for the court, though in many if not most instances restitution is likely to be the means by which the rights of the parties can be given effect to.

Unchallengeable transactions

The Act prescribes a number of transactions and legal acts that cannot be   **15.15** challenged by the young person on the ground that they are prejudicial transactions[61] (though they may, of course, be challenged for other reasons permitted by other legal rules). Most, if not all, are either inappropriate for setting aside or can found some other, more direct, remedy. The transactions that cannot be set aside are as follows:

---

[54] Fraser (3rd ed.), p. 504; *Anderson v. Caution and Husband* (1832) 11 S. 10.
[55] *Rose v. Rose* (1821) 1 S. 154; see also Stair I, vi, 44; Erskine I, vii, 38; Fraser (3rd ed.), at p. 508.
[56] See the 1st edition of this book, at pp. 64–66.
[57] Age of Legal Capacity (Scotland) Act 1991, s. 3(4). This is the statutory formulation of the rule that obtained at common law: Stair I, vi, 44; Erskine I, vii, 47. For a more detailed description of the pre-1991 position see the 1st edition of this book at pp. 63–64.
[58] *ibid.* s. 3(5).
[59] *ibid.*
[60] See the 1st edition of this book at pp. 67–68.
[61] Age of Legal Capacity (Scotland) Act 1991, s. 3(3).

(a) the exercise of testamentary capacity;
(b) the exercise by testamentary writing of any power of appointment;
(c) the giving of consent to the making of an adoption order;
(d) the bringing or defending of, or the taking of any step in, civil proceedings;
(e) the giving of consent to any surgical, medical or dental procedure or treatment;
(f) a transaction in the course of the applicant's trade, business or profession[62];
(g) a transaction into which any other party was induced to enter by virtue of any fraudulent misrepresentation by the applicant as to age or other material fact;
(h) a transaction ratified by the applicant after he or she attained the age of 18 years and in the knowledge that it could be the subject of an application to the court to set it aside[63];
(i) a transaction ratified by the court under section 4 of the 1991 Act, as described immediately below.

Ratification of transactions by the court

15.16   Any transaction that is liable to be set aside under the provisions described above can be ratified by the court before it is entered into, if a joint application by all the parties to the proposed transaction is made to the court to do so.[64] Transactions cannot be ratified by the court retrospectively and there is no obligation on the parties to a proposed transaction involving a person under the age of 18 to seek prior ratification. The aim is to provide a means whereby an adult party who might be unwilling to enter into a transaction because of the potential risk of later reduction can remove the risk before the transaction is entered into: in other words the provision is designed to avoid people being discouraged from transacting with persons over 16 and below 18.

15.17   The procedure is by means of a summary application to the sheriff of the sheriffdom in which any of the parties to the proposed transaction resides, or, where none of the parties resides in Scotland, to the sheriff at Edinburgh; the decision of the sheriff is final and there is no appeal.[65] The sheriff shall not grant the application to ratify the proposed transaction if it appears to the court that an adult, exercising reasonable prudence and in the circumstances of the party to the transaction who is over 16 years but under 18 years of age would not enter into the transaction.[66] This appears to be a lower test than that for the setting aside of the transaction which requires not only that it be one which a reasonably prudent adult would not enter into, but also that the transaction cause or be likely to cause substantial prejudice.[67] Clearly if the transaction is likely to cause substantial prejudice it will not be one which a reasonably prudent adult would enter into (and would not, for that reason, be open to ratification by the court under section 4); but it is conceivable that a transaction might be one which a reasonably prudent adult would not enter into for reasons other than that it is likely to cause substantial prejudice. Such a transaction could not be

---

[62] At common law, such transactions were not open to challenge on the ground of enorm lesion: *McFeetridge v. Stewarts and Lloyds Ltd*, 1913 S.C. 773. It is not always easy to determine whether a particular transaction takes place within the context of a person's trade, business or profession: see *Wall v. Brownlee* (1724) Mor. 9035; *Craig v. Grant* (1732) Mor. 9035; *Macdonald* (1789) Mor. 9038; *Dennistoun v. Mudie* (1850) 12 D. 613.
[63] Again, following the common law: Stair I, vi, 44; Bankton I, vii, 90.
[64] Age of Legal Capacity (Scotland) Act 1991, s. 4(1).
[65] *ibid.* s. 4(3).
[66] *ibid.* s. 4(2).
[67] *ibid.* s. 3(2).

ratified by the court, but nor could it be challenged later by the young person under section 3 unless substantial prejudice did, in fact, occur. If the ratification application is granted by the sheriff, the transaction will then be unchallengeable on the ground that it is a prejudicial transaction.[68]

OTHER ASPECTS OF THE CAPACITY OF CHILDREN

Capacity in delict

The institutional writers do not distinctly treat of the capacity of pupils and minors **15.18** to incur delictual liability. Erskine, however, states the general principle of delictual liability to be that "every one who has the exercise of reason, and so can distinguish between right and wrong, is naturally obliged to make up the damage befalling his neighbour from a wrong committed by himself".[69] The developed Roman law was that the *infans* (*i.e.* child under the age of seven years) was not *doli capax*,[70] and that is followed in the Roman–Dutch tradition by the law of South Africa which holds that children under the age of seven are capable neither of intentional delict nor of negligence.[71] There is no Scottish authority unequivocally laying down a rule for intentional delict,[72] but in view of the affinities of such delict to crime a minimum of seven or now of eight could be justified by comparison with criminal responsibility. With that possible exception the maxim applicable appears to be *neminem in delictis aetas excusat* in the sense that liability depends on rational capacity for discrimination rather than on age. In relation to negligence, that view is supported by authority. In *Campbell v. Ord and Maddison* Lord Justice-Clerk Moncrieff said:

> "Negligence implies a capacity to apprehend intelligently the duty, obligation, or precaution neglected, and that depends to a large degree on the nature of that which is neglected, as well as on the intelligence and maturity of the person said to have neglected it. The capacity to neglect is a question of fact in the individual case, as much so as negligence itself, which is always a question of fact."[73]

It is evident from that passage that the test of capacity for negligence is the subjective one of the mental condition of the person alleged to be negligent. A distinction, perhaps difficult to maintain, is however to be made between whether a person had capacity for negligence and whether he or she was actually negligent ("negligence itself"). To apply the same test to negligence itself as that for capacity for negligence would be to displace the objective test of the conduct of the reasonable man. The view that capacity for delict is a question of fact has been followed in a number of cases in which the court has, if with some reluctance, allowed issues of contributory negligence by very young children to be considered.[74] This position is unaffected by the Age of Legal Capacity (Scotland) Act 1991.[75]

---

[68] Children (Scotland) Act 1995, s. 3(3)(j).

[69] III, i, 13.

[70] Donaldson, *Minors in Roman Law*, p. 86, s. 177.

[71] *ibid.* p. 96, s. 186; McKerron, *The Law of Delict* (3rd ed.), p. 113.

[72] See *Somerville v. Hamilton* (1541) Mor. 8905 in which a six-year-old child was apparently found liable in spuilzie. Stewart however analyses the case as more nearly a claim for unjust enrichment: see Stewart, "Liability for Pupils in Delict", 1989 S.L.T. (News) 404. *Cf. Bryson v. Sommervill* (1565) Mor. 8906 in which a defence to an action of spuilzie was upheld that the defender was 10 and not 14.

[73] (1873) 1 R. 149 at 153.

[74] *Campbell v. Ord and Maddison* above (four-year-old); *Frasers v. Edinburgh Street Tramways Co.* (1882) 10 R. 264 (six-year-old); *Plantza v. Glasgow Corporation*, 1910 S.C. 786 (five-year-old); *Banner's Trs v. Kennedy's Trs*, 1978 S.L.T. (Notes) 83 (five-year-old); *Harvey v. Cairns*, 1989 S.L.T. 107 (six-year-old); *McCluskey v. Wallace*, 1998 S.L.T. 1357 (four-year-old).

[75] Age of Legal Capacity (Scotland) Act 1991, s. 1(3)(c): "Nothing in this Act shall... affect the delictual... responsibility of any person." This may be the answer to the issue raised by Dunlop in 1997 J.L.S.S. 370 in which it was argued that the period of prescription might run from the child's acquiring capacity under the 1991 Act rather than, as before, from the date the child emerges from nonage. See above, n. 39.

Delictual liability of parents

15.19   A parent is not as such liable for the delict of his or her children. It seems, however, to be implicit in *Lewis v. Carmarthen County Council*[76] and *Home Office v. Dorset Yacht Co.*[77] that parents or others who have actual care and control of children may be liable for failure to take reasonable care that those under their charge do not become the occasion of danger to others or cause injury or damage. The limitations are not clear, but it would seem to be necessary both that the injury should have been foreseeable and that the precaution desiderated should have been one that a reasonable person in charge of children or young persons would have taken in the circumstances.[78]

Criminal responsibility

15.20   At one time the minimum age of criminal responsibility was attended with some uncertainty but it is now fixed by statute at eight.[79] The seeming harshness of such an early age is mitigated by the consideration that children under the age of 16 will not normally be prosecuted but will be subject to proceedings before a children's hearing or otherwise dealt with by the reporter.[80] The minimum age applies to all crimes and therefore includes those of strict liability. This position is unaffected by the Age of Legal Capacity (Scotland) Act 1991.[81]

Capacity to marry

15.21   The common law rule was that children attained capacity to marry on the attaining of legal puberty, that is 12 for girls and 14 for boys: pupils could not marry because they were incapable of giving consent.[82] The law was altered in 1929[83] when the age was raised, for both sexes, to 16 at which age it remains. The law is now contained in the Marriage (Scotland) Act 1977, which provides that no person domiciled in Scotland may marry before he or she attains the age of 16.[84] This rule applies no matter where the marriage takes place, and there is an identical rule to govern all marriages that take place in Scotland, no matter the domicile of the parties.[85] Capacity to marry is a personal capacity and does not depend on the capacity of the other party. It follows that while a person domiciled in Scotland cannot marry anywhere before attaining the age of 16, after attaining that age a person domiciled in Scotland may marry someone below that age if the ceremony takes place in a country that allows such a marriage and the other person has personal capacity to enter into such a marriage.[86] Such a marriage will be recognised as valid in this country unless, probably, the age of the other person is so far below 16 as to render recognition contrary to public policy.

15.22   It has been suggested that an under-age marriage could, at common law, be validated by continued cohabitation after both parties had attained the appropriate age,[87] but Clive doubts whether, even if this were correct, such a rule would have survived the enactment of modern statutory provisions.[88] It is clear from

---

[76] [1953] 2 All E.R. 1403.
[77] [1970] A.C. 1004.
[78] *cf. Muir v. Wood and Anr*, 1970 S.L.T. (Notes) 12.
[79] Criminal Procedure (Scotland) Act 1995, s. 41.
[80] See below, Chap. 19.
[81] Age of Legal Capacity (Scotland) Act 1991, s. 1(3)(c): "Nothing in this Act shall... affect the... criminal responsibility of any person."
[82] Stair, I, iv, 6; Erskine, I, vi, 2.
[83] Age of Marriage Act 1929.
[84] Marriage (Scotland) Act 1977, s. 1(1).
[85] *ibid.* s. 1(2).
[86] Anton and Beaumont, *Private International Law* (2nd ed.), p. 437.
[87] *Johnston v. Ferrier* (1770) Mor. 8931; Erskine, I, vi, 2.
[88] Clive (4th ed.), pp. 74–78.

the Marriage (Scotland) Act 1977 that an under-age marriage is void[89] with the result that there is nothing to validate, and the better view today is that continued cohabitation after both parties attain the age of 16 might found a new marriage by cohabitation with habit and repute rather than validating an already existing marriage.[90]

Affinitive marriages
There is one exception to the rule that a person has capacity to marry on **15.23** attaining the age of 16. While the general rule is that a person may not marry those to whom he or she is related within one of the degrees specified in Schedule 1 to the Marriage (Scotland) Act 1977,[91] there are exceptions[92] to the prohibitions on affinitive marriages. A person may marry someone who used to be a step-child or a step-parent of his or hers so long as (a) both parties are over the age of 21 years and (b) the younger of the two had not at any time before attaining the age of 18 lived in the same household as the other party and been treated by the other party as a child of his or her family.[93] A person may marry someone who used to be his or her child-in-law or parent-in-law so long as (a) both parties are over the age of 21 years and (b) both his or her former spouse and the former spouse's other parent (in the case of a person wishing to marry his or her former parent-in-law) or both his or her child and the child's other parent (in the case of a person wishing to marry his or her former son- or daughter-in-law) are now dead.[94]

Registration of births
In terms of the Registration of Births, Deaths and Marriages (Scotland) Act **15.24** 1965, it is the duty of the father or the mother of a child to attend personally at the registration office in order to give the registrar information concerning the birth of the child.[95] Section 99 of the Children (Scotland) Act 1995 amended that provision by adding after the words "father or mother" the additional words "(whether or not they have attained the age of 16 years)". It would seem, therefore, that parenthood alone confers capacity to register the birth of a child and the issue is not referable to age at all.

The 1965 Act also provides for the making of declarations by the father of a **15.25** child who is not married to the mother of that child, and for his registration as the father.[96] The 1995 Act amended this provision also[97] and a person under the age of 16 years now has legal capacity to make the requests, declarations and applications governed by section 18 of the 1965 Act so long as, in the opinion of the registrar or of the sheriff the person understands the nature of the request,

---

[89] s. 1(2).
[90] *AB v. CD*, 1957 S.C. 415; Clive, *op. cit.*, p. 75. The period of cohabitation before both parties are 16 cannot count towards the period required to constitute a marriage, but it might be used to indicate the nature of the relationship after the incapacity disappears: *Kamperman v. McIver*, 1994 S.L.T. 763.
[91] Relationships of consanguinity, affinity or adoption, as there defined. See Clive, *op. cit.*, pp. 23–24 and 76–77.
[92] Introduced into the law by the Marriage (Prohibited Degrees of Relationship) Act 1986, amending the Marriage (Scotland) Act 1977. For a history and examination of this legislation, see Nichols, "Step-Daughters and Mothers-in-Law", 1986 S.L.T. (News) 229.
[93] Marriage (Scotland) Act 1977, s. 2(1A) and Sched. 1.
[94] *ibid.* s. 2(1B) and Sched. 1. See further, Norrie, "Incest and the Forbidden Degrees of Marriage in Scots Law" (1992) 37 J.L.S.S. 216. The Scottish Law Commission proposed (Scot. Law Com. No. 135, *Report on Family Law*, May 1992, at para. 8.13 and draft Bill, cl. 20) scrapping the rules prohibiting marriages between ex-relations-in-law.
[95] Registration of Births, Deaths and Marriages (Scotland) Act 1965, s. 14(1).
[96] *ibid.* s. 18.
[97] 1995 Act, s. 99(3), adding a new s. 18(3) to the 1965 Act.

declaration or application. Without prejudice to the generality of that rule, a person 12 years of age or more shall be presumed to be of sufficient age and maturity to have such understanding: this is a presumption only and a parent over 12 may be found to lack the appropriate understanding. What requires to be understood probably includes the legal effect of the request, declaration or application, in particular that the father making it might find himself thereby subject to alimentary and other obligations towards the child.

Both of the above provisions are given retrospective effect.[98]

Parental responsibilities and parental rights

15.26   The age of the parent does not affect his or her acquisition of parental responsibilities and parental rights,[99] except in so far as it affects the father's marital capacity, but it may affect his or her capacity to act as such. It is provided that a person under the age of 16 years who is him or herself a parent may exercise parental responsibilities and parental rights in relation to his or her child,[1] but this provision does not confer upon a child-parent any capacity he or she would not otherwise have. Rather, it merely clarifies that he or she can act as a parent if, as an individual, he or she has capacity to do so. Capacity to enter into any transaction in the exercise of parental responsibilities and parental rights (*i.e.* capacity of the child-parent to act as his or her child's legal representative) depends on his or her personal capacity to act on his or her own behalf, as determined by the other provisions in the 1991 Act. Fathers below the age of 16 will almost never have parental responsibilities and parental rights in any case (because they will not—if governed by the law of Scotland—be married to the mother and it is highly unlikely that a court would grant them parental responsibilities and parental rights under section 11 of the Children (Scotland) Act 1995[2]). On the other hand, both parents, expressly of whatever age, are given the power to enter into an agreement whereby the father shall have parental responsibilities and parental rights[3]; again, the father's capacity to exercise the responsibilities and rights so acquired will depend on his capacity as determined by the provisions in the 1991 Act.

Other statutory capacities

15.27   Statute lays down a variety of other ages at which a person acquires capacity to perform particular acts and, where these are expressed in years, they are all preserved by the Age of Legal Capacity (Scotland) Act 1991.[4] Examples include section 101 of the Road Traffic Act 1988 (specifying the age of 16 for obtaining a provisional driver's licence, and 17 for driving a car); section 1(1) of the Representation of the People Act 1983 (18 for voting in parliamentary and other elections); section 1(1) of the Law Reform (Miscellaneous Provisions) (Scotland) Act 1980 (18 for jury service); and section 28 of the Children and Young Persons (Scotland) Act 1937 (13 for entering into employment).[5] In addition, section 7 of the Age of Legal Capacity (Scotland) Act 1991 provides that a person may acquire an independent domicile on or after his or her 16th birthday; the Civil

---

[98] Children (Scotland) Act 1995, s. 99(2) and (4).
[99] *ibid.* s. 15(1) defines "parent" as father or mother "of whatever age".
[1] Age of Legal Capacity (Scotland) Act 1991, s. 1(3)(g), as amended by the Children (Scotland) Act 1995, Sched. 4, para. 53.
[2] Though it should be noted that the only circumstance in which the court is able to confer parental responsibilities and parental rights on a person under 16 is—expressly—when the person is the child's parent: Children (Scotland) Act 1995, s. 11(2)(b).
[3] Children (Scotland) Act 1995, s. 4(1).
[4] s. 1(3)(d).
[5] For further examples, see *Stair Memorial Encyclopaedia*, Vol. 3, paras 1210–1258.

Evidence (Family Mediation) (Scotland) Act 1995 provides that a child who is the subject of a family mediation and at the time it took place was capable of understanding the nature and significance of the matters involved has legal capacity to agree that the matters discussed should be admitted as evidence in any civil proceedings[6]; and the Data Protection Act 1998 provides that in Scotland a person under the age of 16 has capacity to exercise any of the rights conferred by that Act where he or she has a general understanding of what it means to exercise that right.[7] The Criminal Law (Consolidation) (Scotland) Act 1995 lays down ages at which young persons can lawfully indulge in particular sexual acts,[8] but this is a matter of policy rather than capacity to consent (for sexual intercourse with a female person without capacity to consent thereto would in all cases be rape).

LEGAL REPRESENTATION OF CHILDREN

Introduction

In the limited circumstances in which a person under 16 years of age has **15.28** legal capacity to enter into a transaction, there is no need for any person to act on behalf of the child in that transaction. Similarly, a person between the ages of 16 and 18 has full legal capacity to enter into any legal transaction on his or her own behalf. However, where, as will be the usual case, a child under 16 does not have legal capacity to enter into a particular transaction, then that child's parent or guardian must exercise their responsibility and right to undertake on the child's behalf acts with legal effect, and to administer the child's property. Their responsibility and right to do so is known as legal representation.[9] As one of the parental responsibilities and parental rights within the meaning of Part I of the Children (Scotland) Act 1995, legal representation inheres in all parents who have parental responsibilities and parental rights under that statute[10]; it inheres also in persons who have parental responsibilities and parental rights by court order[11] or who are appointed guardians by testamentary deed or by court order.[12]

The role of the legal representative

Source and rationale

Legal representation is the modern statutory equivalent of tutory at common **15.29** law, as is made plain by section 5(1) of the Age of Legal Capacity (Scotland) Act 1991 which, as amended by the Children (Scotland) Act 1995,[13] provides as follows:

> "any reference in any rule of law, enactment or document to the tutor of a pupil child shall be construed as a reference to a person entitled to act as a child's legal representative (within the meaning of Part I of the Children (Scotland) Act 1995), and any reference to the tutory of such a child shall be construed as a reference to the entitlement to act as a child's legal representative enjoyed by a person by, under or by virtue of the said Part I".

---

[6] Civil Evidence (Family Mediation) (Scotland) Act 1995, s. 2(2) and (3).
[7] Data Protection Act 1998, s. 66(1). A person of 12 years of age or more is presumed to be of sufficient age and maturity to have such an understanding: s. 66(2).
[8] See Criminal Law (Consolidation) (Scotland) Act 1995, ss. 5–13.
[9] Imposed and granted by s. 1(1)(d) and s. 2(1)(d) of the Children (Scotland) Act 1995.
[10] See ss. 3 and 4.
[11] Under s. 11(2)(b).
[12] Under ss. 7 and 11(2)(h).
[13] Sched. 4, para. 53(4).

The law of tutory is therefore the starting point in determining the role of the legal representative today.

15.30   Although, in the case of tutory, there were feudal antecedents, the Roman law was the primary source of both tutory and curatory in their modern form.[14] The underlying consideration was the necessity, reflected in practically all legal systems, to provide for the protection of the person and the management of the affairs of those who have not reached an age and discretion at which they can be expected to take full responsibility for the protection of their own interests and act with the independence attributed to adults. That protective function is usually thought to belong naturally to parents, in default of whom some substitute must be found. So, for Stair, tutory had its roots in natural or divine law:

> "If there were not positive law, the natural infirmity of pupilage would not want its natural remedies, provided by him, who is the father of the fatherless and layeth his obediential obligations upon those whom, by the law written in their hearts, he hath bound to the performance of these duties."[15]

That reasoning, as Stair recognised, did not apply to curatory for the minor was, in contemplation of the law, much more capable of responsible independent action than was the pupil. Although a minor who had no parents was the subject of a degree of legal protection, his or her acts might have received legal effect without the necessity of the appointment of curators. It is the protective element indicated by Stair in relation to tutory that provides the main rationale for legal representation today.

Parents as legal representatives

15.31   In formal deeds and in legal proceedings the father of a child used commonly to be designed a tutor and administrator-at-law,[16] or as curator, according to whether the child was a pupil or minor. After the Guardianship Act 1973 a similar designation was appropriate to the mother. The usage was ancient and was entirely apt as a description of the exercise of parental power. It was, however, misleading if it is taken to suggest that a distinct office of tutory or curatory rested in the parent, or that parents were subject to all the rules applicable to tutors and curators. In relation to the management of a child's estate and to acts connected therewith, such as the granting of deeds and the taking of legal proceedings, a parent could be (and still can be) superseded in the exercise of his or her administrative and representational powers by an order of the court, but there was no office from which he or she could be removed. So in *Robertson, Petitioners*[17] Lord Justice-Clerk Inglis said of a father:

> "There appears to me to be no room for removing him from the office of administrator-in-law to his son, for there is no such office in the proper sense of the term. It is a position inseparable from the relation of parent and child, and recognised by the municipal law of the country, and all, therefore, that the Court can do is to supersede him in the exercise of his powers derived from that relation, but not to deprive him of any office."[18]

In other words, a parent who acted as tutor and administrator-at-law, or as curator, acted properly *qua* parent and not by virtue of any separate authority. This has

---

[14]   See Montgomery, "Guardian and Ward", in *Scottish Legal History* (Stair Society, Vol. 20), pp. 125–129.

[15]   I, vi, 1.

[16]   The phrase appeared in s. 1(2) of the Trusts (Scotland) Act 1961 until these words were removed by Sched. 2 to the Age of Legal Capacity (Scotland) Act 1991.

[17]   (1865) 3 M. 1077.

[18]   *ibid.* at 1079.

been made plain today in relation to the parent's responsibility and right of legal representation which, statutorily, is one only of the various responsibilities and rights that parents have.[19] A parent who has parental responsibilities and parental rights can act as the child's legal representative because he or she is a parent and parents are given parental responsibilities and parental rights and not because he or she holds a separate office. The responsibility and right can be removed from a parent without affecting that parent's other parental responsibilities and parental rights.

The extent of legal representation

Fraser says[20] that "the office of tutory is strictly one of administration". This **15.32** was not at common law wholly accurate, for the tutor did have a number of rights over the person of the child, such as the right to custody, including the right to determine the child's place of residence and the various powers flowing from custody. In so far as they were inherent in custody these rights over the child's person could be exercised exclusively by the custodian if different from the tutor, except to the extent that they required the consent of the tutor for the application of funds under his control. A question remained, however, of the extent to which the residual powers of a tutor who was not a custodian could be so exercised as to impinge on matters directly affecting the child's person and well-being.[21] The question may still be posed today. Is the legal representative entitled, for example, to consent to the child's medical treatment, because the giving of consent is an act with the legal effect of providing a doctor with a defence to an action for assault and is therefore an aspect of legal representation of the child? Or, because this amounts to an exercise of rights over the child's person, can that be done only by the person—usually, though not always, the same—with the responsibility to safeguard and promote the child's health, development and welfare? The terms of section 5 of the Children (Scotland) Act 1995[22] suggest that this particular matter is one of legal representation, notwithstanding its effects on the person of the child, and this itself indicates that the exercise of the responsibility and right of legal representation may concern matters beyond the administration of the child's estate. This is not altogether surprising when it is remembered that litigation may clearly be instigated by the legal representative even when the effect of any court decree might concern the person of the child, or his or her health, development and welfare, and not just his or her estate. There is, however, no doubt that the main content of the responsibility and right of legal representation is in relation to the child's affairs and his or her property, and the major role of the legal representative is to represent the child in transactions which, because he or she lacks legal capacity, he or she cannot enter into or perform him- or herself. The administrative role of the legal representative is, in so far as it is separate from the representational role, recognised by section 10 of the Children (Scotland) Act 1995. So the role of the legal representative includes both the right to administer the child's property, which might involve entering into contracts and conducting litigation on behalf of the child, and the right to perform other

---

[19] See above, Chap. 8.

[20] at p. 307 (3rd ed.).

[21] *cf.* Norrie, "The *Gillick* Case and Parental Rights in Scots Law", 1985 S.L.T. (News) 157 and Thomson, "The *Gillick* Case and Parental Rights in Scots Law: Another View", 1985 S.L.T. (News) 223.

[22] A person with care and control of a child "may in particular, even although he does not have the parental right [to act as the child's legal representative], give consent to any surgical, medical or dental treatment or procedure".

juristic acts that are necessary for the protection of either the person of the child or his or her property.

15.33   Acts of legal representation performed by persons with that responsibility and right are no longer challengeable on the ground of minority and lesion.[23] It might be perceived that the position of the child has thereby become less secure than it was at common law, where transactions undertaken on behalf of the child could be challenged by the child.[24] The policy of the law today, however, is to give protection to persons under 16 who lack capacity by ensuring that transactions are performed on their behalf by their legal representatives and allowing, where appropriate, a right of personal action against the representative if harm is caused.[25]

The rights and powers of the legal representative

15.34   Before the coming into force of Part I of the Children (Scotland) Act 1995, the "guardian",[26] and before that the tutor or curator, had been within the definition of "trustee" for the purposes of the Trusts (Scotland) Act 1921,[27] the Trusts (Scotland) Act 1961[28] and the Trustee Investments Act 1961[29] and that definition expressly included the parents acting as guardian of a child under the age of 16 years,[30] even although, as explained above, parents did not really hold a separate "office" of guardian.[31] There always was a certain awkwardness in defining a trustee to include a guardian, in particular because guardians did not (and legal representatives do not) have any property rights in the estates with which they are entitled to deal while such property rights are of the essence of trusteeship[32]: a legal representative represents the child and manages the child's estate on his or her behalf, but the child him or herself remains properly the proprietor and titles to property are taken in the name of the child and not of the legal representative.[33] Although guardians were not judicial factors, the same rule is generally applicable to judicial factories where there is a living ward.[34] The assimilation of guardians (in the sense of legal representatives) to trustees did, however, have the advantage that the rights and responsibilities of trustees (and thus of guardians) were set out in some detail in statutory form. Guardians who are entitled to act as legal representatives are no longer within the definition of "trustee" for the purposes of the Trusts Acts,[35] and the statutory obligations

---

[23] Age of Legal Capacity (Scotland) Act 1991, s. 1(5).

[24] See above, paras 1.17–1.19. For further details on reduction for minority and lesion, see the First Edition of this book at pp. 63–68.

[25] Children (Scotland) Act 1995, s. 10. See below, para. 15.47.

[26] In this chapter, unless the context otherwise requires, the word "guardian" is used in the sense previously understood as "tutor" and since understood as "legal representative". This was the primary meaning of the word between the coming into force of the 1991 and the 1995 Acts, though it is not its primary meaning today: see further, above, paras 1.08–1.09 and Chap. 7.

[27] s. 2, as amended by the Age of Legal Capacity (Scotland) Act 1991, Sched. 1, para. 25.

[28] s. 6(1), importing the definition in the 1921 Act.

[29] s. 17(5), importing the definition in the 1921 Act.

[30] This was put beyond doubt by s. 10 of the Guardianship of Infants Act 1925.

[31] Even before 1921, tutors were included in the trust legislation for the purposes of conferring upon them (and others in a fiduciary capacity) the same powers and privileges as trustees: see the Trusts (Scotland) Act 1867. In addition to the trust legislation, common law tutors had been subject to specific statutory regulation (see the Tutors and Curators Act 1696, and the Guardianship of Infants Act 1886) and were, for most purposes, judicial factors within the meaning of the Judicial Factors Act 1849, but none of these provisions applies to the modern legal representative.

[32] *Linton v. Inland Revenue*, 1928 S.C. 209 at 214, *per* Lord President Clyde. See also Norrie and Scobbie, *Trusts*, at p. 2 and Wilson and Duncan, *Trusts, Trustees and Executors* (2nd ed.), p. 15.

[33] *Duff v. Gorrie* (1849) 11 D.1054; *Scott, Petr* (1865) 18 D. 624; *Maconochie* (1857) 19 D. 366; *Taylor v. Duff* (1894) 2 S.L.T. 366 (at 353). This position is expressly preserved by s. 1(3)(e) of the Age of Legal Capacity (Scotland) Act 1991.

[34] Fraser (3rd ed.), p. 205, n. 1. Walker, *Judicial Factors*, p. 83.

[35] Trusts (Scotland) Act 1921, s. 2, as amended by the Children (Scotland) Act 1995, Sched. 4, para. 6. This will include all guardians as understood as parent-substitutes.

of legal representatives are today expressed in much more general terms. Nevertheless these terms create, it is conceived, a trust-like, that is to say a fiduciary, relationship between the legal representative and the child.

The decision whether to enter into, and how to conduct, any transaction lies **15.35** with the child's legal representative, and though the Children (Scotland) Act 1995 contains no general direction to legal representatives as to how they should make their decisions, they will be indirectly governed by the requirement to act in the interests of the child, since any challenge to their actions will be determined on that basis. The right of legal representation exists only in order to allow the holder to fulfil his or her obligation to act as the child's legal representative, and the exercise of the right is valid only in so far as it safeguards the child's health development and, in particular, welfare.[36] In making any major decision in respect of legal representation, the legal representative must have regard so far as practicable to the views (if he or she wishes to express them) of the child concerned, taking account of the child's age and maturity, it being presumed that a child 12 years of age or more is of sufficient age and maturity to form a view, as well as the views of any other person with parental responsibilities and parental rights in relation to the child.[37] The direction to legal representatives in relation to the administration of the child's property, that they act as a reasonable and prudent person would act in their own affairs,[38] does not apply generally to all acts of legal representation but is nevertheless good general guidance, failure to follow which will make it difficult for legal representatives to show that they acted in the interests of the child.

Administration of the child's property

That the legal representative has the responsibility and right to administer **15.36** the child's property on his or her behalf is inherent in the nature of legal representation. It is also implicit in the terms of section 10(1) of the Children (Scotland) Act 1995, which provides that:

"A person acting as a child's legal representative in relation to the administration of the child's property—
   (a) shall be required to act as a reasonable and prudent person would act on his own behalf; and
   (b) subject to any order made under section 11 of this Act, shall be entitled to do anything which the child, if of full age and capacity, could do in relation to that property;
and subject to subsection (2) below, on ceasing to act as legal representative shall be liable to account to the child for his intromissions with the child's property."

While the rights of the guardian and the tutor under the previous law were **15.37** limited by the protective purposes for which they were granted, the powers of the legal representative under the statute are significantly broader and encompass any act which the child if adult could competently do. Though the terms of section 10 are unlimited, it is nevertheless conceived that there are certain implicit limitations on the legal representative's power over the child's property. For one thing, the act must be one that can properly be described as an act of administration. Also, all legal representatives are subject to certain restrictions on their capacity to perform legal transactions on behalf of children, as specified below.[39]

---

[36] Children (Scotland) Act 1995, ss. 1(1)(a) and 2(1)(a).
[37] *ibid.* s. 6(1).
[38] *ibid.* s. 10(1)(a).
[39] See below, paras 15.57–15.58.

Investment

15.38   It is a necessary part of the administration of any estate held for more than a
minimal period of time, and the only means of protecting it against inflation and
other economic dangers, that it be invested property. After mentioning the tutor's
duty of care of the child's person and the duty "to aliment them out of the pupil's
own means, according to the condition thereof; and to educate them for a station
in the commonwealth according to their quality and capacity", Stair lists among
the natural obligations of tutors the management of their wards' affairs

> "with such diligence as provident men use in their own affairs, that nothing
> may be lost but everything improven to the best advantage; in all which they
> are not to exerce voluntary acts of dominion at their choice, as disposing of
> what is secure, but only necessary acts for the preservation and recovery of
> what will or may perish, and for improving the profits of it".[40]

Fraser interpreted that passage and other passages from the institutional writers as
meaning that the object of tutory, with regard to property, was "rather to preserve
than to acquire; to keep the pupil's estate in the same condition as the tutor found it,
so far as consistent with its nature, rather than to attempt by speculations to improve
it, because it can never be improved without risk".[41] The warning against speculation
is apt in the case of a legal representative as it is with trustees,[42] but all improvement
is in a sense speculative and Fraser's interpretation of the authorities does not consist
with their terms.[43] In any event, it is inapplicable to modern conditions in which the
risk of detriment from a legal representative's keeping the child's estate in the same
condition as he or she found it might well be considerably greater than those of
prudent improvement and reinvestment. Though the legal representative is no longer
treated as a trustee, within the meaning of the Trusts Acts, his or her duties and
powers in this respect, as in others, such as protecting and defending the estate, are
analogous to those of trustees. Investment must be suitable to the size of the estate
and for most children their estates will be small. The estates of children with rather
more patrimony are likely today to be held under deed of trust, in which case the
right and duty of investment will fall on the trustees rather than the legal
representative,[44] or be subject to guidance from the Accountant of Court.[45] Further
guidance, though no longer legal obligation, is found in the Trustee Investments
Act 1961, under which investments should be made only after taking financial
advice on the question of whether the investment is satisfactory having regard to
the need for diversification and the suitability of the proposed investment; such
advice should be obtained from a person who is reasonably believed to be qualified
by his or her ability in and practical experience of financial matters, and it may be
given by a person notwithstanding that it was given in the course of that person's
employment as an officer or servant.[46]

---

[40] I, vi, 3.

[41] (3rd ed.), p. 307.

[42] In relation to trustees, see, *e.g.*, *Henderson v. Henderson's Trs* (1900) 2 F. 1295; *Bartlett v.
Barclay's Bank Trust Co. (No. 1)* [1980] 1 All E.R. 139.

[43] It is to be noted that there never was an absolute rule that the child's estate must be preserved: see
Polland and Anr v. Sturrock's Exrs, 1952 S.C. 535, in which it was held that a father could use
part of the child's estate to pay for the child's education, even although he was able to do so from
his own estate. See also *Steele's Trs v. Cooper* (1830) 8 S. 926. The same is true for curators
bonis, to whom similar principles apply: see *B's C.B.*, 1996 S.L.T. (Sh.Ct) 27; *B's C.B.* (1997)
Fam. L.B. 32–6; *D's C.B.*, 1998 S.L.T. 2.

[44] Though the legal representative may have to undertake certain tasks such as discharging trustees
who have resigned. The legal representative may not, however, consent on the child's behalf to
the variation of a trust deed under s. 1 of the Trusts (Scotland) Act 1961.

[45] Under s. 9 of the Children (Scotland) Act 1995. See Robertson, "Children as Inheritors of Property"
(1997) 42 J.L.S.S. 234.

[46] Trustee Investments Act 1961, s. 6.

Aliment from the estate

A legal representative must see that in so far as it is required proper provision **15.39** is made for the aliment of the child from the estate under his or her charge.[47] This duty may sometimes seem to conflict with the legal representative's duty to preserve the child's estate and so not to encroach on capital. On some old authorities, it was held that the child must be alimented only out of the income of the estate and, "except in very singular cases", no more could be given.[48] That doctrine must, however, yield to necessity and if the aliment of the child cannot otherwise be secured the legal representative may encroach upon capital and that may extend, with the authority of the court, to the sale of heritage if aliment "cannot be afforded otherwise".[49] And trust funds in which the child has an interest may be drawn upon for his or her aliment. In *Hamilton*[50] authority was granted for the repayment, out of the capital of the trust estate under a marriage contract, of sums advanced by a mother for the education of her children where she was entitled to the liferent of the whole fund and the children's sole interest was in the capital of the estate. Payment, out of capital, for the aliment and education of the children for a further year was also authorised and leave was reserved to make further applications thereafter. At common law such advances were authorised under the *nobile officium* and could be made only if the interest of the children had vested. By the Trusts (Scotland) Act 1921, however, re-enacting, with some modification, similar provisions of the Trusts (Scotland) Act 1867, the court is empowered to authorise trustees to make advances from capital for the maintenance or education of beneficiaries who are not of full age and to whom the capital of the fund out of which payment is made is destined either absolutely or contingently.[51] It is necessary before such advance can be authorised that it should appear that the income of the fund is insufficient for, or not applicable to, the maintenance or education of the beneficiaries and that the advance is necessary for that purpose. The advance must not be especially prohibited by the trust deed and the rights of the beneficiaries, if contingent, must be contingent only on their survivance. These rules apply only to trustees holding estates on behalf of children, and not to legal representatives administering estates which belong to children: any action by a legal representative will be raised under section 11 of the Children (Scotland) Act 1995.

The child's estate should be applied to his or her aliment only to the extent **15.40** that his or her alimentary needs are not met from other sources.[52] The amount which a parent or other person under an alimentary obligation is liable to contribute to the aliment of a child is now determined by what is reasonable in the circumstances having regard to the respective needs, resources and earning capacities of the obligants and the child and, generally, to all the circumstances of the case.[53] The extent to which a legal representative should apply the child's estate to his or her aliment will therefore depend, *inter alia*, on whether any alimentary liabilities, so determined, are exigible.

---

[47] Erskine, I, vii, 24.
[48] Fraser (3rd ed.), p. 295; *Pearson v. Belshes* (1678) Mor. 16296; *Sandilands v. Tailfer* (1684) Mor. 16300; *Duncanson v. Duncanson* (1715) Mor. 16336; *Kennedy v. Rutherglen* (1860) 22 D. 567.
[49] Stair I, vi, 18; *Gordon v. H.M. Advocate* (1755) Mor. 16356. See also *Polland v. Sturrock's Exrs*, 1952 S.C. 535.
[50] (1859) 21 D. 1379.
[51] Trusts (Scotland) Act 1921, s. 16.
[52] See above, Chap. 13.
[53] Family Law (Scotland) Act 1985, ss. 1(2) and 4.

Contracts

15.41   A child under the age of 16 years has, generally speaking, no contractual capacity[54] and as a result any contract has to be entered into on his or her behalf by his or her legal representative. Doing so is, indeed, the paradigmatic example of the exercise of the responsibility and right of legal representation. At common law the power to enter into contracts belonged to the tutor, but the powers of tutory are now the powers of legal representation.[55] The contracts that tutors could and legal representatives can enter into on behalf of the child are limited in nature to those that are required for the proper administration of the child's property and for the discharge of the legal representative's general responsibility to safeguard and promote the child's health, development and welfare. A legal representative who enters into an entirely unnecessary contract on behalf of the child will doubtless in doing so create valid and enforceable rights and obligations, just as the legal representative does who enters into a contract on disadvantageous terms, though he or she may well, by doing so, open him- or herself to personal liability to the child.[56]

15.42   There are certain contracts that a child under the age of 16 will have capacity to enter into, being those that are both (a) of a kind commonly entered into by persons of his or her age and circumstances and (b) on terms that are not unreasonable.[57] It is not stated in the Age of Legal Capacity (Scotland) Act 1991 whether if the child does have the capacity to enter into a particular contract, the legal representative's power to act on behalf of the child continues or is superseded. Many parents in practice continue to act on behalf of their inexperienced children even in circumstances in which the child could act for him- or herself. While it would be consistent with the legal representative's protective role if the law were to recognise their continued ability to do so until the child reaches the age of 16, it would at the same time be inconsistent with the basis upon which capacity is granted to children under the age of 16, which is to recognise that they no longer need protection in particular circumstances. The matter was resolved by section 15(5) of the Children (Scotland) Act 1995, which provides that

> "Any reference in [Part I] of this Act to a person acting as a legal representative of a child is a reference to that person, in the interests of the child—(a) administering any property belonging to the child and (b) acting in, or giving consent to, any transaction where the child is incapable of so acting or consenting on his own behalf."

In other words, once the child is no longer incapable his or her legal representative loses the legal authority to act on his or her behalf. This is subject to a limited qualification in respect of litigation (considered immediately below) but that does not have general effect. So the parent of a 15-year-old child with capacity has no power as legal representative to use the child's own money to make necessary purchases (*e.g.* of clothing) on the child's behalf. This does not, however, necessarily deny the legal representative of power to perform other transactions having legal effect, if the child has not yet acquired capacity to perform them personally. And the child with capacity may, of course, rely on the general law of agency to grant authority to the person who used to be his or her legal representative (or any other person) to enter contracts on his or her behalf.

---

[54] Age of Legal Capacity (Scotland) Act 1991, s. 1(1). See above, para. 15.03.
[55] *ibid.* s. 5(1). On the powers of tutors, see above, paras 15.29–15.30.
[56] See below, para. 15.47.
[57] Age of Legal Capacity (Scotland) Act 1991, s. 2(1). See above, para. 15.06.

Litigation

The pupil child at common law was not *sui juris*[58] and this proposition now **15.43** applies to children under the age of 16.[59] One of the consequences of a person being in nonage is that, subject to important qualifications,[60] he or she has no *persona standi in judico* and is therefore generally unable to raise or defend actions in his or her own name. The legal representative's right of legal representation finds typical expression here, and actions can and should be raised in the name of the legal representative on behalf of the child, or against the legal representative as representing the child. It is indeed incorrect to libel the child as pursuer (except in circumstances in which the child has no legal representative or for other reason, such as contrary interest or disqualification of the legal representative, the jurisdiction of the court has to be invoked independently of the legal representative) and the correct practice is to name the legal representative and designate him or her as representative of the child.[61] If the child is the defender he or she should be named, with the legal representative named as the second defender. The legal representative is entitled to use his or her discretion in deciding how the action is to be conducted, but he or she must, of course, bear in mind at all times that his or her exercise of the parental right of legal representation is valid only in the fulfilment of the parental responsibilities he or she owes to the child, including the responsibility to safeguard and promote the child's welfare. He or she may validly decide not to pursue an action because the chances of success are low, or to settle, but he or she may not refuse to raise an action for ulterior motives or if the chances are good[62]; nor is the legal representative entitled to waive any legal defences open to the child if he or she is being sued.[63] Losing in litigation does not in itself suggest that the legal representative has acted improperly in raising an action, for that might inhibit legal representatives from pursuing potentially successful claims. A legal representative will not be liable to the child for the expenses of an unsuccessful action unless his or her decision to pursue the case was one that a reasonable and prudent person would not have made on his or her own behalf.[64]

Where a child has legal capacity to sue, or to defend, in any civil proceedings[65] **15.44** then, as explained above, the legal representative loses the power to represent the child in such proceedings. This is, however, subject to the rule introduced by the Children (Scotland) Act 1995 that the child may nevertheless consent to be represented in those proceedings by any person who, had the child lacked that capacity, would have had the responsibility to act as the child's legal representative.[66]

---

[58] Fraser (3rd ed.), p. 204.
[59] Age of Legal Capacity (Scotland) Act 1991, ss. 1(1) and 5(1).
[60] See above, para. 1.14.
[61] Fraser at pp. 270–271. In *Bell v. Trotter's Trs* (1841) 3 D. 380 it was held that "the trustees of A.B." without the trustees being named individually was not a *nomen juris* under which parties can sue or defend an action or use diligence. The trustees or legal representatives must be named.
[62] If he or she does so refuse, the court can appoint a curator *ad litem* on the child raising the action in his or her own name, and the case would then be pursued in the name of the curator: *McConochie v. Binnie* (1847) 9 D. 791; see below, para. 15.60. The rule that a child may raise or defend an action in his or her own name when his or her legal representative refuses to do so even when he or she is not yet 16 years of age, is preserved by s. 1(3)(f)(i) of the Age of Legal Capacity (Scotland) Act 1991, and the court's power to appoint a curator *ad litem* to a child in any civil proceedings is preserved by s. 1(3)(f)(ii).
[63] *Hunter and his Tutor, Petrs* (1739) Mor. 16341.
[64] In *Cunningham's Tutrix*, 1949 S.C. 275 a tutor was awarded expenses out of the child's estate having raised an action for the extension of her powers notwithstanding that the petition was dismissed as unnecessary.
[65] As determined by s. 2(4A) and (4B) of the Age of Legal Capacity (Scotland) Act 1991: see above, para. 15.11.
[66] Children (Scotland) Act 1995, s. 15(6).

Other aspects of legal representation

15.45 Administration of the child's estate, entering into contracts, and conducting litigation on behalf of the child are the major elements of the representational role of the legal representative, but there are others, and the protective aspect of the legal representative's role justifies the wider proposition that he or she may represent the child in any situation in which the child needs protection but is unable legally to act for him- or herself. A legal representative is entitled to grant discharges on behalf of the child, for example to executors or trustees of estates of which the child is a beneficiary.[67] The right to appoint factors and agents is another aspect of legal representation. More generally, any legal act required to protect the child's health, development and welfare falls within the scope of legal representation.

15.46 If the legal representative is unsure whether what he or she proposes to do is a proper exercise of the responsibility and right of legal representation, then it is open to him or her to seek a specific issue order under section 11(2)(e) of the Children (Scotland) Act 1995. The court is expressly empowered under section 11(1) to make an order relating to parental responsibilities, parental rights, guardianship or the administration of the child's property, which is wide enough to allow the order to grant some authority to the legal representative which he or she would not otherwise possess. Such an application might be made whenever the legal representative does not possess, or is unsure whether or not he or she possesses, a power that he or she wants to exercise, or when he or she is unsure whether or not its exercise would be in the interests of the child.[68] Any such application may, however, be dismissed as unnecessary.[69] As with all section 11 applications, the court will regard the welfare of the child involved as its paramount consideration and will not make an order increasing the legal representative's powers unless it is satisfied that it would be better for the child that the order be made than that it not be made.[70] The legal representative's role is, however, limited by its representational, protective and administrative character, and for that reason the court should not grant the legal representative power to do anything that the child, if of full age and capacity, could not do him- or herself. Though the court can make any order it thinks fit under section 11(1), there are some necessary inherent limitations to this: the court could not, it is submitted, authorise the legal representative to make a will on a child's behalf, nor replace the child's consent to his or her own adoption with that of the legal representative.[71]

Liabilities of legal representatives

15.47 Legal representation is a responsibility and right that confers not only powers but also duties and liabilities. The protective aspect of the legal representative's duty has already been mentioned. The exercise of any parental responsibility

---

[67] *Govan v. Richardson* (1633) Mor. 16263; *Dumbreck v. Stevenson* (1861) 4 Macq. 86; *Murray's Trs v. Bloxsom's Trs* (1887) 15 R. 233.

[68] An example of the last situation might involve granting or withholding consent to medical treatment where the balance of welfare is not obvious (such as with sterilisation operations or the withdrawal of life-support treatment).

[69] See, *e.g.*, *Cunningham's Tutrix*, 1949 S.C. 275. That case was raised under s. 5 of the Trusts (Scotland) Act 1921, and in that context the court has been impatient with petitions brought where there was little real doubt that the trustees already had the power sought: see *Marquess of Lothian's C.B.*, 1927 S.C. 579 and *Tennent's Judicial Factor v. Tennent*, 1954 S.C. 215. A legal representative seeking court authority to perform an act clearly within his or her powers may well have to bear the costs of the action personally.

[70] Children (Scotland) Act 1995, s. 11(7). Any residual common law power of the Court of Session to increase the guardian's powers as an exercise of the *nobile officium* is probably subsumed into s. 11.

[71] See further, below, paras 15.57–15.58.

and right is proper only if it does no harm to the interests of the child, and acting against these interests may potentially open the legal representative to personal liability. Though the Trusts Acts do not spell out the nature of a trustee's liabilities to the beneficiaries of a trust, the common law liabilities of trustees do, it is submitted, provide an apt analogy with the situation of the legal representative and child, for both trustee and legal representative stand in an essentially fiduciary position in relation to their charges. The test for a breach of trust is similar to that for determining whether a legal representative has acted properly. In relation to trustees it has been said that the true test for establishing whether there has been a breach of trust is to ask "has it... been shewn that the trustee failed to exercise that degree of diligence which a man of ordinary prudence would exercise in the management of his own affairs?"[72] In relation to the administration of the child's property, the statutory formulation of the legal representative's duty is now expressed in almost identical terms, section 10(1)(a) of the Children (Scotland) Act 1995 providing that the legal representative "shall be required to act as a reasonable and prudent person would act on his own behalf". This imports an objective test: it is nothing to the point how the legal representative would act in relation to his or her own affairs, for the obligation is to act as the reasonable and prudent person would act. Section 10(1) also provides that on ceasing to act as such, the legal representative shall be liable to account to the child for his or her intromissions with the child's property.[73] However, this liability is expressly subject to section 10(2) which states that "No liability shall be incurred by virtue of subsection (1) above in respect of funds which have been used in the proper discharge of the person's responsibility to safeguard and promote the child's health, development and welfare". The liability to account to the child will be incurred, therefore, only if the legal representative uses the child's funds for "improper" purposes: this may be taken to be for purposes other than the prudent administration of the property or the discharge of the legal representative's protective duty to safeguard and promote the child's health, development and welfare. Again the test would appear to be objective, so that it is nothing to the point that the legal representative believed that his or her use of the child's funds was proper when, in fact, it was not so. The liability to account for funds improperly used is a liability to repay to the child the value of these funds, in a manner similar to the liability of a trustee or executor who distributes an estate to persons other than the proper beneficiaries. Again like a trustee, the legal representative cannot set off his or her generally beneficial administration against a loss caused by a single improper act.[74] The child's remedy is to seek damages, or to raise an action for count, reckoning and payment, this latter as a consequence of the legal representative's duty to account and to restore and to refund.[75] The practical effect of both remedies is the same since the level of damages is the extent of the loss, but there are procedural differences, as well as different limitation periods.[76] The remedy may be sought by the child when he or she attains legal capacity to instruct a solicitor,[77] and by any other legal representative of the child or any curator *ad litem* appointed by the

---

[72] *per* Lord Herschell in *Raes v. Meek* (1889) 16 R. (H.L.) 31 at 34. See also Lord Watson in *Learoyd v. Whiteley* (1887) 12 App.Cas. 727 at p. 733; and Lord Atkinson in *Buchanan v. Eaton*, 1911 S.C. (H.L.) 40 at 45.

[73] This liability is personal and cannot be delegated: *Scott v. Occidental Petroleum (Caledonia) Ltd*, 1990 S.L.T. 882.

[74] *Clarke v. Clarke's Trs*, 1925 S.C. 693; Walker, *Civil Remedies*, p. 1072; Norrie and Scobbie, *Trusts*, p. 144.

[75] Stair, I, vi, 21; Children (Scotland) Act 1995, s. 10(1).

[76] See *Hobday v. Kirkpatrick's Trs*, 1985 S.L.T. 197.

[77] See Age of Legal Capacity (Scotland) Act 1991, s. 2(4A) and (4B).

court before then. Indeed any interested party, which would include anyone with care and control of the child, would be able to call the legal representative to account for his or her intromissions with the child's estate.[78] The remedy might be granted if, for example, the legal representative enters into a contract on behalf of the child that proves to be detrimental to the child's interest, or if he or she conducts litigation in a prejudicial manner, or fails to enforce the child's legal rights. The legal transactions themselves will not be challengeable if the legal representative is acting within his or her authority, but he or she will be personally liable to the child if the valid transaction causes loss and his or her actions satisfy the test for liability set out above. At common law, tutors were liable for omissions as well as acts,[79] and though this rule disappeared when tutors were brought within the terms of the Trusts Acts,[80] the application of the new rules to tutors was always awkward and the removal of legal representatives from the terms of the Trusts Acts[81] may be taken to have revived the old rule. A failure to do something, such as the failure to exercise reasonable care, or the failure to call in a debt timeously, might cause real and substantial harm to the child or his or her estate and, quite apart from the conceptual difficulties in distinguishing sensibly between acts and omissions, there is no reason of policy why a legal representative should be able to avoid liability for harmful omissions or neglects. There is certainly no statutory authority for such avoidance in the Children (Scotland) Act 1995.

Auctor in rem suam

15.48   Even before trustees were defined by statute so as to include tutors, it was recognised that the office of tutor had a fiduciary character which required that the tutor should not allow him- or herself to become *auctor in rem suam*.[82] If this rule applies to legal representatives, it would mean that they must not place themselves in a situation in which their interests as an individual might conflict with their responsibilities as a legal representative. Even the mere possibility of such conflict would have to be avoided and questions of fairness or whether an actual advantage was obtained would be irrelevant. "The criterion", said Viscount Dunedin in relation to trustees, "is not what was done, but what might be done".[83] The consequence of breaching this duty is that if a personal advantage is gained by the legal representative then he or she will hold that benefit on a constructive trust for the benefit of the child.[84] However, though the basis of the principle is the fiduciary rather than the trust nature of the relationship, it would appear that these rules no longer apply to legal representatives, since statute now gives them the power to do anything which the child, if of full age and capacity, could do in relation to the child's property[85] and there is no question but that a person, once adult, can transact with the person who used to be their legal representative.[86]

---

[78] Fraser (3rd ed.), p. 421.
[79] Stair, I, vi, 21. Fathers were not liable for omissions and in the case of tutors nominate liability for omissions and liability *in solidum* might be waived in the deed of appointment (Erskine, I, vi, 55 and I, vii, 26).
[80] Under s. 3(d) of the Trusts (Scotland) Act 1921, trustees (and therefore tutors) were liable only for their own acts and intromissions and not for their omissions or the acts and intromissions of co-trustees.
[81] By the Children (Scotland) Act 1995, Sched. 4, para. 6.
[82] Stair I, vi, 17; Erskine, I, vii, 19; Fraser (3rd ed.), pp. 372–389 (and cases cited therein).
[83] *Wright v. Morgan* [1926] A.C. 788 at 798.
[84] *Cherry's Trs v. Patrick*, 1911 2 S.L.T. 313.
[85] Children (Scotland) Act 1995, s. 10(1)(b).
[86] This conclusion differs from that suggested in the 1st edition of this book (at p. 373, n. 27), but the terms of the statute (as, it must be admitted, the terms of the draft Bill being commented upon in the 1st edition) do not indicate that any implicit exception is contained therein. A constructive trust transfers the benefit gained through the transaction from the trustee to the beneficiary, but the policy of the 1995 Act would appear to be to allow the child to seek such a transfer only when he or she has suffered a loss through the transaction and not when the legal representative has acquired a gain therefrom.

Relief from liability

Trustees, by statute,[87] can seek relief from liability in specific circumstances **15.49** but legal representatives are no longer trustees for these, or other, purposes.[88] Nevertheless, the wide terms of section 11 of the Children (Scotland) Act 1995 suggest that the court has the power to make an order relieving a legal representative who is liable to the child for a breach of his or her duty of care wholly or partly therefrom. The court in doing so would be bound to regard the welfare of the child involved as its paramount consideration and would not relieve the legal representative from any liability unless satisfied that it would be better for the child to do so than not to do so.[89] There will be few situations in which it would be in the interests of the child to deprive him or her of a right of recompense from a legal representative who acted wrongfully, but since welfare must be given a wide scope and will include more than merely economic considerations, relief might exceptionally be considered appropriate if that protects and enhances family harmony.

Liability of persons acting as if legal representatives: pro-curatory

It sometimes happens that persons who are not entitled to act as a child's **15.50** legal representatives nevertheless interfere in the child's affairs and purport to undertake acts of administration on behalf of the child. At common law such persons were known as pro-tutors or pro-curators, depending upon whether the child was a pupil or a minor, and they were subject to strict liabilities. There is nothing in the subsequent statutory development to suggest that the liabilities of a person acting as if he or she were a child's legal representative are any less. The term "pro-curator" remains apt as describing the representational role rather than the tutorial role that such persons take on.

By pro-tutors and pro-curators "are understood those who act as tutors or **15.51** curators without having a legal title to the office, whether they sincerely believe themselves tutors, or know that they are not".[90] This is not just a convenient label to describe those who act irregularly in this respect. In a limited, but important, sense pro-curatory is an office, however irregular, recognised by the law. Those who acts as pro-curator not only render themselves liable for what they have done but thereby subject themselves to all the duties of a curator or legal representative and so become, if they neglect these duties, liable for omissions as well as for intromissions. The doctrine goes back to the Roman law and is justified on the view that "he who assumes to himself an office to which he hath no title, ought to be in no better case than one who acts under a proper warrant".[91] At first, however, it was not clear that the Roman law had been received on this matter and in *Swinton v. Notman*[92] in 1665 the court held that the defender, who had been nominated as an overseer but had acted, contrary to the testament, under the name of tutor, should be liable only for his intromissions "seeing he had no law or custom regulating the case." At the same time, however, the court enacted by Act of Sederunt,[93] "that whosoever in time coming meddled with pupils' or minors' means as pro-tutors or pro-curators, should be liable from henceforth as tutors or curators for intromissions and omission". The Act of Sederunt is the foundation of the subsequent law. It has since been provided that "no guardian of a person under the age of 16 years

---

[87] Trusts (Scotland) Act 1921, ss. 29–33.
[88] Children (Scotland) Act 1995, Sched. 4, para. 6, amending s. 2 of the Trusts (Scotland) Act 1921.
[89] Children (Scotland) Act 1995, s. 11(7).
[90] Erskine, I, vii, 28.
[91] *ibid.*
[92] (1665) Mor. 16273.
[93] June 24, 1665 F.

shall be appointed as such except under section 7 of the Children (Scotland) Act 1995".[94] In so far as pro-curatory is an office it is distinct from that of guardianship with the result that this provision does not prevent its arising; and in any case pro-curators are not "appointed."

Commencement

15.52　　　The commencement of pro-curatory is from the first intromission with the child's property and is not, unless on special grounds, drawn back to an earlier time, usually the death of the parents, when the child first became *indefensus*. Where there is room for doubt, there will be reluctance to imply an early commencement if the office has been assumed from friendship or the necessitous circumstances of the child's affairs. If, however, the first act of intromission is shortly after the parent's death, an accounting may be required from the date of death.[95]

Assumption of office

15.53　　　Assumption of the office may sometimes be supported by express words as when someone claims to be the child's legal representative and acts accordingly. A mere verbal pretension to the office, unaccompanied by acts, probably does not infer liability unless, it is thought, where it amounts to a course of holding out from which prejudice to the child results. Where there is a claim to be legal representative, any intromissions with the child's estate can readily be attributed to that character, but where there is no such claim the act must be unequivocally referable to the office before pro-curatory will be inferred.[96] "It is not every management of the affairs of a pupil that will infer a pro-tutory but only such as is *qua* tutor, that is, where one acts under the character of tutor and he is not."[97] So, when trustees intromitted with the share of the estate of a deceased parent, which had been left in trust for his children, it was held that having acted in the character of trustees they did not thereby become pro-tutors.[98] It is no defence to an allegation of pro-curatory that lawful legal representatives were in office and acting. It has been held that that is so, even if the alleged pro-curator acted along with persons entitled to act as the child's legal representative.[99]

Powers, duties and liabilities

15.54　　　By usurping office, the pro-curator brings upon him- or herself all the duties that a lawful holder of the office has. *Qui pro tutore negotia gerit, eandem fidem et diligentiam praestat, quam tutor praestaret.*[1] Indeed, the pro-curator's position is more onerous than that of the lawful legal representative. "It is a familiar maxim in the law, that a pro-tutor or pro-curator is liable in even stricter diligence than the tutor or curator with a legal title".[2] The ambiguity of the pro-curator's situation is acute and perilous. He or she has a duty to act, if that should be necessary to protect or promote the child's interests, but has no active title and so, where the institution of actions or other legal acts are required, he

---

[94] Age of Legal Capacity (Scotland) Act 1991, s. 5(2), as amended by the Children (Scotland) Act 1995, Sched. 4, para. 53(5).

[95] Erskine, above.; *Muir v. Crawfurd* (1697) Mor. 16316.

[96] For cases in which pro-tutory or pro-curatory has been inferred, see *Fowler v. Campbell* (1739). Mor. 16343; *Muir v. Crawfurd*, above; *McDuff v. McDuff* (1637) Mor. 514; *Vanllange v. Kincaid* (1630) Mor. 513 and *Cass v. Ellis* (1671) Mor. 3504.

[97] *Fowler v. Campbell*, above, *per* Lord Kilkerran, cited in *Fulton v. Fulton* (1864) 2 M. 893.

[98] *Fulton v. Fulton*, above.

[99] *Cass v. Ellis*, above.

[1] D. xxvii, 5, 4.

[2] *Fulton v. Fulton*, above, *per* Lord Kinloch (Ordinary) at 896.

or she has no power to carry out that duty.[3] Thus, the pro-curator will be liable for loss occasioned by failure to pursue a debt due to the child but, if he or she does sue, may be met by a plea of "no title to sue".[4] The apparent dilemma of that situation may, however, be circumvented by raising an action in the child's name, and thereafter securing the appointment of a curator *ad litem*.[5] A more intractable problem may be that, while the pro-curator has a duty to employ the child's estate profitably, he or she has no title to grant the deeds that may be necessary for that purpose. It is undecided whether the Court of Session, in the exercise of its *nobile officium*, may relieve a pro-curator who has inadvertently assumed office from the harshness of some of the consequences which that may entail. Any order for relief will however be an order in relation to the administration of a child's property, or possibly in relation to parental responsibilities or parental rights, allowing the court to make such order as it thinks fit under section 11 of the Children (Scotland) Act 1995, though if an application is made relief will be granted on the basis not of the innocence and reasonableness of the pro-curator's actions but on the basis that to do so is in the interests of the child.[6] If relief means that the child's estate loses a claim against the pro-curator it will seldom be the case that the granting of relief could be in the child's interests.[7] Short of that, it appears that the only escape for the pro-curator is to take the steps necessary to bring the office to an end. A pro-curator is liable for all loss to the child's estate resulting from neglect, including loss of interest or other loss flowing from failure to employ the estate profitably.[8] On an accounting, he or she is, however, entitled to credit for moneys of his or her own which have been expended for the child's behoof.[9]

Because a pro-curator has no active title, third parties cannot acquire a good **15.55** title from him or her. All alienations of property, by gift or sale or otherwise, are null even if for value and in a question with a *bona fide* purchaser;[10] and a debtor paying to a pro-curator is not discharged unless he or she can show that the payment was applied *in rem versum* of the child.[11] Stair, however, allows an exception to that where "the person had been long holden and repute tutor".[12] In that case he says that the deed would be likely to be sustained unless it could be reduced on proof of lesion. It is no longer possible to reduce deeds entered into by legal representatives on the ground of lesion,[13] so if Stair is correct even deeds prejudicing the child may remain valid in the circumstances postulated.

Termination of pro-curatory

There can be no pro-curator where there could be no legal representative. **15.56** So pro-curatory ends when the child reaches the age of 16 years,[14] even if the pro-curator continues to manage the property thereafter.[15] The office might also be terminated by death of either the pro-curator or the child. How it is ended,

---

[3] Erskine, I, vii, 28.
[4] *ibid.*; Fraser at p. 564.
[5] See below, para. 15.60.
[6] Children (Scotland) Act 1995, s. 11(7).
[7] It might, however, be possible to envisage an unusual situation in which the child is dependent upon the person who acted as pro-curator, and to hold that person liable would bankrupt him, to the detriment of the child also.
[8] Fraser, above.
[9] Erskine, above; *Gray v. Irving* (1692) Mor. 8927.
[10] Fraser at p. 563; D. xxvii, 5, 2; xxvii, 10, 8.
[11] Erskine, above; *Allan v. Hamilton* (1715) Mor. 5654.
[12] I, vi, 12.
[13] Age of Legal Capacity (Scotland) Act 1991, s. 1(5).
[14] *Cass v. Ellis*, above; D. xxvii, 5, 1.
[15] Any liability for actings after the child attains 16 years of age is as a *negotiorum gestor*.

short of these natural terms, is uncertain. The child can call the pro-curator to account before the natural termination of the office,[16] and unless there are subsequent acts such an accounting probably has the effect of termination. The same effect probably follows where legal representatives (a) put the pro-curator on notice, either expressly or by necessary implication from their actings, that they hold office to his or her exclusion unless, again, there are subsequent acts or (b) take up office subsequent to the act constituting the pro-curatory. Mere abstention from intromissions after the original act cannot, however, bring the office to an end unless, perhaps, the abstention is for a long period and a change in circumstances intervenes; liability for omissions can scarcely be destroyed by inactivity. Whether an intimation of withdrawal from all acts of management serves to terminate the office would seem to depend on whether or not there are legal representatives lawfully in office. If there are, such intimation is, no doubt, effective at least if accompanied by an accounting. If not, however, a bare intimation probably does not suffice. To hold otherwise would be to give pro-curators a power to resign which at common law guardians as legal representatives did not possess and, *a fortiori* of their case, a person who has assumed an office without authority should not be released from it until he or she has secured that the office is lawfully fulfilled. That view consists with the liabilities of pro-curators as noted above.

Powers that legal representatives lack

15.57   While the *raison d'être* of legal representation is to furnish the child with a person *sui juris* who can represent him or her, and undertake legal transactions on his or her behalf, a legal representative is not entitled to perform every sort of legal act on behalf of the child that capax adults could perform on their own behalves, this notwithstanding the terms of section 10(1)(b) of the Children (Scotland) Act 1995 under which the legal representative is entitled to do anything which the child, if of full age and capacity, could do in relation to the child's property. There are a number of acts with legal effect that a legal representative is unable to perform on behalf of the child, even in relation to the child's property, and any purported performance of such an act will be void and of no effect.

15.58   First, a legal representative cannot make a will on behalf of the child. The age for testamentary capacity in modern Scots law is 12 years for both males and females and over both heritable and moveable property[17] and, since the act of testation cannot be carried out on behalf of a child without testamentary capacity, it follows that any child who dies before attaining the age of 12 necessarily dies intestate. The making of a will is the exercise of a most personal discretion and it is something that cannot be delegated to another,[18] and which cannot be performed on one's behalf by another.[19] Secondly, a legal representative cannot consent on behalf of a child who is a beneficiary under a private trust to a variation of its terms or purposes. All persons under the age of 18 are deemed by the Trusts (Scotland) Act 1961 to be incapable of assenting to any proposed variation: this is expressly provided for in relation to persons aged 16 and 17 years[20]; and it is implicitly understood in relation to children under the age of 16 years (because they are in nonage). The result is that in all cases in which the

---

[16] Erskine, above.

[17] Age of Legal Capacity (Scotland) Act 1991, s. 2(2): see further, above, para. 15.07.

[18] *Rintoul's Trs v. Rintoul*, 1949 S.C. 297 at 299, *per* Lord Justice-Clerk Thomson.

[19] Erskine, I, vii, 18; Fraser (3rd ed.), p. 351.

[20] Trusts (Scotland) Act 1961, s. 1(2), as amended by the Age of Legal Capacity (Scotland) Act 1991, Sched. 1, para. 27.

consent of a person under the age of 18 years is required, the court must be asked to grant that consent on that person's behalf under section 1(1) of the 1961 Act. Thirdly, though this has nothing to do with the child's property, a legal representative has no right to consent to the adoption of his or her ward's child or to an order freeing the ward's child for adoption, unless he or she is the guardian of that child and required to consent on that basis. The adoption legislation provides[21] that the court shall not make an adoption order or a freeing order unless satisfied that the parent or guardian has freely and with full understanding of what is involved agreed unconditionally to the making of the order.[22] There is no age limit on the parent's rights and, if the parent is below 16, his or her capacity to consent to adoption, being a consent with legal effect, is determined by the Age of Legal Capacity (Scotland) Act 1991. If the under-16-year-old parent is so young as to be incapable of understanding, or does not satisfy the conditions for capacity to consent in the 1991 Act, this justifies the court dispensing with the parent's agreement[23] rather than giving the parent's legal representative the right to consent on his or her behalf.

CURATORS *AD LITEM* AND CURATORS *BONIS*

Introduction

Curatory was a lesser form of guardianship than was tutory at common law, **15.59** for it was directed at the child's estate rather than his or her person.[24] As we have seen, the Age of Legal Capacity (Scotland) Act 1991 abolished curatory on grounds of age alone.[25] It did not, however, abolish curatory as a legal institution, and that may still be used in other circumstances,[26] so while childhood alone is no longer a sufficient ground for placing one person under the curatory of another, there will remain circumstances in which it is appropriate for a person to be appointed curator of a child. The court may, in any civil proceedings, appoint a curator *ad litem* to a person under the age of 16, and nothing in the 1991 Act prevents this.[27] Where the child is mentally incapax and is likely to remain so into adulthood, or on the failure of the child's legal representative, or when it is considered necessary to supersede the legal representative, the court may appoint, for more general administrative or representative purposes, a curator *bonis*: this power too is unaffected by the 1991 Act.[28] While curators *ad litem* are not limited to children, this remains the main instance in which the appointment will be made; curators *bonis* are similarly not limited to children, but appointment as such may still in some circumstances be considered appropriate. Consequently a brief discussion of the main features of both offices is not inappropriate here. If the appointment is made in order to facilitate or

---

[21] Adoption (Scotland) Act 1978, ss. 16(1) and 18(1).
[22] See further, above, para. 4.29.
[23] Adoption (Scotland) Act 1978, s. 16(2)(a).
[24] Stair, I, vi, 35; Erskine, I, vii, 1; Bell, *Prin.*, s. 2090.
[25] Age of Legal Capacity (Scotland) Act 1991, s. 5(3).
[26] For example, to provide administration and protection of the estates of the mentally *incapax*. Neither was tutory as an institution abolished. The appointment of a tutor-dative over an *incapax* remains competent as a means of protecting or controlling the person of the *incapax*: see *Dick v. Douglas*, 1924 S.C. 787, and more recent cases reported by Ward in "Revival of Tutors-Dative," 1987 S.L.T. (News) 69 and in "Tutors to Adults: Developments", 1992 S.L.T. (News) 325. See *L v. L's Curator ad Litem*, 1997 S.L.T. 167, in which a tutor-dative was appointed expressly to consent to a particular form of medical treatment (opposed, incidentally, by the curator *ad litem*); see also *Britton v. Britton's C.B.*, 1996 S.L.T. 1272, in which a tutor-at-law was appointed to a mentally incapacitated woman.
[27] Age of Legal Capacity (Scotland) Act 1991, s. 1(3)(f)(ii).
[28] *ibid.* s. 1(3)(f)(iv).

regulate the fulfilment of parental responsibilities or the exercise of parental rights, or in relation to guardianship or the administration of a child's property, then the appointment is properly made as an order under section 11(1) of the Children (Scotland) Act 1995; otherwise the court's general protective power can be used to found the appointment. As with legal representatives, curators *ad litem* and curators *bonis* are not absolutely obliged to maintain the value of their wards' estates.[29]

Curators *ad litem*

15.60 The responsibility for instructing the conduct of actions raised on behalf of a child and of defences to actions raised against a child usually rests, of course, with the child's parent or guardian acting as his or her legal representative. There are however a number of circumstances in which a curator *ad litem* will be appointed to take over the management of the case on the child's behalf and supplant legal representatives in that function. "A curator *ad litem* is an officer appointed by the court to act for a child, or for a person labouring under some disability, so that the court may be satisfied that the case has been, and continues to be, properly conducted".[30] At one time the expression "tutor *ad litem*" was often employed and can be found in at least one statute,[31] but "curator" is the modern, and always was the better, usage. There is no personal connection with the child, nor an overall protective function such as the title "tutor" previously suggested. A curator *ad litem* cannot intermeddle with the management of the child's affairs, nor has he or she any responsibility for the child's person or estate except to take care that the case is properly conducted on the child's behalf so that the child's legitimate interests are safeguarded and, so far as may be, promoted.[32] An appointment may be made *ex proprio motu*, or at the request of a party in an appropriate case. There must be a pending *lis* and so an appointment cannot be made before an action is raised, or, in the case of a child defender, before appearance is entered.[33] The following are among the circumstances in which a curator *ad litem* might be appointed:

(1) where the child's parents are dead and he or she has no guardians[34];
(2) where an action has been raised in the child's name alone,[35] and a parent or guardian has not subsequently adopted and so validated the instance[36];
(3) where the action is by, or on behalf of, a child against his or her legal representative[37] or where it is by a legal representative against the child[38];

---

[29] See *B's C.B.*, 1996 S.L.T. (Sh.Ct) 27; *D's C.B.*, 1998 S.L.T. 2.
[30] *Cameron v. Carr's C.B.*, 1998 S.L.T. (Sh.Ct) 22, *per* Sheriff Fitzsimons.
[31] Entail Amendment Act 1848, s. 31.
[32] *Cameron v. Carr's Curator ad Litem* 1998 S.L.T. (Sh.Ct) 22 at 24K. A curator *ad litem* cannot even grant a discharge for moneys decerned in favour of a child and a factor must be appointed for that purpose. See *Pratt v. Knox* (1855) 17 D.1006; *Collins v. Eglinton Iron Co.* (1882) 9 R. 500; *Connolly v. Bent Colliery Co. Ltd* (1897) 24 R. 1172.
[33] *Inglis, Petr* (1855) 17 D. 1005; *Young, Petrs* (1828) 7 S. 220; *Baird, Petrs* (1741) Mor.16346; *Johnston v. Johnston* (1740) Mor. 16346; *Pyper* (1711) Mor. 16330.
[34] *MacNeil v. MacNeil* (1798) Mor. 16384.
[35] This is competent if the child has no legal representative, or if the legal representative is unable (whether by reason of conflict of interest or otherwise) or refuses to bring or defend such proceedings: see Age of Legal Capacity (Scotland) Act 1991, s. 1(3)(f)(i).
[36] *McConochie v. Binnie* (1847) 9 D. 791.
[37] As in, *e.g.*, *Christie's Curator Ad Litem v. Kirkwood*, 1996 S.L.T. 1299.
[38] *MacNeil v. MacNeil* (1798) Mor. 16384; *Keith v. Archer* (1836) 15 S. 116, *per* Lord Balgray at 118; *Paterson v. Sandilands* (1617) Mor. 8968; *Donaldson* (1629) Mor. 16253; *Calderhead's Trs v. Fyfe* (1832) 10 S. 582; *Studd v. Studd* (1880) 8 R. 249; (1883) 10 R. (H.L.) 53.

(4) to protect the interests of the child before a children's hearing at which one or more of the grounds of referral concern the relevant person's alleged abuse or neglect of the child[39];

(5) generally where there is a conflict of interest between the legal representative and the child[40];

(6) where a legal representative is under an incapacity or disability; and

(7) for the purpose of protecting the position of a 16- or 17-year-old child where an application is made to the court under section 1 of the Trusts (Scotland) Act 1961 to provide consent on the child's behalf to a variation of a private trust of which the child is a beneficiary.[41]

The above examples are not exhaustive. An appointment of a curator *ad litem* may be made wherever, in the opinion of the court, the child's interests so require. A parent or guardian, as legal representative, should not, however, be displaced without cause.

A curator *ad litem* makes the declaration *de fideli administratione* and then **15.61** enters on the duties of the office. As an officer of the court the curator may not, it is thought, resign without leave of the court. The appointment may be recalled by the court and comes to an end with the completion of the proceedings to which it relates unless earlier terminated by recall or death.[42]

Curators *bonis*

If a child is left without parents and guardians, or without parents and **15.62** guardians with legal capacity to act as such, or where there are grounds for superseding parents or guardians in the exercise of their responsibilities and rights to act as the child's legal representative, the court may appoint a curator *bonis*. This power of appointment is preserved by section 1(3)(iv) of the Age of Legal Capacity (Scotland) Act 1991 and will usually be made in terms of section 11(1) of the Children (Scotland) Act 1995.

Before the abolition of curatory on the ground of age alone,[43] there was **15.63** some doubt as to the effect of the appointment of a curator *bonis* to a minor child. Fraser[44] suggested that the powers of factors *loco tutoris*[45] and curators *bonis* "are the same over the estate as those of tutors and curators, *in loco* of whom they come". While that was vouched by authority in relation to factors *loco tutoris*[46] it was more doubtful in the case of curators *bonis*. As a court appointment he or she should have had the full powers of a judicial factor rather than the much more limited powers that curators had at common law over minors. Since tutory gave wide powers the problem did not arise with pupil children, and since tutory is now extended to age 16 the problem cannot today arise in relation to children under that age. A curator *bonis* today appointed to a person under the age of 16 will have the full powers of management of the estate, and the responsibilities, that a legal representative[47] and a judicial factor[48] has. In view of the full legal capacity now enjoyed by a person over the age of 16, the

---

[39] *Sloan v. B*, 1991 S.L.T. 530.

[40] *Bogie v. Bogie* (1840) 3 D. 309; *Park's Trs v. Park* (1876) 3 R. 850; *Ross v. Tennant's Trs* (1877) 5 R.182; *Galbraith's Curator Ad Litem v. Stewart*, 1997 S.L.T. 418.

[41] The power to appoint a curator *ad litem* in this situation is preserved by the Age of Legal Capacity (Scotland) Act 1991, s. 1(3)(f)(iii).

[42] On the expenses of a curator *ad litem*, see *L, Petrs (No. 4)*, 1997 S.L.T. 44.

[43] Age of Legal Capacity (Scotland) Act 1991, s. 5(3).

[44] (3rd ed.) at p. 585.

[45] Abolished by the Age of Legal Capacity (Scotland) Act 1991, s. 5(4).

[46] *Robertson v. Elphinstone*, May 28, 1814, F.C. 631; *Paul* (1838) 16 S. 822.

[47] See Children (Scotland) Act 1995, s. 10, discussed above, para. 15.36.

[48] A curator *bonis* is a judicial factor for the purposes of the Judicial Factors Act 1849: s. 1.

appointment of a curator *bonis* to a person of or above that age will be necessary only if he or she is mentally *incapax*.[49]

15.64   Previously the traditional ground for the appointment of a curator *bonis* was that a minor child had been left without parents or guardians, the parents not having nominated by testamentary deed any curators to act after their death. That situation may, of course, still arise today, but in most circumstances the appointment of a guardian under section 11(2)(h) of the Children (Scotland) Act 1995 will probably be considered more appropriate than appointing a curator *bonis*. However, it may exceptionally be considered more appropriate to appoint a curator *bonis* because his or her role is purely administrative and representational while the guardian's role involves the exercise and fulfillment of all the parental responsibilities and parental rights. A single transaction may require a person to represent the child as a matter of urgency, without that person being needed (or willing) to take on the guardianship role of parent-substitute. This might alternatively be achieved by granting the responsibility and right of legal representation to a named individual under section 11(2)(b), with powers limited to the transaction in question. As always, the child's welfare is the determining factor. Other considerations that may point to the aptness of a curator *bonis* include the parent's or guardian's bankruptcy, his or her maladministration with the child's estate (while care of the child's person is satisfactory),[50] or a conflict of patrimonial though not personal interests.[51] The appointment may also be appropriate, and preferable to appointing a legal representative under section 11(2)(b) of the 1995 Act, if it is deemed necessary to ensure that the administrative role is subject to the responsibilities of accounting and supervision contained in the Judicial Factors Act 1849. Likewise there would be advantages if the child were mentally *incapax* and likely to remain so into adulthood, for in that situation the appointment of a curator *bonis* rather than a legal representative would survive the child's attaining majority and thus obviate the need for a fresh appointment.[52]

15.65   The tenure of office of a curator *bonis* comes to an end on his or her death or the death of the child, or when the child, unless mentally *incapax*, attains the age of 16,[53] or by the resignation of the curator, or when the order making the appointment otherwise provides. Further court orders may replace the curator or terminate the curatory without replacement. Such court orders are made under section 11 of the Children (Scotland) Act 1995, and consequently are governed by the welfare of the child as the paramount consideration, no order being made unless better for the child than not making an order, and appropriate account is to be taken of the child's views.[54]

---

[49] As in, *e.g.*, *G's C.B. v. Grampian Health Board*, 1995 S.L.T. 652; *McKechnie's C.B. v. Gribbon*, 1996 S.L.T. 136; *Robertson's C.B. v. Anderson*, 1996 S.L.T. 828.
[50] *McNab v. McNab* (1871) 10 M. 248.
[51] *Earl of Buchan v. Harvey* (1839) 2 D. 275; *Cochrane, Petr* (1891) 18 R. 456.
[52] See, *e.g.*, *B's C.B.* (1997) Fam. L.B. 32–6.
[53] At which age the child can take over the administration of his or her own property: Age of Legal Capacity (Scotland) Act 1991, s. 1(1)(b).
[54] Children (Scotland) Act 1995, s. 11(7).

PART IV

PUBLIC LAW CONSEQUENCES OF THE RELATIONSHIP

CHAPTER 16

LOCAL AUTHORITY CARE OF CHILDREN

Scope of this chapter

Local authorities have a role to play in the upbringing of children in various **16.01** circumstances, primarily when the parent and child relationship has broken down or is threatened with breakdown. Their place in adoption proceedings as adoption agencies has already been noted[1] and their duties in relation to compulsory measures of supervision and emergency protection of children will be examined in some detail later.[2] In addition to these, local authorities have duties to look after children in circumstances in which there is no one else able to do so, and to provide them with accommodation. These duties are, for the most part, governed by Chapter 1 of Part II of the Children (Scotland) Act 1995, and supplemented by the still extant sections of the Social Work (Scotland) Act 1968. This chapter will examine the circumstances in which the duty of local authorities to look after children in their area arises, and the content of their duties and responsibilities towards those children whom they look after. The immediately following chapter will deal with the transference to local authorities of parental rights and responsibilities in relation to particular children.

General duty of local authorities

As part of its duty to enforce and execute the provisions of the Social Work **16.02** (Scotland) Act 1968 and Part II of the Children (Scotland) Act 1995,[3] it is the duty of every local authority to promote social welfare by making available advice, guidance and assistance on such a scale as may be appropriate for its area.[4] In addition, it must prepare and publish plans for the provision of services provided under either the Social Work (Scotland) Act 1968 or the Children (Scotland) Act 1995 for or in respect of children in its area[5] and thereafter from time to time prepare and publish information about these services which are provided by it for or in respect of children in its area or by any other local authority for those children or by voluntary organisations and other persons for those children.[6] In the exercise of any of their functions under Part II of the Children (Scotland) Act 1995, local authorities may request the help of any other local authority, a health board, a National Health Service trust and any person authorised by the Secretary of State; the body requested must comply with the request if it is not incompatible with its own statutory or other duties and obligations and does not unduly prejudice the discharge of any of its functions.[7]

---

[1] See above, Chap. 5.
[2] See below, Chaps 19 and 20.
[3] Social Work (Scotland) Act 1968, s. 1(1), as amended by the Children (Scotland) Act 1995, Sched. 4, para. 15(2).
[4] Social Work (Scotland) Act 1968, s. 12.
[5] Children (Scotland) Act 1995, s. 19.
[6] *ibid.* s. 20.
[7] *ibid.* s. 21.

16.03   It is also the duty of every local authority to (a) safeguard and promote the welfare of children in its area who are in need, and (b) so far as is consistent with that duty, promote the upbringing of such children by their families, by providing a range and level of services appropriate to the children's needs.[8] The service may be provided directly to the child in need or, if provided with a view to safeguarding or promoting the child's welfare, to the child's family or any member of the child's family.[9] A child is "in need" when he or she needs care and attention because (i) he or she is unlikely to achieve or maintain, or to have the opportunity of achieving or maintaining, a reasonable standard of health or development unless there are provided for him or her services by a local authority, (ii) his or her health or development is likely significantly to be impaired, or further impaired, unless such services are so provided, (iii) he or she is disabled, or (iv) he or she is affected adversely by the disability of any other person in his or her family.[10] In providing services to children in need the local authority must have regard, so far as practicable, to each child's religious persuasion, racial origin and cultural and linguistic background.[11] The services may include giving assistance in kind or, in exceptional circumstances, in cash, and these may be given unconditionally or subject to conditions as to repayment.[12] Provision is also made for children affected by disability, whether their own or that of any other person in their family.[13]

Children "looked after" by local authorities[14]
16.04   Local authorities owe various duties, described below, to those children they look after. A child who is "looked after" by a local authority is not necessarily a child who lives in accommodation provided by a local authority, or accommodation away from his or her parents. Regulations expressly provide that a local authority looking after a child may make arrangements for the child to be cared for by his or her own parents or other person who have parental responsibilities in relation to the child.[15] Indeed, the presumption may be that, notwithstanding that a local authority is looking after a child, the child should remain at home. This is because most children who are being looked after by a local authority will satisfy the definition of a child "in need"[16] (which includes children who are unlikely to have the opportunity of achieving or maintaining a reasonable standard of health or development unless in receipt of local authority services), and local authorities have a duty, as noted in the immediately preceding paragraph, to promote the upbringing of children "in need" by their families.[17] The fact that the child comes to be looked after by a local authority will impose duties on that authority,[18] and consequent powers necessary for the fulfilment of their duties, but it has no effect on the child's status nor on the responsibilities and rights that any other person owes to or has over the child, except in so far as any order or requirement through which the child comes to be looked after by a local authority otherwise provides or necessarily involves.

---

[8] Children (Scotland) Act 1995, s. 22(1).
[9] *ibid.* s. 22(3).
[10] *ibid.* s. 93(4)(a).
[11] *ibid.* s. 22(2).
[12] *ibid.* s. 22(3)(b) and (4). No condition of repayment may be imposed on a person in receipt of income support, family credit or an income-based jobseeker's allowance.
[13] *ibid.* ss. 23 and 24.
[14] See *The Children (Scotland) Act 1995: Regulations and Guidance*, Vol. 2, published by the Scottish Office.
[15] Arrangements to Look After Children (Scotland) Regulations 1996 (S.I. 1996 No. 3262), reg. 16(1).
[16] Children (Scotland) Act 1995, s. 93(4).
[17] *ibid.* s. 22(1)(b): this duty exists only in so far as is consistent with the local authority's duty to safeguard and promote the child's welfare.
[18] See below, paras 16.18 *et seq.*.

The question of whether a child is being looked after by a local authority **16.05** depends upon whether or not the child falls within one or other of the categories to be described in the following paragraph, and while in many cases this may appear to be a pure question of fact ("Is the child being provided with accommodation by a local authority?" or "Is the child subject to a supervision requirement?") the more correct way to look upon the issue is as a question of law. The validity of a supervision requirement or the question of whether a warrant or order imposes obligations on a local authority, both circumstances in which, as we will see, a child will be "looked after" by the local authority, are clearly matters of law; so too is the question of whether a local authority is providing a child with accommodation. Once accommodation is provided by a local authority the child remains "looked after" until the provision of accommodation is legally taken over by someone else. So local authority duties to children it is looking after do not terminate if a child is unlawfully removed from accommodation it has provided, or if the child absconds. This question was raised in sharper form than today under the pre-1995 legislation, which dealt with children "in care". Only while a child was "in care" could a parental rights resolution (the precursor to the modern parental responsibilities order) be passed and questions often arose in that context whether a child who, in fact, had been removed from local authority care remained legally "in care".[19] The question might still arise today.[20] Is a local authority obliged, for example, to provide after-care[21] to a child to whom it was providing accommodation shortly before he or she reached school-leaving age but who was unlawfully removed, or who absconded, from that accommodation and was not, in fact, there at the critical date? There would be no doubt that a child, say, subject to a supervision requirement continues to be "looked after" in law by a local authority for these and other purposes even when the local authority is and has been for some time entirely unaware of the child's whereabouts and is, for that reason, in fact fulfilling none of its duties towards the child; and it is submitted that similarly a child continues to be looked after once accommodation has been provided until such time as the provision of accommodation is lawfully taken over, even when in fact the child is not being accommodated.

A child is "looked after" by a local authority whenever (a) the local authority **16.06** is providing the child with accommodation under section 25 of the Children (Scotland) Act 1995, (b) the child is subject to a supervision requirement (whether or not there is a condition of residence attached to the requirement),[22] (c) the child is the subject of an order made, or authorisation or warrant granted by virtue of Chapter 2, 3, 4 or 5 of Part II of the 1995 Act in accordance with which the local authority has responsibilities towards the child (such as a parental responsibilities order, a child protection order or a warrant granted by a children's hearing or a sheriff), and (d) the child is subject to an order made by a court in England and Wales or in Northern Ireland corresponding generally to a Scottish order under which the child would be "looked after".[23] Supervision requirements and warrants and other orders made under Part II of the 1995 Act are dealt with in some detail later and the only class of children requiring further examination here is those who are being provided with accommodation under section 25.

---

[19] See the 1st edition of this book, at pp. 421–423.

[20] Though not for the purposes of making a parental responsibilities order which, as we will see in the following chapter, is no longer dependent on the local authority having a pre-existing relationship with the child.

[21] Under ss. 29 and 30 of the Children (Scotland) Act 1995: see below, paras 16.29–16.31.

[22] Prior to the coming into force of the 1995 Act, a child subject to a supervision requirement was "in care" only for certain specified purposes: see the First Edition of this book at pp. 413–414.

[23] Children (Scotland) Act 1995, s. 17(6). It may be noted that omitted from this list are children who have been freed for adoption, towards whom the local authority have duties under the adoption legislation: see above, paras 4.62–4.63.

Provision of accommodation

16.07   Section 25(1) of the Children (Scotland) Act 1995 imposes upon local authorities an obligation to provide accommodation, which means accommodation for a continuous period of more than 24 hours,[24] for any child (*i.e.* a person under the age of 18[25]) who, residing or having been found within its area, appears to it to require this because of the satisfaction of one or more of the following conditions:

(a) No one has parental responsibility for the child. "Parental responsibility" is not defined but has the same meaning, it is submitted, as "parental responsibilities" which is defined[26] to mean those responsibilities listed in section 1(1) of the 1995 Act.[27] Because the purpose of section 25 is to provide public care for children whose private care would not otherwise be secured, this condition is satisfied only if there is no one who has any of the parental responsibilities or parental rights.

(b) The child has been lost or abandoned. Since the child must be found within the area of the local authority, "lost" means lost to the parent or guardian. "Abandoned" means left to his or her fate[28] but does not require that the circumstances create a likelihood of physical harm to the child. It is abandonment for the person with parental responsibilities to leave a child at a hospital or with a local authority or with any other person who has no duties towards the child other than those incumbent on every person who has the actual care or control of a child.

(c) The person who has been caring for the child is prevented, whether or not permanently and for whatever reason, from providing him or her with suitable accommodation or care. While the word "prevented" suggests at first sight some external influence being brought to bear on the person, the words "for whatever reason" widen out this condition so that it covers any circumstance in which the person is in fact unable to provide suitable accommodation or care. The condition is satisfied if the person is imprisoned, or made homeless, or falls ill, or is no longer able to cope with the child, or for any other reason is unable to care for or provide suitable accommodation for the child. The epithet "suitable" is to be noted, and the duty of the local authority arises when some accommodation can be provided but it is not, in the opinion of the local authority, suitable (judged subjectively, taking account of the needs of the actual child and in the light of its duty to safeguard and promote the child's welfare).

16.08   In addition to falling within one or more of these conditions, the circumstances must indicate that the child, as a result of the condition, "requires" to be accommodated. This imports a degree of necessity into the child's circumstances before the local authority's duty arises. So the local authority's duty does not arise, for example, if the person who has in fact been caring for the child can no longer do so but another person with parental responsibilities and parental rights is willing and able to do so.

16.09   Section 25 also gives the local authority a power, though not a duty, to provide accommodation for any child within its area, or for any person within its area who is at least 18 years of age but not yet 21, if it considers that to do so would safeguard or promote the child's or person's welfare.[29] This allows the

[24] Children (Scotland) Act 1995, s. 25(8).
[25] *ibid.* s. 93(2)(a).
[26] *ibid.* s. 93(1).
[27] See above, para. 8.21.
[28] *Mitchell v. Wright* (1905) 7 F. 568, *per* Lord President Dunedin at 574.
[29] Children (Scotland) Act 1995, s. 25(2) and (3).

authority to provide accommodation even when it is not necessary but in circumstances in which it is of benefit to the child, such as for a short-term period of respite outwith the family home. In determining whether, in the exercise of its discretion, a local authority should provide accommodation to a child who is "in need", as defined in section 93(4)(a), the local authority must, so far as is consistent with its duty to safeguard and promote the welfare of such children in its area, promote the upbringing of such children by their families.[30]

Whether done in response to its duty or to its power, the local authority **16.10** must, before providing the child with accommodation, have regard, so far as practicable, to the views of the child (if he or she wishes to express them), taking account of his or her age and maturity.[31] And, because a decision to provide accommodation to a child will result in the child being "looked after", the local authority are obliged before making such a decision to ascertain the views of the child, his or her parents, any person who is not a parent but who has parental rights in relation to the child and any other person whose views the authority considers relevant, regarding the question of the child being provided with accommodation; in making its decision the local authority must have regard to these views and also to the child's religious persuasion, racial origin and cultural and linguistic background.[32] These duties are particularly important in relation to the local authority providing accommodation as a matter of discretion rather than of obligation and a decision not to provide a child or young person with accommodation would be open to challenge if the authority failed to have such regard to views as the statute requires.

In large measure, section 25 is designed to provide for cases in which parental **16.11** care, or the care of guardians, has failed, whether permanently or temporarily, and there is no one else able and willing to look after the child. The lack of compulsion in these provisions is, however, to be stressed. Means for the taking of compulsory measures of supervision, or for the emergency removal of children to a place of safety, are provided for under Chapters 2 and 3 of Part II of the 1995 Act,[33] and the provisions in Chapter 1, with which we are here concerned, contain no authority to remove a child or keep him or her against the wishes of the parents.[34] Once, however, a child has been provided with accommodation, a power to keep him or her there, correlative to the duty, is, in a question with persons other than those who have parental responsibilities, implied; in a question with those who have parental responsibilities it is expressly excluded.[35]

The appropriate local authority

The duty under section 25 to provide accommodation extends only to children **16.12** within the local government area of the authority to which the duty attaches. Mere physical presence at the time the need for accommodation arises is sufficient irrespective of the child's or parent's domicile, nationality or residence, ordinary or habitual. However, if accommodation is provided in fulfilment of the duty (though not the power) to do so for a child who is ordinarily resident in the area of a local authority other than that providing the accommodation, that local authority must notify the other authority, in writing, that such provision is being made, and the other authority may at any time take over the provision of

---

[30] Children (Scotland) Act 1995, s. 22(1)(b).
[31] *ibid.* s. 25(5). Without prejudice to the generality of that rule, a child 12 years of age or more shall be presumed to be of sufficient age and maturity to form a view.
[32] *ibid.* s. 17(3) and (4).
[33] See below, Chaps 19 and 20.
[34] Subject only to a minor and short-term qualification in s. 25(7): see below, para. 16.15.
[35] Children (Scotland) Act 1995, s. 25(6).

accommodation for the child.[36] The original authority is, it would seem, unable to prevent the other authority taking over the provision of accommodation but it may require the other authority to do so, for a local authority that is providing any service to a child may request help from another local authority in the exercise of any of its functions, including the provision of accommodation, and the authority requested must comply unless to do so would unduly prejudice the discharge of any of its own functions.[37] Where a child, ordinarily resident in the area of one local authority, is provided with accommodation by another local authority, expenditure incurred by the latter is recoverable from the former.[38] In the event of dispute, questions of ordinary residence are to be determined by the Secretary of State.[39]

Type of accommodation

16.13   The local authority may choose which type of accommodation is to be provided for the child,[40] but that decision, like any decision to be made in respect of a child whom it is looking after, must be made having regard to the views of the child and various other persons and to the child's religious persuasion, racial origin and cultural and linguistic background.[41] The obligation here is to be sensitive to the fact that the child's needs and welfare are invariably influenced by these matters. The child might be placed in a domestic setting with a family other than his or her own,[42] with a relative or with any other suitable person, on such terms as to payment, by the authority or otherwise, as the authority may determine.[43] Foster placements are subject to their own detailed regulation, considered later.[44] Alternatively, the local authority may maintain the child in a residential establishment[45] or may make such other arrangements as appear to it to be appropriate.[46] The child may be placed or maintained in England and Wales or in Northern Ireland.[47] Where for any reason it appears to the local authority that it is no longer in a child's best interests to remain in a placement the local authority must make arrangements to terminate the placement as soon as is practicable in the interests of the child.[48] And a local authority may at any

---

[36] Children (Scotland) Act 1995, s. 25(4).

[37] *ibid.* s. 21.

[38] Social Work (Scotland) Act 1968, s. 86(1), as amended by the Children (Scotland) Act 1995, Sched. 4, para. 15(24). The provisions are extended to local authorities in England and Wales.

[39] Social Work (Scotland) Act 1968, s. 86(2).

[40] A consequence of this power to regulate where the child is to live is that, during the time the local authority is entitled to provide accommodation for the child, it will have "rights of custody" within the meaning of the Hague Convention on the Civil Aspects of International Child Abduction (Art. 3 thereof recognises that such rights may be held by institutions as well as by persons), with the result that it may seek the return of a child wrongfully removed outwith the U.K. See further, above, Chap. 11.

[41] Children (Scotland) Act 1995, s. 17(3) and (4). It is the child's and not the parent's religious persuasion that is important here. A very young child cannot, it is submitted, properly be said to have a religious "persuasion", for that word presupposes the ability to be persuaded. Perhaps, however, that is not quite what is meant.

[42] Arrangements to Look After Children (Scotland) Regulations 1996, reg. 16(2), prevents the local authority from placing a child, under s. 25, with his or her own parents or with a person who has parental responsibilities for the child: if it is appropriate to do so the provision of accommodation by the local authority is not necessary.

[43] Children (Scotland) Act 1995, s. 26(1)(a).

[44] See below, Chap. 18.

[45] As defined in s. 93(1). The conduct of residential establishments is governed by the Residential Establishments (Child Care) (Scotland) Regulations 1996 (S.I. 1996 No. 3256): see below, paras 18.25–18.34

[46] Children (Scotland) Act 1995, s. 26(1)(b) and (c).

[47] *ibid.* s. 26(2).

[48] Arrangements to Look After Children (Scotland) Regulations 1996, reg. 19.

time remove a child from a residential establishment in which the child was previously placed, and must do so if requested to do so by the person responsible for the establishment.[49] Its discretion to do so is normally to be exercised bearing in mind that the safeguarding and promoting of the child's welfare is its paramount concern,[50] but it may act inconsistently with this duty if to do so is necessary for the purpose of protecting members of the public, including other children in the residential establishment, from serious harm.[51]

Duration and termination of duty and power to accommodate
Section 25(1) of the 1995 Act obliges local authorities to provide accommo- **16.14** dation to children but it does not oblige parents and guardians to allow their children to be so accommodated. The voluntary nature of the provision of accommodation is preserved by the rule that a local authority may not provide accommodation under section 25 if any person objects, where that person

(a) has parental responsibilities in relation to the child and the parental rights (i) to have the child living with him or her or otherwise to regulate the child's residence and (ii) to control, direct and guide the child's upbringing; and

(b) is willing and able to provide, or to arrange to have provided, accommodation for the child.[52]

The objection of any other person, however willing and able to provide accommodation for the child, is irrelevant. So, for example, a local authority is not prohibited from providing accommodation to a child whose mother has abandoned him or her by the objection of his or her father where he has no parental responsibilities and parental rights in relation to his child. To be effective in terminating a local authority's duty and power to provide accommodation, a willingness on the part of a person with the appropriate parental responsibilities and parental rights must, if the child's fate is not to be left in uncertainty and practical anomalies are to be avoided, be capable of present fulfilment.[53] Accordingly, the parental wish to take over the provision of accommodation for the child terminates the local authority's duty and power to do so if, but only if, to the knowledge of the authority the parent is willing and able immediately to take over the provision of accommodation. "Ability" in this context refers only to the physical possibility of providing accommodation and the absence of any legal constraint in doing so. It does not entitle the local authority to enter into an assessment of the suitability of the accommodation that the parent proposes to provide.[54] It should, however, be noted that the prohibition on providing accommodation in the face of a relevant objection is not absolute. The relevant objection merely removes the local authority's power to provide accommodation under section 25 and it does not remove any power to do so that is referable to any other statutory provision, such as, for example, providing

---

[49] Children (Scotland) Act 1995, s. 32.

[50] *ibid.* s. 17(1)(a).

[51] *ibid.* s. 17(5). A child who is violent to other children, or who seeks to recruit them for immoral purposes, may be removed from a residential establishment notwithstanding that it is contrary to his or her own welfare to do so.

[52] Children (Scotland) Act 1995, s. 25(6)(a).

[53] A parent may give notice that he or she will be willing to take over the provision of accommodation for the child at some specified point in the future. The local authority's duty and power continues until that point, and beyond it if the parent is then no longer willing and able to provide accommodation.

[54] Such an assessment was, on the other hand and as noticed above, implicit in the local authority's original acquisition of the duty to provide accommodation.

residential accommodation under a supervision requirement or keeping the child in a place of safety under a warrant or order made under a provision in another chapter of Part II of the 1995 Act. If the local authority believes that the child's welfare would be threatened by ending the provision of accommodation, it is entitled, and may even be bound, to activate the compulsory or interim measures set out in these chapters to ensure the child's welfare.[55]

16.15 The prohibition on providing accommodation to a child when a person entitled to do so objects does not apply in two circumstances. First, when the child is at least 16 years old and he or she agrees to be provided with accommodation then the authority may do so even against the objection of a person with parental responsibilities and parental rights who is willing and able to provide the child with accommodation.[56] It is considered at that time that the child's wishes to be accommodated are more important than a parent's wishes to terminate the provision of accommodation, and should be given precedence. This rule is, however, redundant in any case, for once the child being accommodated reaches the age of 16 years there is no person with the parental right to have the child living with him or her or otherwise to determine the child's residence, or the parental right to control, direct or guide the child's upbringing and no person, therefore, able relevantly to object to the local authority providing accommodation to the child. Secondly, the authority may provide accommodation in the face of a relevant objection when a person in whose favour a residence order has been made under section 11 of the Children (Scotland) Act 1995 so agrees.[57] A person "in whose favour" a residence order has been made means, normally a person who would not otherwise than under such an order have the parental right to determine the child's residence, for a residence order is never made "in favour" of a person with the right of residence —rather it regulates how that pre-existing right is to be exercised.[58] It is, however, anomalous that the local authority may provide accommodation with the consent of a person who traces his or her right to regulate the child's residence to a court order made under section 11(2)(c) of the 1995 Act but may not do so with the consent of a person whose identical right is traced to section 2(1)(a) of the 1995 Act.[59] This is the only provision in the Children (Scotland) Act 1995 in which a

---

[55] The previous law was contained in s. 15 of the Social Work (Scotland) Act 1968, under which local authorities had a duty to "receive into care" children in circumstances similar to those in which they are now obliged to provide accommodation, but that provision was subject to the qualification that "nothing in this section shall authorise a local authority to keep a child in their care under this section if any parent or guardian desires to take over the care of the child, and the local authority shall in all cases where it appears to them consistent with the welfare of the child so to do, endeavour to secure that the care of the child is taken over" by the parent or guardian (s. 15(3)). In *Central Regional Authority v. B*, 1985 S.L.T. 413 Lord Robertson, citing *Lewisham London Borough Council v. Lewisham Juvenile Court Justices* [1980] A.C. 273, described the effect of this provision as follows: "Difficulty, however, arises where the local authority is of the opinion that return of such a child to the care of the parent would be contrary to the interests and welfare of the child. In such circumstances the local authority must keep the child against the wishes of the parent, under some other statutory power" (1985 S.L.T. at 417). Though the old s. 15(3) specifically referred to the child's welfare while s. 25 of the 1995 Act does not, the result is the same under both provisions since the duties in s. 25 must be carried out by local authorities in a manner consistent with their duties under s. 17(1) and in particular the duty to have the safeguarding and promoting of the child's welfare as their paramount concern: s. 17(1)(a).

[56] Children (Scotland) Act 1995, s. 25(7)(a).

[57] *ibid.* s. 25(7)(b).

[58] See above, para. 9.9.

[59] The issue would arise only when there is more than one person with parental responsibilities and parental rights in relation to the child. If one objects to, and the other agrees to, the local authority providing accommodation for the child then the dispute is resolved in favour of the person agreeing to local authority accommodation if his or her right of residence comes from s. 11(2) but is resolved in favour of the objector (always assuming he or she is willing and able to provide the child with accommodation) if the person agreeing has a right of residence under s. 2.

person with a residence order is treated more favourably than a person with residence rights acquired in other ways, and its rationale is difficult to identify.

Any person who is entitled to object to the local authority providing **16.16** accommodation to the child may at any time remove the child from such accommodation as has been provided by the local authority under section 25.[60] This provision appears to apply even when the child is 16 and agrees to be accommodated, and even when a person with a residence order so agrees.[61] However, when the child is 16 there is, as pointed out above, no person with parental rights over the child and no person, therefore, who is entitled under this provision to remove the child from local authority accommodation. But there remains a potential clash when a person with a residence order consents to the child being accommodated while another person with parental rights who is willing and able to provide accommodation attempts to remove the child from local authority accommodation. The effect of the consent of a person with a residence order in his or her favour is, expressly, to disapply section 25(6)(a) (the prohibition on local authorities providing accommodation), but since the entitlement of a person, who can relevantly object to that provision, to remove the child from accommodation is contained in section 25(6)(b) that entitlement is not disapplied by another person's consent. The result is that the prohibition on the local authority providing accommodation does not apply when the person with a residence order consents (section 25(7)(b)), (in other words, it may still do so) but that it cannot resist a request for the return of the child from another person entitled to object (section 25(6)(b)). Otherwise the provision of accommodation under section 25 becomes compulsory. The only stated circumstance in which the local authority can resist a person who relevantly objects and seeks to remove the child is contained in the second part of section 25(7), under which when the child has been provided with accommodation by one or more local authorities for a continuous period of at least six months the person entitled to object may remove the child only after having given the local authority currently providing the child with accommodation at least 14 days' written notice of his or her intention to remove the child. There is a further clash of principles here, in that the local authority's power to retain the child for 14 days qualifies only the objector's right to remove the child but does not qualify the prohibition on the local authority accommodating the child. This appears to mean that the local authority must not provide accommodation to a child when a person with parental responsibilities who is willing and able to provide accommodation objects,[62] even although that person cannot remove the child from local authority accommodation immediately, because the child has been accommodated for more than six months.[63] However, it is submitted that when a child has been in local authority accommodation for more than six months, the person with parental responsibilities is not "able" to provide accommodation during the 14-day period, because they are not able to remove the child, with the result that all the conditions to make the objection relevant in section 25(6)(a) are not satisfied, thus maintaining the local authority's duty and power to provide accommodation. "Able" in that paragraph includes lack of legal constraint as well as lack of practical ability.

---

[60] Children (Scotland) Act 1995, s. 25(6)(b).

[61] s. 25(7) provides only that s. 25(6)(a) (prohibition on local authorities providing accommodation when person relevantly objects) does not apply in these circumstances. The power to remove a child is found in s. 25(6)(b).

[62] s. 25(6)(a).

[63] s. 25(7), disapplying s. 25(6)(a).

16.17   The resolution of all these difficulties must lie, it is submitted, in the local authority's paramount concern, which is its duty to safeguard and promote the child's welfare.[64] This is so notwithstanding the apparently absolute nature of the prohibition on providing accommodation, on the one hand, and of the non-application of the prohibition, on the other. It was held under provisions now repealed but with similar effect that where a parent or guardian wishes to remove a child from the care of a local authority there is not a positive duty to secure that the child is handed over.[65] As a consequence, it seems that, if the local authority considers that the return of the child would not conflict with the consideration it is bound to give to the welfare of the child and to the child's views,[66] it need take no action unless ordered to do so by the court and, in particular, need not take proceedings to recover the child from third parties, such as foster carers, who have actual control of the child at the time of the parental request.[67] In all cases, however, where it appears to be consistent with the welfare of the child so to do, the local authority must endeavour to secure the return of the child to a person who has parental responsibilities and parental rights in relation to the child and is willing and able to provide or arrange to have provided accommodation for the child.

Duties of local authorities to children they are looking after

16.18   Local authorities' duties towards the children they are looking after are, like their powers to bring children within the abmit of these duties, entirely statutory, contained mostly in the Social Work (Scotland) Act 1968, the Children (Scotland) Act 1995 and subsidiary legislation passed under both.

16.19   Where a child is looked after by a local authority, it must:

    (a) safeguard and promote his or her welfare (which shall, in the exercise of their duty to the child, be its paramount consideration);

    (b) make such use of services available for children cared for by their own parents as appears to the authority reasonable in the child's case; and

    (c) take such steps to promote, on a regular basis, personal relations and direct contact between the child and any person with parental responsibilities in relation to the child as appear to the authority to be, having regard to its duty to safeguard and promote the child's welfare, both practicable and appropriate.[68]

"Personal relations and direct contact" is broader than mere physical contact and might include, in appropriate circumstances, contact by telephone, letters or the exchange of gifts and photographs. The purpose of contact is to preserve the link between the child and those with parental responsibilities and parental rights, and to ease the eventual return home of the child. The less likely such return is, the less appropriate the promotion of regular contact will be. The contact decision may, however, not be within the competence of the local authority, if, for example, the child is within the category of a child being "looked after" because he or she is subject to a supervision requirement or an order or a warrant which contains a condition as to contact. In these circumstances the duty of the local authority is to permit such contact as the terms of the condition requires.

---

[64] s. 17(1)(a).

[65] *Krishnan v. London Borough Council of Sutton* [1970] Ch. 181.

[66] Children (Scotland) Act 1995, s. 17(1)(a), (3) and (4).

[67] See comments on *Krishnan* in *Lewisham London Borough Council v. Lewisham Juvenile Court Justices* [1980] A.C. 273.

[68] Children (Scotland) Act 1995, s. 17(1). Partly in order to allow the local authority to fulfil this final duty, any person who has parental responsibilities in relation to the child is obliged to notify the local authority of any change of his or her address: failure to do so is, indeed, an offence (s. 18).

Before making any decision, whether contact or otherwise, with respect to a **16.20** child whom it is looking after, or is proposing to look after, a local authority must, so far as is reasonably practicable, ascertain the views of the child,[69] his or her parents,[70] any person who is not the child's parent but who has parental rights in relation to the child, and any other person whose views the authority considers to be relevant[71]; and in making any such decision the local authority must have regard:

(a) to the views of the child concerned (if he or she wishes to express them);

(b) to such views as it has been able to ascertain of any of the other persons whose views had to be sought; and

(c) to the child's religious persuasion, racial origin and cultural and linguistic background.[72]

The duty is to have regard to these matters, but the decision is, of course, governed by the child's welfare.

Most children who satisfy the criteria for becoming children who are looked **16.21** after by a local authority will also come within the definition of children who are "in need".[73] This will impose the additional duties on local authorities to provide a range and level of services appropriate to the child's needs in order to safeguard and promote his or her welfare, and to promote the upbringing of such children by their families.[74]

The local authority is absolved from its duties mentioned above where this **16.22** is necessary for the purpose of protecting members of the public from serious harm (whether or not physical harm).[75] It is implicit that the source of the harm is the child him or herself. "Members of the public" mean any person other than the local authority or their agencies or employees, and include other children who are being looked after by the local authority, whether in a domestic or a residential setting.[76]

Care plans and reviews of children's cases

Even before a child begins to be looked after by a local authority, the authority **16.23** must, so far as is reasonably practicable, make a care plan to address the immediate and longer-term needs of the child with a view to safeguarding and promoting his or her welfare.[77] In drawing up the care plan for a child who is being accommodated by a local authority, the authority must obtain and record in writing information specified in the regulations.[78] In making a care plan, the

---

[69] There is no presumption here, as there is in various other statutory provisions, that a child 12 years of age or more is capable of forming a view. The child's capacity to do so is a question of fact, but a mistaken assessment of that fact leaves any decision made open to challenge.

[70] "Parent" is not defined and is not limited, therefore, to the parent with parental responsibilities and parental rights. It will include the unmarried father, the adoptive parent and the person presumed parent under s. 5 of the Law Reform (Parent and Child) (Scotland) Act 1986, or deemed or made parent under ss. 27–30 of the Human Fertilisation and Embryology Act 1990.

[71] Children (Scotland) Act 1995, s. 17(3).

[72] *ibid.* s. 17(4).

[73] *i.e.* children who are in need of care and attention because (i) he or she is unlikely to achieve or maintain, or to have the opportunity of achieving or maintaining, a reasonable standard of health or development unless there are provided for him or her services by a local authority; (ii) his or her health or development is likely significantly to be impaired, or further impaired, unless such services are so provided; (iii) he or she is disabled; or (iv) he or she is affected adversely by the disability of any other person in his or her family: s. 93(4).

[74] Children (Scotland) Act 1995, s. 22.

[75] *ibid.* s. 17(5).

[76] See n. 51 above.

[77] Arrangements to Look After Children (Scotland) Regulations 1996 (S.I. 1996 No. 3262), reg. 3(1).

[78] *ibid.* reg. 3(2) and Sched. 1.

local authority must have regard to the nature of the service to be provided, alternative courses of action, whether the local authority should seek a change in the child's status,[79] the arrangements which need to be made for the time when the child would or will no longer be looked after by the local authority, the views that have to be obtained under section 17(4) of the 1995 Act, the child's religious persuasion, racial origin and cultural and linguistic background, and any further matters relating to the child as appear to the authority to be relevant for the making of the care plan.[80] Additionally, if the child is to be accommodated by the local authority, issues of contact, health, education and the appropriateness of any residential establishment must be given regard in the care plan,[81] and the matters to be included in the plan must include the local authority's immediate and longer-term plans for the child, details of services to be provided and the respective responsibilities of the local authority, the child, any person with parental responsibility for the child and any "relevant person".[82]

16.24   If a child has been placed in accommodation by a local authority, the case of the child must be reviewed within six weeks of the date of the placement, there must be a second review within three months of the first review, and thereafter the child's case must be reviewed within six months of the previous review.[83] If the child is being looked after by a local authority but is not being accommodated by it, the first review of the child's case must be within three months of the date on which the authority began to look after the child, with subsequent reviews within six months of the previous review.[84] In addition, reviews must be held if the child's case is being referred to the reporter for a review of a supervision requirement that the child is subject to.[85] In carrying out any review, the care plan must be considered and revised as appropriate.[86]

Health requirements

16.25   So far as is reasonably practicable a local authority shall before placing a child looked after by it (i) ensure that arrangements are made for the child to be examined by a registered medical practitioner, and (ii) obtain from the practitioner who has carried out the examination a written assessment of the state of health of the child and his or her need for health care, this unless the child has been so examined and such assessment has been made within a period of three months immediately preceding the date the child began to be looked after by it.[87] During the placement the local authority must ensure that arrangements are made for the child to be provided with health services, including medical and dental care and treatment.[88] If, however, the child is capable of consenting to his or her own medical treatment or examination,[89] then any examination or treatment provided under the present rules may be carried out only if the child consents.[90]

---

[79] Adoption is the only legal procedure which changes a child's formal status.
[80] Arrangements to Look After Children (Scotland) Regulations 1996, reg. 4.
[81] *ibid.* reg. 5.
[82] *ibid.* reg. 6 and Sched. 2. "Relevant person" is defined as in s. 93(2)(b) of the Children (Scotland) Act 1995.
[83] *ibid.* reg. 9(1).
[84] *ibid.* reg. 9(2).
[85] *ibid.* reg. 9(3).
[86] *ibid.* reg. 8.
[87] *ibid.* reg. 13(1).
[88] *ibid.* reg. 13(2).
[89] Under the terms of s. 2(4) of the Age of Legal Capacity (Scotland) Act 1991.
[90] Arrangements to Look After Children (Scotland) Regulations 1996, reg. 13(3).

Recovery of maintenance contributions

Where a child is being looked after by a local authority or, tautologously, is **16.26** the subject of a supervision requirement made by a children's hearing which requires the child concerned to reside in a place or places other than his or her own home,[91] the local authority acquires thereby obligations, discussed above, including necessarily the obligation to maintain the child. Contributions in respect of the child may be exacted from any natural[92] person who has parental responsibilities, within the meaning of section 1(3) of the Children (Scotland) Act 1995 in relation to the child if the child is under 16 and from the child him or herself if he or she is over 16.[93]

Visiting expenses of parents, etc.

A local authority may make payments to any parent, relative or other person **16.27** connected with a child who is being looked after by the authority in respect of travelling, subsistence or other expenses incurred in visiting the child if it appears to the authority that the parent, relative or other person would not otherwise be able to visit the child without undue hardship and that the circumstances warrant the making of the payments.[94] Like payments may be made in like circumstances to any parent, relative or other person connected with a child who had been looked after by the authority for the purposes of that person attending the funeral of the child.[95]

Death of child

If a child who is being looked after by a local authority dies, the local authority **16.28** must forthwith notify the Secretary of State and, so far as reasonably practicable, notify each parent of the child, except those with whom the child was living at the time of his or her death.[96] The local authority may cause to be buried or cremated the body of any deceased person who, immediately before his or her death, was a child being looked after by the authority.[97] The authority is not, however, to arrange for cremation where that is not in accordance with the practice of the deceased person's religious persuasion.[98] Expenses incurred under this provision and not reimbursed under the social security legislation may be recovered from the estate of the deceased person or from any person who was liable to maintain the deceased immediately before his or her death.[99]

After-care

In fulfilling their duty towards children whom they look after, local authorities **16.29** have the duty to provide advice and assistance with a view to preparing the child for when he or she is no longer looked after by a local authority.[1] This is a matter that must be part of the child's care plan.[2]

---

[91] Such a child would be "looked after" by a local authority in any case: Social Work (Scotland) Act 1968, s. 83A and Children (Scotland) Act 1995, s. 17(6)(b).
[92] This word is otiose since it is only natural persons who can have parental responsibilities, within the meaning of s. 1(3) of the 1995 Act, in relation to a child: s. 15(4).
[93] Social Work (Scotland) Act 1968, s. 78(1) and (2), as amended by the Children (Scotland) Act 1995, Sched. 4, para. 15(17).
[94] Social Work (Scotland) Act 1968, s. 29(1), as amended by the Children (Scotland) Act 1995, Sched. 4, para. 15(13).
[95] Social Work (Scotland) Act 1968, s. 29(2), as so amended.
[96] Arrangements to Look After Children (Scotland) Regulations 1996, reg. 15.
[97] Social Work (Scotland) Act 1968, s. 28(1), as amended by the Children (Scotland) Act 1995, Sched. 4 para. 15(12). *Cf.* the English decision of *R. v. Gwynedd County Council, ex p. B and Anr* [1992] All E.R. 317.
[98] *ibid.*
[99] Social Work (Scotland) Act 1968, s. 28(2).
[1] Children (Scotland) Act 1995, s. 17(2).
[2] Arrangements to Look After Children (Scotland) Regulations 1996, reg. 4.

16.30   Where it comes to the knowledge of a local authority that there is in its area any child over school age who at the time when he or she ceased to be of that age or at any subsequent time was, but no longer is, being looked after by a local authority it is the duty of the authority, unless satisfied that the welfare of the child does not so require, to advise, guide or assist the child until he or she has attained the age of 19.[3] If such a person within the area of a local authority is between the ages of 19 and 21 he or she may apply to the authority for the provision of advice, guidance and assistance and the authority may, unless it is satisfied that the person's welfare does not require it, grant that application.[4] Assistance under both these provisions may include assistance in kind or in cash.[5] Where a child to whom these provisions apply ceases to be looked after by a local authority and proposes to reside in the area of another authority the authority which was looking after the child must inform the local authority for the area in which the child proposes to reside, provided that the child consents to its doing so.[6]

16.31   Where a person, who is over school age but has not attained the age of 21, and at the time when he or she ceased to be of school age or at any subsequent time he or she was, but is no longer, looked after by a local authority, the authority may make grants to the person to enable him or her to meet expenses connected with his or her receiving education or training, as well as contributions to the costs of accommodation and maintenance in any place near the place where he or she may be employed or seeking employment or in receipt of education or training.[7] These contributions or grants may be continued beyond the person's 21st birthday until the completion of any course of education or training on which a person was engaged when he or she attained the age of 21 or on which he or she had previously been engaged and which he or she resumes as soon as practicable after an interruption occasioned by any circumstance.[8]

Enforcement of duty

16.32   Although the question of judicial intervention while a child is being looked after by a local authority has been discussed in a number of English cases,[9] there is no authority in Scotland on enforcement of the duty to accommodate or otherwise look after a child. As the duty on the local authority to accommodate arises only where "it appears to them" that the conditions stipulated in section 25(1) of the Children (Scotland) Act 1995 exist, a *bona fide* decision on whether a child should be accommodated cannot be challenged on its merits, but relief will be available by way of judicial review in the Court of Session if, in an appropriate case, the question has not been considered or if failure or refusal is coloured by irregularity or impropriety (such as the failure to have regard to the child's views or to the views of any other person which ought to have been taken into account), or represents a decision which no reasonable authority could in the circumstances have reached. If there is a clear contravention of the statute

---

[3] Children (Scotland) Act 1995, s. 29(1).
[4] *ibid.* s. 29(2).
[5] *ibid.* s. 29(3).
[6] *ibid.* s. 29(4).
[7] *ibid.* s. 30(1) and (2).
[8] *ibid.* s. 30(3).
[9] See, most recently, *R. v. East Sussex County Council, ex p. Tandy* [1998] 2 All E.R. 769, in which the House of Lords held that, once a statutory duty is established, perceived lack of resources does not provide a defence to a failure to fulfil that duty. (The House of Lords did not, indeed, accept that local authorities suffered from a lack of resources and indicated instead that they should divert resources from discretionary expenditure to mandatory expenditure.)

a convenient remedy is provided by summary petition to the Court of Session to order specific performance of the local authority's statutory duty,[10] and procedure by action for declarator and implement, available in the sheriff court as well as the Court of Session, is probably also competent.[11] Local authority duties to look after children do not in themselves relate to parental responsibilities or parental rights,[12] with the result that a remedy is not available under section 11 of the Children (Scotland) Act 1995, and that the statutory direction to the court in section 11(7) of that Act to regard the welfare of the child as the paramount consideration does not apply. Nevertheless, a local authority's actions in relation to children it is looking after are legitimate only in so far as the child's welfare is its paramount concern. Negligence in carrying out its duties in relation to child care does not normally expose the local authority to civil liability to the child or his or her parents[13] but it will sometimes be just and reasonable to impose a duty of care on social workers and other members of the local authority's staff. So it was held in a case in which the act complained of (placing a child who had a history of sexually abusing other children with foster carers who had specifically indicated that they could not, for the protection of their own children, take such children) was so unreasonable as to fall outwith the ambit of discretion conferred.[14]

---

[10] Court of Session Act 1988, s. 45.

[11] *Hardie v. Walker*, 1948 S.C. 674.

[12] Though it was held in the sheriff court under the Law Reform (Parent and Child) (Scotland) Act 1986 that an action of delivery by parents against a local authority which was retaining the child against the parent's wishes was "an action relating to parental rights", and so could be resisted if the return of the child were not shown by the parents to be in the interests of the child: *M v. Dumfries and Galloway Regional Council*, 1991 S.C.L.R. 481. This was expressly departed from by Sheriff Principal Nicholson in *City of Edinburgh District Council v. M*, 1996 S.L.T. (Sh.Ct) 112 and no longer represents the law: see further, above, para. 9.57.

[13] *X v. Bedfordshire County Council* [1995] 2 A.C. 633.

[14] *W v. Essex County Council* [1998] 2 F.L.R. 278.

CHAPTER 17

TRANSFERENCE TO LOCAL AUTHORITY OF PARENTAL
RIGHTS AND RESPONSIBILITIES

INTRODUCTORY

17.01 Since 1948[1] local authorities[2] have been empowered, under certain conditions, to take over the parental rights and responsibilities in respect of children within their local government area. Such a transference of responsibilities has the effect of barring the parents and guardians of the child from exercising any of the relevant parental rights and responsibilities, and of vesting in the local authority full powers in relation to the upbringing of the child. The relationship thus created between the local authority and the child has been likened to adoption,[3] but there are a number of points of distinction, both practical and legal. An approximation to the natural relationship of parent and child, such as adoption seeks to promote, can be achieved by the body to which parental rights and responsibilities are transferred only indirectly by delegation to foster carers or, in a modified and necessarily incomplete form, by institutional care; the guarantee of permanency associated with adoption is lacking; the transfer of responsibilities and rights, although considerable, is more limited than with adoption; the status of the child is unaffected and links with the natural parents may more often be maintained than with adoption. There is, moreover, a difference in purpose. The restructuring of the child's life on what is intended to be a secure basis is integral to the adoption process whereas the transference of parental rights and responsibilities is rather a device for the protection of the child while that restructuring takes place. Adoption is the creation of a (legal) parent-child relationship which is complete for almost all legal purposes, while the transference of parental rights and responsibilities does not create such a relationship except for the purposes of bringing up the child—the other consequences of the parent-child relationship, for example in relation to succession, apply as before to the parent. In sum, the child's relationship to his or her parents is affected only in respect of the rights and responsibilities that are referable to the day-to-day care and the long-term upbringing of the child. The purpose of the transference is not to bring an end to the parent–child relationship, but to ensure that that relationship does not unduly prejudice the child. An appreciation of its protective character is the key to an understanding of some of its features.

17.02 Prior to the coming into force of Part II of the Children (Scotland) Act 1995[4] the transference of parental rights and responsibilities was effected under section 16 of the Social Work (Scotland) Act 1968. Under that provision a local authority could in certain circumstances assume to itself, by an essentially administrative process, the parental rights and powers that a particular parent possessed over a

---

[1] Children Act 1948, s. 2.
[2] *i.e.* under present legislation, councils constituted under s. 2 of the Local Government etc. (Scotland) Act 1994: 1994 Act, s. 183(2).
[3] *Re AB (An Infant)* [1954] 2 Q.B. 385.
[4] On April 1, 1997. All references in this chapter are, unless otherwise stated, to the 1995 Act.

child. This was achieved simply by the local authority passing a resolution **17.02** to that effect, which transfered the relevant rights and powers held by the parent in respect of whom the resolution was passed to the local authority itself. It was possible to assume one parent's parental rights and powers while leaving the other parent's untouched, though that would be unusual; it was not, however, possible to pass a resolution in respect of a child unless that child was already statutorily in the "care" of the local authority.[5] The procedure was frequently, though not invariably, a prelude to adoption. There was no need for any court process before the resolution was made, and the assumption of parental rights and powers took effect immediately. However, if the parent wished to challenge it this could be done by counter-notice the result of which was to put the onus on the local authority to take the matter to the sheriff court within 14 days for confirmation of the resolution, failing which the resolution fell.[6] These provisions were all repealed in Schedule 5 to the Children (Scotland) Act 1995, and are replaced with an entirely new procedure,[7] governed by Chapter 4 of Part II of the 1995 Act, under which a local authority which wishes to take over the parental responsibilities and parental rights relating to a child (*i.e.* a person under the age of 18 years)[8] may apply to the sheriff court for a "parental responsibilities order". Such an order has the effect of transferring to the local authority the appropriate parental rights and responsibilities relating to the child in respect of whom the order is made. The new rules represent a radical reshaping of the statutory procedure for local authority acquisition of parental responsibilities and parental rights.[9]

MAKING THE ORDER

Making the application

A parental responsibilities order may be made by a sheriff on an application **17.03** by a local authority.[10] Before making such an application, the local authority which is considering this option must (because the effect of the order is that the child will be "looked after" by it) ascertain the views regarding whether to make the application of the child, of his or her parents, of any person who is not a parent of the child but who has parental rights in relation to the child, and any other person whose views the authority consider to be relevant.[11] In making its decision whether to apply for a parental responsibilities order the local authority must have regard so far as practicable to these views and to the child's religious persuasion, racial origin and cultural and linguistic background.[12] There is no requirement on the local authority to explore alternatives to seeking a parental responsibilities order (as there is, for example, before it makes any arrangements

---

[5] The artificial concept of "care" had become progressively more recondite before 1995 and has now been abolished completely.

[6] For full details of the process, see the 1st edition of this work, at Chap. 16.

[7] Following the recommendations of the *Child Care Law Review* (Scottish Office, October 1990), and the approach adopted in England under the Children Act 1989.

[8] s. 93(2)(a).

[9] See *The Children (Scotland) Act 1995: Regulations and Guidance*, Vol. 3 (Scottish Office).

[10] s. 86(1).

[11] s. 17(3), which applies when the local authority is "proposing to look after" a child.

[12] s. 17(4).

for the child's adoption[13]) but given the far-reaching effects of the order on the child's relationship with his or her parents or guardians the local authority is unlikely to be able to persuade the sheriff that it would be better for the child that the order be made than that none be made at all unless alternatives have been explored and been found less likely to meet the child's needs.[14]

Appointment of a curator *ad litem* and reporting officer

17.04   After the local authority has made the application for a parental responsibilities order, the sheriff must appoint a curator *ad litem* and reporting officer and, if he considers it appropriate in the circumstances, may appoint the same person to both offices.[15] The appointee does not need to be a member of the panel of curators *ad litem* and reporting officers.[16] A reporting officer may, on cause shown, be appointed prior to the lodging of the application.[17]

17.05   The duties of the reporting officer are as follows:

(a)   to witness any agreement executed within the United Kingdom by a relevant person to the making of a parental responsibilities order in respect of the child and lodge the agreement in process;

(b)   to ascertain that each relevant person who can be found understands that the effect of a parental responsibilities order would be to transfer his or her parental responsibilities and rights;

(c)   to ascertain whether there is any person other than those mentioned in the application upon whom notice of the application should be served;

(d)   to confirm that each relevant person who can be found understands the implications of a parental responsibilities order; and

(e)   to confirm that each relevant person who can be found understands that he or she may apply to the sheriff for a variation or discharge of a parental responsibilities order and understands the appropriate procedure for so applying.[18]

The reporting officer must report in writing on these matters to the sheriff within four weeks from the date of the interlocutor appointing the reporting officer, or within such other period as the sheriff in his discretion may allow.[19]

17.06   The curator *ad litem* must have regard to the welfare of the child as his or her paramount duty and must perform the following functions:

(a)   generally safeguard the interests of the child who is the subject of the application and ensure that consideration has been given to the interests of the child for the purposes of section 6 of the Adoption (Scotland) Act 1978[20];

(b)   ascertain whether the facts stated in the application are correct, except where investigation of such facts falls within the duties of the reporting officer;

---

[13] Adoption (Scotland) Act 1978, s. 6A, as inserted by the Children (Scotland) Act 1995, s. 96.

[14] It is in any case part of the child's plan, which must be drawn up for every child being looked after by a local authority (which includes children subject to parental responsibilities orders): Arrangements to Look After Children (Scotland) Regulations 1996 (S.I. 1996 No. 3262), reg. 4(1)(b).

[15] Act of Sederunt (Child Care and Maintenance Rules 1997) (hereinafter "AS 1997"), r. 2.39(1).

[16] *ibid.* r. 2.39(2).

[17] *ibid.* r. 2.39(3).

[18] *ibid.* r. 2.40(1).

[19] *ibid.*

[20] This imposes upon the curator *ad litem* the duty to take account of those factors a court considering an adoption application would consider in relation to the child's welfare: see above, paras 4.68 *et seq.*

(c)   ascertain from the child whether he or she wishes to express a view and, where the child indicates a wish to express a view, ascertain that view;

(d)   ascertain whether a parental responsibilities order would safeguard and promote the welfare of the child; and

(e)   report on the current circumstances and care of the child.[21]

The curator *ad litem* must report in writing on these matters to the sheriff within four weeks from the date of the interlocutor appointing the curator, or within such period as the sheriff in his discretion may allow.[22] Subject to any order made by the sheriff, the views of the child ascertained by the curator *ad litem* may, if the curator considers it appropriate, be conveyed to the sheriff orally.[23]

The hearing

When the reports of the reporting officer and the curator *ad litem* have been **17.07** received by the court, the sheriff must order a diet of hearing to be fixed,[24] and this must be intimated in correct form by the applicant (a) to any relevant person[25] whose whereabouts are known to him and whose agreement to the making of the parental responsibilities order is required or must be dispensed with, and (b) in the case of a child whose father is not married to the mother, to any person whose whereabouts are known to the applicant and who claims to be the father of the child but who is not the child's guardian and in respect of whom no order relating to parental rights has been made.[26] If no person entitled to appear appears and wishes to be heard, the sheriff may make the parental responsibilities order,[27] and if a person entitled to appear does appear and wishes to be heard, the sheriff may hear him or her or may order a further diet to be fixed at which the person may be heard; evidence given at any such diet is to be given in the presence of the applicant or the applicant's (*i.e.* the local authority's) solicitor.[28] After hearing the evidence and allowing such further procedure as he thinks appropriate, the sheriff must make an order granting or refusing the application.[29]

Criteria for making the order

Before making the order, the sheriff must be satisfied that one or other of **17.08** the following two circumstances exists:

(1)   That every relevant person agrees to the making of the order unconditionally, freely and with full understanding of what is involved.[30] There was no analogous provision in the Social Work (Scotland) Act 1968, which was primarily concerned with forfeiture of parental rights rather than their voluntary surrender. It will seldom be appropriate for a local authority to apply for a parental responsibilities order when there is a parent or guardian able to provide proper care for the child, and the policy of the law is strongly to discourage the voluntary surrender of parental responsibilities and parental rights. However, this provision might appropriately be used in the case of a child whose parents recognise and accept their own

---

[21] A.S. 1997, r. 2.40(2).
[22] *ibid.*
[23] *ibid.* r. 2.40(3).
[24] *ibid.* r. 2.42(1).
[25] Defined in the Children (Scotland) Act 1995, s. 86(4): see below, para. 17.10.
[26] *ibid.* r. 2.42(2).
[27] *ibid.* r. 2.43(3).
[28] *ibid.* r. 2.42(4).
[29] *ibid.* r. 2.43(1).
[30] Children (Scotland) Act 1995, s. 86(2)(a).

inability to fulfil their parental responsibilities. If there is a relevant person who does not agree unconditionally to the making of the order, the order cannot be made unless, in relation to that person, there exists one or more of the four circumstances specified in the paragraph below.

(2)   That each relevant person is a person who:

(i)   is not known, cannot be found or is incapable of giving agreement; or

(ii)   is withholding such agreement unreasonably[31]; or

(iii)   has persistently failed, without reasonable cause, to fulfil one or other of the following parental responsibilities in relation to the child, that is to say the responsibility to safeguard and promote the child's health, development and welfare or, if the child is not living with him or her, the responsibility to maintain personal relations and direct contact with the child on a regular basis; or

(iv)   has seriously ill-treated the child, whose reintegration into the same household as that person is, because of the serious ill-treatment or for other reasons, unlikely.[32] These conditions are identical to the grounds upon which parental agreement to adoption can be dispensed with by the court under section 16 or section 18 of the Adoption (Scotland) Act 1978, and a full discussion of the meaning of these conditions in that context can be found in Chapter 4. It should be remembered, however, that the purpose and nature of adoption is very different from the purpose and nature of a parental responsibilities order, the one being lifelong while the other is limited to the upbringing of the child, and the conditions must be interpreted and applied by the court in such a way as reflects this. It may well, for example, be unreasonable for a parent to withhold agreement to a parental responsibilities order but not be unreasonable for that parent to withhold consent to adoption (if, *e.g.*, the parental responsibilities order is designed to deal with a long-term but essentially temporary problem).

The onus lies on the applicant to prove the existence of one or other of the conditions but the sheriff is not obliged to make the order even when that onus is discharged.[33] In determining whether to make the order, having been satisfied that a condition for its granting exists, the sheriff must regard the welfare of the child throughout his or her childhood as his paramount consideration.[34] In addition, he must, taking account of the age and maturity of the child concerned and so far as practicable, (i) give the child an opportunity to indicate whether he or she wishes to express views, (ii) if the child does wish to express views give him or her an opportunity to do so, and (iii) have regard to such views as the child may express; a child of 12 years of age or more is presumed to be of sufficient age and maturity to form a view.[35] Where the child has indicated his or her wish to express views, the sheriff may order such procedural steps to be taken as he considers appropriate to ascertain the views of the child, and he is prohibited from making a parental responsibilities order unless an opportunity has been given for the views of the child to be obtained or heard.[36] Where the

---

[31] See *Glasgow City Council v. M*, February 12, 1999.
[32] s. 86(2)(b).
[33] "The sheriff *may* make an order": s. 86(1).
[34] s. 16(1).
[35] s. 16(2).
[36] A.S. 1997, r. 2.41(1).

views of the child have been recorded in writing, the sheriff may direct that such a written record shall (a) be sealed in an envelope marked "Views of the Child—Confidential"; (b) be available to a sheriff only; (c) not be opened by any person other than a sheriff; and (d) not form a borrowable part of the process.[37] If the child is subject to a supervision requirement the sheriff must, before deciding whether to make a parental responsibilities order, consider a report of the children's hearing drawn up at a review hearing called to provide advice in respect of the proposed application for a parental responsibilities order.[38] He must also take into consideration the report of the curator *ad litem* and the reporting officer. The sheriff must not make a parental responsibilities order unless he considers that it would be better for the child that it be made than that no order should be made at all.[39] This requires the applicant to show some positive benefit to the child from the making of the order or some disadvantage from a failure to make the order. If there is no such benefit or disadvantage then the sheriff ought not to make the order.[40] It is open to the sheriff to make an order under section 11 of the 1995 Act on an application for a parental responsibilities order[41] if he considers that it would better meet the needs of the child to have rights and responsibilities transferred to a natural person rather than an institution like a local authority. If, concurrently, applications are made both by relatives of the child under section 11 and by the local authority under section 86, the sheriff should, where possible, deal with them both together and, it is submitted, the Court of Session should not hear an application under section 11 while an application under section 86 is pending before a sheriff.

The condition founded upon by the local authority must be satisfied in respect **17.09** of each "relevant person" (as defined in the following paragraph), and the parental responsibilities order cannot be made if one of the conditions is satisfied in relation to one relevant person but neither is satisfied in relation to any other relevant person. This is a change from the position under the 1968 Act, under which the local authority resolution was passed in respect of a particular parent or guardian, and it did not affect the rights and duties of other parents and guardians.[42] The current provisions, on the other hand, provide that the order is made in relation to the child rather than the individual parents and it may be made only when one or other of the conditions is satisfied in respect of each relevant person. This emphasises that a parental responsibilities order should be sought only when there is no appropriate person willing or able properly to look after the child. A parental responsibilities order cannot be made which removes one parent's rights and responsibilities but allows the other parent's rights and responsibilities to continue.

Meaning of "relevant person"

Either condition must be satisfied in respect of each "relevant person" in **17.10** relation to the child. This is defined as "a parent of a child or a person who for the time being has parental rights in relation to the child".[43] It is to be noted that

---

[37] A.S. 1997, r. 2.41(2).

[38] s. 73(4)(c), (13) and (14) and A.S. 1997, r. 2.42(5).

[39] s. 16(3) and (4)(b)(i).

[40] Prior to the introduction of the "no-order" principle the sheriff had rather more discretion and even in the absence of positive benefit to the child he was entitled to confirm the local authority resolution assuming parental rights and powers if he considered it appropriate to do so. *cf. City of Glasgow Council v. M*, 1998 S.L.T. 1413 where the sheriff was held entitled to refuse to confirm the local authority resolution in the absence of any identifiable benefit in the order or identifiable disadvantage from the absence of the transference of parental rights and powers. The application of the no-order principle prohibits the sheriff from making the order unless it can be shown to his satisfaction that there is benefit in the order or disadvantage in not making the order.

[41] s. 11(3)(b).

[42] See the 1st edition of this work at p. 434.

[43] s. 86(4).

the word "parent" is not defined for the purposes of Part II of the 1995 Act. In the present context the word is probably[44] to be limited to those parents who have at least some parental rights and responsibilities which can be transferred, for if the parents have none it is difficult to see what interest they have in attempting to prevent the local authority from acquiring parental rights and responsibilities.[45] This interpretation would exclude any parent who has no parental responsibilities or parental rights, such as an unmarried father who lacks a section 11 order or a section 4 agreement granting him any such responsibility or right, a married father or mother whose whole parental responsibilities and parental rights have been removed by an order under section 11(2)(a) of the 1995 Act, and the parent of a child who is the subject of an order under section 18 of the Adoption (Scotland) Act 1978 freeing him or her for adoption.[46] "A person who for the time being has parental rights in relation to the child" includes the child's guardian, and will cover any person who, not being a parent,[47] has any one or more[48] of the rights listed in section 2(1) of the 1995 Act, such as any person in whose favour a residence order has been made, and the unmarried father or any other person who has a right of contact with the child under an order made in terms of section 11(2)(d).[49]

EFFECT OF THE ORDER

Introduction

17.11 Somewhat surprisingly, there is no provision in either the Children (Scotland) Act 1995 or the regulations spelling out in detail the effect that a parental responsibilities order has, though an effect broadly similar to that under the old legislation[50] may be assumed. The Act itself gives some indication of the consequences of the order, but in a number separate provisions; and some important matters are left entirely to implication.

Effect on parental responsibilities and parental rights

17.12 On the making of a parental responsibilities order the relevant person's parental responsibilities and parental rights are, it may be supposed, extinguished. This was presumed to be the effect under the 1968 Act, although it is (expressly)

---

[44] The alternative is to define "parent" as "parent" and hold that the withholding of consent by a parent without parental responsibilities and parental rights is (nearly) always unreasonable, so opening the way for dispensation with their consent.

[45] This is in contradistinction to an adoption order which affects the whole parent–child relationship and therefore gives an interest to parents who lack parental responsibilities and parental rights to agree to adoption or have their agreement dispensed with. As will be seen, below, para. 17.12, a parental responsibilities order has effect only in respect of parental rights and responsibilities and it leaves other aspects of the parent–child relationship untouched.

[46] It is expressly provided that the parent of a child who is the subject of a parental responsibilities order retains the right to agree to or decline to agree to an adoption order or an order freeing the child for adoption (s. 86(3)) but there is no analogous provision to the effect that the parent of a child free for adoption retains the right to agree or to decline to agree to the making of a parental responsibilities order. Nor is there any basis upon which an implication can be drawn from the terms of the Adoption (Scotland) Act 1978 that such a right survives a freeing order. It is, however, difficult to imagine circumstances in which a parental responsibilities order would be appropriate over a child freed for adoption.

[47] The "or" in the definition of "relevant person" is clearly disjunctive.

[48] s. 103(1).

[49] Contact rights might be acquired under various provisions in Pt II of the 1995 Act (such as, *e.g.*, as a condition attached to a child protection order under s. 58, a child assessment order under s. 55(5), and a supervision requirement under s. 70(5)(b)). None of these, however, creates the "parental right" of contact such as would make a person entitled to contact with the child a "relevant person" for present purposes. See further, above, para. 9.11.

[50] See the 1st edition of this work, at pp. 432–436.

not the effect of a care order made by the English courts under the Children Act 1989.[51] Nevertheless, it is implicit in the terminology of "transference" used throughout Chapter 4 of Part II of the 1995 Act, and it can also be assumed from the procedural similarities between this process and the adoption process. The order is described as an order transferring to the local authority which applied for it (but only during such period as the order remains in force) "the appropriate parental rights and responsibilities relating to a child".[52] This phrase is defined to mean "all parental rights and responsibilities" subject to certain specified exceptions. It is unclear whether "parental rights and responsibilities" is limited to the parental responsibilities and parental rights listed in sections 1 and 2 of the 1995 Act, though it certainly includes these.[53] The specified exceptions are not responsibilities or rights of this type, which suggests that the phrase "parental rights and responsibilities" as used in Chapter 4 of Part II is intended to be wider than the phrases "parental responsibilities" and "parental rights" as defined for the purposes of Part I. The rights and responsibilities which are transferred are, it is conceived, all those incidental to, or associated with, the exercise of parental powers for the nurture and well-being of the child and the protection of his or her person or property.[54] There are, however, other aspects of parenthood, commonly referred to as "rights" or "responsibilities" which may or may not come within the range of rights and responsibilities transferred by the order. The test, it is submitted, is whether the right or responsibility is referable to the upbringing of the child. So succession "rights" of parents are unaffected. In relation to the parents' right and duty to attend a children's hearing, this disappears on the making of a parental responsibilities order, not only because that right and duty comes within the phrase "parental rights and responsibilities" but also because the parent is no longer within the definition of "relevant person"[55] for these purposes.[56] It is less clear whether "parental rights and responsibilities" includes the duty of aliment.[57] There is no provision in the 1995 Act analogous to the now repealed section 17(6) of the Social Work (Scotland) Act 1968 to the effect that the person whose parental rights are removed is not thereby relieved of any liability to contribute to the maintenance of the child, and the amended provision for contributions towards the maintenance of children "looked after" by local authorities is expressly limited to persons with parental responsibilities.[58] It could be argued that

---

[51] Under that legislation, a person with parental responsibility does not cease to have that responsibility solely because some other person subsequently acquires parental responsibility (s. 2(6)), though on the making of a care order the local authority acquires the power to determine the extent to which a parent or guardian may meet his or her parental responsibility for the child (s. 33(3)(b)).

[52] s. 86(1).

[53] Though s. 15(4) provides that references in Pt I of the Act to a "person" holding parental responsibilities or parental rights are references to natural persons only, this does not prevent local authorities acquiring, under Pt II, responsibilities and rights of the same nature as those described in ss. 1 and 2.

[54] Although, in contrast with the English definition of parental responsibility (Children Act 1989, s. 3(1)), there is no express reference to property in the Scottish provisions, the reference to legal representation in both s. 1 and s. 2 is sufficient to embrace administration of the child's property as well as the care of his or her person.

[55] s. 93(2). It should be remembered that "relevant person" as defined for children's hearings is different from "relevant person" as defined for parental responsibilities orders.

[56] In *City of Glasgow Council v. M*, 1998 S.L.T. 1413 the Inner House accepted (at 1416L) that the right and duty of parents to attend a children's hearing transferred from a parent to a local authority on the assumption of parental rights and powers under the 1968 Act. The effect remains the same today under the 1995 Act.

[57] The terms of the Child Support Act 1991 clearly preclude local authorities being liable for child support.

[58] Social Work (Scotland) Act 1968, s. 78(1), as amended by the Children (Scotland) Act 1995, Sched. 4, para. 15(17).

alimentary obligations are within the meaning of the phrase "parental rights and responsibilities" and are therefore removed from the parent and imposed on the local authority by the making of a parental responsibilities order. It is, however, submitted that in the absence of express provision to the contrary, the alimentary and child support obligations of the parents remain. These are not directly upbringing powers, but responsibilities designed to ensure that the child's proper upbringing is secured. By obtaining a parental responsibilities order the local authority will itself acquire certain financial responsibilities, but that is no justification for absolving the parent from his or her own financial obligations towards the child.

Exceptions

17.13   The local authority in whose favour a parental responsibilities order has been made does not obtain the right to agree to or to decline to agree to the making (whether under English and Welsh, Northern Irish, or Scottish legislation) of an adoption order, the making of an order freeing the child for adoption, or the making of an order vesting parental responsibilities and parental rights in a person who intends to adopt the child abroad.[59] These rights remain with the person to whom they attached before the making of the order.

Effect on the local authority

17.14   Where a parental responsibilities order is made as respects a child, it is the duty of the local authority which applied for it to fulfil the transferred responsibilities owed to the child while the order remains in force.[60] The "transferred responsibilities" includes as a minimum the parental responsibilities listed in section 1(1) of the 1995 Act: so the authority becomes bound: (i) to safeguard and promote the child's health, development and welfare; (ii) to provide, in a manner appropriate to the stage of development of the child direction and guidance; (iii) to maintain personal relations and direct contact with the child on a regular basis[61]; and (iv) to act as the child's legal representative. It is implicit that the local authority may also exercise the parental rights which section 86(1) describes as being transferred to the local authority. The use of the words "transferred" in section 87(1) and "transferring" in section 86(1) initially suggests that the local authority obtains only those responsibilities and rights that the relevant person had immediately before the order was made, for in principle there cannot be "transferred" from a person to a local authority that which the person does not have.[62] However, the better interpretation of section 86(3) is that the local authority acquires under the order all parental rights and responsibilities apart from those expressly excepted. The effect of the order, in other words, is to remove from each of the relevant persons such parental responsibilities and parental rights as they have and to confer on the local authority all parental rights and responsibilities. It is unfortunate that this important point has been left to implication, though the implication would seem to be inevitable.

17.15   In addition to these duties, because a child who is the subject of a parental responsibilities order is a child who is "looked after" by the local authority,[63] the local authority will also be subject to the duties in section 17(1), that is to

---

[59] s. 86(3).
[60] s. 87(1).
[61] It is difficult to see how an artificial entity like a local authority can "maintain personal relations and direct contact with the child on a regular basis", but this may be taken to oblige the local authority to ensure that one of its officers or employees does so.
[62] Under the Social Work (Scotland) Act 1968 this was explicit in the terms of s. 16(3) thereof.
[63] s. 17(6)(c).

say, the duty to safeguard and promote the child's welfare; the duty to make use of such services available to children cared for by their own parents as appears reasonable; and the duty to take practical and appropriate steps to promote personal relations and direct contact between the child and those with parental responsibilities. This last is inept in relation to children subject to a parental responsibilities order since all parental responsibilities will have been transferred to the local authority itself and since contact is specifically dealt with in section 88.[64] A child who is the subject of a parental responsibilities order will almost invariably be characterised as a "child in need",[65] with the result that the local authority also becomes subject to the two duties in section 22. The first of these is to provide a range and level of services appropriate to the child's needs in order to safeguard and promote his or her welfare; merely to seek a parental responsibilities order does not in itself fulfil this obligation but is designed to give the local authority the means by which it may be fulfilled. The second is to promote the upbringing of children in need by their families, so far as is consistent with the first duty. Given the need for the order in the first place, this duty has little substantive content except, perhaps, to encourage the local authority to aim for the child's eventual reintegration into his or her family.

On acquiring parental rights and responsibilities, the local authority acquires **17.16** thereby what are described as "rights of custody" for the purposes of the Hague Convention on International Child Abduction[66]: this means that if the child is wrongfully removed to a jurisdiction outwith the United Kingdom, the local authority can seek the child's immediate and summary return.[67]

Transfer of residence to others and return to local authority

It might be thought that the transference of parental rights and responsibilities **17.17** would, by itself, be sufficient authority for the local authority to allow the child to reside with another person if that were consistent with their duty to fulfil the responsibility of safeguarding and promoting the child's health, development and welfare.[68] The matter is, however, put beyond doubt by a specific provision that notwithstanding the making of a parental responsibilities order as respects a child, the local authority may allow, either for a fixed period or until the authority otherwise determines, the child to reside with a parent, guardian, relative or friend where it appears to the authority that so to allow would be for the benefit of the child.[69] There is no definition of the word "parent" for this or any

---

[64] See below, paras 7.22–7.28.

[65] *i.e.* a child who is in need of care and attention because (i) he or she is unlikely to achieve or maintain, or to have the opportunity of achieving or maintaining, a reasonable standard of health or development unless there are provided for him or her services by a local authority; (ii) his or her health or development is likely significantly to be impaired, or further impaired, unless such services are so provided; (iii) he or she is disabled; or (iv) he or she is affected adversely by the disability of any other person in his or her family: s. 93(4).

[66] That this might be so is recognised in the terms of the Hague Convention itself: Hague Convention, Art. 3.

[67] On the Hague Convention, see above, Chap. 11.

[68] s. 1(1)(a) and s. 87(1).

[69] s. 87(2). See also the Arrangements to Look After Children (Scotland) Regulations 1996 (S.I. 1996 No. 3262), reg. 16, which permits a local authority looking after a child (which includes children subject to a parental responsibilities order) to make arrangements for the child to be cared for by his or her own parent or a person with parental responsibilities. Other than during attempts to rehabilitate the child back with his or her family, it will be an unusual case in which a parent or guardian of a child over whom a parental responsibilities order has been proved necessary will be allowed to continue to look after the child, but an appropriate example is found in *Re T (A Minor) (Care or Supervision Order)* [1994] 1 F.L.R. 103 in which a local authority with parental responsibility allowed a six month old child to remain for the time being with parents who were incapable of making proper plans for the child but who posed no immediate threat to the child's well-being.

other purpose in Part II of the 1995 Act, and though it may sometimes appropriately be defined to exclude the unmarried father,[70] in the present context, reading the words *"ejusdem generis"* with the words "guardian, relative or friend of the child" which immediately follow it, there would be no reason so to restrict it. "Parent" means parent, whether adoptive or genetic or presumed[71] or deemed[72] and it includes the parent who had previously but, due to the making of a parental responsibilities order, no longer has parental responsibilities or parental rights. Nor is the word "guardian" defined, either here or elsewhere in the Act but its normal meaning of parent-substitute appointed as guardian by a parent or guardian under section 7 or by the court under section 11(2)(h) is apt in the present context. "Relative or friend" means a person with some existing connection to the child, whether of blood or affinity in the former case or affection in the latter. In addition to this express provision, one of the rights obtained by the local authority under the order is to "regulate the child's residence"[73] the generality of which would allow the local authority to permit the child to reside elsewhere than with a parent, guardian, relative or friend. That right is not, however, unqualified. It must be exercised bearing in mind the local authority's obligation to safeguard and promote the child's welfare,[74] as well as the other duties in section 17,[75] and where the child is not to be accommodated in a residential setting the provisions in the Fostering of Children (Scotland) Regulations 1996[76] must be satisfied. There is nothing to prevent the local authority transferring the day-to-day care of the child to another local authority for the purpose of the fulfilment of their duties to look after and accommodate the child[77] and, if requested to do so, the other local authority is obliged to comply with the request provided it is compatible with their own statutory or other duties and obligations and does not unduly prejudice the discharge of any of their own functions.[78] There is express provision permitting the local authority to arrange for a child whom they are looking after[79] to be placed with a person in England and Wales or in Northern Ireland, or to be maintained in any accommodation in which a local authority in these countries are statutorily permitted to maintain children.[80] Notwithstanding that the local authority allows the child to reside with another person, parental rights and responsibilities remain at all times with the local authority which applied for and obtained the parental responsibilities order, though the other person has responsibility to do what is reasonable in all the circumstances to safeguard the child's health, development and welfare and may in particular give consent to any surgical, medical or dental treatment or procedure.[81]

17.18   The local authority in whose favour a parental responsibilities order has been made and who have permitted the child to reside with a parent, guardian, relative or friend under section 87(2) may at any time call for the return to them

---

[70] As, *e.g.*, in s. 86(4).

[71] Under the Law Reform (Parent and Child) (Scotland) Act 1986.

[72] Under the Human Fertilisation and Embryology Act 1990.

[73] s. 2(1)(a).

[74] s. 17(1)(a).

[75] In particular the duty to promote direct contact on a regular basis between the child and parent, which could be frustrated by allowing the child to reside at such a distance away from the parent that direct contact becomes practically impossible.

[76] S.I. 1996 No. 3263.

[77] For example if a residential establishment suitable to the child's needs is situated in the area of the other authority.

[78] s. 21(1) and (2).

[79] Which includes the child who is the subject of a parental responsibilities order: s. 17(6)(c).

[80] s. 26(2).

[81] s. 5.

of the child.[82] It may do so only if the notice to that effect is in writing and specifies a time, though no time-limit is laid down. It is an offence to fail to comply with this notice.[83] In its terms, this provision does not apply to cases in which the child is permitted, under the exercise of the general power such as is mentioned in section 2(1)(a), to reside with someone other than a parent, guardian, relative or friend, with the result that to rely on the general power to regulate residence necessarily carries with it a loosening of the statutory control that the local authority have over the child's whereabouts.

Other consequences

Apart from the matters relating to the upbringing of the child, the parent– **17.19** child relationship is unaffected by the making of a parental responsibilities order. For example the order has no effect on the status of the child, whose domicile and nationality remain as they were immediately before the making of the order. So too, as has already been pointed out, succession rights are unaffected, as are the rules relating to the law of incest, the forbidden degrees of marriage, and entitlement to damages under the Damages (Scotland) Act 1976. The parents retain their status for the purposes of the prohibitions upon parents contained in the Child Abduction Act 1984. On the other hand, the parent loses title to raise an action under section 11 of the Children (Scotland) Act 1995 during the currency of a parental responsibilities order.[84] However, it remains competent for a person whose title is not removed by the provisions in section 11(3) and (4) to seek a residence or a contact order in respect of a child who is subject to a parental responsibilities order, and competent for the court to make a residence or contact order, though any rights arising thereby may not be exercised in such a way as is inconsistent with the parental responsibilities order.[85]

Offences

It is a criminal offence for any person, knowingly and without lawful authority **17.20** or reasonable excuse, to do any of the following acts during the currency of a parental responsibilities order:

(i)   to fail to comply with a notice[86] requiring the return of the child to the local authority which has allowed the child to reside with a parent, guardian, relative or friend;

(ii)   to harbour or conceal a child who has run away or been taken away or whose return has been required by notice as in (i) above; or

(iii) to induce, assist or incite a child to run away or stay away from the place where he or she is being looked after or who takes away such a child from that place.[87]

Summary conviction renders the offender liable to a fine not exceeding level 5 on the standard scale or to imprisonment for a term not exceeding six months, or to both. A local authority which at the child's request provides the child with a refuge in a residential establishment both controlled or managed by it and designated by it for this purpose or which arranges for a person whose household has been approved for this purpose to provide the child with refuge in that household has not committed an offence under the above provisions so long as

---

[82] s. 87(3).
[83] s. 89(a).
[84] s. 11(3)(a)(iii) and (4)(d).
[85] s. 3(4).
[86] Served under s. 87(3).
[87] s. 89.

the child appears to it to be at risk of harm, and the same is true of a person who carries on, or is employed in the management of, a registered residential establishment so long as the local authority within whose area the establishment is situated has given its approval to the use of the establishment for these purposes.[88]

Conditions attached to the order

17.21   In making a parental responsibilities order the sheriff may impose such conditions as he considers appropriate.[89] This might include, for example, conditions as to the child's residence, education, medical treatment or even (at least in relation to younger children) the religious observances to which the child is to be exposed. A condition could determine the length of time the order is to last. The sheriff might also include conditions as to contact between the child and any other person, and this matter is dealt with below. The power of the sheriff to impose conditions is unqualified and he may therefore direct the local authority as to the nature of the care it provides, such as requiring it to accommodate the child in a particular residential establishment or to provide certain specified services to the child; the sheriff may even specify the long-term plan that he considers should be followed for the child, determining matters such as the time-scale for the child's reintegration back to his or her family.[90] In the generality of cases, however, it would be inappropriate for sheriffs to impose such detailed and rigid conditions and it will usually be in the interests of children subject to parental responsibilities orders for local authorities to be allowed such flexibility as enables them to respond immediately to rapidly changing circumstances without having to return to court seeking a variation of the order every time a new situation arises. Conditions should not require adherence to care plans but should deal only with discrete aspects of the child's day-to-day care and long-term upbringing.

Contact arrangements

17.22   During the currency of a parental responsibilities order, the local authority must allow the child reasonable contact with (a) each person who, immediately before the making of the parental responsibilities order, was a relevant person[91] as respects the child, (b) any person in whose favour a residence order or contact order was in force immediately before the making of the parental responsibilities order,[92] and (c) any person who was entitled to have the child residing with him or her under an order by a court of competent jurisdiction.[93] Though the child must be allowed reasonable contact with the stated persons, there is nothing to prevent the local authority allowing the child contact with other persons such as siblings, grandparents, foster carers and friends, so long as the authority is of the view that to do so is not inconsistent with its paramount concern, which is to safeguard and promote the welfare of the child.

---

[88] s. 38(3).

[89] s. 86(5) and A.S. 1997, r. 2.43(1).

[90] *cf.* the position in England where, on the making of a care order, the court has no power to direct the exercise of local authority functions: see *Berkshire County Council v. B* [1997] 1 F.L.R. 171, *per* Hale J. at 174D and *Re C (Interim Care Order: Assessment)* [1996] 2 F.L.R. 708, *per* Butler-Sloss L.J. at 711G.

[91] As defined in s. 86(4).

[92] This paragraph is tautologous of para. (a) since any such person would be a relevant person in any case by dint of having parental rights in relation to the child.

[93] s. 88(2). Paragraph (c) overlaps para. (b) and its practical effect is therefore limited to orders of courts outwith Scotland.

The wording of section 88(2) suggests that it is primarily for the local **17.23** authority to determine what reasonable contact is. "Reasonable" is to be determined according to all relevant factors, including in particular the wishes of the child, the welfare of the child, the long-term plans for the child, and the nature of the relationship between the child and the appropriate person. The local authority is obliged, in making decisions in relation to contact, to ascertain the views of the child, of his or her parents, and of any other person whose views the authority considers to be relevant.[94] In making the decision relating to contact the local authority must have regard so far as practicable to these views and to the child's religious persuasion, racial origin and cultural and linguistic background[95]; this suggests that the child should be allowed such contact as will preserve exposure to these aspects of his or her background. The duty to safeguard and promote the welfare of the child is here, as elsewhere, the local authority's paramount concern[96] but the fact that the obligation is to "allow" reasonable contact suggests that the presumption should be in favour of continued contact, at least with the named categories, and that this should be limited or denied altogether only when, in the light of the obligation to safeguard and promote the child's welfare, continued contact can no longer be considered to be "reasonable". This presumption is strengthened by the provision requiring local authorities to promote the upbringing of children in need (which will include nearly every child who is the subject of a parental responsibilities order) by their families.[97] It would be an infringement of Article 8 of the European Convention on Human Rights (the right to respect for family life) for the local authority to refuse to allow contact between the child and his or her family for no legitimate reason.[98]

Application to sheriff for contact order

If any person with an interest believes that reasonable contact is not being **17.24** or will not be permitted, or that what the local authority claim is reasonable is not in fact so, or if the local authority feels that it cannot otherwise resolve a dispute between itself and a person seeking contact with the child as to what is "reasonable" contact, application may be made to the sheriff for an order relating to contact between the child and any named person.[99] Such application can be made at the time of the application for the making of a parental responsibilities order,[1] or at any time while it is in force, and the sheriff may make such order even where no application has been made to him in that regard.[2] This provision is stated to apply whenever a parental responsibilities order is being made or is in force as respects a child,[3] but a necessary limitation is that the sheriff may make an order regulating contact only when a matter relating to the parental responsibilities order is before him, such as when he is considering whether to make the order under section 86(1), or is reviewing the order under section 86(5). It is submitted that this is the extent of the sheriff's power under this provision

---

[94] s. 17(3). This provision also mentions "any person who is not a parent [of the child] but who has parental rights in relation to [the child]" but there is no such person (apart from the local authority itself) during the currency of the parental responsibilities order.

[95] s. 17(4).

[96] s. 17(1).

[97] s. 22(1)(b).

[98] See *Olson v. Sweden (No. 2)* (1994) 17 E.H.R.R. 134.

[9] s. 88(3).

[1] An example under the similar English provisions can be found in *Re D and H (Care: Termination of Contact)* [1997] 1 F.L.R. 841.

[2] s. 88(4).

[3] s. 88(1).

to act *ex proprio motu* and that in particular he cannot make an order relating to contact if the need for such an order comes to his attention in some other process, such as for example a referral for proof from the children's hearing, even when the referred child is the suject of a parental responsibilities order: to hold otherwise would be to confuse two quite separate processes and indeed to usurp the role of the children's hearing. That consideration does not, however, apply to applications under section 11 and the sheriff may, it is submitted, impose or vary contact conditions on a parental responsibilities order in such proceedings[4] (just as he may make a section 11 order in an application under section 86(1)).

17.25 The sheriff may make such order as he considers appropriate as to the contact, if any, which is to be allowed between the child and any person specified in the order.[5] There is no limitation on whom the sheriff may specify in the contact order, for he may regulate contact between the child and "any person",[6] which includes (i) a person who has not applied for the order and (ii) a person who has no title to apply for the order. The sheriff has a wide discretion to make any order that he considers appropriate as to contact, but in coming to his decision, he is obliged to regard the child's welfare as his paramount consideration, to have regard to the views of the child, and to make no order unless he considers that to do so would be better for the child than making no order at all.[7] The presumption in favour of continued contact between the child and the persons with whom the local authority should allow contact is as applicable to the sheriff's decision as to the local authority's decision, but the words of Butler-Sloss L.J. are apposite: "The presumption of contact... has always to be balanced against the long-term welfare of the child and, particularly, where he will live in the future. Contact must not be allowed to destabilise or endanger the arrangements for the child and in many cases the plans for the child will be decisive."[8]

17.26 An application for a contact order may be made by the child, by the appropriate authority (*i.e.* the local authority to which parental rights and responsibilities have been transferred) or by "any person with an interest" (*i.e.* a person with a legitimate concern for the welfare of, or established connection with, the child). The child's capacity to make the application is governed by the Age of Legal Capacity (Scotland) Act 1991, sections 2(4A) and (4B) and if he or she lacks that capacity application may be made on his or her behalf by his or her legal representative. During the currency of the parental responsibilities order the local authority is, of course, the child's legal representative and so it can make the application either in its own name or on behalf of the child. The terms of the application should make it clear in which capacity the local authority is acting. Since the person whose parental responsibilities and parental rights have been removed will often be the person with whom contact would be most appropriate, there is no exclusion of that person's title to seek a contact order under section 88, as there is, for example, in section 11(3). Persons whose responsibilities and rights are removed by a parental responsibilities order are excluded from using the private law provisions in Part I to obtain back some of these responsibilities and rights in order to prevent the public law provisions in

---

[4] The class of persons with title to seek an order under s. 11 is different from the class of persons able to seek contact under s. 88.

[5] s. 88(3).

[6] *ibid.*

[7] s. 16(1)–(3). These provisions are not expressly stated to apply to contact orders under s. 88, but s. 16(1) applies to any decision of the sheriff and s. 16(2) and (3) apply when the sheriff is considering whether to make, vary or discharge a parental responsibilities order (s. 16(4)(b)(i)). An order relating to contact is either a part of the making of a parental responsibilities order or is the variation thereof.

[8] *Re B (Minors) (Termination of Contact: Paramount Consideration)* [1993] Fam. 301 at 311.

Part II being subverted. That consideration does not apply in the present context and the fact that a person whose responsibilities and rights are removed by a parental responsibilities order is one of those with whom the child is to be allowed reasonable contact[9] clearly gives that person interest to make an application under this provision.[10]

Any order made as respects contact may contain such conditions as the **17.27** sheriff considers appropriate.[11] These might relate to whether contact be supervised or unsupervised, or to the place, times, or frequency of contact, or whether it should be increased, decreased, or terminated. The sheriff may be as specific or as unspecific in these matters as he considers appropriate in the circumstances of the case, taking account of the need to regard the welfare of the child as paramount and taking appropriate account of the child's views. On the same basis, the sheriff may vary or discharge the order on the application of the child, the local authority, or any person with an interest.[12]

Termination of contact order

A contact order is dependent for its existence on the parental responsibilities **17.28** order to which it relates and it follows that when the latter ceases to have effect, so does the former (if it has not previously been discharged).[13] Any contact order made under section 11(2)(d), which will have been suspended during the currency of the parental responsibilities order, will be reactivated on the termination of the parental responsibilities order, unless that termination is as a result of the child's age or the sheriff makes a further order under section 11(2).

Variation and termination of parental responsibilities order

There are a number of different ways in which a parental responsibilities **17.29** order can be brought to an end. The consequences of termination on parental responsibilities and parental rights relating to the child vary depending on how the order comes to an end.

Court order

The sheriff may vary or discharge the parental responsibilities order on the appli- **17.30** cation of the local authority, of the child, of any person who immediately before the making of the order is a relevant person, or of any other person claiming an interest.[14] On an application for variation or discharge, the sheriff may appoint a curator *ad litem* who shall have regard to the welfare of the child as his or her paramount duty and shall (a) investigate the facts as contained in the application, (b) investigate the care of the child with regard to the promotion of his or her welfare throughout his or her life[15]; (c) ascertain from the child whether he or she wishes to express a view and, where the child does so wish, ascertain that view; and (d) report in writing thereon to the sheriff within four weeks from the date of the interlocutor appointing the curator, or within such other period as the sheriff in his discretion may allow.[16] The sheriff must regard

---

[9] s. 88(2)(a).
[10] In *Boyle v. U.K.* (1995) 19 E.H.R.R. 179 the European Commission of Human Rights had held that the pre-1989 English position that an uncle accused of sexually abusing a child had no title to apply to a court for a contact order was a violation of the right to respect for family life protected by Art. 8 of the European Convention on Human Rights. Given that the rule was altered by the Children Act 1989, the U.K. Government reached a settlement with the applicant and the European Court of Human Rights gave no judgment.
[11] s. 86(5).
[12] *ibid.*
[13] s. 88(6).
[14] s. 86(5) and A.S. 1997, r. 2.44(1). See r. 2.44(2) for the details that the application must contain.
[15] Notwithstanding that the sheriff's consideration of the child's welfare extends only to the child's childhood.
[16] A.S. 1997, r. 2.44(3).

the welfare of the child throughout his or her childhood as his paramount consideration, must take account of the child's views, and must not make any order unless he considers that it would be better for the child that the order be made than that none should be made at all.[17] In the present context the "no-order" or "minimum intervention" principle does not require no interference with existing orders but with the child's life, with the result that the onus lies on those opposing the discharge of the order. The sheriff's discretion appears in all other respects to be unfettered and he may discharge the order when a party merely seeks its variation, or vary it when discharge is sought. Unless the sheriff makes any other order[18] the effect of the discharge is to restore the status quo ante, with the restoration of parental responsibilities and parental rights to those who possessed them before the order was made and this is a matter that the sheriff must take into account in determining whether to discharge the order. Similarly, if there are extant section 11 orders which might have their effect restored by the termination of a parental responsibilities order the sheriff ought to give consideration to the question of whether they too need to be varied or terminated.

Child attaining 18 years

17.31   "Child" for the purposes of a parental responsibilities order is defined as a person under the age of 18 years[19] and if it has not been discharged earlier the order terminates when the child reaches that age.[20] It is, however, to be noted that on a child attaining the age of 16 years all the parents' and guardians' parental responsibilities except that to provide guidance come to an end,[21] as do all their parental rights.[22] The effect of a parental responsibilities order is not, it is submitted, to maintain on behalf of the local authority all these responsibilities and rights until the child who is subject to such an order is 18, otherwise the statute would have provided for them having more rights than parents. The order may last until the child is 18, but its effect can vary with time, just as the effect of the parent–child relationship varies with time. It follows that the local authority loses those responsibilities and rights in relation to a child that a parent would lose on the child's 16th birthday. On the other hand, the duties incumbent on a local authority contained in sections 17 and 22[23] remain until the child's 18th birthday[24] and it can be assumed that the local authority also retains the rights necessary to fulfil its duties under these sections. No other parental responsibilities or parental rights are reactivated by the termination of an order on the child's attaining the age of 18.

Adoption

17.32   The parental responsibilities order terminates automatically if the child becomes the subject (whether under English and Welsh, Northern Irish, or Scottish legislation) of an adoption order, the making of an order freeing the child for adoption, or the making of an order vesting parental responsibilities and parental rights in a person who intends to adopt the child abroad.[25] The

---

[17] s. 16(1)–(3) and (4)(b)(i). The procedure to be followed where the child wishes to express a view is the same as when the original application for the parental responsibilities order is made: A.S. 1997, r. 2.44(4).

[18] Which he may do under s. 11: s. 11(3)(b).

[19] s. 93(2)(a).

[20] s. 86(6)(a).

[21] s. 1(2).

[22] s. 2(7).

[23] See above, paras 16.18–16.22.

[24] s. 93(2)(a). The aftercare provisions contained in ss. 29 and 30 apply even beyond the child's 18th birthday: see above, paras 16.29–16.31.

[25] s. 86(6)(b).

making of any of these orders has the effect of vesting the relevant responsibilities and rights in either adoptive or prospective adoptive parents or adoption agencies.

Hague Convention

If an order is made for the child's return to his or her habitual residence under **17.33** the Hague Convention on the Civil Aspects of International Child Abduction, as given effect to in our law by the Child Abduction and Custody Act 1985,[26] the parental responsibilities order is terminated.[27] A decision under the 1985 Act may be made by any court in England and Wales or Northern Ireland or Scotland and its effect is to require that the child be returned "forthwith" to the country of his or her habitual residence in order that the authorities there may determine the child's long-term future. If a child who is subject to that decision is also the subject in Scotland of a parental responsibilities order (which, in practice, will be unusual) the order for return will remove the need for the parental responsibilities order to continue in effect. In this situation also, the status quo ante is restored in relation to the parental responsibilities and parental rights that persons have over the child, except in so far as they are qualified by the order for return.

European Convention

The European Convention on Recognition and Enforcement of Decisions **17.34** Concerning Custody of Children, also given effect to in this country by the Child Abduction and Custody Act 1985,[28] allows for the registration of foreign custody decisions in courts in the United Kingdom, and such registration has the effect of rendering these foreign decisions as enforceable here as analogous domestic decisions. If this occurs (anywhere in the U.K.) in respect of a "custody" decision, though not an "access" decision,[29] then any parental responsibilities order in respect of the child to whom the decision relates is terminated.[30] Again, this will be an unusual case but the rationale is that the effect of the decision being registered will be to remove the need for the protection afforded by the parental responsibilities order. The status quo ante, as qualified by the effect of the registered foreign custody decision, is restored.

APPEALS

The Children Act 1989 provides[31] for an appeal to the High Court from decisions **17.35** of magistrates' courts in England and Wales making orders placing children in the care of local authorities. Even before the coming into force of the Children Act 1989, when the vesting in local authorities of parental responsibilities was achieved by local authority resolution, the Children Act 1975 had provided an appeal to the High Court from decisions in England and Wales on the lapse or determination of resolutions.[32] The Houghton Committee,[33] upon which much of the 1975 Act was based, had recommended a right of appeal from decisions upholding local authority resolutions assuming parental rights in terms which, if only by implication, suggested that fresh statutory provision was necessary

---

[26] See above, paras 11.19–11.36.
[27] s. 86(6)(c).
[28] See above, paras 11.10–11.15.
[29] See Child Abduction and Custody Act 1985, s. 25(2).
[30] s. 86(6)(d).
[31] s. 94.
[32] ss. 58 and 63(3).
[33] Cmnd. 5107, p. 46, para. 159; p. 106, rec. 33.

in order to achieve that result in Scotland as well as in England and Wales. No right of appeal was, however, enacted for Scotland in the Children Act 1975 in respect of decisions relating to local authority assumption of parental rights and powers under the Social Work (Scotland) Act 1968, nor has any right of appeal been enacted in respect of parental responsibilities orders under the Children (Scotland) Act 1995. The omission of appeal provisions from Chapter 4 of Part II of the 1995 Act contrasts not only with the English provisions but also with the provisions in Chapters 2 and 3 of Part II of the 1995 Act.[34] There is difficulty only as regards appeals on the merits. Appeals to the sheriff principal in respect of local authority assumption of parental rights and powers under the 1968 Act had been entertained without the question of competency being raised,[35] but are difficult to reconcile with the principles generally applicable to appeals in summary applications. Despite the wide terms of section 27 of the Sheriff Courts (Scotland) Act 1907 by which appeals are governed, the statutory requirement that a matter is to be determined by the sheriff normally is taken to exclude by implication the appellate jurisdiction of the sheriff principal. A distinction is drawn for this purpose between "the sheriff" and "the sheriff court". Where the matter at issue is referred to the decision of the sheriff (as is the case with Chapter 4 of Part II of the 1995 Act) it may be decided by the sheriff or the sheriff principal but not, except in the sense that one may take over from the other, by both.[36] As section 86(1) requires "the sheriff" to be satisfied appeal to the sheriff principal would normally be regarded as incompetent. However, in *Central Regional Council v. B*,[37] decided under the 1968 Act although the issue

---

[34] See below, paras 19.96 *et seq.* Similarly, the Adoption (Scotland) Act 1978 contains no provisions for appeal, though there has never been any doubt as to the competency of appealing against the making of an adoption order, or against other decisions in that process.

[35] *Central Regional Council v. Mailley*, 1977 S.L.T. (Sh.Ct) 36. The application in that case, if properly analysed, raised, however, jurisdictional questions that are an exception to the general rule. No comment was made in the appeal in *Lothian Regional Council v. H*, 1982 SLT (Sh.Ct) 65. In *Strathclyde Regional Council v. McNair*, 1980 S.L.T. (Sh.Ct) 16 and *Strathclyde Regional Council v. T*, 1984 S.L.T. (Sh.Ct) 18 the appeals were heard under express reservation of the general question of competency.

[36] *Allen and Sons (Billposting) Ltd v. Edinburgh Corporation*, 1909 SC 70, *per* Lord Justice-Clerk Macdonald at 74 and Lord Low at 75; *Ross-shire County Council v. Macrae-Gilstrat*, 1930 SC 808, *per* Lord Sands at 812; *Balderston v. Richardson* (1841) 3D 597; *Parish of Strichen v. Goodwillie*, 1908 S.C. 835. *Obiter dicta* to the contrary in *Leitch v. Scottish Legal Burial Society* (1870) 9 M. 40 cannot be reconciled with these authorities, while the decision in *Magistrates of Portobello v. Magistrates of Edinburgh* (1882) 10 R. 130 turns on its own statutory peculiaries and, in particular, the fact that the statutory provisions on jurisdiction in Scotland were related to provisions conferring jurisdiction on "the county court" in England. Each statute must be considered on its own terms (*ibid., per* Lord Justice-Clerk Moncreiff at 137; *Kaye v. Hunter*, 1958 SC 208 *per* Lord President Clyde at 211-212). *Bone v. School Board of Parish of Sorn* (1886) 13 R. 768 and *Fleming v. Dickson* (1862) 1 M. 188 are authority for the view that the sheriff principal may intervene so as to take over the case where the sheriff has dealt with interlocutory matters but has not given final judgment. By s. 4(1) of the Sheriff Courts (Scotland) Act 1971 the word "sheriff", which formerly included "sheriff substitute" (Sheriff Courts (Scotland) Act 1907, s. 3(a)) now includes "sheriff principal". The burden of the authorities is that the conferring of a new statutory jurisdiction on "the sheriff" excludes the appellate jurisdiction of the sheriff principal unless there is a peculiarity of the statute making it clear that "the sheriff court" was intended. The conferring of jurisdiction on the sheriff is also a factor tending to exclude the appellate jurisdiction of the Court of Session, but in that context it is not conclusive (*Arcari v. Dumbarton County Council*, 1948 S.C. 62). The fact that it is the sheriff who has to be satisfied (as is the case in s. 86(2)) also tends to exclude review (cf. the interpetation of "in the opinion of the court or tribunal making the award" in *Todd v. Todd and Anr*, 1966 S.L.T. 50). *Arcari* is not authority against that view as the point, although open, appears to have been neither argued nor considered). See also *Rodenhurst v. Chief Constable, Grampian Police*, 1992 S.L.T. 104 (Court of Five Judges) in which *Arcari* was followed, *Allen & Sons (Billposting)* was distinguished, and *Kaye v. Hunter* was overruled.

[37] 1985 S.L.T. 413.

remains the same under the 1995 Act, the opinions of the judges clearly contemplated appeal from the sheriff to the sheriff principal, and in the case of Lord Stewart expressly so.[38] That case is also authority for the proposition that appeal from the sheriff court to the Court of Session is competent, unless expressly restricted (which it is not by the 1995 Act).[39]

There was never the same doubt as to the competency of appeals other than **17.36** on the merits of the case. Where the sheriff has exceeded his jurisdiction or failed to exercise it, there is a right of appeal to the sheriff principal.[40] That is probably also true of instances of incompetency, of breaches of natural justice, and of fundamental irregularity of procedure. Moreover, the jurisdiction of the Court of Session to review decisions both of administrative bodies and of inferior courts on grounds extrinsic to the merits remains unimpaired[41] and in the latter case may, where appropriate, be invoked by way of appeal as well as by reduction.[42]

EXTRATERRITORIAL AND INTERNATIONAL ASPECTS

The order discussed in this chapter raises, for the most part, no extraterritorial **17.37** questions or questions of international private law. It is domestic in character, being concerned with the regulation within Scotland of an aspect of local authority involvement in the upbringing of children. Some incidental questions of the application of foreign law and matters of jurisdiction, recognition and enforcement do, however, require consideration.

Application of foreign law

On the question of making a parental responsibilities order and also of issues **17.38** of title to seek variation or termination, it is necessary to ascertain who the child's parents, or those who have parental responsibilities and parental rights in relation to the child, are. That question, and also questions of the child's legitimacy which may arise in association with it, are, normally, referable to the law of the child's domicile as the personal law by which his or her status is determined.[43] So, for example, the question of the nature of the relationship between a child and his or her father who is not married to the mother may be referable to the child's domicile. Except that for that purpose any reference to the child's domicile, origin, residence or nationality is irrelevant. The only territorial requirement is the jurisdictional one relating to the sheriff court.[44] In *Re M (Care Orders: Jurisdiction)*,[45] it was held that jurisdiction of the English court to make a public law order for the protection of children was based on the presence of the child in England and the fact that he was habitually resident in Scotland was irrelevant (except that that fact denied the English court jurisdiction

---

[38] 1985 S.L.T. 413 at 422.

[39] See also *Marr & Sons v. Lindsay* (1881) 8 R. 784; *Magistrates of Portobello v. Magistrates of Edinburgh* (1882) 10 R. 130. Appeal from the sheriff was also taken to the Court of Session in *Lothian Regional Council v. AJF & Anr*, March 18, 1997; *City of Glasgow Council v. M*, 1998 S.L.T. 1413; and *North Lanarkshire Council v. C*, 1999 S.L.T. 238.

[40] *Leitch v. Scottish Legal Burial Society* (1870) 9 M. 40; *Roxburgh County Council v. Dalrymple's Trs* (1894) 21 R. 1063; *Leggat v. Burgh of Barrhead* (1902) 10 Sh.CtRep. 7 at 11.

[41] *Dalgleish v. Leitch* (1889) 2 White 302; *Penny v. Scott* (1894) 22 R. 5; *Heddle v. Magistrates of Leith* (1898) 25 R. 801; *Moss's Empires v. Assessor for Glasgow*, 1917 S.C. (H.L.) 1, *per* Lord Kinnear at 6. See also Walker, *Civil Remedies*, at pp. 163–172.

[42] *Allen and Sons (Billposting) Ltd v. Edinburgh Corporation*, above.

[43] See above, para. 3.69. The law of the domicile may, however, in the absence of proof to the contrary, be assumed to be the same as the law of Scotland.

[44] The sheriff whose court district includes any area of which the applicant is the local authority has jurisdiction to make a parental responsibilities order. The appropriate local authority is probably determined by the presence in its area of the child.

[45] [1997] 1 F.L.R. 456.

to make a private law order).[46] In *Re R (Care Orders: Jurisdiction)*,[47] jurisdiction was accepted on the same basis in the case of a child habitually resident outwith the United Kingdom.

Extraterritorial enforcement—criminal jurisdiction

17.39   Problems may arise where a child who is the subject of a parental responsibilities order is outwith Scotland, as may happen legally (*e.g.* where he or she is placed in foster care or in residential accommodation in England and Wales or Northern Ireland[48] or where, while still the subject of the order, he or she is permitted to reside with another person[49]) as well as where he or she absconds or is illegally removed. In relation to children taken outwith the United Kingdom the local authority may seek their return under the provisions of the Hague Convention on International Child Abduction, on the basis that the parental responsibilities order gives them "rights of custody" as there defined.[50] Scottish criminal sanctions may, moreover, be applicable. As was noted earlier in this chapter,[51] it is an offence in the case of a child in respect of whom a parental responsibilities order has been made to harbour or conceal a child who has run away or been taken away or knowingly to induce, assist or incite the child to run away or stay away. It is also an offence if a person with whom the child has been permitted to reside fails to comply with a notice requiring the return of the child. The jurisdiction of the Scottish courts and the application of Scots law depend on whether the offence can be treated as having been committed in Scotland. If the child has been taken away or induced, assisted or incited to run away while in Scotland, the offence has clearly been committed here even if the destination to which the child has been taken is furth of Scotland. If, however, the acts take place for the first time when the child is already outwith Scotland (*e.g.* if he or she is taken away from foster carers with whom he or she has been boarded out in England, or if the offence consists solely in harbouring or concealing outwith Scotland) the Scottish courts have no jurisdiction.[52]

Recognition and enforcement of analogous rights arising outside Scotland

17.40   Although contained in separate statutes, legislative provision for the transference to local authorities of parental rights and responsibilities follows a similar pattern throughout the United Kingdom. On the principle of reciprocity indicated in *Obers v. Paton's Trustees*,[53] a Scottish court would, it is submitted, be bound to recognise the care orders made in favour of an English, Welsh or Northern Irish authority under the Children Act 1989 and to grant appropriate remedies for their enforcement, by ordering delivery or otherwise, if the child were in Scotland. In the case of children who are being looked after by a local authority, are subject to an emergency protection order, or are in police protection, the courts in England and Wales and in Northern Ireland may make recovery orders[54] when a child is removed or has run away from a responsible person or is missing: in that case the order has effect in Scotland as if it had been made by the Court of Session and as if that court had had jurisdiction to make it.[55] Some

---

[46] It was left undecided whether the English court had a public law jurisdiction to make an order over a child habitually resident in England but not physically present there.
[47] [1995] 1 F.L.R. 711.
[48] s. 26(2).
[49] s. 87(2).
[50] See above, para. 11.22.
[51] Above, para. 17.20.
[52] *H.M. Advocate v. Witherington* (1881) 8 R. (J.) 41.
[53] (1897) 24 R. 719.
[54] Children Act 1989, s. 50.
[55] *ibid*. s. 50(13).

parallel may be drawn with the enforcement of residence orders but the arguments for the enforcement of rights arising under legislation in other parts of the United Kingdom corresponding to section 86 of the Children (Scotland) Act 1995 lie *a fortiori*[56] of those applying to the recognition and enforcement of foreign residence orders and the jurisdictional tests on which the recognition of these orders largely depends are inept in the context of local authority rights and responsibilities.

Institutions or legal regimes outwith the United Kingdom may have features **17.41** similar to the transference of parental rights and responsibilities in this country but an exact parallel is not to be expected. In questions of recognition and enforcement much will turn on the particular features of the foreign system. Despite the lack of a common pattern and the impossibility of appeal to the intention of a common legislature, it is submitted that the principles applicable are, however, broadly similar to those applicable to cases arising within the United Kingdom except that the analogy with residence orders and, in some instances, with adoption, may be more apt than in the United Kingdom context. In general, and subject to the controls of public policy and the welfare test, there would seem to be no objection to giving effect to measures taken according to the law of the place where the child was at the time of the making of the order or equivalent act, although restraints imposed by the law of the child's domicile may also require to be considered.

---

[56] A residence order is always open to judicial review on a change of circumstances whereas, where a child has been made subject to a parental responsibilities order, the court will be slow to intervene and indeed in the latter case will do so only to prevent clear abuse or in other exceptional circumstances.

CHAPTER 18

FOSTERING, RESIDENTIAL AND
TEMPORARY CARE OF CHILDREN

Scope of this chapter

18.01   Previous chapters have examined how the parent and child relationship is created by an adoption order,[1] and a parental order following a surrogacy arrangement,[2] as well as the duties owed by local authorities to children they are looking after,[3] and how parental rights and responsibilities are transferred to local authorities.[4] The immediately following chapters will examine in what circumstances compulsory measures of supervision can be exercised over children,[5] and the orders giving interim protection to children at risk of harm.[6] This chapter is concerned with the control of temporary arrangements for the care and well-being of children through fostering and other forms of temporary care. Fostering is always, and temporary care may be, on a residential basis but the law controls both that and the non-residential care of children. This chapter will examine, first private fostering arrangements, secondly different forms of local authority provision for the care of children (including fostering as an aspect thereof) and thirdly the controlled forms of non-residential child care, that is child minding and day care of young children.

PRIVATE FOSTERING OF CHILDREN

Introduction

18.02   Fostering may take one of two forms: (1) it may be the subject of private arrangement, or (2) it may be the means by which a local authority fulfils its duty to look after children. Each form is the subject of separate statutory regulation. In both cases it is convenient to speak of "foster children" and "foster parents" although in the case of private arrangements the relevant statute employs the term "foster child" but not "foster parent"[7] while the reverse is true of local authority fostering. The term "foster carer" is becoming more widely used[8] and is adopted in this work in both contexts as more accurately reflecting the nature of the relationship between carer and child. Private arrangements will be considered immediately hereafter, while fostering as a means whereby local authorities accommodate children whom they are looking after is considered later.[9]

---

[1] Above, Chaps 4 and 5.
[2] Above, Chap. 6.
[3] Above, Chap. 16.
[4] Above, Chap. 17.
[5] Above, Chap. 19.
[6] Above, Chap. 20.
[7] The Regulations do, however, refer in this context to "foster parent": see Foster Children (Private Fostering) (Scotland) Regulations 1985 (S.I. 1985 No. 1798).
[8] See, *e.g.*, the Fostering of Children (Scotland) Regulations 1996 (S.I. 1996 No. 3263). The term is also preferred in the Scottish Office *Children (Scotland) Act 1995, Regulations and Guidance*, Vol. 2, p. 46. Some local authorities employ the phrase "community carers".
[9] Below, paras 18.21 *et seq.*

Private arrangements for the care, on a residential but temporary or at least uncertain basis, of children by those who have no parental responsibilities or parental rights in relation to the child, hereinafter referred to as "fostering", **18.03** are governed by the Foster Children (Scotland) Act 1984.[10] Before 1968, the legislation dealing with the fostering of children had been concerned with the control of fostering only where it was undertaken for reward. That concern had its origin in the gross abuses associated in the nineteenth century with "baby farming". Experience had, however, shown that abuses might arise even where the care of a child is undertaken without reward or provision for reward. Moreover, difficulties might often occur in ascertaining whether or not there was an element of reward in a fostering arrangement. The Social Work (Scotland) Act 1968[11] remedied these defects by removing most of the references to reward. The only relevance of "reward" remaining in the 1984 Act is that a person who maintains a foster child for reward is deemed for the purposes of the Life Assurance Act 1774 to have no interest in the life of the child[12] (with the result that any policy taken out by him or her on the life of the child is void).

The relationship between foster carer and foster child is not a parent and child relationship in the full sense but, though it does not involve parental **18.04** responsibilities and parental rights, it does involve obligations of care on the part of the foster carer. Any person who has the care or control of a child but does not have parental responsibilities or parental rights in relation to the child has the responsibility to do what is reasonable in all the circumstances to safeguard the child's health, development and welfare, and in fulfilling that responsibility the person may give consent to the child's surgical, medical or dental treatment or procedure.[13] Foster carers who ordinarily have charge of or control over the child will also be "relevant persons" for the purposes of proceedings before the children's hearings.[14]

Meaning of "foster child"

A foster child, within the meaning of the Foster Children (Scotland) Act 1984, is a child below the upper limit of compulsory school age whose care is **18.05** undertaken by a person who is not a relative or guardian of the child.[15] "Relative" means a grandparent, brother, sister, uncle or aunt, whether of the full blood or half blood or by affinity, and includes, where the child is illegitimate, the father of the child and any person who would be a relative if the child were the legitimate child of his or her father and mother.[16] "Guardian" is not defined, but, in the absence of indication to the contrary, may be taken to mean a person who has been appointed to be guardian of the child, either under section 7 of the Children (Scotland) Act 1995 (testamentary deed of a deceased parent or guardian) or section 11(2)(h) thereof (court order), or under any predecessor of these provisions. This definition of "foster child" is wide and would, if unqualified, embrace many who would not in ordinary usage be so described. It is, however, qualified in a number of respects. First, a child is not a foster child for the purpose of the statutory provisions at present under consideration while he or

---

[10] This Act consolidates legislation, most of which was previously contained in the Children Act 1958, as amended. The 1958 Act was repealed by the 1984 Act.

[11] Sched. 1, para. 2(1), amending the Children Act 1958, s. 2(1).

[12] Foster Children (Scotland) Act 1984, s. 18.

[13] Children (Scotland) Act 1995, s. 5(1). See further, above, paras 8.15–8.16.

[14] *ibid.* s. 93(2)(b). Carers in a private fostering arrangement clearly do not act as such by reason only of employment.

[15] *ibid.* s. 1, as amended by the Children Act 1989, Sched. 12, para. 41.

[16] *ibid.* s. 21(1).

she is being looked after[17] by a local authority or is boarded out by an education authority.[18] Secondly,[19] a child is not a foster child while he or she is in the care[20] of any person

    (a) in premises in which any parent, adult relative or guardian of his or her is, for the time being, residing;

    (b) in any residential establishment[21];

    (c) in any school within the meaning of the Education (Scotland) Act 1980[22];

    (d) in any hospital or in any nursing home registered or exempted from registration under the Nursing Homes Registration (Scotland) Act 1938;

    (e) in any home or institution maintained by a public or local authority; or

    (f) if he or she has been in that person's care for a period of less than 28 days and that person does not intend to undertake his or her care for any longer period. The effect of this is that, subject to the other qualifications, a child falls into the category of a foster child if his or her care is undertaken by another person for 28 days or more. Control of foster carers, and thus protection of foster children, is available before the completion of 28 days if the foster carer's intention is to care for the child beyond that time. Otherwise the provisions of the Act do not apply, so preserving the general policy that casual short-term arrangements should not be subject to local authority supervision.

18.06   Thirdly, a child is not a foster child while he or she is in the care of any person in compliance with a supervision order within the meaning of the Children and Young Persons Act 1969 in England and Wales, or a supervision requirement (under Part II of the Children (Scotland) Act 1995), or a probation order.[23] Fourthly, a child is not a foster child while he or she is liable to be detained, or subject to guardianship, under the Mental Health (Scotland) Act 1984.[24] And fifthly, a child is not a foster child while he or she is placed in the care and possession of prospective adopters under arrangements made by an adoption agency.[25]

The child's age

18.07   Although it is only children below the upper limit of compulsory school age who come within the statutory definition of "foster child", a child who is already a foster child and who has attained that age will remain subject to the protection

---

[17] Within the meaning of s. 17 of the Children (Scotland) Act 1995: Foster Children (Scotland) Act 1984, s. 2(6), as inserted by the 1995 Act, Sched. 4, para. 35(2).

[18] Foster Children (Scotland) Act 1984, s. 2(1), as amended by the Children (Scotland) Act 1995, Sched. 4, para. 35(2). Education authorities in England and Wales appear to be contemplated. The provision for children who are looked after by local authorities covers children fostered by Scottish local authorities.

[19] Foster Children (Scotland) Act 1984, s. 2(2).

[20] Care is undertaken when it is in fact provided but the continuity of a period of care is not interrupted by a weekend break spend at the parents' home: *Surrey County Council v. Battersby* [1965] 2 Q.B. 194.

[21] *i.e.* an establishment managed by a local authority, voluntary organisation or any other person which provides residential accommodation for the purposes of the Social Work (Scotland) Act 1968 or of Pt II of the Children (Scotland) Act 1995, whether for reward or not: Foster Children (Scotland) Act 1984, s. 21(1).

[22] Where, however, a child below the upper limit of the compulsory school age resides, during school holidays, in a school other than a local authority school for a period exceeding one month, he or she is for most purposes of the Act, a foster child: Foster Children (Scotland) Act 1984, s. 16.

[23] Foster Children (Scotland) Act 1984, s. 2(3).

[24] *ibid.* s. 2(4).

[25] *ibid.* s. 2(5).

of the Act unless (a) he or she would, apart from the age limit, have ceased to be a foster child: or (b) he or she has reached the age of 18; or (c) he or she is living elsewhere than with the person with whom he or she was living when he or she attained the upper age limit.[26]

Disqualification

Unless the disqualifying fact has been disclosed to the local authority and **18.08** its written consent obtained, no one may maintain a foster child if[27]:

(a) an order has been made against him or her under the Foster Children (Scotland) Act 1984 or the Foster Children Act 1980 removing a child from his or her care;

(b) a child has been removed from his or her care by virtue of an order made under the Children and Young Persons legislation[28] or a supervision requirement made under the Social Work (Scotland) Act 1968 or section 70 of the Children (Scotland) Act 1995;

(c) he or she has been convicted of any of certain specified offences against children and young persons,[29] or has been placed on probation or discharged absolutely or conditionally for any such offence;

(d) his or her parental rights and powers with respect to a child have been vested in a local authority[30] or his or her parental rights and responsibilities have been transferred to a local authority by an order under section 86 of the Children (Scotland) Act 1995;

(e) a local authority has made an order under the Nurseries and Child Minders Regulation Act 1948[31] refusing or cancelling his or her registration under the Act or the registration of any premises occupied by him or her;

(f) an order has been made under any of the Adoption Acts[32] for the removal of a "protected child" who was being kept or was about to be received by him or her; or

(g) he or she is disqualified from fostering a child privately, within the meaning of the Children Act 1989, by regulations made under section 68 of that Act.[33]

The disqualification extends to any person living in the same premises as the person disqualified or in premises at which he or she is employed.[34] Any disqualified person who maintains a foster child commits an offence,[35] but it is a defence for anyone disqualified by virtue of living in premises in which a disqualified person lives or is employed to show that he or she did not know and had no reasonable ground for believing that a disqualification applied to that person.[36]

---

[26] Foster Children (Scotland) Act 1984, s. 17.

[27] *ibid*. s. 7, as amended by the Children Act 1989, Sched. 12, para. 43 and the Children (Scotland) Act 1995, Sched. 4, para. 35(4).

[28] Children and Young Persons Acts 1933 and 1969 or the Children and Young Persons (Scotland) Act 1937.

[29] Specified in Sched. 1 to the Criminal Procedure (Scotland) Act 1995, or in the corresponding statutory provisions for England and Wales (Children and Young Persons Act 1933, Sched. 1).

[30] Under s. 16 of the Social Work (Scotland) Act 1968, or under s. 2 of the Children Act 1948 or ss. 2 or 3 of the Child Care Act 1980.

[31] s. 1(3) or (4) or s. 5.

[32] Adoption Act 1958, s. 43; Adoption Act 1976, s. 34; Adoption (Scotland) Act 1978, s. 34. The "protected child" provisions have been repealed from the 1978 Act.

[33] Sched. 15 to the Children Act 1989 repeals many of the English statutory provisions mentioned above. Orders made under them remain valid.

[34] Foster Children (Scotland) Act 1984, s. 7(2).

[35] *ibid*. s. 15(1)(c).

[36] *ibid*. s. 15(2).

Visiting of foster children

18.09   The duty is laid upon the local authority of securing the welfare of foster children within its area.[37] Presence within the area is sufficient to give rise to the duty and there is no additional residential or other qualification. In order to fulfil its duty, the local authority is required to cause foster children to be visited from time to time by its officers where it considers such a course to be necessary or expedient. The officers making such visits are required to give such advice as to care and maintenance as may appear to be necessary.[38] Regulations provide[39] that a foster child is to be visited within one week of the placement or within one week of notice being given to the local authority under section 5(2), and thereafter (i) in the case of a child who has lived with the foster parent for less than one year at intervals of not more than three months, (ii) in any other case at intervals of not more than six months, (iii) and in all cases on such occasions as the local authority considers necessary. It is an offence to refuse to allow the visiting of any foster child by a duly authorised officer of a local authority,[40] and such refusal shall be treated, for the purposes of an application for a child assessment order,[41] as giving the local authority reasonable cause to suspect that the child is being so treated or so neglected that he or she is suffering, or is likely to suffer, significant harm.[42]

Notification

By prospective foster carers

18.10   A prerequisite of the discharge by the local authority of its duty in relation to foster children is that it should have sufficient knowledge of private fostering arrangements. Accordingly, anyone who proposes to maintain as a foster child a child not already in his or her care is required to give written notice not less than two weeks before he or she receives the child unless the child is received in an emergency.[43] The notice must be given to the local authority in whose area the premises in which the child is to be kept are situated and must specify these premises.[44] If a foster child is received in an emergency, the foster carer must give written notice not later than one week after reception.[45] Similarly, anyone who has in his or her care a child previously outwith the statutory definition of a foster child who becomes a foster child (*e.g.* if there has been a parent, or adult relative, or guardian residing in the premises and he or she leaves) must give written notice not later than one week after that event.[46] The duty to give notice does not apply if the child has within the last three months been maintained as a foster child by the same foster carer but ceased to be a foster child while in that person's care or on removal from his or her care.[47]

---

[37] Foster Children (Scotland) Act 1984, s. 3(1).
[38] *ibid.* s. 3(2). This might include, *e.g.*, the provision of assistance to the foster carer in dealing with any problems caused by the fact that the child has a different religious, racial, cultural or linguistic background, as was recognised in *Osborne v. Matthan (No. 2)*, 1998 S.L.T. 1264
[39] Foster Children (Private Fostering) (Scotland) Regulations 1985, reg. 7.
[40] Foster Children (Scotland) Act 1984, s. 15(1)(b)(i).
[41] Under s. 55 of the Children (Scotland) Act 1995.
[42] Foster Children (Scotland) Act 1984, s. 13, as amended by the Crime and Punishment (Scotland) Act 1997, Sched. 1, para. 1.
[43] Foster Children (Scotland) Act 1984, s. 5(1).
[44] *ibid.* s. 5(3).
[45] *ibid.* s. 5(2).
[46] *ibid.*
[47] *ibid.* s. 5(6).

By foster carers

Certain additional duties of notification are laid on foster carers. If there is a **18.11**
permanent change of address, or of the premises in which a foster child is kept,
written notice must be given not less than two weeks before or, in the case of
emergency, not later than one week after the change.[48] The new address or
premises must be specified. The notice must be given to the local authority for
the area in which the premises in which the child was kept before the change
were situated. If, however, the new premises are in the area of another local
authority, the authority to which notice was given must pass on such particulars as are known to it of the name, sex and date and place of birth of the child
and the name and address of every person who is a parent or guardian, or acts as
a guardian, of the child, or from whom the child was received. Any person
maintaining or proposing to maintain a foster child is required to furnish
these particulars so far as known to him or her, at the request of the local
authority.[49] Written notice must be given within 48 hours of the death of a
foster child or of his or her removal from the care of the foster carer, and that
notice must be given to the person from whom the child was received as well as
to the local authority. It must state, if known, the name and address of the
person, if any, into whose care the child has been removed or received. The
duty to give such notice applies in cases where the child removes him- or
herself as well as to cases where he or she is taken away by another but it
does not apply if, on removal, the child ceases to be a foster child. In the
latter event the foster carer must, however, at the request of the local
authority, give the same particulars as would have been required to be stated
in the notice.[50]

By parents

As well as the statutory obligation on foster carers to notify the local authority, **18.12**
the regulations[51] also provide that, except in an emergency, the parent of a child
whom it is proposed will become a foster child must give notice of the proposed
fostering to the local authority in whose area the premises in which the child is
to be kept are situated, not less than two weeks before the date on which the
child becomes a foster child. Where a child is placed with a foster carer in an
emergency, or becomes a foster child while in the care and possession of a
person with whom he or she has been placed, the parent of the child must give
notice thereof to the local authority in whose area the premises in which the
child is to be kept are situated, not later than one week after the child is placed
with the foster carer or becomes a foster child.[52] The notice must specify in
writing the premises in which the child is to be or is being kept, and the local
authority may require any additional information it considers necessary to
determine whether the placement is or will be appropriate to the child's needs.[53]
"Parent" in this context includes a guardian or relative of the child who has care
and possession of the child and who is proposing to place the child with a foster
carer.[54]

---

[48] Foster Children (Scotland) Act 1984, s. 5(4).
[49] *ibid.* s. 5(5).
[50] *ibid.* s. 6.
[51] Foster Children (Private Fostering) (Scotland) Regulations 1985, reg. 3(1).
[52] *ibid.* reg. 3(2).
[53] *ibid.* reg. 3(3).
[54] *ibid.* reg. 3(4).

Exemptions and offences

18.13 A local authority may exempt anyone from the duty of giving notice. The exemption may be granted as regards all or any such notices for a specified period and may be revoked at any time by notice in writing.[55] It is an offence for anyone to fail to give notice or information or to fail to give the notice timeously or to fail to give the information within a reasonable time, or knowingly to make or to cause or procure another to make any false or misleading statement in the notice or information.[56] It is also an offence to cause to be published or knowingly to publish an advertisement indicating that a person will undertake or will arrange for the care and maintenance of a child which does not state that person's name and address.[57]

Requirements and prohibitions

18.14 Where anyone keeps or proposes to keep foster children in premises used while the children are kept there, wholly or mainly for that purpose, the local authority may impose on him or her requirements as to:

(a) the number, age and sex of the foster children who may be kept at any one time on the premises or any part thereof;
(b) the accommodation and equipment to be provided for the children;
(c) the medical arrangements to be made for protecting the health of the children;
(d) the giving of particulars of the person for the time being in charge of children;
(e) the number, qualifications or experience of the persons employed in looking after the children;
(f) the keeping of records.[58]

These requirements must, after such time as the authority may specify, be complied with whenever a foster child is kept on the premises.[59] Requirements imposed under (b)–(f) above may, however, be limited by the authority so as to apply only if the number of foster children kept on the premises exceeds a specified number.[60] If, within the specified time, a requirement is not complied with, the local authority may prohibit the keeping of foster children in the premises thereafter.[61]

18.15 Under the above provisions a prohibition is competent only after a requirement has been imposed and there has been failure to comply with it within the time specified. Where foster children are already being kept in the premises, that is the only way in which a prohibition can be made against keeping these children there. In the case, however, of a child who is not already kept as a foster child in the premises, the local authority may, without the necessity of imposing any requirements in advance, prohibit the keeping of that child there as a foster child if it is of the opinion that it would be detrimental to the child to be kept there by the person proposing to do so.[62] Similarly, if the premises are not for the time being used for the keeping of a foster child by the person who proposes to keep a foster child there, a prohibition, on like grounds, may be made against keeping any foster child there.[63] It is to be noted that the question of detriment

---

[55] Foster Children (Scotland) Act 1984, ss. 5(7) and 6(4).
[56] *ibid*. s. 15(1)(a).
[57] *ibid*. ss. 14 and 15(1)(f).
[58] *ibid*. s. 9(1).
[59] *ibid*. s. 9(3).
[60] *ibid*. s. 9(2).
[61] *ibid*. s. 10(2).
[62] *ibid*. s. 10(1).
[63] *ibid*.

to the child is to be considered in relation not only to the premises but also to the foster carer. Both the physical suitability of the premises and the capacity and resources of the foster carer to care for a child there may therefore be taken into account.

Any requirement or prohibition must be imposed by a notice in writing **18.16** addressed to the person on whom it is imposed.[64] Failure to comply with a requirement or contravention of a prohibition is an offence.[65]

Inspection

The power to impose requirements and make prohibitions would be largely **18.17** nugatory without a power of inspection; so any officer of a local authority authorised to visit foster children may inspect any premises in the area of the authority in which foster children are to be, or are being kept.[66] He must, if asked to do so, produce a document showing his authorisation. The document must be duly authenticated, but the manner of authentication is not specified. It is an offence to refuse to allow inspection[67] and such refusal gives the local authority reasonable cause to suspect that the child is suffering significant harm for the purposes of an application for a child assessment order, in the same way as does refusal to allow a foster child to be visited.[68]

Appeal against requirement or prohibition

Within 14 days from the date on which he or she was notified of a requirement **18.18** or prohibition an aggrieved person may appeal to the sheriff; where the appeal is against a requirement, the requirement shall not have effect while the appeal is pending.[69] The notice of a requirement or prohibition must contain a statement informing the person to whom it is directed of his or her right to appeal and of the time within which he or she may do so. If the court allows the appeal it may, instead of cancelling the requirement or prohibition, vary it or allow more time for compliance, or, where an absolute prohibition has been imposed, substitute a prohibition against use of the premises, after a time specified by the court, unless there is compliance with such specified requirements as the local authority had power to impose.[70] Any requirement or prohibition specified or substituted by the court shall be deemed for the purposes of the Act other than appeal to have been imposed by the local authority.[71] In England and Wales provision is made for an appeal to the High Court,[72] but there is no Scottish provision for an appeal from the sheriff's decision. Such an appeal may, however, be open on principles already discussed,[73] even in the absence of express statutory provision, either to the sheriff principal or direct to the Court of Session.

Cancellation of requirement or prohibition

It has been specifically enacted for England and Wales that a local authority **18.19** may, if it thinks fit, cancel, on the ground that it is no longer justified, a prohibition (other than a prohibition made in respect of non-compliance with a requirement) and may do so either of its own motion or on the application of the person on

---

[64] Foster Children (Scotland) Act 1984, s. 10(3).
[65] *ibid.* s. 15(1)(d).
[66] *ibid.* s. 8.
[67] *ibid.* s. 15(1)(b)(ii).
[68] *ibid.* s. 13; above, para. 18.09.
[69] *ibid.* s. 11(1).
[70] *ibid.* s. 11(2).
[71] *ibid.* s. 11(3).
[72] Children Act 1989, s. 94.
[73] Above, para. 17.35

whom the prohibition was imposed.[74] There is no corresponding provision for Scotland. Accordingly, there can be no right to apply for a cancellation and no right to appeal against refusal to accede to an application for cancellation. It is thought, however, that the power to make a prohibition carries with it, as a facultative power, an implied power to revoke.

Removal of foster children

18.20 The sanctions attaching to the maintaining of foster children by disqualified persons and to non-compliance with requirements and contravention of prohibitions do not give any direct protection to the child. Provision is accordingly made that if a sheriff is satisfied on the complaint of a local authority that a foster child is being kept, or is about to be received (a) by any person who is unfit to have his or her care, or (b) in contravention of a disqualification imposed by the Act or of a prohibition from keeping foster children or a foster child imposed by a local authority, or (c) in any premises or any environment detrimental or likely to be detrimental to the child, he may make an order for removal of the child to a place of safety[75] until the child can be restored to a parent, relative or guardian, or until other arrangements can be made with respect to him or her.[76] On proof that there is imminent danger to the health or well-being of the child, the power to make such an order may be exercised by a justice of the peace acting on the application of a person authorised to visit foster children.[77] Where an order is made on the ground that a prohibition imposed by a local authority has been contravened, it may require the removal from the premises of all the foster children kept there.[78] It is an offence to refuse to comply with an order for the removal of any child or obstruct any person in the execution of such an order.[79] Any child removed under these provisions is regarded as requiring the provision of accommodation on the ground that the person who has been caring for him or her is prevented from providing suitable accommodation, with the result that the local authority has a duty to provide that child with accommodation.[80] The implication from the fact that a child in a place of safety requires accommodation is that he or she should be removed from the place of safety to suitable accommodation as soon as possible, unless the place of safety is itself suitable accommodation. In any event, the local authority must, if practicable, inform a parent or guardian of the child, or any person who acts as his or her guardian, of his or her removal.[81] In addition, the interim protection measures contained in Part II of the Children (Scotland) Act 1995[82] may be utilised in appropriate circumstances.

LOCAL AUTHORITY FOSTERING

Introduction

18.21 The only kind of fostering so far considered has been the private fostering arrangement. The term may, however, also be used to describe one of the ways in which local authorities may discharge their duty to provide accommodation for children whom they look after. In fulfilling their duties to foster children,

---

[74] Children Act 1989, s. 69(4).
[75] As defined in s. 21(1) of the Foster Children (Scotland) Act 1984.
[76] Foster Children (Scotland) Act 1984, s. 12(1).
[77] *ibid*. s. 12(2).
[78] *ibid*. s. 12(3).
[79] *ibid*. s. 15(1)(e).
[80] *ibid*. s. 12(5).
[81] *ibid*. s. 12(6).
[82] Described in detail below, Chap. 20.

local authorities must have as their paramount concern their duty to safeguard and promore the child's welfare and must take such steps to promote, on a regular basis, personal relations and direct contact between the child and any person with parental responsibilities in relation to him or her as appear to the local authority to be, having regard to its paramount concern, both practicable and reasonable.[83] Before making any decision, whether to place a child with foster carers or to alter that arrangement, the local authority must, so far as reasonably practicable, ascertain the views of the child, his or her parents, any other person who has parental rights in relation to the child, and any other person whose views the authority considers to be relevant regarding the matter to be decided.[84] In making any such decision, a local authority must have regard, so far as practicable, to (i) the views (if he or she wishes to express them) of the child concerned, taking account of his or her age and maturity, (ii) such views as it has been able to ascertain of the persons mentioned in the preceding sentence, and (iii) the child's religious persuasion, racial origin and cultural and linguistic background.[85] The last-mentioned obligation requires the local authority to take these matters into account in determining a placement, but it does not oblige it to provide a placement with persons of the same racial, cultural or linguistic background as the child. The Scottish Office Guidance goes too far, it is submitted, when it says "where a child is placed with foster carers, his or her carers must be of the same religious persuasion as the child or must undertake to bring him or her up in his or her religious persuasion".[86] The obligation in the Act is to "have regard" to these matters and this is fulfilled if the local authority gives them appropriate weight in the decision-making process and within the context of the child's welfare being paramount, bearing in mind that disruption to patterns of religious observances to which the child is accustomed is likely to interfere with the child's welfare.[87]

The Fostering of Children (Scotland) Regulations 1996

Section 5(3) of the Social Work (Scotland) Act 1968 provides for the making **18.22** of regulations regarding the provision by local authorities of accommodation for children looked after by them. It is noteworthy and in contrast to the legislation on private fostering, which is applicable to a variety of residential arrangements including those in which the element of a domestic setting is lacking,[88] that the scope of the regulations here under consideration is confined to cases where the child lives as a member of the family of the person with whom he or she is placed. Residential accommodation provided by local authorities or voluntary organisations otherwise than by placing in a domestic familial context is the subject of separate statutory treatment, considered shortly.

The regulations,[89] which came into operation on April 1, 1997, make **18.23** provision for the appointment and composition of fostering panels,[90] whose functions are to consider the suitability of prospective foster carers and to make

---

[83] Children (Scotland) Act 1995, s. 17(1). This is subject to any condition of contact contained in the order under which the child becomes a looked after child.

[84] *ibid.* s. 17(3).

[85] *ibid.* s. 17(4).

[86] *The Children (Scotland) Act 1995: Regulations and Guidance* (Scottish Office), Vol. 2, p. 6.

[87] Examples where following the Scottish Office Guidance on this point would be detrimental to the child are not difficult to envisage: the child might have been removed from his or her family because of the physical and emotional dangers their adherence to an extreme sect has created for the child.

[88] Above, para. 18.02.

[89] Fostering of Children (Scotland) Regulations 1996 (S.I. 1996 No. 3263). See *The Children (Scotland) Act 1995: Regulations and Guidance* (Scottish Ofice), Vol. 2, Chap. 3.

[90] Fostering of Children (Scotland) Regulations 1996, regs 4 and 5.

recommendations to the local authority thereupon[91]; for the approval of foster carers by a local authority[92]; reviews and termination of approval[93]; for the entering into agreements between the local authority with the foster carers regarding the foster carer's obligations[94]; and for the payment of allowances to foster carers, which may be subject to such conditions as the local authority considers necessary, taking into account the needs and circumstances of the foster carer with whom the child is placed.[95] The regulations also detail the arrangements to be made by a local authority for the placing in a foster placement of a child looked after by it[96]; the nature and terms of the foster placement agreement which must be entered into between the local authority and the foster carer[97]; the limitations on the composition of the household of the prospective foster carer[98]; and the circumstances in which emergency and immediate placements of children with foster carers can be made.[99] The regulations also make provision[1] for local authorities, either individually or jointly, to enter into arrangements with voluntary organisations, whereby the voluntary organisations discharge on the local authorities' behalf their duties in relation to fostering under the regulations.

Restrictions on removal

18.24   The absence of statutory provision detailing when a local authority may terminate or vary a foster placement indicates that the matter lies entirely within its discretion (subject always to its general duties under section 17(1)–(5) of the Children (Scotland) Act 1995[2]). The freedom with which a local authority may terminate a foster placement reflects the view that foster carers are the agents or delegates of the authority which is looking after the child and that restrictions on the power to secure the return of the child would fetter the authority's exercise of its responsibility to those whom it is looking after and so put the welfare of the child at risk. The criticism may, on the other hand, be made that the way is open to arbitrary disturbance of long-standing arrangements and to administrative abuse and that the legitimate interests of foster carers are insufficiently protected. It is submitted, however, that arbitrary action or abuse of powers is open to judicial review on application to the Court of Session.

Provision of residential accommodation

Residential establishments

18.25   Maintaining a child in a residential establishment is the principal alternative to fostering by which a local authority may discharge its duty to provide accommodation for a child looked after by it . The term "residential establishment", in relation to a place in Scotland, means an establishment, by whomever

---

[91] Fostering of Children (Scotland) Regulations 1996, reg. 6.
[92] *ibid*. reg. 7.
[93] *ibid*. reg. 10.
[94] *ibid*. reg. 8 and Sched. 2.
[95] *ibid*. reg. 9.
[96] *ibid*. regs 10–15.
[97] *ibid*. reg. 12(2) and Sched. 3.
[98] *ibid*. reg. 12(4) and (5). The household must comprise a man and a woman living together and acting jointly, or a man or a woman living alone and acting alone, or a person living with relatives who are not concerned with the care of the child.
[99] *ibid*. regs 13 and 14.
[1] *ibid*. reg. 16.
[2] See above, para. xx.xx.
[3] Children (Scotland) Act 1995, s. 26(1)(b).

managed, which provides residential accommodation for children for the purposes of the Social Work (Scotland) Act 1968 or the Children (Scotland) Act 1995.[4] These purposes include promoting social welfare in Scotland, and in the present context a residential establishment may be classed as an establishment that provides residential accommodation for the purpose of promoting the welfare of children (including children in need of compulsory measures of supervision within the meaning of section 70 of the 1995 Act).

Duty to provide

It is the duty of a local authority to provide and maintain such residential **18.26** and other establishments as may be required for its functions under either the Social Work (Scotland) Act 1968 or Part II of the Children (Scotland) Act 1995.[5] These functions include the looking after of children and the provision of accommodation to them.[6] A local authority is not, however, obliged to provide all such establishments itself but may join with another local authority in so doing, or may secure the provision of such establishments by voluntary organisations or other persons, including other local authorities.[7] In any event local authorities, in providing accommodation for children in their care, are not restricted to residential establishments that they themselves may manage, but, by arrangement with the managers, may use establishments managed by others.[8]

Regulations

Under the Social Work (Scotland) Act 1968[9] the Secretary of State has made **18.27** regulations for the conduct of residential and other establishments and for securing the welfare of persons resident and accommodated in them.[10] Importantly, the regulations provide[11] that the managers of a residential establishment must have in place appropriate procedures to be followed in the vetting of staff in relation to their suitability to work in the establishment, both prior to their appointment and regularly thereafter. Further regulations[12] make provision concerning the care plans to be drawn up for children looked after by local authorities, whether in residential accommodation or otherwise,[13] notifications by the local authority on the placement of a child,[14] review of children's cases,[15] and monitoring and termination of placements.[16]

Registration

Anyone other than a local authority or government department which carries **18.28** on a residential establishment must be registered with the local authority,[17] or, if

---

[4] Children (Scotland) Act 1995, s. 93(1). See also Social Work (Scotland) Act 1968, s. 94(1).

[5] Social Work (Scotland) Act 1968, s. 59(1), as amended by the Children (Scotland) Act 1995, Sched. 4, para. 15(15).

[6] Children (Scotland) Act 1995, ss. 17 and 25. For details, see above, Chap. 16. The local authority is also obliged to give effect to supervision requirements (s. 71(1)), which may include a condition of residence (s. 70(3)(a)).

[7] Social Work (Scotland) Act 1968, s. 59(2).

[8] Children (Scotland) Act 1995, s. 93(1).

[9] ss. 5 and 60.

[10] Residential Establishments—Child Care (Scotland) Regulations 1996 (S.I. 1996 No. 3256).

[11] *ibid.* reg. 8.

[12] Arrangements to Look After Children (Scotland) Regulations 1996 (S.I. 1996 No. 3262): considered further, above, paras 16.23–16.24.

[13] *ibid.* regs 3–6.

[14] *ibid.* reg. 7.

[15] *ibid.* reg. 8.

[16] *ibid.* regs 18 and 19.

[17] Social Work (Scotland) Act 1968, s. 61, as amended by the Registered Establishments (Scotland) Act 1987, s. 1 and substituted by the Children (Scotland) Act 1995, s. 34(2). Any grant-aided school or independent school which performs the functions of a residential establishment may, but is not required to, apply for registration: s. 61A, as inserted by the Registered Establishments (Scotland) Act 1987, s. 2(1).

the Secretary of State so directs, in respect of any establishment or class of establishments, with the Secretary of State.[18] Unless there are grounds for refusal the authority must, on receipt of an application, register the applicant in respect of the establishment named. The registration authority, whether the local authority or the Secretary of State, may refuse to register the applicant if satisfied that:

(a) the applicant, or any person employed or proposed to be employed by him or her in the management of the establishment, is not a fit person whether by reason of age or otherwise to carry on or be employed by an establishment of that description; or

(b) for reasons connected with situation, construction, state of repair, accommodation, staffing or equipment, the establishment or any premises used in connection with it are not fit to be used for an establishment of that description; or

(c) the way in which it is proposed to conduct the establishment is such as not to provide services or facilities reasonably required by persons resorting to an establishment of that kind.[19]

18.29   Registration may be cancelled at any time, (a) on any ground that would entitle the authority to refuse an application for registration; or (b) on the ground that the registered person has either failed to notify the local authority of a change in manager[20] or been convicted of an offence under the present section or under any of the regulations made under Part III of the 1968 Act relating to the conduct of an establishment; or (c) on the ground that any other person has been convicted of such an offence in respect of that establishment; or (d) on the ground that the annual fee[21] for the continuation of registration has not been paid on the due date.[22] The person in respect of whom an establishment is registered must comply with such reasonable conditions with regard to the proper operation of the establishment as the local authority may impose, and these conditions must include conditions as to the maximum number of persons who may be accommodated at any one time in the establishment and the categories of person who may be admitted to the establishment.[23] The local authority may impose new conditions or vary any existing conditions.[24] Provision is made for appeal to an appeal tribunal[25] against the imposition of conditions on registration or subsequently.[26]

18.30   In the event of the death of the registered person, his or her executor or widow or any other member of his or her family may, for a period not exceeding four weeks from the death or such longer period as the local authority may sanction, carry on the establishment without being registered.[27]

18.31   Notice stating the grounds on which it is intended to refuse or cancel registration must be given to the person affected who may, within 14 days, inform the authority in writing of his or her desire to show cause why the registration should not be refused or cancelled, and if that is done an opportunity

---

[18] Social Work (Scotland) Act 1968, s. 63.
[19] *ibid.* s. 62(3).
[20] Which he or she is obliged to do under s. 62(4).
[21] For which see s. 64A, as added by the Registered Establishments (Scotland) Act 1987, s. 6(1).
[22] Social Work (Scotland) Act 1968, s. 62(4C), as similarly added (s. 3).
[23] *ibid.* s. 62(5).
[24] *ibid.* s. 62(5A), as similarly added.
[25] Established under Sched. 5.
[26] Social Work (Scotland) Act 1968, s. 63A as inserted by the Registered Establishments (Scotland) Act 1987, s. 4.
[27] *ibid.* s. 62(8).

of being heard must be given.[28] Provision is made for appeal to an appeal tribunal[29] against refusal or cancellation of registration.[30]

Removal of occupants

Where an establishment is carried on by an unregistered person, other than **18.32** the person authorised to carry it on at the death of a registered person, or where notice to cancel a registration has been given, the local authority with which the person carrying on the establishment is registered, or ought to be registered, may remove all, or any, of the persons for whom accommodation is being provided, and that power may be exercised although the time for appeal has not expired or although an appeal is pending.[31] The Secretary of State may, where the person carrying on the establishment is, or ought to be, registered with him, require the local authority in whose area the establishment is situated to act and he may, in any case of urgent necessity, exercise that power in respect of any establishment.[32] Any person authorised by the local authority may, on producing, if required, a duly authenticated document showing his authority, enter premises in which the establishment in question is being carried on in order that the local authority's function in removing the persons accommodated may be performed.[33] It is an offence to obstruct the exercise of that power.[34]

Particulars to be furnished, visitation and inspection

A person in charge of an establishment is obliged to furnish such particulars **18.33** of the establishment and the persons accommodated, or to be accommodated, in it as the Secretary of State may prescribe.[35] A duly authorised officer of a local authority may, at all reasonable times, enter any establishment where the person carrying it on is or ought to be registered for the purpose of making such examination as he thinks necessary into the state and management of the place and the condition and treatment of the persons in it and for the purpose of inspecting any records or registers which are required to be kept there; like powers of entry and inspection may be exercised in respect of any place which the officer has reasonable cause to believe is being used as an establishment in respect of which the person carrying it on is or ought to be registered.[36] The local authority has a duty to see that persons in establishments in their area are visited from time to time in the interests of their well-being; and any person authorised by a local authority is empowered to enter any establishment for the purpose of visiting the persons in the establishment and that power extends to entering establishments outside the area of the authority for the purpose of visiting children who are being looked after by the authority, or who are receiving assistance from it.[37] It is an offence to obstruct the exercise of the powers of inspection and visitation.[38] It is the duty of a local authority to review the case of a child who is being accommodated by them within six weeks of the date of

---

[28] Social Work (Scotland) Act 1968, s. 64(1), (2) and (3).
[29] Established under Sched. 5.
[30] *ibid.* s. 64(4).
[31] *ibid.* s. 65(1).
[32] *ibid.* s. 65(1) and (2).
[33] *ibid.* s. 65(3).
[34] *ibid.* s. 65(4), as amended by the Registered Establishments (Scotland) Act 1987, s. 7.
[35] *ibid.* s. 66(1) and (2).
[36] *ibid.* s. 67, as substituted by the Children (Scotland) Act 1995, s. 34(6). Scottish Office Circulars SWSG 9/90 and SWSG 7/96 suggest that a minimum of two visits *per* year, one unannounced, would be the normal expectation.
[37] *ibid.* s. 68, as amended by the Children (Scotland) Act 1995, Sched. 4, para. 15(16).
[38] *ibid.* ss. 67(1), 6(5) and 68(3).

the placement, thereafter within three months of the first review and thereafter within six months of each preceding review.[39]

Secure accommodation

18.34 A form of residential establishment provided by local authorities is secure accommodation, that is to say accommodation for children in places from which they are prevented leaving. A child may be placed in secure accommodation with the authority of a children's hearing,[40] or a court,[41] or, if subject to a supervision requirment which does not contain such authorisation or if being looked after by a local authority under Chapters 1 or 4 of Part II of the Children (Scotland) Act 1995, by agreement between the chief social work officer and the person in charge of the accommodation,[42] or if taken there as a place of safety.[43] The Secure Accommodation (Scotland) Regulations 1996[44] provide for the review of the case of each child kept in secure accommodation within seven days of the child's placement there, at such times thereafter as appears to the chief social work officer and the person in charge necessary or appropriate in the light of the child's progress, and in any event at intervals of not more than three months.[45] These regulations also provide for approval of the accommodation by the Secretary of State,[46] for the safeguarding and promotion of the welfare of the child and for the provision of the child's education, development and control.[47]

CHILD-MINDING AND DAY CARE OF YOUNG CHILDREN

18.35 Child-minding and day care (*i.e.* any form of care or activity supervised by a responsible person and provided for children during the day, whether or not it is provided on a regular basis[48]) may take a wide variety of forms. Some are free from statutory control, for example where children are cared for during the day in a dwelling-house under a private arrangement that makes no provision for reward or where children over eight are so cared for even if for reward. Establishments provided for the purposes of the Social Work (Scotland) Act 1968 or of the Children (Scotland) Act 1995 that receive children on a non-residential basis are subject to the same controls in respect of the registration of the person by whom they are carried on, of their management and conduct and of the treatment of persons in them as have just been noted in connection with residential establishments.[49] Every local authority must, at least once every three years, review the provision of day care within its area made for children under the age of eight by the local authority and by persons required to register as persons who provide day care. Child-minding and day care of children under eight (other than local authority day care but including care in certain voluntary establishments, carried on by persons also registrable under the Social Work

---

[39] Arrangements to Look After Children (Scotland) Regulations 1996, reg. 9(1).
[40] Children (Scotland) Act 1995, s. 70(9).
[41] Criminal Procedure (Scotland) Act 1995, Pts V and XI.
[42] Secure Accommodation (Scotland) Regulations 1996, (S.I. 1996 No. 3255), regs 6 and 7.
[43] *ibid.* reg. 9. The maximum period during which a child may be kept in secure accommodation without the authority of a children's hearing or a sheriff is an aggregate of 72 hours (whether or not consecutive) in any period of 28 consecutive days: *ibid.* reg. 5.
[44] above.
[45] *ibid.* reg. 15.
[46] *ibid.* reg. 3.
[47] *ibid.* reg. 4 and Pt II of the Residential Establishments (Child Care) (Scotland) Regulations 1996 (S.I. 1996 No. 3256).
[48] Children Act 1989, s. 79(b).
[49] Social Work (Scotland) Act 1968, s. 61(1), as substituted by the Children (Scotland) Act 1995, s. 34(2).

(Scotland) Act 1968) is regulated by Part X of the Children Act 1989.[50] It effects control through a system of registration and inspection, which forms the subject-matter of the following paragraphs.

Register of child-minders and register of persons who provide day care

Every local authority is required to keep a register (which must be open to **18.36** inspection by members of the public at all times and which may be kept by means of a computer[51]) of (a) persons who act as child-minders on domestic premises within the authority's area, and (b) persons who provide day care for children under the age of eight on premises other than domestic premises within that area.[52] A child-minder is a person who looks after, in a domestic setting,[53] one or more children under the age of eight for reward for more than two hours in any day[54]; though excluded from this definition are parents, relatives, persons having parental responsibilities (within the meaning of section 1 of the Children (Scotland) Act 1995) in relation to the child, foster parents, and nannies[55] employed for the child.[56] Anyone who provides day care for one or more children under the age of eight for more than two hours in any day in other than a domestic setting, and whether or not for reward, is registrable as a person who provides day care for children.[57]

Refusal of registration

A local authority may refuse to register an applicant for registration as a **18.37** child-minder if:

(a) the applicant, or any person looking after or likely to be looking after any children in any premises on which the applicant is or is likely to be child-minding, is not fit to look after children under the age of eight[58]; or

(b) any person living or likely to be living at any premises on which the applicant is or is likely to be child-minding, or any person employed or likely to be employed on those premises, is not fit to be in the proximity of children under the age of eight[59]; or

(c) the local authority is satisfied that any premises on which the applicant is or is likely to be child-minding are not fit to be used for looking after children under the age of eight, whether because of their condition or the condition of any equipment used on the premises or for any reason connected with their situation, construction, or size.[60]

A local authority may refuse to register an applicant for registration as a **18.38** person who provides day care for children if:

---

[50] As applied to Scotland by s. 108(11). See Sutherland, "Child Law: Radical Change or Woeful Neglect?", 1991 S.L.T. (News) 447.

[51] Children Act 1989, s. 71(15).

[52] *ibid*. s. 71(1).

[53] "Domestic premises" means any premises which are wholly or mainly used as a private dwelling; and "premises" includes any vehicle: s. 71(12).

[54] *ibid*. s. 71(2)(a).

[55] "A person acts as a nanny for a child if she is employed to look after the child by (a) a parent of the child, (b) a person who is not a parent of the child but who is a person having parental responsibilities (within the meaning of section 1 of the Children (Scotland) Act 1995) relating to the child, or (c) a person who is a relative of the child and who has assumed responsibility for his care": *ibid*. s. 71(13), as applied to Scotland by s. 79(e) (as amended by the Children (Scotland) Act 1995, Sched. 4, para. 48(4)).

[56] *ibid*. ss. 71(4), (5) and (6) and 79.

[57] *ibid*. s. 71(1)(b) and (2)(b).

[58] *ibid*. s. 71(7).

[59] *ibid*. s. 71(8).

[60] *ibid*. s. 71(11).

(a) it is satisfied that any person looking after, or likely to be looking after, any children on the premises to which the application relates is not fit to look after children under the age of eight[61]; or

(b) it is satisfied that any person living or likely to be living at the premises to which the application relates, or any person employed or likely to be employed, at these premises, is not fit to be in the proximity of children under the age of eight[62]; or

(c) it is satisfied that the premises to which the application relates are not fit to be used for looking after children under the age of eight, whether because of their condition or the condition of any equipment used on the premises or for any reason connected with their situation, construction, or size.[63]

Requirements that may be imposed

18.39   Either at the time of registration or at any time thereafter the local authority may impose requirements upon applicants to be child-minders or persons providing day care. The requirements in both cases shall be such reasonable requirements as the local authority considers appropriate, and it may be added to, varied, or removed at any time.[64] If the local authority considers it appropriate to impose requirements on the applicant, it must impose certain specified requirements, described below; and if in addition it imposes other requirements, those other requirements must not be incompatible with any of those that must be imposed.[65]

Specified requirements for child-minders[66]

18.40   In imposing requirements on a registered child-minder, the local authority shall:

(a) specify the maximum number of children, or the maximum number of children within specified age groups, whom he or she may look after when acting as a child-minder. In determining the maximum number of children under this provision the authority shall take account of the number of other children who may at any time be on any premises on which the person concerned acts, or is likely to act, as a child-minder[67];

(b) require him or her to secure that any premises on which he or she looks after any child, and the equipment used in those premises, are adequately maintained and kept safe;

(c) require him or her to keep a record of the name and address of any child looked after by him or her on any premises within the authority's area, and of any person who assists in looking after any such child, and of any person living or likely to be living at those premises; and

(d) require him or her to notify the authority in writing of any change in the persons mentioned above.

---

[61] Children Act 1989, s. 71(9).
[62] *ibid.* s. 71(10).
[63] *ibid.* s. 71(11).
[64] *ibid.* s. 72(1) and (6) and s. 73(1) and (8).
[65] *ibid.* ss. 72(5) and 73(7).
[66] *ibid.* s. 72(2).
[67] *ibid.* s. 72(4).

Specified requirements for persons providing day care[68]

In imposing requirements on a person registered as a person providing day **18.41** care the local authority shall:

(a) specify the maximum number of children, or the maximum number of children within specified age groups, who may be looked after on the premises. In determining the maximum number of children to be specified the authority shall take account of the number of other children who may at any time be on the premises[69];

(b) require him or her to secure that the premises, and the equipment used in them, are adequately maintained and kept safe;

(c) require him or her to notify the authority of any change in the facilities which he or she provides or in the period during which he or she provides them;

(d) specify the number of persons required to assist in looking after children on the premises;

(e) require him or her to keep a record of the name and address of (i) any child looked after on the registered premises, (ii) any person who assists in looking after any such child, and (iii) any person who lives, or is likely at any time to be living, at those premises; and

(f) require him or her to notify the authority of any change in the persons mentioned above.

Cancellation of registration

Registration of child-minders or of persons providing day care may be **18.42** cancelled by the local authority at any time if,

(a) it appears to them that the circumstances of the case are such that they would be justified in refusing to register the person in the first place;

(b) the care provided is, in the opinion of the authority, seriously inadequate having regard to the needs of the child or children[70];

(c) the person has contravened or failed to comply with any requirement imposed[71]; or

(d) the person has failed to pay any annual fee under Schedule 9 within the prescribed time.[72]

In addition, registration of persons providing day care may be cancelled if it appears to the local authority that the circumstances of the case are such that it would be justified in refusing to register the applicant with respect to any premises.[73]

Protection of children in an emergency

The sheriff has the power to make an order, on the application of the local **18.43** authority, cancelling registration, or varying, removing or imposing any additional requirements on a registered person, if it appears to the sheriff that a child being looked after by that person is suffering or is likely to suffer significant

---

[68] Children Act 1989, s. 73(3).

[69] *ibid.* s. 73(6).

[70] In relation to this provision the local authority must have regard, amongst other things, to the child's religious persuasion, racial origin, and cultural and linguistic background: s. 74(6).

[71] Registration may not be cancelled on this ground where the requirement is to carry out repairs or make alterations or additions, and they have not been carried out or made, but the time set for complying with the requirements has not expired: s. 74(4).

[72] Children Act 1989, s. 74(1) and (2).

[73] *ibid.* s. 74(3).

harm.[74] Any such cancellation, variation, removal or imposition shall have effect from the date on which the order is made.[75] Notice must be served by the local authority on the registered person.[76]

Inspection

18.44   Any person authorised by a local authority may at any reasonable time enter (a) any domestic premises in the area of the authority on which child-minding is at any time carried on, or (b) any premises within its area on which day care for children under the age of eight is at any time provided,[77] or (c) any premises within its area in which the local authority has reasonable cause to believe that a child is being looked after in contravention of the provisions of the Act.[78] Such a person may inspect the children being looked after there, the arrangements for their welfare and any statutory records relating to them.[79] Every local authority must exercise its power to inspect at least once a year.[80] A duly authenticated document showing authority to enter and inspect must be produced if required.[81] It is an offence to obstruct the exercise of the power of inspection.[82]

18.45   In addition to the power of the local authority, the Secretary of State may also cause to be inspected premises on which any person is acting as a child-minder or in respect of which a person is registered as a person who provides day care.[83]

Appeals

18.46   Not less than 14 days before taking any of the steps described above, the authority concerned shall send to the applicant for registration or registered person notice of its intention to take the step, with reasons and a statement of their rights to object or appeal.[84] Where the recipient of the notice wishes to object he or she must be afforded the opportunity to do so.[85] If the step is nevertheless taken the person aggrieved thereby may appeal to the sheriff.[86] If he allows the appeal, the sheriff may impose requirements, cancel requirements or vary those appealed against.[87] The appeal is by way of summary application to the sheriff and must be brought within 21 days of the date of the step to which the appeal relates.[88]

Offences

18.47   It is an offence for a person, without reasonable cause, to provide day care for children under the age of eight on any premises within the area of a local authority without being registered.[89] If a person acts as a child-minder on domestic premises within the area of a local authority without being registered,

---

[74] Children Act 1989, ss. 75(1) and 79(a).
[75] *ibid.* s. 75(2).
[76] *ibid.* s. 75(4).
[77] *ibid.* s. 76(1).
[78] *ibid.* s. 76(2).
[79] *ibid.* s. 76(3). The right to inspect records includes the right to have access to, inspect and check the operation of any computer in use in connection with the records in question: s. 76(5).
[80] *ibid.* s. 76(4).
[81] *ibid.* s. 76(6).
[82] *ibid.* s. 76(7).
[83] *ibid.* s. 80, as applied to Scotland by s. 108(11).
[84] *ibid.* s. 77(1) and (2).
[85] *ibid.* s. 77(3).
[86] *ibid.* ss. 77(6) and 79(a).
[87] *ibid.* ss. 77(8) and (9).
[88] *ibid.* s. 77(10).
[89] *ibid.* s. 78(1) and (2).

the local authority may serve an enforcement notice on him or her,[90] which will have effect for a period of one year beginning with the date on which it is served[91]; if a person to whom an enforcement notice relates continues, without reasonable excuse, to act as a child-minder, he or she shall be guilty of an offence,[92] this whether or not the subsequent contravention occurs within the area of the authority which served the enforcement notice.[93] It is also an offence to contravene any requirement imposed.[94]

---

[90] Children Act 1989, s. 78(3) and (4).
[91] *ibid.* s. 78(5).
[92] *ibid.* s. 78(6).
[93] *ibid.* s. 78(7).
[94] *ibid.* s. 78(8).

CHAPTER 19

CHILDREN'S HEARINGS

INTRODUCTORY

19.01 Children may be made subject to compulsory measures of supervision by a children's hearing imposing in respect of them supervision requirements made under section 70 of the Children (Scotland) Act 1995. The children's hearing system[1] was introduced by Part III of the Social Work (Scotland) Act 1968 on the recommendation of the Kilbrandon Committee, which had been appointed to consider the provision of the law of Scotland relating to the treatment of "juvenile delinquents and juveniles in need of care and protection or beyond parental control" and, in particular, the powers and procedures of the tribunals who deal with such juveniles.[2] Part II of the Children (Scotland) Act 1995[3] substantially re-enacts Part III of the 1968 Act and, though some important revisions were made, the underlying philosophy of the system was not changed. In particular, the procedures to be followed and the possible outcomes available remain applicable both to children who, through neglect or ill-treatment, are in need of care and protection and to children who have committed offences. The underlying concept is that in both categories the fundamental need of the child is for protection, guidance, treatment or control which can be achieved only by compulsory intervention. The commission of an offence, no less than danger to the child's health, safety or well-being, is therefore seen as a symptom of need calling for a caring rather than a punitive response. In offence-based cases the emphasis will often and inevitably be on control, while in the cases brought on non-offence grounds it will more often be on protection. In both categories guidance and treatment may, according to circumstances, be appropriate.

19.02 The changes introduced by the 1968 Act were, perhaps, less radical than is sometimes represented. The measures of care actually available under the 1968 legislation, although different in form, were not materially different in substance from their predecessors; and nor are the measures of supervision available under the 1995 Act. Even the use of measures of care or supervision, rather than of punishment, in relation to children who have committed offences is not a major innovation in principle. It was implicit in the obligation, previously laid upon courts dealing with offences committed by juveniles, to have regard to the welfare of the child.[4] The radical changes were in the personnel and machinery of administration, the composition of the decision-making tribunals, and procedures.

---

[1] See generally Kearney, *Children's Hearings and the Sheriff Court* (1987) and Norrie, *Children's Hearings in Scotland* (1997).

[2] See *Report on Children and Young Persons, Scotland*, Cmnd. 2306 (1964): a summary of the conclusions and recommendations contained in this Report can be found in the *Stair Memorial Encyclopaedia of the Laws of Scotland*, Vol. 3, paras 1278–1281, and in Lockyer and Stone, *Juvenile Justice in Scotland* (1998) at Chaps 1 and 2.

[3] All references in this chapter are to this Act, unless otherwise stated. Pt II came into force on April 1, 1997.

[4] Children and Young Persons (Scotland) Act 1937, s. 49(1), repealed by the Criminal Procedure (Scotland) Act 1975, Sched. 10.

The children's hearing and the reporter

The key elements in the current system are a lay tribunal, known as the **19.03**
children's hearing, and an official charged with arranging and bringing cases
before the children's hearing, known as the reporter.

A children's hearing consists of a chairman and two other members and **19.04**
must include both a man and a woman.[5] Its membership is chosen from the
members of children's panels constituted for each local authority area.[6] The
members of panels are appointed by the Secretary of State who has an unfettered
discretion as to whom he may appoint.[7] In practice, however, appointments are
made from those nominated by Children's Panel Advisory Committees
(CPACs)[8], upon whom a duty is laid to submit names of possible panel members
and to advise the Secretary of State as required on the suitability of persons
referred to him as possible members.[9] Once appointed, panel members may be
removed only by the Secretary of State with the consent of the Lord President.[10]
The selection of the chairman and members of any given hearing rests with the
chairman of the children's panel, or, in his or her absence, the deputy chairman
or by the operation of standing arrangements made by the chairman after
consulting the Principal Reporter and such members of the panel as he or she
may think fit.[11] No principles of selection are laid down, but the chairman of the
panel is obliged to keep any standing arrangements which he or she has made
under review and from time to time to engage in consultations about their
operation.[12]

Reporters are employed by the Scottish Children's Reporter Administration **19.05**
(SCRA)[13] and they are prohibited from being employed in any capacity by local
authorities, except where consent is given in individual cases by SCRA[14]. The
term "reporter" means the Principal Reporter and any officer of SCRA to whom
he has delegated any of his functions under section 131(1) of the Local Government
etc. (Scotland) Act 1994[15]. Throughout the Children (Scotland) Act 1995 the term
"Principal Reporter" is used, but that is defined in section 93(1) thereof in the
same way as "reporter" has been defined here. SCRA is responsible for the
management of reporters, including their discipline and removal from office and
their deployment throughout Scotland for the purposes of performing their duties.[16]
Reporters (*i.e.* officers to whom the Principal Reporter has delegated his functions)
must comply with any instructions or guidance given by the Principal Reporter.[17]
If dismissed from office by SCRA, the Principal Reporter or any other reporter
may appeal to the Secretary of State against such dismissal.[18]

Children and relevant persons

A child for the purposes of the children's hearing system is a person who **19.06**
either (a) is less than 16 years of age, or (b) if currently subject to a supervision
requirement is less than 18 years of age, or (c) is a person who has been referred

---

[5] s. 39(5).
[6] s. 39(1).
[7] Sched. 1, para. 1.
[8] Formed in accordance with Sched. 1, paras. 3–7.
[9] Sched. 1, para. 6.
[10] Tribunals and Inquiries Act 1992, s. 7(1)(e) and Sched. 1, para. 61(a).
[11] Children's Hearings (Scotland) Rules 1996 (S.I. 1996 No. 3261), r. 10(1) (hereinafter the "1996 Rules").
[12] *ibid.* r. 10(2).
[13] Local Government etc. (Scotland) Act 1994, s. 128(4) and (5).
[14] Children (Scotland) Act 1995, s. 40(2).
[15] s. 40(5).
[16] Local Government etc. (Scotland) Act 1994, s. 128(7)
[17] *ibid.* s. 131(2).
[18] *ibid.* s. 129(1).

to a children's hearing, under regulations made under section 33, by a court in England and Wales or in Northern Ireland, or (d) has been referred to a children's hearing on the basis of failure to attend school regularly and, though over the age of 16, is not yet of school leaving age[19]. The hearing must, at the commencement of the proceedings, make inquiry as to the child's age and shall proceed with the hearing only if the child declares that he or she is a child or they so determine; they may at any time before the conclusion of the proceedings accept a declaration by the child, or make a fresh determination, as to his or her age[20]. The age declared or determined by the children's hearing to be the age of the person brought before them shall be deemed to be the true age of that person[21] and no decision reached, order continued, warrant granted or requirement imposed by a children's hearing shall be invalidated by any subsequent proof that the age of the person brought before them had not been correctly declared to the hearing or determined by them.[22]

19.07   The "relevant person" in relation to the child has various duties and powers, including in particular the duty to attend at all stages of the children's hearing, the right to deny grounds of referral, the right to call for a review of a supervision requirement, and the power to appeal against any decision of the hearing. The "relevant person" is defined as follows:

> (a)   any person enjoying parental responsibilities or parental rights under Part I of the Children (Scotland) Act 1995,
> (b)   any person in whom parental responsibilities or rights are vested by, under or by virtue of the 1995 Act, and
> (c)   any person who appears to be a person who ordinarily (and other than by reason only of his employment) has charge of, or control over, the child.[23]

Whether a person comes into category (a) or (b) will be established by examining the legal relationship between the referred child and the person[24]; category (c), containing elements of fact as well as of law, is rather more problematical. It is designed to give an interest in the proceedings to those persons who play a significant part in the child's upbringing, such as the unmarried father, grandparent or other relative who lives with the child and takes a share in his or her upbringing. "Charge of, or control over the child" does not require any pre-existing legal or genetic relationship between the person and the child and is solely a question of fact. Section 94 of the Social Work (Scotland) Act 1968 gave similar interest[25] to any person who "has for the time being the custody or charge of or control over the child". This was more clearly a factual test than the current legislation suggests, with its reference to "ordinarily" having charge of or control over the child. Nevertheless it is submitted that the test is primarily factual under the current legislation and that a person is a relevant person if, in fact, that person ordinarily looks after or controls (other than by reason of employment) the child's day-to-day upbringing.[26] It follows that a person may

---

[19] s. 93(2)(b).
[20] s. 47(1).
[21] s. 47(2).
[22] s. 47(3).
[23] s. 93(2).
[24] In *Chapman, Petr*, May 21, 1997 Lord Hamilton held that a father who had been awarded by a foreign court certain rights of contact and consultation, including the right to consent to emergency medical treatment, was not a relevant person since these were not parental responsibilities or parental rights under the Children (Scotland) Act 1995. This should not be taken to mean that parents who trace their responsibilities and rights to a foreign legal system will never be relevant persons, but rather that they must have responsibilities and rights analogous to those contained in Pt I of the 1995 Act.
[25] By defining "guardian".
[26] Whether foster carers can be considered relevant persons is explored in Norrie, *Children's Hearings in Scotland* (1997) at pp. 12–13. It is submitted there that, in some circumstances at least, long-term foster carers can properly be described as ordinarily having charge of or control over the children in their care.

move in and out of the category of "relevant person" depending on whether the test is satisfied at the appropriate time. In *S v. Lynch*[27] an unmarried father was looking after his child at the date of the hearing at which he denied grounds of referral, but by the time of the hearing before the sheriff to establish the grounds of referral the child had been summarily removed from his charge and control by her mother. The sheriff held that he was no longer a "guardian" under the terms of the then extant Social Work (Scotland) Act 1968 and this was upheld by the First Division on the basis that the statute required the person to have charge of or control over the child "for the time being". This decision would not be reached on those facts under the terms of the present legislation, where the father could be described as "ordinarily" having charge of or control over the child even when at particular and critical moments in time, due to extraordinary events (such as the child's kidnapping) he loses physical possession.[28] The use of the term "ordinarily" makes the concept of "relevant person" rather more stable than the definition of "guardian" under the 1968 Act, for it will be more difficult for a person to become a relevant person by taking over charge of or control over the child for a short or limited period of time.

Restriction on prosecution of children

The policy of Part II of the 1995 Act is to take children out of the prosecution **19.08** process. So it is provided that no child is to be prosecuted for any offence except on the instructions of the Lord Advocate, or at his instance.[29] Private prosecution is, therefore, altogether excluded and a complaint by a procurator fiscal can be preferred only on the Lord Advocate's instructions. No court other than the High Court of Justiciary and the sheriff court has jurisdiction.[30] As all public prosecutions on solemn procedure are at the instance of the Lord Advocate, the indictment is, from this standpoint, itself conclusive of the competency of the proceedings. In summary cases, however, competency can be determined only by reference to the Lord Advocate's instructions. These may be verbal and in general terms covering various kinds of offences.[31] In the absence of challenge they are presumed to have been given and to embrace the case in question.[32] General instructions have, in fact, been issued[33] in relation to children of 13 years of age and over. They provide for prosecution of children of that age group if the case falls into any of the following categories and the procurator fiscal, in his discretion, decides to follow that course rather than to refer the case to the reporter:

(a) Offences which require by law to be prosecuted on indictment or which are so serious as normally to give rise to solemn proceedings on the instructions of the Lord Advocate in the public interest.

(b) Offences alleged to have been committed by children aged 15 years or over which in the event of conviction oblige or permit a court to order disqualification from driving.

(c) Offences alleged to have been committed by children as described in section 31(1) of the Social Work (Scotland) Act 1968.

---

[27] 1997 S.L.T. 1377.

[28] The First Division in *S v. Lynch* also held that the reason why the charge or control was lost was irrelevant. The circumstances will now be pertinent in determining whether the person "ordinarily" has charge of or contol over the child.

[29] Social Work (Scotland) Act 1968, s. 31(1).

[30] *ibid.*

[31] *M v. Dean*, 1974 S.L.T. 229.

[32] *ibid.*

[33] Aug. 3, 1987.

As the matter is entirely one for the Lord Advocate's instructions, the above categories may, of course, be varied or withdrawn by him at any time either generally or in relation to a particular case. The sole question in relation to any prosecution is whether, at the time it is instituted, it comes within the terms of instructions by the Lord Advocate then in force. Children under the age of 13 are not to be prosecuted except with the prior express authority of the Lord Advocate.

Investigation and transmission of information

19.09   The satisfactory operation of any system of care and protection of children largely depends on the adequacy of the means for ascertaining cases in which compulsory measures of supervision may be necessary and for the transmission of information to the appropriate authorities so that action can be taken. The reporter's role is central but, although once information is received he has certain investigatory duties,[34] he is, nearly always, dependent initially on information supplied by others. Accordingly the 1995 Act provides that where any person has reasonable cause to believe that compulsory measures of supervision may be necessary in respect of a child, he or she may (and if a police officer he or she must) give to the reporter such information about the child as he or she has been able to discover.[35] Moreover, where a local authority receives information suggesting that compulsory measures of supervision may be necessary in respect of a child, it is obliged, unless satisfied that they are unnecessary, to cause inquiries to be made into the case and, if it appears that compulsory measures of supervision may be required in respect of the child, to give to the reporter such information about the child as it has been able to discover.[36] The obligation appears to be incumbent on the local authority no matter from what source the information is received, and may be taken to have been imposed because Parliament envisaged a sifting function for local authorities where information came into their hands rather than directly into the hands of the reporter. As a consequence, however, there may be delay in information reaching the reporter while the authority investigates the information and considers, or even attempts, measures alternative to compulsory measures of supervision. That consequence is somewhat mitigated if the statutory requirement that information must be transmitted whenever it appears that compulsory measures of supervision "may" be necessary in respect of the child is strictly observed. To the local authority is given the judgment, in cases in which it receives information, of whether there may be a need for compulsory measures but not of whether there is an actual need. Accordingly, it is obliged to transmit information whenever the view that compulsory measures of supervision are required could reasonably be entertained even if in its judgment alternative measures, or no action, would be preferable. The obligation is incumbent on the local authority as such and therefore on all its agencies which may become possessed of such information, for example not only the social work department but also the education department, local authority schools and local authority medical services. The wording used is in contrast with that applied to the reporter, who is charged with taking a preliminary decision on whether compulsory measures of supervision "are" necessary in respect of the child.[37] The central role of the reporter is, therefore, preserved in cases in which information is first received by a local authority, as well as in other cases, but only if the limitations on the local authority's function are scrupulously observed.

---

[34] Below, para. 19.32.
[35] s. 53(2).
[36] s. 53(1).
[37] s. 56(6).

Referral from court

Where it appears to a court in relevant proceedings that any of the conditions **19.10** for referral, except that the child has committed an offence, is satisfied in respect of a child, it may refer the matter to the reporter, specifying the condition.[38] The reporter must then make such investigations as he or she thinks appropriate and, if he or she considers that compulsory measures of supervision are necessary, arrange a children's hearing at which the condition specified will be treated as grounds of referral established in an application to the sheriff.[39] "Relevant proceedings" are (a) an action for divorce, or judicial separation or for declarator of marriage, nullity of marriage, parentage or non-parentage; (b) proceedings relating to parental responsibilities or parental rights within the meaning of Part I of the 1995 Act; (c) proceedings for an adoption order under the Adoption (Scotland) Act 1978 or for an order under section 18 of that Act declaring a child free for adoption; and (d) proceedings for an offence under section 35, section 41 or section 42(3) of the Education (Scotland) Act 1980.[40] In addition, a criminal court which has convicted a person of certain offences may refer the child victim or any child who is or is likely to become a member of the same household as the offender to the reporter and certify that the offence is a ground established for the purpose of a referral to the children's hearing.[41]

Children arrested by police

If a child has been arrested and detained in a place of safety but it is decided **19.11** that charges are not to be proceeded with, the reporter must be informed and, unless he or she considers that compulsory measures of supervision are not required in relation to the child (in which case he or she must direct that the child shall no longer be kept in a place of safety[42]), he or she must arrange a children's hearing to which he or she shall refer the case.[43] That children's hearing must begin not later than the third day after the reporter received the information,[44] during which time the child may be kept in the place of safety.[45] The children's hearing may (i) grant a warrant if the conditions for a section 66 warrant[46] are satisfied and (ii) direct the reporter to arrange a children's hearing for consideration and determination of the child's case.[47] If a warrant is granted, the child may nevertheless be released where the reporter, having regard to the welfare of the child, considers that (a) the conditions for the granting of the warrant are no longer satisfied or (b) the child is not in need of compulsory measures of supervision.[48]

CONDITIONS OF NEED FOR COMPULSORY MEASURES OF SUPERVISION

The grounds of referral

The question arises of whether a child is in need of compulsory measures of **19.12** supervision only if certain conditions specified in the Act are satisfied.[49] This form of wording is used to emphasise that the satisfaction of any of the conditions

---

[38] s. 54(1).
[39] s. 54(3).
[40] s. 54(2).
[41] Criminal Procedure (Scotland) Act 1995, s. 48(1): see further, below, para. 19.18.
[42] s. 63(3).
[43] s. 63(1).
[44] s. 63(2).
[45] s. 63(4).
[46] See below, 20.11.
[47] s. 63(5).
[48] s. 63(6). See further, para. 20.18.
[49] s. 52(1).

does not in itself answer the question, but merely requires (i) the reporter to decide whether or not to arrange a children's hearing, and (ii) the hearing to decide whether or not compulsory measures of supervision are required in the particular circumstances of the case. There is no presumption that compulsory measures of supervision are required simply because one or more of the conditions in section 52(2) have been satisfied.[50] Although the matter could have been more clearly expressed, the conditions are, it is thought, exhaustive of the circumstances in which compulsory measures of supervision may be applied and there is no residual power to hold a child to be in need of compulsory measures of supervision on grounds extraneous to the specified conditions.[51] The conditions are as follows:

(a) The child is beyond the control of any relevant person

19.13   It is the responsibility and the right of relevant persons to safeguard and promote the child's health, development and welfare and to provide appropriate guidance and direction to the child.[52] In order to do so, the relevant person must be able to control the child and an inability on the part of the relevant person to exercise that control, for whatever reason, may potentially harm the child, giving rise to the question of whether compulsory measures are required. The control that should be exercised varies in particular cases with the particular needs and circumstances of individual children.[53] Problems may arise in applying this condition to older children, since the extent of control which a parent or other relevant person may exercise over a child becomes progressively more uncertain the older the child becomes. In cases of older children it is thought that the child's conduct must not only show that there is an absence of control but must also be actually, or potentially, harmful to the child or to others so as to make the exercise of parental control appropriate.

(b) The child is falling into bad associations or is exposed to moral danger

19.14   The 1968 Act, as originally passed, required that this should be caused "through lack of parental care", but these words were removed in 1975[54] and they do not appear in the current legislation. Bad associations are not defined, nor is moral danger. Any association which may be harmful to the child's welfare in any, not only in its moral, aspect may be regarded as bad. Moral danger is commonly equiparated with the risk of sexual corruption,[55] but there is no warrant for restricting it to such cases. The mere commission of an offence does not, but the exposure to circumstances from which a habitual pattern of criminal conduct is likely to follow probably does, indicate moral danger.[56] There are obvious hazards and difficulties in going beyond recognised categories such as sexual corruption and criminality, but a wide scope is clearly intended. Thus, exposure of a child to scenes of habitual drunkenness may involve moral danger or at least indicate that the child is falling into bad associations. Similarly, circumstances in which the child is likely to indulge in solvent abuse or to

---

[50] Indeed the presumption is rather the reverse: s. 16(3) provides that where a children's hearing are considering whether to make or are reviewing a supervision requirement, no requirement shall be made unless the children's hearing consider that it would be better for the child that the requirement be made than that none be made at all.

[51] *H* v. *Harkness*, 1998 S.L.T. 1431.

[52] ss. 1 and 2.

[53] See *D* v. *Kelly*, 1995 S.L.T. 1220.

[54] Children Act 1975, Sched. 3, para. 54(a).

[55] As in, *e.g.*, *Sloan* v. *B*, 1991 S.L.T. 530 and *F* v. *Kennedy (No. 2)*, 1993 S.L.T. 1284.

[56] *cf. B* v. *Kennedy*, 1987 S.L.T. 765.

develop the habit of taking drugs or drinking to excess may be regarded as obnoxious to this condition.[57] The question of moral danger is to be approached in a practical fashion and is to be answered by reference to the whole circumstances, including the conduct of the child, actual or anticipated, and the existence of arrangements for the care of the child or their absence. The question to be considered is whether those circumstances create a reasonable apprehension of harm to the child.[58] Some regard must be had to the way of life in the community in which the child has been brought up. Thus, the English court held that a 13-year-old girl domiciled in Nigeria, who lived in England with a Nigerian to whom she had been married in Nigeria under a form of marriage potentially polygamous, was not thereby to be regarded as exposed to moral danger.[59] While, however, it is wrong to ignore the way of life in which the child has been brought up, it is submitted that it is equally wrong to regard it as necessarily conclusive. The proper question is not one of what is permitted by the way of life in which the child has been brought up—the whole ground of complaint may be that he or she has been brought up in a way of life that involves moral danger—but whether the circumstances alleged to constitute exposure to moral danger are regarded as morally unobjectionable by the community to which by upbringing or present association the child is most closely connected. Even, however, if that question can be answered in the affirmative, it is no more than an element to be taken into account. In some cases it will be a strong factor and even conclusive. In others, the conduct in question may be so repugnant to the moral notions generally prevailing in the forum that the latter must prevail.

(c) The child is likely (i) to suffer unnecessarily; or (ii) to be impaired seriously in his health or development, due to a lack of parental care

Parental care is undefined but is, it is submitted, to be understood as the care **19.15** that requires to be provided to a child by a person (whether a parent or not) who is subject to the parental responsibilities listed in section 1 of the 1995 Act and in particular the responsibility to safeguard and promote the child's health, development and welfare. Likelihood qualifies the whole condition and so, where it is likely that a child will experience a lack of parental care which is in turn likely to cause him or her to suffer unnecessarily or to be impaired seriously in his or her health or development, the condition is satisfied even if the child has never been in the care of his or her parents.[60] The likelihood of relevant lack of parental care may be inferred from past habits and mode of life of the parents which resulted in the neglect of other children if these habits and mode of life still persist.[61] In a rather different context[62] the House of Lords has held[63] that the word "likely" does not mean "probable"[64] or "more likely than not" but means, rather, to indicate a "real possibility" of harm: this definition may well be appropriate here also. All the circumstances of the case are to be taken into account in determining whether there is a likelihood of harm.[65] There may be difficulty in forecasting the precise form of damage which may be caused by a lack of care[66] but the ground is estabished if some serious impairment is likely to follow the lack of parental care.

---

[57] As well as being a ground of referral in itself under s. 52(2)(j) or (k).
[58] *Constanda v. M*, 1997 S.L.T. 1396, *per* Lord Coulsfield at 1400I–J.
[59] *Mohamed v. Knott* [1968] 2 All E.R. 563.
[60] *McGregor v. L*, 1981 S.L.T. 194.
[61] *ibid.* And see the English case of *D (A Minor) v. Berkshire County Council* [1987] 1 All E.R. 20, HL.
[62] s. 31(2)(a) of the (English) Children Act 1989.
[63] *Re H & Ors (Minors) (Sexual Abuse: Standard of Proof)* [1996] 1 All E.R. 1.
[64] See also *Newham London Borough Council v. AG* [1993] 1 F.L.R. 281.
[65] See *H v. Lees, D v. Orr*, 1994 S.L.T. 908 and *M v. Normand*, 1995 S.L.T. 1284 which, though criminal cases, make pertinent comment on likelihood of harm.
[66] *H v. Harkness*, 1998 S.L.T. 1431, *per* Lord Coulsfield at 1435I.

19.16   Impairment of health or development is apt to cover mental or emotional conditions as well as physical. Parental refusal of consent to necessary medical or surgical treatment is clearly within this condition.[67]

19.17   Lack of parental care is to be assessed objectively from the standpoint of its effect on the child and the question is whether the child is likely to be harmed because he or she was being deprived of the care that was reasonably to be expected of a reasonable parent.[68] The mental disposition of a parent or relevant person does not require to be considered. The condition is concerned with defining circumstances in which a child may be in need of compulsory measures of supervision and that need is not affected by the fact that the lack of care does not flow from a blameworthy disposition on the part of the parent or relevant person. Accordingly, this condition may be invoked where lack of care exists although the parent or relevant person, by reason of psychosis, mental deficiency or illness, or other incapacity or circumstance over which he or she has no control, is unable to do better. A contrast may be drawn between lack of parental care in this context and "wilful neglect" which is the criterion for the commission of a criminal offence under section 12 of the Children and Young Persons (Scotland) Act 1937.

(d) The child is a child in respect of whom any of the offences mentioned in Sched. 1 to the Criminal Procedure (Scotland) Act 1995 has been committed.

19.18   The scheduled offences are as follows: (i) any offence under Part I of the Criminal Law (Consolidation) (Scotland) Act 1995 (*i.e.* sexual offences), (ii) any offence under sections 12, 15, 22, or 33 of the Children and Young Persons (Scotland) Act 1937, (iii) any other offence involving bodily injury to a child under the age of 17 years, and (iv) any offence involving the use of lewd, indecent or libidinous practice or behaviour towards a child under the age of 17 years. It is of no relevance that the offence was committed outwith Scotland and could not, therefore, found a competent criminal charge in a Scottish court: the ground of referral is established when there has been conduct amounting to a scheduled offence and the statutory reference to Schedule 1 is not a reference to particular crimes but a means of identifying or characterising the conduct struck at.[69] Where any person is convicted of having committed a Schedule 1 offence or (tautologously) the offence of incest with a person aged 17 years or over[70] or an offence under section 21 of the Children and Young Persons (Scotland) Act 1937[71] the court may refer the child victim to the reporter and certify that the commission of the offence shall be treated as a ground established for the purposes of referral to the children's hearing.[72] A conviction is not, however, a prerequisite for the existence of this ground and a child may be referred under this paragraph as in need of compulsory measures of supervision although a prosecution is pending,[73] or is not brought, or is brought and fails.[74] Proceedings to find the ground established are, however, undesirable while a prosecution is pending and so, in such cases, referral may be postponed if the interim safety of the child can be otherwise secured, though only in very special and extraordinary circumstances. Postponement, if permitted, must not be for an unduly long or

---

[67] *Finlayson, Applicant*, 1989 S.C.L.R. 601.
[68] *D* v. *Kelly*, 1995 S.L.T. 1220.
[69] *S* v. *Kennedy*, 1996 S.L.T. 1087, *per* Lord Murray at 1093H.
[70] Which is itself a scheduled offence.
[71] Vagrants preventing children from receiving education.
[72] Criminal Procedure (Scotland) Act 1995, s. 48. This also applies to children who are members of the same household as the offender, which is a ground of referral under s. 52(2)(f): see below, para. 19.21.
[73] As in *Ferguson v. P*, 1989 S.L.T. 681.
[74] *cf. Kennedy v. B*, 1992 S.C.L.R. 55.

indefinite time, such as "until after any criminal proceedings have taken place" and any decision to postpone must take account of how the child is to be protected during the delay.[75] If delay is undesirable from the point of view of the child, it is no bar to the hearing, or to the sheriff deciding whether the ground of referral is established, that the evidence will be rehearsed before being presented in any criminal trial.[76] The sheriff has no power to exclude part only of the evidence that the reporter seeks to present to the court in support of grounds of referral, in order to avoid prejudice.[77]

Proof for the purpose of establishing this ground (and the following two **19.19** grounds also) is on the civil and not the criminal standard, notwithstanding that it involves proof of a criminal offence.[78] The identity of the offender is not in issue under this ground, and it is sufficient that the commission of the offence be proved even if the perpetrator cannot be identified.[79] The essence of this ground is whether the offence took place in relation to the child and not who the perpetrator was: "it is concerned with offences and not offenders"[80] (in contrast with ground (f) below). Consequently it is unnecessary to identify the offender[81]: in *S v. Kennedy*[82] it was held that the sheriff was not entitled to make a finding of fact that the offender was "probably" the child's stepfather. Only the conditions for the existence of the offence, and the fact that it was committed in relation to the child, need be shown.[83] Being civil proceedings, a husband or wife is, in principle, a compellable witness as to the commission of the offence by the other spouse.[84]

(e) The child is, or is likely to become, a member of the same household as a child in respect of whom any of the offences referred to in paragraph (d) above has been committed.

As with paragraph (d) above, the identity of the offender is not in issue **19.20** under this condition and it is sufficient that the commission of the offence be proved even if the perpetrator cannot be identified. But it must in addition be proved that the child referred "is a member of the same household" as the victim of the offence.[85] In determining membership of a household for this ground of referral (and for the following two grounds also) the test is membership of the household regarded as a family unit and not whether at a particular time the child has lived, or is likely to live, in the same house[86]: the test is "membership of" rather than "living in" the household. And a household continues to be the same household even if one of the original members has separated from it

---

[75] *Ferguson v. P*, 1989 S.L.T. 681.
[76] *ibid.*
[77] *P v. Kennedy*, 1995 S.L.T. 476.
[78] *McGregor v. D*, 1977 S.C. 330.
[79] *Kennedy v. F*, 1985 S.L.T. 22; *McGregor v. K*, 1982 S.L.T. 293.
[80] *S. v. Kennedy*, 1987 S.L.T. 667, *per* Lord Justice-Clerk Ross at 669L.
[81] Nor, indeed, is it necessary to identify the precise offence. Though usually this will be a practical necessity, it is possible to establish that a child has been a victim of a scheduled offence such as unlawful sexual intercourse even when it cannot be determined whether the offence is one under s. 3 or s. 4 of the Sexual Offences (Scotland) Act 1976: *M v. Kennedy*, 1996 S.L.T. 434.
[82] above.
[83] So in *B v. Harris*, 1990 S.L.T. 208 where the *mens rea* necessary for assault was missing, there was no crime and therefore no ground of referral.
[84] Since spouses of parties became competent witnesses there is little doubt that in civil cases the general rule that a witness who is competent is also compellable applies to them. See Wilkinson, *The Scottish Law of Evidence* (1986) at 152. There is no rule of law that says that a husband or a wife who gives evidence cannot be asked questions that might tend to incriminate their spouse: *Bates v. H.M. Advocate*, 1989 S.L.T. 701 at 703D, *per* Lord Justice-Clerk Ross.
[85] *Ferguson v. S*, 1992 S.C.L.R. 866.
[86] *McGregor v. H*, 1983 S.L.T. 626.

permanently, and even if new members join it, through birth or otherwise.[87] A child may be a member of the same household as another child even when the latter died some years before the former's birth,[88] so long as the household remains, in essence, the same as it was at the previous time: it is a question of circumstances whether the household is the same, and it is a matter of fact and degree.[89] Where grounds of referral under this heading have been established after proof in relation to one child in the household a certified copy interlocutor of the sheriff affords sufficient proof of the commission of the offence for the purpose of proceedings relating to the other children in the same household.[90] However, if the earlier grounds of referral have been accepted before the sheriff and proof is consequently dispensed with, the interlocutor is not sufficient proof of the commission of the offence and if denied in proceedings relating to other children in the same household the offence must be proved by evidence.[91]

(f) The child is, or is likely to become, a member of the same household as a person who has committed any of the offences mentioned in Schedule 1 to the Criminal Procedure (Scotland) Act 1995

19.21   It is not necessary for this condition that the child be the victim of the offence. A conviction is prima facie evidence of the commission of an offence[92] and may be used in circumstances in which the provisions for certification that the ground is established, noted under para. (d) above, do not apply.[93] For this condition, identification of the offender will normally be a practical necessity but if it can, in fact, be shown that the offence has been committed by someone in the household, then that will be sufficient even if the perpetrator cannot be identified. Under this condition it would be competent for the sheriff, in finding the ground established, to make a finding in fact concerning the identity of the offender.[94] The standard of proof was previously a matter of contention. Opinions were reserved in *S v. Kennedy*[95] as to whether the criminal standard of proof was required: it was argued that while the civil standard may be appropriate when identity is not in issue (as under conditions (d) and (e) above) different considerations may well come into play when identity is in issue.[96] The matter was put beyond doubt in *Harris v. F*[97] in which it was held by the Second Division that the standard of proof to be applied in determining the existence of all conditions except that contained in section 32(2)(g) of the 1968 Act (now section 52(2)(i)) was the civil standard, i.e. balance of probability.[98] It is expressly provided that the criminal standard is to be applied in relation to section 52(2)(i)[99]: "[T]he

---

[87] *A v. Kennedy*, 1993 S.L.T. 1188. See Norrie, "The Meaning of 'Household' in Referrals to Children's Hearings", 1993 S.L.T. (News) 192.

[88] *ibid*. The phrase "child is... a member" must be read to include "child who was a member" in order to give effect to the purpose of the statute and to provide protection when it is needed.

[89] *ibid*. See also *Kennedy v. R's Curator ad Litem*, 1993 S.L.T. 295 in which it was held that a temporary separation, or one designed purely to avoid the establishment of this ground, would not be sufficient to break up a household if the ties of affection and regular contact which hold the parties together still continue. See also *Templeton v. E*, 1998 S.C.L.R. 672.

[90] *McGregor v. H*, 1983 S.L.T. 626.

[91] *Milan v. Constanda*, December 4, 1998.

[92] Law Reform (Miscellaneous Provisions) (Scotland) Act 1968, s. 10. See *MacKenzie v. Mackay*, 1989 S.L.T. 810.

[93] *i.e.* where the referred child is not him or herself the victim of the offence.

[94] *S. v. Kennedy*, 1987 S.L.T. 667, *per* Lord Justice-Clerk Ross at 669E.

[95] above.

[96] *ibid*. at 669L and 671K.

[97] 1991 S.L.T. 242.

[98] Opinions were reserved on whether the standard of proof of the commission of a criminal offence was the civil or the criminal standard when such matters arose in ordinary civil proceedings.

[99] s. 68(3)(b).

proper inference to be drawn from that provision is that a distinction is being taken between a ground of referral based on section [52)†)(i)] and all other grounds of referral... The reasonable implication must be that a different and lesser standard of proof will be applicable in the case of all other grounds of referral... *expressio unius est exclusio alterius.*"[1] It follows from this, and it has been held, that an acquittal is not conclusive proof of the absence of this ground: a failure to prove something beyond reasonable doubt does not mean that it cannot be established on a balance of probabilities.[2] "Household" is to be defined as in condition (e) above.

(g) The child is, or is likely to become, a member of the same household as a person in respect of whom an offence under sections 1–3 of the Criminal Law (Consolidation) (Scotland) Act 1995 (incest and intercourse with a child by step-parent or person in position of trust) has been committed by a member of that household

When the 1968 Act was originally passed, it was not a ground of referral **19.22** that a child was a member of the same household as a victim of a scheduled offence; this was added as a ground in 1975.[3] Incest was not a scheduled offence unless committed against a child and this condition therefore had practical relevance between 1975 and 1986 for children[4] who were members of the same household as adult victims. However, since the passing of the Incest and Related Offences (Scotland) Act 1986 the offences mentioned in this condition are all scheduled offences regardless of the age of the victim. Thus any child who is a member of the same household as a child in respect of whom the crime of incest has been committed will fall under paragraph (e), and any child who is a member of the same household as the person who committed the crime of incest will fall under paragraph (f) even if the person in respect of whom the offence was committed is not a child. This ground exists if, in addition to ground (e) or (f) or both existing, the victim and the perpetrator are members of the same household as the referred child, and it therefore adds nothing to the protection that can be afforded to children in need of compulsory measures of supervision. "Household" is defined as in condition (e) above.

(h) The child has failed to attend school regularly without reasonable excuse

The wording of this condition is perplexing not so much for what is said as **19.23** for what is omitted. It can, it is submitted, apply only to children of school age but the absence of an express limitation to that effect is surprising (*cf.* the previous English provisions[5] which were in contrast on this point). Normally only children of school age can be the subject of compulsory measures of supervision but, exceptionally, they may be older[6]: they will, of course, frequently be younger. The definitions of "school" and "reasonable excuse" given in the Education (Scotland) Act 1980 seem appropriate but are not expressly incorporated. The wording is, however, open to a construction that is at least as wide as these definitions. The condition can, it is submitted, apply only to a child for whom attendance at school is the means selected by his or her parent for providing

---

[1] *Harris v. F*, above, *per* Lord Justice-Clerk Ross at 245F.

[2] *Kennedy v. B*, 1992 S.C.L.R. 55.

[3] Children Act 1975, Sched. 3, para. 54(c).

[4] Until 1995, only female children.

[5] Children and Young Persons Act 1969, s. 1(2)(e). This was repealed by the Children Act 1989, Sched. 15. The current English provisions do not contain a long and detailed list of conditions for a child being in need of compulsory measures of supervision, adopting instead a much more generally worded scheme: see Children Act 1989, s. 31.

[6] See above, para. 19.06.

efficient education; it is to be remembered that other means are open.[7] The onus of proving reasonable excuse probably rests on the child or relevant person.[8] It is a reasonable excuse that the child has been excluded from his or her school by an exclusion order issued by the rector which was made on the basis of an allegation of misconduct that was neither established nor admitted; a different conclusion might be reached if it is established that the exclusion order had been necessary due to the misconduct of the child.[9] Provision is made for the proof of attendance and other matters by documents.[10]

19.24   Where a child of school age has failed to attend a public school regularly the education authority may refer the child to the reporter[11] who may then consider taking proceedings under this condition. In addition, where a parent is prosecuted in respect of a failure to secure the child's regular attendance at a public school or a failure to comply with an attendance order or a failure to permit a medical examination where it is alleged that the child has been prevented by sickness from attending school or receiving education, the court may, if satisfied that the ground of referral exists and whether or not the parent is convicted, refer the matter to the reporter.[12] If the court does so, the condition specified shall be treated as if it had been a ground of referral established under section 68.[13] In that event some of the difficulties of interpretation noted above are avoided.

(i) The child has committed an offence

19.25   This is the most frequent ground on which children are referred to children's hearings. It differs from the others in that, in proceedings before the sheriff for a finding that the ground is established, the standard of proof is expressly that required in criminal procedure, *i.e.* beyond reasonable doubt.[14] This higher standard cannot be avoided by referring the child on the basis that his or her commission of criminal offences amounts to exposure to moral danger (the ground of referral contained in s. 52(2)(b)).[15] It would be different if the commission of offences was merely part of a wider picture which in essence amounted to another ground of referral: in that case even the offences could be proved on the civil rather than the criminal standard.[16] It is, however, only the standard of proof that is affected by referring the child under this condition. Proceedings under this condition, as under others, are not criminal proceedings; although essentially *sui generis* they are more akin to civil than to criminal proceedings.[17]

19.26   There is a conclusive presumption that no child under the age of eight years can be guilty of an offence.[18] It follows that no child under eight can be referred to a children's hearing under this condition.[19] Whether a child over that age has the *mens rea* necessary to commit an offence may sometimes be a question of difficulty. There is old authority for the view that a pupil child cannot be guilty

---

[7] Education (Scotland) Act 1980, s. 30.
[8] *Kennedy v. Clark*, 1970 J.C. 55. See above, paras 12.07 *et seq.*
[9] *D v. Kennedy*, 1988 S.L.T. 55.
[10] Education (Scotland) Act 1980, s. 86, which applies to "any legal proceedings".
[11] Education (Scotland) Act 1980, s. 36(3), as amended by the Children (Scotland) Act 1995, Sched. 4, para. 28(2).
[12] Children (Scotland) Act 1995, s. 54(1) and (2).
[13] For which, see below, paras 19.63 *et seq.*
[14] s. 68(3)(b).
[15] *Constanda v. M*, 1997 S.L.T. 1396.
[16] *ibid. per* Lord President Rodger at 1398D–F.
[17] *McGregor v. T & Anr*, 1975 S.L.T. 76.
[18] Criminal Procedure (Scotland) Act 1995, s. 41.
[19] *Merrin v. S*, 1987 S.L.T. 193.

art and part in a crime committed by his or her parent if he or she acted at the parent's command.[20] However, rules designed for the avoidance of punishment are not altogether apt in the context of compulsory measures of supervision, and in any case if the parent's guilt is established then condition (b)[21] will almost certainly be established and the child's case can be referred on that basis.

If a child has been prosecuted in a criminal court and pleads guilty to or is **19.27** found guilty of an offence that court may, except where the offence is one the sentence for which is fixed by law, remit the case to a children's hearing for disposal. If it does so the court's jurisdiction ceases and the case stands referred to the children's hearing.[22] A certificate of the plea or finding of guilt signed by the clerk of court is conclusive evidence for the purposes of the remit of the commission of the offence,[23] with the result that there is no need to seek the child's and relevant persons' acceptance of the ground at the commencement of the hearing. The court may make such a remit: (i) where a child is not already subject to a supervision requirement; (ii) after obtaining and considering the advice of a children's hearing as to the treatment of a child who is already subject to a supervision requirement; or (iii) after obtaining and considering such advice in relation to a person not subject to a supervision requirement who is over the age of 16 and is not within six months of attaining the age of 18, but in this case only if the advice obtained is to the effect that such a remit should be made. For the purposes of disposal of the case the Act applies to a person in category (iii) as if he or she were a child.[24]

(j) The child has misused alcohol or any drug, whether or not a controlled drug within the meaning of the Misuse of Drugs Act 1971
This condition can be traced to Article 33 of the UN Convention on the Rights **19.28** of the Child, under which States are obliged to take appropriate steps to protect children from the dangers of illicit use of drugs. The important word in this condition is "misused". The taking of drugs for proper medicinal purposes and, perhaps, the taking of alcohol in a responsibly supervised social environment will not satisfy the condition. For a child to become inebriated through alcohol use will invariably be a misuse, as will any use of drugs for other than medicinal purposes.

(k) The child has misused a volatile substance by deliberately inhaling its vapour, other than for medical purposes
This condition concerns "glue sniffing" and inhaling the vapours of similar **19.29** intoxicating substances.

(l) The child is being provided with accommodation by a local authority under section 25, or is subject to a parental responsibilities order obtained under section 86, of the Children (Scotland) Act 1995 and, in either case, his or her behaviour is such that special measures are necessary for his or her adequate supervision in his or her interests or the interests of others
In carrying out its duties to provide accommodation for children,[25] or when **19.30** a parental responsibilities order has been made in its favour,[26] it sometimes happens that a local authority believes that special measures must be adopted,

[20] *John Rae*, Jan. 1, 1662; Mackenzie, I, v; Hume, Comm., I, 49 and 50. The concept of pupillarity remains relevant for the criminal law: see Age of Legal Capacity (Scotland) Act 1991, s. 1(3)(c).
[21] Above, para. 19.14.
[22] Criminal Procedure (Scotland) Act 1995, s. 49.
[23] *ibid.* s. 50(1).
[24] Children (Scotland) Act 1995, s. 50(2).
[25] See above, paras 16.07 *et seq.*
[26] See above, Chap. 17.

such as restraining the child in secure accommodation. If this is necessary either in the child's own interests or in the interests of others (*e.g.* if the child poses some threat to others) then this condition is satisfied and the question arises of whether the child is in need of compulsory measures of supervision.

PROCEDURES BEFORE THE HEARING

Interim protection of the child

19.31   While it is not required by the scheme of the Act that any interim measures be taken before the children's hearing convenes, this may sometimes be desirable, for need may arise to secure the safety of a child pending consideration of his or her case by the reporter and the children's hearing. This is achieved primarily by removing a child to a place of safety either under a warrant or under a child protection order. The rules and procedures governing these orders are examined later.[27]

Initial action by reporter

19.32   On receipt of information about a case that may require a children's hearing to be arranged (*i.e.* a case of a child who may be in need of compulsory measures of supervision) there are several ways in which, after making such initial investigation as he or she may think necessary, the reporter may proceed with the case.[28] As he or she is required to proceed only with cases that may require a children's hearing to be arranged, he or she must first decide whether a case on which information is received falls into that category. Unless it is clear that the information either does not disclose any case appropriate for action by him or her or is already sufficient to enable him or her to decide how to proceed, an initial investigation is then indicated so as to enable a proper choice to be made among the options which are open to the reporter. For the purposes of making this initial investigation the reporter may request from the local authority a report on the child and on such circumstances concerning the child as appear to him or her to be relevant; and the local authority is obliged to supply such a report, which may contain such information, from any person whomsoever, as the reporter or the local authority thinks fit.[29] Having investigated the case, the reporter must decide whether or not a children's hearing requires to be arranged. This is not the same question as whether or not grounds of referral exist in relation to the child, for it is open to the reporter to conclude that, though grounds do exist, nevertheless the child is not in need of compulsory measures of supervision. It is only when he or she is satisfied both (i) that at least one of the grounds of referral exists and (ii) that compulsory measures of supervision are necessary that the obligation to arrange a children's hearing arises.[30] If the reporter decides that a children's hearing does not require to be arranged, he or she may not at any other time, on the basis solely of the information obtained during the initial investigation, arrange a children's hearing[31]; this does not, however, preclude a subsequent reference to the reporter based on new evidence. The reporter must inform the child, any relevant person, and the person who brought the case to his or her notice, or any of those persons, of his or her decision not to arrange a children's hearing[32] and may, if he or she considers it appropriate, refer the case to the local authority with a view to its making arrangements for the advice, guidance and assistance of the child and his or her family in accordance with Chapter 1 of Part II of the 1995 Act.[33]

---

[27] Below, Chap. 20.
[28] s. 56(1).
[29] s. 56(2).
[30] s. 65(1).
[31] s. 56(5).
[32] s. 56(4)(a).
[33] s. 56(4)(b).

Where, on the other hand, it appears to the reporter that compulsory measures **19.33** of supervision are necessary in respect of the child, he or she must arrange a children's hearing to which he or she shall refer the case for consideration and determination.[34] Having arranged a children's hearing the reporter must, if he or she has not already done so, request a report on the child and his or her circumstances from the local authority and he or she may request such additional information as he or she thinks fit.[35] If the reference to the reporter came from a local authority or a police officer, the reporter must inform the local authority or the chief constable of his or her decision to arrange a children's hearing.[36] The reporter's discretion is wide and unfettered. There is no means by which a case can be referred to a children's hearing except on his or her decision. He or she is not, however, master of the process in the way that a public prosecutor is. If it appears to the reporter that a child is in need of compulsory measures of supervision, he or she must arrange a children's hearing and once a hearing has been arranged the case cannot be withdrawn or abandoned by the reporter. It is thought that this stage is reached as soon as there is an overt act indicating that a hearing has been arranged, such as notification to the child or relevant person, or a request for the statutory report from a local authority.

Business meetings

The reporter may, in his or her discretion, arrange a "business meeting" **19.34** with members of the children's panel from which the children's hearing is to be constituted, in order to obtain such direction or guidance in relation to the performance of his or her functions in relation to the proceedings of a particular case as they think appropriate.[37] The business meeting is a meeting between the reporter and three panel members, at least one of whom must be male and at least one of whom must be female.[38] Neither the child nor the relevant person has a right to attend this meeting, but they must be given notice, not later than four working days before the date of the meeting (i) that it has been arranged and of the matters which may be considered and determined by the meeting, (ii) that they have a right to make their views on these matters known to the reporter, and (iii) that the reporter has a duty to present these views to the meeeting.[39] A copy of the grounds of referral and of any document or information relevant to the matters to be considered at the business meeting must be given to the panel members, the relevant persons, any safeguarder and the child.[40]

There are three matters which are open to a business meeting to consider.[41] **19.35** First, it may consider whether notice of the children's hearing is to be given by the reporter to a person as a "relevant person": in other words, the business meeting may give advice to the reporter as to who should be regarded as a relevant person. It should be noted, however, that the actual decision falls to the children's hearing, who may disagree with the advice given by the business meeting. Since the reporter has a duty to notify all relevant persons of the arranging of a children's hearing (thereby protecting their right and duty to attend) an error on the part of the business meeting, if acted upon by the reporter, will be appealable.[42] Secondly, the business meeting may determine whether

---

[34] s. 56(6).
[35] s. 56(7).
[36] Children's Hearings (Scotland) Rules 1996 (S.I. 1996 No. 3261), r. 3(2).
[37] s. 64.
[38] 1996 Rules, r. 4(1).
[39] s. 64(2) and 1996 Rules, r. 4(3) and (4).
[40] 1996 Rules, r. 4(3)(c). This is the only requirement to provide the child with documentation.
[41] *ibid*. r. 4(2).
[42] See further, Norrie, *Children's Hearings in Scotland* (1997) at pp. 42–43.

the reporter should give notice to the child that he or she is released from the obligation to attend the children's hearing. It is not the business meeting which has the power to release the child from that obligation, but only the children's hearing[43] and so it remains open to the children's hearing to require the child's attendance even when the child has been informed that he or she need not attend. Thirdly, the business meeting may determine whether the reporter should inform a relevant person that it is considered unreasonable to require his or her attendance or that his or her attendance is unnecessary for the proper consideration of the case. Again, it is the children's hearing rather than the business meeting which has the sole power to relieve the relevant person of the obligation to attend[44] and so it remains open to the children's hearing to disagree with the advice given by the business meeting and to require the relevant person's attendance.

19.36   Once a determination has been made by a business meeting, or it has given guidance or direction to the reporter, the reporter must, as soon as reasonably practicable, give written notice of the determination, guidance or direction to the child, the relevant person and any safeguarder.[45]

Notification of hearings and supply of documents
19.37   When the reporter arranges a children's hearing, he or she is obliged to notify those with a right and a duty to attend that he or she has done so, and must also supply various documents to the participants.

19.38   The panel members must be notified of the hearing wherever practicable at least seven days before the date of the hearing[46] and, as soon as reasonably practicable, but wherever practicable not later than three days before the date of the hearing, they must be given a copy of any of the following which is relevant:

    (a) a report of a local authority on the child and his or her social background;
    (b) a statement of the grounds of referral;
    (c) any judicial remit or reference or any reference by a local authority;
    (d) any supervision requirement to which the child is subject;
    (e) any report prepared by any safeguarder[47] appointed in the case; and
    (f) any views of the child given in writing to the reporter.[48]

Additionally, any other information or document which is material to the consideration of the case must be made available to members of the children's hearing before the hearing.[49]

19.39   The relevant persons must be given written notice, if their whereabouts are known and not later than seven days before the date of the hearing,[50] of their right and obligation to attend and of the date, time and place of the hearing.[51] Any document given to or information made available to the chairman and members of the children's hearing must at the same time (unless previously supplied) be given to or made available to each relevant person[52] but not,

---

[43] s. 45(2) grants the power to "a children's hearing": the business meeting is limited to directing that the child should be informed of such a release.
[44] Under s. 45(8): see below. para. 19.46.
[45] 1996 Rules, r. 4(8).
[46] *ibid.* r. 5(1).
[47] See below, paras 19.53 –19.54.
[48] 1996 Rules, r. 5(1).
[49] *ibid.* r. 5(2).
[50] Unless the hearing is arranged on an emergency basis, in which case the notice must be given as soon as reasonably practicable and if it cannot be given in writing it may be given orally: *ibid.* r. 7(5).
[51] *ibid.* r. 7(1) and (4).
[52] *ibid.* r. 5(3).

noticeably, the child. Additionally, notification of the right to attend, together with copies of the documents and other information sent to members of the children's hearing, must be sent to any father of the child referred who is living with the mother of the child.[53] Any person provided with papers under any of these provisions must return them to the reporter at the end of the hearing.[54]

The child must receive notice of the hearing not less than seven days before **19.40** the hearing and in that notice he or she must be informed of his or her right and obligation to attend, and of the date, time and place of the hearing.[55] Notification is not achieved by sending notice to the address from which the child has been removed to a place of safety.[56] The child must also be informed of the entitlement to indicate whether or not he or she wishes to express views, of the entitlement to express views, and of the fact that if views are expressed to the reporter he or she will convey them to the members of the children's hearing, to any relevant person and to any safeguarder.[57] The reporter is obliged to send to the child, not less than seven days before the date of the hearing, a statement of the grounds of referral.[58] The requirement to notify is absolute regardless of age, despite its inevitably notional character in the case of very young children. The reporter has no discretion in respect of notification or of securing attendance, but if a hearing decide to release the child from the obligation to attend at a subsequent hearing or the reporter has been advised by a business meeting to give notice to the child that he or she is released from the obligation to attend the requirement to secure the attendance of the child is clearly superseded so far as the hearing for which the release is granted is concerned.

If a safeguarder has been appointed by a children's hearing,[59] the reporter **19.41** must inform that person of the date, time and place of the hearing at the same time and in the same manner as notice is given to the relevant person, and the safeguarder must also be given a statement of the reasons for his or her appointment.[60] The reporter must also send to the safeguarder any information or documentation made available to the members of the children's hearing regardless of the date of the safeguarder's appointment in the proceedings.[61]

The chief social work officer of the appropriate local authority must be **19.42** notified of the date, time and place of the hearing, and of the name, date of birth and address, so far as is known, of the child whose case is to be considered at the hearing.[62]

CONDUCT OF THE HEARING

Privacy of hearing: persons present

A children's hearing is conducted in private and the general rule is that no **19.43** person other than one whose presence is necessary for the proper consideration of the case, or whose presence is permitted by the chairman, shall be present.[63] It appears that it is for the hearing as a whole to decide whether a person's presence is necessary for the proper consideration of the case, should that be in

---

[53] 1996 Rules, rr. 5(3) and 7(3).
[54] *ibid.* r. 5(7).
[55] *ibid.* r. 6(1).
[56] *Sloan* v. *B*, 1991 S.L.T. 530, *per* Lord President Hope at 540I
[57] 1996 Rules, r. 6(4).
[58] *ibid.* r. 18(1)(b).
[59] See below, paras 19.53–19.54.
[60] 1996 Rules, r. 14(2).
[61] *ibid.* r. 14(5).
[62] *ibid.* r. 8.
[63] s. 43(1).

dispute, and that the chairman has a discretion to admit other persons. The general rule is, however, subject to a number of qualifications.

The child

19.44 Under the 1968 Act, the child was placed under a duty to attend his or her own children's hearing,[64] but that statute was remarkably silent on his or her right to attend. However, in *Sloan v. B*, Sheriff Kelbie expressed himself "satisfied that the corollary of the obligation on the child to attend and listen to the explanation is a right to be there and to hear the explanation",[65] and this was surely correct. The matter has now been put beyond doubt and the 1995 Act confers upon the child an absolute right, and imposes upon the child a qualified duty, to attend at all stages of the hearing.[66] This includes those portions of the hearing at which grounds of referral are put, at which the hearing gives consideration to the case, and at which the members of the hearing make and explain their decision. The child's right to attend must be read in the light of his or her duty to attend—it is not a right that gives the child a choice whether to exercise it but rather is one that imposes an obligation on everyone else to allow the child to be present. The qualification to the duty is that the child may be released from the obligation to attend where the children's hearing are satisfied in a case concerned with Schedule 1 offences that the attendance of the child is not necessary for the just hearing of that case or, in any case, where the hearing are satisfied that it would be detrimental to the interests of the child to be present at the hearing of the case.[67] Although not specifically provided for in the statute, it is necessary that certain decisions extrinsic to the merits (*e.g.* on the granting of warrants) should be made in the absence of the child and also of the relevant person. It appears from the terms of the provisions on consideration of a child's case in his or her absence that, except in the cases for which specific statutory provision is made, such consideration may be incompetent even if the requisite measures to secure attendance have been taken and have failed or if the child has waived his or her right to attend and the hearing does not consider his or her attendance necessary. Hearings should, therefore, make positive and recorded decisions to consider the case in the child's absence, specifying the statutory ground upon which they do so.

19.45 Release of the child from the obligation to attend does not take away the child's right to attend,[68] and this right is further protected in these circumstances by the requirement in the rules that, where release is granted, the reporter must inform the child that he or she has a right to attend if he or she so wishes.[69] Nor does release of the child from the obligation to attend relieve the chairman of the obligation in section 65(4) to explain the grounds to the child.[70] In other words, while the child may be released from the obligation to attend, the chairman must still explain to the child the grounds of referral. Allowing the child not to attend the part of the hearing at which the grounds are explained would deny the chairman the opportunity to fulfil his or her obligation to explain and would, therefore, be incompetent unless the child were too young to understand and reference to the sheriff is required in any case under section 65(9)(a).[71] It follows

---

[64] Social Work (Scotland) Act 1968, s. 40(1).
[65] 1991 S.L.T. 530 at 534–535. This part of Sheriff Kelbie's judgment was not criticised by the First Division when the case reached that court.
[66] s. 45(1).
[67] s. 45(2).
[68] s. 45(2) is expressly "without prejudice" to s. 45(1)(a).
[69] 1996 Rules, r. 6(3).
[70] s. 45(2) is expressly stated to be "without prejudice to… s. 65(4)".
[71] See below, para. 19.59.

that the power to release the understanding child from the obligation to attend can be exercised only in relation to the other stages of the hearing, that is to say the consideration of the case and its disposal, and any review subsequent to the imposition of a supervision requirement, or in relation to the granting or continuing of a warrant.

The relevant person

Each relevant person[72] has the right to attend at all stages of a children's **19.46** hearing.[73] The relevant person's right to be present carries with it a duty to attend at all stages unless the hearing are satisfied that it would be unreasonable to require his or her attendance or that his or her attendance is unnecessary for the proper consideration of the case[74]; it is an offence to fail to comply with that obligation.[75] The genetic father of a child who is not a relevant person[76] is also entitled to attend the hearing so long as he is living with the genetic mother.[77] He is entitled to receive all the documents that the reporter must make available to the relevant person; but his right to be present is designed solely to permit him to take part in the discussion of his child's case and he has neither standing to accept or deny grounds of referral, nor title to appeal any decision made by the children's hearing or to call for a review of any supervision requirement made or continued. Whether such a father is living with the mother or not is a question of fact and there is no requirement that they be living together "as husband and wife". It would seem that the parents must be living together at the date of the hearing to give the non-relevant person father the right to attend.[78]

When parental responsibilities and parental rights have been removed from **19.47** a relevant person by a parental responsibilities order under section 86 of the Children (Scotland) Act 1995,[79] that person is no longer a relevant person in relation to the child and his or her right to attend any children's hearing disappears.[80] Since the effect of a parental responsibilities order is to transfer parental rights and responsibilities from the relevant person to the local authority[81] it would seem that the right (and duty) to attend the children's hearing will pass from the relevant persons to the officers of the relevant local authority as from the time the parental responsibilities order is made and will remain with them until such time as that order comes to an end.

The children's hearing have the power to exclude any relevant person or **19.48** that person's representative, or both, from any part or parts of the hearing for so long as is necessary in the interests of the child, where they are satisfied that (i) they must do so in order to obtain the views of the child in relation to the case before the hearing or (ii) the presence of the person or persons in question is causing, or is likely to cause, significant distress to the child.[82] On the same grounds they may also exclude the non-relevant person father who has a right

---

[72] Defined above, para. 19.07.
[73] s. 45(8)(a).
[74] s. 45(8)(b).
[75] s. 45(9).
[76] Usually a father who is not and has never been married to the mother of the child.
[77] 1996 Rules, rr. 12(1) and 5(3).
[78] Where the child is also living with the parents it will be a highly unusual case that the father is not a relevant person: this provision is, in practice, limited to cases in which the child is living apart from his or her parents and gives the father an equal right of attendance (but not of participation) to the mother.
[79] For details of which, see above, Chap. 17.
[80] Unless, perhaps, as a genetic father living with the mother he can rely on r. 12 to give him the right to attend.
[81] See above, para. 17.14.
[82] s. 46(1).

to attend under rule 12.[83] Excluding a relevant person is a matter entirely within the discretion of the hearing, and the decision lies with all three members and not just the chairman alone; it is a decision in which the child's welfare is the hearing's paramount consideration.[84] The power to exclude cannot be used to avoid explaining the grounds of referral to the relevant person, though there would seem to be nothing to prevent the hearing from excluding the relevant person while the explanation is given to the child, so long as they then seek acceptance of the grounds from the relevant person separately. If a relevant person or his or her representative has been excluded the chairman is obliged, after the exclusion has ended, to explain to the person who was so excluded the substance of what took place in his or her absence.[85] The "substance" of what took place is the generality of the discussion and the procedure and not the detail.

Other persons

19.49   Any member of the Council on Tribunals or of its Scottish committee and *bona fide* representatives of a newspaper or news agency have a right to attend,[86] and any constable, prison officer or other person duly authorised who has in his or her lawful custody a person who has to attend a children's hearing is entitled to be present at the hearing for the purpose of escorting that person.[87] None of these people takes an active part in the hearing. Safeguarders appointed by the hearing under section 41 are entitled to be present,[88] and they do take an active part. Also, any child whose case comes before a children's hearing and any relevant person who attends that children's hearing may each be accompanied by one person for the purpose of assisting the child or the relevant person in the discussion of the case.[89] A single person may represent both the child and a relevant person, or may represent more than one relevant person.[90] Journalists and representatives of relevant persons (but not, it would seem, the child's representative[91]) can be excluded if (i) it is necessary to do so, in the interests of the child, in order to obtain the views of the child in relation to the case before the hearing or (ii) the presence of the person in question is causing, or is likely to cause, significant distess to the child.[92] Once the exclusion has ended the chairman of the hearing must (in the case of representatives) and may (in the case of journalists) explain the substance of what took place during the exclusion.[93]

19.50   Rules also provide for the discretionary admission by the chairman of the hearing of certain other categories of persons. The categories are:

(a)   the chairman and members of the Children's Panel Advisory Committee and the clerk to the CPAC of the local authority;

(b)   any members or possible members of children's panels whose attendance is required at children's hearings for the purpose of their training and their instructors;

---

[83]   1996 Rules, r. 12(1).
[84]   s. 16(1).
[85]   s. 46(2).
[86]   s. 43(3).
[87]   1996 Rules, r. 12(2).
[88]   *ibid.* r. 14(3).
[89]   *ibid.* r. 11(1) and (2).
[90]   *ibid.* r. 11(3).
[91]   *Quaere* whether a person who represents both the child and the relevant person can be excluded.
[92]   ss. 43(4) (journalists) and 46(1) (representatives).
[93]   ss. 43(5) and 46(2).

   (c) any student engaged in formal education or training in social work or
       any person engaged in research relating to children who may be in
       need of compulsory measures of supervision;
   (d) any other person whose presence at the hearing may in the opinion of
       the chairman be justified by special circumstances.[94]

Paragraph (d) is designed to allow the presence of those who, in the opinion
of the chairman, have a significant interest in the child's well-being or have
something relevant to contribute to the consideration of the case which will
help the hearing determine wherein the child's interests lie. In *L v. H*[95]
Lord Justice-Clerk Ross expressed the hope that an unmarried father who
regularly exercised rights of access to the child would be permitted to attend
the hearing under this provision. None of these people, except those in
paragraph (d), takes an active part in the hearing but all are, of course, subject
to the rules of confidentiality that apply to everyone else. The chairman
must take all reasonable steps to ensure that the number of persons present
at any one time is kept to a minimum[96] but as he or she cannot, of course,
exclude the persons who have a right to attend, that injunction is little more
than a guide as to the way in which his or her discretionary powers of
admission should be exercised.

Offence of publication
    It is an offence for any person to publish any matter in respect of proceedings **19.51**
at a children's hearing, or before a sheriff in a case within the children's hearing
system, or at any appeal, which is intended to, or is likely to, identify any child
concerned in the proceedings or appeal, or an address or school as being that of
any such child.[97] The prohibition extends to publication in England and Wales
and in Northern Ireland[98] and it protects not only the referred child but also any
other child concerned in the proceedings, such as a child witness.[99] This offence
may be committed by any person and not just (as was the case under the 1968
Act[1]) by newspaper publishers and broadcasters. It is a defence for the accused
to prove that he or she did not know and had no reason to suspect that the
published matter was intended, or was likely, to identify the child or, as the case
may be, the address or school.[2] The sheriff in any proceedings before him, the
Court of Session in any appeal, or the Secretary of State in relation to any
proceedings at a children's hearing may, in the interests of justice and to such
extent as they consider appropriate, dispense with the requirement that there be
no publication of the child's identity, address or school.[3] The sheriff and the
Court of Session are obliged, in deciding whether to do so, to regard the child's
welfare as paramount[4] with the result that, in these cases, dispensation can be
given only in the interests of justice to the child.[5]

---

[94] 1996 Rules, r. 13.
[95] 1996 S.L.T. 612. See also *Chapman, Petr*, May 21, 1997, OH.
[96] s. 43(2).
[97] s. 44(1).
[98] s. 105(8).
[99] See *McArdle v. Orr*, 1994 S.L.T. 463.
[1] Social Work (Scotland) Act 1968, s. 58.
[2] s. 44(3).
[3] s. 44(5).
[4] s. 16(1).
[5] See Norrie, *Children's Hearings in Scotland* (1997) at pp. 63–64. On different statutory provisions,
   it was held in England that the welfare of the child was not paramount: *Oxfordshire County
   Council v. L and F* (1997) 1 F.L.R. 235.

Securing the attendance of the child

19.52   The reporter is charged with the responsibility of securing the child's attendance at the hearing of his or her case, including hearings to which the case is continued subsequent to the first hearing.[6] The child must be notified that his or her case has been referred to a children's hearing,[7] and must attend in accordance with that notification.[8] In order to allow the reporter to fulfil his or her duty of securing the child's attendance at a children's hearing, he or she may make application to the children's hearing seeking the issuing of a warrant to keep the child in a place of safety and to bring him or her before a children's hearing.[9] In cases in which the child has failed to attend a hearing a warrant can be issued by the children's hearing, either on the application of the reporter or of their own motion, to find the child, to keep him or her in a place of safety and to bring him or her before a children's hearing.[10] These warrants are considered in more detail elsewhere.[11]

Appointment of a safeguarder

19.53   In any proceedings at a children's hearing the hearing[12] must give consideration to the question of whether it is necessary to appoint a person to safeguard the interests of the child in the proceedings and, if they do so consider, they must make such an appointment on such terms and conditions as appear appropriate.[13] The reasons for the decision to make such an appointment must be stated by the hearing.[14] The legislation does not specify the circumstances in which it would be appropriate to appoint a safeguarder,[15] except that it must be necessary to safeguard the interests of the child in the proceedings. Such necessity might arise if there is a conflict of interests between the child and the relevant person, or because the child needs independent advice in the course of the proceedings and might not otherwise get it, or because the hearing believes that a safeguarder might be able to identify, and indicate to the hearing, wherein the child's interests lie, or because this is the best way to allow the child the opportunity to express views.[16]

19.54   Once appointed, the safeguarder is obliged to draw up a report in writing on the case of the child,[17] and though it is not specified what matters should be covered by this report, it is expected to contain a recommendation as to what disposal the hearing should make in the interests of the child. In order to assist in the performance of the safeguarder's function, he or she is entitled to receive from the reporter, regardless of the date of his or her appointment as safeguarder, any information or document which has been made available to the members of the hearing.[18] The report drawn up by the safeguarder must be given to the reporter, who must make it available to the members of the hearing and all the relevant persons.[19] The safeguarder is entitled to be present throughout the

---

[6] s. 45(3).
[7] See above, para. 19.40.
[8] s. 45(1).
[9] s. 45(4).
[10] s. 45(5).
[11] See below, paras 20.09–20.10.
[12] And not just the chairman, as was the position under s. 34A of the Social Work (Scotland) Act 1968.
[13] s. 41(1).
[14] s. 41(3).
[15] Under s. 34A of the Social Work (Scotland) Act 1968 appointment was expressly limited to situations in which there was a conflict of interests between the child and his or her parent.
[16] r. 15(4)(c) of the 1996 Rules envisages that one of the functions of the safeguarder is to elicit and transmit the views of the child.
[17] 1996 Rules, r. 14(4).
[18] *ibid.* r. 14(5).
[19] *ibid.* r. 5(1)(e) and (3).

hearing[20] and the children's hearing must endeavour to obtain the views of any safeguarder who attends on what arrangements would be in the best interests of the child.[21] Once the hearing have made a decision, the safeguarder must be given written notice of the decision, plus a copy of the statement of reasons therefor.[22] The safeguarder has a right of appeal against the decision, on behalf of the child.[23]

Commencement of the hearing: explanation of the grounds

The procedure at any children's hearing is as the chairman in his or her **19.55** discretion determines.[24] There is, nevertheless, a statutory structure that must be followed. The hearing commences with an explanation given to the child and the relevant person of the grounds stated by the reporter for the referral of the case. It is the chairman's duty to give the explanation and he or she should do so at the opening of the proceedings on the referral.[25] The purpose of this explanation is to ascertain whether the grounds are accepted in whole or in part by the child and the relevant person. The Act is silent as to how the duty is to be discharged adequately where the grounds of referral raise legal issues of difficulty or complexity nor is any means provided for securing that such issues do not pass undetected. Grounds of referral are not defined but there is, by implication, a clear reference to the conditions which have to be satisfied if it is to be held that a child may be in need of compulsory measures of supervision,[26] and the relevant rules have been made on that basis.[27] The grounds of referral in any given case are the conditions which it is claimed are satisfied in respect of the child together with the facts stated as supporting that claim. They are a composite of law and fact.

Subsequent procedure depends on the response to the explanation of the **19.56** grounds of referral. Where the child and all the relevant persons who attend the hearing accept the grounds, the hearing proceeds to a consideration of the case.[28] If either the child or any of the relevant persons does not accept the grounds, the hearing must, unless they decide to discharge the referral, direct the reporter to make an application to the sheriff for a finding as to whether the grounds are established.[29] That is required wherever there is not explicit acceptance; absence of dispute is not enough, although a statement that the grounds are not disputed may be open to construction as an acceptance.

It may happen that the grounds are accepted by one or more of the parties **19.57** only in part. In that situation, the hearing has a choice of:

(a) proceeding with the hearing, if it considers it appropriate to do so, in respect of the grounds accepted by the child and relevant persons, or

(b) directing the reporter to make an application to the sheriff for a finding as to whether such grounds as are not accepted are established, or

(c) discharging the referral.[30]

---

[20] 1996 Rules, r. 14(3).
[21] *ibid*. rr. 20(3)(d), 22(3)(c) and 26(1).
[22] *ibid*. rr. 21(1), 22(7) and 26(1).
[23] See below, para. 19.96.
[24] 1996 Rules, r. 10(3).
[25] s. 65(4).
[26] s. 52.
[27] 1996 Rules, r. 17.
[28] s. 65(5).
[29] s. 65(7).
[30] *ibid*.

19.58   If partial acceptance of the grounds is to be such as to enable the hearing, if it thinks it appropriate to do so, to proceed, it must, it is submitted, extend to an admission of both law and fact sufficient to justify the conclusion that the child may be in need of compulsory measures of supervision—that is to say, the facts accepted must be sufficient to show that at least one of the conditions on which the reporter relies is satisfied. Anything short of that means that the competency of the hearing's applying compulsory measures of supervision is not accepted or that facts sufficient to form a basis for disposal of the case, other than by discharge, are not accepted, or both. In either of these events, there is a clear barrier to the hearing's proceeding. It is not, however, necessary that the legal incidents of a condition should be accepted in the terms set out by the reporter. The emphasis is on the facts rather than on legal refinements although the facts must disclose that a condition is satisfied. Accordingly, if the grounds of referral relate to the commission by the child of an offence, the grounds are accepted in part if it is accepted that an offence was committed and stated facts sufficient to amount to the commission of an offence are also accepted. The case may then proceed before the hearing although it is not accepted that the particular offence libelled by the reporter was committed.[31] If, for example, the grounds of referral are that the child committed the offence of theft, and the child and relevant person accept that an offence was committed but claim it was reset, there is an acceptance in part which is sufficient to entitle the hearing to proceed provided facts sufficient to amount at least to reset are also accepted. Likewise, the hearing may proceed if assault is alleged but only breach of the peace and facts sufficient to support that offence are admitted. That hearings, as a result, may be faced with questions outwith the competence of a lay tribunal is a defect in the system for which the only remedy is that, whenever there is doubt, an application should be made to the sheriff.[32]

Lack of understanding

19.59   It may also happen that a child will not be capable of understanding an explanation of the grounds of referral, or in fact does not understand any explanation that has been given. In either of these events the hearing must, unless it decides to discharge the referral, direct the reporter to make an application to the sheriff for a finding as to whether any of the grounds has been established.[33] A decision that the child will not be capable of understanding can be made in the absence of any examination of the child but this should be done only in the clearest of cases, such as with very young children. A determination that the child has not understood presupposes that the chairman has attempted to give an explanation and should not, therefore, be made in the absence of such an attempt (or, *a fortiori*, in the absence of the child[34]). The provision is supererogatory where the child does not accept a ground of referral. Its purpose would seem to be to require an application to be made where the child, although he or she did not understand the explanation, was nonetheless willing to accept the ground, and so to reduce the risk of acceptances based on deficient understanding. There is no corresponding provision for the case of a relevant person who is incapable of understanding or does not understand the explanation; but a relevant person who is incapable of understanding cannot, it is submitted, accept and a relevant person who, although not lacking in capacity, does not

---

[31] *cf. McGregor v. D*, 1977 S.C. 330 which, although concerned with the sheriff's decision on whether grounds of referral were established, turns on issues which are largely similar.

[32] On which, see below, paras 19.63 *et seq.*

[33] s. 65(9).

[34] See *Sloan v. B*, 1991 S.L.T. 530.

understand must, unless he or she indicates to the contrary, be taken as not accepting.[35] Capacity to understand is to be presumed in the case of an adult and on the assumption that the explanation is adapted to the age and intellectual development of the child, the same is true of a child, other than a child clearly too young to understand any explanation.[36] It is, however, desirable, if not mandatory, that the hearing should ascertain whether or not an explanation has in fact been understood by the child. There is no provision for the case where a child's lack of understanding relates to only part of the grounds of referral. It is attractive to regard such a case as one of non-acceptance of that part, but as the Act treats the explanation as a whole, it would appear, on a strict construction, that failure to understand any part of it affects the whole and so requires the making of an application to the sheriff for a finding as to whether any of the grounds has been established.

Non-attendance

In the event of non-attendance by a relevant person, his or her acceptance is **19.60** not required[37] and the hearing may proceed to a consideration of the case in his or her absence (so long as the other appropriate acceptances are obtained). Where the child does not attend it would in some cases be advantageous if the hearing could treat his or her non-attendance as indicating that he or she did not accept the grounds of referral and so direct the reporter to make an application to the sheriff forthwith. The Act, however, contemplates that acceptance or non-acceptance should follow on the chairman's explanation, and that before a hearing can either proceed with a case or make an application to the sheriff the child must have appeared before it, which can be secured by the granting of a warrant,[38] and have had an opportunity of accepting or not accepting the grounds of referral. The requirment on the chairman to give an explanation to a child who may be able to understand cannot be avoided by releasing the child from the obligation to attend the hearing at which an explanation is to be given. Section 45(2), which allows such release, is expressly stated to be "without prejudice to... section 65(4)", which requires the chairman to give an explanation. It follows that such release should not be granted in relation to hearings at which acceptance of the grounds of referral is sought, except in the case of children who clearly will not understand any explanation offered. *Sloan v. B*[39] might be taken to suggest that an older child can be released from the obligation to attend this part of the hearing in circumstances in which the relevant person denies the grounds of referral—for that denial will necessitate an application to the sheriff in any case. However, any release would invariably be granted before the hearing at which grounds of referral are explained and before, therefore, it is known whether or not the relevant person is denying the grounds—before, that it, it is known whether a release would be competent or not. The implication from *Sloan* (if it was ever correct[40]) does not, it is submitted, survive the coming into force of the 1995 Act.

---

[35] See Kearney, *Children's Hearings and the Sheriff Court* (1987) at p. 110.

[36] While the child 12 years of age or over is presumed to be of sufficient age and maturity to express views (s. 16(2)) and, it may be assumed, to understand an explanation, it should be remembered (i) that that presumption is a rebuttable presumption of fact and (ii) its existence does not imply a contrary presumption in the case of children under the age of 12. In all cases it is a question of fact whether the child understands or is capable of understanding and each child should be assessed individually.

[37] s. 65(10).

[38] See below, para. 20.09.

[39] 1991 S.L.T. 530.

[40] This was doubted in Norrie, "Excluding Children from Children's Hearings", 1993 S.L.T. (News) 67.

Keeping the child in a place of safety

19.61   If the children's hearing are unable to dispose of the case, for example because the grounds of referral have been denied or not understood, and either (i) there is reason to believe that the child may not attend at any hearing of his or her case or (ii) there is reason to believe that the child may fail to comply with a requirement to attend at a clinic, hospital or other establishment for further investigation or (iii) it is necessary that the child should be kept in a place of safety in order to safeguard and promote his or her welfare, then it may, either *ex proprio motu* or on the motion of the reporter, grant a warrant which will be authority to a person named in the warrant to find and keep, or to keep, the child in a place of safety for a period not exceeding 22 days after the warrant is granted and to bring the child before a children's hearing at such times as may be specified in the warrant.[41] The warrant may contain such conditions as the children's hearing thinks necessary or expedient, including conditions relating to medical treatment and contact.[42] When granting a warrant the children's hearing may order that the place of safety at which the child is to be kept shall not be disclosed to any person or class of persons specified in the order.[43] A warrant under this provision may be continued by the children's hearing, on cause shown by the reporter, for such period not exceeding 22 days as appears to the children's hearing to be necessary,[44] and the total length of time a child can be kept in a place of safety under this provision is 66 days.[45] At any time prior to the expiry of a warrant granted under section 66 the reporter may apply to the sheriff for a warrant to keep the child in the place of safety after such expiry.[46] The warrant may be granted by the sheriff only on cause shown and must specify the date on which it will expire; it may contain any condition or requirement that could be contained in a section 66 warrant granted by the children's hearing.[47]

Transference of case

19.62   A children's hearing in one local authority's area may transfer the case to a children's hearing in the area of another where it is satisfied that the case could be better considered by a children's hearing in that other area.[48] If this is done, grounds of referral accepted or established do not require to be further accepted or established.[49] Such transfer will be appropriate where the child is resident in the area of the other local authority, because a supervision requirement made by a hearing constituted from the children's hearing from one local government area imposes an obligation to give effect to it only on that local authority and not on any other.[50]

APPLICATION TO THE SHERIFF

Introduction

19.63   The policy of the Act is to separate the body that decides what compulsory measures to take concerning the child, and the body that decides whether there are grounds on which such measures can lawfully be taken.[51] Consequently, if

---

[41] s. 66(1)–(3).
[42] s. 66(4). These matters are discussed more fully below, para. 20.12.
[43] s. 66(7).
[44] s. 66(5).
[45] s. 66(8).
[46] s. 67(1).
[47] s. 67(2).
[48] s. 48(1).
[49] s. 48(2).
[50] ss. 71 and 93(1) (definition of "relevant local authority").
[51] *per* Lord President Hope in *Sloan v. B*, 1991 S.L.T. 530 at 548D–E.

either the child or the relevant person or both does not accept the grounds of referral, or if the child will not or did not understand the explanation of the grounds of referral, the hearing must direct the reporter to apply to the sheriff for a finding of whether or not the grounds of referral are established.[52] If a hearing directs the reporter to make an application to the sheriff it is the duty of the chairman to explain to the child and the relevant person the purpose for which the application to the sheriff is being made and to inform the child that he or she is under an obligation to attend the hearing of the application.[53] The reporter must make the application within seven days.[54] There is no prescription of the sheriff court to which application is to be made except that where the ground of referral is that the child has committed an offence the application must be made to the sheriff who would have jurisdiction if the child were being prosecuted for that offence.[55] In other cases, the matter would appear to be at the discretion of the reporter, or, if the hearing so direct, of the hearing. The court which will normally be appropriate is, however, that of the sheriff court district within which the hearing is held, or, at least, a sheriff court situated in the local authority area within which the hearing took place.[56] A plea of *forum non conveniens* may not be altogether apt in proceedings bounded by the confines of a self-contained statutory scheme but the court retains, it is submitted, power to control extreme instances of choice of forum which amount to an abuse of process. The sheriff has no statutory authority to conduct any part of the proceedings outside the sheriff court district within which the court is situated, but the reporter may apply to the *nobile officium* of the Court of Session for a direction that the hearing or part of it should be held elsewhere, if good reasons for the exercise of that power exists.[57] The hearing before the sheriff must commence within 28 days of the lodging of the application[58] but thereafter, in order to allow time for further inquiry or for any other necessary cause, the sheriff may, either on his own motion or on the motion of any party, continue the hearing for such reasonable time as he may in the circumstances consider necessary.[59] A hearing at which all parties are present or at least have full opportunity of being present must take place within the prescribed time and accordingly the statutory requirement is not met if a diet fixed for a competent time is adjourned to a date outwith the 28-day period in circumstances which effectively deprive a party of such opportunity.[60] It is essential to such opportunity that there should be effective procedure at the diet fixed or at least that the prospect of effective procedure should not be precluded by unilateral action in advance. It is not, however, necessary that a consideration of the merits of the

---

[52] s. 65(7) and (9).

[53] s. 65(8).

[54] Act of Sederunt (Child Care and Maintenance Rules) 1997 (S.I. 1997 No. 291) (hereinafter "A.S. 1997"), r. 3.45(1).

[55] s. 68(3)(a).

[56] *Sloan, Petr*, 1991 S.L.T. 527 at 529D, *per* Lord President Hope. In *L. v. McGregor*, 1980 S.L.T. 17 it was held that it was competent for the reporter to apply to any court within, at least, the area of his local authority and perhaps beyond. Reporters are no longer tied in to local authorities, though children's panels are.

[57] *Sloan, Petr*, above, at 529D, *per* Lord President Hope. In this case the application was refused, the grounds advanced (that it would be contrary to the interests of certain child witnesses, who had been removed from their homes in Orkney to the mainland, to return to Orkney, and prejudicial to certain adult witnesses, including professional people, to require them to travel to Orkney) not being sufficient to persuade the court to direct that the proceedings before the sheriff be conducted elsewhere. Authority was however give for evidence of certain children to be taken elsewhere within the sheriffdom within which the sheriff was empowered to act.

[58] s. 68(2).

[59] A.S. 1997, r. 3.49.

[60] *H v. Mearns*, 1974 S.L.T. 184.

case should be commenced.[61] As the sheriff's power to continue the case is subordinated to the requirement for a hearing within 28 days,[62] that requirement is, it is submitted, mandatory and cannot be waived by the parties. At the hearing, which must be in chambers,[63] a reporter may appear although not legally qualified, and the child and the relevant person may be represented. Lay, as well as legal, representation appears to be competent for the child and relevant person.[64] The sheriff has the same duty and power as the children's hearing to consider and arrange separate representation for the child where this is necessary in the child's interests.[65] Any safeguarder appointed by the sheriff has the powers and duties at common law of a curator *ad litem* in respect of the child and is entitled to receive from the reporter copies of the application, all productions, and any papers which were before the hearing.[66] The role of a safeguarder appointed by the sheriff probably comes to an end when the proceedings before the sheriff end[67] (unlike the role of a safeguarder appointed by the hearing, which continues until a dispositive decision has been made and even, if an appeal is lodged, beyond then).

19.64   The child has a right to attend the hearing of the application and also the duty to do so, unless (i) the obligation to attend is dispensed with by the sheriff on the ground (in a case involving a scheduled offence) that the child's attendance is not necessary for the just hearing of that application and (in all cases) that it would be detrimental to the interests of the child for him or her to be present at the hearing of the application[68] or (ii) the sheriff has excluded the child from any stage of the proceedings because the nature of the case or of any evidence to be given is such that the sheriff is satisfied that it is in the interests of the child that he or she should not be present at any stage of the proceedings.[69] If the child fails to attend the hearing of the application at which his or her attendance has not been dispensed with, the sheriff may grant an order to find and keep the child, which order will be authority for bringing him or her before the sheriff and for his or her detention in a place of safety for a period not exceeding 14 days or until disposal of the application by the sheriff, whichever is the earlier.[70]

19.65   Once an application has been made to the sheriff, the reporter is entitled to request any prosecutor to supply him or her with any evidence lawfully obtained in the course of, and held by the prosecutor in connection with, the investigation of a crime or suspected crime, whenever the evidence is such that it might assist the sheriff in determining the application.[71] The evidence may relate to a crime or suspected crime committed by the child or against the child or by or against another member of the child's household. The prosecutor is obliged to comply with this request, unless he or she reasonably believes that it is necessary to retain the evidence for the purposes of the proceedings in respect of the crime, whether these proceedings have commenced or not.[72]

---

[61] *H v. Mearns*, 1974 S.L.T. 184.
[62] A.S. 1997, r. 3.49.
[63] s. 93(5).
[64] s. 68(4).
[65] s. 41.
[66] A.S. 1997, r. 3.8.
[67] See Norrie, *Children's Hearings in Scotland* (1997), p. 84.
[68] s. 68(4) and (5).
[69] A.S. 1997, r. 3.47(5).
[70] s. 68(6) and (7).
[71] s. 53(4).
[72] s. 53(4) and (5).

Relevancy and competency

Although the reporter may abandon the application in part as well as in **19.66** whole,[73] and the sheriff, either on his own motion or on the application of any party, may allow amendment of any statement supporting the conditions of the grounds of referral,[74] there is no general jurisdiction to dismiss the application as irrelevant.[75] It does not, however, follow from the lack of a preliminary jurisdiction on relevancy, that where an application is tainted with radical incompetency apparent on the face of the record, a sheriff must hear evidence before dismissing it. In such cases he is entitled *in limine* to refuse to exercise a jurisdiction which *ex hypothesi* of the incompetency he does not have, although reservation of the question of competency, until after the evidence has been heard, may often be convenient and desireable. In *L v. McGregor*[76] the sheriff entertained a plea on the grounds of no jurisdiction (and repelled it) and was not criticised for doing so by the Court of Session; and in *Merrin v. S*[77] the sheriff sustained a plea to the competency without hearing evidence on the basis that the child involved was under eight years of age and the ground of referral was that he had committed an offence. However, a sharp distinction arises between cases of this type, where the incompetency cannot be put right and the sheriff would be unable, whatever the evidence, to hold the ground of referral established, and other cases, where the alleged incompetency arises merely through a defect in procedure that can be put right. In all cases falling into the latter class it is the duty of the sheriff, unless he dispenses with the evidence under section 68(8), to hear all the evidence tendered by the reporter in respect of all the grounds so far as that evidence is competent and relevant to the statement of facts contained in the grounds of referral.[78] Where in the course of the hearing of an application made because the grounds were not accepted or were accepted only in part the child and the relevant person now accept any of the grounds of referral to which the application relates the sheriff must, and where in the course of the hearing of an application made because the child will not or did not understand the grounds of referral and the relevant person accepts any of the grounds of referral the sheriff may, dispense with hearing the evidence that relates to that ground and deem the ground to be established, unless he is satisfied that, in all the circumstances of the case, the evidence should be heard.[79] If the case is one involving a ground of referral that the child has committed an offence, then at the conclusion of the reporter's evidence the sheriff must consider whether sufficient evidence has been led to establish that the condition is satisfied and he must give all the parties an opportunity to be heard on the question of sufficiency of evidence.[80] Where he is not satisfied that sufficient evidence has been led, he shall make a finding to that effect; where he is satisfied that sufficient evidence has been led, the child, relevant person and any safeguarder appointed under section 41 may give evidence and call witnesses with regard to the condition in question.[81]

---

[73] A.S. 1997, r. 3.46(1).
[74] *ibid.* r. 3.48.
[75] *McGregor v. D*, 1977 S.C. 330.
[76] 1980 S.L.T. 17. See also *H v. Mearns*, 1974 S.L.T. 184; *McGregor v. L*, 1983 S.L.T. (Sh.Ct) 7.
[77] 1987 S.L.T. 193.
[78] A.S. 1997, r. 3.47(1); *McGregor v. D*, 1977 S.C. 330; *Sloan v. B*, 1991 S.L.T. 530 at 546, *per* Lord President Hope.
[79] s. 68(8).
[80] A.S. 1997, r. 3.47(2).
[81] *ibid.* r. 3.47(3) and (4).

Proof

19.67   The proceedings, which are essentially *sui generis*[82] and not in any proper sense adversarial, are governed by the statute[83] and Act of Sederunt.[84] They are civil rather than criminal in character even when the grounds relate to the commission of an offence, though they are "civil proceedings of a special type",[85] and therefore the ordinary rules of civil procedure do not apply. The central consideration is, within the limits imposed by the Act and subordinate legislation, to achieve "a simplicity of procedure avoiding, as far as possible, technicalities of legal process which will, on the one hand, enable the requisite action in the interest and for the benefit of the child to be taken by panels of laymen while, at the same time, provide an effective and simple structure within which the purpose of the legislation can be secured".[86] Many of the basic rules of evidence apply.[87] However, it has been stated that the principles of natural justice have to yield to the interests of the child[88] and, even before the rule was statutorily altered, it had been held by the First Division that hearsay evidence should be admissible in a children's hearing case.[89] The court said this:

> "The proceedings in front of the sheriff on referral are self-contained civil proceedings *sui generis* in which it must be borne in mind at all times that the principal purpose is to ascertain what is necessary to be done in the interests of the child. In our opinion it would be quite wrong for this objective to be thwarted by the application of rigid rules of evidence or procedure just because such rigidity may be appropriate in other kinds of proceedings."[90]

19.68   Statute has now provided that in any civil proceedings (which is defined to include any hearing by the sheriff under section 68 of the 1995 Act except in so far as the ground of referral is the commission by the child of an offence) evidence shall not be excluded solely on the ground that it is hearsay.[91] In cases based on the commission of an offence hearsay evidence is also sometimes admitted, in circumstances laid down in the Criminal Procedure (Scotland) Act 1995.[92] Where, however, a child is rejected as a witness because of his or her inability to distinguish truth from falsehood[93] evidence cannot be led of his or her extrajudicial hearsay statements.[94] It is also provided that (except in offence-based cases) facts can be held to be proved on the balance of probabilities even when the evidence is not corroborated.[95]

---

[82] *McGregor v. D*, above, *per* Lord President Emslie at 336; *F v. Kennedy*, 1992 S.C.L.R. 750, *per* Lord Justice-Clerk Ross at 775A.
[83] Children (Scotland) Act 1995, Pt II.
[84] Act of Sederunt (Child Care and Maintenance Rules) 1997 (S.I. 1997 No. 291), Chap. 3, Pt VII.
[85] *Harris v. F*, 1991 S.L.T. 242 at 245B, *per* Lord Justice-Clerk Ross.
[86] *McGregor v. D*, 1977 S.C. 330 at 339, *per* Lord Cameron.
[87] *Kennedy v. B*, 1973 S.L.T. 38, *per* Lord Justice-Clerk Grant at 41.
[88] *Kennedy v. A*, 1986 S.L.T. 358.
[89] *W v. Kennedy*, 1988 S.L.T. 583.
[90] *ibid.* at 585–586. See also *K v. Kennedy*, 1992 S.C.L.R. 386.
[91] Civil Evidence (Scotland) Act 1988, s. 2.
[92] Criminal Procedure (Scotland) Act 1995, ss. 259–260.
[93] See *M v. Kennedy*, 1993 S.C.L.R. 69; *M v. Ferguson*, 1994 S.C.L.R. 487, *L v. L*, 1996 S.L.T. 767. And see Sheldon, "Children's Evidence, Competency and the New Hearsay Provisions", 1997 S.L.T. (News) 1.
[94] *F v. Kennedy (No. 1)*, 1992 S.C.L.R. 139; *M v. Ferguson*, 1994 S.C.L.R. 487; *Sanderson v. McManus*, 1996 S.L.T. 750, IH; *AR v. JGR*, December 30, 1998. It is, however, competent to lead evidence of the fact that the child made statements, though this is no evidence of the content of the statements: *Sanderson v. McManus*, 1997 S.L.T. 629.
[95] Civil Evidence (Scotland) Act 1988, s. 1.

In so far as the rules against evidence of character and similar fact are in **19.69** point, they apply as they would in civil rather than in criminal proceedings. When the ground of referral is that the child has committed an offence, proof is on the criminal standard[96] (*i.e.* proof beyond reasonable doubt). In any other case, as previously explained,[97] proof is on a balance of probabilities. Questions have, however, sometimes been raised of whether a higher standard applies where the ground of referral relates to the commission of offences by persons other than the child.[98] There is authority for the view that where allegations of certain types of criminal conduct are made in civil proceedings they require to be proved, if not on the criminal standard, at least by evidence of a clear and strongly persuasive kind.[99] The view taken in England is that the inherent probability or improbability of an event is itself a matter to be taken into account when weighing the probabilities and deciding whether, on balance, the event occurred.[1] "The more improbable the event", it has been said, "the stronger must be the evidence that it did occur before, on the balance of probabilities, its occurence will be established".[2] This tautology has been criticised because of its implicit assumption that serious abuse is less likely to occur than minor abuse and that therefore more skepticism should be shown when serious than when minor allegations are made,[3] and there is much strength in this criticism. Nevertheless it does resolve the conflict of authority which had arisen in England as to whether a higher standard than the balance of probabilities was appropriate in order to establish sexual abuse,[4] and it does accord with the comment of the Second Division in *B v. Kennedy*,[5] in which the English approach[6] was construed

---

[96] s. 68(3)(b).

[97] Above, para. 19.19.

[98] *i.e.* under the conditions specified in s. 52(2)(d), (e), (f) or (g).

[99] *Arnot v. Burt* (1872) 11 M. 62, *per* Lord Neaves at 74, where the criminal standard was said to be applicable to cases of fraudulent conduct. *cf.* "Fraud is a thing that must be clearly and conclusively established" (*Cullen's Tr v. Johnston* (1865) 3 M. 935, *per* Lord President McNeill at 937–938); and again in the case of fraud: "The case will require to be made out by very clear evidence" (*Wink v. Speirs* (1867) 6 M. 77, *per* Lord Justice-Clerk Patton at 80). It is clear, however, that these dicta cannot be applied to all instances of criminal conduct arising in the course of civil proceedings. It is, for example, an everyday incident of civil practice that contraventions of the Road Traffic Acts are proved on the ordinary civil standard. It is intelligible that a court should require strong evidence to prove allegations of conduct which would amount to the commission of a seriously reprehensible crime, but there is also justice in Sir Rupert Cross's observation that "very strong reason is required to justify the imposition of the standard of proof appropriate to a criminal charge in a civil case, and it is open to question whether that reason has ever been convincingly stated": *Evidence* (3rd ed.) at 99. See also *Buick v. Jaglar*, 1973 S.L.T. (Sh.Ct) 6. In the U.S., the Supreme Court held in *Santosky v. Kramer*, 455 U.S. 743 (1982) that it was unconstitutional for a state to adopt a standard less than one of "clear and convincing evidence" in child protection cases, and in New South Wales the burden statutorily lies between the balance of probabilities and beyond reasonable doubt: s. 70(2) of the Children (Care and Protection) Act 1987 provides that the child protection agency must prove that "it is very highly probable that the child is in need of care". However, in both these jurisdictions this standard must be satisfied in relation to a finding that State intervention in the child's life is necessary, and not simply in relation to a finding that a ground for intervention exists.

[1] See Cross and Tapper on *Evidence* (8th ed.), pp. 169–171.

[2] *per* Lord Nichols in *Re H & Ors (Minors) (Sexual Abuse: Standard of Proof)* [1996] 1 All E.R. 1.

[3] Keating, "Shifting Standards in the House of Lords" (1996) 8 Child & Fam. L.Q. 157 at 160.

[4] In *Re G (A Minor) (Sexual Abuse: Standard of Proof)* [1987] 1 W.L.R. 1461 at 1466 and in *Re W (Minors) (Sexual Abuse: Standard of Proof)* [1994] 1 F.L.R. 419 at 429 suggestions were made that a higher standard was appropriate; the ordinary civil standard of balance of probabilities was held appropriate in *H v. H and C (Child Abuse: Evidence)* [1989] 3 All E.R. 740 at 745, *Re M (A Minor) (Appeal No 2)* [1994] 1 F.L.R. 59 at 67 and *Re W*, above, at 424.

[5] 1987 S.L.T. 765.

[6] In particular the words of Denning L.J. in *Hornal v. Neuberger Products Ltd* [1957] 1 Q.B. 247 at 258 that "the more serious the allegation the higher the degree of probability that is required". The Second Division found this to be "unfortunately phrased": 1987 S.L.T. at 768H.

"as meaning that the weight of evidence required to tip the scales may vary with the gravity of the allegation to be proved. For example, the weight of evidence required to prove fraud in a civil case may be greater than that required to prove a breach of contract." But in the end, as was emphasised, "the standard of proof is fixed as 'the balance of probabilities'... [Apart from commission of an offence by the child] the ordinary civil law standard applies to all other grounds".[7] The appellant's contention that the sheriff should have applied a higher standard of proof than the balance of probabilities was expressly rejected. Clearly the trier of fact in a civil case may be more reluctant to believe an allegation of serious criminal conduct than an allegation of negligence or breach of contract, and that reluctance will enter into his assessment of the probabilities, but if at the end of the day the balance of probability is that the criminal conduct took place he must hold it proved. Such reluctance as may be appropriate in the ordinary civil case may not, however, be apt to an application to hold grounds of referral established. It is one thing to treat with caution or reserve allegations of crime made by one party against another; it is another and more questionable matter to entertain the same scruples where the protection of a third party—the child—is at issue. The purpose of the statute will be best achieved if attention focuses without further elaboration on proof on a balance of probabilities.

19.70   Any person can be excluded while any child is giving evidence if the sheriff is satisfied that this is necessary in the interests of the child giving evidence and either (a) he must do so in order to obtain the evidence of the child or (b) the presence of the person in question is causing or is likely to cause significant distress to the child.[8]

Fresh matters

19.71   The grounds of referral are inevitably based on past events. It is to these events that the evidence will, in the main, be directed and on proof of which the establishment of the grounds of referral will depend. Where, however, a ground of referral involves consideration of an existing or future state of affairs, and in particular where it involves consideration of the future welfare of the child, it is competent to lead evidence of facts as at the date of the proof before the sheriff and such facts, if proved, must be taken into account.[9] In these circumstances, an adjournment should be granted if necessary to avoid prejudice caused by the introduction of new matter. The plea of *res judicata* has no place in applications of this kind and if an earlier episode is relied upon by the reporter, "the sheriff is entitled and indeed bound to hear evidence relating to it".[10] Where the grounds of referral relate to a state of affairs obtaining over a period of time and include incidents which had been finally disposed of in previous proceedings as well as a later incident, evidence must be heard on all the facts stated, the earlier incidents cannot be treated as *res judicata*,[11] and the eventual decision must, it is submitted, be based on the totality of circumstances. A party is entitled to make an unsworn statement which may be taken into account and, if accepted, is entitled to have some weight given to it.[12]

---

[7] 1987 S.L.T. at 768I–J.

[8] A.S. 1997, r. 3.47(6).

[9] *Kennedy v. B and Anr*, 1972 S.C. 128. That case was concerned with a referral under s. 32(2)(c) of the Social Work (Scotland) Act 1968 (lack of parental care - now contained in s. 52(2)(c) of the 1995 Act), but its reasoning seems to be applicable to all the conditions in s. 52(2) that are expressed in the present or future, as opposed to the past tense (*i.e.* conditions (a)–(g) and (l), but not (h), (i), (j) or (k)). In *Kennedy v. R's Curator ad Litem*, 1993 S.L.T. 295 it was held that a parent was entitled to dispute the grounds of referral because circumstances had changed since the hearing, even if he or she had accepted the grounds at the hearing itself.

[10] *per* Lord Hunter in *Kennedy v. S*, 1986 S.L.T. 679 at 681J, relying on the authority of *McGregor v. D*, 1981 S.L.T. (Notes) 97.

[11] *ibid.*

[12] *Kennedy v. B and Anr*, above.

Competency of witnesses

A relevant person is a competent and compellable witness at the instance of **19.72** the reporter where the ground of referral is that the child has committed an offence[13] and there is no reason that, subject where appropriate to a privilege against self-incrimination, he or she should not be similarly competent and compellable in relation to other grounds. Neither the common law rule that an accused person is not a competent witness for the prosecution or the defence in the proceedings against him nor its statutory modifications have any application in the context of proceedings for the establishment of a ground of referral and there is no barrier to the invocation of the principle that anyone is a competent witness unless of a class specifically excluded by law and, if competent, is compellable. Where, however, it is alleged that the child has committed an offence the privilege against self-incrimination would, unless waived, constitute an obstacle to the child's effective use as a witness for the reporter and the resemblance to criminal proceedings may, in any event, be thought to be sufficient to make such a course undesirable. There would seem to be no objection to the reporter's calling him or her as a witness in relation to any other ground. A spouse is a competent and compellable witness as to the commission of an offence by the other spouse, and there is no privilege to refuse to answer questions that might tend to incriminate one's spouse. A child is competent only if capable of telling the difference between truth and falsehood and likely, therefore, to give trustworthy evidence; if adjudged so capable the child must be admonished to tell the truth.[14]

Scope and effect of decisions

At the conclusion of the hearing the sheriff is required to give his decision **19.73** orally.[15] A copy of the subsequent interlocutor embodying the decision must be transmitted by the sheriff clerk to the child, the relevant person, any safeguarder and the reporter. The sheriff may, when giving his decision or within seven days thereafter, issue a note of the reasons for his decision,[16] but there is no absolute requirement that he do so. The absence of a note may in some cases deprive the hearing of information (*e.g.* on the truthfulness of statements by the child or relevant person) that would be useful for the further consideration of the case. Where the sheriff decides that none of the grounds in respect of which the application was made has been established he must dismiss the application, discharge the referral in respect of those grounds, and recall, discharge or cancel any order, warrant or direction under Chapter 3 of Part II of the 1995 Act which relates to the child in respect of those grounds.[17] The children's hearing can in that event proceed with the case only in respect of grounds, if any, which were accepted. Where the sheriff after hearing the evidence or dispensing with the evidence finds that any of the grounds in respect of which the application was made is or should be deemed to be established, he must remit the case to the reporter to make arrangements for a children's hearing to consider and determine the case.[18] It is noteworthy that the sheriff is not empowered in that event to discharge the referral in respect of any grounds which have not been established, and that it is the child's case that is remitted for consideration and determination. The inference would seem to be that consideration by the children's hearing is

---

[13] *McGregor v. T and Anr*, 1975 S.L.T. 71.

[14] *M v. Kennedy*, 1993 S.C.L.R. 69; *L v. L*, 1998 S.L.T. 672; *AR v. JGR*, December 30, 1998.

[15] A.S. 1997, r. 3.51(1).

[16] A.S. 1997, r. 3.51(3).

[17] s. 68(9).

[18] s. 68(10)(a).

not to be too closely tied to the established grounds of referral, though clearly the hearing are not entitled to put reliance on any ground that the sheriff had held not to be established. The sheriff may at any time, on the application of any party or on his own motion, allow amendment of any statement supporting the conditions of the grounds of referral.[19] Where in a ground of referral it is alleged that an offence has been committed by or against any child, the sheriff may find that any other offence established by the facts has been committed.[20] It may be assumed that this is subject to the implicit qualification that any offence against the child found established falls within the ambit of the conditions of section 52(2) to which the grounds relate. In *McGregor v. A*[21] it was held that the rule[22] merely permits the sheriff to find that the facts establish some other offence and does not require him to do so. However, given the terms of the rule, it is difficult to conceive of any sound principle upon which, if the facts establish some relevant offence other than that libelled, the sheriff could, if invited to do so, decline so to find.[23]

19.74   In addition to finding a ground of referral established, the sheriff may, if he is satisfied that the child's best interests require that he or she be kept in a place of safety or that there is reason to believe that the child will run away before the sitting of the children's hearing, issue an order requiring that the child be kept in a place of safety.[24] If the sheriff is satisfied that either of the criteria for authorising the child to be kept in secure accommodation[25] is fulfilled, he may provide that the child shall be liable to be placed and kept in secure accommodation within a residential establishment at such time as the person in charge of the establishment, with the agreement of the chief social work officer of the relevant local authority, considers necessary.[26] The order keeping the child in a place of safety ceases to have effect on the expiry of three days beginning with the day on which the child is first kept in a place of safety or, if earlier, on the consideration of the child's case by a children's hearing.[27]

19.75   Neither the Court of Session nor the sheriff has any power to direct the hearing as to how it should dispose of the case, and in *Kennedy v. A*[28] the Second Division held that the sheriff had no power even to indicate some of the factors which he considered that the hearing ought to take into account when coming to a decision on the merits of the case. The powers of the Court of Session are similarly constrained. But neither court is, it is thought, precluded from drawing the hearing's attention to aspects of its decision or the reasons for it which may assist in the hearing's disposal and it may, in particular, sometimes be helpful for the sheriff to indicate evidence he has accepted or rejected and the weight he has attached to it. There is, however, no requirement to do so.

---

[19] A.S. 1997, r. 3.48, reversing the rule in *McGregor v. D*, 1977 S.C. 330.

[20] A.S. 1997, r. 3.50; *McGregor v. D*, above; *McGregor v. A*, 1982 S.L.T. 45; *M v. Kennedy*, 1986 S.L.T. 434.

[21] above.

[22] Then contained in the similarly worded r. 10 of the Social Work (Sheriff Court Procedure Rules) 1971.

[23] It is a sufficient *ratio* for *McGregor v. A* that the reporter had not invited the sheriff to consider such a course and that on appeal the point was not raised in the stated case.

[24] s. 68(10)(b).

[25] Listed in s. 70(10).

[26] s. 68(11).

[27] s. 68(12).

[28] 1986 S.L.T. 358.

Further application to the sheriff

If the sheriff finds the grounds of referral to be established the case is referred **19.76** back to the children's hearing for consideration and disposal, and there is no provision in the Act for further applications to the sheriff to resolve matters of dispute which arise after the establishment of the grounds. It follows that it is for the hearing to resolve such disputes within the context of determining how to dispose of the case.[29] This is so except when the dispute concerns the original grounds of referral. If the sheriff has previously found that a ground of referral exists in an application under section 68[30] then an application can be made to the sheriff for a review of the sheriff's original findings by the child or any of the relevant persons[31] (but by no one else). Such an application can be made only when the applicant claims (a) to have evidence which was not considered by the sheriff on the original application, being evidence the existence or significance of which might materially have affected the determination of the original application; (b) that such evidence is likely to be credible and reliable and would have been admissible in relation to the ground of referral which was found to be established on the original application; and (c) that there is a reasonable explanation for the failure to lead such evidence on the original application.[32] If the sheriff is not satisfied that any of the claims are established he must dismiss the application and where he is satisfied that the claims made are established then he must consider the evidence.[33]

Having considered the evidence, and heard such parties as wish to make **19.77** representations, the sheriff must give his decision orally at the conclusion of the hearing.[34] If he is satisfied that any ground of referral stated in the original application is established he may remit the case under section 68(10) to the reporter to arrange a children's hearing.[35] If he finds that none of the original grounds is established he must discharge the referral,[36] and if the child is subject to a supervision requirement in respect of the referral the sheriff may order that it be terminated either immediately or on such date as he may specify.[37] That date must not, it is submitted, be later than the date on which a review of the supervision requirement would be required.[38] If termination of the supervision requirement is postponed, the sheriff may vary the requirement in any way he thinks fit or vary any condition attached to it or any requirement to keep the child's address secret or any determination by the children's hearing as to when the supervision requirement is to be reviewed.[39] Where termination is ordered by the sheriff, he must also consider whether, after such termination, the child concerned will still require supervision or guidance; and where he considers that such supervision or guidance will be necessary he shall direct a local authority to provide it.[40] The local authority is obliged to provide that supervision or guidance but that duty is regarded as being discharged where supervision or guidance is offered but the child, being of sufficient age and maturity to understand what is being offered, is unwilling to accept it.[41]

---

[29] See further, Norrie, "Children's Hearings, New Evidence, and the Nobile Officium" 1994 S.L.G. 4.
[30] But not in any other circumstance, such as when the grounds of referral were accepted.
[31] s. 85.
[32] s. 85(3).
[33] s. 85(5) and (6).
[34] A.S. 1997, rr. 3.64 and 3.51.
[35] s. 85(6)(b).
[36] s. 85(6)(a).
[37] s. 85(7). See also *L, Petrs*, 1993 S.L.T. 1310 and 1342.
[38] See further, Norrie, *Children's Hearings in Scotland* (1997) at 152–153.
[39] s. 85(8).
[40] s. 85(9).
[41] s. 85(10).

19.78   If the sheriff determines that the grounds of referral which are being reviewed have not been made out, but that the evidence establishes that other grounds do exist then, as well as discharging the original referral, he may, instead of terminating the supervision requirement to which the child is subject, remit the case to the reporter to arrange a children's hearing for the consideration and determination of the case.[42]

CONSIDERATION AND DISPOSAL OF THE CASE

Considering the case

19.79   If grounds of referral are accepted or established, the children's hearing must then proceed to a consideration of these grounds, the social background report which the local authority is obliged to furnish and such other relevant information including other reports as may be available[43]; and, in discussion with the child (unless he or she is incapable of participating) any relevant person, any safeguarder appointed under section 41 of the Act and any representative if attending the hearing, they must consider on what course they should decide in the child's best interests.[44] The children's hearing, taking account of the age and maturity of the child must, so far as practicable, give the child an opportunity to indicate whether he or she wishes to express his or her views; if the child indicates a wish to express views the children's hearing must not make any decision unless an opportunity has been given for the views of the child to be obtained or heard and they have had regard to such views as have been expressed.[45] There is no provision for resolution of disputes on the factual basis of reports or statements and allegations made during the discussion of the child's case. Ascertainment of facts as well as expression of opinion is, however, in so far as relevant to his or her report, within the province of the compiler of any report and the hearing are, it is submitted, entitled, if they think fit, to accept the report-compiler's findings as to the facts even if these have been challenged. Where, however, challenge raises doubts as to the accuracy of the report on an important matter, further investigation will often be appropriate and, in any event, a hearing ought not to proceed on factual contents of a report that are inconsistent with grounds of referral accepted or established.

19.80   There was previously some doubt as to the scope of the matter which a hearing is entitled to take into account in deciding whether a child is in need of compulsory measures of supervision and on the consequent disposal. In *K v. Finlayson*[46] it was contended on behalf of the reporter that, once the grounds of referral had been accepted or established, "the hearing then has absolute power to take any steps they considered to be in the child's best interests—and without having any further regard to any limitation in their discussion". The sheriff[47] held however that, where a ground of referral had been disputed and established, the hearing were bound to interpret the relevant statutory condition for the application of compulsory measures of care in the context of what had been held by the court to be established and were not entitled to look at other matters.[48] A decision of a hearing based on any grounds other than those accepted or

---

[42] s. 85(7)(b). See further, Norrie, *op. cit.*, p. 154.
[43] s. 69(1).
[44] Children's Hearings (Scotland) Rules 1996, r. 20(3).
[45] *ibid.* r. 15(1) and (3) and s. 16(2). For the purpose of this rule, a child of 12 years of age or more shall be presumed to be of sufficient age and maturity to form a view: r. 15(5).
[46] 1974 S.L.T. (Sh.Ct) 51. For comment and criticism see Grant, "More Bridges, but More Gaps", 1974 S.L.T. (News) 213.
[47] Isabel L. Sinclair, Q.C.
[48] 1974 S.L.T. (Sh.Ct) at 53.

established was, in her opinion, *ultra vires* of their powers.[49] It seems that the sheriff meant not merely that the hearing could not rely on facts which would appropriately have formed the subject-matter of an entirely different ground for referral involving another condition, but that it was illegitimate for the hearing to have regard to any facts and circumstances not stated in grounds of referral accepted or established. That view and the reporter's contention are both, it is submitted, somewhat extreme. The difficulty stems from some ambiguity in the statute about the role, in decisions on disposal, of the "grounds of referral" on the one hand and the wider aspects of the child's "case" on the other. At times the grounds of referral are stressed. Thus where the child and relevant person accept grounds in part, the hearing are empowered if they consider it proper to proceed "in respect of those grounds which are accepted"[50]; where a sheriff decides that none of the grounds has been established he discharges the referral "in respect of those grounds"[51] (leaving, as already noted, the hearing to proceed in respect of the grounds, if any, which were accepted); and where grounds of referral are accepted or established, the children's hearing proceed to consider "those grounds".[52] On the other hand, where the sheriff is satisfied that any of the grounds has been established, it is the child's "case" that he remits for consideration and determination by a hearing.[53] Facts unnecessary to ground the referral may, nonetheless, be relevant to a consideration of the child's case. If that were not so, the requirement that the hearing consider the social background report supplied by the local authority and such other relevant information as may be available to them[54] and the power given to continue a case for further investigation of the case[55] would scarcely be intelligible. The policy of the Act is that the hearing should explore what is in the interests of the child free from any narrow constraints. *K v. Finlayson* was disapproved by the First Division in *O v. Rae*,[56] in which Lord President Hope, speaking for the court, said:

> "The information to which [the hearing] must have regard in terms of section 43(1)[57] includes the grounds of referral accepted or established. But it may extend well beyond what may have been stated in these grounds. This is because the hearing must have regard also to a report obtained from the local authority under section 39(4)[58] on the child and his social background. As that subsection points out, this report may contain information from any such person as the reporter or the local authority may think fit. Furthermore they are entitled, in terms of section 43(1), to have regard to 'such other relevant information as may be available to them.' [Counsel for the appellants] said that this information must be confined to information which was relevant to the grounds for the referral, but in our opinion that interpretation is not consistent with the express purpose of the subsection. Its purpose is to enable the children's hearing to consider what is in the best interests of the child. The test of relevancy in this context, therefore, is whether the information is relevant to a consideration of what course should be taken in the child's best interests."[59]

---

[49] 1974 S.L.T. (Sh.Ct) at 54.
[50] s. 56(6).
[51] s. 68(9).
[52] s. 69(1).
[53] s. 68(10).
[54] s. 69(1).
[55] s. 69(2).
[56] 1993 S.L.T. 570. See Norrie, "In Defence of *O v. Rae*", 1995 S.L.T. (News) 353. Mitchell considers the case indefensible: 1997 SCOLAG 9.
[57] Now s. 69(1) of the 1995 Act.
[58] Now s. 56(7) of the 1995 Act.
[59] 1993 S.L.T. 570–574H.

19.81   Nevertheless the grounds of referral have a central role. "While they [the hearing] have reports and submissions before them, the hard core of the material upon which their decision is based is the grounds of referral."[60] The grounds of referral should not be set in antithesis to the child's case or divorced from it. They are the grounds of referral "of the case". They indicate what the case referred is and if the hearing take account of matters which have no substantial connection with the grounds of referral accepted or established, or, *a fortiori*, elements of the grounds of referral that the sheriff has found not established,[61] they embark on a consideration of what is essentially a different case. In that way the grounds of referral control the hearing's consideration but, within the limits as indicated, the hearing are free to explore all matters connected with the case and so take into account a wide range of facts and circumstances which are not detailed in, but flow from, or are related to, the grounds of referral. Moreover, facts and circumstances which are purely dispositive in character, in that they have no relevance to any ground on which the case was or might have been referred but bear only on the appropriate form of disposal, may be taken into account without restriction.

19.82   As a consequence of the grounds of referral being central to the hearing's consideration, an appeal by the reporter from a sheriff's finding that one or more grounds has not been established while another ground has been is not in any sense of the word "academic". The hearing are required by section 69(1) to consider the grounds of referral accepted or established in order to come to a decision as to what is best for the child. It is in light of that, and any reports obtained under section 56(7), that they proceed to consider how to dispose of the case of the child.[62] Likewise an application may be made to the sheriff to determine some incident of the ground, even although the ground itself is accepted, whenever that incident would be relevant to the subsequent disposal of the case. So in *M v. Kennedy*[63] the ground of referral (that the child had been the victim of unlawful sexual intercourse) was accepted by the parents, which was sufficient to found the children's hearing's jurisdiction, but an application was made to the sheriff to determine whether the unlawful act had taken place in the family home, since this was not accepted by the parents but would strongly influence the appropriate disposal of the case by the children's hearing.

Criteria of decisions

19.83   In making their decisions the children's hearing are bound by the principles in section 16 of the 1995 Act,[64] that is to say (i) the welfare of the child throughout his or her childhood shall be their paramount consideration; (ii) they must, taking account of the age and maturity of the child so far as practicable give him or her an opportunity to indicate whether he or she wishes to express views, if he or she does so wish, to give him or her an opportunity to express them, and must have regard to such views as may be expressed; and (iii) they must make no requirement or order unless they consider that it would be better for the child that the requirement or order be made than that none should be made at all.[65] The welfare principle applies whenever a children's hearing are deciding any matter with respect to the child; the requirement to take account of the child's views applies when the childrens' hearing are considering whether to make or

---

[60] *Kennedy v. B*, 1973 S.L.T. 38, *per* Lord Justice-Clerk Grant at 40.
[61] *M v. Kennedy* 1993 S.L.T. 431.
[62] *per* Lord Justice-Clerk Ross in *Harris v. F*, 1991 S.L.T. 242 at 246F.
[63] above.
[64] Sometimes called the three overarching principles.
[65] s. 16(1)-(3).

are reviewing a supervision requirement, or are considering whether to grant or continue a warrant, or are engaged in providing advice to a sheriff who is considering whether to continue a child protection order, or are drawing up a report when it is proposed that the child be adopted[66]; the no order presumption applies when the children's hearing are considering whether to make or are reviewing a supervision requirement or are considering whether to grant or continue a warrant.[67]

Qualifications to the welfare test

While the welfare of the child will usually be the determining, and should **19.84** never be a subordinate, consideration, it does not follow that it is the sole consideration and in some circumstances there may be need to reconcile the child's interests with other claims. It is provided that where, for the purpose of protecting members of the public from serious harm (whether or not physical harm) a children's hearing consider it necessary to make a decision which would not be consistent with their affording paramountcy to the child's welfare, they may make that decision.[68] This, or any other, consideration can, however, be taken into account only as an aspect of the child's need for protection, guidance, treatment or control and so conflict with the child's interest is likely to be avoided. A child who has committed an offence (to take the strongest example, although others do suggest themselves, for example where the child is beyond the control of his or her parents) may be in need of control, not only in his or her own interests but in the interests of the protection of the public.

It is the child's welfare throughout his or her childhood that is the hearing's **19.85** paramount consideration and this means that the hearing must do their best to take a long-term view of what will be in the interests of the child. This might include, in appropriate cases, making decisions which will either assist or inhibit local authority plans for the adoption of the child. The statutory bar in the adoption legislation on anyone other than an adoption agency "making arrangements" for the adoption of a child[69] does not, it is submitted, cover decisions of the children's hearings.[70]

Available disposals

Having considered the child's case, three main options are open to the **19.86** children's hearing:

(a) to discharge the referral;
(b) to continue the case to a subsequent hearing;
(c) to make a supervision requirement.

The first of these options is appropriate where the hearing decides that no further action is required[71]; the second where it considers that further investigation of the case is necessary to complete the consideration of the case[72]; and the third

---

[66] If the child has indicated a wish to express views the hearing cannot make any decision unless the opportunity has been given to the child to express those views: A.S. 1997, r. 15(3)(b).
[67] s. 16(4).
[68] s. 16(5).
[69] Adoption (Scotland) Act 1978, s. 11(1).
[70] s. 73(13), which requires the children's hearing to draw up a report on any adoption plans, obliges the hearing to give consideration to these plans and it is implicit that they may make their decision in the light of, and in order to further, these plans. It follows that this provision must be taken to have overruled the sheriff court decisions (if they were ever good law) in *A v. Children's Hearing for Tayside Region*, 1987 S.L.T. (Sh.Ct) 126 and *M v. Children's Hearing for Strathclyde Region*, 1988 S.C.L.R. 592, in which it had been held that it was *ultra vires* of children's hearings to make decisions expressly to facilitate adoptions. See further, Norrie, *Children's Hearings in Scotland* (1997), pp. 99–100.
[71] s. 69(12).
[72] s. 69(3).

where it decides that the child is in need of compulsory measures of supervision.[73] Where a referral is discharged, any order, direction or warrant under Chapter 2 or 3 of Part II of the 1995 Act in respect of the child's case will cease to have effect.[74] Where a case is continued for further investigation, the child may be required to attend or reside at any clinic, hospital or other establishment during a period not exceeding 22 days,[75] and if he or she fails to fulfil that requirement the children's hearing may, either on an application by the reporter or on their own motion, grant a warrant which shall be authority to find the child, to remove the child to a place of safety and keep him or her there, and to take the child from the place of safety to the clinic, hospital or other establishment for the purposes of the investigation required under section 69(3).[76] This warrant can be granted for such period as appears to the children's hearing to be appropriate, provided that no warrant shall permit the keeping of a child in a place of safety after the earlier of (i) the expiry of 22 days after the warrant is granted or (ii) the day on which the subsequent hearing of the child's case by a children's hearing begins.[77] The children's hearing may also grant a warrant on continuing the case where they are satisfied that (a) keeping the child in a place of safety is necessary in the interests of safeguarding or promoting the welfare of the child or (b) there is reason to believe that the child may not attend the subsequent hearing of his or her case; this warrant will cease to have effect on the earlier of (a) the expiry of 22 days after the warrant is granted or (b) the day on which the subsequent hearing of the child's case by a children's hearing begins.[78] Though there is no provision for the continuation of a warrant granted under section 69, there would seem to be nothing to prevent a continued hearing, which again continues the hearing, from granting a new warrant under the same provisions (if the same, or another, ground for granting it exists). The warrant may contain such conditions as appear to the children's hearing to be necessary or expedient and they may, in particular, make conditions relating to medical treatment or contact.[79]

Making a supervision requirement

19.87   Where, after consideration of the case, the children's hearing are satisfied that the child is in need of compulsory measures of supervision, they may make a supervision requirement.[80] That requirement may require the child (a) to reside at any place or places specified in the requirement and (b) to comply with any condition contained in the requirement.[81] When making a supervision requirement, the children's hearing may require that any place where the child is to reside in accordance with the supervision requirement shall not be disclosed to any specified person or class of persons.[82] The wording of this provision suggests that this requirement can be made only when the child is required to reside at a place or places as one of the terms of the supervision requirement. The children's hearing may also make a determination that the supervision requirement be reviewed at such time during the duration of the requirement as they determine.[83] This allows the children's hearing to specify a date on or

---

[73] s. 70(1).
[74] s. 69(13).
[75] s. 69(3).
[76] s. 69(4) and (5).
[77] s. 69(6).
[78] s. 69(7) and (8).
[79] s. 69(9). See further, below, para. 20.17.
[80] s. 70(1).
[81] s. 70(3).
[82] s. 70(6).
[83] s. 70(7).

before which the reporter must arrange a review. It may be that the specified date may be uncertain, so long as it is reasonably certain to occur, but it is probably incompetent to specify a review on the occurrence of an uncertain event, such as "once the child has shown he can attend school regularly".[84] The children's hearing may specify in the requirement that the child shall be liable to be placed and kept in secure accommodation during such period as the person in charge of the establishment, with the agreement of the chief social work officer considers necessary where (a) they are satisfied that it is necessary to make a supervision requirement which includes a requirement that the child reside in a named residential establishment and (b) they are satisfied that the child (i) having previously absconded is likely to abscond again unless kept in secure accommodation and, if he or she does abscond, it is likely that his or her physical, mental or moral welfare will be at risk or (ii) is likely to injure him or herself unless he or she is kept in such accommodation.[85]

Requirement to reside

A children's hearing may require the child to reside in a place where he or she is to be under the charge or control of a person who is not a relevant person only when (i) it has received and considered a report of a local authority on the child and his or her social background, together with recommendations from that authority on the needs of the child and the suitability of the proposed place to meet those needs and (ii) the local authority has confirmed to the hearing that in compiling the report it carried out the procedures and gathered the information prescribed in the Fostering of Children (Scotland) Regulations 1996.[86] If the child is required to reside in a specified place that place may be in England or Wales; and the supervision requirement will be authority for the person in charge of the place where the child is to reside to restrict the child's liberty to such extent as that person may consider appropriate, having regard to the terms of the requirement.[87] The place must be expressly named.[88] Any requirement that the child resides at a specified place prevents the exercise of any existing parental responsibility or parental right in any way that would be incompatible with the terms of the supervision requirement[89] and it supersedes, during its currency, any court order regulating the child's residence in so far as that order is inconsistent with the terms of the supervision requirement.[90] A local authority may recommend that a child be required to reside with foster carers only when the requirements for approval of foster carers in the Fostering of Children (Scotland) Regulations 1996 have been satisfied.[91] Where as a result of the making or variation of a supervision requirement, a child has been required to reside in a residential establishment or other specified place but the local authority are unable to make immediate arrangements for the child's reception in that establishment or place, they may arrange for the child to be temporarily accommodated in some other suitable place for any period not exceeding 22 days

19.88

---

[84] See further, Norrie, *Children's Hearings in Scotland* (1997), pp. 136–137.
[85] s. 70(9) and (10).
[86] Children's Hearings (Scotland) Rules 1996, r. 20(6).
[87] s. 70(4).
[88] *R v. Children's Hearing for Borders Region*, 1984 S.L.T. 65.
[89] s. 3(4).
[90] *Aitken v. Aitken*, 1978 S.L.T. 183. This was decided under the 1968 Act, but there is nothing in the 1995 Act that suggests the position is changed. The court retains jurisdiction to make orders under s. 11 of the 1995, but the implementation of any such order is postponed in so far as inconsistent with a supervision requirement until the requirement is terminated or varied.
[91] Fostering of Children (Scotland) Regulations 1996 (S.I. 1996 No. 3263), r. 15.

commencing on the date of the children's hearing.[92] If the local authority cannot ensure that the child will be received into the named establishment or place within the 22-day period, they must refer the child's case to the reporter on the ground that the supervision requirement ought to be reviewed[93]; this hearing must be arranged as soon as is reasonably practicable and in any event within seven days of the reporter receiving the reference.[94] If the sitting of the children's hearing occurs after the expiry of the period of 22 days from the making or varying of the supervision requirement, that period is deemed to extend until the hearing sits.[95] It is the duty of the local authority to ensure that the child is conveyed to the place where he or she is required to reside.[96]

Other conditions attached to supervision requirements

19.89   The discretion of the children's hearing is unfettered in the conditions that they may attach to a supervision requirement, except that the condition must require something of the child. Any condition imposed must be expressed in clear and unambiguous terms[97] and specified in the relevant form: a passage in the statement of reasons is not a condition.[98] In every case in which a supervision requirement is made the children's hearing are obliged to consider whether to impose a condition which regulates the contact with the child that any specified person or class of persons is to have.[99] Any such condition supersedes any other legal right of contact enjoyed by another person, to the extent that the exercise of that right would be inconsistent with the condition in the supervision requirement,[1] and though a person dissatisfied with the contact they are being permitted retains title to seek a court order altering the position[2] any order made is suspended insofar as it is inconsistent with the terms of the supervision requirement. If no condition relating to contact is made, the matter lies in the hands of those who must give effect to the supervision requirement, that is to say, the local authority.[3]

19.90   It is provided that a condition attached to a supervision requirement may require the child to submit to any medical or other examination or treatment, but that is expressly made subject to section 90 of the 1995 Act.[4] That provision preserves the right under section 2(4) of the Age of Legal Capacity (Scotland) Act 1991 of the child who is old enough to consent to his or her own medical treatment[5] to do so and it further provides that where a condition requiring a

---

[92] Children's Hearings (Transmission of Information etc.) (Scotland) Regulations 1996 (S.I. 1996 No. 3261), r. 4(1).

[93] *ibid.* r. 4(2).

[94] *ibid.* r. 4(3).

[95] *ibid.* r. 4(3)(b).

[96] *ibid.* r. 5.

[97] *D v. Strathclyde Regional Council*, 1991 S.C.L.R. 185 at 186F.

[98] *Kennedy v. M*, 1995 S.L.T. 717.

[99] s. 70(2) and (5)(b).

[1] s. 3(4); *D v. Strathclyde Regional Council*, 1985 S.L.T. 114.

[2] Prior to 1995 the court could not make an access order during the subsistence of a supervision requirement: *D v. Strathclyde Regional Council*, above; *A v. G*, 1996 S.L.T. (Sh.Ct) 123. However, under the Children (Scotland) Act 1995, the responsibility and right of contact exists independently of any other right and can be regulated independently—with the result that a contact order may be made during the currency of a supervision requirement, but its effect suspended. See further, above, paras 9.13 and 19.88.

[3] s. 71. Because a child subject to a supervision requirement is deemed to be "looked after" by the local authority (s. 17(6)(b)), that local authority is under an obligation to take such steps to promote, on a regular basis, personal relations and direct contact between the child and any person with parental responsibilities in relation to the child as appear to it to be, having regard to its obligation to safeguard and promote the child's welfare, both practicable and reasonable: s. 17(1)(c). The welfare consideration gives the local authority power to refuse contact whenever it believes that this would not be in the interests of the child.

[4] s. 70(5)(a).

[5] See above, para. 15.09.

child to submit to any examination or treatment but the child has capacity under section 2(4), the examination or treatment shall only be carried out if the child consents. It follows that a condition that the capable child submit to examination or treatment is not authority for the carrying out of the examination or treatment— a breach of the condition by the child will necessitate a review of the supervision requirement but does not in itself justify any physical action to force the child to submit. If the child is too young to consent him or herself, consent must be given by someone with parental responsibilities and parental rights (*e.g.* the relevant person) and a condition attached to a supervision requirement imposed upon the child does not replace that person's consent.[6]

Implementation of supervision requirements

The carrying of supervision requirements into effect is entrusted to the local **19.91** authority for whose area the children's panel from which the children's hearing which imposed the supervision requirement was formed[7] and a child subject to a supervision requirement is treated as being "looked after" by that local authority.[8] This means that the local authority must (a) safeguard and promote the child's welfare (which shall, in the exercise of its duties to the child, be its paramount concern), (b) make such use of services available for children cared for by their own parents as appears to the authority reasonable in the child's case, and (c) take such steps to promote, on a regular basis, personal relations and direct contact between the child and any person with parental responsibilities in relation to him or her as appears to it to be, having regard to duty (a), both practicable and reasonable.[9] In addition, if the child remains "looked after" at the time when he or she ceased to be of school age or at any subsequent time, then once that child is no longer "looked after" by the local authority it is bound, unless satisfied that the child's welfare does not require it, to advise, guide and assist that child until the age of 19; and it may do so until the child is 21.[10] That assistance may include assistance in kind or in cash.[11] Where the performance of the local authority's duties requires or would be facilitated by the variation or discharge of the supervision requirement, the proper course is for the local authority to recommend a review.[12] There are some disadvantages in the placing of the duty to carry out the requirement on local authorities. There is a weakening of control by the hearing in that those responsible for the implementation of the requirement are not directly answerable to the hearing. While there is no difficulty in the placing of children in residential establishments managed by voluntary bodies, as these are in some degree subject to local authority supervision,[13] there is a disincentive to the use of other voluntary agencies. Where, on the other hand, a placement is made with, or caring functions entrusted to, a voluntary agency or private individual, or even where the child is placed in a residential establishment managed by a voluntary organisation, problems may thereby be created for the effective discharge by the local authority of their duties. Such problems are mitigated in cases of urgent necessity by the power given to the chief social work officer of the relevant local authority to direct in the interests of the child required to reside in a specified place, or of the other children in that place, that a child required to reside in that place be transferred to another

[6] See further, Norrie, *Children's Hearings in Scotland* (1997), pp. 118–120.
[7] ss. 71 and 93(1).
[8] s. 17(6)(b).
[9] s. 17(1).
[10] s. 29(1) and (2).
[11] s. 29(3).
[12] See below, para. 19.93.
[13] See above, paras 18.25 *et seq.*

place.[14] The power is personal to the chief social work officer with the consequence that a direction given by anyone other than his deputy is invalid. As the interests of the child under the supervision requirement, and of the other children, are alternatives, the power may be exercised where the interests of the child and the other children conflict provided it is in the interests either of the child or the other children for this to be done and provided, as always, there is urgent necessity. The reference to "another place" is wide enough to cover any location, including the child's own home. No means, however, is provided for enforcing a direction if the place is outwith the control or supervision of the local authority. Where a transfer is made under this power, the child's case must be reviewed within seven days.[15]

Cessation of supervision requirement

19.92   It is consistent with the caring purposes for which supervision requirements are designed that they should not be of a determinate duration. The intention is that a child should remain under supervision so long as his or her need for compulsory measures of supervision so requires.[16] The Act contains, however, no positive stipulation for determining that need. The matter is, instead, expressed negatively. No child shall continue to be subject to a supervision requirement for any period longer than is necessary in the interests of promoting or safeguarding his or her welfare.[17] Subject to variation or continuation of the supervision requirement, no supervision requirement shall remain in force for a period longer than one year.[18] In addition a supervision requirement ceases to have effect when the child attains the age of 18 years.[19] The reporter must arrange a children's hearing to review any supervision requirement where, if a review has not been called, the supervision requirement will expire within three months[20] and where he or she does so the children's hearing must consider whether, if the supervision requirement is not continued, the child still requires supervision or guidance; and where a children's hearing consider such supervision or guidance is necessary, it shall be the duty of the local authority to provide such supervision or guidance as the child is willing to accept.[21] If the reporter fails to arrange a review then the supervision requirement ceases to have effect on the anniversary of its being imposed, or as the case may be on the child's 18th birthday. That result appears to be mandatory since the Act contains no provision for excuse or failure on the part of the reporter.

Review of supervision requirement

19.93   The hearing's control over the operation of supervision requirements is maintained by the provisions for review. As the decision of a hearing on review is, like other decisions of the hearing, open to appeal, a safeguard is at the same time provided against the oppressive continuance of supervision requirements. It is the duty of the reporter to ensure that any review is duly held and to make any arrangements incidental to that review.[22] The powers of a hearing reviewing a supervision requirement are, by and large, contermimous with their powers when originally deciding whether to make such a requirement: they may (a)

---

[14] s. 72(1).
[15] s. 72(2).
[16] See *Report of the Kilbrandon Committee*, Chap. IX, para. 197.
[17] s. 73(1).
[18] s. 73(2).
[19] s. 73(3).
[20] s. 73(8)(a)(v).
[21] s. 73(12).
[22] s. 73(8)(b).

continue the review to a subsequent hearing; (b) terminate the requirement; (c) vary the requirement; (d) insert in the requirement any requirement which could have been imposed by them under section 70(3) (*i.e.* a residence or other condition); or (e) continue the requirement, with or without such variation or insertion.[23] A supervision requirement must be reviewed in the following circumstances:

(1) Where a local authority so recommends.[24] The local authority is obliged to refer the case of the child to the reporter in a number of circumstances: (i) whenever it is satisfied that the current supervision requirement ought to be varied or terminated; (ii) where it is satisfied that a condition in the supervision requirement is not being fulfilled; (iii) where it is satisfied that the best interests of the child would be served by its applying under section 86 of the 1995 Act for a parental responsibilities order, or applying under section 18 of the Adoption (Scotland) Act 1978 for an order freeing the child for adoption, or placing the child for adoption[25]; or (iv) whenever it is aware that an adoption application has been or is about to be made in respect of the child under section 12 of the Adoption (Scotland) Act 1978.[26] Where a review is arranged because of grounds (iii) or (iv) the hearing, in addition to reviewing the child's case and irrespective of the outcome of the review, must also draw up a report which shall provide advice in respect of the proposed application or proposed placing for adoption for any court which may subsequently require to come to a decision, and any court which receives such a report must consider it before coming to a decision in the matter.[27]

(2) At the request of the child or relevant person.[28] A review may be required by either the child or any relevant person at any time after three months from the imposition or last continuation of the supervision requirement, whether varied then or not.[29]

(3) Whenever the children's hearing has required that a review be held within a specified time.[30] It may make such a requirement whenever it makes a supervision requirement.[31]

(4) Whenever the reporter has received notice that a relevant person intends to take the child to live outwith Scotland.[32] The relevant person is obliged to give such a notice not later than 28 days before so taking the child,[33] but there is no sanction laid down in the Act for failure to do so.

(5) Where the child has been transferred in case of urgent necessity.[34] This provision is discussed above.[35]

(6) Where a referral is made in respect of a child who is already subject to a supervision requirement.[36] Though the statute is ambiguous on the point, it would appear that the obligation to review the case of a child

---

[23] s. 73(9).
[24] s. 73(8)(a)(i).
[25] s. 73(4).
[26] s. 73(5).
[27] s. 73(13) and (14).
[28] s. 73(8)(a)(ii).
[29] s. 73(6).
[30] s. 73(8)(a)(iii).
[31] s. 70(7). See above, para. 19.87.
[32] s. 73(8)(a)(iv).
[33] s. 73(7).
[34] s. 72(1).
[35] Above, para. 19.91.
[36] s. 65(3).

currently under supervision arises only when the new grounds are accepted or established and not when the referral is made and the grounds are denied or not understood.[37]

(7) Where a child who has absconded from a place of safety is returned.[38] If a child who is subject to a supervision requirement and is being kept in a place of safety under any provision in the 1995 Act, but he or she absconds from that place and, on being apprehended and returned the person in charge of the place is unwilling or unable to take the child back, the child must be brought before a children's hearing for a review of the supervision requirement.[39]

(8) After a child has been kept in secure accommodation for three months.[40] In addition, if the child has been liable to be kept in secure accommodation for more than six weeks but has not at any time during these six weeks been placed in secure accommodation, either the child or the relevant person may require the reporter to arrange a review hearing, which must be held within 21 days of the receipt by the reporter of the notice.[41]

(9) Where the child is placed for adoption by an adoption society.[42] In this event the children's hearing must both review the child's case and, irrespective of the outcome of that review, draw up a report for the court of the same nature as the report drawn up when a local authority requires a review for similar reasons.[43]

Recovery of fugitive children

19.94　　　If a child absconds from a place of safety in which he or she is being kept under Part II of the 1995 Act, or a residential establishment in which he or she is required to reside under the terms of a supervision requirement, or from a person who has control over him or her by virtue of a supervision requirement while he or she is being taken to or temporarily taken away from such a residential establishment, then that child may be arrested without warrant in any part of the United Kingdom and taken to the place of safety or the residential establishment.[44] Where a court is satisfied that there are reasonable grounds for believing that the child is within any premises, it may, where there is such a power of arrest, grant a warrant authorising a constable to enter those premises and search for the child using reasonable force if necessary.[45] A child who at the end of a period of leave from a place of safety or residential establishment fails to return there shall be taken for the purposes of this provision to have absconded.[46] It appears from the absence of any other relvant provision that these provisions are intended to cover the case of the child who *ab initio* refuses to surrender him or herself to, or is withheld by his or her parents from, the place of safety or residential establishment, but they are ill-expressed for that purpose. If the occupier of the place of safety or residential establishment is unwilling or unable to receive the child, that circumstance must be intimated

---

[37] See further, Norrie, *Children's Hearings in Scotland* (1997), pp. 137–139.
[38] s. 82(1).
[39] See further, below, para. 19.94.
[40] Secure Accommodation (Scotland) Regulations 1996, r. 11.
[41] *ibid.* r. 12.
[42] Adoption (Scotland) Act 1978, s. 22A(1) and (2), as added by the Children (Scotland) Act 1995, Sched. 2, para. 15.
[43] Adoption (Scotland) Act 1978, s. 22A(3).
[44] s. 82(1).
[45] *ibid.*
[46] s. 82(2).

forthwith to the reporter,[47] and the child must be kept in a place of safety until, if he or she is subject to a supervision requirement, he or she can be brought before a children's hearing for the review of that requirement or, in any other case, the reporter has considered whether compulsory measures of supervision are required for the child.[48]

Harbouring of children

It is an offence for a person (i) knowingly to assist or induce a child to **19.95** abscond in circumstances which render the child liable to arrest under the provisions described in the previous paragraph; (ii) knowingly and persistently to attempt to induce a child to abscond in such circumstances; (iii) knowingly to harbour or conceal a child who has so absconded; or (iv) knowingly to prevent a child from returning to a place of safety or residential establishment in which the child is required to reside or to a person who has control over him or her while he or she is being taken to or temporarily taken from such a place of safety or residential establishment.[49]

APPEALS

Appeal to sheriff

Jurisdiction and procedure

An appeal to the sheriff lies at the instance of the child or the relevant person **19.96** or both but not of the reporter against any decision of a children's hearing.[50] The appeal must be taken within a period of three weeks beginning with the date of the decision appealed against[51] and is to be heard in chambers.[52] The date of the hearing is to be included in the computation of the three-week period with the result that it terminates at midnight on the 20th day after the date of the decision.[53] The provision has been repealed that on special cause shown the sheriff may in his discretion hear an appeal notwithstanding that it was not lodged in time.[54] As soon as reasonably practicable after an appeal has been lodged, the sheriff must consider whether it is necessary to appoint a safeguarder and may at that stage or at any later stage appoint a safeguarder.[55]

Despite the apparent generality of the words "any decision", appeals may **19.97** be taken only against decisions disposing of a referral or reviewing a supervision requirement or on the granting or renewing of warrants. Decisions that relate merely to steps in procedure may not be appealed. Accordingly there is no appeal against a direction to make an application to the sheriff for a finding as to whether the grounds of referral are established rather than to discharge the referral,[56] nor against a decision to exclude a relevant person or a representative from part of the hearing, or to require the child to reside or attend at a hospital

---

[47] s. 82(4).
[48] s. 82(5).
[49] s. 83.
[50] s. 51(1). A safeguarder may sign the appeal on the child's behalf: AS 1997, r. 3.53(3). See, *e.g.*, *Catto v. Pearson*, 1990 S.L.T. (Sh.Ct) 77.
[51] s. 51(1)(a).
[52] s. 93(5).
[53] *S, Appellants*, 1979 S.L.T. (Sh.Ct) 37.
[54] Act of Sederunt (Statutory Appeals) 1981 (S.I. 1981 No. 1591), para. 2(2) (repealed by the Sheriff Court Summary Applications Rules 1993). In *Thomson, Petr*, 1998 S.L.T. 1066 a petition to the *nobile officium* to allow an appeal out of time was dismissed.
[55] s. 41(1) and AS 1997, r. 3.7(1).
[56] *H v. McGregor*, 1973 S.C. 95; *M v. Kennedy*, 1995 S.L.T. 123 at 125L.

or clinic for further investigation. A decision to discharge a referral is, however, an appealable decision[57]; and, although usually neither child nor relevant person would have an interest or wish to appeal such a decision, cases are conceivable, especially where there is a conflict of interest between the child and the relevant person, in which the child, in particular, might competently use the appellate process to secure the protection of compulsory measures of supervision which the hearing, by a decision to discharge the referral or terminate the supervision requirement, had denied him or her[58]; and a relevant person might likewise seek such measures where a child was beyond his or her control. An appeal in respect of the grant of a warrant must be disposed of within three days of the lodging of the appeal and if that is not done the warrant forthwith ceases to have effect.[59]

19.98   The Act provides that the child, or the relevant person, or both (or all), shall be heard by the sheriff where an appeal is made.[60] The correct interpretation of that is, it is submitted, that each must be heard if they so wish. It appears to be accepted that the reporter is the contradictor in an appeal[61], and that is consistent with the right given to the reporter, acting on behalf of a children's hearing, to initiate an appeal from the sheriff's decision to the sheriff principal or the Court of Session.[62] If that is correct the reporter must also be heard. The duty is laid on the reporter of ensuring that all reports and statements available to the hearing, along with the reports of their proceedings and the reason for the decision of the hearing, are lodged with the sheriff clerk.[63] The duty of making, or causing to be made, a report of the hearing's decision and a statement in writing of the reasons for it is laid upon the chairman.[64] The statement of reasons should be a clear statement of the material considerations to which the children's hearing had regard in its decision and it must be intelligible to the persons to whom it is addressed—including those who were not present at the hearing—and it must deal with all the substantial questions which were the subject of the decision.[65] It is not sufficient merely to refer to the information and recommendations before, and the procedure at, the hearing, and to state that the decision was taken on that basis.[66] The sheriff may hear evidence for or on behalf of the parties in relation to the decision, he may examine the reporter and authors or compilers of any reports or statements, and he may call for any further report which he considers may assist him in deciding the appeal.[67] Under that power there is no warrant for examining any member of the hearing other than the chairman, but it may sometimes be useful to do so and, although no means of compulsion are available, there is nothing in the Act which excludes it.

---

[57] *H v. McGregor*, above, at 100, *per* Lord Wheatley.

[58] In *Thomson, Petr*, 1998 S.L.T. 1066 the 17-year-old petitioner sought authority to appeal out of time a decision of a children's hearing to terminate a supervision requirement, in order that, for the purposes of sentencing by a criminal court, he could still be treated as a "child". The prayer of the petition was refused. *Cf. Anderson v. McGlennan*, 1998 S.C.C.R. 552, in which a 17-year-old who was subject to a supervision requirement had wrongly been treated by a criminal court as an adult for the purposes of sentencing.

[59] s. 51(8). "Three days" means three calendar days and not three court days and they begin to run on the day after the warrant is granted: *B v. Kennedy*, 1992 S.L.T. 870.

[60] s. 51(1)(b).

[61] See the role played by the reporter in *K v. Finlayson*, 1974 SLT (Sh.Ct) 51.

[62] s. 51(11) and (12).

[63] s. 51(2).

[64] Children's Hearings (Scotland) Rules 1996, r. 10(5).

[65] *per* Lord President Hope in *Kennedy v. M*, 1995 S.L.T. 717 at 723H, citing his own comments in *DH and JH v. Kennedy*, December 20, 1991, unreported.

[66] *K v. Finlayson*, 1974 S.L.T. (Sh.Ct) 51 at 54.

[67] s. 51(3) and A.S. 1997, r. 3.56(3).

Disposal

Where the sheriff is satisfied that the decision of the hearing is not justified **19.99** in all the circumstances of the case, he must allow the appeal[68]; otherwise he must hold that it has failed. He must give his decision orally either at the conclusion of the appeal or on such day as he appoints.[69] At the time of giving his decision or within seven days thereafter the sheriff may issue a note of the reasons for his decision and he must do so if he decides either to remit the case back to the hearing or to substitute his own disposal for that of the children's hearing.[70] There was at one time controversy about the scope of the ground on which a sheriff may reverse a hearing's decision, one view being that the matter is at large for the sheriff, the other that some error on the part of the hearing going beyond what may be the legitimate subject-matter of difference of opinion must be shown.[71] The former view derives some support from the powers of examination and of calling for further reports given to the sheriff and from the requirement that he be satisfied that the decision was not justified "in all the circumstances of the case", but it is submitted that the latter view is to be preferred. In *D v. Sinclair*[72] Sheriff Mowat said:

> "a sheriff should not interfere with the determination simply because he felt another form of treatment might be preferable. ... Accordingly, I consider that a sheriff should not allow an appeal unless there was some flaw in the procedure adopted by the hearing or he was satisfied that the hearing had not given proper consideration to some factor in the case."

The key lies in the words "not justified", as they appear in section 51(5). The sheriff cannot merely substitute his own opinion for that of the hearing but must, if the appeal is to be allowed, have some grounds on which the hearing's decision can justly be impugned. Irregularity in the conduct of the case is a ground of appeal from the sheriff to the sheriff principal or to the Court of Session under section 51(11),[73] from which it can be inferred that irregularity in the conduct of the case is among the grounds on which a decision of the children's hearing may be appealed to the sheriff under s. 51(1).[74] Error of law and lack of clarity in the hearing's statement of reasons are also grounds of appeal,[75] as is the decision being one that no reasonable children's hearing would have reached on the information which was properly before them.[76]

Where the appeal fails, the sheriff confirms the decision of the hearing.[77] **19.100** If the appeal is against the granting of a warrant and he allows the appeal, he must recall the warrant[78] and if the child is subject to a supervision requirement with a condition that the child be liable to be kept in secure accommodation he must direct that that condition shall cease to have effect.[79] Where the appeal succeeds the sheriff may, as he thinks fit:

---

[68] s. 51(5).
[69] A.S. 1997, r. 3.58(1).
[70] *ibid.* r. 3.58(2) and (3).
[71] See Grant, "The Legal Safeguards for the Rights of the Child and Parents in the Children's Hearing System", 1975 J.R. 209.
[72] 1973 S.L.T. (Sh.Ct) 47 at 48.
[73] See below, para. 19.103.
[74] *M v. Kennedy,* 1995 S.L.T. 123, *per* Lord President Hope at 126E.
[75] *D v. Strathclyde Regional Council,* 1991 S.C.L.R. 185.
[76] *O v. Rae,* 1993 S.L.T. 570, *per* Lord President Hope at 575I.
[77] s. 51(4).
[78] s. 51(5)(a).
[79] s. 51(5)(b).

    (a) remit the case with reasons for his decision to the children's hearing for reconsideration of its decision;

    (b) discharge the child from any further hearing or other proceedings in relation to the grounds for referral of the case; or

    (c) substitute for the disposal of the children's hearing any requirement which could be imposed by it as a disposal of the case.[80]

Criminal proceedings arising out of the same *species facti* are not, it is submitted, "proceedings in relation to the grounds for referral of the case".

Frivolous appeals

19.101 Although decisions at the review of a supervision requirement are appealable, there is a risk that repeated appeals against such decisions might become an abuse. Accordingly, if the sheriff is satisfied that an appeal against the decision of the hearing at a review is frivolous, he may order that no subsequent appeal against a decision to continue (with or without variation) the supervision requirement in question shall lie until the expiration of 12 months beginning with the date of the order.[81]

Effect of pending appeal

19.102 A supervision requirement, if made, remains in force pending an appeal unless the hearing, on the application of the child or relevant person, suspends it.[82] The considerations which militate against appeals from decisions on mere steps in procedure do not, in the main, apply to decisions not to suspend a requirement pending appeal and these are, it is submitted, themselves appealable. An application to suspend can be made only after an appeal is lodged[83] and it must be in writing.[84]

Appeal to sheriff principal or Court of Session

19.103 An appeal on a point of law, or in respect of any irregularity in the conduct of the case, lies to the sheriff principal from any decision of the sheriff on applications for findings in relation to the grounds of referral[85] and on appeals from decisions of hearings; and lies to the Court of Session from any such decision and, with leave of the sheriff principal, from any decision of the sheriff principal.[86] Appeal is by way of stated case and may be at the instance of a child or relevant person or both or of a reporter acting on behalf of a children's hearing.[87] The application to the sheriff or the sheriff principal to state a case must be made within a period of 28 days beginning with the date of his decision.[88] No new evidence can be placed before the appeal court since that would not bear upon any irregularity in the conduct of the case.[89] On deciding the appeal, the sheriff principal or as the case may be the Court of Session must remit the case to the sheriff for disposal in accordance with such directions as the court may give.[90] No other, or further, appeal is competent beyond the Court of Session.[91]

---

[80] s. 51(5)(c).
[81] s. 51(7).
[82] s. 51(9) and (10); *Kennedy v. M*, 1995 S.L.T. 717. *Cf. Stirling v. D*, 1995 S.L.T. 1089.
[83] Children's Hearings (Scotland) Rules 1996, r. 23(6).
[84] *ibid.* r. 23(1).
[85] Made under either s. 65 or s. 85.
[86] s. 51(11).
[87] s. 51(12).
[88] s. 51(13).
[89] *Stirling v. R*, 1996 S.C.L.R. 191 (Notes).
[90] s. 51(14).
[91] s. 51(11)(b).

CHAPTER 20

INTERIM PROTECTION OF CHILDREN

Scope of this chapter

20.01 Long-term provision for the care and protection of children can be made through the children's hearing system, through the making of a parental responsibilities order or the making of either an adoption order or an order freeing a child for adoption. All these issues are dealt with in detail elsewhere. This chapter will examine the various provisions in Part II of the Children (Scotland) Act 1995 whereby protection can be afforded children on an interim or emergency basis, together with those provisions designed to ensure that long- term care and protection is not frustrated by non-co-operation or by absconsion. Both the children's hearing and the sheriff may grant warrants to apprehend children and keep them in a place of safety after a child has been referred to a children's hearing, and these provisions will be examined first. There will then follow a discussion of child assessment orders, child protection orders and exclusion orders, all of which may only be granted by the sheriff.

The overarching principles

20.02 Section 16 of the Children (Scotland) Act 1995 sets out three principles which apply throughout Part II of the Act. Most of the warrants and orders to be discussed in this chapter can be made only after the children's hearing or the sheriff has applied these principles. While it is now common to refer to these principles as "the overarching principles", this should not be taken to imply that they are all of equal weight. The first is predominant, the third amounts to a rebuttable presumption, and the second is in reality a rule derived from the proposition that, where appropriate, children should be listened to.

20.03 First and foremost, the welfare of the child throughout his or her childhood is the hearing's or court's paramount consideration. This applies where a children's hearing decide or a court determines, under Part II of the Act, any matter with respect to a child.[1] As with orders under section 11 in Part I,[2] this does not mean that welfare is the only consideration but rather that it is the most important consideration and is likely, in most cases, to determine the issue to be resolved. If, however, for the purpose of protecting members of the public from serious harm (whether or not physical harm) a children's hearing or a court considers it necessary to make a decision or determination which would not be consistent with their affording paramountcy to the welfare of the child throughout his or her childhood they may make that decision or determination.[3]

---

[1] s. 16(1).

[2] See above, Chap. 10. One noticeable difference between the welfare principle as expressed in s. 11(7) and as expressed in s. 16(1) is that in the former there is no time-frame given within which welfare is to be assessed; in s. 16(1) welfare throughout the child's childhood is to be assessed. "Childhood", one assumes, relates to the period in which a person is legally a child, as defined in s. 93(2).

[3] s. 16(5).

20.04   Secondly, a children's hearing or a sheriff, taking account of the age and maturity of the child concerned, shall so far as practicable, (i) give the child an opportunity to indicate whether he or she wishes to express his or her views; (ii) if he or she does so wish, give the child an opportunity to express them; and (iii) have regard to such views as may be expressed.[4] Without prejudice to that generality, a child 12 years of age or more is presumed to be of sufficient age and maturity to form a view. This provision applies in the following circumstances:

(a) the children's hearing (i) is considering whether to make or are reviewing a supervision requirement, (ii) is considering whether to grant a warrant under section 66(1) or its continuation under section 66(5), or a warrant under either 69(4) or (7), (iii) is engaged in providing advice on the continuation of a child protection order or (iv) is drawing up a report concerning the adoption of the child[5]; and

(b) the sheriff is considering (i) whether to make, vary or discharge a parental responsibilities order, a child assessment order or an exclusion order, (ii) whether to vary or discharge a child protection order, (iii) whether to grant a warrant under section 67, or (iv) on appeal from a decision of a children's hearing, whether to substitute his own disposal for that of the children's hearing.[6]

Where the child has indicated a wish to express views, the children's hearing and the sheriff may not make any decision or make any order or disposal as is mentioned above unless an opportunity has been given for the child's views to be obtained or heard.[7]

20.05   Thirdly, no requirement or order shall be made with respect to the child concerned unless the children's hearing, or as the case may be the sheriff, considers that it would be better for the child that the requirement or order be made than that none should be made at all.[8] This application of the "no-order presumption"[9] applies when (a) the children's hearing is considering whether to make or is reviewing a supervision requirement or is considering whether to grant a warrant under section 66(1), a continuation thereof under section 66(5), or a warrant under section 69(4) or (7) and (b) the sheriff is considering (i) whether to make, vary or discharge a parental responsibilities order, a child assessment order or an exclusion order, (ii) whether to vary or discharge a child protection order, (iii) whether to grant a warrant under section 67, or (iv) on appeal from a decision of a children's hearing, whether to substitute his own disposal for that of the children's hearing.[10] As with section 11 orders, the "no-order presumption" has the effect that the onus lies on the person seeking the order to persuade the sheriff or the children's hearing that the order should be made or, as the case may be, continued.

---

[4] s. 16(2). See also Act of Sederunt (Child Care and Maintenance Rules) 1997 (S.I. 1997 No. 291) (hereinafter "A.S. 1997"), r. 3.5 and Children's Hearings (Scotland) Rules 1996 (S.I. 1996 No. 3261) (hereinafter "1996 Rules"), r. 15.

[5] Other circumstances are listed in the 1996 Rules, r. 15(2).

[6] s. 16(4).

[7] 1996 Rules, r. 15(3)(b) and A.S. 1997, r. 3.5(1)(b).

[8] s. 16(3).

[9] See above, para. 10.38 in relation to this principle as it applies in s. 11 of the 1995 Act.

[10] s. 16(4).

WARRANTS TO DETAIN CHILD IN PLACE OF SAFETY

Introduction

Warrants, issued or granted under any provision in Part II of the Children **20.06**
(Scotland) Act 1995, provide authority to apprehend the child subject to the warrant
and detain him or her in a place of safety[11] and they may be implemented as if
they were warrants for the apprehension of an accused person issued by a court of
summary jurisdiction; and any enactment or rule of law applying to such a warrant
shall apply in like manner to a warrant under the 1995 Act.[12] A child who absconds
from a place of safety may be arrested without further warrant in any part of the
United Kingdon and taken back to the place of safety; and a court which is satisfied
that there are reasonable grounds for believing that the child is within any premises
may, where the child is liable to such arrest, grant a warrant authorising a constable
to enter those premises and search for the child using reasonable force if necessary.[13]
A child who at the end of a period of leave from a place of safety fails to return
there shall be taken to have absconded for these purposes.[14] It is an offence for
any person knowingly to assist or induce, or persistently attempt to induce, a
child to abscond from a place of safety, to harbour or conceal a child who has so
absconded, or to prevent a child from returning to a place of safety.[15] However, a
local authority is not "harbouring" a child where the child appears to it to be at
risk of harm and at the child's request it provides him with a refuge in a residential
establishment or arrange for refuge to be provided in an approved household.[16]

If a child has been taken to a place of safety which is a residential **20.07**
establishment under a warrant or order and subsequent to its issue the chief
social work officer of the relevant local authority and the person in charge of
the residential establishment are satisfied that the criteria for the granting of secure
accommodation authorisation are fulfilled,[17] the child may be placed and kept
in secure accommodation. The reporter and relevant person[18] must be informed
forthwith.[19] A children's hearing must be arranged within 72 hours if the warrant
is granted under sections 66, 68, or 69, and if granted by a sheriff under section 67
an application to the sheriff must be made within 72 hours.[20]

Conditions may be attached to warrants granted by a children's hearing under **20.08**
sections 63, 66 and 69, but not under section 45. The sheriff may attach conditions
to warrants granted under section 67.

Warrant to secure child's attendance (section 45)

A child referred to a children's hearing has a right and also a duty to attend **20.09**
at all stages of the hearing,[21] though he or she may be relieved of that duty in
certain circumstances.[22] It is the reporter who has the responsibility for securing
the attendance of the child at the hearing of his or her case by a children's

---

[11] "Place of safety" is defined in s. 93(1) as "(a) a residential or other establishment provided by a
local authority; (b) a community house within the meaning of section 53 of the Children Act
1989; (c) a police station; or (d) a hospital, surgery or other suitable place, the occupier of which
is willing temporarily to receive the child".

[12] s. 84.

[13] s. 82(1).

[14] s. 82(2).

[15] s. 83.

[16] s. 38(1).

[17] s. 70(9) and (10).

[18] *i.e.* the person, as defined in s. 93(1), with the right and duty to attend children's hearings: see
above, para. 19.07

[19] Secure Accommodation (Scotland) Regulations 1996, r. 9(1).

[20] *ibid.* r. 9(2).

[21] s. 45(1).

[22] s. 45(2). See above, para. 19.44.

hearing[23] and on the application of the reporter the children's hearing, if satisfied on cause shown that it is necessary for it to do so, may issue a warrant to find the child, keep him or her in a place of safety, and bring him or her to a hearing.[24] Though this provision is not worded in terms of likelihood that the child will fail to attend,[25] that is its effect since the warrant may be issued only when the reporter shows cause why it is necessary to do so for the purpose of fulfilling his or her responsibility for securing the attendance of the child. The hearing must be satisfied that it is "necessary" to issue the warrant, by which is meant it must be persuaded that the child is unlikely to attend a hearing unless a warrant to bring him or her to a hearing is issued. In addition, if a hearing has been arranged at which the child was obliged to attend, in accordance with notice in proper form,[26] but the child has failed to attend, then that children's hearing may issue a warrant to find the child, keep him or her in a place of safety, and bring him or her to a subsequent hearing.[27] The children's hearing may issue a warrant under this provision on its own motion, as well as on the application of the reporter. Under the wording of the Act, neither the reason for the child's failure to attend nor the likelihood of that failure recurring is relevant, though in practice a warrant is unlikely to be issued unless there is a fear that the non-attendance will be repeated at a subsequent hearing and any known reason for non-attendance may indicate how realistic that fear is. A children's hearing cannot, it is submitted, issue a warrant under section 45(5) if a child has failed to attend a hearing from which he or she has previously been relieved of the obligation to attend.[28] If the hearing wishes to see the child in that circumstance, it must either withdraw the release previously given and continue the hearing for the child to attend at some later date or, if it is persuaded that the child will not attend at the later hearing even if the legal obligation to do so is reimposed and if the reporter so moves, issue a warrant under section 45(4).

20.10   A warrant issued under either section 45(4) or section 45(5) is authority to keep the child in a place of safety either until the expiry of seven days from the day the child was first taken to the place of safety or, if earlier, the day on which a children's hearing first sit to consider the child's case.[29] If the child cannot be brought to a children's hearing immediately on being found in pursuance of a section 45 warrant, then the reporter must, whenever practicable, arrange a children's hearing to sit on the first working day after the child was so found.[30]

Warrant when hearing unable to dispose of case (section 66)

20.11   Where a children's hearing has been arranged but it is unable to dispose of the case, it may grant a warrant which will be authority to keep the child in a place of safety and to bring the child to a children's hearing in the event of the sheriff finding the grounds established.[31] The grounds upon which a warrant may be granted under section 66 are that: (i) there is reason to believe that the child may not attend at any hearing of his or her case; (ii) there is reason to believe that the child may fail to comply with a requirement to attend, or reside

---

[23] s. 45(3).

[24] s. 45(4). This is the only provision under which the children's hearing is not permitted to grant a warrant *ex proprio motu*.

[25] *cf.* s. 66(2)(a) and s. 69(7)(b).

[26] See 1996 Rules, r. 6.

[27] s. 45(5).

[28] Under s. 45(2). *Cf.* s. 68(6), under which the sheriff may grant an order to find and keep the child who has failed to attend the hearing of a s. 68 application: this power is expressly limited to situations in which the child has not been relieved of the obligation to attend.

[29] s. 45(6).

[30] s. 45(7).

[31] s. 66.

at any clinic, hospital, or other establishment for the purposes of further investigation to allow a children's hearing to complete their investigation of the child's case; or (iii) it is necessary that the child should be kept in a place of safety in order to safeguard or promote his or her welfare.[32]

The warrant granted under section 66(1) may require any person named in **20.12** the warrant (i) to find and to keep or, as the case may be, to keep the child in a place of safety; and (ii) to bring the child before a children's hearing at such times as may be specified in the warrant.[33] The child cannot be kept in a place of safety for longer than 22 days.[34] The warrant may contain such conditions as the children's hearing thinks necessary or expedient and in particular it may require the child to submit to any medical or other examination or treatment, and may regulate the contact that the child is to have with any other person while the child is being kept in the place of safety.[35] Any condition that the child submit to medical or other examination or treatment is qualified by the terms of section 90,[36] which provides that the child's capacity to consent to any surgical, medical or dental procedure or treatment remains to be determined by section 2(4) of the Age of Legal Capacity (Scotland) Act 1991 and that where a condition contained in a warrant granted under section 66 (or section 69, as discussed below) requires a child to submit to examination or treatment, that examination or treatment may only be carried out on a child who has capacity under the 1991 Act when that child consents. In other words, a child who is old enough to understand (in the opinion of the medical practitioner) the nature and consequences of the examination or treatment required by the condition in the warrant may refuse to submit to such examination or treatment, and any that is carried out in the face of such refusal will be an assault against the child. If the child does not have capacity to consent or refuse under the 1991 Act, then a condition in a warrant granted under section 66 does not provide the authority required for the examination or treatment to go ahead: power to give that authority still rests with those who have parental responsibilities and parental rights, and a requirement that the child "submits" to medical treatment does not replace that power.

Where the children's hearing which grants or continues a section 66 warrant **20.13** is satisfied that either of the criteria for authorising the child to be kept in secure accommodation[37] is satisfied, it may authorise the child to be kept there, at such times as the person in charge of that establishment, with the agreement of the chief social work officer of the relevant local authority,[38] considers necessary.[39] The children's hearing may also order that the place of safety at which the child is to be kept shall not be disclosed to any person or class of persons specified in the order.[40]

Continuation of a section 66 warrant

A warrant granted by a children's hearing under section 66(1) allows a child **20.14** to be kept in a place of safety for a maximum period of 22 days,[41] though the hearing may specify a shorter period, if this is appropriate in the child's interests.

---

[32] s. 66(2).
[33] s. 66(3).
[34] s. 66(3)(a). The warrant can, however, be continued under s. 66(5): see below, para. 20.14.
[35] s. 66(4).
[36] s. 66(4)(a).
[37] Listed in s. 70(10).
[38] For which, see s. 93(1).
[39] s. 66(6).
[40] s. 66(7).
[41] s. 66(3)(a).

At any time prior to the expiry of the 22 days, the warrant may, on an application to the children's hearing on cause shown by the reporter, be continued in force, whether with or without variation of any condition, by the children's hearing for a further period not exceeding 22 days.[42] There is no limit to the number of times that the warrant can be continued, but the total length of time during which the child can be kept in a place of safety under a warrant granted and continued under section 66 is 66 days.[43]

Warrant for further detention granted by sheriff

20.15   The reporter may apply to the sheriff for a warrant to keep the child in a place of safety after a warrant granted and continued by the children's hearing under section 66 has expired.[44] Such an application may also be made at the same time as, or during, the hearing of an application for the establishment of the grounds of referral.[45] The sheriff may grant such a warrant on cause shown, and he must specify the date on which the warrant will expire. The warrant may contain any requirement or condition that a warrant granted by a children's hearing under section 66 might contain, including secure accommodation authorisation and non-disclosure of the child's address.[46] There is no stated limit to the number of consecutive warrants that can be granted under this provision, though it will seldom be in the child's interests to be kept in a place of safety, waiting to be brought to a children's hearing, for even as long as 66 days. Parliament's intention in setting time-limits must be taken to be that referrals be disposed of without unnecessary delay.[47]

Warrant on continuation of hearing (section 69)

20.16   A children's hearing which, after considering the case of a child, continues that case to a subsequent hearing for further investigation may grant a warrant under one or other of two separate subsections. First, it may grant a warrant requiring that the child be taken to and kept in a place of safety until the next hearing if (i) keeping the child in a place of safety is necessary in the interests of safeguarding or promoting the welfare of the child; or (ii) there is reason to believe that the child may not attend the subsequent hearing of his or her case.[48] Such a warrant ceases to have effect at the end of 22 days after it was granted or, if earlier, on the day a hearing convenes to consider the continued case.[49] There is no provision for the renewal of a warrant granted under section 69(7),[50] which is designed to ensure that a continued hearing takes place within as short a period of time as possible. However, the continued hearing may decide again to continue the case on the ground that the investigations are not yet complete or that further investigations are required, and a further warrant may be granted under this provision. Secondly, if the children's hearing has continued the case for further investigation and, for the purposes of such investigation, required the child to attend, or to reside at, any clinic, hospital or other establishment,[51] but the child thereafter fails to attend or reside for investigation as required, a

---

[42] s. 66(5).
[43] s. 66(8).
[44] s. 67(1) and A.S. 1997, rr. 3.41–3.43.
[45] s. 67(4).
[46] s. 67(2) and (3).
[47] *per* Lord President Emslie in *Humphries, Petr*, 1982 S.L.T. at 481.
[48] s. 69(7).
[49] s. 69(8).
[50] *cf.* the renewal provisions concerning warrants granted under s. 66, considered above.
[51] s. 69(3).

warrant may be granted by the children's hearing, with or without an application to that effect by the reporter.[52] The effect of this warrant is to give authority (a) to find the child, (b) to remove the child to a place of safety and keep him or her there, and (c) where the place of safety is not the clinic, hospital or other establishment referred to in the requirement to attend, to take the child from the place of safety to that named place for the purposes of the investigation.[53] Such a warrant cannot authorise the keeping of a child in a place of safety for any more than 22 days after the granting of the warrant or after the beginning of the subsequent hearing, whichever is earlier.[54]

A warrant granted under either section 69(4) or section 69(7) may contain **20.17** such conditions as appear to the children's hearing to be necessary or expedient, and may in particular require the child to submit to any medical or other examination or treatment and may regulate contact between the child and any specified person or class of persons.[55] The children's hearing in granting a warrant under section 69(4) or (7) may order that the place of safety at which the child is to be kept shall not be disclosed to any person or class of persons specified in the order.[56] Where it is satisfied that either of the criteria for authorising the child to be kept in secure accommodation[57] is satisfied, the children's hearing may authorise the child to be kept there at such times as the person in charge of that establishment, with the agreement of the chief social work officer of the relevant local authority, considers necessary.[58]

Warrant after child arrested by police (section 63)

If the reporter is informed that the child is in a place of safety after having **20.18** been apprehended by the police and detained in a place of safety in terms of section 43(5) of the Criminal Procedure (Scotland) Act 1995, the reporter must, unless he or she considers that compulsory measures of supervision are not required in relation to the child,[59] arrange a children's hearing to which he or she shall refer the case.[60] The child may be kept in the place of safety until the commencement of the hearing.[61] That hearing, which must begin not later than the third day after the reporter received the information,[62] (i) must consider whether to grant a warrant to keep the child in a place of safety,[63] and (ii) may direct the reporter to arrange a children's hearing in order to put grounds of referral to the child.[64] The effect of a warrant granted under section 63, and the terms and conditions on which it can be granted, are the same as with a warrant granted under section 66,[65] which includes its time-limits, conditions, continuations, secure accommodation authorisations and non-disclosure of child's whereabouts; the grounds upon which a section 63 warrant may be granted are identical to the grounds upon which a section 66 warrant is granted.[66] There

---

[52] s. 69(4).
[53] s. 69(5).
[54] s. 69(6).
[55] s. 69(9).
[56] s. 69(10).
[57] Listed in s. 70(10).
[58] s. 69(11).
[59] In which case, the reporter shall direct that the child shall no longer be kept in a place of safety: s. 63(3).
[60] s. 63(1).
[61] s. 63(4).
[62] s. 63(2).
[63] s. 63(5)(a).
[64] s. 63(5)(b).
[65] s. 63(5), referring to s. 66(3)–(8).
[66] s. 63(5)(a), referring to the conditions in s. 66(2).

are, however, two differences between a section 63 warrant and a section 66 warrant. First, the termination of a warrant granted under section 63 by the expiry of 66 days does not activate the sheriff's power to grant an additional warrant under section 67, as he may do on the termination of a warrant granted and continued under section 66.[67] Secondly, a child may not be kept in a place of safety in accordance with a warrant granted under section 63 where the reporter, having regard to the welfare of the child, considers that, whether as a result of a change in the circumstances of the case or of further information relating to the case having been received, either the conditions for the granting of the warrant no longer exist or the child is not in need of compulsory measures of supervision.[68] There is no equivalent provision for the release of a child from a place of safety during the currency of a warrant granted under section 66.

Appeals

20.19   A children's hearing's decision to issue or grant a warrant is an appealable decision, and any appeal must be disposed of within three days of having been lodged, failing which the warrant will cease to have effect.[69] An appeal from the sheriff to the sheriff principal or the Court of Session is competent against his decision on appeal from a children's hearing[70] but, not being a decision listed in section 51(11), it would seem that a sheriff's decision to grant a warrant under section 67 is not appealable.[71]

CHILD ASSESSMENT ORDERS

Introduction

20.20   It may happen that medical examination or assessment of a child is necessary in order to obtain evidence upon which the care and protection measures contained in the Children (Scotland) Act 1995 can be based. Often such examination is of an intimate nature and, because all medical examination is an assault unless founded upon either consent or necessity, it is important that proper authorisation be obtained. One difficulty, however, is that the person with the right and power to consent on behalf of a child is very often the person against whom suspicions of ill-treatment of the child have been raised. Before the coming into force of Part II of the Children (Scotland) Act 1995 medical examination or assessment of children in such circumstances was sometimes carried out without proper authorisation, specifically in order to gain evidence to back up these suspicions. Now, however, following the model established by section 43 of the English Children Act 1989,[72] there is a procedure to be followed, for section 55 of the 1995 Act allows the sheriff to grant an order for an assessment of the state of a child's health or development or of the way in which he or she has been treated, and it authorises the removal of the child to the place where the assessment is to be carried out, and the keeping of the child

---

[67] s. 67(1) expressly refers to s. 66 warrants only and there is no reference in s. 63 to this provision.
[68] s. 63(6).
[69] s. 51(8).
[70] s. 51(11)(a)(i) and (b).
[71] The question of what decisions made by the sheriff under Pt II of the Act are appealable is rather confused by the listing of certain decisions in s. 51(11). It is open to argument that all other decisions, such as those to grant child assessment orders or exclusion orders, are appealable on general principles. Warrants granted under s. 67 might well be different since warrants granted by children's hearings are expressly made appealable and *expressio unius est exclusio alterius*.
[72] For a (rather negative) appraisal of how the child assessment order has worked in England, see Dickens, "Assessment and the Control of Social Work: Analysis of Reasons for the Non-use of the Child Assessment Order" (1993) J.S.W.F.L. 88; Lavery, "The Child Assessment Order: A Reassessment" (1996) 8 C.F. L.Q. 41.

there or elsewhere. While this is not limited to medical assessments and might include, for example, psychological, educational, emotional and even social assessments, it is likely that the greatest use of the child assessment order will be in acquiring evidence as to the state of the child's health or development. The evidence thus acquired may be used to found other child protection measures.

Grounds for granting a child assessment order

A sheriff may grant an order for an assessment of the state of a child's health **20.21** or development, or of the way in which he or she has been treated, on the application of a local authority if he is satisfied that *each* of the following three conditions are made out:

(1) The local authority has reasonable cause to suspect that the child in respect of whom the order is sought is being so treated (or neglected) that he or she is suffering, or is likely to suffer, significant harm.[73] What amounts to reasonable cause to suspect will depend upon the circumstances, but it must be remembered that the purpose of the order is to allow a testing of suspicion: it follows that the level of suspicion required should not be set too high. It is likely that only in cases in which there is no cause whatsoever to suspect that the child is suffering will this provision not be satisfied. Significant harm is harm that is serious and not of a minor, superficial or transient nature. It may be physical or emotional.

(2) Such assessment of the child is required in order to establish whether or not there is reasonable cause to believe that the child is so treated (or neglected). If the information can be acquired in a way that does not require the legal force of a child assessment order, and it is practicable so to acquire the information, then the child assessment order is not "required".

(3) Such assessment is unlikely to be carried out, or be carried out satisfactorily, unless the order is granted.[74]

Application is made in Form 45 in the Schedule to the Act of Sederunt **20.22** (Child Care and Maintenance Rules) 1997,[75] and the sheriff must grant or refuse the application after hearing the parties and allowing such further procedure as he thinks fit.[76] The order itself is made in Form 46 of the Act of Sederunt. If the sheriff considers it necessary to appoint a person to safeguard the interests of the child in the proceedings, he must do so on such terms and conditions as appear appropriate.[77] The role of a safeguarder appointed in such circumstances would appear to come to an end when the proceedings come to an end, that is to say when the sheriff has made his determination whether or not to make a child assessment order.

Effect of a child assessment order

The child assessment order lasts for a specified period of time, not exceeding **20.23** seven days, and it will commence on a date that must be specified in the order.[78] Comprehensive assessment of a child's emotional or psychological state will

---

[73] The refusal to allow the visiting of a foster child within the meaning of the Foster Children (Scotland) Act 1984 or the inspection of premises in which a person is authorised to keep foster children amounts to reasonable cause for this purpose: Foster Children (Scotland) Act 1984, s. 13.

[74] s. 55(1).

[75] A.S. 1997, r. 3.25.

[76] *ibid*. r. 3. 27.

[77] s. 41(1).

[78] s. 55(3)(a) and (b).

seldom be possible within that time-scale, suggesting again that the primary purpose of child assessment orders will be in relation to medical examination. The order will require any person in a position to produce the child to (i) produce him or her to any authorised person, (ii) permit that person or any other authorised person to carry out an assessment in accordance with the order and (iii) comply with any other condition in the order.[79] The order must be carried out by an authorised person (that is an officer of the local authority who sought the order, or any person authorised by the local authority, to perform the assessment in accordance with the terms of the order).[80] In order to carry out the assessment the child may if necessary be taken to any place at which the assessment is to be carried out and the order may authorise the child to be kept at that place, or any other place, for such period of time as may be specified in the order.[81] If a child is taken to a place for the carrying out of an assessment the order must contain such directions as the sheriff considers appropriate as to the contact the child is to have with any other person while at the place of assessment.[82] In addition, the child will be treated as being "looked after" by the local authority,[83] which imposes on the authority the duty to safeguard and promote the child's welfare, to make use of such services available for children cared for by their own parents as appear to the authority reasonable, and to take such steps to promote, on a regular basis, personal relations and direct contact between the child and any person with parental responsibilities as appear to it to be both practicable and reasonable, taking account of the child's welfare.[84] The local authority must also have regard, in making any decisions in relation to the child, to the child's religious persuasion, racial origin and cultural and linguistic background.[85]

20.24   These provisions leave the practical effect of the child assessment order in some obscurity. In particular it is not clear what effect the making of the order has on the general requirement to obtain consent to medical or other examination or assessment. In other words, does the order authorise assessment in the absence of, or even against, the consent of the person with the legal power to grant consent (so replacing that consent) or does it direct that person to give consent which remains required? In relation to the child who has capacity to grant or withhold consent to medical, dental or surgical treatment or procedure (which will cover most—but not all[86]—forms of assessment of health or development) the making of a child assessment order does not prejudice that child's capacity to do so.[87] It is expressly provided, in addition and without prejudice to the generality of the rule just mentioned, that where a child has such capacity, any examination or treatment to which the child is required to submit in terms of a warrant or a supervision requirement, may be carried out only if the child consents.[88] This additional provision does not, rather surprisingly, (and in contrast to the position in England[89]) refer to child assessment orders but that omission

---

[79] s. 55(3)(c).
[80] s. 55(3)(d) and (6).
[81] s. 55(4).
[82] s. 55(5). Contact arrangements may be made even although there is a supervision requirement in place but it is unclear whether, if inconsistent with that requirement, they can be given effect to. On the same point in relation to child protection orders, see below, para. 20.35, n. 17.
[83] s. 17(6).
[84] s. 17(1).
[85] s. 17(4).
[86] A psychological assessment, for example, is unlikely to come within that phrase.
[87] s. 90.
[88] *ibid*.
[89] Children Act 1989, s. 43(8).

does not, it is submitted, affect the rule that a capable child remains capable even in the face of a child assessment order. It follows from this that a child assessment order cannot be given effect to if the child refuses to submit to it and the child is of sufficient mental maturity to understand the nature and consequences of the proposed assessment.[90] The matter must, however, be different when the child has no such capacity, for otherwise the whole purpose of the order would be frustrated. When the child has no capacity, consent to medical treatment or examination requires to be given by the parent or guardian, and it is their refusal that will render the order necessary, by satisfying the condition for the granting of the order that the assessment "is unlikely to be carried out... unless the order is granted".[91] In this circumstance, therefore, the order does replace the consent otherwise required, and the person authorised to carry out the order may perform the assessment in the absence of the parent's or guardian's consent.

Child assessment orders and child protection orders
The conditions for the granting of a child protection order laid down in **20.25** section 57 (to be discussed shortly) are stricter than the conditions for the granting of a child assessment order in section 55, for it must be shown under section 57 that there are reasonable grounds to believe that the child is suffering significant harm (or, under section 57(2), that the local authority has reasonable grounds to suspect that the child is being or will be so treated, and that they are attempting to make inquiries but that those inquiries are being frustrated by access to the child being unreasonably denied), while it must be shown under section 55 that there is reasonable cause to suspect significant harm and that the assessment is necessary to test that suspicion. The child protection order is designed, as the child assessment order is not, to deal with cases in which the threat to the child is believed to be immediate or imminent. The form of application for a child assessment order[92] contains a section in which the applicant must give reasons why a child protection order is not being sought. Nevertheless there may well be cases in which, while attempting to establish that it has reasonable cause to suspect, the local authority actually establishes reasonable grounds to believe that the child is suffering significant harm (or reasonable grounds to suspect such harm, together with an unreasonable denial of access to the child). It is therefore provided that if, in an application for a child assessment order, the conditions for a child protection order are shown to be satisfied then a child protection order under section 57 must be made rather than a child assessment order.[93] The apparently mandatory terms of this provision suggest that the sheriff has no discretion but must make the child protection order if the conditions in section 57 are found to be satisfied in an application under section 55. This, however, should be read in light of section 57 itself, which provides that the sheriff "may make" a child protection order if the conditions for its granting are established. It is submitted that the words "shall make" as they appear in section 55(2) should be interpreted to mean that the sheriff must treat an application made under section 55 as if it were an application under section 57, thereby permitting the sheriff the discretion contained in the latter section. This, admittedly, involves some violence to the actual terms of the statute, but the alternative of giving the sheriff a discretion to make an order under section 57 when the application is made under section 57 but obliging him to make an order under section 57

---

[90] See further, Lockyer and Stone, *Juvenile Justice in Scotland* (1998), p. 120.
[91] s. 55(1)(c).
[92] A.S. 1997, Form 45.
[93] s. 55(2).

when the application is made under section 55 is ludicrous and an interpretation which avoids that result is to be preferred.[94] Were this interpretation to be rejected, sheriffs would be obliged to make an order under section 57 even when, had the application been made under section 57 itself, the sheriff would have refused the order on grounds relating to the child's welfare and the availability of a child assessment order would, as Lockyer and Stone, point out,[95] be restricted to cases in which the local authority have reasonable cause to suspect but not reasonable grounds to believe that a child is suffering significant harm. The distinctions between "reasonable cause to suspect" (as used in section 55(1)), "reasonable grounds to believe" (as used in section 57(1)), and "reasonable grounds to suspect" (as used in section 57(2)) are too subtle to have any real substance. The problem may, however, be academic since the terms and conditions of the order made under section 57 remain within the discretion of the sheriff, and if he feels, in an application made under section 55 that he must make an order under section 57 but that it would be contrary to the child's interests to remove him or her from home, he may word the order in terms of requiring merely that the child be produced to the applicant.[96] A condition of assessment might be added to achieve all that an assessment order itself would achieve.

CHILD PROTECTION ORDERS

Introduction

20.26   Prior to the coming into force of the Children (Scotland) Act 1995, emergency protective measures that could not wait until a children's hearing was convened were governed by section 37 of the Social Work (Scotland) Act 1968, under which a court or justice of the peace could issue an order authorising the removal of a child to a place of safety.[97] Deficiencies in this system were identified in the Clyde Report[98] and new procedures were put into place by sections 57–61 of the Children (Scotland) Act 1995, which govern the granting and the effect of a child protection order. It is an offence, making the offender liable on summary conviction to a fine not exceeding level three on the standard scale, for any person intentionally to obstruct any person who is acting either under a child protection order or under an authorisation by a justice of the peace under section 61(1) or section 61(2) or to obstruct a constable removing a child to a place of safety under section 61(5).[99]

Grounds for granting a child protection order

20.27   A child protection order may be applied for under either section 57(1) or section 57(2). Any person (including a local authority) may apply for a child protection order under section 57(1); alternatively a local authority, but no other

---

[94] A factor telling against this proposed interpretation, however, is the wording of s. 76(8), which in relation to an application for an exclusion order provides a similar rule to that contained in s. 55(2), except that it is provided that the sheriff "may" rather than "shall" make an order under s. 57. The principle behind the rule in both provisions is the same but the fact that different words are used might be taken to indicate a parliamentary intention that the provisions are to have a different effect. The policy behind such an intention is, however, obscure.

[95] *op. cit.*, p. 121.

[96] s. 57(4)(a).

[97] For a discussion, see the 1st edition of this book at pp. 457–462.

[98] *Report of the Inquiry into the Removal of Children From Orkney in February 1991*: H.C. Papers 1992–93, No. 195. For a discussion of the events leading to the Clyde Inquiry and the development of the proposals in that inquiry and therafter, see Lockyer and Stone, *Juvenile Justice in Scotland* (1998), esp. at pp. 94–101 and 119–120.

[99] s. 81. S. 61 is considered below, paras 20.52–20.56.

person may apply under section 57(2). The effect of the order, if granted, is the same whichever subsection is used to base the application, as are the matters it may authorise and the procedures that its implementation activates.

Reasonable grounds for believing harm

Any person, whether a local authority, a parent or other relative, a constable, **20.28** or even the child him or herself may apply to the sheriff for a child protection order, which may be granted if the following two conditions are satisfied:

> "(a) there are reasonable grounds to believe that a child—
> (i) is being so treated (or neglected) that he is suffering significant harm; or
> (ii) will suffer such harm if he is not removed to and kept in a place of safety, or if he does not remain in the place where he is then being accommodated (whether or not he is resident there); and
> (b) an order under this section is necessary to protect that child from such harm (or such further harm)."[1]

Paragraph (a) requires that the sheriff be satisfied that there is evidence sufficient to found a reasonable belief that the child is being or will be significantly harmed. Sub-paragraph (i) concerns the way that some other person is presently acting towards the child. The words "is being treated" suggest a continuing state of affairs brought about by someone other than the child and it does not cover either significant harm caused by the child's own acts or omissions, or harm caused to the child in the past. It cannot be said, it is submitted, of a child who was beaten some time in the past that he or she "is being treated" unless, perhaps, the injuries are still being suffered from.[2] Sub-paragraph (ii) concerns future harm and is capable of covering both significant harm that another person will cause to the child in the future and harm which is being or will be caused by the child him or herself. Harm inflicted upon the child in the past (whether by the child or some other person) may well provide reasonable grounds for believing that it will be repeated, particularly if the treatment is continuing. So the fact that a parent has beaten a child in the past will give reasonable grounds for believing that the child "will suffer" harm only if it is reasonable to believe that the beating may be repeated. A child may be presently harming him or herself, say, by abusing alcohol or drugs, or by associating with thieves or prostitutes: such actions may clearly give reasonable grounds to believe that the child will suffer significant harm if not removed to a place of safety and kept there. In relation to either sub-paragraph, the harm that the child must be suffering or threatened with must be "significant" harm, that is to say harm of a not minor, transient or superficial nature. It may be physical or psychological or, perhaps, social (for a child who is anti-social does him or herself harm).[3] "The categories of harm are never closed."[4] The subjecting of the child to any sexual activity is likely always to be considered significant harm, as is any physical assault that causes bruising or lesions or involved the use of implements. There is, however, no necessary connection between "significant harm" and harm that could lead to a criminal charge against the perpetrator: the latter does not require to be "signficant".

---

[1] s. 57(1).

[2] But even then, since the purpose of the child protection order is to provide necessary protection from immediate harm, the words should not be interpreted to cover harm that has already occurred.

[3] The (English) Children Act 1989 defines "harm" to mean "ill-treatment or the impairment of health or development": s. 31(9). There is no definition of "harm" in the Scottish statute but it would, it is submitted, include developmental impairment.

[4] Freeman, *Children, their Families and the Law* (Macmillan, 1992), p. 93.

Emotional harm will be significant when it can properly be described as trauma; distress and upset will not usually be sufficient. Harm will always be significant when it is more serious than the potential trauma that removal from home will almost inevitably cause a child.

20.29   Under paragraph (b), the sheriff must be satisfied that the making of a child protection order is "necessary" to protect the child from the actual or threatened significant harm. If the harm is not such as to require, in the eyes of the reasonable person, immediate action to protect the child from any continuation of the harm, then the making of the order cannot be said to be "necessary". This does not mean that the child protection order must be shown to be the only possible way in which the child can be protected. Rather the word "necessary" has, it is submitted, a somewhat looser meaning, and this condition will be fulfilled when the child protection order is shown to be either the only, or the most efficacious, or in the circumstances the most appropriate, means of protecting the child. Necessity must be interpreted in the light of a continuing risk to the child, for the whole point of the order is to give immediate protection to the child from risk. So even when significant harm has been unquestionably caused, a child protection order will not be necessary unless there is a likelihood of the harm continuing or being repeated. The no-order principle in section 16(4) does not apply to the sheriff's decision whether to make a child protection order, but it is implicit in the concept of necessity that the order will be made only when it is capable of achieving some protective benefit.

Frustration of inquiries

20.30   A child protection order might also be made (though in this case on the application only of a local authority) on the satisfaction of all of the following conditions:

    (i)   that the local authority has reasonable grounds to suspect that a child is being or will be so treated (or neglected) that he or she is suffering or will suffer significant harm;

    (ii) that it is making or causing to be made inquiries to allow it to decide whether it should take any action to safeguard the welfare of the child; and

    (iii) that those inquiries are being frustrated by access to the child being unreasonably denied, the authority having reasonable cause to believe that such access is required as a matter of urgency.[5]

20.31   It has been held in England[6] that since it is reasonable to expect a parent to allow suspicions of sexual abuse to be properly investigated, a refusal to do so may in itself justify the court in holding that the risk of significant harm results from a failure in parenting. Applying this reasoning to the very differently worded Scottish provisions runs the risk of confusing the first and the third of the conditions which a local authority must satisfy in seeking a child protection order on this ground. Unreasonable denial of access to a child ought not, it is submitted, in itself give reasonable grounds to suspect that the child is suffering significant harm. The structure of section 57(2) suggests that the suspicion must arise independently of, and prior to, the local authority making inquiries which are subsequently being frustrated by unreasonable denial of access.

---

5 s. 57(2).
6 *Re B (A Minor) (Interim Care Order: Criteria)* [1993] Fam. Law 335.

The sheriff's decision

On receipt of an application for a child protection order, the sheriff, having **20.32** considered the grounds of the application and the supporting evidence,[7] must forthwith[8] grant or refuse it.[9] The sheriff is not entitled to appoint a safeguarder at this stage in the proceedings in order to assist him or to safeguard the interests of the child.[10] The sheriff retains a discretion and he is not obliged to grant the order sought, even when the conditions are satisfied. He is guided in the exercise of that discretion by section 16(1), under which the welfare of the child is his paramount consideration. This may well indicate that no order should be made if, for example, it appears that the implementation of the order would be likely to do more harm (perhaps psychological) to the child than good. The granting of a child protection order can quite conceivably be both necessary to protect a child from significant harm and at the same time be against the welfare of the child. The removal of a child from familiar surroundings might sometimes be so traumatic and cause such distress to the child as to be a greater, psychological, injury than the physical harm it is designed to protect the child from. It is common experience for children to express a preference to remain in a highly unsatisfactory home than to be summarily removed to the alien environment most children would regard a residential establishment or even a foster home to be, and their opinions are not to be dismissed lightly on that matter. This is not, of course, to deny that in some cases the child's welfare will indeed require immediate removal of the child from a source of risk, whatever their own wishes and feelings. The sheriff's decision whether or not to grant a child protection order is not appealable.[11]

Matters authorised

A child protection order is designed to be flexible and to give a range of **20.33** options for the protection of the child, it being recognised that the child may be protected by means other than simply the removal of the child from his or her home. Therefore, the child protection order may do any of the following:

(a) Require any person in a position to do so to produce the child to the applicant.

(b) Authorise the removal of the child by the applicant to a place of safety, and the keeping of the child at that place. The reference to "removal" suggests that this paragraph cannot be used when the child is already in a place of safety, but is to be used only to take a child to a place of safety and keep him or her there.

(c) Authorise the prevention of the removal of the child from any place where he or she is being accommodated. This covers (but is not limited to) the situation of the child already in a place of safety. The word "removal" should, it is submitted, be interpreted to include removal of the child by the child him or herself from the place of safety (otherwise a child already at a place of safety before a child protection order was made could not be prevented from leaving on his or her own initiative).

---

[7] Lockyer and Stone, *op. cit.*, p. 119 point out that "an imperative of [these] provisions is to increase the demand for prima facie 'evidence' before an initial order to remove a child can be granted. The Form [A.S. 1997, r. 3.30 and Forms 47 and 48] suggests that the evidence take the form of 'reports, statements, affidavits or other evidence produced'".

[8] Kearney (Butterworths *Scottish Family Law Service*, at para. C.1814) suggests that a few hours' delay to check some important matter is permissible.

[9] A.S. 1997, r. 3.31.

[10] s. 41(2).

[11] s. 51(15)(a).

(d) Provide that the location of any place of safety in which the child is being kept should not be disclosed to any person or class of person specified in the order.[12]

20.34 The order may be subject to such terms and conditions as the sheriff considers appropriate.[13] Once made, the applicant must, as soon as practicable, inform both the local authority and the reporter of the making of the child protection order,[14] and serve a copy of the order and notice that it has been made on the child and any other person named in the application.[15] The applicant is authorised to act only when he reasonably believes that it is necessary to safeguard or promote the welfare of the child to do so.[16] If the applicant acts without this belief then he is acting without statutory authority and can be subject to liability therefor. Though it is likely to be difficult to establish lack of reasonable belief that the implementation of a child protection order is unnecessary when a sheriff has granted it on the basis that it is necessary, this is not impossible, such as, for example, when the original source of danger to the child has died or been removed to police custody since the granting of the order.

Directions as to contact

20.35 The sheriff is obliged to give consideration in all cases in which a child protection order is made to the question of whether it is necessary to give a direction as to contact between the child and any specified person or class of persons.[17] The direction given by the sheriff may require that contact be permitted between the child and another person, or may prohibit it, or may subject it to such conditions as the sheriff considers appropriate to safeguard and promote the welfare of the child.[18] Different arrangements can be made for different people.[19] A direction under section 58(1) does not regulate contact in the way that a contact order made under section 11 does but rather is in the nature of a direction to the applicant to allow contact between the child and another person (typically but not necessarily a person with a pre-existing responsibility and right of contact). A direction cannot be given to a person who is not an applicant and if the applicant is not the person who will be looking after the child then a direction under this section will seldom be appropriate. The sheriff is obliged to consider the matter of contact, whether requested to do so or not but, perhaps suprisingly, he is not obliged to give a direction, even when he considers that the direction is "necessary".[20] This is designed to ensure flexibility in the child's interests. The philosophy here, as in other parts of the 1995 Act, is that the court should get involved in directing children's lives only when to do so would be better for the child than not to do so. Necessity might arise, for example, when the applicant is minded not to allow contact and the sheriff is of the view that contact would be in the child's interests, or when the applicant cannot reach an

---

[12] s. 57(4).
[13] *ibid.*
[14] s. 57(5).
[15] A.S. 1997, r. 3.32.
[16] s. 57(6).
[17] s. 58(1). The requirement that the sheriff must give consideration to this matter and that he may make an order if he considers it necessary indicates that his powers to do so are not circumscribed by a pre-existing supervision requirement. The normal rule that a supervision requirement is given precedence over an inconsistent s. 11 order is probably inappropriate in the present context. The immediacy of the need for, and the short-term nature of, a child protection order should be given precedence over an inconsistent supervision requirement.
[18] s. 58(2).
[19] s. 58(3).
[20] s. 58(1) says that the sheriff "shall" consider whether a direction as to contact is necessary, and when he considers that it is necessary he "may" give the direction.

agreement with a person who is seeking to have contact with the child about the extent or nature of that contact. When the applicant is the person who will be looking after the child it is good practice for sheriffs to enquire of the applicant what arrangements for contact they would be minded to make in the absence of any direction. It will be "necessary" to give a direction only when the proposed arrangements are not, in the sheriff's opinion, satisfactory and the child's interest requires that better arrangements be made or when, for whatever reason, the child's interests require that the arrangements be put on a formal footing under the authority of a court order.

Directions as to parental responsibilities and parental rights

A child protection order does not confer parental responsibilities and 20.36 parental rights on the applicant, even for the short period of its operation, and these remain with whomsoever had them before the making of the order. Nevertheless the applicant may, at the same time as applying for the child protection order itself, apply to the sheriff for a direction as to the exercise or fulfilment of any parental responsibilities or parental rights.[21] Only very rarely will the applicant be a person with parental responsibilities or parental rights and so any direction given will not be directed towards the applicant (as is the case with a direction as to contact), but towards the person whose fulfilment or exercise of parental responsibilities or parental rights is to be regulated. The purpose is to provide directions as to how these responsibilities and rights should be carried out. The directions may in particular be in relation to medical examination, assessment or treatment.[22] This does not allow the sheriff to authorise examination, assessment or treatment, nor can he authorise the applicant to carry it out:[23] rather the sheriff may simply direct the parent or guardian to exercise their parental responsibilities and parental rights in a particular manner. Kearney[24] suggests that the sheriff may direct the applicant local authority to exercise parental responsibilities and parental rights, such as the responsibility and right to consent to medical treatment. While the practicalities of this are attractive, there is nothing in the Act which suggests that a child protection order transfers parental responsibilities and parental rights to the local authority and a direction that they exercise that which they do not have would seem to be incompetent. It is submitted that the direction must be to a person with parental responsibilities and parental rights, directing them to consent to the child's medical examination, assessment or treatment. Such a direction, however, would have practical content only when the person retains the right to provide such consent. Such a direction will not, therefore, be competent in relation to many older children, for a person with parental responsibilities and parental rights can consent only when the child cannot consent or refuse on his or her own behalf.[25] Section 90 of the 1995 Act preserves the child's capacity to consent or refuse consent under section 2(4) of the Age of Legal Capacity (Scotland) Act 1991 and a direction made under section 58(4) does not replace the capable child's consent.

---

[21] s. 58(4).

[22] s. 58(5).

[23] For child assessment orders, see s. 55, discussed above, paras 20.20–20.25. It may be noted that the sheriff cannot make a child assessment order on an application for a child protection order, nor do any of the actions authorised by a child protection order cover medical examination or treatment (even when the ground upon which the order was granted is frustration of inquiries). A child subject to a child protection order is, however, "looked after" by a local authority (s. 17(6)), which therefore has a duty to safeguard and promote the child's welfare.

[24] Butterworths *Scottish Family Law Service*, para. 1816.

[25] See above, para. 8.50.

20.37   Any direction to those with parental responsibilities and parental rights as to how they should exercise these responsibilities and rights is to be given only when the sheriff considers that such a direction is necessary to safeguard or promote the welfare of the child.[26] The direction may be granted subject to such conditions as the sheriff thinks appropriate, and in particular he must bear in mind in coming to his decision the duration of the order[27]: a child protection order is designed to last only for the shortest possible period of time, and it follows that directions made in connection with it should not, except in cases of immediate necessity, deal irrevocably with matters of long-term consequence. In all cases it will be for the applicant to show the existence of such a necessity.

Duration of directions
20.38   The direction, whether relating to contact or to parental responsibilities or parental rights, cannot survive without the child protection order to which it is attached and the direction will cease to have effect whenever the order ceases to have effect, for whatever reason.[28] So any direction given, like the child protection order itself, can last for a maximum of eight working days, and will come to an end earlier if the order is terminated earlier. The sheriff may vary or set aside a direction while continuing the child protection order at a review under section 60(7), as discussed below, and a children's hearing may vary it at an initial review under section 59(4), also discussed below.

Review of a child protection order
20.39   Once a child protection order, which authorises either (i) the removal of a child from his or her home and the keeping of the child in a place of safety, or (ii) the prevention of the removal of the child from any specified place, has been implemented, that order must be reviewed not later than on the second working day after its implementation, either by the sheriff on application under section 60(7) or, if no such application has been made, by an initial children's hearing under section 59 convened solely for the purpose of determining whether the child protection order should be continued. In addition, if an initial hearing has been held and the child protection order is continued, an application to the sheriff may be made within two working days of that continuation, for the same purpose.[29]

Review by a children's hearing
20.40   If a child has been taken to a place of safety or is prevented from being removed, and remains there on the second working day after having been taken there then, so long as the reporter has not received intimation that an application has been made to the sheriff to have the order set aside or varied, a children's hearing must be arranged by the reporter to conduct an initial hearing into the question of whether the child protection order should be continued.[30] That hearing must sit on the second working day[31] after the order was implemented[32] and the terms of that requirement are such that it would be incompetent to hold the hearing on any other day, such as the day before, even when that is practicable.

---

[26] s. 58(6).
[27] *ibid.*
[28] s. 58(7)
[29] s. 60(8)(b).
[30] s. 59(1).
[31] "Working day" is defined in s. 93(1) to be every day except Saturdays and Sundays, December 25th and 26th, and January 1st and 2nd. All other public holidays count as working days.
[32] s. 59(3).

Failure to hold a children's hearing on the second working day will bring the child protection order to an end, for the order can survive beyond that day only if a hearing continues it under section 59(4).[33]

The initial children's hearing is subject to the same rules of constitution and **20.41** procedure as a substantive hearing, except that its role is more limited. It can make no dispositive decision, nor review any supervision requirement to which the child is already subject.[34] Rather, the initial hearing is limited to considering two questions: whether it is satisfied that the conditions for the making of the child protection order, set out in section 57(1) or (2), exist or not and, if so, whether the order should be continued, with or without a variation in its terms until the commencement of the children's hearing on the eighth working day.[35] While the children's hearing may vary the terms of the order, and the terms of any direction the sheriff makes under section 58 (which includes withdrawing the direction), the wording of section 59(4) does not permit the hearing to impose a direction in the absence of any made by the sheriff.[36]

Review by a sheriff before initial hearing

If an application to the sheriff to set aside or vary the child protection order has **20.42** been made before the sitting of the children's hearing on the second working day after the order has been implemented then no such children's hearing may take place,[37] and the review will be conducted by the sheriff.[38] The applicant may be either one or more of: (a) the child to whom the order or direction relates; (b) a person having parental rights over the child; (c) a relevant person; (d) any person to whom notice of the application for the order was given by virtue of the rules[39]; or (e) the applicant for the child protection order itself.[40] The sheriff must determine the application within three working days of its being made.[41] If he has not determined the application by then, the child protection order ceases to have effect.[42] The applicant is required to send notice of the application to the reporter,[43] since if notice is not given to the reporter of an application to the sheriff to set aside or vary the child protection order within two working days of its implementation, the reporter is obliged to arrange an initial children's hearing in terms of section 59, as described above. The sheriff must hear the parties to the application and, if he or she wishes to make representations, the reporter.[44] In addition, any person on whom service of the order is made may appear or be represented at the hearing of the application.[45]

---

[33] s. 60(6)(a).
[34] The provision in s. 65(3) requiring a review of a supervision requirement when a child is referred under new grounds does not apply to the initial hearing since, at this stage, there are no new grounds, and in any case the initial hearing has no power to "dispose" of the case.
[35] s. 59(4).
[36] "The terms of the order" include its terms and conditions imposed under s. 57(4) but do not include any direction made under s. 58 in conjunction with the order. One practical result of this is that if the sheriff fails to give a direction as to contact, the initial hearing may not do so either, and during the child protection order that matter rests with the person in charge of the child: if, as will be the normal case, this is a local authority, it must exercise its powers in this respect having regard to the principles in s. 17(1) and in particular the duty to promote direct contact between the child and any person with parental responsibilities, but always having as its paramount concern its duty to safeguard and promote the child's welfare. That paramount concern might in some cases oblige the local authority to prevent contact taking place. If contact is sought, then the sheriff at a review rather than a hearing's review has the appropriate power.
[37] s. 59(1)(c).
[38] s. 60(8)(a).
[39] See A.S. 1997, r. 3.12.
[40] s. 60(7).
[41] s. 60(8).
[42] s. 60(2).
[43] s. 60(9).
[44] s. 60(11) and A.S. 1997, r. 3.33(4).
[45] A.S. 1997, r. 3.33(3).

20.43   After hearing the parties to the action and having allowed such further procedure as he thinks fit, the sheriff must make his decision[46] and, where the sheriff so directs, intimation of that decision must be given by the applicant to such persons as the sheriff directs.[47] The decision to be made is whether or not the conditions for the making of a child protection order under section 57 are satisfied or, where the application relates only to the variation or cancellation of a section 58 direction, whether that direction should be varied or cancelled.[48] Where the sheriff finds that the conditions in section 57 are satisfied, he "may" do any of the following acts:

    (a) confirm or vary the order, or any term or condition on which it was granted;

    (b) confirm or vary any direction given, in relation to the order, under section 58;

    (c) give a new direction under section 58; or

    (d) continue in force the order and any such direction until the commencement of the children's hearing on the eighth working day after its implementation.[49]

An unstated option is for the sheriff not to continue the order.[50] Where the sheriff finds that the conditions in section 57 are not satisfied he "shall" recall the child protection order and cancel any direction given.[51] This refers to all the conditions in section 57, including conditions as to its form such as are contained in section 57(3).

Review by sheriff after initial hearing

20.44   An application to the sheriff may also be made within two working days after the children's hearing has continued the child protection order under section 59(4), effectively giving a second review.[52] The rules, procedures and outcomes described above in relation to applications made before the sitting of the children's hearing apply here in the same way, except that the sheriff will have at his disposal the reasons why the children's hearing considered it appropriate to continue the order, and for that reason it will seldom, if ever, be appropriate for the reporter to arrange an advice hearing as considered immediately below.

Advice hearings

20.45   The reporter may arrange a children's hearing (to which the normal rules of attendance and procedure apply) after an application has been made to the sheriff, but before the sheriff has determined the application, for variation or setting aside of a child protection order, the purpose being that the hearing may provide the sheriff with advice to assist him in his determination of the application.[53] The nature of the advice given is entirely for the children's hearing itself to

---

[46] A.S. 1997, r. 3.33(4).

[47] A.S. 1997, r. 3.33(6).

[48] s. 60(11).

[49] s. 60(12).

[50] Section 16(4)(b) refers to the sheriff "considering... whether to discharge a child protection order". He has no discretion when he finds the conditions not satisfied, and so these words indicate the existence of a discretion to discharge when the conditions are held to be establshed. In addition, there is no doubt that an initial children's hearing, on finding the conditions for the granting of a child protection order are satisfied, does have the power not to continue the order (otherwise the words "may continue" in section 59(4) would have to mean "shall continue") and it is unlikely that the statute intended to give the sheriff a lesser discretion than the hearing.

[51] s. 60(13).

[52] s. 60(8)(b).

[53] s. 60(10).

decide, but it should be directed towards the question of whether it remains in the child's best interests for the child protection order to be continued (if the application is to set aside the order) or whether its terms and conditions are appropriate (if the application is to vary the order or any directions given in connection with it). The sheriff is not, of course, obliged to accept the advice, but it is implicit that he must take it into account in reaching his decision. The statute gives no guidance to the reporter as to how and when to exercise his or her discretion to arrange this advice hearing, and often the matter will be determined by the availability of time: the arranging of this hearing does not interrupt the running of the three working days within which the sheriff must determine the application and on that time-scale it will seldom be possible for a children's hearing to give sufficiently deep consideration to the child's circumstances to be able to say anything very useful.

Termination of child protection order

The eighth working day hearing

In no circumstance can a child protection order ever remain effective beyond **20.46** the eighth working day after it was implemented, and on the eighth working day a children's hearing must be held[54] (unless the reporter has decided that this is unnecessary[55]) at which grounds of referral will be put to the child and relevant person for acceptance or denial. The order comes to an end on the commencement of this hearing.[56] If it is considered necessary for the child to remain in a place of safety thereafter, the children's hearing may grant a warrant, as discussed above, under either section 66(1) or section 69(7), or make a supervision requirement naming a place of safety as the child's residence.

Non-implementation of the order

The child protection order will cease to have effect if no attempt to implement **20.47** it is made within 24 hours of making the order.[57] Implementation occurs on the day the child is removed to a place of safety, if that is what the child protection order authorises,[58] and on the day the child protection order is made when it authorises the prevention of the removal of the child from the place where he or she is being accommodated.[59] It is difficult to see how the applicant can attempt to implement the non-disclosure of the child's whereabouts if no one attempts to find this out and it is submitted that here too implementation occurs on the day that the order is made. The applicant can be said to make an attempt to implement the order when he takes necessary steps directed to that end, and the nature of the attempt will vary with the nature of the order. The attempt might not be successful until after 24 hours have passed, but that does not bring the order to an end so long as the attempt commences before then.

Non-continuation or recall

The child protection order will also come to an end if, after it has been **20.48** reviewed, it is not continued by the initial hearing,[60] or, implicitly, if the initial hearing that ought to have been held to review the order has not been held on

---

[54] s. 65(2).
[55] s. 60(6)(c).
[56] s. 60(6)(e).
[57] s. 60(1).
[58] s. 59(5)(a).
[59] s. 59(5)(b).
[60] s. 60(6)(a).

the second working day. The order comes to an end in the former case at the conclusion of the initial children's hearing and in the latter case at the end of the second working day. If an application has been made to the sheriff to review the child protection order, either before or after an initial hearing, the order comes to an end if the sheriff fails to determine that application within three working days of it having been made[61] or if he recalls the child protection order having found that the conditions for its granting are not (or are no longer) satisfied.[62]

Release from a place of safety by reporter

20.49   If the reporter decides not to refer the child to a children's hearing on the eighth working day, the child protection order comes to an end on the notification by the reporter to the person who implemented the order of this decision.[63] This does not, however, preclude the reporter from thereafter deciding to arrange a children's hearing at any other time under section 65(1).[64] In addition, but only before the children's hearing or the sheriff has conducted a review of the child protection order, if the reporter considers that the conditions for the granting of the child protection order or the giving of the directions are no longer satisfied, and he or she notifies the person who implemented the order that he or she so considers, the child protection order ceases to have effect.[65] The reporter can reach the view that the child should be released either because he or she has received further information relating to the case or because of a change in the circumstances of the case.[66] Again, in these circumstances, it remains open to the reporter to arrange a children's hearing under section 65(1) (*i.e.* not necessarily on the eighth working day after the child protection order was implemented), for section 60(3) and (6)(d) are directed solely to the question of whether the child should be kept in a place of safety and not whether a children's hearing should be arranged to consider his or her case.

Appeals

20.50   It is expressly provided that there is no appeal to the sheriff principal or the Court of Session from any decision of the sheriff in granting or refusing to grant a child protection order, nor any appeal to the sheriff from the decision of a children's hearing continuing a child protection order.[67] It is surprising that there is no reference at all in the Act to an appeal against a sheriff's decision to continue or to vary or to recall a child protection order, nor to an appeal against a children's hearing's decision not to continue the order. Appeal against the sheriff's decision on review of a child protection order under section 60 might be argued to be incompetent since section 51(11) lists the decisions that are appealable but does not mention decisions under section 60: *expressio unius est exclusio alterius*. However, it is by no means clear that section 51(11) is intended to be an exhaustive list of decisions made under Part II that are appealable.[68] Decisions of children's hearings not to continue a child protection order, being "any decision of a children's hearing", other than one continuing a child protection order,[69] might therefore be appealable. If this is so, then the appeal will

---

[61] s. 60(2).

[62] s. 60(6)(b) and (13).

[63] s. 60(6)(c).

[64] See further, Norrie, *Children's Hearings in Scotland*, pp. 212–213.

[65] s. 60(3), (4) and (6)(d).

[66] s. 60(3). Whenever such notice is given, the reporter must also notify the sheriff: s. 60(5).

[67] s. 51(15).

[68] So, *e.g.*, there is no reference to decisions under s. 76 to make an exclusion order, nor indeed any reference in that section to appeals. Yet appeal from such a decision is clearly envisaged by s. 29(9) of the Legal Aid (Scotland) Act 1986, as substituted by s. 92 of the Children (Scotland) Act 1995.

[69] s. 51(1)(a) and (15).

be to the sheriff and the ground will be that the decision was not justified in all the circumstances of the case. The only option open to the sheriff upholding an appeal is to remit the case with reasons for his decision to the children's hearing for reconsideration of their decision,[70] which seems a clumsy procedure when the emergency protection of a child from significant harm is at stake. Nor is the question of title to appeal against a hearing's decision not to continue a child protection order clear. The reporter may appeal decisions of the sheriff, but only "on behalf of the children's hearing",[71] and he or she cannot, it is submitted, appeal to the sheriff "on behalf of the children's hearing" a decision of the children's hearing not to continue a child protection order. The same difficulties do not arise in relation to relevant persons, the child, and the child's safeguarder.[72] It will be a highly unusual case in which a relevant person wishes to appeal against a decision not to continue a child protection order, but more plausible might be a child, or his or her safeguarder, seeking the protection that non-continuation of the order denies the child. The authority under section 57 to keep a child in a place of safety comes to an end on the recall or non-continuation of the child protection order and does not continue pending an appeal,[73] but a child seeking the protection of a child protection order may seek refuge under the terms of section 38 for up to seven days. All these difficulties would be avoided if the terms of section 51(15)(a) ("a decision of the sheriff on an application under section 57") were interpreted to mean the whole process instigated by section 57 and governed by sections 57 to 60 and not just the initial application, and if the terms of section 51(15)(b) ("a decision of a children's hearing continuing a child protection order") were interpreted to mean "a decision on whether to continue a child protection order". The child protection order procedure would thereby be entirely contained within the provisions of sections 57 to 60 and no appeals beyond the reviews discussed above would be permitted. This is, it is submitted, the intendment of the Act.

EMERGENCY PROTECTION IN THE ABSENCE OF A SHERIFF

It may sometimes happen that either a sheriff is not available to grant a child **20.51** protection order or it appears that a child's safety can be secured only by his or her immediate and summary removal from a source of potential danger. In these circumstances a child protection order, though designed to be granted quickly, might not be available quite quickly enough. Section 61 of the Children (Scotland) Act 1995 attempts to resolve that difficulty by permitting a justice of the peace to grant authorisations to do certain of the acts which could be authorised by a child protection order, and by permitting police officers to remove a child from an immediate source of danger. The provisions in section 61 are simpler than those relating to child protection orders and have no reviews or appeals, nor indeed any requirement to refer the case to a children's hearing thereafter, but they are designed to be holding measures only, until a child protection order can be sought (which does, of course, involve such a requirement). As early as is consistent with the protection and welfare of the child, after these measures have been taken the child must (taking account of his or her age and maturity) be informed of the reason why emergency measures have been taken and be given an opportunity to express views.[74] The applicant

---

[70] s. 51(5)(c)(i). The other options in s. 51(5) are inapplicable to the circumstances.
[71] s. 51(12)(b).
[72] Though since the sheriff in making a child protection order cannot appoint a safeguarder (s. 41(2)) a safeguarder will be in office only if the child was currently in the system before the child protection order was made.
[73] *cf. Stirling* v. *D*, 1995 S.L.T. 1089.
[74] Emergency Child Protection Measures (Scotland) Regulations 1996, reg. 13.

must allow reasonable contact, if in accordance with the welfare of the child, between the child and any relevant person or any person with whom the child was living immediately before the taking of emergency protection measures, and contact may be allowed with any other person.[75]

Justice of the peace authorisations

20.52   When the conditions specified in either section 57(1) or section 57(2) for the granting of a child protection order are satisfied, but it is not practicable in the circumstances to obtain such an order from a sheriff, then, so long as the justice of the peace is satisfied that had a child protection order been granted it is probable that it would have contained either an authorisation to remove the child to a place of safety and to keep the child there or an authorisation to prevent the removal of a child from any place where he or she is being accommodated, the justice of the peace may grant an authorisation which may do one or more of the following:

(a) require any person in a position to do so to produce the child to the applicant;

(b) prevent any person from removing a child from a place where he is then being accommodated;

(c) authorise the applicant to remove the child to a place of safety and to keep him there until the expiration of the authorisation.[76]

In addition, the rules permit the applicant to withhold the location of any place of safety in which the child is being kept from the relevant person or any other person with whom the child was residing immediately before the authorisation of the justice of the peace, if the applicant considers it necessary to do so in order to safeguard the welfare of the child.[77]

20.53   The act or acts authorised must be performed within 12 hours of the authorisation having been granted, otherwise the authorisation falls,[78] and in any case the authorisation must be implemented as soon as reasonably practicable.[79] The authorisation itself ceases to have effect 24 hours after having been granted or, if earlier, on the disposal of an application for a child protection order.[80] As soon as reasonably practicable after taking the steps authorised, the applicant must take such steps as are reasonably practicable to inform (a) any relevant person, (b) any person with whom the child was residing, (c) where not the applicant, the local authority in whose area the child was residing, (d) where not the applicant, the local authority in whose area the child is ordinarily resident, (e) where not the applicant, the local authority in whose area the child was residing immediately before the grant of the authorisation, and (f) the reporter of the following matters: (i) the grant of the authorisation and the steps taken to implement it, (ii) the place of safety where the child is being kept, (iii) the reasons for the granting of the authorisation, and (iv) any other step the applicant takes to safeguard the child's welfare.[81]

Emergency protection by a constable

20.54   A child may be removed from, or kept away from, a source of immediate danger by a police officer who has reasonable cause to believe that the conditions

---

[75] Emergency Child Protection Measures (Scotland) Regulations 1996, reg. 16.
[76] s. 61(1)–(3).
[77] Emergency Child Protection Measures (Scotland) Regulations 1996, reg. 10.
[78] Children (Scotland) Act 1995, s. 61(4)(a). The applicant must thereafter inform various people: Emergency Child Protection Measures (Scotland) Regulations 1996, reg. 11.
[79] Emergency Child Protection Measures (Scotland) Regulations 1996, reg. 7.
[80] s. 61(4)(b).
[81] Emergency Child Protection Measures (Scotland) Regulations 1996, regs 8 and 9.

in section 57(1) for the granting of a child protection order exist but it is not practicable in the circumstances for him or her to obtain a child protection order.[82] But he or she can remove or keep a child only when to do so is necessary to protect the child from significant harm. The necessity must be immediate, otherwise the provisions concerning authorisations by a justice of the peace can be utilised, or a child protection order sought. A police officer can, for example, step in and remove a child to a place of safety if he or she witnesses the child being assaulted by his or her parents, or if a child is brought to a female and child unit at a police station in a distressed state, or if the police officer comes across a child who has been expelled from the family home in conditions that create a risk of significant harm. It should be noted that where, further to emergency protection measures, a child is taken to a police station as a place of safety, the constable keeping him or her there must as soon as reasonably practicable take the child to another type of place of safety and keep the child in that other place.[83] As soon as reasonably practicable after a child has been removed to a place of safety under this provision, the constable must take such steps as are reasonably practicable to inform (a) any relevant person, (b) any person other than a relevant person with whom the child was residing, (c) the local authority in whose area the place of safety is situated, (d) the local authority in whose area the child is ordinarily resident, (e) the local authority in whose area the child was residing immediately before being removed to a place of safety, and (f) the reporter of the following matters: (i) the removal of the child to a place of safety, (ii) the place of safety where the child is being kept, (iii) the reasons for the removal to a place of safety and (iv) any other steps taken to safeguard the child's welfare.[84] The address of the place of safety and details of other steps taken can be withheld from the relevant person and persons with whom the child was residing if the constable considers it necessary in order to safeguard the welfare of the child.[85]

The child may be kept in a place of safety only so long as the conditions for **20.55** activating section 61(5) remain satisfied[86] and in any event a child taken to or kept in a place of safety by a police officer under the terms of section 61(5), may be kept there only for a maximum period of 24 hours after first being removed or kept from the source of danger.[87]

Release by reporter

As with child protection orders, the reporter has ultimate control over whether **20.56** a child is kept in a place of safety, and the child cannot be kept in a place of safety or prevented from being removed from such a place either by a justice of the peace or by a constable if the reporter is of the view either (i) in cases of authorisation by a justice of the peace that the conditions for its granting in section 61(1) are not satisfied, or (ii) in cases of emergency removal and keeping by a constable that the conditions specified in section 61(5) for the exercise of that power of removal are not satisfied, or (iii) in either case that it is no longer in the best interests of the child that he or she be kept in a place of safety or prevented from being removed from the place where he or she is being accommodated.[88] It remains open to the reporter to refer the case of a child released to a children's hearing under section 65(1).[89]

---

[82] Children (Scotland) Act 1995, s. 61(5).
[83] Emergency Child Protection Measures (Scotland) Regulations 1996, reg. 15.
[84] *ibid.* regs 3 and 4.
[85] *ibid.* reg. 5.
[86] *ibid.* reg. 6. Except, for obvious reasons, the unavailability of the sheriff.
[87] s. 61(6).
[88] s. 61(8).
[89] And, indeed, release by the reporter does not prevent any person seeking a child protection order under s. 57(1).

EXCLUSION ORDERS

Introduction

20.57   The protection of a child will often be achieved by separating the child from
the adult who poses a threat to his or her well-being. Until the coming into force
of Part II of the Children (Scotland) Act 1995, if the threatening adult lived in
the same household as the child that separation could be achieved only by
removing the child from his or her home, either by means of emergency
provisions (place of safety orders or warrants) or by means of more long-term
protective measures (supervision requirements with conditions of residence away
from the source of danger). It had long been recognised that the removal of a
child from his or her home environment would itself in most, if not all, cases be
a traumatic experience for the child and in some cases that trauma could counter
or even outweigh any good the removal was designed to achieve. It was seen as
a failing in the law that there was no procedure, similar to that contained in the
Matrimonial Homes (Family Protection) (Scotland) Act 1981, for the exclusion
of an abuser from the child's home.[90] These issues were addressed by the 1995
Act and sheriffs now have the power to grant exclusion orders, on the application
of a local authority, excluding named individuals from the child's family home
if this is necessary for the protection of the child.[91]

Exclusion orders and child protection orders

20.58   Local authorities have the choice of whether to seek an exclusion order or a
child protection order, though there is little indication in the Act as to when it
would be appropriate for them to seek one rather than the other. Their decision
is, however, governed by the requirement in section 17(3) to ascertain the views
of the child, his or her parents, any other person who has parental rights in
relation to the child, and any other person whose views the authority consider
to be relevant;[92] the requirement in section 17(4) to have regard to these views
and to the child's religious persuasion, racial origin and cultural and linguistic
background also applies. There are at least two considerations which may in
practice encourage local authorities to seek a child protection order rather than
an exclusion order. First, the burden of proof is rather less under section 57
than under section 76, in that the condition to be established for a child protection
order is, as has been seen, "reasonable grounds for believing" that the child is
suffering significant harm while the condition to be established for an exclusion
order is, as will be seen below, that the child is actually suffering significant
harm as a matter of fact rather than as a matter of belief. And secondly, there are
a number of defences to the granting of exclusion orders which do not apply to
child protection orders, so that even when the conditions for both orders can be
satisfied by the applicant local authority, the inclination may well be to seek the
order which cannot be defended rather than the order which can be.

20.59   If, in an application for an exclusion order, the conditions for the granting of
a child protection order are established, the sheriff may make a child protection
order as if the application had been made under section 57.[93] It is difficult to

---

[90] See White Paper: *Scotland's Children: Proposals for Child Care Policy and Law*, Cm. 2286
      (August 1993).

[91] ss. 76–80.

[92] This requirement applies whenever the local authority is making any decision with respect to a
      child whom it is looking after or is proposing to look after (s. 17(3)). A child is "looked after" by a
      local authority when he or she is subject to an order made, or authorisation or warrant granted, by
      virtue of Chaps 2, 3 or 4 of Pt II of the 1995 Act (s. 17(6)(c)). Seeking either an exclusion order or
      a child protection order means that the local authority is "proposing to look after" the child.

[93] s. 76(8).

envisage a situation in which proof that the child is suffering significant harm did not also amount to proof of a reasonable ground to believe that the child is suffering significant harm, and it follows that in virtually every case in which the conditions for an exclusion order are met, the conditions for a child protection order will also have been met, giving the sheriff the choice of which order to make. In addition, the local authority may fail to establish that the conditions for an exclusion order have been met, but nevertheless succeed in satisfying the conditions for a child protection order: in that case too the sheriff may treat the application as if it had been made under section 57. The sheriff has a discretion and he is not obliged to treat the application as one for a child protection order even when the conditions for the granting of such an order have been made out.[94]

Exclusion orders and the Matrimonial Homes (Family Protection) (Scotland) Act 1981

    The provisions in sections 76–80 of the Children (Scotland) Act 1995 are to a **20.60** large extent modelled on those in the Matrimonial Homes (Family Protection) (Scotland) Act 1981. Under section 4 of that Act the court may, on application by either spouse to a marriage (and, if the court has granted occupancy rights to a cohabitant, either cohabitant[95]) grant an order excluding the spouse or cohabitant from the "matrimonial home". The court must do so "if it appears to the court that the making of the order is necessary for the protection of the applicant or of any child of the family from any conduct or threatened or reasonably apprehended conduct of the non-applicant spouse which is or would be injurious to the physical or mental health of the applicant or child".[96] So this provision too might be used for the protection of children. There are, however, a number of major differences between exclusion orders under the 1981 Act and those under the 1995 Act. First, applications under the 1981 Act may be made by a member of the child's family seeking to protect her or himself together with the child while under the 1995 Act orders may be applied for only by an outside agency seeking to impose protection upon the child. Secondly, if the making of the order is found to be necessary then the court "shall" make the order under the 1981 Act, but the sheriff "may" make the order under the 1995 Act. Thirdly, if the applicant for an exclusion order requests that a power of arrest be attached to a matrimonial interdict under the 1981 Act this must be granted[97] while the court has a discretion to refuse to attach a power or arrest to an interdict under the 1995 Act, the applicant having the onus of proving why it is necessary to attach a power of arrest. And fourthly, the three overarching principles in section 16 apply in relation to the 1995 Act but not the 1981 Act, under which, for example, the welfare of the child is not expressed to be the court's paramount consideration.

Grounds for granting an exclusion order

    The sheriff[98] may grant an exclusion order on the application of a local authority[99] **20.61** if he is satisfied, in relation to the child, of *all* of the following three conditions:

---

[94] *cf.* the provision in s. 55(2) in relation to assessment orders, discussed above, para. 20.25.

[95] Matrimonial Homes (Family Protection) (Scotland) Act 1981, s. 18.

[96] For a more detailed discussion of this provision than is appropriate here, see Clive, *Husband and Wife* (4th ed.), pp. 271–277.

[97] s. 15(1).

[98] That is to say, the sheriff within whose sheriffdom the family home is situated: s. 80(2).

[99] Oddly, in the first reported application for an exclusion order, *Russell v. W*, 1998 Fam. L.R. 25, the applicant was a named individual employed by a local authority. Somewhat surprisingly no issue was taken to this and all parties, and the sheriff, seem to have assumed that the employee, though named as an individual, represented the local authority. While this is clearly competent in relation to child protection orders, it is submitted that with exclusion orders (and indeed child protection orders applied for under s. 57(2)) the better approach is for the local authority to be named as the applicant.

(1) That the child has suffered, is suffering, or is likely to suffer, significant harm as a result of any conduct, or any threatened or reasonably apprehended conduct, of the named person. "Significant harm" has the same meaning as with child protection orders.[1] It has been held that it may be reasonably apprehended that a Schedule 1 offender will repeat his offences if he has repeated them in the past, on separate occasions with some years between, against children over whom he was in a position of trust, and where the offender refuses to acknowledge his guilt, with the result that no work could be done with him during his period of imprisonment nor assessment carried out of the likelihood of his reoffending.[2] In the absence of circumstances such as these it is unlikely that the fact that a person is a Schedule 1 offender will alone be sufficient to create a reasonable apprehension of risk to the child.[3]

(2) That the making of an exclusion order against the named person (i) is necessary for the protection of the child, irrespective of whether the child is for the time being residing in the family home; and (ii) would better safeguard the child's welfare than the removal of the child from the family home. It must be shown by the applicant that the exclusion order is "necessary", but this word is not to be interpreted to mean that the exclusion order can be granted only when no other order (such as a child protection order) is available to protect the child, for otherwise exclusion orders could never be granted. Rather it must be shown that without this order or any other order the child's welfare would be at risk. It is submitted that an exclusion order is "necessary" when it is the most appropriate of the available means of protecting the child from significant harm, or likely to be the most efficacious.[4] It is implicit in the concept of "necessity" that an exclusion order is an alternative to a child protection order and that it will not usually be appropriate to seek both at the same time. It is, however, to be remembered that a child protection order need not remove a child to a place of safety. If it does not do so then a sheriff may, it is submitted, make both a child protection order and an exclusion order at the same time.[5] Similarly, an exclusion order may be "necessary" even during the currency of a supervision requirement which contains a condition that the child have no contact with the named person, if there are reasons to believe that that condition might not be complied with.[6]

(3) That, if an order is made, there will be a person specified in the application who is capable of taking responsibility for the provision of appropriate care for the child and any other member of the family who requires such care and who is, or will be, residing in the family home.[7] An exclusion order will not, therefore, be appropriate in cases in which the threat to the child comes from his or her only carer, or both or all of the carers.

---

[1] See above, para. 20.28.
[2] *Russell v. W,* above.
[3] It may be noted that until the 1995 Act, the fact that a person was a Sched. 1 offender was sufficient cause to remove the child from his or her home under a place of safety order granted under s. 37 of the Social Work (Scotland) Act 1968. It is no longer considered sufficient cause for the granting of a child protection order under s. 57 of the 1995 Act and it should not be considered sufficient cause to exclude a person from the child's home under s. 76.
[4] See Clive, *Husband and Wife* (4th ed.) at pp. 272–273 for a discussion of the meaning of "necessity" under the 1981 Act.
[5] *cf.* the (English) Children Act 1989, s. 44A(10) under which an exclusion order falls if the child has been removed by the applicant from his or her home and kept for longer than a period of 24 hours.
[6] *Russell v. W,* above.
[7] s. 76(2). This person is called the "appropriate person": s. 76(2)(c).

The sheriff will make the order granting or refusing the application for an exclusion order after hearing parties and allowing such further procedure as he thinks fit.[8] If he considers it necessary to appoint a person to safeguard the interests of the child in the proceedings, the sheriff must make such an appointment.[9] It would appear that the appointment comes to an end when the proceedings come to an end, that is to say when the sheriff has determined whether or not to grant an exclusion order.

Effect of the order

The effect of an exclusion order is to prevent the named person from entering **20.62** the child's family home (including garden and grounds) over which the order has been made, and to suspend any right of occupancy, whether as owner, tenant or otherwise that the named person has in that home.[10] The excluded person (known as the "named person") may enter the family home only with the express permission of the local authority. The "family home" is the place where the child ordinarily resides with a person who has parental responsibilities in relation to the child.[11] The order may exclude any named person from the child's family home, and it is not limited to a relative of the child, nor to someone who would otherwise be living in the home with the child. On the application of either the named person or the local authority, the sheriff may make the exclusion order, or any ancillary order, subject to such terms and conditions as he considers appropriate.[12]

Interim orders

The final determination by the sheriff of the application for an exclusion **20.63** order cannot be made until such time as the person to be excluded has been given an opportunity to be heard by the sheriff, either personally or through a representative, and the sheriff has given consideration to the views expressed by any person notified of the application.[13] As a consequence, a final exclusion order is not practicable as a means of providing emergency protection for the child. The immediate exclusion of someone causing significant harm to a child is, however, permitted on an interim basis, where the conditions for the granting of an exclusion order are met but the requirement for the affording of an opportunity to the person to be excluded to express views have not been fulfilled.[14] Where an interim order has been made on this basis a hearing must take place not later than three working days thereafter at which the sheriff may, before finally determining the application, confirm or vary the order or any of its terms or conditions, or recall it.[15] In addition, where the opportunity to express views has been given the sheriff may at any point prior to the final determination of the application grant an interim order.[16] An interim order granted under section 76(6) or an order granted under section 76(5) continuing an interim order made under section 76(4) has the same effect as a final order pending the final determination of the application.[17]

---

[8] A.S. 1997, r. 3.37.
[9] s. 41(1).
[10] s. 77(1).
[11] s. 76(12) and (13).
[12] s. 77(7).
[13] s. 76(3).
[14] s. 76(4).
[15] s. 76(5) and A.S. 1997, r. 3.36.
[16] s. 76(6).
[17] s. 76(7).

Defences

20.64   Following closely the terms in section 4(3) of the Matrimonial Homes
(Family Protection) (Scotland) Act 1981, the sheriff is prohibited from making
an exclusion order in circumstances in which it would be unjustifiable and
unreasonable to do so, taking account of certain matters, specified below.[18] An
exclusion order may well be "necessary" but at the same time be "unjustifiable
or unreasonable", because while necessity is to be looked at from the point of
view of the child, the defences require to be looked at from the point of view of
the adult the exclusion of whom the local authority is seeking.[19] An exclusion
order might be considered unjustifiable or unreasonable when some other order
is available. This cannot, however, be regarded as an automatic conclusion,
otherwise there would always be a defence to an exclusion order since a child
protection order will always be available as an alternative. Rather, what is
required is that the sheriff weighs up the respective interests of the child and the
adult, and the respective effects that the different orders would have on both. If
the detriment to the adult is disproportionate to the benefit to the child (bearing
in mind, in making that assessment, that the child's welfare is the court's
paramount consideration) then an exclusion order is likely to be considered
unjustifiable or unreasonable.

20.65   The whole circumstances of the case are to be taken into account by the
sheriff in determining whether it would be unjustifiable or unreasonable to make
an exclusion order,[20] but the Act specifies certain matters which must always be
taken into account[21]:

> (1)   The conduct of the members of the child's family (whether in relation to
>   each other or otherwise). The conduct must refer to conduct which
>   indicates whether members of the child's family are able to protect the
>   child from the risk posed by the person the local authority are seeking to
>   exclude, or are, for example, likely to collude with the excluded person.[22]
>
> (2)   The respective needs and financial resources of the members of that
>   family. Every member of a child's family needs accommodation and
>   it will seldom be reasonable (though it may, depending upon one's
>   perception of justice, be justifiable) to exclude a person from his or
>   her home when he or she has nowhere else to go. The reference to
>   financial resources allows the sheriff to take account of the ability of
>   the potentially excluded person to pay for alternative accommodation.
>   The needs and financial resources of a person who is not a member of
>   the child's family[23] are not relevant here even when that is the person
>   who poses the risk to the child.
>
> (3)   The extent (if any) to which (i) the family home and (ii) any relevant
>   item in that home is used in connection with a trade, business or
>   profession by any member of the family.

Where the family home (i) is or is part of an agricultural holding or (ii) is let or
is a home in respect of which possession is given, to a named person (whether
alone or with any other person) by an employer as an incident of employment,

---

[18]   s. 76(9).
[19]   On this point under the 1981 Act, see Clive, *op. cit.*, p. 274.
[20]   s. 76(9)(a).
[21]   s. 76(10).
[22]   *cf. Berry* v. *Berry*, 1988 S.L.T. 650 in relation to the equivalent provision in the 1981 Act.
[23]   "Family" means any person who has parental responsibilities for the child and any other person
       with whom the child has been living: ss. 76(12) and 93(1).

then, in deciding whether an exclusion order would be unjustifiable or unreasonable the sheriff must take account of any requirement (and the likely consequences, in light of that requirement, of the exclusion of the named person from the family home) that the potentially excluded person reside in the child's home and the likelihood of that person losing his or her entitlement to live there if the exclusion order is made.[24]

Ancillary orders

The sheriff may make orders ancillary to the exclusion order if and in so far **20.66** as he thinks fit.[25] This differs somewhat from the provisions in the Matrimonial Homes (Family Protection) (Scotland) Act 1981, under which the sheriff is obliged to make some of these orders whenever he is requested to do so.[26] Here, the matter lies entirely in the discretion of the sheriff (though subject, as always, to the overarching principles in section 16) and they may be made subject to such terms and conditions as the sheriff thinks appropriate.[27] The orders are as follows[28]:

(1) A warrant for the summary ejection of the named (*i.e.* the excluded) person from the home. If this warrant is granted in the absence of the named person, the sheriff may give directions as to the preservation of any of that person's goods and effects which remain in the family home.[29]

(2) An interdict prohibiting the named person from entering the home without the express permission of the local authority. This is necessary if a power of arrest is to be attached under section 78 (discussed shortly).

(3) An interdict prohibiting the removal by the named person of any relevant item specified in the interdict from the home, except either (i) with the written consent of the local authority, or of an appropriate person,[30] or (ii) by virtue of a subsequent order of the sheriff.

(4) An interdict prohibiting the named person from entering or remaining in a specified area in the vicinity of the home.

(5) An interdict prohibiting the taking by the named person of any step of a kind specified in the interdict in relation to the child.

(6) An order regulating the contact between the child and the named person. The sheriff may make this order irrespective of whether there has been an application for such an order.[31] It may also be made even when a supervision requirement over the child is in force. The suggestion to the contrary by the sheriff in *Russell v. W*[32] fails, it is respectfully submitted, to take account of the facts (i) that "contact" as used in Part I of the 1995 Act is a parental responsibility and parental right and is very different from the factual nature of "contact" in section 77(5), and (ii) that the responsibility and right of contact is different in its nature from "access" under the pre-1995 legislation and at common law.[33] Any inconsistency between the sheriff's order regulating contact

---

[24] s. 76(9)(b) and (11).
[25] s. 77(2).
[26] Matrimonial Homes (Family Protection) (Scotland) Act 1981, s. 4(4).
[27] s. 77(7).
[28] s. 77(3)
[29] s. 77(5).
[30] *i.e.* the person specified in the order as being responsible for the care of the child during the currency of the exclusion order: s. 76(2)(c).
[31] s. 77(6).
[32] 1998 Fam. L.R. 25 at paras 382–397.
[33] See above, paras 8.39 and 9.13.

and the provisions of a supervision requirement are resolved by giving the supervision requirement precedence.[34]

The sheriff may make any other order which he considers is necessary for the proper enforcement of any of the first three above-mentioned remedies.[35]

20.67   None of these ancillary orders (except that listed in (2) above) will be granted or made if the named (*i.e.* excluded) person satisfies the sheriff that it is unnecessary to do so.[36] "Unnecessary" means unnecessary in light of the threat to the child. So, for example, a warrant for the summary ejection of the excluded person from the child's home will be unnecessary if that person agrees to leave the home voluntarily and there is reason to believe that he or she will do so, or the person is not presently living there, in circumstances in which that removes the risk to the child. It will be unnecessary to grant any of the listed interdicts in situations in which there is no suggestion that the excluded person will perform any of the acts that can be interdicted.

Powers of arrest

20.68   The sheriff may, at his own hand or on application by the local authority either when the exclusion order is applied for or at any time during its currency, attach a power of arrest to any interdict which has been granted ancillary to the exclusion order itself.[37] By this means, but only by this means, an exclusion order can be backed up by police powers. If this is deemed necessary, an interdict should be sought at the same time as the exclusion order is sought, for an exclusion order without an interdict cannot have a power of arrest attached. The effect of a power of arrest is that a constable may arrest without warrant the named person if he has reasonable cause for suspecting that person to be in breach of the interdict to which the power of arrest is attached.[38] If this happens and the arrested person is not released immediately on the ground that the constable in charge of the police station to which he or she is taken is satisfied that there is no likelihood of that person further breaching the interdict,[39] and the procurator fiscal decides that no criminal proceedings are to be taken,[40] the person arrested must, wherever practicable, be brought before the sheriff sitting as a court of summary criminal jurisdiction for the district in which he or she was arrested not later than in the course of the first day after the arrest, other than a Saturday, Sunday or court holiday.[41] The sheriff may detain the person for a period not exceeding two days.[42]

Duration, variation and recall of exclusion order

20.69   Unless brought to an end earlier, an exclusion order ceases to have effect six months after it was made.[43] This applies to the final order made on an application under section 76(1), an interim order made under section 76(6) and a continuation granted under section 76(5) of an interim order made under section 76(4).[44] The

---

[34] Such inconsistency should indicate to the local authority that they should refer the case of the child to the reporter to arrange a review of the supervision requirement under s. 73(8)(a)(i). This conclusion is different from that reached (above, para. 20.35, n. 17) in relation to child protection orders, but the emergency context there justifies a different approach.
[35] s. 77(3).
[36] s. 77(4).
[37] s. 78(1)–(3).
[38] s. 78(6).
[39] s. 78(7).
[40] s. 78(10).
[41] s. 78(11).
[42] s. 78(13).
[43] s. 79(1).
[44] s. 76(12).

order will cease to have effect prior to the date six months after having been made in the following circumstances:

(1) If the sheriff on making the order directed that it should cease on some prior date.

(2) If the sheriff recalls the order. Application can be made to the sheriff for the variation or recall of an exclusion order and any order made ancillary to it.[45] Title to seek a recall inheres in the local authority, the named (*i.e.* the excluded) person, an appropriate person[46] or the spouse or partner[47] of the named person, if that spouse or partner is not excluded from the family home and is not an appropriate person. It is noticeable that the child is not given title to seek the recall of an exclusion order, which may be considered anomalous given that children must be given an opportunity to express views on the making of the order, and its variation or recall.

(3) If the named person's spouse or partner or the person looking after the child becomes no longer entitled to occupy the child's home. This might include, for example, the termination of a lease or the sale of the house during the currency of the exclusion order: it is appropriate to bring the order to an end in these circumstances since the child will no longer practically be able to live in the house from which the person is excluded.

Appeals

There is no provision in the Act expressly granting a right of appeal to the **20.70** sheriff principal or to the Court of Session from a decision of the sheriff to grant (or refuse) an exclusion order, though normal principles of appeal will apply.[48]

---

[45] s. 79(3) and A.S. 1997, r. 3.40.

[46] *i.e.* the person specified in the order as being responsible for the care of the child during currency of the exclusion order: s. 76(2)(c).

[47] Defined as persons who live together in a family home as if they were husband and wife: s. 79(4).

[48] It is assumed in s. 92 in the legal aid provisions that there is an appeal from the sheriff in relation to exclusion orders.

CHILD SUPPORT CALCULATIONS

EXAMPLE 1

Appendix 1

Maintenance Requirement as Calculated by theFirst Child Support Officer

Section 11 and paragraph 1(1) of Schedule 1 to the CS Act 1991 provides, along with regulations 3 and 4 of CS (MASC) 1992 (S.I. 1992 No. 1815), that the maintenance requirement for B and C is the sum of prescribed amounts of income support rates for the qualifying children and, if appropriate, the parent with care, less any child benefit.

The prescribed amounts are based on the amounts applicable at the effective date (reg. 3 (2) of CS (MASC) 1992).

In Mrs A's case the prescribed amounts were calculated as:

	£
Income Support applicable amount for an adult aged 25+ Para. 1(3)(b) of Sched. 1 to the Act; Reg. 3(1)(b) of CS (MASC) 1992 as amended by CS (MATP) 1994	46.50
Income Support applicable amount for the children: B aged 5	15.95
C aged 2 Para. 1(3)(a) of Sched. 1 to the Act; Reg. 3 (1)(a) of CS (MASC) 1992	15.95
Income Support Family Premium Para. 1(3)(c) of Sched. 1 to the Act; Reg. 3(1)(c) of CS (MASC) 1992	10.25
Income Support Lone Parent Premium Para. 1(3)(c) of Sched. 1 to the Act; Reg. 3(1)(d) of CS (MASC) 1992	5.20
Total:	**93.85**
Less Child Benefit Paras 1(2) and (4) of Sched. 1 to the Act and reg. 4 of CS (MASC) 1992	**18.85**
Maintenance requirement	**£75.00**

*as at September 1996

Appendix 2

Net Income of Mr A as Calculated by the First Child Support Officer

Regulation 7 of CS (MASC) 1992 provides for the calculation of the absent parent's net income.

Paragraphs 1 and 2 of Schedule 1 to CS (MASC) 1992 as amended by the CS and IS (Amendment) Regs 1995, relate to earnings of an employed earner.

Paragraph 1(3) of the same Schedule states that for the purposes of calculating assessable income, a person's net income shall be the gross earnings less any amounts deducted in respect of income tax, national insurance contributions and one half of any payments made to an occupational or personal pension scheme, or, where that scheme is intended partly to provide a capital sum to discharge a mortgage secured on the parents' home, 37.5 per cent of any such sums.

Subject to sub-paragraphs 2(2)–(4) of Schedule 1 of CS(MASC) 1992, as amended by the CS and IS (Amendment) Regs 1995, paragraph 2(1) provides that the amount of earnings to be taken into account for the purpose of calculating net income shall be calculated or estimated by reference to the average earnings at the relevant week. This shall have regard to such evidence as is available in relation to that person's earnings during such period as appears appropriate to the child support officer. This shall begin no earlier than eight weeks before the relevant week and end no later than the date of the assessment and for the purposes of that calculation or estimate, the child support officer may consider evidence of that person's cumulative earnings during the period beginning with the start of the year of assessment in which the relevant week falls and ending with a date no later than the date of the assessment.

The MEF was sent to Mr A on April 4, 1996. It is to be "treated as having been sent" on April 6, 1996. This is two days after posting (not counting Sundays or bank holidays) as laid down in regulation 1(6)(b) of CS (MAP) 1992.

The "relevant week" is the period of seven days immediately preceding the date on which the MEF is treated as having been sent (reg. 1(2) of CS (MASC) 1992). The relevant week was therefore March 30, 1996 to April 5, 1996.

The child support officer used the earnings for the period January 20, 1996 to April 12, 1996, which included the relevant week.

Mr A is paid on a four-weekly basis, *i.e.* lunar monthly, and therefore the calculations have been based on these periods.

The calculation of net income was as follows:

PERIOD 1 (20/01/96 – 16/02/96)

		£
Gross Wage		1, 251.32
Income Tax	less	17.94
National Insurance Contribution	less	88.22
Occupational Pension (50% x £56.31)	less	28.16
	Total	1,117.00

PERIOD 2 (17/02/96 – 15/03/96)		£
Gross Wage		1, 373.40
Income Tax	less	203.95
National Insurance Contribution	less	98.23
Occupational Pension (50% x £93.50)	less	30.90
	Total	1,040.32

PERIOD 3 (16/03/96 – 12/04/96)		£
Gross Wage		2,077.78
Income Tax	less	373.92
National Insurance Contribution	less	134.11
Occupational Pension (50% x £93.50)	less	46.75
		1,523.00

The net weekly earnings calculation was made as follows:

£3,680.32 ÷ 12 = £306.69

Net Income   £306.69

Appendix 3

Net Income of Mrs A as Calculated by the First Child Support Officer

Regulations 7 and 8 of CS (MASC) 1992 provide for the calculation of the parent with care's net income.

Paragraphs 1 and 2 of Schedule 1 to CS (MASC) 1992, as amended by the CS and IS (Amendment) Regs 1995, relate to earnings of an employed earner. Paragraph 6 of the same Schedule relates to benefit payments.

Paragraph 1(3) of the same Schedule states that for the purposes of calculating assessable income, a person's net income shall be the gross earnings less any amounts deducted in respect of income tax, national insurance contributions and one half of any payments made to an occupational or personal pension scheme, or, where that scheme is intended partly to provide a capital sum to discharge a mortgage secured on the parents' home, 37.5 per cent of any such sums.

Subject to sub-paragraphs 2(2)–(4) of Schedule 1 of CS (MASC) 1992, as amended by the CS and IS (Amendment) Regs 1995, paragraph 2(1) provides that the amount of earnings to be taken into account for the purpose of calculating net income shall be calculated or estimated by reference to the average earnings at the relevant week. This shall have regard to such evidence as is available in relation to that person's earnings during such period as appears appropriate to the child support officer. This may begin no earlier than eight weeks before the relevant week and end no later than the date of the assessment and for the purposes of that calculation or estimate, the child support officer may consider evidence of that person's cumulative earnings during the period beginning with the start of the year of assessment in which the relevant week falls and ending with a date no later than the date of the assessment.

The MAF was received on January 17, 1996. The "relevant week" is the period of seven days immediately preceding the date on which the MAF is submitted to the Secretary of State (reg. 1(2) of CS (MASC) 1992). The relevant week was therefore January 10, 1996 to January 16, 1996.

The child support officer used the earnings for the period January 1, 1996 to January 31, 1996, which included the relevant week.

The calculation of net income was as follows:
Month 1 (31/01/96)

		£
Gross Wage		965.79
Income Tax	less	132.66
National Insurance Contribution	less	76.44
Occupational Pensions (50% x £nil)	less	nil
	Total	756.69

The net weekly earnings calculation was made as follows:

£756.69 x 12 ÷ 52 = £174.62

	£
Mrs A also receives one parent benefit weekly	6.30

Therefore, the net income calculation was:	£
Net Weekly Income	174.62
One Parent Benefit	6.30
Total	180.92

Net Income **£180.92**

Appendix 4

Exempt Income of Mr A as Calculated by the First Child Support Officer

Under the provisions of regulation 9 of CS (MASC) 1992, as amended by the CS and IS (Amendment) Regs 1995, the amount to be included in the calculation of Mr A's exempt income was calculated as follows:

	£
Income Support applicable amount for an adult aged 25+ Reg. 9(1)(a) of CS (MASC) 1992	46.50
Income Support applicable amount for the child: aged 2 months Reg. 9(1)(g)(i) of CS (MASC) 1992	15.95
Income Support Family Premium Reg. 9(1)(f) of CS (MASC) 1992	10.25
Housing Costs Reg. 9(1)(b) and paras 1(b) and 3(5) of Sched. 3 to CS (MASC) 1992	47.76

Exempt Income **£120.46**

The housing costs calculation is shown below

Monthly mortgage interest	£154.82 per month
Monthly endowment premium	£52.15 per month

£154.82 + £52.15 = £206.97

Regulation 16(b) of CS (MASC) 1992 states that where the housing costs are paid on a monthly basis the amount shall be multiplied by 12, and divided by 52. Therefore in Mr A's case the calculation was made as follows:

£206.97 x 12 ÷ 52 = **£47.76**

Appendix 5

Exempt Income of Mrs A asCcalculated by the First Child Support Officer

Under the provisions of regulations 9 and 10 of CS (MASC) 1992, as amended by the CS and IS (Amendment) Regs 1995, the amount to be included in the calculation of Mrs A's exempt income was calculated as follows:

	£
Income Support applicable amount for an adult aged 25+	46.50
Reg. 9(1)(a) of CS (MASC) 1992	
Income Support applicable amount for the children:	
B aged 5	15.95
C aged 2	15.95
Reg. 9(1)(g)(i) of CS (MASC) 1992	
Income Support Family Premium	10.25
Income Support Lone Parent Premium	5.20
Reg. 9(1)(f) of CS (MASC) 1992	
Housing Costs*	49.15
Reg. 9(1)(b) and paras 1(b)	
and 3(5) of Sched. 3 to CS (MASC) 1992	

Exempt Income   **£143.00**

*The housing costs calculation is shown below.

Monthly mortgage interest	£155.01 per month
Monthly endowment premium	£ 58.00 per month

£155.01 + £58.00 = £213.01

Regulation 16(b) of CS (MASC) 1992 states that where the housing costs are paid on a monthly basis the amount shall be multiplied by 12, and divided by 52. Therefore in Mrs A's case the calculation was made as follows:

£213.01 x 12 ÷ 52 = £49.16

Appendix 6

Maintenance Assessment as Calculated by the First Child Support Officer

Paragraph 2 of Schedule 1 to the CS Act 1991 provides for the calculation of the maintenance assessment.

First, the calculation as in para. 2(1) must be made. This is:

$(A + C) \times P$, where —

A = the absent parent's assessable income (£186.23)
C = the parent with care's assessable income (37.92)
P = 0.5 (as prescribed in reg. 5 (b) of CS (MASC) 1992)

In this case, the calculation was/is:

$(£186.23 + £37.92) \times 0.5 = £112.08$

This figure is more than the maintenance requirement of £75.00, which means that the provisions of paragraph 2(3) of Schedule 1 to the CS Act 1991 will apply. The maintenance assessment will therefore consist of a basic element and an additional element/maximum additional element.

Paragraphs 3 and 4 of Schedule 1 to the CS Act 1991 provide for the calculation of a basic and an additional element.

(i) The basic element is calculated by applying the formula:

$A \times G \times P = BE$ (Basic Element)

G is determined by applying the formula: $\dfrac{MR}{(A + C) \times P}$

i.e. $\dfrac{£75.00}{(186.23 + £37.92) \times 0.5}$ $= 0.6691947$

(ii) The additional element is calculated by applying the formula:

$(1 - G) \times A \times R = AE$ (Additional Element)

A = the absent parent's assessable income
C = the parent with care's assessable income
MR = the maintenance requirement figure
P = 0.5 (CS (MASC) 1992, reg. 5(b))

R   =   0.20 (2 qualifying children) (CS (MASC) 1992, reg. 6 (1) as amended by CS (MATP) Regs 1994)

In this case:
A   =   £186.23
C   =   £37.92
MR =   £75.00
G   =   0.6691947

Therefore:

(a) The basic element was £186.23 x 0.6691947 x 0.50 resulting in the figure of £62.31.

(b) The additional element was (1 – 0.6691947) x £186.23 x 0.20 resulting in the figure of £12.32.

Paragraph 4(3) of Schedule 1 to the CS Act 1991 provides for the calculation of the maximum amount of additional element.

The maximum amount of additional element is calculated by applying the formula:

$$Z \times Q \times \frac{(A)}{(A + C)}$$

Where:

A and C have the same value as shown earlier in this appendix.

Z   =   1.5 (CS (MASC) 1992, reg. 6(2)(a) as amended by the CS and IS (Amendment) Regs 1995).

Q   =   the age allowance plus family premium for each child in the maintenance requirement.

In this case the amount of £52.40 (CS (MASC), reg. 6(2)(b))

Therefore, the maximum amount of additional element was £65.30.

i.e.   1.5   x   £52.40   x $\dfrac{£186.23}{£224.15}$

The maintenance assessment = basic element + lesser of additional element <u>or</u> maximum additional element, *i.e.*   £62.31 + £12.32   =   £74.63

Maintenance assessment   **£74.63**

Appendix 7

Protected Income of Mr A as Calculated by the First Child Support Officer

Regulation 11 of CS (MASC) 1992, as amended by CS (MATP) 1994 and the CS and IS (Amendment) Regs, lays down the items that are to be included in an absent parent's protected income calculation.

In Mr A's case, these were as follows:

	£
Income Support applicable amount for a couple aged 18+ Reg. 11(1)(a)(i)/ Reg. 11 (1)(a)(ii) of CS (MASC) 1992	73.00
Income Support applicable amount for the child xx aged 2 months Reg. 11 (1)(g)(i) of CS (MASC) 1992	15.95
Income Support Family Premium Reg. 11 (1)(f) of CS (MASC) 1992	10.25
Housing Costs* Reg. 11 (1)(b) and paragraph 1 (b) of Sched. 3 to CS (MASC) 1992	35.73
Council Tax# Reg. 11(1)(j) of CS (MASC) 1992	10.31
Standard Margin Reg. 11(1)(k) of CS (MASC) 1992	<u>30.00</u>

	Sub-Total	175.24

Plus 15% of the residue after deducting the sub-total shown above from Mr A's disposable income,
i.e. £317.14 – £175.24
= £141.90 x 15%   21.29
Reg. 11(1)(1) of CS (MASC) 1992

Total Protected Income   **£196.53**

However, in accordance with regulation 11 (6) of CS (MASC) 1992, as amended by the CS and IS (Amendment) Regs 1995, if the protected income level of an absent parent is less than 70 per cent of his net income then his protected income shall be 70 per cent of his net income.

In this case:

	£
Protected income before adjustment	196.53
70% of Mr A's net income	214.68
Therefore, Mr A's protected income is	214.68
Total Protected Income	**214.68**

*The housing costs are calculated as follows:

Monthly mortgage interest	£154.82 per month

---

*See Housing Costs above.

Regulation 16(b) of CS (MASC) 1992 states where the housing costs are paid on a monthly basis the amount shall be multiplied by 12, and divided by 52, therefore in Mr A's case the calculation was made as follows:

£154.82 x 52 ÷ 12 = £35.73

\# The council tax calculation is calculated as follows:

Annual amount £536.00

£536.00 ÷ 52 = £10.31

EXAMPLE 2 — MR & MRS SG

Appendix 1

Maintenance Requirement as Calculated by the Second Child Support Officer

Section 11 and paragraph 1 (1) of Schedule 1 to the CS Act 1991 provides, along with regulations 3 and 4 of CS (MASC) 1992, that the maintenance requirement for D and E is the sum of prescribed amounts of income support rates for the qualifying children and, if appropriate, the parent with care, less any child benefit.

The prescribed amounts are based on the amounts applicable at the effective date (reg. 3 (2) of CS (MASC) 1992).

In Mrs G's case the prescribed amounts were calculated as:

	£
Income Support applicable amount for an adult aged 25+ Para. 1(3)(b) of Sched. 1 to the CS Act 1991; Reg. 3(1)(b) of CS (MASC) 1992 as amended by CS (MATP) 1994	47.90
Income Support applicable amount for the children: D aged 5 E aged 3 Para. 1(3)(a) of Sched. 1 to the CS Act 1991; Reg. 3(1)(a) of CS (MASC) 1992	16.45 16.45
Income Support Family Premium Para. 1(3)(c) of Sched. 1 to the CS Act 1991; Reg. 3(1)(c) of CS (MASC) 1992	10.55
Income Support Lone Parent Premium Para. 1(3)(c) of Sched. 1 to the CS Act 1991 Reg. 3(1)(d) of CS (MASC) 1992	5.20
Total	**96.55**

Less Child Benefit   19.60
Paras 1(2) and (4) of Sched. 1 to the CS Act 1991
and reg. 4 of CS (MASC) 1992

Maintenance requirement   **£76.95**

Appendix 2

Net Income of Mr G as Calculated by the Second Child Support Officer

Regulation 7 of CS (MASC) 1992 provides for the calculation of the absent parent's net income.

Paragraphs 1 and 2 of Schedule 1 to CS (MASC) 1992, as amended by CS and IS (Amendment) Regs 1995, relate to earnings of an employed earner.

Paragraph 1(3) of Schedule 1 to CS (MASC) 1992 as amended by CS and IS (Amendment) Regs 1995 states that for the purposes of calculating assessable income, a person's net income shall be the gross earnings less any amounts deducted in respect of income tax, national insurance contributions and one half of any payments made to an occupational or personal pension scheme, or, where that scheme is intended partly to provide a capital sum to discharge a mortgage secured on the parent's home, 37.5 per cent of any such sums.

Subject to paragraphs 2(2)–(4) of Schedule 1 of CS (MASC) 1992 as amended by CS and IS (Amendment) Regs 1995, paragraph 2(1) provides that the amount of earnings to be taken into account for the purpose of calculating net income shall be calculated or estimated by reference to the average earnings at the relevant week. This shall have regard to such evidence as is available in relation to that person's earnings during such period as appears appropriate to the child support officer. This may begin no earlier than eight weeks before the relevant week and end no later than the date of assessment and for the purposes of that calculation or estimate, the child support officer may consider evidence of that person's cumulative earnings during the period beginning with the start of the year of assessment in which the relevant week falls and ending with a date no later than the date of assessment.

The MEF was sent to Mr G on April 23, 1996. It is to be "treated as having been sent" on April 25, 1996. This is two days after posting (not counting Sundays or bank holidays) as laid down in regulation 1(6)(b) of CS (MAP) 1992.

The "relevant week" is the period of seven days immediately preceding the date on which the MEF is treated as having been sent (reg. 1(2) of CS (MASC) 1992 and CS(MA) 1995). The relevant week was therefore April 18, 1996 to April 24, 1996.

The child support officer used the earnings for the period, month ending March 25, 1996 to April 25, 1996, which included the relevant week.

The calculation of net income was as follows:

MONTH 1 (25/03/96)

		£
Gross Wage		2,175.84
Income Tax	less	524.91
National Insurance Contribution	less	170.54
Occupational Pension (50% x £57.73)	less	28.87
	Total	1,451.52

MONTH 2 (25/04/96)

		£
Gross Wage		2,175.84
Income Tax	less	526.20
National Insurance Contribution	less	176.00
Occupational Pension (50% x £57.73)	less	28.87
	Total	1,444.77

The net monthly earnings calculation was:

	£
Month 1 Total	1,451.52
Month 2 Total	1,444.77
	2,896.29

The net weekly earnings calculation was made as follows:

£2,896.29 x 6 ÷ 52 = £334.19

Mr G also receives bonus payments. In accordance with Schedules 1(1)(a), (3) and 2(2) to CS (MASC) 1992 the amount received in the last 52 weeks was totalled (notional tax and national insurance deducted) and then calculated as a weekly average.

£2,419.00 + £318.00 =		£2,737.00
£2,737.00 x 24% =		£ 656.88
£2,737.00 x 10% =		£ 273.70
	Total	**£ 930.58**
£2,737.00 – £930.58 =		£1,806.42
£1,806.42 ÷ 52 =		£ 34.74

Therefore, the net income calculation was:

	£
Net weekly income	334.19
Plus bonus payments (average weekly amount)	34.74
Net Income	**£368.93**

Appendix 3

Net income of Mrs G as Calculated by the Second Child Support Officer

Regulations 7 and 8 of CS (MASC) 1992 provides for the calculation of the parent with care's net income.

Paragraphs 1 and 2 of Schedule 1 to CS (MASC) 1992, as amended by CS and IS (Amendment) Regs 1995, relate to earnings of an employed earner. Paragraph 6 of Schedule 1 to CS (MASC) 1992 relates to benefit payments.

Paragraph 1(3) of Schedule 1 to CS (MASC) 1992 as amended by CS and IS (Amendment) Regs 1995 states that for the purposes of calculating assessable income, a person's net income shall be the gross earnings less any amounts deducted in respect of income tax, national insurance contributions and one half of any payments made to an occupational or personal pension scheme, or, where that scheme is intended partly to provide a capital sum to discharge a mortgage secured on the parents home, 37.5 per cent of any such sums.

Subject to paragraphs 2(2)–(4) of Schedule 1 to CS (MASC) 1992 as amended by CS and IS (Amendment) Regs 1995, paragraph 2(1) provides that the amount of earnings to be taken into account for the purpose of calculating net income shall be calculated or estimated by reference to the average earnings at the relevant week. This shall have regard to such evidence as is available in relation to that person's earnings during such period as appears appropriate to the child support officer. This may begin no earlier than eight weeks before the relevant week and end no later than the date of the assessment and, for the purposes of that calculation or estimate, the child support officer may consider evidence of that person's cumulative earnings during the period beginning with the start of the year of assessment in which the relevant week falls and ending with a date no later than the date of the assessment.

The MAF was received on April 15, 1996. The "relevant week" is the period of seven days immediately preceding the date on which the MAF is submitted to the Secretary of State (reg. 1(2) of CS (MASC) 1992 as amended by CS (MA) 1993 and 1995). The relevant week was therefore April 8, 1996 to April 14, 1996.

The child support officer used the earnings for the period month ending March 31, 1996 to April 30, 1996, which included the relevant week.

The calculation of net income was as follows :

MONTH 1 (31/03/96) £

			£
Gross Wage			518.19
Income Tax		less	0.00
National Insurance Contribution		less	26.85
Occupational Pension (50% x £31.09)		less	15.55
	Total		475.79

MONTH 2 (30/04/96) £

			£
Gross Wage			518.19
Income Tax		less	13.60
National Insurance Contribution		less	26.13
Occupational Pension (50% x £31.09)		less	15.55
	Total		462.91

The net monthly earnings calculation was:	£
Month 1 Total	475.79
Month 2 Total	462.91
	938.70

The net weekly earnings calculation was made as follows :

£938.70 x 6 ÷ 52 = £108.31

Mrs G also receives Family Credit weekly	47.17

Mrs G also receives One Parent Benefit weekly	6.30

Therefore, the net income calculation was:

	£
Net weekly income	108.31
Family Credit	47.17
One Parent Benefit	6.30
Net Income	**£161.78**

Appendix 4

Exempt Income of Mr G as Calculated by the Second Child Support Officer

Under the provisions of regulation 9 of CS (MASC) 1992, as amended by CS and IS (Amendment) Regs 1995 and CS (MA)) 1993 and 1995, the amount to be included in the calculation of Mr G's exempt income was:

	£
Income Support applicable amount for an adult aged 25+ Reg. 9(1)(a) of CS (MASC) 1992	47.90

Income Support applicable amount for the children:	
D aged 5	4.79
E aged 3	4.79
Reg. 9(1)(g)(i) of CS(MASC) 1992 **£16.45 x 2.04/7**	

Income Support Family Premium Reg. 9(1)(f) of CS (MASC) 1992 **£10.55 x 2.04/7**	3.07

Income Support Lone Parent Premium Reg. 9(1)(c) of CS (MASC) 1992 **£5.20 x 2.04/7**	1.52

Housing Costs Reg. 15(4) of CS (MASC) 1992 as amended by CS and IS (Amendment) Regs 1995 and CS (MA) 1995 Reg. 9(1)(b) of CS (MASC) 1992	nil

Exempt Income	**£62.07**

Regulation 15(4), substituted under the designation of regulation 15(10) by CS and IS (Amendment) Regs 1995 and redesignated as regulation 15(4) by CS (MA) 1995, states that:

A parent shall be treated as having no housing costs where he is a non-dependant member of a household and is not responsible for meeting housing costs except to another member, or other members, of that household.

Regulation 1(2) of CS (MASC) 1992 defines a non-dependant. Non-dependant means a person who is a non-dependant for the purposes of either:
(a) Regulation 3 of the Income Support Regulations; or
(b) Regulation 3 of the Housing Benefit Regulations,

or who would be a non-dependant for those purposes if another member of the household in which he is living were entitled to income support or housing benefit as the case may be.

Paragraph 4 of Schedule 3 to CS (MASC) 1992 provides that housing costs shall only be included where:

(a) they are incurred in relation to the parents' home;

(b) the parent is responsible for those costs; and

(c) the liability to meet those costs is to a person other than a member of the same household.

Mr G was treated as having no housing costs for exempt income purposes as he was living as a non-dependant in the household of a close relative or friend.

He was not responsible for meeting the housing costs such as rent or mortgage, etc., for the property for the purposes of income support and housing benefit legislation.

Appendix 5

Exempt income of Mrs G as Calculated by the Second Child Support Officer

Under the provisions of regulation 9 of CS (MASC) 1992 as amended by CS and IS (Amendment) Regs 1995 and CS (MA) 1993 and 1995 and regulation 10 of CS (MASC) 1992 as amended by CS (MA) 1993, and CS and IS (Amendment) Regs 1995, the amount to be included in the calculation of Mrs G's exempt income was:

	£
Income Support applicable amount for an adult aged 25+	47.90
Income Support applicable amount for the children:	
D aged 5	11.66
E aged 3	11.66

Reg. 9(1)(g)(i) of CS (MASC) 1992

Income Support Family Premium   7.48
Reg. 9(1)(f) of CS (MASC) 1992

Income Support Lone Parent Premium   3.68
Reg. 9(1)(c) of CS (MASC) 1992

Housing Costs*   nil
Reg. 9 (1)(b) of CS (MASC) 1992

Exempt Income   **£82.38**

* The housing costs calculation is nil as it was confirmed that Mrs G was not
paying the mortgage on the property she was residing in.

Appendix 6A

*The Notional Maintenance Assessment for Mr G as Calculated by the Second
Child Support Officer*

Paragraph 2 of Schedule 1 to the CS Act 1991 provides for the calculation of
the maintenance assessment.

First, the calculation as in paragraph 2(1) must be made. This is:

$(A + C)$ x P, where—

$A =$ the absent parent's assessable income (£306.86)
$C =$ the parent with care's assessable income (£79.40)
$P =$ 0.5 (as prescribed in reg. 5(b) of CS (MASC) 1992)

In this case, the calculation was:

$(£306.86 + £79.40)$ x 0.5 = £193.13

The figure is more than the maintenance requirement of £79.95, which means
that the provisions of paragraph 2(3) of Schedule 1 to the CS Act 1991 will
apply. The maintenance assessment will therefore consist of a basic element
and an additional element/maximum additional element.

(i) The basic element is calculated by applying the formula:

   A x G x P = BE (Basic Element)
   G is determined by applying the formula: $\dfrac{MR}{(A + C) \times P}$

i.e. $\dfrac{£76.95}{(£306.86 + £79.40) \times 0.5}$ $=$ 0.3984362

(ii) The additional element is calculated by applying the formula:

$(1- G) \times A \times R = AE$ (Additional Element)

A	the absent parent's assessable income
C	the parent with care's assessable income
MR	the maintenance requirement figure
P	0.5 (CS (MASC) 5(b))
R	0.20 (2 qualifying children) (CS (MASC) 1992, reg. 6(1) as amended by CS (MATP) 1994)

In this case:

A	=	£306.86
C	=	£79.40
MR	=	£76.95
G	=	£0.3984362

Therefore :

(a) The basic element was £306.86 x 0.3984362 x 0.50 resulting in the figure of £61.13.

(b) The additional element was (1 – 0.3984362) x £306.86 x 0.20 resulting in the figure of £36.92.

Paragraph 4(3) of Schedule 1 to the CS Act 1991 provides for the calculation of the maximum amount of additional element.

The maximum amount of additional element is calculated by applying the formula:

$$Z \times Q \times \frac{(A)}{(A + C)}$$

Where:
A and C have the same value as shown earlier in this appendix.

Z	=	1.5	(Regulation 6(2)(a) of CS (MASC) 1992 as amended by CS and IS (Amendment) Regs 1995)
Q	=		the age allowance plus family premium for each child in the maintenance requirement.

In this case the amount of £54.00 (regulation 6(2)(b) of CS (MASC) 1992).

Therefore, the maximum amount of additional element was £64.35.

i.e.   1.5   x   £54.00 x $\dfrac{£306.86}{£386.26}$

The maintenance assessment = basic element + lesser of additional element <u>or</u> maximum additional element, *i.e.*   £61.13 + £36.92 = £98.05.

Maintenance assessment   **£98.05**

Appendix 6B

The Notional Maintenance Assessment of Mrs G as Calculated by the Second Child Support Officer

Paragraph 2 of Schedule 1 to the CS Act 1991 provides for the calculation of the maintenance assessment.

First, the calculation as in paragraph 2(1) must be made. This is:

$(A + C) \times P$ where —

    A = the parent with care's assessable income (£79.40)
    C = the absent parent's assessable income   (£306.86)
    P = 0.5 (as prescribed in reg. 5(b) of the CS (MASC) Regs 1992)

In this case, the calculation was:

$(£79.40 + £306.86) \times 0.5 = £193.13$

This figure is more than the maintenance requirement of £76.95, which means that the provisions of paragraph 2(3) of Schedule 1 to the CS Act 1991 will apply. The maintenance assessment will therefore consist of a basic element and an additional element/maximum additional element.

Paragraphs 3 and 4 of Schedule 1 to the CS Act 1991 provide for the calculation of a basic and an additional element.

(i) The basic element is calculated by applying the formula:

    $A \times G \times P = BE$ (Basic Element)
    G is determined by applying the formula: $\dfrac{MR}{(A + C) \times P}$

i.e. $\dfrac{£76.95}{(£79.40 + £306.86) \times 0.5}$

(ii) The additional element is calculated by applying the formula:

    $(1 - G) \times A \times R = AE$ (Additional Element)
    A   the parent with care's assessable income
    C   the absent parent's assessable income
    MR   the maintenance requirement figure
    P   0.5 (CS (MASC) Reg. 5(b))
    R   0.20 (2 qualifying children)(CS (MASC) 1992, reg. 6(1) as amended by CS (MATP) 1992)

In this case :
A = £ 79.40
C = £306.86
MR = £ 76.95
G = £0.3984362

Therefor :

(a) The basic element was £79.40 x 0.3984362 x 0.50 resulting in the figure of £15.82.

(b) The additional element was (1 − 0.3984362) x £79.40 x 0.20 resulting in the figure of £9.55.

Paragraph 4(3) of Schedule 1 to the CS Act 1991 provides for the calculation of the maximum amount of the additional element.

The maximum amount of additional element is calculated by applying the formula:

$$Z \times Q \times \frac{(A)}{(A+C)}$$

Where:
A and C have the same value as shown earlier in this appendix.

$Z = 1.5$ (CS (MASC) 1992, reg. 6(2)(a) as amended by CS and IS (Amendment) Regs 1995)

$Q = $ the age allowance plus family premium for each child in the maintenance requirement.

In this case the amount of £54.00 (CS (MASC) 1992, reg. 6(2)(b))

Therefore, the maximum amount of additional element was £16.65
i.e. 1.5 x £54.00 x $\frac{£79.40}{£386.26}$

The maintenance assessment = basic element + lesser of additional element <u>or</u> maximum additional element, *i.e.* £15.82 + £9.55 = £25.37.

Maintenance assessment £25.37

Appendix 6C

Maintenance Assessment Calculation (Shared Care)

In Mr G's case the child support officer calculated that he had care of D and E for 2.04 nights per week, *i.e.* 106 nights per year on average.

Therefore Mr G was responsible for paying maintenance and the following formula, as stated in regulation 20(4) of CS (MASC) 1992, was used to work out the amount of maintenance he should pay:

$$T = X - \left((X+Y) \times \frac{J}{7 \times L}\right)$$

where:

T   is the amount of child support payable;

X   is the amount of child support maintenance which would be payable by the parent who is treated as an absent parent, assessed under Schedule 1 to the CS Act 1991 as if paragraphs 6 and 7 of that Schedule did not apply, and, where the other parent is an absent parent, as if the value of C was the assessable income of the other parent;

Y   is:
   (i)   the amount of child support maintenance assessed under Schedule 1 to the CS Act 1991 payable by the other parent if he is an absent parent or which would be payable if he were an absent parent, and for the purposes of such calculation the value of C shall be the assessable income of the parent treated as an absent parent in accordance with regulation 20(2) of CS (MASC) 1992 ; **or**

   (ii) if there is no such other parent, shall be NIL ;

J   is the total of the weekly average number of nights for which day-to-day care is provided by the person who is treated as the absent parent in respect of each child included in the maintenance assessment and shall be calculated to two decimal places.

L   is the number of children who are included in the maintenance assessment in question.

Regulation 20(6) of CS (MASC) 1992 states that the liability to pay any amount calculated under paragraph 20(4) shall be subject to the provision made for protected income and minimum payments under paragraphs 6 and 7 of Schedule 1 to the CS Act 1991.

In this case:

$$T = \pounds 98.05 - (\ (98.05 + 25.37) \quad x \quad \frac{4.08}{7 \times 2}\ )$$

$$T = \pounds 98.05 - (123.42 \times 0.2914285)$$

$$T = \pounds 98.05 - \pounds 35.97 = \pounds 62.08$$

T = £62.08

Appendix 7

Protected Income of Mr G as Calculated by the Second Child Support Officer

Regulation 11 of CS (MASC) 1992 as amended by CS (MATP) 1992, and CS and IS (Amendment) Regs 1995 and CS (MA) 1995, lays down the items that are to be included in an absent parent's protected income calculation.

In Mr G's case, these were as follows: £
Income Support applicable amount for an adult aged 25+   47.90
Reg. 11(1)(a)(i) of CS (MASC) 1992

Income Support applicable amount for the children
D aged 5   4.79
E aged 3   4.79
Reg. 11(1)(g)(i) of CS (MASC) 1992
£16.45 x 2.04/7

Income Support Family Premium   3.07
Reg. 11(1)(f) of CS (MASC) 1992
£10.55 x 2.04/7

Income Support Lone Parent Premium   1.52
Reg. 11(1)(c) of CS (MASC) 1992
£5.20 x 2.04/7

Housing Costs   32.00
Reg. 11(1)(b) of CS (MASC) 1992 as amended by CS and IS
(Amendment) Regs 1995 and CS(MA) 1995
Reg. 15(4) of CS (MASC) 1992 as amended by CS and
IS (Amendment) Regs 1995 and CS(MA) 1995

Standard Margin   <u>30.00</u>
Reg. 11(1)(k) of CS (MASC) 1992
as amended by CS (MATP) 1994

    Sub-Total   124.07
Plus 15% of the residue after deducting the sub-total shown above from Mr G's
disposable income,

i.e. £368.93 – £124.07
= £244.86 x 15%   36.73
Reg. 11(1)(1) of CS (MASC) 1992 as amended by CS (MATP) 1994 and CS
and IS (Amendment) Regs 1995

Total Protected Income   **£160.80**

However, in accordance with regulation 11(6) of CS (MASC) 1992 as amended
by CS and IS (Amendment) Regs 1995, if the protected income level of an
absent parent is less than 70 per cent of his net income then his protected income
shall be 70 per cent of his net income.

Regulation 11(6) of CS (MASC) 1992 as added by CS and IS, (Amendment)
Regs 1995 states "if the application of the above provisions of this regulation
would result in the protected income level of an absent parent being less than
70 per centum of his net income, as calculated in accordance with regulation 7,
those provisions shall not apply in his case and instead his protected income
level shall be 70 per centum of his net income as so calculated".

In this case: £
Protected income before adjustment   160.80

70% of Mr G's net income   258.25

Therefore, Mr G's protected income is   258.25

Total Protected Income   **£258.25**

Regulation 15(10) of CS (MASC) 1992 was redesignated as regulation 15(4) of CS (MASC) 1992 by CS and IS (Amendment) Regs 1995 and states that:

A parent shall be treated as having no housing costs where he is a non-dependant member of a household and is not responsible for meeting housing costs except to another member, or other members, of that household.

Regulation 1(2) of CS (MASC) 1992 defines a non-dependant. Non-dependant means a person who is a non-dependant for the purposes of either:

(a) Regulation 3 of the Income Support Regulations; or

(b) Regulation 3 of the Housing Benefit Regulations,

or who would be a non-dependant for those purposes if another member of the household in which he is living were entitled to income support or housing benefit as the case may be.

Paragraph 4 of Schedule 3 to CS (MASC) 1992 provides that housing costs shall only be included where:

(a) they are incurred in relation to the parent's home;

(b) the parent is responsible for those costs; and

(c) the liability to meet those costs is to a person other than a member of the same household.

The words in regulation 11(1)(b) of CS (MASC) 1992 were substituted for regulation 15(5) by regulation 46(2)(b) of CS and IS (Amendment) Regs 1995 as from April 18, 1995. From January 22, 1996, the words in regulation 11(1)(b) were substituted by regulation 43(2) of CS (MA) 1995, and state that:

The amount of housing costs for an absent parent who is a non-dependant, and is treated as having no housing costs by regulation 15(4), will be the non-dependant amount which would be calculated for him/her under paragraphs (1), (2) and (9) of regulation 63 of the Housing Benefit Regulations, if he were a non-dependant in respect of whom a calculation were to be made under those paragraphs (disregarding any other provision of that regulation).

As Mr. G has a gross weekly income of £502.11 (see appendix 2), his allowance in respect of housing costs for protected income purposes was £32.00.

Appendix 8

*Details of Shared Care Data as Provided by Mr G and and Mrs G and Data
used by Second Child Support Officer*

Month	Mr G No. of nights	Child support officer Calculation	Child support officer No. of nights
April 1996	11	11	10
May 1996	7	7	6
June 1996	9	9	9
July 1996	17	17	17
August 1996	9	9	9
September	3	3	3
October	6	6	6
November	8	8	8
December	20	18	10
Jan 1997	8	6	6
February	n/k	6	7
March	n/k	6	7

Appendix 9

Amounts used Within the Various Assessments

E/D	18/06/96	20/08/96	01/10/96	13/01/97
M.R	£76.95	£76.95	£76.95	£76.95
NI.PWC	£161.78	£173.30	£173.30	£0.00
NI.AP	£368.93	£368.93	£368.93	£368.93
EI.PWC	£82.38	£82.38	£82.38	£0.00
EI.AP	£62.07	£62.07	£93.24	£93.24
AI.PWC	£79.40	£90.92	£90.92	£0.00
AI.AP	£306.86	£306.86	£275.69	£275.69
M.A	£62.08	£60.35	£55.03	£71.79
DI.AP	£368.93	£368.93	£551.75	£551.75
PI.AP	£258.25	£258.25	£258.25	£258.25
M.P	**£62.08**	**£60.35**	**£55.03**	**£71.79**

Key

E/D	Effective Date
M.R	Maintenance Requirement
AP	Absent Parent
PWC	Parent With Care
NI	Net Income
EI	Exempt Income
DI	Disposable Income
PI	Protected Income
M.P	Maintenance Payable
M.A	Maintenance Assessment

INDEX